THE
HOTEL
GUIDE 2014

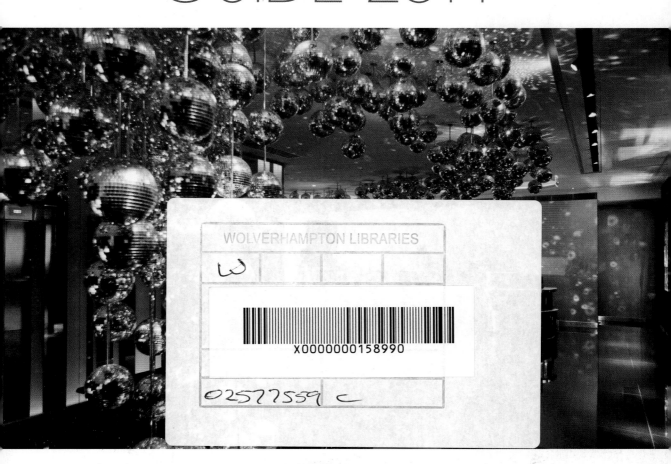

AA Lifestyle Guides

Published by AA Publishing, a trading name of AA Media Limited, whose registered office is Fanum House, Basing View, Basingstoke, Hampshire RG21 4EA.
Registered number 06112600

47th edition September 2013.
First published by the Automobile Association as the Hotel and Restaurant Guide, 1967
© AA Media Limited 2013.

Assessments of AA inspected establishments are based on the experience of the Hotel and Restaurant Inspectors on the occasion(s) of their visit(s) and therefore descriptions given in this guide necessarily contain an element of subjective opinion which may not reflect or dictate a reader's own opinion on another occasion. See 'AA Star Classification' in the preliminary section for a clear explanation of how, based on our Inspectors' inspection experiences, establishments are graded. If the meal or meals experienced by an Inspector or Inspectors during an inspection fall between award levels the restaurant concerned may be awarded the lower of any award levels considered applicable.

AA Media Limited strives to ensure accuracy of the information in this guide at the time of printing. Due to the constantly evolving nature of the subject matter the information is subject to change. AA Media Limited will gratefully receive any advice from our readers of any necessary updated information.

Please contact:
Advertising Sales Department: advertisingsales@theAA.com
Editorial Department: lifestyleguides@theAA.com
AA Hotel Scheme Enquiries: 01256 844455

Typesetting and Repro by Servis Filmsetting Ltd, Stockport
Printed in Italy by Printer Trento SRL, Trento

This directory is compiled by AA Lifestyle Guides; managed in the Librios Information Management System and generated by the AA establishment database system.

A CIP catalogue record for this book is available from the British Library.

ISBN: 978-0-7495-7474-1

A04980

Maps prepared by the Mapping Services Department of AA Publishing.

Maps © AA Media Limited 2013.

Contains Ordnance Survey data © Crown copyright and database right 2013. Licence number 100021153.

 Land & Property Services. This is based upon Crown Copyright and is reproduced with the permission of Land & Property Services under delegated authority from the Controller of Her Majesty's Stationery Office. © Crown copyright and database rights 2013 Licence number 100,363. Permit number 130023

 Ordnance Survey Ireland's National Mapping Agency Republic of Ireland mapping based on © Ordnance Survey Ireland/ Government of Ireland Copyright Permit number MP000913.

Information on National Parks in England provided by the Countryside Agency (Natural England).

Information on National Parks in Scotland provided by Scottish Natural Heritage.

Information on National Parks in Wales provided by The Countryside Council for Wales.

Contents

Welcome to the Guide	4
How to Use the Guide	6
Hotels of the Year	11
AA Star Classifications & Rosette Awards	20
Additional Information	24
Island Getaways	26
Hotel Groups	33
England	47
London	244
Isle of Man	483
Channel Islands	484
Scotland	498
Scottish Islands	552
Wales	560
Ireland	590
Gibraltar	621
County Maps	624
Atlas Section	626
Readers' Report Forms	651

Welcome to the Guide

We know that people use the AA Hotel Guide for finding many different types of accommodation for a variety of reasons, and as the AA inspects such a wide range of establishments, we hope that this guide will prove an invaluable asset in helping you to find just the right place.

Updated every year, the AA Hotel Guide 2014 includes many old favourites, as well as plenty of new places to stay across Britain.

Who's in the Guide?

From the most opulent and sophisticated of London's elite hotels to personally run small hotels in the British countryside; from the practical and convenient budget hotel aimed at the business or air traveller, to the luxurious country house hotel catering for leisure and sporting guests, *The AA Hotel Guide 2014* has it all. All year round our specially trained team of expert inspectors are visiting, grading and advising the hotels that appear in this guide. Each one is judged on its presentation, quality of accommodation, leisure and sporting facilities, food operation, service, hospitality, conference facilities and cleanliness; and then rated according to our Classification System (see page 24).

Any hotel applying for AA recognition receives an annual unannounced visit to check standards. If the hotel changes hands, the new owners must reapply for classification, as AA recognition is not transferable.

Our inspectors have also chosen their Hotels of the Year, for England, Scotland, Wales, Northern Ireland and the Republic of Ireland, as well as Hotel Group and Small Hotel Group of the Year.

Red Stars and Inspectors' Choice

All of the hotels in this guide should be of a high standard, but some are a cut above, and these are specially selected by our inspectors. At these establishments you can expect a little more of everything: more comfort,

more facilities, more extras, and more attention. From 2 red stars to 5 red stars, these are the best of British hotels. Every Red Star hotel is highlighted as an INSPECTORS' CHOICE, but these are not the only places that are singled out in this way.

Rosettes

Most of the hotels in this guide have their own restaurants, and a large proportion of them serve food that has attained the award of AA Rosettes; including some that have reached the four and five Rosette level, making them among the finest restraurants in the world. These are regularly visited by the AA inspectorate and awarded Rosettes strictly on the basis of the inspector's experience alone.

Some of the establishments in the guide are known as Restaurants with Rooms. Most will have been awarded AA Rosettes for their food, and the accommodation they offer meets the required AA standard, making them worthy of inclusion in this guide.

Anonymous Inspection

All hotel and restaurant inspections are made anonymously, and the inspector always pays his or her own bill (rather than it being paid by the establishment). After taking a meal or staying overnight at the hotel, the inspector will announce to a member of staff and ask to speak to the manager, or the chef, in the case of a Rosette visit.

Tell us what you think

We welcome your feedback about the hotels included in this guide, and about the guide itself. A Readers' Report form appears at the back of the guide, so please write in, or e-mail us at: lifestyleguides@theaa.com.

The hotels, along with guest accommodation, pubs, golf courses, days out and restaurants feature on The AA website: theAA.com, and on a number of AA mobile apps.

How to Use the Guide

1 LOCATION

Town listed alphabetically within country (the county name appears under the town name)

2 MAP REFERENCE

Map page number followed by a 2-figure National Grid reference (see also page 9)

3 HOTEL NAME

Where the name appears in *italic* type the information that follows has not been confirmed by the establishment for 2014

4 GRADING

Hotels are listed in star rating and merit score order within each location (for full explanation of ratings and awards see page 24)
★ Star rating
% Merit score
◉ Rosette award

5 TYPE OF HOTEL

(see opposite)

6 HOTEL LOGO

If a symbol appears here it represents a hotel group or consortium (See pages 33–41)

7 PICTURE

Optional photograph supplied by the establishment

8 ADDRESS AND CONTACT DETAILS

9 DIRECTIONS

Brief details of how to find the hotel

10 DESCRIPTION

Written by the AA inspector at the time of the last visit

11 ROOMS

Number of rooms and prices (see page 8)

12 FACILITIES

Additional facilities including those for children and for leisure activities

13 CONFERENCE

Conference facilities as available (see page 8)

14 NOTES

Additional information (see pages 8–9)

1 **3** **4** **5** **7** **2** **6**

HELMSLEY   Map 19 SE66
North Yorkshire

Black Swan Hotel   LOGO
★★★★ 77% ◉◉ HOTEL

☎ 01439 770466
Market Place YO62 5BJ
8 — **e-mail:** enquiries@blackswan-helmsley.co.uk
web: www.blackswan-helmsley.co.uk
9 — **dir:** A1 junct 49, A168, A170 east, hotel 14m from Thirsk

10 — People have been visiting this establishment for over 200 years and it has become a landmark that dominates the market square. The hotel is renowned for its hospitality and friendliness; many of the staff are long-serving and dedicated. The bedrooms are stylish and include a junior suite and feature rooms. Dinner in the award-winning restaurant is the highlight of any stay. The hotel has a Tearoom and Patisserie that is open daily.

11 — **Rooms** 45 (4 fmly) ⌇ **S** £150-£222; **D** £198-£270 (incl.
12 — bkfst)* **Facilities** STV FTV Wi-fi Xmas New Year
Conf Class 30 Board 26 Thtr 50 Del from £165*
Parking 50 **Notes** LB Civ Wed 130

13   **14**

KEY TO SYMBOLS AND ABBREVIATIONS	
★	Black stars
★	Red stars – indicate AA Inspectors' Choice
@	AA Rosettes – indicate an AA award for food
%	Inspectors' Merit score (see page 6)
A	Associate Hotels (see this page)
O	Hotel due to open during the currency of the guide
U	Star rating not confirmed (see this page)
Fmly	Number of family rooms available
GF	Ground floors rooms available
♠	Bedrooms with walk-in showers available
Smoking	Number of bedrooms allocated for smokers
pri facs	Bedroom with separate private facilities (Restaurant with Rooms only)
S	Single room
D	Double room
*	2013 prices
fr	From
incl. bkfst	Breakfast included in the price
FTV	Freeview television
STV	Satellite television
Wi-fi	Wireless network connection
↳	High speed internet connection (bedrooms)
HL	Hearing loop installed
Air con	Air conditioning
⊗	Heated indoor swimming pool
⊸	Outdoor swimming pool
⊸	Heated outdoor swimming pool
♫	Entertainment
Child facilities	Children's facilities (see page 8)
Xmas/New Year	Special programme for Christmas/New Year
⚲	Tennis court
♣	Croquet lawn
⚑	Golf course
CONF	Conference facilities
Thtr	Number of theatre style seats
Class	Number of classroom style seats
Board	Number of boardroom style seats
⊗	No dogs allowed (guide dogs for the blind and assist dogs should be allowed)
No children	Children cannot be accommodated
RS	Restricted opening time
Civ Wed	Establishment licensed for civil weddings (+ maximum number of guests at ceremony)
LB	Special leisure breaks available
Spa	Hotel has its own spa

Types of Hotel

The majority of establishments in this guide come under the category of Hotel; other categories are listed below.

TOWN HOUSE HOTEL A small, individual city or town centre property, which provides a high degree of personal service and privacy.

COUNTRY HOUSE HOTEL These are quietly located in a rural area.

SMALL HOTEL Has fewer than 20 bedrooms and is owner-managed.

METRO HOTEL A hotel in an urban location that does not offer an evening meal.

BUDGET HOTEL These are usually purpose-built modern properties offering inexpensive accommodation. Often located near motorways and in town or city centres.

RESTAURANT WITH ROOMS This category of accommodation is now assessed under the AA's Guest Accommodation scheme, therefore, although they continue to have an entry in this guide, we do not include their star rating. Most Restaurants with Rooms have been awarded AA Rosettes for their food and the rooms will meet the required AA standard. For more detailed information about any Restaurant with Rooms please consult *The AA Bed and Breakfast Guide* or see **www.theAA.com/bed-and-breakfast-and-hotel**.

A These are establishments that have not been inspected by the AA, but which have been inspected by the national tourist boards in Britain and Northern Ireland. An establishment marked as "Associate" has paid to belong to the AA Associate Hotel Scheme and therefore receives a limited entry in the guide. Descriptions of these hotels can be found on **theAA.com**.

U A small number of hotels in the guide have this symbol because their star classification was not confirmed at the time of going to press. This may be due to a change of ownership or because the hotel has only recently joined the AA rating scheme.

AA Advertised
These establishments are not rated or inspected by theAA, but are displayed for purely advertising purposes only.

O These hotels were not open at the time of going to press, but will open in late 2013, or in 2014.

Merit Score (%)

AA inspectors supplement their reports with an additional quality assessment of everything the hotel provides, including hospitality, based on their findings as a 'mystery guest'. This wider ranging quality assessment results in an overall Merit Score which is shown as a percentage beside the hotel name. When making your selection of hotel accommodation this enables you to see at a glance that a three star hotel with a Merit Score of 79% offers a higher standard overall than one in the same star classification but with a Merit Score of 69%. To gain AA recognition, a hotel must achieve a minimum score of 50%.

AA Awards

Every year the AA presents a range of awards to the finest AA-inspected and rated hotels from England, Scotland, Wales and the Republic of Ireland. The Hotel of the Year is our ultimate accolade and is awarded to those hotels that are recognised as outstanding examples in their field. Often innovative, the winning hotels always set high standards in hotel keeping. The winners for all the 2013–2014 awards are listed on pages 11–16.

Rooms

Each entry shows the total number of en suite rooms available (this total will include any annexe rooms). The total number may be followed by a breakdown of the type of rooms available, i.e. the number of annexe rooms; number of family rooms (fmly); number of ground-floor rooms (GF); number of rooms available for smokers.

Bedrooms in an annexe or extension are only noted if they are at least equivalent in quality to those in the main building, but facilities and prices may differ. In some hotels all bedrooms are in an annexe or extension.

If the hotel has highspeed or broadband internet access in the bedrooms, this may be chargeable.

Prices

Prices are per room per night and are provided by the hoteliers in good faith. These prices are indications and not firm quotations. * indicates 2013 prices. Many hotels have special rates so it is worth looking at their websites for the latest information.

Payment

Credit cards may be subject to a surcharge – check when booking if this is how you intend to pay.

Children

Child facilities may include baby intercom, baby sitting service, playroom, playground, laundry, drying/ironing facilities, cots, high chairs or special meals. In some hotels children can sleep in parents' rooms at no extra cost – check when booking.

If 'No children' is indicated, a minimum age may be also given e.g. No children 4yrs indicates that no children under 4 years of age would be accepted.

Some hotels, although accepting children, may not have any special facilities for them.

Leisure breaks (LB)

Some hotels offer special leisure breaks. The cost of these may differ from those quoted in this guide and availability may vary through the year.

Parking

We indicate the number of parking spaces available for guests. This may include covered parking. Please note that some hotels make a charge for the use of their car park.

Civil Weddings (Civ Wed)

Indicates that the establishment holds a civil wedding licence, and we indicate the number of guests that can be accommodated at the ceremony.

Conference Facilities

We include three types of meeting layouts – Theatre, Classroom and Boardroom style and include the maximum number of delegates for each. The price shown is the maximum 24-hour rate per delegate. Please note that as arrangements vary between a hotel and a business client, VAT may or may not be included in the price quoted in the guide. We also show if Wi-fi connectivity is available, but please check with the hotel that this is suitable for your requirements.

Dogs

Although many hotels allow dogs, they may be excluded from some areas of the hotel and some breeds, particularly those requiring an exceptional licence, may not be acceptable at all. Under the Equality Act 2010 access should be allowed for guide dogs and assistance dogs. Please check the hotel's policy when making your booking.

Entertainment (♫)

This indicates that live entertainment will be available at least once a week all year. Some hotels provide live entertainment only in summer or on special occasions.

Hotel logos

If an establishment belongs to a hotel group or consortium their logo is included in their entry (see pages 33–41).

Map references

Each town is given a map reference – the map page number and a two-figure map reference based on the National Grid. For example: **Map 05 SU 48**:

05 refers to the page number of the map section at back of the guide

SU is the National Grid lettered square (representing 100,000sq metres) in which the location will be found

4 is the figure reading across the top or bottom of the map page

8 is the figure reading down at each side of the map page

Restricted service

Some hotels have restricted service (RS) during quieter months, usually during the winter, and at this time some of the listed facilities will not be available. If your booking is out-of-season, check with the hotel and enquire specifically.

Smoking regulations

If a bedroom has been allocated for smokers, the hotel is obliged to clearly indicate that this is the case. If either the freedom to smoke, or to be in a non-smoking environment is important to you, please check with the hotel when you book.

Spa

For the purposes of this guide the word Spa in an entry indicates that the hotel has its own spa which is either managed by themselves or outsourced to an external management company. Facilities will vary but will include a minimum of two treatment rooms. Any specific details are also given, and these are as provided to us by the establishment (i.e. steam room, beauty therapy etc).

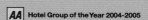

Hotels of the Year

ENGLAND

GRAVETYE MANOR
EAST GRINSTEAD, West Sussex page 159
★★★★ ⊚⊚⊚

Gravetye was built in 1598 by Richard Infield for his bride, Katherine; their carved portraits are still set over the fireplace. In 1884 the manor was bought by William Robinson, the notable gardener. He oversaw the creation of the stunning gardens, for which the property has become world-famous, and lived here until his death in 1935. In 1958, Peter Herbert arrived, and Gravetye Manor became a hotel. Over time it become one of the most renowned country house hotels in the country.

Peter Herbert retired in 2004, and in 2010 the hotel was bought by Jeremy Hosking who has invested heavily in the property, leading to a sympathetic restoration which has retained all the charm of the building, along with many original features.

The 17 beautifully appointed bedrooms have rich soft furnishings and delightful antiques. En suites are stylish, and boast luxury toiletries among other thoughtful extras. The stunning oak-panelled day rooms are filled with antiques. Roaring fires, fresh flowers and beautiful soft furnishings make the perfect backdrop for afternoon tea and pre-dinner drinks.

The oak panelled restaurant boasts 3 AA Rosettes and uses plenty of produce from the hotel's walled kitchen garden.

One outstanding feature of this Relais & Chateau property, is excellent customer care. Managing director, Andrew Thomason, has a wealth of experience in quality hotels, and leads his friendly team by example.

LONDON

DUKES HOTEL
LONDON SW1 page 272
★★★★★ ⊚⊚⊚

This St James' Hotel first opened its doors just over a century ago. Enjoying a discreet location in a private courtyard, it's only a stone's throw from Piccadilly, Green Park, Buckingham Palace and London's main shopping and theatre districts. Over the last 3 years, Dukes has been transformed physically, culturally and ethically, until it is a match for any top 5 Star hotel in London.

Bedrooms and suites have been carefully refurbished to reflect an elegant sophisticated design and also retain the classic vintage décor. Linens are crisp; throws and soft furnishings are in rich sophisticated colour schemes; and marble en suites boast an excellent range of luxury toiletries and extra touches.

Day rooms include a smart drawing room, where afternoon tea is served; a stunning Perrier-Jouët Lounge; Thirty Six by Nigel Mendham Restaurant, and the world-renowned Dukes Martini Bar. Links with James Bond creator, Ian Fleming, along with the skills and passion of award-winning bar tender, Alessandro Palazzi, have helped make Dukes Martini Bar one of the busiest and most popular bars in London. There's also a cognac and cigar garden where guests can retire, should they wish to smoke a cigar from the wide choice available. The hotel also has a small health club offering gym, steam room and beauty treatments.

Under the directorship of Debrah Dhugga, the hotel boasts an excellent team of staff who offer impeccable levels of service and professional but friendly hospitality.

SCOTLAND

CRINGLETIE HOUSE
PEEBLES page 540
★★★★ ⊕⊕⊕

This soft red stone baronial house is the perfect Country House hotel. Sitting in 28 acres of well tended grounds, it has its own walled kitchen garden and supposedly the oldest Yew hedge in Scotland.

The owners, Mrs & Mrs van Houdt, have completely refurbished the hotel to an excellent standard during their tenure. This includes installing a lift and creating facilities for less able guests as well as re-styling the 12 delightful bedrooms, while still retaining the character and original features.

Public areas are calm and relaxing, with roaring open fires adding an extra touch of comfort. The ceiling of the first floor dining room is hand painted with some very tasteful murals, purportedly by the original owner and continuously updated, and the room has views of the gardens. This formal style room is an elegant haven of tranquillity for food lovers.

Under the management of husband and wife team, Vivienne and Patric (they previously ran the Horseshoe Inn down the road, where they achieved huge acclaim), the levels of service at the hotel have been raised to a new level. Staff training is carried out each week by Vivienne and it's already paid dividends, while Patric's food is at the top end of 3 AA Rosette cooking, showing flair, imagination and some wonderful culinary skills.

Overall the hotel is well managed with outstanding quality and design and has also won awards for accessibility. It is a worthy contender for this award.

WALES

LLANGOED HALL
LLYSWEN page 580
★★★★ ⊕⊕

Set against the backdrop of the Black Mountains and the Wye Valley, Llangoed Hall has recently seen a dramatic transformation. The new owners have substantially invested in the property and not only returned it to its former glory, but also enhanced much of the history, style and ethos which Sir Bernard Ashley, widower of the designer, Laura Ashley, had lovingly produced.

Bedrooms have been painstakingly redesigned; new fabrics and décor, as well as furnishings, fixtures and fittings have been lovingly sought out to provide rooms with every modern comfort without losing the superior qualities and comforts that the house boasted in its heyday.

Day rooms too have undergone a transformation with every detail considered; there is new glassware, crockery, cutlery and fine linens, along with other necessary accessories, many from Royal Charter manufacturers.

The grounds and gardens have been given a complete refreshment, including a new drive (heated would you believe!), while careful planning and planting has provided a contemporary kitchen garden, and grounds now fit for the grandest expectations.

The directors have invested heavily in people as well. Nick Brodie is the new head chef, and a new front of house team is in place. Service and hospitality standards are excellent and Llangoed, is now once again back on the map as a great British country house hotel.

NORTHERN IRELAND

REPUBLIC OF IRELAND

THE MERCHANT HOTEL
BELFAST page 593
★★★★★ 85% ⊛⊛

This impressive hotel is a worthy first winner of AA Hotel of the Year for Northern Ireland.

Located in the historic Cathedral Quarter of the city centre of Belfast, this smart, stylish hotel used to be the Ulster Bank head office; more recently there has been a further extension to the building to add further bedrooms, spa and a jazz bar. Bedrooms come in two types, Victorian and Contemporary. The first room type is very traditional whilst the latter is more modern, and spacious. All rooms are beautifully decorated and sumptuous.

The Great Room is at the heart of the hotel and is stunning, with the original architecture all lovingly restored – the gold and deep red colour scheme – and the whole ambience of this regal room lends itself well to dinner and afternoon tea services. The cocktail bar is renowned for an amazing cocktail and drinks list and service there is impeccable. Burt's is a jazz bar with live jazz playing every weekend. If neither of these options appeals, there is a lively pub operation called The Cloth Ear, which is run separately to the main hotel. If arriving by car, valet parking is usefully provided with prompt efficiency.

The team are very hospitable and helpful and true to form in this friendly city, they are always willing to engage the guest in conversation.

CASTLEKNOCK HOTEL & COUNTRY CLUB
CASTLEKNOCK page 604
★★★★ 82% ⊛

Castleknock Hotel & Country Club is the perfect property for a wide variety of guests and patrons. It is an inviting and vibrant property, balancing conference, leisure and golf business, set in an idyllic location; 15 minutes from Dublin City and 25 minutes from Dublin Airport. There are 138 guest bedrooms including 114 standard guest bedrooms, 20 recently refurbished executive guest bedrooms and 4 suites.

A variety of restaurants and bars is presented, offering anything from a pasta dish in the contemporary Brasserie followed by a glass of wine in the open-plan modern Fionn Uisce Bar; to a perfectly cooked rump of Cooley lamb in the elegant award-winning Park Restaurant, preceded by a romantic cocktail in the stylish Lime Tree Bar.

The Tonic Health & Day Spa is a recent addition, offering guests an extensive range of therapies in luxurious treatment rooms. There's also an 18-metre swimming pool with great views of the golf course, lake and countryside. The centre has a baby pool, toddler pool, sauna, steam room and jacuzzi.

An 18-hole golf course is located on the grounds, and there are hi-tech meeting rooms with natural daylight, air-conditioning and a capacity for up to 500 delegates. Castleknock can accommodate over 400 for a large banquet in the main ballroom, and has catered for a wide variety of national and international sports teams.

Service is exceptional, with a natural and honest approach.

Hotel Group of the Year

MACDONALD HOTELS

Macdonald hotels comprise 45 properties located across the UK, each with its own individual charm and character. The company continues to focus on delivering quality accommodation and facilities and outstanding customer experience. Between them these 45 hotels have over 40 AA Rosettes.

Macdonald Hotels has also invested heavily in developing staff potential through training and personal development, and encourages hotels to work closely where they can with their local community and organizations.

ENGLAND

ANSTY, Warwickshire	Macdonald Ansty Hall
ASCOT, Berkshire	Macdonald Berystede Hotel & Spa
BATH, Somerset	Macdonald Bath Spa
BIRMINGHAM, West Midlands	Macdonald Burlington Hotel
BOTLEY, Hampshire	Macdonald Botley Park, Golf & Spa
CAMBERLEY, Surrey	Macdonald Frimley Hall Hotel & Spa
CHESTER, Cheshire	Macdonald New Blossoms Hotel
GRASMERE, Cumbria	Macdonald Swan Hotel
GUISBOROUGH, N Yorkshire	Gisborough Hall
HEMEL HEMPSTEAD, Hertfordshire	The Bobsleigh Hotel
LONGHORSLEY, Northumberland	Macdonald Linden Hall, Golf & Country Club
LYMINGTON, Hampshire	Macdonald Elmers Court Hotel & Resort
LYMM, Cheshire	The Lymm Hotel
MANCHESTER	Macdonald Townhouse Manchester
	Macdonald Manchester Hotel
MARLOW, Buckinghamshire	Macdonald Compleat Angler
OXFORD, Oxfordshire	Macdonald Randolph Hotel
PRESTON, Lancashire	Macdonald Tickled Trout
PUDDINGTON, Cheshire	Macdonald Craxton Wood Hotel
STRATFORD-UPON-AVON, Warwickshire	
	Macdonald Alveston Manor
	Macdonald Swan's Nest Hotel
TARPORLEY, Cheshire	Macdonald Portal Hotel Golf & Spa
WANSFORD, Cambridgeshire	The Haycock Hotel
WATERMILLOCK, Cumbria	Macdonald Leeming House
WHITCHURCH, Shropshire	Macdonald Hill Valley Spa, Hotel & Golf
WIGAN, Greater Manchester	Macdonald Kilhey Court Hotel
WINDERMERE, Cumbria	Macdonald Old England Hotel & Spa
WINDSOR, Berkshire	Macdonald Windsor Hotel
WOODSTOCK, Oxfordshire	Macdonald Bear Hotel

SCOTLAND

ABERFOYLE, Stirling	Macdonald Forest Hills Hotel & Resort
AVIEMORE, HIghland	Macdonald Highlands Hotel
EAST KILBRIDE, South Lanarkshire	Macdonald Crutherland House
EDINBURGH	The Roxburghe Hotel
	Macdonald Holyrood Hotel
INVERURIE, Aberdeenshire	Macdonald Pittodrie House
KINLOCH RANNOCH, Perth & Kinross	
	Macdonald Loch Rannoch Hotel
NORTH BERWICK, East Lothian	Macdonald Marine Hotel & Spa
PEEBLES, Scottish Borders	Macdonald Cardrona Hotel, Golf & Spa
POLMONT, Falkirk	Macdonald Inchyra Hotel and Spa
ST ANDREWS, Fife	Macdonald Rusacks Hotel
UPHALL, West Lothian	Macdonald Houstoun House

WALES

SWANSEA	The Dragon Hotel

Macdonald Compleat Angler, Marlow

Gisborough Hall, Guisborough

RED CARNATION HOTELS

THE
RED CARNATION
HOTEL COLLECTION

Red Carnation Hotels' mission statement is "To provide exceptional, memorable hospitality by meeting or exceeding guest expectations and creating an environment in our hotels where our guests, as well as our employees, refer to our hotels as their "home away from home".

This international hotel group is predominantly London based with six hotels in the capital; other UK properties include two in Dorset and two in Guernsey.

Red Carnation also won this award in 2007, but we consider them to be such strong and exceptional candidates that it was appropriate to give them the honour of this award a second time.

The Milestone Hotel, London

ENGLAND

EVERSHOT, DORSET	Summer Lodge Country House Hotel
	The Acorn Inn
LONDON	The Rubens at the Palace
	The Chesterfield Mayfair
	The Milestone Hotel
	The Montague on the Gardens
	No 41
	The Egerton House Hotel

CHANNEL ISLANDS

ST PETER PORT, GUERNSEY	The Old Government House Hotel & Spa
	The Duke of Richmond Hotel

The Chesterfield Mayfair, London

The Egerton House Hotel, London

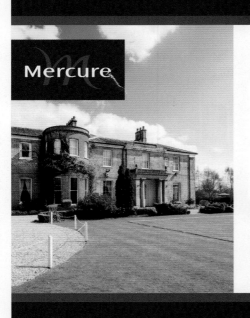

AA Assessment

In collaboration with VisitBritain, VisitScotland and VisitWales, the AA developed Common Quality Standards for inspecting and rating accommodation. These standards and rating categories are now applied throughout the British Isles.

Any hotel applying for AA recognition receives an unannounced visit from an AA inspector to check standards. AA inspectors pay as a guest for their inspection visit, they do not accept free hospitality of any kind. Although AA inspectors do not stay overnight at Budget Hotels, they do carry out regular visits to verify standards and procedures.

A guide to some of the general expectations for each star classification is as follows:

★ One Star

Polite, courteous staff providing a relatively informal yet competent style of service, available during the day and evening to receive guests

- At least one designated eating area open to residents for breakfast
- If dinner is offered it should be on at least five days a week, with last orders no earlier than 6.30pm
- Television in bedroom
- Majority of rooms en suite, bath or shower room available at all times

★★ Two Star

As for one star, plus

- At least one restaurant or dining room open to residents for breakfast (and for dinner at least five days a week)
- Last orders for dinner no earlier than 7pm
- En suite or private bath or shower and WC

★★★ Three Star

- Management and staff smartly and professionally presented and usually uniformed
- A dedicated receptionist on duty at peak times
- At least one restaurant or dining room open to residents and non-residents for breakfast and dinner whenever the hotel is open
- Last orders for dinner no earlier than 8pm
- Remote-control television, direct-dial telephone
- En suite bath or shower and WC

★★★★ Four Star

- A formal, professional staffing structure with smartly presented, uniformed staff anticipating and responding to your needs or requests. Usually spacious, well-appointed public areas
- Reception staffed 24 hours by well-trained staff
- Express checkout facilities where appropriate
- Porterage available on request
- Night porter available
- At least one restaurant open to residents and non-residents for breakfast and dinner seven days per week, and lunch to be available in a designated eating area
- Last orders for dinner no earlier than 9pm
- En suite bath with fixed overhead shower and WC

AA Rosette Awards

Out of the many thousands of restaurants in the UK, the AA identifies over 2,000 as the best. The following is an outline of what to expect from restaurants with AA Rosette Awards.

⊛ Excellent local restaurants serving food prepared with care, understanding and skill, using good quality ingredients.

⊛⊛ The best local restaurants, which aim for and achieve higher standards, better consistency and where a greater precision is apparent in the cooking. There will be obvious attention to the selection of quality ingredients.

⊛⊛⊛ Outstanding restaurants that demand recognition well beyond their local area.

⊛⊛⊛⊛ Amongst the very best restaurants in the British Isles, where the cooking demands national recognition.

⊛⊛⊛⊛⊛ The finest restaurants in the British Isles, where the cooking stands comparison with the best in the world.

★★★★★ Five Star

- Luxurious accommodation and public areas with a range of extra facilities. First time guests shown to their bedroom
- Multilingual service
- Guest accounts well explained and presented
- Porterage offered
- Guests greeted at hotel entrance, full concierge service provided
- At least one restaurant open to residents and non-residents for all meals seven days per week
- Last orders for dinner no earlier than 10pm
- High-quality menu and wine list
- Evening service to turn down the beds. Remote-control television, direct-dial telephone at bedside and desk, a range of luxury toiletries, bath sheets and robes. En suite bathroom incorporating fixed overhead shower and WC

★ Inspectors' Choice

Each year we select the best hotels in each rating. These hotels stand out as the very best in the British Isles, regardless of style. Red Star hotels appear in highlighted panels throughout the guide. Inspectors' Choice Restaurants with Rooms are establishments that have been awarded the highest accommodation rating under the AA Guest Accommodation scheme.

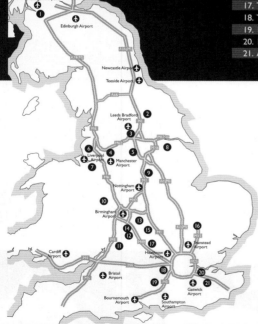

Additional information

Hints on booking your stay

It's always worth booking as early as possible, particularly for the peak holiday period from the beginning of June to the end of September. Bear in mind that Easter and other public holidays may be busy too and in some parts of Scotland, the ski season is a peak holiday period.

Some hotels will ask for a deposit or full payment in advance, especially for one-night bookings. Some hotels charge half-board (bed, breakfast and dinner) whether you require the meals or not, while others may only accept full-board bookings. Not all hotels will accept advance bookings for bed and breakfast, overnight or short stays. Some will not take reservations from mid week.

Once a booking is confirmed, let the hotel know at once if you are unable to keep your reservation. If the hotel cannot re-let your room you may be liable to pay about two-thirds of the room price (a deposit will count towards this payment).

In Britain a legally binding contract is made when you accept an offer of accommodation, either in writing or by telephone, and illness is not accepted as a release from this contract. You are advised to take out insurance against possible cancellation, for example AA Single Trip Insurance (telephone 0800 975 5819).

Booking online

Locating and booking somewhere to stay can be a time-consuming process, but you can search quickly and easily online for a place that best suits your needs. Simply visit **theAA.com** to search for full details of over 5,700 quality rated hotels and B&Bs in Great Britain and Ireland. Check availability and click on the 'Book it' button.

Prices

The AA encourages the use of the Hotel Industry Voluntary Code of Booking Practice, which aims to ensure that guests know how much they will have to pay and what services and facilities are included, before entering a financially binding agreement. If the price has not previously been confirmed in writing, guests should be given a card stipulating the total obligatory charge when they register at reception.

Facilities for disabled guests

The Equality Act 2010 provides legal rights for disabled people including access to goods, services and facilities, and means that service providers may have to consider making adjustments to their premises. For more information about the Act see: https://www.gov.uk/government/policies/creating-a-fairer-and-more-equal-society. or https://www.gov.uk/definition-of-disability-under-equality-act-2010

The establishments in this guide should be aware of their obligations under the Act. We recommend that you always

Bank and Public Holidays 2014

New Year's Day	1st January
Good Friday	18th April
Easter Monday	21st April
Early May Bank Holiday	5th May
Spring Bank Holiday	26th May
Summer Bank Holiday (Scotland)	5th August
Summer Bank Holiday	25th August
St Andrew's Day (Scotland)	30th November
Christmas Day	25th December
Boxing Day	26th December

telephone in advance to ensure that the establishment you have chosen has appropriate facilities.

Please note: AA inspectors are not accredited to make inspections under the National Accessibility Scheme. We indicate in entries if an establishment has ground floor rooms, walk-in showers and whether the hotel has a hearing loop system; and if a hotel tells us that they have disabled facilities this is included in the description.

Licensing Laws

Licensing laws differ in England, Wales, Scotland, the Republic of Ireland, the Isle of Man, the Isles of Scilly and the Channel Islands. Public houses are generally open from mid morning to early afternoon, and from about 6 or 7pm until 11pm, although closing times may be earlier or later and some pubs are open all afternoon. Unless otherwise stated, establishments listed are licensed to serve alcohol. Hotel residents can obtain alcoholic drinks at all times, if the licensee is prepared to serve them. Non-residents eating at the hotel restaurant can have drinks with meals. Children under 14 may be excluded from bars where no food is served. Those under 18 may not purchase or consume alcoholic drinks.

Club licence means that drinks are served to club members only, 48 hours must lapse between joining and ordering.

The Fire Precautions Act does not apply to the Channel Islands, Republic of Ireland, or the Isle of Man, which have their own rules. As far as we are aware, all hotels listed in Great Britain have applied for and not been refused a fire certificate.

For information on Ireland see page 592.

Island
Getaways

BY MARIE-CLAIRE DILLON

Think of islands – think beaches, sea and stunning scenery. Forget tropical heat, coconuts and being stranded like Robinson Crusoe, some of the most beautiful islands are closer than you might imagine. The British Isles are made up of somewhere between 1,000 and 5,000 islands (depending on how you define one) from Scotland's 841 sq-mile Isle of Lewis and Harris to tiny uninhabited islets just off shore. In fact, only around 140 of the islands are populated (the majority are Scottish), but many that are inhabited are home to AA-rated hotels, some with full leisure facilities, luxury accommodation and AA Rosette awarded restaurants, providing great options for your perfect island getaway.

Easy Escapes

These days, you can even reach some islands by car. The largest Welsh island, the Isle of Angelsey, is connected to north-west Wales by the Britannia Bridge, while a road bridge also links the mainland village of Kyle to the Isle of Skye – although you may still prefer to travel the traditional way, by boat. Hayling Island, east of Portsmouth on England's south coast, is only a 320-yard drive over the water. The five-star Isle of Eriska Hotel, Spa & Golf in the Scottish Highlands is located on its own private tidal island, connected by a short road bridge to the mainland.

Skye draws visitors from far and wide, who come to appreciate the rugged beauty of the Cuillin mountains, the mild climate and the Gaelic language. Some revel in climbing the peaks, land sailing or going on energetic walks, while others simply relax on the beach, admire the golden eagles, take in the panoramic views or play a spot of golf. Skye's Duisdale House Hotel, built in 1865 as a private home and then used as a hunting lodge, is now a contemporary boutique hotel attracting visitors from both the UK and abroad with its two-AA Rosette restaurant, 35 acres of gardens and luxuriously furnished rooms. Most guests

Duisdale Hotel and Gardens, Isle of Skye

take advantage of the fine dining during their stay, but the restaurant and bar are well patronised by locals, too. Known for its hospitality and high levels of customer care, almost all the Duisdale's staff are local to Skye and pass on their enthusiasm for the island to their visitors. Owners Anne Gracie and Ken Gunn go one step further to please their guests at the Duisdale and the nearby Toravaig House Hotel (which they also own), by offering unique sailing experiences: "We have our own luxury yacht, Solus a Chuain, which is available exclusively for guests of both hotels to enjoy day trips around the small Hebridean islands off Skye." Anne and Ken themselves act as captain and crew, making the most of the relatively short peak season to interact with their guests.

The Georgian Bulkeley Hotel on the Isle of Anglesey enjoys a prime location in the heart of the 13th-century town of Beaumaris. This is another island offering breathtaking mountain vistas, and from the Bulkeley lucky guests can look upon the Menai Strait and Snowdonia National Park over the water. Surrounded by the Irish Sea, Anglesey's rural coastline is an Area of Outstanding Natural Beauty and the lovely sandy beach at Beaumaris is just yards from the hotel. During your visit, you might want to explore the World Heritage Site of Beaumaris Castle, try your hand at sea fishing or take afternoon tea in the Bulkeley's garden.

A Little More Effort

England's largest island and its second-most populated is the Isle of Wight, off the south coast and accessible by ferry, hovercraft or catamaran from Lymington, Southampton and Portsmouth, with journey times ranging from 10 to 40 minutes. Holiday-makers are attracted to the numerous beaches, sightings of red squirrels and the 67-mile Coastal Path, as well as the regattas at Cowes, and Blackgang Chine, one of the world's oldest theme parks. On the island's south side is the Victorian spa town of Ventnor, which overlooks the English Channel and benefits from a mild maritime climate, enabling subtropical plants to flourish. The coastal town's Royal Hotel has been welcoming guests since 1832, including Queen Victoria, who used to take afternoon tea here when she wasn't at Osborne House. Full of character. The Royal has a mainly British clientele, catering for families and couples, and is busiest during the summer months. The hotel's two-AA Rosette Appuldurcombe Restaurant makes use of local produce and fresh fish from the bay to entice both guests and non-residents, while the Riviera Terrace, perched on the cliff-top gardens with stunning views of the sea, is perfect for an alfresco lunch or picnic. The Royal also sees itself as part of the local community, supporting local events and providing meeting facilities for the island's businesses.

A Real Retreat

The Isles of Scilly form an archipelago 28 miles from Land's End on the south-western tip of the Cornish peninsula and enjoy one of the warmest climates in the UK. They are known as a paradise for native and rare migrant birds, including puffins, stonechats and storm petrels. The smallest inhabited island is Bryher (0.5 sq miles) and can be reached by flying (by plane or helicopter) or sailing to St. Mary's or Tresco and then boarding a connecting boat. The rugged island is crisscrossed with paths and is home to deserted white sandy beaches. Popular activities here include island hopping, watersports and snorkelling in the clear waters. Set in a picturesque and secluded cove, the Hell Bay (open Mar-

Oct) is the Scillies' highest rated hotel, providing an oasis of calm with its relaxed atmosphere, Caribbean-style decor and spa treatments. The Hell Bay features a heated outdoor swimming pool, tennis court, large terrace and three-AA Rosette restaurant. The majority of patrons are from the UK – predominantly families during peak season and couples at other times; being a seasonal business, the staff live in hotel accommodation or elsewhere on the island.

Under 100 miles from England's south coast and about 30 miles from Normandy, the Channel Islands are accessible by ferry from France or the UK, or by plane from many British and European airports. The Old Government House Hotel & Spa in Guernsey's capital of St Peter Port dates to 1796 when it was the official residence of the Governor of the Bailiwick. A hotel since 1858, the business benefits from its historic location, the wealth of local produce and seafood, fresh sea air and a varied landscape of beaches, cliffs and woodland. As well as an outdoor pool and health club, the Old Government House offers a spa, a two-AA Rosette restaurant and rooms with sea views. Andrew Chantrell, the General Manager, explains: "Guernsey offers so much in the way of history, heritage and culture, which is a massive draw to visitors. We are very lucky that our hotel appeals to a wide number of different markets, from the business traveller to leisure guests and families looking for a 'home away from home' and the opportunity to relax, as well as explore all that Guernsey has to offer." Almost three-quarters of guests are from the UK, with the rest mainly visiting from Europe. With its narrow roads and low speed limits, Guernsey is a safe and laid-back destination for visitors. Andrew also believes that the hotel has an important part to play in the local community: "... whether it be by supporting local charities, opening up to school and college students for them find out more about careers in hospitality, or by simply playing an active role in local groups and associations."

Relax and Unwind

Many of the UK's islands are self-sufficient, close-knit communities whose economies are often heavily reliant on tourism. Island hotels can be at the mercy of the unpredictable British weather and the short summer season, but islands are, on the whole, an attractive year-round option. Visitors to islands are united in their desire to experience something a bit different and escape from urban life for a few days, to get away from the hum of motorways and instead be lured by the promise of peace and quiet, beautiful landscapes, nature and being close to the sea. The simple act of staying on an island, even one close to home, can make you feel like you're a world away.

The Hell Bay, Isles of Scilly

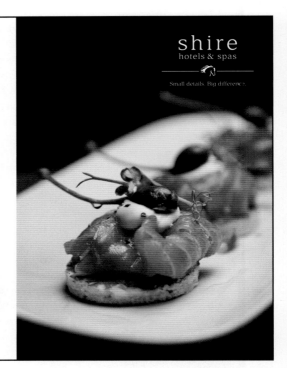

Perfect breaks
with Menzies Hotels

From country breaks to city breaks, golf breaks to spa breaks.
Whatever break you're booking, a stay in a Menzies Hotel
will be unforgettable.

15 distinctive different hotels around the UK offering luxurious surroundings,
excellent facilities with some of the country's biggest attractions close by.

Book online for our best rate guarantee, see our website for further details
www.menzieshotels.co.uk/about/best-rate-guarantee

www.menzieshotels.co.uk

MenziesHotels
You're in a good place

Proud to sponsor
WE ARE
MACMILLAN.
CANCER SUPPORT

Aberdeen
Glasgow
Irvine
Derby
Stourport on Severn
Birmingham
Cambridge
Flitwick
Stratford-upon-Avon
Luton
Swindon
London
Gatwick
Bournemouth

Hotel Groups Information

APEX HOTELS	**Apex Hotels** A group of contemporary four star hotels. One in Dundee, four in Edinburgh and three in London. Spa and gym facilities are available at a number of the hotels.	*0845 365 0000* *www.apexhotels.co.uk*
"bespoke" HOTELS	**Bespoke** A growing group of personally managed three and four star hotels in leisure locations.	*0844 815 9833* *www.bespokehotels.com*
Best Western	**BEST WESTERN** Britain's largest consortia group has over 280 independently owned and managed hotels, modern and traditional, in the two, three and four star range. Many have leisure facilities and rosette awards.	*08457 76 76 76* *www.bestwestern.co.uk*
Best Western PREMIER	**BEST WESTERN Premier** These hotels are selected for their beautiful settings, range of facilities and enhanced levels of service. There are currently 7 BEST WESTERN Great Britain hotels that have achieved Premier status. These join over 45 BEST WESTERN Premier accredited hotels across Europe and Asia.	*08457 76 76 76* *www.bestwestern.co.uk*
Best Western PLUS	**Best Western Plus** 13 independently owned and managed hotels that offer that little something extra in the three and four star range. Some of these hotels have AA Rosette awards.	*08457 76 76 76* *www.bestwestern.co.uk*
Bewleys Hotels.com	**Bewley's Hotels** Part of the Moran Hotel Group. A privately owned group of high quality, contemporary three star hotels in key locations in the UK and Ireland.	*0845 234 5959* *www.bewleyshotels.com*
Brend Hotels	**Brend** A privately owned group of 11 three and four star hotels in Devon and Cornwall.	*01271 344 496* *www.brend-hotels.co.uk*
Campanile	**Campanile** An American owned and French managed company, Campanile has 17 properties in the UK offering modern accommodation in budget hotels.	*www.campanile.com*
CHOICE HOTELS EUROPE	**Choice** Choice has four different brands in the UK: Clarion and Quality Hotels are three and four star hotels, Comfort Inns are two and three star hotels, and Sleep Inns are budget hotels.	*0800 44 44 44* *www.choicehotelseurope.com*
CLASSIC BRITISH HOTELS	**Classic British Hotels** An exclusive upmarket collection of four star and quality three star independent hotels throughout the UK, noted for its comforts, fine dining, spas, golf and event facilities.	*0845 070 7090* *www.classicbritishhotels.com*
CLASSIC LODGES	**Classic Lodges** A small group of three and four star hotels.	*0845 603 8892* *www.classiclodges.co.uk*
MILLENNIUM HOTELS AND RESORTS MILLENNIUM · COPTHORNE	**Copthorne** Part of the Millennium and Copthorne group, with 12 three and four star hotels in primary provincial locations as well as London.	*0800 41 47 41* *www.millenniumhotels.com*
Cotswold Inns & Hotels	**Cotswold Inns & Hotels** Charming three and four star small hotels located in the Cotswolds.	*www. cotswold-inns-hotels.co.uk*

Hotel Groups Information *continued*

CROWNE PLAZA HOTELS & RESORTS	**Crowne Plaza** Four star hotels predominantly found in key city centre locations.	*0871 423 4876* *www.crowneplaza.co.uk*
DAYS INN	**Days Inn** Good quality modern budget hotels with good coverage across the UK.	*0800 028 0400* *www.daysinn.com*
DE VERE Hotels & Resorts	**De Vere Hotels & Resorts** A group of four star hotels with good coverage across the UK.	*0845 375 2808* *www.devere.co.uk*
EDEN HOTEL COLLECTION	**Eden Hotel Collection** A privately owned collection of individual hotels, featuring award winning dining in quality surroundings.	*0845 351 0980* *www.edenhotelcollection.com*
English Lakes Hotels Resorts & Venues	**English Lakes Hotels** A collection of individually styled four star hotels located in and around the Lake District.	*015394 33773* *www.englishlakes.co.uk*
EXCLUSIVE HOTELS	**Exclusive Hotels** A small privately owned group of luxury five and four star hotels, all located in the south of England.	*01276 471 774* *www.exclusivehotels.co.uk*
FBD Hotels & Resorts	**FBD Hotels & Resorts** An Irish owned and operated group offering quality hotels in convenient locations.	*353 (0)1 428 2400* *www.fdbhotels.com*
fOCUS hotels	**Focus Hotels** A group of three star hotels in both city and country locations across England. All offer Wi-fi and a number have spa facilities.	*0844 225 1625* *www.focushotels.co.uk*
FOUR PILLARS HOTELS	**Four Pillars Hotels** A group of mainly four star hotels located in Oxfordshire and Gloucestershire. Most hotels have leisure facilities and all offer free Wi-Fi.	*0800 374 692* *www.four-pillars.co.uk*
GUOMAN HOTELS	**Guoman Hotels** A collection of large hotels in London, all four star, with the exception of The Royal Horseguards which has five stars.	*www.gouman.com*
Hallmark	**Hallmark Hotels** A collection of seven hotels that provide comfortable accommodation; some have leisure facilities.	*0113 307 6760* *www.hallmarkhotels.co.uk*
Hand PICKED HOTELS	**Hand Picked Hotels** A group of 17 predominantly four star, high quality country house hotels, with a real emphasis on quality food. Some provide stylish spa facilities.	*0845 458 0901* *www.handpickedhotels.co.uk*
HB HILLBROOKE HOTELS	**Hillbrooke Hotels** A growing portfolio of hotels and inns under the banner 'Quirky Luxury'. Excellent locations, comfortable surroundings, relaxed informal service.	*hillbrookehotels.co.uk*
Holiday Inn	**Holiday Inn** A major international group with many hotels across the UK.	*0871 423 4896* *www.holidayinn.co.uk*
Holiday Inn Express	**Holiday Inn Express** A major international hotel brand with over 100 hotels across the UK.	*www.hiexpress.co.uk*
Hotel du Vin & Bistro	**Hotel du Vin** A small expanding group of high quality four star hotels, that places a strong emphasis on its destination restaurant concept and appealing menus.	*0845 365 4438* *www.hotelduvin.com*
ibis	**Ibis** A growing chain of modern budget hotels with properties across the UK.	*www.ibishotel.com*

WHAT YOU EXPECTED:

WHAT YOU DID NOT:

MERCURE WHITE HART SALISBURY

DISCOVER
MERCURE

Mercure

LE CLUB ACCOR
HOTELS

JOIN OUR GLOBAL LOYALTY PROGRAM
AT ACCORHOTELS.COM

MERCURE.COM
OVER 70 HOTELS IN THE UK
AND 700 WORLDWIDE.

Hotel Groups Information *continued*

THE INDEPENDENTS HOTEL ASSOCIATION	**The Independents** A consortium of independently owned, mainly two, three and four star hotels across Britain.	0844 800 9965 www.theindependents.co.uk
IRELAND'S BLUE BOOK	**Ireland's Blue Book** A collection of country houses, historic hotels, castles and restaurants throughout Ireland.	00 353 1 676 9914 www.irelands-blue-book.ie
IRISH COUNTRY HOTELS	**Irish Country Hotels** A collection of family-run hotels, located all across Ireland.	00 353 1 295 8900 (local) 0818 281 281 www.irishcountryhotels.com
LAKE DISTRICT HOTELS	**Lake District Hotels** A small collection of hotels situated in some of the most beautiful parts of the Lake District countryside and in Lakeland towns.	0800 840 1240 www.lakedistricthotels.net
LEGACY HOTELS	**Legacy Hotels** A small group of three and four star hotels growing its coverage across the UK.	0844 411 9011 www.legacy-hotels.co.uk
Leisureplex	**Leisureplex** A group of 20 two star hotels located in many popular seaside resorts.	08451 305 888 www.leisureplex.co.uk
MACDONALD HOTELS & RESORTS	**Macdonald** A large group of predominantly four star hotels, both traditional and modern in style and located across the UK. Many hotels enjoy rural settings and state-of-the-art spa facilities	0844 879 9000 www.macdonaldhotels.co.uk
Malmaison	**Malmaison** A growing brand of modern, luxurious city centre hotels that provide deeply comfortable bedrooms, exciting restaurants and carefully selected wine lists.	0845 365 4247 www.malmaison.com
MANOR HOUSE HOTELS	**Manor House** Located throughout Ireland, this group offers a selection of independent, high quality country and manor house hotels.	00 353 1 295 8900 (local) 0818 281 281 www.manorhousehotels.com
Marriott.	**Marriott** This international brand has four and five star hotels in primary locations. Most are modern and have leisure facilities with a focus on activities such as golf.	00800 1927 1927 www.marriott.co.uk
MAYBOURNE HOTEL GROUP	**Maybourne Hotels** A hotel group representing the prestigious London five star hotels – The Berkeley, Claridge's and The Connaught.	020 7107 8800 (Head Office) www.maybourne.com
MenziesHotels	**Menzies Hotels** A group of predominantly four star hotels in key locations across the UK.	0845 850 3013 www.menzieshotels.co.uk
Mercure	**Mercure Hotels** A large group of three and four star hotels throughout England, Scotland and Wales.	0871 663 0627 www.mercure.com
MILLENNIUM MILLENNIUM · COPTHORNE	**Millennium** Part of the Millennium and Copthorne group with 7 high-quality four star hotels, mainly in central London.	0800 41 47 41 www.millenniumhotels.com
MORAN HOTELS	**Moran Hotels** A privately owned group with 4 four star Moran Hotels, and 6 three star Bewley's Hotels. All have strategic locations in the UK and Ireland.	00 353 1 459 3650 www.moranhotels.com
NEW FOREST HOTELS	**New Forest Hotels** A collection of properties situated in the New Forest National Park, each with its own distinct character. All have an AA Rosette award for culinary excellence.	0800 44 44 41 www.newforesthotels.co.uk

Hotel Groups Information *continued*

Novotel Part of French group Accor, Novotel provides mainly modern three star hotels and a new generation of four star hotels in key locations throughout the UK.	0871 663 0626 www.novotel.com	
Old English Inns A large collection of former coaching inns that are mainly graded at two and three stars.	0845 608 6040 www.oldenglishinns.co.uk	
Park Inn by Radisson A fresh, energetic hotel group suitable for business and leisure guests, offering comfortable accommodation and excellent meeting and conference facilities.	www.parkinn.co.uk	
Park Plaza Hotels A European based group increasing its presence in the UK with quality four star hotels in primary locations.	0800 169 6128 www.parkplaza.com	
Peel Hotels A group of mainly three and four star hotels located across the UK.	0845 601 7335 www.peelhotels.co.uk	
Premier Inns The largest and fastest growing budget hotel group with over 600 hotels offering quality, modern accommodation in key locations throughout the UK and Ireland. Each hotel is located adjacent to a family restaurant and bar.	0871 527 8000 www.premierinn.com	
Pride of Britain A consortium of privately owned high quality British hotels, often in the country house style, many of which have been awarded Red Stars and AA Rosettes.	0800 089 3929 www.prideofbritainhotels.com	
Prima Hotels A small hotel group which currently has 6 four star hotels. Five hotels are in England and one is in Scotland.	www.primahotels.co.uk	
Principal Hayley A collection of luxury properties from Victorian grandeur to iconic city centre hotels.	0844 824 6171 www.ph-hotels.com	
Puma Hotels Formerly Barcelo UK, Puma Hotels Collection operates 20 four star hotels in locations across the UK.	0800 652 8413 www.pumahotels.co.uk	
QHotels A hotel group with 21 individually styled four star hotels across the UK.	0845 241 9783 www.qhotels.co.uk	
Radisson Blu A recognised international brand increasing its hotels in the UK and Ireland, and offering high-quality four star hotels in key locations. (Formerly known as Radisson SAS).	0800 374 411 www.radissonblu.com	
Ramada A large hotel group with many properties throughout the UK in three brands – Ramada Plaza, Ramada and Ramada Hotel & Resort.	0845 2070 100 www.ramada.co.uk	

Hotel Groups Information *continued*

THE RED CARNATION HOTEL COLLECTION	**Red Carnation** A unique collection of prestigious four and five star hotels in Dorset and the Channel Islands providing luxurious surroundings and attentive service.	*www.redcarnationhotels.com*
RELAIS & CHATEAUX	**Relais et Chateaux** An international consortium of rural, privately owned hotels, mainly in the country house style.	*00800 2000 0002* *www.relaischateaux.com*
RENAISSANCE. HOTELS & RESORTS	**Renaissance** One of the Marriott brands, Renaissance is a collection of individual hotels offering comfortable guest rooms, quality cuisine and good levels of service.	*00800 1927 1927* *www.marriott.co.uk*
RICHARDSON HOTELS	**Richardson Hotels** A group of 5 three and four star hotels located in Cornwall and Devon, plus one hotel in Lancashire.	*www.richardsonhotels.co.uk*
RF THE ROCCO FORTE COLLECTION	**Rocco Forte Hotels** A small group of luxury hotels spread across Europe. Owned by Sir Rocco Forte, with three hotels in the UK, all situated in major city locations.	*0870 458 4040* *www.roccofortehotels.com*
	Scotland's Hotels of Distinction A consortium of independent Scottish hotels in the three and four star range.	*www.hotels-of-distinction.com*
Sheraton	**Sheraton** Represented in the UK by a small number of four and five star hotels in London and Scotland.	*www.starwoodhotels.com*
shire hotels & spas	**Shire** A small group of four star hotels which feature spa facilities and well-equipped bedrooms ideal for both business and leisure guests.	*www.shirehotels.com*
SLH slh.com	**Small Luxury Hotels of the World** Part of an international consortium of mainly privately owned hotels, often in the country house style.	*0800 037 1888* *www.slh.com*
T A HOTEL COLLECTION	**TA Hotel Collection** A privately owned collection of three and four star hotels across Suffolk	*01728 452176* *www.tahotelcollection.co.uk*
THE CIRCLE	**The Circle** A consortium of independently owned, mainly two and three star hotels, across Britain.	*0845 345 1965* *www.circlehotels.co.uk*
thistle	**Thistle** A large group of 31 hotels across the UK with a significant number in London.	*0871 376 9099* *www.thistle.com*
Warner Leisure Hotels JUST FOR GROWN-UPS	**Warner Leisure Hotels** A collection of 3 and 4 star country hotels and villages, exclusively for adults. Renowned for their restaurants, daytime activities and live entertainment.	*0844 871 4523* *www.warnerleisurehotels.co.uk*
WELCOMEBREAK	**Welcome Break** Good quality, modern, budget accommodation at motorway services.	*01908 299 700* *www.welcomebreak.co.uk*

Great hotels, great locations

Find yours...

You choose: From Brighton to Edinburgh, select from 31 ideally located hotels

London calling: Our 9 hotels in central London all include free Wi-Fi

New look: We've invested in refurbishment, from bedrooms to modern lounges

Simply delicious: New menu, seasonal ingredients, taste the difference

Travel well, visit **thistle.com**

thistle

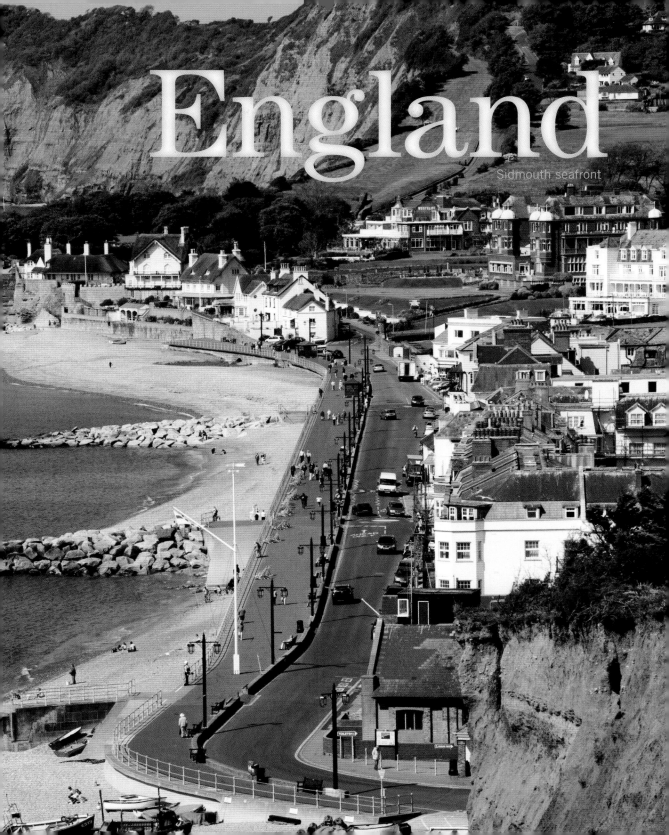

England

Sidmouth seafront

A

Oxford Abingdon Four Pillars Hotel

★★★ 77% HOTEL

☎ 01235 553456
Marcham Rd OX14 1TZ
e-mail: abingdon@four-pillars.co.uk
web: www.four-pillars.co.uk/abingdon
dir: A34 at junct with A415, in Abingdon, turn right at rdbt, hotel on right

On the outskirts of Abingdon, this busy commercial hotel is well located for access to major roads. The bedrooms are comfortable and well equipped with extras such as safes and trouser presses. All day refreshments are offered in the stylish lounge and conservatory.

Rooms 66 (5 fmly) (32 GF) ⚡ **Facilities** FTV Wi-fi ⌕
Xmas New Year **Conf** Class 80 Board 40 Thtr 140
Parking 85 **Notes** ⊗ Civ Wed 120

Upper Reaches Hotel

★★★ 72% HOTEL

☎ 01235 522536 & 462143
Thames St OX14 3JA
e-mail:
reservations@upperreaches-abingdon.co.uk
web: www.upperreaches-abingdon.co.uk
dir: From A415 in Abingdon follow Dorchester signs, turn left just before bridge over Thames

Built from Abingdon Abbey's old corn mill, the hotel enjoys an attractive location. It offers well-appointed rooms, individually styled and with a wide range of amenities. The aptly named Millrace Restaurant is situated in the ancient mill house which still features a working wheel, and the river can be seen flowing beneath.

Rooms 31 (5 GF) **Facilities** FTV Fishing Xmas New Year **Parking** 60 **Notes** ⊗

Premier Inn Abingdon

BUDGET HOTEL

☎ 0871 527 8014
Marcham Rd OX14 1AD
web: www.premierinn.com
dir: On A415. Approx 0.5m from A34 at Abingdon South junct (Marcham Interchange)

High quality, budget accommodation ideal for both families and business travellers. Spacious, en suite bedrooms feature tea and coffee making facilities, and Freeview TV in most hotels. Internet access and Wi-fi are available for a small fee. The adjacent family restaurant features a wide and varied menu. See also the Hotel Groups pages.

Rooms 27

Mercure Blackburn Dunkenhalgh Hotel & Spa

★★★★ 73% HOTEL

☎ 01254 398021
Blackburn Rd, Clayton-le-Moors BB5 5JP
e-mail: H6617@accor.com
web: www.mercure.com
dir: M65 junct 7, left at rdbt, left at lights, hotel 100yds on left

Set in delightfully tended grounds yet only a stone's throw from the M65, this fine mansion has conference and banqueting facilities that attract the wedding and corporate markets. The state-of-the-art thermal suite allows guests to relax and take life easy. Bedrooms come in a variety of styles, sizes and standards; some are located away from the main hotel building.

Rooms 175 (119 annexe) (36 fmly) (43 GF) ⚡
Facilities Spa STV Wi-fi HL ☃ Gym Thermal suite Aerobics studio Xmas New Year **Conf** Class 200 Board 100 Thtr 400 **Services** Lift **Parking** 400
Notes ⊗ Civ Wed 300

Sparth House Hotel

★★★ 74% SMALL HOTEL

☎ 01254 872263
Whalley Rd, Clayton Le Moors BB5 5RP
e-mail: mail.sparth@btinternet.com
web: www.sparthhousehotel.co.uk
dir: A6185 to Clitheroe along Dunkenhalgh Way, right at lights onto A678, left at next lights, A680 to Whalley. Hotel on left after 2 sets of lights

This 18th-century listed building sits in three acres of well-tended gardens. Bedrooms come in a choice of styles, from the cosy modern rooms ideal for business guests, to the spacious classical rooms - including one with furnishings from one of the great cruise liners. Public rooms feature a panelled restaurant and plush lounge bar.

Rooms 16 (3 fmly) **S** £69.70-£80; **D** £91.50-£110 (incl. bkfst)* **Facilities** FTV Wi-fi **Conf** Class 50 Board 40 Thtr 160 Del from £95 to £105* **Parking** 50 **Notes** ⊗ Civ Wed

ADDINGHAM
West Yorkshire   Map 19 SE05

Craven Heifer

◉◉ RESTAURANT WITH ROOMS

☎ 01943 830106
Main St LS29 0PL
e-mail: info@wellfedpubs.co.uk

The Craven Heifer is located close to the town of Skipton and boasts themed rooms based on Yorkshire celebrities. The bar is a traditional "Dalesway" Inn with stone and oak floors, open fires, leather seating, real ale and outstanding food with a wine list to complement as well. A warm and very friendly welcome from well informed staff is guaranteed.

Rooms 7

ALBURGH
Norfolk   Map 13 TM28

The Dove Restaurant with Rooms

◉◉ RESTAURANT WITH ROOMS

☎ 01986 788315
Holbrook Hill IP20 0EP
e-mail: info@thedoverestaurant.co.uk
dir: Between Harleston & Bungay at junct A143 & B1062

A warm welcome awaits at this restaurant with rooms. Bedrooms are pleasantly decorated, furnished with pine pieces and have modern facilities. Public rooms include a lounge area with a small bar, and a smart restaurant with well-spaced tables and excellent food.

Rooms 2 (1 fmly)

ALCESTER
Warwickshire   Map 10 SP05

Kings Court Hotel

★★★ 77% HOTEL

☎ 01789 763111
Kings Coughton B49 5QQ
e-mail: info@kingscourthotel.co.uk
web: www.kingscourthotel.co.uk
dir: 1m N on A435

This privately owned hotel dates back to Tudor times and the bedrooms in the original house have oak beams. Most guests are accommodated in the well-appointed modern wings. The bar and restaurant offer very good dishes from interesting menus. The hotel is licensed to hold civil ceremonies and the pretty garden is ideal for summer weddings.

Rooms 61 (57 annexe) (2 fmly) (30 GF) ↖
Facilities FTV Wi-fi ↕ Gym Xmas New Year
Conf Class 60 Board 40 Thtr 100 Del from £110 to £125 **Parking** 200 **Notes** Civ Wed 100

ALDEBURGH
Suffolk   Map 13 TM45

Brudenell Hotel   T|A|HOTEL
                                      COLLECTION

★★★★ 85% ◉◉ HOTEL

☎ 01728 452071
The Parade IP15 5BU
e-mail: info@brudenellhotel.co.uk
web: www.brudenellhotel.co.uk
dir: A12, A1094. In town, right into High St. Hotel on seafront adjoining Fort Green car park

Situated at the far end of the town centre just a step away from the beach, this hotel has a contemporary appearance, enhanced by subtle lighting and quality soft furnishings. Many of the bedrooms have superb sea views; they include deluxe rooms with king-sized beds and superior rooms suitable for families. The informal restaurant showcases skilfully prepared dishes that use fresh, seasonal produce, especially local fish, seafood and game.

Rooms 44 (17 fmly) ↖ **S** £100-£120; **D** £130-£335 (incl. bkfst) **Facilities** STV Wi-fi Xmas New Year **Conf** Class 20 Board 20 Thtr 20 Del from £165 to £185* **Services** Lift **Parking** 18 **Notes** LB

Wentworth Hotel

★★★ 88% ◉◉ HOTEL   **A**

☎ 01728 452312
Wentworth Rd IP15 5BD
e-mail: stay@wentworth-aldeburgh.co.uk
web: www.wentworth-aldeburgh.com
dir: A12 onto A1094, 6m to Aldeburgh, with church on left, left at bottom of hill

Wentworth Hotel is a delightful, privately-owned building overlooking the beach. The attractive, well-maintained public rooms include three stylish lounges as well as a cocktail bar and elegant restaurant. Bedrooms are smartly decorated with co-ordinated fabrics and have many thoughtful touches; some rooms have superb sea views. Several very spacious Mediterranean-style rooms are located across the road.

Rooms 35 (7 annexe) (2 fmly) (5 GF) **Facilities** FTV Wi-fi Xmas New Year **Conf** Class 12 Board 12 Thtr 15 **Parking** 30

The White Lion Hotel   T|A|HOTEL
                                   COLLECTION

★★★ 88% ◉ HOTEL

☎ 01728 452720
Market Cross Place IP15 5BJ
e-mail: info@whitelion.co.uk
web: www.whitelion.co.uk
dir: A12 onto A1094, follow signs to Aldeburgh at junct on left. Hotel on right

A popular 15th-century hotel situated at the quiet end of town overlooking the sea. Bedrooms are pleasantly decorated and thoughtfully equipped, many rooms have lovely sea views. Public areas include two lounges and an elegant restaurant, where locally-caught fish and seafood are served. There is also a modern brasserie.

Rooms 38 (1 fmly) **Facilities** STV Wi-fi Xmas New Year **Conf** Class 50 Board 50 Thtr 120 **Parking** 15 **Notes** Civ Wed 100

A

ALDERLEY EDGE   Map 16 SJ87
Cheshire

Alderley Edge Hotel
★★★★ 79% ◉◉◉ HOTEL

☎ 01625 583033
Macclesfield Rd SK9 7BJ
e-mail: sales@alderleyedgehotel.com
web: www.alderleyedgehotel.com
dir: From A34 in Alderley Edge onto B5087 towards Macclesfield. Hotel 200yds on right

This well-furnished hotel, with its charming grounds, was originally a country house built for one of the region's 'cotton kings'. The bedrooms and suites are attractively furnished, offering excellent quality and comfort. The welcoming bar and adjacent lounge lead into the conservatory restaurant where imaginative, memorable food and friendly, attentive service are highlights of any visit.

Rooms 50 (4 fmly) (6 GF) ➧ **S** £99.50-£400;
D £135-£400* **Facilities** STV Wi-fi ➧ Child facilities
Conf Class 40 Board 30 Thtr 120 Del from £150*
Services Lift **Parking** 90 **Notes** LB ⊗ Closed 1 Jan
RS 25-26 Dec Civ Wed 114

Premier Inn Alderley Edge
BUDGET HOTEL

☎ 0871 527 8016
Congleton Rd SK9 7AA
web: www.premierinn.com
dir: From N: M56 junct 6, A538 towards Wilmslow, onto A34 towards Birmingham. From S: M6 junct 17, A534 towards Congleton, onto A34 towards Manchester. Hotel adjacent to De Trafford Arms

High quality, budget accommodation ideal for both families and business travellers. Spacious, en suite bedrooms feature tea and coffee making facilities, and Freeview TV in most hotels. Internet access and Wi-fi are available for a small fee. The adjacent family restaurant features a wide and varied menu. See also the Hotel Groups pages.

Rooms 37

ALDERMINSTER   Map 10 SP24
Warwickshire

INSPECTORS' CHOICE

Ettington Park Hotel   Hand PICKED HOTELS
★★★★ ◉◉
COUNTRY HOUSE HOTEL

☎ 01789 450123 & 0845 072 7454
CV37 8BU
e-mail: ettingtonpark@handpicked.co.uk
web: www.handpickedhotels.co.uk/ettingtonpark
dir: Off A3400, 5m S of Stratford, just outside Alderminster

Set in 40-acre grounds in the picturesque Stour Valley, Ettington Park offers the best of both worlds - the peace of the countryside and easy access to main roads and motorway networks. Bedrooms are spacious and individually decorated; views include the delightful grounds and gardens, or the historic chapel. Luxurious day rooms extend to the period drawing room, the oak-panelled dining room with inlays of family crests, a range of contemporary meeting rooms and an indoor leisure centre.

Rooms 48 (20 annexe) (5 fmly) (10 GF) ➧
S £125-£327; **D** £135-£337 (incl. bkfst)
Facilities STV Wi-fi ➧ ➧ ➧ Clay pigeon shooting
Archery Sauna Steam room Xmas New Year
Conf Class 48 Board 48 Thtr 90 Del from £145 to £180 **Services** Lift **Parking** 100 **Notes** LB ⊗
Civ Wed 96

ALDERSHOT   Map 5 SU85
Hampshire

Potters International Hotel
★★★ 68% HOTEL

☎ 01252 344000
1 Fleet Rd GU11 2ET
e-mail: reservations@pottersinthotel.com
dir: Access via A325 & A321 towards Fleet

This modern hotel is located within easy reach of Aldershot. Extensive air-conditioned public areas include ample lounge areas, a pub and a more formal restaurant; there are also conference rooms and a very good leisure club. Bedrooms, mostly spacious, are well equipped and have been attractively decorated and furnished.

Rooms 103 (9 fmly) (9 GF) **Facilities** STV Wi-fi ➧
Gym Beauty treatment room **Conf** Class 250
Board 100 Thtr 400 Del from £125 to £165
Services Lift **Parking** 120 **Notes** ⊗

Premier Inn Aldershot
BUDGET HOTEL

☎ 0871 527 8018
7 Wellington Av GU11 1SQ
web: www.premierinn.com
dir: M3 junct 4, A331. A325 through Farnborough. Pass Barons BMW then Queens Rdbt. Adjacent to Willems Park Brewers Fayre

High quality, budget accommodation ideal for both families and business travellers. Spacious, en suite bedrooms feature tea and coffee making facilities, and Freeview TV in most hotels. Internet access and Wi-fi are available for a small fee. The adjacent family restaurant features a wide and varied menu. See also the Hotel Groups pages.

Rooms 60

ALDWARK   Map 19 SE46
North Yorkshire

Aldwark Manor Golf & Spa Hotel   QHOTELS
★★★★ 77% HOTEL

☎ 01347 838146
YO61 1UF
e-mail: aldwarkmanor@qhotels.co.uk
web: www.qhotels.co.uk
dir: A1/A59 towards Green Hammerton, then B6265 Little Ouseburn. Follow signs for Aldwark Bridge/ Manor. A19 through Linton-on-Ouse

Mature parkland forms the impressive backdrop for this rambling 19th-century mansion, with the River Ure flowing gently through the hotel's own 18-hole

A

golf course. Bedrooms vary - the main-house rooms are traditional and those in the extension are modern in design. Impressive conference and banqueting facilities and a stylish, very well equipped leisure club are available.

Rooms 54 (6 fmly) **Facilities** Spa FTV Wi-fi ⓢ ♨ 18 Putt green Gym Health & beauty Xmas New Year **Conf** Class 100 Board 80 Thtr 240 **Services** Lift **Parking** 150 **Notes** ⊗ Civ Wed 140

ALFRISTON	Map 6 TQ50
East Sussex	

Deans Place
★★★ 86% ⑳⑳ HOTEL

☎ 01323 870248
Seaford Rd BN26 5TW
e-mail: mail@deansplacehotel.co.uk
web: www.deansplacehotel.co.uk
dir: Exit A27 between Eastbourne & Brighton, signed Alfriston & Drusillas Zoo Park. S through village towards Seaford

Situated on the southern fringe of the village, this friendly hotel is set in attractive gardens. Bedrooms vary in size and are well appointed with good facilities. A wide range of food is offered including an extensive bar menu and a fine dining option in Harcourt's Restaurant.

Rooms 36 (4 fmly) (8 GF) **S** £47.50-£107.50; **D** £90-£160 (incl. bkfst)* **Facilities** FTV Wi-fi ⚲ Putt green ⚑ Boules Xmas New Year **Conf** Class 100 Board 60 Thtr 200 Del from £150 to £180* **Parking** 100 **Notes** Civ Wed 150

The Star Alfriston
★★★ 77% ⑳ HOTEL

☎ 01323 870495
BN26 5TA
e-mail: bookings@thestaralfriston.co.uk
dir: 2m from A27, at Drusillas rdbt follow Alfriston signs. Hotel on right in centre of High St

Built in the 13th century and reputedly one of the country's oldest inns, this charming establishment is ideally situated for walking the South Downs or exploring the Sussex coast. Bedrooms, including two feature rooms and a mini suite, are traditionally decorated but with comfortable, modern facilities. Public areas include cosy lounges with open log fires, a bar and a popular restaurant serving a wide choice of dishes using mainly local produce. Guests can also enjoy luxury spa treatments by appointment.

Rooms 37 (1 fmly) (11 GF) **S** £70-£90; **D** £99-£135 (incl. bkfst)* **Facilities** FTV Wi-fi Xmas New Year **Conf** Class 60 Board 46 Thtr 85 Del from £125 to £145* **Parking** 35 **Notes** LB Civ Wed 120

ALMONDSBURY	Map 4 ST68
Gloucestershire	

Aztec Hotel & Spa
★★★★ 80% ⑳ HOTEL   shire
hotels & spas

☎ 01454 201090
Aztec West Business Park, Almondsbury BS32 4TS
e-mail: aztec@shirehotels.com
web: www.aztechotelbristol.com

(For full entry see Bristol)

ALNWICK	Map 21 NU11
Northumberland	

See also **Embleton**

White Swan Hotel
★★★ 80% HOTEL   CLASSIC
LODGES
the sign of a great hotel

☎ 01665 602109
Bondgate Within NE66 1TD
e-mail: info.whiteswan@classiclodges.co.uk
web: www.classiclodges.co.uk
dir: From A1 follow town centre signs. Hotel in town centre near Bondgate Tower

Situated in the heart of the historic town, this charming 300-year-old coaching inn still retains many authentic period features. The Olympic Suite Dining Room, with its original oak panelling and stained glass windows salvaged from the *RMS*

Olympic (sister ship of the ill fated *Titanic*) blends well with the modern Hardy's bistro. All the bedrooms are stylishly appointed and well equipped.

Rooms 56 (5 fmly) (11 GF) **Facilities** FTV Wi-fi Xmas New Year **Conf** Class 50 Board 40 Thtr 150 **Parking** 25 **Notes** ⊗ Civ Wed 150

ALSTON	Map 18 NY74
Cumbria	

Lovelady Shield Country House Hotel
★★★ 82% ⑳⑳ COUNTRY HOUSE HOTEL

☎ 01434 381203 & 381305
CA9 3LF
e-mail: enquiries@lovelady.co.uk
dir: 2m E, signed off A689 at junct with B6294

Located in the heart of the Pennines close to England's highest market town, this delightful country house is set in three acres of landscaped gardens. Accommodation is provided in stylish, thoughtfully equipped bedrooms. Carefully prepared meals are served in the elegant dining room and there is a choice of appealing lounges with log fires in the cooler months.

Rooms 10 (1 fmly) **Facilities** Wi-fi Xmas New Year **Conf** Class 12 Board 12 **Parking** 20 **Notes** Civ Wed 100

Alston House
RESTAURANT WITH ROOMS

☎ 01434 382200
Townfoot CA9 3RN
e-mail: alstonhouse@fsmail.net
web: www.alstonhouse.co.uk
dir: On A686 opposite Spar garage

Located at the foot of the town, this family-owned restaurant with rooms provides well-equipped, stylish and comfortable accommodation. The kitchen serves both modern and traditional dishes with flair and creativity. Alston House runs a café during the day serving light meals and afternoon teas.

Rooms 7 (3 fmly)

A

ALTON
Hampshire
Map 5 SU73

The Anchor Inn

@ @ RESTAURANT WITH ROOMS

☎ 01420 23261
Lower Froyle GU34 4NA
e-mail: info@anchorinnatlowerfroyle.co.uk
dir: From A3 follow Bentley signs & inn signs

The Anchor Inn is located in the tranquil village of Lower Froyle. Luxury rooms are designed to reflect the traditional English inn style with charming decor, pictures and a selection of books. The restaurant welcomes both residents and the public with classic pub cooking, in impressive surroundings, with wooden floors and period furnishings.

Rooms 5

ALTRINCHAM
Greater Manchester
Map 15 SJ78

Mercure Altrincham Bowden Hotel

★★★ 78% HOTEL

☎ 0161 928 7121 & 941 1866
Langham Rd, Bowdon WA14 2HT
e-mail: enquiries@hotels-altrincham.com
web: www.hotels-altrincham.com
dir: A556 towards Manchester, into Park Rd at lights, hotel 1m on right

Situated within easy access of Manchester and the Airport, this hotel offers comfortable and well equipped bedrooms. Public areas include the Café Bar and The Restaurant, both serving a good choice of dishes. A well-equipped leisure centre has an indoor heated pool, spa, sauna and comprehensive air-conditioned gym. There is free Wi-fi throughout.

Rooms 87 (8 fmly) (13 GF) **Facilities** FTV Wi-fi ⓒ supervised Gym Sauna Steam room Xmas New Year **Conf** Board 40 Thtr 140 **Parking** 125 **Notes** Civ Wed 125

Premier Inn Manchester Altrincham

BUDGET HOTEL

☎ 0871 527 8738
Manchester Rd WA14 4PH
web: www.premierinn.com
dir: From N: M60 junct 7, A56 towards Altrincham. From S: M6 junct 19, A556 then A56 towards Sale

High quality, budget accommodation ideal for both families and business travellers. Spacious, en suite bedrooms feature tea and coffee making facilities, and Freeview TV in most hotels. Internet access and Wi-fi are available for a small fee. The adjacent family restaurant features a wide and varied menu. See also the Hotel Groups pages.

Rooms 46

ALVESTON
Gloucestershire
Map 4 ST68

Alveston House Hotel

★★★ 81% HOTEL

☎ 01454 415050
Davids Ln BS35 2LA
e-mail: info@alvestonhousehotel.co.uk
web: www.alvestonhousehotel.co.uk
dir: M5 junct 14 from N or junct 16 from S, on A38

In a quiet area with easy access to the city and a short drive from both the M4 and M5, this smartly presented hotel provides an impressive combination of good service, friendly hospitality and a relaxed atmosphere. The comfortable bedrooms are well equipped for both business and leisure guests. The restaurant offers carefully prepared fresh food, and the pleasant bar and conservatory area is perfect for enjoying a pre-dinner drink.

Rooms 29 (1 fmly) (6 GF) ✆ **S** £85-£120; **D** £120-£135 (incl. bkfst)* **Facilities** FTV Wi-fi ⌇ Beauty treatments Xmas New Year **Conf** Class 48 Board 50 Thtr 85 Del from £135 to £150* **Parking** 75 **Notes** LB Civ Wed 75

AMBLESIDE
Cumbria
Map 18 NY30

***See also* Elterwater**

Waterhead Hotel

English Lakes
Hotels Resorts & Venues

★★★★ 78% @ TOWN HOUSE HOTEL

☎ 015394 32566
Lake Rd LA22 0ER
e-mail: waterhead@englishlakes.co.uk
web: www.englishlakes.co.uk
dir: A591 to Ambleside. Hotel opposite Waterhead Pier

With an enviable location opposite the bay, this well-established hotel offers contemporary and comfortable accommodation with CD/DVD players, plasma screens and internet access. There is a bar with a garden terrace overlooking the lake and a stylish restaurant serving classical cuisine with a modern twist. Staff are very attentive and friendly. Guests can enjoy full use of the leisure facilities at a nearby hotel.

Rooms 41 (3 fmly) (7 GF) **Facilities** FTV Wi-fi ⌇ Free use of leisure facilities at sister hotel (1m) Xmas New Year **Conf** Class 30 Board 26 Thtr 40 **Parking** 43 **Notes** Civ Wed 80

Rothay Manor

★★★ 83% @ HOTEL

☎ 015394 33605
Rothay Bridge LA22 0EH
e-mail: hotel@rothaymanor.co.uk
web: www.rothaymanor.co.uk/aa
dir: In Ambleside follow signs for Coniston (A593). Hotel 0.25m SW of Ambleside opposite rugby pitch

A long-established hotel, this attractive listed building built in Regency style, is a short walk from both the town centre and Lake Windermere. Spacious bedrooms, including suites, family rooms and rooms with balconies, are comfortably equipped and furnished to a very high standard. Public areas include a choice of lounges, a spacious restaurant and conference facilities.

Rooms 19 (2 annexe) (7 fmly) (3 GF) ✆ **S** £85-£110; **D** £99-£180 (incl. bkfst)* **Facilities** STV Wi-fi Free use of nearby leisure centre Free fishing permit Xmas New Year **Conf** Board 18 Thtr 22 **Parking** 45 **Notes** ⊗ Closed 2-17 Jan

Save on hotels. Book at **theAA.com/hotel**

ALT – AND 53 ENGLAND

BEST WESTERN Ambleside Salutation Hotel

★★★ 83% HOTEL

☎ 015394 32244
Lake Rd LA22 9BX
e-mail: ambleside@hotelslakedistrict.com
web: www.hotelslakedistrict.com
dir: A591 to Ambleside, onto one-way system, Wansfell Rd into Compston Rd. Right at lights into village

A former coaching inn, this hotel lies in the centre of the town. Bedrooms are tastefully appointed and thoughtfully equipped; many boast balconies and fine views. Inviting public areas include an attractive restaurant and a choice of comfortable lounges for relaxing. For the more energetic there is a swimming pool and small gym, and for relaxation a spa and treatment rooms.

Rooms 53 (12 annexe) (4 fmly) (1 GF) ⌇ **S** £60-£79; **D** £118-£158 (incl. bkfst)* **Facilities** Spa Wi-fi ⊗ Gym Sauna Steam room Xmas New Year **Conf** Class 36 Board 26 Thtr 80 Del from £161 to £192* **Services** Lift **Parking** 53 **Notes** LB Closed 15-16 Dec

Regent Hotel

★★★ 82% HOTEL

☎ 015394 32254
Waterhead Bay LA22 0ES
e-mail: info@regentlakes.co.uk
dir: M6 junct 36, 1m S on A591

This attractive holiday hotel, situated close to Waterhead Bay, offers a warm welcome. Bedrooms come in a variety of styles, including three suites and five bedrooms in the garden wing. Public areas are contemporary and comfortable; the light, airy restaurant is the setting for hearty, enjoyable meals.

Rooms 30 (7 fmly) (7 GF) ⌇ **S** £75-£149; **D** £85-£159 (incl. bkfst) **Facilities** FTV Wi-fi New Year **Parking** 39 **Notes** Closed 19-27 Dec

---

AMESBURY
Wiltshire   Map 5 SU14

Holiday Inn Salisbury - Stonehenge

★★★★ 75% ◉ HOTEL

☎ 0845 241 3535
Midsummer Place, Solstice Park SP4 7SQ
e-mail: reservations@hisalisbury-stonehenge.co.uk
web: www.hisalisbury-stonehenge.co.uk
dir: Exit A303, follow signs into Solstice Park. Hotel adjacent to service area

This hotel of striking modern design is located on the A303 very close to Stonehenge. All bedrooms have been appointed to the highest standards with unique headboards, air conditioning and broadband connection included in the generous amenities. Fluffy towels and powerful showers are provided in the modern bathrooms. The Solstice Bar and Grill is open from 7am-11pm and offers a range of snacks and meals.

Rooms 103 (24 fmly) (8 GF) ⌇ **D** £49-£160* **Facilities** FTV Wi-fi Xmas New Year **Conf** Class 20 Board 20 Thtr 25 Del from £120 to £190* **Services** Lift Air con **Parking** 168 **Notes** LB ⊗

ANDOVER
Hampshire   Map 5 SU34

Esseborne Manor

★★★ 80% ◉◉ HOTEL

☎ 01264 736444
Hurstbourne Tarrant SP11 0ER
e-mail: info@esseborne-manor.co.uk
web: www.esseborne-manor.co.uk
dir: Halfway between Andover & Newbury on A343, 1m N of Hurstbourne Tarrant

Set in two acres of well-tended gardens, this attractive manor house is surrounded by the open countryside of the North Wessex Downs. Bedrooms are delightfully individual and are split between the main house, an adjoining courtyard and separate garden cottage. There's a wonderfully relaxed atmosphere throughout, and public rooms combine elegance with comfort.

Rooms 19 (8 annexe) (5 fmly) (6 GF) ⌇ **S** £95-£130; **D** £125-£250 (incl. bkfst) **Facilities** STV FTV Wi-fi ☕ ☕ New Year **Conf** Class 40 Board 30 Thtr 60 Del from £135 to £155 **Parking** 50 **Notes** LB Civ Wed 100

Quality Hotel Andover

Ⓤ

☎ 01264 369111
Micheldever Rd SP11 6LA
e-mail: andover@quality-hotels.co.uk
dir: At A303 & A3093 junct. At 1st rdbt 1st exit, at 2nd rdbt 1st exit. Left immediately before Total petrol station, left again

Currently the rating for this establishment is not confirmed. This may be due to a change of ownership or because it has only recently joined the AA rating scheme. For further details please see the AA website: theAA.com

Rooms 49 (36 annexe) (13 GF) ⌇ **Facilities** Wi-fi **Conf** Class 60 Board 60 Thtr 180 Del £85 **Parking** 100 **Notes** Civ Wed 85

A

ANDOVER *continued*

Premier Inn Andover

BUDGET HOTEL

☎ 0871 527 8020
West Portway Industrial Estate, Joule Rd SP10 3UX
web: www.premierinn.com
dir: From A303 follow A342/A343 signs. Hotel at rdbt junct of A342 & A343 adjacent to Portway Inn Brewers Fayre

High quality, budget accommodation ideal for both families and business travellers. Spacious, en suite bedrooms feature tea and coffee making facilities, and Freeview TV in most hotels. Internet access and Wi-fi are available for a small fee. The adjacent family restaurant features a wide and varied menu. See also the Hotel Groups pages.

Rooms 50

ANSTY
Warwickshire   **Map 11 SP48**

Macdonald Ansty Hall

★★★★ 77% ⚜ HOTEL

☎ 0844 879 9031
Main Rd CV7 9HZ
e-mail: ansty@macdonald-hotels.co.uk
web: www.macdonald-hotels.co.uk/anstyhall
dir: M6 junct 2 onto B4065 signed Ansty. Hotel 1.5m on left

Dating back to 1678, this Grade II listed Georgian house is set in eight acres of attractive grounds and woodland. The hotel enjoys a central yet tranquil location. Spacious bedrooms feature a traditional decorative style and a range of extras. Rooms are divided between the main house and the newer annexe. Macdonald Hotels is the AA Hotel Group of the Year 2013-14.

Rooms 62 (39 annexe) (4 fmly) (22 GF) **Facilities** FTV Wi-fi ↕ Xmas New Year **Conf** Class 60 Board 60 Thtr 150 **Services** Lift **Parking** 100 **Notes** Civ Wed 100

APPLEBY-IN-WESTMORLAND   **Map 18 NY62**
Cumbria

Appleby Manor Country House Hotel

★★★★ 78% ⚜ COUNTRY HOUSE HOTEL

☎ 017683 51571
Roman Rd CA16 6JB
e-mail: reception@applebymanor.co.uk
web: www.applebymanor.co.uk
dir: M6 junct 40, A66 towards Brough. Take Appleby turn, immediately right. 0.5m to hotel

This imposing country mansion is set in extensive grounds amid stunning Cumbrian scenery. The Dunbobbin family and their experienced staff ensure a warm welcome and attentive service. The thoughtfully equipped bedrooms vary in style and include the impressive Heelis Suite; some rooms also have patio areas. The bar offers a wide range of malt whiskies and the restaurant serves carefully prepared meals.

Rooms 30 (7 annexe) (9 fmly) (10 GF) 🐾
D £150-£240 (incl. bkfst)* **Facilities** FTV Wi-fi ↕ ③ Putt green Steam room Spa bath Sauna Table tennis Pool table New Year **Conf** Class 25 Board 28 Thtr 38 Del from £140 to £180* **Parking** 51 **Notes** LB ⊗ Closed 24-26 Dec RS 6-13 Jun Civ Wed 60

ARLINGHAM   **Map 4 SO71**
Gloucestershire

The Old Passage Inn

⚛ ⚛ RESTAURANT WITH ROOMS

☎ 01452 740547
Passage Rd GL2 7JR
e-mail: oldpassage@btconnect.com
dir: A38 onto B4071 through Frampton on Severn. 4m to Arlingham, through village to river

Delightfully located on the very edge of the River Severn, this relaxing restaurant with rooms combines high quality food with an air of tranquillity. Bedrooms and bathrooms are decorated in a modern style and include a range of welcome extras such as air conditioning and a well-stocked mini-bar. The menu offers a wide range of seafood and shellfish dishes including crab, oysters and lobsters from Cornwall (kept alive in seawater tanks). An outdoor terrace is available in warmer months.

Rooms 3

ARUNDEL   **Map 6 TQ00**
West Sussex

Premier Inn Arundel

BUDGET HOTEL

☎ 0871 527 8022
Crossbush Ln BN18 9PQ
web: www.premierinn.com
dir: At junct of A27 &A284, 1m E of Arundel

High quality, budget accommodation ideal for both families and business travellers. Spacious, en suite bedrooms feature tea and coffee making facilities, and Freeview TV in most hotels. Internet access and Wi-fi are available for a small fee. The adjacent family restaurant features a wide and varied menu. See also the Hotel Groups pages.

Rooms 30

The Town House

⚛ ⚛ RESTAURANT WITH ROOMS

☎ 01903 883847
65 High St BN18 9AJ
e-mail: enquiries@thetownhouse.co.uk
web: www.thetownhouse.co.uk
dir: A27 to Arundel, into High Street, establishment on left at top of hill

This is an elegant, Grade II-listed Regency building overlooking Arundel Castle, just a short walk from the shops and centre of the town. Bedrooms and public areas retain the building's unspoilt character. The ceiling in the dining room is particularly spectacular and originated in Florence in the 16th century.

Rooms 4

ASCOT   **Map 6 SU96**
Berkshire

Coworth Park

★★★★★ 86% ⚜⚜⚜
COUNTRY HOUSE HOTEL

☎ 01344 876600
London Rd SL5 7SE
e-mail: info.coworthpark@dorchestercollection.com
dir: M25 junct 13 S onto A30 Egham/Bagshot. Past Wentworth Golf Club turn right at lights onto Blacknest Rd (A329) hotel on left

Set in 240 acres of stunning parkland, Coworth Park is part of the luxury Dorchester Collection, sister to The Dorchester in London. The hotel offers luxurious guest rooms and suites, polo grounds, stables and a spa. Children are well cared for too, with a 'Kids Concierge' who can arrange a wide variety of activities for them. The hotel maintains a strong 'green' policy, as does

A

the kitchen team where local quality suppliers are a priority. Casual dining is available in the popular Barn restaurant, in a converted stable block, while the delightfully elegant Restaurant Coworth Park serves Modern British dishes.

Rooms 70 (40 fmly) (27 GF) ♠ D £235-£520 (incl. bkfst)* Facilities Spa STV FTV Wi-fi ↕ ☉ ☕ 🍴 Gym Polo Equestrian centre Archery Laser clays Falconry Duck herding ♫ Xmas New Year Child facilities Conf Class 54 Board 40 Thtr 100 Del from £325 to £545* Services Lift Air con Parking 100 Notes LB ⊗ Civ Wed 250

Macdonald Berystede Hotel & Spa

 MACDONALD HOTELS & RESORTS

★★★★ 78% ⊛ HOTEL

☎ 0844 879 9104
Bagshot Rd, Sunninghill SL5 9JH
e-mail:
general.berystede@macdonald-hotels.co.uk
web: www.macdonald-hotels.co.uk/berystede
dir: A30, B3020 (Windmill Pub). 1.25m to hotel on left just before junct with A330

This impressive Victorian mansion, close to Ascot Racecourse, offers executive bedrooms that are spacious, comfortable and particularly well equipped. Public rooms include a cosy bar and an elegant restaurant which serves creative dishes. The impressive self-contained conference centre and spa facility appeal to both conference and leisure guests. Macdonald Hotels is the AA Hotel Group of the Year 2013-14.

Rooms 126 (61 fmly) (33 GF) Facilities Spa STV Wi-fi ↕ ☉ ♨ Gym Leisure complex (thermal & beauty treatments) Outdoor garden spa Xmas New Year Conf Class 220 Board 150 Thtr 330 Services Lift Parking 200 Notes Civ Wed 300

Brockenhurst Hotel

★★ 67% HOTEL

☎ 01344 621912
Brockenhurst Rd SL5 9HA
e-mail: info@brockenhurst.com
dir: On A330 (near Ascot racecourse), pass course on left, right at mini rdbt, 0.5m, hotel on right

Sitting in well kept grounds and gardens, this hotel is conveniently located in a leafy suburb in south Ascot, a short distance from the railway station. Bedrooms are comfortable, and each is individually designed to reflect the hotel's unique character. Dinner is served in the contemporary dining room and offers a good range of home cooked dishes. Parking is available at this property.

Rooms 10 (3 fmly) Facilities Wi-fi Parking 30 Notes ⊗

Premier Inn Ascot

 Premier Inn

BUDGET HOTEL

☎ 0871 527 8024
London Rd SL5 8DR
web: www.premierinn.com
dir: M3 junct 3, A322 signed Bracknell & Ascot, follow Ascot signs. At next rdbt 1st exit to Bracknell. Hotel on right after lights. Or M4 junct 6 follow Ascot/A322 signs. Racecourse on left, at rdbt follow Bracknell/A329 signs. Hotel on right after lights

High quality, budget accommodation ideal for both families and business travellers. Spacious, en suite bedrooms feature tea and coffee making facilities, and Freeview TV in most hotels. Internet access and Wi-fi are available for a small fee. The adjacent family restaurant features a wide and varied menu. See also the Hotel Groups pages.

Rooms 28

Crab Manor

⊛⊛ RESTAURANT WITH ROOMS

☎ 01845 577286
YO7 3QL
dir: A1(M) junct 49, on outskirts of village

This stunning 18th-century Grade II listed Georgian manor is located in the heart of the North Yorkshire Dales. Each bedroom is themed around the world's most famous hotels and each is uniquely designed with high quality furnishings, beautiful wallpaper, and thoughtful extras. Scandinavian log cabins are also available within the grounds, which have their own terrace with hot tubs. There is a comfortable lounge bar where guests can relax in the Manor before enjoying dinner next door in the Crab & Lobster Restaurant, which specialises in fresh local seafood. The attractive gardens offer a lovely backdrop, and provide a pleasant place in which to relax.

Rooms 14 (6 annexe) (3 fmly)

Callow Hall Hotel

★★★ 82% ⊛⊛ HOTEL

☎ 01335 300900
Mappleton Rd DE6 2AA
e-mail: info@callowhall.co.uk
dir: Telephone for directions

This delightful, creeper-clad, early Victorian house, set on a 44-acre estate, enjoys views over Bentley Brook and the Dove Valley. The atmosphere is relaxed

and welcoming, and some of the bedrooms in the main house have comfortable sitting areas. Public rooms feature high ceilings, ornate plaster work and antique furniture. The elegant restaurant offers accomplished cuisine.

Rooms 16 (1 fmly) (2 GF) ♠ Facilities FTV Wi-fi ↕ 🍴 Xmas New Year Conf Class 40 Board 20 Thtr 40 Del from £195* Parking 20 Notes Civ Wed 100

The Royal Hotel

★★★ 63% HOTEL

☎ 01530 412833
Station Rd LE65 2GP
e-mail: reservations@royalhotelashby.com
web: www.royalhotelashby.com
dir: A42 junct 13, A511 towards Ashby-de-la-Zouch. A511 on Nottingham Rd to Station Rd & Main Rd into town. Left at rdbt, left & left again

This Grade II listed Regency building retains much of its original character. The bedrooms, although varying in size are comfortable and well equipped; one room has a four-poster bed. The Castle Room Restaurant overlooks the lovely landscaped gardens, and staff are friendly and efficient.

Rooms 34 (4 fmly) S £55-£60; D £60-£75 (incl. bkfst)* Facilities STV Wi-fi Conf Class 26 Board 26 Thtr 70 Parking 200 Notes ⊗ Civ Wed 70

Premier Inn Ashby De La Zouch

 Premier Inn

BUDGET HOTEL

☎ 0871 527 8026
Flagstaff Island LE65 1DS
web: www.premierinn.com
dir: M1 junct 23a, follow A42 (M42), Tamworth & Birmingham signs. Hotel at rdbt at A42 junct 13. (NB for Sat Nav use LE65 1JP)

High quality, budget accommodation ideal for both families and business travellers. Spacious, en suite bedrooms feature tea and coffee making facilities, and Freeview TV in most hotels. Internet access and Wi-fi are available for a small fee. The adjacent family restaurant features a wide and varied menu. See also the Hotel Groups pages.

Rooms 40

A

ASHFORD   Map 7 TR04
Kent

INSPECTORS' CHOICE

Eastwell Manor

★★★★ ⍟⍟ HOTEL

☎ 01233 213000 & 213020
Eastwell Park, Boughton Lees TN25 4HR
e-mail: enquiries@eastwellmanor.co.uk
dir: M20 junct 9, follow Faversham A251 signs. On
A251 hotel on left on entering Boughton Lees

Set in 62 acres of landscaped grounds, this lovely
hotel dates back to the Norman Conquest and
boasts a number of interesting features, including
carved wood-panelled rooms and huge baronial
stone fireplaces. Accommodation is divided
between the manor house and the courtyard mews
cottages. The luxury Pavilion Spa in the grounds
has an all-day brasserie, and award-winning fine
dining is offered in the main restaurant.

Rooms 62 (39 annexe) (2 fmly) (15 GF) 🐾
S £50-£85; **D** £85-£450 (incl. bkfst)* **Facilities** Spa
FTV Wi-fi ⍟ ↻ ↨ 9 ⍟ Putt green ⌣ Gym Boules
♫ Xmas New Year **Conf** Class 70 Board 60
Thtr 180 **Services** Lift **Parking** 200 **Notes** LB ⊗
Civ Wed 450

Ashford International Hotel

★★★★ 81% HOTEL   QHOTELS

☎ 01233 219988
Simone Weil Av TN24 8UX
e-mail: ashford@qhotels.co.uk
web: www.qhotels.co.uk
dir: M20 junct 9, exit for Ashford/Canterbury. Left at
1st rdbt, hotel 200mtrs on left

Situated just off the M20 and with easy links to the
Eurotunnel, Eurostar and ferry terminals, this hotel
has been stunningly appointed. The slick, stylishly
presented bedrooms are equipped with the latest
amenities. Public areas include the spacious Horizons
Wine Bar and Restaurant serving a competitively
priced menu, and Quench Sports Bar for relaxing
drinks. The Reflections leisure club boasts a pool,

fully-equipped gym, spa facilities and treatment
rooms.

Rooms 179 (29 fmly) (57 GF) 🐾 **Facilities** Spa Wi-fi
⍟ Gym Aroma steam room Rock sauna Feature
shower Ice fountain Xmas New Year **Conf** Class 180
Board 26 Thtr 400 **Services** Lift Air con **Parking** 400
Notes Civ Wed 400

Holiday Inn Ashford - Central

★★★ 77% HOTEL   Holiday Inn

☎ 08771 9429001
Canterbury Rd TN24 8QQ
e-mail: reservations-ashford@ihg.com
web: www.holidayinn.co.uk
dir: A28, at 2nd lights turn left. Hotel approx 90mtrs
on right

Ideally situated within easy reach of Eurostar and
Eurotunnel terminals and a short drive to historic
Canterbury, this popular hotel offers stylish facilities
for both business and leisure travellers. Comfortable,
well-equipped bedrooms vary in size and include
spacious family rooms with modern sofa beds. Public
areas include a casual restaurant, lounges, bar and
attractive garden area.

Rooms 103 (40 fmly) (50 GF) (12 smoking)
Facilities STV Wi-fi Xmas **Conf** Class 64 Board 40
Thtr 120 **Parking** 120 **Notes** ⊗ Civ Wed 130

Premier Inn Ashford Central

BUDGET HOTEL   Premier Inn

☎ 0871 527 8030
Hall Av, Orbital Park, Sevington TN24 0GN
web: www.premierinn.com
dir: M20 junct 10 S'bound; 4th exit at rdbt. (N'bound:
1st exit onto A2070 signed Brenzett). Hotel on right at
next rdbt

High quality, budget accommodation ideal for both
families and business travellers. Spacious, en suite
bedrooms feature tea and coffee making facilities,
and Freeview TV in most hotels. Internet access and
Wi-fi are available for a small fee. The adjacent
family restaurant features a wide and varied menu.
See also the Hotel Groups pages.

Rooms 60

Premier Inn Ashford (Eureka Leisure Park)

BUDGET HOTEL

☎ 0871 527 8028
Eureka Leisure Park TN25 4BN
web: www.premierinn.com
dir: M20 junct 9, take 1st exit on left

Rooms 74

Premier Inn Ashford North

BUDGET HOTEL

☎ 0871 527 8032
Maidstone Road (A20), Hothfield Common TN26 1AP
web: www.premierinn.com
dir: M20 junct 9, A20 follow Lenham signs. Hotel
between Ashford & Charing

Rooms 60

The Wife of Bath

⍟⍟ RESTAURANT WITH ROOMS

☎ 01233 812232
4 Upper Bridge St, Wye TN25 5AF
e-mail: relax@thewifeofbath.com
dir: 4m NE of Ashford. M20 junct 9, A28 for
Canterbury, 3m right to Wye

The Wife of Bath is set in the medieval village of Wye
which is close to Dover, Canterbury and Ashford.
Bedrooms are tastefully decorated and provide guests
with comfortable accommodation; each is equipped
with LCD TVs and DVD players (a range of DVDs is
available). The stylish restaurant, with a small
separate bar area, is open for lunch and dinner daily;
a cooked or continental breakfast is served here in
the morning. Free Wi-fi is available throughout.

Rooms 5 (2 annexe) (1 fmly)

ASHINGTON   Map 21 NZ28
Northumberland

Premier Inn Ashington

BUDGET HOTEL   Premier Inn

☎ 0871 527 8034
Queen Elizabeth Country Park, Woodhorn NE63 9AT
web: www.premierinn.com
dir: From A1 follow signs to Morpeth then Woodhorn
Colliery Museum/Ashington. Through Ashington. Hotel
in Queen Elizabeth II Country Park

High quality, budget accommodation ideal for both
families and business travellers. Spacious, en suite
bedrooms feature tea and coffee making facilities,
and Freeview TV in most hotels. Internet access and
Wi-fi are available for a small fee. The adjacent

A

family restaurant features a wide and varied menu. See also the Hotel Groups pages.

Rooms 20

ASPLEY GUISE
Bedfordshire   Map 11 SP93

BEST WESTERN Moore Place Hotel

★★★ 79% HOTEL

☎ 01908 282000
The Square MK17 8DW
e-mail: business@mooreplace.com
web: www.mooreplace.com
dir: M1 junct 13, A507 signed Aspley Guise & Woburn Sands. Hotel on left in village square

This impressive Georgian house, set in delightful gardens in the village centre, is very conveniently located for the M1. Bedrooms do vary in size, but consideration has been given to guest comfort, with many thoughtful extras provided. There is a wide range of meeting rooms and private dining options.

Rooms 62 (27 annexe) (2 fmly) (16 GF) 🐾
Facilities FTV Wi-fi ↕ **Conf** Class 24 Board 20 Thtr 50 Del from £130 to £155* **Parking** 70 **Notes** Civ Wed 65

ATHERSTONE
Warwickshire   Map 10 SP39

Chapel House Restaurant With Rooms

◉ RESTAURANT WITH ROOMS

☎ 01827 718949
Friar's Gate CV9 1EY
e-mail: info@chapelhouse.eu
web: www.chapelhouse.eu
dir: A5 to town centre, right into Church St. Right into Sheepy Rd, left into Friar's Gate

Sitting next to the church, this 18th-century town house offers excellent hospitality and service while the cooking, using much local produce, is very notable. Bedrooms are well equipped and lounges are extensive; there is also a delightful walled garden for guests to use.

Rooms 11

ATTLEBOROUGH
Norfolk   Map 13 TM09

Sherbourne House Hotel

★★★ 77% SMALL HOTEL

☎ 01953 454363
8 Attleborough Rd NR17 2JX
e-mail: stay@sherbourne-house.co.uk
web: www.sherbourne-house.co.uk
dir: A11 from London/Thetford towards Attleborough, through town centre, pass church on right, next left, hotel on right after 500mtrs

Built in 1740 this fine manor house is set among beautifully landscaped gardens and is a short walk from the historic market town of Attleborough. Much of the house has been refurbished and many of the original features sympathetically restored. Bedrooms are spacious, comfortable and there is a light-filled conservatory lounge for guests. An extensive dinner menu is available in the evenings and freshly prepared breakfasts are served in the charming breakfast room overlooking the gardens. Wi-fi is available throughout the property and the hotel is ideally placed for visitors to Snetterton motor racing circuit.

Rooms 8 (1 fmly) (1 GF) **S** fr £50; (incl. bkfst)*
Facilities FTV Wi-fi **Conf** Class 18 Board 22 Thtr 30 Del £100* **Parking** 20

AUSTWICK
North Yorkshire   Map 18 SD76

The Traddock

◉ ◉ RESTAURANT WITH ROOMS

☎ 015242 51224
LA2 8BY
e-mail: info@thetraddock.co.uk
dir: From Skipton take A65 towards Kendal, 3m after Settle turn right signed Austwick, cross hump back bridge, 100yds on left

Situated within the Yorkshire Dales National Park and a peaceful village environment, this fine Georgian country house with well-tended gardens offers a haven of calm and good hospitality. There are two comfortable lounges with real fires and fine furnishings, as well as a cosy bar and an elegant dining room serving fine cuisine. Bedrooms are individually styled with many homely touches.

Rooms 12 (2 fmly)

AXBRIDGE
Somerset   Map 4 ST45

The Oak House

◉ ◉ RESTAURANT WITH ROOMS

☎ 01934 732444
The Square BS26 2AP
e-mail: info@theoakhousesomerset.com
dir: M5 junct 22, A38 N, turn right towards Axbridge & Cheddar

This impressive restaurant with rooms is located in the middle of the village and has undergone a considerable transformation in recent years. It now provides a relaxed, high quality experience, whether guests are coming to enjoy the restaurant or to stay in one of the nine bedrooms above. Hospitality and service are delivered in an efficient and helpful manner by a young and enthusiastic team. The kitchen has a serious approach and delivers delightful dishes full of flavour, utilising the best quality produce.

Rooms 9 (2 fmly)

AXMINSTER
Devon   Map 4 SY29

See also **Colyford**

Fairwater Head Hotel

★★★ 77% ◉ HOTEL

☎ 01297 678349
Hawkchurch EX13 5TX
e-mail: stay@fairwaterheadhotel.co.uk
web: www.fairwaterheadhotel.co.uk
dir: From B3165 (Crewkerne to Lyme Regis road) follow Hawkchurch signs

This elegant Edwardian country house provides a perfect location for anyone looking for a peaceful break. Surrounded by extensive gardens and rolling countryside, the setting guarantees relaxation. Bedrooms are located both within the main house and the garden wing, and all provide good levels of comfort. Public areas are very appealing and include lounge areas, a bar and an elegant restaurant. Food is a highlight with excellent local produce prepared with care and skill.

Rooms 16 (4 annexe) (8 GF) 🐾 **S** £117-£177; **D** £135-£195 (incl. bkfst)* **Facilities** FTV Wi-fi Library Xmas New Year **Conf** Class 25 Board 20 Thtr 35 Del from £152 to £186* **Parking** 30 **Notes** LB Closed 1-30 Jan Civ Wed 50

A

AYCLIFFE
Co Durham   Map 19 NZ22

The County
RESTAURANT WITH ROOMS

☎ 01325 312273
12 The Green DL5 6LX
e-mail: info@thecountyaycliffevillage.com
dir: A1(M) junct 59, A167 towards Newton Aycliffe. In Aycliffe turn onto village green

Located overlooking the pretty village green yet convenient for the A1, the focus here is on fresh, home-cooked meals, real ales and friendly service. There is a relaxed atmosphere in the bar area, and the restaurant where attractive artwork is displayed. The bedrooms in the smart townhouse next door are all furnished to a high standard.

Rooms 7

AYLESBURY
Buckinghamshire   Map 11 SP81

INSPECTORS' CHOICE

Hartwell House Hotel, Restaurant & Spa
★★★★ ◉◉ HOTEL

☎ 01296 747444
Oxford Rd HP17 8NR
e-mail: info@hartwell-house.com
web: www.hartwell-house.com
dir: From S: M40 junct 7, A329 to Thame, then A418 towards Aylesbury. After 6m, through Stone, hotel on left. From N: M40 junct 9 for Bicester. A41 to Aylesbury, A418 to Oxford for 2m. Hotel on right

This beautiful, historic house is set in 90 acres of unspoilt parkland. The grand public rooms are truly magnificent, and feature many fine works of art. The service standards are very high; guests will find that the staff offer attentive and traditional hospitality without stuffiness. There is an elegant, award-winning restaurant where carefully prepared dishes use the best local produce. Bedrooms are spacious, elegant and very comfortable. Most are in the main house, but some, including suites, are in

the nearby, renovated coach house, which also houses an excellent spa.

Rooms 46 (16 annexe) (3 fmly) (10 GF) ↑ **S** £175; **D** £290–£700 (incl. bkfst)* **Facilities** Spa STV Wi-fi ☆ ⊙ supervised ⌣ 🦢 Gym Sauna Steam rooms ♫ Xmas New Year **Conf** Class 40 Board 40 Thtr 100 Del from £225* **Services** Lift **Parking** 91 **Notes** LB No children 4yrs RS Xmas/New Year Civ Wed 120

Holiday Inn Aylesbury
★★★ 78% HOTEL

☎ 01296 734000
Aston Clinton Rd HP22 5AA
e-mail: aylesbury@ihg.com
web: www.hiaylesburyhotel.co.uk
dir: M25 junct 20, follow A41. Hotel on left on entering Aylesbury

Situated to the south of town, this hotel is conveniently located for local businesses and the town centre. Public areas are extensive, including the well-equipped health club and a superb range of meeting rooms. Bedrooms are comfortable and are equipped with a host of extras.

Rooms 139 (45 fmly) (69 GF) (8 smoking) **S** £49–£135; **D** £59–£145* **Facilities** Spa STV Wi-fi ⊙ supervised Gym Steam room Sauna Dance studio Gym New Year **Conf** Class 50 Board 50 Thtr 120 Del from £99 to £135* **Services** Air con **Parking** 160 **Notes** LB ⊗ Civ Wed 120

Premier Inn Aylesbury
BUDGET HOTEL   Premier Inn

☎ 0871 527 8036
Buckingham Rd HP19 9QL
web: www.premierinn.com
dir: From Aylesbury on A413 towards Buckingham. Hotel in 1m on left adjacent to lights

High quality, budget accommodation ideal for both families and business travellers. Spacious, en suite bedrooms feature tea and coffee making facilities, and Freeview TV in most hotels. Internet access and Wi-fi are available for a small fee. The adjacent family restaurant features a wide and varied menu. See also the Hotel Groups pages.

Rooms 64

AYNHO
Northamptonshire   Map 11 SP53

Cartwright Hotel
★★★ 79% HOTEL

☎ 01869 811885
1-5 Croughton Rd OX17 3BE
e-mail: cartwright@oxfordshire-hotels.co.uk
dir: M40 junct 10, A43, B4100 to Aynho

This former coaching inn is located between Banbury and Oxford, making it ideally located for visiting the many tourist attractions the area has to offer including Blenheim Palace and the circuit at Silverstone. The hotel features individually designed bedrooms which range from double to executive, and premiere standards with flat-screen digital TVs and complimentary Wi-fi. Secure parking is available.

Rooms 21 (12 annexe) (2 fmly) (12 GF) ↑ **S** £65–£120; **D** £75–£175 (incl. bkfst)* **Facilities** FTV Wi-fi Xmas New Year **Conf** Class 40 Board 20 Thtr 60 Del from £135 to £150* **Parking** 15 **Notes** LB ⊗

BABBACOMBE

See Torquay

BACTON
Norfolk   Map 13 TG33

The Keswick Hotel
★★★ 70% ◉ HOTEL

☎ 01692 650468
Walcott Rd NR12 0LS
e-mail: margaret@keswickhotelbacton.co.uk
web: www.keswickhotelbacton.co.uk
dir: On B1159 (coast road)

A small personally run hotel situated by the sea within easy driving distance of the Broads and north Norfolk coastline. The individually decorated bedrooms are pleasantly appointed, have modern facilities and either sea or countryside views. Public areas include a cosy lounge bar with plush sofas, a further lounge area, a restaurant and a conservatory.

Rooms 9 (1 fmly) (3 GF) **S** £49.95; **D** £49.95–£79.95 (incl. bkfst) **Facilities** FTV Wi-fi **Conf** Del from £160 to £180 **Parking** 75 **Notes** No children

B

BAGSHOT
Surrey   Map 6 SU96

INSPECTORS' CHOICE

Pennyhill Park Hotel & The Spa

★★★★★ ◉◉◉◉◉
COUNTRY HOUSE HOTEL

☎ 01276 471774 & 486150
London Rd GU19 5EU
e-mail: enquiries@pennyhillpark.co.uk
web: www.pennyhillpark.co.uk
dir: M3 junct 3, follow signs to Camberley. On A30 between Bagshot & Camberley

This delightful country-house hotel, set in 120-acre grounds, provides every modern comfort. The stylish bedrooms are individually designed and have impressive bathrooms. Leisure facilities include a jogging trail, a golf course and a state-of-the-art spa with a thermal sequencing experience, ozone-treated swimming and hydrotherapy pools along with a comprehensive range of therapies and treatments. The Latymer restaurant, overseen by Chef Michael Wignall, has become a true dining destination in its own right. The cooking is outstanding and great care is made to source first-rate ingredients, much from local suppliers. There is an eight-seater chef's table for enjoying the tasting menu while watching the action in the kitchen. In addition there are other eating options, and lounges and bars to relax in.

Rooms 123 (97 annexe) (6 fmly) (26 GF) 🐾
D £205-£1250* **Facilities** Spa STV Wi-fi ⊙ ⊰ ⅃ 9
⅊ Fishing ⤵ Gym Archery Clay shooting Plunge pool Turkish steam room Rugby/football pitch ♫ Xmas New Year **Conf** Class 108 Board 55 Thtr 140 Del £425* **Services** Lift **Parking** 500 **Notes** LB Civ Wed 140

Premier Inn Bagshot
BUDGET HOTEL

☎ 0871 527 8040
1 London Rd GU19 5HR
web: www.premierinn.com
dir: On A30 (London Rd) just before junct with A322 (Bracknell Rd). Adjacent to Cricketers Beefeater

High quality, budget accommodation ideal for both families and business travellers. Spacious, en suite bedrooms feature tea and coffee making facilities, and Freeview TV in most hotels. Internet access and Wi-fi are available for a small fee. The adjacent family restaurant features a wide and varied menu. See also the Hotel Groups pages.

Rooms 39

BAINBRIDGE
North Yorkshire   Map 18 SD99

INSPECTORS' CHOICE

Yorebridge House

◉ ◉ RESTAURANT WITH ROOMS

☎ 01969 652060
DL8 3EE
e-mail: enquiries@yorebridgehouse.co.uk
dir: A648 to Bainbridge. Yorebridge House N of centre on right before river

Yorebridge House is situated by the river on the edge of Bainbridge, in the heart of the North Yorkshire Dales. In the Victorian era this was a schoolmaster's house and school, but this building now offers luxury boutique-style accommodation. Each bedroom is individually designed with high quality furnishings and thoughtful extras. All rooms have stunning views of the Dales and some have their own terrace with hot tubs. There is a comfortable lounge bar where guests can relax before enjoying dinner in the attractive and elegant dining room.

Rooms 11 (4 annexe) (11 fmly)

BALDOCK
Hertfordshire   Map 12 TL23

Days Inn Stevenage North - A1

BUDGET HOTEL

☎ 01462 730598
Baldock Extra Motorways, A1(M) Junction 10, Radwell SG7 5TR
e-mail: stevenage.hotel@welcomebreak.co.uk
dir: A1(M) junct 10 Baldock Extra Services

This modern, purpose built accommodation offers smartly appointed, well-equipped bedrooms, with good power showers. There is a choice of adjacent food outlets where guests may enjoy breakfast, snacks and meals. See also the Hotel Groups pages.

Rooms 62 (14 fmly) (30 GF) (8 smoking)

BALSALL COMMON
West Midlands   Map 10 SP27

Nailcote Hall

★★★★ 76% ◉ HOTEL

☎ 024 7646 6174
Nailcote Ln, Berkswell CV7 7DE
e-mail: info@nailcotehall.co.uk
web: www.nailcotehall.co.uk
dir: On B4101

This 17th-century house, set in 15 acres of grounds, boasts a 9-hole championship golf course and Roman bath-style swimming pool amongst its many facilities. The bedrooms are spacious and elegantly furnished. The eating options are the fine dining restaurant where smart casual dress is required, or The Piano Bar where more informal meals are served.

Rooms 40 (19 annexe) (2 fmly) (15 GF) **Facilities** STV FTV Wi-fi ⊙ supervised ⅃ 9 ⅊ Putt green ⤵ Gym ♫ Xmas New Year **Conf** Class 80 Board 44 Thtr 140 **Services** Lift **Parking** 200 **Notes** ⊗ Civ Wed 120

BALSALL COMMON *continued*

Premier Inn Balsall Common (Near NEC)

BUDGET HOTEL

☎ 0871 527 8042
Kenilworth Rd CV7 7EX
web: www.premierinn.com
dir: M42 junct 6, A45 towards Coventry for 0.5m.
A452 signed Leamington/Kenilworth. In 3m hotel on
right

High quality, budget accommodation ideal for both
families and business travellers. Spacious, en suite
bedrooms feature tea and coffee making facilities,
and Freeview TV in most hotels. Internet access and
Wi-fi are available for a small fee. The adjacent
family restaurant features a wide and varied menu.
See also the Hotel Groups pages.

Rooms 42

BAMBURGH	Map 21 NU13
Northumberland	

Waren House Hotel

★★★ 85% ◉ COUNTRY HOUSE HOTEL

☎ 01668 214581
Waren Mill NE70 7EE
e-mail: enquiries@warenhousehotel.co.uk
web: www.warenhousehotel.co.uk
dir: 2m E of A1 turn onto B1342 to Waren Mill, at
T-junct turn right, hotel 100yds on right

This delightful Georgian mansion is set in six acres of
woodland and offers a welcoming atmosphere and
views of the coast. The individually themed bedrooms
and suites include many with large bathrooms. Good,
home-cooked food is served in the elegant dining
room. A comfortable lounge and library are also
available.

Rooms 15 (4 annexe) (3 GF) **S** £90-£120;
D £190-£200 (incl. bkfst & dinner)* **Facilities** FTV
Wi-fi ♨ Xmas New Year **Conf** Class 16 Board 16
Parking 20 **Notes** LB No children 14yrs

Victoria Hotel

★★★ 81% ◉ HOTEL

☎ 01668 214431
Front St NE69 7BP
e-mail:
enquiries@thevictoriahotelbamburgh.co.uk

Set on the delightful village green and overlooked by
Bamburgh Castle, this hotel offers bedrooms with
high quality furnishings and modern conveniences
including LCD TV, a hairdryer, trouser press and
complimentary refreshment tray. Bailey's Bar and

Restaurant offers locally sourced food on menus
served throughout the day. The staff pay great
attention to detail and the hotel makes an ideal base
from which to tour this beautiful area of
Northumberland.

Rooms 36 (3 fmly) (2 GF) ⌇ **S** £35-£55; **D** £70-£95
(incl. bkfst)* **Facilities** FTV Wi-fi Xmas New Year
Conf Class 20 Board 12 Thtr 25 Del from £80 to
£100* **Parking** 20 **Notes** LB Civ Wed 40

The Lord Crewe

★★★ 81% HOTEL

☎ 01668 214243 & 214613
Front St NE69 7BL
e-mail: enquiries@lordcrewe.co.uk
dir: Just below castle

Located in the heart of the village in the shadow of
impressive Bamburgh Castle, this hotel has been
developed from an old inn. Public areas combine
modern and traditional very well and include a choice
of lounges, a cosy bar and a smart contemporary
Italian restaurant. Bedrooms vary in size, but all are
well equipped and offer expected amenities.

Rooms 17 **Facilities** FTV Wi-fi **Parking** 20 **Notes** ⊗
No children 5yrs Closed 25-26 Dec & 6 Jan-1 Feb

BAMPTON	Map 5 SP30
Oxfordshire	

Biztro at Wheelgate House

RESTAURANT WITH ROOMS

☎ 01993 851151 & 07747 466151
Wheelgate House, Market Square OX18 2JH
e-mail: enquiries@wheelgatehouse.co.uk
web: www.wheelgatehouse.co.uk
dir: In village centre opposite war memorial

This restaurant with rooms is set in the pretty village
of Bampton at the edge of the Cotswolds, and extends
a warm and friendly welcome awaits. Bedrooms are
individual in design offering a cosy experience. The
ground floor is 'Biztro' where breakfast is served daily
along with lunches and dinners available from
Tuesday to Saturday.

Rooms 3

BANBURY	Map 11 SP44
Oxfordshire	

BEST WESTERN PLUS Wroxton House Hotel

★★★ 85% ◉ HOTEL

☎ 01295 730777
Wroxton St Mary OX15 6QB
e-mail: reservations@wroxtonhousehotel.com
dir: M40 junct 11, A422 signed Banbury & Wroxton.
Approx 3m, hotel on right on entering Wroxton

Dating in part from 1649, this partially thatched hotel
is set just off the main road. Bedrooms, either created
from cottages or situated in a contemporary wing, are
comfortable and well equipped with Wi-fi and LCD
TVs. The public areas are open plan and the low-
beamed Restaurant 1649 has a peaceful atmosphere
for dining.

Rooms 32 (3 annexe) (5 fmly) (8 GF) ⌇ **S** £67-£102;
D £79-£112* **Facilities** FTV Wi-fi ♨ Xmas New Year
Child facilities **Conf** Class 40 Board 40 Thtr 90
Del from £129 to £142* **Parking** 60 **Notes** LB ⊗
Civ Wed 90

Mercure Banbury Whately Hall Hotel

★★★ 77% HOTEL

☎ 01295 253261
Banbury Cross OX16 0AN
e-mail: h6633@accor.com
web: www.mercure.com
dir: M40 junct 11, straight over 2 rdbts, left at 3rd,
0.25m to Banbury Cross, hotel on right

Dating back to 1677, this historic inn boasts many
original features such as stone passages, priests'
holes and a fine wooden staircase. Spacious public
areas include the oak-panelled restaurant, which
overlooks the attractive well-tended gardens, a choice
of lounges and a traditional bar. Smartly appointed
bedrooms vary in size and style but all are
thoughtfully equipped.

Rooms 69 (6 fmly) (2 GF) **Facilities** FTV Wi-fi Xmas
New Year **Conf** Class 40 Board 40 Thtr 120
Services Lift **Parking** 52 **Notes** ⊗ Civ Wed 150

Save on hotels. Book at **theAA.com/hotel**

BAL – BAR   61   ENGLAND

B

Premier Inn Banbury

BUDGET HOTEL

☎ 0871 527 8044
Warwick Rd, Warmington OX17 1JJ
web: www.premierinn.com
dir: From N: M40 junct 12, B4451, B4100 towards
Warmington. From S: M40 junct 11, A423, A422,
B4100. Hotel adjacent to Wobbly Wheel Brewers Fayre

High quality, budget accommodation ideal for both
families and business travellers. Spacious, en suite
bedrooms feature tea and coffee making facilities,
and Freeview TV in most hotels. Internet access and
Wi-fi are available for a small fee. The adjacent
family restaurant features a wide and varied menu.
See also the Hotel Groups pages.

Rooms 39

BARKING   Map 6 TQ48
Greater London

Ibis London East Barking

BUDGET HOTEL

ibis

☎ 020 8477 4100
Highbridge Rd IG11 7BA
e-mail: H2042@accor.com
web: www.ibishotel.com
dir: Exit Barking from A406 or A13

Modern, budget hotel offering comfortable
accommodation in bright and practical bedrooms.
Breakfast is self-service and dinner is available in
the restaurant. See also the Hotel Groups pages.

Rooms 86 (26 GF)

Premier Inn Barking

BUDGET HOTEL

Premier Inn

☎ 0871 527 8048
Highbridge Rd IG11 7BA
web: www.premierinn.com
dir: A13 onto A406 signed Barking/Ilford. At Barking,
exit at Tesco/A406 slip road. Hotel on left

High quality, budget accommodation ideal for both
families and business travellers. Spacious, en suite
bedrooms feature tea and coffee making facilities,
and Freeview TV in most hotels. Internet access and
Wi-fi are available for a small fee. The adjacent
family restaurant features a wide and varied menu.
See also the Hotel Groups pages.

Rooms 88

BARLBOROUGH   Map 16 SK47
Derbyshire

Ibis Sheffield North

BUDGET HOTEL

ibis

☎ 01246 813222
Tallys End, Chesterfield Rd S43 4TX
e-mail: H3157@accor.com
web: www.ibishotel.com
dir: M1 junct 30. Towards A619, right at rdbt towards
Chesterfield. Hotel immediately left

Modern, budget hotel offering comfortable
accommodation in bright and practical bedrooms.
Breakfast is self-service and dinner is available in
the restaurant. See also the Hotel Groups pages.

Rooms 86 (22 fmly) **Conf** Board 18 Thtr 35

BARNARD CASTLE   Map 19 NZ01
Co Durham

The Morritt

★★★★ 82% @@ HOTEL

☎ 01833 627232
Greta Bridge DL12 9SE
e-mail: relax@themorritt.co.uk
web: www.themorritt.co.uk
dir: Exit A1 (A1(M)) at Scotch Corner onto A66
W'bound towards Penrith. Greta Bridge 9m on left

In the heart of beautiful Teesdale, this 17th-century
former coaching house, with connections to Dickens,
is full of character and is a popular meeting place.
The bar area has two amazing Dickens murals - one
newly created in 2012 to commemorate Dickens'
200th birthday. The hotel has equally impressive
traditional values, apparent in its service, locally-
sourced food and individually styled rooms. Added
relaxation in the way of unparalleled pampering and
treatments in the adjoining new spa, The Garage, are
now available.

Rooms 26 (6 annexe) (2 fmly) (4 GF) 🐾 **S** £85-£169;
D £110-£200 (incl. bkfst)* **Facilities** Spa FTV Wi-fi ॐ
Xmas New Year **Conf** Class 60 Board 50 Thtr 200
Del from £145 to £224* **Parking** 40 **Notes** LB
Civ Wed 200

BARNBY MOOR   Map 16 SK68
Nottinghamshire

Ye Olde Bell Hotel & Restaurant

★★★★ 78% HOTEL

☎ 01777 705121
DN22 8QS
e-mail: enquiries@yeoldebell-hotel.co.uk
web: www.yeoldebell-hotel.co.uk
dir: A1(M) south near junct 34, exit Barnby Moor or
A1(M) north exit A620 Retford. Hotel on A638 between
Retford & Bawtry

Ye Olde Bell is a 17th-century coaching inn situated
in the rural village of Barnby Moor near Retford.
Public rooms have a wealth of original character such
as traditional log fires, ornate plaster work and wood
panelling. The tastefully appointed bedrooms have
superb co-ordinated soft furnishings and many
thoughtful touches.

Rooms 57 (8 annexe) (5 fmly) (8 GF) 🐾 **Facilities** FTV
Wi-fi ॐ Gym Hair salon Beauty treatment salon Xmas
New Year **Conf** Class 100 Board 50 Thtr 250
Del from £99 to £145* **Parking** 200 **Notes** ⊗
Civ Wed 250

B

BARNET
Greater London
Map 6 TQ29

Savoro Restaurant with Rooms

◉ RESTAURANT WITH ROOMS

☎ 020 8449 9888
206 High St EN5 5SZ
e-mail: savoro@savoro.co.uk
web: www.savoro.co.uk
dir: M25 junct 23, A1000. Establishment in crescent behind Hadley Green Jaguar Garage

Set back from the main high street, the traditional frontage of this establishment belies the stylishly modern bedrooms and well designed bathrooms within. The award-winning restaurant is an additional bonus.

Rooms 11 (2 fmly)

BARNHAM BROOM
Norfolk
Map 13 TG00

Barnham Broom Hotel, Golf & Restaurant

★★★★ 78% ◉◉ HOTEL

☎ 01603 759393
NR9 4DD
web: www.barnham-broom.co.uk
dir: A11/A47 towards Swaffham, follow brown tourist signs

Situated in a peaceful rural location just a short drive from Norwich, this hotel offers contemporary style bedrooms that are tastefully furnished and thoughtfully equipped. The Sports Bar serves a range of snacks and meals throughout the day, or guests can choose from the carte menu in Flints Restaurant. There are also extensive leisure, conference and banqueting facilities.

Rooms 46 (5 fmly) (22 GF) ♦ **S** £60-£205;
D £80-£225 (incl. bkfst)* **Facilities** Spa STV Wi-fi ⟍ ⟳ supervised ⚓ 36 ⚘ Putt green Gym Squash Sauna Steam room Personal trainers Xmas New Year **Conf** Class 100 Board 50 Thtr 150 Del from £130 to £165* **Services** Air con **Parking** 150 **Notes** LB ⊗ Civ Wed 150

BARNSLEY
South Yorkshire
Map 16 SE30

Tankersley Manor

★★★★ 77% HOTEL

☎ 01226 744700
Church Ln S75 3DQ
e-mail: tankersleymanor@qhotels.co.uk
web: www.qhotels.co.uk

(For full entry see Tankersley)

Premier Inn Barnsley Central M1 Jct 37

BUDGET HOTEL

☎ 0871 527 9204
Gateway Plaza, Sackville St S70 2RD
web: www.premierinn.com
dir: M1 junct 37, A628 (Dodworth Rd) signed Barnsley. In approx 1m 2nd exit at rdbt into Shambles St, car park entrance on left

High quality, budget accommodation ideal for both families and business travellers. Spacious, en suite bedrooms feature tea and coffee making facilities, and Freeview TV in most hotels. Internet access and Wi-fi are available for a small fee. The adjacent family restaurant features a wide and varied menu. See also the Hotel Groups pages.

Rooms 110

BARNSTAPLE
Devon
Map 3 SS53

The Imperial Hotel

★★★★ 75% HOTEL

☎ 01271 345861
Taw Vale Pde EX32 8NB
e-mail: reservations@brend-imperial.co.uk
web: www.brend-imperial.co.uk
dir: M5 junct 27/A361 to Barnstaple. Follow town centre signs, passing Tesco. Straight on at next 2 rdbts. Hotel on right

This smart and attractive hotel is pleasantly located at the centre of Barnstaple and overlooks the River Taw. Staff are friendly and offer attentive service. The comfortable bedrooms are of various sizes; some have balconies and many enjoy river views. Afternoon tea is available in the lounge, and the appetising cuisine is freshly prepared.

The Imperial Hotel

Rooms 63 (8 annexe) (9 fmly) (4 GF) ♦ **S** £89-£199; **D** £99-£199* **Facilities** FTV Wi-fi ⟍ Leisure facilities at sister hotel Xmas New Year **Conf** Class 40 Board 30 Thtr 60 **Services** Lift **Parking** 80 **Notes** LB ⊗ Civ Wed 50

See advert on opposite page

The Barnstaple Hotel

★★★ 80% HOTEL

☎ 01271 376221
Braunton Rd EX31 1LE
e-mail: reservations@barnstaplehotel.co.uk
web: www.barnstaplehotel.co.uk
dir: Outskirts of Barnstaple on A361

This well-established hotel enjoys a convenient location on the edge of town. Bedrooms are spacious and well equipped, many with access to a balcony overlooking the outdoor pool and garden. A wide choice is offered from various menus based on local produce, served in the Brasserie Restaurant. There is an extensive range of leisure and conference facilities.

Rooms 60 (4 fmly) (17 GF) ♦ **S** £64-£110;
D £72-£120* **Facilities** FTV Wi-fi ⟍ ⟳ ⚘ Gym Beauty treatment room Saunas Chill out sanctuary Xmas New Year Child facilities **Conf** Class 100 Board 50 Thtr 250 **Parking** 250 **Notes** LB ⊗ Civ Wed 150

Save on hotels. Book at **theAA.com/hotel**

BAR 63 ENGLAND

The Park Hotel

★★★ 78% HOTEL

☎ 01271 372166
Taw Vale EX32 9AE
e-mail: reservations@parkhotel.co.uk
web: www.parkhotel.co.uk
dir: A361 to Barnstable, 0.5m from town centre.
Opposite Rock Park

Enjoying views across the park and within easy
walking distance of the town centre, this modern
hotel offers a choice of bedrooms in both the main
building and the Garden Court, just across the car
park. Public rooms are open-plan in style and the
friendly staff offer attentive service in a relaxed
atmosphere.

Rooms 40 (17 annexe) (3 fmly) (2 GF) ↱ S £57-£75;
D £67-£85* **Facilities** FTV Wi-fi ☉ Leisure facilities
available at sister hotel Xmas New Year
Conf Class 50 Board 30 Thtr 80 **Parking** 100
Notes LB ⊗ Civ Wed 100

The Royal & Fortescue Hotel

★★★ 78% HOTEL

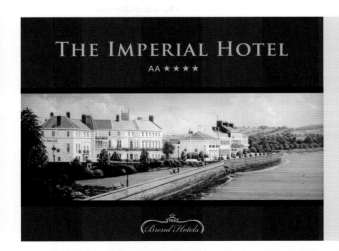

☎ 01271 342289
Boutport St EX31 1HG
e-mail: reservations@royalfortescue.co.uk
web: www.royalfortescue.co.uk
dir: From A361 onto Barbican Rd signed town centre,
right into Queen St, left into Boutport St, hotel on left

Formerly a coaching inn, this friendly and convivial
hotel is conveniently located in the centre of town.
Bedrooms vary in size and all are decorated and
furnished to a consistently high standard. In addition
to the formal restaurant, guests can take snacks in
the popular coffee shop or dine more informally in The
Bank, a bistro and café bar.

Rooms 49 (4 fmly) (4 GF) ↱ S £58-£123;
D £73-£153* **Facilities** FTV Wi-fi ☉ Leisure facilities
available at sister hotel Xmas New Year
Conf Class 25 Board 25 Thtr 25 **Services** Lift
Parking 40 **Notes** LB ⊗

Premier Inn Barnstaple

BUDGET HOTEL

☎ 0871 527 8052
Whiddon Dr, off Eastern Av EX32 8RY
web: www.premierinn.com
dir: Exit A361 (North Devon Link Rd) towards
Barnstaple. Right at Portmore rdbt

High quality, budget accommodation ideal for both
families and business travellers. Spacious, en suite
bedrooms feature tea and coffee making facilities,
and Freeview TV in most hotels. Internet access and
Wi-fi are available for a small fee. The adjacent
family restaurant features a wide and varied menu.
See also the Hotel Groups pages.

Rooms 40

B

B

BARROW-IN-FURNESS
Cumbria
Map 18 SD26

Clarence House Country Hotel & Restaurant

★★★★ 73% ◉◉ HOTEL

☎ 01229 462508
Skelgate, Dalton-in-Furness LA15 8BQ
e-mail: clarencehsehotel@aol.com
web: www.clarencehouse-hotel.co.uk
dir: A590 through Ulverston & Lindal, 2nd exit at rdbt & 1st exit at next. Follow signs to Dalton, hotel at top of hill on right

This hotel is located in ornamental grounds with unrestricted countryside views. Bedrooms are individually themed with those in the main hotel being particularly stylish and comfortable. The public rooms are spacious and also furnished to a high standard. The popular conservatory restaurant and contemporary brasserie offer well-prepared dishes from extensive menus. There is a delightful barn conversion that is ideal for weddings.

Rooms 19 (12 annexe) (1 fmly) (5 GF) **Facilities** FTV Wi-fi ♫ New Year **Conf** Class 40 Board 15 Thtr 100 **Parking** 40 **Notes** Closed 25-26 Dec Civ Wed 100

Abbey House Hotel

★★★ 79% HOTEL

☎ 01229 838282 & 0844 826 2091
Abbey Rd LA13 0PA
e-mail: enquiries@abbeyhousehotel.com
dir: From A590 follow signs for Furness General Hospital & Furness Abbey. Hotel approx 100yds on left

Set in its own gardens, this smart hotel provides stylish public areas, as well as extensive function and conference facilities. The well-equipped bedrooms vary in style - the more traditional rooms are in the main house while a more contemporary style of accommodation can be found in the extension. Service is friendly and helpful.

Rooms 61 (4 annexe) (6 fmly) (2 GF) ⚓ **Facilities** STV FTV Wi-fi ♫ Xmas New Year **Conf** Class 120 Board 80 Thtr 300 **Services** Lift **Parking** 100 **Notes** Civ Wed 120

Clarke's Hotel

★★★ 74% HOTEL

☎ 01229 820303
Rampside LA13 0PX
e-mail: bookings@clarkeshotel.co.uk
dir: A590 to Ulverston then A5087, take coast road for 8m, turn left at rdbt into Rampside

This smart, well-maintained hotel enjoys a peaceful location on the south Cumbrian coast, overlooking

Morecambe Bay. The tastefully appointed bedrooms come in a variety of sizes and are thoughtfully equipped, particularly for the business guest. Inviting public areas include an open-plan bar and a brasserie offering freshly prepared food throughout the day.

Rooms 14 (1 fmly) **Facilities** FTV **Parking** 50

BARTON
Lancashire
Map 18 SD53

Barton Grange Hotel

★★★★ 79% HOTEL

☎ 01772 862551
Garstang Rd PR3 5AA
e-mail: stay@bartongrangehotel.com
web: www.bartongrangehotel.co.uk
dir: M6 junct 32, follow Garstang (A6) signs for 2.5m. Hotel on right

Situated close to the M6, this modern, stylish hotel benefits from extensive public areas that include leisure facilities with a swimming pool, sauna and gym. Comfortable, well-appointed bedrooms include executive rooms and family rooms, as well as attractive accommodation in an adjacent cottage. The unique Walled Garden Bistro offers all-day eating.

Rooms 51 (8 annexe) (4 fmly) (4 GF) ⚓ **S** £50-£90; **D** £60-£120* **Facilities** STV Wi-fi ♫ ⊙ Gym Sauna Xmas New Year **Conf** Class 100 Board 80 Thtr 300 **Services** Lift **Parking** 250 **Notes** LB ⊗ Civ Wed 300

BARTON-ON-SEA
Hampshire
Map 5 SZ29

Pebble Beach

◉ RESTAURANT WITH ROOMS

☎ 01425 627777
Marine Dr BH25 7DZ
e-mail: mail@pebblebeach-uk.com
dir: A35 from Southampton onto A337 to New Milton, left into Barton Court Av to clifftop

Situated on the clifftop the restaurant at this establishment boasts stunning views towards The Needles. Bedrooms and bathrooms, situated above the restaurant, are well equipped and provide a range of accessories to enhance guest comfort. A freshly cooked breakfast is served in the main restaurant.

Rooms 4

BASILDON
Essex
Map 6 TQ78

Holiday Inn Basildon

★★★ 81% HOTEL

☎ 0871 942 9003 & 01268 824000
Waterfront Walk, Festival Leisure Park SS14 3DG
e-mail: reservations-basildon@ihg.com
web: www.hibasildonhotel.co.uk
dir: From A127 take A176/Basildon Billericay exit. Follow brown signs to Festival Leisure Park

This modern hotel sits alongside the river in a convenient location in the heart of town. It enjoys delightful views and is ideally placed for leisurely walks beside the river or for easy access to the town. The contemporary bedrooms are comfortable and particularly well equipped, with safes, Wi-fi and flat-screen TVs. There are a host of other facilities including a range of meeting rooms and leisure facilities, as well as a car park.

Rooms 148 (10 fmly) (8 GF) (16 smoking) **Facilities** STV Wi-fi ♫ Free use of nearby leisure club to over 18's New Year **Conf** Class 80 Board 80 Thtr 300 **Services** Lift Air con **Parking** 152 **Notes** ⊗ Civ Wed 300

Chichester Hotel

★★★ 77% HOTEL

☎ 01268 560555
Old London Rd, Wickford SS11 8UE
e-mail: reception@chichester-hotel.com
web: www.chichester-hotel.com
dir: Signed from A129 between Wickford & Rayleigh

Set in landscaped gardens and surrounded by farmland, this friendly hotel has been owned and run by the same family for over 25 years. Spacious bedrooms are located around an attractive courtyard, and each is pleasantly decorated and thoughtfully equipped. Public rooms include a cosy lounge bar and a smart restaurant.

Rooms 35 (32 annexe) (12 fmly) (17 GF) **S** £48-£72; **D** £48-£72* **Facilities** FTV Wi-fi **Parking** 150 **Notes** ⊗

Premier Inn Basildon (East Mayne)

BUDGET HOTEL

☎ 0871 527 8054
Felmores, East Mayne SS13 1BW
web: www.premierinn.com
dir: M25 junct 29 , A127 towards Southend, take A132 S signed Basildon & Wickford at Neverdon exit. Hotel on left

High quality, budget accommodation ideal for both families and business travellers. Spacious, en suite bedrooms feature tea and coffee making facilities, and Freeview TV in most hotels. Internet access and Wi-fi are available for a small fee. The adjacent family restaurant features a wide and varied menu. See also the Hotel Groups pages.

Rooms 32

Premier Inn Basildon (Festival Park)

BUDGET HOTEL

☎ 0871 527 8056
Festival Leisure Park, Pipps Hill Road South, Off Cranes Farm Rd SS14 3WB
web: www.premierinn.com
dir: M25 junct 9, A217 towards Basildon. Take A17. Hotel just off A1235 adjacent to David Lloyd Leisure Club

Rooms 64

Premier Inn Basildon South

BUDGET HOTEL

☎ 0871 527 8060
High Rd, Fobbing, Stanford-Le-Hope SS17 9NR
web: www.premierinn.com
dir: M2 junct 30/31, A13 towards Southend. 10m to Five Bells Rdbt junct with A176. Right into Fobbing High Rd. Hotel on left

Rooms 61

BASINGSTOKE   **Map 5 SU65**
Hampshire

INSPECTORS' CHOICE

Tylney Hall Hotel

★★★★ ◉◉ HOTEL

☎ 01256 764881
RG27 9AZ
e-mail: sales@tylneyhall.com
web: www.tylneyhall.com

(For full entry see Rotherwick)

Oakley Hall Hotel

★★★★ 83% ◉ COUNTRY HOUSE HOTEL

☎ 01256 783350
Rectory Rd RG23 7EL
e-mail: enquiries@oakleyhall-park.com
web: www.oakleyhall-park.com
dir: M3 junct 7, follow Basingstoke signs. In 500yds before lights turn left onto A30 towards Oakley, immediately right onto unclass road towards Oakley. In 3m left at T-junct into Rectory Rd. Left onto B3400. Hotel signed 1st on left

An impressive drive leads to this country house which benefits from delightful country views across north Hampshire. Built in 1795, it was once owned by the Bramston family who were friends of Jane Austen. An ideal wedding venue, Oakley Hall also has an excellent range of conference facilities, and is a great place to spend a relaxing leisure break. The bedrooms are spacious; many are located in the impressively restored courtyard and are particularly well equipped; there is also the delightful Garden Cottage. Service is delivered by a friendly team, and cuisine is contemporary and satisfying.

Rooms 18 (18 annexe) (8 fmly) (18 GF) 📶
Facilities FTV Wi-fi Clay pigeon shooting Xmas New Year **Conf** Class 82 Board 50 Thtr 300 Del from £145 to £195* **Services** Air con **Parking** 100 **Notes** ⊗ Civ Wed 100

Audleys Wood Hotel

★★★★ 80% ◉◉ HOTEL

☎ 01256 817555
Alton Rd RG25 2JT
e-mail: audleyswood@handpicked.co.uk
web: www.handpickedhotels.co.uk/audleyswood
dir: M3 junct 6. From Basingstoke take A339 towards Alton, hotel on right

A long sweeping drive leads to what was once a Victorian hunting lodge. This traditional country-house hotel offers bedrooms with flat-screen TVs and MP3 player connections. Smart and traditional public areas have log fires, and the dining options include the award-winning Simonds Room and a contemporary conservatory with a small minstrels' gallery.

Rooms 72 (23 fmly) (34 GF) **Facilities** STV FTV Wi-fi HL 🍴 Xmas New Year **Conf** Class 80 Board 60 Thtr 200 Del from £160 to £235 **Parking** 60 **Notes** ⊗ Civ Wed 100

The Hampshire Court Hotel

★★★★ 79% HOTEL

☎ 01256 319700
Centre Dr, Chineham RG24 8FY
e-mail: hampshirecourt@qhotels.co.uk
web: www.qhotels.co.uk
dir: Off A33 (Reading road) behind Chineham Shopping Centre via Great Binfields Rd

This hotel boasts a range of smart, comfortable and stylish bedrooms, and leisure facilities that are unrivalled locally. Facilities include indoor and outdoor tennis courts, two swimming pools, a gym and a number of treatment rooms.

Rooms 90 (6 fmly) 📶 **Facilities** Spa STV Wi-fi ⌕ HL 🏊 🏌 Gym Steam room Sauna Exercise studios Xmas New Year **Conf** Class 800 Board 60 Thtr 1500 **Services** Lift **Parking** 220 **Notes** Civ Wed 1500

Basingstoke Country Hotel

PUMA HOTELS
COLLECTION

★★★★ 76% ◉ HOTEL

☎ 01256 764161
Scures Hill, Nately Scures, Hook RG27 9JS
e-mail: basingstokecountry.mande@pumahotels.co.uk
web: www.pumahotels.co.uk
dir: M3 junct 5, A287 towards Newnham. Left at lights. Hotel 200mtrs on right

This popular hotel is close to Basingstoke, and its country location ensures a peaceful stay. Bedrooms are available in a number of styles - all have air conditioning, Wi-fi, in-room safes and hairdryers. Guests have a choice of dining in the formal restaurant, or for lighter meals and snacks there is a relaxed café and a smart bar. Extensive wedding, conference and leisure facilities complete the picture.

Rooms 100 (26 GF) **Facilities** Spa STV Wi-fi 🏊 supervised Gym Sauna Solarium Steam room Dance studio Beauty treatments New Year **Conf** Class 85 Board 80 Thtr 240 **Services** Lift Air con **Parking** 200 **Notes** RS 24 Dec-2 Jan Civ Wed 90

B

BASINGSTOKE *continued*

Apollo Hotel

★★★★ 71% ❀ HOTEL

☎ 01256 796700
Aldermaston Roundabout RG24 9NU
e-mail: admin@apollohotels.com
web: www.apollohotels.com
dir: M3 junct 6. Follow ring road N towards Newbury.
Follow A340 (Aldermaston) signs. Hotel on rdbt, 5th
exit into Popley Way for access

This modern hotel provides well-equipped
accommodation and spacious public areas, appealing
to both the leisure and business guest. Facilities
include a smartly appointed leisure club, a business
centre, along with a good choice of formal and
informal eating in two restaurants; Vespers is the fine
dining option.

Rooms 125 (32 GF) **Facilities** Spa FTV Wi-fi ↕ ⊗
supervised Gym Sauna Steam room **Conf** Class 196
Board 30 Thtr 255 **Services** Lift Air con **Parking** 200
Notes ⊗ Civ Wed 100

Holiday Inn Basingstoke

★★★ 79% HOTEL

☎ 0871 942 9004
Grove Rd RG21 3EE
e-mail: reservations-basingstoke@ihg.com
web: www.hibasingstokehotel.co.uk
dir: On A339 (Alton road) S of Basingstoke

Located conveniently on the southern approach to
Basingstoke and close to the M3, this modern,
comfortable hotel offers well-equipped, air-
conditioned bedrooms. There is a busy Conference
Academy on site. The staff are friendly throughout the
hotel. Free parking is available.

Rooms 86 (1 fmly) (43 GF) ↜ **Facilities** STV FTV Wi-fi
↕ Complimentary passes available at nearby leisure
centre Xmas New Year **Conf** Class 70 Board 70
Thtr 140 **Services** Air con **Parking** 150 **Notes** ⊗
Civ Wed 140

Premier Inn Basingstoke Central

BUDGET HOTEL

☎ 0871 527 8062
Basingstoke Leisure Park, Worting Rd RG22 6PG
web: www.premierinn.com
dir: M3 junct 6, A339 towards Newbury. A340 follow
brown Leisure Park signs. At next rdbt right onto
B3400 (Churchill Way West). Right on next rdbt into
Leisure Park. Hotel adjacent to Spruce Goose
Beefeater

High quality, budget accommodation ideal for both
families and business travellers. Spacious, en suite
bedrooms feature tea and coffee making facilities,
and Freeview TV in most hotels. Internet access and
Wi-fi are available for a small fee. The adjacent
family restaurant features a wide and varied menu.
See also the Hotel Groups pages.

Rooms 71

BASLOW
Derbyshire   Map 16 SK27

INSPECTORS' CHOICE

Fischer's Baslow Hall

★★★ ❀❀❀ HOTEL

☎ 01246 583259
Calver Rd DE45 1RR
e-mail: reservations@fischers-baslowhall.co.uk
web: www.fischers-baslowhall.co.uk
dir: On A623 between Baslow & Calver

Located at the end of a chestnut tree-lined drive on
the edge of the Chatsworth Estate, in marvellous
gardens, this beautiful Derbyshire manor house
offers sumptuous accommodation and facilities.
Staff provide very friendly and personally attentive
service. There are two styles of bedroom available -
traditional, individually-themed rooms in the main
house and spacious, more contemporary-styled
rooms with Italian marble bathrooms in the Garden
House. The cuisine is excellent and may prove the
highlight of any stay.

Rooms 11 (5 annexe) (4 GF) ↜ **S** £105-£145;
D £155-£225 (incl. bkfst)* **Facilities** FTV Wi-fi ↕ HL

Conf Board 15 Thtr 20 Del from £205 to £225*
Parking 40 **Notes** LB ⊗ No children 12 yrs Closed
25-26 Dec RS 31 Dec Civ Wed 38

Cavendish Hotel

★★★ 87% ❀❀ HOTEL

☎ 01246 582311
DE45 1SP
e-mail: info@cavendish-hotel.net
web: www.cavendish-hotel.net
dir: M1 junct 29/A617 W to Chesterfield & A619 to
Baslow. Hotel in village centre, off main road

This stylish property, dating back to the 18th century,
is delightfully situated on the outskirts of the
Chatsworth Estate. Elegantly appointed bedrooms
offer a host of thoughtful amenities, while
comfortable public areas are furnished with period
pieces and paintings. Guests have a choice of dining
in either the informal conservatory Garden Room or
the elegant Gallery Restaurant.

Rooms 24 (3 fmly) (2 GF) **S** £133-£177;
D £169-£219* **Facilities** FTV Wi-fi ↕ Putt green Xmas
New Year **Conf** Class 8 Board 18 Thtr 25
Del from £205 to £235* **Parking** 50 **Notes** LB ⊗
RS 25 Dec evening

Save on hotels. Book at **theAA.com/hotel**

BAS – BAT   67   ENGLAND

BASSENTHWAITE
Cumbria

Map 18 NY23

INSPECTORS' CHOICE

Armathwaite Hall Country House & Spa

★★★★ ◉ COUNTRY HOUSE HOTEL

☎ 017687 76551
CA12 4RE
e-mail: reservations@armathwaite-hall.com
web: www.armathwaite-hall.com
dir: M6 junct 40/A66 to Keswick rdbt then A591 signed Carlisle. 8m to Castle Inn junct, turn left. Hotel 300yds

Enjoying fine views over Bassenthwaite Lake, this impressive mansion, dating from the 17th century, is situated amid 400 acres of deer park. The comfortably furnished bedrooms and well-appointed bathrooms are complemented by a choice of public rooms that have many original features. The spa is an outstanding asset to the leisure facilities; it offers an infinity pool, thermal suite, sauna, state-of-the-art gym, treatments, exercise classes and a hot tub overlooking the landscaped gardens.

Rooms 46 (8 fmly) (8 GF) ⟨ **Facilities** Spa STV Wi-fi ⟨ supervised ⟨ Fishing ⟨ Gym Archery Clay shooting Quad & mountain bikes Falconry Xmas New Year **Conf** Class 50 Board 60 Thtr 200 **Services** Lift **Parking** 100 **Notes** Civ Wed 150

BEST WESTERN PLUS Castle Inn

★★★★ 77% HOTEL

☎ 017687 76401
CA12 4RG
e-mail: reservations@castleinncumbria.co.uk
web: www.castleinncumbria.co.uk
dir: A591 to Carlisle, pass Bassenthwaite village on right. Hotel on left of T-junct

Overlooking some of England's highest fells and Bassenthwaite Lake, this fine hotel is ideally situated for exploring Bassenthwaite, Keswick and the Lake District. The accommodation, extensive leisure facilities and friendly service are certainly strong points here. Ritson's Restaurant and Laker's Lounge offer a range of dishes using locally sourced meats from the fells; managed, sustainable fish stocks; and international and seasonal ingredients.

Rooms 42 (4 fmly) (9 GF) ⟨ **Facilities** FTV Wi-fi ⟨ supervised ⟨ Putt green Gym Sauna Steam room Xmas New Year **Conf** Class 108 Board 60 Thtr 200 **Parking** 120 **Notes** ⊗ Civ Wed 180

The Pheasant

★★★ 86% ◉ HOTEL

☎ 017687 76234
CA13 9YE
e-mail: info@the-pheasant.co.uk
web: www.the-pheasant.co.uk
dir: Midway between Keswick & Cockermouth, signed from A66

Enjoying a rural setting, within well-tended gardens, on the western side of Bassenthwaite Lake, this friendly 500-year-old inn is steeped in tradition. The attractive oak-panelled bar has seen few changes over the years, and features log fires and a great selection of malt whiskies. The individually decorated bedrooms are stylish and thoughtfully equipped.

Rooms 15 (2 annexe) (2 GF) **S** £95-£120; **D** £130-£200 (incl. bkfst)* **Facilities** FTV Wi-fi ⟨ New Year **Parking** 40 **Notes** LB No children 12yrs Closed 25 Dec

BATH
Somerset

Map 4 ST76

See also **Colerne & Hinton Charterhouse**

B

Macdonald Bath Spa

★★★★★ 87% ◉◉ HOTEL

☎ 0844 879 9106 & 01225 444424
Sydney Rd BA2 6JF
e-mail: sales.bathspa@macdonald-hotels.co.uk
web: www.macdonaldhotels.co.uk/bathspa
dir: A4, left onto A36 at 1st lights. Right at lights after pedestrian crossing left into Sydney Place. Hotel 200yds on right

A delightful Georgian mansion set amidst seven acres of pretty landscaped grounds, just a short walk from the many and varied delights of the city centre. A timeless elegance pervades the gracious public areas and bedrooms. Facilities include a popular leisure club, a choice of dining options and a number of meeting rooms. Macdonald Hotels is the AA Hotel Group of the Year 2013-14.

Rooms 129 (3 fmly) (17 GF) ⟨ **S** £265-£699; **D** £265-£699 **Facilities** Spa STV FTV Wi-fi ⟨ ⟨ ⟨ Gym Thermal suite Outdoor hydro pool Whirlpool Xmas New Year **Conf** Class 100 Board 50 Thtr 130 Del from £175 to £195 **Services** Lift Air con **Parking** 160 **Notes** LB ⊗ Civ Wed 130

The Royal Crescent Hotel

★★★★★ 83% ◉◉◉ HOTEL

☎ 01225 823333
16 Royal Crescent BA1 2LS
e-mail: info@royalcrescent.co.uk
dir: From A4, right at lights. 2nd left into Bennett St, into The Circus, 2nd exit into Brock St

The Royal Crescent Hotel is set in a number of houses in the famous Royal Crescent, and is one of the country's most interesting and historic places to stay. Bedrooms offer a range of suites and sizes, all have individual style and character, many have views across the city, and all are most comfortably appointed. Public rooms make the most of the character of the house and are styled in keeping with the elegance of the period. The hotel has a superb spa and range of leisure facilities, as well as a number of meeting rooms and private dining venues. The bar and Dower House restaurant offer the very best of contemporary dining and are not to be missed. Ingredients are sourced locally where possible, and elegantly presented by Head Chef David Campbell and his team.

Rooms 45 (8 fmly) (7 GF) ⟨ **S** £229-£955; **D** £249-£975 (incl. bkfst)* **Facilities** Spa STV FTV Wi-fi ⟨ ⟨ ⟨ Gym 1920s river launch Xmas New Year

continued

B

BATH *continued*

Conf Class 20 Board 20 Thtr 50 Del from £258 to £324* **Services** Lift Air con **Parking** 27 **Notes** LB Civ Wed 50

The Bath Priory Hotel, Restaurant & Spa

★★★★★ 82% ❀❀❀ HOTEL

☎ 01225 331922
Weston Rd BA1 2XT
e-mail: mail@thebathpriory.co.uk
web: www.thebathpriory.co.uk
dir: Adjacent to Victoria Park

The Bath Priory Hotel is a country house set in four acres of beautiful grounds. It features a luxury spa and award-winning, multi-AA Rosetted restaurant. The Priory Restaurant is under the direction of Head Chef, Sam Moody. Sam and his team deliver food that is derived from modern European cuisine, created from the very finest local produce and seasonal fruit, vegetable and herbs from the property's own garden. Opening onto the leafy gardens, the Mediterranean-style spa features an indoor heated swimming pool with a pool-side sauna and modern steam pod. Luxury beauty treatments are also available by appointment. Luxurious bedrooms have elegant decor and free Wi-Fi access. All rooms feature period furniture and spacious en suite bathrooms with fluffy bathrobes and designer toiletries.

Rooms 33 (6 annexe) (6 fmly) (1 GF) ⚑
S £170-£1030; **D** fr £210 (incl. bkfst)* **Facilities** Spa STV Wi-fi ❄ ⚓ ⚑ Gym Steam pod Sauna Xmas New Year **Conf** Class 25 Board 25 Thtr 32 **Parking** 40 **Notes** LB Civ Wed 70

Combe Grove Manor Hotel

★★★★ 78% ❀❀ COUNTRY HOUSE HOTEL

☎ 01225 834644
Brassknocker Hill, Monkton Combe BA2 7HS
e-mail: combegrovemanor@pumahotels.co.uk
web: www.pumahotels.co.uk
dir: Exit A36 at Limpley Stoke onto Brassknocker Hill. Hotel 0.5m up hill on left

Set in over 80 acres of gardens, this Georgian mansion commands stunning views over Limpley Stoke Valley. Most bedrooms are in the Garden Lodge, a short walk from the main house. The superb range of indoor and outdoor leisure facilities includes a beauty clinic with holistic therapies, golf, tennis and two pools. The Eden Brasserie is in the cellar (please note that the narrow steps may prove a problem for less able guests).

Rooms 42 (33 annexe) (5 fmly) (8 GF) **Facilities** Spa STV Wi-fi ⚓ supervised ⚓ ⚓ 5 ⚓ Putt green ⚑ Gym Squash Driving range Xmas New Year **Conf** Class 60 Board 30 Thtr 90 **Parking** 150 **Notes** ⊗ Civ Wed 50

Francis Hotel Bath - MGallery

★★★★ 76% HOTEL

☎ 01225 424105 & 338970
Queen Square BA1 2HH
e-mail: h6636@accor.com
web: www.francishotel.com
dir: M4 junct 18/A46 to Bath junct. 3rd exit onto A4, right into George St, left into Gay St into Queen Sq. Hotel on left

Overlooking Queen Square in the centre of the city, this elegant Georgian hotel is within walking distance of Bath's many attractions. The public rooms provide a variety of areas where guests can eat, drink and relax - from the informal café-bar to a more formal restaurant, to the traditional lounge. Bedrooms have air conditioning.

Rooms 98 (17 fmly) (5 smoking) ⚑ **S** £119-£314; **D** £119-£314* **Facilities** Wi-fi HL Xmas New Year **Conf** Class 40 Board 30 Thtr 80 **Services** Lift Air con **Parking** 40 **Notes** LB ⊗ Civ Wed 100

The Queensberry Hotel

★★★ ❀❀❀ HOTEL

☎ 01225 447928
Russel St BA1 2QF
e-mail: reservations@thequeensberry.co.uk
web: www.thequeensberry.co.uk
dir: 100mtrs from the Assembly Rooms

This charming family-run hotel, situated in a quiet residential street near the city centre, consists of four delightful townhouses. The spacious bedrooms offer deep armchairs, marble bathrooms and a range of modern comforts. Sumptuously furnished sitting rooms add to The Queensberry's appeal and allow access to the very attractive and peaceful walled gardens. The Olive Tree is a stylish restaurant that combines Georgian opulence with contemporary simplicity. Innovative menus are based on best quality ingredients and competent cooking. Valet parking proves a useful service.

Rooms 29 (2 fmly) (2 GF) ⚑ **S** £125-£190; **D** £130-£255* **Facilities** FTV Wi-fi **Conf** Class 12 Board 25 Thtr 35 Del from £195 to £265* **Services** Lift **Parking** 6 **Notes** ⊗

Abbey Hotel Bath

★★★ 79% ❀❀❀ HOTEL

☎ 01225 461603
1 North Pde BA1 1LF
e-mail: reservations@abbeyhotelbath.co.uk
web: www.abbeyhotelbath.co.uk
dir: M 4 junct 18/A46 for approx 8m. At rdbt right onto A4 for 2m. Once past Morrisons stay in left lane & turn left at lights. Over bridge & right at lights. Over rdbt & right at lights. Hotel at end of road

Perfectly located in the heart of Bath and just a two minute stroll to the famous Abbey, this popular hotel now has new owners who are transforming the hotel to a well balanced mix of a relaxing welcome with professional, helpful service in newly refurbished contemporary surroundings. The impressive new

B

Brasserie offers an excellent range of the highest quality dishes with something to suit all tastes. In the warmer months, outdoor seating on the front terrace is the ideal location for coffee or lunch.

Rooms 60 (7 fmly) (3 GF) ✎ **S** £90–£130; **D** £120–£200* **Facilities** Wi-fi ☾ Xmas New Year **Services** Lift **Notes** LB

Haringtons Hotel

★★★ 78% METRO HOTEL

☎ 01225 461728 & 445883
8-10 Queen St BA1 1HE
e-mail: post@haringtonshotel.co.uk
web: www.haringtonshotel.co.uk
dir: A4 into George St, into Milsom St. 1st right into Quiet St, 1st left into Queen St

Dating back to the 18th century, this hotel is situated in the heart of the city and provides all the expected modern facilities and comforts. Although a full dinner in a restaurant is not offered, the comfortably furnished lounge is light and airy and open throughout the day for light snacks and refreshments. A warm welcome is assured from the proprietors and staff, making this a delightful place to stay.

Rooms 13 (3 fmly) ✎ **S** £69–£170; **D** £79–£170 **Facilities** STV FTV Wi-fi **Conf** Class 10 Board 12 Thtr 18 **Parking** 11 **Notes** ⊗

Wentworth House Hotel

★★ 69% HOTEL

☎ 01225 339193
106 Bloomfield Rd BA2 2AP
e-mail: stay@wentworthhouse.co.uk
web: www.wentworthhouse.co.uk
dir: A36 towards Bristol at railway arches, hotel on right

This hotel is located on the outskirts of Bath yet is within walking distance of the city centre. Bedrooms vary in size and style; ground-floor rooms have their own conservatory seating area, some have four-posters and one has superb city views. The dinner menu features authentic home-cooked Indian dishes. There is a garden, which has a pool to enjoy in fine weather.

Rooms 20 (2 fmly) (6 GF) **S** £60–£100; **D** £65–£135 (incl. bkfst) **Facilities** STV FTV Wi-fi ☘ Xmas **Conf** Class 40 Board 35 Del from £95 to £135* **Parking** 19 **Notes** ⊗ No children 7yrs

Carfax Hotel

★★ ⓐ TOWN HOUSE HOTEL

☎ 01225 462089
13-15 Great Pulteney St BA2 4BS
e-mail: reservations@carfaxhotel.co.uk
dir: A36 onto Great Pulteney St

Comprising three Georgian town houses, this hotel has been welcoming guests for over 70 years. The individually designed bedrooms, of varying sizes, include TV with Sky channels and radios. A comprehensive range of dishes is offered at breakfast, and Sunday lunch is served. The hotel is not licensed.

Rooms 30 (5 fmly) (4 GF) **Facilities** FTV Wi-fi **Conf** Class 18 Board 12 Thtr 30 **Services** Lift **Parking** 13 **Notes** ⊗

Holiday Inn Express Bath

BUDGET HOTEL

☎ 01225 303000
Lower Bristol Rd, Brougham Hayes BA2 3QU
e-mail: info@expressbath.co.uk
web: www.hiexpress.co.uk/bath
dir: From A4, right into Bathwick St, over rdbt onto Pulteney Rd. Into Claverton St, straight over at next rdbt (Lower Bristol Rd). Hotel opposite Sainsburys

A modern hotel ideal for families and business travellers. Fresh and uncomplicated, the spacious rooms include Sky TV, power shower and tea and coffee-making facilities. Continental buffet breakfast is included in the room rate; other meals may be taken at the nearby family pub or restaurant. See also the Hotel Groups pages.

Rooms 126 (33 fmly) (31 GF) ✎ **Conf** Class 10 Board 15 Thtr 15

Bailbrook House Hotel

ⓤ

☎ 01225 855100
Eveleigh Ave, London Rd West BA1 7JD
e-mail: reception.bailbrook@handpicked.co.uk
web: www.bailbrookhouse.co.uk
dir: M4 junct 18/A46, at bottom of long hill take slip road to city centre. At rdbt take 1st exit. London Road West. Hotel 200mtrs on left

This property has undergone a £10 million refurbishment and renovation, and is now under new ownership of Hand Picked Hotels. Located within its own 20 acres of grounds, it offers free on-site parking and is just 1.5 miles from the city centre. Bailbrook House is made up of an historic main Georgian mansion house and the adjacent contemporary

Bailbrook Court. The hotel provides a fine dining restaurant, brasserie, three lounges and a conservatory bar. At the time of going to print the hotel was still undergoing development and is scheduled to open in August 2013; please see theAA.com for up-to-date information.

Rooms 94

Milsoms Bath

RESTAURANT WITH ROOMS

☎ 01225 750128
24 Milsom St BA1 1DG
e-mail: bath@milsomshotel.co.uk
dir: M4 junct 18, A46 (Bath), 3m, through Pennsylvania. 3rd exit at rdbt onto A420 (Bristol). 1st left signed Hamswell/Park & Ride, left at junct towards Lansdown. Right at next T-junct. 5th right into George St. 1st left into Milsom St

Located at the end of the main street in busy, central Bath, this stylish restaurant with rooms offers a range of comfortable, well-equipped accommodation. The ground-floor Loch Fyne Restaurant serves an excellent selection of dishes at both lunch and dinner with an emphasis on freshest quality fish and shellfish. A good selection of hot and cold items is also available in the same restaurant at breakfast.

Rooms 9

BATTLE	Map 7 TQ71
East Sussex	

Powder Mills Hotel

★★★ 81% ⓐ HOTEL

☎ 01424 775511
Powdermill Ln TN33 0SP
e-mail: powdc@aol.com
web: www.powdermillshotel.com
dir: M25 junct 5, A21 towards Hastings. At St Johns Cross take A2100 to Battle. Pass Abbey on right, 1st right into Powdermills Ln. 1m, hotel on right

A delightful 18th-century country-house hotel set amidst 150 acres of landscaped grounds with lakes and woodland. The individually decorated bedrooms are tastefully furnished and thoughtfully equipped; some rooms have sun terraces with lovely views over the lake. Public rooms include a cosy lounge bar, music room, drawing room, library, restaurant and conservatory.

Rooms 40 (10 annexe) (5 GF) ✎ **S** £100–£115; **D** £110–£140 (incl. bkfst)* **Facilities** STV FTV Wi-fi ☾ ☘ ⚒ Fishing Jogging trails Woodland walks Clay pigeon shooting Xmas New Year **Conf** Class 50 Board 16 Thtr 250 Del from £140 to £150* **Parking** 101 **Notes** LB Civ Wed 100

B

BATTLE *continued*

Brickwall Hotel

★★★ 78% HOTEL

☎ 01424 870253 & 870339
The Green, Sedlescombe TN33 0QA
e-mail: info@brickwallhotel.com
web: www.brickwallhotel.com
dir: A21 on B2244 at top of Sedlescombe Green

This is a well-maintained Tudor house, which is situated in the heart of a pretty village overlooking the green. The spacious public rooms feature a lovely wood-panelled restaurant with a wealth of oak beams, a choice of lounges and a smart bar. Bedrooms are pleasantly decorated and some have garden views.

Rooms 24 (2 fmly) (17 GF) ➤ S £49-£69; D £89-£129 (incl. bkfst)* **Facilities** Wi-fi ➤ Xmas New Year **Conf** Class 40 Board 30 Thtr 30 **Parking** 40 **Notes** LB

Leeford Place

★★ 72% HOTEL

☎ 01424 772863
Mill Ln, Whatlington TN33 0ND
e-mail: info@leefordplace.co.uk
dir: A21 towards Hastings, right at Whatlington Rd by Royal Oak, Leeford Place is 0.5m on right

Smartly appointed, privately owned hotel situated in a peaceful rural location on the outskirts of Battle. The spacious bedrooms are individually decorated, tastefully furnished and equipped with modern facilities. Public rooms include a smart conservatory, an attractive lounge bar, a cosy restaurant and large banqueting suite.

Rooms 18 S £45-£105; D £65-£105 (incl. bkfst)*
Facilities FTV Wi-fi Beauty Salon **Parking** 50
Notes LB Civ Wed 120

BEAMINSTER	Map 4 ST40
Dorset	

BridgeHouse

★★★ 81% ◉◉ HOTEL

☎ 01308 862200
3 Prout Bridge DT8 3AY
e-mail: enquiries@bridge-house.co.uk
web: www.bridge-house.co.uk
dir: A3066 to Beaminster, hotel 100yds from town square

Dating back to the 13th century, this property offers friendly and attentive service. The stylish bedrooms feature finest Italian cotton linens, flat-screen TVs and Wi-fi. There are five types of room to choose from, including four-poster and coach house rooms. Smartly presented public areas include the Georgian

dining room, cosy bar and adjacent lounge. There's also a breakfast room and the Beaminster Brasserie with its alfresco eating area under a canopy overlooking the attractive walled garden.

Rooms 13 (4 annexe) (2 fmly) (4 GF) ➤ **Facilities** FTV Wi-fi ➤ Xmas New Year **Conf** Class 14 Board 10 Thtr 24 **Parking** 20 **Notes** Civ Wed 100

BEANACRE	Map 4 ST96
Wiltshire	

Beechfield House Hotel, Restaurant & Gardens

★★★ 85% ◉ COUNTRY HOUSE HOTEL

☎ 01225 703700
SN12 7PU
e-mail: reception@beechfieldhouse.co.uk
web: www.beechfieldhouse.co.uk
dir: M4 junct 17, A350 S, bypass Chippenham, towards Melksham. Hotel on left in Beanacre

This is a charming, privately-owned hotel set within eight acres of beautiful grounds that has its own arboretum. Bedrooms are individually styled and include four-poster rooms, and ground-floor rooms in the coach house. Relaxing public areas are comfortably furnished and there is a beauty salon with a range of pampering treatments available. At dinner there is a very good selection of carefully prepared dishes with an emphasis on seasonal and local produce.

Rooms 24 (9 fmly) (4 GF) ➤ S £100-£215; D £125-£235 (incl. bkfst)* **Facilities** FTV Wi-fi ➤ ➤ Beauty treatment room Xmas New Year **Conf** Class 60 Board 45 Thtr 100 **Parking** 70 **Notes** LB Civ Wed 70

BEAULIEU	Map 5 SU30
Hampshire	

The Montagu Arms Hotel

★★★★ 82% ◉◉◉ HOTEL

☎ 01590 612324 & 624467
Palace Ln SO42 7ZL
e-mail: reservations@montaguarmshotel.co.uk
web: www.montaguarmshotel.co.uk
dir: M27 junct 2, follow signs for Beaulieu. In Dibden Purlieu right at rdbt. Hotel on left in Beaulieu

Situated at the heart of this charming village and surrounded by glorious New Forest scenery, the Montagu Arms dates back to 1742, and still retains the character of a traditional country house. The individually designed bedrooms include some with four-posters. Public rooms include a choice of two dining options: the informal Monty's brasserie serving home-cooked classics, and the stylish, award-winning Terrace Restaurant. Much produce comes from the kitchen garden project which saw a derelict piece of

land to the rear transformed to produce organic fruit, vegetables and herbs plus free-range eggs from the hens. In warmer weather there is a sheltered alfresco eating area overlooking the pretty terraced garden. Complimentary use of leisure and spa facilities is available to guests at a sister hotel six miles away.

Rooms 22 (3 fmly) ➤ S £164-£239; D £228-£378 (incl. bkfst)* **Facilities** FTV Wi-fi ➤ Complimentary use of spa in Brockenhurst Xmas New Year **Conf** Class 16 Board 26 Thtr 50 **Del** from £165 to £195* **Parking** 86 **Notes** ⊗ Civ Wed 100

Beaulieu Hotel

★★★ 80% ◉ HOTEL

NEW FOREST HOTELS

☎ 023 8029 3344 & 0800 444441
Beaulieu Rd SO42 7YQ
e-mail: beaulieu@newforesthotels.co.uk
web: www.newforesthotels.co.uk
dir: M27 junct 1, A337 towards Lyndhurst. Left at lights, through Lyndhurst, right onto B3056, hotel in 3m

Located in the heart of the beautiful New Forest National Park and close to Beaulieu Road railway station, this popular, small hotel provides an ideal base for exploring the area. Once a coaching inn, the hotel now particularly welcomes families; children will delight in seeing the ponies on the doorstep. Bedrooms, all with free Wi-fi and flat-screen TVs, range from cosy Keeper rooms to Crown rooms which also have four-posters and iPod docking stations. The relaxing Exbury Restaurant has doors that lead out onto the patio area and the landscaped gardens, and alfresco eating is possible in the summer.

Rooms 28 (7 annexe) (5 fmly) (4 GF) ➤ S £114; D £187 (incl. bkfst)* **Facilities** FTV Wi-fi ➤ HL ⊗ Steam room Xmas New Year **Conf** Class 100 Board 100 Thtr 250 **Del** £132 **Services** Lift **Parking** 60 **Notes** LB Civ Wed 200

The Master Builders at Bucklers Hard

★★★ 77% HOTEL

☎ 01590 616253
Buckler's Hard SO42 7XB
e-mail: enquiries@themasterbuilders.co.uk
web: www.themasterbuilders.co.uk
dir: M27 junct 2, follow Beaulieu signs. At T-junct left onto B3056, 1st left to Buckler's Hard. Hotel 2m on left before village

A tranquil historic riverside setting creates the backdrop for this delightful property. The main house bedrooms are full of historical features and of individual design, and in addition there are some bedrooms in the newer wing. Public areas include a popular bar and guest lounge, whilst grounds are an ideal location for alfresco dining in the summer months. Award-winning cuisine is served in the stylish dining room.

Rooms 26 (18 annexe) (4 fmly) (8 GF) **S** £130-£205; **D** £130-£205 (incl. bkfst)* **Facilities** FTV Wi-fi ⌕ Xmas New Year **Conf** Class 30 Board 20 Thtr 40 Del from £150 to £185* **Parking** 40 **Notes** Civ Wed 100

BECCLES
Suffolk   Map 13 TM48

Waveney House Hotel

★★★ 83% HOTEL

☎ 01502 712270
Puddingmoor NR34 9PL
e-mail: enquiries@waveneyhousehotel.co.uk
web: www.waveneyhousehotel.co.uk
dir: From A146 onto Common Lane North, left into Pound Rd, left into Ravensmere, right onto Smallgate, right onto Old Market, continue to Puddingmoor

An exceptionally well presented, privately owned hotel situated by the River Waveney on the edge of this busy little market town. The stylish public rooms include a smart lounge bar and a contemporary-style restaurant with views over the river. The spacious bedrooms are attractively decorated with co-ordinated fabrics and have many thoughtful touches.

Rooms 12 (3 fmly) **Facilities** FTV Wi-fi Xmas New Year **Conf** Class 100 Board 50 Thtr 160 **Parking** 45 **Notes** ⊗ Civ Wed 80

BEDFORD
Bedfordshire   Map 12 TL04

The Bedford Swan Hotel

★★★★ 75% ⊛ HOTEL

☎ 01234 346565
The Embankment MK40 1RW
e-mail: info@bedfordswanhotel.co.uk
web: www.bedfordswanhotel.co.uk
dir: Towards Bedford - A421 or A1M/A428

This historic hotel successfully combines original features with modern comforts. The bedrooms ooze style and quality; the needs of the modern traveller are catered for. The award-winning River Room Restaurant offers a varied choice of freshly prepared dishes. The hotel also offers meeting and function rooms, spa facilities and secure parking.

Rooms 113 (10 fmly) (12 smoking) **S** £79-£199; **D** £79-£199 (incl. bkfst) **Facilities** Spa STV FTV Wi-fi ⌕ ⊗ Xmas New Year **Conf** Class 40 Board 60 Thtr 250 **Services** Lift Air con **Parking** 80 **Notes** LB Civ Wed 250

The Barns Hotel

★★★★ 74% HOTEL

☎ 0844 855 9101
Cardington Rd MK44 3SA
e-mail: foh@barnshotelbedford.co.uk
web: www.barnshotelbedford.co.uk
dir: M1 junct 13, A421, approx 10m to A603 Sandy/ Bedford exit, hotel on right at 2nd rdbt

A tranquil location on the outskirts of Bedford, friendly staff and well-equipped bedrooms all combine to make this a good choice. Cosy day rooms and two informal bars add to the hotel's appeal, while large windows in the restaurant make the most of the view over the river. The original barn houses the conference and function suite.

Rooms 49 (18 GF) ⌕ **S** £69-£152; **D** £84-£167* **Facilities** Wi-fi Free use of local leisure centre (1m) New Year **Conf** Class 40 Board 40 Thtr 120 Del from £125 to £155* **Parking** 90 **Notes** LB ⊗ Civ Wed 90

B

B

BEDFORD *continued*

Woodland Manor Hotel

★★★ 71% HOTEL

☎ 01234 363281

Green Ln, Clapham MK41 6EP
e-mail: reception@woodlandmanorhotel.co.uk
dir: A6 towards Kettering. Clapham N of town centre. On entering village 1st right into Green Ln. Hotel 200mtrs on right

Sitting in acres of wooded grounds and gardens, this secluded Grade II listed, Victorian manor house offers a warm welcome. The hotel has spacious bedrooms and ample parking plus meeting rooms that are suitable for a variety of occasions. Public areas include a cosy bar and a smart restaurant, where traditional English dishes, with a hint of French flair, are served.

Rooms 34 (3 annexe) (6 fmly) (3 GF) ☜ **S** £40-£70; **D** £50-£110* **Facilities** STV FTV Wi-fi ⌂ **Conf** Class 25 Board 22 Thtr 80 Del from £130 to £140* **Parking** 60 **Notes** LB Civ Wed 80

Park Inn by Radisson Bedford

park inn
by Radisson

★★★ 68% HOTEL

☎ 01234 799988 & 799900

2 St Marys St MK40 1DZ
e-mail: info.bedford@rezidorparkinn.com
dir: B531, left A5141/Cauldwell St, right St Mary's St then left into Duck Mill Lane

This modern hotel sits alongside the river in a convenient location in the heart of town and enjoys delightful views. The comfortable bedrooms are contemporary in style and particularly well equipped, with safes, Wi-fi and flat-screen TVs. The hotel also offers a host of other facilities including leisure facilities and a range of meeting rooms.

Rooms 120 (1 fmly) (16 GF) **Facilities** FTV Wi-fi Gym Beauty treatment room Cardio vascular equipment Xmas New Year **Conf** Class 200 Board 160 Thtr 450 **Services** Lift Air con **Parking** 72 **Notes** ⊗ Civ Wed 100

Premier Inn Bedford (Priory Marina)

BUDGET HOTEL

☎ 0871 527 8066

Priory Country Park, Barkers Ln MK41 9DJ
web: www.premierinn.com
dir: M1 junct 13, A421, A6, A428 signed Cambridge. Cross River Ouse, right at next rdbt into Barkers Lane. Follow Priory Country Park signs. Hotel adjacent to Priory Marina Beefeater

High quality, budget accommodation ideal for both families and business travellers. Spacious, en suite bedrooms feature tea and coffee making facilities, and Freeview TV in most hotels. Internet access and Wi-fi are available for a small fee. The adjacent family restaurant features a wide and varied menu. See also the Hotel Groups pages.

Rooms 57

BELTON   Map 11 SK93
Lincolnshire

De Vere Belton Woods

DE VERE
HOTELS

★★★★ 75% HOTEL

☎ 01476 593200

NG32 2LN
e-mail: belton.woods@devere-hotels.com
web: www.devere.co.uk
dir: A1 to Gonerby Moor Services. B1174 towards Great Gonerby. At top of hill turn left towards Manthorpe/Belton. At T-junct turn left onto A607. Hotel 0.25m on left

Beautifully located amidst 475 acres of picturesque countryside, this is a destination venue for lovers of sport, especially golf, as well as a relaxing executive retreat for seminars. Comfortable and well-equipped accommodation complements the elegant and spacious public areas, which provide a good choice of drinking and dining options.

Rooms 136 (136 fmly) (68 GF) ☜ **Facilities** Spa STV FTV Wi-fi ⌂ HL ☒ supervised ₤ 45 ☋ Putt green ⛳ Gym Squash Outdoor activity centre ♫ Xmas New Year **Conf** Class 180 Board 80 Thtr 270 **Services** Lift **Parking** 350 **Notes** Civ Wed 80

BEMBRIDGE   Map 5 SZ68
Isle of Wight

Bembridge Coast Hotel

Warner Leisure Hotels
JUST FOR GROWN-UPS

★★★ 80% HOTEL

☎ 01983 873931

Fishermans Walk PO35 5TH
dir: A3055 Ryde to Sandown, approx 1.5m, left at lights into Carpenters Rd to St Helens. At mini-rdb 2nd exit onto A3395 signed Bembridge. In Bembridge follow one-way system to right, left after bakery into Forelands Rd. 1m, left into Lane End Rd. Follow to end, right to hotel entrance

This hotel occupies a delightfully peaceful location on the east coast of the Isle of Wight in 23-acre grounds. The accommodation is comfortable, and there are a number of rooms with sea views for which a small supplementary charge applies. A full activities itinerary ensures that guests can make the most of what the hotel, and this beautiful island, has to offer. The helpful reservations team can also arrange ferry bookings from the UK mainland. Please note that this is an adults-only (over 21 years) hotel.

Rooms 250 (76 GF) ☜ **Facilities** Spa FTV Wi-fi HL ☒ supervised ☋ Putt green ⛳ Gym ♫ Xmas New Year **Services** Lift **Parking** 244 **Notes** ⊗ No children 21yrs

---

BERWICK-UPON-TWEED   Map 21 NT95
Northumberland

Queens Head

★★★ 78% SMALL HOTEL

☎ 01289 307852

Sandgate TD15 1EP
e-mail: info@queensheadberwick.co.uk
dir: A1 towards centre & town hall, into High St. Right at bottom to Hide Hill

This small hotel is situated in the town centre, close to the old walls of this former garrison town. Bedrooms provide many thoughtful extras as standard. Dining remains a strong aspect with a carte menu that offers an impressive choice of tasty, freshly prepared dishes served in the comfortable lounge or dining room.

Rooms 6 (1 fmly) ☜ **S** £57.50-£75; **D** £80-£90* **Facilities** STV FTV Wi-fi ⌂ **Notes** ⊗

Save on hotels. Book at **theAA.com/hotel**

BED – BEX   73   ENGLAND

B

BEVERLEY
East Riding of Yorkshire   Map 17 TA03

Beverley Tickton Grange Hotel
★★★ 82% ◉◉ HOTEL

☎ 01964 543666
Tickton HU17 9SH
e-mail: info@ticktongrange.co.uk
dir: 3m NE on A1035

A charming Georgian country house situated in four acres of private grounds and attractive gardens. Bedrooms are individually designed and decorated to a high specification. Pre-dinner drinks may be enjoyed in the comfortable library lounge, prior to enjoying fine, modern British cooking in the restaurant. The hotel has excellent facilities for both weddings and business conferences.

Rooms 20 (3 annexe) (2 fmly) (4 GF) **S** £85-£115; **D** £118-£175 (incl. bkfst)* **Facilities** STV FTV Wi-fi Gym **Conf** Class 100 Board 80 Thtr 200 Del from £123.95 to £159* **Parking** 90 **Notes** ⊗ RS 25-29 Dec Civ Wed 200

BEST WESTERN Lairgate Hotel
★★★ 72% HOTEL

Best Western

☎ 01482 882141
30/32 Lairgate HU17 8EP
e-mail: lairgate@bestwestern.co.uk
dir: A63 towards town centre. Hotel 220yds on left, follow one-way system

Located just off the market square, this pleasing Georgian hotel has been appointed to offer stylish accommodation. Bedrooms are elegant and well equipped, and public rooms include a comfortable lounge, a lounge bar, and restaurant with a popular sun terrace.

Rooms 30 (1 fmly) (8 GF) ⚑ **S** £70-£90; **D** £98-£140 (incl. bkfst)* **Facilities** FTV Wi-fi New Year **Conf** Class 20 Board 20 Thtr 20 **Parking** 18 **Notes** LB ⊗ Closed 26 Dec & 1 Jan RS 25 Dec Civ Wed 70

BEWDLEY
Worcestershire   Map 10 SO77

Mercure Kidderminster Hotel
★★★ HOTEL

Mercure

☎ 0844 815 9033
Habberley Rd DY12 1LA
e-mail: info@mercurekidderminster.co.uk
web: www.jupiterhotels.co.uk
dir: A456 towards Kidderminster to ring road, follow signs to Bewdley. Pass Safari Park then exit A456/Town Centre, take sharp right after 200yds onto B4190, hotel 400yds on right

Currently the rating for this establishment is not confirmed. This may be due to a change of ownership or because it has only recently joined the AA rating scheme.

Rooms 44 **Conf** Class 120 Board 60 Thtr 350

BEXHILL
East Sussex   Map 6 TQ70

The Cooden Beach Hotel
★★★ 80% HOTEL

☎ 01424 842281
Cooden Beach TN39 4TT
e-mail: rooms@thecoodenbeachhotel.co.uk
web: www.thecoodenbeachhotel.co.uk
dir: A259 towards Bexhill. Signed at rdbt in Little Common Village. Hotel at end of road in Cooden, just past railway station

This privately owned hotel is situated in private gardens which have direct access to the beach. With a train station within walking distance the location is perfectly suited for both business and leisure guests. Bedrooms are comfortably appointed, and public areas include a spacious restaurant, lounge, bar and leisure centre with swimming pool.

Rooms 41 (8 annexe) (10 fmly) (4 GF) ⚑ **S** £40-£70; **D** £80-£160 (incl. bkfst)* **Facilities** FTV Wi-fi ⬡ Gym Sauna Steam room Spa bath Beauty treatment room ♫ Xmas New Year **Conf** Class 40 Board 40 Thtr 150 Del £135* **Parking** 60 **Notes** LB Civ Wed 160

BEXLEY
Greater London   Map 6 TQ47

Bexleyheath Marriott Hotel
★★★★ 75% HOTEL

Marriott

☎ 020 8298 1000
1 Broadway DA6 7JZ
e-mail: bexleyheath@marriotthotels.co.uk
web: www.bexleyheathmarriott.co.uk
dir: M25 junct 2/A2 towards London. Exit at Black Prince junct onto A220, signed Bexleyheath. Left at 2nd lights into hotel

Well positioned for access to major road networks, this large, modern hotel offers spacious, air-conditioned bedrooms with a comprehensive range of extra facilities. Planters Bar is a popular venue for pre-dinner drinks and offers guests a choice of lighter dining, although a more formal restaurant is also available. The hotel boasts a well-equipped leisure centre and undercover parking.

Rooms 142 (44 fmly) (26 GF) ⚑ **Facilities** Spa STV FTV Wi-fi ⬡ HL ⬡ supervised Gym Steam room Xmas New Year **Conf** Class 120 Board 34 Thtr 250 Del from £125 to £145* **Services** Lift Air con **Parking** 78 **Notes** ⊗ Civ Wed 80

Holiday Inn London - Bexley
★★★ 78% HOTEL

Holiday Inn

☎ 0871 942 9006 & 01322 625513
Black Prince Interchange, Southwold Rd DA5 1ND
e-mail: bexley@ihg.com
web: www.hilondonbexleyhotel.co.uk
dir: M25 junct 2, A2 towards London. Exit at Black Prince Interchange (signed Bexley, Bexleyheath, A220, A223). Hotel on left

This hotel is within easy access of London and the Kent countryside; only 10 minutes from the famous Bluewater Shopping Centre and 15 minutes from Brands Hatch motor racing circuit. All bedrooms are air conditioned; suites are available. The hotel has a range of meeting rooms.

Rooms 107 (17 fmly) (33 GF) (8 smoking) **S** £69-£199; **D** £69-£199* **Facilities** STV FTV Wi-fi ⬡ Fitness room Xmas New Year **Conf** Class 42 Board 50 Thtr 120 Del from £125* **Services** Lift Air con **Parking** 200 **Notes** LB ⊗ Civ Wed 100

B

BIBURY
Gloucestershire
Map 5 SP10

Swan Hotel
★★★★ 73% ❀ HOTEL

Cotswold
Inns & Hotels

☎ 01285 740695
GL7 5NW
e-mail: info@swanhotel.co.uk
web: www.cotswold-inns-hotels.co.uk/swan
dir: 9m S of Burford A40 onto B4425. 6m N of
Cirencester A4179 onto B4425

This hotel, built in the 17th century as a coaching
inn, is set in peaceful and picturesque surroundings.
It provides well-equipped and smartly presented
accommodation, including four luxury cottage suites
set just outside the main hotel. The elegant public
areas are comfortable and have feature fireplaces.
There is a choice of dining options to suit all tastes.

Rooms 22 (4 annexe) (1 fmly) ↖ **S** £150-£210;
D £170-£370 (incl. bkfst)* **Facilities** FTV Wi-fi
Fishing Xmas New Year **Conf** Class 50 Board 32
Thtr 80 **Services** Lift **Parking** 22 **Notes** Civ Wed 110

Bibury Court Hotel
★★★ 85% ❀❀ COUNTRY HOUSE HOTEL

☎ 01285 740337 & 741171
GL7 5NT
e-mail: hello@biburycourt.com
web: www.biburycourt.com
dir: On B4425, 6m N of Cirencester (A4179). 8m S of
Burford (A40), entrance by River Coln

Dating back to Tudor times, this elegant manor is the
perfect antidote to the hustle and bustle of the
modern world. Public areas have abundant charm
and character, while bedrooms are spacious and offer
traditional quality with modern comforts. A choice of
interesting dishes is available in the conservatory at
lunchtime, whereas dinner is served in the more
formal restaurant. Staff are friendly and helpful.

Rooms 18 (3 fmly) (1 GF) ↖ **S** £95-£345; **D** £95-£345
(incl. bkfst)* **Facilities** FTV Wi-fi Fishing ⛵ Xmas
New Year **Conf** Class 50 Board 30 Thtr 50
Del from £200 to £250* **Parking** 40 **Notes** LB
Civ Wed 80

BIDEFORD
Devon
Map 3 SS42

Yeoldon House Hotel
★★★ 77% ❀ SMALL HOTEL

☎ 01237 474400
Durrant Ln, Northam EX39 2RL
e-mail: yeoldonhouse@aol.com
web: www.yeoldonhousehotel.co.uk
dir: A39 from Barnstaple over River Torridge Bridge.
At rdbt right onto A386 towards Northam, 3rd right
into Durrant Lane

In a tranquil location with superb views over
attractive grounds and the River Torridge, is this
charming Victorian house. The well-equipped
bedrooms are individually decorated and some have
balconies with breathtaking views. The public rooms
are full of character with many interesting features
and artefacts. The daily-changing dinner menu offers
imaginative dishes.

Rooms 10 **S** £85-£90; **D** £125-£145 (incl. bkfst)
Facilities FTV Wi-fi **Parking** 20 **Notes** LB Closed
24-27 Dec Civ Wed 50

The Royal Hotel
★★★ 74% HOTEL

(Brend Hotels)

☎ 01237 472005
Barnstaple St EX39 4AE
e-mail: reservations@royalbideford.co.uk
web: www.royalbideford.co.uk
dir: At eastern end of old Bideford Bridge

A quiet and relaxing hotel, the Royal is set near the
river within a five-minute walk of the busy town

centre and the quay. The bright, well maintained
public areas retain much of the charm and style of
the hotel's 16th-century origins, particularly n the
wood-panelled Kingsley Suite. Bedrooms are well
equipped and comfortable. The meals at dinner and
the lounge snacks are appetising.

Rooms 32 (2 fmly) (2 GF) ↖ **S** £55-£120;
D £75-£120* **Facilities** FTV Wi-fi ☒ Xmas New Year
Conf Class 100 Board 100 Thtr 100 **Services** Lift
Parking 70 **Notes** LB ⊗ Civ Wed 130

Durrant House Hotel
★★★ Ⓐ HOTEL

☎ 01237 472361
Heywood Rd, Northam EX39 3QB
e-mail: info@durranthousehotel.com
dir: A39 to Bideford, over New Torridge Bridge, right
at rdbt, hotel 500yds on right

This large hotel offers bedrooms with Italian-marble
bathrooms, and the facilities include a hospitality
tray, hairdryer, TV, clock radio and an iron with
ironing board; superior rooms have wonderful views of
the Torridge estuary and Taw Valley, plus rain
showers, sofas and luxury toiletries. The fine dining,
oak-panelled Olive Tree Restaurant offers dishes
based on locally sourced produce.

Rooms 125 (25 fmly) (14 GF) **Facilities** FTV Wi-fi ↖
Gym Sauna ♫ Xmas New Year **Conf** Class 100
Board 80 Thtr 350 **Services** Lift **Parking** 200
Notes Civ Wed 100

BIGBURY-ON-SEA
Devon
Map 3 SX64

Henley Hotel
★★ 83% SMALL HOTEL

☎ 01548 810240
TQ7 4AR
e-mail: thehenleyhotel@btconnect.com
dir: Through Bigbury, past Golf Centre into Bigbury-
on-Sea. Hotel on left

Henley Hotel is an Edwardian building complete with
its own private cliff path to a sandy beach, and
stunning views from an elevated position. Family run,
it is a perfect choice for guests wishing to escape to a
peaceful retreat. Personal service, friendly hospitality
and food cooked with care using local, fresh produce
combine to make this an uncomplicated and special
place to stay.

Rooms 6 **S** £85; **D** £120-£145 (incl. bkfst)*
Facilities FTV Wi-fi **Parking** 9 **Notes** LB No children
12yrs Closed Nov-Mar

BILDESTON   Map 13 TL94
Suffolk

INSPECTORS' CHOICE

The Bildeston Crown

★★★ ☺☺☺ HOTEL

☎ 01449 740510
104 High St IP7 7EB
e-mail: hayley@thebildestoncrown.co.uk
web: www.thebildestoncrown.co.uk
dir: A12 junct 31, B1070 towards Hadleigh. At
T-junct left onto A1141, right onto B1115. Hotel
0.5m

The Bildeston Crown is a charming Grade II former
coaching inn situated in a peaceful village. Public
areas feature beams, exposed brickwork and oak
floors, with contemporary style décor. There is a
choice of bars, a lounge and a restaurant. The
individually designed bedrooms, including a
romantic four-poster room, have lovely co-ordinated
fabrics and modern facilities that include Musicast
systems and internet access via Wi-fi and
LAN. Food here is the real focus and certainly a
draw; both the chef and the owner, who is a farmer,
are very conscious of reducing 'food miles'; top
quality produce such as Red Poll beef (from the
owner's own farm), locally reared lamb, pork and
seasonal game appear on the menus. Accomplished
technical skills achieve award-winning results.

Rooms 13 🐾 **S** £80-£195; **D** £100-£195 (incl.
bkfst)* **Facilities** STV FTV Wi-fi Xmas New Year
Conf Class 25 Board 16 Thtr 40 Del from £100 to
£125* **Services** Lift **Parking** 30 **Notes** LB
Civ Wed 50

BILLINGHAM   Map 19 NZ42
Co Durham

INSPECTORS' CHOICE

Wynyard Hall Hotel

★★★★ ☺☺☺ HOTEL

☎ 01740 644811
Wynyard TS22 5NF
e-mail: enq@wynyardhall.co.uk
web: www.wynyardhall.co.uk
dir: A19, A1027 towards Stockton. At rdbt take
B1274 (Junction Rd). At next rdbt take A177
(Durham Rd). Right onto Wynyard Rd signed
Wolviston. Left into estate

Drive though the gates, over the lion bridge and
Wynyard Hall will immediately impress with its
grandeur and elegance. The opulent public areas
are as much a feature of the property as are the
grounds and gardens. The individually designed
bedrooms and suites are stunning, with a
combination of modern and period style furniture.
The elegant, award-winning Duke of Wellington
restaurant is also impressive, to the tune of three
AA Rosettes. The Essential Time Treatment Suite
offers many relaxing therapies and beauty
treatments. As a wedding venue the hall provides
the option for a civil ceremony, or a religious service
in the chapel, followed by a memorable reception.

Rooms 25 (9 annexe) (1 fmly) (9 GF) 🐾
S £180-£240; **D** £180-£240 (incl. bkfst)*
Facilities Spa FTV Wi-fi ◊ 🏊 Clay pigeon shooting
Archery Hawk walk Boot camp Xmas New Year
Conf Class 240 Board 50 Thtr 300
Del from £191.50 to £211.50* **Services** Lift
Parking 500 **Notes** LB ☻ Civ Wed 150

BILSBORROW   Map 18 SD53
Lancashire

Premier Inn Preston North

BUDGET HOTEL

☎ 0871 527 8912
Garstang Rd PR3 0RN
web: www.premierinn.com
dir: 4m from M6 junct 32 on A6 towards Garstang.
7m from Preston

High quality, budget accommodation ideal for both
families and business travellers. Spacious, en suite
bedrooms feature tea and coffee making facilities,
and Freeview TV in most hotels. Internet access and
Wi-fi are available for a small fee. The adjacent
family restaurant features a wide and varied menu.
See also the Hotel Groups pages.

Rooms 40

BINGLEY   Map 19 SE13
West Yorkshire

Five Rise Locks Hotel & Restaurant

★★★ 75% ☺ SMALL HOTEL

☎ 01274 565296
Beck Ln BD16 4DD
e-mail: info@five-rise-locks.co.uk
dir: From Main St into Park Rd, in 0.5m left into Beck
Ln

A warm welcome and comfortable accommodation
awaits guests at this impressive Victorian building.
Bedrooms are of a good size and feature homely
extras. The restaurant offers imaginative dishes and
the bright breakfast room overlooks open countryside.

Rooms 9 (2 GF) **S** £69; **D** £92-£115 (incl. bkfst)*
Facilities FTV Wi-fi **Conf** Class 16 Board 18 Thtr 25
Del from £110 to £150* **Parking** 20 **Notes** LB Closed
6-14 May

Mercure Bradford North Hotel

★★★ HOTEL

☎ 0844 815 9004
Bradford Rd BD16 1TU
e-mail: info@mercurebradford.co.uk
web: www.jupiterhotels.co.uk
dir: From M62 junct 26 onto M606, at rdbt follow
signs for A650 Skipton/Keighley, hotel 2m from
Shipley.

Currently the rating for this establishment is not
confirmed. This may be due to a change of ownership
or because it has only recently joined the AA rating
scheme.

Rooms 103 **Conf** Class 328 Board 246 Thtr 560

B

BIRCHANGER GREEN MOTORWAY SERVICE AREA (M11)
Essex
Map 6 TL52

Days Inn Bishop's Stortford - M11

BUDGET HOTEL

☎ 01279 656477

CM23 5QZ
e-mail: birchanger.hotel@welcomebreak.co.uk
web: www.welcomebreak.co.uk
dir: M11 junct 8

This modern building offers accommodation in smart, spacious and well-equipped bedrooms, suitable for families and business travellers, and all with en suite bathrooms. Continental breakfast is available and other refreshments may be taken at the nearby family restaurant. See also the Hotel Groups pages.

Rooms 60 (12 fmly) (29 GF) (8 smoking)

BIRKENHEAD
Merseyside
Map 15 SJ38

The RiverHill Hotel

★★★ 85% HOTEL

☎ 0151 653 3773

Talbot Rd, Prenton CH43 2HJ
e-mail: reception@theriverhill.co.uk
web: www.theriverhill.co.uk
dir: M53 junct 3, A552. Left onto B5151 at lights, hotel 0.5m on right

Pretty lawns and gardens provide the setting for this friendly, privately owned hotel. Its convenient location and attractive grounds make it a popular wedding venue. The comfortable bedrooms are equipped with a wealth of extras; ground floor, family, and four-poster rooms are available. Well-cooked meals and substantial breakfasts are served in the elegant restaurant overlooking the garden.

Rooms 14 (1 fmly) **S** £50-£69.75; **D** £75-£89.50*
Facilities FTV Wi-fi Free use of local leisure facilities
Conf Class 30 Board 52 Thtr 50 **Parking** 32 **Notes** ⊗
Civ Wed 40

Premier Inn Wirral (Greasby)

BUDGET HOTEL

☎ 0871 527 9176

Greasby Rd, Greasby, Wirral CH49 2PP
web: www.premierinn.com
dir: 9m from Liverpool city centre. 2m from M53 junct 2. Just off B5139

High quality, budget accommodation ideal for both families and business travellers. Spacious, en suite bedrooms feature tea and coffee making facilities, and Freeview TV in most hotels. Internet access and Wi-fi are available for a small fee. The adjacent family restaurant features a wide and varied menu. See also the Hotel Groups pages.

Rooms 30

BIRMINGHAM
West Midlands
Map 10 SP08

See also Bromsgrove, Lea Marston, Oldbury & Sutton Coldfield

Hotel du Vin Birmingham

★★★★ 78% ◎ ◎
TOWN HOUSE HOTEL

☎ 0844 736 4250

25 Church St B3 2NR
e-mail: info@birmingham.hotelduvin.com
web: www.hotelduvin.com
dir: M6 junct 6/A38(M) to city centre, over flyover. Keep left & exit at St Chads Circus signed Jewellery Quarter. At lights & rdbt take 1st exit, follow signs for Colmore Row, opposite cathedral. Right into Church St, across Barwick St. Hotel on right

The former Birmingham Eye Hospital has become a chic and sophisticated hotel. The stylish, high-ceilinged rooms, all with a wine theme, are luxuriously appointed and feature stunning bathrooms, sumptuous duvets and Egyptian cotton sheets. The Bistro offers relaxed dining and a top-notch wine list, while other attractions include a champagne bar, a wine boutique and a health club.

Rooms 66 ☇ **Facilities** Spa STV Wi-fi Gym Steam room Sauna Xmas New Year **Conf** Class 40 Board 40 Thtr 84 **Services** Lift Air con **Notes** Civ Wed 84

Birmingham Marriott Hotel

★★★★ 78% HOTEL

☎ 0121 452 1144

12 Hagley Rd, Five Ways B16 8SJ
web: www.birminghammarriott.co.uk
dir: Leebank Middleway to Five Ways rdbt, 1st left then right. Follow signs for hotel

Situated in the suburb of Edgbaston, this Edwardian hotel is a prominent landmark on the outskirts of the city centre. Air-conditioned bedrooms are decorated in a comfortable, modern style and provide a comprehensive range of extra facilities. Public rooms include the contemporary, brasserie-style West 12 Bar and Restaurant.

Rooms 104 **Facilities** Spa STV Wi-fi ⌇ ⌘ Gym Steam room **Conf** Board 35 Thtr 80 **Services** Lift Air con **Parking** 50 **Notes** ⊗ Civ Wed 60

Macdonald Burlington Hotel

★★★★ 76% HOTEL

☎ 0844 879 9019 & 0121 643 9191

Burlington Arcade, 126 New St B2 4JQ
e-mail: events.burlington@macdonald-hotels.co.uk
web: www.macdonaldhotels.co.uk/burlington
dir: M6 junct 6, A38, follow city centre signs

The Burlington's original Victorian grandeur - the marble and iron staircases and the high ceilings - blend seamlessly with modern facilities. Bedrooms are equipped to a good standard and public areas include a stylish bar and coffee lounge. The Berlioz Restaurant specialises in innovative dishes using fresh produce. Macdonald Hotels is the AA Hotel Group of the Year 2013-14.

Rooms 114 (6 fmly) ☇ **Facilities** STV Wi-fi ⌇ HL New Year **Conf** Class 200 Board 80 Thtr 500 **Services** Lift **Notes** Closed 24-26 Dec Civ Wed 400

Novotel Birmingham Centre

★★★★ 75% HOTEL

☎ 0121 643 2000

70 Broad St B1 2HT
e-mail: h1077@accor.com
web: www.novotel.com
dir: M6 junct 6, A38(M) (Aston Expressway), A456 towards Kidderminster

This large, modern, purpose-built hotel benefits from an excellent city centre location, with the bonus of secure parking. Bedrooms are spacious, modern and well equipped especially for business users; four rooms have facilities for less able guests. Public

B

areas include the Garden Brasserie, function rooms and a fitness room.

Rooms 148 (148 fmly) ☀ **Facilities** Wi-fi ⌘ Gym Fitness room Cardiovascular equipment Sauna Steam room New Year **Conf** Class 120 Board 90 Thtr 300 **Services** Lift Air con **Parking** 53

Radisson Blu Hotel Birmingham

★★★★ 74% HOTEL

☎ 0121 654 6000

12 Holloway Circus, Queensway B1 1BT

e-mail: info.birmingham@radissonblu.com

dir: Through A38 underpass, left, merge into Suffolk St Queensway. Hotel on corner of Holloway Circus Queensway

This modern glass structure of 39 floors sits in the heart of the city dominating the area with its conceptual design. The interior continues the modern look and feel - public areas have wooden floors, leather seating and a stylish Italian restaurant. The bedrooms are individually appointed with bold colours and designer pieces of furniture. The small gym, sauna suite and spa areas add to the hotel's impressive facilities.

Rooms 211 **Facilities** Spa STV FTV Wi-fi ⌘ HL Gym Sauna **Conf** Class 48 Board 40 Thtr 130 **Services** Lift Air con **Notes** ⊗ Civ Wed 130

Menzies Strathallan

★★★★ 73% HOTEL

☎ 0121 455 9777

225 Hagley Rd, Edgbaston B16 9RY

e-mail: strathallan@menzieshotels.co.uk

web: www.menzies-hotels.co.uk

dir: From A38 follow signs for ICC into Broad St, towards Five Ways island, take underpass to Hagley Rd. Hotel 1m

Located just a few minutes from the city's central attractions and with the benefit of excellent parking, this hotel provides a range of comfortable and well-equipped bedrooms. A modern lounge bar and contemporary restaurant offer a good range of dining options.

Rooms 135 (36 fmly) ☀ **Facilities** FTV Wi-fi ⌘ Gym Xmas New Year **Conf** Class 90 Board 50 Thtr 170 **Services** Lift **Parking** 120 **Notes** ⊗ Civ Wed 100

Copthorne Hotel Birmingham

★★★★ 71% HOTEL

☎ 0121 200 2727

Paradise Circus B3 3HJ

e-mail: reservations.birmingham@millenniumhotels.co.uk

web: www.millenniumhotels.co.uk

dir: M6 junct 6, city centre A38(M). After Queensway Tunnel follow International Convention Centre signs. At Paradise Circus island take right lane. Hotel in centre

This hotel is one of the few establishments in the city that benefits from its own car park. Bedrooms are spacious and come in a choice of styles, all with excellent facilities. Guests can choose to eat in the Bugis Street Brasserie which offers traditional Chinese, Singaporean and Malay cuisine.

Rooms 211 **Facilities** FTV Wi-fi ⌘ Gym Xmas New Year **Conf** Class 120 Board 30 Thtr 200 **Services** Lift **Parking** 78 **Notes** ⊗ Civ Wed 150

Malmaison Birmingham

★★★ 83% ◉ HOTEL

☎ 0121 246 5000

1 Wharfside St, The Mailbox B1 1RD

e-mail: birmingham@malmaison.com

web: www.malmaison.com

dir: M6 junct 6, A38 towards Birmingham. Hotel within The Mailbox, signed from A38

The 'Mailbox' development, of which this stylish and contemporary hotel is a part, incorporates the very best in fashionable shopping outlets, an array of restaurants and ample parking. The air-conditioned bedrooms are stylishly decorated and feature comprehensive facilities. Public rooms include a contemporary bar and brasserie which prove a hit with guests and locals alike. Gymtonic, and a Petit Spa offering rejuvenating treatments are also available.

Rooms 189 **Facilities** Wi-fi Gym **Conf** Class 40 Board 24 Thtr 50 **Services** Lift Air con

BEST WESTERN Westley Hotel

★★★ 82% HOTEL

☎ 0121 706 4312

80-90 Westley Rd, Acocks Green B27 7UJ

e-mail: reservations@westley-hotel.co.uk

dir: A41 signed Birmingham on Solihull by-pass, to Acocks Green. At rdbt, 2nd exit B4146 (Westley Rd). Hotel 200yds on left

Situated in the city suburbs and conveniently located for the N.E.C. and the airport, this friendly hotel

provides well-equipped, smartly presented bedrooms. In addition to the main restaurant, there is also a lively bar and brasserie together with a large function room.

Rooms 37 (11 annexe) (3 fmly) (3 GF) **S** £55-£95; **D** £75-£110 (incl. bkfst) **Facilities** STV Wi-fi ⌘ New Year **Conf** Class 80 Board 50 Thtr 200 Del from £159 to £209 **Parking** 150 **Notes** ⊗ Civ Wed 200

Thistle Birmingham City

thistle

★★★ 81% HOTEL

☎ 0871 376 9005

St Chads, Queensway B4 6HY

e-mail: birminghamcity@thistle.co.uk

web: www.thistle.com/birminghamcity

dir: From M6 junct 6 onto Aston Expressway towards city centre, after 1m exit A38 signed Jewellery Quarter. Hotel on left

Thistle Birmingham City benefits from a central location and is convenient for both the motorway network and nearby extensive parking facilities. Bedrooms range in size and style with most bedrooms providing air conditioning, along with a host of thoughtful guest extras. A modern comfortable lounge bar links to a terrace area.

Rooms 133 (3 fmly) **Facilities** STV Wi-fi Xmas New Year **Conf** Class 90 Board 35 Thtr 180 **Services** Lift **Notes** ⊗ Civ Wed 170

Holiday Inn Birmingham City

Holiday Inn

★★★ 80% HOTEL

☎ 0871 942 9008 & 0121 634 6202

Smallbrook Queensway B5 4EW

e-mail: reservations@hibirmingham.co.uk

web: www.holidayinn.co.uk

dir: M6 junct 6, A38(M) to city centre, keep left after flyover & two underpasses. 2nd left into Suffolk Place. 1st right into St Jude's Passage

This is a large hotel in the city centre with extensive meeting rooms and a business centre. The lounge bar with a roof terrace is a popular meeting place. The Albany Restaurant offers lunch and dinner, and room service is available.

Rooms 241 (8 fmly) ☀ **S** £49-£189; **D** £49-£189 **Facilities** FTV Wi-fi ⌘ HL **Conf** Class 300 Board 150 Thtr 600 Del from £99 to £189 **Services** Lift Air con **Parking** 8

BIRMINGHAM *continued*

B

Holiday Inn Birmingham M6 Jct 7

★★★ 75% HOTEL

☎ 0871 942 9009 & 0121 357 7303
Chapel Ln, Great Barr B43 7BG
e-mail: birminghamgreatbarr@ihg.com
web: www.holidayinn.co.uk
dir: M6 junct 7, A34 signed Walsall. Hotel 200yds on right across carriageway in Chapel Ln

Situated in pleasant surroundings, this modern hotel offers well-equipped and comfortable bedrooms. Public areas include the popular Traders restaurant and a comfortable lounge where a menu is available to guests all day. There is also 24-hour room service; a courtyard patio and a garden.

Rooms 190 (44 fmly) (67 GF) **S** £29–£110; **D** £39–£120* **Facilities** STV FTV Wi-fi ℘ ⊕ supervised Gym Beauty treatment room Xmas New Year **Conf** Class 75 Board 50 Thtr 160 Del from £99 to £145* **Services** Air con **Parking** 250 **Notes** LB Civ Wed 160

Edgbaston Palace Hotel

★★★ 73% HOTEL

☎ 0121 452 1577
198-200 Hagley Rd, Edgbaston B16 9PQ
e-mail: enquiries@edgbastonpalacehotel.com
dir: M5 junct 3 N, A456 for 4.3m. Hotel on right

Dating back to the 19th century, this Grade II listed Victorian property has bedrooms that are modern, well appointed and offer good comfort levels. The hospitality is warm, personal and refreshing. Supervised children under 18 are welcome.

Rooms 48 (21 annexe) (3 fmly) (16 GF) **Facilities** FTV Wi-fi **Conf** Class 70 Board 60 Thtr 200 **Parking** 70 **Notes** ⊗

Ramada Encore Birmingham City Centre

★★★ 73% HOTEL

☎ 0121 622 8800
Ernerst Street/Holloway Head B1 1NS
e-mail: reservations@encorebirmingham.co.uk
web: www.encorebirmingham.co.uk
dir: M6 junct 6/A38, merge onto A5127, follow A38 onto A41 exit onto Suffolk Queensway, at rdbt take 4th exit onto Holloway Head

Located in the heart of the city, this hotel offers stylish and comfortable accommodation. 'The Hub' is a smart, modern, open plan bar and restaurant with a choice of seating areas, that offers a full dining menu all day. Secure on-site parking is a plus.

Rooms 131 (11 fmly) **Facilities** STV Wi-fi ℘ Xmas New Year **Conf** Class 10 Board 20 Thtr 30 **Services** Lift **Parking** 24 **Notes** ⊗

Great Barr Hotel & Conference Centre

★★★ 67% HOTEL

☎ 0121 357 1141
Pear Tree Dr, Newton Rd, Great Barr B43 6HS
e-mail: sales@thegreatbarrhotel.com
web: www.thegreatbarrhotel.com
dir: M6 junct 7, at Scott Arms x-rds right towards West Bromwich (A4010) Newton Rd. Hotel 1m on right

This busy hotel, situated in a leafy residential area, is particularly popular with business clients; the hotel has excellent, state-of-the-art training and seminar facilities. There is a traditional oak-panelled bar and formal restaurant. The bedrooms are appointed to a good standard and have the expected amenities.

Rooms 92 (6 fmly) **S** £45-£85; **D** £55-£125 (incl. bkfst)* **Facilities** STV Wi-fi ℘ **Conf** Class 90 Board 60 Thtr 200 **Parking** 200 **Notes** ⊗ RS BH (restaurant may close) Civ Wed 200

Park Inn by Radisson Birmingham Walsall, M6 Jct 9

★★★ 66% HOTEL

☎ 01922 639100
Bescot Crescent WS1 4SE
e-mail: reservations.walsall@rezidorparkinn.com
dir: M6 junct 9 (signed Wednesbury), A461 (signed Walsall). At lights right onto A4148 (signed Ring Road, Birmingham, A34). At lights right into Bescot Cres (signed Bescot Stadium) pass stadium, hotel on left. (NB use WS1 4SA for Sat Nav)

This hotel is set just off the motorway and within easy reach of all the attractions around Birmingham, including the NEC. The bedrooms are bright and modern; all have air conditioning and spacious work desks. There are family rooms, twin rooms and double rooms. The spacious Hub Bar and Restaurant is the venue for a hot buffet breakfast. A meeting room and a fitness suite are also available.

Rooms 121 (6 fmly) ℘ **Facilities** Wi-fi Gym **Conf** Board 20 Thtr 30 Del from £105 to £145 **Services** Lift Air con **Parking** 74 **Notes** ⊗ Closed 24-27 Dec

Campanile Birmingham

BUDGET HOTEL

☎ 0121 359 3330
Chester St, Aston B6 4BE
e-mail: birmingham@campanile.com
web: www.campanile.com
dir: Adjacent to rdbt at junct of A4540 & A38

This modern building offers accommodation in smart, well-equipped bedrooms, all with en suite bathrooms. Refreshments may be taken at the informal bistro. See also the Hotel Groups pages.

Rooms 110 (5 fmly) **Conf** Class 100 Board 100 Thtr 250

B

Holiday Inn Express Birmingham City Centre

BUDGET HOTEL

☎ 0845 1126151
65 Lionel St B3 1JE
e-mail: enquiries@hiexpressbirminghamcitycentre.co.uk
web: www.hiexpress.com/exb'minghamc
dir: A38 to City Centre until Paradise Circus, take 4th exit on Queensway, 1st left into Lionel St, hotel on right

A modern hotel ideal for families and business travellers. Fresh and uncomplicated, the spacious rooms include Sky TV, power shower and tea and coffee-making facilities. Continental buffet breakfast is included in the room rate; other meals may be taken at the nearby family pub or restaurant. See also the Hotel Groups pages.

Rooms 120 (80 fmly) ➤ **Conf** Class 16 Board 16 Thtr 30

Holiday Inn Express Birmingham - South A45

BUDGET HOTEL

☎ 0121 289 3333
1270 Coventry Rd, Yardley B25 8BS
e-mail: reservations@hiex-birmingham.co.uk

Rooms 83 ➤ **D** £45-£149 (incl. bkfst)*
Conf Board 16 Thtr 24 Del from £110 to £159*

Ibis Birmingham Bordesley Circus

BUDGET HOTEL

☎ 0121 506 2600
1 Bordesley Park Rd, Bordesley B10 0PD
e-mail: H2178@accor.com
web: www.ibishotel.com

Modern, budget hotel offering comfortable accommodation in bright and practical bedrooms. Breakfast is self-service and dinner is available in the restaurant. See also the Hotel Groups pages.

Rooms 87 (15 GF) ➤

Ibis Birmingham City Centre

BUDGET HOTEL

☎ 0121 622 6010
Arcadian Centre, Ladywell Walk B5 4ST
e-mail: h1459@accor-hotels.com
web: www.ibishotel.com
dir: From motorways follow city centre signs. Then follow Bullring or Indoor Market signs. Hotel adjacent to market

Rooms 159 (5 fmly) **Conf** Class 60 Board 50 Thtr 120

Ibis Birmingham Holloway Circus

BUDGET HOTEL

☎ 0121 622 4925
55 Irving St B1 1DH
e-mail: H2092@accor.com
web: www.ibishotel.com
dir: From M6 take A38 (City Centre), left after 2nd tunnel. Right at rdbt, 4th left (Sutton St) into Irving St. Hotel on left

Rooms 51 (26 GF)

Premier Inn Birmingham Broad St Canal Side

BUDGET HOTEL

☎ 0871 527 8078
20 Bridge St B1 2JH
web: www.premierinn.com
dir: M6 junct 6, A38(M) towards city centre. Follow signs for city centre/ICC/A456 (Broad St). Left at Hyatt Hotel, hotel on right at bottom of Bridge St

High quality, budget accommodation ideal for both families and business travellers. Spacious, en suite bedrooms feature tea and coffee making facilities, and Freeview TV in most hotels. Internet access and Wi-fi are available for a small fee. The adjacent family restaurant features a wide and varied menu. See also the Hotel Groups pages.

Rooms 83

Premier Inn Birmingham Broad Street (Brindley Place)

BUDGET HOTEL

☎ 0871 527 8076
80 Broad St B15 1AU
web: www.premierinn.com
dir: M6 junct 6, A38(M) (Aston Expressway). Follow City Centre, ICC & NIA signs into Broad St. Right into Sheepcote St. 2nd left at rdbt into Essington St. Hotel on left. (NB for Sat Nav use B16 8AL)

Rooms 62

Premier Inn Birmingham Central East

BUDGET HOTEL

☎ 0871 527 8080
Richard St, Aston, Waterlinks B7 4AA
web: www.premierinn.com
dir: M6 junct 6, signed city centre. A38(M) signed A4540 (ring road). At rdbt 1st exit 50mtrs left into Richard St, hotel on left (barrier access to car park)

Rooms 61

Premier Inn Birmingham Central (Hagley Road)

BUDGET HOTEL

☎ 0871 527 8082
Hagley Rd B16 9NY
web: www.premierinn.com
dir: M6 junct 6, A38(M) (Aston Express Way). Follow city centre, ICC & NIA signs, into Broad St. From M5 junct 3, A456 for approx 3m, hotel on left

Rooms 62

Premier Inn Birmingham City Centre (Waterloo Street)

BUDGET HOTEL

☎ 0871 527 8074
3-6 Waterloo St B2 5PG
web: www.premierinn.com
dir: M6 junct 6, A38 (Corporation St). Follow West Bromwich/A41 signs. Merge into St Chad's Queensway. 2nd exit for Great Charles St Queensway, becomes Livery St. Left into Waterloo St

Rooms 109

Premier Inn Birmingham (Great Barr/M6 Jct 7)

BUDGET HOTEL

☎ 0871 527 8072
Birmingham Rd, Great Barr B43 7AG
web: www.premierinn.com
dir: M6 junct 7, A34 towards Walsall. Hotel on left behind Beacon Harvester

Rooms 32

B

BIRMINGHAM *continued*

Premier Inn Birmingham South (Hall Green)

BUDGET HOTEL

☎ 0871 527 8092
Stratford Rd, Hall Green B28 9ES
web: www.premierinn.com
dir: M42 junct 4, A34 towards Shirley signed Birmingham. Straight on at 6 rdbts. At 7th rdbt 4th exit. Hotel on left

Rooms 51

Novotel Birmingham Airport

★★★★ 72% HOTEL

☎ 0121 782 7000 & 782 4111
B26 3QL
e-mail: H1158@accor.com
web: www.novotel.com
dir: M42 junct 6, A45 to Birmingham, signed to airport. Hotel opposite main terminal

This smartly decorated hotel with air conditioning throughout its public areas and bedrooms benefits from being less than a minute's walk from the main terminal of Birmingham International Airport. Spacious bedrooms are comfortable and modern bathrooms are stylish with powerful showers. The Elements bar and restaurant provides a great atmosphere for meals and a fitness room is available on site. Long stay car parking packages can be arranged at this location.

Rooms 195 (24 fmly) ⚑ **Facilities** STV Wi-fi ♨ Gym Fitness room **Conf** Class 10 Board 20 Thtr 35 **Services** Lift Air con

---

Ibis Birmingham Airport

BUDGET HOTEL

☎ 0121 780 5800
Ambassador Rd, Bickenhill, Solihull B26 3AW
e-mail: H6359@accor.com
dir: M42 junct 6, A45 follow signs to Birmingham Airport

Modern, budget hotel offering comfortable accommodation in bright and practical bedrooms. Breakfast is self-service and dinner is available in the restaurant. See also the Hotel Groups pages.

Rooms 162 (2 fmly) ⚑ **D** £42-£165*

Crowne Plaza Birmingham NEC

CROWNE PLAZA
HOTELS & RESORTS

★★★★ 78% HOTEL

☎ 0871 942 9160
National Exhibition Centre, Pendigo Way B40 1PS
e-mail: necroomsales@ihg.com
web: www.cpbirminghamnec.hotel.co.uk
dir: M42 junct 6, follow signs for NEC, take 2nd exit on left, South Way for hotel entrance 50mtrs on right

On the doorstep of the NEC and overlooking Pendigo Lake, this hotel has contemporary design and offers well-equipped bedrooms with air conditioning. Bedrooms have ample working space and high-speed internet access (for an additional charge). Eating options include the modern Pendigo Restaurant overlooking the lake, the bar and 24-hour room service.

Rooms 242 (13 fmly) **Facilities** STV Wi-fi HL Gym Sauna **Conf** Class 140 Board 56 Thtr 200 **Services** Lift Air con **Parking** 348 **Notes** ⊗

BEST WESTERN PREMIER Moor Hall Hotel & Spa

Best Western
PREMIER

★★★★ 77% HOTEL

☎ 0121 308 3751
Moor Hall Dr, Four Oaks B75 6LN
e-mail: mail@moorhallhotel.co.uk
web: www.moorhallhotel.co.uk

(For full entry see Sutton Coldfield)

Nailcote Hall

CLASSIC
BRITISH HOTELS

★★★★ 76% ⊛ HOTEL

☎ 024 7646 6174
Nailcote Ln, Berkswell CV7 7DE
e-mail: info@nailcotehall.co.uk
web: www.nailcotehall.co.uk

(For full entry see Balsall Common)

Arden Hotel & Leisure Club

★★★ 74% HOTEL

☎ 01675 443221
Coventry Rd, Bickenhill B92 0EH
e-mail: enquiries@ardenhotel.co.uk
dir: M42 junct 6, A45 towards Birmingham. Hotel 0.25m on right, just off Birmingham International railway island

This smart hotel neighbouring the NEC, offers modern rooms and well-equipped leisure facilities. After dinner in the formal restaurant, the place to relax is the spacious lounge area. A buffet breakfast is served in the bright and airy Meeting Place.

Rooms 216 (6 fmly) (6 GF) (12 smoking) **S** £50-£150; **D** £55-£175 **Facilities** Spa STV Wi-fi ☉ supervised Gym Beautician ♬ New Year **Conf** Class 40 Board 60 Thtr 200 Del from £95 to £195 **Services** Lift **Parking** 300 **Notes** LB Closed 25-28 Dec Civ Wed 100

Premier Inn Birmingham NEC/Airport

Premier Inn

BUDGET HOTEL

☎ 0871 527 8086
Off Bickenhill Parkway, National Exhibition Centre B40 1QA
web: www.premierinn.com
dir: M42 junct 6 signed NEC. Turn right towards North Way. Follow Premier Inn signs. Hotel on left at 5th rdbt

High quality, budget accommodation ideal for both families and business travellers. Spacious, en suite bedrooms feature tea and coffee making facilities, and Freeview TV in most hotels. Internet access and Wi-fi are available for a small fee. The adjacent family restaurant features a wide and varied menu. See also the Hotel Groups pages.

Rooms 199

Premier Inn Bishop Auckland

BUDGET HOTEL

☎ 0871 527 8096
West Auckland Rd DL14 9AP
web: www.premierinn.com
dir: From S: A1 junct 58, left onto A68 signed Corbridge/Bishop Auckland. At 1st rdbt 2nd exit onto A6072 signed Shildon. Straight on at 4 rdbts, follow Shildon/Bishop Auckland signs. Hotel approx 1m on left

High quality, budget accommodation ideal for both families and business travellers. Spacious, en suite bedrooms feature tea and coffee making facilities, and Freeview TV in most hotels. Internet access and Wi-fi are available for a small fee. The adjacent family restaurant features a wide and varied menu. See also the Hotel Groups pages.

Rooms 49

B

BISHOP'S STORTFORD   Map 6 TL42
Hertfordshire

Down Hall Country House Hotel

★★★★   77%   HOTEL

☎ 01279 731441
Hatfield Heath CM22 7AS
e-mail: reservations@downhall.co.uk
web: www.downhall.co.uk
dir: A1060, at Hatfield Heath keep left. Right into lane opposite Hunters Meet restaurant, left at end, follow signs

Imposing country-house hotel set amidst 100 acres of mature grounds in a peaceful location just a short drive from Stansted Airport. Bedrooms are generally quite spacious; each one is pleasantly decorated, tastefully furnished and equipped with modern facilities. Public rooms include a choice of restaurants, a cocktail bar, two lounges and leisure facilities.

Rooms 99 (20 GF) 🐾 **Facilities** FTV Wi-fi 🔲 ♨ 🚲 Giant chess Whirlpool Sauna Snooker room Gym equipment Xmas New Year **Conf** Class 140 Board 68 Thtr 200 **Services** Lift **Parking** 150 **Notes** Civ Wed 150

Great Hallingbury Manor Hotel

 LEGACY HOTELS

U

☎ 01279 506475
Tilekiln Green, Great Hallingbury CM22 7TJ
e-mail: info@greathallingburymanor.co.uk
dir: M11 junct 8 rdbt take exit to B1256, turn immediately right at petrol station. Under bridge, sharp left bend, continue for 500yds. Hotel on left.

Currently the rating for this establishment is not confirmed. This may be due to a change of ownership or because it has only recently joined the AA rating scheme. For further details please see the AA website: theAA.com

Rooms 33 **S** £55-£110; **D** £69-£140 **Conf** Class 120 Board 30 Thtr 180

Days Hotel London Stansted - M11

 Welcome Break

BUDGET HOTEL

☎ 01279 213900
M11 Motorway, Junction 8, Old Dunmow Rd CM23 5QZ
dir: Adjacent to M11 junct 8

This modern building offers accommodation in smart, spacious and well-equipped bedrooms, suitable for families and business travellers, and all with en suite

---

bathrooms. There is an attractive lounge area and a dining room where breakfast is served and other refreshments may be taken. See also the Hotel Groups pages.

Rooms 77 (16 fmly) (16 GF) (8 smoking) 🐾

BISHOPSTEIGNTON   Map 3 SX97
Devon

Cockhaven Manor Hotel   THE INDEPENDENTS
HOTEL ASSOCIATION

★★   72%   HOTEL

☎ 01626 775252
Cockhaven Rd TQ14 9RF
e-mail: cockhaven@btconnect.com
web: www.cockhavenmanor.com
dir: A380 towards Torquay, A381 towards Teignmouth. Left at Metro Motors. Hotel 500yds on left

Cockhaven Manor is a friendly, family-run inn that dates back to the 16th century. Bedrooms are well equipped and many enjoy views across the beautiful Teign estuary. A choice of dining options is offered, and traditional and interesting dishes, along with locally caught fish, prove popular.

Rooms 12 (2 fmly) **S** £50-£65; **D** £60-£90 (incl. bkfst) **Facilities** FTV Wi-fi Petanque **Conf** Class 50 Board 30 Thtr 50 Del from £63.50 to £70* **Parking** 50 **Notes** LB Closed 25-26 Dec Civ Wed 100

BLACKBURN   Map 18 SD62
Lancashire

See also Langho

Mercure Blackburn Foxfields Country Hotel

 Mercure

★★★   74%   HOTEL

☎ 01254 822556
Whalley Rd, Billington, Clitheroe BB7 9HY
e-mail: enquiries@hotels-blackburn.com
web: www.hotels-blackburn.com
dir: Just off A59

This modern hotel is easily accessible from major road networks. Bedrooms are comfortable and spacious, and include some suites and others with separate dressing areas. Facilities include a good-sized swimming pool, a small gym and conference suites. The hotel is also a popular wedding venue, and its traditional restaurant serves an interesting range of cuisine.

Rooms 44 (16 annexe) (27 fmly) (13 GF) (8 smoking) **Facilities** STV FTV Wi-fi 🔲 Gym Sauna Steam room Xmas New Year **Conf** Class 60 Board 60 Thtr 140 **Parking** 194 **Notes** Civ Wed 200

Premier Inn Blackburn North West

 Premier Inn

BUDGET HOTEL

☎ 0871 527 8098
Myerscough Rd, Balderstone BB2 7LE
web: www.premierinn.com
dir: M6 junct 31, A59 towards Clitheroe. Hotel opposite British Aerospace, adjacent to Boddington Arms

High quality, budget accommodation ideal for both families and business travellers. Spacious, en suite bedrooms feature tea and coffee making facilities, and Freeview TV in most hotels. Internet access and Wi-fi are available for a small fee. The adjacent family restaurant features a wide and varied menu. See also the Hotel Groups pages.

Rooms 20

Premier Inn Blackburn South

BUDGET HOTEL

☎ 0871 527 8100
Off Eccleshill Rd, Riversway Dr, Lower Darwen BB3 0SN
web: www.premierinn.com
dir: At M65 junct 4

Rooms 43

BLACKPOOL   Map 18 SD33
Lancashire

The Imperial Hotel   PUMA HOTELS
COLLECTION

★★★★   72%   HOTEL

☎ 01253 623971
North Promenade FY1 2HB
e-mail: imperialblackpool@pumahotels.co.uk
web: www.pumahotels.co.uk
dir: M55 junct 2, A583 (North Shore), follow signs to North Promenade. Hotel on seafront, north of tower

Enjoying a prime seafront location, this grand Victorian hotel offers smartly appointed, well-equipped bedrooms and spacious, elegant public areas. Facilities include a smart leisure club, a comfortable lounge, the No 10 bar and an attractive split-level restaurant that overlooks the seafront. Conferences and functions are extremely well catered for.

Rooms 180 (16 fmly) **Facilities** Spa STV Wi-fi 🔲 supervised Gym Xmas New Year **Conf** Class 280 Board 70 Thtr 600 **Services** Lift **Parking** 150 **Notes** Civ Wed 200

B

BLACKPOOL *continued*

BEST WESTERN Carlton Hotel

★★★ 78% HOTEL

Best Western

☎ 01253 628966
282-286 North Promenade FY1 2EZ
e-mail: mail@carltonhotelblackpool.co.uk
web: www.bw-carltonhotel.co.uk
dir: M6 junct 32, M55 follow signs for North Shore. Between Blackpool Tower & Gynn Square

Enjoying a prime seafront location, this hotel offers bedrooms that are attractively furnished in modern style. Public areas include a choice of bar lounge and seafront lounges. Well cooked meals are served in the elegant Caesar's restaurant; extensive function facilities are available.

Rooms 58 (9 fmly) **S** £45-£75; **D** £55-£115 (incl. bkfst) **Facilities** STV FTV Wi-fi Xmas **Conf** Class 40 Board 40 Thtr 90 Del from £95 to £135 **Services** Lift **Parking** 43 **Notes** LB ⊗ Civ Wed 80

Carousel Hotel

★★★ 77% HOTEL

☎ 01253 402642
663-671 New South Prom FY4 1RN
e-mail: carousel.reservations@sleepwellhotels.com
web: www.sleepwellhotels.com
dir: From M55 follow signs to airport, pass airport to lights. Turn right, hotel 100yds on right

This friendly seafront hotel, close to the Pleasure Beach, offers smart, contemporary accommodation. Bedrooms are comfortably appointed and have a modern, stylish feel to them. An airy restaurant and a spacious bar/lounge both overlook the Promenade. The hotel has good conference and meeting facilities and its own car park.

Rooms 92 (22 fmly) **Facilities** FTV Wi-fi Xmas New Year **Conf** Class 30 Board 40 Thtr 100 **Services** Lift **Parking** 46 **Notes** ⊗ Civ Wed 150

The Claremont Hotel

★★ 78% HOTEL

☎ 0844 811 5570
270 North Promenade FY1 1SA
e-mail: reservations@choice-hotels.co.uk
dir: M55 junct 3 follow sign for promenade. Hotel beyond North Pier

Conveniently situated, the Claremont is a popular family holiday hotel. Bedrooms are bright and attractively decorated, and extensive public areas include a spacious air-conditioned restaurant which offers a good choice of dishes. There is a well equipped, supervised children's play room, and entertainment is provided during the season.

Rooms 143 (50 fmly) **Facilities** FTV Wi-fi Beauty treatments Xmas New Year **Conf** Class 300 Board 75 Thtr 530 Del from £79.50 to £100* **Services** Lift **Parking** 40 **Notes** ⊗

The Viking Hotel

★★ 75% HOTEL

☎ 0844 811 5570
479 South Promenade FY4 1AY
e-mail: reservations@choice-hotels.co.uk
dir: M55 junct 3, follow Pleasure Beach signs

Located close to the centre of the South Promenade, this establishment offers well equipped accommodation and a warm welcome. Meals are served in the attractive sea view restaurant and entertainment is available in the renowned 'Talk of the Coast' night club. Leisure facilities at sister hotels are also available free of charge.

Rooms 100 (10 GF) **Facilities** FTV Wi-fi Cabaret club Xmas New Year **Services** Lift **Parking** 50 **Notes** ⊗ No children 18yrs

The Cliffs Hotel

★★ 74% HOTEL

☎ 0844 811 5570 & 01253 595559
Queens Promenade FY2 9SG
e-mail: reservations@choice-hotels.co.uk
dir: M55 junct 3, follow Promenade signs. Hotel just after Gynn rdbt

This large, privately owned and extremely popular hotel is within easy reach of the town centre. The bedrooms, including spacious family rooms, vary in size. Public areas offer an all-day coffee shop, a smart restaurant and a family room where children are entertained.

Rooms 163 (47 fmly) **Facilities** FTV Wi-fi supervised Gym Beauty treatments Sauna Xmas New Year **Conf** Class 210 Board 50 Thtr 475 Del from £79.50 to £100.50* **Services** Lift **Parking** 30 **Notes** ⊗ Civ Wed 100

Hotel Sheraton

★★ 72% HOTEL

☎ 01253 352723
54-62 Queens Promenade FY2 9RP
e-mail: email@hotelsheraton.co.uk
web: www.hotelsheraton.co.uk
dir: 1m N from Blackpool Tower towards Fleetwood

This family-owned and run hotel is situated at the quieter, northern end of the promenade. Public areas include a choice of spacious lounges with sea views, a heated indoor swimming pool and a large function suite where popular dancing and cabaret evenings are held. The smartly appointed bedrooms come in a range of sizes and styles.

Rooms 104 (45 fmly) (15 smoking) **Facilities** Table tennis Darts Xmas New Year **Conf** Class 100 Board 150 Thtr 200 **Services** Lift **Parking** 20 **Notes** ⊗

Queens Hotel

★★ 72% HOTEL

Leisureplex

☎ 01253 342015 & 336980
469-471 South Promendae FY4 1AY
e-mail: reservations@queenshotelblackpool.alex.hallett@
web: www.leisureplex.co.uk

Situated on the South promenade overlooking the Irish Sea, close to the South Pier and Pleasure Beach. The bedrooms are well equipped and some rooms have lovely sea views. The spacious public areas include a choice of lounges, a range of bars, a conservatory and a large dining room as well as a refurbished 300-seat theatre bar.

Rooms 107 (8 fmly) **S** £36-£49; **D** £58-£81* **Facilities** FTV Wi-fi HL supervised Xmas New Year **Conf** Class 60 Board 60 Thtr 80 Del from £72 to £82* **Services** Lift **Parking** 55 **Notes** LB ⊗ Closed Jan

B

Headlands Hotel

★★ 71% HOTEL

☎ 01253 341179
611-613 South Promenade FY4 1NJ
e-mail: info@theheadlandsblackpool.co.uk
dir: From end of M55 follow South Promenade signs

This friendly, family-owned hotel stands on the South Promenade, close to the Pleasure Beach and many of the town's major attractions. Bedrooms are traditionally furnished and many enjoy sea views. There is a choice of lounges and live entertainment is provided regularly. Home-cooked food is served in the panelled dining room.

Rooms 41 (10 fmly) ✹ **S** £35-£50; **D** £50-£100 (incl. bkfst & dinner) **Facilities** FTV Wi-fi Darts Games room Pool Snooker ♬ Xmas New Year **Services** Lift **Parking** 38 **Notes** Closed 2-15 Jan

Alumhurst Hotel

★★ 50% HOTEL

☎ 01253 620959 & 07746 191023
13-15 Charnley Rd FY1 4PE
e-mail: alumhursthotel@btconnect.com
web: www.alumhursthotel.com
dir: End of M55 take urban route to central parking area (red). Follow to end, right to exit, left into Central Drive. Follow round to Debenhams then right & 1st left

Close to the Winter Gardens and Blackpool's multiplicity of attractions, this personally-managed hotel has been in the Francis family for 40 years, and offers a range of room options. Premier and traditional rooms are comfortable and well presented, but it is the 'retro 70's' rooms that stand out. These offer the expected comfort along with clever nostalgic touches such as Goblin Teasmades, cabinet TVs, 70's magazines and décor, and wind-up alarm clocks. There's also a bar and lounge with pool, darts, a jukebox, TV and fruit machines. The bar also has an area dedicated to 'Old Blackpool'.

Rooms 32 (9 fmly) (7 smoking) **S** £41-£70; **D** £72-£90 (incl. bkfst)* **Facilities** FTV Wi-fi ✅ Fishing Gym Sauna **Services** Lift **Parking** 6 **Notes** LB ⊗ Closed mid Nov-Mar

Lyndene Hotel

★★ Ⓐ HOTEL

☎ 01253 346779
303/315 Promenade FY1 6AN
e-mail: enquiries@lyndenehotel.com
web: www.lyndenehotel.com

Family run for over 20 years, this hotel is on the promenade and offers bedrooms with LCD flat-screen TVs, safes and hospitality trays; some rooms are on the ground floor. Public rooms include two air-conditioned lounges, two restaurants and an outside seating area and sun terrace. Entertainment is offered every evening.

Rooms 140 (60 fmly) (12 GF) (140 smoking) ✹ **Facilities** FTV Wi-fi ♬ Xmas New Year **Services** Lift **Parking** 70 **Notes** ⊗ No children 5yrs

The Craig-y-Don Hotel

Ⓤ

☎ 01253 624249
211-213 Central Promenade FY1 5DL
e-mail: craig-y-donhotel@btconnect.com
web: www.craig-y-don.com
dir: On promenade, 2/3m past Blackpool Pleasure Beach

Currently the rating for this establishment is not confirmed. This may be due to a change of ownership or because it has only recently joined the AA rating scheme. For further details please see the AA website: theAA.com

Rooms 38 (28 fmly) (7 GF) ✹ **S** £30-£50; **D** £50-£70 (incl. bkfst)* **Facilities** FTV Wi-fi ♬ Xmas New Year **Services** Lift **Notes** LB ⊗ RS Nov-May wknds only

New Guilderoy Hotel

Ⓤ

☎ 01253 351547
57-59 Holmfield Rd, North Shore FY2 9RU
e-mail: simon_connelly@yahoo.com

Currently the rating for this establishment is not confirmed. This may be due to a change of ownership or because it has only recently joined the AA rating scheme. For further details please see the AA website: theAA.com

Rooms 15 **S** £25-£40; **D** £40-£75 (incl. bkfst)*
Notes Closed occasional dates out of season

Hotel Ibis Styles Blackpool

 fOCUShotels

BUDGET HOTEL

☎ 01253 752478
Talbot Square FY1 1ND
e-mail: H9148@accor.com
web:
dir: M55 junct 4, follow signs for A583 Blackpool North Shore, approx 4m to seafront. Property on right opposite North Pier entrance

Modern, budget hotel offering comfortable accommodation in bright and practical bedrooms. Breakfast is self-service and dinner is available in the restaurant. See also the Hotel Groups pages.

Rooms 90 (4 fmly) ✹ **S** £44-£94; **D** £49-£99 (incl. bkfst)

Premier Inn Blackpool Airport

 Premier Inn

BUDGET HOTEL

☎ 0871 527 8106
Squire Gate Ln FY4 2QS
web: www.premierinn.com
dir: M55 junct 4, A5230, left at 1st rdbt towards airport. Hotel just before Squires Gate rail station

High quality, budget accommodation ideal for both families and business travellers. Spacious, en suite bedrooms feature tea and coffee making facilities, and Freeview TV in most hotels. Internet access and Wi-fi are available for a small fee. The adjacent family restaurant features a wide and varied menu. See also the Hotel Groups pages.

Rooms 39

B

BLACKPOOL *continued*

Premier Inn Blackpool (Bispham)

BUDGET HOTEL

☎ 0871 527 8102
Devonshire Rd, Bispham FY2 0AR
web: www.premierinn.com
dir: M55 junct 4, A583. At 5th lights turn right
(Whitegate Drive). Approx. 4.5m onto A587
(Devonshire Rd)

Rooms 40

Premier Inn Blackpool Central

BUDGET HOTEL

☎ 0871 527 8108
Yeadon Way, South Shore FY1 6BF
web: www.premierinn.com
dir: M55 junct 4 to Blackpool, straight on at last
island onto Yeaden Way. Follow signs for Central Car
Park/Coach Area. Left at Total garage

Rooms 82

Premier Inn Blackpool East (M55 Jct 4)

BUDGET HOTEL

☎ 0871 527 8110
Whitehills Park, Preston New Rd FY4 5NZ
web: www.premierinn.com
dir: Just off M55 junct 4. 1st left off rdbt. Hotel on
right

Rooms 81

BLAKENEY	Map 13 TG04
Norfolk	

The Blakeney Hotel

★★★★ 76% ☻ HOTEL

☎ 01263 740797
The Quay NR25 7NE
e-mail: reception@blakeneyhotel.co.uk
web: www.blakeneyhotel.co.uk
dir: From A148 between Fakenham & Holt, take
B1156 to Langham & Blakeney

A traditional, privately-owned hotel situated on the
quayside with superb views across the estuary and
the salt marshes to Blakeney Point. Public rooms
feature an elegant restaurant, ground-floor lounge, a
bar and a first-floor sun lounge overlooking the
harbour. Bedrooms are smartly decorated and
equipped with modern facilities. The leisure area is a
real feature with pool, sauna, steam room and mini-
gym.

Rooms 63 (16 annexe) (20 fmly) (17 GF) ⟆
S £79-£155; **D** £158-£334 (incl. bkfst & dinner)*
Facilities FTV Wi-fi ⟆ HL ⟆ Gym Billiards Snooker
Table tennis Sauna Steam room Spa bath Xmas New
Year **Conf** Class 100 Board 100 Thtr 150
Del £145.20* **Services** Lift **Parking** 60 **Notes** LB

INSPECTORS' CHOICE

Morston Hall

★★★ ☻☻☻ HOTEL

☎ 01263 741041
Morston, Holt NR25 7AA
e-mail: reception@morstonhall.com
web: www.morstonhall.com
dir: 1m W of Blakeney on A149 (King's Lynn to
Cromer road)

This delightful 17th-century country-house hotel
enjoys a tranquil setting amid well-tended gardens.
The comfortable public rooms offer a choice of
attractive lounges and a sunny conservatory, while
the elegant dining room is the perfect setting to
enjoy Galton Blackiston's award-winning cuisine.
The spacious bedrooms are individually decorated
and stylishly furnished with modern opulence.

Rooms 13 (6 annexe) (7 GF) ⟆ **S** £200-£240;
D £310-£360 (incl. bkfst & dinner)* **Facilities** STV
FTV Wi-fi ⟆ New Year **Conf** Class 20 Board 16
Del from £260* **Parking** 40 **Notes** LB Closed
1 Jan-last Fri in Jan & 2 days Xmas

Blakeney Manor Hotel

★★ 78% HOTEL

☎ 01263 740376
The Quay, Holt NR25 7ND
e-mail: reception@blakeneymanor.co.uk
web: www.blakeneymanor.co.uk
dir: Exit A149 at Blakeney towards Blakeney Quay.
Hotel at end of quay between Mariner's Hill & Friary
Hills

An attractive Norfolk flint building overlooking
Blakeney Marshes close to the town centre and
quayside. The bedrooms are located in flint-faced
barns in a courtyard adjacent to the main building.
The spacious public rooms include a choice of

lounges, a conservatory, a popular bar and a large
restaurant offering an interesting choice of dishes.

Rooms 35 (28 annexe) (26 GF) **Facilities** Wi-fi Xmas
New Year **Parking** 40 **Notes** No children 14yrs

BLEADON	Map 4 ST35
Somerset	

Premier Inn Weston-Super-Mare

BUDGET HOTEL

☎ 0871 527 9154
Bridgwater Rd, Lympsham BS24 0BP
web: www.premierinn.com
dir: M5 junct 22, A38 (Bristol Rd) signed Weston-
Super-Mare. At 1st rdbt take 1st exit into Bridgewater
Rd (A370). Approx 2m to hotel

High quality, budget accommodation ideal for both
families and business travellers. Spacious, en suite
bedrooms feature tea and coffee making facilities,
and Freeview TV in most hotels. Internet access and
Wi-fi are available for a small fee. The adjacent
family restaurant features a wide and varied menu.
See also the Hotel Groups pages.

Rooms 24

BLETCHINGDON	Map 11 SP51
Oxfordshire	

The Oxfordshire Inn

★★★ 64% HOTEL

☎ 01869 351444
Heathfield Village OX5 3DX
e-mail: staff@oxfordshireinn.co.uk
web: www.oxfordshireinn.co.uk
dir: M40 junct 9, A34 towards Oxford, A4027 towards
Bletchingdon. Hotel signed 0.7m on right

A converted farmhouse with additional outbuildings
that is located close to major motorway networks. The
accommodation is set around an open courtyard, and
includes suites that have four-poster beds. There is a
spacious bar and restaurant.

Rooms 28 (4 fmly) (15 GF) **S** £59-£99; **D** £59-£119*
Facilities Wi-fi Putt green Golf driving range Xmas
New Year **Conf** Class 80 Board 30 Thtr 140
Del from £79 to £125* **Parking** 50

B

BODMIN
Cornwall   Map 2 SX06

Trehellas House Hotel & Restaurant
★★★ 74% ◉ SMALL HOTEL

☎ 01208 72700
Washaway PL30 3AD
e-mail: enquiries@trehellashouse.co.uk
web: www.trehellashouse.co.uk
dir: A389 from Bodmin towards Wadebridge. Hotel on right 0.5m beyond road to Camelford

This 18th-century former posting inn retains many original features and provides comfortable accommodation. Bedrooms are located in both the main house and adjacent coach house - all provide the same high standards. An interesting choice of cuisine, with an emphasis on locally-sourced ingredients, is offered in the impressive slate-floored restaurant.

Rooms 12 (7 annexe) (2 fmly) (5 GF) **Facilities** FTV Wi-fi ⤵ Xmas New Year **Conf** Board 20 Thtr 20 **Parking** 32

Westberry Hotel
★★ 81% HOTEL

☎ 01208 72772
Rhind St PL31 2EL
e-mail: westberry@btconnect.com
web: www.westberryhotel.net
dir: On ring road off A30 & A38. St Petroc's Church on right, at mini rdbt turn right. Hotel on right

This popular hotel is conveniently located for both Bodmin town centre and the A30. The bedrooms are attractive and well equipped, and a spacious bar lounge and billiard room are also provided. The restaurant serves a variety of dishes, ranging from bar snacks to a more extensive carte menu.

Rooms 20 (8 annexe) (2 fmly) (6 GF) ⤳ **S** £48-£68; **D** £48-£78 (incl. bkfst) **Facilities** STV FTV Wi-fi ⤵ **Conf** Class 80 Board 80 Thtr 100 **Parking** 30 **Notes** LB

Premier Inn Bodmin
BUDGET HOTEL

☎ 0871 527 8112
Launceston Rd PL31 2AR
web: www.premierinn.com
dir: From A30 S'bound exit onto A389, hotel 0.5m on right. N'bound exit onto A38, follow A389 signs. Left at T-junct

High quality, budget accommodation ideal for both families and business travellers. Spacious, en suite bedrooms feature tea and coffee making facilities, and Freeview TV in most hotels. Internet access and Wi-fi are available for a small fee. The adjacent family restaurant features a wide and varied menu. See also the Hotel Groups pages.

Rooms 44

BOGNOR REGIS
West Sussex   Map 6 SZ99

The Russell Hotel
★★★ 75% HOTEL

☎ 01243 871300
King's Pde PO21 2QP
e-mail: reservations.russell@visionhotels.co.uk
dir: A27 follow signs for town centre, hotel on seafront

Situated in a pleasant location close to the seafront, the Russell Hotel offers large and well-appointed bedrooms; some are fully accessible and many have sea views. This hotel also caters for visually impaired people, their families, friends and their guide dogs, as well as offering a warm welcome to business and leisure guests. There are of course special facilities for the guide dogs. Leisure facilities are also available.

Rooms 40 (5 fmly) ⤳ **D** £49-£99 (incl. bkfst)* **Facilities** FTV ⊗ supervised Putt green Gym ♫ Xmas New Year **Conf** Class 60 Board 40 Thtr 100 Del from £69 to £149* **Services** Lift **Parking** 6 **Notes** LB Civ Wed 80

The Inglenook
★★★ 70% SMALL HOTEL

☎ 01243 262495 & 265411
255 Pagham Rd, Nyetimber PO21 3QB
e-mail: reception@the-inglenook.com
dir: A27 into Vinnetrow Rd, left at Walnut Tree, hotel 2.5m on right

This 16th-century inn retains much of its original character, including exposed beams throughout. Bedrooms are individually decorated and vary in size. There is a cosy lounge, a well-kept garden and a bar that offers a popular evening menu and convivial atmosphere. The restaurant, overlooking the garden, also serves enjoyable cuisine.

Rooms 18 (1 fmly) (2 GF) ⤳ **S** £55-£75; **D** £80-£200 (incl. bkfst)* **Facilities** STV FTV Wi-fi Xmas New Year **Conf** Class 50 Board 50 Thtr 100 Del from £110* **Parking** 35 **Notes** LB Civ Wed 80

The Royal Norfolk Hotel
★★ 76% HOTEL   Leisureplex

☎ 01243 826222
The Esplanade PO21 2LH
e-mail: royalnorfolk@leisureplex.co.uk
web: www.leisureplex.co.uk
dir: From A259 follow Longford Rd through lights to Canada Grove to T-junct. Right, take 2nd exit at rdbt. Hotel on right

Located on the seafront, but set back behind well-tended lawns and gardens, is this fine Regency hotel. The bedrooms are traditionally furnished and provide guests with modern comforts. There are sea views from the bar and restaurant, as well as the lounges.

Rooms 60 (3 fmly) (7 GF) ⤳ **S** £38-£56; **D** £62-£98 (incl. bkfst)* **Facilities** FTV Wi-fi ♫ Xmas New Year **Services** Lift **Parking** 35 **Notes** LB ⊗ Closed 2 Jan-14 Feb

Premier Inn Bognor Regis
BUDGET HOTEL

☎ 0871 527 8114
Shripney Rd PO22 9PA
web: www.premierinn.com
dir: From A27 & A29 rdbt junct follow Bognor Regis signs. Approx 4m, hotel on left

High quality, budget accommodation ideal for both families and business travellers. Spacious, en suite bedrooms feature tea and coffee making facilities, and Freeview TV in most hotels. Internet access and Wi-fi are available for a small fee. The adjacent family restaurant features a wide and varied menu. See also the Hotel Groups pages.

Rooms 24

B

BOLTON   **Map 15 SD70**
Greater Manchester

Egerton House Hotel

★★★ 81% ◉ HOTEL

☎ 01204 307171
Blackburn Rd, Egerton BL7 9SB
e-mail: reservation@egertonhouse-hotel.co.uk
web: www.egertonhouse-hotel.co.uk
dir: M61, A666 (Bolton road), pass ASDA on right.
Hotel 2m on just after war memorial on right

Peace and relaxation come as standard at this popular, privately owned hotel that sits in acres of well-tended woodland gardens. Public rooms are stylishly appointed and have an inviting, relaxing atmosphere. Many of the individually styled, attractive guest bedrooms enjoy delightful garden views. Conferences and meetings are well catered for.

Rooms 29 (7 fmly) **Facilities** FTV Wi-fi ⏃ Xmas New Year **Conf** Class 90 Board 60 Thtr 150 **Parking** 135 **Notes** ❀ Civ Wed 140

Mercure Bolton Georgian House Hotel

★★★ HOTEL

☎ 0844 815 9029
Manchester Rd, Blackrod BL6 5RU
e-mail: info@mercurebolton.co.uk
web: www.jupiterhotels.co.uk
dir: M61 junct 6, follow Blackrod A6027 signs. 200yds turn right onto A6 signed Chorley. Hotel 0.5m on right

Currently the rating for this establishment is not confirmed. This may be due to a change of ownership or because it has only recently joined the AA rating scheme.

Rooms 91 **Conf** Class 100 Board 60 Thtr 300

Mercure Bolton Last Drop Village Hotel & Spa

★★★ 74% HOTEL

☎ 01204 591131
Hospital Rd, Bromley Cross BL7 9PZ
e-mail: h6634@accor.com
web: www.mercure.com
dir: 3m N of Bolton off B5472

MercureBolton Last Drop Village Hotel & Spa is a collection of 18th-century farmhouses set on cobbled streets with various shops and a local pub. Extensive self-contained conference rooms, a modern health and beauty spa and breathtaking views of the West Pennine Moors make this a popular choice with both corporate and leisure guests. The bedrooms are well equipped and spacious.

Rooms 128 (10 annexe) (29 fmly) (20 GF)
Facilities Spa FTV Wi-fi ⏃ Gym Craft shops Thermal suite Rock sauna Steam bath Bio sauna Xmas New Year **Conf** Class 300 Board 95 Thtr 700 **Services** Lift **Parking** 400 **Notes** Civ Wed 500

Premier Inn Bolton (Reebok Stadium)

BUDGET HOTEL

☎ 0871 527 8116
Arena Approach 3, Horwich BL6 6LB
web: www.premierinn.com
dir: M61 junct 6, right at rdbt, left at 2nd rdbt

High quality, budget accommodation ideal for both families and business travellers. Spacious, en suite bedrooms feature tea and coffee making facilities, and Freeview TV in most hotels. Internet access and Wi-fi are available for a small fee. The adjacent family restaurant features a wide and varied menu. See also the Hotel Groups pages.

Rooms 74

Premier Inn Bolton West

BUDGET HOTEL

☎ 0871 527 8118
991 Chorley New Rd, Horwich BL6 4BA
web: www.premierinn.com
dir: M61 junct 6, follow dual carriageway signed Bolton/Horwich (Reebok Stadium on left). Hotel at 2nd rdbt

Rooms 60

BOLTON ABBEY   **Map 19 SE05**
North Yorkshire

INSPECTORS' CHOICE

The Devonshire Arms Country House Hotel & Spa

★★★★ HOTEL

☎ 01756 710441 & 718111
BD23 6AJ
e-mail: res@devonshirehotels.co.uk
web: www.thedevonshirearms.co.uk
dir: On B6160, 250yds N of junct with A59

With stunning views of the Wharfedale countryside this beautiful hotel, owned by the Duke and Duchess of Devonshire, dates back to the 17th century. Bedrooms are elegantly furnished; those in the old part of the house are particularly spacious and have four-posters and fine antiques. The sitting rooms are delightfully cosy with log fires, and the dedicated staff deliver service with a blend of friendliness and professionalism. The Burlington Restaurant offers accomplished cuisine, while the Brasserie provides a lighter alternative.

Rooms 40 (1 fmly) (17 GF) 🏹 **Facilities** Spa STV Wi-fi ⏃ ⏃ supervised 🎣 Fishing 💪 Gym Classic cars Falconry Laser pigeon shooting Fly fishing Cricket Xmas New Year **Conf** Class 80 Board 30 Thtr 90 **Parking** 150 **Notes** Civ Wed 90

B

BOREHAMWOOD Map 6 TQ19
Hertfordshire

Ibis London Elstree Borehamwood

BUDGET HOTEL

☎ 020 8736 2600
Elstree Way WD6 1JY
e-mail: H6186@accor.com
dir: M25 junct 23, A1, exit at Borehamwood, take
A5135 (Elstree Way)

Modern, budget hotel offering comfortable
accommodation in bright and practical bedrooms.
Breakfast is self-service and dinner is available in
the restaurant. See also the Hotel Groups pages.

Rooms 122 (16 fmly) (16 GF)

Premier Inn London Elstree/Borehamwood

BUDGET HOTEL

☎ 0871 527 8654
Warwick Rd WD6 1US
web: www.premierinn.com
dir: Exit A1 signed Borehamwood onto A5135 (Elstree
Way). Pass BP Garage, left into Warwick Rd

High quality, budget accommodation ideal for both
families and business travellers. Spacious, en suite
bedrooms feature tea and coffee making facilities,
and Freeview TV in most hotels. Internet access and
Wi-fi are available for a small fee. The adjacent
family restaurant features a wide and varied menu.
See also the Hotel Groups pages.

Rooms 120

BOROUGHBRIDGE Map 19 SE36
North Yorkshire

BEST WESTERN Crown Hotel

★★★ 77% HOTEL

☎ 01423 322328
Horsefair YO51 9LB
e-mail: sales@crownboroughbridge.co.uk
web: www.crownboroughbridge.co.uk
dir: A1(M) junct 48 towards Boroughbridge. Hotel 1m

Situated in the centre of town but convenient for the
A1(M), The Crown provides a full leisure complex,
conference rooms and a secure car park. Bedrooms
are well appointed. A wide range of well-prepared
dishes can be enjoyed in both the restaurant and bar.

Rooms 37 (3 fmly) (2 GF) **S** £75-£105; **D** £90-£145
(incl. bkfst) **Facilities** FTV Wi-fi ⬙ HL ⬙ supervised
Gym Xmas New Year **Conf** Class 80 Board 80 Thtr 150
Parking 60 **Notes** LB ⊛ Civ Wed 120

The Crown Inn

◉ RESTAURANT WITH ROOMS

☎ 01423 322300
Roecliffe YO51 9LY
e-mail: info@crowninnroecliffe.com
web: www.crowninnroecliffe.com
dir: A1(M) junct 48, follow signs for Boroughbridge. At
rdbt exit towards Roecliffe & brown tourist signs

The Crown is a 16th-century coaching inn providing
an excellent combination of traditional charm and
modern comforts. Service is friendly and professional
and food is a highlight of any stay. The kitchen team
use the finest of Yorkshire produce from the best local
suppliers to create a weekly-changing seasonal
menu. Bedrooms are attractively furnished with
stylish en suite bathrooms.

Rooms 4 (1 fmly)

BORROWDALE Map 18 NY21
Cumbria

See also **Keswick & Rosthwaite**

Lodore Falls Hotel

LAKE DISTRICT HOTELS

★★★★ 74% HOTEL

☎ 017687 77285 & 0800 840 1246
CA12 5UX
e-mail: lodorefalls@lakedistricthotels.net
web: www.lakedistricthotels.net/lodorefalls
dir: M6 junct 40, A66 to Keswick, B5289 to
Borrowdale. Hotel on left

This impressive hotel has an enviable location
overlooking Derwentwater. The bedrooms, many with
lake or fell views, are comfortably equipped; family
rooms and suites are also available. The dining room,
bar and lounge areas are appointed to a very high
standard. One of the treatments in the hotel's Elemis
Spa actually makes use of the Lodore Waterfall.

Rooms 69 (11 fmly) ⬙ **S** £112-£118; **D** £188-£198
(incl. bkfst) **Facilities** Spa STV FTV Wi-fi ⬙ ⬙ ⬙
Fishing Gym Squash Sauna Xmas New Year
Conf Class 90 Board 45 Thtr 200 Del from £145
Services Lift **Parking** 103 **Notes** LB Civ Wed 130

Borrowdale Gates Country House Hotel

★★★ 85% COUNTRY HOUSE HOTEL

☎ 017687 77204
CA12 5UQ
e-mail: hotel@borrowdale-gates.com
dir: From A66 follow B5289 for approx 4m. Turn right
over bridge, hotel 0.25m beyond village

This friendly hotel is peacefully located in the
Borrowdale Valley, close to the village but in its own
three acres of wooded grounds. Public rooms include
comfortable lounges and a restaurant with picture
postcard views. Bedrooms and their en suites have
benefited from investment and refurbishment with
very good results.

Rooms 25 (2 fmly) (9 GF) ⬙ **S** £65-£120;
D £130-£200 (incl. bkfst)* **Facilities** FTV Wi-fi ⬙
Xmas New Year **Services** Lift **Parking** 29 **Notes** LB
Closed 5-31 Jan

Leathes Head Hotel

★★★ 81% ◉ HOTEL

☎ 017687 77247 & 77650
CA12 5UY
e-mail: reservations@leatheshead.co.uk
dir: 3.5m from Keswick on B5289 (Borrowdale road).
Hotel on left 0.25m before Grange Bridge

A fine Edwardian building, with lovely gardens, set in
the heart of the unspoilt Borrowdale Valley. The
hospitality and customer care are really outstanding
here. The bedrooms have commanding views and the
award-winning food, including a wonderful Cumbrian
breakfast, will not disappoint.

Rooms 11 (2 fmly) (3 GF) ⬙ **D** £142-£244 (incl. bkfst
& dinner)* **Facilities** FTV Wi-fi **Parking** 16 **Notes** No
children 15yrs Closed late Nov-mid Feb

B

BORROWDALE *continued*

Borrowdale Hotel

LAKE DISTRICT HOTELS

★★★ 80% HOTEL

☎ 017687 77224
CA12 5UY
e-mail: borrowdale@lakedistricthotels.net
dir: 3m from Keswick, on B5289 at S end of Lake Derwentwater

Situated in the beautiful Borrowdale Valley overlooking Derwentwater, this traditionally styled hotel guarantees a friendly welcome. Extensive public areas include a choice of lounges, traditional dining room, lounge bar and popular conservatory which serves more informal meals. Bedrooms vary in style and size, including two that are suitable for less able guests.

Rooms 40 (2 fmly) (4 GF) **Facilities** STV FTV Wi-fi Leisure facilities available at nearby sister hotel Xmas New Year **Conf** Class 30 Board 24 Thtr 80 **Parking** 30

BOSCASTLE Map 2 SX09
Cornwall

The Wellington Hotel

★★★ 78% ◉◉ HOTEL

☎ 01840 250202
The Harbour PL35 0AQ
e-mail: info@wellingtonhotelboscastle.com
web: www.wellingtonhotelboscastle.com
dir: A30/A395 at Davidstowe follow Boscastle signs. B3266 to village. Right into Old Rd

This 16th-century coaching inn is very much a landmark in Boscastle and has been providing rest and relaxation for weary travellers for many years. There is character in abundance which adds to its engaging charm and personality. The Long Bar is popular with visitors and locals alike and features a delightful galleried area. The stylish bedrooms come in varying sizes, including the spacious Tower Rooms; all provide contemporary comforts and the expected necessities. In addition to the bar menus, The Waterloo Restaurant is the elegant setting for accomplished cuisine.

Rooms 14 (1 fmly) **S** £45-£55; **D** £75-£155 (incl. bkfst)* **Facilities** FTV Wi-fi Xmas New Year **Conf** Class 40 Board 24 Thtr 50 Del from £100 to £200* **Parking** 14 **Notes** LB

BOSHAM Map 5 SU80
West Sussex

The Millstream Hotel & Restaurant

★★★ 85% ◉◉ HOTEL

☎ 01243 573234
Bosham Ln PO18 8HL
e-mail: info@millstreamhotel.com
web: www.millstreamhotel.com
dir: 4m W of Chichester on A259, left at Bosham rdbt. After 0.5m right at T-junct signed to church & quay. Hotel 0.5m on right

Lying in the idyllic village of Bosham, this attractive hotel provides comfortable, well-equipped and tastefully decorated bedrooms. Many guests regularly return here for the relaxed atmosphere created by the notably efficient and friendly staff. Public rooms include a cocktail bar that opens onto the garden, and a pleasant award-winning restaurant where varied and freshly prepared cuisine can be enjoyed. The new Markwick's Brasserie Restaurant is open all day for coffee, snacks, light lunches and dinners.

Rooms 35 (2 annexe) (2 fmly) (9 GF) **S** £99-£109; **D** £159-£179 (incl. bkfst)* **Facilities** FTV Wi-fi Painting & Bridge breaks ♫ Xmas New Year **Conf** Class 20 Board 20 Thtr 45 **Parking** 44 **Notes** LB ⊗ Civ Wed 75

BOSTON Map 12 TF34
Lincolnshire

Poacher's Country Hotel

★★★ 82% HOTEL

☎ 01205 290310
Swineshead Rd, Kirton Holme PE20 1SQ
e-mail: enquiries@poachershotel.co.uk
dir: Just off A52, exit at A52/A17 rdbt

The Poachers, dating back to the 1800s, has undergone a total transformation over the last few years, yet retains most of its original character. The open-plan, contemporary public areas are bright and inviting. The bedrooms are smartly appointed and have flat-screen TVs and many thoughtful touches.

Rooms 14 (1 fmly) (8 GF) **Facilities** FTV Wi-fi Xmas New Year **Conf** Class 150 Board 50 Thtr 175 **Parking** 55 **Notes** ⊗ Civ Wed 200

Supreme Inns Boston

★★★ 78% HOTEL

☎ 01205 822804
Donnington Rd, Bicker Bar Roundabout PE20 3AN
e-mail: enquiries@supremeinns.co.uk
web: www.supremeinns.co.uk
dir: At rdbt junct of A52 & A17

Situated south west of Boston and surrounded by the Lincolnshire Fens, this modern, purpose-built hotel offers well equipped bedrooms that have flat-screen TVs and internet access. Food is available in the restaurant or all day in the relaxing bar area. Wedding, private dinner and conference facilities are all available.

Rooms 55 (27 GF) **Facilities** FTV Wi-fi Xmas New Year **Conf** Board 35 Thtr 60 **Parking** 65 **Notes** ⊗ Civ Wed 60

Best Western White Hart Hotel and Eatery

★★★ 77% HOTEL

☎ 01205 311900
1-5 High St, Bridge Foot PE21 8SH
e-mail: whitehartboston@bpcmail.co.uk

The White Hart Hotel is well appointed and attractive, and is conveniently located in the centre of this market town with great views of the 700-year-old St Botolph's Church, known as the Boston Stump, from its riverside location. The hotel has spacious public areas including the Riverside Restaurant for evening meals, and the lively Courtyard Bar which is open for brunch, lunch and afternoon tea. There is a wonderful outside area for relaxing, eating and drinking. Conferences and weddings are catered for. Off-street parking in a private car park is also available.

Rooms 26 **Facilities** FTV Wi-fi HL Xmas New Year **Conf** Class 26 Board 26 Thtr 80 Del £142* **Parking** 35 **Notes** ⊗ Civ Wed 80

Boston West Hotel

★★★ 73% HOTEL

☎ 01205 292969 & 290670
Hubberts Bridge PE20 3QX
e-mail: info@bostonwesthotel.co.uk
dir: A1121 signed Boston, hotel on left after speed camera

A modern, purpose-built hotel situated in a rural location on the outskirts of town. The smartly appointed bedrooms are spacious and thoughtfully equipped; some rooms have balconies with stunning countryside views. Public rooms include a restaurant and a large open-plan lounge bar which overlooks the golf course.

Rooms 24 (5 fmly) (12 GF) **S** £49-£60; **Facilities** FTV Wi-fi ⅃ 18 Putt green Driving range New Year **Conf** Class 60 Board 40 Thtr 80 **Services** Lift **Parking** 24 **Notes** ⊗ Civ Wed 110

Premier Inn Boston

BUDGET HOTEL

☎ 0871 527 8120
Wainfleet Rd PE21 9RW
web: www.premierinn.com
dir: A52, 300yds E of junct with A16 (Boston/Grimsby road)

High quality, budget accommodation ideal for both families and business travellers. Spacious, en suite bedrooms feature tea and coffee making facilities, and Freeview TV in most hotels. Internet access and Wi-fi are available for a small fee. The adjacent family restaurant features a wide and varied menu. See also the Hotel Groups pages.

Rooms 54

BOTLEY   Map 5 SU51
Hampshire

Macdonald Botley Park, Golf & Spa

★★★★ 76% ⚙ COUNTRY HOUSE HOTEL

☎ 01489 780 888 & 0844 879 9034
Winchester Rd, Boorley Green SO32 2UA
e-mail: botleypark@macdonald-hotels.co.uk
web: www.macdonald-hotels.co.uk/botleypark
dir: M27 junct 7, A334 towards Botley. At 1st rdbt left, pass M&S store, over at next 5 mini rdbts. At 6th mini rdbt turn right. In 0.5m hotel on left

This modern and spacious hotel sits peacefully in the midst of its own 176-acre parkland golf course. Bedrooms are comfortably appointed with a good range of extras, and extensive leisure facilities are on offer. Attractive public areas include a relaxing restaurant and the more informal Swing and Divot

Bar. Macdonald Hotels is the AA Hotel Group of the Year 2013-14.

Rooms 130 (30 fmly) (44 GF) 🐾 **Facilities** Spa STV Wi-fi ⅃ ⚘ ⅃ 18 ⚘ Putt green Gym Squash Dance studio Xmas New Year **Conf** Class 180 Board 100 Thtr 450 **Services** Air con **Parking** 250 **Notes** ⊗ Civ Wed 400

BOURNEMOUTH   Map 5 SZ19
Dorset

***See also* Christchurch**

Bournemouth Highcliff Marriott Hotel

★★★★ 80% ⚙⚙ HOTEL

☎ 01202 557702
St Michaels Rd, West Cliff BH2 5DU
e-mail: mhrs.bohbm.ays@marriotthotels.co.uk
web: www.bournemouthhighcliffmarriott.co.uk
dir: A338 into Bournemouth then BIC signs to West Cliff Rd. 2nd right into St Michaels Rd. Hotel at end of road on left

Originally built as a row of coastguard cottages, this establishment has expanded over the years into a very elegant and charming hotel. Impeccably maintained throughout, many of the bedrooms have sea views. An excellent range of leisure, business and conference facilities are offered, as well as private dining and banqueting rooms. The hotel also has direct access to the Bournemouth International Centre.

Rooms 160 (19 annexe) (22 fmly) (4 GF) (8 smoking) 🐾 **Facilities** STV FTV Wi-fi ⚘ ⅃ ⚘ Putt green Gym Beautician Beauty treatment room ♫ Xmas New Year **Conf** Class 180 Board 90 Thtr 350 **Services** Lift Air con **Parking** 80 **Notes** ⊗ Civ Wed 250

Menzies East Cliff Court

MenziesHotels

★★★★ 78% HOTEL

☎ 01202 554545
East Overcliff Dr BH1 3AN
e-mail: eastcliff@menzieshotels.co.uk
web: www.menzieshotels.co.uk
dir: From M3, M27 towards Bournemouth on A338 (leads onto Wessex Way), follow signs to East Cliff, hotel on seafront

Enjoying panoramic views across the bay, this popular hotel offers bedrooms that are modern and contemporary in style; they are appointed to a very high standard, and many have the benefit of balconies and sea views. Stylish public areas include a range of inviting lounges, a spacious restaurant and a selection of conference rooms.

Rooms 67 (4 fmly) (2 GF) (5 smoking) **Facilities** FTV Wi-fi ⚘ Full leisure facilities at adjacent Menzies

Carlton Xmas New Year **Conf** Class 80 Board 50 Thtr 120 Del from £99* **Services** Lift **Parking** 45 **Notes** Civ Wed 250

B

The Green House

★★★★ 77% ⚙ TOWN HOUSE HOTEL

☎ 01202 498900
4 Grove Rd BH1 3AX
e-mail: reception@thegreenhousehotel.com

This hotel has a clear commitment to the environment which goes beyond just energy efficient lighting; everything has been designed and built to be sympathetic to the environment. The beautifully appointed bedrooms and bathrooms demonstrate the 'green' principle from the locally-made 100% wool carpets and solid wood furniture to the wallpapers and paint that have been used. The ingredients used for the menus are locally sourced and organic.

Rooms 32 (3 fmly) (6 GF) 🐾 **Facilities** FTV Wi-fi ⚘ Xmas New Year **Conf** Class 40 Board 40 Thtr 100 **Services** Lift **Parking** 32 **Notes** ⊗ Civ Wed 100

Menzies Hotels Bournemouth - Carlton

MenziesHotels

★★★★ 75% ⚙ HOTEL

☎ 01202 552011
East Overcliff BH1 3DN
e-mail: carlton@menzieshotels.co.uk
web: www.menzieshotels.co.uk
dir: From M3, M27 towards Bournemouth on A338 (leads onto Wessex Way), follow signs to East Cliff, hotel on seafront

Enjoying a prime location on the East Cliff, and with views of the Isle of Wight and Dorset coastline, the Carlton has attractive gardens and pool area. Most of the spacious bedrooms enjoy sea views. Leisure facilities include an indoor and outdoor pool as well as a gym. Guests can enjoy an interesting range of carefully prepared dishes in Frederick's restaurant. The conference and banqueting facilities are varied.

Rooms 76 (17 fmly) (8 GF) (9 smoking) 🐾 **Facilities** STV FTV Wi-fi ⚘ ⅃ ⚘ Gym Hair & beauty salon Xmas New Year **Conf** Class 110 Board 50 Thtr 250 Del from £109* **Services** Lift **Parking** 87 **Notes** ⊗ Civ Wed 200

B

BOURNEMOUTH *continued*

Hermitage Hotel

★★★★ 74% ◎ HOTEL

☎ 01202 557363
Exeter Rd BH2 5AH
e-mail: info@hermitage-hotel.co.uk
web: www.hermitage-hotel.co.uk
dir: A338 (Ringwood), follow signs for BIC & pier.
Hotel directly opposite

Occupying an impressive location overlooking the seafront, at the heart of the town centre, the Hermitage offers friendly and attentive service. The majority of the smart bedrooms are comfortably appointed and all are very well equipped; many rooms have sea views. The wood-panelled lounge provides an elegant and tranquil area, as does the restaurant where well-prepared and interesting dishes are served.

Rooms 74 (11 annexe) (9 fmly) (7 GF) ▶
Facilities FTV Wi-fi ⟲ Xmas New Year **Conf** Class 60 Board 60 Thtr 180 **Services** Lift **Parking** 58 **Notes** ⊗

Park Central Hotel

★★★★ 73% ◎◎ HOTEL

☎ 01202 203600
Exeter Rd BH2 5AJ
e-mail: reception@parkcentralhotel.co.uk
dir: A338, A35 (St Pauls Rd). At rdbt 3rd exit onto B3066 (Holdenburst Rd). Straight on at 3 rdbts, hotel on right opposite Bournemouth International Centre

Located opposite Bournemouth International Centre, this modern, contemporary hotel is in a good location and has sea views. The bedrooms are comfortable and attractively furnished. The menu features creative modern ideas based on intuitive combinations of well-sourced raw materials featuring, of course a great deal of seafood. A pre-theatre menu is also available, but be sure to book as this can prove very popular.

Rooms 50 (6 fmly) (7 GF) ▶ **S** £58-£120; **D** £69-£160 (incl. bkfst) **Facilities** FTV Wi-fi ⟲ ♫ Xmas New Year **Services** Lift **Parking** 29 **Notes** ⊗

Norfolk Royale Hotel

★★★★ 72% HOTEL

PEEL HOTELS PLC

☎ 01202 551521
Richmond Hill BH2 6EN
e-mail:
gm@norfolkroyale-hotel-bournemouth.com
web: www.thenorfolkhotel.co.uk
dir: A338 into Bournemouth take Richmond Hill exit to A347 Wimborne, turn left at top into Richmond Hill. Hotel on right

Easily recognisable by its wrought iron balconies, this Edwardian hotel is conveniently located for the centre of the town. Most of the bedrooms are contained in a modern wing at the side of the building, overlooking the pretty landscaped gardens. There is a car park at rear of the hotel.

Rooms 95 (23 fmly) (9 GF) ▶ **Facilities** Spa STV Wi-fi ⟲ HL ⟳ Membership of nearby health club ♫ Xmas New Year **Conf** Class 50 Board 40 Thtr 150 Del from £145 to £195* **Services** Lift **Parking** 95 **Notes** ⊗ Civ Wed 150

Hallmark Bournemouth

★★★★ 71% HOTEL

☎ 01202 751000
Durley Chine Rd, West Cliff BH2 5JS
e-mail: bournemouth.sales@hallmarkhotels.co.uk
dir: A338 follow signs to West Cliff & BIC, hotel on right

This property is conveniently located and offers a friendly atmosphere and attentive service. The comfortable bedrooms are tastefully appointed and are suitable for both business and leisure guests. The restaurant and bar serve a good choice of dishes, and the well-appointed leisure area is popular with both residents and locals alike. There is also a good range of conference facilities and meeting rooms.

Rooms 78 (12 annexe) ▶ **Facilities** Spa FTV Wi-fi ⟳ Gym Sauna Steam room Aromatherapy Ice zone Xmas New Year **Conf** Class 80 Board 40 Thtr 250 **Services** Lift **Parking** 80 **Notes** Civ Wed 200

Cumberland Hotel

★★★ 88% ◎◎ HOTEL

☎ 01202 290722 & 298350
East Overcliff Dr BH1 3AF
e-mail: info@cumberlandbournemouth.co.uk
dir: A35 towards East Cliff & beaches, right onto Holdenhurst Rd, straight over 2 rdbts, left at junct to East Overcliff Drive, hotel on seafront

A purpose built, art deco hotel where many of the bedrooms are appointed in keeping with the hotel's original character. Front-facing bedrooms have balconies with superb sea views. The comfortable

public areas are spacious and striking in their design. The Mirabelle Restaurant and the Ventana Bar offer cuisine prepared from local produce.

Rooms 102 (20 fmly) **S** £29.50-£90; **D** £59-£180 (incl. bkfst) **Facilities** FTV Wi-fi ⟲ ⟳ ⤵ Gym Squash Sauna Beauty treatment room Xmas New Year **Conf** Class 180 Board 40 Thtr 250 Del from £50 to £110 **Services** Lift **Parking** 50 **Notes** LB Civ Wed 100

BEST WESTERN The Connaught Hotel

★★★ 85% ◎◎ HOTEL

Best Western

☎ 01202 298020
West Hill Rd, West Cliff BH2 5PH
e-mail: reception@theconnaught.co.uk
web: www.theconnaught.co.uk
dir: Follow Town Centre West & BIC signs

Conveniently located on the West Cliff, close to the BIC, beaches and town centre, this privately-owned hotel offers well equipped, neatly decorated rooms, some with balconies. The hotel boasts a very well-equipped leisure complex with a large pool and gym. Breakfast and dinner offer imaginative dishes made with quality local ingredients.

Rooms 82 (27 annexe) (9 fmly) ▶ **S** £50-£80; **D** £60-£140 (incl. bkfst) **Facilities** Spa FTV Wi-fi ⟲ ⟳ supervised Gym Sauna Steam room Beauty therapies Xmas New Year **Conf** Class 60 Board 35 Thtr 180 Del from £85 to £165 **Services** Lift **Parking** 66 **Notes** LB ⊗ Civ Wed 200

See advert on opposite page

B

Hotel Miramar

★★★ 82% HOTEL

☎ 01202 556581
East Overcliff Dr, East Cliff BH1 3AL
e-mail: sales@miramar-bournemouth.com
web: www.miramar-bournemouth.com
dir: From Wessex Way rdbt into St Pauls Rd, right at
next rdbt. 3rd exit at next rdbt, 2nd exit at next rdbt
into Grove Rd. Hotel car park on right

Conveniently located on the East Cliff, this Edwardian
hotel enjoys glorious sea views. The Miramar was a
favoured destination of famed author JRR Tolkien,
who often stayed here. The bedrooms are comfortable
and well equipped, and there are spacious public
areas and a choice of lounges. The friendly staff and
a relaxing environment are noteworthy here.

Rooms 43 (6 fmly) ⏻ **S** £39.95-£74.95;
D £79.90-£149.90 (incl. bkfst)* **Facilities** FTV Wi-fi ⏻

HL ♫ Xmas New Year **Conf** Class 50 Board 50
Thtr 200 Del from £100 to £150* **Services** Lift
Parking 80 **Notes** LB Civ Wed 110

Langtry Manor - Lovenest of a King

★★★ 82% HOTEL

☎ 0844 3725 432 & 01202 553887
Derby Rd, East Cliff BH1 3QB
e-mail: lillie@langtrymanor.com
web: www.langtrymanor.co.uk
dir: A31/A338, 1st rdbt by rail station turn left. Over
next rdbt, 1st left into Knyveton Rd. Hotel opposite

Retaining a stately air, this property was originally
built in 1877 by Edward VII for his mistress Lillie
Langtry. The individually furnished and decorated
bedrooms include several with four-poster beds.
Enjoyable cuisine is served in the magnificent dining
hall that displays several large Tudor tapestries.
There is an Edwardian banquet on Saturday evenings.

Rooms 20 (8 annexe) (2 fmly) (3 GF) **Facilities** FTV
Wi-fi Free use of health club (200yds) ♫ Xmas New
Year **Conf** Class 60 Board 40 Thtr 100 **Parking** 30
Notes Civ Wed 100

BEST WESTERN Hotel Royale

★★★ 80% HOTEL

☎ 01202 554794
16 Gervis Rd BH1 3EQ
e-mail: reservations@thehotelroyale.com
web: www.thehotelroyale.com
dir: M27 junct 1, A31 onto A338 to Bournemouth,
follow signs for East Cliff & seafront. Over 2 rdbts
into Gervis Rd. Hotel on right

Located on the East Cliff, just a short walk from the
seafront and local shops and amenities, is this
privately owned hotel. Public areas are contemporary

in style, and facilities include a small health club and
spacious function rooms. Bedrooms are comfortable
and well furnished.

Rooms 64 (8 annexe) (22 fmly) (8 GF) ⏻ **S** £29-£75;
D £39-£120 (incl. bkfst)* **Facilities** STV FTV Wi-fi ⏻
⏻ Xmas New Year **Conf** Class 60 Board 40 Thtr 100
Del from £89 to £135* **Services** Lift **Parking** 80
Notes LB ⏻

The Chine

★★★ 80% HOTEL

☎ 01202 396234 & 0845 337 1550
Boscombe Spa Rd BH5 1AX
e-mail: reservations@fjbhotels.co.uk
web: www.fjbcollection.co.uk
dir: Follow BIC signs, A338/Wessex Way to St Pauls
rdbt. 1st exit, to next rdbt, 2nd exit signed Eastcliff,
Boscombe, Southbourne. Next rdbt, 1st exit into
Christchurch Rd. After 2nd lights, right into
Boscombe Spa Rd

Benefiting from superb views, this popular hotel is set
in delightful gardens with private access to the
seafront and a sandy beach that stretches for miles;
it is just a five-minute drive from the shops and
entertainments of the town centre. The excellent
range of facilities includes an indoor pool, a seasonal
outdoor pool, jacuzzi, gym and sauna. There are also
children's facilities and dedicated entertainers during
the school holidays. The spacious bedrooms, some
with balconies, are well appointed and thoughtfully
equipped. The Seaview Restaurant and Gallery
Brasserie are popular eating options.

Rooms 83 (23 annexe) (16 fmly) (8 GF) **Facilities** STV
Wi-fi ⏻ supervised ⏻ supervised ⏻ Gym Games
room Children's indoor play area Xmas New Year
Conf Class 70 Board 40 Thtr 140 **Services** Lift
Parking 55 **Notes** ⏻ Civ Wed 120

BOURNEMOUTH *continued*

Elstead Hotel

★★★ 80% HOTEL

☎ 01202 293071
Knyveton Rd BH1 3QP
e-mail: info@the-elstead.co.uk
web: www.the-elstead.co.uk
dir: A338 (Wessex Way) to St Pauls rdbt, left & left again

Ideal as a base for business and leisure travellers, this popular hotel is conveniently located for the town centre, seafront and BIC. An impressive range of facilities is offered, including meeting rooms, an indoor leisure centre and comfortable lounges.

Rooms 50 (15 fmly) **Facilities** Wi-fi ☜ supervised Gym Steam room Pool & snooker tables Xmas New Year **Conf** Class 60 Board 40 Thtr 80 **Services** Lift **Parking** 40 **Notes** Civ Wed 60

The Riviera Hotel

★★★ 79% HOTEL

☎ 01202 763653
Burnaby Rd, Alum Chine BH4 8JF
e-mail: info@rivierabournemouth.co.uk
web: www.rivierabournemouth.co.uk
dir: A338, follow signs to Alum Chine

The Riviera offers a range of comfortable, well-furnished bedrooms and bathrooms. Welcoming staff provide efficient service delivered in a friendly manner. In addition to a spacious lounge with regular entertainment, there are indoor and outdoor pools, all just a short walk from the beach.

Rooms 73 (4 annexe) (25 fmly) (11 GF) ☕ **Facilities** FTV Wi-fi ☜ ☚ Games room Sauna Spa bath Treatments available ♪ Xmas New Year **Conf** Class 120 Board 50 Thtr 180 **Services** Lift **Parking** 45 **Notes** Civ Wed 160

Royal Exeter Hotel

★★★ 79% HOTEL

☎ 01202 438000
Exeter Rd BH2 5AG
e-mail: enquiries@royalexeterhotel.com
web: www.royalexeterhotel.com
dir: Opposite Bournemouth International Centre

Ideally located opposite the Bournemouth International Centre, and convenient for the beach and town centre, this busy hotel caters for both business and leisure guests. Public areas are smart, and there's a modern open-plan lounge bar and restaurant, together with an exciting adjoining bar complex.

Rooms 54 (13 fmly) (12 smoking) **Facilities** FTV Wi-fi Gym ♪ **Conf** Class 40 Board 40 Thtr 100 **Services** Lift **Parking** 50 **Notes** LB ⊗

See advert on opposite page

Hinton Firs Hotel

★★★ 77% HOTEL

☎ 01202 555409
Manor Rd, East Cliff BH1 3ET
e-mail: info@hintonfirshotel.co.uk
web: www.hintonfirshotel.co.uk
dir: A338, W at St Paul's rdbt, over next 2 rdbts, fork left to side of church. Hotel on next corner

This family-owned hotel is very friendly and is conveniently located on East Cliff, just a short stroll from the sea. The smart, well-appointed bedrooms are light and airy. There are family rooms and also one bedroom with a wet room, that is suitable for less able guests. The leisure facilities include indoor and outdoor pools, a sauna, beauty treatments and

supervised children's activities in the school holidays. There is also a spacious lounge, a restaurant and bar.

Rooms 52 (6 annexe) (12 fmly) (3 GF) ☕ **Facilities** FTV Wi-fi ☜ ☚ ♪ Xmas New Year **Conf** Class 20 Board 15 Thtr 60 **Services** Lift **Parking** 40 **Notes** LB ⊗

Suncliff Hotel

★★★ 77% HOTEL

☎ 01202 291711 & 298350
29 East Overcliff Dr BH1 3AG
e-mail: info@sunclliffbournemouth.co.uk
dir: A338/A35 towards East Cliff & beaches, right into Holdenhurst Rd, straight over 2 rdbts, left at junct into East Overcliff Drive, hotel on seafront

Enjoying splendid views from the East Cliff and catering mainly for leisure guests, this friendly hotel offers a range of facilities and services. Bedrooms are well equipped and comfortable, and many have sea views. Public areas include a large conservatory, an attractive bar and pleasant lounges.

Rooms 97 (29 fmly) (14 GF) ☕ **S** £22-£129; **D** £44-£249 (incl. bkfst)* **Facilities** Wi-fi ☜ ☚ Gym Squash Sauna Table tennis ♪ Xmas New Year **Conf** Class 70 Board 60 Thtr 100 Del from £89 to £109* **Services** Lift **Parking** 62 **Notes** LB Civ Wed 80

Cliffeside Hotel

★★★ 76% HOTEL

☎ 01202 555724 & 298350
East Overcliff Dr BH1 3AQ
e-mail: info@cliffesidebournemouth.co.uk
dir: A35, A338 to East Cliff & beaches, right into Holdenhurst Rd, over next 2 rdbts, at junct left into East Overcliff Drive, hotel on left

Benefiting from an elevated position on the seafront and just a short walk from town, it's no wonder that this friendly hotel has many returning guests. Bedrooms and public areas are attractively appointed, many with sea views. The Atlantic Restaurant offers guests a fixed-price menu.

Rooms 62 (5 fmly) (2 GF) ☕ **S** £35-£85; **D** £59-£155 (incl. bkfst)* **Facilities** Wi-fi ☜ ☚ Gym Squash Sauna Beauty treatment room ♪ Xmas New Year **Conf** Class 70 Board 40 Thtr 120 **Services** Lift **Parking** 72 **Notes** LB Civ Wed 120

B

Hotel Piccadilly

★★★ 75% HOTEL

☎ 01202 298024
25 Bath Rd BH1 2NN
e-mail: enquiries@hotelpiccadilly.co.uk
dir: From A338 take 1st exit rdbt, signed East Cliff. 3rd exit at next rdbt signed Lansdowne, 3rd exit at next rdbt into Bath Rd

This hotel offers a friendly welcome to guests, many of whom return on a regular basis, particularly for the superb ballroom dancing facilities and small break packages which are a feature here. Bedrooms are smartly decorated, well maintained and comfortable. Dining in the attractive restaurant is always popular and dishes are freshly prepared and appetising.

Rooms 45 (2 fmly) (5 GF) **S** £35-£55; **D** £70-£120 **Facilities** FTV Wi-fi Ballroom 🎵 Xmas New Year **Conf** Class 50 Board 50 Thtr 140 Del from £60 to £90* **Services** Lift **Parking** 45 **Notes** ⊗ Civ Wed 200

Trouville Hotel

★★★ 75% HOTEL

☎ 01202 552262
Priory Rd BH2 5DH
e-mail: reception@trouvillehotel.com
dir: Follow Town Centre West signs. Exit at rdbt signed BIC/West Cliff/Beaches. 2nd exit at next rdbt, left at next rdbt. Hotel on left near end of Priory Rd

Located near Bournemouth International Centre, the seafront and the shops, this hotel has the advantage of indoor leisure facilities and a large car park. Bedrooms are generally a good size with comfortable furnishings, and there are plenty of family rooms. The air-conditioned restaurant offers a daily changing menu.

Rooms 99 (19 annexe) (21 fmly) (6 GF) 🐾 **S** £49.95-£64.95; **D** £99.90-£129.90* **Facilities** FTV Wi-fi ⌕ ❄ Gym Sauna 🎵 Xmas New Year **Conf** Class 100 Board 80 Thtr 250 **Services** Lift **Parking** 70 **Notes** Civ Wed 130

Mayfair Hotel

★★★ 74% HOTEL

☎ 01202 551983
27 Bath Rd BH1 2NW
e-mail: info@themayfair.com
web: www.themayfair.com
dir: Exit A338 at St Pauls Rd (Asda rdbt), right into Holdenhurst Rd, 3rd exit from Lansdowne rdbt

Occupying a central location in the heart of Bournemouth and within walking distance of both the town centre and the seafront, this hotel offers guests comfortable, modern accommodation. There is a spacious restaurant and bar area, plus a pleasant outdoor patio and function room.

Rooms 40 (6 fmly) (1 GF) **Facilities** Wi-fi Ballroom dancing programme on request Xmas New Year **Conf** Class 40 Board 30 Thtr 60 Del from £90 to £110* **Services** Lift **Parking** 30 **Notes** ⊗ Civ Wed 80

Hotel Collingwood

★★★ 71% HOTEL

☎ 01202 557575
11 Priory Rd, West Cliff BH2 5DF
e-mail: info@hotel-collingwood.co.uk
web: www.hotel-collingwood.co.uk
dir: A338 left at West Cliff sign, over 1st rdbt, left at 2nd rdbt. Hotel 500yds on left

This privately owned and managed hotel is situated close to the BIC. Bedrooms are airy, with the emphasis on comfort. An excellent range of leisure facilities is available and the public areas are spacious and welcoming. Pinks Restaurant offers carefully prepared cuisine and a fixed-price, five-course dinner.

Rooms 53 (16 fmly) (6 GF) 🐾 **S** £35-£65; **D** £70-£130 (incl. bkfst)* **Facilities** FTV Wi-fi ❄ Gym Steam room Sauna Games room Snooker room 🎵 Xmas New Year **Conf** Class 60 Board 20 Thtr 100 Del from £70 to £90* **Services** Lift **Parking** 55 **Notes** LB

Durley Dean Hotel

★★★ 68% HOTEL

☎ 01202 557711
West Cliff Rd BH2 5HE
e-mail: reservations@durleydean.co.uk
dir: Into Bournemouth, follow signs for Westcliff. Onto Durley Chine Rd South to next rdbt, hotel at 2nd exit on left

Situated close to the seafront on the West Cliff, this modern hotel has bedrooms which vary in size and style. There is a restaurant, a comfortable bar and several meeting rooms. Parking is also a bonus.

Rooms 117 (36 fmly) (6 GF) **Facilities** FTV Wi-fi ⌕ ❄ Gym 🎵 Xmas New Year **Conf** Class 40 Board 40 Thtr 150 **Services** Lift **Parking** 30 **Notes** ⊗ Civ Wed 200

B

BOURNEMOUTH *continued*

Burley Court Hotel

★★★ 63% HOTEL

☎ 01202 552824 & 556704
Bath Rd BH1 2NP
e-mail: info@burleycourthotel.co.uk
dir: Exit A338 at St Paul's rdbt, take 3rd exit at next
rdbt into Holdenhurst Rd. 3rd exit at next rdbt into
Bath Rd, over crossing, 1st left

Located on Bournemouth's West Cliff, this established
hotel is well located and convenient for the town and
beaches. Bedrooms are pleasantly furnished and
decorated in bright colours. A daily-changing menu is
served in the spacious dining room.

Rooms 38 (8 fmly) (4 GF) **Facilities** ᵪ Xmas
Conf Class 15 Board 15 Thtr 30 **Services** Lift
Parking 35 **Notes** Closed 30 Dec-14 Jan RS 15-31 Jan

Tower House Hotel

★★ 76% HOTEL

☎ 01202 290742
West Cliff Gardens BH2 5HP
e-mail: towerhouse.hotel@btconnect.com

A popular family owned and run hotel on the West
Cliff. The owners and their staff are friendly and
helpful. The bedrooms are comfortable and well
maintained and the hotel provides good off-road
parking.

Rooms 32 (12 fmly) (3 GF) ⬧ **S** £25-£49; **D** £50-£98
(incl. bkfst)* **Facilities** FTV Wi-fi Xmas New Year
Services Lift **Parking** 30 **Notes** Closed 2-31 Jan

Devon Towers Hotel

★★ 74% HOTEL   *Leisureplex*

☎ 01202 553863
58-62 St Michael's Rd, West Cliff BH2 5ED
e-mail:
devontowers.bournemouth@alfatravel.co.uk
web: www.leisureplex.co.uk
dir: A338 into Bournemouth, follow signs for BIC. Left
into St. Michaels Rd at top of hill. Hotel 100mtrs on
left

Located in a quiet road within walking distance of the
West Cliff and shops, this hotel appeals to the budget
leisure market. The four-course menus offer plenty of
choice and entertainment is featured most evenings.
The bar and lobby area provide plenty of space for
relaxing.

Rooms 60 (8 GF) ⬧ **S** £36-£47; **D** £58-£80 (incl.
bkfst)* **Facilities** FTV ♫ Xmas New Year
Services Lift **Parking** 6 **Notes** LB ⊗ Closed Jan-mid
Feb (ex Xmas) RS mid-end Feb, Mar & Nov

Durley Grange Hotel

★★ 74% HOTEL

☎ 01202 554473
6 Durley Rd, West Cliff BH2 5JL
e-mail: reservations@durleygrange.com
web: www.durleygrange.com
dir: A338/Bournemouth West rdbt. Over next rdbt, 1st
left into Sommerville Rd & right into Durley Rd

Located in a quiet area, the town and beaches are all
in walking distance of this welcoming, friendly hotel.
Bedrooms are brightly decorated, comfortable and
well equipped. There is an indoor pool and sauna for
all-year round use, and enjoyable meals are served in
the smart dining room. Parking is a plus.

Rooms 52 (8 fmly) (4 GF) ⬧ **S** £49-£71; **D** £98-£142
(incl. bkfst & dinner) **Facilities** Wi-fi ⊛ Sauna ♫
Xmas New Year **Services** Lift **Parking** 35 **Notes** LB ⊗

Ullswater Hotel

★★ 71% HOTEL

☎ 01202 555181
West Cliff Gardens BH2 5HW
e-mail: enquiries@ullswater-hotel.co.uk
web: www.ullswater-hotel.co.uk
dir: In Bournemouth follow signs to West Cliff. Hotel
just off Westcliff Rd

Ullswater Hotel is a welcoming family-run
establishment conveniently located for the city and
the seafront. The well-equipped bedrooms vary in
size, and the charming lounge bar and dining room
are very smart. Cuisine is hearty and homemade,
offering a good choice from the daily-changing menu.

Rooms 42 (8 fmly) (2 GF) ⬧ **S** £35-£55; **D** £55-£95
(incl. bkfst)* **Facilities** FTV Wi-fi ↳ Snooker room

Table tennis ♫ Xmas New Year **Conf** Class 30
Board 24 Thtr 40 Del from £60 to £105 **Services** Lift
Parking 12 **Notes** LB

Bourne Hall Hotel

★★ 62% HOTEL

☎ 01202 299715
14 Priory Rd, West Cliff BH2 5DN
e-mail: info@bournehall.co.uk
web: www.bournehall.co.uk
dir: M27, A31 from Ringwood into Bournemouth on
A338 (Wessex Way). Follow signs to BIC, onto West
Cliff. Hotel on right

This friendly, comfortable hotel is conveniently
located close to the Bournemouth International Centre
and the seafront. Bedrooms are well equipped, some
located on the ground floor and some with sea views.
In addition to the spacious lounge, there are two bars
and a meeting room. A daily-changing menu is
offered in the dining room.

Rooms 48 (9 fmly) (5 GF) ⬧ **Facilities** FTV Wi-fi Free
leisure facilities for guests at Marriott Highcliff Hotel
♫ Xmas New Year **Conf** Class 60 Board 40 Thtr 130
Services Lift **Parking** 35

Premier Inn Bournemouth Central

BUDGET HOTEL

☎ 0871 527 8124
Westover Rd BH1 2BZ
web: www.premierinn.com
dir: M27 junct 1, A31. Left at Ashley Heath junct.
A338 towards Bournemouth. At rdbt 1st exit. At next
rdbt 3rd exit (Holdenhurst Rd). At next rdbt 3rd exit
(Bath Rd). At next rdbt 3rd exit onto Bath Hill. At next
rdbt into Westover Rd, right into Hinton Rd, hotel on
right

High quality, budget accommodation ideal for both
families and business travellers. Spacious, en suite
bedrooms feature tea and coffee making facilities,
and Freeview TV in most hotels. Internet access and
Wi-fi are available for a small fee. The adjacent
family restaurant features a wide and varied menu.
See also the Hotel Groups pages.

Rooms 120

B

Premier Inn Bournemouth East

BUDGET HOTEL

☎ 0871 527 8126
47 Christchurch Rd, Boscombe BH1 3PA
web: www.premierinn.com
dir: M27 junct 1, A31, 9m, left at Ashley Heath junct, take A338 signed Bournemouth. At 1st rdbt take 1st exit into Saint Paul's Rd. At 2nd rdbt 1st exit onto Christchurch Rd. Hotel on right

Rooms 20

Premier Inn Bournemouth Westcliffe

BUDGET HOTEL

☎ 0871 527 8128
Poole Rd BH2 5QU
web: www.premierinn.com
dir: M27 junct 1, A31. At Ashley Heath junction, left. Take A338 signed Bournemouth. At Bournemouth West rdbt 1st exit signed Ring Road, West Cliff. At next rdbt (St Michael's) 3rd exit (signed Westbourne) into Poole Rd. Hotel on right

Rooms 101

BOURTON-ON-THE-WATER   Map 10 SP12
Gloucestershire

Chester House Hotel

★★★ 73% SMALL HOTEL

☎ 01451 820286
Victoria St GL54 2BU
e-mail: info@chesterhousehotel.com
dir: On A429 between Northleach & Stow-on-the-Wold

Chester House Hotel occupies a secluded but central location in this delightful Cotswold village. Bedrooms, some at ground floor level, are situated in the main house and adjoining coach house. The public areas are stylish, light and airy. Breakfast is taken in the main building whereas dinner is served in the attractive restaurant just a few yards away.

Rooms 22 (10 annexe) (3 fmly) (8 GF) ↾ **S** £95-£130; **D** £95-£130 (incl. bkfst)* **Facilities** FTV Wi-fi Beauty therapist New Year **Parking** 18 **Notes** Closed 7 Jan-1 Feb

---

BOWNESS ON WINDERMERE

See **Windermere**

BOXWORTH   Map 12 TL36
Cambridgeshire

Days Inn Cambridge - A1

BUDGET HOTEL

☎ 01954 267176
Cambridge Extra Services, Junction A14/M11 CB3 8WU
e-mail: cambridge.hotel@welcomebreak.co.uk
dir: A14/M11 Cambridge Extra Services

This modern, purpose built accommodation offers smartly appointed, well-equipped bedrooms, with good power showers. There is a choice of adjacent food outlets where guests may enjoy breakfast, snacks and meals. See also the Hotel Groups pages.

Rooms 82 (14 fmly) (40 GF) (19 smoking)

BRACKNELL   Map 5 SU86
Berkshire

Coppid Beech

★★★★ 74% ⚜ HOTEL

☎ 01344 303333
John Nike Way RG12 8TF
e-mail: sales@coppidbeech.com
web: www.coppidbeech.com
dir: M4 junct 10 take Wokingham/Bracknell onto A329. In 2m take B3408 to Binfield, at lights turn right. Hotel 200yds on right

This chalet designed hotel offers extensive facilities and includes a ski-slope, ice rink, nightclub, health club and Bier Keller. Bedrooms range from suites to standard rooms - all are impressively equipped. A choice of dining is offered; there's a full bistro menu available in the Keller, and for more formal dining, Rowan's restaurant provides award-winning cuisine.

Rooms 205 (6 fmly) (16 GF) **S** £70-£205; **D** £90-£250* **Facilities** STV Wi-fi ⊗ Gym Beauty treatment room Ice rink Dry ski slope Snow boarding Freestyle park ♫ New Year **Conf** Class 161 Board 24 Thtr 350 Del from £150 to £185* **Services** Lift Air con **Parking** 350 **Notes** LB ⊗ Civ Wed 200

Stirrups Country House

★★★ 82% HOTEL

☎ 01344 882284
Maidens Green RG42 6LD
e-mail: reception@stirrupshotel.co.uk
web: www.stirrupshotel.co.uk
dir: 3m N on B3022 towards Windsor

Situated in a peaceful location between Maidenhead, Bracknell and Windsor, this hotel has high standards of comfort particularly in the bedrooms; some rooms have a small sitting room area. There is a popular bar, a restaurant, function rooms and delightful grounds.

Rooms 30 (4 fmly) (2 GF) ↾ **S** £79-£87; **D** £79-£87* **Facilities** STV Wi-fi ⊗ New Year **Conf** Class 50 Board 40 Thtr 100 Del from £170* **Services** Lift **Parking** 100 **Notes** LB ⊗ Civ Wed 100

Premier Inn Bracknell Central

BUDGET HOTEL

☎ 0871 527 8132
Wokingham Rd RG42 1NA
web: www.premierinn.com
dir: M4 junct 10, A329(M) (Bracknell) to lights. 1st left, 3rd exit rdbt by Morrisons to town centre. Left at rdbt, left at next rdbt. Hotel on left

High quality, budget accommodation ideal for both families and business travellers. Spacious, en suite bedrooms feature tea and coffee making facilities, and Freeview TV in most hotels. Internet access and Wi-fi are available for a small fee. The adjacent family restaurant features a wide and varied menu. See also the Hotel Groups pages.

Rooms 60

Premier Inn Bracknell (Twin Bridges)

BUDGET HOTEL

☎ 0871 527 8130
Downshire Way RG12 7AA
web: www.premierinn.com
dir: M4 junct 10, A329(M) towards Bracknell. Straight on at mini rdbt. At Twin Bridges rdbt take 2nd exit. Hotel on right adjacent to Downshire Arms Beefeater

Rooms 28

B

BRADFORD
West Yorkshire   Map 19 SE13

See also **Gomersal & Shipley**

BEST WESTERN PLUS Cedar Court Hotel

★★★★ 71% HOTEL

☎ 01274 406606
Mayo Av, Off Rooley Ln BD5 8HZ
e-mail: sales@cedarcourtbradford.co.uk
dir: M62 junct 26, M606, to end of motorway, take 1st left

This purpose built, modern hotel is conveniently located just off the motorway and close to the city centre and the airport. The hotel boasts extensive function and conference facilities, a well-equipped leisure club and an elegant restaurant. Bedrooms are comfortably appointed for both business and leisure guests.

Rooms 131 (7 fmly) (23 GF) **Facilities** STV FTV Wi-fi ⓧ Gym Steam room Sauna Solarium New Year **Conf** Class 300 Board 100 Thtr 800 **Services** Lift **Parking** 350 **Notes** ⊗ Civ Wed 550

Midland Hotel

PEEL HOTELS PLC

★★★ 80% HOTEL

☎ 01274 735735
Forster Square BD1 4HU
e-mail: info@midland-hotel-bradford.com
web: www.peelhotels.co.uk
dir: M62 junct 26, M606, past ASDA, left at rdbt onto A650. Through 2 rdbts & 2 lights. Follow A6181/Haworth signs. Up hill, next left into Manor Row. Hotel 400mtrs

Ideally situated in the heart of the city, this grand Victorian hotel provides modern, very well equipped accommodation and comfortable, spacious day rooms. Ample parking is available in what was once the city's railway station, and a Victorian walkway linking the hotel to the old platform can still be used today.

Rooms 90 (5 fmly) (10 smoking) ⓡ **S** £65-£110; **D** £75-£165 (incl. bkfst)* **Facilities** STV FTV Wi-fi ⓧ New Year **Conf** Class 150 Board 100 Thtr 450 Del from £116* **Services** Lift **Parking** 60 **Notes** LB Civ Wed 450

BEST WESTERN Bradford Guide Post Hotel

★★★ 75% HOTEL

☎ 0844 332 0459 & 01274 607866
Common Rd, Low Moor BD12 0ST
e-mail: sue.barnes@guideposthotel.net
web: www.guideposthotel.net
dir: From M606 rdbt take 2nd exit. At next rdbt take 1st exit (Cleckheaton Rd). 0.5m, turn right at bollard into Common Rd

Situated south of the city, this hotel offers attractively styled, modern, comfortable bedrooms. The restaurant offers an extensive range of food using fresh, local produce; lighter snack meals are served in the bar. There is also a choice of well-equipped meeting and function rooms. There is disabled access to the hotel, restaurant and one function room.

Rooms 42 (10 fmly) (13 GF) ⓡ **Facilities** FTV Wi-fi ⓧ Complimentary use of nearby swimming & gym facilities **Conf** Class 80 Board 60 Thtr 120 **Parking** 100 **Notes** Civ Wed 120

Campanile Bradford

Campanile

★★★ 73% HOTEL

☎ 01274 683683
6 Roydsdale Way, Euroway Estate BD4 6SA
e-mail: bradford@campanile.com
web: www.campanile.com
dir: M62 junct 26 into M606. Exit Euroway Estate East into Merrydale Rd, right onto Roydsdale Way

This modern building offers accommodation in smart, well-equipped bedrooms, all with en suite bathrooms. Refreshments may be taken at the informal bistro.

Rooms 130 (37 fmly) (22 GF) (8 smoking) **Facilities** STV FTV Wi-fi **Conf** Class 100 Board 100 Thtr 300 **Services** Lift **Parking** 200 **Notes** Civ Wed 170

Premier Inn Bradford Central

BUDGET HOTEL

☎ 0871 527 9306
Vicar Ln BD1 5LD
dir: M62 junct 24, M606, at junct 3 take 4th exit into Rooley Ln (A6177) towards Ring Rd/A650/Leeds/A647. In 1m 1st exit into Wakefield Rd towards City Centre. Follow Wakefield Rd/A650 signs. Straight on a 2 rdbts, right into Vicar Ln

High quality, budget accommodation ideal for both families and business travellers. Spacious, en suite bedrooms feature tea and coffee making facilities, and Freeview TV in most hotels. Internet access and Wi-fi are available for a small fee. The adjacent

family restaurant features a wide and varied menu. See also the Hotel Groups pages.

Rooms 118

BRADFORD-ON-AVON
Wiltshire   Map 4 ST86

Widbrook Grange

★★★ 75% COUNTRY HOUSE HOTEL

☎ 01225 864750 & 863173
Trowbridge Rd, Widbrook BA15 1UH
e-mail: stay@widbrookgrange.com
web: www.widbrookgrange.com
dir: 1m SE from Bradford on A363, hotel diagonally opposite Bradford Marina & Arabian Stud

This former farmhouse, built as a model farm in the 18th century, has been carefully renovated to provide modern comforts, suitable for both business and leisure guests. Some bedrooms are in the main house, but most are in adjacent converted buildings, and these rooms have their own courtyard entrance and many are located on the ground floor. The lounges offer a good level of comfort. French influenced cuisine is served in the refurbished brasserie where friendly staff provide a personal and relaxed service.

Rooms 20 (15 annexe) (6 fmly) (13 GF) ⓡ **Facilities** FTV Wi-fi ⓧ ⓧ Gym Children's weekend play room Beauty treatments New Year **Conf** Class 35 Board 25 Thtr 50 **Parking** 50 **Notes** Closed 24-30 Dec Civ Wed 50

BRAINTREE
Essex   Map 7 TL72

White Hart Hotel

OldEnglish

★★★ 67% HOTEL

☎ 01376 321401
Bocking End CM7 9AB
e-mail: whitehart.braintree@greeneking.co.uk
web: www.oldenglish.co.uk
dir: Exit A120 towards town centre. Hotel at B1256 & Bocking Causeway junct

This 18th-century former coaching inn is conveniently located in the heart of the bustling town centre. The smartly appointed public rooms include a large lounge bar, a restaurant and meeting rooms. The pleasantly decorated bedrooms have co-ordinated fabrics and many thoughtful touches.

Rooms 31 (8 fmly) **Facilities** FTV Wi-fi Xmas New Year **Conf** Class 16 Board 24 Thtr 40 **Parking** 52 **Notes** ⊗ Civ Wed 35

Premier Inn Braintree (A120)

BUDGET HOTEL

☎ 0871 527 8138
Cressing Rd, Galley's Corner CM77 8GG
web: www.premierinn.com
dir: On A120 (Stansted to Braintree link road).
Adjacent to Mulberry Tree Brewers Fayre

High quality, budget accommodation ideal for both
families and business travellers. Spacious, en suite
bedrooms feature tea and coffee making facilities,
and Freeview TV in most hotels. Internet access and
Wi-fi are available for a small fee. The adjacent
family restaurant features a wide and varied menu.
See also the Hotel Groups pages.

Rooms 60

Premier Inn Braintree (Freeport Village)

BUDGET HOTEL

☎ 0871 527 8140
Fowlers Farm, Cressing Rd CM77 8DH
web: www.premierinn.com
dir: M11 junct 8, follow signs to A120 Colchester &
Freeport Shopping Village. At Galley's Corner rdbt, 4th
exit, left into Wyevale Garden Centre. Hotel adjacent

Rooms 47

BRAITHWAITE Map 18 NY22
Cumbria

The Cottage in the Wood

◉◉ RESTAURANT WITH ROOMS

☎ 017687 78409
Whinlatter Pass CA12 5TW
e-mail: relax@thecottageinthewood.co.uk
dir: M6 junct 40, A66 W. After Keswick exit for
Braithwaite via Whinlatter Pass (B5292),
establishment at top of pass

This charming property sits on wooded hills with
striking views of Skiddaw, and is conveniently placed
for Keswick. The owners provide excellent hospitality
in a relaxed manner. The award-winning food, freshly
prepared and locally sourced, is served in the bright
and welcoming conservatory restaurant that has
stunning views. The comfortable bedrooms are well
appointed and have many useful extras.

Rooms 9

BRAMPTON Map 21 NY56
Cumbria

INSPECTORS' CHOICE

Farlam Hall Hotel

★★★ ◉◉ HOTEL

☎ 016977 46234
CA8 2NG
e-mail: farlam@relaischateaux.com
web: www.farlamhall.co.uk
dir: On A689 (Brampton to Alston). Hotel 2m on left
(not in Farlam village)

This delightful country house has a history dating
back to 1428, although the building today is very
much the result of alterations carried out in the
mid-19th century. The hotel is run by a friendly
family team and their enthusiastic staff, and is set
in beautifully landscaped Victorian gardens
complete with an ornamental lake and stream.
Lovingly restored over many years, it provides very
high standards of comfort and hospitality. Gracious
public rooms invite relaxation, and much thought
has gone into the beautiful bedrooms, many of
which are simply stunning. Nearby are Hadrian's
Wall and the Northern Pennines Area of
Outstanding Natural Beauty, which both provide
endless opportunities for walking and sightseeing.

Rooms 12 (1 annexe) (2 GF) ♦ **S** £160-£190;
D £300-£360 (incl. bkfst & dinner)* **Facilities** FTV
Wi-fi ♦ ♨ New Year **Conf** Class 24 Board 12
Thtr 24 Del from £180* **Parking** 25 **Notes** LB No
children 5yrs Closed 24-30 Dec & 4-17 Jan
Civ Wed 45

BRANCASTER STAITHE Map 13 TF74
Norfolk

The White Horse

★★★ 80% ◉◉ HOTEL

☎ 01485 210262
PE31 8BY
e-mail: reception@whitehorsebrancaster.co.uk
web: www.whitehorsebrancaster.co.uk
dir: On A149 (coast road) midway between
Hunstanton & Wells-next-the-Sea

A charming hotel situated on the north Norfolk coast
with contemporary bedrooms in two wings, some
featuring an interesting cobbled fascia. Each room is
attractively decorated and thoughtfully equipped.
There is a large bar and a lounge area leading
through to the conservatory restaurant, with stunning
tidal marshland views across to Scolt Head Island.

Rooms 15 (8 annexe) (4 fmly) (8 GF) ♦ **S** £60-£160;
D £95-£210 (incl. bkfst)* **Facilities** FTV Wi-fi ♦ Xmas
New Year **Parking** 60

BRANDON Map 11 SP47
Warwickshire

Mercure Coventry Brandon Hall Hotel & Spa

★★★★ 74% ◉ HOTEL

☎ 024 7654 6000
Main St CV8 3FW
e-mail: h6625@accor.com
web: www.mercure.com
dir: A45 towards Coventry S. After Peugeot-Citroen
garage on left, at island take 5th exit to M1 South/
London (back onto A45). After 200yds, immediately
after Texaco garage, left into Brandon Ln, hotel after
2.5m

An impressive tree-lined avenue leads to this 17th-
century property which sits in 17 acres of grounds.
The hotel provides a peaceful and friendly sanctuary
away from the hustle and bustle. The bedrooms
provide comfortable facilities and a good range of
extras for guest comfort. There is a Spa Naturel with
health, beauty and fitness facilities in a separate
building.

Rooms 120 (30 annexe) (10 fmly) (50 GF) ♦
Facilities Spa STV Wi-fi ♦ Gym Steam room Sauna
Xmas New Year **Conf** Class 120 Board 112 Thtr 280
Services Lift **Parking** 200 **Notes** Civ Wed 280

B

BRANDS HATCH
Kent
Map 6 TQ56

Thistle Brands Hatch
thistle

★★★★ 77% HOTEL

☎ 0871 376 9008
DA3 8PE
e-mail: brandshatch@thistle.co.uk
web: www.thistle.com/brandshatch
dir: M25 junct 3, follow signs for Brands Hatch. Hotel on left of racing circuit entrance

Ideally situated overlooking Brands Hatch race track and close to the major road networks (M20/M25). The open-plan public areas include a choice of bars, large lounge and a restaurant. Bedrooms are stylishly appointed and well equipped for both leisure and business guests. Extensive meeting rooms and Otium leisure facilities are also available.

Rooms 121 (5 fmly) (60 GF) (6 smoking) **S** £60-£120; **D** £70-£160* **Facilities** Spa STV FTV Wi-fi HL ⊗ Gym Xmas New Year **Conf** Class 120 Board 60 Thtr 270 Del from £99 to £149 **Parking** 200 **Notes** LB Civ Wed 200

BRANKSOME

See **Poole**

BRANSCOMBE
Devon
Map 4 SY18

The Bulstone Hotel

★★ 71% HOTEL

☎ 01297 680446
High Bulstone EX12 3BL
e-mail: bulstone@aol.com
web: www.childfriendlyhotels.com
dir: A3052 (Exeter to Lyme Regis road) at Branscombe Cross follow brown hotel sign

Situated in a peaceful location close to the beautiful east Devon coast, this family-friendly hotel is ideally placed for a relaxing break with plenty of attractions within easy reach. All bedrooms comprise a main bedroom and separate children's room, each being practically furnished and equipped. Additional facilities include a playroom, a snug lounge, and the dining room where enjoyable home-cooked meals are offered. There is no charge for children under ten, and children's tea is at 5pm.

Rooms 7 (7 fmly) (4 GF) **Facilities** FTV Wi-fi Children's playroom Xmas New Year **Conf** Class 25 Board 25 **Services** Air con **Parking** 25 **Notes** ⊗

BREADSALL
Derbyshire
Map 11 SK33

Breadsall Priory, A Marriott Hotel & Country Club
Marriott

★★★★ 73% ⊛ COUNTRY HOUSE HOTEL

☎ 01332 832235
Moor Rd, Morley DE7 6DL
web: www.marriottbreadsallpriory.co.uk
dir: A52 to Derby, at Pentagon rdbt 3rd exit towards A61/Chesterfield. At 3rd rdbt take 3rd exit & 1st left into village, left at church into Moor Rd. Hotel 1.5m on left

This extended mansion house is set in 400 acres of parkland and well-tended gardens. The smart bedrooms are mostly contained in the modern wing. There is a vibrant café-bar, a more formal restaurant and a large room-service menu. The extensive leisure facilities include two golf courses and a swimming pool. Dinner in the Priory Restaurant is a highlight.

Rooms 112 (100 annexe) (40 fmly) **Facilities** Spa STV Wi-fi ⊗ ⊗ ⅃ 36 ⛳ Putt green ⊛ Gym Health, beauty & hair salon Dance studio Leisure club Xmas New Year **Conf** Class 50 Board 36 Thtr 120 **Services** Lift **Parking** 300 **Notes** ⊗ Civ Wed 100

BRENTFORD
Greater London

Premier Inn London Kew
Premier Inn

BUDGET HOTEL PLAN 1 C3

☎ 0871 527 8670
52 High St TW8 0BB
web: www.premierinn.com
dir: At junct of A4 (M4), A205 & A406, Chiswick rdbt, take A205 towards Kew & Brentford. 200yds right fork onto A315 (High St), for 0.5m. Hotel on left

High quality, budget accommodation ideal for both families and business travellers. Spacious, en suite bedrooms feature tea and coffee making facilities, and Freeview TV in most hotels. Internet access and Wi-fi are available for a small fee. The adjacent family restaurant features a wide and varied menu. See also the Hotel Groups pages.

Rooms 141

BRENTWOOD
Essex
Map 6 TQ59

Marygreen Manor Hotel
CLASSIC BRITISH HOTELS

★★★★ 75% ⊛⊛ HOTEL

☎ 01277 225252
London Rd CM14 4NR
e-mail: info@marygreenmanor.co.uk
web: www.marygreenmanor.co.uk
dir: M25 junct 28, onto A1023 over 2 sets of lights, hotel on right

This 16th-century house was built by Robert Wright, who named the house 'Manor of Mary Green' after his young bride. Public rooms exude character and have a wealth of original features that include exposed beams, carved panelling and the impressive Tudors Restaurant. Bedrooms are tastefully decorated and thoughtfully equipped.

Rooms 44 (40 annexe) (35 GF) ⤳ **S** £70-£160; **D** £70-£240* **Facilities** STV FTV Wi-fi ↘ **Conf** Class 20 Board 25 Thtr 50 Del from £139 to £159* **Parking** 100 **Notes** ⊗ Civ Wed 60

De Rougemont Manor

★★★★ 72% HOTEL

☎ 01277 226418 & 220483
Great Warley St CM13 3JP
e-mail: info@derougemontmanor.co.uk
web: www.derougemontmanor.co.uk
dir: M25 junct 29, A127 to Southend then B186 towards Great Warley

Expect a warm welcome at this family owned and managed hotel, situated on the outskirts of Brentwood just off the M25. The stylish bedrooms are divided between the main hotel and a bedroom wing; each one is tastefully appointed and well equipped. Public rooms include a smart lounge bar, restaurant and a choice of seating areas.

Rooms 74 (10 annexe) (8 fmly) (16 GF) ⤳ **S** £79-£99; **D** £119-£169 (incl. bkfst)* **Facilities** FTV Wi-fi ↘ ↘ ⛳ Gym 3-acre nature reserve Xmas New Year **Conf** Class 120 Board 16 Thtr 200 Del from £150 to £170* **Services** Lift Air con **Parking** 200 **Notes** LB ⊗ Civ Wed 90

Save on hotels. Book at **theAA.com/hotel**

BRA – BRI 99 ENGLAND

B

Holiday Inn Brentwood

★★★ 80% HOTEL

☎ 0871 942 9012
Brook St CM14 5NF
e-mail: reservations-brentwoodm25@ihg.com
web: www.holidayinn.co.uk
dir: Exit M25 junct 28 (or A12 at M25 interchange). Follow signs to Brentwood/A1023. Hotel 200yds on left

Ideally located just off the M25, this hotel is only 40 minutes from central London and 25 minutes from Stansted Airport, making it the perfect choice for business and leisure travellers alike. The public areas are smartly appointed; the health and fitness club has an indoor swimming pool.

Rooms 149 (28 fmly) (43 GF) **Facilities** STV FTV Wi-fi ᕹ HL ☺ Gym New Year **Conf** Class 60 Board 50 Thtr 140 **Services** Lift Air con **Parking** 276 **Notes** ⊗ Civ Wed 70

Premier Inn Brentwood

BUDGET HOTEL

☎ 0871 527 8142
Brentwood House, 169 Kings Rd CM14 4EF
web: www.premierinn.com
dir: From S: M25 junct 28 take A1023 (or from N: at Brook Street rdbt 2nd exit onto A1023). Right at lights into Kings Rd, at rdbt 2nd exit into Kings Rd

High quality, budget accommodation ideal for both families and business travellers. Spacious, en suite bedrooms feature tea and coffee making facilities, and Freeview TV in most hotels. Internet access and Wi-fi are available for a small fee. The adjacent family restaurant features a wide and varied menu. See also the Hotel Groups pages.

Rooms 122

BRIDGNORTH
Shropshire
Map 10 SO79

The Old Vicarage Hotel

★★★ 83% ◉◉ SMALL HOTEL

☎ 01746 716497
Worfield WV15 5JZ
e-mail: admin@oldvicarageworfield.co.uk
web: www.oldvicarageworfield.com
dir: Exit A454 approx 3.5m NE of Bridgnorth, 5m S of Telford's southern business area. Follow brown signs

This delightful property is set in acres of wooded farmland in a quiet and peaceful area of Shropshire. Service is friendly and helpful, and customer care is one the many strengths of this charming small hotel.

The well-equipped bedrooms are individually appointed, and thoughtfully and luxuriously furnished. The lounge and conservatory are the perfect places to enjoy a pre-dinner drink or the complimentary afternoon tea. The restaurant is a joy, serving award-winning modern British cuisine in elegant surroundings.

Rooms 14 (4 annexe) (1 fmly) (2 GF) **Facilities** FTV Wi-fi ᕹ ✦ New Year **Conf** Class 40 Board 30 Thtr 60 **Parking** 30 **Notes** Civ Wed 60

BRIDGWATER
Somerset
Map 4 ST23

Walnut Tree Hotel

★★★ 77% HOTEL

☎ 01278 662255
North Petherton TA6 6QA
e-mail: reservations@walnuttreehotel.com
web: www.walnuttreehotel.com
dir: M5 junct 24. Follow North Petherton signs. 1.3m. Hotel in village centre

Popular with both business and leisure guests, this 18th-century former coaching inn is conveniently located within easy reach of the M5. The spacious and smartly decorated bedrooms are well furnished to ensure a comfortable and relaxing stay. An extensive selection of dishes is offered in either the restaurant, or the more informal setting of the bistro.

Rooms 30 (3 fmly) (3 GF) ♠ **S** £79-£114; **D** £98-£128 (incl. bkfst)* **Facilities** FTV Wi-fi ᕹ Gym New Year **Conf** Class 60 Board 50 Thtr 100 Del from £135* **Parking** 70 **Notes** LB ⊗ Civ Wed 100

Apple Tree Hotel

★★★ 71% HOTEL

☎ 01278 733238
Keenthorne TA5 1HZ
e-mail: reservations@appletreehotel.com
web: www.appletreehotel.com

(For full entry see Nether Stowey)

Premier Inn Bridgwater

BUDGET HOTEL

☎ 0871 527 8148
Express Park, Bristol Rd TA6 4RR
web: www.premierinn.com
dir: M5 junct 23, A38 to Bridgwater. Hotel on right in 2m

High quality, budget accommodation ideal for both families and business travellers. Spacious, en suite bedrooms feature tea and coffee making facilities, and Freeview TV in most hotels. Internet access and Wi-fi are available for a small fee. The adjacent family restaurant features a wide and varied menu. See also the Hotel Groups pages.

Rooms 40

BRIDLINGTON
East Riding of Yorkshire
Map 17 TA16

Expanse Hotel

★★★ 75% HOTEL

☎ 01262 675347
North Marine Dr YO15 2LS
e-mail: reservations@expanse.co.uk
web: www.expanse.co.uk
dir: Follow North Beach signs, pass under railway arch for North Marine Drive. Hotel at bottom of hill

This traditional seaside hotel overlooks the bay and has been in the same family's ownership for many years. Service is relaxed and friendly and the modern bedrooms are well equipped. Comfortable public areas include a conference suite, a choice of bars and an inviting lounge. Complimentary Wi-fi is available.

Rooms 47 (5 fmly) **S** fr £29.95; **D** £59.90-£128 (incl. bkfst)* **Facilities** FTV Wi-fi ♫ Xmas New Year **Conf** Class 50 Board 50 Thtr 180 **Services** Lift **Parking** 17 **Notes** LB ⊗ Civ Wed 140

BRIDPORT
Dorset
Map 4 SY49

Bridge House Hotel
THE INDEPENDENTS
HOTEL ASSOCIATION

★★★ 71% METRO HOTEL

☎ 01308 423371
115 East St DT6 3LB
e-mail: info@bridgehousebridport.co.uk
web: www.bridgehousebridport.co.uk
dir: From A35 follow town centre signs, hotel 200mtrs on right

A short stroll from the town centre, this 18th-century Grade II listed property offers well-equipped bedrooms that vary in size. In addition to the main lounge, there is a small bar-lounge and a separate breakfast room. An interesting range of home-cooked meals is provided in the wine bar and brasserie.

Rooms 10 (3 fmly) ⌂ **S** £69-£75; **D** £98-£150 (incl. bkfst)* **Facilities** FTV Wi-fi New Year **Conf** Class 20 Board 15 Thtr 36 **Parking** 13 **Notes** LB

Haddon House Hotel
★★★ 68% HOTEL

☎ 01308 423626 & 425323
West Bay DT6 4EL
e-mail: info@haddonhousehotel.co.uk
web: www.haddonhousehotel.co.uk
dir: At Crown Inn rdbt take B3157 (West Bay Rd), hotel 0.5m on right at mini-rdbt

This attractive, creeper-clad hotel offers good standards of accommodation and is situated a few minutes' walk from the seafront and the quay. A friendly and relaxed style of service is provided. An extensive range of dishes, from lighter bar snacks to main meals, is on offer in the Tudor-style restaurant.

Rooms 12 (2 fmly) (2 GF) **Facilities** FTV Wi-fi ⌂ New Year **Conf** Class 20 Board 26 Thtr 60 **Parking** 40 **Notes** ⊗

BRIGHOUSE
West Yorkshire
Map 16 SE12

Holiday Inn Leeds - Brighouse
Holiday Inn

★★★ 81% HOTEL

☎ 0871 942 9013 & 01484 404 500
Clifton Village HD6 4HW
e-mail: brighouse@ihg.com
web: www.hileedsbrighousehotel.co.uk
dir: M62 junct 25, A644 signed Brighouse. Remain in right lane, 1st right, hotel at next left

A modern hotel built from traditional Yorkshire stone, and easily accessible from the M62. The bedrooms are spacious and include executive rooms. Other facilities include a leisure club, meeting rooms and ample parking.

Rooms 94 (14 fmly) (43 GF) **Facilities** STV FTV Wi-fi ⌂ HL ⌂ supervised Gym Steam room Xmas New Year **Conf** Class 120 Board 50 Thtr 200 Del from £110 to £150 **Services** Air con **Parking** 197 **Notes** Civ Wed 200

Premier Inn Huddersfield North

Premier Inn

BUDGET HOTEL

☎ 0871 527 8530
Wakefield Rd HD6 4HA
web: www.premierinn.com
dir: M62 junct 25, A644 signed Huddersfield, Dewsbury & Wakefield. Hotel 500mtrs up hill on right

High quality, budget accommodation ideal for both families and business travellers. Spacious, en suite bedrooms feature tea and coffee making facilities, and Freeview TV in most hotels. Internet access and Wi-fi are available for a small fee. The adjacent family restaurant features a wide and varied menu. See also the Hotel Groups pages.

Rooms 71

BRIGHTON & HOVE
East Sussex
Map 6 TQ30

See also Steyning

Hotel du Vin Brighton
Hotel du Vin & Bistro

★★★★ 77% ◎◎
TOWN HOUSE HOTEL

☎ 01273 718588
2-6 Ship St BN1 1AD
e-mail: info@brighton.hotelduvin.com
web: www.hotelduvin.com
dir: From A23 follow seafront/city centre signs. Right at seafront, right into Middle St. Follow to end bear right into Ship St. Hotel on right

This tastefully converted mock-Tudor building occupies a convenient location in a quiet side street close to the seafront. The individually designed bedrooms have a wine theme, and all are comprehensively equipped. Public areas offer a spacious split-level bar, an atmospheric and locally popular restaurant, plus useful private dining and meeting facilities.

Rooms 49 (2 fmly) (4 GF) **Facilities** STV Wi-fi ♫ Xmas New Year **Conf** Class 50 Board 60 Thtr 80 **Services** Air con **Notes** Civ Wed 120

Thistle Brighton
thistle

★★★★ 77% HOTEL

☎ 01273 206700
King's Rd BN1 2GS
e-mail: brighton@thistle.co.uk
web: www.thistlehotels.com/brighton
dir: A23 to seafront. At rdbt turn right, hotel 200yds on right

Situated overlooking the sea and within easy reach of the town's many attractions, this hotel is built around an atrium and offers air-conditioned rooms including luxury suites. The restaurant provides stunning sea views, and a comfortable, spacious lounge and bar offer a full range of drinks, light refreshments and meals. The Otium Health & Fitness Club has a pool, sauna and gym facilities plus health and beauty treatments.

Rooms 210 (29 fmly) ⌂ **D** £89-£219* **Facilities** STV FTV Wi-fi HL ⌂ supervised Sauna Solarium Beauty treatment room Xmas New Year **Conf** Class 180 Board 120 Thtr 300 Del from £138* **Services** Lift Air con **Parking** 68 **Notes** LB Civ Wed 300

Save on hotels. Book at **theAA.com/hotel**

BRI 101 ENGLAND

B

Mercure Brighton Seafront Hotel

★★★★ HOTEL

☎ 0844 815 9061
149 Kings Rd BN1 2PP
e-mail: info@mercurebrighton.co.uk
web: www.jupiterhotels.co.uk
dir: A23 follow signs for seafront. Right at Brighton Pier rdbt. Hotel on right, just after West Pier

Currently the rating for this establishment is not confirmed. This may be due to a change of ownership or because it has only recently joined the AA rating scheme.

Rooms 117 **Conf** Class 160 Board 185 Thtr 455

The Old Ship Hotel

PUMA HOTELS
COLLECTION

★★★★ 70% HOTEL

☎ 01273 329001
King's Rd BN1 1NR
e-mail: oldship@pumahotels.co.uk
web: www.pumahotels.co.uk
dir: A23 to seafront, right at rdbt along Kings Rd. Hotel 200yds on right

This historic hotel enjoys a stunning seafront location and offers guests elegant surroundings to relax in. Bedrooms are well designed, with modern facilities ensuring comfort. Many original features have been retained, including the Paganini Ballroom. Facilities include a sleek bar, alfresco dining and a variety of conference rooms.

Rooms 152 **Facilities** STV Wi-fi Xmas New Year **Conf** Class 100 Board 35 Thtr 250 **Services** Lift Parking 40 **Notes** Civ Wed 150

BEST WESTERN Princes Marine

★★★ 78% HOTEL

☎ 01273 207660
153 Kingsway BN3 4GR
e-mail: princesmarine@bestwestern.co.uk
dir: Right at Brighton Pier, follow seafront for 2m. Hotel 200yds from King Alfred leisure centre

This friendly hotel enjoys a seafront location and offers spacious, comfortable bedrooms equipped with a good range of facilities including free Wi-fi. There is a stylish restaurant, modern bar and selection of roof-top meeting rooms with sea views. Limited parking is available at the rear.

Rooms 48 (4 fmly) ⬧ **S** £51.50-£127.50; **D** £74-£155 (incl. bkfst) **Facilities** STV FTV Wi-fi ⬧ **Conf** Class 40 Board 40 Thtr 70 Del from £123 to £150 **Services** Lift Parking 30 **Notes** LB ⊗

BEST WESTERN Brighton Hotel

Best Western

★★★ 75% METRO HOTEL

☎ 01273 820555
143/145 King's Rd BN1 2PQ
e-mail: info@thebrightonhotel.com
web: www.thebrightonhotel.co.uk
dir: M23 onto A23 to pier. Right at rdbt, hotel just past West Pier

This friendly hotel is well placed in a prime seafront location close to the historic West Pier. The contemporary bedrooms are spaciously appointed and well equipped. The lounge, bar and restaurant are sunny, bright and comfortable with great sea views. Dinner is not available in the restaurant but a 24-hour room service menu is in place, and restaurants are within easy walking distance. Parking facilities, though limited, are a real bonus in this area of town.

Rooms 55 (6 fmly) ⬧ **S** £45-£110; **D** £50-£250* **Facilities** FTV Wi-fi ⬧ **Conf** Class 30 Board 40 Thtr 70 Del from £119 to £149* **Services** Lift Parking 10 **Notes** LB ⊗ Civ Wed 140

The Kings Hotel

★★★ 72% METRO HOTEL

☎ 01273 820854
139-141 Kings Rd BN1 2NA
e-mail: info@kingshotelbrighton.co.uk
dir: Follow signs to seafront. At Brighton Pier rdbt take 3rd exit & drive west (seafront on left). Hotel adjacent to West Pier

Located on the seafront adjacent to West Pier, this Grade II listed, Regency building has been restored to offer contemporary accommodation. Although the hotel does not provide a full dinner service, light snacks are available throughout the day and evening in the public areas and also in the guests' bedrooms. There is limited parking space which is a bonus in Brighton.

Rooms 90 (3 fmly) (6 GF) ⬧ **S** £45-£110; **D** £50-£250* **Facilities** FTV Wi-fi **Conf** Class 25 Board 30 Thtr 70 Del from £119 to £149* **Services** Lift **Notes** LB

Queens Hotel

★★★ 70% HOTEL

☎ 01273 321222 & 0800 970 7570
1-3 King's Rd BN1 1NS
e-mail: info@queenshotelbrighton.com
dir: A23 to Brighton town centre, follow signs for seafront. At Brighton Pier right onto seafront, hotel 500mtrs

This hotel has a fantastic location with views of the beach and pier. The modern bedrooms and bathrooms are spacious, and many benefit from uninterrupted

sea views. All bedrooms have LCD TVs and free Wi-fi. There is a spacious bar and restaurant area plus fully equipped spa, gym and swimming pool.

Rooms 94 (28 fmly) **S** £59-£229; **D** £59-£349 (incl. bkfst) **Facilities** Spa FTV Wi-fi ⬧ HL ⬧ supervised Gym Beauty salon **Conf** Class 50 Board 50 Thtr 150 Del from £100 to £175 **Services** Lift **Notes** ⊗ Civ Wed 120

Umi Brighton Hotel

★★★ 70% HOTEL

☎ 01273 323221
64 King's Rd BN1 1NA
e-mail: reservations@umibrighton.co.uk
dir: On A259 adjacent to Brighton Centre

Umi Hotel is located right in the heart of Brighton on the seafront with just a short walk to the Pier, Station and City Centre. Bedrooms are modern in style and include free Wi-fi access, all seafront bedrooms benefit from excellent uninterrupted sea views. The little Bay Restaurant has a theatre style theme and offers a good range of dishes at very affordable prices, both a cooked and continental breakfast is served here daily. There is a Coffee Republic on site.

Rooms 78 (20 fmly) (1 GF) **S** £50-£155; **D** £55-£255 (incl. bkfst)* **Facilities** FTV Wi-fi ⬧ HL Free use of leisure centre in Queens Hotel **Conf** Class 20 Board 20 Thtr 20 Del from £99 to £199* **Services** Lift **Notes** ⊗

Ambassador Brighton

★★ 69% METRO HOTEL

☎ 01273 676869
22-23 New Steine, Marine Pde BN2 1PD
e-mail: info@ambassadorbrighton.co.uk

At the heart of bustling Kemp Town, overlooking the attractive garden square next to the seaside, this well-established property has a friendly and relaxing atmosphere. Bedrooms are well equipped and vary in size, with the largest having the best views. A small lounge with a separate bar is available.

Rooms 24 (9 fmly) (3 GF) (2 smoking) **Facilities** STV FTV Wi-fi ⬧ HL

BRIGHTON & HOVE *continued*

Preston Park Hotel

★★ 67% HOTEL

☎ 01273 507853
216 Preston Rd BN1 6UU
e-mail: manager@prestonparkhotel.co.uk
dir: On A23 towards town centre. 5 mins from Preston
Park train station

This hotel enjoys a convenient roadside location on
the outskirts of Brighton. Bedrooms are modern in
style and well provisioned for both the leisure and
business guest. Freshly prepared meals are offered in
the spacious Sussex Bar (open 24 hours to residents)
and in the more intimate and relaxing restaurant.
Guests can enjoy a drink on the patio in summer.

Rooms 33 (4 fmly) **Facilities** Gym Xmas New Year
Conf Class 80 Board 80 Thtr 200 Del from £120 to
£160 **Parking** 60 **Notes** Civ Wed 150

The De Vere Grand, Brighton

Ⓤ

☎ 01273 224300
King's Rd BN1 2FW
e-mail: reservations@grandbrighton.co.uk
web: www.devere-hotels.co.uk/thegrand
dir: On A259 adjacent to Brighton Centre

Currently the rating for this establishment is not
confirmed. We are working with the management /
owners whilst works and changes take place to
achieve an AA star rating. For further details please
see the AA website: theAA.com

Rooms 201 (60 fmly) ➧ **S** £89-£109; **D** £109-£139
(incl. bkfst)* **Facilities** STV Wi-fi Gym ♫ Xmas New
Year **Conf** Class 450 Board 60 Thtr 750 Del from £140
to £185* **Services** Lift **Parking** 50 **Notes** LB
Civ Wed 800

Ibis Brighton City Centre

BUDGET HOTEL

☎ 01273 986800
88 92 Queens Rd BN1 3XE
e-mail: h6444@accor.com

Modern, budget hotel offering comfortable
accommodation in bright and practical bedrooms.
Breakfast is self-service and dinner is available in
the restaurant. See also the Hotel Groups pages.

Premier Inn Brighton City Centre

BUDGET HOTEL

☎ 0871 527 8150
144 North St BN1 1RE
web: www.premierinn.com
dir: From A23 follow signs for city centre. Right at
lights near Royal Pavilion, take road ahead on left
(runs adjacent to Pavilion) into Church St, 1st left
into New Rd leading North St

High quality, budget accommodation ideal for both
families and business travellers. Spacious, en suite
bedrooms feature tea and coffee making facilities,
and Freeview TV in most hotels. Internet access and
Wi-fi are available for a small fee. The adjacent
family restaurant features a wide and varied menu.
See also the Hotel Groups pages.

Rooms 160

BRISTOL
Bristol   **Map 4 ST57**

Aztec Hotel & Spa

★★★★ 80% ⊛ HOTEL

☎ 01454 201090
Aztec West Business Park, Almondsbury BS32 4TS
e-mail: aztec@shirehotels.com
web: www.aztechotelbristol.com
dir: Access via M5 junct 16 & M4

Situated close to Cribbs Causeway shopping centre
and major motorway links, this stylish hotel offers
comfortable, very well-equipped bedrooms and suites.
Built in a Nordic style, public rooms boast log fires
and vaulted ceilings. Leisure facilities include a
popular gym and good size pool. The Quarter Jacks
Restaurant Bar & Lounge offers relaxed informal
dining with a focus on simply prepared, quality
regional foods. The hotel has a spa with a gym, pool,
children's pool, whirlpool, sauna, steam room and a
range of treatments.

Rooms 128 (8 fmly) (29 GF) **S** £90-£150;
D £90-£150* **Facilities** Spa STV Wi-fi HL ☺ Gym
Steam room Sauna Children's splash pool Activity
studio New Year **Conf** Class 120 Board 36 Thtr 200
Del from £145 to £185* **Services** Lift **Parking** 240
Notes LB ⊗ Civ Wed 120

Bristol Marriott Royal Hotel

★★★★ 80% ⊛ HOTEL

☎ 0117 925 5100
College Green BS1 5TA
web: www.bristolmarriottroyal.co.uk
dir: Adjacent to cathedral

A truly stunning hotel located in the centre of the city,
next to the cathedral. Public areas are particularly
impressive with luxurious lounges and a leisure club.
Dining options include the informal Terrace, and the
really spectacular restaurant adjacent to the
champagne bar. The spacious bedrooms have the
benefit of air conditioning, comfortable armchairs
and marble bathrooms.

Rooms 242 (23 GF) (6 smoking) ➧ **Facilities** Wi-fi ฿
HL ☺ Gym Hair & beauty salon Beauty treatment
rooms **Conf** Class 180 Board 60 Thtr 300
Services Lift Air con **Parking** 190 **Notes** ⊗
Civ Wed 200

Hotel du Vin Bristol

★★★★ 76% ⊛
TOWN HOUSE HOTEL

☎ 0844 7364 252
The Sugar House, Narrow Lewins Mead BS1 2NU
e-mail: info.bristol@hotelduvin.com
web: www.hotelduvin.com
dir: From A4 follow city centre signs. After 400yds
pass Rupert St NCP on right. Hotel on opposite
carriageway

This hotel is part of one of Britain's most innovative
hotel groups, offering high standards of hospitality
and accommodation. Housed in a Grade II listed,
converted 18th-century sugar refinery, it provides
great facilities with a modern, minimalist design. The
bedrooms are exceptionally well designed and the
bistro offers an excellent menu and wine list.

Rooms 40 (10 fmly) ➧ **S** £129-£189; **D** £129-£189*
Facilities STV FTV Wi-fi ฿ ♫ New Year **Conf** Class 36
Board 34 Thtr 72 Del from £175 to £245*
Services Lift **Parking** 9 **Notes** Civ Wed 65

Bristol Marriott City Centre

★★★★ 76% HOTEL

☎ 0117 929 4281
Lower Castle St BS1 3AD
web: www.bristolmarriottcitycentre.co.uk
dir: M32 follow signs to Broadmead, take slip road to
large rdbt, take 3rd exit. Hotel on right

Situated at the foot of the picturesque Castle Park,
this mainly business-orientated hotel is well placed

for the city centre. Executive and deluxe bedrooms have high speed internet access. In addition to a coffee bar and lounge menu, the Mediterrano Restaurant offers an interesting selection of well-prepared dishes.

Rooms 300 (135 fmly) **Facilities** STV FTV Wi-fi 🖏 🕄 Gym Steam room Sauna Spa pool Xmas New Year **Conf** Class 280 Board 40 Thtr 600 **Services** Lift Air con **Notes** ⊗ Civ Wed 700

The Grand, Bristol   thistle
★★★★ 75% HOTEL

☎ 0871 376 9042
Broad St BS1 2EL
e-mail: thegrand@thistle.co.uk
web: www.thistle.com/thegrand
dir: In city centre pass The Galleries. 3rd right into Broad St

This large hotel is situated in the heart of the city, and benefits from its own secure parking. Bedrooms are well equipped and comfortably appointed, and include a number of Premium Executive rooms. The public areas include leisure and therapy treatment rooms and there is an impressive range of conference and banqueting facilities.

Rooms 182 (10 fmly) 🐾 **Facilities** Spa STV Wi-fi 🕄 supervised Gym Steam room Sauna Solarium Xmas New Year **Conf** Class 250 Board 40 Thtr 600 **Services** Lift Air con **Parking** 150 **Notes** ⊗ Civ Wed 500

Holiday Inn Bristol Filton
★★★★ 74% HOTEL   *Holiday Inn*

☎ 0871 942 9014
Filton Rd, Hambrook BS16 1QX
e-mail: bristol@ihg.com
web: www.hibristolfiltonhotel.co.uk
dir: M4 junct 19/M32 junct 1/A4174 towards Filton & Bristol. Hotel 800yds on left

With easy access of both the M4 and M5 this is, understandably, a popular hotel with business guests. Public areas are spacious and relaxing with a wide choice of comfortable seating options. There are two restaurants - Sampans with a selection of dishes from the Far East, and the more traditional Junction Restaurant. Bedrooms vary in size, but all are well furnished and well equipped. A large car park, leisure facilities and range of conference rooms are all available.

Rooms 211 (40 fmly) (70 GF) (2 smoking) **Facilities** STV FTV Wi-fi 🖏 🕄 supervised Fishing Gym Beauty treatment room Sauna Xmas New Year **Conf** Class 180 Board 75 Thtr 250 Del from £99 to £165* **Services** Lift Air con **Parking** 250 **Notes** ⊗ Civ Wed 250

Mercure Bristol Holland House Hotel & Spa

★★★★ 74% HOTEL

☎ 0117 968 9900
Redcliffe Hill BS1 6SQ
e-mail: h6698@accor.com
web: www.mercure.com
dir: M4 junct 19 towards city centre, follow signs A4 then A370, take A38 Redcliffe Hill. Hotel opposite St Mary Redcliffe Church

This modern hotel, just a ten-minute walk from Bristol Temple Meads, has striking, contemporary style throughout, and offers some impressive facilities including a spa, a fitness suite and meeting rooms. The hotel has a green-bicycle service for guests. Bedrooms are stylishly designed with large plasma screen TVs, comfortable beds and free internet access. Dining is offered in the Phoenix Restaurant and bar.

Rooms 275 (59 fmly) (44 GF) 🐾 **S** £59-£99; **D** £59-£99* **Facilities** Spa FTV Wi-fi 🖏 Gym Free bike rental Xmas New Year **Conf** Class 150 Board 80 Thtr 220 Del from £109 to £155* **Services** Lift Air con **Parking** 140 **Notes** LB ⊗ Civ Wed 220

Mercure Bristol North The Grange

★★★★ 74% COUNTRY HOUSE HOTEL

☎ 0844 815 9063
Northwoods, Winterbourne BS36 1RP
e-mail: gm.mercurebristolnorthgrange@jupiterhotels.co.uk
web: www.jupiterhotels.co.uk
dir: A38 towards Filton/Bristol. At rdbt 1st exit into Bradley Stoke Way, at lights 1st left into Woodlands Ln, at 2nd rdbt left into Tench Ln. In 1m left at T-junct, hotel 200yds on left

Built in the 19th century and surrounded by 18 acres of attractive grounds, this is a pleasant hotel situated only a short drive from the city centre. The bedrooms are spacious and well equipped; there is a leisure centre with a pool plus a range of meeting facilities. The conservatory bar has a terrace which makes a delightful place to enjoy a drink under the shade of a 200-year-old cedar tree. The hotel is popular as a wedding venue.

Rooms 68 (20 fmly) (22 GF) **Facilities** Spa STV FTV Wi-fi 🕄 supervised 🍴 Gym Sauna Xmas New Year **Conf** Class 120 Board 134 Thtr 150 Del from £125 to £160* **Parking** 150 **Notes** Civ Wed 150

Radisson Blu Hotel Bristol   *Radisson*
★★★★ 73% HOTEL   **B**

☎ 01179 349500
Broad Qauy BS1 4BY
dir: Telephone for directions (NB use BS1 4AQ for Sat Nav)

This city centre hotel is in a great location, with views of the harbour and offering impressive facilities. The contemporary, spacious bedrooms, with stylish bathrooms, have floor-to-ceiling windows; the 17th-floor split-level, maisonette suites feature a bedroom and an upstairs living area. The Filini Restaurant offers Italian and Sardinian cuisine and enjoys views across the city, and the bar, opening out onto Bristol's main shopping and business area, is the place to relax with a coffee, a cocktail or light meal. There is a range of meeting rooms and a spa.

Rooms 176 (1 fmly) (4 smoking) 🐾 **Facilities** STV FTV Wi-fi 🖏 Gym 🎵 Xmas New Year **Conf** Class 60 Board 40 Thtr 120 **Services** Lift Air con **Notes** ⊗ Civ Wed 100

DoubleTree by Hilton Bristol City Centre   fOCUShotels
★★★★ 72% HOTEL

☎ 0117 926 0041
Redcliffe Way BS1 6NJ
e-mail: sales@focusbristol.co.uk
web: www.doubletree.hilton.com
dir: 1m from M32. 400yds from Temple Meads BR station, before church

This large modern hotel is situated in the heart of the city centre and offers spacious public areas and ample parking. Bedrooms are well equipped for both business and leisure guests. Dining options include a relaxed bar and a unique kiln restaurant where a good selection of freshly prepared dishes is available.

Rooms 201 🐾 **S** £69-£165; **D** £69-£165 **Facilities** FTV Wi-fi 🖏 Gym Xmas New Year **Conf** Class 120 Board 75 Thtr 300 Del from £99 to £175 **Services** Lift Air con **Parking** 150 **Notes** LB ⊗ Civ Wed 250

BRISTOL *continued*

Holiday Inn Bristol City Centre

★★★★ 72% HOTEL

☎ 0117 924 5000
Bond St BS1 3LE
e-mail: reservations@hibristolcity.co.uk
dir: M4 junct 19/M32 into city centre. At Cabot Circus veer onto Bond St, hotel on right

Located right in the heart of the city centre and within easy walking distance of all local attractions, this modern and stylish hotel offers a range of high quality bedrooms and bathrooms with the executive rooms and suites being especially comfortable. Guests have use of a small gym area and receive a discounted rate at the adjacent NCP. The restaurant and bar overlook the busy centre and offer a range of freshly prepared dishes to suit all tastes.

Rooms 155 (51 fmly) (13 smoking) ✆ **S** fr £89.95; **D** fr £89.95* **Facilities** STV FTV Wi-fi ☝ Gym Xmas New Year **Conf** Class 76 Board 62 Thtr 150 Del from £110 to £165* **Services** Lift Air con **Parking** 70 **Notes** LB ⊗ Civ Wed 130

Mercure Brigstow Bristol

★★★★ 72% HOTEL

☎ 0117 929 1030
5-7 Welsh Back BS1 4SP
e-mail: H6548@accor.com
web: www.mercure.com
dir: From the centre follow Baldwin St then right into Queen Charlotte St

In a prime position on the river this handsome purpose-built hotel is designed and finished with care. The shopping centre and theatres are within easy walking distance. The stylish bedrooms are extremely well equipped, including plasma TV screens in the bathrooms. There is an integrated state-of-the-art conference and meeting centre, and a smart restaurant and bar overlooking the harbour. Guests have complimentary use of a squash and health club, plus free internet access.

Rooms 116 ✆ **S** £65-£165; **D** £65-£165* **Facilities** STV FTV Wi-fi ☝ Gym Free access to nearby gym & squash courts New Year **Conf** Class 40 Board 30 Thtr 85 Del from £150 to £190* **Services** Lift Air con **Notes** LB Civ Wed 80

Novotel Bristol Centre

★★★★ 71% HOTEL

☎ 0117 976 9988
Victoria St BS1 6HY
e-mail: H5622@accor.com
web: www.novotel.com
dir: At end of M32 follow signs for Temple Meads station to rdbt. Final exit, hotel immediately on right

This city centre hotel provides smart, contemporary style accommodation. Most of the bedrooms demonstrate the Novotel 'Novation' style with unique swivel desk, internet access, air-conditioning and a host of extras. The hotel is convenient for the mainline railway station and also has its own car park.

Rooms 131 (20 fmly) ✆ **Facilities** STV Wi-fi ☝ HL Gym Sauna Steam room **Conf** Class 70 Board 35 Thtr 210 **Services** Lift **Parking** 100 **Notes** ⊗ Civ Wed 100

BEST WESTERN Henbury Lodge Hotel

★★★ 80% ◉◉ HOTEL

☎ 0117 950 2615
Station Rd, Henbury BS10 7QQ
e-mail: info@henburyhotel.com
web: www.henburyhotel.com
dir: M5 junct 17/A4018 towards city centre, 3rd rdbt right into Crow Ln. At end turn right, hotel 200mtrs on right

This quietly located hotel is popular with both business and leisure guests. Bedrooms, in a wide range of shapes and sizes, are divided between the main house and a converted stable block; all are comfortably furnished and equipped. The small and friendly team offer a very personal welcome and many guests here are regulars. Dinner and breakfast are taken in the stylish restaurant where high quality local produce is used.

Rooms 20 (9 annexe) (4 fmly) (6 GF) **S** £89-£99; **D** £99-£119 (incl. bkfst)* **Facilities** FTV Wi-fi ☝ **Conf** Class 15 Board 20 Thtr 20 Del £159* **Parking** 20 **Notes** LB ⊗ Closed 22 Dec-9 Jan

The Avon Gorge Hotel

★★★ 77% ◉ HOTEL

☎ 0117 973 8955
Sion Hill, Clifton BS8 4LD
e-mail: rooms@theavongorge.com
dir: From S: M5 junct 19, A369 to Clifton Toll, over suspension bridge, 1st right into Sion Hill. From N: M5 junct 18A, A4 to Bristol, under suspension bridge, follow signs to bridge, exit Sion Hill

This is a delightful terraced property overlooking the Clifton Suspension Bridge. It offers bedrooms of varying shapes and sizes with either views across the river or of Clifton Village. Meals can be taken in the contemporary Bridge Café restaurant where a range of carefully prepared, tempting dishes is available. There is a limited amount of free parking space at the rear of the hotel or on-street (no restrictions) in the vicinity.

Rooms 75 (8 fmly) **S** £69-£105; **D** £89-£150 (incl. bkfst) **Facilities** STV Wi-fi ☝ Xmas New Year **Conf** Class 40 Board 30 Thtr 100 Del from £125 to £180 **Services** Lift **Parking** 25 **Notes** LB Civ Wed 100

Holiday Inn Bristol Airport

★★★ 74% HOTEL

☎ 01934 861123
A38 Bridgwater Rd, Cowslip Garden, Wrington BS40 5RB
e-mail: reservations@hibristolairport.co.uk
web: www.hibristolairport.co.uk
dir: From Bristol, W on A38. Hotel 3m from Bristol International Airport on right

While ideally located for Bristol Airport, this modern hotel is also an ideal base for exploring the areas surrounding Bath, Bristol and Wells; many attractions are within easy reach. The bedrooms and bathrooms are generally spacious and well equipped. Guests can dine throughout the day on a range of lounge meals, including room service, while in the evening an additional selection of tempting dishes is offered in the restaurant.

Rooms 80 (4 fmly) (12 GF) (12 smoking) ✆ **S** £59-£99; **D** £69-£119* **Facilities** FTV Wi-fi ☝ HL Gym **Conf** Class 20 Board 24 Thtr 60 Del from £120 to £160* **Services** Lift Air con **Parking** 100 **Notes** LB ⊗

Rodney Hotel

★★★ 68% ◉ HOTEL

☎ 0117 973 5422
4 Rodney Place, Clifton BS8 4HY
e-mail: rodney@cliftonhotels.com
dir: Off Clifton Down Rd

With easy access from the M5, this attractive, listed building in Clifton is conveniently close to the city centre. The individually decorated bedrooms provide a useful range of extra facilities for the business traveller; the public areas include a smart bar and small restaurant offering enjoyable and carefully prepared dishes. A pleasant rear garden provides additional seating in the summer months.

Rooms 31 (1 fmly) (2 GF) **Facilities** FTV Wi-fi **Conf** Class 20 Board 20 Thtr 30 **Parking** 10 **Notes** LB Closed 22 Dec-3 Jan RS Sun Civ Wed 40

BEST WESTERN Victoria Square Hotel

★★ 79% HOTEL

☎ 0117 973 9058
Victoria Square, Clifton BS8 4EW
e-mail: info@victoriasquarehotel.co.uk
dir: M5 junct 19, follow Clifton signs. Over suspension/toll bridge, right into Clifton Down Rd. Left into Merchants Rd then into Victoria Square

This welcoming hotel offers high quality, individual bedrooms and bathrooms in a variety of shapes and sizes. Well located, the hotel is just one mile from the city centre and a two-minute stroll from the heart of Clifton village. The atmosphere is relaxed, and guests have a choice of dining options - from lighter meals in the bar to a range of imaginative dishes in the main restaurant.

Rooms 41 (20 annexe) (3 fmly) (3 GF) ⟨ **S** £59-£79; **D** £69-£129 (incl. bkfst)* **Facilities** FTV Wi-fi **Conf** Class 15 Board 20 Thtr 30 **Parking** 15 **Notes** ⊗

Clifton Hotel

★★ 76% HOTEL

☎ 0117 973 6882
St Pauls Rd, Clifton BS8 1LX
e-mail: clifton@cliftonhotels.com
web: www.cliftonhotels.com/bristolhotels/clifton
dir: M32 follow Bristol/Clifton signs, along Park St. Left at lights into St Pauls Rd

This popular hotel offers a relaxed, friendly service and very well equipped bedrooms. There is a welcoming lounge by the reception, and in summer months drinks and meals can be enjoyed on the terrace. Racks Bar and Restaurant offers an interesting selection of modern dishes in informal surroundings. There is some street parking, but for a small charge, secure garage parking is available.

Rooms 59 (2 fmly) (12 GF) ⟨ **S** £50-£83; **D** £61-£101* **Facilities** STV FTV Wi-fi **Services** Lift **Parking** 12 **Notes** LB

Ibis Bristol Centre (AKA Harbourside)

BUDGET HOTEL

☎ 0117 9897200
Explore Ln BS1 5TY
e-mail: H5547-GM@accor.com
dir: Off A4 in harbourside district

Modern, budget hotel offering comfortable accommodation in bright and practical bedrooms. Breakfast is self-service and dinner is available in the restaurant. See also the Hotel Groups pages.

Rooms 182 (2 fmly)

Ibis Bristol Temple Meads

BUDGET HOTEL

☎ 0117 954 3600
Avon St BS2 0PS
e-mail: H6593@accor.com
dir: M4 junct 19, M32, follow Temple Meads train station signs. Left after underpass

Rooms 141 (7 fmly) ⟨ **D** £27-£89* **Conf** Class 12 Board 12 Thtr 12

Premier Inn Bristol Airport (Sidcot)

BUDGET HOTEL

☎ 0871 527 8154
Bridgwater Rd, Winscombe BS25 1NN
web: www.premierinn.com
dir: Between M5 junct 21 & 22 (9m from Bristol Airport), onto A371 towards Banwell, Winscombe to A38. Right at lights, Hotel 300yds on left

High quality, budget accommodation ideal for both families and business travellers. Spacious, en suite bedrooms feature tea and coffee making facilities, and Freeview TV in most hotels. Internet access and Wi-fi are available for a small fee. The adjacent family restaurant features a wide and varied menu. See also the Hotel Groups pages.

Rooms 31

Premier Inn Bristol (Alveston)

BUDGET HOTEL

☎ 0871 527 8152
Thornbury Rd, Alveston BS35 3LL
web: www.premierinn.com
dir: Just off M5. From N: exit at junct 14 onto A38 towards Bristol. From S: exit at junct 16 onto A38 towards Gloucester

Rooms 75

Premier Inn Bristol City Centre (Haymarket)

BUDGET HOTEL

☎ 0871 527 8156
The Haymarket BS1 3LR
web: www.premierinn.com
dir: M4 junct 19, M32 towards city centre. Through 2 sets of lights, at 3rd lights turn right, to rdbt, take 2nd exit. Hotel on left

Rooms 224

Premier Inn Bristol City Centre King St

BUDGET HOTEL

☎ 0871 527 8158
Llandoger Trow, King St BS1 4ER
web: www.premierinn.com
dir: A38 into city centre. Left onto B4053 Baldwin St. Right into Queen Charlotte St, follow one-way system, bear right at river. Hotel on right

Rooms 60

Premier Inn Bristol Cribbs Causeway

BUDGET HOTEL

☎ 0871 527 8160
Cribbs Causeway, Catbrain Ln BS10 7TQ
web: www.premierinn.com
dir: M5 junct 17, A4018. 1st left at rdbt into Lysander Rd. Right into Catbrain Hill, leads to Catbrain Lane

Rooms 106

Premier Inn Bristol East (Emersons Green)

BUDGET HOTEL

☎ 0871 527 8162
200/202 Westerleigh Rd, Emersons Green BS16 7AN
web: www.premierinn.com
dir: M4 junct 19 onto M32 junct 1, left onto A4174 (Avon Ring Rd). Hotel at 3rd rdbt

Rooms 67

B

BRISTOL *continued*

Premier Inn Bristol Filton

BUDGET HOTEL

☎ 0871 527 8164
Shield Retail Park, Gloucester Road North, Filton BS34 7BR
web: www.premierinn.com
dir: M5 junct 16, A38 signed Filton/Patchway. Pass airport & Royal Mail on right. Left at 2nd rdbt, 1st left into retail park

Rooms 62

Premier Inn Bristol South

BUDGET HOTEL

☎ 0871 527 8166
Hengrove Leisure Park, Hengrove Way BS14 0HR
web: www.premierinn.com
dir: From city centre take A37 to Wells & Shepton Mallet. Right onto A4174. Hotel at 3rd lights

Rooms 56

BRIXHAM	Map 3 SX95
Devon	

Quayside Hotel

★★★ 75% ⏺ HOTEL

☎ 01803 855751
41-49 King St TQ5 9TJ
e-mail: reservations@quaysidehotel.co.uk
web: www.quaysidehotel.co.uk
dir: A380, at 2nd rdbt at Kinkerswell towards Brixham on A3022

With views over the harbour and bay, this hotel was formerly six cottages, and the public rooms retain a certain cosiness and intimacy. These include the lounge, residents' bar and Ernie Lister's public bar. Freshly-landed fish features on the menus, alongside a number of creative and skilfully prepared dishes, served in the well-appointed restaurant. Good food is also available in the public bar. The owners and their team of local staff provide friendly and attentive service.

Rooms 29 (2 fmly) 🐾 **Facilities** FTV Wi-fi ♫ Xmas New Year **Conf** Class 18 Board 18 Thtr 25 **Parking** 30

Berry Head Hotel

★★★ 75% HOTEL

☎ 01803 853225
Berry Head Rd TQ5 9AJ
e-mail: stay@berryheadhotel.com
dir: From marina, 1m, hotel on left

From its stunning cliff-top location, this imposing property dates back to 1809, and has spectacular views across Torbay. Public areas include two comfortable lounges, an outdoor terrace, and a swimming pool, together with a bar serving a range of popular dishes. Many of the bedrooms have the benefit of splendid sea views.

Rooms 32 (7 fmly) **Facilities** FTV Wi-fi ⏺ ⛵ Petanque Sailing Deep sea fishing Yacht charter ♫ Xmas New Year **Conf** Class 250 Board 40 Thtr 300 **Services** Lift **Parking** 200 **Notes** Civ Wed 200

BROADWAY	Map 10 SP03
Worcestershire	

The Lygon Arms

★★★★ 82% ⏺⏺ HOTEL PUMA HOTELS COLLECTION

☎ 01386 852255
High St WR12 7DU
e-mail: thelygonarms@pumahotels.co.uk
web: www.pumahotels.co.uk
dir: From Evesham take A44 signed Oxford, 5m. Follow Broadway signs. Hotel on left

A hotel with a wealth of historic charm and character, the Lygon Arms dates back to the 16th century. There is a choice of restaurants, a stylish cosy bar, an array of lounges and a smart spa and leisure club. Bedrooms vary in size and style, but all are thoughtfully equipped and include a number of contemporary rooms as well as a cottage in the grounds.

Rooms 78 (16 fmly) (17 GF) **Facilities** Spa STV FTV Wi-fi ♨ ⏺ supervised ⏺ ⛵ Gym Beauty treatments ♫ Xmas New Year **Conf** Class 42 Board 30 Thtr 100 **Parking** 200 **Notes** Civ Wed 100

Dormy House Hotel

★★★★ 80% ⏺⏺ HOTEL

☎ 01386 852711
Willersey Hill WR12 7LF
e-mail: reservations@dormyhouse.co.uk.
web: www.dormyhouse.co.uk
dir: 2m E of Broadway off A44, at top of Fish Hill turn for Saintbury/Picnic area. In 0.5m turn left, hotel on left

Dormy House is a converted 17th-century farmhouse set in extensive grounds, with stunning views over Broadway. Some rooms are in an annexe at ground-floor level, and some have a contemporary style. The best traditions are retained - customer care, real fires, comfortable sofas and afternoon teas. Dinner features an interesting choice of dishes created by a skilled kitchen brigade.

Rooms 40 (21 annexe) (8 fmly) (21 GF) 🐾
D £250-£350 (incl. bkfst) **Facilities** Spa STV FTV Wi-fi ♨ ⏺ Gym Nature & jogging trail Bicycle hire Champagne nail bar Xmas New Year **Parking** 90 **Notes** LB ⊗

See advert on opposite page

The Broadway Hotel

★★★ 80% HOTEL

☎ 01386 852401
The Green, High St WR12 7AA
e-mail: info@broadwayhotel.info
web: www.cotswold-inns-hotels.co.uk/broadway
dir: Follow signs to Evesham, then Broadway

The Broadway Hotel is a half-timbered Cotswold stone property, built in the 15th century as a retreat for the Abbots of Pershore. It combines modern, attractive decor with original charm and character. Bedrooms are tastefully furnished and well equipped while public rooms include a relaxing lounge, cosy bar and charming restaurant; alfresco all-day dining in summer months proves popular.

Rooms 19 (1 fmly) (3 GF) **S** £120-£160; **D** £160-£220 (incl. bkfst)* **Facilities** FTV Wi-fi Xmas New Year **Parking** 20

Russell's

◉◉ RESTAURANT WITH ROOMS

☎ 01386 853555
20 High St WR12 7DT
e-mail: info@russellsofbroadway.co.uk
dir: Opposite village green

Situated in the centre of a picturesque Cotswold village this restaurant with rooms makes a great base for exploring local attractions. The superbly appointed bedrooms, each with its own character, have air conditioning and a wide range of extras for guests. The cuisine is a real draw here with freshly-prepared, local produce skilfully utilised.

Rooms 7 (3 annexe) (4 fmly)

BROCKENHURST   Map 5 SU30
Hampshire

INSPECTORS' CHOICE

Rhinefield House Hotel Hand PICKED HOTELS
BUILT FOR PLEASURE

★★★★ ◉◉ HOTEL

☎ 01590 622922 & 0845 072 7516
Rhinefield Rd SO42 7QB
e-mail: rhinefieldhouse@handpicked.co.uk
web: www.handpickedhotels.co.uk/rhinefieldhouse
dir: A35 towards Christchurch. 3m from Lyndhurst turn left to Rhinefield, 1.5m to hotel

This stunning 19th-century, mock-Elizabethan mansion is set in 40 acres of beautifully

landscaped gardens and forest. Bedrooms are spacious and great consideration is given to guest comfort. The elegant and award-winning Armada Restaurant is richly furnished, and features a fireplace carving (nine years in the making) that is worth taking time to admire. If the weather permits, the delightful terrace is just the place for enjoying alfresco eating.

Rhinefield House Hotel

Rooms 50 (10 fmly) (18 GF) **Facilities** Spa STV Wi-fi ↕ HL ③ ↘ ♨ ⤵ Gym Hydrotherapy pool Plunge pool Steam room Sauna Xmas New Year **Conf** Class 72 Board 56 Thtr 160 Del from £155 to £175 **Services** Lift **Parking** 100 **Notes** ⊗ Civ Wed 130

BROCKENHURST *continued*

B

Careys Manor Hotel & Senspa

★★★★ 84% ◉◉ HOTEL

☎ 01590 624467
SO42 7RH
e-mail: stay@careysmanor.com
web: www.careysmanor.com
dir: M27 junct 3, M271, A35 to Lyndhurst. A337 towards Brockenhurst. Hotel on left after Beaulieu sign

This smart property offers a host of facilities that include an Oriental-style spa and leisure suite with an excellent range of unusual treatments, and three contrasting restaurants that offer a choice of Thai, French or modern British cuisine. Many of the spacious and well appointed bedrooms have balconies overlooking the gardens. Extensive function and conference facilities are also available.

Rooms 79 (61 annexe) (31 GF) **D** £158-£338 (incl. bkfst)* **Facilities** Spa FTV Wi-fi ⓑ ⓧ ⓨ Gym Steam room Beauty therapists Hydrotherapy pool Xmas New Year **Conf** Class 70 Board 40 Thtr 120 Del from £150* **Services** Lift **Parking** 180 **Notes** LB ⓧ No children 16yrs Civ Wed 100

The Balmer Lawn Hotel

★★★★ 80% ◉ HOTEL

☎ 01590 623116
Lyndhurst Rd SO42 7ZB
e-mail: info@balmerlawnhotel.com
dir: Just off A337 from Brockenhurst towards Lymington

Situated in the heart of the New Forest, this peacefully located hotel provides comfortable public rooms and a wide range of bedrooms. A selection of carefully prepared and enjoyable dishes is offered in the spacious restaurant. The extensive function and leisure facilities make this popular with both families and conference delegates.

Rooms 50 (10 fmly) ⓡ **S** £75-£99; **D** £129-£350* **Facilities** FTV Wi-fi ⓧ ⓧ ⓨ Gym Squash Indoor leisure suite Beauty treatment room Sauna ♫ Xmas New Year **Conf** Class 76 Board 48 Thtr 150 **Services** Lift **Parking** 100 **Notes** Civ Wed 120

THE PIG

★★★ ◉◉ COUNTRY HOUSE HOTEL

☎ 01590 622354 & 0845 077 9494
Beaulieu Rd SO42 7QL
e-mail: info@thepighotel.com
dir: At Brockenhurst onto B3055 (Beaulieu Road). 1m on left up private road

A delightful country house where the focus is very much on the food, with the chef, gardener and forager working as a team to create menus of seasonal, locally sourced produce; all ingredients are found within a 15-mile radius. The result of such a policy is that menus change daily, and sometimes even more frequently! The stylish dining room is an authentically reproduced Victorian greenhouse, and alfresco eating is possible as there is a wood-fired oven in the courtyard. The bedrooms have eclectic furnishings, good beds and views of either the forest or the garden; two suites with private courtyards are available.

Rooms 26 (10 annexe) (2 fmly) (10 GF) ⓡ **D** £129-£259* **Facilities** STV FTV Wi-fi ⓑ ⓧ ⓨ Beauty treatment room Xmas New Year **Conf** Board 14 Del £225* **Parking** 20

Cloud Hotel

★★ SMALL HOTEL

☎ 01590 622165 & 622354
Meerut Rd SO42 7TD
e-mail: enquiries@cloudhotel.co.uk
web: www.cloudhotel.co.uk
dir: M27 junct 1 signed New Forest, A337 through Lyndhurst to Brockenhurst. On entering Brockenhurst 1st right. Hotel 300mtrs

This charming hotel enjoys a peaceful location on the edge of the village. The bedrooms are bright and comfortable with pine furnishings and smart en suite facilities. Public rooms include a selection of cosy lounges, a delightful rear garden with outdoor seating and a restaurant specialising in home-cooked, wholesome English food.

Rooms 18 (1 fmly) (2 GF) ⓡ **S** £83-£90; **D** £124-£180 (incl. bkfst)* **Facilities** FTV Wi-fi Xmas **Conf** Class 12 Board 12 Thtr 40 Del from £165 to £180 **Parking** 20 **Notes** LB ⓧ No children 12yrs Closed 27 Dec-12 Jan

B

Watersplash Hotel

★★ 65% HOTEL

☎ 01590 622344
The Rise SO42 7ZP
e-mail: bookings@watersplash.co.uk
web: www.watersplash.co.uk
dir: M3 junct 13/M27 junct 1/A337 S through Lyndhurst & Brockenhurst. The Rise on left, hotel on left

This popular, welcoming hotel that dates from Victorian times has been in the same family for over 40 years. It is in a great location close to the centre of Brockenhurst, and the delights of the New Forest are easily accessible. The bedrooms are pleasantly appointed and come in a range of sizes. The public rooms are spacious and comfortable, and include a pleasant bar. There is a well-tended garden, and good parking facilities.

Rooms 23 (6 fmly) (2 GF) 🕏 **Facilities** FTV Wi-fi ⚲ Beauty & massage therapist Xmas New Year Child facilities **Conf** Class 20 Board 20 Thtr 80 **Parking** 29

BROMBOROUGH	Map 15 SJ38
Merseyside	

Premier Inn Wirral (Bromborough)

BUDGET HOTEL

☎ 0871 527 9172
High St, Bromborough Cross CH62 7EZ
web: www.premierinn.com
dir: On A41 (New Chester Rd), 2m from M53 junct 5

High quality, budget accommodation ideal for both families and business travellers. Spacious, en suite bedrooms feature tea and coffee making facilities, and Freeview TV in most hotels. Internet access and Wi-fi are available for a small fee. The adjacent family restaurant features a wide and varied menu. See also the Hotel Groups pages.

Rooms 32

BROMLEY	
Greater London	

BEST WESTERN Bromley Court Hotel

★★★ 77% HOTEL PLAN 1 H1

☎ 020 8461 8600
Bromley Hill BR1 4JD
e-mail: enquiries@bromleycourthotel.co.uk
web: www.bromleycourthotel.co.uk
dir: N of town centre, off A21. Private drive opposite Volkswagen garage on Bromley Hill

Set amid three acres of grounds, this smart hotel enjoys a peaceful location, in a residential area on the outskirts of town. Well maintained bedrooms are smartly appointed and thoughtfully equipped. The contemporary-style restaurant offers a good choice of meals in comfortable surroundings. Extensive facilities include a leisure club and a good range of meeting rooms.

Rooms 115 (4 fmly) 🕏 **S** £85-£120; **D** £95-£130 (incl. bkfst)* **Facilities** STV FTV Wi-fi ⚲ Gym Steam room Spa pool **Conf** Class 70 Board 40 Thtr 150 Del from £155 to £165* **Services** Lift Air con **Parking** 86 **Notes** LB ⊗ Civ Wed 130

BROMSGROVE	Map 10 SO97
Worcestershire	

Holiday Inn Birmingham - Bromsgrove

★★★★ 73% HOTEL

☎ 01527 576600 & 0871 942 9142
Kidderminster Rd B61 9AB
e-mail: info@hi-birminghambromsgrove.co.uk
dir: From S: M5 junct 5, A38 to Bromsgrove 2m. At rdbt left, B4091,1.5m. Left at 2nd rdbt A448. Hotel 0.5m on left. From N: M5 junct 4, A38/Bromsgrove for 2m. Through lights, straight on at rdbt. Filter right at lights. Right at 2nd rdbt onto A448. Hotel 0.5m on left

Public areas in this striking building are comfortable and spacious. A selection of meeting rooms is available, along with function suites, a courtyard garden and plenty of natural light. Bedrooms come in a variety of styles - some are more compact than others but all offer an excellent working environment for the business guest. Leisure facilities include a steam room, sauna, pool and gym. There is an extensive car park.

Rooms 110 (11 fmly) (31 GF) **S** £50-£130; **D** £50-£130* **Facilities** Spa STV FTV Wi-fi ⚲ HL ⚙ Gym Sauna Steam room Xmas **Conf** Class 120 Board 50 Thtr 220 Del from £99 to £139 **Services** Lift Air con **Parking** 220 **Notes** LB ⊗ Civ Wed 180

Premier Inn Bromsgrove Central

BUDGET HOTEL

☎ 0871 527 8168
Birmingham Rd B61 0BA
web: www.premierinn.com
dir: M42 junct 1 (S'bound access only) or M5 junct 4 S'bound or M5 junct 5 N'bound onto A38 towards Bromsgrove. Hotel adjacent to Guild Brewers Fayre. (NB for Sat Nav use B60 1GJ)

High quality, budget accommodation ideal for both families and business travellers. Spacious, en suite bedrooms feature tea and coffee making facilities, and Freeview TV in most hotels. Internet access and Wi-fi are available for a small fee. The adjacent family restaurant features a wide and varied menu. See also the Hotel Groups pages.

Rooms 78

Premier Inn Bromsgrove South (Worcester Road)

BUDGET HOTEL

☎ 0871 527 8170
Worcester Rd, Upton Warren B61 7ET
web: www.premierinn.com
dir: M5 junct 5, A38 towards Bromsgrove, 1.2m. Or M42 junct 1, A38 S, cross over A448

Rooms 27

B

BROOK (NEAR CADNAM)   Map 5 SU21
Hampshire

The Bell Inn
★★★ 82% ◉ HOTEL

☎ 023 8081 2214
SO43 7HE
e-mail: bell@bramshaw.co.uk
web: www.bellinnbramshaw.co.uk
dir: M27 junct 1 onto B3079, hotel 1.5m on right

The inn is part of the Bramshaw Golf Club and has tailored its style to suit this market, but it is also an ideal base for visiting the New Forest. Bedrooms are comfortable and attractively furnished, and the public areas, particularly the welcoming bar, have a cosy and friendly atmosphere.

Rooms 27 (2 annexe) (1 fmly) (8 GF) **Facilities** FTV Wi-fi ↕ 54 Putt green Xmas New Year **Conf** Class 20 Board 30 Thtr 50 **Parking** 150 **Notes** ⊗ Civ Wed 50

BROXTON   Map 15 SJ45
Cheshire

De Vere Carden Park
★★★★ 85% ◉ HOTEL   DE VERE HOTELS

☎ 01829 731000
Carden Park CH3 9DQ
e-mail: reservations.carden@devere-hotels.com
web: www.cardenpark.co.uk
dir: M56 junct 15, M53 Chester. Take A41 signed Whitchurch. 8m. At Broxton rdbt right onto A534 (signed Wrexham). Hotel 1.5m on left

This impressive Cheshire estate dates back to the 17th century and consists of 1,000 acres of mature parkland. The hotel offers a choice of dining options along with superb leisure facilities that include golf courses, a fully equipped gym, a swimming pool and popular spa. Spacious, thoughtfully equipped bedrooms have excellent business and in-room entertainment facilities.

Rooms 196 (83 annexe) (24 fmly) (68 GF) **Facilities** Spa STV Wi-fi ⓣ supervised ↕ 36 ⌣ Putt green Gym Archery Quad bikes Off-roading Bike & walking trails Laser clay shooting Xmas New Year **Conf** Class 240 Board 125 Thtr 400 **Services** Lift **Parking** 700 **Notes** Civ Wed 375

BRYHER   Map 2 SV81
Cornwall (Isles of Scilly)

Hell Bay
★★★★ 80% ◉◉◉ HOTEL

☎ 01720 422947
TR23 0PR
e-mail: contactus@hellbay.co.uk
web: www.hellbay.co.uk
dir: Access by boat from Penzance, plane from Exeter, Newquay or Land's End

Located on the smallest of the inhabited islands of the Scilly Isles on the edge of the Atlantic, this hotel makes a really special destination. The owners have filled the hotel with original works of art by artists who have connections with the islands, and the interior is decorated in cool blues and greens creating an extremely restful environment. The contemporary bedrooms are equally stylish, and many have garden access and stunning sea views. Eating here is a delight, and naturally seafood features strongly on the award-winning, daily-changing menus.

Rooms 25 (25 annexe) (3 fmly) (15 GF) ⌂
S £168.75-£400; **D** £270-£640 (incl. bkfst & dinner)*
Facilities STV FTV Wi-fi ↕ ↖ ↕ 7 ⌣ ↘ Gym Beauty treatment room **Conf** Class 36 Board 36 Thtr 36 **Notes** LB Closed Nov-Feb

BUCKHURST HILL   Map 6 TQ49
Essex

Premier Inn Loughton/ Buckhurst Hill
 Premier Inn

BUDGET HOTEL

☎ 0871 527 8686
High Rd IG9 5HT
web: www.premierinn.com
dir: M25 junct 26 towards Loughton. A121 into Buckhurst Hill (approx 5m), hotel on left

High quality, budget accommodation ideal for both families and business travellers. Spacious, en suite bedrooms feature tea and coffee making facilities, and Freeview TV in most hotels. Internet access and Wi-fi are available for a small fee. The adjacent family restaurant features a wide and varied menu. See also the Hotel Groups pages.

Rooms 49

BUCKINGHAM   Map 11 SP63
Buckinghamshire

Villiers Hotel
★★★★ 73% ◉◉ HOTEL   CLASSIC BRITISH HOTELS

☎ 01280 822444
3 Castle St MK18 1BS
e-mail: villiers@oxfordshire-hotels.co.uk
web: www.oxfordshire-hotels.co.uk
dir: M1 junct 13 (N) or junct 15 (S) follow signs to Buckingham. Castle St by Old Town Hall

Guests can enjoy a town centre location with a high degree of comfort at this 400-year-old former coaching inn. Relaxing public areas feature flagstone floors, oak panelling and real fires whilst bedrooms are modern, spacious and equipped to a high level. Diners can unwind in the atmospheric bar before taking dinner in the award-winning restaurant.

Rooms 49 (4 fmly) (3 GF) **S** £75-£120; **D** £110-£160 (incl. bkfst)* **Facilities** STV FTV Wi-fi Xmas New Year **Conf** Class 120 Board 80 Thtr 250 Del from £138 to £165* **Services** Lift **Parking** 52 **Notes** LB ⊗ Civ Wed 180

BEST WESTERN Buckingham Hotel
 Best Western

★★★ 76% HOTEL

☎ 01280 822622
Buckingham Ring Rd MK18 1RY
e-mail: info@thebuckinghamhotel.co.uk
dir: A421 to Buckingham, take ring road S towards Brackley & Bicester. Hotel on left

A purpose-built hotel, which offers comfortable and spacious rooms with well designed working spaces for business travellers. There are also extensive conference facilities. The open-plan restaurant and bar offer a good range of dishes, and the well-equipped leisure suite is popular with guests.

Rooms 70 (6 fmly) (31 GF) **S** £41-£67; **D** £41-£77* **Facilities** STV FTV Wi-fi ⓣ supervised Gym Sauna Steam room Xmas New Year **Conf** Class 60 Board 60 Thtr 200 Del from £120* **Parking** 200 **Notes** Civ Wed 120

Save on hotels. Book at **theAA.com/hotel**

BRO – BUR 111 ENGLAND

B

BUDE
Cornwall   Map 2 SS20

Falcon Hotel

★★★ 80% HOTEL

☎ 01288 352005
Breakwater Rd EX23 8SD
e-mail: reception@falconhotel.com
web: www.falconhotel.com
dir: Exit A39 to Bude, then Widemouth Bay. Hotel on right over canal bridge

Dating back to 1798, this long-established hotel boasts delightful walled gardens, ideal for afternoon teas. Bedrooms offer high standards of comfort and quality; there is also a four-poster room complete with spa bath. A choice of menus is offered in the elegant restaurant and the friendly bar. The hotel has an impressive function room.

Rooms 29 (7 fmly) ✎ **S** £62.50-£72.50; **D** £125-£145 (incl. bkfst)* **Facilities** STV FTV Wi-fi ☙ 🛁 🎵 New Year **Conf** Class 50 Board 50 Thtr 200 Del from £99.50 to £125 **Services** Lift **Parking** 40 **Notes** LB ⊗ RS 25 Dec Civ Wed 160

Hartland Hotel

★★★ 78% HOTEL

☎ 01288 355661
Hartland Ter EX23 8JY
e-mail: info@hartlandhotelbude.com
dir: Exit A39 to Bude, follow town centre signs. Left into Hartland Terrace opposite Boots the Chemist. Hotel at seaward end of road

This long established hotel has an enduring and timeless elegance with a reassuring sense of tradition. Its location is a wonderful asset, overlooking Summerleaze Beach with panoramic views of the town and coast. The comfortable bedrooms are individually styled and a number have four-poster beds and wonderful sea views. The spacious public areas include a convivial bar, lounges and an attractive dining room where a varied menu is on offer. An outdoor pool is available for lazing away the summer days.

Rooms 28 (2 fmly) **S** £64-£70; **D** £112-£122 (incl. bkfst)* **Facilities** FTV ☙ ✫ 🎵 Xmas New Year **Services** Lift **Parking** 30 **Notes** LB Closed mid Nov-Etr (ex Xmas & New Year)

The Cliff Hotel at Bude

★★ 76% HOTEL

☎ 01288 353110
Maer Down, Crooklets Beach EX23 8NG
e-mail: cliff_hotel@btconnect.com
web: www.cliffhotel.co.uk
dir: A39 through Bude, left at top of High St, pass Sainsburys, 1st right between golf course, over x-rds, premises at end on right

Overlooking the sea from a clifftop location, this friendly and efficient establishment provides spacious, well-equipped bedrooms. The various public areas include a bar and lounge and an impressive range of leisure facilities. Delicious dinners and tasty breakfasts are available in the attractive dining room.

Rooms 15 (15 fmly) (8 GF) **S** £39.95-£44.95; **D** £79.90-£89.90 (incl. bkfst)* **Facilities** FTV Wi-fi ⊗ 🏊 Putt green Gym **Parking** 25 **Notes** LB Closed Nov-Mar

Hotel Penarvor

★★ 74% SMALL HOTEL

☎ 01288 352036
Crooklets Beach EX23 8NE
e-mail: stay@hotelpenarvor.co.uk
dir: A39 towards Bude for 1.5m. At 2nd rdbt turn right, pass shops. Top of hill, left signed Crooklets Beach

Adjacent to the golf course and overlooking Crooklets Beach, this family owned hotel has a relaxed and friendly atmosphere. Bedrooms vary in size but are all equipped to a similar standard. An interesting selection of dishes, using fresh local produce is available in the restaurant, and bar meals are also provided.

Rooms 16 (6 fmly) (3 GF) ✎ **S** £38-£45; **D** £76-£90 (incl. bkfst)* **Facilities** FTV Wi-fi **Parking** 20 **Notes** LB Closed 24-28 Dec

BURFORD
Oxfordshire   Map 5 SP21

The Bay Tree Hotel

★★★★ 73% ⊛ HOTEL

Cotswold Inns & Hotels

☎ 01993 822791
Sheep St OX18 4LW
e-mail: info@baytreehotel.info
web: www.cotswold-inns-hotels.co.uk/bay-tree
dir: A40 or A361 to Burford. From High St turn into Sheep St, next to old market square. Hotel on right

The modern decorative style combines seamlessly with features from this delightful inn's long history. Bedrooms are tastefully furnished and some have four-poster or half-tester beds. Public areas consist of a character bar, a sophisticated airy restaurant, a selection of meeting rooms and an attractive walled garden.

Rooms 21 (13 annexe) (2 fmly) (3 GF) **S** £160-£170; **D** £180-£270 (incl. bkfst)* **Facilities** Wi-fi 🛁 Xmas New Year **Conf** Class 12 Board 25 Thtr 40 **Parking** 50 **Notes** Civ Wed 90

B

BURFORD *continued*

The Lamb Inn

★★★ 83% SMALL HOTEL

☎ 01993 823155
Sheep St OX18 4LR
e-mail: info@lambinn-burford.co.uk
web: www.cotswold-inns-hotels.co.uk/lamb
dir: A40 into Burford, downhill, 1st left into Sheep St,
hotel last on right

This enchanting old inn is just a short walk from the
centre of this delightful Cotswold village. Inside an
abundance of character and charm is found in the
cosy lounge with log fire, and intimate bar with
flagged floors. An elegant restaurant offers locally
sourced produce in carefully prepared dishes.
Bedrooms, some with original features, are
comfortable and well appointed.

Rooms 17 (1 fmly) (4 GF) **S** £150-£170; **D** £160-£310
(incl. bkfst)* **Facilities** Wi-fi Xmas New Year

The Bull at Burford

 RESTAURANT WITH ROOMS

☎ 01993 822220
105 High St OX18 4RG
e-mail: info@bullatburford.co.uk
dir: In town centre

Situated in the heart of a pretty Cotswold town, The
Bull was originally built in 1475 as a rest house for
the local priory. It now has stylish, attractively
presented bedrooms that reflect plenty of charm and
character. Dinner is a must and the award-winning
restaurant has an imaginative menu along with an
excellent choice of wines. Lunch is served daily and
afternoon tea is popular. There is a residents' lounge,
and free Wi-fi is available.

Rooms 15 (2 annexe) (1 fmly)

BURGESS HILL Map 6 TQ31
West Sussex

Premier Inn Burgess Hill

BUDGET HOTEL

☎ 0871 527 8172
Charles Av RH15 9AG
web: www.premierinn.com
dir: M25 junct 7, M23, A23. Left at Burgess Hill follow
A2300 signs. At rdbt 2nd exit onto A2300. At next rdbt
4th exit onto A273, straight on at next 2 rdbts, at 3rd
rdbt (Tesco) 1st left. Hotel 2nd left

High quality, budget accommodation ideal for both
families and business travellers. Spacious, en suite
bedrooms feature tea and coffee making facilities,
and Freeview TV in most hotels. Internet access and

Wi-fi are available for a small fee. The adjacent
family restaurant features a wide and varied menu.
See also the Hotel Groups pages.

Rooms 60

BURLEY Map 5 SU20
Hampshire

Moorhill House Hotel

NEW FOREST HOTELS

★★★ 79%
COUNTRY HOUSE HOTEL

☎ 01425 403285 & 0800 444 441
BH24 4AH
e-mail: moorhill@newforesthotels.co.uk
web: www.newforesthotels.co.uk
dir: M27, A31, follow signs to Burley, through village,
up hill, right opposite school & cricket grounds

Situated deep in the heart of the New Forest and
formerly a grand gentleman's residence, this
charming hotel offers a relaxed and friendly
environment. Bedrooms, of varying sizes, are smartly
decorated. A range of facilities is provided and guests
can relax by walking around the extensive grounds.
Both dinner and breakfast offer a choice of
interesting and freshly prepared dishes.

Rooms 31 (13 fmly) (3 GF) 🐾 **S** £114; **D** £187 (incl.
bkfst)* **Facilities** FTV Wi-fi ♨ HL ⏲ ♨ Badminton
(Apr-Sep) Sauna Xmas New Year **Conf** Class 60
Board 65 Thtr 120 Del £132 **Parking** 50 **Notes** LB
Civ Wed 80

BURNHAM Map 6 SU98
Buckinghamshire

Burnham Beeches Hotel

corus hotels

★★★★ 76% HOTEL

☎ 0844 736 8603
Grove Rd SL1 8DP
e-mail: sales.burnhambeeches@corushotels.com
web: www.corushotels.com/burnham-beeches
dir: M40 junct 2, A355 towards Slough, right at 2nd
rdbt, 1st right to Grove Rd

Set in attractive mature grounds on the fringes of
woodland, this extended Georgian manor house has
spacious, comfortable and well-equipped bedrooms.
Public rooms include a cosy lounge/bar offering all-
day snacks and an elegant wood-panelled restaurant
that serves interesting cuisine; there are also
conference facilities, a fitness centre and pool.

Rooms 82 (22 fmly) (12 GF) 🐾 **S** £99-£210;
D £109-£220 (incl. bkfst)* **Facilities** FTV Wi-fi ⏲ ♨
♨ Gym Beauty treatment room Xmas New Year
Conf Class 80 Board 60 Thtr 150 Del from £160 to
£265* **Services** Lift **Parking** 150 **Notes** LB ⊗
Civ Wed 120

The Grovefield House Hotel

CLASSIC LODGES
the sign of a great hotel

★★★★ 73% HOTEL

☎ 01628 603131
Taplow Common Rd SL1 8LP
e-mail: info.grovefield@classiclodges.co.uk
web: www.classiclodges.co.uk
dir: M4 junct 7, A4 towards Maidenhead. Next rdbt
right under rail bridge. Straight over mini rdbt,
garage on right. 1.5m, hotel on right

Set in its own spacious grounds, the Grovefield is
conveniently located for Heathrow Airport as well as
Slough and Maidenhead. Accommodation is spacious
and well presented and most rooms have views over
the attractive gardens. Public areas include a range
of meeting rooms, a comfortable bar/lounge area and
Hamilton's restaurant.

Rooms 40 (5 fmly) (7 GF) **Facilities** Putt green
Fishing ♨ Xmas New Year **Conf** Class 80 Board 80
Thtr 180 **Services** Lift **Parking** 155
Notes Civ Wed 200

BURNHAM MARKET Map 13 TF84
Norfolk

The Hoste

★★★★ 79% HOTEL

☎ 01328 738777
The Green PE31 8HD
e-mail: reception@thehoste.com
web: www.thehoste.com
dir: Signed on B1155, 5m W of Wells-next-the-Sea

A stylish, privately-owned inn situated in the heart of
a bustling village close to the north Norfolk coast. The
extensive public rooms feature a range of dining
areas that include a conservatory with plush
furniture, a sunny patio and a traditional pub. The
tastefully furnished and thoughtfully equipped
bedrooms are generally very spacious and offer a high
degree of comfort.

B

The Hoste

Rooms 34 (7 GF) **Facilities** Spa STV Wi-fi Beauty treatment rooms Xmas New Year **Conf** Class 40 Board 16 Thtr 25 **Services** Air con **Parking** 45

See advert below

BURNLEY
Lancashire — Map 18 SD83

Holiday Inn Express Burnley

BUDGET HOTEL

☎ 01282 855955 & 855963
M65 Jct 10, 55 Pendle Way BB12 0TJ
dir: M65 junct 10, 3rd exit at rdbt, Pendle Way, hotel on right

A modern hotel ideal for families and business travellers. Fresh and uncomplicated, the spacious rooms include Sky TV, power shower and tea and coffee-making facilities. Continental buffet breakfast is included in the room rate; other meals may be taken at the nearby family pub or restaurant. See also the Hotel Groups pages.

Rooms 102 (67 fmly) (4 GF) 🐾 **Conf** Class 28 Board 28 Thtr 70

Premier Inn Burnley

BUDGET HOTEL

Premier Inn

☎ 0871 527 8174
Queen Victoria Rd BB10 3EF
web: www.premierinn.com
dir: M65 junct 12, 5th exit at rdbt, 1st exit at rdbt, keep in right lane at lights, 2nd exit at next rdbt, 3rd at next rdbt, under bridge, left before football ground

High quality, budget accommodation ideal for both families and business travellers. Spacious, en suite bedrooms feature tea and coffee making facilities, and Freeview TV in most hotels. Internet access and Wi-fi are available for a small fee. The adjacent family restaurant features a wide and varied menu. See also the Hotel Groups pages.

Rooms 43

BURNSALL
North Yorkshire — Map 19 SE06

Red Lion Hotel & Manor House

★★ 78% HOTEL

☎ 01756 720204
By the Bridge BD23 6BU
e-mail: redlion@daelnet.co.uk
web: www.redlion.co.uk
dir: On B6160 between Grassington & Bolton Abbey

This delightful 16th-century Dales' inn stands adjacent to a five-arch bridge over the scenic River Wharfe. Stylish, comfortable bedrooms are individually decorated, and well equipped. Public areas include a tasteful lounge, traditional oak-

panelled bar, and impressive function rooms. The elegant restaurant makes good use of fresh local ingredients. Additional bed and breakfast based accommodation is available in the Manor House.

Rooms 25 (15 annexe) (5 fmly) (4 GF) **Facilities** FTV Wi-fi Fishing Xmas New Year **Conf** Class 50 Board 25 Thtr 60 **Parking** 80 **Notes** Civ Wed 125

The Devonshire Fell

❀❀ RESTAURANT WITH ROOMS

☎ 01756 729000 & 718111
BD23 6BT
e-mail: manager@devonshirefell.co.uk
web: www.devonshirefell.co.uk
dir: On B6160, 6m from Bolton Abbey rdbt, A59 junct

Located on the edge of the attractive village of Burnsall, this establishment offers comfortable, well-equipped accommodation in a relaxing atmosphere. There is an extensive menu featuring local produce, and meals can be taken either in the bar area or the more formal restaurant. A function room with views over the valley is also available.

Rooms 12 (2 fmly)

B

BURRINGTON   Map 3 SS61
(NEAR PORTSMOUTH ARMS STATION)
Devon

INSPECTORS' CHOICE

Northcote Manor

★★★ ◉◉ COUNTRY HOUSE HOTEL

☎ 01769 560501
EX37 9LZ
e-mail: rest@northcotemanor.co.uk
web: www.northcotemanor.co.uk
dir: From A377 opposite Portsmouth Arms, into
hotel drive (NB do not enter Burrington village)

A warm and friendly welcome is assured at this
beautiful country-house hotel, built in 1716 and
surrounded by 20 acres of grounds and woodlands.
Guests can enjoy wonderful views over the Taw
River Valley while relaxing in the delightful
environment created by the attentive staff. A meal
in either the intimate, more formal Manor House
Restaurant or the Walled Garden Restaurant will
prove a highlight; each offers menus of the finest
local produce used in well-prepared dishes.
Bedrooms, including some suites, are individually
styled, spacious and well appointed.

Rooms 16 (2 fmly) (3 GF) ⬧ **Facilities** FTV Wi-fi ⬧
⬧ Xmas New Year **Conf** Class 50 Board 30 Thtr 80
Del from £170 **Parking** 50 **Notes** Civ Wed 100

BURTON UPON TRENT   Map 10 SK22
Staffordshire

Mercure Burton Upon Trent Newton Park

★★★★ COUNTRY HOUSE HOTEL

☎ 0844 815 9018
Newton Solney DE15 0SS
e-mail: info@mercureburton.co.uk
web: www.jupiterhotels.co.uk
dir: On B5008 past Repton to Newton Solney. Hotel on
left

Currently the rating for this establishment is not
confirmed. This may be due to a change of ownership

or because it has only recently joined the AA rating
scheme.

Rooms 50 **Conf** Class 70 Board 60 Thtr 100

Three Queens Hotel

★★★ 78% ◉ HOTEL

☎ 01283 523800 & 0845 230 1332
One Bridge St DE14 1SY
e-mail: hotel@threequeenshotel.co.uk
web: www.threequeenshotel.co.uk
dir: On A511 in Burton upon Trent at junct of Bridge
St & High St. Town side of Old River Bridge

Located in the centre of the town close to the river,
this smartly presented hotel provides an appealing,
high quality base from which to tour the area.
Bedrooms come in a mix of styles that include
spacious duplex suites and executive rooms located
in the original Jacobean heart of the building. Smart
day rooms include the medieval styled Grill
Restaurant, a modern bar and a contemporary
breakfast room. A warm welcome is assured from the
professional staff.

Rooms 38 (7 smoking) **Facilities** STV FTV Wi-fi ⬧
Xmas New Year **Conf** Class 40 Board 30 Thtr 60
Services Lift Air con **Parking** 55 **Notes** ⊗

Holiday Inn Express Burton upon Trent

BUDGET HOTEL

☎ 01283 504300
2nd Av, Centrum 100 DE14 2WF
e-mail: reservations@exhiburton.co.uk
web: www.exhiburton.co.uk
dir: From A38 Branston exit take A5121 signed Town
Centre. At McDonalds rdbt, turn left into 2nd Avenue.
Hotel on left

A modern hotel ideal for families and business
travellers. Fresh and uncomplicated, the spacious
rooms include Sky TV, power shower and tea and
coffee-making facilities. Continental buffet breakfast
is included in the room rate; other meals may be
taken at the nearby family pub or restaurant. See also
the Hotel Groups pages.

Rooms 82 (47 fmly) (14 GF) (3 smoking) ⬧
S £55-£95; D £55-£95 (incl. bkfst)* **Conf** Class 30
Board 25 Thtr 60 Del from £85 to £105*

Premier Inn Burton upon Trent Central

BUDGET HOTEL

☎ 0871 527 9280
Wellington Rd DE14 2WD
dir: Exit A38 at Branston junction onto A5121 to
Burton on Trent. Straight on at lights. At rdbt take 3rd
exit, hotel on left

High quality, budget accommodation ideal for both
families and business travellers. Spacious, en suite
bedrooms feature tea and coffee making facilities,
and Freeview TV in most hotels. Internet access and
Wi-fi are available for a small fee. The adjacent
family restaurant features a wide and varied menu.
See also the Hotel Groups pages.

Rooms 64

Premier Inn Burton upon Trent East

BUDGET HOTEL

☎ 0871 527 8176
Ashby Road East DE15 0PU
web: www.premierinn.com
dir: 2m E of Burton upon Trent on A50

Rooms 34

BURY   Map 15 SD81
Greater Manchester

Red Hall Hotel

★★★ 80% HOTEL

☎ 01706 822476
Manchester Rd, Walmersley BL9 5NA
e-mail: info@red-hall.co.uk
dir: M66 junct 1, A56. Over motorway bridge, hotel
approx 300mtrs on right

Originally a farmhouse, this hotel, located in the
picturesque village of Warmersley on the outskirts of
Ramsbottom, is just off the M66, making it ideal for
business and leisure guests alike. Bedrooms are
contemporary and well equipped. There is a
restaurant and lounge bar, plus meeting and event
facilities.

Rooms 37 (2 fmly) (18 GF) ⬧ S £45-£105;
D £45-£105* **Facilities** STV Wi-fi Xmas New Year
Conf Class 60 Board 30 Thtr 140 **Services** Lift
Parking 100 **Notes** Civ Wed

Save on hotels. Book at **theAA.com/hotel**

BUR – BUX 115 ENGLAND

B

Premier Inn Bury

BUDGET HOTEL

☎ 0871 527 9294

5 Knowsley Place, Duke St BL9 0EJ

web: www.premierinn.com

dir: M66 junct 2, A58 towards Bolton & Bury. At rdbt in Bury centre follow A58 (Angouleme Way). Left in Knowsley St, hotel on left

High quality, budget accommodation ideal for both families and business travellers. Spacious, en suite bedrooms feature tea and coffee making facilities, and Freeview TV in most hotels. Internet access and Wi-fi are available for a small fee. The adjacent family restaurant features a wide and varied menu. See also the Hotel Groups pages.

BURY ST EDMUNDS
Suffolk Map 13 TL86

The Angel Hotel

★★★★ 88% ◉◉ TOWN HOUSE HOTEL

☎ 01284 714000

Angel Hill IP33 1LT

e-mail: staying@theangel.co.uk

web: www.theangel.co.uk

dir: From A134, left at rdbt into Northgate St. Continue to lights, right into Mustow St, left into Angel Hill. Hotel on right

The Angel Hotel is an impressive building situated just a short walk from the town centre. One of the hotel's more notable guests over the last 400 years was Charles Dickens, who is reputed to have written part of *The Pickwick Papers* while in residence. The hotel offers a range of individually designed bedrooms that include a selection of four-poster rooms and a suite.

Rooms 80 (5 fmly) (22 GF) ⚓ **D** £120-£340 (incl. bkfst)* **Facilities** FTV Wi-fi Xmas **Conf** Board 16 Del from £150* **Services** Lift **Parking** 20

Ravenwood Hall Hotel

★★★ 88% ◉◉ COUNTRY HOUSE HOTEL

☎ 01359 270345

Rougham IP30 9JA

e-mail: enquiries@ravenwoodhall.co.uk

web: www.ravenwoodhall.co.uk

dir: 3m E from A14 junct 45. Hotel on left

Ravenwood Hall is a delightful 15th-century property set in seven acres of woodland and landscaped gardens. The building has many original features including carved timbers and inglenook fireplaces. The spacious bedrooms are attractively decorated, tastefully furnished with well-chosen pieces, and equipped with many thoughtful touches. Public rooms

include an elegant restaurant and a smart lounge bar with an open fire.

Rooms 14 (7 annexe) (5 GF) ⚓ **Facilities** Wi-fi ⚒ ⚓ Shooting, fishing & horse riding can be arranged Xmas New Year **Conf** Class 80 Board 40 Thtr 130 **Parking** 150 **Notes** Civ Wed 130

BEST WESTERN Priory Hotel

★★★ 82% ◉ HOTEL

☎ 01284 766181

Mildenhall Rd IP32 6EH

e-mail: reservations@prioryhotel.co.uk

web: www.prioryhotel.co.uk

dir: From A14 take Bury St Edmunds W slip road. Follow signs to Brandon. At mini-rdbt turn right. Hotel 0.5m on left

An 18th-century Grade II listed building set in landscaped grounds on the outskirts of town. The attractively decorated, tastefully furnished and thoughtfully equipped bedrooms are split between the main house and garden wings, which have their own sun terraces. Public rooms feature a smart restaurant, a conservatory dining room and a lounge bar.

Rooms 36 (29 annexe) (1 fmly) (30 GF) ⚓ **S** £76-£84; **D** £88-£102 (incl. bkfst) **Facilities** FTV Wi-fi Xmas New Year **Conf** Class 24 Board 30 Thtr 75 Del from £135 to £147 **Parking** 60 **Notes** LB Civ Wed 75

The Grange Hotel

★★★ 77% ◉ COUNTRY HOUSE HOTEL

☎ 01359 231260

Barton Rd, Thurston IP31 3PQ

e-mail: info@grangecountryhousehotel.com

web: www.grangecountryhousehotel.com

dir: A14 junct 45 towards Gt Barton, right at T-junct. At x-rds left into Barton Rd to Thurston. At rdbt, left after 0.5m, hotel on right

A Tudor-style country-house hotel situated on the outskirts of town. The individually decorated bedrooms have co-ordinated fabrics and many thoughtful touches; some rooms have nice views of the gardens. Public areas include a smart lounge bar, two private dining rooms, the Garden Restaurant and banqueting facilities.

Rooms 18 (5 annexe) (1 fmly) (3 GF) ⚓ **S** £79.50; **D** £130 (incl. bkfst)* **Facilities** FTV Wi-fi Beauty treatment room Xmas New Year **Conf** Class 40 Board 30 Thtr 135 Del from £102.50 to £142.50* **Parking** 100 **Notes** LB Civ Wed 150

BUXTON
Derbyshire Map 16 SK07

The Palace Hotel

★★★★ 71% HOTEL PUMA HOTELS COLLECTION

☎ 01298 22001

Palace Rd SK17 6AG

e-mail: palace@pumahotels.co.uk

web: www.pumahotels.co.uk

dir: M6 junct 20, follow M56/M60 signs to Stockport then A6 to Buxton, hotel adjacent to railway station

This impressive Victorian hotel is located on the hill overlooking the town. Public areas are traditional and elegant in style, and include chandeliers and decorative ceilings. The bedrooms are spacious and equipped with modern facilities, and The Dovedale Restaurant provides modern British cuisine. Good leisure facilities are available.

Rooms 122 (18 fmly) **Facilities** Spa Wi-fi ⊗ supervised Gym Beauty facilities Xmas New Year **Conf** Class 125 Board 80 Thtr 350 **Services** Lift **Parking** 180 **Notes** Civ Wed 100

BEST WESTERN Lee Wood Hotel

★★★ 82% ◉ HOTEL

☎ 01298 23002

The Park SK17 6TQ

e-mail: reservations@leewoodhotel.co.uk

web: www.leewoodhotel.co.uk

dir: From town centre take A5004 NE, hotel 150mtrs beyond University of Derby (Buxton Campus)

This elegant Georgian hotel offers high standards of comfort and hospitality. The individually furnished bedrooms are generally spacious, with all of the expected modern conveniences. There is a choice of two comfortable lounges and a conservatory restaurant. The quality cooking, good service and fine hospitality are noteworthy.

Rooms 39 (5 annexe) (4 fmly) **S** £50-£95; **D** £60-£130 **Facilities** STV FTV Wi-fi ⚒ Gym Serenity beauty & wellbeing New Year **Conf** Class 65 Board 40 Thtr 120 Del from £110 to £150 **Services** Lift **Parking** 50 **Notes** LB Civ Wed 120

C

CADNAM
Hampshire   Map 5 SU31

Bartley Lodge Hotel
★★★ 85% ◉ HOTEL   NEW FOREST HOTELS

☎ 023 8081 2248 & 0800 444 441
Lyndhurst Rd SO40 2NR
e-mail: bartley@newforesthotels.co.uk
web: www.newforesthotels.co.uk
dir: M27 junct 1 at 1st rdbt 1st exit, at 2nd rdbt 3rd
exit onto A337. Hotel sign on left

This 18th-century former hunting lodge is very quietly
situated, yet is just minutes from the M27. Bedrooms
vary in size but all are well equipped. There is a
selection of small lounge areas, a cosy bar and an
indoor pool, together with a small fitness suite. The
Crystal dining room offers a tempting choice of well
prepared dishes.

Rooms 40 (15 fmly) (4 GF) ⬩ S £119; **D** £197 (incl.
bkfst)* **Facilities** FTV Wi-fi ♗ HL ⬧ Sauna Xmas
New Year **Conf** Class 60 Board 60 Thtr 120
Del £141.60 **Parking** 60 **Notes** LB Civ Wed 80

CALNE
Wiltshire   Map 4 ST97

The Lansdowne Hotel
★★★ 64% HOTEL

☎ 01249 812488
The Strand SN11 0EH
e-mail: reservations@lansdownestrand.co.uk
dir: From Chippenham take A4 signed Calne. Straight
on at 2 rdbts, hotel in town centre

Situated in a picturesque market town, The
Lansdowne was built in the 16th century as a
coaching inn, and it still retains much of the charm
and character of that era. Bedrooms are spacious and
furnished in a traditional style. Guests can enjoy
dinner in the pleasant bistro, in either of the bar
areas, or choose from a varied room-service menu. An
outdoor courtyard seating area is also available.

Rooms 26 (2 fmly) ⬩ S £40-£55; **D** £65-£85 (incl.
bkfst)* **Facilities** FTV Wi-fi **Conf** Class 60 Board 50
Thtr 60 Del from £80 to £110* **Parking** 15 **Notes** ⊗
RS 25 Dec

CAMBER
East Sussex   Map 7 TQ91

The Gallivant Hotel
★★★ 75% ◉ HOTEL

☎ 01797 225057
New Lydd Rd TN31 7RB
e-mail: enquiries@thegallivanthotel.com
web: www.thegallivanthotel.com
dir: M29 junct 10 to A2070, left Camber Road before
Rye. Hotel located on left in Camber Village

The Gallivant Hotel is located right on the edge of
Camber Sands and just a short drive from the historic
town of Rye. Following a complete refurbishment this
hotel offers guests modern, coastal-styled
accommodation with light airy décor and
reconditioned driftwood furniture. Rooms are well
equipped and ideal for both business and leisure
guests. There is a bar and The Beach Bistro, an
award-wining restaurant that serves food daily. The
large function suite is open year round and is perfect
for parties or weddings. Guests can walk directly
opposite the hotel onto the sand dunes and beach.

Rooms 18 (4 fmly) (18 GF) S £115-£170;
D £115-£170 (incl. bkfst)* **Facilities** FTV Wi-fi ♗
Xmas New Year **Conf** Class 50 Board 30 Thtr 100
Del £220 **Parking** 20 **Notes** LB Civ Wed 150

CAMBERLEY
Surrey   Map 6 SU86

See also Yateley

Macdonald Frimley Hall
Hotel & Spa

★★★★ 80% ◉◉ HOTEL

☎ 0844 879 9110
Lime Av GU15 2BG
e-mail:
sales.frimleyhall@macdonald-hotels.co.uk
web: www.macdonaldhotels.co.uk/frimleyhall
dir: M3 junct 3, A321 follow Bagshot signs. Through
lights, left onto A30 signed Camberley & Basingstoke.
To rdbt, 2nd exit onto A325, take 5th right

The epitome of classic English elegance, Macdonald
Frimley Hall Hotel is an ivy-clad Victorian manor
house set in two acres of immaculate grounds in the
heart of Surrey. The bedrooms and public areas are
smart and have a modern decorative theme. The hotel
boasts an impressive health club and spa with
treatment rooms, a fully equipped gym and heated
indoor swimming pool. Macdonald Hotels is the AA
Hotel Group of the Year 2013-14.

Rooms 98 (15 fmly) ⬩ S £89-£179; **D** £99-£189*
Facilities Spa FTV Wi-fi ♗ HL ⬧ Gym Technogym

Sauna Steam room Relaxation room Xmas New Year
Conf Class 100 Board 60 Thtr 250 Del from £160 to
£240* **Parking** 150 **Notes** LB Civ Wed 220

Lakeside International
★★★ 73% HOTEL

☎ 01252 838000
Wharf Rd, Frimley Green GU16 6JR
e-mail: info@lakesideinthotel.com
dir: Exit A321 at mini-rdbt turn into Wharf Rd.
Lakeside complex on right

This hotel, geared towards the business market,
enjoys a lakeside location with noteworthy views.
Bedrooms are modern, comfortable and with a range
of facilities. Public areas are spacious and include a
residents' lounge, bar, games room, a smart
restaurant and an established health and leisure
club.

Rooms 98 (1 fmly) (31 GF) ⬩ S £74-£121;
D £84-£141 (incl. bkfst)* **Facilities** FTV Wi-fi ⬧ Gym
Squash Sauna Steam room **Conf** Class 100 Board 40
Thtr 120 **Services** Lift **Parking** 250 **Notes** LB ⊗
Civ Wed 100

The Ely
★★★ 70% HOTEL   OldEnglish

☎ 01252 860444
London Road (A30), Blackwater GU17 9LJ
e-mail: ely.yateley@newbridgeinns.co.uk
dir: M3 junct 4A, A327 towards Yateley. Right onto
A30

This establishment benefits from being conveniently
located close to Camberley and the M3. Bedrooms are
particularly spacious and families are well catered
for. A variety of enjoyable, substantial dishes are
available throughout the day with the addition of a
specials board in the evening. The range of options at
breakfast is impressive. There is ample free parking
on site and free Wi-fi throughout the hotel.

Rooms 35

Premier Inn Camberley
BUDGET HOTEL

☎ 0871 527 9322
Park St GU15 3SG
dir: M3 junct 4, A331 towards Camberley. In 2m, at
major junct into right lane, 4th exit signed A30. For
parking, in 1m, right into Southern Rd for Atrium Car
Park

High quality, budget accommodation ideal for both
families and business travellers. Spacious, en suite
bedrooms feature tea and coffee making facilities,
and Freeview TV in most hotels. Internet access and
Wi-fi are available for a small fee. The adjacent

family restaurant features a wide and varied menu. See also the Hotel Groups pages.

Rooms 95

Premier Inn Sandhurst
BUDGET HOTEL

☎ 0871 527 8958
221 Yorktown Rd, College Town, Sandurst GU47 0RT
web: www.premierinn.com
dir: M3 junct 4, A331 to Camberley. At large rdbt take A321 towards Bracknell. At 3rd lights, hotel on left

Rooms 40

CAMBORNE   Map 2 SW63
Cornwall

Premier Inn Camborne
BUDGET HOTEL

☎ 0871 527 9308
Treswithian Rd TR14 7NF
dir: From M5 (S) junct 31, A30 to Bodmin, then to Redruth, follow signs to Camborne. Left onto A3047, to rdbt, 1st exit to hotel

High quality, budget accommodation ideal for both families and business travellers. Spacious, en suite bedrooms feature tea and coffee making facilities, and Freeview TV in most hotels. Internet access and Wi-fi are available for a small fee. The adjacent family restaurant features a wide and varied menu. See also the Hotel Groups pages.

Rooms 65

CAMBOURNE   Map 12 TL35
Cambridgeshire

The Cambridge Belfry
★★★★ 80% HOTEL

☎ 01954 714600
Back St CB3 6BW
e-mail: cambridgebelfry@qhotels.co.uk
web: www.qhotels.co.uk
dir: M11 junct 13, A428 towards Bedford, follow signs to Cambourne. Exit at Cambourne, keep left. Left at rdbt, hotel on left

This exciting hotel, built beside the water, is located at the gateway to Cambourne Village and Business Park. Contemporary in style throughout, the hotel boasts state-of-the-art leisure facilities, including Reflections Spa offering a range of therapies and treatments, and extensive conference and banqueting rooms. There are two eating options - the Bridge Restaurant and the Brooks Brasserie. Original artwork is displayed throughout the hotel.

Rooms 120 (30 GF) ✎ **Facilities** Spa FTV Wi-fi ⚐ HL 🕲 ♨ Gym Beauty treatments Xmas New Year **Conf** Class 70 Board 70 Thtr 250 **Services** Lift **Parking** 200 **Notes** Civ Wed 200

CAMBRIDGE   Map 12 TL45
Cambridgeshire

Hotel Felix
★★★★ 80% ◉◉ HOTEL

☎ 01223 277977
Whitehouse Ln CB3 0LX
e-mail: help@hotelfelix.co.uk
web: www.hotelfelix.co.uk
dir: M11 junct 13. From A1 N, take A14 onto A1307. At 'City of Cambridge' sign left into Whitehouse Ln

A beautiful Victorian mansion set amidst three acres of landscaped gardens, this property was originally built in 1852 for a surgeon from the famous Addenbrookes Hospital. The contemporary-style bedrooms have carefully chosen furniture and many thoughtful touches, whilst public rooms feature an open-plan bar, the adjacent Graffiti restaurant and a small quiet lounge.

Rooms 52 (5 fmly) (26 GF) ✎ **S** £170-£210; **D** £205-£320 (incl. bkfst)* **Facilities** STV Wi-fi ⚐ Xmas New Year **Conf** Class 36 Board 34 Thtr 60 **Services** Lift **Parking** 90 **Notes** LB Civ Wed 60

Hotel du Vin Cambridge
★★★★ 77% ◉
TOWN HOUSE HOTEL

☎ 01223 227330
15-19 Trumpington St CB2 1QA
e-mail: info.cambridge@hotelduvin.com
web: www.hotelduvin.com
dir: M11 junct 11 Cambridge S, pass Trumpington Park & Ride on left. Hotel 2m on right after double rdbt

This beautiful building, which dates back in part to medieval times, has been transformed to enhance its many quirky architectural features. The bedrooms and suites, some with private terraces, have the company's trademark monsoon showers and Egyptian linen. The French-style bistro has an open-style kitchen and the bar is set in the unusual labyrinth of

vaulted cellar rooms. There is also a library, specialist wine tasting room and private dining room.

Rooms 41 (3 annexe) (6 GF) **Facilities** STV Wi-fi Xmas New Year **Conf** Class 18 Board 18 Thtr 30 **Services** Lift Air con **Parking** 24

C

Menzies Cambridge Hotel & Golf Club   MenziesHotels
★★★★ 77% ◉ HOTEL

☎ 01954 249988
Bar Hill CB23 8EU
e-mail: cambridge@menzieshotels.co.uk
web: www.menzieshotels.co.uk
dir: M11 junct 13, A14, follow signs for Huntingdon. Take B1050 (Bar Hill), hotel 1st exit on rdbt

The Menzies Cambridge Hotel is ideally situated amidst 200 acres of open countryside, just five miles from the university city of Cambridge. Public rooms include a brasserie restaurant and the popular Gallery Bar. The contemporary-style bedrooms are smartly decorated and equipped with a good range of useful facilities. The hotel also has a leisure club, swimming pool and golf course.

Rooms 136 (35 fmly) (68 GF) (12 smoking) **Facilities** STV Wi-fi ⚐ 🕲 ♨ 18 ♨ Putt green Gym Hair & beauty salon Steam room Sauna Xmas New Year **Conf** Class 90 Board 45 Thtr 200 **Services** Lift **Parking** 200 **Notes** Civ Wed 200

BEST WESTERN PLUS The Gonville Hotel
★★★★ 76% HOTEL

☎ 01223 366611 & 221111
Gonville Place CB1 1LY
e-mail: all@gonvillehotel.co.uk
web: www.gonvillehotel.co.uk
dir: M11 junct 11, on A1309 follow city centre signs. At mini rdbt right into Lensfield Rd, over junct with lights. Hotel 25yds on right

This is a well-established hotel situated on the inner ring road, a short walk across the green from the city centre. The air-conditioned public areas are cheerfully furnished, and include a lounge bar and brasserie. Bedrooms are well appointed and appealing, offering a good range of facilities for both corporate and leisure guests.

Rooms 80 (2 fmly) (8 GF) ✎ **S** £76.30-£204; **D** £83.30-£229 (incl. bkfst)* **Facilities** FTV Wi-fi ⚐ HL New Year **Conf** Class 30 Board 30 Thtr 50 **Services** Lift Air con **Parking** 80 **Notes** LB RS 24-29 Dec Civ Wed 50

C

CAMBRIDGE *continued*

The Varsity Hotel & Spa

★★★★ 76% HOTEL

☎ 01223 306030
Thompson's Ln CB5 8AQ
e-mail: info@thevarsityhotel.co.uk
dir: M11 junct 13, pass Park & Ride, next rdbt 1st left, right at next junct into Bridge St, right into Thompou's Lane

Situated close to the River Cam and occupying a central location, The Varsity Hotel is a stylish property. The bedrooms are smartly decorated and have all the expected facilities including power showers, CD players and free internet access. The River Bar, to the side of the hotel, has a buzzing atmosphere and offers a range of popular dishes. The hotel has a health club and spa and a roof top bar.

Rooms 48 (2 fmly) ✎ **S** £110-£390; **D** £120-£590 (incl. bkfst)* **Facilities** Spa FTV Wi-fi ☝ Gym Sauna Steam room Valet parking New Year **Conf** Class 40 Board 30 Thtr 60 **Services** Lift Air con **Notes** Civ Wed 60

Cambridge City Hotel

★★★★ 75% HOTEL

☎ 01223 464491
20 Downing St CB2 3DT
web: www.cambridgecityhotel.co.uk
dir: From M11 (either junct 11, 12 or 13). Follow signs to city centre then Grand Arcade car park. Hotel adjacent. Or from A14 take Cambridge exit, onto Huntingdon Rd, follow one-way system

Located in the heart of the city, this hotel enjoys an enviable position, with many of the universities and the town centre within easy walking distance. It is located adjacent to the Grand Arcade shopping centre, and on-site parking, although limited, is a plus. The hotel offers modern accommodation and large open-plan public areas; a fitness room and several conference rooms are also available.

Rooms 198 **Facilities** STV Wi-fi ☝ HL Gym Sauna New Year **Conf** Class 70 Board 50 Thtr 250 **Services** Lift Air con **Parking** 70 **Notes** ⊗ Civ Wed 250

BEST WESTERN PLUS
Cambridge Quy Mill Hotel

★★★ 84% ◉◉ HOTEL

☎ 01223 293383 & 378118
Church Rd, Stow Cum Quy CB25 9AF
e-mail: info@cambridgequymill.co.uk
web: www.cambridgequymill.co.uk
dir: Exit A14 at junct 35, E of Cambridge, onto B1102 for 50yds. Entrance opposite church

Set in open countryside, this 19th-century former watermill is conveniently situated for access to Cambridge. Bedroom styles differ, yet each room is smartly appointed and brightly decorated; superior, spacious courtyard rooms are noteworthy. Well-designed public areas include several spacious bar/lounges, with a choice of casual and formal eating areas; service is both friendly and helpful. There is a smart leisure club with state-of-the-art equipment, as well as a health spa.

Rooms 51 (30 annexe) (1 fmly) (24 GF) ✎ **Facilities** Spa FTV Wi-fi ☝ HL ☁ Gym New Year **Conf** Class 30 Board 24 Thtr 80 **Parking** 90 **Notes** Closed 24-25 Dec RS 26 Dec Civ Wed 80

Arundel House Hotel

★★★ 81% HOTEL

☎ 01223 367701
Chesterton Rd CB4 3AN
e-mail: info@arundelhousehotels.co.uk
web: www.arundelhousehotels.co.uk
dir: In city centre on A1303

Overlooking the River Cam and enjoying views of open parkland, this popular and smart hotel was originally a row of townhouses dating from Victorian times. Bedrooms are attractive and have a special character. The smart public areas feature a conservatory for informal snacks, a spacious bar and an elegant restaurant for more serious dining.

Rooms 103 (22 annexe) (7 fmly) (14 GF) **S** £75-£115; **D** £95-£145 (incl. bkfst)* **Facilities** FTV Wi-fi ☝ New Year **Conf** Class 24 Board 22 Thtr 50 Del from £145* **Parking** 70 **Notes** LB ⊗ Closed 25-26 Dec

Holiday Inn Cambridge

★★★ 79% HOTEL

☎ 0871 942 9015
Lakeview, Bridge Rd, Impington CB24 9PH
e-mail: reservations-cambridge@ihg.com
web: www.hicambridgehotel.co.uk
dir: 2.5m N, on N side of rdbt junct A14 & B1049

A modern, purpose-built hotel conveniently situated just off the A14 junction, a short drive from the city centre. Public areas include a popular bar, the Junction Restaurant and a large open-plan lounge. Bedrooms come in a variety of styles and are suited to both business and leisure guests alike.

Rooms 161 (14 fmly) (75 GF) **S** £90-£195; **D** £95-£195* **Facilities** Spa STV Wi-fi ☝ HL ☁ supervised Gym **Conf** Class 40 Board 45 Thtr 120 Del from £110 to £180* **Services** Air con **Parking** 175 **Notes** LB ⊗ Civ Wed 100

The Lensfield Hotel

★★★ 77% METRO HOTEL

☎ 01223 355017
53-57 Lensfield Rd CB2 1EN
e-mail: reservations@lensfieldhotel.co.uk
web: www.lensfieldhotel.co.uk
dir: M11 juncts 11,12 or 13, follow signs to city centre. Access via Silver St, Trumpington St, left into Lensfield Rd

Located close to all the city's attractions, this constantly improving hotel provides a range of attractive bedrooms, equipped with thoughtful extras. Comprehensive breakfasts are taken in an elegant dining room and a comfortable bar and cosy foyer lounge are also available.

Rooms 28 (3 fmly) (4 GF) **S** £72-£120; **D** £110-£132 (incl. bkfst)* **Facilities** Spa STV FTV Wi-fi ☝ HL Fitness suite **Services** Air con **Parking** 5 **Notes** LB ⊗ Closed last 2 wks in Dec-4 Jan

Centennial Hotel

★★★ 71% HOTEL

☎ 01223 314652
63-71 Hills Rd CB2 1PG
e-mail: reception@centennialhotel.co.uk
dir: M11 junct 11, A1309 to Cambridge. Right Into Brooklands Ave to end. Left, hotel 100yds on right

This friendly hotel is convenient for the railway station and town centre. Well-presented public areas include a welcoming lounge, a relaxing bar and restaurant on the lower-ground level. Bedrooms are generally spacious, well maintained and thoughtfully equipped with a good range of facilities; several rooms are available on the ground floor.

Rooms 39 (1 fmly) (7 GF) 🐾 **Facilities** FTV Wi-fi 🐾
Conf Class 25 Board 25 Thtr 25 **Parking** 28 **Notes** ⊗
Closed 23 Dec-1 Jan

Ashley Hotel

★★ 81% METRO HOTEL

☎ 01223 350059 & 367701
74-76 Chesterton Rd CB4 1ER
e-mail: info@arundelhousehotels.co.uk
dir: On city centre ring road

Expect a warm welcome at this delightful Victorian
property situated just a short walk from the River
Cam. The smartly decorated bedrooms are generally
quite spacious and equipped with a good range of
useful extras. Breakfast is served at individual tables
in the smart lower ground floor dining room.

Rooms 16 (5 fmly) (5 GF) **S** £75-£95; **D** £75-£95 (incl.
bkfst)* **Facilities** FTV Wi-fi 🐾 **Parking** 12 **Notes** ⊗
Closed 24-26 Dec

Helen Hotel

★★ 80% METRO HOTEL

☎ 01223 246465
167-169 Hills Rd CB2 2RJ
e-mail: enquiries@helenhotel.co.uk
dir: On A1307, 1.25m from city centre (south side). At
Cherry-Hinton Rd junct, opposite Homerton College

This extremely well maintained, privately owned hotel
is situated close to the city centre and a range of
popular eateries. Public areas include a smart lounge
bar with plush sofas and a cosy breakfast room.
Bedrooms are pleasantly decorated with co-ordinated
fabrics and have many thoughtful touches.

Rooms 19 (2 fmly) (2 GF) **Facilities** STV Wi-fi
Parking 12 **Notes** ⊗ Closed Xmas & New Year

Premier Inn Cambridge (A14 Jct 32)

BUDGET HOTEL

☎ 0871 527 8186
Ring Fort Rd CB4 2GW
web: www.premierinn.com
dir: A14 junct 32, follow B1049/city centre signs. At
1st lights left into Kings Hedges Rd, 2nd left into
Ring Fort Rd

High quality, budget accommodation ideal for both
families and business travellers. Spacious, en suite
bedrooms feature tea and coffee making facilities,
and Freeview TV in most hotels. Internet access and
Wi-fi are available for a small fee. The adjacent
family restaurant features a wide and varied menu.
See also the Hotel Groups pages.

Rooms 154

CANNOCK   Map 10 SJ91
Staffordshire

Premier Inn Cannock (Orbital)

BUDGET HOTEL

☎ 0871 527 8190
Eastern Way WS11 8XR
web: www.premierinn.com
dir: N'bound: M6 (Toll) junct 7, A5. At rdbt 1st exit
(A5), 4th exit onto A460, 1st exit. S'bound: (no access
from M6 Toll). M6 junct 11, A460 signed Cannock. At
next 2 rdbts take 3rd exit. At next rdbt 1st exit onto
service road. Hotel adjacent to Orbital Brewers Fayre

High quality, budget accommodation ideal for both
families and business travellers. Spacious, en suite
bedrooms feature tea and coffee making facilities,
and Freeview TV in most hotels. Internet access and
Wi-fi are available for a small fee. The adjacent
family restaurant features a wide and varied menu.
See also the Hotel Groups pages.

Rooms 21

Premier Inn Cannock South

BUDGET HOTEL

☎ 0871 527 8192
Watling St WS11 1SJ
web: www.premierinn.com
dir: At junct of A5 & A460, 2m from M6 juncts 11 &
12

Rooms 60

CANTERBURY   Map 7 TR15
Kent

Castle House

★★★ 71% METRO HOTEL

☎ 01227 761897
28 Castle St CT1 2PT
dir: Next to Canterbury Castle

Conveniently located in the city centre opposite the
imposing ruins of the ancient Norman castle; part of
the building dates back to the 1730s. Bedrooms are
spacious, all with en suite facilities and many useful
extras, such as Wi-fi. There is a walled garden in
which to relax during the warmer months.

Rooms 15 **S** £65-£120; **D** £70-£180*

Holiday Inn Express Canterbury

BUDGET HOTEL

☎ 01227 865000
A2 Dover Rd, Upper Harbledown CT2 9HX
e-mail: operations@exbhi-canterbury.co.uk
web: www.hiexpresscanterbury.co.uk
dir: M2 junct 7, take A2 towards Dover. 4m. Hotel
access via Texaco service area

A modern hotel ideal for families and business
travellers. Fresh and uncomplicated, the spacious
rooms include Sky TV, power shower and tea and
coffee-making facilities. Continental buffet breakfast
is included in the room rate; other meals may be
taken at the nearby family pub or restaurant. See also
the Hotel Groups pages.

Rooms 89 (38 GF) **S** £55-£125; **D** £55-£125 (incl.
bkfst)* **Conf** Class 20 Board 10 Thtr 36

CARBIS BAY

See St Ives (Cornwall)

CARLISLE   Map 18 NY35
Cumbria

Hallmark Hotel Carlisle

★★★★ 74% HOTEL

☎ 01228 531951 & 633503
Court Square CA1 1QY
e-mail: carlisle.reservations@hallmarkhotels.co.uk
dir: M6 junct 43, to city centre, then follow road to left
& railway station

This hotel is at the heart of the town, opposite the
railway station. Most of the bedrooms have benefited
from an investment programme, and the smart
ground-floor areas include a popular bar and
restaurant. A number of meeting rooms are available
and at the rear of the hotel is a small car park.

Rooms 70 (3 fmly) 🐾 **Facilities** FTV Wi-fi Xmas New
Year **Conf** Class 100 Board 30 Thtr 240 **Services** Lift
Parking 26 **Notes** ⊗ Civ Wed 200

C

C

CARLISLE *continued*

Crown Hotel

★★★ 83% ⊛ HOTEL

☎ 01228 561888
Station Rd, Wetheral CA4 8ES
e-mail: info@crownhotelwetheral.co.uk
web: www.crownhotelwetheral.co.uk
dir: M6 junct 42, B6263 to Wetheral, right at village shop, car park at rear of hotel

Set in the attractive village of Wetheral, with landscaped gardens to the rear, this hotel is well suited to both business and leisure guests. Bedrooms vary in size and style and include two apartments in an adjacent house ideal for long stays. A choice of dining options is available, with the popular Waltons Bar an informal alternative to the main restaurant.

Rooms 51 (2 annexe) (10 fmly) (3 GF) ☔
Facilities Spa STV Wi-fi HL ⓢ supervised Gym Squash Children's splash pool Steam room Beauty room Sauna Dance studio Xmas New Year
Conf Class 90 Board 50 Thtr 175 **Parking** 55
Notes Civ Wed 120

The Crown & Mitre

★★★ 72% HOTEL

PEEL HOTELS PLC

☎ 01228 525491
4 English St CA3 8HZ
e-mail: info@crownandmitre-hotel-carlisle.com
web: www.crownandmitre-hotel-carlisle.com
dir: A6 to city centre, pass station on left. Right into Blackfriars St. Rear entrance at end

Located in the heart of the city, this Edwardian hotel is close to the cathedral and a few minutes' walk from the castle. Bedrooms vary in size and style, from smart executive rooms to more functional standard rooms. Public rooms include a comfortable lounge area and the lovely bar with its feature stained-glass windows.

Rooms 95 (20 annexe) (4 fmly) (11 smoking) ☔
S £60-£75; **D** £70-£100* **Facilities** STV FTV Wi-fi ↕ ⓢ Xmas New Year **Conf** Class 250 Board 50 Thtr 400 **Del** from £100 to £140* **Services** Lift **Parking** 42 **Notes** Civ Wed 200

Ibis Carlisle

BUDGET HOTEL

ibis

☎ 01228 518000
Portlands, Botchergate CA1 1RP
e-mail: H3443@accor.com
web: www.ibis.com
dir: M6 junct 42/43 follow signs for city centre. Hotel on Botchergate

Modern, budget hotel offering comfortable accommodation in bright and practical bedrooms. Breakfast is self-service and dinner is available in the restaurant See also the Hotel Groups pages.

Rooms 102 (17 fmly) ☔

Premier Inn Carlisle Central

BUDGET HOTEL

Premier Inn

☎ 0871 527 8210
Warwick Rd CA1 2WF
web: www.premierinn.com
dir: M6 junct 43, on A69

High quality, budget accommodation ideal for both families and business travellers. Spacious, en suite bedrooms feature tea and coffee making facilities, and Freeview TV in most hotels. Internet access and Wi-fi are available for a small fee. The adjacent family restaurant features a wide and varied menu. See also the Hotel Groups pages.

Rooms 44

Premier Inn Carlisle Central North

BUDGET HOTEL

☎ 0871 527 8212
Kingstown Rd CA3 0AT
web: www.premierinn.com
dir: M6 junct 44, A7 towards Carlisle, hotel 1m on left

Rooms 49

Premier Inn Carlisle (M6 Jct 42)

BUDGET HOTEL

☎ 0871 527 8206
Carleton CA4 0AD
web: www.premierinn.com
dir: Just off M6 junct 42, S of Carlisle

Rooms 61

Premier Inn Carlisle (M6 Jct 44)

BUDGET HOTEL

☎ 0871 527 8208
Parkhouse Rd CA3 0HR
web: www.premierinn.com
dir: M6 junct 44, A7 signed Carlisle. Hotel on right at 1st set of lights

Rooms 127

CARTMEL	**Map 18 SD37**
Cumbria	

Aynsome Manor Hotel

★★★ 81% ⊛ COUNTRY HOUSE HOTEL

☎ 015395 36653
LA11 6HH
e-mail: aynsomemanor@btconnect.com
dir: M6 junct 36, A590 signed Barrow-in-Furness towards Cartmel. Left at end of road, hotel before village

Dating back, in part, to the early 16th century, this manor house overlooks the fells and the nearby priory. Spacious bedrooms, including some courtyard rooms, are comfortably furnished. Dinner in the elegant restaurant features local produce whenever possible, and there is a choice of lounges to relax in.

Rooms 12 (2 annexe) (2 fmly) ☔ **S** £80-£95; **D** £90-£125 (incl. bkfst) **Facilities** FTV Wi-fi New Year **Parking** 20 **Notes** LB Closed 2-31 Jan RS Sun

INSPECTORS' CHOICE

L'enclume

◎ ◎ ◎ ◎ ◎ RESTAURANT WITH ROOMS

☎ 015395 36362
Cavendish St LA11 6PZ
e-mail: info@lenclume.co.uk
dir: From A590 turn left for Cartmel before Newby Bridge

L'enclume is a delightful 13th-century property in the heart of a lovely village offering 21st-century cooking that makes it a definite destination for foodies. Simon Rogan cooks imaginative and adventurous food in this stylish restaurant. Individually designed, modern, en suite rooms vary in size and style, and are either in the main property or dotted about the village only a few moments' walk from the restaurant.

Rooms 17 (11 annexe) (3 fmly)

CASTLE CARY
Somerset   Map 4 ST63

The George Hotel

★★ 65% HOTEL

☎ 01963 350761
Market Place BA7 7AH
e-mail: castlecarygeorge@aol.co.uk
dir: A303 onto A371. Signed Castle Cary, 2m on left

This 15th-century coaching inn provides well-equipped bedrooms that are, in general, spacious. Most rooms are at the back of the house and therefore enjoy a quiet aspect; some are on the ground floor and one is suitable for less able guests. Diners can choose to eat in the more formal dining room, or in one of the two cosy bars.

Rooms 17 (5 annexe) (1 fmly) (5 GF) 🐾
Facilities Wi-fi ᑫ Xmas New Year **Conf** Class 40 Board 20 Thtr 50 **Parking** 7 **Notes** LB

The Pilgrims

◎ RESTAURANT WITH ROOMS

☎ 01963 240600
Lovington BA7 7PT
e-mail: jools@thepilgrimsatlovington.co.uk
web: www.thepilgrimsatlovington.co.uk
dir: On B3153, 1.5m E of lights on A37 at Lydford

This popular establishment describes itself as 'the pub that thinks it's a restaurant', which is pretty accurate. With a real emphasis on fresh, local and carefully prepared produce, both dinner and breakfast are the focus of any stay here. In addition, the resident family proprietors provide a friendly and relaxed atmosphere. Comfortable and well-equipped bedrooms are available in the adjacent, converted cider barn.

Rooms 5 (5 annexe)

CASTLE COMBE
Wiltshire   Map 4 ST87

Manor House Hotel and Golf Club

★★★★★ 83% ◎ ◎ ◎
COUNTRY HOUSE HOTEL

☎ 01249 782206
SN14 7HR
e-mail: enquiries@manorhouse.co.uk
web: www.manorhouse.co.uk
dir: M4 junct 17 follow Chippenham signs onto A420 Bristol, then right onto B4039. Through village, right after bridge. Useful to follow brown tourism signs to Castle Combe Racing Circuit

This delightful hotel is situated in a secluded valley adjacent to a picturesque village, where there have been no new buildings for 300 years. There are 365 acres of grounds to enjoy, complete with an Italian garden and an 18-hole golf course. Bedrooms, some in the main house and some in a row of stone cottages, have been superbly furnished, and public rooms include a number of cosy lounges with roaring fires. Service is a pleasing blend of professionalism

---

and friendliness. The award-winning food utilises top quality local produce.

Rooms 48 (26 annexe) (8 fmly) (12 GF) 🐾
D £205-£650* **Facilities** STV Wi-fi ᑫ 18 ⛳ Putt green Fishing ⚓ Jogging track Hot air ballooning Giant games on lawns Xmas New Year **Conf** Class 84 Board 40 Thtr 120 **Del** £320* **Parking** 100
Notes Civ Wed 110

CASTLE DONINGTON

See **East Midlands Airport**

CASTLEFORD
West Yorkshire   Map 16 SE42

Premier Inn Castleford M62 Jct 31

BUDGET HOTEL

☎ 0871 527 8216
Pioneer Way WF10 5TG
web: www.premierinn.com
dir: M62 junct 31, A655 towards Castleford, right at 1st lights, then left

High quality, budget accommodation ideal for both families and business travellers. Spacious, en suite bedrooms feature tea and coffee making facilities, and Freeview TV in most hotels. Internet access and Wi-fi are available for a small fee. The adjacent family restaurant features a wide and varied menu. See also the Hotel Groups pages.

Rooms 62

Premier Inn Castleford M62 Jct 32

BUDGET HOTEL

☎ 0871 527 8218
Colarado Way WF10 4TA
web: www.premierinn.com
dir: M62 junct 32, follow signs for Xscape. Hotel adjacent to Xscape complex

Rooms 119

C

CAVENDISH
Suffolk   Map 13 TL84

The George
⊛ RESTAURANT WITH ROOMS

☎ 01787 280248
The Green CO10 8BA
e-mail: thegeorgecavendish@gmail.com
web: www.thecavendishgeorge.co.uk
dir: A1092 into Cavendish, The George next to village green

The George is situated in the heart of the pretty village of Cavendish and has five very stylish bedrooms. The front-facing rooms overlook the village; the comfortable, spacious bedrooms retain many of their original features. The award-winning restaurant is very well appointed and dinner should not be missed. Guests are guaranteed to receive a warm welcome, attentive friendly service and great food.

Rooms 5 (1 fmly)

CHADDESLEY CORBETT
Worcestershire   Map 10 SO87

INSPECTORS' CHOICE

Brockencote Hall Country House Hotel

★★★★ ⊛⊛⊛ COUNTRY HOUSE HOTEL

☎ 01562 777876
DY10 4PY
e-mail: info@brockencotehall.com
web: www.brockencotehall.com
dir: A38 to Bromsgrove, off A448 towards Kidderminster

Glorious countryside extends all around this magnificent mansion, and grazing sheep can be seen from the conservatory. Not surprisingly, relaxation comes high on the list of priorities here. Despite its very English location the hotel's owner actually hails from Alsace and the atmosphere is very much that of a provincial French château. The spacious, chandeliered dining room is a popular venue for accomplished classical French cuisine which has modern British influences.

Rooms 21 (4 fmly) (5 GF) ☏ **Facilities** FTV Wi-fi ⇘ ⛲ Fishing ⛄ Xmas New Year **Conf** Class 35 Board 35 Thtr 80 **Parking** 60 **Notes** ⊗ Civ Wed 95

CHAGFORD
Devon   Map 3 SX78

INSPECTORS' CHOICE

Gidleigh Park
★★★★★ ⊛⊛⊛⊛⊛
COUNTRY HOUSE HOTEL

☎ 01647 432367
TQ13 8HH
e-mail: gidleighpark@gidleigh.co.uk
web: www.gidleigh.com
dir: From Chagford, right at Lloyds Bank into Mill St. After 150yds fork right. 2m to end

Built in 1928 as a private residence for an Australian shipping magnate and set in 107 acres of lovingly tended grounds, this world-renowned hotel retains a timeless charm and a very endearing, homely atmosphere. The individually styled bedrooms are sumptuously furnished; some with separate seating areas, some with balconies and many enjoying panoramic views. There are spa suites, a loft suite which is ideal for families, and the stunning thatched Pavilion in the grounds. The latter has two bedrooms, two bathrooms, a lounge and kitchen diner. The spacious public areas feature antique furniture, beautiful flower arrangements and magnificent artwork. The award-winning cuisine created by Michael Caines, together with the top quality wine list, will make a stay here a truly memorable experience.

Rooms 24 (4 fmly) (4 GF) ☏ **S** £320-£1170; **D** £345-£1195 (incl. bkfst)* **Facilities** STV FTV Wi-fi ⛲ Putt green Fishing ⛄ Bowls Xmas New Year **Conf** Class 22 Board 18 Thtr 22 **Parking** 45 **Notes** LB

C

CHARD
Somerset   Map 4 ST30

Cricket St Thomas Hotel   Warner Leisure Hotels
                                      JUST FOR GROWN-UPS

★★★★ 72% @ COUNTRY HOUSE HOTEL

☎ 01460 30111
TA20 4DD
e-mail: cricket.sales@bourne-leisure.co.uk
dir: M5 junct 25, A358 towards Chard, A30 to
Crewkerne. Hotel 3m from Chard

This Grade II listed house has an interesting history
including the fact that Lord Nelson and Lady
Hamilton were frequent visitors. The hotel is set in
splendid parkland, with colourful gardens, lakes, and
a unique woodland area. Various holiday packages
are available, and there are extensive leisure
facilities, as well as live entertainment and various
dining venues, including Fenocchi's, with an Italian-
themed menu. The bedrooms are spacious and well
appointed. Please note that this is an adults-only
(over 21 years) hotel.

Rooms 239 (84 GF) ➧ **Facilities** Spa FTV Wi-fi HL ⊗
➧ Putt green ⊛ Gym Rifle shooting Archery ♫ Xmas
New Year **Conf** Class 50 Board 25 Thtr 80
Services Lift **Parking** 351 **Notes** ⊗ No children 18yrs
Civ Wed 80

Lordleaze Hotel   THE INDEPENDENTS
                             HOTEL ASSOCIATION

★★★ 77% HOTEL

☎ 01460 61066
Henderson Dr, Forton Rd TA20 2HW
e-mail: info@lordleazehotel.com
web: www.lordleazehotel.com
dir: A358 from Chard, left at St Mary's Church to
Forton & Winsham on B3162. Follow signs to hotel

Conveniently and quietly located, this hotel is close to
the Devon, Dorset and Somerset borders, and only
minutes from Chard. All bedrooms are well equipped
and comfortable. The friendly lounge bar has a wood-
burning stove and serves tempting bar meals. The
conservatory restaurant offers more formal dining.

Rooms 25 (2 fmly) (7 GF) ➧ **Facilities** FTV Wi-fi Xmas
New Year **Conf** Class 60 Board 40 Thtr 180
Parking 55 **Notes** Civ Wed 100

CHARINGWORTH
Gloucestershire   Map 10 SP13

Charingworth Manor Hotel   CLASSIC
                                       LODGES
                                       the sign of a great hotel

★★★★ 75% @
COUNTRY HOUSE HOTEL

☎ 01386 593555
Charingworth Manor GL55 6NS
e-mail:
gm.charingworthmanor@classiclodges.co.uk
web: www.classiclodges.co.uk/charingworthmanor

This 14th-century manor house retains many original
features including flagstone floors, exposed beams
and open fireplaces. The house has a beautiful
setting in 50 acres of grounds and has been carefully
extended to provide high quality accommodation and
a delightful, small leisure facility. Spacious bedrooms
are furnished with period pieces and modern
amenities.

Rooms 26 (18 annexe) (2 fmly) (12 GF) **Facilities** ⊗
➩ ⊛ Gym Sauna Steam room Solarium Xmas New
Year **Conf** Class 30 Board 40 Thtr 80 **Parking** 50
Notes Civ Wed 60

CHARMOUTH
Dorset   Map 4 SY39

Fernhill Hotel

★★★ 81% HOTEL

☎ 01297 560492
Fernhill DT6 6BX
e-mail: mail@fernhill-hotel.co.uk
web: www.fernhill-hotel.co.uk
dir: A35 onto A3052 to Lyme Regis. Hotel 0.25m on
left

Fernhill is a small, friendly hotel on top of a hill in
well-tended grounds. It boasts an outdoor pool and
treatment rooms, together with elegant public areas.
Each of the comfortable bedrooms is individually
styled and many have views of the Char Valley and
beyond. The menus are based on seasonal, locally
sourced produce.

Rooms 10 (1 fmly) ➧ **S** £90-£140; **D** £120-£170
(incl. bkfst)* **Facilities** FTV Wi-fi ⊗ ⊰ Fishing
Holistic treatment centre Air/Massage baths Xmas
Child facilities **Conf** Class 20 Board 24 Thtr 60
Del from £168 to £237.50* **Parking** 30 **Notes** LB ⊗
Closed 31 Dec-30 Jan Civ Wed 100

CHARNOCK RICHARD
MOTORWAY SERVICE AREA (M6)
Lancashire   Map 15 SD51

Days Inn Charnock Richard - M6
                                            Welcome
                                            Break

BUDGET HOTEL

☎ 01257 791746
Welcome Break Service Area PR7 5LR
e-mail: charnockhotel@welcomebreak.co.uk
web: www.welcomebreak.co.uk
dir: Between junct 27 & 28 of M6 N'bound. 500yds
from Camelot Theme Park via Mill Lane

This modern building offers accommodation in smart,
spacious and well-equipped bedrooms, suitable for
families and business travellers, and all with en suite
bathrooms. Continental breakfast is available and
other refreshments may be taken at the nearby family
restaurant. See also the Hotel Groups pages.

Rooms 100 (68 fmly) (32 GF) (20 smoking)
Conf Class 16 Board 24 Thtr 40

CHATHAM
Kent   Map 7 TQ76

Holiday Inn Rochester - Chatham
                                             Holiday Inn

★★★ 78% HOTEL

☎ 0871 942 9069 & 07736 746421
Maidstone Rd ME5 9SF
e-mail: christopher.ross@ihg.com
web: www.hirochesterhotel.co.uk
dir: M2 junct 3 or M20 junct 6, then A229 for
Chatham

A modern, well-equipped hotel close to Rochester,
Canterbury and the historic Chatham Dockyards.
Bedrooms, including family rooms, are comfortable
and spacious; all have air conditioning and
broadband access. Public facilities include a lounge,
bar and modern restaurant. There is a gym, indoor
pool, sauna, spa and an impressive self-contained
conference centre.

Rooms 149 (29 fmly) (53 GF) (16 smoking)
Facilities STV FTV Wi-fi ⊗ ⊗ supervised Gym Beauty
treatment room Steam room Sauna Pilates & beauty
evenings **Conf** Class 45 Board 45 Thtr 100
Services Lift Air con **Parking** 200 **Notes** ⊗
Civ Wed 100

C

CHATHAM *continued*

Ramada Encore Chatham

★★★ 70% HOTEL

☎ 01634 891677
Western Av, Chatham Historic Dockyard ME4 4NT
e-mail: operations@encorechatham.co.uk
web: www.encorechatham.co.uk
dir: Follow signs for Chatham Historic Dockyard

Located in the historic dockyard and just minutes from the town centre, this hotel offers stylish, comfortable accommodation. The smart open-plan bar and restaurant are modern in design and provide a choice of seating areas; a full menu is on offer all day and in the evening. Free Wi-fi is available throughout the public areas, and there is a meeting room.

Rooms 90 (14 fmly) (8 smoking) 🐾 **Facilities** STV FTV Wi-fi HL **Conf** Class 12 Board 12 Thtr 20 **Services** Lift Air con **Parking** 60 **Notes** ⊗

INSPECTORS' CHOICE

Doxford Hall Hotel & Spa

★★★★ ◉◉ COUNTRY HOUSE HOTEL

☎ 01665 589700 & 589707
NE67 5DN
e-mail: info@doxfordhall.com
dir: 8m N of Alnwick just off A1, signed Christon Bank & Seahouses. Take B6347 follow signs for hotel

A beautiful country-house hotel set in a private estate, surrounded by countryside and convenient for visiting nearby historic towns and attractions. Bedrooms are spacious and luxuriously furnished, each named after Northumbrian Castles. The dining room and lounges are very attractive. There is an impressive grand staircase and beautiful wood throughout the hotel. The spa adds to the range of facilities.

Rooms 31 (1 fmly) (11 GF) 🐾 **S** £80-£200; **D** £125-£280 (incl. bkfst)* **Facilities** Spa FTV Wi-fi ➘ HL 🐾 supervised Gym Sauna Steam room Spa bath Xmas New Year **Conf** Class 100 Board 22 Thtr 250 Del from £140 to £160* **Services** Lift **Parking** 100 **Notes** LB Civ Wed 250

Premier Inn Manchester (Cheadle)

BUDGET HOTEL

☎ 0871 527 8728
Royal Crescent SK8 3FE
web: www.premierinn.com
dir: Exit A34 at Cheadle Royal rdbt behind TGI Friday's

High quality, budget accommodation ideal for both families and business travellers. Spacious, en suite bedrooms feature tea and coffee making facilities, and Freeview TV in most hotels. Internet access and Wi-fi are available for a small fee. The adjacent family restaurant features a wide and varied menu. See also the Hotel Groups pages.

Rooms 65

Pontlands Park

★★★ 81% HOTEL

☎ 01245 476444
West Hanningfield Rd, Great Baddow CM2 8HR
e-mail: sales@pontlandsparkhotel.co.uk
web: www.heritageleisure.co.uk
dir: A12, A130 , A1114 to Chelmsford. 1st exit at rdbt, 1st slip road on left. Left towards Great Baddow, 1st left into West Hanningfield Rd. Hotel 400yds on left

A Victorian country-house hotel situated in a peaceful rural location amidst attractive landscaped grounds. The stylishly furnished bedrooms are generally quite spacious; each is individually decorated and equipped with modern facilities. The elegant public rooms include a tastefully furnished sitting room, a cosy lounge bar, smart conservatory restaurant and an intimate dining room.

Rooms 35 (10 fmly) (11 GF) **S** £80-£138.50; **D** £80-£152 (incl. bkfst)* **Facilities** FTV Wi-fi 🐾 ➘ Gym Beauty room **Conf** Class 40 Board 40 Thtr 100 Del from £153 to £165* **Parking** 100 **Notes** ⊗ Closed 24-26 Dec Civ Wed 100

County Hotel

★★★ 80% ◉ HOTEL

☎ 01245 455700
29 Rainsford Rd CM1 2PZ
e-mail: kloftus@countyhotelgroup.co.uk
web: www.countyhotelgroup.co.uk
dir: From town centre, past rail & bus station. Hotel 300yds left beyond lights

This popular hotel is ideally situated within easy walking distance of the railway station, bus depot and town centre. Stylish bedrooms offer spacious comfort and plentiful extras including free Wi-fi. There are a smart restaurant, bar and lounge as well as sunny outdoor terraces for making the most of warm weather. The hotel also has a range of meeting rooms and banqueting facilities.

Rooms 50 🐾 **S** £50-£95; **D** £75-£170* **Facilities** FTV Wi-fi HL Xmas New Year **Conf** Class 84 Board 64 Thtr 160 Del from £130 to £180* **Services** Lift **Parking** 80 **Notes** LB ⊗ Closed 27-30 Dec Civ Wed 80

BEST WESTERN Ivy Hill

★★★ 79% HOTEL

☎ 01277 353040 & 355111
Writtle Rd, Margaretting CM4 0EH
e-mail: sales@ivyhillhotel.co.uk
web: www.heritageleisure.co.uk
dir: Just off A12 junct 14. Hotel on left at top of slip road

A smartly appointed hotel conveniently situated just off the A12. The spacious bedrooms are tastefully decorated, have co-ordinated fabrics and all the expected facilities. Public rooms include a choice of lounges, a cosy bar, a smart conservatory and restaurant, as well as a range of conference and banqueting facilities.

Rooms 33 (5 fmly) (11 GF) **S** £90-£128.50; **D** £90-£142 (incl. bkfst)* **Facilities** FTV Wi-fi ➘ **Conf** Class 80 Board 40 Thtr 180 Del from £135 to £146* **Parking** 200 **Notes** ⊗ Closed 24-26 Dec Civ Wed 100

Save on hotels. Book at **theAA.com/hotel**

CHA – CHE 125 ENGLAND

BEST WESTERN Atlantic Hotel

★★★ 77% HOTEL

☎ 01245 268168
New St CM1 1PP
e-mail: info@atlantichotel.co.uk
dir: From Chelmsford rail station, left into Victoria Rd, left at lights into New St, hotel on right

Ideally situated just a short walk from the railway station with its quick links to London, this modern, purpose-built hotel has contemporary-style bedrooms equipped with modern facilities. The open-plan public areas include Sapori Ristorante, an Italian restaurant, a lounge bar and a conservatory.

Rooms 59 (3 fmly) (27 GF) **Facilities** FTV Wi-fi Gym Complimentary use of facilities at Fitness First ♫ **Conf** Class 40 Board 10 Thtr 15 Del from £145 to £175 **Services** Air con **Parking** 60 **Notes** ⊗ Closed 23 Dec-3 Jan

Premier Inn Chelmsford (Boreham)

BUDGET HOTEL

☎ 0871 527 8220
Main Rd, Boreham CM3 3HJ
web: www.premierinn.com
dir: M25 junct 28, A12 to Colchester, B1137 to Boreham

High quality, budget accommodation ideal for both families and business travellers. Spacious, en suite bedrooms feature tea and coffee making facilities, and Freeview TV in most hotels. Internet access and Wi-fi are available for a small fee. The adjacent family restaurant features a wide and varied menu. See also the Hotel Groups pages.

Rooms 78

Premier Inn Chelmsford (Springfield)

BUDGET HOTEL

☎ 0871 527 8222
Chelmsford Service Area, Colchester Rd, Springfield CM2 5PY
web: www.premierinn.com
dir: At A12 junct 19, Chelmsford bypass, signed Chelmsford Service Area

Rooms 61

CHELMSFORD Map 10 SO92
Gloucestershire

Ellenborough Park

★★★★★ 86% ⧜⧜⧜
COUNTRY HOUSE HOTEL

C

☎ 01242 545454
Southam Rd GL52 3NH
e-mail: info@ellenboroughpark.com
dir: A46 right after 3m onto B4079, merges with A435, 4m, over 3 rdbts, left onto Southam Lane, right onto Old Road, right onto B4632, hotel on right

Set on the original Cheltenham Racecourse estate, this impressive hotel dates in part from the 16th century and has been beautifully restored. The Nina Campbell-designed bedrooms and suites are spread across the main house and adjacent buildings, and all feature superb beds, a great range of modern amenities, and luxurious bathrooms. The stylish Indian-themed spa has a gym and outdoor heated pool. There are two dining options; the modern Brasserie offers a country house menu, while the elegant, oak-panelled Beaufort dining room is more formal and offers a high standard of classic cuisine.

Rooms 62 (44 annexe) (20 GF) ⧜ **S** fr £230; **D** fr £230 (incl. bkfst)* **Facilities** Spa STV FTV Wi-fi ⧖ ⧖ ⧖ Gym Xmas New Year **Conf** Class 70 Board 40 Thtr 120 Del from £245 to £285* **Services** Lift Air con **Parking** 130 **Notes** LB Civ Wed 120

WHAT YOU EXPECTED:

WHAT YOU DID NOT:

CHELTENHAM *continued*

The Greenway Hotel & Spa

★★★★ 82% ◉◉ COUNTRY HOUSE HOTEL

☎ 01242 862352
Shurdington GL51 4UG
e-mail: info@thegreenway.co.uk
web: www.thegreenwayhotelandspa.com
dir: From Cheltenham centre 2.5m S on A46

This hotel, with a wealth of history, is peacefully located in a delightful setting within easy reach of the many attractions of the Cotswolds and also the M5. The Manor House bedrooms are luxuriously appointed - traditional in style yet with plasma TVs and internet access. The tranquil Coach House rooms, in the converted stable block, have direct access to the beautiful grounds. The attractive dining room overlooks the sunken garden and is the venue for excellent food, proudly served by dedicated and attentive staff.

Rooms 19 (6 annexe) (1 fmly) ➧ **S** £110-£195; **D** £169-£399 **Facilities** Spa FTV Wi-fi ⓢ ⬥ Gym Xmas New Year **Conf** Board 18 Thtr 50 Del from £155 to £216 **Parking** 30 **Notes** LB Civ Wed 60

The Cheltenham Chase Hotel

★★★★ 80% HOTEL

☎ 01452 519988
Shurdington Rd, Brockworth GL3 4PB
e-mail: cheltenhamreservations@qhotels.co.uk
web: www.qhotels.co.uk
dir: M5 junct 11a onto A417 Cirencester. 1st exit A46 to Stroud, hotel 500yds on left.

Conveniently positioned for Cheltenham, Gloucester, and the M5, this hotel is set in landscaped grounds with ample parking. Bedrooms are spacious with attractive colour schemes and excellent facilities; executive rooms and suites benefit from air conditioning. Public areas include an open-plan bar/lounge, Hardey's restaurant, extensive meeting and functions rooms and a well-equipped leisure club.

Rooms 122 (19 fmly) (44 GF) ➧ **S** £95-£145; **D** £105-£155 (incl. bkfst)* **Facilities** Spa STV FTV Wi-fi ⓢ Gym Steam room Sauna Xmas New Year **Conf** Class 160 Board 80 Thtr 350 Del from £135 to £165 **Services** Lift Air con **Parking** 240 **Notes** LB ⊗ Civ Wed 344

Cheltenham Park Hotel

PUMA HOTELS COLLECTION

★★★★ 79% ◉ HOTEL

☎ 01242 222021
Cirencester Rd, Charlton Kings GL53 8EA
e-mail: cheltenhampark@pumahotels.co.uk
web: www.pumahotels.co.uk
dir: On A435, 2m SE of Cheltenham near Lilley Brook Golf Course

Located south of Cheltenham, this attractive Georgian property is set in its own landscaped gardens, adjacent to Lilley Brook Golf Course. All the bedrooms, whether premium or standard, are spacious and well equipped for both business and leisure guests. The hotel has an impressive health and leisure club with the latest gym equipment plus a pool, steam room and beauty salon; extensive meeting facilities are available. The Lakeside Restaurant serves carefully prepared cuisine.

Rooms 152 (119 annexe) **Facilities** STV Wi-fi ⓢ supervised Gym Beauty treatment rooms Xmas New Year **Conf** Class 180 Board 110 Thtr 320 **Parking** 170 **Notes** ⊗ Civ Wed 100

Thistle Cheltenham Hotel

thistle

★★★★ 78% HOTEL

☎ 0871 376 9013
Gloucester Rd GL51 0TS
e-mail: cheltenham@thistle.co.uk
web: www.thistlehotels.com/cheltenham
dir: M5 junct 11, A40 signed Cheltenham, at 1st rdbt take 2nd exit. Hotel immediately on left

Conveniently located for easy access to the M5, this large hotel offers a good range of dining options in addition to extensive leisure facilities. Bedrooms and bathrooms are well equipped and provide good ease of use for both the business and leisure guest. Ample parking and a range of conference rooms are provided.

Rooms 122 (9 fmly) (40 GF) ➧ **Facilities** FTV Wi-fi HL ⓢ ⬥ Gym Sauna Steam room Xmas New Year **Conf** Class 220 Board 45 Thtr 400 Del from £125 to £155* **Services** Lift **Parking** 300 **Notes** ⊗ Civ Wed 300

Hotel du Vin Cheltenham

Hotel du Vin & Bistro

★★★★ 77% ◉ HOTEL

☎ 0844 7364 254
Parabola Rd GL50 3AQ
e-mail: info@cheltenham.hotelduvin.com
web: www.hotelduvin.com
dir: M5 junct 11, follow signs for city centre. At rdbt opposite Morgan Estate Agents take 2nd left, 200mtrs to Parabola Rd

This hotel, in the Montpellier area of the town, has spacious public areas that are packed with stylish features. The pewter-topped bar has comfortable seating and the spacious restaurant has the Hotel du Vin trademark design; alfresco dining is possible on the extensive terrace area. Bedrooms are very comfortable, with Egyptian linen, deep baths and power showers. The spa is the ideal place to relax and unwind. Although parking is limited, it is a definite bonus. Service is friendly and attentive.

Rooms 49 (2 fmly) (5 GF) ➧ **D** £99-£750* **Facilities** Spa STV Wi-fi **Conf** Class 24 Board 24 Thtr 30 **Services** Lift Air con **Parking** 26 **Notes** Civ Wed 60

Mercure Cheltenham Queen's Hotel

Mercure

★★★★ 77% HOTEL

☎ 01242 514754
The Promenade GL50 1NN
e-mail: h6632@accor.com
web: www.mercure.com
dir: Follow town centre signs. Left at Montpellier Walk rdbt. Entrance 500mtrs right

With its spectacular position at the top of the main promenade, this landmark hotel is an ideal base from which to explore the charms of this Regency spa town and also the Cotswolds. Bedrooms are very comfortable and include two beautiful four-poster rooms. Smart public rooms include the popular Gold Cup bar and a choice of dining options.

Rooms 84 (15 fmly) ➧ **Facilities** STV Wi-fi HL Xmas New Year **Conf** Class 60 Board 40 Thtr 100 **Services** Lift Air con **Parking** 70 **Notes** Civ Wed 100

See advert on page 125

George Hotel

★★★ 80% ◉ ◉ HOTEL

☎ 01242 235751
St Georges Rd GL50 3DZ
e-mail: hotel@stayatthegeorge.co.uk
web: www.stayatthegeorge.co.uk
dir: M5 junct 11 follow town centre signs. At 2nd
lights left into Gloucester Rd, past rail station over
mini-rdbt. At lights right into St Georges Rd. Hotel
0.75m on left

A genuinely friendly, privately-owned hotel occupying
part of a Regency terrace, just two-minutes walk from
the town centre. The contemporary interior is elegant
and stylish, and the well-equipped, modern bedrooms
offer a relaxing haven; individually designed junior
suites and deluxe double rooms are available. Lunch
or dinner can be enjoyed in the lively atmosphere of
Monty's Brasserie, perhaps followed by an evening in
the vibrant cocktail bar which hosts live
entertainment on Friday and Saturday evenings.

Rooms 31 (1 GF) ✿ **S** £90; **D** £100 (incl. bkfst)*
Facilities STV Wi-fi Complimentary membership to
local health club Live music at wknds ♫
Conf Class 18 Board 24 Thtr 30 Del £140*
Parking 30 **Notes** LB ⊗ RS 24-26 Dec

BEST WESTERN Cheltenham Regency Hotel

★★★ 79% HOTEL

☎ 01452 713226 & 0845 194 9867
Gloucester Rd, Staverton GL51 0ST
e-mail: info@cheltenhamregency.co.uk
dir: M5 junct 11 onto A40 to Cheltenham. Left at rdbt,
hotel 1m on left

This hotel provides high standards of quality and
comfort. The bedrooms are large and include several
suites; all are very well equipped and ideal for both
business and leisure guests. A good selection of
carefully prepared dishes is available from either the
extensive lounge/bar menu, or a more formal offering
can be found in the main restaurant.

Rooms 47 (2 fmly) (16 GF) ✿ **Facilities** FTV Wi-fi ↳
Xmas New Year **Conf** Class 90 Board 80 Thtr 170
Services Lift Air con **Parking** 120 **Notes** LB ⊗
Civ Wed 140

The Royal George Hotel

OldEngl◆sh

★★★ 71% HOTEL

☎ 01452 862506
Birdlip GL4 8JH
e-mail: royalgeorge.birdlip@greeneking.co.uk
web: www.oldenglish.co.uk
dir: M5 junct 11A take A417 towards Cirencester. At
Air Balloon rdbt take 2nd exit then 1st right into
Birdlip, hotel on right

This attractive property, built around a 17th-century
Cotswold house, has been sympathetically converted
and extended to become a pleasant and friendly
hotel. The bedrooms, including a four-poster room,
are spacious and comfortably furnished with modern
facilities. The public areas have been designed to
create a traditional English pub with the bar leading
onto a terrace that overlooks extensive lawns.

Rooms 34 (4 fmly) (12 GF) **Facilities** ♫ Xmas
Conf Class 60 Board 40 Thtr 90 **Notes** ⊗ Civ Wed 80

Premier Inn Cheltenham Central

BUDGET HOTEL

☎ 0871 527 8224
374 Gloucester Rd GL51 7AY
web: www.premierinn.com
dir: M5 junct 11, A40 (Cheltenham). Follow dual
carriageway to end, straight on at 1st rdbt, right at
2nd rdbt

High quality, budget accommodation ideal for both
families and business travellers. Spacious, en suite
bedrooms feature tea and coffee making facilities,
and Freeview TV in most hotels. Internet access and
Wi-fi are available for a small fee. The adjacent
family restaurant features a wide and varied menu.
See also the Hotel Groups pages.

Rooms 43

Premier Inn Cheltenham West

BUDGET HOTEL

☎ 0871 527 8226
Tewkesbury Rd, Uckington GL51 9SL
web: www.premierinn.com
dir: M5 junct 10 (S'bound exit only), A4019, hotel in
2m. Or M5 junct 11, A40 towards Cheltenham. At
Benhall Rdbt left onto A4103 (Princess Elizabeth Way)
follow racecourse signs. At rdbt left onto A4019
signed Tewkesbury/M5 North. Hotel opposite
Sainsburys

Rooms 40

CHENIES   **Map 6 TQ09**
Buckinghamshire

The Bedford Arms Hotel

★★★ 79% ◉ COUNTRY HOUSE HOTEL

C

☎ 01923 283301
WD3 6EQ
e-mail: contact@bedfordarms.co.uk
web: www.bedfordarms.co.uk
dir: M25 junct 18, A404 towards Amersham, hotel
signed after 2m on right

This attractive, 19th-century country inn enjoys a
peaceful rural setting. Comfortable bedrooms are
decorated in traditional style and feature a range of
thoughtful extras. Each room is named after a
relation of the Duke of Bedford, whose family has an
historic association with the property. There are two
bars, a lounge and a cosy, wood-panelled restaurant.

Rooms 18 (8 annexe) (2 fmly) (8 GF) ✿ **Facilities** STV
FTV Wi-fi ↳ **Conf** Class 16 Board 24 Thtr 50
Parking 60 **Notes** RS 27 Dec-4 Jan Civ Wed 55

CHERTSEY   **Map 6 TQ06**
Surrey

Hamilton's

◉ RESTAURANT WITH ROOMS

☎ 01932 560745
23 Windsor St KT16 8AY
e-mail: bookings@hamiltons23.com
dir: M25 junct 11 St Peters Way (A317). At rdbt 1st
exit, Chertsey Rd (A317), next rdbt 2nd exit into Free
Prae Rd, then Pound Rd. Left into London St, opposite
church

Hamilton's is an intimate and attractive building
close to the cricket ground. The en suite rooms are
beautifully appointed and equipped with all modern
amenities. The restaurant offers a fine dining menu
on selected days of the week while a freshly cooked
breakfast ensures a good start to the day. Free
parking is available.

Rooms 5

C

CHESHUNT
Hertfordshire
Map 6 TL30

Cheshunt Marriott Hotel

★★★★ 74% HOTEL

☎ 01992 451245
Halfhide Ln, Turnford, Broxbourne EN10 6NG
web: www.cheshuntmarriott.co.uk
dir: Exit A10 at Broxbourne, right & right again at rdbt, hotel on right at next rdbt

This popular suburban hotel has an attractive courtyard garden, overlooked by many of the guest bedrooms. All bedrooms are spacious and air conditioned. Public areas include a small, unsupervised leisure facility, along with the busy Washington Bar and Restaurant.

Rooms 143 (37 fmly) (39 GF) **Facilities** STV Wi-fi ⊿ ⊕ Gym Xmas New Year **Conf** Class 72 Board 56 Thtr 150 Del from £120 to £165* **Services** Lift Air con **Parking** 200 **Notes** ⊗ Civ Wed 120

CHESSINGTON
Greater London
Map 6 TQ16

Holiday Inn London - Chessington

★★★★ 72% HOTEL

☎ 01372 734600
Leatherhead Rd KT9 2NE
e-mail: enquiries@holidayinnchessington.co.uk
web: www.holidayinnchessington.co.uk
dir: Follow signs for Chessington World of Adventures. Hotel at North Car Park entrance

In a convenient location just off the M25 (junction 9), two miles from the A3 and just 12 miles from London, this hotel is, of course, ideal for those visiting Chessington World of Adventures and the zoo. The bedrooms are safari-themed and include family rooms with a separate sleeping area for children with their own TV. The Merula Bar and lounge is a great place to relax, and guests can eat in the Langata brasserie. The leisure facilities are extensive and there's ample parking.

Rooms 150 (56 fmly) (6 smoking) ⁉ **Facilities** Spa STV FTV Wi-fi ⊕ supervised Gym Sauna Steam room Xmas New Year **Conf** Class 150 Board 70 Thtr 300 **Services** Lift Air con **Parking** 120 **Notes** ⊗ Civ Wed 100

Premier Inn Chessington

BUDGET HOTEL

☎ 0871 527 8228
Leatherhead Rd KT9 2NE
web: www.premierinn.com
dir: M25 junct 9, A243 towards Kingston-upon-Thames for approx 2m. Hotel adjacent to Chessington World of Adventures

High quality, budget accommodation ideal for both families and business travellers. Spacious, en suite bedrooms feature tea and coffee making facilities, and Freeview TV in most hotels. Internet access and Wi-fi are available for a small fee. The adjacent family restaurant features a wide and varied menu. See also the Hotel Groups pages.

Rooms 42

CHESTER
Cheshire
Map 15 SJ46

See also **Puddington**

INSPECTORS' CHOICE
The Chester Grosvenor

★★★★★ ⊕⊕⊕⊕ HOTEL

☎ 01244 324024
Eastgate CH1 1LT
e-mail: reservations@chestergrosvenor.com
dir: A56 follow signs for city centre hotels. On Eastgate St next to the Eastgate clock

Located within the Roman walls of the city, this Grade II listed, half-timbered building is the essence of Englishness. Furnished with fine fabrics and queen or king-size beds, the suites and bedrooms are of the highest standard, each designed with guest comfort as a priority. The eating options are the art deco La Brasserie, a bustling venue awarded 2 AA Rosettes; the Arkle Bar and Lounge for morning coffee, light lunches, afternoon tea and drinks; plus the fine dining restaurant, Simon Radley at The Chester Grosvenor, which offers creative cuisine with flair and style, and has been awarded 4 AA Rosettes. The hotel has a luxury spa and small fitness centre.

Rooms 80 (7 fmly) ⁉ **S** fr £159; **D** fr £169 (incl. bkfst)* **Facilities** Spa STV FTV Wi-fi ⊿ HL Gym New Year **Conf** Class 100 Board 50 Thtr 250 Del from £195* **Services** Lift Air con **Notes** LB ⊗ Closed 25 Dec RS Sun & Mon Civ Wed 250

Rowton Hall Country House Hotel & Spa

★★★★ 81% ֎ HOTEL

☎ 01244 335262
Whitchurch Rd, Rowton CH3 6AD
e-mail: reception@rowtonhallhotelandspa.co.uk
web: www.rowtonhallhotel.co.uk
dir: M56 junct 12, A56 to Chester. At x-rds left onto A41 towards Whitchurch. Approx 1m, follow hotel signs

This delightful Georgian manor house, set in mature grounds, retains many original features such as a superb carved staircase and several eye-catching fireplaces. Bedrooms vary in size but all have been stylishly fitted and have impressive en suites. Public areas include a smart leisure centre, extensive function facilities and a striking restaurant that serves imaginative dishes.

Rooms 37 (4 fmly) (8 GF) ✎ **S** £85-£235; **D** £85-£235 **Facilities** Spa FTV Wi-fi ☺ ☻ ⚒ Gym Sauna Steam room Xmas New Year **Conf** Class 48 Board 50 Thtr 170 Del from £125 to £250 **Parking** 200 **Notes** LB Civ Wed 170

Grosvenor Pulford Hotel & Spa

★★★★ 78% ֎ HOTEL

☎ 01244 570560
Wrexham Rd, Pulford CH4 9DG
e-mail: reservations@grosvenorpulfordhotel.co.uk
web: www.grosvenorpulfordhotel.co.uk
dir: M53, A55 at junct signed A483 Chester/Wrexham & North Wales. Left onto B5445, hotel 2m on right

Set in a rural location, this modern, stylish hotel features a magnificent spa with a large Roman-style swimming pool. Among the range of bedrooms are several executive suites, and others that have spiral staircases leading to the bedroom sections. A smart brasserie restaurant and bar provides a wide range of imaginative dishes in a relaxed atmosphere.

Grosvenor Pulford Hotel & Spa

Rooms 73 (10 fmly) (21 GF) ✎ **Facilities** Spa STV FTV Wi-fi ☺ HL ☻ ⚒ Gym Steam room Sauna Xmas New Year **Conf** Class 100 Board 60 Thtr 220 Del from £117 to £150* **Services** Lift **Parking** 200 **Notes** Civ Wed 200

BEST WESTERN PREMIER Queen Hotel

★★★★ 78% HOTEL

☎ 01244 305000
City Rd CH1 3AH
e-mail: queenhotel@feathers.uk.com
web: www.feathers.uk.com
dir: Follow signs for railway station, hotel opposite

This hotel is ideally located opposite the railway station and just a couple minutes' walk from the city. Public areas include a restaurant, small gym, waiting room bar, separate lounge and Roman-themed gardens. Bedrooms are generally spacious and reflect the hotel's Victorian heritage.

Rooms 218 (11 fmly) (12 GF) ✎ **S** £79-£189; **D** £79-£199 **Facilities** STV FTV Wi-fi ☺ HL Gym Beauty treatment room Table tennis ♬ Xmas New Year **Conf** Class 150 Board 60 Thtr 400 Del from £125 to £185 **Services** Lift **Parking** 150 **Notes** LB ֎ Civ Wed 400

Macdonald New Blossoms Hotel

★★★★ 74% HOTEL

☎ 01244 323186 & 0844 8799113
St John St CH1 1HL
e-mail: events.blossoms@macdonald-hotels.co.uk
web: www.macdonaldhotels.co.uk/blossoms
dir: M53 junct 12 follow city centre signs for Eastgate, through pedestrian zone, hotel on left

Ideally located to explore the historic city of Chester, this is a modern and contemporary hotel. Bedrooms range from executive to feature four-poster rooms, with many retaining the charm of the original Victorian building. A stylish brasserie restaurant and bar offer an informal dining experience. Macdonald Hotels is the AA Hotel Group of the Year 2013-14.

Rooms 67 (1 fmly) **Facilities** Wi-fi Xmas New Year **Conf** Class 50 Board 40 Thtr 90 **Services** Lift **Notes** ֎

Mercure Chester Abbots Well Hotel

 C

★★★★ 74% HOTEL

☎ 0844 815 9001
Whitchurch Rd, Christleton CH3 5QL
e-mail: gm.mercurechester@jupiterhotels.co.uk
web: www.jupiterhotels.co.uk
dir: A41 (Whitchurch) hotel on right in 200mtrs

This smart, modern hotel is located just a short drive from the city centre; with extensive meeting and function facilities, a well-equipped leisure club and ample parking, it is a popular conference venue. Bedrooms vary in size and style but all are well equipped for both business and leisure guests. Food is served in the airy restaurant and also in the large open-plan bar lounge.

Rooms 126 (6 fmly) (58 GF) ✎ **S** £65-£169; **D** £65-£169* **Facilities** STV Wi-fi ☺ ☻ Gym Xmas New Year **Conf** Class 80 Board 60 Thtr 230 Del from £100 to £200* **Services** Lift **Parking** 160 **Notes** LB ֎ Civ Wed 180

BEST WESTERN Westminster Hotel

★★★ 82% HOTEL

☎ 01244 317341
City Rd CH1 3AF
e-mail: westminsterhotel@feathers.uk.com
web: www.feathers.uk.com
dir: A56, 3m to city centre, left signed rail station. Hotel opposite station, on right

Situated close to the railway station and city centre, the Westminster is an established hotel. It has an attractive Tudor-style exterior, while bedrooms are brightly decorated with a modern theme; family rooms are available. There is a choice of bars and lounges, and the dining room serves a good range of dishes.

Rooms 75 (5 fmly) (5 GF) **Facilities** FTV Wi-fi Free gym facilities at sister hotel Xmas New Year **Conf** Class 60 Board 40 Thtr 150 Del from £99 to £129* **Services** Lift **Notes** ֎ Civ Wed 100

C

CHESTER *continued*

Mill Hotel & Spa Destination

★★★ 80% HOTEL

☎ 01244 350035
Milton St CH1 3NF
e-mail: reservations@millhotel.com
web: www.millhotel.com
dir: M53 junct 12, A56, left at 2nd rdbt (A5268), 1st left, 2nd left

This hotel is a stylish conversion of an old corn mill, and enjoys an idyllic canalside location near to the inner ring road and close to the city centre. The bedrooms come in a variety of styles, and public rooms are spacious and comfortable. There are several dining options, and meals are often served on a broad-beam boat that cruises Chester's canal system, to and from the hotel. A well-equipped leisure centre is also provided.

Rooms 1128 (49 annexe) (57 fmly) ⊛ **S** £73-£93; **D** £95-£140 (incl. bkfst)* **Facilities** Spa STV FTV Wi-fi HL ⊛ supervised Gym Aerobic studio Hairdresser Sauna Steam room Kinesis studio ♬ Xmas New Year **Conf** Class 36 Board 30 Thtr 100 Del from £125 to £135* **Services** Lift **Parking** 120 **Notes** LB ⊛

Holiday Inn Chester South

★★★ 77% HOTEL

☎ 0871 942 9019 & 01244 688770
Wrexham Rd CH4 9DL
e-mail: reservations-chester@ihg.com
web: www.hichestersouthhotel.co.uk
dir: Near Wrexham junct on A483

Located close to the A55 and opposite the Park & Ride for the city centre, this hotel offers spacious and comfortable accommodation. Meals can be taken in the attractive bar or in the restaurant. There is also a well-equipped leisure club for residents, and extensive conference facilities are available.

Rooms 143 (21 fmly) (71 GF) **S** £59-£149; **D** £69-£159* **Facilities** STV FTV Wi-fi HL ⊛ supervised Gym Beauty treatment room Xmas New Year **Conf** Class 70 Board 70 Thtr 100 Del from £105 to £170* **Services** Lift Air con **Parking** 150 **Notes** LB ⊛ Civ Wed 50

Brookside Hotel

★★★ 72% HOTEL

☎ 01244 381943 & 390898
Brook Ln CH2 2AN
e-mail: info@brookside-hotel.co.uk
web: www.brookside-hotel.co.uk
dir: M53 junct 12, A56 towards Chester, A41. 0.5m left signed Newton (Plas Newton Ln). 0.5m right into Brook Ln. Hotel 0.5m. Or from Chester inner ring road follow A5116/Ellesmere Port/Hospital signs (keep in right lane to take right fork). Immediately left. At mini-rdbt 2nd right

This hotel is conveniently located in a residential area just north of the city centre. The attractive public areas consist of a foyer lounge, a small bar and a split-level restaurant. The homely bedrooms are thoughtfully furnished and some feature four-poster beds.

Rooms 26 (9 fmly) (4 GF) **Facilities** Wi-fi **Conf** Class 20 Board 12 **Parking** 20 **Notes** ⊛ Closed 20 Dec-3 Jan

Holiday Inn Express at Chester Racecourse

BUDGET HOTEL

☎ 0870 9904065 & 01244 327900
The Racecourse, New Crane St CH1 2LY
e-mail: hotel@chester-races.com
web: www.hiexpress.com/exchesterrac
dir: M53, A483 (Wrexham). Follow ring road & signs for A548. Right into New Crane St. Hotel 0.5m on left at racecourse

A modern hotel ideal for families and business travellers. Fresh and uncomplicated, the spacious rooms include Sky TV, power shower and tea and coffee-making facilities. Continental buffet breakfast is included in the room rate; other meals may be taken at the nearby family pub or restaurant. See also the Hotel Groups pages.

Rooms 97 (66 fmly) (4 GF) **Conf** Class 30 Board 25 Thtr 20

Premier Inn Chester Central (North)

BUDGET HOTEL

☎ 0871 527 8230
76 Liverpool Rd CH2 1AU
web: www.premierinn.com
dir: M53 junct 12, A56. At 2nd rdbt right signed A41 to Chester Zoo. At 1st lights left into Heath Rd, leads into Mill Ln. Under small rail bridge. Hotel at end on right

High quality, budget accommodation ideal for both families and business travellers. Spacious, en suite bedrooms feature tea and coffee making facilities, and Freeview TV in most hotels. Internet access and Wi-fi are available for a small fee. The adjacent family restaurant features a wide and varied menu. See also the Hotel Groups pages.

Rooms 31

Premier Inn Chester Central (South East)

BUDGET HOTEL

☎ 0871 527 8232
Caldy Valley Rd, Boughton CH3 5PR
web: www.premierinn.com
dir: M53 junct 12, A56 to Chester. At 1st lights onto A41 (Whitchurch). At 2nd rdbt rd exit into Caldy Valley Rd (Huntington). Hotel on right

Rooms 94

Premier Inn Chester City Centre

BUDGET HOTEL

☎ 0871 527 8234
20-24 City Rd CH1 3AE
web: www.premierinn.com
dir: M53 junct 12, follow A56/Chester City Centre
signs. At rdbt 1st exit onto A5268 (St Oswalds Way)
follow railway station signs. At Bar's Rdbt 1st exit.
Hotel on right

Rooms 120

Oddfellows

◉ RESTAURANT WITH ROOMS

☎ 01244 895700
20 Lower Bridge St CH1 1RS
e-mail: reception@oddfellowschester.com

Surrounded by designer shops and only a few
minutes' walk from the Chester Rows, old meets new
at this stylish Georgian mansion. The upper ground
floor comprises a walled garden with ornamental
moat, Arabian tents, a roofed patio, a cocktail bar
with an excellent wine selection, a bustling brasserie
and an Alice in Wonderland tea room. Fine dining,
featuring local produce, is skilfully prepared in the
brasserie restaurant and a sumptuous 'members'
lounge is also available to diners and resident
guests. Bedrooms have the wow factor with super
beds and every conceivable guest extra. Conference
facilities are also available.

Rooms 18 (14 annexe)

CHESTERFIELD	**Map 16 SK37**
Derbyshire	

Casa Hotel

★★★★ 82% ◉ ◉ HOTEL

☎ 01246 245999
Lockoford Ln S41 7JB
e-mail: enquiries@casahotels.co.uk
web: www.casahotels.co.uk
dir: M1 junct 29 to A617 Chesterfield/A61 Sheffield,
1st exit at rdbt, hotel on left

A luxurious hotel with a contemporary Spanish theme
throughout. The stylish bedrooms feature air
conditioning, Hypnos beds and bathrooms with
rainshowers. Some also have jacuzzi baths and two
have balconies with hot tubs. Cocina Restaurant
offers appealing menus featuring ingredients from
the hotel's own organic farm. The conference and
events facilities are excellent and complimentary
Wi-fi is offered.

Rooms 100 (6 fmly) ☛ **S** £90-£125; **D** £99-£140
(incl. bkfst)* **Facilities** STV FTV Wi-fi ⤵ HL Gym New
Year **Conf** Class 140 Board 50 Thtr 280 **Services** Lift
Air con **Parking** 200 **Notes** LB ⊗ Civ Wed 280

Ringwood Hall Hotel   THE INDEPENDENTS
HOTEL ASSOCIATION

★★★ 86% HOTEL

☎ 01246 280077
Brimington S43 1DQ
e-mail: reception@ringwoodhallhotel.com
web: www.ringwoodhallhotel.com
dir: M1 junct 30, A619 to Chesterfield through
Staveley. Hotel on left

A beautifully presented Georgian manor house set in
29 acres of peaceful grounds, between the M1 and
Chesterfield. The stylish bedrooms include 'Feature
Rooms' and three apartments within the grounds.
Public areas include comfortable lounges, the
Markham Bar and a Cocktail Lounge. The health and
fitness club has a pool, sauna, steam room and gym.

Rooms 74 (10 annexe) (32 fmly) (32 GF) ☛
S £70-£98; **D** £90-£128 (incl. bkfst)* **Facilities** FTV
Wi-fi ⤵ Gym Steam room Sauna Xmas New Year
Conf Class 80 Board 60 Thtr 250 Del from £100*
Parking 150 **Notes** LB Civ Wed 250

Sandpiper Hotel   THE INDEPENDENTS
HOTEL ASSOCIATION

★★★ 68% HOTEL

☎ 01246 450550
Sheffield Rd, Sheepbridge S41 9EH
e-mail: sue@sandpiperhotel.co.uk
web: www.sandpiperhotel.co.uk
dir: M1 junct 29, A617 to Chesterfield then A61 to
Sheffield. 1st exit take Dronfield/Unstone sign. Hotel
0.5m on left

Conveniently situated for both the A61, the M1, and
Chesterfield, this modern hotel offers comfortable and
well-furnished bedrooms. Public areas are situated in
a separate building across the car park, and include
a cosy bar and open-plan restaurant, serving a range
of interesting and popular dishes.

Rooms 46 (11 fmly) (16 GF) **S** £40-£55; **D** £40-£60*
Facilities FTV Wi-fi ⤵ New Year **Conf** Class 35
Board 35 Thtr 100 Del from £100* **Services** Lift
Parking 120 **Notes** LB Civ Wed 90

The Chesterfield Hotel

★★★ 62% HOTEL

☎ 01246 271 141
Malkin St S41 7UA
e-mail: res-chesterfield@metroinns.co.uk
dir: M1 junct 29, A617 through town centre follow
signs rail station

Ideally situated within walking distance of the town
centre and within sight of Chesterfield's famous
crocked spire, this railway hotel offers comfortable
accommodation along with bars, lounges and leisure
facilities. On-site free car parking available.

Rooms 73 ☛ **S** £30-£52; **D** £40-£62 (incl. bkfst)*
Facilities FTV Wi-fi ⊘ Gym **Conf** Class 100 Board 56
Thtr 200 Del from £80 to £100* **Services** Lift
Parking 50 **Notes** Civ Wed 50

Ibis Chesterfield

BUDGET HOTEL

☎ 01246 221333
Lordsmill St S41 7RW
e-mail: h3160@accor.com
web: www.ibishotel.com
dir: M1 junct 29/A617 to Chesterfield. 2nd exit at 1st
rdbt. Hotel on right at 2nd rdbt

Modern, budget hotel offering comfortable
accommodation in bright and practical bedrooms.
Breakfast is self-service and dinner is available in
the restaurant. See also the Hotel Groups pages.

Rooms 86 (21 fmly) (8 GF) **Conf** Board 12 Thtr 25

Premier Inn Chesterfield North

BUDGET HOTEL

☎ 0871 527 8238
Tapton Lock Hill, off Rotherway S41 7NJ
web: www.premierinn.com
dir: Adjacent to Tesco, at A61 & A619 rdbt, 1m N of
city centre

High quality, budget accommodation ideal for both
families and business travellers. Spacious, en suite
bedrooms feature tea and coffee making facilities,
and Freeview TV in most hotels. Internet access and
Wi-fi are available for a small fee. The adjacent
family restaurant features a wide and varied menu.
See also the Hotel Groups pages.

Rooms 60

C

C

CHESTERFIELD *continued*

Premier Inn Chesterfield West

BUDGET HOTEL

☎ 0871 527 8240
Baslow Rd, Eastmoor S42 7DA
web: www.premierinn.com
dir: M1 junct 29, A617. At next rdbt 2nd exit. At next rdbt 1st exit into Markham Rd. At next rdbt 2nd exit into Wheatbridge Rd, left into Chatsworth Rd. 2.5m to hotel

Rooms 23

CHICHESTER
West Sussex   Map 5 SU80

The Goodwood Hotel

★★★★ 81% ◉◉ HOTEL

☎ 01243 775537
PO18 0QB
e-mail: reservations@goodwood.com
web: www.goodwood.com

(For full entry see Goodwood)

The Millstream Hotel & Restaurant

★★★ 85% ◉◉ HOTEL

☎ 01243 573234
Bosham Ln PO18 8HL
e-mail: info@millstreamhotel.com
web: www.millstreamhotel.com

(For full entry see Bosham)

Crouchers Country Hotel & Restaurant

★★★ 80% ◉◉ HOTEL

☎ 01243 784995
Birdham Rd PO20 7EH
e-mail: crouchers@btconnect.com
dir: From A27 (Chichester bypass) onto A286 towards West Wittering, 2m, hotel on left between Chichester Marina & Dell Quay

This friendly, family-run hotel, situated in open countryside, is just a short drive from the harbour. The stylish and well-equipped bedrooms are situated in a separate barn, coach house and stable block, and include four-poster rooms and rooms with patios that overlook the fields. The modern oak-beamed restaurant, with country views, serves award-winning cuisine.

Rooms 26 (23 annexe) (2 fmly) (15 GF) **Facilities** STV FTV Wi-fi Xmas New Year **Conf** Class 80 Board 50 Thtr 80 Del from £110 to £115* **Parking** 80 **Notes** Civ Wed 70

The Ship Hotel

★★★ 78% ◉ HOTEL

☎ 01243 778000
57 North St PO19 1NH
e-mail: enquiries@theshiphotel.net
dir: From A27, onto inner ring road to Northgate. At Northgate rdbt left into North St, hotel on left

This well-presented Grade II listed, Georgian property occupies a prime position at the top of North Street. The stylish bedrooms have flat-screen TVs, Egyptian cotton linen and high-speed Wi-fi access. The bar and restaurant are contemporary venues for enjoying meals and refreshments which are served all day. The hotel is just a few minutes' away from the famous Festival Theatre; and Goodwood, for motorsport and horse racing, is also close by.

Rooms 36 (2 fmly) **Facilities** FTV Wi-fi ↘ Xmas New Year **Conf** Class 50 Board 30 Thtr 50 **Services** Lift **Parking** 35 **Notes** ⊗ Civ Wed 70

Premier Inn Chichester

BUDGET HOTEL

☎ 0871 527 8242
Chichester Gate Leisure Park, Terminus Rd PO19 8EL
web: www.premierinn.com
dir: A27 towards city centre. Follow Terminus Road Industrial Estate signs. Left at 1st lights, left at next lights into Chichester Gate Leisure Park. Hotel on right

High quality, budget accommodation ideal for both families and business travellers. Spacious, en suite bedrooms feature tea and coffee making facilities, and Freeview TV in most hotels. Internet access and Wi-fi are available for a small fee. The adjacent family restaurant features a wide and varied menu. See also the Hotel Groups pages.

Rooms 83

CHIEVELEY
Berkshire   Map 5 SU47

The Crab at Chieveley

◉◉ RESTAURANT WITH ROOMS

☎ 01635 247550
Wantage Rd RG20 8UE
e-mail: info@crabatchieveley.com
dir: 1.5m W of Chieveley on B4494

The individually themed bedrooms at this former pub have been appointed to a very high standard and include a full range of modern amenities. Ground-floor rooms have a small private patio area complete with a hot tub. The warm and cosy restaurant offers an extensive and award-winning range of fish and seafood dishes.

Rooms 14 (5 annexe)

CHILDER THORNTON
Cheshire   Map 15 SJ37

Brook Meadow

bespoke

★★★ 73% HOTEL

☎ 0151 339 9350
Health Ln CH66 7NS
e-mail: reservations.brookmeadow@ohiml.com
web: www.oxfordhotelsandinns.com
dir: M53 junct 5, A41, right onto A550, 2nd right into Heath Ln

This delightful country hotel, set in its own lovely gardens, is within easy reach of Liverpool, Chester, the M53 and M56. Bedrooms are tastefully decorated and well equipped; the bathrooms have spa baths, and there is a comfortable lounge. The dining room has a conservatory which overlooks the grounds. Two function suites are available.

Rooms 25 (7 fmly) (7 GF) **Facilities** FTV Wi-fi Xmas New Year **Conf** Class 60 Board 60 Thtr 180 **Services** Lift Air con **Parking** 80 **Notes** ⊗ Civ Wed 160

Premier Inn Wirral (Childer Thornton)

BUDGET HOTEL

☎ 0871 527 9174
New Chester Rd CH66 1QW
web: www.premierinn.com
dir: M53 junct 5, A41 towards Chester. Hotel on right (same entrance as Burleydam Garden Centre)

High quality, budget accommodation ideal for both families and business travellers. Spacious, en suite bedrooms feature tea and coffee making facilities, and Freeview TV in most hotels. Internet access and Wi-fi are available for a small fee. The adjacent

Save on hotels. Book at **theAA.com/hotel**

CHE – CHO 133 ENGLAND

C

family restaurant features a wide and varied menu. See also the Hotel Groups pages.

Rooms 31

BEST WESTERN PLUS Angel Hotel

★★★ 80% HOTEL

☎ 01249 652615
Market Place SN15 3HD
e-mail: reception@angelhotelchippenham.co.uk
web: www.angelhotelchippenham.co.uk
dir: Follow tourist signs for Bowood House. Under railway arch, follow 'Borough Parade Parking' signs. Hotel adjacent to car park

Several impressive buildings combine to make this smart and comfortable hotel. The well-equipped bedrooms vary from those in the main house where character is the key, to the smart executive-style, courtyard rooms. The lounge and restaurant are bright and modern, and offer an imaginative carte and an all-day menu.

Rooms 50 (35 annexe) (3 fmly) (12 GF) **S** £79.85-£115.85; **D** £99.85-£125.85 (incl. bkfst) **Facilities** STV FTV Wi-fi ↻ ⊗ Gym **Conf** Class 50 Board 50 Thtr 100 **Parking** 50 **Notes** LB

Stanton Manor Hotel

★★★ 79% ⊚ HOTEL

☎ 01666 837552
SN14 6DQ
e-mail: reception@stantonmanor.co.uk
web: www.stantonmanor.co.uk

(For full entry see Stanton St Quintin)

Premier Inn Chippenham

BUDGET HOTEL

☎ 0871 527 8244
Cepen Park, West Cepen Way SN14 6UZ
web: www.premierinn.com
dir: M4 junct 17, A350 towards Chippenham. Hotel at 1st main rdbt

High quality, budget accommodation ideal for both families and business travellers. Spacious, en suite bedrooms feature tea and coffee making facilities, and Freeview TV in most hotels. Internet access and Wi-fi are available for a small fee. The adjacent family restaurant features a wide and varied menu. See also the Hotel Groups pages.

Rooms 79

Three Ways House

★★★ 82% ⊚ HOTEL

☎ 01386 438429
Mickleton GL55 6SB
e-mail: reception@puddingclub.com
web: www.threewayshousehotel.com
dir: In Mickleton centre, on B4632 (Stratford-upon-Avon to Broadway road

Built in 1870, this charming hotel has welcomed guests for over 100 years and is home to the world famous Pudding Club, formed in 1985 to promote traditional English puddings. Individuality is a hallmark here, as reflected in a number of the bedrooms that have been designed around a pudding theme. Public areas are stylish and include the air-conditioned restaurant, lounges and meeting rooms.

Rooms 48 (7 fmly) (14 GF) ↻ **S** £88-£125; **D** £145-£240 (incl. bkfst)* **Facilities** FTV Wi-fi ↻ ♫ Xmas New Year **Conf** Class 40 Board 35 Thtr 100 Del from £130* **Services** Lift **Parking** 37 **Notes** LB Civ Wed 100

Noel Arms Hotel

"bespoke" HOTELS

★★★ 77% HOTEL

☎ 01386 840317
High St GL55 6AT
e-mail: reception@noelarmshotel.com
web: www.noelarmshotel.com
dir: Exit A44 onto B4081 to Chipping Campden, 1st right down hill into town. Hotel on right

This historic 14th-century hotel has a wealth of character and charm, and retains original features. The bedrooms are very individual in style, and all have high levels of comfort and interesting interior design. Such distinctiveness is also evident throughout the public areas, which include the popular bar, coffee shop, conservatory lounge and attractive restaurant.

Rooms 28 (1 fmly) (8 GF) **Facilities** Wi-fi Use of spa at sister hotel (charged) Xmas New Year **Conf** Class 40 Board 40 Thtr 80 **Parking** 28 **Notes** Civ Wed 100

The Kings

⊚ ⊚ RESTAURANT WITH ROOMS

☎ 01386 840256 & 841056
The Square GL55 6AW
e-mail: info@kingscampden.co.uk
dir: In centre of town square

Located in the centre of this delightful Cotswold town, The Kings effortlessly blends a relaxed and friendly welcome with efficient service. Bedrooms and bathrooms come in a range of shapes and sizes, all are appointed to high levels of quality and comfort. Dining options, whether in the main restaurant or the comfortable bar area, serve a tempting menu to suit all tastes, from light salads and pasta to meat and fish dishes.

Rooms 19 (5 annexe) (3 fmly)

Wild Thyme Restaurant with Rooms

⊚ ⊚ RESTAURANT WITH ROOMS

☎ 01608 645060
10 New St OX7 5LJ
e-mail: enquiries@wildthymerestaurant.co.uk
dir: On A44 in town centre off market square

Located in the bustling Cotswold market town of Chipping Norton, this restaurant with rooms offers three en suite bedrooms that are individually designed, well equipped and have many thoughtful extras. The restaurant serves exciting modern British food along with relaxed and friendly service.

Rooms 3

Premier Inn Chorley North

BUDGET HOTEL

☎ 0871 527 8246
Malthouse Farm, Moss Ln, Whittle-le-Woods PR6 8AB
web: www.premierinn.com
dir: M61 junct 8 onto A674 (Wheelton), 400yds on left into Moss Ln

High quality, budget accommodation ideal for both families and business travellers. Spacious, en suite bedrooms feature tea and coffee making facilities, and Freeview TV in most hotels. Internet access and Wi-fi are available for a small fee. The adjacent family restaurant features a wide and varied menu. See also the Hotel Groups pages.

Rooms 81

CHORLEY *continued*

Premier Inn Chorley South

BUDGET HOTEL

☎ 0871 527 8248
Bolton Rd PR7 4AB
web: www.premierinn.com
dir: From N: M61 junct 8, A6 to Chorley. From S: M6
junct 27 follow Standish signs. Left onto A5106 to
Chorley, A6 towards Preston. Hotel 0.5m on right

Rooms 29

| CHRISTCHURCH | Map 5 SZ19 |
| Dorset | |

Christchurch Harbour Hotel

★★★★ 82% ◉◉ HOTEL

☎ 01202 483434
95 Mudeford BH23 3NT
e-mail: christchurch@harbourhotels.co.uk
web: www.christchurch-harbour-hotel.co.uk
dir: On A35 to Christchurch onto A337 to Highcliffe.
Right at rdbt, hotel 1.5m on left

Delightfully situated on the side of Mudeford Quay
close to sandy beaches, and conveniently located for
Bournemouth Airport and the BIC, this hotel boasts
an impressive spa and leisure facility. The bedrooms
are particularly well appointed and stylishly finished,
many have excellent views, and some have balconies.
Guests can eat in the award-winning Harbour
Restaurant, or the waterside Rhodes South.

Rooms 64 (2 fmly) (14 GF) ✦ **Facilities** Spa FTV Wi-fi
↻ ❄ Gym Steam room Sauna Exercise classes
Hydrotherapy pool Xmas New Year **Conf** Class 20
Board 30 Thtr 100 **Services** Lift **Parking** 55 **Notes** ⊗
Civ Wed 100

Captain's Club Hotel and Spa

★★★★ 81% ◉◉ HOTEL

☎ 01202 475111
Wick Ferry, Wick Ln BH23 1HU
e-mail: enquiries@captainsclubhotel.com
web: www.captainsclubhotel.com
dir: B3073 to Christchurch. On Fountain rdbt take 5th
exit (Sopers Ln) 2nd left (St Margarets Ave) 1st right
onto Wick Ln

The Captain's Club Hotel is situated in the heart of
the town on the banks of the River Stour at
Christchurch Quay, and only ten minutes from
Bournemouth. All bedrooms, including the suites and
apartments, have views overlooking the river. Guests
can relax in the hydrotherapy pool, enjoy a spa
treatment or enjoy the cuisine in Tides Restaurant.

Rooms 29 (12 fmly) ✦ **S** fr £199; **D** £249 (incl.
bkfst)* **Facilities** Spa STV FTV Wi-fi ↻ Hydrotherapy
pool Sauna Dry flotation ⏀ **Conf** Class 72 Board 64
Thtr 140 **Services** Lift Air con **Parking** 41 **Notes** LB
Civ Wed 100

Premier Inn Christchurch East

BUDGET HOTEL

☎ 0871 527 8250
Somerford Rd BH23 3QG
web: www.premierinn.com
dir: In Christchurch from A35 & B3059 rdbt junct take
B3059 (Somerford Rd)

High quality, budget accommodation ideal for both
families and business travellers. Spacious, en suite
bedrooms feature tea and coffee making facilities,
and Freeview TV in most hotels. Internet access and
Wi-fi are available for a small fee. The adjacent
family restaurant features a wide and varied menu.
See also the Hotel Groups pages.

Rooms 102

Premier Inn Christchurch West

BUDGET HOTEL

☎ 0871 527 8252
Barrack Rd BH23 2BN
web: www.premierinn.com
dir: From A338 take A3060 towards Christchurch. Left
onto A35. Hotel on right

Rooms 41

| CHURT | Map 5 SU83 |
| Surrey | |

BEST WESTERN Frensham Pond Hotel

★★★ 81% ◉ HOTEL

☎ 01252 795161
Bacon Ln GU10 2QB
e-mail: info@frenshampondhotel.co.uk
web: www.frenshampondhotel.co.uk
dir: A3 onto A287. 4m left at 'Beware Horses' sign.
Hotel 0.25m

This 15th-century house occupies a superb location
on the edge of Frensham Pond. The bedrooms are
mainly spacious, and the superior, garden annexe
rooms have their own patio and air conditioning. The
contemporary bar and lounge offers a range of
snacks, and the leisure club has good facilities.

Rooms 51 (12 annexe) (14 fmly) (27 GF) **S** £55-£130;
D £55-£130* **Facilities** STV FTV Wi-fi ❄ Gym Squash
Steam room Sauna Xmas New Year **Conf** Class 45
Board 40 Thtr 120 Del from £95 to £155*
Parking 120 **Notes** LB ⊗ Civ Wed 130

Save on hotels. Book at **theAA.com/hotel**

CHO – CLA 135 ENGLAND

C

INSPECTORS' CHOICE

Barnsley House

★★★★ ◉ ◉ COUNTRY HOUSE HOTEL

☎ 01285 740000
Barnsley GL7 5EE
e-mail: info@barnsleyhouse.com
dir: 4m NE of Cirencester on B4425

This delightful Cotswold country house has been appointed to provide the highest levels of quality, comfort and relaxation. Individually styled bedrooms come in a range of shapes and sizes, from the large character rooms in the main house to the more contemporary-style stable rooms; all rooms have garden views and are packed with guest extras and little luxuries, including plasma TVs in the bathrooms. The delightful gardens, originally designed in the late 1950s by previous owner and award-winning gardener Rosemary Verey and her husband, include a fruit and vegetable area which is the home of much of the produce used in the delicious cuisine on offer in Potager Restaurant. In the grounds is the Garden Spa with treatment rooms, sauna, steam room and an outdoor hydrotherapy pool. The hotel also has a cinema.

Rooms 18 (12 annexe) (10 GF) **S** £262-£642;
D £280-£660 (incl. bkfst)* **Facilities** Spa STV FTV Wi-fi ◊ ♨ ☙ Cinema Bicycles Hydrotherapy pool Relaxation rooms Xmas New Year **Conf** Class 20 Board 18 Thtr 30 Del £300* **Parking** 30 **Notes** ⊗ No children 14yrs Civ Wed 100

The Crown of Crucis

★★★ 77% HOTEL

☎ 01285 851806
Ampney Crucis GL7 5RS
e-mail: reception@thecrownofcrucis.co.uk
web: www.thecrownofcrucis.co.uk
dir: A417 to Fairford, hotel 2.5m on left

This delightful hotel consists of two buildings; one a 16th-century coaching inn, which houses the bar and restaurant, and a more modern bedroom block which surrounds a courtyard. Rooms are attractively appointed and offer modern facilities; the restaurant serves a range of imaginative dishes.

Rooms 25 (2 fmly) (13 GF) **S** £85-£155; **D** £115-£155 (incl. bkfst) **Facilities** FTV Wi-fi ◊ New Year **Conf** Class 50 Board 40 Thtr 100 **Parking** 82 **Notes** LB RS 25-26 Dec Civ Wed 90

Corinium Hotel & Restaurant

★★★ Ⓐ SMALL HOTEL

☎ 01285 659711
12 Gloucester St GL7 2DG
e-mail: info@coriniumhotel.co.uk
web: www.coriniumhotel.co.uk
dir: From A417/A419/A429 towards Cirencester. A435 at rdbt. After 500mtrs turn left at lights, then 1st right, car park on left

This delightful 16th-century small hotel is quietly situated just five minutes walk from town, and is an ideal base from which to explore the Cotswolds. The Corinium has a locally renowned restaurant offering modern British cuisine, as well as a cosy bar full of Cotswold charm. Other benefits include free Wi-fi throughout hotel, an attractive secluded garden for alfresco dining and ample free parking.

Rooms 15 (2 fmly) (2 GF) **S** £55-£80; **D** £65-£120 (incl. bkfst)* **Facilities** FTV Wi-fi **Conf** Class 30 Board 34 Thtr 70 Del from £95 to £125* **Parking** 30 **Notes** LB

Premier Inn Clacton-on-Sea

Premier Inn

BUDGET HOTEL

☎ 0871 527 8254
Crown Green Roundabout, Colchester Rd, Trending CO16 9AA
web: www.premierinn.com
dir: A12, A120 towards Harwich. In 4m take A133 to Clacton-on-Sea. Hotel off Weeley Rdbt

High quality, budget accommodation ideal for both families and business travellers. Spacious, en suite bedrooms feature tea and coffee making facilities, and Freeview TV in most hotels. Internet access and Wi-fi are available for a small fee. The adjacent family restaurant features a wide and varied menu. See also the Hotel Groups pages.

Rooms 40

Ardencote Manor Hotel & Spa

★★★★ 80% ◉ ◉ HOTEL

☎ 01926 843111
The Cumsey, Lye Green Rd, Claverdon CV35 8LT
e-mail: hotel@ardencote.com
web: www.ardencote.com
dir: Off A4189. In Claverdon follow signs for Shrewley & brown tourist signs for Ardencote Manor, approx 1.5m

Originally built as a gentleman's residence around 1860, this hotel is set in 83 acres of landscaped grounds. Public rooms include a choice of lounge areas, a cocktail bar and conservatory breakfast room. Main meals are served in the Lodge Restaurant, a separate building with a light contemporary style, which sits beside a small lake. An extensive range of leisure and conference facilities is provided and bedrooms are smartly decorated and tastefully furnished.

Rooms 110 (10 fmly) (30 GF) ❦ **S** £90-£110; **D** £115-£165 (incl. bkfst) **Facilities** Spa STV FTV Wi-fi ◊ HL ③ ⦂ ♨ 9 ♨ ☙ Gym Squash Sauna Steam room Dance studio Xmas New Year **Conf** Class 70 Board 50 Thtr 175 Del from £130 to £180 **Services** Lift Air con **Parking** 350 **Notes** ⊗ Civ Wed 150

C

CLEARWELL
West: Gloucestershire
Map 4 SO50

Tudor Farmhouse Hotel & Restaurant

★★★ 79% @@ HOTEL

☎ 01594 833046
High St GL16 8JS
e-mail: info@tudorfarmhousehotel.co.uk
web: www.tudorfarmhousehotel.co.uk
dir: A4136 onto B4228, through Coleford, right into
Clearwell, hotel on right just before War Memorial
Cross

Dating from the 13th century, this idyllic former
farmhouse retains a host of original features
including exposed stonework, oak beams, wall
panelling and wonderful inglenook fireplaces.
Bedrooms have great individuality and style and are
located either in the main house or in converted
buildings in the grounds. Creative menus offer quality
cuisine, served in the intimate, candlelit restaurant.

Rooms 23 (18 annexe) (3 fmly) (10 GF) 🛏
S £95-£195; **D** £95-£210 (incl. bkfst)* **Facilities** STV
FTV Wi-fi ⮑ HL Xmas New Year **Conf** Class 20
Board 12 Thtr 30 Del £135* **Parking** 30 **Notes** LB
Closed 2-5 Jan

The Wyndham Arms Hotel

★★★ 68% @ HOTEL

☎ 01594 833666
GL16 8JT
e-mail: nigel@thewyndhamhotel.co.uk
dir: Exit B4228, in village centre on B4231

The history of this charming village inn can be traced
back over 600 years. It has exposed stone walls,
original beams and an impressive inglenook fireplace
in the friendly bar. Most bedrooms are in a modern
extension, while the other rooms, in the main house,
are more traditional in style. A range of dishes is
offered in the bar or restaurant.

Rooms 18 (12 annexe) (3 fmly) (6 GF) **S** £45-£65;
D £75-£140 (incl. bkfst)* **Facilities** FTV Wi-fi ⮑ Xmas
Conf Class 30 Board 22 Thtr 56 Del from £90 to
£110* **Parking** 52 **Notes** LB Closed 1st wk Jan
Civ Wed 80

CLECKHEATON
West Yorkshire
Map 19 SE12

Premier Inn Bradford South

BUDGET HOTEL

☎ 0871 527 8136
Whitehall Rd, Dye House Dr BD19 6HG
web: www.premierinn.com
dir: On A58 at intersection with M62 & M606

High quality, budget accommodation ideal for both
families and business travellers. Spacious, en suite
bedrooms feature tea and coffee making facilities,
and Freeview TV in most hotels. Internet access and
Wi-fi are available for a small fee. The adjacent
family restaurant features a wide and varied menu.
See also the Hotel Groups pages.

Rooms 40

CLEETHORPES
Lincolnshire
Map 17 TA30

Kingsway Hotel

★★★ 77% HOTEL

☎ 01472 601122
Kingsway DN35 0AE
e-mail: reception@kingsway-hotel.com
web: www.kingsway-hotel.com
dir: Exit A180 at Grimsby, to Cleethorpes seafront.
Hotel at Kingsway & Queen Parade junct (A1098)

This seafront hotel has been in the same family for
four generations and continues to provide traditional
comfort and friendly service. The lounges are
comfortable and good food is served in the pleasant
dining room. The bedrooms are bright and nicely
furnished - most are comfortably proportioned.

Rooms 49 🛏 **S** £79-£92; **D** £96-£109 (incl. bkfst)*
Facilities STV FTV Wi-fi **Conf** Board 18 Thtr 22
Services Lift **Parking** 50 **Notes** ⊗ No children 5yrs
Closed 25-26 Dec

CLIMPING
West Sussex
Map 6 SU90

INSPECTORS' CHOICE

Bailiffscourt Hotel & Spa

★★★ @@ HOTEL

☎ 01903 723511
Climping St BN17 5RW
e-mail: bailiffscourt@hshotels.co.uk
web: www.hshotels.co.uk
dir: A259, follow Climping Beach signs. Hotel 0.5m
on right

This delightful, moated, 'medieval manor', has the
appearance of having been in existence for
centuries, but in fact only dates back to the 1920s.
It was built for Lord Moyne, a member of the
Guinness family, who wanted to create an ancient
manor house. It became a hotel just over 60 years
ago and sits in 30 acres of delightful parkland that
leads to the beach. Bedrooms vary from
atmospheric feature rooms with log fires, oak
beams and four-poster beds to spacious, stylish
and contemporary rooms located in the grounds.
The Tapestry Restaurant serves award-winning
classic European cuisine, and in summer the
Courtyard is the place for informal light lunches
and afternoon tea. Superb facilities are to be found
in the hotel's health spa.

Rooms 39 (30 annexe) (25 fmly) (16 GF) 🛏 (incl.
bkfst & dinner) **Facilities** Spa STV FTV Wi-fi ⮑ ⊛
⚡ ♨ ♨ Gym Sauna Steam room Dance/Fitness
studio Yoga/Pilates/Gym inductions Xmas New Year
Conf Class 20 Board 26 Thtr 40 Del from £180*
Parking 80 **Notes** LB Civ Wed 75

CLOVELLY
Devon Map 3 SS32

Red Lion Hotel
★★ 76% HOTEL

☎ 01237 431237
The Quay EX39 5TF
e-mail: redlion@clovelly.co.uk
web: www.clovelly.co.uk
dir: Exit A39 at Clovelly Cross onto B3237. Pass visitor centre, 1st left by white rails to harbour

'Idyllic' is the only word to describe the harbour-side setting of this charming 18th-century inn, with the famous fishing village forming a spectacular backdrop. Bedrooms are stylish and enjoy delightful views. The inn's relaxed atmosphere is conducive to switching off from the pressures of modern life, even when the harbour comes alive with the activities of the local fishermen during the day.

Rooms 17 (6 annexe) (5 fmly) (2 GF) ➤
S £68-£91.50; **D** £136-£147 (incl. bkfst)*
Facilities FTV Wi-fi Sea fishing Diving Tennis can be arranged Xmas New Year **Parking** 11 **Notes** LB Civ Wed 70

New Inn
★★ 72% HOTEL

☎ 01237 431303
High St EX39 5TQ
e-mail: newinn@clovelly.co.uk
web: www.clovelly.co.uk
dir: At Clovelly Cross, exit A39 onto B3237. Follow down hill for 1.5m. Right at sign 'All vehicles for Clovelly'

Famed for its cobbled descent to the harbour, this fascinating fishing village is a traffic-free zone. Consequently, luggage is conveyed by sledge or donkey to this much-photographed hotel. Carefully renovated bedrooms and public areas are smartly presented with quality, locally-made furnishings. Meals may be taken in the elegant restaurant or the popular Upalong bar.

Rooms 8 (2 fmly) ➤ **S** £58-£61.50; **D** £116-£123 (incl. bkfst)* **Facilities** FTV Wi-fi Sea fishing Diving Tennis can be arranged Xmas New Year **Notes** LB Civ Wed 50

CLOWNE
Derbyshire Map 16 SK47

Hotel Van Dyk
★★★★ 76% ⊛ SMALL HOTEL

☎ 01246 810219
Worksop Rd S43 4TD
e-mail: marcus@hotelvandyk.co.uk
dir: M1 junct 30, 2nd right towards Worksop, 2nd rdbt 1st exit, 3rd rdbt straight over. Through lights, hotel 100yds on right

A sympathetic renovation has resulted in a small vibrant boutique-style hotel where staff are always on hand to offer friendly and welcoming service. Accommodation is luxurious and equipped with many thoughtful extras. Bowdens Restaurant offers fine dining and makes the ideal setting for a memorable evening; alternatively there's Southgate Grill for those looking for a more casual eating option.

Rooms 15 (4 fmly) **Facilities** FTV Wi-fi ♫ Xmas New Year **Conf** Class 50 Board 60 Thtr 200 **Parking** 78 **Notes** ⊗ Civ Wed 250

COBHAM
Surrey Map 6 TQ16

Premier Inn Cobham
BUDGET HOTEL

☎ 0871 527 8256
Portsmouth Rd, Fairmile KT11 1BW
web: www.premierinn.com
dir: M25 junct 10, A3 towards London, A245 towards Cobham. In Cobham town centre left onto A307 (Portsmouth Rd). Hotel on left

High quality, budget accommodation ideal for both families and business travellers. Spacious, en suite bedrooms feature tea and coffee making facilities, and Freeview TV in most hotels. Internet access and Wi-fi are available for a small fee. The adjacent family restaurant features a wide and varied menu. See also the Hotel Groups pages.

Rooms 48

COCKERMOUTH
Cumbria Map 18 NY13

The Trout Hotel
★★★★ 79% HOTEL

☎ 01900 823591
Crown St CA13 0EJ
e-mail: reservations@trouthotel.co.uk
web: www.trouthotel.co.uk
dir: Adjacent to Wordsworth House

Dating back to 1670, this privately owned hotel has an enviable setting on the banks of the River Derwent. The well-equipped bedrooms, some contained in a wing overlooking the river, are comfortable and mostly spacious. The Terrace Bar & Bistro, serving food all day, has a sheltered patio area. There is also a cosy bar, a choice of lounge areas and an attractive, traditional-style dining room that offers a good choice of set-price dishes.

Rooms 49 (4 fmly) (15 GF) ➤ **S** £95-£118; **D** £120-£249* **Facilities** STV Wi-fi ⌕ Fishing Xmas New Year **Conf** Class 20 Board 20 Thtr 25 **Parking** 40 **Notes** Civ Wed 60

C

COCKERMOUTH *continued*

Shepherds Hotel

★★★ 75% HOTEL

☎ 0845 459 9770

Lakeland Sheep & Wool Centre, Egremont Rd CA13 0QX

e-mail: info@argyllholidays.com

web: www.shepherdshotel.co.uk

dir: At junct of A66 & A5086 S of Cockermouth, entrance off A5086, 200mtrs from rdbt

This hotel is modern in style and offers thoughtfully equipped accommodation. It is well situated for the Northern Lakes area and has good road links. The restaurant, open all day, serves a wide variety of meals and snacks; the Black Rock dishes are recommended. Free Wi-fi is available in the bedrooms.

Rooms 26 (4 fmly) (13 GF) **Facilities** STV FTV Wi-fi ⌨ Pool table Small children's play area **Conf** Class 30 Board 30 Thtr 40 **Services** Lift **Parking** 100 **Notes** Closed 25-26 Dec & 6-20 Jan

---

| COGGESHALL | Map 7 TL82 |
| Essex | |

White Hart Hotel

★★★ 74% HOTEL

OldEngl sh

☎ 01376 561654

Market End CO6 1NH

e-mail: 6529@greeneking.co.uk

web: www.oldenglish.co.uk

dir: From A12 through Kelvedon & onto B1024 to Coggeshall

The White Hart Hotel is a delightful inn situated in the centre of this bustling market town. Bedrooms vary in size and style; each one offers good quality and comfort with extras such as CD players, fruit and mineral water. The heavily beamed public areas include a popular bar serving a varied menu, a large restaurant offering European style cuisine and a cosy residents' lounge.

Rooms 18 (1 fmly) (18 smoking) **Facilities** STV FTV ♬ Xmas **Conf** Class 10 Board 22 Thtr 30 **Parking** 47 **Notes** LB

| COLCHESTER | Map 13 TL92 |
| Essex | |

Wivenhoe House Hotel

★★★★ 87% ❀❀ HOTEL

☎ 01206 863666

Wivenhoe Park CO4 3SQ

e-mail: info@wivenhoehouse.co.uk

web: www.wivenhoehouse.co.uk

dir: From A12 take exit signed Colchester. Follow A133 towards Clacton. Take B1027 for Wivenhoe, right on Boundry Rd, right on Park Rd, signed

A superb building which forms part of Essex University, the property has been totally refurbished. The bedrooms are split between the main building and the more contemporary extension; each one has been individually decorated, furnished to a very high standard and has modern technology. Public rooms include the Signatures fine dining restaurant and a modern brasserie; there is also a choice of lounges with plush furnishings.

Rooms 40 (6 fmly) ⌨ **Facilities** STV FTV Wi-fi ⌨ Xmas New Year **Conf** Class 81 Board 20 Thtr 140 Del £155* **Services** Lift **Parking** 40 **Notes** Civ Wed

---

Crowne Plaza Resort Colchester - Five Lakes

★★★★ 78% ❀ HOTEL

☎ 01621 868888

Colchester Rd CM9 8HX

e-mail: enquiries@cpcolchester.co.uk

web: www.cpcolchester.co.uk

(For full entry see Tolleshunt Knights)

Stoke by Nayland Hotel, Golf & Spa

★★★★ 75% ❀❀ HOTEL

☎ 01206 262836 & 265835

Keepers Ln, Leavenheath CO6 4PZ

e-mail: sales@stokebynayland.com

web: www.stokebynaylandclub.com

dir: Exit A134 at Leavenheath onto B1068, hotel 0.75m on right

This hotel is situated on the edge of Dedham Vale, an Area of Outstanding Natural Beauty, in 300 acres of undulating countryside with lakes and two golf courses. The spacious bedrooms are attractively decorated and equipped with modern facilities, including ISDN lines. Free Wi-fi is available throughout. Public rooms include the Spikes bar, a conservatory, a lounge, a smart restaurant, conference and banqueting suites. The superb Peake Spa and Fitness Centre offers extensive facilities including health and beauty treatments.

Rooms 80 (4 fmly) (26 GF) **Facilities** Spa STV FTV Wi-fi ⌨ ⌕ supervised ⬇ 36 Putt green Fishing Gym Squash Driving range Snooker tables ♬ Xmas New Year **Conf** Class 300 Board 60 Thtr 450 Del from £119 to £139* **Services** Lift **Parking** 335 **Notes** ⊗ Civ Wed 200

BEST WESTERN Marks Tey Hotel

★★★★ 71% HOTEL

☎ 01206 210001

London Rd, Marks Tey CO6 1DU

e-mail: info@marksteyhotel.co.uk

web: www.marksteyhotel.co.uk

dir: Off A12/A120 junct signed Marks Tey/Stansted. At rdbt follow Stanway signs. Follow over A12, at next rdbt take 1st exit. Hotel on left

Best Western Marks Tey Hotel is a purpose-built hotel situated just off the A12 on the outskirts of Colchester. Public rooms include a brasserie restaurant, a choice of lounges, a bar and a conservatory. Bedrooms come in a variety of styles; each one is smartly furnished and equipped with modern facilities. The hotel also has conference and leisure facilities.

Rooms 110 (57 GF) **Facilities** FTV Wi-fi ⌨ ⌕ supervised ⬦ Gym Steam room Beauty treatments Sauna Xmas New Year **Conf** Class 100 Board 60 Thtr 200 **Services** Lift **Parking** 200 **Notes** ⊗ Civ Wed 160

The North Hill Hotel

★★★ 82% ❀❀ HOTEL

☎ 01206 574001

51 North Hill CO1 1PY

e-mail: info@northhillhotel.com

dir: Follow directions for town centre, down North Hill, hotel on left

This hotel is situated in the centre of this historic town. The contemporary open-plan public areas include a small lounge bar and the Green Room restaurant. The smartly appointed bedrooms are modern and well equipped with large flat-screen TVs and many thoughtful touches.

Rooms 17 (3 fmly) (1 GF) ⌨ **S** fr £64.50; **D** fr £89.50 (incl. bkfst)* **Facilities** FTV Wi-fi Xmas New Year **Conf** Class 25 Board 20 Thtr 30 Del from £125* **Notes** ⊗

Holiday Inn Colchester

★★★ 82% HOTEL *Holiday Inn*

☎ 0871 942 9020
Abbotts Ln, Eight Ash Green CO6 3QL
web: www.hicolchesterhotel.co.uk
dir: Exit A12 at junct with A1124, follow Halstead signs. 0.25m, hotel at rdbt on left

This hotel is situated three miles from Colchester and is ideally located just off the A12 in a quiet village setting. All bedrooms are air conditioned and have high-speed internet access. Trader's bar and grill offers a relaxed and informal environment; a range of conference rooms can cater for meetings and weddings.

Rooms 109 (25 fmly) (54 GF) **Facilities** Spa STV Wi-fi ⓢ supervised Gym Health club Xmas New Year **Conf** Class 60 Board 50 Thtr 120 **Services** Air con **Parking** 130 **Notes** ⊗ Civ Wed 100

BEST WESTERN The Rose & Crown Hotel

★★★ 80% HOTEL *Best Western*

☎ 01206 866677
East St CO1 2TZ
e-mail: info@rose-and-crown.com
web: www.rose-and-crown.com
dir: From A12 follow Rollerworld signs, hotel by level crossing

This delightful 14th-century coaching inn is situated close to the shops and is full of charm and character. Public areas feature a wealth of exposed beams and timbered walls, and includes the contemporary East St Grill. Although the bedrooms vary in size, all are stylishly decorated and equipped with many thoughtful extras suitable for both business and leisure guests; luxury executive rooms are available.

Rooms 39 (3 fmly) (12 GF) **Facilities** Wi-fi **Conf** Class 50 Board 45 Thtr 100 Del from £125 to £145 **Services** Lift **Parking** 50 **Notes** ⊗ Civ Wed 80

The George Hotel

★★★ 75% HOTEL *"bespoke"*

☎ 01206 578494 & 0843 1787 153
116 High St CO1 1TD
e-mail: reservations.thegeorgehotel@bespokehotels.com
web: www.bespokehotels.com
dir: In town centre, 200yds from Town Hall

Ideally situated in the centre of town, this 500-year-old establishment has much to offer. The medieval cellar has, preserved behind glass, evidence of the Roman road than once ran through this town. The individually decorated bedrooms are equipped with a range of amenities. There's a popular lounge in which to relax and enjoy good food and real ales. The Bubbles Wine Bar offers an alternative to the traditional lounge.

Rooms 47 (7 fmly) **Facilities** FTV Wi-fi **Conf** Class 40 Board 34 Thtr 70 **Parking** 50 **Notes** ⊗

Premier Inn Colchester (A12)

BUDGET HOTEL

☎ 0871 527 8260
Ipswich Rd CO4 9WP
web: www.premierinn.com
dir: From A12 exit at Colchester Nrth/A1232 junct off towards Colchester. Hotel on right, 200yds from rdbt. (NB for Sat Nav use CO4 9TD)

High quality, budget accommodation ideal for both families and business travellers. Spacious, en suite bedrooms feature tea and coffee making facilities, and Freeview TV in most hotels. Internet access and Wi-fi are available for a small fee. The adjacent family restaurant features a wide and varied menu. See also the Hotel Groups pages.

Rooms 60

Premier Inn Colchester Central

BUDGET HOTEL

☎ 0871 527 8258
Cowdray Av CO1 1UT
web: www.premierinn.com
dir: From Ipswich A12 junct 29. At rdbt onto A1232 (Ipswich road). At 2nd rdbt 2nd exit onto A133 (Cowdray Ave). Hotel approx 0.5m on right

Rooms 20

COLEFORD	Map 4 SO51
Gloucestershire	

Bells Hotel & The Forest of Dean Golf Club

★★★ 70% HOTEL

☎ 01594 832583
Lords Hill GL16 8BE
e-mail: enquiries@bells-hotel.co.uk
dir: 0.25m from Coleford. Off B4228

Set in its own grounds, with an 18-hole golf course, this purpose-built establishment offers a range of facilities. Bedrooms vary in style and space, and a number are on the ground floor. There is a small gym, and a comfortable bar and lounge which is available until late. The hotel's club house, just yards away, has a bar with all-day meals and snacks, a restaurant, a games/TV room and conference and function rooms.

Rooms 53 (12 fmly) (36 GF) (5 smoking) ⌕
Facilities FTV Wi-fi ⓛ 18 Putt green Bowling green Short mat bowling room ♫ Xmas New Year **Conf** Class 250 Board 100 Thtr 350 **Parking** 100 **Notes** LB ⊗ Civ Wed 150

C

COLERNE	Map 4 ST87
Wiltshire	

INSPECTORS' CHOICE

Lucknam Park Hotel & Spa

★★★★★ ❀❀❀
COUNTRY HOUSE HOTEL

☎ 01225 742777
SN14 8AZ
e-mail: reservations@lucknampark.co.uk
web: www.lucknampark.co.uk
dir: M4 junct 17, A350 towards Chippenham, then A420 towards Bristol for 3m. At Ford left to Colerne, 3m, right at x-rds, entrance on right

Approaching this Palladian mansion along a magnificent mile-long avenue of beech and lime trees, builds a wonderful sense of anticipation. Surrounded by 500 acres of parkland and beautiful gardens, the hotel offers a wealth of choices ranging from pampered relaxation within the indulgent spa, complete with an innovative new Well-Being centre, to more energetic equestrian pursuits. Elegant bedrooms and suites are split between the main building and adjacent courtyard, all of which exude quality, individuality and comfort. Dining options range from the informal Brasserie (awarded 1 AA Rosette), to the formal and very accomplished main restaurant, The Park (with 3 AA Rosettes), where skilled, sincere and engaging staff contribute to a memorable experience. For anyone with a passion for food, the recently opened Cookery School is also worth investigating.

Rooms 42 (18 annexe) (16 GF) ⌕ **S** £345-£1170; **D** £345-£1170* **Facilities** Spa STV FTV Wi-fi ⓛ ⓢ ⓛ ⓛ Gym Cross country course Mountain bikes Equestrian centre Cookery school Xmas New Year **Conf** Class 24 Board 24 Thtr 60 **Parking** 80 **Notes** LB ⊗ Civ Wed 110

C

COLESHILL
Warwickshire   Map 10 SP28

Grimstock Country House Hotel

★★★ 74% COUNTRY HOUSE HOTEL

☎ 01675 462121
Gilson Rd, Gilson B46 1LJ
e-mail: enquiries@grimstockhotel.co.uk
web: www.grimstockhotel.co.uk
dir: Exit A446 at rdbt onto B4117 to Gilson, hotel
100yds on right

This privately owned hotel is convenient for
Birmingham International Airport and the NEC, and
benefits from a peaceful rural setting. Bedrooms are
spacious and comfortable. Public rooms include two
restaurants, a wood-panelled bar, good conference
facilities and a gym featuring the latest
cardiovascular equipment.

Rooms 44 (1 fmly) (13 GF) **S** £60-£95; **D** £75-£125
(incl. bkfst)* **Facilities** FTV Wi-fi ⓑ Gym Xmas New
Year **Conf** Class 60 Board 50 Thtr 100 Del from £125
to £145* **Parking** 100 **Notes** Civ Wed 100

COLTISHALL
Norfolk   Map 13 TG21

Norfolk Mead Hotel

★★★★ 77% ⓐ COUNTRY HOUSE HOTEL

☎ 01603 737531
Church Loke NR12 7DN
e-mail: info@norfolkmead.co.uk
web: www.norfolkmead.co.uk
dir: Coltishall village, go right with petrol station on
left, 200 yds church on right, go down driveway

This beautiful hotel enjoys a peaceful location and is
set in its own extensive grounds, while still being a
short walk to the pretty village of Coltishall. A major
renovation has been completed in 2013, so the new
bedrooms are all beautifully designed, and the public
areas are very well appointed. Afternoon tea can be
enjoyed in the walled garden on finer days and the
cosy bar is very comfortable. There is an award-
winning restaurant, which benefits from garden and
river views.

Rooms 13 (2 annexe) (2 fmly) (1 GF) ⓡ **S** £115-£165;
D £125-£175 (incl. bkfst)* **Facilities** FTV Wi-fi ⓑ ⓢ
Xmas New Year **Conf** Class 20 Board 20 Thtr 40
Del from £200 to £250* **Parking** 40 **Notes** ⊗
Civ Wed 40

COLYFORD
Devon   Map 4 SY29

Swallows Eaves Hotel

★★ 85% SMALL HOTEL

☎ 01297 553184
Swan Hill Rd EX24 6QJ
e-mail: info@swallowseaves.co.uk
web: www.swallowseaves.co.uk
dir: On A3052 between Lyme Regis & Sidmouth, in
village centre, opposite post office store

Close to the Devon and Dorset border, this intimate
and welcoming hotel is ideally located for exploring
this beautiful area. The relaxed atmosphere is
matched with attentive service. Comfortable
bedrooms come complete with Egyptian cotton
bedding and large fluffy towels. Local produce
features on the menu which is offered in the stylish
Reeds restaurant.

Rooms 7 (1 GF) ⓡ **S** £75-£85; **D** £95-£135 (incl.
bkfst)* **Facilities** FTV Wi-fi Xmas **Conf** Thtr 20
Parking 18 **Notes** LB ⊗ No children 14yrs

CONSETT
Co Durham   Map 19 NZ15

BEST WESTERN Derwent Manor Hotel

★★★ 75% HOTEL

☎ 01207 592000
Allensford DH8 9BB
e-mail: reservations.derwentmanor@ohiml.com
web: www.bw-derwentmanorhotel.co.uk
dir: On A68

This hotel, built in the style of a manor house, is set
in open grounds overlooking the River Derwent.
Spacious bedrooms, including a number of suites, are
comfortably equipped. A popular wedding venue,
there are also extensive conference facilities and an
impressive leisure suite. The Grouse & Claret bar
serves a wide range of drinks and light meals, and
Guinevere's restaurant offers the fine dining option.

Rooms 48 (29 fmly) (26 GF) ⓡ **S** £50-£115;
D £65-£130 (incl. bkfst)* **Facilities** STV FTV Wi-fi ⓑ
ⓢ supervised Gym Xmas New Year **Conf** Class 200
Board 60 Thtr 300 Del from £125 to £150*
Services Lift **Parking** 100 **Notes** LB Civ Wed 300

COPTHORNE

See **Gatwick Airport**

CORBY
Northamptonshire   Map 11 SP88

Premier Inn Corby

BUDGET HOTEL

☎ 0871 527 8264
1 Little Colliers Field NN18 8TJ
web: www.premierinn.com
dir: M1 junct 19, A14 E'bound. Exit at junct 7, left at
rdbt onto A43. At next rdbt left onto A6003. Hotel at
next rdbt (NB for Sat Nav use NN18 9EX)

High quality, budget accommodation ideal for both
families and business travellers. Spacious, en suite
bedrooms feature tea and coffee making facilities,
and Freeview TV in most hotels. Internet access and
Wi-fi are available for a small fee. The adjacent
family restaurant features a wide and varied menu.
See also the Hotel Groups pages.

Rooms 56

CORFE CASTLE
Dorset   Map 4 SY98

Mortons House Hotel

★★★ 86% ⓐⓐ HOTEL

☎ 01929 480988
49 East St BH20 5EE
e-mail: stay@mortonshouse.co.uk
web: www.mortonshouse.co.uk
dir: On A351 between Wareham & Swanage

Set in delightful gardens and grounds with excellent
views of Corfe Castle, this impressive building dates
back to Tudor times. The oak-panelled drawing room
has a roaring log fire in cooler months, and an
interesting range of enjoyable cuisine is available in
the well-appointed dining room. Bedrooms, many with
views of the castle, are comfortable and well
equipped.

Rooms 21 (7 annexe) (2 fmly) (7 GF) ⓡ **S** £85-£120;
D £160 (incl. bkfst)* **Facilities** FTV Wi-fi HL Xmas
New Year Child facilities **Conf** Class 45 Board 20
Thtr 45 Del from £135 to £155* **Parking** 40 **Notes** LB
⊗ Civ Wed 60

Save on hotels. Book at **theAA.com/hotel**

COL – COV 141 ENGLAND

C

CORLEY
MOTORWAY SERVICE AREA (M6)
Warwickshire
Map 10 SP38

Days Inn Corley - NEC - M6

BUDGET HOTEL

☎ 01676 543800
Junction 3-4, M6 North, Corley CV7 8NR
e-mail: corley.hotel@welcomebreak.co.uk
dir: On M6 between juncts 3 & 4 N'bound

This modern building offers accommodation in smart, spacious and well-equipped bedrooms, suitable for families and business travellers, and all with en suite bathrooms. Continental breakfast is available and other refreshments may be taken at the nearby family restaurant. See also the Hotel Groups pages.

Rooms 50 (13 fmly) (24 GF) (8 smoking)

CORNHILL-ON-TWEED
Northumberland
Map 21 NT83

Tillmouth Park Country House Hotel

★★★ 87% ◉ COUNTRY HOUSE HOTEL

☎ 01890 882255
TD12 4UU
e-mail: reception@tillmouthpark.f9.co.uk
web: www.tillmouthpark.co.uk
dir: Exit A1(M) at East Ord rdbt at Berwick-upon-Tweed. Take A698 signed Cornhill & Coldstream. Hotel 9m on left

An imposing mansion set in landscaped grounds by the River Till. Gracious public rooms include a stunning galleried lounge with a drawing room adjacent. The quiet, elegant dining room overlooks the gardens, whilst lunches and early dinners are available in the bistro. Bedrooms retain much traditional character and include several magnificent master rooms.

Rooms 14 (2 annexe) (2 fmly) (2 GF) (4 smoking)
S £79-£215; **D** £165-£235 (incl. bkfst)* **Facilities** FTV Wi-fi Game shooting Fishing New Year **Conf** Class 20 Board 20 Thtr 50 Del £195* **Parking** 50 **Notes** LB Closed 3 Jan-1 Apr Civ Wed 50

CORSE LAWN
Gloucestershire
Map 10 SO83

INSPECTORS' CHOICE

Corse Lawn House Hotel

★★★ ◉◉ HOTEL

☎ 01452 780771
GL19 4LZ
e-mail: enquiries@corselawn.com
web: www.corselawn.com
dir: On B4211 5m SW of Tewkesbury

This gracious Grade II listed Queen Anne house, in 12 acres of grounds, has been home to the Hine family for more than thirty years. Aided by an enthusiastic and committed team, the family continues to preside over all aspects of the hotel, creating a wonderfully relaxed environment. Bedrooms offer a reassuring mix of comfort and quality, and include four-poster rooms. In both The Restaurant and The Bistro the impressive cuisine is based on excellent produce, much of it locally sourced.

Rooms 19 (2 fmly) (5 GF) **S** £75-£100;
D £120-£160 (incl. bkfst)* **Facilities** STV FTV Wi-fi Badminton Table tennis New Year **Conf** Class 30 Board 25 Thtr 50 Del from £130 to £150* **Parking** 62 **Notes** LB Closed 24-26 Dec Civ Wed 70

CORSHAM
Wiltshire
Map 4 ST87

Guyers House Hotel

★★★ 79% ◉◉ HOTEL

☎ 01249 713399
Pickwick SN13 0PS
dir: A4 between Pickwick & Corsham

This privately owned hotel retains the charm and ambiance of a country house. The bedrooms are well appointed in keeping with the style of the house, and equipped with all modern amenities. The award-winning restaurant is the ideal place for an intimate dinner or a family gathering; alfresco dining is possible when the weather is favourable. The gardens

are a feature and are open to the public on certain days under the National Garden Scheme. The hotel is conveniently located for easy access to Bath.

Rooms 37 (13 GF) **S** £80-£101; **D** £100-£120 (incl. bkfst)* **Facilities** FTV Wi-fi Gym Xmas **Conf** Class 34 Board 24 Thtr 75 Del £135* **Parking** 60 **Notes** Closed 30 Dec-3 Jan Civ Wed

COVENTRY
West Midlands
Map 10 SP37

See also **Meriden & Nuneaton**

BEST WESTERN PLUS Windmill Village Hotel

★★★★ 79% HOTEL

☎ 02476 404040
Birmingham Rd, Allesley CV5 9AL
e-mail: reservations@windmillvillagehotel.co.uk
dir: A45, close to Coventry City Centre

This modern hotel is conveniently located on the outskirts of Coventry and is a short drive from Birmingham and the NEC. Bedrooms are all very attractively presented and most rooms have views over the hotel's challenging golf course. The leisure facilities are first rate and include a very well-equipped gym and a swimming pool. Business guests are well catered for with a range of conference facilities including business suites, and free Wi-fi is available throughout the hotel.

Rooms 105 (35 annexe) (10 fmly) (39 GF) **Facilities** Spa FTV Wi-fi supervised 18 Putt green Gym Beautry treatment room Xmas New Year **Conf** Class 140 Board 60 Thtr 400 **Services** Lift **Parking** 400 **Notes** Civ Wed 100

Holiday Inn Coventry

★★★ 78% HOTEL

☎ 0871 942 9021 & 024 7658 7420
Hinckley Rd CV2 2HP
e-mail: reservations-coventrym6@ihg.com
web: www.holidayinn.co.uk
dir: M6 junct 2. Hotel on A4600

Situated close to the city centre and major motorway networks, this hotel offers comfortable and modern accommodation. Facilities include the Spirit Leisure Suite, Traders Restaurant, spacious lounges where food is served all day, and extensive conference services.

Rooms 158 (11 fmly) (64 GF) (16 smoking)
S £139-£159; **Facilities** STV Wi-fi HL supervised Gym Steam room Sauna Aqua aerobic classes Zumba classes New Year **Conf** Class 120 Board 105 Thtr 350 Del from £99 to £155 **Services** Lift Air con **Parking** 246 **Notes** LB Civ Wed 200

C

COVENTRY *continued*

Novotel Coventry

★★★ 77% HOTEL

☎ 024 7636 5000
Wilsons Ln CV6 6HL
e-mail: h0506@accor-hotels.com
web: www.novotel.com
dir: M6 junct 3. Follow signs for B4113 towards
Longford & Bedworth. 3rd exit on large rdbt

Novotel Coventry is a modern hotel convenient for
Birmingham, Coventry and the motorway network,
offering spacious, well-equipped accommodation. The
bright brasserie has extended dining hours,
alternatively there is an extensive room-service menu.
Family rooms and a play area make this a child-
friendly hotel, and there is also a selection of meeting
rooms.

Rooms 98 (25 GF) 🐾 **S** £40–£139; **D** £50–£149
Facilities STV Wi-fi **Conf** Class 100 Board 40 Thtr 200
Del from £105 to £145 **Services** Lift **Parking** 120
Notes Civ Wed 50

Ibis Coventry Centre

BUDGET HOTEL

☎ 024 7625 0500
Mile Ln, St John's Ringway CV1 2LN
e-mail: H2793@accor.com
web: www.ibishotel.com
dir: A45, A4114 signed Jaguar Assembly Plant. At
inner ring road towards ring road S. Exit junct 5 for
Mile Lane

Modern, budget hotel offering comfortable
accommodation in bright and practical bedrooms.
Breakfast is self-service and dinner is available in
the restaurant. See also the Hotel Groups pages.

Rooms 89 (5 fmly) (25 GF)

Ibis Coventry South

BUDGET HOTEL

☎ 024 7663 9922
Abbey Rd, Whitley CV3 4LF
e-mail: H2094@accor.com
web: www.ibishotel.com
dir: Signed from A46/A423 rdbt. Take A423 towards
A45. Follow signs for Racquets Health Club & Jaguar
Engineering Plant. 1st exit from Jaguar rdbt, hotel at
end of lane by The Racquets

Rooms 51 (51 annexe) (25 GF) **Conf** Class 20
Board 16 Thtr 20

Premier Inn Coventry (Binley/A46)

BUDGET HOTEL

☎ 0871 527 8268
Rugby Rd, Binley Woods CV3 2TA
web: www.premierinn.com
dir: M6 junct 2 follow Warwick, A46 & M40 signs.
Follow 'All traffic' signs, under bridge onto A46. Left
at 1st rdbt to Binley. Hotel on right at next rdbt

High quality, budget accommodation ideal for both
families and business travellers. Spacious, en suite
bedrooms feature tea and coffee making facilities,
and Freeview TV in most hotels. Internet access and
Wi-fi are available for a small fee. The adjacent
family restaurant features a wide and varied menu.
See also the Hotel Groups pages.

Rooms 76

Premier Inn Coventry City Centre

BUDGET HOTEL

☎ 0871 527 8272
Belgrade Plaza, Bond St CV1 4AH
web: www.premierinn.com
dir: A4053 (ring road) junct 9, follow Belgrade Plaza
car park signs. Hotel in same complex

Rooms 119

Premier Inn Coventry City Centre (Earlsdon Park)

BUDGET HOTEL

☎ 0871 527 9318
Earlsdon Park CV1 3BH
dir: From Coventry ring road follow Ikea signs. Hotel
adjacent to Coventry RFC on Butts Rd. Parking in
multi storey adjacent

Rooms 100

Premier Inn Coventry East (Ansty)

BUDGET HOTEL

☎ 0871 527 8274
Coombe Fields Rd, Ansty CV7 9JP
web: www.premierinn.com
dir: M6 junct 2, B4065 towards Ansty. After village
right onto B4029 signed Brinklow. Right into Coombe
Fields Rd, hotel on right

Rooms 27

Premier Inn Coventry (M6 Jct 2)

BUDGET HOTEL

☎ 0871 527 8266
Gielgud Way, Cross Point Business Park CV2 2SZ
web: www.premierinn.com
dir: M6 junct 2 towards Coventry onto A4600
(Hinckley road). At rdbt 1st exit into Parkway, left at
next rdbt into Olivier Way. At next rdbt straight on into
retail park towards cinema, hotel on right

Rooms 48

Premier Inn Coventry South (A45)

BUDGET HOTEL

☎ 0871 527 8270
Kenpas Highway CV3 6PB
web: www.premierinn.com
dir: M6 junct 2, A46. Follow A45 towards Birmingham

Rooms 37

COWES   Map 5 SZ49
Isle of Wight

BEST WESTERN New Holmwood Hotel

★★★ 77% HOTEL

☎ 01983 292508
Queens Rd, Egypt Point PO31 8BW
e-mail: reception@newholmwoodhotel.co.uk
dir: From A3020 at Northwood Garage lights, left &
follow to rdbt. 1st left then sharp right into Baring
Rd, 4th left into Egypt Hill. At bottom turn right, hotel
on right

Just by the Esplanade, this hotel has an enviable
outlook. Bedrooms are comfortable and very well
equipped, and the light and airy, glass-fronted
restaurant looks out to sea and serves a range of
interesting meals. The sun terrace is delightful in the
summer and there is a small pool area.

Rooms 26 (1 fmly) (9 GF) 🐾 **Facilities** STV FTV Wi-fi
❄ Xmas New Year **Conf** Class 60 Board 50 Thtr 100
Parking 20 **Notes** Civ Wed 50

Save on hotels. Book at **theAA.com/hotel**

COV – CRI 143 ENGLAND

CRAMLINGTON
Northumberland
Map 21 NZ27

Premier Inn Newcastle Gosforth/Cramlington

BUDGET HOTEL

☎ 0871 527 8788
Moor Farm Roundabout, Off Front St, Annitsford NE23 7QA
web: www.premierinn.com
dir: At rdbt junct of A19 & A189, S of Cramlington

High quality, budget accommodation ideal for both families and business travellers. Spacious, en suite bedrooms feature tea and coffee making facilities, and Freeview TV in most hotels. Internet access and Wi-fi are available for a small fee. The adjacent family restaurant features a wide and varied menu. See also the Hotel Groups pages.

Rooms 40

CRAWLEY

See Gatwick Airport

CREWE
Cheshire
Map 15 SJ75

Crewe Hall
★★★★ 80% ◉ HOTEL

☎ 01270 253333
Weston Rd CW1 6UZ
e-mail: crewehall@qhotels.co.uk
web: www.qhotels.co.uk
dir: M6 junct 16, A500 to Crewe. Take A5020. 1st exit at next rdbt to Crewe. Hotel 150yds on right

Standing in 500 acres of mature grounds, this historic hall dates back to the 17th century, yet retains an elaborate interior with Victorian-style architecture. Bedrooms are spacious, well equipped and comfortable with traditionally styled suites in the main hall and modern rooms in the west wing. Afternoon tea is served in The Sheridan Lounge and The Brasserie Restaurant and Bar is contemporary and has a relaxed atmosphere. The health and beauty spa ensure that the hotel is a popular choice with both corporate and leisure guests.

Rooms 117 (91 annexe) (5 fmly) (35 GF)
Facilities Spa STV Wi-fi ◊ ⊛ ⌇ Gym Enclosed events field **Conf** Class 172 Board 96 Thtr 364 **Services** Lift **Parking** 500 **Notes** ⊗ Civ Wed 180

Hunters Lodge Hotel
★★★ 78% HOTEL

☎ 01270 539100
Sydney Rd, Sydney CW1 5LU
e-mail: info@hunterslodge.co.uk
web: www.hunterslodge.co.uk
dir: M6 junct 16. 1m from Crewe station, off A534

Dating back to the 18th century, the hotel has been extended and modernised. Accommodation, mainly located in adjacent well-equipped bedroom wings, includes family and four-poster rooms. Imaginative dishes are served in the spacious restaurant, and the popular bar also offers a choice of tempting meals. Service throughout is friendly and efficient.

Rooms 57 (4 fmly) (31 GF) (2 smoking) **S** £55-£60; **D** £77-£87 (incl. bkfst) **Facilities** STV FTV Wi-fi ◊ Gym **Conf** Class 100 Board 80 Thtr 160 Del from £118.80 to £136.35 **Parking** 240 **Notes** ⊗ RS Sun Civ Wed 130

Premier Inn Crewe Central

BUDGET HOTEL

☎ 0871 527 8276
Weston Rd CW1 6FX
web: www.premierinn.com
dir: M6 junct 16, A500, at rdbt 3rd exit onto A5020 (Old Park Rd). At next rdbt 2nd exit into Western Rd, at next rdbt 3rd exit, hotel on left

High quality, budget accommodation ideal for both families and business travellers. Spacious, en suite bedrooms feature tea and coffee making facilities, and Freeview TV in most hotels. Internet access and Wi-fi are available for a small fee. The adjacent family restaurant features a wide and varied menu. See also the Hotel Groups pages.

Rooms 20

Premier Inn Crewe West

BUDGET HOTEL

☎ 0871 527 8278
Coppenhall Ln, Woolstanwood CW2 8SD
web: www.premierinn.com
dir: At junct of A530 & A532, 9m from M6 junct 16 N'bound

Rooms 42

CRICK
Northamptonshire
Map 11 SP57

Holiday Inn Rugby - Northampton

★★★ 73% HOTEL

☎ 0871 942 9059 & 01788 824800
M1 Junction 18 NN6 7XR
e-mail: rugbyhi@ihg.com
web: www.hirugbyhotel.co.uk
dir: 0.5m from M1 junct 18

Situated in pleasant surroundings, located just off the M1, this modern hotel offers well-equipped and comfortable bedrooms. Public areas include the popular Traders restaurant and a lounge where an all-day menu is available. The Spirit Health Club provides indoor swimming and a good fitness facility.

Rooms 90 (19 fmly) (42 GF) (12 smoking)
Facilities STV Wi-fi ⊛ Gym New Year **Conf** Class 90 Board 64 Thtr 170 **Services** Lift Air con **Parking** 250 **Notes** Civ Wed

Ibis Rugby

ibis

BUDGET HOTEL

☎ 01788 824331
Parklands NN6 7EX
e-mail: H3588@accor.com
web: www.ibishotel.com
dir: M1 junct 18, follow Daventry/Rugby A5 signs. At rdbt 3rd exit signed DIRFT East. Hotel on right

Modern, budget hotel offering comfortable accommodation in bright and practical bedrooms. Breakfast is self-service and dinner is available in the restaurant. See also the Hotel Groups pages.

Rooms 111 (47 fmly) (12 GF) **Conf** Class 25 Board 25 Thtr 30

C

C

CRICKLADE
Wiltshire — Map 5 SU09

Cricklade House
★★★ 79% ◎◎ HOTEL

☎ 01793 750751
Common Hill SN6 6HA
e-mail: reception@crickladehotel.co.uk
web: www.crickladehotel.co.uk
dir: A419 onto B4040. Left at clock tower. Right at rdbt. Hotel 0.5m up hill on left

A haven of peace and tranquillity with spectacular views, this hotel is set in over 30 acres of beautiful countryside. Bedrooms vary in size and style; there are main building rooms and courtyard rooms - all offer high levels of comfort and quality. Public areas include an elegant lounge, dining room and a Victorian-style conservatory that runs the full length of the building. The extensive leisure facilities include a 9-hole golf course, an indoor pool and a gym.

Rooms 47 (21 annexe) (2 fmly) (5 GF) **Facilities** STV FTV Wi-fi ⊗ ♨ 9 ⌣ Gym Aromatherapy Beautician Xmas New Year **Conf** Class 60 Board 42 Thtr 120 Del from £130 to £156* **Parking** 100 **Notes** Civ Wed 120

See advert on opposite page

CROMER
Norfolk — Map 13 TG24

Sea Marge Hotel
★★★ 87% ◎◎ HOTEL

☎ 01263 579579
16 High St, Overstrand NR27 0AB
e-mail: seamarge@mackenziehotels.com
dir: A140 from Norwich then A149 to Cromer, B1159 to Overstrand. Hotel in village centre

An elegant Grade II listed Edwardian mansion perched on the clifftop amidst pretty landscaped gardens which lead down to the beach. Bedrooms are tastefully decorated and thoughtfully equipped; many have superb sea views. Public rooms offer a wide choice of areas in which to relax, including Frazer's restaurant and a smart lounge bar.

Rooms 25 (6 annexe) (6 fmly) (2 GF) ↖ **S** fr £97; **D** fr £154 (incl. bkfst)* **Facilities** FTV Wi-fi ♨ Xmas New Year **Conf** Class 55 Board 30 Thtr 70 Del from £120 **Services** Lift **Parking** 50 **Notes** LB

The Cliftonville Hotel
★★★ 77% HOTEL

☎ 01263 512543
Seafront NR27 9AS
e-mail: reservations@cliftonvillehotel.co.uk
web: www.cliftonvillehotel.co.uk
dir: From A149 (coast road), 500yds from town centre, N'bound on clifftop by sunken gardens

The Cliftonville Hotel is an imposing Edwardian hotel situated on the main coast road with stunning views of the sea. Public areas feature a magnificent staircase, minstrels' gallery, coffee shop, lounge bar, a further residents' lounge, Boltons Bistro and an additional restaurant. The pleasantly decorated bedrooms are generally quite spacious and have lovely sea views.

Rooms 30 (2 fmly) **S** £70-£95; **D** £140-£190 (incl. bkfst)* **Facilities** FTV Wi-fi Xmas New Year **Conf** Class 100 Board 60 Thtr 150 **Services** Lift **Parking** 20 **Notes** LB

Hotel de Paris
★★ 74% HOTEL

Leisureplex

☎ 01263 513141
High St NR27 9HG
e-mail: deparis.cromer@alfatravel.co.uk
web: www.leisureplex.co.uk
dir: Enter Church St (one way) after lights left straight into Jetty St, car park at end on left

An imposing, traditional-style resort hotel, situated in a prominent position overlooking the pier and beach. The bedrooms are pleasantly decorated and equipped with a good range of useful extras; many rooms have lovely sea views. The spacious public areas include a large lounge bar, restaurant, games room and a further lounge.

Rooms 63 (8 fmly) ↖ **Facilities** FTV Wi-fi Games room ♫ Xmas New Year **Services** Lift **Parking** 14 **Notes** ⊗ Closed Jan-Feb RS Mar, Nov & Dec

CROOKLANDS
Cumbria — Map 18 SD58

Crooklands Hotel
★★★ 78% HOTEL

☎ 015395 67432
LA7 7NW
e-mail: reception@crooklands.com
web: www.crooklands.com
dir: M6 junct 36 onto A65. Left at rdbt. Hotel 1.5m on right past garage

Although only a stone's throw from the M6, this hotel enjoys a peaceful rural location. Housed in a converted 200-year-old farmhouse, the restaurant retains many original features such as the beams and stone walls. Bedrooms are a mix of modern and traditional and vary in size. The hotel is a popular stop-over for both leisure and corporate guests travelling between England and Scotland.

Rooms 30 (3 fmly) (14 GF) **Facilities** FTV Wi-fi New Year **Conf** Class 50 Board 40 Thtr 80 **Services** Lift **Parking** 80 **Notes** ⊗ Closed 24-28 Dec

C

CROSTHWAITE
Cumbria   Map 18 SD49

Damson Dene Hotel
★★★ 73% HOTEL

☎ 015395 68676
LA8 8JE
e-mail: info@damsondene.co.uk
web: www.bestlakesbreaks.co.uk
dir: M6 junct 36, A590 signed Barrow-in-Furness, 5m right onto A5074. Hotel on right in 5m

A short drive from Lake Windermere, this hotel enjoys a tranquil and scenic setting. Bedrooms include a number with four-poster beds and jacuzzi baths. The spacious restaurant serves a daily-changing menu, with some of the produce coming from the hotel's own kitchen garden. Real fires warm the lounge in the cooler months, and leisure facilities are available.

Rooms 40 (3 annexe) (7 fmly) (9 GF) **S** £82-£102; **D** £124-£164 (incl. bkfst)* **Facilities** Spa Wi-fi ⊙ Gym Beauty salon Xmas New Year **Conf** Class 60 Board 40 Thtr 140 Del from £115 to £135* **Parking** 45 **Notes** LB Civ Wed 120

CROYDON
Greater London   Map 6 TQ36

Croydon Park Hotel
★★★★ 73% HOTEL

☎ 020 8680 9200
7 Altyre Rd CR9 5AA
e-mail: info@croydonparkhotel.com
dir: 3-min walk from East Croydon Station

This hotel is located in the heart of the town centre, a 3-minute walk to East Croydon train station and with easy access to both Gatwick Airport and central London. Bedrooms vary in style, but all are comfortably appointed. The two dining options are Whistlers Bar with a menu available throughout the day, and Oscars Brasserie with a daily buffet and carte menu. Conference and leisure facilities are available.

Rooms 211 (36 fmly) (6 GF) (15 smoking) **Facilities** FTV Wi-fi � ⊙ supervised Gym Squash Sauna Solarium Xmas New Year **Conf** Class 100 Board 30 Thtr 220 Del from £130 to £145* **Services** Lift Air con **Parking** 91 **Notes** ⊗ Civ Wed 220

Hallmark Hotel Croydon
★★★★ 73% HOTEL

☎ 020 8680 1999
Purley Way CR9 4LT
e-mail:
croydon.reservations@hallmarkhotels.co.uk
dir: Follow A23 & Central London signs. Hotel on left adjacent to Airport House

This hotel (formerly the Aerodrome Hotel) sits in a prime location and offers comfortably appointed bedrooms, all with LCD TVs and free Wi-fi throughout. Following a refurbishment programme, public areas are stylish and modern in their design and include a spacious open-plan bar and brasserie. Ideal for both the leisure and corporate market, there are a number of fully-equipped meeting and conference facilities.

Rooms 110 ⊮ **Facilities** STV FTV Wi-fi ⅋ Xmas New Year **Conf** Class 60 Board 36 Thtr 170 Del from £125 to £140* **Notes** Civ Wed

Selsdon Park Hotel & Golf Club
★★★★ 73% HOTEL

☎ 020 8657 8811
Addington Rd, Sanderstead CR2 8YA
e-mail:
selsdonpark.reception@principal-hayley.com
dir: 3m SE of Croydon, off A2022

Surrounded by 200 acres of mature parkland with its own 18-hole golf course, this imposing Jacobean mansion is less than 20 minutes from central London. The hotel's impressive range of conference rooms along with the spectacular views of the North Downs countryside, make this a popular venue for both weddings and meetings. The leisure facilities are impressive.

Rooms 199 (19 fmly) (33 GF) **Facilities** Spa STV Wi-fi ⊙ ⅄ ⅃ 18 ⅊ Putt green ⅁ Gym Squash Xmas **Conf** Class 250 Board 100 Thtr 350 **Services** Lift **Parking** 300 **Notes** ⊗ Civ Wed 350

Coulsdon Manor Hotel
★★★★ 70% HOTEL

☎ 020 8668 0414
Coulsdon Court Rd, Coulsdon CR5 2LL
e-mail: reservations.coulsdon@ohiml.com
web: www.oxfordhotelsandinns.com
dir: M23/25 junct 7, A23 for 2.5m, B2030 for 1m, left onto Coulsdon Rd, then 0.5m to hotel

This delightful Victorian manor house is peacefully set amidst 140 acres of landscaped parkland, complete with its own professional 18-hole golf course. Bedrooms are spacious and comfortable, whilst public areas include a choice of lounges and an elegant restaurant serving carefully prepared, imaginative food.

Rooms 37 (4 fmly) **S** £65-£145; **D** £75-£155 **Facilities** STV FTV Wi-fi ⅃ 18 ⅁ Putt green Gym Squash Aerobic studio Steam room Sauna Xmas New Year **Conf** Class 90 Board 70 Thtr 180 Del from £140 to £160 **Services** Lift **Parking** 200 **Notes** LB Civ Wed 100

South Park Hotel
★★★ 73% HOTEL

☎ 020 8688 5644
3-5 South Park Hill Rd, South Croydon CR2 7DY
e-mail: reception@southparkhotel.co.uk
web: www.southparkhotel.co.uk
dir: Follow A235 to town centre. At Coombe Rd lights turn right (A212) towards Addington, 0.5m to rdbt take 3rd exit into South Park Hill Rd, hotel on left

This intimate hotel has easy access to rail and road networks and some off-street parking is available. Attractively decorated bedrooms vary in size and offer a good range of in-room facilities. Public areas consist of a bar and lounge with large sofas and an informal dining area where meals are served.

Rooms 30 (2 fmly) (9 GF) **Facilities** FTV Wi-fi **Conf** Class 50 Board 30 Thtr 60 **Parking** 15 **Notes** ⊗

Holiday Inn Express London - Croydon

BUDGET HOTEL

☎ 020 8253 1200
1 Priddys Yard, Off Frith Rd CRO 1TS
e-mail: gm@exhicroydon.com
web: www.hiexpress.com/london-croydon
dir: From A235 into Lower Coombe St, at rdbt 1st exit, at next rdbt 2nd exit onto dual carriageway, right to Centrale Shopping Centre, under car park, follow to right, 1st left

A modern hotel ideal for families and business travellers. Fresh and uncomplicated, the spacious rooms include Sky TV, power shower and tea and coffee-making facilities. Continental buffet breakfast is included in the room rate; other meals may be taken at the nearby family pub or restaurant. See also the Hotel Groups pages.

Rooms 156 (62 fmly) 🐾 **Conf** Class 30 Board 30 Thtr 60

Premier Inn Croydon South

BUDGET HOTEL

☎ 0871 527 8280
104 Coombe Rd CRO 5RB
web: www.premierinn.com
dir: M25 junct 7, A23 to Purley, A235 to Croydon. Pass Tree House pub on left. Right at lights onto A212

High quality, budget accommodation ideal for both families and business travellers. Spacious, en suite bedrooms feature tea and coffee making facilities, and Freeview TV in most hotels. Internet access and Wi-fi are available for a small fee. The adjacent family restaurant features a wide and varied menu. See also the Hotel Groups pages.

Rooms 39

Premier Inn Croydon West

BUDGET HOTEL

☎ 0871 527 8282
The Colonnades Leisure Park, 619 Purley Way CRO 4RQ
web: www.premierinn.com
dir: From N: M1, M25, A23 towards Croydon. From S: M25 junct 7, A23 towards Purley Way, 8m, hotel close to junct with Waddon Way

Rooms 84

CUCKFIELD   Map 6 TQ32
West Sussex

INSPECTORS' CHOICE

Ockenden Manor Hotel & Spa

★★★ ◉◉◉ HOTEL

☎ 01444 416111
Ockenden Ln RH17 5LD
e-mail: reservations@ockenden-manor.com
web: www.hshotels.co.uk
dir: A23 towards Brighton. 4.5m left onto B2115 towards Haywards Heath. Cuckfield 3m. Ockenden Lane off High St. Hotel at end

This charming 16th-century property enjoys fine views of the South Downs. The individually designed bedrooms and suites offer high standards of accommodation, some with unique historic features. Public rooms, retaining much original character, include an elegant sitting room with all the elements in place for a relaxing afternoon in front of the fire. Imaginative, noteworthy cuisine is the highlight to any stay. The beautiful rooms and lovely garden make Ockenden a popular wedding venue. The hotel has a spa, situated in a walled garden, that offers a pool, hot tub, spa bath, rain shower, floatation room, gym, sauna, steam room plus health and beauty treatments.

Rooms 28 (6 annexe) (4 fmly) (4 GF) 🐾
S £147-£250; **D** £190-£495 (incl. bkfst)*
Facilities Spa STV FTV Wi-fi 🕸 🎾 🏊 Gym Floatation tank Xmas New Year **Conf** Class 20 Board 26 Thtr 50 Del from £294 to £354*
Services Lift **Parking** 98 **Notes** LB Civ Wed 150

CULLOMPTON   Map 3 ST00
Devon

Padbrook Park

★★★ 78% HOTEL

☎ 01884 836100
EX15 1RU
e-mail: info@padbrookpark.co.uk
dir: 1m from M5 junct 28, follow brown signs

This purpose-built hotel is part of a golf and leisure complex located in the Culm Valley, just one mile from the M5. Set in 100 acres of parkland with an 18-hole golf course, Padbrook Park has a friendly, relaxed atmosphere and a contemporary feel. A variety of room types is available, including family, inter-connecting, superior and deluxe rooms.

Rooms 40 (4 fmly) (11 GF) **Facilities** STV FTV Wi-fi 🐾 HL ⚓ 18 Putt green Fishing Gym 3 rink bowling centre Crazy golf 🎵 Xmas New Year **Conf** Class 150 Board 50 Thtr 200 **Services** Lift **Parking** 250 **Notes** 🚫 Civ Wed 2000

DAGENHAM   MAP 6 TQ48
Greater London

Premier Inn London Dagenham

BUDGET HOTEL

☎ 0871 527 9364
Chequers Corner, 2 New Rd RM9 6YS
web: www.premierinn.com
dir: M25 junct 30/A13 signed Barking. Continue on A13 through underpass then flyover, following directions to Central London, Barking & Docklands. Left off A13 - Dagenham East. At rdbt 4th exit, then left at traffic signals onto A1306 Dagenham. Continue at traffic signals. Inn on left

High quality, budget accommodation ideal for both families and business travellers. Spacious, en suite bedrooms feature tea and coffee making facilities, and Freeview TV in most hotels. Internet access and Wi-fi are available for a small fee. The adjacent family restaurant features a wide and varied menu. See also the Hotel Groups pages.

Rooms 80

D

D

DARLINGTON
Co Durham

Map 19 NZ21

Rockliffe Hall

★★★★★ ◉◉◉ HOTEL

☎ 01325 729999
Rockliffe Park, Hurworth-on-Tees DL2 2DU
e-mail: enquiries@rockliffehall.com
web: www.rockliffehall.com
dir: A66 towards Darlington, A167, through
Hurworth-on-Tees. In Croft-on-Tees left into
Hurworth Rd

This impressive hotel enjoys a peaceful setting on a
restored 18th-century estate on the banks of the
River Tees. Luxurious, spacious bedrooms,
contemporary in style, are split between the original
old hall, the new hall and Tiplady Lodge. Dining
options include The Orangery, The Clubhouse and
The Brasserie. A state-of-the-art spa and
championship golf course, with a first-class club
house, complete the picture.

Rooms 61 (5 fmly) (17 GF) ➤ **S** £135-£270;
D £170-£305* **Facilities** Spa STV FTV Wi-fi ↕ ③ ♨
18 Putt green Fishing Gym Nordic walking ♫ Xmas
New Year **Conf** Class 100 Board 30 Thtr 180
Del from £185 to £215 **Services** Lift **Parking** 200
Notes ⊗ Civ Wed 180

See advert on opposite page

Headlam Hall

★★★★ 80% ◉◉ HOTEL

☎ 01325 730238
Headlam, Gainford DL2 3HA
e-mail: admin@headlamhall.co.uk
web: www.headlamhall.co.uk
dir: 2m N of A67 between Piercebridge & Gainford

This impressive Jacobean hall lies in farmland north-
east of Piercebridge and has its own 9-hole golf
course. The main house retains many historical
features, including flagstone floors and a pillared
hall. Bedrooms are well proportioned and traditionally
styled; a converted coach house contains the more
modern rooms. There are extensive conference
facilities, and the hotel is popular as a wedding
venue. There is a stunning spa complex with a 14-
metre pool, an outdoor hot spa, drench shower, sauna
and steam room. There is also a gym with the latest
cardio and resistance equipment, and five treatment
rooms offering a range of therapies and beauty
treatments.

Rooms 39 (22 annexe) (4 fmly) (9 GF) ➤
S £100-£145; **D** £125-£175 (incl. bkfst)*
Facilities Spa STV FTV Wi-fi ↕ ③ ♨ 9 ♨ Putt green
Fishing ♨ Gym New Year **Conf** Class 40 Board 40
Thtr 120 Del from £145* **Services** Lift **Parking** 80
Notes LB Closed 24-26 Dec Civ Wed 150

Bannatyne Hotel Darlington

★★★★ 75% HOTEL

☎ 01325 365858
Southend Av DL3 7HZ
e-mail: enquiries.darlingtonhotel@bannatyne.co.uk
dir: From S: A1(M) junct 57, A66(M) signed
Darlington. 2nd rdbt 2nd exit into Grange Rd. 3rd left
into Southend Ave. From N: A1(M) junct 58, A68
signed Darlington, left at 1st rdbt, 2nd rdbt 2nd exit
into Carmel Rd N, into Carmel Rd S. Left at 4th rdbt
into Grange Rd, 3rd left

This hotel, with excellent parking, is close to the town
centre and provides well-equipped accommodation
with Wi-fi in all areas. Public areas include the
brasserie-style bar and restaurant, Maxine's, plus
good function, conference and wedding facilities. Free
use of Bannatyne's Spa and gym (just five minutes
away) is also available to guests. Very friendly
hospitality is assured from the young and
enthusiastic team at this hotel.

Rooms 60 (4 fmly) (11 GF) ➤ **S** £60-£85; **D** £70-£120
(incl. bkfst)* **Facilities** FTV Wi-fi ↕ Xmas New Year
Conf Class 60 Board 60 Thtr 120 **Services** Lift
Parking 50 **Notes** LB ⊗ Civ Wed 120

BEST WESTERN Walworth Castle Hotel

★★★ 75% HOTEL

☎ 01325 485470
Walworth DL2 2LY
e-mail: enquiries@walworthcastle.co.uk
web: www.walworthcastle.co.uk
dir: A1(M) junct 58 follow signs to Corbridge. Left at
The Dog pub. Hotel on left after 2m

This 12th-century castle is privately owned and has
been tastefully converted. Accommodation is offered
in a range of styles, including an impressive suite
and more compact rooms in an adjoining wing.
Dinner can be taken in the fine dining Hansards
Restaurant or the more relaxed Farmer's Bar. This is a
popular venue for conferences and weddings.

Rooms 32 (14 annexe) (4 fmly) (8 GF) ➤ **S** fr £78;
D fr £97 (incl. bkfst)* **Facilities** Spa FTV Wi-fi ↕ ♨
Beauty rooms Hair salon Xmas New Year
Conf Class 60 Board 40 Thtr 120 **Parking** 100
Notes ⊗ Civ Wed 100

Save on hotels. Book at theAA.com/hotel

DAR 149 ENGLAND

Hall Garth Hotel, Golf and Country Club

★★★ 75% HOTEL

☎ 01325 300400
Coatham Mundeville DL1 3LU
e-mail: gm@hallgarthdarlington.co.uk
web: www.hallgarthdarlington.co.uk
dir: A1(M) junct 59, A167 towards Darlington. After 600yds left at top of hill, hotel on right

Peacefully situated in grounds that feature a golf course, this hotel is just a few minutes from the motorway network. The well-equipped bedrooms come in various styles - it's worth asking for one of the trendy, modern rooms. Public rooms include relaxing lounges, a fine-dining restaurant and a separate pub. The extensive leisure and conference facilities are an important focus here.

Rooms 56 (16 annexe) (3 fmly) (1 GF) **Facilities** Spa STV FTV Wi-fi ↕ ✑ supervised ♨ 9 Putt green Gym Steam room Beauty salon Sauna Spa Xmas New Year **Conf** Class 160 Board 80 Thtr 250 **Parking** 150 **Notes** Civ Wed 170

Premier Inn Darlington

BUDGET HOTEL

☎ 0871 527 8286
Morton Park Way, Morton Park DL1 4PJ
web: www.premierinn.com
dir: A1(M) junct 57, A66(M), A66 towards Teeside. At 3rd rdbt left onto B6280. Hotel on right. From N: A1(M) junct 57 onto A167, A1150, A66 towards Darlington, right onto B6280. Hotel on right

High quality, budget accommodation ideal for both families and business travellers. Spacious, en suite bedrooms feature tea and coffee making facilities, and Freeview TV in most hotels. Internet access and Wi-fi are available for a small fee. The adjacent family restaurant features a wide and varied menu. See also the Hotel Groups pages.

Rooms 58

DARTFORD
Kent

Map 6 TQ57

Rowhill Grange Hotel & Utopia Spa

★★★★ 81% ◉◉ HOTEL

☎ 01322 615136
Wilmington DA2 7QH
e-mail: admin@rowhillgrange.co.uk
web: www.rowhillgrange.co.uk
dir: M25 junct 3 take B2173 to Swanley, then B258 to Hextable

Set in nine acres of mature woodland this hotel enjoys a tranquil setting, yet is accessible to road networks. Bedrooms are stylishly and individually decorated; many have four-poster or sleigh beds. The elegant lounge is popular for afternoon teas, and the leisure and conference facilities are impressive. There is a smart, conservatory restaurant and also a more informal brasserie.

Rooms 38 (8 annexe) (4 fmly) (3 GF) ⚲ **Facilities** Spa STV FTV Wi-fi ↕ ✑ ⤸ Gym Beauty treatment Hair salon Aerobic studio Japanese therapy pool Xmas New Year **Conf** Class 64 Board 34 Thtr 160 **Services** Lift **Parking** 150 **Notes** ⊗ Civ Wed 150

Campanile Dartford

BUDGET HOTEL

☎ 01322 278925
1 Clipper Boulevard West, Crossways Business Park DA2 6QN
e-mail: dartford@campanile.com
web: www.campanile.com
dir: Follow signs for Ferry Terminal from Dartford Bridge

This modern building offers accommodation in smart, well-equipped bedrooms, all with en suite bathrooms. Refreshments may be taken at the informal bistro. See also the Hotel Groups pages.

Rooms 125 (14 fmly) **Conf** Class 30 Board 30 Thtr 40

Premier Inn Dartford

BUDGET HOTEL

☎ 0871 527 9328
Halcrow Av DA1 5FX
dir: M25 junct 1A , A206 towards Erith. At next rdbt right to Bridge Business Park. At next rdbt left towards Power Station. Hotel 300yds on left

High quality, budget accommodation ideal for both families and business travellers. Spacious, en suite bedrooms feature tea and coffee making facilities, and Freeview TV in most hotels. Internet access and Wi-fi are available for a small fee. The adjacent family restaurant features a wide and varied menu. See also the Hotel Groups pages.

Rooms 60

D

DARTMOUTH
Devon   Map 3 SX85

The Dart Marina Hotel

★★★★ 78% ⊛ HOTEL

☎ 01803 832580 & 837120
Sandquay Rd TQ6 9PH
e-mail: reservations@dartmarina.com
web: www.dartmarina.com
dir: A3122 from Totnes to Dartmouth. Follow road
which becomes College Way, before Higher Ferry.
Hotel sharp left in Sandquay Rd

Boasting a stunning riverside location with its own
marina, this is a special place to stay. Bedrooms vary
in style, all have wonderful views, while some have
private balconies to sit and soak up the atmosphere.
The stylish public areas take full advantage of the
waterside setting with opportunities to dine alfresco.
In addition to the Wildfire Bar & Bistro, the River
Restaurant is the venue for accomplished cooking.

Rooms 49 (4 annexe) (4 fmly) (4 GF) ⟡ **S** £95-£155;
D £140-£200 (incl. bkfst)* **Facilities** Spa Wi-fi ⟳
Gym Canoeing Sailing Xmas New Year **Services** Lift
Parking 50 **Notes** LB Civ Wed 40

Royal Castle Hotel

★★★ 81% HOTEL

☎ 01803 833033
11 The Quay TQ6 9PS
e-mail: enquiry@royalcastle.co.uk
web: www.royalcastle.co.uk
dir: In centre of town, overlooking Inner Harbour

At the edge of the harbour, this imposing 17th-
century former coaching inn is filled with charm and
character. Bedrooms are well equipped and
comfortable, and many have harbour views. A choice
of quiet seating areas is offered in addition to both
the traditional and contemporary bars. A variety of
eating options is available, including the main
restaurant which has lovely views.

Rooms 25 (3 fmly) ⟡ **Facilities** FTV Wi-fi ⌁ ♫ Xmas
New Year **Conf** Class 30 Board 20 Thtr 50 **Parking** 15
Notes Civ Wed 80

Stoke Lodge Hotel

★★★ 74% HOTEL

☎ 01803 770523
Stoke Fleming TQ6 0RA
e-mail: mail@stokelodge.co.uk
web: www.stokelodge.co.uk
dir: 2m S A379

This family-run hotel continues to attract returning
guests and is set in three acres of gardens and
grounds with lovely views across to the sea. A range
of leisure facilities is offered including both indoor
and outdoor pools, along with a choice of comfortable
lounges. Bedrooms are pleasantly appointed. The
restaurant offers a choice of menus and an
impressive wine list.

Rooms 25 (5 fmly) (7 GF) ⟡ **S** £73-£76; **D** £99-£131
(incl. bkfst) **Facilities** FTV Wi-fi ⟳ ⥀ ⟳ Putt green
Table tennis Pool & Snooker tables Sauna Xmas New
Year **Conf** Class 60 Board 30 Thtr 80 Del from £85 to
£110 **Parking** 50 **Notes** LB

DARWEN
Lancashire   Map 15 SD62

The Whitehall Hotel

★★★ 77% HOTEL

☎ 01254 701595
off Ross St BB3 2JU
e-mail: info@whitehallhotel.uk.com
dir: M61, A666 (Bolton Road) through Egerton. Turn
right at Whitehall Park. From N: M65 junct 4 past
Darwen town

This privately owned hotel is nestled at the base of
the West Pennine Moor close to Bolton and
Blackburn. Bedrooms are spacious and are equipped
for both business and leisure guests. Public areas
include a traditional lounge alongside a very modern
dining room that offers a range of dishes to suit all
tastes. Secure parking is available to the front of the
hotel.

Rooms 17 (3 fmly) (8 GF) ⟡ **S** £60-£90; **D** £70-£140
(incl. bkfst) **Facilities** FTV Wi-fi Gym Fitness classes
Xmas New Year **Conf** Class 80 Board 40 Thtr 110
Del from £130 to £160 **Parking** 70 **Notes** LB ⊗
Civ Wed 120

DAVENTRY
Northamptonshire   Map 11 SP56

INSPECTORS' CHOICE

Fawsley Hall

★★★★ ⊛⊛ ⊛ HOTEL

☎ 01327 892000
Fawsley NN11 3BA
e-mail: reservations@fawsleyhall.com
web: www.fawsleyhall.com
dir: A361 S of Daventry, between Badby &
Charwelton, hotel signed (single track lane)

Dating back to the 15th century, this delightful hotel
is peacefully located in beautiful gardens designed
by 'Capability' Brown. Spacious, individually
designed bedrooms and stylish public areas are
beautifully furnished with antique and period
pieces. The different wings of the house - Tudor,
Georgian and Victorian - all have their distinct
identity. For a true sense of the past, why not stay in
the Queen's Suite, where Elizabeth I is documented
to have slept in 1575. Afternoon tea is served in the
impressive Great Hall, and dinner is available in the
award-winning fine-dining Equilibrium Restaurant.
Seating just 16 people, the intimate restaurant has
huge original beams and stonework, an impressive
inglenook fireplace and candlelit tables dressed in
fine white linen. The other eating option is the more
relaxed Bess's Brasserie. The hotel has its own
cinema and The Grayshot Spa features an ozone
pool, treatment rooms and fitness studio.

Rooms 58 (14 annexe) (2 GF) **S** £185-£190;
D £185-£495 (incl. bkfst)* **Facilities** Spa STV Wi-fi
⟳ ⥀ ⥁ Gym Health & beauty treatment rooms
Fitness studio 29-seat cinema Xmas New Year
Conf Class 64 Board 40 Thtr 120 **Parking** 140
Notes LB Civ Wed 120

Save on hotels. Book at **theAA.com/hotel**

DAR – DED 151 ENGLAND

D

Daventry Court Hotel

PUMA HOTELS
COLLECTION

★★★★ 72% HOTEL

☎ 01327 307000

Sedgemoor Way NN11 0SG
e-mail: daventry@pumahotels.co.uk
web: www.pumahotels.co.uk
dir: M1 junct 16, A45 to Daventry, at 1st rdbt turn
right signed Kilsby/M1(N). Hotel on right in 1m

This modern, striking hotel overlooking Drayton Water
boasts spacious public areas that include a good
range of banqueting, meeting and leisure facilities. It
is a popular venue for conferences. Bedrooms are
suitable for both business and leisure guests.

Rooms 155 (17 fmly) **Facilities** STV Wi-fi
supervised Gym Steam room Health & beauty salon
Xmas New Year **Conf** Class 200 Board 100 Thtr 600
Services Lift **Parking** 350 **Notes** Civ Wed 280

Premier Inn Daventry

BUDGET HOTEL

Premier Inn

☎ 0871 527 8288

High St, Weedon NN7 4PX
web: www.premierinn.com
dir: M1 junct 16, A45 towards Daventry. Through
Upper Heyford & Flore. Hotel on left before Weedon &
A5 junct

High quality, budget accommodation ideal for both
families and business travellers. Spacious, en suite
bedrooms feature tea and coffee making facilities,
and Freeview TV in most hotels. Internet access and
Wi-fi are available for a small fee. The adjacent
family restaurant features a wide and varied menu.
See also the Hotel Groups pages.

Rooms 47

DAWLISH
Devon

Map 3 SX97

Langstone Cliff Hotel

THE INDEPENDENTS
HOTEL ASSOCIATION

★★★ 78% HOTEL

☎ 01626 868000

Dawlish Warren EX7 0NA
e-mail: reception@langstone-hotel.co.uk
web: www.langstone-hotel.co.uk
dir: 1.5m NE off A379 (Exeter road) to Dawlish Warren

A family-owned and run hotel, the Langstone Cliff
Hotel offers a range of leisure, conference and
function facilities. Bedrooms, many with sea views
and balconies, are spacious, comfortable and well
equipped. The hotel has a number of attractive
lounges and a well-stocked bar. Dinner is served,
often carvery style, in the restaurant.

Rooms 66 (4 annexe) (52 fmly) (10 GF)
Facilities STV FTV Wi-fi Gym Table tennis
Golf practice area Hair & beauty salon Therapy room
Ballroom Xmas New Year **Conf** Class 200 Board 80
Thtr 400 **Services** Lift **Parking** 200
Notes Civ Wed 400

DEAL
Kent

Map 7 TR35

Dunkerleys Hotel & Restaurant

★★★ 80% HOTEL

☎ 01304 375016

19 Beach St CT14 7AH
e-mail: info@dunkerleys.co.uk
web: www.dunkerleys.co.uk
dir: From M20 or M2 follow signs for A258 Deal. Hotel
close to Pier

This hotel is centrally located and on the seafront.
Bedrooms are furnished to a high standard with a
good range of amenities. The restaurant and bar offer
a comfortable and attractive environment in which to
relax and to enjoy the cuisine that makes the best use
of local ingredients. Service throughout is friendly
and attentive.

Rooms 16 (2 fmly) **S** £65-£100; **D** £80-£150 (incl.
bkfst) **Facilities** FTV Wi-fi Xmas New Year **Notes** LB
RS Sun eve & Mon

DEDDINGTON
Oxfordshire

Map 11 SP43

Deddington Arms

★★★ 75% HOTEL

☎ 01869 338364

Horsefair OX15 0SH
e-mail: deddarms@oxfordshire-hotels.co.uk
web: www.oxfordshire-hotels.co.uk
dir: From S: M40 junct 10/A43. 1st rdbt left to Aynho
(B4100) & left to Deddington (B4031). From N: M40
junct 11 to hospital & Adderbury on A4260, then to
Deddington

This charming and friendly old inn is conveniently
located off the market square. The well-equipped
bedrooms are comfortably appointed and situated
either in the main building or a purpose-built
courtyard wing. The bar is full of character, and the
delightful restaurant enjoys a well-deserved
reputation locally.

Rooms 27 (4 fmly) (10 GF) (2 smoking) **S** £65-£95;
D £65-£140 (incl. bkfst)* **Facilities** STV FTV Wi-fi
Xmas New Year **Conf** Class 20 Board 25 Thtr 40
Del from £130 to £165 **Parking** 36 **Notes** LB

DEDHAM
Essex

Map 13 TM03

INSPECTORS' CHOICE

Maison Talbooth

★★★ COUNTRY HOUSE HOTEL

PRIDE OF BRITAIN
HOTELS

☎ 01206 322367

Stratford Rd CO7 6HN
e-mail: maison@milsomhotels.co.uk
web: www.milsomhotels.com
dir: A12 towards Ipswich, 1st turn signed Dedham,
follow to left bend, turn right. Hotel 1m on right

Warm hospitality and quality service are to be
expected at this Victorian country-house hotel,
which is situated in a peaceful rural location
amidst pretty landscaped grounds overlooking the
Stour River Valley. Public areas include a
comfortable drawing room where guests may take
afternoon tea or snacks. Residents are chauffeured
to the popular Le Talbooth Restaurant just a mile
away for dinner. The spacious bedrooms are
individually decorated and tastefully furnished with
lovely co-ordinated fabrics and many thoughtful
touches.

Rooms 12 (1 fmly) (5 GF) **D** £210-£420 (incl.
bkfst)* **Facilities** Spa STV Wi-fi Xmas
Conf Class 20 Board 16 Thtr 30 **Parking** 40
Notes LB Civ Wed 50

D

DEDHAM *continued*

milsoms

★★★ 81% ◉ SMALL HOTEL

☎ 01206 322795
Stratford Rd CO7 6HW
e-mail: milsoms@milsomhotels.com
web: www.milsomhotels.com
dir: 6m N of Colchester off A12, follow Stratford St Mary/Dedham signs. Turn right over A12, hotel on left

Situated in the Dedham Vale, an Area of Outstanding Natural Beauty, this is the perfect base to explore the countryside on the Essex/Suffolk border. This establishment is styled along the lines of a contemporary 'gastro bar' combining good food served in an informal atmosphere, with stylish and well-appointed accommodation.

Rooms 15 (3 fmly) (4 GF) **D** £120-£200 (incl. bkfst)*
Facilities STV Wi-fi Use of spa at nearby sister hotel Maison Talbooth ♫ Xmas **Conf** Board 24
Del from £155* **Parking** 90 **Notes** LB

DELPH Map 16 SD90
Greater Manchester

The Saddleworth Hotel

★★★★ 84% COUNTRY HOUSE HOTEL

☎ 01457 871888
Huddersfield Rd OL3 5LX
e-mail: enquiries@thesaddleworthhotel.co.uk
web: www.thesaddleworthhotel.co.uk
dir: M62 junct 21, A640 towards Huddersfield. At Junction Inn take A6052 towards Delph; at White Lion left onto unclassified road; in 0.5m left on A62 towards Huddersfield. Hotel 0.5m on right

Situated in nine acres of landscaped gardens and woodlands in the Castleshaw Valley, this lovingly restored 17th-century building, once a coaching station, has stunning views. The hotel offers comfort and opulence together with a team of staff who provide delightful customer care. Antique pieces have been acquired from far and wide, and no expense has been spared to provide guests with the latest up-to-date facilities. The restaurant, with black table linen and crystal glassware, offers an award-winning, fashionably understated, modern European menu.

Rooms 16 (8 annexe) (4 fmly) (4 GF) **S** £80-£110;
D £130-£350 (incl. bkfst) **Facilities** FTV Wi-fi ♫ ⊰
Gym Xmas New Year **Conf** Class 40 Board 40 Thtr 150
Del from £150 **Parking** 140 **Notes** LB ⊗ Civ Wed 250

DERBY Map 11 SK33
Derbyshire

See also Morley

Hallmark Derby

★★★★ 79% HOTEL

☎ 01332 345894
Midland Rd DE1 2SQ
e-mail: derby.reservations@hallmarkhotels.co.uk
web: www.hallmarkhotels.co.uk
dir: Opposite rail station

This early Victorian hotel situated opposite Derby Midland Station provides very comfortable accommodation. The executive rooms are ideal for business travellers as they are equipped with writing desks and high speed internet access. Public rooms include a comfortable lounge and a popular restaurant. Service is skilled, attentive and friendly. There is also a walled garden and private parking.

Rooms 102 **S** £69-£140; **D** £79-£150* **Facilities** Wi-fi ♫ Xmas New Year **Conf** Class 50 Board 35 Thtr 150
Services Lift **Parking** 70 **Notes** ⊗ Civ Wed 150

Menzies Derby - Mickleover Court

MenziesHotels

★★★★ 77% HOTEL

☎ 01332 521234
Etwall Rd, Mickleover DE3 0XX
e-mail: mickleovercourt@menzieshotels.co.uk
web: www.menzieshotels.co.uk
dir: A50 towards Derby, exit at junct 5. A516 towards Derby, take exit signed Mickleover

Located close to Derby, this modern hotel is well suited to both the conference and leisure markets. Bedrooms are spacious, air conditioned, well equipped and include some smart executive rooms and suites. The well presented leisure facilities are amongst the best in the region.

Rooms 99 (20 fmly) (5 smoking) ⊷ **Facilities** STV FTV Wi-fi ♫ ⊙ Gym Beauty salon Steam room Xmas New Year **Conf** Class 106 Board 70 Thtr 200 **Services** Lift Air con **Parking** 270 **Notes** Civ Wed 150

Breadsall Priory, A Marriott Hotel & Country Club

 Marriott.

★★★★ 73% ◉ COUNTRY HOUSE HOTEL

☎ 01332 832235
Moor Rd, Morley DE7 6DL
web: www.marriottbreadsallpriory.co.uk

(For full entry see Breadsall)

Holiday Inn Derby Riverlights

Holiday Inn

★★★★ 73% HOTEL

☎ 01332 412644 & 412533
Derby Riverlights, Mortledge DE1 2AY
e-mail: reservations@hiderby.co.uk
dir: M1 junct 25, A52 to Derby. Follow signs to City Centre/Westfield Shopping Centre. Hotel on Morledge on right by bus station

With a central location adjacent to the Westfield Shopping Centre, this new hotel is ideal for both business and leisure guests. The lobby area is a four storey atrium. The stylish bedrooms are well equipped, and there is air conditioning throughout. The contemporary restaurant, Stresa, offers Italian cooking in a relaxed environment; complimentary Wi-fi is available throughout the property. Discounted rates for guests are offered at the Riverside car park.

Rooms 105 (11 smoking) ⊷ **Facilities** FTV Wi-fi ♫ HL Gym **Conf** Class 60 Board 50 Thtr 130 **Services** Lift Air con **Notes** Civ Wed 120

Ramada Encore Derby

★★★ 75% HOTEL

☎ 0844 801 3680
Locomotive Way, Pride Park DE24 8PU
e-mail: admin@encorederby.co.uk
web: www.encorederby.co.uk
dir: M1 junct 25, A52 towards Derby. Telephone for detailed directions

This hotel offers stylish and comfortable accommodation. The Hub is a smart, modern, open-plan bar and restaurant with a choice of seating areas - it offers an extensive menu throughout the day. Secure on-site parking is available, and the hotel is within walking distance of Derby railway station.

Rooms 112 (16 fmly) ⊷ **Facilities** STV Wi-fi HL Gym Sauna **Conf** Class 40 Board 20 Thtr 60 **Services** Lift Air con **Parking** 110 **Notes** ⊗

Save on hotels. Book at **theAA.com/hotel**

DED – DEV 153 ENGLAND

Hallmark Inn

★★★ 74% METRO HOTEL

☎ 01332 292000
Midland Rd DE1 2SL
e-mail: europeanreception@hallmarkhotels.co.uk
web: www.hallmarkhotels.co.uk
dir: City centre, 200yds from railway station

This is a contemporary hotel, offering quality accommodation plus a lounge bar, free Wi-fi and free parking. Situated just 100 metres from the railway station and not far from the city centre.

Rooms 87 (18 fmly) **S** £59-£120; **D** £69-£129*
Facilities FTV Wi-fi **Conf** Class 20 Board 30 Thtr 60
Services Lift **Parking** 90 **Notes** LB ⊗

Littleover Lodge Hotel

★★★ 72% HOTEL

☎ 01332 510161
222 Rykneld Rd, Littleover DE23 4AN
e-mail: enquiries@littleoverlodge.co.uk
web: www.littleoverlodge.co.uk
dir: A38 towards Derby approx 1m on left slip lane signed Littleover/Mickleover/Findon, take 2nd exit off island marked Littleover 0.25m on right

Situated in a rural location this friendly hotel offers modern bedrooms with direct access from the car park. Two styles of dining are available - an informal carvery operation which is very popular locally, and a more formal restaurant which is open for lunch and dinner each day. Service is excellent with the long serving staff being particularly friendly.

Rooms 16 (3 fmly) (6 GF) **Facilities** STV Wi-fi 🎵
Xmas New Year **Parking** 75 **Notes** Civ Wed 100

Premier Inn Derby East

BUDGET HOTEL

☎ 0871 527 8292
The Wyvern, Stanier Way DE21 6BF
web: www.premierinn.com
dir: M1 junct 25, A52 towards Derby. After 6.5m exit for Wyvern/Pride Park. 1st exit at rdbt (A52 Nottingham), straight on at next rdbt. Hotel on left

High quality, budget accommodation ideal for both families and business travellers. Spacious, en suite bedrooms feature tea and coffee making facilities, and Freeview TV in most hotels. Internet access and Wi-fi are available for a small fee. The adjacent family restaurant features a wide and varied menu. See also the Hotel Groups pages.

Rooms 83

Premier Inn Derby North West

BUDGET HOTEL

☎ 0871 527 8294
95 Ashbourne Rd, Mackworth DE22 4LZ
web: www.premierinn.com
dir: Exit M1 junct 25 onto A52 towards Derby. At Pentagon Island straight ahead towards city centre. Follow A52/Ashbourne signs into Mackworth

Rooms 22

Premier Inn Derby South

BUDGET HOTEL

☎ 0871 527 8296
Foresters Leisure Park, Osmaston Park Rd DE23 8AG
web: www.premierinn.com
dir: M1 junct 24, A6 towards Derby. Left onto A5111 (ring road), hotel in 2m

Rooms 27

Premier Inn Derby West

BUDGET HOTEL

☎ 0871 527 8298
Manor Park Way, Uttoxeter New Rd DE22 3HN
web: www.premierinn.com
dir: M1 junct 25, A38 W towards Burton upon Trent (approx 15m). Left at island (city hospital), right at lights, 3rd exit at city hospital island

Rooms 66

Days Inn Donington - A50

BUDGET HOTEL

☎ 01332 799666
Welcome Break Services, A50 Westbound DE72 2WA
e-mail: derby.hotel@welcomebreak.co.uk
web: www.welcomebreak.co.uk
dir: M1 junct 24/24a, onto A50 towards Stoke/Derby. Hotel between juncts 1 & 2

This modern building offers accommodation in smart, spacious and well-equipped bedrooms, suitable for families and business travellers, and all with en suite bathrooms. Continental breakfast is available and other refreshments may be taken at the nearby family restaurant. See also the Hotel Groups pages.

Rooms 47 (38 fmly) (17 GF) (9 smoking)
Conf Class 20 Board 40 Thtr 40

The Bear Hotel

★★★ 80% ◉◉ HOTEL

☎ 01380 722444
Market Place SN10 1HS
e-mail: info@thebearhotel.net
web: www.thebearhotel.net
dir: In town centre, follow Market Place signs

Tracing its history back over three centuries, this friendly establishment occupies a prominent position in a bustling town. Staff and management are keen to please and offer friendly and hospitable service. The bedrooms are pleasantly appointed and have flat-screen TVs and broadband connection. The hotel has two restaurants - Lambtons Restaurant for fine dining, and the Lawrence Room Bistro open for lunch; in summer there is a courtyard for alfresco dining. The hotel is a popular venue for conferences and weddings. Please note that there is restricted service on Christmas Day and Boxing Day - accommodation is not available.

Rooms 25 (5 fmly) 🐾 **Facilities** Wi-fi 🎵
Conf Class 55 Board 48 Thtr 110 **Services** Lift
Parking 14 **Notes** ⊗ RS 25-26 Dec Civ Wed 100

D

DIDCOT
Oxfordshire   Map 5 SU59

Premier Inn Oxford South (Didcot)

BUDGET HOTEL

☎ 0871 527 8868
Milton Heights, Milton OX14 4TX
web: www.premierinn.com
dir: On A4130. Just off A34 at Milton interchange, between Oxford & Newbury

High quality, budget accommodation ideal for both families and business travellers. Spacious, en suite bedrooms feature tea and coffee making facilities, and Freeview TV in most hotels. Internet access and Wi-fi are available for a small fee. The adjacent family restaurant features a wide and varied menu. See also the Hotel Groups pages.

Rooms 83

DISS
Norfolk   Map 13 TM18

The Scole Inn

★★★ 67% HOTEL   OXFORD
HOTELS & INNS

☎ 01379 740481
Ipswich Rd, Scole IP21 4DR
e-mail: scoleinn.reservations@ohiml.com
web: www.oxfordhotelsandinns.com
dir: A140, Diss rdbt signed Scole, left at T-junct, hotel on left

A charming 17th-century inn situated in the heart of the village where King Charles II and highwayman John Belcher are said to have stayed. Bedrooms come in a variety of styles; each one is pleasantly decorated and well equipped. The hotel retains a wealth of original features such as exposed brickwork, huge open fires and a superb carved wooden staircase. The public areas include a bar, restaurant and lounge bar.

Rooms 23 (12 annexe) (2 fmly) (7 GF) **Facilities** Wi-fi ♫ Xmas New Year **Conf** Class 26 Board 35 Thtr 45 **Parking** 60

DOGMERSFIELD
Hampshire   Map 5 SU75

INSPECTORS' CHOICE

Four Seasons Hotel Hampshire

★★★★★ ◉◉ COUNTRY HOUSE HOTEL

☎ 01252 853000
Dogmersfield Park, Chalky Ln RG27 8TD
e-mail: reservations.ham@fourseasons.com
dir: M3 junct 5 onto A287 Farnham. After 1.5m left for Dogmersfield, hotel 0.6m on left

This Georgian manor house, set in 500 acres of rolling grounds and English Heritage listed gardens, offers the upmost in luxury and relaxation, just an hour from London. The spacious and stylish bedrooms are particularly well appointed and offer up-to-date technology. Fitness and spa facilities include nearly every conceivable indoor and outdoor activity, in addition to luxurious pampering. An elegant restaurant, a healthy eating spa café and a trendy bar are popular venues.

Rooms 133 (23 GF) ♠ **Facilities** Spa STV Wi-fi ⊗ ♨ Fishing ⚑ Gym Clay pigeon shooting Bikes Canal boat Falconry Horse riding Jogging trails ♫ Xmas New Year **Conf** Class 110 Board 60 Thtr 260 **Services** Lift Air con **Parking** 165 **Notes** Civ Wed 200

DONCASTER
South Yorkshire   Map 16 SE50

BEST WESTERN PREMIER Mount Pleasant Hotel

★★★★ 80% ◉ HOTEL

☎ 01302 868696 & 868219
Great North Rd DN11 0HW
e-mail: reception@mountpleasant.co.uk
web: www.mountpleasant.co.uk

(For full entry see Rossington)

Ramada Encore Doncaster Airport

★★★ 74% HOTEL

☎ 01302 718520
Robin Hood Airport DN9 3RH
e-mail: reception@encoredoncaster.co.uk
web: www.encoredoncaster.co.uk
dir: M180 junct 1, follow signs for airport

Conveniently situated only a few minutes' walk from the main terminal at Robin Hood Airport, this purpose-built hotel is an good base for both the business and the leisure traveller. The air-conditioned bedrooms are spacious and bright, with power shower rooms. Public areas include the Hub Bar and Lounge. Secure parking is available on site.

Rooms 102 (36 fmly) (3 GF) (8 smoking) ♠ **Facilities** STV FTV Wi-fi ♫ HL **Conf** Class 20 Board 20 Thtr 40 **Services** Lift Air con **Parking** 144 **Notes** ⊗

Park Inn by Radisson Doncaster

★★★ 68% HOTEL

☎ 01302 760710
Decoy Bank S DN4 5PD
e-mail: info.doncaster@rezidorparkinn.com
dir: Telephone for directions

Situated in a thriving business park close to the city centre, this modern, contemporary hotel offers comfortable, spacious accommodation with individual climate control and complimentary Wi-fi, and is convenient for the A1 (north and south) and M18. A. An air-conditioned meeting room is available, and on-site parking is a real plus.

Rooms 85 (12 fmly) (21 GF) ♠ **Facilities** FTV Wi-fi Xmas New Year **Conf** Class 50 Board 50 Thtr 144 **Services** Lift Air con **Parking** 92

Campanile Doncaster   Campanile

BUDGET HOTEL

☎ 01302 370770
Doncaster Leisure Park, Bawtry Rd DN4 7PD
e-mail: doncaster@campanile.com
web: www.campanile.com
dir: Follow signs to Doncaster Leisure Centre, left at rdbt before Dome complex

This modern building offers accommodation in smart, well-equipped bedrooms, all with en suite bathrooms. Refreshments may be taken at the informal bistro. See also the Hotel Groups pages.

Rooms 50 (25 GF) **D** £39-£70* **Conf** Class 15 Board 15 Thtr 25

Holiday Inn Express Doncaster

BUDGET HOTEL
- -
☎ 01302 314100
Catesby Business Park, Bullrush Grove DN4 8SJ
e-mail: doncaster@holidayinnexpress.org.uk
web: www.hiexpress.com/doncaster
dir: M18 junct 3, A6182, left at 1st rdbt into Woodfield Way, straight over next rdbt, hotel on left

A modern hotel ideal for families and business travellers. Fresh and uncomplicated, the spacious rooms include Sky TV, power shower and tea and coffee-making facilities. Continental buffet breakfast is included in the room rate; other meals may be taken at the nearby family pub or restaurant. See also the Hotel Groups pages.

Rooms 94 (63 fmly) (16 GF) (14 smoking) 🐾
Conf Class 16 Board 20 Thtr 40

Premier Inn Doncaster Central

BUDGET HOTEL
- -
☎ 0871 527 8302
High Fishergate DN1 1QZ
web: www.premierinn.com
dir: Off A630 (Church Way)

High quality, budget accommodation ideal for both families and business travellers. Spacious, en suite bedrooms feature tea and coffee making facilities, and Freeview TV in most hotels. Internet access and Wi-fi are available for a small fee. The adjacent family restaurant features a wide and varied menu. See also the Hotel Groups pages.

Rooms 140

Premier Inn Doncaster Central East

BUDGET HOTEL
- -
☎ 0871 527 8304
Doncaster Leisure Park, Herten Way DN4 7NW
web: www.premierinn.com
dir: M18 junct 3, signed Doncaster racecourse. Left into Whiterose Way (B&Q on left). Straight on at rdbt into Wilmington Dr, right at next rdbt into Lakeside Boulevard. At next rdbt 2nd exit. Straight on at next rdbt, hotel ahead

Rooms 47

Premier Inn Doncaster (Lakeside)

BUDGET HOTEL
- -
☎ 0871 527 8300
Wilmington Dr, Doncaster Carr DN4 5PJ
web: www.premierinn.com
dir: M18 junct 3, A6182. Hotel near junct with access road

Rooms 42

DORCHESTER	Map 4 SY69
Dorset	

The Wessex Royale Hotel   THE INDEPENDENTS
HOTEL ASSOCIATION

★★★ 74% HOTEL
- -
☎ 01305 262660
High West St DT1 1UP
e-mail: info@wessexroyalehotel.co.uk
web: www.wessexroyalehotel.co.uk
dir: From A35 follow town centre signs. Straight on, hotel at top of hill on left

This centrally situated Georgian townhouse dates from 1756 and successfully combines historic charm with modern comforts. The restaurant is a relaxed location for enjoying innovative food, and the hotel offers the benefit of a smart conservatory, ideal for functions. Limited courtyard parking is available.

Rooms 27 (2 annexe) (2 fmly) (2 GF) **Facilities** STV FTV Wi-fi ⬦ **Conf** Class 40 Board 40 Thtr 80 **Parking** 11 **Notes** ⊗ Closed 23-30 Dec

DORCHESTER (ON THAMES)	Map 5 SU59
Oxfordshire	

White Hart Hotel

★★★ 74% HOTEL
- -
☎ 01865 340074
High St OX10 7HN
e-mail: whitehart@oxfordshire-hotels.co.uk
web: www.oxfordshire-hotels.co.uk
dir: M40 junct 6, take B4009 through Watlington & Benson to A4074. Follow signs to Dorchester. Hotel on right

Period charm and character are plentiful throughout this 17th-century coaching inn, which is situated in the heart of a picturesque village. The spacious bedrooms are individually decorated and thoughtfully equipped. Public rooms include a cosy bar, a choice of lounges and an atmospheric restaurant, complete with vaulted timber ceiling.

Rooms 28 (4 annexe) (2 fmly) (9 GF) 🐾 **Facilities** FTV Wi-fi ⬦ Xmas New Year **Conf** Class 20 Board 18 Thtr 30 **Parking** 36 **Notes** ⊗

George Hotel

★★ 68% HOTEL
- -
☎ 01865 340404
25 High St OX10 7HH
e-mail: georgedorchester@relaxinnz.co.uk
dir: M40 junct 6 onto B4009 through Watlington & Benson. Take A4074 at BP petrol station, follow Dorchester signs. Hotel on left

Located on the quaint High Street, The George is directly opposite the stunning abbey. Once a coaching inn, this historic property provides comfortable accommodation in the main house and also in a separate building which was once the stable. The food is freshly prepared and can be enjoyed in the formal beamed restaurant, in the more relaxed Potboys Bar with open fires, or in the garden in warmer months. Complimentary Wi-fi is available throughout.

Rooms 24 (15 annexe) (1 fmly) (10 GF) 🐾 S £65-£85; **D** £65-£120 (incl. bkfst)* **Facilities** FTV Wi-fi Beauty treatment room Xmas New Year **Conf** Class 20 Board 24 Thtr 40 Del from £100 to £135* **Parking** 50 **Notes** LB ⊗

DORKING	Map 6 TQ14
Surrey	

Mercure Boxhill Burford Bridge Hotel

★★★★ 76% ◉◉ HOTEL
- -
☎ 01306 884561
Burford Bridge, Box Hill RH5 6BX
e-mail: h6635@accor.com
web: www.mercure.com
dir: M25 junct 9, A245 towards Dorking. Hotel approx 5m on A24

Steeped in history, this hotel was reputedly where Lord Nelson and Lady Hamilton met for the last time, and it is said that the landscape around the hotel has inspired many poets. The hotel has a contemporary feel throughout. The grounds, running down to the River Mole, are extensive, and there are good transport links to major centres, including London. The elegant Emlyn Restaurant offers a modern award-winning menu.

Rooms 57 (22 fmly) (3 GF) **Facilities** Wi-fi ⬦ 🎵 Xmas New Year **Conf** Class 80 Board 60 Thtr 120 **Parking** 130 **Notes** ⊗ Civ Wed 200

D

D

DORKING *continued*

Mercure Dorking White Horse Hotel

★★★ 73% HOTEL

☎ 01306 881138
High St RH4 1BE
e-mail: h6637@accor.com
web: www.mercure.com
dir: M25 junct 9, A24 S towards Dorking. Hotel in town centre

The hotel was first established as an inn in 1750, although parts of the building date back as far as the 15th century. Its town centre location and Dickensian charm have long made this a popular destination for travellers. There are beamed ceilings, open fires and four-poster beds; more contemporary rooms can be found in the garden wing.

Rooms 78 (41 annexe) (2 fmly) (5 GF) **S** £45-£95; **D** £50-£114* **Facilities** FTV Wi-fi Discount at local leisure centre Xmas New Year **Conf** Class 30 Board 30 Thtr 50 Del from £90 to £145* **Parking** 73 **Notes** LB

DORRIDGE	Map 10 SP17
West Midlands	

The Forest

◉◉ RESTAURANT WITH ROOMS

☎ 01564 772120
25 Station Rd B93 8JA
e-mail: info@forest-hotel.com
web: www.forest-hotel.com
dir: In town centre near station

This very individual and stylish restaurant with rooms is well placed for routes to Birmingham, Stratford-upon-Avon and Warwick. The individually designed bedrooms are very well equipped with modern facilities, and imaginative food is served in the bars and intimate restaurant. A warm welcome is assured.

Rooms 12

DOVER	Map 7 TR34
Kent	

BEST WESTERN PLUS Dover Marina Hotel

★★★★ 75% HOTEL

☎ 01304 203633
Dover Waterfront CT17 9BP
e-mail: reservations@dovermarinahotel.co.uk
web: www.dovermarinahotel.co.uk
dir: M20 junct 13, A20 to Dover, straight on at 2 rdbts, at 3rd take 2nd exit into Union St. Cross swing bridge, next left into Marine Pde/Waterloo Cres. Hotel 200yds on left

An attractive terraced waterfront hotel overlooking the harbour that offers a wide range of facilities including meeting rooms, health club, hairdresser and beauty treatments. Some of the tastefully decorated bedrooms have balconies, some have broadband access and many of the rooms have superb sea views. Public rooms include a large, open-plan lounge bar and a smart bistro restaurant.

Rooms 81 (5 fmly) 🐾 **Facilities** STV FTV Wi-fi Gym Beauty treatment room Xmas New Year **Conf** Class 60 Board 50 Thtr 110 **Services** Lift **Notes** ⊗ Civ Wed 100

Wallett's Court Country House Hotel & Spa

★★★★ 72% ◉◉ HOTEL

☎ 01304 852424   & 0800 035 1628
West Cliffe, St Margarets-at-Cliffe CT15 6EW
e-mail: wc@wallettscourt.com
web: www.wallettscourt.com
dir: From Dover take A258 towards Deal. 1st right to St Margarets-at-Cliffe & West Cliffe, 1m on right opposite West Cliffe church

A lovely Jacobean manor situated in a peaceful location on the outskirts of town. Bedrooms in the original house are traditionally furnished whereas the rooms in the courtyard buildings are more modern; all are equipped to a high standard. Public rooms include a smart bar, a lounge and a restaurant that utilises local organic produce. An impressive spa facility is housed in converted barn buildings in the grounds.

Rooms 16 (13 annexe) (2 fmly) (7 GF) **Facilities** Spa FTV Wi-fi 🎣 ⛳ Putt green 🏌 Gym Treatment suite Aromatherapy massage Beauty therapy Golf pitching range New Year **Conf** Class 25 Board 16 Thtr 25 **Parking** 30 **Notes** Closed 24-26 Dec Civ Wed

Ramada Hotel Dover

★★★★ 70% HOTEL

☎ 01304 821230
Singledge Ln, Whitfield CT16 3EL
e-mail: reservations@ramadadover.co.uk
web: www.ramadadover.co.uk
dir: From M20 follow signs to A2 towards Canterbury. Turn right after Whitfield rdbt. From A2 towards Dover, turn left before Whitfield rdbt

A modern purpose-built hotel situated in a quiet location between Dover and Canterbury, close to the ferry port and seaside. The open-plan public areas are contemporary in style and include a lounge, a bar and The Olive Tree Restaurant. The stylish bedrooms are simply decorated with co-ordinated soft furnishings and many thoughtful extras.

Rooms 68 (19 fmly) (68 GF) 🐾 **S** £60-£164; **D** £60-£164 **Facilities** STV FTV Wi-fi 🌀 HL Gym Xmas New Year **Conf** Class 25 Board 20 Thtr 400 Del from £99 to £150* **Parking** 110 **Notes** LB ⊗ Civ Wed

Premier Inn Dover (A20)

BUDGET HOTEL

☎ 0871 527 8310
Folkestone Rd CT15 7AB
web: www.premierinn.com
dir: A20 to Dover. Through tunnel, take 2nd exit onto B2011. 1st left at rdbt. In 1m hotel on left

High quality, budget accommodation ideal for both families and business travellers. Spacious, en suite bedrooms feature tea and coffee making facilities, and Freeview TV in most hotels. Internet access and Wi-fi are available for a small fee. The adjacent family restaurant features a wide and varied menu. See also the Hotel Groups pages.

Rooms 64

Premier Inn Dover East

BUDGET HOTEL

☎ 0871 527 8308
Jubilee Way, Guston Wood CT15 5FD
web: www.premierinn.com
dir: At rdbt junct of A2 & A258

Rooms 40

Save on hotels. Book at **theAA.com/hotel**

DOR – DUM 157 ENGLAND

Premier Inn Dover (Eastern Ferry Terminal)

BUDGET HOTEL

☎ 0871 527 8306
Marine Court, Marine Pde CT16 1LW
web: www.premierinn.com
dir: In town centre adjacent to ferry terminal. M20 junct 13 onto A20 for 8.2m

Rooms 100

INSPECTORS' CHOICE

The Marquis at Alkham

◉ ◉ ◉ RESTAURANT WITH ROOMS

☎ 01304 873410 & 822945
Alkham Valley Rd, Alkham CT15 7DF
e-mail: info@themarquisatalkham.co.uk
web: www.themarquisatalkham.co.uk
dir: A256 from Dover, at rdbt 1st exit into London Rd, left into Alkham Rd, Alkham Valley Rd. Establishment 1.5m after sharp bend

Located between Dover and Folkestone, this modern, contemporary restaurant with rooms offers luxury accommodation with modern features - flat screen TVs, Wi-fi, power showers and bathrobes to name but a few. All the stylish bedrooms are individually designed and have fantastic views of the Kent Downs. The award-winning restaurant, open for lunch and dinner, specialises in modern British cuisine guided by Head Chef Charlie Lakin. Both continental and a choice of cooked breakfasts are offered.

Rooms 10 (3 fmly)

DOWNHAM MARKET   Map 12 TF60
Norfolk

Castle Hotel

★★★ 77% HOTEL

☎ 01366 384311
High St PE38 9HF
e-mail: howards@castle-hotel.com
dir: M11 take A10 for Ely into Downham Market. Hotel opposite lights on corner of High St

This popular coaching inn is situated close to the centre of town and has been welcoming guests for over 300 years. Well-maintained public areas include a cosy lounge bar and two smartly appointed restaurants. Inviting bedrooms, some with four-poster beds, are attractively decorated, thoughtfully equipped, and have bright, modern decor.

Rooms 12 (2 fmly) **S** £85-£99; **D** £85-£140 (incl. bkfst) **Facilities** Wi-fi ◊ New Year **Conf** Class 30 Board 40 Thtr 60 Del from £110 to £130 **Parking** 26 **Notes** LB

DOWN THOMAS   Map 3 SX55
Devon

Langdon Court Hotel & Restaurant

★★★★ 74% ◉ ◉ HOTEL

☎ 01752 862358
Adams Ln PL9 0DY
e-mail: enquiries@langdoncourt.com
dir: From Plymouth follow Kingsbridge signs Elberton rdbt. Signs to Langdon Court

This hotel has a super location, set in seven acres of grounds and away from the traffic and hubbub of the city; a Grade II listed building, this Tudor Mansion in steeped in history and is very stylish. There are some excellent gardens and the hotel is developing their own vineyard. Bedrooms are stylishly appointed, and comfortably furnished. The restaurant and bar areas offer enjoyable dining featuring fresh and local produce.

Rooms 16 (3 fmly) ↖ **S** £89-£109; **D** £109-£199 (incl. bkfst) **Facilities** STV FTV Wi-fi ◊ Xmas New Year **Conf** Class 20 Board 20 Thtr 60 Del frcm £159 to £189 **Parking** 60 **Notes** LB ⊗ Civ Wed 100

DRIFFIELD (GREAT)   Map 17 TA05
East Riding of Yorkshire

BEST WESTERN Bell Hotel

★★★ 79% HOTEL

☎ 01377 256661
46 Market Place YO25 6AN
e-mail: bell@bestwestern.co.uk
web: www.bw-bellhotel.co.uk
dir: From A164, right at lights. Car park 50yds on left behind black railings

This 250-year-old hotel incorporates the old corn exchange and the old town hall. It is furnished with antique and period pieces, and contains many items of local historical interest. The bedrooms vary in size, but all offer modern facilities and some have their own sitting rooms. The hotel has a relaxed and very friendly atmosphere. There is a spa and gym providing a very good range of facilities and treatments.

Rooms 16 (3 GF) ↖ **S** £76-£96; **D** £98-£120 (incl. bkfst) **Facilities** Spa FTV Wi-fi ◊ ⊛ Gym Squash Masseur Snooker ♫ New Year **Conf** Class 100 Board 40 Thtr 150 **Services** Lift **Parking** 18 **Notes** LB ⊗ No children 16yrs Closed 25 Dec & 1 Jan RS 24 & 26 Dec Civ Wed 120

DUDLEY   Map 10 SO99
West Midlands

Copthorne Hotel Merry Hill - Dudley

★★★★ 73% HOTEL

☎ 01384 482882
The Waterfront, Level St, Brierley Hill DY5 1UR
e-mail: reservations.merryhill@millenniumhotels.co.uk
web: www.millenniumhotels.co.uk/copthornedudley
dir: Follow signs for Merry Hill Centre

This hotel enjoys a waterfront location and is close to the Merry Hill Shopping Mall. Polished marble floors, rich fabrics and striking interior design are all in evidence in the stylish public areas. Bedrooms are spacious and some have Connoisseur status, which includes the use of a private lounge. A modern leisure centre with pool occupies the lower level.

Rooms 138 (14 fmly) **Facilities** Spa STV Wi-fi ◊ HL ⊛ supervised Gym Aerobics Beauty/massage therapists Steam room Sauna Dance studio ♫ Xmas New Year **Conf** Class 240 Board 60 Thtr 570 Del from £99 to £175* **Services** Lift **Parking** 100 **Notes** ⊗ Civ Wed 400

DUMBLETON   Map 10 SP03
Gloucestershire

Dumbleton Hall Hotel

★★★ 79% COUNTRY HOUSE HOTEL

☎ 01386 881240
WR11 7TS
e-mail: dh@pofr.co.uk
web: www.dumbletonhall.co.uk
dir: M5 junct 9/A46. 2nd exit at rdbt signed Evesham. Through Beckford for 1m, turn right signed Dumbleton. Hotel at S end of village

Standing on the site of a 16th-century building also known as Dumbleton Hall, the current mansion, surrounded by 19 acres of landscaped gardens and parkland, was built in the mid-18th century. Panoramic views of the Vale of Evesham can be seen from every window, and the spacious public rooms make this an ideal venue for weddings, conferences or just as a hideaway retreat. The individually designed bedrooms vary in size and layout; one room is adapted for less able guests.

Rooms 34 (9 fmly) **Facilities** Wi-fi ⚓ Xmas New Year **Conf** Class 60 Board 60 Thtr 100 **Services** Lift **Parking** 60 **Notes** Civ Wed 100

D

DUNSTABLE
Bedfordshire
Map 11 TL02

Premier Inn Dunstable/ Luton

BUDGET HOTEL

☎ 0871 527 8330
350 Luton Rd LU5 4LL
web: www.premierinn.com
dir: M1 junct 11, follow Dunstable signs. At 1st rdbt turn right. Hotel on left on A505

High quality, budget accommodation ideal for both families and business travellers. Spacious, en suite bedrooms feature tea and coffee making facilities, and Freeview TV in most hotels. Internet access and Wi-fi are available for a small fee. The adjacent family restaurant features a wide and varied menu. See also the Hotel Groups pages.

Rooms 42

Premier Inn Dunstable South (A5)

BUDGET HOTEL

☎ 0871 527 8332
Watling St, Kensworth LU6 3QP
web: www.premierinn.com
dir: M1 junct 9 towards Dunstable on A5, hotel on right after Packhorse pub

Rooms 40

DUNWICH
Suffolk
Map 13 TM47

The Ship at Dunwich
★★ 81% ❀ SMALL HOTEL

☎ 01728 648219 & 07921 061060
St James St IP17 3DT
e-mail: info@shipatdunwich.co.uk
dir: From N: A12, exit at Blythburgh onto B1125, then left to village. Inn at end of road. From S: A12, turn right to Westleton. Follow signs for Dunwich

A delightful inn situated in the heart of this quiet village, surrounded by nature reserves and heathland, and just a short walk from the beach. Public rooms feature a smart lounge bar with an open fire and real ales on tap. The comfortable bedrooms are traditionally furnished; some rooms have lovely views across the sea or marshes.

Rooms 15 (4 annexe) (4 fmly) (4 GF) Facilities FTV Xmas New Year Parking 15

DURHAM
Co Durham
Map 19 NZ24

Ramside Hall Hotel
★★★★ 79% ❀ HOTEL

☎ 0191 386 5282
Carrville DH1 1TD
e-mail: mail@ramsidehallhotel.co.uk
web: www.ramsidehallhotel.co.uk
dir: A1(M) junct 62, A690 to Sunderland. Straight on at lights. 200mtrs after rail bridge turn right

With its proximity to the motorway and delightful parkland setting, this establishment combines the best of both worlds - convenience and tranquillity. The hotel boasts 27 holes of golf, a choice of lounges, two eating options and two bars. Bedrooms are furnished and decorated to a very high standard and include two very impressive presidential suites.

Rooms 80 (10 fmly) (28 GF) Facilities STV Wi-fi ⚷ 27 Putt green Steam room Sauna Golf academy Driving range ♫ Xmas New Year Conf Class 160 Board 40 Thtr 500 Services Lift Parking 500 Notes Civ Wed 500

Durham Marriott Hotel, Royal County
★★★★ 78% HOTEL

☎ 0191 386 6821
Old Elvet DH1 3JN
e-mail: mhrs.xvudm.frontdesk@marriotthotels.com
web: www.durhammarriottroyalcounty.co.uk
dir: From A1(M) junct 62, A690 to Durham, over 1st rdbt, left at 2nd rdbt left at lights, hotel on left

In a wonderful position on the banks of the River Wear, the hotel's central location makes it ideal for visiting the attractions of this historic city. The building was developed from a series of Jacobean town houses. The bedrooms are tastefully styled. Eating options include the County Restaurant, for formal dining, and the Cruz Restaurant.

Rooms 150 (8 annexe) (10 fmly) (15 GF) (2 smoking) ⚷ Facilities Spa STV FTV Wi-fi ⚷ HL ⚷ supervised Gym Turkish steam room Plunge pool Sanarium Tropical fun shower Conf Class 50 Board 50 Thtr 120 Services Lift Parking 76 Notes Civ Wed 120

Radisson Blu Durham
★★★★ 77% HOTEL

☎ 0191 372 7200
Framwellgate Waterside DH1 5TL
e-mail: info.durham@radissonblu.com

Situated on the River Wear this smart hotel is a short walk from the city centre and the castle. The stylish

accommodation includes business class rooms and a range of suites; most rooms have views of the cathedral and the old part of the city. Filini Restaurant serves Italian cuisine, and the PACE Health Club has an indoor pool, steam room, sauna, gym and five treatment rooms. The impressive conference facilities include a business centre.

Rooms 207 (8 fmly) ⚷ Facilities Spa STV Wi-fi ⚷ ⚷ Gym New Year Conf Class 200 Board 120 Thtr 450 Services Lift Air con Parking 130 Notes ⊗ Civ Wed 80

Honest Lawyer Hotel
★★★ 82% ❀ HOTEL

☎ 0191 378 3780
Croxdale Bridge, Croxdale DH1 3SP
e-mail: enquiries@honestlawyerhotel.com
dir: A1(M) junct 61, A688 towards Bishops Auckland. Right at rdbt (continue on A688), right at next rdbt onto A167 towards Durham. In 2.5m hotel on right

This hotel offers a mixture of smart motel-style bedrooms along with six junior suites in the main building that have four-poster beds. 40" LCD TVs, power showers and complimentary Wi-fi are provided as standard. Bailey's Bar & Restaurant, with its open kitchen, offers a seasonally changing menu and friendly service. There are good transportation links to Durham and the motorway.

Rooms 46 (40 annexe) (6 fmly) (40 GF) Facilities FTV Wi-fi ⚷ ♫ Xmas New Year Conf Class 27 Board 24 Thtr 50 Services Air con Parking 150 Notes Civ Wed 40

Premier Inn Durham City Centre

BUDGET HOTEL

☎ 0871 527 8338
Freemans Place, Walkergate DH1 1SQ
web: www.premierinn.com
dir: A1(M) junct 62, A690 (Leazes Rd) towards city centre. In Durham follow Watergate signs, under bridge immediately left into Walkergate (one way). Back under A690, hotel on right

High quality, budget accommodation ideal for both families and business travellers. Spacious, en suite bedrooms feature tea and coffee making facilities, and Freeview TV in most hotels. Internet access and Wi-fi are available for a small fee. The adjacent family restaurant features a wide and varied menu. See also the Hotel Groups pages.

Rooms 103

Premier Inn Durham East

BUDGET HOTEL

☎ 0871 527 8340
Broomside Park, Belmont Industrial Estate DH1 1GG
web: www.premierinn.com
dir: A1(M) junct 62, A690 W towards Durham. In 1m
left. Hotel on left

Rooms 40

Premier Inn Durham North

BUDGET HOTEL

☎ 0871 527 8342
adj. Arnison Retail Centre, Pity Me DH1 5GB
web: www.premierinn.com
dir: A1 junct 63, A167 to Durham. Straight on at 5
rbts, left at 6th rbt. Hotel on right after 200yds

Rooms 60

DUXFORD	Map 12 TL44
Cambridgeshire	

Duxford Lodge Hotel
THE INDEPENDENTS
HOTEL ASSOCIATION

★★★ 77% ◉ HOTEL

☎ 01223 836444
Ickleton Rd CB22 4RT
e-mail: admin@duxfordlodgehotel.co.uk
web: www.duxfordlodgehotel.co.uk
dir: M11 junct 10, onto A505 to Duxford. 1st right at
rdbt, hotel 0.75m on left

A warm welcome is assured at this attractive red-
brick hotel in the heart of a delightful village. Public
areas include a cosy relaxing bar, separate lounge,
and an attractive restaurant, where an excellent and
imaginative menu is offered. The bedrooms are well
appointed, comfortable and smartly furnished.

Rooms 15 (4 annexe) (2 fmly) (4 GF) **Facilities** FTV
Wi-fi **Conf** Class 20 Board 26 Thtr 45 **Parking** 34
Notes Closed 25 Dec-2 Jan Civ Wed 50

EASINGTON	Map 19 NZ71
North Yorkshire	

The Grinkle Park Hotel
CLASSIC
LODGES
the sign of a great hotel

★★★★ 74%
COUNTRY HOUSE HOTEL

☎ 01287 640515
TS13 4UB
e-mail: info.grinklepark@classiclodges.co.uk
web: www.classiclodges.co.uk
dir: Take A171 from Guisborough towards Whitby.
Hotel signed on left

Grinkle Park Hotel is a 19th-century baronial hall
situated between the North Yorkshire Moors and the
coast, and surrounded by 35 acres of parkland, and
gardens where peacocks roam. It retains many
original features including fine wood panelling, and
the bedrooms are individually designed. The
comfortable lounge and bar have welcoming log fires,
while the Camelia Room is ideal for smaller weddings
and private dining.

Rooms 20 (1 fmly) **Facilities** Wi-fi ☺ ☝ Xmas New
Year **Conf** Class 80 Board 40 Thtr 120 **Parking** 150
Notes ⊗ Civ Wed 150

EASINGWOLD	Map 19 SE56
North Yorkshire	

George Hotel
THE CIRCLE

★★ 76% SMALL HOTEL

☎ 01347 821698
Market Place YO61 3AD
e-mail: info@the-george-hotel.co.uk
web: www.the-george-hotel.co.uk
dir: From A19 midway between York & Thirsk, into
Easingwold

A friendly welcome awaits at this former coaching inn
that faces the Georgian market square. Bedrooms are
very comfortably furnished and well equipped, and
the mews rooms have their own external access. An
extensive range of well-produced food is available
both in the bar and restaurant. There are two
comfortable lounges and complimentary use of a
local fitness centre.

Rooms 15 (2 fmly) (6 GF) ⬟ **S** £80-£90; **D** £90-£110
(incl. bkfst)* **Facilities** FTV Wi-fi Complimentry use of
local fitness centre New Year **Conf** Board 12
Del from £95 to £135* **Parking** 10 **Notes** LB ⊗

EAST GRINSTEAD	Map 6 TQ33
West Sussex	

AA HOTEL OF THE YEAR FOR ENGLAND

INSPECTORS' CHOICE

Gravetye Manor Hotel

★★★★ ◉ ◉ ◉
COUNTRY HOUSE HOTEL

☎ 01342 810567
Vowels Ln, West Hoathly RH19 4LJ
e-mail: info@gravetyemanor.co.uk
web: www.gravetyemanor.co.uk
dir: B2028 to Haywards Heath. 1m after Turners
Hill fork left towards Sharpthorne, 1st left into
Vowels Lane

Gravetye Manor is a beautiful Elizabethan mansion,
built in 1598 and enjoying a tranquil setting. One
of the first country house hotels in Britain, it
remains an excellent example of its type. Bedrooms
and bathrooms have been sympathetically
refurbished with style and luxurious finishing
touches. The day rooms, each with oak panelling,
fresh flower arrangements and open fires, create a
relaxing atmosphere. Cuisine is excellent and
makes use of local suppliers and producers. Guests
should take time to explore the impressive gardens
and grounds; a perfect spot for afternoon tea.
Gravetye Manor is the AA Hotel of the Year for
England, 2013-2014.

Rooms 17 ⬟ **S** £240-£430; **D** £240-£550 (incl.
bkfst)* **Facilities** FTV Wi-fi ⬚ Fishing ☝ Deer
stalking Xmas New Year **Conf** Board 15 Del £350*
Parking 20 **Notes** ⊗ No children 7yrs Civ Wed 60

E

E

EAST GRINSTEAD *continued*

The Felbridge Hotel & Spa

★★★★ 86% ◎◎ HOTEL

☎ 01342 337700
London Rd RH19 2BH
e-mail: sales@felbridgehotel.co.uk
dir: From W: M23 junct 10, follow signs to A22. From N: M25 junct 6. Hotel on A22 at Felbridge

This hotel is within easy of the M25 and Gatwick as well as Eastbourne and the glorious south coast. All bedrooms are beautifully styled and offer a wealth of amenities. Diners can choose from the Bay Tree Brasserie, Anise Fine Dining Restaurant or contemporary QUBE Bar. Facilities include a selection of modern meeting rooms, the luxurious Chakra Spa and swimming pool.

Rooms 120 (16 fmly) (53 GF) 📞 **S** £79-£160; **D** £79-£160* **Facilities** Spa STV FTV Wi-fi ⬇ ⓣ ♨ Gym Sauna Steam room Hairdresser Xmas New Year **Conf** Class 120 Board 100 Thtr 500 Del from £120 **Services** Air con **Parking** 300 **Notes** LB ⊗ Civ Wed 150

See advert on opposite page

Premier Inn East Grinstead

BUDGET HOTEL

☎ 0871 527 8348
London Rd, Felbridge RH19 2QR
web: www.premierinn.com
dir: M25 junct 6. Hotel at junction of A22 & A264

High quality, budget accommodation ideal for both families and business travellers. Spacious, en suite bedrooms feature tea and coffee making facilities, and Freeview TV in most hotels. Internet access and Wi-fi are available for a small fee. The adjacent family restaurant features a wide and varied menu. See also the Hotel Groups pages.

Rooms 41

EAST MIDLANDS AIRPORT	Map 11 SK42
Leicestershire	

The Priest House Hotel

★★★★ 80% ◎◎ HOTEL

☎ 01332 810649
Kings Mills DE74 2RR
e-mail: thepriesthouse@handpicked.co.uk
web: www.handpickedhotels.co.uk/thepriesthouse
dir: M1 junct 24, A50, take 1st slip road signed Castle Donington. Right at lights, hotel in 2m

A historic hotel peacefully situated in a picturesque riverside setting. Public areas include a fine dining restaurant, a modern brasserie and conference rooms. Bedrooms are situated in both the main building and converted cottages, and the executive rooms feature state-of-the-art technology.

Rooms 42 (18 annexe) (5 fmly) (16 GF) 📞 **S** £89-£119; **D** £99-£129 (incl. bkfst) **Facilities** STV FTV Wi-fi ⬇ HL Fishing Xmas New Year **Conf** Class 40 Board 40 Thtr 120 Del from £135 to £165 **Parking** 200 **Notes** LB ⊗ Civ Wed 120

BEST WESTERN PREMIER Yew Lodge Hotel & Spa

★★★★ 78% ◎◎ HOTEL

☎ 01509 672518
Packington Hill DE74 2DF
e-mail: info@yewlodgehotel.co.uk
web: www.yewlodgehotel.co.uk
dir: M1 junct 24. Follow signs to Loughborough & Kegworth on A6. On entering village, 1st right, after 400yds hotel on right

This smart, family-owned hotel is close to both the motorway and airport, yet is peacefully located. Modern, stylish bedrooms and public areas are thoughtfully appointed and smartly presented. The restaurant serves interesting dishes, while lounge service and extensive conference facilities are available. A very well equipped spa and leisure centre complete the picture.

Rooms 103 (22 fmly) 📞 **Facilities** Spa STV FTV Wi-fi ⬇ HL ⓣ Gym Beauty therapy suite Steam room Sauna Power plate Xmas New Year **Conf** Class 150 Board 84 Thtr 330 **Services** Lift **Parking** 180 **Notes** Civ Wed 260

Radisson Blu Hotel East Midlands Airport

★★★★ 77% HOTEL

☎ 01509 670575
Herald Way, Pegasus Business Park DE74 2TZ
e-mail: sales.eastmidlandsairport@radissonblu.com
web: www.radissonblu.co.uk/hotel-eastmidlandsairport
dir: S'bound: M1 junct 24/A453 exit to East Midlands Airport. N'bound: M1 junct 23A/A453 exit to East Midlands Airport

Located moments from East Midlands Airport, a shuttle service operates between the terminal and the hotel (Charges apply. Please contact the hotel in advance.) The impressive atrium and popular bar provide a good area in which to relax, while the Runway brasserie provides a contemporary venue for dining, with a good menu offering quality local produce. Bedrooms are tastefully furnished in a contemporary style, taking inspiration from nature and the environment throughout all rooms. An indoor pool and fitness suite with spa treatments is also available. Ample secure car parking is available for car users.

Rooms 218 (9 fmly) 📞 **S** £69-£159; **D** £69-£159* **Facilities** Spa STV FTV Wi-fi ⬇ HL ⓣ Gym **Conf** Class 148 Board 50 Thtr 350 Del from £125 to £165* **Services** Lift Air con **Parking** 350 **Notes** LB Civ Wed 350

Save on hotels. Book at **theAA.com/hotel**

EAS 161 ENGLAND

Thistle East Midlands Airport   thistle

★★★★ 77% HOTEL

☎ 0871 376 9015
DE74 2SH
e-mail: eastmidlandsairport@thistle.co.uk
web: www.thistle.com/eastmidlandsairport
dir: On A453, at entrance to East Midlands Airport

This large, two-storey purpose-built hotel is conveniently located next to East Midlands Airport with easy access to the M1 and M42. Bedrooms are quiet and generally spacious. Substantial public areas include the popular Lord Byron bar, a comprehensive range of meeting rooms and an Otium health and leisure club.

Rooms 164 (8 fmly) (78 GF) ⚐ **Facilities** STV FTV Wi-fi ᖇ HL 🕙 supervised Gym Sauna Steam room Spa bath Xmas New Year **Conf** Class 140 Board 54 Thtr 250 Del from £99 to £135* **Services** Air con **Parking** 350 **Notes** Civ Wed 250

Premier Inn East Midlands Airport

BUDGET HOTEL

☎ 0871 527 8350
Pegasus Business Park, Herald Way DE74 2TQ
web: www.premierinn.com
dir: From S: M1 junct 23a, A453 signed to airport. From N: M1 junct 24, A456 signed to airport. Hotel on Pegasus Business Park

High quality, budget accommodation ideal for both families and business travellers. Spacious, en suite bedrooms feature tea and coffee making facilities, and Freeview TV in most hotels. Internet access and Wi-fi are available for a small fee. The adjacent

family restaurant features a wide and varied menu. See also the Hotel Groups pages.

Rooms 80

EASTBOURNE   Map 6 TV69
East Sussex

The Grand Hotel

★★★★★ 85% ⑩⑩ HOTEL

☎ 01323 412345
King Edward's Pde BN21 4EQ
e-mail: reservations@grandeastbourne.com
web: www.grandeastbourne.com
dir: On seafront W of Eastbourne, 1m from railway station

This famous Victorian hotel offers high standards of service and hospitality, and is in close proximity to both the beach and the South Downs National Park. The extensive public rooms feature a magnificent Great Hall, with marble columns and high ceilings, where guests can relax and enjoy afternoon tea. The spacious bedrooms provide high levels of comfort; many with stunning sea views and a number with private balconies. Guests can choose fine dining in The Mirabelle, or the Garden Restaurant, and there are bars as well as superb spa and leisure facilities.

The Grand Hotel

Rooms 152 (20 fmly) (4 GF) ⚐ **S** £200–£570; **D** £230–£600 (incl. bkfst)* **Facilities** Spa STV Wi-fi ᖇ HL 🕙 supervised ⚘ supervised Putt green Gym Snooker table 𝄞 Xmas New Year Child facilities **Conf** Class 200 Board 40 Thtr 350 **Services** Lift **Parking** 80 **Notes** LB Civ Wed 300

Langham Hotel

★★★ 82% ⑩ HOTEL

☎ 01323 731451
Royal Pde BN22 7AH
web: www.langhamhotel.co.uk
dir: Follow seafront signs. Hotel 0.5m E of pier

This popular hotel is situated in a prominent position with superb views of the sea and pier. Bedrooms are pleasantly decorated, and equipped with modern facilities. Superior rooms, some with four-poster beds are stylish and offer sea views. The spacious public rooms include the Grand Parade bar, a lounge and a fine dining conservatory restaurant. The hotel has 40 additional secure, charged-for parking spaces within 350 yards on Fridays, Saturdays and Sundays.

Rooms 81 (2 fmly) ⚐ **Facilities** STV FTV Wi-fi ᖇ 𝄞 Xmas New Year **Conf** Class 40 Board 30 Thtr 80 Del from £90 to £110* **Services** Lift **Parking** 5 **Notes** ⊗ Civ Wed 140

E

EASTBOURNE *continued*

Hydro Hotel

★★★ 82% HOTEL

☎ 01323 720643
Mount Rd BN20 7HZ
e-mail: sales@hydrohotel.com
dir: From pier/seafront, right along Grand Parade. At
Grand Hotel follow Hydro Hotel sign. Into South Cliff,
200mtrs

This well-managed and popular hotel enjoys an
elevated position with views of attractive gardens
and the sea beyond. The spacious bedrooms are
attractive and well equipped. In addition to the
comfortable lounges, guests also have access to
fitness facilities and a hairdressing salon. Service is
both professional and efficient throughout.

Rooms 84 (3 fmly) (3 GF) **Facilities** FTV Wi-fi ⚡ Putt
green 🏖 Beauty room Hair salon 3/4 size snooker
table Xmas New Year **Conf** Class 90 Board 40
Thtr 140 **Services** Lift **Parking** 40 **Notes** RS 24-28 &
30-31 Dec Civ Wed 120

BEST WESTERN Lansdowne Hotel

★★★ 79% HOTEL

☎ 01323 725174 & 745483
King Edward's Pde BN21 4EE
e-mail: reception@lansdowne-hotel.co.uk
web: www.bw-lansdownehotel.co.uk
dir: At W end of seafront opposite Western Lawns

Enjoying an enviable position at the quieter end of the
parade, this hotel overlooks the Western Lawns and
Wish Tower, and is just a few minutes' walk from
many of the town's attractions. Public rooms include
a variety of lounges, a range of meeting rooms, and
games rooms. Bedrooms are attractively decorated
and many offer sea views. The hotel has a wheelchair
lift near the front entrance that operates between the
pavement and one of the ground-floor public rooms.

Rooms 102 (10 fmly) (7 smoking) 🛏 **S** £62-£90;
D £115-£199 (incl. bkfst) **Facilities** FTV Wi-fi 🏓 Table
tennis Pool table 2 Snooker tables Xmas New Year
Conf Class 40 Board 40 Thtr 80 Del from £99 to £135
Services Lift **Parking** 22 **Notes** LB Civ Wed 60

The Devonshire Park Hotel

★★★ 79% HOTEL

☎ 01323 728144
27-29 Carlisle Rd BN21 4JR
e-mail: info@devonshire-park-hotel.co.uk
web: www.devonshire-park-hotel.co.uk
dir: Follow signs to seafront, exit at Wish Tower. Hotel
opposite Congress Theatre

A handsome family-run hotel handily placed for the
seafront and theatres. Attractively furnished rooms
are spacious and comfortable; many boast king-size
beds and all are equipped with Wi-fi and satellite TV.
Guests can relax in the well presented lounges, the
cosy bar or, when the weather's fine, on the garden
terrace.

Rooms 35 (8 GF) 🛏 **Facilities** STV Wi-fi Xmas New
Year **Services** Lift **Parking** 25 **Notes** LB ⊗ No
children 12yrs

New Wilmington Hotel

★★★ 75% HOTEL

☎ 01323 721219
25-27 Compton St BN21 4DU
e-mail: info@new-wilmington-hotel.co.uk
web: www.new-wilmington-hotel.co.uk
dir: A22 to Eastbourne seafront. Right along
promenade to Wish Tower. Right, then left at end of
road, hotel 2nd on left

This friendly, family-run hotel is conveniently located
close to the seafront, the Congress Theatre and
Winter Gardens. Public rooms are well presented and
include a cosy bar, a small comfortable lounge and a
spacious restaurant. Bedrooms are comfortably
appointed and tastefully decorated; family and
superior bedrooms are available.

Rooms 40 (14 fmly) (3 GF) 🛏 **Facilities** STV FTV Wi-fi
🐾 🎵 Xmas New Year **Conf** Class 20 Board 20 Thtr 40
Services Lift **Parking** 3 **Notes** Closed 3 Jan-mid Feb

Chatsworth Hotel

★★★ 74% HOTEL

☎ 01323 411016 & 748700
Grand Pde BN21 3YR
e-mail: chatsworth@lionhotelsltd.com
web: www.lionhotelsltd.com
dir: M23 then A27 to Polegate. A2270 into
Eastbourne, follow seafront signs. Hotel near pier

Within minutes of the town centre and pier, this
attractive Edwardian hotel is located on the seafront.
The public areas consist of the Chatsworth Bar, a
cosy lounge and the Devonshire Restaurant.
Bedrooms, many with sea views, are traditional in
style and have a range of facilities. Service is friendly
and helpful throughout.

Rooms 45 (2 fmly) 🛏 **S** £52-£62; **D** £82-£105 (incl.
bkfst) **Facilities** Spa STV FTV Wi-fi Gym Hairdresser
Sauna Massage Beauty treatments 🎵 Xmas New
Year **Conf** Class 60 Board 40 Thtr 100 Del from £110
to £135 **Services** Lift **Notes** LB ⊗ Civ Wed 140

Albany Lions Hotel

★★★ 73% HOTEL

☎ 01323 722788 & 748700
Grand Pde BN21 4DJ
e-mail: albany@lionhotelsltd.com
dir: From town centre follow Seafront/Pier signs

This hotel, close to the bandstand, has a seafront
location that is within walking distance of the main
town shopping. A carvery dinner is served in the
restaurant, which has great sea views from most
tables, and a relaxing drink or afternoon tea can be
enjoyed in the sun lounge.

Rooms 61 (5 fmly) 🛏 **S** £48-£60; **D** £72-£95 (incl.
bkfst) **Facilities** STV FTV Wi-fi Hairdresser Massage
🎵 Xmas New Year **Conf** Class 60 Board 40 Thtr 120
Del from £100 to £125 **Services** Lift **Notes** LB ⊗

Mansion Lions Hotel

★★★ 66% HOTEL

☎ 01323 727411 & 748700
Grand Pde BN21 3YS
e-mail: mansion@lionhotelsltd.com
dir: From town centre follow Seafront/Pier signs. Hotel
on seafront

Directly overlooking the beach, this Victorian hotel is
only two minutes' walk from the magnificent pier, the
shopping centre and bandstand. The well-equipped
bedrooms are spacious, comfortably furnished and
some have sea views. An enjoyable four-course
evening meal and a filling breakfast are served in the
stylish Hartington Restaurant. There is an attractive
lounge, and a pretty garden can be found at the back
of the hotel.

Rooms 108 (6 fmly) (4 GF) ⚓ **S** £48-£60; **D** £72-£105 (incl. bkfst)* **Facilities** STV Wi-fi ♫ Xmas New Year **Conf** Class 80 Board 40 Thtr 150 Del from £100 to £125 **Services** Lift **Notes** LB ⊗ Closed 2-31 Jan Civ Wed 150

Queens Hotel

★★ 76% HOTEL

Leisureplex

☎ 01323 722822

Marine Pde BN21 3DY
e-mail: queens.eastbourne@alfatravel.co.uk
web: www.leisureplex.co.uk
dir: Follow signs for seafront, hotel opposite pier

Popular with tour groups, this long-established hotel enjoys a central, prominent seafront location overlooking the pier. Spacious public areas include a choice of lounges, and regular entertainment is also provided. Bedrooms are suitably appointed and equipped.

Rooms 122 (5 fmly) ⚓ **Facilities** Wi-fi Snooker ♫ Xmas New Year **Services** Lift **Parking** 50 **Notes** ⊗ Closed Jan (ex New Year) RS Nov, Feb-Mar

Alexandra Hotel

★★ 75% HOTEL

☎ 01323 720131

King Edwards Pde BN21 4DR
e-mail: alexandrahotel@mistral.co.uk
web: www.alexandrahotel.mistral.co.uk
dir: On seafront at junct of Carlisle Road & King Edward Parade

Located at the west end of the town, opposite the Wishing Tower, this hotel boasts panoramic views of the sea from many rooms. Bedrooms vary in size but are comfortable with good facilities for guests. A warm welcome is guaranteed at this long-standing, family run establishment.

Rooms 38 (2 fmly) (3 GF) **S** £33-£47; **D** £66-£94 (incl. bkfst)* **Facilities** FTV Wi-fi ♫ Xmas New Year **Services** Lift **Notes** ⊗ Closed Jan & Feb RS Mar

Congress Hotel

★★ 75% HOTEL

☎ 01323 732118

31-41 Carlisle Rd BN21 4JS
e-mail: reservations@congresshotel.co.uk
web: www.congresshotel.co.uk
dir: From Eastbourne seafront W towards Beachy Head. Right at Wishtower into Wilmington Sq, cross Compton St, hotel on left

An attractive Victorian property ideally located close to the seafront, Wish Tower and Congress Theatre. The bedrooms are bright and spacious. Family rooms are available plus there are facilities for less mobile

guests. Entertainment is provided in a large dining room that has a dance floor and bar.

Rooms 62 (6 fmly) (8 GF) ⚓ **S** £33-£48; **D** £66-£96 (incl. bkfst) **Facilities** FTV Wi-fi HL Games room ♫ Xmas New Year **Services** Lift **Parking** 12 **Notes** LB RS Jan-Feb

The Palm Court

★★ 74% HOTEL

☎ 01323 725811

15 Burlington Place BN21 4AR
e-mail: thepalmcourt@btconnect.com
web: www.thepalmcourthotel.co.uk
dir: From pier, W along seafront, Burlington Place 5th right

This family-run hotel is ideally situated close to the seafront and local theatres. The well appointed public areas include the lounge, spacious bar and stylish restaurant. Bedrooms vary in size but all offer plenty of handy accessories, comfortable furnishings and bright modern bathrooms. Good mobility facilities are provided.

Rooms 38 (5 GF) ⚓ **S** £38-£45; **D** £76-£90 (incl. bkfst) **Facilities** FTV Wi-fi Xmas New Year **Services** Lift **Notes** LB ⊗

The Afton Hotel

★★ 69% HOTEL

☎ 01323 733162

2-8 Cavendish Place BN21 3EJ
e-mail: info@aftonhotel.com
dir: From A22, A27 or A259, follow seafront signs. Hotel by pier

This friendly family-run hotel is ideally located in the centre of town, opposite the pier and close to the shopping centre. Bedrooms vary in size but are all comfortable and well co-ordinated. The spacious restaurant serves traditional home cooking. A full programme of entertainment is provided.

Rooms 54 (3 fmly) (2 GF) ⚓ **S** £25-£40; **D** £50-£80 (incl. bkfst)* **Facilities** Wi-fi ♫ Xmas New Year **Conf** Class 50 Board 50 Thtr 100 **Services** Lift **Notes** LB

Savoy Court Hotel

★★ 68% HOTEL

☎ 01323 723132

11-15 Cavendish Place BN21 3EJ
e-mail: info@savoycourthotel.co.uk
web: www.savoycourthotel.co.uk
dir: M25 junct 6, A22 to Eastbourne. Hotel 50mtrs from pier

Located close to the pier and within easy walking distance of the beaches and open-air bandstand this hotel offers bedrooms that are pleasantly decorated and furnished. The public areas include a cosy lounge and spacious bar/lounge for relaxing at the end of the day.

Rooms 29 (3 fmly) (5 GF) **S** £35-£55; **D** £50-£80 (incl. bkfst) **Facilities** FTV Wi-fi ♫ Xmas New Year **Conf** Class 40 Board 30 Thtr 60 Del from £65 to £90 **Services** Lift **Notes** LB ⊗

West Rocks Hotel

★★ 61% HOTEL

☎ 01323 725217

Grand Pde BN21 4DL
dir: West end of seafront

Ideally located near to the pier and bandstand, this hotel is only a short walk from the town centre. Bedrooms vary in size, with many offering stunning sea views. Guests have the choice of two comfortable lounges and a bar.

Rooms 47 (8 fmly) (6 GF) **S** £30-£55; **D** £60-£120 (incl. bkfst) **Facilities** FTV Wi-fi HL ♫ Xmas New Year **Conf** Class 45 Board 30 Thtr 75 Del from £70 to £120 **Services** Lift **Notes** LB ⊗ Closed 3 Jan-20 Feb

Premier Inn Eastbourne

BUDGET HOTEL

☎ 0871 527 8352

Willingdon Dr BN23 8AL
web: www.premierinn.com
dir: From A22 or A27 at Polegate, take bypass signed Eastbourne (A22). Continue to Shinewater rdbt. Left towards Langney. Hotel 0.25m on left

High quality, budget accommodation ideal for both families and business travellers. Spacious, en suite bedrooms feature tea and coffee making facilities, and Freeview TV in most hotels. Internet access and Wi-fi are available for a small fee. The adjacent family restaurant features a wide and varied menu. See also the Hotel Groups pages.

Rooms 47

E

EASTBOURNE *continued*

Premier Inn Eastbourne (Polegate)

BUDGET HOTEL

☎ 0871 527 8354
Hailsham Rd, Polegate BN26 6QL
web: www.premierinn.com
dir: At rdbt junct of A22 & A27

Rooms 40

EASTLEIGH	Map 5 SU41
Hampshire	

Holiday Inn Southampton - Eastleigh M3 Jct 13

★★★ 82% HOTEL

☎ 0871 942 9075
Leigh Rd SO50 9PG
e-mail: reservations-eastleigh@ihg.com
web: www.hisouthamptoneastleighhotel.co.uk
dir: M3 junct 13, right at lights, follow signs to Eastleigh, hotel on right

Located close to the M3 and convenient for Southampton Airport and the New Forest, this hotel is suitable for both the business and leisure traveller. All bedrooms have air conditioning and work desks as standard, but there are also executive rooms and suites with extra facilities. Junction Restaurant serves international dishes and there is a cocktail lounge. The popular leisure area includes a swimming pool, jacuzzi, aerobics studio, steam room, sauna and beauty treatments.

Rooms 129 (3 fmly) (27 GF) **Facilities** Spa FTV Wi-fi ↕ HL ⊕ Gym Whirlpool spa Steam room Sauna Personal trainer Studio **Conf** Class 60 Board 50 Thtr 120 **Services** Lift Air con **Parking** 175 **Notes** ⊗ Civ Wed 100

Premier Inn Southampton (Eastleigh)

BUDGET HOTEL

☎ 0871 527 8994
Leigh Rd SO50 9YX
web: www.premierinn.com
dir: M3 junct 13, A335 towards Eastleigh. Hotel on right

High quality, budget accommodation ideal for both families and business travellers. Spacious, en suite bedrooms feature tea and coffee making facilities, and Freeview TV in most hotels. Internet access and Wi-fi are available for a small fee. The adjacent family restaurant features a wide and varied menu. See also the Hotel Groups pages.

Rooms 60

EDGWARE	Map 6 TQ19
Greater London	

Premier Inn London Edgware

BUDGET HOTEL

☎ 0871 527 8652
435 Burnt Oak Broadway HA8 5AQ
web: www.premierinn.com
dir: M1 junct 4, A41, A5 towards Edgware. 3m to hotel

High quality, budget accommodation ideal for both families and business travellers. Spacious, en suite bedrooms feature tea and coffee making facilities, and Freeview TV in most hotels. Internet access and Wi-fi are available for a small fee. The adjacent family restaurant features a wide and varied menu. See also the Hotel Groups pages.

Rooms 111

EGGESFORD	Map 3 SS61
Devon	

Fox & Hounds Country Hotel

★★★ 75% ֎ HOTEL

☎ 01769 580345
EX18 7JZ
e-mail: relax@foxandhoundshotel.co.uk
web: www.foxandhoundshotel.co.uk
dir: M5 junct 27, A361 towards Tiverton. Take B3137 signed Witheridge. After Nomans Land follow signs for Eggesford Station. Hotel 50mtrs up hill from station

Situated midway between Exeter and Barnstaple, in the beautiful Taw Valley, this extensively developed hotel was originally a coaching inn dating back to the 1800s. Many of the comfortable, elegant bedrooms have lovely countryside views. Good cooking utilises excellent local produce and can be enjoyed in either restaurant or the convivial bar. For fishing enthusiasts, the hotel has direct access to the River Taw, and equipment and tuition can be provided if required.

Rooms 19 (6 fmly) (3 GF) ↖ **S** £62-£75; **D** £128-£150 (incl. bkfst)* **Facilities** FTV Wi-fi ↕ Fishing Health & beauty suite Hair salon Xmas New Year **Conf** Class 60 Board 60 Thtr 100 Del from £87 to £112* **Parking** 100 **Notes** LB Civ Wed 130

EGHAM	Map 6 TQ07
Surrey	

Great Fosters

★★★★ 83% HOTEL

☎ 01784 433822
Stroude Rd TW20 9UR
e-mail: reception@greatfosters.co.uk
web: www.greatfosters.co.uk
dir: From A30 (Bagshot to Staines), right at lights by Wheatsheaf pub into Christchurch Rd. Straight on at rdbt (pass 2 shop parades on right). Left at lights into Stroude Rd. Hotel 0.75m on right

This Grade II listed mansion dates back to the 16th century. The main house rooms are very much in keeping with the house's original style but are, of course, up-to-date with modern amenities. The stables and cloisters provide particularly stylish and luxurious accommodation. A stimulating range of award-winning cuisine can be enjoyed in the newly launched dining rooms, The Estate Grill and The Tudor Room. The beautiful public rooms, including the Terrace during the Summer months, provide the perfect setting for afternoon tea and cocktails. A host of meeting and event facilities provide the setting for a range of individual events.

Rooms 43 (22 annexe) (1 fmly) (13 GF) ↖ **D** £185-£450 **Facilities** STV Wi-fi ↕ ⊹ ⏛ ⛳ Xmas New Year **Conf** Class 72 Board 50 Thtr 150 Del from £275 to £325 **Parking** 200 **Notes** ⊗ Civ Wed 180

---

the runnymede-on-thames

★★★★ 81% HOTEL

☎ 01784 220600
Windsor Rd TW20 0AG
e-mail: info@therunnymede.co.uk
web: www.therunnymede.co.uk
dir: M25 junct 13, onto A308 towards Windsor

Enjoying a peaceful location beside the River Thames, this large modern hotel, with its excellent range of facilities, balances both leisure and corporate business. The extensive function suites, together with spacious lounges and stylish, well laid-out bedrooms are impressive. Superb spa facilities are available, and the good food and beverage venues offer wonderful river views.

Rooms 181 (19 fmly) ↖ **Facilities** Spa STV Wi-fi ↕ HL ⊕ supervised ⊹ supervised ⏛ ⛳ Gym Dance studio Children's play area River boat hire Group treatment suite ♫ Xmas New Year **Conf** Class 250 Board 76 Thtr 300 **Services** Lift Air con **Parking** 300 **Notes** ⊗ Civ Wed 140

Save on hotels. Book at **theAA.com/hotel**

EAS – EMS 165 ENGLAND

ELLESMERE PORT
Cheshire · Map 15 SJ47

Mercure Chester North Woodhey House Hotel

★★★ 71% HOTEL

☎ 0151 339 5121
Berwick Road West / Welsh Rd, Little Sutton CH66 4PS
e-mail:
enquiries@woodheyhouse-hotel-chester.com
web: www.woodheyhouse-hotel-chester.com
dir: A41 S, right at 2nd set of lights onto A550 towards Queensferry. Hotel 1m on left

Located in a quiet rural setting, yet within easy reach of the M53, this hotel is an ideal stop-off for both business and leisure guests. All bedrooms are well equipped, and the day rooms are stylishly appointed. They include a bar, restaurant and a very good range of meeting and conference facilities. The hotel also has an indoor pool, gym and steam room.

Rooms 75 (8 fmly) (23 GF) ↙ **Facilities** FTV Wi-fi ✪ Gym Sauna Steam room Xmas New Year **Conf** Class 120 Board 80 Thtr 250 **Services** Lift **Parking** 150 **Notes** Civ Wed 100

ELTERWATER
Cumbria · Map 18 NY30

Langdale Hotel & Spa

★★★★ 81% ⊛⊛ COUNTRY HOUSE HOTEL

☎ 015394 38014 & 38012
LA22 9JD
e-mail: info@langdale.co.uk
web: www.langdale.co.uk
dir: In Langdale Valley W of Ambleside

Founded on the site of an abandoned 19th-century gunpowder works, this modern hotel is set in 35 acres of woodland and waterways. Comfortable bedrooms, many with spa baths, vary in size. Extensive public areas include a choice of stylish restaurants, conference and leisure facilities and an elegant bar with an interesting selection of snuff. There is also a traditional pub run by the hotel just along the main road.

Rooms 56 (51 annexe) (4 fmly) (25 GF) ↙ **S** £109-£275; **D** £109-£275 (incl. bkfst)* **Facilities** Spa STV FTV Wi-fi ✪ supervised ⌒ Fishing Gym Steam room Solarium Aerobics studio Health & beauty salon Cycle hire Xmas New Year **Conf** Class 40 Board 35 Thtr 80 Del from £145* **Parking** 65 **Notes** ⊗ Civ Wed 65

New Dungeon Ghyll Hotel

★★★ 74% HOTEL

☎ 015394 37213
Great Langdale, Ambleside LA22 9JX
e-mail: enquiries@dungeon-ghyll.com
web: www.dungeon-ghyll.com
dir: From Ambleside follow A593 towards Coniston for 3m, at Skelwith Bridge right onto B5343 towards 'The Langdales'

This friendly hotel enjoys a tranquil, idyllic position at the head of the valley, set among the impressive peaks of Langdale. Bedrooms vary in size and style, but all the rooms are brightly decorated and smartly furnished. Bar meals are served all day, and dinner can be enjoyed in the restaurant overlooking the landscaped gardens; there is also a cosy lounge/bar.

Rooms 22 (1 fmly) (4 GF) ↙ **Facilities** FTV Wi-fi ↘ Xmas New Year **Conf** Class 30 Board 20 Thtr 20 **Parking** 30 **Notes** ⊗

ELY
Cambridgeshire · Map 12 TL58

Lamb Hotel

OldEnglish

★★★ Ⓐ HOTEL

☎ 01353 663574
2 Lynn Rd CB7 4EJ
e-mail: lamb.ely@oldenglishinns.co.uk
web: www.oldenglish.co.uk
dir: From A10 into Ely, hotel in town centre

The Lamb Hotel is a 15th-century former coaching inn situated in the heart of this popular market town. The hotel offers a combination of light, modern and traditional public rooms, while the bedrooms provide contemporary standards of accommodation. Food is available throughout the hotel - the same menu is provided in the bar and restaurant areas.

Rooms 31 (4 fmly) **S** £40-£85; **D** £60-£105 (incl. bkfst)* **Facilities** FTV Wi-fi HL Xmas New Year **Conf** Class 30 Board 30 Thtr 70 **Parking** 14

EMBLETON
Northumberland · Map 21 NU22

Dunstanburgh Castle Hotel

★★ 85% HOTEL

☎ 01665 576111
NE66 3UN
e-mail: stay@dunstanburghcastlehotel.co.uk
web: www.dunstanburghcastlehotel.co.uk
dir: From A1 take B1340 to Denwick past Rennington & Masons Arms. Right signed Embleton

The focal point of the village, this friendly, family-run hotel has a dining room and grill room that offer different menus, plus a cosy bar and two lounges. In addition to the main bedrooms, a barn conversion houses three stunning suites, each with a lounge and gallery bedroom above.

Rooms 32 (12 annexe) (6 fmly) ↙ **S** £56.50-£64.50; **D** £95-£113 (incl. bkfst)* **Facilities** Wi-fi **Parking** 33 **Notes** Closed Dec-Jan

EMSWORTH
Hampshire · Map 5 SU70

Brookfield Hotel

CLASSIC
BRITISH HOTELS

★★★ 80% HOTEL

☎ 01243 373363
Havant Rd PO10 7LF
e-mail: bookings@brookfieldhotel.co.uk
dir: From A27 onto A259 towards Emsworth. Hotel 0.5m on left

This well-established family-run hotel has spacious public areas with popular conference and banqueting facilities. Bedrooms are in a modern style, and comfortably furnished. The popular Hermitage Restaurant offers a seasonally changing menu and an interesting wine list.

Rooms 39 (6 fmly) (12 GF) ↙ **S** £65-£95; **D** £65-£120* **Facilities** STV FTV Wi-fi ↘ New Year **Conf** Class 50 Board 50 Thtr 100 Del from £149.95 to £174.95* **Parking** 80 **Notes** ⊗ Civ Wed 100

E

EMSWORTH *continued*

36 on the Quay

◉ ◉ ◉ RESTAURANT WITH ROOMS

☎ 01243 375592 & 372257
47 South St PO10 7EG

Occupying a prime position with far-reaching views over the estuary, this 16th-century house is the scene for some accomplished and exciting cuisine. The elegant restaurant occupies centre stage with peaceful pastel shades, local art and crisp napery together with glimpses of the bustling harbour outside. The contemporary bedrooms offer style, comfort and thoughtful extras.

Rooms 6 (1 annexe)

ENFIELD
Greater London   Map 6 TQ39

Royal Chace Hotel

★★★★ 77% ◉ HOTEL

☎ 020 8884 8181
The Ridgeway EN2 8AR
e-mail: reservations@royalchacehotel.co.uk
dir: M25 junct 24, A1005 towards Enfield. Hotel 3m on right

This professionally run, privately owned hotel enjoys a peaceful location with open fields to the rear. Public rooms are smartly appointed; the ground-floor Kings Restaurant is particularly appealing with its warm colour schemes and friendly service. Bedrooms are well presented and thoughtfully equipped.

Rooms 92 (5 fmly) (32 GF) 🐾 **Facilities** FTV Wi-fi 🎾 Gym New Year **Conf** Class 100 Board 40 Thtr 250 **Parking** 200 **Notes** ⊛ RS Sun eve Civ Wed 220

Comfort Hotel Enfield

BUDGET HOTEL

☎ 020 8366 3511

52 Rowantree Rd EN2 8PW
e-mail: reservations@comfortenfield.co.uk
web: www.comfortenfield.co.uk
dir: M25 junct 24 follow signs for A1005 towards Enfield. Hospital on left, across mini-rdbt, 3rd left onto Bycullah Rd, 2nd left into Rowantree Rd

This hotel is situated in a quiet residential area, close to the centre of Enfield. Comfortable accommodation is provided in the thoughtfully equipped bedrooms, which include ground floor and family rooms. Public areas include a cosy bar and lounge, conference and function rooms and the smart Etruscan Restaurant. See also the Hotel Groups pages.

Rooms 34 (26 annexe) (3 fmly) **S** £35-£89; **D** £50-£99* **Conf** Class 24 Board 30 Thtr 65 Del from £110 to £125*

Premier Inn Enfield

BUDGET HOTEL

☎ 0871 527 8374
Innova Park, Corner of Solar Way EN3 7XY
web: www.premierinn.com
dir: M25 junct 25, A10 towards London, left into Bullsmoor Lane & Mollison Ave. Over rdbt, right at lights into Innova Science Park

High quality, budget accommodation ideal for both families and business travellers. Spacious, en suite bedrooms feature tea and coffee making facilities, and Freeview TV in most hotels. Internet access and Wi-fi are available for a small fee. The adjacent family restaurant features a wide and varied menu. See also the Hotel Groups pages.

Rooms 160

EPPING
Essex   Map 6 TL40

BEST WESTERN The Bell Hotel

★★★ 75% HOTEL

☎ 01992 573138
High Rd, Bell Common CM16 4DG
e-mail: reservations@bellhotelepping.com
web: www.bellhotelepping.com
dir: M11 junct 7, B1393 to Epping. Hotel on right past town centre

This hotel enjoys a convenient location on the outskirts of the town centre, close to the M25 and M1. The nearby tube station allows for quick access to London. There is a range of bedroom styles, all attractively presented and featuring LCD TVs and free Wi-fi. Public areas include a cosy bar and a popular restaurant, along with well-equipped conference facilities.

Rooms 79 (5 fmly) (38 GF) (10 smoking) **S** £60-£90; **D** £70-£110* **Facilities** FTV Wi-fi ♨ Xmas New Year **Conf** Class 50 Board 50 Thtr 85 Del from £99 to £145 **Parking** 80 **Notes** LB ⊛ Civ Wed 60

EPSOM
Surrey   Map 6 TQ26

Holiday Inn Express London - Epsom Downs

BUDGET HOTEL

☎ 01372 755200
Langley Vale Rd KT18 5LG
e-mail: epsom@holidayinnexpress.org.uk
dir: Just off M25 junct 9

A modern hotel ideal for families and business travellers. Fresh and uncomplicated, the spacious rooms include Sky TV, power shower and tea and coffee-making facilities. Continental buffet breakfast is included in the room rate; other meals may be taken at the nearby family pub or restaurant. See also the Hotel Groups pages.

Rooms 120 (90 fmly) (37 GF) 🐾 **S** £69-£299; **D** £69-£299 (incl. bkfst) **Conf** Class 20 Board 12 Thtr 20

Premier Inn Epsom Central

BUDGET HOTEL

☎ 0871 527 8376
2-4 St Margarets Dr, off Dorking Rd KT18 7LB
web: www.premierinn.com
dir: M25 junct 9, A24 towards Epsom, hotel on left, just before town centre

High quality, budget accommodation ideal for both families and business travellers. Spacious, en suite bedrooms feature tea and coffee making facilities, and Freeview TV in most hotels. Internet access and Wi-fi are available for a small fee. The adjacent family restaurant features a wide and varied menu. See also the Hotel Groups pages.

Rooms 58

Premier Inn Epsom North

BUDGET HOTEL

☎ 0871 527 8380
272 Kingston Rd, Ewell KT19 0SH
web: www.premierinn.com
dir: M25 junct 8, A217 towards Sutton. A240 towards Ewell. At Beggars Hill rdbt 2nd exit into Kingston Rd

Rooms 29

ERMINGTON   Map 3 SX65
Devon

Plantation House

◉ RESTAURANT WITH ROOMS

☎ 01548 831100 & 830741
Totnes Rd PL21 9NS
e-mail: info@plantationhousehotel.co.uk

Peacefully situated within the picturesque South Hams, this former Parish rectory now provides an intimate and relaxing base from which to explore the locale. Quality, comfort and individuality are hallmarks throughout, with bedrooms offering impressive standards and a host of thoughtful extras. The stylish bathrooms come equipped with cosseting towels, robes and under-floor heating. A drink beside the crackling log fire is the ideal prelude to dinner, where skill and passion underpin menus focussing upon wonderful local produce. Breakfast is equally enjoyable, with superb eggs provided by the resident hens.

Rooms 8

ESCRICK   Map 16 SE64
North Yorkshire

The Parsonage Country House Hotel

★★★ 79% ◉ COUNTRY HOUSE HOTEL

☎ 01904 728111
York Rd YO19 6LF
e-mail: reservations@parsonagehotel.co.uk
web: www.parsonagehotel.co.uk
dir: A64 onto A19 (Selby). Follow to Escrick. Hotel by St Helens Church

This 19th-century, former parsonage has been carefully restored and extended, and is situated in six acres of gardens. Bedrooms are smartly appointed and well equipped for both business and leisure guests. Public areas include an elegant restaurant, conference facilities and a choice of attractive lounges. Cloisters Spa is located in the formal gardens and includes a swimming pool, jacuzzi, sauna, steam room, aromatherapy salt room and an excellent Health Club. Please note that the Spa and Health Club is for adults aged 18+ only.

Rooms 50 (13 annexe) (4 fmly) (9 GF) (8 smoking) **Facilities** Spa STV Wi-fi ⊗ Putt green Gym Sauna Steam room Aromatherapy room Xmas New Year **Conf** Class 80 Board 50 Thtr 240 Del from £135 to £140* **Services** Lift **Parking** 120 **Notes** ⊗ Civ Wed 150

EVERSHOT   Map 4 ST50
Dorset

INSPECTORS' CHOICE

Summer Lodge Country House Hotel, Restaurant & Spa

THE RED CARNATION HOTEL COLLECTION

★★★★ ◉◉◉ COUNTRY HOUSE HOTEL

☎ 01935 482000
DT2 0JR
e-mail: summer@relaischateaux.com
dir: 1m W of A37 halfway between Dorchester & Yeovil

This picturesque hotel is situated in the heart of Dorset and is the ideal retreat for getting 'away from it all', and it's worth arriving in time for the excellent afternoon tea. Bedrooms are appointed to a very high standard; each is individually designed, with upholstered walls and a wealth of luxurious facilities. Expect plasma screen TVs, DVD players, radios, air conditioning and Wi-fi access, plus little touches such as homemade shortbread, fresh fruit and scented candles. The delightful public areas include a sumptuous lounge complete with an open fire, and the elegant restaurant where the cuisine continues to be the high point of any stay. Red Carnation Hotels is the AA Small Hotel Group of the Year 2013-14.

Rooms 25 (15 annexe) (6 fmly) (2 GF) **S** £235-£650; **D** £235-£650 (incl. bkfst)* **Facilities** Spa STV FTV Wi-fi ⊗ ⊗ ⊗ Gym Sauna Xmas New Year **Conf** Class 16 Board 16 Thtr 24 Del from £375 to £575* **Services** Air con **Parking** 41 **Notes** LB Civ Wed 30

George Albert Hotel

★★★ 81% ◉ HOTEL

☎ 01935 483430
Wardon Hill DT2 9PW
e-mail: enquiries@gahotel.co.uk
dir: On A37 (between Yeovil & Dorchester). Adjacent to Southern Counties Shooting Ground

Situated mid-way between Dorchester and Yeovil, this hotel has much to offer for both business and leisure guests. The bedrooms offer impressive levels of comfort and many also have wonderful views across the Dorset countryside. Stylish public areas include extensive function rooms, a relaxing lounge, and a choice of dining options. Additional facilities include a karting track and clay pigeon shooting.

Rooms 39 (3 fmly) ⊗ **Facilities** FTV Wi-fi ⊗ Shooting Clay pigeon Kart track Xmas New Year **Conf** Class 60 Board 90 Thtr 250 Del from £120 to £130* **Services** Lift Air con **Parking** 200 **Notes** ⊗ Civ Wed 405

EVESHAM   Map 10 SP04
Worcestershire

Northwick Hotel

★★★ 83% HOTEL

☎ 01386 40322
Waterside WR11 1BT
e-mail: enquiries@northwickhotel.co.uk
dir: A46 onto A44, over lights, right at next lights onto B4035. Past hospital, hotel on right

Located close to the centre of the town, this hotel benefits a good position overlooking the River Avon and adjacent park. The bedrooms are traditional in style and have broadband access; one room has been adapted to provide disabled access. Public areas offer a choice of drinking options, a restaurant and function and meeting rooms.

Rooms 29 (4 fmly) (1 GF) ⊗ **Facilities** STV FTV Wi-fi ⊗ New Year **Conf** Class 150 Board 80 Thtr 240 Del £140 **Parking** 110 **Notes** ⊗ Closed 25-28 Dec Civ Wed 70

Dumbleton Hall Hotel

★★★ 79% COUNTRY HOUSE HOTEL

☎ 01386 881240
WR11 7TS
e-mail: dh@pofr.co.uk
web: www.dumbletonhall.co.uk

(For full entry see Dumbleton)

E

EVESHAM continued

The Evesham Hotel

★★★ 77% HOTEL

☎ 01386 765566
Coopers Ln, Off Waterside WR11 1DA
e-mail: reception@eveshamhotel.com
web: www.eveshamhotel.com
dir: M5 junct 9, A46 to Evesham. At rdbt on entering Evesham, take B4184 towards town, right at new bridge lights, 800yds, right into Coopers Ln

Dating from 1540 and set in extensive grounds, this delightful hotel has well-equipped accommodation that includes a selection of quirkily themed rooms, including Alice in Wonderland, Egyptian, and Aquarium (which has a tropical fish tank in the bathroom). A reputation for food is well deserved, with a particularly strong choice for vegetarians. Children are welcome and toys are always available.

Rooms 39 (2 fmly) (11 GF) 🐾 **S** £82-£92; **D** £133-£143 (incl. bkfst) **Facilities** FTV Wi-fi 🌐 Putt green 🏌 New Year **Conf** Class 12 Board 12 Thtr 12 Del £149* **Parking** 50 **Notes** LB Closed 25-26 Dec

Premier Inn Evesham

BUDGET HOTEL

☎ 0871 527 8384
Evesham Country Park, A46 Trunk Rd, Twyford WR11 4TP
web: www.premierinn.com
dir: At rdbt junct of A46(T) & A4184 at N end of Evesham bypass. Adjacent to Evesham Country Park

High quality, budget accommodation ideal for both families and business travellers. Spacious, en suite bedrooms feature tea and coffee making facilities, and Freeview TV in most hotels. Internet access and Wi-fi are available for a small fee. The adjacent family restaurant features a wide and varied menu. See also the Hotel Groups pages.

Rooms 40

EXETER
Devon

Map 3 SX99

Mercure Exeter Southgate Hotel & Spa

★★★★ 73% HOTEL

☎ 01392 412812
Southernhay East EX1 1QF
e-mail: h6624@accor.com
web: www.mercure.com
dir: M5 junct 30, 3rd exit (Exeter), 2nd left towards city centre, 3rd exit at next rdbt, hotel 2m on right

Centrally located and with excellent parking, The Southgate offers a diverse range of leisure and business facilities. Public areas are pleasantly spacious with comfortable seating in the bar and lounge; there is also a pleasant terrace. The bedrooms, in differing sizes, are well equipped and have modern facilities.

Rooms 154 (6 fmly) (23 GF) 🐾 **Facilities** FTV Wi-fi 🌐 🌐 supervised Gym Sauna Spa bath New Year **Conf** Class 70 Board 50 Thtr 150 **Services** Lift **Parking** 101 **Notes** ⊗ Civ Wed 80

The Rougemont Hotel, Exeter

thistle

★★★★ 72% HOTEL

☎ 0871 376 9018
Queen St EX4 3SP
e-mail: exeter@thistle.co.uk
web: www.thistlehotels.com/exeter
dir: M5 junct 30 follow signs to services at 1st rdbt, 1st left towards city centre. In city centre follow Museum/Central Station signs. Hotel opposite

Centrally located, this elegant hotel is well situated for those visiting the city for business or leisure. There is a charming, old-fashioned atmosphere here, with traditional hospitality to the fore. All bedrooms offer high levels of comfort and a number of suites are available. A choice of bars is provided - the convivial Drakes Bar or the smart and more formal cocktail bar.

Rooms 98 (4 fmly) 🐾 **Facilities** STV Wi-fi HL Xmas **Conf** Class 110 Board 70 Thtr 250 **Services** Lift **Parking** 24 **Notes** ⊗ Civ Wed 200

BEST WESTERN Lord Haldon Country Hotel

★★★ 77% HOTEL

☎ 01392 832483
Dunchideock EX6 7YF
e-mail: enquiries@lordhaldonhotel.co.uk
web: www.lordhaldonhotel.co.uk
dir: M5 junct 31, A30, 1st exit, follow signs through Ide to Dunchideock

Set amid rural tranquillity, this is an attractive country house where guests are assured of a warm welcome from the professional team of staff, and the well-equipped bedrooms are comfortable; many have stunning views. The daily-changing menu features skilfully cooked dishes with most of the produce sourced locally.

Rooms 25 (3 fmly) 🐾 **Facilities** FTV Wi-fi 🌐 Xmas New Year **Conf** Class 100 Board 40 Thtr 250 **Parking** 120 **Notes** Civ Wed 120

The Devon Hotel

Brend Hotels

★★★ 77% HOTEL

☎ 01392 259268
Exeter Bypass, Matford EX2 8XU
e-mail: reservations@devonhotel.co.uk
web: www.devonhotel.co.uk
dir: M5 junct 30 follow Marsh Barton Ind Est signs on A379. Hotel on Marsh Barton rdbt

Within easy access of the city centre, the M5 and the city's business parks, this smart Georgian hotel offers modern, comfortable accommodation. The Carriages Bar and Brasserie is popular with guests and locals alike, offering a wide range of dishes as well as a carvery at both lunch and dinner. Service is friendly and attentive, and extensive meeting and business facilities are available.

Rooms 40 (40 annexe) (2 fmly) (11 GF) 🐾 **S** £74-£94; **D** £94-£104* **Facilities** FTV Wi-fi 🌐 Xmas New Year **Conf** Class 80 Board 40 Thtr 150 **Parking** 250 **Notes** LB ⊗ Civ Wed 100

Save on hotels. Book at **theAA.com/hotel**

EVE – EXE 169 ENGLAND

E

Queens Court Hotel

★★★ 75% ◎◎ HOTEL

☎ 01392 272709
6-8 Bystock Ter EX4 4HY
e-mail: enquiries@queenscourt-hotel.co.uk
web: www.queenscourt-hotel.co.uk
dir: Exit dual carriageway at junct 30 onto B5132
(Topsham Rd) towards city centre. Hotel 200yds from
Central Station

Quietly located within walking distance of the city
centre, this privately owned hotel is a listed, early
Victorian property that provides friendly hospitality.
The smart public areas and contemporary bedrooms
are tastefully furnished, and the stylish and
attractive Olive Tree restaurant offers an award-
winning selection of dishes. Rooms are available for
conferences, meetings, weddings and parties.
Complimentary parking is available in a public car
park directly opposite the hotel entrance.

Rooms 18 (1 fmly) **Facilities** FTV Wi-fi **Conf** Class 30
Board 30 Thtr 60 **Services** Lift **Notes** ⊗ Closed Xmas
& New Year RS 25-30 Dec Civ Wed 60

Barton Cross Hotel & Restaurant

★★★ 71% ◎ HOTEL

☎ 01392 841245
Huxham, Stoke Canon EX5 4EJ
e-mail: bartonxhuxham@aol.com
web: www.thebartoncrosshotel.co.uk
dir: From A396, 0.5m to Stoke Canon, 3m N of Exeter

17th-century charm combined with 21st-century
luxury perfectly sums up the appeal of this lovely
country hotel. The bedrooms are spacious, tastefully
decorated and well maintained. Public areas include
the cosy first-floor lounge and the lounge/bar with its
warming log fire. The restaurant offers a seasonally
changing menu of consistently enjoyable cuisine.

Barton Cross Hotel & Restaurant

Rooms 9 (2 fmly) (2 GF) (2 smoking) **Facilities** STV
FTV Wi-fi ◊ Xmas New Year **Conf** Class 20 Board 20
Thtr 20 **Parking** 35 **Notes** LB

See advert below

Gipsy Hill Hotel

THE INDEPENDENTS
HOTEL ASSOCIATION

★★★ 71% HOTEL

☎ 01392 465252
Gipsy Hill Ln, Monkerton EX1 3RN
e-mail: stay@gipsyhillhotel.co.uk
web: www.gipsyhillhotel.co.uk
dir: M5 junct 29 towards Exeter. Right at 1st rdbt,
right again at next rdbt. Hotel 0.5m on right

Located on the edge of the city, with easy access to
the M5 and the airport, this popular hotel is set in
attractive, well-tended gardens and boasts far-
reaching country views. The hotel offers a range of
conference and function rooms, comfortable
bedrooms and modern facilities. An intimate bar and
lounge are adjacent to the elegant restaurant.

Rooms 37 (17 annexe) (4 fmly) (12 GF) 🐾
Facilities STV FTV Wi-fi ◊ Xmas New Year
Conf Class 80 Board 80 Thtr 300 Del from £100 to
£140 **Parking** 60 **Notes** ⊗ Civ Wed 160

EXETER continued

Premier Inn Exeter Central St Davids

BUDGET HOTEL

☎ 0871 527 9278
Bonhay Rd EX4 4BG
web: www.premierinn.com
dir: M5 junct 31, A30 towards Bodmin & Oakehampton. Exit onto A377 towards Exeter & Crediton. Hotel on left

High quality, budget accommodation ideal for both families and business travellers. Spacious, en suite bedrooms feature tea and coffee making facilities, and Freeview TV in most hotels. Internet access and Wi-fi are available for a small fee. The adjacent family restaurant features a wide and varied menu. See also the Hotel Groups pages.

Rooms 102

Premier Inn Exeter (Countess Wear)

BUDGET HOTEL

☎ 0871 527 8386
398 Topsham Rd EX2 6HE
web: www.premierinn.com
dir: 2m from M5 junct 30/A30 junct 29. Follow signs for Exeter & Dawlish (A379). On dual carriageway take 2nd slip road on left at Countess Wear rdbt. Hotel adjacent to Beefeater

Rooms 44

Chi Restaurant & Bar with Accommodation

RESTAURANT WITH ROOMS

☎ 01626 890213
Fore St, Kenton EX6 8LD
e-mail: enquiries@chi-restaurant.co.uk
web: www.chi-restaurant.co.uk
dir: 5m S of Exeter. M5 junct 30, A379 towards Dawlish, in village centre

This former pub has been spectacularly transformed into a chic and contemporary bar, allied with a stylish Chinese restaurant. Dishes are beautifully presented with an emphasis on quality produce and authenticity, resulting in a memorable dining experience. Bedrooms are well equipped and all provide good levels of space and comfort, along with modern bathrooms.

Rooms 5 (1 fmly)

EXFORD
Somerset
Map 3 SS83

Crown Hotel

★★★ 79% ◉ HOTEL

☎ 01643 831554
TA24 7PP
e-mail: info@crownhotelexmoor.co.uk
web: www.crownhotelexmoor.co.uk
dir: M5 junct 25, follow Taunton signs. Take A358 from Taunton, then B3224 via Wheddon Cross to Exford

Guest comfort is certainly the hallmark here. Afternoon tea is served in the lounge beside a roaring fire, and tempting menus in the bar and restaurant are all part of the charm of this delightful old coaching inn that specialises in breaks for shooting and other country sports. Bedrooms retain a traditional style yet offer a range of modern comforts and facilities, many have views of this pretty moorland village.

Rooms 16 (3 fmly) ✱ **S** £65-£79; **D** £105-£159 (incl. bkfst)* **Facilities** FTV Wi-fi ♨ Xmas New Year **Conf** Board 15 **Parking** 30 **Notes** LB

EXMOUTH
Devon
Map 3 SY08

Royal Beacon Hotel

★★★ 79% HOTEL

☎ 01395 264886
The Beacon EX8 2AF
e-mail: info@royalbeacon.co.uk
web: www.royalbeaconhotel.co.uk
dir: From M5 onto A376 & Marine Way. Follow seafront signs. On Imperial Rd left at T-junct then 1st right. Hotel 100yds on left

This elegant Georgian property sits in an elevated position overlooking the town and has fine views of the estuary towards the sea. Bedrooms are individually styled and many have sea views. Public areas include a well stocked bar, a cosy lounge, an impressive function suite, and a choice of restaurants where freshly prepared and enjoyable cuisine is offered.

Rooms 52 (17 annexe) (2 fmly) (8 GF) ✱ **Facilities** FTV Wi-fi ♨ Xmas New Year **Conf** Class 100 Board 60 Thtr 160 **Services** Lift **Parking** 28 **Notes** ⊗ Civ Wed 160

Cavendish Hotel

Leisureplex

★★ 71% HOTEL

☎ 01395 272528
11 Morton Crescent, The Esplanade EX8 1BE
e-mail: cavendish.exmouth@alfatravel.co.uk
web: www.leisureplex.co.uk
dir: Follow seafront signs, hotel in centre of large crescent

Situated on the seafront, this terraced hotel attracts many groups from around the country. With fine views out to sea, the hotel is within walking distance of the town centre. The bedrooms are neatly presented, and front-facing rooms are always popular. Entertainment is provided on most evenings during the summer.

Rooms 78 (3 fmly) (21 GF) ✱ **Facilities** FTV Wi-fi Snooker ♫ Xmas New Year **Services** Lift **Parking** 25 **Notes** ⊗ Closed Dec-Jan (ex Xmas) RS Nov & Mar

---

EYE
Suffolk
Map 13 TM17

The Cornwallis Hotel

bespoke

★★★★ 74% ◉ HOTEL

☎ 01379 870326 & 08444 146524
Rectory Rd, Brome IP23 8AJ
e-mail: reservations.cornwallis@ohiml.com
web: www.oxfordhotelsandinns.com
dir: 50yds from A140 (Norwich to Ipswich road)

Peacefully situated just off the A140 at the end of a tree lined lane in 23 acres of wooded grounds, this charming Grade II listed property has a wealth of original character such as exposed beams, open fireplaces and wood carvings. Public rooms include a 15th-century Tudor bar, a lounge, a conservatory and a fine-dining restaurant. The individually designed bedrooms are tastefully appointed and have lovely views of the gardens.

Rooms 16 (5 annexe) (1 fmly) (3 GF) **Facilities** FTV Wi-fi Xmas New Year **Conf** Class 50 Board 30 Thtr 70 **Parking** 100 **Notes** ⊗ Civ Wed 80

FALFIELD
Gloucestershire   Map 4 ST69

BEST WESTERN The Gables Hotel

★★★ 73% HOTEL

☎ 01454 260502
Bristol Rd GL12 8DL
e-mail: mail@thegablesbristol.co.uk
web: www.thegablesbristol.co.uk
dir: M5 junct 14 N'bound. Left at end of sliproad. Right onto A38, hotel 300yds on right

Conveniently located, just a few minutes from the motorway this establishment is ideally suited to both business and leisure guests, with easy access to Cheltenham, Gloucester, Bristol and Bath. Bedrooms are spacious and well equipped. Relaxing public areas consist of a light and airy bar and restaurant where meals and all-day snacks are available; a more formal restaurant is open for dinner. There is also a range of meeting rooms.

Rooms 46 (4 fmly) (18 GF) **S** £60-£99; **D** £60-£110 (incl. bkfst)* **Facilities** FTV Wi-fi ⓑ New Year **Conf** Class 90 Board 50 Thtr 200 Del from £125 to £155* **Parking** 104 **Notes** LB ⊗ Civ Wed 150

FALMOUTH
Cornwall   Map 2 SW83

See also **Mawnan Smith**

The Royal Duchy Hotel

★★★★ 78% ⍟⍟ HOTEL

☎ 01326 313042
Cliff Rd TR11 4NX
e-mail: reservations@royalduchy.com
web: www.royalduchy.com
dir: On Cliff Rd, along Falmouth seafront

Staff at this hotel, which looks out over the sea and towards Pendennis Castle, create a very friendly environment. The comfortable lounge and cocktail bar are well appointed and just the place for a light lunch. Leisure facilities include a beauty salon, and meeting rooms are also available. The award-winning Terrace Restaurant serves carefully prepared dishes, and guests can sit on the sea-facing terrace in warmer weather. The bedrooms vary in size and aspect, and many have sea views. Babysitting is happily arranged for families with small children and babies.

The Royal Duchy Hotel

Rooms 43 (6 fmly) (1 GF) **S** £80-£115; **D** £140-£350 (incl. bkfst)* **Facilities** FTV Wi-fi ⓑ ⓖ Games room Sauna Hot stone therapy beds Beauty treatment room ♬ Xmas New Year Child facilities **Conf** Thtr 50 **Services** Lift **Parking** 50 **Notes** LB ⊗ Civ Wed 100

See advert below

The Greenbank Hotel

★★★★ 76% ⍟⍟ HOTEL

☎ 01326 312440
Harbourside TR11 2SR
e-mail: reception@greenbank-hotel.co.uk
web: www.greenbank-hotel.co.uk
dir: A39 to Falmouth, left at Ponsharden rdbt onto North Parade. 500yds past Falmouth Marina on the Harbourfront

Located by the marina, and with its own private quay dating from the 17th century, The Greenbank Hotel has a strong maritime theme throughout. Set at the water's edge, the lounge, restaurant and many bedrooms all benefit from harbour views. The restaurant provides a choice of interesting and enjoyable dishes.

Rooms 60 (5 fmly) ⓡ **S** £89-£129; **D** £145-£235 (incl. bkfst)* **Facilities** FTV Wi-fi ⓑ Private beach & quay Xmas New Year **Conf** Class 30 Board 50 Thtr 90 Del from £140 to £160* **Services** Lift **Parking** 8 **Notes** LB ⊗ Civ Wed 90

FALMOUTH *continued*

St Michael's Hotel and Spa

★★★★ 75% ☻ HOTEL

☎ 01326 312707
Gyllyngvase Beach, Seafront TR11 4NB
e-mail: info@stmichaelshotel.co.uk
dir: A39 into Falmouth, follow beach signs, at 2nd
mini-rdbt into Pennance Rd. Take 2nd left & 2nd left
again

Overlooking the bay, this hotel is in an excellent
position and commands lovely views. It is appointed
in a fresh, contemporary style that reflects its location
by the sea. The Flying Fish restaurant has a great
atmosphere and a real buzz about it. The light and
bright bedrooms, some with balconies, are well
equipped. There are excellent leisure facilities
including a fitness and health club together with a
spa offering many treatments. The attractive gardens
also provide a place to relax and unwind.

Rooms 61 (8 annexe) (7 fmly) (12 GF) ♠
Facilities Spa FTV Wi-fi ☜ ♨ Gym Sauna Steam
room Aqua aerobics Fitness classes Xmas New Year
Conf Class 150 Board 50 Thtr 200 **Parking** 30
Notes ⊗ Civ Wed 80

BEST WESTERN Penmere Manor Hotel

★★★ 79% HOTEL

☎ 01326 211411
Mongleath Rd TR11 4PN
e-mail: reservations@penmere.co.uk
web: www.penmere.co.uk
dir: Exit A39 at Hillhead rdbt, over double mini rdbt.
After 0.75m left into Mongleath Rd

Set in five acres on the outskirts of town, this
Georgian manor house was originally built for a ship's
captain. Now a family-owned hotel it provides friendly
service and a good range of facilities. Bedrooms vary
in size and are located in the manor house and the
garden wing. Various menus are available in the bar
and the smart restaurant. There is a health and
beauty centre offering a wide range of treatments and
the water in the indoor pool is UV filtered.

Rooms 37 (12 fmly) (13 GF) ♠ **Facilities** FTV Wi-fi ☜
↘ Gym Sauna New Year **Conf** Class 20 Board 30
Thtr 60 **Parking** 50 **Notes** Closed 22-27 Dec

Falmouth Hotel

RICHARDSON HOTELS

★★★ 77% ☻ HOTEL

☎ 01326 312671 & 0800 019 3121
Castle Beach TR11 4NZ
e-mail: reservations@falmouthhotel.com
web: www.falmouthhotel.com
dir: A30 to Truro then A390 to Falmouth. Follow signs
for beaches, hotel on seafront near Pendennis Castle

This spectacular beach-front Victorian property
affords wonderful sea views from many of its
comfortable bedrooms, some of which have their own
balconies. Spacious public areas include a number of
inviting lounges, a choice of dining options and an
impressive range of leisure facilities.

Rooms 71 (16 fmly) ♠ **Facilities** Spa FTV Wi-fi ↘ ☜
Putt green Gym Beauty salon & Therapeutic rooms
Xmas New Year **Conf** Class 150 Board 100 Thtr 250
Del £110 **Services** Lift **Parking** 120
Notes Civ Wed 250

Penmorvah Manor

★★★ 73% HOTEL

☎ 01326 250277
Budock Water TR11 5ED
e-mail: reception@penmorvah.co.uk
web: www.penmorvah.co.uk
dir: A39 to Hillhead rdbt, take 2nd exit. Right at
Falmouth Football Club, through Budock. Hotel
opposite Penjerrick Gardens

Situated within two miles of central Falmouth, this
extended Victorian manor house is a peaceful
hideaway, set in six acres of private woodland and
gardens. Penmorvah is well positioned for visiting the
local gardens, and offers many garden-tour breaks.
Dinner features locally sourced, quality ingredients
such as Cornish cheeses, meat, fish and game.

Rooms 27 (1 fmly) (10 GF) ♠ **S** £70; **D** £105 (incl.
bkfst)* **Facilities** FTV Wi-fi **Conf** Class 100 Board 56
Thtr 250 Del from £100* **Parking** 80 **Notes** LB Closed
31 Dec-Jan Civ Wed 120

Membly Hall Hotel

★★ 71% HOTEL

☎ 01326 312869
Sea Front, Cliff Rd TR11 4NT
e-mail: memblyhallhotel@tiscali.co.uk
dir: A39 to Falmouth. Follow seafront & beaches signs

Located conveniently on the seafront and enjoying
splendid views, this family-run hotel offers friendly
service. Bedrooms are pleasantly spacious and well

equipped. Carefully prepared and enjoyable meals are
served in the spacious dining room. Live
entertainment is provided on some evenings and
there is also a sauna and spa pool.

Rooms 35 (3 fmly) (6 GF) ♠ **Facilities** FTV Wi-fi ⛱
Gym Indoor short bowls Table tennis Pool table Sauna
Spa pool ♫ New Year **Conf** Class 130 Board 60
Thtr 150 **Services** Lift **Parking** 30 **Notes** ⊗ Closed
Xmas week RS Dec-Jan

Madeira Hotel

Leisureplex

★★ 69% HOTEL

☎ 01326 313531
Cliff Rd TR11 4NY
e-mail: madeira.falmouth@alfatravel.co.uk
web: www.leisureplex.co.uk
dir: A39 (Truro to Falmouth), follow tourist 'Hotels'
signs to seafront

This popular hotel offers splendid sea views and a
pleasant, convenient location, which is close to the
town. Extensive sun lounges are popular haunts from
which to enjoy the views, while additional facilities
include an oak-panelled cocktail bar. Bedrooms,
many with sea views, are available in a range of
sizes.

Rooms 50 (8 fmly) (7 GF) **Facilities** FTV ♫ Xmas New
Year **Services** Lift **Parking** 11 **Notes** ⊗ Closed
Dec-Feb (ex Xmas) RS Nov & Mar

FAREHAM   **Map 5 SU50**
Hampshire

Solent Hotel & Spa

shire

★★★★ 80% ☻ HOTEL

☎ 01489 880000
Rookery Av, Whiteley PO15 7AJ
e-mail: solent@shirehotels.com
web: www.solenthotel.com
dir: M27 junct 9, hotel on Solent Business Park

Close to the M27 with easy access to Portsmouth, the
New Forest and other attractions, this smart,
purpose-built hotel enjoys a peaceful location.
Bedrooms are spacious and very well appointed and
there is a well-equipped spa with health and beauty
facilities.

Rooms 115 (9 fmly) (39 GF) **S** £90-£150;
D £90-£150* **Facilities** Spa STV Wi-fi ↘ HL ☜ ♨
Gym Steam room Sauna Children's splash pool
Activity studio Xmas New Year **Conf** Class 100
Board 80 Thtr 200 Del from £145 to £185*
Services Lift **Parking** 200 **Notes** LB ⊗ Civ Wed 160

Holiday Inn Fareham - Solent

★★★ 79% HOTEL

☎ 0871 942 9028
Cartwright Dr, Titchfield PO15 5RJ
e-mail: fareham@ihg.com
web: www.holidayinn.co.uk
dir: M27 junct 9, follow signs for A27. Over Segensworth rdbt 1.5m, left at next rdbt

This hotel is well positioned and attracts both the business and leisure markets. Bedrooms are spacious and smart, and stylish public areas include a number of conference rooms. Beauty treatments are available in the leisure area which has a swimming pool, aerobics studio and gym.

Rooms 124 (4 fmly) (72 GF) **S** £66-£210; **D** £66-£210 (incl. bkfst)* **Facilities** FTV Wi-fi ↕ HL ⊙ supervised Gym Sauna Beauty treatment rooms **Conf** Class 64 Board 45 Thtr 140 Del from £135 to £200* **Services** Air con **Parking** 160 **Notes** ⊗ Civ Wed 100

Lysses House Hotel

★★★ 74% HOTEL

☎ 01329 822622
51 High St PO16 7BQ
e-mail: lysses@lysses.co.uk
web: www.lysses.co.uk
dir: M27 junct 11 follow Fareham signs, stay in left lane to Delme rdbt. At rdbt 3rd exit into East St, follow into High St. Hotel at top on right

This attractive Georgian hotel is situated on the edge of the town in a quiet location and provides spacious and well-equipped accommodation. There are conference facilities, and a lounge bar serving a range of snacks together with the Richmond Restaurant that offers imaginative cuisine.

Rooms 21 (2 fmly) (7 GF) **Facilities** FTV Wi-fi Free entry to nearby LA Fitness **Conf** Class 42 Board 28 Thtr 95 **Services** Lift **Parking** 30 **Notes** ⊗ Closed 25 Dec-1 Jan RS 24 Dec & BHs Civ Wed 100

Red Lion Hotel

★★★ 70% HOTEL

☎ 01329 822640
East St PO16 0BP
e-mail: redlion.fareham@oldenglishinns.co.uk

This hotel, which was formerly a coaching inn, is conveniently located within a few moments' walk of the market town of Fareham. An array of substantial hot and cold meals is served throughout the day in the bright informal restaurant and bar area. Bedrooms provide good comfort levels, and the hotel has pretty gardens and benefits from barrier operated parking.

Rooms 46 **Conf** Class 60 Board 40 Thtr 100

Premier Inn Fareham

BUDGET HOTEL

☎ 0871 527 8396
Southampton Rd, Park Gate SO31 6AF
web: www.premierinn.com
dir: M27 junct 9, follow Fareham West, A27 signs. (NB for Sat Nav use SO31 6BZ)

High quality, budget accommodation ideal for both families and business travellers. Spacious, en suite bedrooms feature tea and coffee making facilities, and Freeview TV in most hotels. Internet access and Wi-fi are available for a small fee. The adjacent family restaurant features a wide and varied menu. See also the Hotel Groups pages.

Rooms 41

BEST WESTERN Sudbury House Hotel & Conference Centre

★★★ 74% ⊛ HOTEL

☎ 01367 241272
London St SN7 8AA
e-mail: events@sudburyhouse.co.uk
web: www.sudburyhouse.co.uk
dir: From A420, follow Folly Hill signs

Situated on the edge of the Cotswolds and in nine acres of pleasant grounds, this hotel offers spacious and well-equipped bedrooms that are attractively decorated in warm colours. Dining options include the comfortable restaurant for a good selection of carefully presented dishes, and the bar for lighter options; a comprehensive room-service menu is also available.

Rooms 49 (2 fmly) (10 GF) ⟟ **S** £55-£99; **D** £65-£109 (incl. bkfst)* **Facilities** FTV Wi-fi ↲ Gym Boules New Year **Conf** Class 40 Board 34 Thtr 100 Del from £109 to £155* **Services** Lift **Parking** 100 **Notes** LB Civ Wed 160

Aviator

★★★★ 81% ⊛ HOTEL

☎ 01252 555890
Farnborough Rd GU14 6EL
e-mail: enquiries@aviatorbytag.com
web: www.aviatorbytag.com
dir: A325 to Aldershot, 3m, hotel on right

A striking property with a modern, sleek interior overlooking Farnborough airfield and located close to the main transport networks. This hotel is suitable for both the business and leisure travellers. The bedrooms have are well designed and provide complimentary Wi-fi. Both the Brasserie and the Deli source local ingredients for their menus.

Rooms 169 ⟟ **Facilities** STV Wi-fi ↕ Gym Exercise studio Xmas New Year **Conf** Class 30 Board 40 Thtr 110 Del from £240 to £280* **Services** Lift Air con **Parking** 169 **Notes** ⊗ Civ Wed 150

Holiday Inn Farnborough

★★★ 81% HOTEL

☎ 0871 942 9029 & 01252 894300
Lynchford Rd GU14 6AZ
e-mail: reservations-farnborough@ihg.com
web: www.hifarnboroughhotel.co.uk
dir: M3 junct 4, A325 through Farnborough towards Aldershot. Hotel on left at The Queen's rdbt

This hotel occupies a perfect location for events in Aldershot and Farnborough with ample parking on site and easy access to the M3. Modern bedrooms provide good comfort levels, and internet access is provided throughout. Leisure facilities comprise a swimming pool, gym and beauty treatment rooms. Smart meeting rooms are also available.

Rooms 142 (31 fmly) (35 GF) **Facilities** Spa STV Wi-fi ↕ ⊙ supervised Gym Sauna Steam room Beauty room ♬ Xmas New Year **Conf** Class 80 Board 60 Thtr 180 Del from £100 to £250* **Services** Air con **Parking** 170 **Notes** Civ Wed 180

FARNBOROUGH *continued*

Premier Inn Farnborough

BUDGET HOTEL

☎ 0871 527 8398
Ively Rd, Southwood GU14 0JP
web: www.premierinn.com
dir: M3 junct 4a, A327 to Farnborough. Hotel on left at 5th rdbt (Monkey Puzzle Rdbt)

High quality, budget accommodation ideal for both families and business travellers. Spacious, en suite bedrooms feature tea and coffee making facilities, and Freeview TV in most hotels. Internet access and Wi-fi are available for a small fee. The adjacent family restaurant features a wide and varied menu. See also the Hotel Groups pages.

Rooms 62

FARNHAM   Map 5 SU84
Surrey

BEST WESTERN Frensham Pond Hotel

★★★ 81% ☻ HOTEL

☎ 01252 795161
Bacon Ln GU10 2QB
e-mail: info@frenshampondhotel.co.uk
web: www.frenshampondhotel.co.uk

(For full entry see Churt)

Mercure Farnham Bush Hotel

Mercure

★★★ 77% HOTEL

☎ 01252 715237
The Borough GU9 7NN
e-mail: H6621@accor.com
web: www.mercure.com
dir: M3 junct 4, A31, follow town centre signs. At East Street lights turn left, hotel on right

Dating back to the 17th century, this extended former coaching inn is attractively presented and has a courtyard and a lawned garden. The bedrooms are well appointed, with quality fabrics and good facilities. The public areas include the panelled Oak Lounge, a smart cocktail bar and a conference facility in an adjoining building.

Rooms 94 (3 fmly) (27 GF) **Facilities** FTV Wi-fi Xmas **Conf** Class 80 Board 30 Thtr 140 **Parking** 70 **Notes** Civ Wed 90

FAWKHAM GREEN   Map 6 TQ56
Kent

Brandshatch Place Hotel & Spa

HandPICKED HOTELS
BUILT FOR PLEASURE

★★★★ 80% ☻☻ HOTEL

☎ 01474 875000
Brands Hatch Rd, Fawkham Green DA3 8NQ
e-mail: brandshatchplace@handpicked.co.uk
web: www.handpickedhotels.co.uk/brandshatchplace
dir: M25 junct 3, A20 West Kingsdown. Left at paddock entrance/Fawkham Green sign. 3rd left signed Fawkham Rd. Hotel 500mtrs on right

This charming 18th-century Georgian country house close to the famous racing circuit offers stylish and elegant rooms. Bedrooms are appointed to a very high standard, offering impressive facilities and excellent levels of comfort and quality. The hotel also features a comprehensive leisure club with substantial crèche facilities.

Rooms 38 (12 annexe) (1 fmly) (6 GF) ⚡ **S** £79-£163; **D** £89-£173 (incl. bkfst)* **Facilities** Spa FTV Wi-fi ⇘ ☜ ⚐ Gym Squash Aerobic dance studio Sauna Steam room Xmas New Year Child facilities **Conf** Class 60 Board 50 Thtr 160 Del from £140 to £175* **Services** Lift **Parking** 100 **Notes** LB ⊗ Civ Wed 110

FELIXSTOWE   Map 13 TM33
Suffolk

The Brook Hotel

★★★ 77% HOTEL

☎ 01394 278441
Orwell Rd IP11 7PF
e-mail: welcome@brookhotel.com

The Brook Hotel is a modern, well furnished building ideally situated in a residential area close to the town centre and the sea. Public areas include a lounge bar, a large open-plan restaurant with a bar area and a residents' lounge. Bedrooms are generally quite spacious; each one is pleasantly decorated and equipped with modern facilities.

Rooms 25 (5 fmly) (3 GF) ⚡ **Facilities** FTV Wi-fi ♫ Xmas New Year **Conf** Class 60 Board 60 Thtr 100 **Parking** 20 **Notes** LB ⊗ Civ Wed 150

Marlborough Hotel

★★ 72% HOTEL

☎ 01394 285621
Sea Front IP11 2BJ
e-mail: hsm@marlborough-hotel-felix.com
web: www.marlborough-hotel-felix.com
dir: From A14 follow 'Docks' signs. Over Dock rdbt, rail crossing & lights. Left at T-junct. Hotel 400mtrs on left

Situated on the seafront, overlooking the beach and just a short stroll from the pier and town centre, this traditional resort hotel offers a good range of facilities including the smart Rattan Restaurant, Flying Boat Bar and L'Aperitif lounge. The pleasantly decorated bedrooms come in a variety of styles; some have lovely sea views.

Rooms 48 (1 fmly) ⚡ **Facilities** STV Wi-fi ⇘ Pool table Xmas New Year **Conf** Class 60 Board 40 Thtr 80 **Services** Lift **Parking** 16 **Notes** ⊗

FERNDOWN   Map 5 SU00
Dorset

Premier Inn Bournemouth/Ferndown

BUDGET HOTEL

☎ 0871 527 8122
Ringwood Rd, Tricketts Cross BH22 9BB
web: www.premierinn.com
dir: Off A348 just before Tricketts Cross rdbt

High quality, budget accommodation ideal for both families and business travellers. Spacious, en suite bedrooms feature tea and coffee making facilities, and Freeview TV in most hotels. Internet access and Wi-fi are available for a small fee. The adjacent family restaurant features a wide and varied menu. See also the Hotel Groups pages.

Rooms 32

Save on hotels. Book at **theAA.com/hotel**

FAR – FOL 175 ENGLAND

FLAMBOROUGH Map 17 TA27
East Riding of Yorkshire

North Star Hotel

★★ 80% SMALL HOTEL

☎ 01262 850379
North Marine Dr YO15 1BL
e-mail: info@thenorthstarhotel.co.uk
web: www.thenorthstarhotel.co.uk
dir: B1229 or B1255 to Flamborough. Follow signs for North Landing along North Marine Dr. Hotel 100yds from sea

Standing close to the North Landing of Flamborough Head, this family-run hotel overlooks delightful countryside, and provides excellent accommodation and caring hospitality. A good range of fresh local food, especially fish, is available in both the bar and the dining room.

Rooms 7 🐾 **Parking** 60 **Notes** ⊗ Closed Xmas RS Nov-Etr

FLEET Map 5 SU85
Hampshire

The Lismoyne Hotel

🆄

☎ 01252 628555
45 Church Rd GU51 4NE
e-mail: info@lismoynehotel.com
dir: M3 junct 4a follow signs for Fleet. Pass railway station over lights into shopping area. Right into Church Rd, hotel on left

Currently the rating for this establishment is not confirmed. This may be due to a change of ownership or because it has only recently joined the AA rating scheme. For further details please see the AA website: theAA.com

Rooms 62 (4 fmly) (28 GF) 🐾 **S** £62.50-£97.50; **D** £72.50-£117.50 (incl. bkfst)* **Facilities** FTV Wi-fi ⋫ **Conf** Class 46 Board 60 Thtr 145 Del from £180 to £210* **Parking** 100 **Notes** LB Civ Wed

FLEET Map 5 SU75
MOTORWAY SERVICE AREA (M3)
Hampshire

Days Inn Fleet - M3

BUDGET HOTEL

☎ 01252 815587
Fleet Services GU51 1AA
e-mail: fleet.hotel@welcomebreak.co.uk
web: www.welcomebreak.co.uk
dir: Between junct 4a & 5 southbound on M3

This modern building offers accommodation in smart, spacious and well-equipped bedrooms, suitable for families and business travellers, and all with en suite bathrooms. Continental breakfast is available and other refreshments may be taken at the nearby family restaurant. See also the Hotel Groups pages.

Rooms 59 (46 fmly) (5 smoking)

FLITWICK Map 11 TL03
Bedfordshire

Menzies Hotels Woburn Flitwick Manor

★★★★ 76% ⊛ COUNTRY HOUSE HOTEL

☎ 01525 712242
Church Rd MK45 1AE
e-mail: flitwick@menzieshotels.co.uk
web: www.menzieshotels.co.uk
dir: M1 junct 12, follow signs for Flitwick, turn left into Church Rd, hotel on left

With its picturesque setting in acres of gardens and parkland, yet only minutes by car from the motorway, this lovely Georgian house combines the best of both worlds, being both accessible and peaceful. Bedrooms are individually decorated and furnished with period pieces; some are air conditioned. Cosy and intimate, the lounge and restaurant give the hotel a home-from-home feel.

Rooms 18 (1 fmly) (5 GF) (1 smoking) **Facilities** STV FTV Wi-fi ⋫ ⛳ Putt green ⛳ Xmas New Year **Conf** Class 30 Board 22 Thtr 50 **Parking** 18 **Notes** Civ Wed 50

FOLKESTONE Map 7 TR23
Kent

BEST WESTERN Clifton Hotel

★★★ 77% HOTEL

☎ 01303 851231
The Leas CT20 2EB
e-mail: reservations@thecliftonhotel.com
dir: M20 junct 13, 0.25m W of town centre on A259

This privately-owned Victorian-style hotel occupies a prime location, looking out across the English Channel. The bedrooms are comfortably appointed and most have views of the sea. Public areas include a traditionally furnished lounge, a popular bar serving a good range of beers and several well-appointed conference rooms.

Rooms 80 (5 fmly) 🐾 **Facilities** FTV Wi-fi Games room Xmas New Year **Conf** Class 36 Board 32 Thtr 80 **Services** Lift

The Southcliff Hotel

★★ 72% HOTEL

☎ 01303 850075
22-26 The Leas CT20 2DY
e-mail: sales@thesouthcliff.co.uk
web: www.thesouthcliff.co.uk
dir: M20 junct 13, follow signs for The Leas. Left at rdbt onto Sandgate Rd, right at Blockbusters, right at end of road, hotel on right

Located on the town's panoramic promenade with a bird's eye view of the sea, this historical Victorian hotel is perfectly located for cross channel connections and is only minutes from the town centre. The bedrooms are spacious and airy with some boasting balconies and sea views. Enjoy dinner in the spacious restaurant or relax in the contemporary bar. Parking is available by arrangement.

Rooms 68 🐾 **Facilities** FTV Wi-fi ♫ Xmas New Year **Conf** Class 120 Board 50 Thtr 200 **Services** Lift **Notes** ⊗

F

FOLKESTONE *continued*

Premier Inn Folkestone (Channel Tunnel)

BUDGET HOTEL

☎ 0871 527 8400
Cherry Garden Ln CT19 4AP
web: www.premierinn.com
dir: M20 junct 13. Follow Folkestone, A20 signs. At lights turn right, hotel on right

High quality, budget accommodation ideal for both families and business travellers. Spacious, en suite bedrooms feature tea and coffee making facilities, and Freeview TV in most hotels. Internet access and Wi-fi are available for a small fee. The adjacent family restaurant features a wide and varied menu. See also the Hotel Groups pages.

Rooms 79

Rocksalt Rooms

◉◉ RESTAURANT WITH ROOMS

☎ 01303 212070
2 Back St CT19 6NN
e-mail: info@rocksaltfolkestone.co.uk
dir: M20 junct 13 follow signs to harbour (A259). At harbour left onto Fish Market

Overlooking the busy harbour, crowded with small leisure boats, and having wonderful sea views, Rocksalt enjoys a great location in Folkestone. Bedrooms are stylish, well appointed with original antique beds and equipped with a host of thoughtful little extras. Continental breakfasts are delivered promptly to the guests' rooms each morning, and dinner is served in the award-winning restaurant that has panoramic views.

Rooms 4 (1 fmly)

FOREST ROW   Map 6 TQ43
East Sussex

INSPECTORS' CHOICE

Ashdown Park Hotel & Country Club

★★★★ ◉◉ HOTEL

☎ 01342 824988
Wych Cross RH18 5JR
e-mail: reservations@ashdownpark.com
web: www.ashdownpark.com
dir: A264 to East Grinstead, then A22 to Eastbourne. 2m S of Forest Row at Wych Cross lights. Left to Hartfield, hotel on right 0.75m

Situated in 186 acres of landscaped gardens and parkland, this impressive country house enjoys a peaceful countryside setting in the heart of the Ashdown Forest. Bedrooms are individually styled and decorated. Public rooms include a restored 18th-century chapel, ideal for exclusive meetings and wedding parties, plus three drawing rooms, a cocktail bar and the award-winning Anderida Restaurant. The extensive indoor and outdoor leisure facilities include the Country Club and Spa plus an 18-hole, par 3 golf course and driving range.

Rooms 106 (12 fmly) (16 GF) ➤ **S** £200-£480; **D** £230-£510 (incl. bkfst)* **Facilities** Spa FTV Wi-fi ➤ HL ☺ ♨ 18 🏌 Putt green 💪 Gym Aerobics Snooker Clay pigeon Archery Falconry Cycling Xmas New Year **Conf** Class 70 Board 40 Thtr 160 **Parking** 200 **Notes** LB Civ Wed 150

FORMBY   Map 15 SD30
Merseyside

Formby Hall Golf Resort & Spa

★★★★ 77% HOTEL

☎ 01704 875699
Southport Old Rd L37 0AB
e-mail: gm@formbyhallgolfresort.co.uk
web: www.formbyhallgolfresort.co.uk
dir: A565 to 2nd rdbt, follow brown signs

This hotel offers modern, boutique-style bedrooms with state-of-the-art facilities, some with excellent views over the championship golf course. The lavish spa offers peace and tranquillity along with a superbly equipped gym. Two golf courses and a driving range also add to the hotel's outstanding facilities. The Brasserie is an informal eating option and guests can enjoy a relaxing drink in the 19th Hole bar.

Rooms 62 (10 fmly) (29 GF) ➤ **Facilities** Spa STV FTV Wi-fi ➤ HL ☺ ♨ 18 Putt green Gym Kinesis studio Driving range Short ball area 🎵 Xmas New Year **Conf** Class 60 Board 40 Thtr 300 **Services** Lift Air con **Parking** 457 **Notes** ⊗ Civ Wed 100

FOWEY   Map 2 SX15
Cornwall

The Fowey Hotel

★★★★ 74% ◉ HOTEL   RICHARDSON HOTELS
Where memories are made

☎ 01726 832551
The Esplanade PL23 1HX
e-mail: reservations@thefoweyhotel.co.uk
web: www.thefoweyhotel.co.uk
dir: A30 to Okehampton, continue to Bodmin. Then B3269 to Fowey for 1m, on right bend left junct then right into Dagands Rd. Hotel 200mtrs

This attractive hotel stands proudly above the estuary, with marvellous views of the river from the public areas and the majority of the bedrooms. High standards are evident throughout, augmented by a relaxed and welcoming atmosphere. There is a spacious bar, elegant restaurant and smart drawing room. Imaginative dinners make good use of quality local ingredients.

Rooms 37 (2 fmly) ➤ **S** £59-£165; **D** £59-£219 (incl. bkfst)* **Facilities** FTV Wi-fi 💪 Xmas New Year **Conf** Class 60 Board 20 Thtr 100 **Services** Lift **Parking** 20 **Notes** LB Civ Wed 120

FRADDON　　Map 2 SW95
Cornwall

Premier Inn Newquay (A30/ Fraddon)

BUDGET HOTEL

☎ 0871 527 8816
Penhale Round TR9 6NA
web: www.premierinn.com
dir: On A30, 2m S of Indian Queens

High quality, budget accommodation ideal for both families and business travellers. Spacious, en suite bedrooms feature tea and coffee making facilities, and Freeview TV in most hotels. Internet access and Wi-fi are available for a small fee. The adjacent family restaurant features a wide and varied menu. See also the Hotel Groups pages.

Rooms 40

FRANKBY　　Map 15 SJ28
Merseyside

Hillbark Hotel & Spa
★★★★★ 85% ◉◉◉ HOTEL

☎ 0151 625 2400
Royden Park CH48 1NP
e-mail: enquiries@hillbarkhotel.co.uk
web: www.hillbarkhotel.co.uk
dir: M53 junct 3, A552 (Upton), right onto A551 (Arrowe Park Rd). 0.6m at lights left into Arrowe Brook Rd. 0.5m on left

Originally built in 1891 on Bidston Hill, this Elizabethan-style mansion was actually moved, brick by brick, to its current site in 1931. The house now sits in a 250-acre woodland estate and enjoys delightful views towards the River Dee and to hills in North Wales. Bedrooms are luxuriously furnished and well equipped, while elegant day rooms are richly styled. There is a choice of restaurants including the fine dining restaurant and a spa.

Rooms 18 (1 fmly) ↕ **S** £140-£680; **D** £160-£700 (incl. bkfst)* **Facilities** Spa STV FTV Wi-fi ↕ ↩ Gym Cinema Library Games room Children's play area Xmas New Year Child facilities **Conf** Class 300 Board 60 Thtr 750 Del from £170* **Services** Lift **Parking** 160 **Notes** LB ⊗ Civ Wed 500

FRESHWATER　　Map 5 SZ38
Isle of Wight

Albion Hotel
★★★ 71% HOTEL

☎ 01983 755755
PO40 9RA
e-mail: info@albion-hotel.net

In an idyllic location on the island's southern heritage coast, the Albion Hotel is right on the seafront with stunning views of Freshwater Bay. The bedrooms and bathrooms are spacious and offer guests modern, comfortable accommodation; many rooms have balconies. Breakfast and dinner are served in the traditionally styled restaurant that also enjoys lovely views.

Rooms 41 **Conf** Class 30 Board 40 Thtr 60 **Notes** Closed Nov-Apr

FROME　　Map 4 ST74
Somerset

Premier Inn Frome

BUDGET HOTEL

☎ 9871 527 8404
Commerce Park, Jenson Av BA11 2LD
web: www.premierinn.com
dir: M4 junct 18, A46 follow Warminster & Frome signs. Hotel off A361 (Frome bypass) in Commerce Park

High quality, budget accommodation ideal for both families and business travellers. Spacious, en suite bedrooms feature tea and coffee making facilities, and Freeview TV in most hotels. Internet access and Wi-fi are available for a small fee. The adjacent family restaurant features a wide and varied menu. See also the Hotel Groups pages.

Rooms 40

GARFORTH　　Map 16 SE43
West Yorkshire

BEST WESTERN PLUS Milford Hotel

★★★ 83% HOTEL

☎ 01977 681800
A1 Great North Rd, Peckfield LS25 5LQ
e-mail: enquiries@mlh.co.uk
web: www.mlh.co.uk
dir: On A63, 1.5m W of A1(M) junct 42 & 4.5m E of M1 junct 46

This friendly, family owned and run hotel is conveniently situated, and provides very comfortable, modern accommodation. The air-conditioned bedrooms are particularly spacious and well equipped, and ten boutique-style superior rooms are available. Public areas include a relaxing lounge area, the contemporary Watermill Restaurant and lounge bar which has a working waterwheel.

Rooms 46 (13 GF) **S** £39-£109; **D** £39-£109* **Facilities** FTV Wi-fi ↕ Xmas New Year **Conf** Class 35 Board 30 Thtr 60 Del from £120 to £125* **Services** Air con **Parking** 80 **Notes** LB Civ Wed 80

GARSTANG　　Map 18 SD44
Lancashire

BEST WESTERN Garstang Country Hotel & Golf Centre

★★★ 79% HOTEL

☎ 01995 600100
Garstang Rd, Bowgreave PR3 1YE
e-mail: reception@garstanghotelandgolf.com
web: www.garstanghotelandgolf.com
dir: M6 junct 32 take 1st right after Shell garage on A6 onto B6430. 1m, hotel on left

This smart, purpose-built hotel enjoys a peaceful location alongside its own 18-hole golf course. Comfortable and spacious bedrooms are well equipped for both business and leisure guests, while inviting public areas include a restaurant and a choice of bars - one serving food.

Rooms 32 (16 GF) ↕ **S** £64-£79; **D** £78-£108 (incl. bkfst)* **Facilities** STV FTV Wi-fi ↕ 18 Putt green Golf driving range Xmas New Year **Conf** Class 150 Board 80 Thtr 250 Del from £75 to £95* **Services** Lift **Parking** 172 **Notes** LB ⊗ Civ Wed 200

G

Newcastle Gateshead Marriott Hotel MetroCentre

★★★★ 76% HOTEL

☎ 0191 493 2233
MetroCentre NE11 9XF
e-mail: reservations.newcastle.england.
metrocentre@marriotthotels.co.uk
web: www.newcastlemarriottmetrocentre.co.uk
dir: From N exit A1 at MetroCentre exit, take 'Other Routes'. From S exit A1 at MetroCentre exit, turn right

Set just off the A1 and on the doorstep of the popular Metro shopping centre, this stylish purpose-built hotel provides modern amenities including a leisure centre, conference facilities and an informal stylish restaurant offering a range of dining styles. All bedrooms are smartly laid out and thoughtfully equipped to suit both the business traveller and the leisure guest.

Rooms 150 (147 fmly) **Facilities** Spa STV FTV Wi-fi ⌁ HL ⓢ Gym Health & beauty clinic Dance studio Hairdresser Spinning studio Sauna Steam room **Conf** Class 172 Board 48 Thtr 400 **Services** Lift Air con **Parking** 300 **Notes** ⊗ Civ Wed 100

Eslington Villa Hotel

★★★ 82% ◉ HOTEL

☎ 0191 487 6017 & 420 0666
8 Station Rd, Low Fell NE9 6DR
e-mail: home@eslingtonvilla.co.uk
dir: From A1(M) exit for Team Valley Trading Estate. Right at 2nd rdbt along Eastern Av. Left at car show room, hotel 100yds on left

Set in a residential area, this smart hotel combines a bright, contemporary atmosphere with the period style of a fine Victorian villa. The overall ambience is relaxed and inviting. Chunky sofas grace the cocktail lounge, while tempting dishes can be enjoyed in either the classical dining room or modern conservatory overlooking the Team Valley.

Rooms 17 (2 fmly) (3 GF) **S** £59.50-£79.95;
D £69.50-£99.50 (incl. bkfst)* **Facilities** FTV Wi-fi
Conf Class 30 Board 25 Thtr 36 Del from £99 to £119* **Parking** 28 **Notes** LB ⊗ Closed 25-26 Dec RS BHs

Ramada Encore Newcastle - Gateshead

★★★ 77% HOTEL

☎ 0191 481 3600
Hawks Rd, Gateshead Quays NE8 3AD
web: www.encorenewcastlegateshead.co.uk
dir: Located Gateshead Quays

A modern, purpose-built hotel located at the Gateshead Quays. Bedrooms are well appointed and comfortable with well-presented en suites. Public areas are open-plan with a relaxed all-day menu serving food in all locations. A small gym and off-road parking are added benefits.

Rooms 200 (75 fmly) ⌇ **Facilities** FTV Wi-fi ⌁ HL Gym **Conf** Class 14 Board 18 Thtr 20 Del from £120 to £140* **Services** Lift **Parking** 70 **Notes** ⊗

Premier Inn Newcastle (Metro Centre)

BUDGET HOTEL

☎ 0871 527 8792
Derwent Haugh Rd, Swalwell NE16 3BL
web: www.premierinn.com
dir: From A1 & A694 junct into Derwent Haugh Rd. 1m N of Metro Centre

High quality, budget accommodation ideal for both families and business travellers. Spacious, en suite bedrooms feature tea and coffee making facilities, and Freeview TV in most hotels. Internet access and Wi-fi are available for a small fee. The adjacent family restaurant features a wide and varied menu. See also the Hotel Groups pages.

Rooms 69

Premier Inn Newcastle South

BUDGET HOTEL

☎ 0871 527 8806
Lobley Hill Rd NE11 9NA
web: www.premierinn.com
dir: A1 onto A692

Rooms 42

Premier Inn Newcastle (Team Valley)

BUDGET HOTEL

☎ 0871 527 8794
Maingate, Kingsway North, Team Valley NE11 0BE
web: www.premierinn.com
dir: A1 onto B1426 signed Team Valley (S'bound) or Teams/Consett (N'bound). Take Gateshead exit at rdbt. At bottom of hill straight on at rdbt. Hotel opposite

Rooms 115

See also **Dorking, East Grinstead & Reigate**

INSPECTORS' CHOICE

Langshott Manor

★★★★ ◉◉◉
COUNTRY HOUSE HOTEL

☎ 01293 786680
Langshott Ln RH6 9LN
e-mail: admin@langshottmanor.com
dir: From A23 take Ladbroke Rd, off Chequers rdbt to Langshott, after 0.75m hotel on right

On the outskirts of town this charming timber-framed Tudor manor house is set amidst beautifully landscaped grounds with an ancient moat. The stylish public areas feature a choice of inviting lounges with polished oak panelling, exposed beams and crackling log fires. Each bedroom - whether in the manor itself or in one of three mews buildings in the grounds - has been designed with flair and imagination. Expect sumptuous furnishings, Egyptian linens, flat-screen TVs and bathrooms with deep baths and power showers. The Mulberry restaurant overlooks a picturesque pond and offers an imaginative menu.

Rooms 22 (15 annexe) (2 fmly) (8 GF) ⌇
S £99-£199; **D** £109-£399* **Facilities** FTV Wi-fi ⌁ Xmas New Year **Conf** Class 20 Board 22 Thtr 40 Del from £198 to £304* **Parking** 25 **Notes** ⊗ Civ Wed 60

G

Sofitel London Gatwick

★★★★　77% ⊛　HOTEL

☎ 01293 567070　& 555000
North Terminal RH6 0PH
e-mail: h6204-re@accor.com
dir: M23 junct 9, follow to 2nd rdbt. Hotel straight ahead

One of the closest hotels to the airport, this modern, purpose-built hotel is located only minutes from the terminals. Bedrooms are contemporary and all are air conditioned. Guests have a choice of eating options including a French-style café, a brasserie and an oriental restaurant.

Rooms 518 (19 fmly) **Facilities** FTV Wi-fi ⇘ Gym **Conf** Class 150 Board 90 Thtr 300 Del from £135 to £160* **Services** Lift Air con **Parking** 565 **Notes** ⊗

Crowne Plaza London - Gatwick Airport

★★★★　75%　HOTEL

☎ 01293 608608
Langley Dr RH11 7SX
e-mail: info@cpgatwick.co.uk
web: www.cpgatwick.co.uk
dir: M23 junct 10, 3rd exit at rdbt & 3rd exit at next rdbt. At lights take 3rd exit at rdbt

Ideally located for Gatwick Airport, this contemporary hotel offers comfortable and well-furnished rooms suitable for both leisure and business travellers. Elite Health and Fitness Centre is the leisure centre which houses a stunning indoor swimming pool. Cube Restaurant & Bar offers a relaxed dining experience and the Gallery Sports Bar, an informal alternative. The hotel also has extensive conference facilities.

Rooms 294 (15 fmly) (6 GF) **Facilities** STV FTV Wi-fi ⇘ 🏊 supervised Gym Saunas Steam room Xmas New Year **Conf** Class 110 Board 40 Thtr 230 **Services** Lift Air con **Parking** 200 **Notes** ⊗ Civ Wed 150

Ramada Plaza London Gatwick

★★★★　75%　HOTEL

☎ 01293 561186
Tinsley Ln, Three Bridges RH10 8XH
e-mail: gm@ramadahotelgatwick.co.uk
web: www.ramadaplazalondongatwick.co.uk
dir: M25 junct 7, M23 signed Brighton, exit junct 10 signed Crawley, then A2011 to 1st rdbt. Hotel on left

This modern purpose-built hotel is just four miles from the airport with easy access to the M23. The spacious bedrooms are comfortably appointed and well equipped; some family rooms are available. Air-conditioned public areas include a brightly appointed

Arts Restaurant, first-floor conference centre and Sebastian Coe health club.

Rooms 151 (31 fmly) 🐾 **Facilities** STV Wi-fi ⇘ HL Gym New Year **Conf** Class 120 Board 90 Thtr 200 **Services** Lift Air con **Parking** 160 **Notes** ⊗ Civ Wed 100

Holiday Inn London Gatwick Worth

★★★★　74%　HOTEL

☎ 01293 884806
Crabbet Park, Turners Hill Rd, Worth RH10 4SS
e-mail: info@higatwickworth.co.uk
web: www.higatwickworth.co.uk
dir: M23 junct 10/A264 Copthorne Way at rdbt last exit towards Three Bridges. 1st left along Old Hollow, right at end of lane then 1st right into Crabbet Park

This purpose-built hotel is ideally placed for access to Gatwick Airport. The bedrooms are spacious and suitably appointed with good facilities. Public areas consist of a light and airy bar area and a brasserie-style restaurant offering good value meals. Guests have use of the superb leisure club next door.

Rooms 118 (39 fmly) (56 GF) 🐾 **S** fr £50; **D** fr £50* **Facilities** FTV Wi-fi ⇘ HL Use of gym & pool next door (chargeable) Xmas New Year **Conf** Class 80 Board 80 Thtr 250 **Services** Lift Air con **Parking** 150 **Notes** LB ⊗ Civ Wed 60

Copthorne Hotel London Gatwick

MILLENNIUM
HOTELS AND RESORTS
MILLENNIUM • COPTHORNE

★★★★　72%　HOTEL

☎ 01342 348800　& 348888
Copthorne Way RH10 3PG
e-mail: sales.gatwick@millenniumhotels.co.uk
web: www.millenniumhotels.co.uk
dir: On A264, 2m E of A264/B2036 rdbt

Situated in a tranquil position, the Copthorne is set in 100 acres of wooded, landscaped gardens containing jogging tracks, a putting green and a petanque pit. The sprawling building is built around a 16th-century farmhouse and has comfortable bedrooms; many are air conditioned. There are three dining options, ranging from the informal bar and carvery to the more formal Lion d'Or.

Rooms 227 (10 fmly) (122 GF) **Facilities** STV Wi-fi ⇘ HL 🏊 🎾 Gym Squash Aerobic studio Jogging trail Xmas New Year **Conf** Class 60 Board 48 Thtr 155 **Parking** 300 **Notes** ⊗ Civ Wed 100

Copthorne Hotel Effingham Gatwick

MILLENNIUM
HOTELS AND RESORTS
MILLENNIUM • COPTHORNE

★★★★　71%　HOTEL

☎ 01342 714994
West Park Rd RH10 3EU
e-mail: sales.effingham@millenniumhotels.co.uk
web: www.millenniumhotels.co.uk
dir: M23 junct 10, A264 towards East Grinstead. Over rdbt, at 2nd rdbt left onto B2028. Effingham Park on right

A former stately home, set in 40 acres of grounds, this hotel is popular for conference and weekend functions. The main restaurant is an open-plan brasserie serving modern continental cuisine, and snacks are also available in the bar. Bedrooms are spacious and well equipped. Facilities include a golf course and a leisure club.

Rooms 122 (9 fmly) (20 GF) 🐾 **Facilities** Spa STV Wi-fi HL 🎾 ⛳ 9 🏌 Putt green 🏋 Gym Aerobic & Dance studios Xmas New Year **Conf** Class 450 Board 250 Thtr 800 **Services** Lift **Parking** 500 **Notes** ⊗ Civ Wed 600

Menzies Hotels London Gatwick - Chequers

MenziesHotels

★★★★　70%　HOTEL

☎ 01293 766750
Brighton Rd RH6 8PH
e-mail: chequers@menzieshotels.co.uk
web: www.menzieshotels.co.uk
dir: M23 junct 9, A23 towards Redhill. At 'Longbridge' rdbt take 3rd exit signed Horley/A23. 1m to Sainsburys/Shell rdbt. Take 1st exit, hotel on right

Menzies Chequers is a popular hotel located close to the town centre and also convenient for Gatwick Airport; original parts of the building date back to the 1750s. Bedrooms are comfortable and well equipped with good facilities. Dining areas include a contemporary restaurant and the traditional Chequers pub. Secure parking is available.

Rooms 104 (10 fmly) (46 GF) (6 smoking) 🐾 **Facilities** FTV Wi-fi ⇘ Xmas New Year **Conf** Class 30 Board 32 Thtr 80 **Services** Lift **Parking** 140 **Notes** ⊗

G

GATWICK *continued*

Stanhill Court Hotel

★★★ 82% HOTEL

☎ 01293 862166
Stanhill Rd, Charlwood RH6 0EP
e-mail: enquiries@stanhillcourthotel.co.uk
web: www.stanhillcourthotel.co.uk
dir: N of Charlwood towards Newdigate

This hotel dates back to 1881 and enjoys a secluded location of 35 acres of well-tended grounds with views over the Downs. Bedrooms are individually furnished and decorated, and many have four-poster beds. Public areas include a library, a bright Spanish-style bar and a traditional wood-panelled restaurant. Extensive and varied function facilities make this a popular wedding venue.

Rooms 34 (2 fmly) (1 GF) ⚓ **D** £59-£120*
Facilities FTV Wi-fi ⓑ ☀ Xmas New Year
Conf Del from £150 to £179.95* **Parking** 150
Notes LB ⊗ Civ Wed 150

Holiday Inn London – Gatwick Airport

★★★ 78% HOTEL

☎ 0871 942 9030 & 01293 787648
Povey Cross Rd RH6 0BA
web: www.higatwickairporthotel.co.uk
dir: M23 junct 9, follow Gatwick, then Reigate signs. Hotel on left after 3rd rdbt

Situated close to the airport, this modern hotel provides air conditioned, smart accommodation with facilities suiting both the business and leisure guest. There is a restaurant and bar, and a variety of conference rooms plus a supporting business centre. Park and Fly stays are popular.

Rooms 216 (13 fmly) (37 GF) (22 smoking)
Facilities STV Wi-fi ⓑ **Conf** Class 100 Board 70
Thtr 210 **Services** Lift Air con **Parking** 600

Ibis London Gatwick Airport

BUDGET HOTEL

☎ 01293 590300
London Rd, County Oak RH10 9GY
e-mail: H1889@accor.com
web: www.ibis.com
dir: M23 junct 10, A2011 towards Crawley. Onto A23 left towards Crawley/Brighton. Hotel on left

Modern, budget hotel offering comfortable accommodation in bright and practical bedrooms. Breakfast is self-service and dinner is available in the restaurant. See also the Hotel Groups pages.

Rooms 141 **S** £33-£82; **D** £33-£82*

Premier Inn Crawley East

BUDGET HOTEL

☎ 0871 527 8412
Crawley Av, Gossops Green RH10 8BA
web: www.premierinn.com
dir: M23 junct 11, A23 towards Crawley & Gatwick Airport

High quality, budget accommodation ideal for both families and business travellers. Spacious, en suite bedrooms feature tea and coffee making facilities, and Freeview TV in most hotels. Internet access and Wi-fi are available for a small fee. The adjacent family restaurant features a wide and varied menu. See also the Hotel Groups pages.

Rooms 83

Premier Inn Crawley (Pound Hill)

BUDGET HOTEL

☎ 0871 527 8410
Balcombe Rd, Worth RH10 3NL
web: www.premierinn.com
dir: M23 junct 10, B2036 S towards Crawley

Rooms 41

Premier Inn Crawley South (Goffs Park)

BUDGET HOTEL

☎ 0871 527 8414
45 Goffs Park Rd RH11 8AX
web: www.premierinn.com
dir: M23 junct 11, A23 towards Crawley. At 2nd rdbt take 3rd exit for town centre, then 2nd right into Goffs Park Rd

Rooms 49

Premier Inn Gatwick Airport Central

BUDGET HOTEL

☎ 0871 527 8406
Longbridge Way, North Terminal RH6 0NX
web: www.premierinn.com
dir: M23 junct 9/9A towards North Terminal, at rdbt take 3rd exit, hotel on right

Rooms 219

Premier Inn Gatwick Airport North

BUDGET HOTEL

☎ 0871 527 9354
Crossway, Gatwick North Terminal RH6 0PH
web: www.premierinn.com
dir: M23 junct 9. Follow signs for Gatwick North Terminal, at North Terminal rdbt enter at Arrivals Road (2nd exit), turn right onto Northway (Drop Off point), hotel is on right.

Rooms 630

Premier Inn Gatwick Airport South

BUDGET HOTEL

☎ 0871 527 8408
London Rd, Lowfield Heath RH10 9ST
web: www.premierinn.com
dir: M23 junct 9a towards North Terminal rdbt. Follow A23 & Crawley signs. Hotel in 2m

Rooms 102

Premier Inn Gatwick Manor Royal

BUDGET HOTEL

☎ 0871 527 9214
Crawley Business Quarter, Fleming Way RH10 9DF
web: www.premierinn.com
dir: M23 junct 10, A2011 (Crawley Ave). At rdbt 4th exit onto A23 (London Rd), at rdbt right into Fleming Way. Hotel 300yds on left

Rooms 180

GERRARDS CROSS   Map 6 TQ08
Buckinghamshire

The Bull Hotel

★★★★ 76% ◉ HOTEL

☎ 01753 885995
Oxford Rd SL9 7PA
e-mail: bull@sarova.co.uk
dir: M40 junct 2 follow Beaconsfield on A355. After 0.5m 2nd exit at rdbt signed A40 Gerrards Cross for 2m. The Bull on right

Dating from the 17th-century, this former inn has been extensively refurbished to provide smart, well-equipped bedrooms. Public areas include the popular bar and Beeches Restaurant, serving a wide variety of dishes to suit all tastes. In addition there is the informal Jack Shrimpton bar offering snacks and bar meals. Attractive gardens and a good range of function rooms make this a popular wedding and events venue.

Save on hotels. Book at **theAA.com/hotel**

GAT – GLE 181 ENGLAND

Rooms 150 (15 fmly) (19 GF) Facilities FTV Wi-fi
Use of private leisure facilities Xmas New Year
Conf Class 108 Board 40 Thtr 180 **Services** Lift
Parking 150 **Notes** Civ Wed 114

GILLINGHAM
Kent
Map 7 TQ76

Premier Inn Gillingham Business Park

BUDGET HOTEL

☎ 0871 527 8416
Will Adams Way ME8 6BY
web: www.premierinn.com
dir: M2 junct 44, A278 to A2. Left at Tesco. Hotel at next rdbt

High quality, budget accommodation ideal for both families and business travellers. Spacious, en suite bedrooms feature tea and coffee making facilities, and Freeview TV in most hotels. Internet access and Wi-fi are available for a small fee. The adjacent family restaurant features a wide and varied menu. See also the Hotel Groups pages.

Rooms 46

Premier Inn Gillingham/Rainham

BUDGET HOTEL

☎ 0871 527 9268
High St, Rainham ME8 7JE
web: www.premierinn.com
dir: M25 junct 2 (Canterbury/Dover/A2), A2 to M2 (Dover). Exit at junct 4 (Rainham/Medway Tunnel), straight on at 2 rdbts. At 3rd rdbt take 3rd exit (Rainham High St). Hotel on right at 3rd lights

Rooms 26

GIRTON
Cambridgeshire
Map 12 TL46

Premier Inn Cambridge North (Girton)

BUDGET HOTEL

☎ 0871 527 8188
Huntingdon Rd CB3 0DR
web: www.premierinn.com
dir: A14 junct 31 follow signs towards Cambridge. Pass BP garage, next right. Hotel adjacent to Traveller's Rest Beefeater

High quality, budget accommodation ideal for both families and business travellers. Spacious, en suite bedrooms feature tea and coffee making facilities, and Freeview TV in most hotels. Internet access and Wi-fi are available for a small fee. The adjacent

family restaurant features a wide and varied menu. See also the Hotel Groups pages.

Rooms 20

GISBURN
Lancashire
Map 18 SD84

Stirk House Hotel

★★★ 82% ◉ HOTEL

☎ 01200 445581
BB7 4LJ
e-mail: reservations@stirkhouse.co.uk
web: www.stirkhouse.co.uk
dir: W of village, on A59. Hotel 0.5m on left

This delightful historic hotel enjoys a peaceful location in its own grounds, amid rolling countryside. Extensive public areas include excellent conference and banqueting facilities, a leisure centre and an elegant restaurant. The stylish bedrooms and suites vary in size and style but all are comfortable and well equipped. Hospitality is warm and friendly, and service attentive.

Rooms 32 (11 annexe) (2 fmly) (10 GF)
Facilities STV Wi-fi supervised Gym Beauty treatment room Aromatherapy Personal training Kick boxing New Year **Conf** Class 150 Board 45 Thtr 200 **Del** £108* **Parking** 100 **Notes** Civ Wed 95

GLAZEBROOK
Cheshire
Map 15 SJ69

The Rhinewood Country House Hotel

★★★ 77% HOTEL

☎ 0161 775 5555
Glazebrook Ln WA3 5BB
e-mail: info@therhinewoodhotel.co.uk
dir: M6 junct 21, A57 towards Irlam. Left at Glazebrook sign, hotel 0.25m on left

This privately owned hotel stands in spacious landscaped gardens a short drive from Manchester and Warrington. The attractively presented bedrooms are well equipped. There is a popular restaurant and the stylish bar is ideal for more informal dining. Facilities include conference and function rooms and the hotel is a popular wedding venue.

Rooms 32 (4 fmly) (16 GF) (8 smoking) **Facilities** STV Wi-fi Complimentary membership at nearby health spa Xmas **Conf** Class 70 Board 40 Thtr 100 **Parking** 120 **Notes** Civ Wed 100

GLENRIDDING
Cumbria
Map 18 NY31

The Inn on the Lake

LAKE DISTRICT HOTELS

★★★★ 78% ◉◉ HOTEL

☎ 017684 82444 & 0800 840 1245
Lake Ullswater CA11 0PE
e-mail: innonthelake@lakedistricthotels.net
web: www.lakedistricthotels.net/innonthelake
dir: M6 junct 40, A66 to Keswick. At rdbt take A592 to Ullswater Lake. Along lake to Glenridding. Hotel on left on entering village

In a picturesque lakeside setting, this restored Victorian hotel is a popular leisure destination as well as catering for weddings and conferences. Superb views can be enjoyed from the bedrooms and from the garden terrace where afternoon teas are served during warmer months. There is a popular pub in the grounds, and moorings for yachts are available to guests. Sailing tuition can be arranged.

Rooms 47 (20 fmly) (1 GF) **S** fr £109; **D** fr £244 (incl. bkfst)* **Facilities** FTV Wi-fi Putt green Gym Sauna 9 hole pitch & putt course Xmas New Year **Conf** Class 42 Board 30 Thtr 100 Del from £168* **Services** Lift **Parking** 100 **Notes** LB Civ Wed 110

BEST WESTERN Glenridding Hotel

★★★ 77% HOTEL

☎ 017684 82228 & 82289
CA11 0PB
e-mail: glenridding@bestwestern.co.uk
dir: N'bound M6 junct 36, A591 Windermere then A592, for 14m. S'bound M6 junct 40, A592 for 13m

This friendly hotel benefits from a picturesque location in the village centre, and many rooms have fine views of the lake and fells. Public areas are extensive and include a choice of dining options including Ratchers Restaurant and a café. Leisure facilities are available along with a conference room and a garden function room.

Rooms 36 (7 fmly) (8 GF) **Facilities** STV Wi-fi Sauna Snooker Table tennis Xmas New Year **Conf** Class 30 Board 24 Thtr 30 **Services** Lift **Parking** 30 **Notes** Civ Wed 120

G

GLOSSOP	Map 16 SK09
Derbyshire	

Wind in the Willows Hotel

★★ 85% COUNTRY HOUSE HOTEL

☎ 01457 868001
Derbyshire Level SK13 7PT
e-mail: info@windinthewillows.co.uk
dir: 1m E of Glossop on A57, turn right opposite Royal Oak, hotel 400yds on right

This impressive house sits in peaceful grounds with lovely views of the Peak District National Park. Individually furnished bedrooms are in keeping with the Victorian style of the house. Beautiful original oak panelling and crackling log fires add to the charm of the lounges and dining room. There is also a conference suite that is perfect for meetings, private dining or special occasions.

Rooms 12 ↰ **S** £95-£125; **D** £159-£189 (incl. bkfst)
Facilities FTV Wi-fi ↓ Xmas New Year **Conf** Class 12 Board 16 Thtr 40 **Parking** 16 **Notes** LB ⊗ No children 10yrs

---

GLOUCESTER	Map 10 SO81
Gloucestershire	

Hallmark Hotel Gloucester

★★★★ 73% HOTEL

☎ 01452 525653
Matson Ln, Robinswood Hill GL4 6EA
e-mail:
gloucester.reservations@hallmarkhotels.co.uk
web: www.hallmarkhotels.co.uk/gloucester
dir: A40 towards Gloucester onto A38. 1st exit at 4th rdbt (Painswick Rd). Right onto Matson Lane

Ideally located for exploring the Cotswolds and Gloucester, this hotel offers well-appointed bedrooms and relaxing public areas. The large leisure club has a well-equipped gym, squash courts and pool. Complimentary Wi-fi is available throughout.

Rooms 95 ↰ **Facilities** FTV Wi-fi ↓ ⊛ supervised ⌇ Gym Squash Beauty salon Xmas New Year **Conf** Class 150 Board 18 Thtr 220 **Parking** 150 **Notes** Civ Wed 120

Hatton Court

★★★ 82% HOTEL

☎ 01452 617412
Upton Hill, Upton St Leonards GL4 8DE
e-mail: res@hatton-court.co.uk
web: www.hatton-court.co.uk
dir: From Gloucester on B4073 (Painswick road). Hotel at top of hill on right

Built in the style of a 17th-century Cotswold manor house and set in seven acres of well-kept gardens, this hotel is popular with both business and leisure guests. It stands at the top of Upton Hill and commands truly spectacular views of the Severn Valley. The bedrooms, including a four-poster room, are comfortable and tastefully furnished with many extra facilities. The elegant Tara Restaurant offers varied menus, and outdoor seating in summer; there is also a bar and foyer lounge.

Rooms 45 (28 annexe) (6 fmly) ↰ **S** £60-£300; **D** £65-£350 (incl. bkfst)* **Facilities** FTV Wi-fi HL ⍢ Gym Xmas New Year **Conf** Class 100 Board 60 Thtr 200 Del from £99 to £159* **Parking** 80 **Notes** LB Civ Wed 120

Mercure Gloucester, Bowden Hall Hotel

★★★ HOTEL

☎ 0844 815 9077
Bondend Ln, Upton St Leonards GL4 8ED
e-mail: info@mercuregloucester.co.uk
web: www.jupiterhotels.co.uk
dir: A417/A38/Gloucester. At rdbt take 2nd exit. At 2nd lights left onto Abbeymead Ave (becomes Metz Way). 1.5m, 3rd left onto Upton Lane, left into Bondend Rd, then left into Bondend Lane. Hotel at end

Currently the rating for this establishment is not confirmed. This may be due to a change of ownership or because it has only recently joined the AA rating scheme.

Rooms 72 **Conf** Class 70 Board 30 Thtr 120

Hatherley Manor

★★★ 79% HOTEL

☎ 01452 730217
Down Hatherley Ln GL2 9QA
e-mail: reservations@hatherleymanor.com
web: www.hatherleymanor.com
dir: A38 into Down Hatherley Lane, signed. Hotel 600yds on left

Within easy striking distance of the M5, Gloucester, Cheltenham and the Cotswolds, this stylish 17th-century manor, set in attractive grounds, remains popular with both business and leisure guests. Bedrooms are well appointed and offer contemporary comforts. A particularly impressive range of meeting and function rooms is available.

Rooms 50 (5 fmly) (18 GF) **S** £65-£280; **D** £65-£280 **Facilities** FTV Wi-fi Xmas New Year **Conf** Class 90 Board 75 Thtr 400 Del from £120 to £185 **Parking** 250 **Notes** LB Civ Wed 300

Holiday Inn Gloucester - Cheltenham

★★★ 77% HOTEL

☎ 0871 942 9034
Crest Way, Barnwood GL4 3RX
e-mail: reservations-gloucester@ihg.com
web: www.holidayinn.co.uk
dir: A40 to Gloucester. At rdbt take 2nd exit signed A417/Cirencester. At next rdbt take 2nd exit then 1st left

This hotel is conveniently located close to the M5, and within easy driving distance of both Gloucester and Cheltenham. Bedrooms vary in size from the larger, well-equipped executive rooms to smaller style standard doubles. A good selection of dining options is available in either the lounge/bar, the relaxing restaurant or via room service. Guests can also enjoy the well-equipped leisure facilities.

Rooms 125 (25 fmly) (61 GF) (6 smoking) **D** £50-£160* **Facilities** Spa STV FTV Wi-fi ↓ ⊛ Gym Dance studio New Year **Conf** Class 50 Board 60 Thtr 140 Del from £110 to £175* **Services** Air con **Parking** 200 **Notes** LB ⊗ Civ Wed 120

Premier Inn Gloucester (Barnwood)

BUDGET HOTEL

☎ 0871 527 8456
Barnwood GL4 3HR
web: www.premierinn.com
dir: M5 junct 11, A40 towards Gloucester. At 1st rdbt A417 towards Cirencester, at next rdbt take 4th exit

High quality, budget accommodation ideal for both families and business travellers. Spacious, en suite bedrooms feature tea and coffee making facilities, and Freeview TV in most hotels. Internet access and Wi-fi are available for a small fee. The adjacent family restaurant features a wide and varied menu. See also the Hotel Groups pages.

Rooms 83

Premier Inn Gloucester Business Park

BUDGET HOTEL

☎ 0871 527 8462
Gloucester Business Park, Brockworth GL3 4AJ
web: www.premierinn.com
dir: M5 junct 11a, A417 towards Cirencester. At Brockworth Rdbt follow Gloucester Business Park signs, onto dual carriageway (Valiant Way). At next rdbt left into Delta Way. Hotel adjacent to Tesco

Rooms 48

Premier Inn Gloucester (Little Witcombe)

BUDGET HOTEL

☎ 0871 527 8458
Witcombe GL3 4SS
web: www.premierinn.com
dir: M5 junct 11a, A417 signed Cirencester. At 1st exit turn right onto A46 towards Stroud & Witcombe. Left at next rdbt by Crosshands pub

Rooms 39

Premier Inn Gloucester (Longford)

BUDGET HOTEL

☎ 0871 527 8460
Tewkesbury Rd, Longford GL2 9BE
web: www.premierinn.com
dir: M5 junct 11, A40 towards Gloucester & Ross-on-Wye. Hotel on A38 towards Gloucester

Rooms 60

Premier Inn Gloucester North

BUDGET HOTEL

☎ 0871 527 8464
Tewkesbury Rd, Twigworth GL2 9PG
web: www.premierinn.com
dir: On A38, 1m N from junct with A40

Rooms 50

The Wharf House Restaurant with Rooms

⊚ RESTAURANT WITH ROOMS

☎ 01452 332900
Over GL2 8DB
e-mail: thewharfhouse@yahoo.co.uk
web: www.thewharfhouse.co.uk
dir: From A40 between Gloucester & Highnam exit at lights for Over. Establishment signed

The Wharf House was built to replace the old lock cottage and, as the name suggests, it is located at the very edge of the river; it has pleasant views and an outdoor terrace. The bedrooms and bathrooms have been decorated and appointed to high levels of quality and comfort, and there are plenty of guest extras. Seasonal, local produce can be enjoyed both at breakfast and dinner in the delightfully relaxing restaurant.

Rooms 7 (1 fmly)

GODALMING   Map 6 SU94
Surrey

Premier Inn Godalming

BUDGET HOTEL

☎ 0871 527 8466
Guildford Rd GU7 3BX
web: www.premierinn.com
dir: Exit A3 onto A3000 signed Godalming. 1m to rdbt, turn right into Guildford Rd towards Godalming. Hotel on left in 500yds

High quality, budget accommodation ideal for both families and business travellers. Spacious, en suite bedrooms feature tea and coffee making facilities, and Freeview TV in most hotels. Internet access and Wi-fi are available for a small fee. The adjacent family restaurant features a wide and varied menu. See also the Hotel Groups pages.

Rooms 17

GOLANT   Map 2 SX15
Cornwall

Cormorant Hotel & Restaurant

★★★ 81% ⊛⊛ HOTEL

☎ 01726 833426
PL23 1LL
e-mail: relax@cormoranthotel.co.uk
web: www.cormoranthotel.co.uk
dir: A390 onto B3269 signed Fowey. In 3m left to Golant, through village to end of road, hotel on right

This hotel focuses on traditional hospitality, attentive service and good food. All the bedrooms enjoy views of the river, and guests can expect goose and down duvets, flat-screen digital TVs and free Wi-fi access. Breakfast and lunch may be taken on the terrace which overlooks the river.

Rooms 14 (4 GF) ↖ **S** £70-£200; **D** £70-£250 (incl. bkfst)* **Facilities** FTV Wi-fi ↕ ↺ Xmas New Year **Parking** 20 **Notes** LB ⊗ No children 16yrs

G

GOMERSAL   Map 19 SE22
West Yorkshire

Gomersal Park Hotel

★★★ 79% HOTEL   CLASSIC BRITISH HOTELS

☎ 01274 869386
Moor Ln BD19 4LJ
e-mail: enquiries@gomersalparkhotel.com
web: www.gomersalparkhotel.com
dir: A62 to Huddersfield. At junct with A65, by Greyhound Pub right, after 1m take 1st right after Oakwell Hall

Constructed around a 19th-century house, this stylish, modern hotel enjoys a peaceful location and pleasant grounds. Deep sofas ensure comfort in the open-plan lounge, and imaginative meals are served in the popular Brasserie 101. The well-equipped bedrooms provide high quality and comfort. Extensive public areas include a well-equipped leisure complex and pool, and a wide variety of air-conditioned conference rooms.

Rooms 100 (3 fmly) (32 GF) **Facilities** FTV Wi-fi ↺ supervised Gym **Conf** Class 130 Board 60 Thtr 250 **Services** Lift **Parking** 150 **Notes** Civ Wed 200

GOODRINGTON

See Paignton

GOODWOOD   Map 6 SU81
West Sussex

The Goodwood Hotel

★★★★ 81% ◉◉ HOTEL

☎ 01243 775537
PO18 0QB
e-mail: reservations@goodwood.com
web: www.goodwood.com
dir: Off A285, 3m NE of Chichester

Set at the centre of the 12,000-acre Goodwood Estate, this attractive hotel boasts extensive indoor and outdoor leisure facilities, along with a range of meeting rooms plus conference and banqueting facilities. Bedrooms are furnished to a consistently high standard, including a luxury suite located in the old coaching inn, and Executive rooms, each with a patio. Eating options include the Richmond Arms which sources produce extensively from the estate farm; The Richmond Arms Bar, and the Goodwood Bar and Grill. Overnight guests can also choose to dine in The Kennels, a private members' clubhouse.

Rooms 91 (17 fmly) (47 GF) 🅿 **Facilities** Spa STV FTV Wi-fi ⬚ ♨ 18 ⛳ Putt green Gym Golf driving range Sauna Steam room Fitness studio Xmas New Year **Conf** Class 60 Board 50 Thtr 150 Del from £160 to £220* **Parking** 150 **Notes** Civ Wed 120

GOOLE   Map 17 SE72
East Riding of Yorkshire

Lowther Hotel

★★★ 80% HOTEL

☎ 01405 767999
Aire St DN14 5QW
web: www.lowtherhotel.co.uk
dir: M62 junct 36, A614, follow town centre signs. At clock tower rdbt right into Aire St. Hotel at end on left

A beautifully restored Georgian Grade II* listed building that combines historic features with contemporary design. Set in a unique location, overlooking the port yet within easy reach of motorway links. The bedrooms are stylish, well equipped and have free Wi-fi. Public areas include Bar Absolut and The Burlington Restaurant, and the impressive Mural Rooms are perfect for weddings, conferences and meetings. Private parking is also available.

Rooms 14 (1 fmly) **Facilities** FTV Wi-fi 🎵 Xmas New Year **Conf** Class 90 Board 50 Thtr 90 **Parking** 30 **Notes** ⊗ Civ Wed 90

Premier Inn Goole

BUDGET HOTEL

☎ 0871 527 8468
Rawcliffe Rd, Airmyn DN14 8JS
web: www.premierinn.com
dir: M62 junct 36, A614 signed Rawcliffe. Hotel immediately on left

High quality, budget accommodation ideal for both families and business travellers. Spacious, en suite bedrooms feature tea and coffee making facilities, and Freeview TV in most hotels. Internet access and Wi-fi are available for a small fee. The adjacent family restaurant features a wide and varied menu. See also the Hotel Groups pages.

Rooms 41

GORDANO SERVICE AREA (M5)   Map 4 ST57
Somerset

Days Inn Bristol West - M5

BUDGET HOTEL

☎ 01275 373709 & 373624
BS20 7XG
e-mail: gordano.hotel@welcomebreak.co.uk
web: www.welcomebreak.co.uk
dir: M5 junct 19, follow signs for Gordano Services

This modern building offers accommodation in smart, spacious and well-equipped bedrooms, suitable for families and business travellers, and all with en suite bathrooms. Continental breakfast is available and other refreshments may be taken at the nearby family restaurant. See also the Hotel Groups pages.

Rooms 60 (52 fmly) (29 GF) (10 smoking)
Conf Board 10

GORING   Map 5 SU68
Oxfordshire

The Miller of Mansfield

◉◉ RESTAURANT WITH ROOMS

☎ 01491 872829
High St RG8 9AW
e-mail: reservations@millerofmansfield.com
web: www.millerofmansfield.com
dir: M40 junct 7, S on A329 towards Benson, A4074 towards Reading, B4009 towards Goring. Or M4 junct 12, S on A4 towards Newbury. 3rd rdbt onto A340 to Pangbourne. A329 to Streatley, right at lights onto B4009 into Goring

The frontage of this former coaching inn hides sumptuous rooms with a distinctive and individual style, an award-winning restaurant that serves appealing dishes using locally sourced ingredients, and a comfortable bar, which serves real ales, fine wines, afternoon tea and a bar menu for a quick bite to eat.

Rooms 13 (2 fmly)

GORLESTON ON SEA   Map 13 TG50
Norfolk

The Pier Hotel

★★★ 85% HOTEL

☎ 01493 662631
Harbourmouth, South Pier NR31 6PL
e-mail: bookings@pierhotelgorleston.co.uk
dir: From A47 W of Great Yarmouth take A12 signed
Lowestoft. At 3rd rdbt 1st left (Beccles Rd) signed
Gorleston. At rdbt 2nd left (Church Rd). Next rdbt 1st
left (Baker St). Right into Pier Plain, then Pier Walk to
Pier Gdns

Ideally situated on the seafront this hotel offers
smartly appointed bedrooms that are thoughtfully
equipped and have a good range of useful extras;
some rooms have superb sea views. The public areas
include a large restaurant and a conservatory, which
leads to a terrace and bar.

Rooms 21 (1 fmly) ⚑ **Facilities** STV FTV Wi-fi 🐾 ♫
New Year **Parking** 14 **Notes** ⊗

GOSFORTH   Map 18 NY00
Cumbria

Westlakes Hotel

★★★ 81% HOTEL

☎ 019467 25221
CA20 1HP
e-mail: info@westlakeshotel.co.uk
web: www.westlakeshotel.co.uk
dir: From A595 take B5344 signed Seascale. Hotel
entrance 1st right

Located amid the stunning scenery of the western
lakes and within easy striking distance of a whole
array of visitor attractions, the hotel offers
accommodation of a high standard, with many
thoughtful extras provided. High quality food is
served in the restaurant with relaxed and friendly
service led by the hands-on owners and their team.
There are excellent walking opportunities from this
hotel.

Rooms 10 (4 annexe) (1 GF) ⚑ **S** £65-£88;
D £80-£109.75 (incl. bkfst)* **Facilities** FTV Wi-fi
Conf Class 30 Board 30 Thtr 50 Del from £125 to
£140* **Parking** 15 **Notes** ⊗

GRANGE-OVER-SANDS   Map 18 SD47
Cumbria

Netherwood Hotel

★★★ 80% HOTEL

☎ 015395 32552
Lindale Rd LA11 6ET
e-mail: enquiries@netherwood-hotel.co.uk
web: www.netherwood-hotel.co.uk
dir: On B5277 before station

This imposing hotel stands in terraced grounds and
enjoys fine views of Morecambe Bay, also popular as
a conference and wedding venue. Good levels of
hospitality and service ensure all guests are well
looked after. Bedrooms vary in size but all are well
furnished and have smart modern bathrooms.
Magnificent woodwork is a feature of the public
areas.

Rooms 34 (5 fmly) ⚑ **S** £70-£100; **D** £160-£180
(incl. bkfst) **Facilities** Spa FTV Wi-fi ⊙ supervised 🏊
Gym Beauty salon Steam room Sunbed Fitness centre
New Year **Conf** Class 150 Board 60 Thtr 150
Del from £120 to £160 **Services** Lift **Parking** 100
Notes LB Civ Wed 200

Cumbria Grand Hotel

★★★ 70% HOTEL

☎ 015395 32331
LA11 6EN
e-mail: salescumbria@strathmorehotels.com
dir: M6 junct 36, A590 & follow Grange-over-Sands
signs

Set within extensive grounds, this large hotel offers
fine views over Morecambe Bay and caters well for a

mixed market. Public areas are pure nostalgia, and
include a grand dining room and fine ballroom.
Bedrooms are comfortably equipped and some have
views of the bay.

Rooms 122 (10 fmly) (25 GF) ⚑ **S** £35-£109;
D £55-£168 (incl. bkfst)* **Facilities** STV Wi-fi 🏌 Putt
green Snooker & pool table Table tennis ♫ Xmas New
Year **Services** Lift **Parking** 75 **Notes** LB

See advert on page 501

See advert on page 501

INSPECTORS' CHOICE

Clare House

★★ ◉ HOTEL

☎ 015395 33026 & 34253
Park Rd LA11 7HQ
e-mail: info@clarehousehotel.co.uk
web: www.clarehousehotel.co.uk
dir: A590 onto B5277, through Lindale into Grange,
keep left, hotel 0.5m on left past Crown Hill & St
Paul's Church

A warm, genuine welcome awaits guests at this
delightful hotel, proudly run by the Read family for
over 40 years. Situated in its own secluded
gardens, it provides a relaxed haven in which to
enjoy the panoramic views across Morecambe Bay.
The stylish bedrooms and public areas are
comfortable and attractively furnished. Skilfully
prepared dinners and hearty breakfasts are served
in the elegant dining room.

Rooms 18 (4 GF) ⚑ **S** £74-£93; **D** £148-£186 (incl.
bkfst & dinner)* **Facilities** FTV Wi-fi 🏊 **Parking** 18
Notes ⊗ Closed mid Dec-late Mar

G

GRANTHAM
Lincolnshire

Map 11 SK93

Ramada Grantham
★★★★ 72% HOTEL

☎ 01476 593000
Swingbridge Rd NG31 7XT
e-mail: info@ramadagrantham.co.uk
web: www.ramadagrantham.co.uk
dir: Exit A1 at Grantham/Melton Mowbray junct onto A607. From N: 1st exit at mini rdbt, hotel on right. From S: at rdbt 2nd exit. Next left at T-junct. At mini rdbt 2nd exit. Hotel on right

A modern, purpose-built hotel ideally placed for touring the area. Bedrooms are spacious, smartly decorated and equipped with modern facilities. Public rooms include a large open-plan lounge/bar area with comfortable seating and an intimate restaurant as well as conference and banqueting facilities. The property also has smart leisure facilities.

Rooms 89 (44 GF) (2 smoking) **S** £39–£106; **D** £45–£125* **Facilities** FTV Wi-fi ⓧ Gym Steam room Sauna Xmas New Year **Conf** Class 90 Board 60 Thtr 200 Del from £110 to £125* **Parking** 102 **Notes** LB ⊗ Civ Wed 200

Premier Inn Grantham
BUDGET HOTEL

☎ 0871 527 8470
A1/607 Junction, Harlaxton Rd NG31 7UA
web: www.premierinn.com
dir: A1 onto A607. N'bound: hotel on right. S'bound: under A1, hotel on left

High quality, budget accommodation ideal for both families and business travellers. Spacious, en suite bedrooms feature tea and coffee making facilities, and Freeview TV in most hotels. Internet access and Wi-fi are available for a small fee. The adjacent family restaurant features a wide and varied menu. See also the Hotel Groups pages.

Rooms 59

GRASMERE
Cumbria

Map 18 NY30

Rothay Garden Hotel
★★★★ 84% ◉◉ HOTEL

☎ 015394 35334
Broadgate LA22 9RJ
e-mail: stay@rothaygarden.com
web: www.rothaygarden.com
dir: A591, opposite Swan Hotel, into Grasmere, 300yds on left

On the edge of the village, and sitting in two acres of riverside gardens, Rothay Garden offers an impressive combination of stylish design and luxurious comfort. Bedrooms include five Loft Suites, each named after one of the fells they overlook. Sun lounges and balconies on the upper floor rooms, are a real feature. The garden spa is the perfect way to relax with steam, sauna, heated relaxing beds and a hydrotherapy pool. There is a chic lounge bar and an elegant dining room, and the friendly staff provide attentive service.

Rooms 30 (3 fmly) (8 GF) ❧ **S** £107–£162; **D** £214–£364 (incl. bkfst & dinner) **Facilities** FTV Wi-fi ⓧ HL Hydro spa pool Sauna Aromatherapy room Infra red loungers Reflexology Xmas New Year **Parking** 38 **Notes** LB No children 5yrs

Daffodil Hotel
★★★★ 82% HOTEL

☎ 015394 63550
Keswick Rd LA22 9PR
e-mail: stay@daffodilhotel.com
web: www.daffodilhotel.com
dir: M6 junct 36 then A591, past Windermere & Ambleside. Hotel on left on entering Grasmere

Daffodil Hotel provides very high levels of service, comfort and luxury in a beautiful location on the edge of Grasmere, within easy walking distance of the village. Most rooms have either a lake or a valley view, several with private balconies, and are equipped to very high standards.

Rooms 78 (11 fmly) ❧ **S** £120–£210; **D** £130–£220 (incl. bkfst)* **Facilities** Spa FTV Wi-fi ⓧ HL Sauna Steam room Tepidarium Xmas New Year **Conf** Class 160 Board 42 Thtr 200 Del from £130 to £250* **Services** Lift Air con **Parking** 96 **Notes** LB Civ Wed 200

Wordsworth Hotel & Spa
★★★★ 81% ◉◉ HOTEL

☎ 015394 35592
Stock Ln LA22 9SW
e-mail: enquiry@thewordsworthhotel.co.uk
web: www.thewordsworthhotel.co.uk
dir: Off A591. In centre of village adjacent to St Oswald's Church

This historic hotel, ideally situated in the heart of Grasmere provides high levels of style and luxury. The bedrooms are equipped with smart furnishings, comfortable beds with Egyptian cotton linens, and quality accessories. Guests can enjoy fine dining in the modernised Signature Restaurant which boasts stylish and elegant decor, and for a less formal dining experience, light meals and fine ales are offered in the Dove Bistro. The hotel has a heated swimming pool, and the sauna and spa make the ideal place for relaxation.

Rooms 40 (2 fmly) (3 GF) ❧ **S** £80–£100; **D** £110–£160 (incl. bkfst) **Facilities** Spa FTV Wi-fi ⓧ ⓧ ⓧ Gym Beauty treatment room Mixed sauna Nail bar Xmas New Year **Conf** Class 50 Board 40 Thtr 100 Del from £180 to £240 **Services** Lift **Parking** 60 **Notes** LB Civ Wed 100

Oak Bank Hotel
★★★ 81% ◉◉ HOTEL

☎ 015394 35217
Broadgate LA22 9TA
e-mail: info@lakedistricthotel.co.uk
web: www.lakedistricthotel.co.uk
dir: N'bound: M6 junct 36 onto A591 to Windermere, Ambleside, then Grasmere. S'bound: M6 junct 40 onto A66 to Keswick, A591 to Grasmere

Privately owned and personally run by friendly proprietors, Oak Bank is a Victorian house in the charming village of Grasmere. Bedrooms are well-equipped and include one with a four-poster bed, as well as a suite with jacuzzi bath. In colder weather, welcoming log fires burn in the comfortable lounges. The restaurant has a conservatory extension overlooking the garden, and there is also a pleasant bar.

Rooms 14 (1 GF) ❧ **S** £82.75–£140; **D** £105.50–£416 (incl. bkfst & dinner) **Facilities** FTV Wi-fi Use of nearby leisure facilities New Year **Parking** 14 **Notes** LB Closed 2-6 Jan, 3-15 Aug, 21-26 Dec

Save on hotels. Book at **theAA.com/hotel**

GRA 187 ENGLAND

BEST WESTERN Grasmere Red Lion Hotel

★★★ 80% HOTEL

☎ 015394 35456
Red Lion Square LA22 9SS
e-mail: reservations@grasmereredlionhotel.co.uk
dir: From A591, signed Grasmere Village. Hotel in village centre

This modernised and extended 18th-century coaching inn, located in the heart of the village, offers spacious well-equipped rooms and a number of meeting and conference facilities. A range of pub meals complement the more formal Courtyard Restaurant. The comfortable lounge area is ideal for relaxing, and for the more energetic guest there is a pool and gym.

Rooms 49 (10 fmly) ⚡ **Facilities** STV Wi-fi ⊛ Gym Sauna Steam room Spa bath Xmas New Year **Conf** Class 24 Board 28 Thtr 60 **Services** Lift **Parking** 35

Gold Rill Country House Hotel

★★★ 79% HOTEL

☎ 015394 35486
Red Bank Rd LA22 9PU
e-mail: reception@goldrill.co.uk
web: www.goldrill.co.uk
dir: A591 into village centre, turn into road opposite St Oswald's Church. Hotel 300yds on left

This popular hotel enjoys a fine location on the edge of the village with spectacular views of the lake and surrounding fells. Attractive bedrooms - some with balconies - are tastefully decorated and many have separate, comfortable seating areas. The hotel boasts a private pier, an outdoor heated pool and a putting green. Public areas include a well-appointed restaurant and choice of lounges.

Rooms 32 (7 annexe) (2 fmly) (11 GF) ⚡ **S** £56-£93; **D** £112-£202 (incl. bkfst & dinner)* **Facilities** FTV Wi-fi ↗ Putt green New Year **Parking** 35 **Notes** LB ⊗ Closed mid Dec-mid Jan (ex New Year)

Macdonald Swan Hotel

★★★ 77% ⊛ HOTEL

☎ 0844 879 9120
LA22 9RF
e-mail:
sales/oldengland@macdonald-hotels.co.uk
web: www.macdonaldhotels.co.uk
dir: M6 junct 36, A591 towards Kendal, A590 to Keswick through Ambleside. Hotel on right on entering village

Close to Dove Cottage and occupying a prominent position on the edge of the village, this 300-year-old inn is mentioned in Wordsworth's poem, *The Waggoner*. Attractive public areas are spacious and comfortable, and bedrooms are equally stylish, some have CD players. A good range of bar meals is available, while the elegant restaurant offers more formal dining. Macdonald Hotels is the AA Hotel Group of the Year 2013-14.

Rooms 37 (2 fmly) (21 GF) ⚡ **Facilities** FTV Wi-fi HL Xmas New Year **Conf** Class 20 Board 30 Thtr 40 **Parking** 45 **Notes** Civ Wed 60

GRASSINGTON   Map 19 SE06
North Yorkshire

Grassington House

⊛ ⊛ RESTAURANT WITH ROOMS

☎ 01756 752406
5 The Square BD23 5AQ
e-mail: bookings@grassingtonhousehotel.co.uk
web: www.grassingtonhousehotel.co.uk
dir: A59 into Grassington, in town square opposite post office

Located in the square of the popular village of Grassington this beautifully converted Georgian house is personally run by owners John and Sue. Delicious food, individually designed bedrooms and warm hospitality ensure an enjoyable stay. There is a stylish lounge bar looking out to the square and the restaurant is split between two rooms; here guests will find the emphasis is on fresh, local ingredients and attentive, yet friendly service.

Rooms 9 (2 fmly)

GRAVESEND   Map 6 TQ67
Kent

Premier Inn Gravesend (A2/Singlewell)

BUDGET HOTEL

☎ 0871 527 8472
Hevercourt Rd, Singlewell DA12 5UQ
web: www.premierinn.com
dir: At Gravesend East exit on A2

High quality, budget accommodation ideal for both families and business travellers. Spacious, en suite bedrooms feature tea and coffee making facilities, and Freeview TV in most hotels. Internet access and Wi-fi are available for a small fee. The adjacent family restaurant features a wide and varied menu. See also the Hotel Groups pages.

Rooms 31

G

Premier Inn Gravesend Central

BUDGET HOTEL

☎ 0871 527 8474
Wrotham Rd DA11 7LF
web: www.premierinn.com
dir: A2 onto A227 towards town centre, 1m to hotel

Rooms 36

GRAYS
Essex
Map 6 TQ67

Park Inn by Radisson Thurrock

★★★ 72% HOTEL

☎ 01708 719988
High Rd, North Stifford RM16 5UE
e-mail: info.thurrock@rezidorparkinn.com
dir: M25 junct 30/31, follow A13 towards Brentwood/
Southend, A1012 (Grays), hotel is 1st exit on rdbt

This hotel is conveniently located just 20 minutes
from London, and is within close proximity of the
Lakeside Shopping Centre and Dartford. It is a
Georgian manor house set in landscaped gardens
that offers comfortable bedrooms with satellite TV
and Wi-fi. There is a range of modern meeting rooms,
a sport-themed bar and a large Regency restaurant
which is open for lunch and dinner daily; hot dishes
and a continental buffet are on offer at breakfast. The
hotel is a popular wedding venue.

Rooms 97 (18 fmly) (48 GF) (2 smoking) 🐾
Facilities STV FTV Wi-fi ⚘ Xmas New Year
Conf Class 134 Board 185 Thtr 445 **Services** Air con
Parking 60 **Notes** ⊗ Civ Wed 150

GREAT BIRCHAM
Norfolk
Map 13 TF73

The Kings Head Hotel

★★★ 86% ◉ HOTEL

☎ 01485 578265 & 572846
PE31 6RJ
e-mail: info@thekingsheadhotel.co.uk
web: www.thekingsheadhotel.co.uk

A delightful family-run hotel situated in the heart of
this north Norfolk village close to Royal Sandringham.
The property is very contemporary, yet still retains
much of its original character. The spacious
bedrooms are tastefully appointed and equipped with
modern facilities. Public rooms inlude a lounge, bar,
restaurant and further dining room.

Rooms 12 **Facilities** FTV Wi-fi ⚘ Xmas **Conf** Class 30
Board 20 Thtr 40 **Parking** 30 **Notes** Civ Wed 80

GREAT CHESTERFORD
Essex
Map 12 TL54

The Crown House

★★★ 72% HOTEL

☎ 01799 530515 & 530257
CB10 1NY
e-mail: reservations@crownhousehotel.com
web: www.crownhousehotel.com
dir: From N: M11 at junct 9 (from S junct 10) follow
signs for Saffron Walden, then Great Chesterford
(B1383)

This Georgian coaching inn, situated in a peaceful
village close to the M11, has been sympathetically
restored and retains much original character. The
bedrooms are well equipped and individually
decorated; some rooms have delightful four-poster
beds. Public rooms include an attractive lounge bar,
an elegant oak-panelled restaurant and an airy
conservatory.

Rooms 18 (10 annexe) (1 fmly) (5 GF) **Facilities** FTV
Wi-fi ⚘ New Year **Conf** Class 14 Board 12 Thtr 30
Parking 30 **Notes** Closed 27-30 Dec Civ Wed 60

GREAT MILTON
Oxfordshire
Map 5 SP60

INSPECTORS' CHOICE

Le Manoir Aux Quat' Saisons

★★★★★ ◉◉◉◉◉ HOTEL

☎ 01844 278881
Church Rd OX44 7PD
e-mail: lemanoir@blanc.co.uk
web: www.manoir.com
dir: From A329 2nd right to Great Milton Manor,
hotel 200yds on right

Even though Le Manoir is now very much part of the
British scene, its iconic chef patron, Raymond
Blanc, still fizzes with new ideas and projects. His
first loves are his kitchen and his garden and the
vital link between them. The fascinating grounds
feature a Japanese tea garden and two acres of
vegetables and herbs that supply the kitchen with
an almost never-ending supply of top-notch
produce. Even the car park has a stunning
artichoke sculpture. The kitchen is the epicentre,
with outstanding cooking highlighting freshness
and seasonality. Bedrooms in this idyllic 'grand
house on a small scale' are either in the main
house or around an outside courtyard; all offer the
highest levels of comfort and quality, have
magnificent marble bathrooms and are equipped
with a host of thoughtful extra touches. For
something really special there is the 15th-century
dovecot with a stunning upper-floor bedroom and a
bathroom below. La Belle Epoque is the private
dining room, ideal for weddings, celebrations and
corporate events.

Rooms 32 (23 annexe) (13 GF) **Facilities** STV FTV
Wi-fi ⚘ Cookery school Water gardens Bikes Spa
treatment Xmas New Year **Conf** Board 20 Thtr 24
Parking 60 **Notes** ⊗ Civ Wed 50

Save on hotels. Book at **theAA.com/hotel**

GRA – GRE 189 ENGLAND

GREAT TOTHAM
Essex · Map 7 TL81

The Bull at Great Totham

◎◎ RESTAURANT WITH ROOMS

☎ 01621 893385 & 894020
2 Maldon Rd CM9 8NH
e-mail: reservations@thebullatgreattotham.co.uk
dir: Exit A12 at Witham junct to Great Totham

A 16th-century coaching inn located in the village of Great Totham, The Bull is now a very stylish restaurant with rooms that offers en suite bedrooms with satellite TVs with Freeview; Wi-fi is available throughout. Guests can enjoy dinner in the gastro-pub or in the award-winning, fine dining restaurant, The Willow Room.

Rooms 4

GREAT YARMOUTH
Norfolk · Map 13 TG50

Imperial Hotel

THE INDEPENDENTS
HOTEL ASSOCIATION

★★★★ 75% ◎ HOTEL

☎ 01493 842000
North Dr NR30 1EQ
e-mail: reservations@imperialhotel.co.uk
web: www.imperialhotel.co.uk
dir: Follow signs to seafront, turn left. Hotel opposite Waterways

This friendly, family-run hotel is situated at the quieter end of the seafront within easy walking distance of the town centre. Bedrooms are attractively decorated with co-ordinated soft furnishings and many thoughtful touches; most rooms have superb sea views. Public areas include the smart Savoie Lounge Bar and the Rambouillet Restaurant.

Rooms 39 (4 fmly) ✎ **S** £85-£140; **D** £95-£160 (incl. bkfst) **Facilities** FTV Wi-fi ⇲ New Year **Conf** Class 40 Board 30 Thtr 140 Del from £120 to £200 **Services** Lift **Parking** 50 **Notes** LB Civ Wed 140

Furzedown Hotel

★★★ 79% HOTEL

☎ 01493 844138
19-20 North Dr NR30 4EW
e-mail: paul@furzedownhotel.co.uk
web: www.furzedownhotel.co.uk
dir: At end of A47 or A12, towards seafront, left, hotel opposite Waterways

Expect a warm welcome at this family-run hotel situated at the northern end of the seafront overlooking the town's Venetian Waterways. Bedrooms are pleasantly decorated and thoughtfully equipped; many rooms have superb sea views. The stylish public areas include a comfortable lounge bar, a smartly appointed restaurant and a cosy TV room.

Rooms 20 (11 fmly) **Facilities** FTV Wi-fi New Year **Conf** Class 80 Board 40 Thtr 75 **Parking** 30

Comfort Hotel Great Yarmouth

★★★ 75% HOTEL

☎ 01493 855070 & 850044

Albert Square NR30 3JH
e-mail: sales@comfortgreatyarmouth.co.uk
web: www.comfortgreatyarmouth.co.uk
dir: From seafront left at Wellington Pier into Kimberley Terr. Left into Albert Sq, hotel on left

A large hotel situated in the quieter end of town, just off the seafront and within easy walking distance of the town centre. The pleasantly decorated, well-equipped bedrooms are generally quite spacious and include Wi-fi. Public rooms include a comfortable lounge, a bar and smart brasserie-style restaurant.

Rooms 50 (6 fmly) (3 GF) **S** £39-£59; **D** £59-£99 (incl. bkfst)* **Facilities** FTV Wi-fi ⇲ Xmas **Conf** Class 50 Board 30 Thtr 120 Del £82.50 **Parking** 15 **Notes** ⊗ Civ Wed 120

The Prom Hotel

★★★ 75% HOTEL

☎ 01493 842308
77 Marine Pde NR30 2DH
e-mail: info@promhotel.co.uk

Ideally situated on the seafront close to the bright lights and attractions of Marine Parade. The open-plan public areas include a smart lounge bar with views of the sea, and a relaxed restaurant; guests also have the use of a further quieter lounge bar with plush seating. The modern contemporary bedrooms are smartly appointed and have many thoughtful touches; many rooms have lovely sea views.

Rooms 25 (1 fmly) ✎ **S** £75-£90; **D** £90-£115 (incl. bkfst)* **Facilities** STV FTV Wi-fi ⇲ Xmas

Knights Court Hotel

★★★ 72% HOTEL

☎ 01493 843089 & 07748 501009
22 North Dr NR30 4EW
e-mail: enquiries@knights-court.co.uk
dir: From A12 & A47 rdbt, A149 to seafront

Knights Court is a small privately-owned hotel situated on the seafront overlooking the beach. The smartly appointed bedrooms are comfortable and well equipped; many of the rooms have lovely sea views. Breakfast and dinner are served in the stylish dining room and there is a cosy lounge bar with views of the beach.

Rooms 20 (5 fmly) ✎ **S** fr £49; **D** fr £70 (incl. bkfst)* **Facilities** STV FTV Wi-fi ⇲ **Conf** Class 40 Board 20 Thtr 40 **Parking** 22 **Notes** LB ⊗

G

GREAT YARMOUTH *continued*

Burlington Palm Hotel

★★★ 71% HOTEL

☎ 01493 844568
11 North Dr NR30 1EG
e-mail: enquiries@burlington-hotel.co.uk
web: www.burlington-hotel.co.uk
dir: A12 to seafront, left at Marine Lodge. Hotel near tennis courts

This privately owned hotel is situated at the quiet end of the resort, overlooking the sea. Bedrooms come in a variety of sizes and styles; they are pleasantly decorated and well equipped, and many have lovely sea views. The spacious public rooms include a range of seating areas, a choice of dining rooms, two bars and a heated indoor swimming pool.

Rooms 69 (9 fmly) (1 GF) ✷ **Facilities** FTV Wi-fi ⊛ Xmas **Conf** Class 60 Board 30 Thtr 120 Del from £75 to £90 **Services** Lift **Parking** 70 **Notes** ⊗ Closed 28 Dec-2 Jan

See advert on opposite page

The Waverley Hotel

★★★ 70% HOTEL

☎ 01493 853388
32-34 Princes Rd NR30 2DG
e-mail: thewaverleyhotel.gy@gmail.com

The Waverley is situated in a side road adjacent to the seafront and close to the local amenities. The property has been totally refurbished by the current owner to a very good standard. Public rooms include a large lounge bar, foyer and spacious restaurant. Bedrooms are contemporary in style and have a good range of extra facilities.

Rooms 47 (2 fmly) ✷ **S** £35-£50; **D** £55-£80 (incl. bkfst)* **Facilities** FTV Wi-fi Xmas New Year **Conf** Class 60 Board 60 Thtr 60 Del from £90 to £250* **Services** Lift **Notes** LB ⊗

The Nelson Hotel

★★★ 66% HOTEL

☎ 01493 855551
1 Marine Pde NR30 3AG
e-mail: johnrushworth@theukholidaygroup.com
dir: On right of Marine Parade, opposite Sealife Centre

The Nelson Hotel is ideally situated overlooking the sea, close to the pier and just a short stroll from the town centre and local amenities. It is ideal for both business and leisure guests, and all of the bedrooms are well equipped, while some rooms have lovely sea views. Public areas include a lounge with plush sofas, a bar and a separate dining room.

Rooms 50 (10 fmly) ✷ **S** £45-£60; **D** £70-£90 (incl. bkfst)* **Facilities** FTV Wi-fi ♫ Xmas New Year **Conf** Class 60 Board 60 Thtr 100 Del £65* **Services** Lift **Notes** LB ⊗ Closed 2 Jan-end Feb

New Beach Hotel

★★ 69% HOTEL *Leisureplex*

☎ 01493 332300
67 Marine Pde NR30 2EJ
e-mail: newbeach.gtyarmouth@alfatravel.co.uk
web: www.leisureplex.co.uk
dir: Follow signs to seafront. Hotel facing Britannia Pier

This Victorian building is centrally located on the seafront, overlooking Britannia Pier and the sandy beach. Bedrooms are pleasantly decorated and equipped with modern facilities; many have lovely sea views. Dinner is taken in the restaurant which doubles as the ballroom, and guests can also relax in the bar or sunny lounge.

Rooms 77 (4 fmly) **S** £35-£45; **D** £56-£88 (incl. bkfst)* **Facilities** Wi-fi ♫ Xmas New Year **Services** Lift **Notes** LB ⊗ Closed Dec-Feb (ex Xmas) RS Nov & Mar

Andover House

⊚⊚ RESTAURANT WITH ROOMS

☎ 01493 843490
28-30 Camperdown NR30 3JB
e-mail: info@andoverhouse.co.uk
web: www.andoverhouse.co.uk
dir: Opposite Wellington Pier turn into Shadingfield Close, right into Kimberley Terrace, follow into Camperdown. Property on left

A lovely three-storey Victorian town house which features a series of contemporary spaces that include a large open-plan lounge bar, a brasserie-style restaurant serving modern British cuisine, a cosy lounge and a smart sun terrace. Bedrooms are tastefully appointed with co-ordinated soft furnishings and have many thoughtful touches.

Rooms 20

GREAT YELDHAM Map 13 TL73
Essex

The White Hart

⊚⊚ RESTAURANT WITH ROOMS

☎ 01787 237250
Poole St CO9 4HJ
e-mail: mjwmason@yahoo.co.uk
dir: On A1017 in village

A large timber-framed character building houses the main restaurant and bar areas while the bedrooms are located in the converted coach house; all are smartly appointed and well equipped with many thoughtful extras. A comfortable lounge-bar area and beautifully landscaped gardens provide areas for relaxation. Locally sourced produce is used in the main house restaurant, popular with local residents and guests alike.

Rooms 11 (2 fmly)

Save on hotels. Book at **theAA.com/hotel**

GRE – GRI 191 ENGLAND

GREENFORD
Greater London

Premier Inn London Greenford

BUDGET HOTEL PLAN 1 C4

☎ 0871 527 8658
Western Av UB6 8TE
web: www.premierinn.com
dir: From A40 (Western Avenue) E'bound, exit at Perivale. Right, left at 2nd lights. Hotel opposite Hoover Building

High quality, budget accommodation ideal for both families and business travellers. Spacious, en suite bedrooms feature tea and coffee making facilities, and Freeview TV in most hotels. Internet access and Wi-fi are available for a small fee. The adjacent family restaurant features a wide and varied menu. See also the Hotel Groups pages.

Rooms 39

GREETHAM
Rutland   Map 11 SK91

Greetham Valley

★★★ 75% HOTEL

☎ 01780 460444
Wood Ln LE15 7SN
e-mail: info@greethamvalley.co.uk
web: www.greethamvalley.co.uk
dir: A1/B668. Left towards Greetham, Cottesmore & Oakham. Left at x-rds after 0.5m, follow brown signs to golf club entrance

Spacious bedrooms with storage facilities designed for golfers, offer high levels of comfort and many

have superb views over the two golf courses. Meals are taken in the clubhouse restaurants with a choice of informal or more formal styles. A beauty suite and extensive conference facilities are ideal for both large and small groups.

Rooms 35 (17 GF) ⚓ **S** £67-£95; **D** £67-£95 (incl. bkfst)* **Facilities** FTV Wi-fi ⚡ 45 Putt green Fishing Gym 4x4 off-road course Archery centre Bowls green Driving range Petanque New Year **Conf** Class 150 Board 80 Thtr 280 Del £117 **Services** Lift **Parking** 300 **Notes** LB ⊗ Civ Wed 200

GRIMSBY
Lincolnshire   Map 17 TA21

Millfields Hotel

★★★ Ⓐ HOTEL

☎ 01472 356068
53 Bargate DN34 5AD
e-mail: info@millfieldshotel.co.uk
web: www.millfieldshotel.co.uk
dir: A180, right at KFC rdbt then left at next rdbt. Right at 2nd lights & right onto Bargate, hotel 0.5m on left after Wheatsheaf pub

Dating from 1879 this hotel is surrounded by its own grounds and caters for both leisure and business guests. The bedrooms are individually designed and there is a four-poster room. The contemporary Orangery Restaurant offers both carte and traditional bar menus. The hotel has extensive leisure facilities.

Rooms 27 (4 annexe) (7 fmly) (13 GF) ⚓ **S** £75-£95; **D** £85-£175 (incl. bkfst)* **Facilities** FTV Wi-fi Gym Squash Sauna Steam room Hairdresser Beauty salon Aromatherapist **Conf** Class 25 Board 25 Thtr 50 Del £125* **Parking** 75 **Notes** LB Civ Wed 50

Premier Inn Grimsby

BUDGET HOTEL

☎ 0871 527 8478
Europa Park, Appian Way, off Gilbey Rd DN31 2UT
web: www.premierinn.com
dir: M180 junct 5, A180 towards town centre. At 1st rdbt take 2nd exit. 1st left, left at mini rdbt into Appian Way

High quality, budget accommodation ideal for both families and business travellers. Spacious, en suite bedrooms feature tea and coffee making facilities, and Freeview TV in most hotels. Internet access and Wi-fi are available for a small fee. The adjacent family restaurant features a wide and varied menu. See also the Hotel Groups pages.

Rooms 40

G

G

GRIMSTON — Map 12 TF72
Norfolk

INSPECTORS' CHOICE

Congham Hall Country House Hotel

★★★ ◉◉ COUNTRY HOUSE HOTEL

☎ 01485 600250
Lynn Rd PE32 1AH
e-mail: info@conghamhallhotel.co.uk
dir: At A149/A148 junct, NE of King's Lynn, take
A148 towards Fakenham for 100yds. Right to
Grimston, hotel 2.5m on left

An elegant 18th-century Georgian manor set amid
30 acres of mature landscaped grounds and
surrounded by parkland. The inviting public rooms
provide a range of tastefully furnished areas in
which to sit and relax. Imaginative cuisine is served
in the Orangery Restaurant which has an intimate
atmosphere and panoramic views of the gardens.
The bedrooms, tastefully furnished with period
pieces, have modern facilities and many thoughtful
touches.

Rooms 26 (6 annexe) (12 GF) 🐾 **D** fr £135 (incl.
bkfst)* **Facilities** Wi-fi 🕸 🏌 Putt green 🦌 Xmas
New Year **Conf** Class 12 Board 28 Thtr 50
Parking 50 **Notes** Civ Wed 100

GRINDLEFORD — Map 16 SK27
Derbyshire

The Maynard

★★★ 81% ◉◉ HOTEL

☎ 01433 630321
Main Rd S32 2HE
e-mail: info@themaynard.co.uk
dir: A625 from Sheffield to Castleton. Left into
Grindleford on B6521. Hotel on left after Fox House
Hotel

This building, dating back over 100 years, is situated
in a beautiful and tranquil location yet within easy
reach of Sheffield and the M1. The bedrooms are
contemporary in style and offer a wealth of
accessories. The Peak District views from the
restaurant and garden are stunning.

Rooms 10 (1 fmly) **Facilities** FTV Wi-fi 🕸
Conf Class 60 Board 40 Thtr 120 **Parking** 60
Notes Civ Wed 140

GUILDFORD — Map 6 SU94
Surrey

Holiday Inn Guildford

★★★★ 73% HOTEL

☎ 0871 942 9036
Egerton Rd GU2 7XZ
e-mail: reservations-guildford@ihg.com
web: www.higuildfordhotel.co.uk
dir: A3 to Guildford. Exit at sign for Research Park/
Onslow Village. 3rd exit at 1st rdbt, 2nd exit at 2nd
rdbt

This hotel is in a convenient location just off the A3
and within a 25 minute-drive of the M25. Public
areas are stylish, and on-site facilities include a
swimming pool and gym. The accommodation is
spacious and comfortable and caters well for both the
business and leisure markets. A number of well-
equipped meeting rooms is available. There is ample
free parking.

Rooms 168 (89 fmly) (66 GF) 🐾 **Facilities** Spa STV
FTV Wi-fi 🕸 HL 🌀 Gym Fitness studio Beauty
treatments **Conf** Class 100 Board 60 Thtr 180
Services Air con **Parking** 230 **Notes** ⊗ Civ Wed 180

Premier Inn Guildford Central

BUDGET HOTEL

☎ 0871 527 8482
Parkway GU1 1UP
web: www.premierinn.com
dir: M25 junct 10, follow Portsmouth (A3) signs. Exit
for Guildford Centre/Leisure Complex (A322/A320/
A25). Turn left, hotel on left

High quality, budget accommodation ideal for both
families and business travellers. Spacious, en suite
bedrooms feature tea and coffee making facilities,
and Freeview TV in most hotels. Internet access and
Wi-fi are available for a small fee. The adjacent
family restaurant features a wide and varied menu.
See also the Hotel Groups pages.

Rooms 87

Premier Inn Guildford (Worplesdon)

BUDGET HOTEL

☎ 0871 527 8480
Perry Hill GU3 3RY
web: www.premierinn.com
dir: A3 onto A322 towards Bagshot. In Worplesdon,
hotel on right. Or from M3 junct 3, A322 S towards
Guildford. In Worplesdon hotel on left

Rooms 19

GUISBOROUGH — Map 19 NZ61
North Yorkshire

Gisborough Hall

★★★★ 79% ◉◉ HOTEL

☎ 0844 879 9149 & 01287 593999
Whitby Ln TS14 6PT
e-mail: general.gisboroughhall@macdonald-hotels.
co.uk
web: www.gisborough-hall.co.uk
dir: A171, follow signs for Whitby to Waterfall rdbt,
3rd exit into Whitby Ln, hotel 500yds on right

Dating back to the mid-19th century, this elegant
country house provides a pleasing combination of
original features and modern facilities. Bedrooms,
including four-poster and family rooms, are richly
furnished. The elegant Drawing Room is welcoming
and has an open fire, whilst the opulent G Bar &
Bistro provides a contemporary alternative. Excellent
food is served in Chaloner's Restaurant. Macdonald
Hotels is the AA Hotel Group of the Year 2013-14.

Rooms 71 (2 fmly) (12 GF) **S** £89-£167; **D** £99-£177
(incl. bkfst)* **Facilities** Spa STV FTV Wi-fi 🕸 HL 🌀 🦌
Sauna Xmas New Year **Conf** Class 150 Board 32
Thtr 400 Del from £135 to £165* **Services** Lift
Parking 180 **Notes** LB Civ Wed 250

Premier Inn Middlesborough South (Guisborough)

BUDGET HOTEL

☎ 0871 527 8772
Middlesbrough Rd, Upsall TS14 6RW
web: www.premierinn.com
dir: Off A171 towards Whitby

High quality, budget accommodation ideal for both families and business travellers. Spacious, en suite bedrooms feature tea and coffee making facilities, and Freeview TV in most hotels. Internet access and Wi-fi are available for a small fee. The adjacent family restaurant features a wide and varied menu. See also the Hotel Groups pages.

Rooms 20

HADLEY WOOD   Map 6 TQ29
Greater London

West Lodge Park Hotel

★★★★ 81% ⊛ HOTEL

☎ 020 8216 3900 ＆ 8216 3903
Cockfosters Rd EN4 0PY
e-mail: westlodgepark@bealeshotels.co.uk
web: www.bealeshotels.co.uk
dir: On A111, 1m S of M25 junct 24

A stylish country house set in stunning parkland and gardens, yet only 12 miles from central London and a few miles from the M25. Bedrooms are individually decorated in traditional style and offer excellent facilities. Annexe rooms feature air-conditioning and have access to an outdoor patio area. Public rooms include the award-winning Cedar Restaurant, cosy bar area and separate lounge.

Rooms 59 (13 annexe) (1 fmly) (11 GF) ✎ **S** £115; **D** £165-£275* **Facilities** STV FTV Wi-fi Putt green ⛳ Free use of nearby leisure club ♬ New Year **Conf** Class 30 Board 30 Thtr 64 Del from £199 to £225* **Services** Lift **Parking** 200 **Notes** LB ⊗ Civ Wed 72

HADLOW   Map 6 TQ65
Kent

Hadlow Manor Hotel

★★★ 77% HOTEL

☎ 01732 851442
Goose Green TN11 0JH
e-mail: dc@hadlowmanor.co.uk
dir: On A26 (Maidstone to Tonbridge road). 1m E of Hadlow

This is a friendly, independently owned country-house hotel, ideally situated between Maidstone and Tonbridge. Traditionally styled bedrooms are spacious and attractively furnished with many amenities. Public areas include a sunny restaurant, bar and lounge. The gardens are delightful and there's a seated area ideal for relaxation in warmer weather. Meeting and banqueting facilities are available.

Rooms 29 (2 fmly) (8 GF) **S** fr £59; **D** fr £69* **Facilities** STV FTV Wi-fi New Year **Conf** Class 90 Board 103 Thtr 200 Del from £110* **Parking** 120 **Notes** ⊗ Civ Wed 200

HADNALL   Map 15 SJ52
Shropshire

Saracens at Hadnall

⊛⊛ RESTAURANT WITH ROOMS

☎ 01939 210877
Shrewsbury Rd SY4 4AG
e-mail: reception@saracensathadnall.co.uk
web: www.saracensathadnall.co.uk
dir: M54 onto A5 towards Shrewsbury, take A49 towards Whitchurch. In Hadnall, property diagonally opposite church

This Georgian Grade II listed former farmhouse and village pub has been tastefully converted into a very smart restaurant with rooms, without any loss of original charm and character. The bedrooms are thoughtfully equipped. Skilfully prepared meals are served in either the elegant dining room or the adjacent conservatory, where there is a glass-topped well.

Rooms 5

HAGLEY   Map 10 SO98
Worcestershire

Premier Inn Hagley

BUDGET HOTEL

☎ 0871 527 8484
Birmingham Rd DY9 9JS
web: www.premierinn.com
dir: M5 junct 3, A456 towards Kidderminster (dual carriageway). Hotel visible on opposite side of road. At next rdbt double back follow A456 Birmingham signs. Hotel on left

High quality, budget accommodation ideal for both families and business travellers. Spacious, en suite bedrooms feature tea and coffee making facilities, and Freeview TV in most hotels. Internet access and Wi-fi are available for a small fee. The adjacent family restaurant features a wide and varied menu. See also the Hotel Groups pages.

Rooms 40

HALIFAX   Map 19 SE02
West Yorkshire

Holdsworth House Hotel

★★★★ 75% ⊛⊛ HOTEL

☎ 01422 240024
Holdsworth HX2 9TG
e-mail: info@holdsworthhouse.co.uk
web: www.holdsworthhouse.co.uk
dir: From town centre take A629 towards Keighley. 1.5m right at garage, into Shay Ln. Hotel on right after 1m

This delightful 17th-century Jacobean manor house, set in well-tended gardens, offers individually decorated, thoughtfully equipped bedrooms. Public rooms, adorned with beautiful paintings and antique pieces, include a choice of inviting lounges and superb conference and function facilities. Dinner provides the highlight of any stay and is served in the elegant restaurant by friendly, attentive staff.

Rooms 40 (2 fmly) (15 GF) ✎ **S** fr £75; **D** fr £85 (incl. bkfst)* **Facilities** FTV Wi-fi New Year **Conf** Class 75 Board 50 Thtr 150 Del from £125* **Parking** 60 **Notes** LB Civ Wed 120

H

H

HALIFAX *continued*

The White Swan Hotel

★★★ 74% HOTEL

☎ 01422 355541
Princess St HX1 1TS
e-mail: info@whiteswanhalifax.com
dir: Adjacent to Town Hall

The White Swan is a well established hotel noted for its friendly staff. Located in the heart of the town it offers comfortable, well-equipped bedrooms plus conference and function facilities. The lounge area is ideal for relaxing, and for the more energetic guest there is a small fitness room.

Rooms 40 (2 fmly) **Facilities** STV FTV Wi-fi Gym New Year **Conf** Class 35 Board 35 Thtr 80 **Services** Lift **Parking** 9

Premier Inn Halifax

BUDGET HOTEL

☎ 0871 527 8486
Salterhebble Hill, Huddersfield Rd HX3 0QT
web: www.premierinn.com
dir: Just off M62 junct 24 on A629 towards Halifax

High quality, budget accommodation ideal for both families and business travellers. Spacious, en suite bedrooms feature tea and coffee making facilities, and Freeview TV in most hotels. Internet access and Wi-fi are available for a small fee. The adjacent family restaurant features a wide and varied menu. See also the Hotel Groups pages.

Rooms 31

Premier Inn Halifax Town Centre

BUDGET HOTEL

☎ 0871 527 9348
Broad Street Plaza HX1 1YA
web: www.premierinn.com

Rooms 100

The Halland Forge Hotel

★★ 71% HOTEL

☎ 01825 840456
BN8 6PW
e-mail: info@hallandforgehotel.co.uk
web: www.hallandforgehotel.co.uk
dir: On A22 at junct with B2192, 4.5m S of Uckfield

Conveniently located, this hotel offers comfortable annexed accommodation with parking spaces directly outside the bedrooms. Public areas include a spacious lounge bar, attractive outdoor seating (weather permitting) and an informal restaurant serving generous portions at dinner. An attractively presented room is available for private dining, special occasions or for meetings by prior arrangement.

Rooms 20 (20 annexe) (2 fmly) (8 GF) **Conf** Class 20 Board 26 Thtr 45 **Parking** 70 **Notes** ⊗

The Carlton Mitre Hotel

★★★★ 74% HOTEL PLAN 1 B1

☎ 020 8979 9988 & 8783 3505
Hampton Court Rd KT8 9BN
e-mail: info@carltonhotels.co.uk
dir: M3 junct 1 follow signs to Sunbury & Hampton Court Palace. At Hampton Court Palace rdbt right, hotel on right

This hotel, dating back in parts to 1655, enjoys an enviable setting on the banks of the River Thames opposite Hampton Court Palace. The riverside restaurant and Edge bar/brasserie command wonderful views as well as spacious terraces for alfresco dining. Bedrooms are spacious and elegant with excellent facilities. Parking is limited.

Rooms 36 (2 fmly) (12 GF) **Facilities** STV FTV Wi-fi ⌨ Xmas New Year **Conf** Class 60 Board 40 Thtr 120 **Services** Lift Air con **Parking** 13 **Notes** ⊗ Civ Wed 100

See **Manchester Airport**

Park Inn by Radisson Harlow

park inn *by Radisson*

★★★ 70% HOTEL

☎ 01279 829988
Southern Way CM18 7BA
e-mail: info.harlow@rezidorparkinn.com
web: www.parkinn.co.uk/hotel-harlow
dir: M11 junct 7, A414 towards Harlow, 1st exit at 1st rdbt then 1st left

Bedrooms are comfortably appointed with flat-screen TVs, Wi-fi and safes included. The RBG Restaurant dining concept offers a versatile format and service is attentive and unfussy. Conference facilities and convenient parking complete the picture.

Rooms 119 (2 fmly) (60 GF) **Facilities** FTV Wi-fi ⓢ Gym Beauty treatment room Dance studio & classes Xmas New Year **Conf** Class 110 Board 80 Thtr 200 **Services** Air con **Parking** 100 **Notes** ⊗ Civ Wed 180

Harpenden House Hotel

CLASSIC BRITISH HOTELS

★★★★ 74% HOTEL

☎ 01582 449955
18 Southdown Rd AL5 1PE
e-mail: reservations@harpendenhouse.co.uk
web: www.harpendenhouse.co.uk
dir: M1 junct 10 left at rdbt. Next rdbt right onto A1081 to Harpenden. Over 2 mini rdbts, through town centre. Next rdbt left, hotel 200yds on left

This attractive Grade II listed Georgian building overlooks East Common. The hotel gardens are particularly attractive and the public areas are stylishly decorated, including the restaurant which has an impressive ceiling. Some of the bedrooms and a large suite are located in the original house but most of the accommodation is in the annexe.

Rooms 78 (61 annexe) (13 fmly) (2 GF) **S** £72-£169; **D** £82-£169* **Facilities** Wi-fi Complimentary use of local leisure centre **Conf** Class 60 Board 60 Thtr 150 Del from £120 to £175* **Parking** 80 **Notes** LB ⊗ RS wknds & BHs Civ Wed 120

Save on hotels. Book at **theAA.com/hotel**

HAL – HAR 195 ENGLAND

HARROGATE
North Yorkshire
Map 19 SE35

See also **Knaresborough**

INSPECTORS' CHOICE

Rudding Park Hotel, Spa & Golf

★★★★ ◉ HOTEL

☎ 01423 871350
Rudding Park, Follifoot HG3 1JH
e-mail: reservations@ruddingpark.com
web: www.ruddingpark.co.uk
dir: From A61 at rdbt with A658 take York exit, follow signs to Rudding Park

Set in beautiful parkland, Rudding Park dates from the early 19th century. Interiors are stylishly contemporary and elegant, with luxurious bedrooms; the new Follifoot wing features stunning suites and bedrooms with spas. Carefully prepared meals and Yorkshire tapas are served in the contemporary Clocktower, which has a striking pink chandelier. The stylish bar and conservatory lead to a generous terrace which is perfect for eating alfresco. The grandeur of the mansion house and grounds make this a popular wedding venue. The hotel has an impressive spa, gym, private cinema and extensive conference facilities, plus an adjoining 18-hole, par 72 golf course and driving range.

Rooms 90 (15 fmly) (31 GF) ⟟ **S** £123-£500; **D** £144-£530 (incl. bkfst)* **Facilities** Spa STV FTV Wi-fi ⟟ ↯ supervised ↧ 18 Putt green Gym Driving range Jogging trail Sauna Hammam ♪♪ Xmas New Year **Conf** Class 150 Board 40 Thtr 300 Del from £160 to £278* **Services** Lift **Parking** 250 **Notes** ⊗ Civ Wed 300

Hotel du Vin Harrogate

★★★★ 80% ◉◉
TOWN HOUSE HOTEL

☎ 01423 856800
Prospect Place HG1 1LB
e-mail: info@harrogate.hotelduvin.com
web: www.hotelduvin.com
dir: A1(M) junct 47, A59 to Harrogate, follow town centre signs to Prince of Wales rdbt, 3rd exit, remain in right lane. Right at lights into Albert St, right into Prospect Place

This town house was created from eight Georgian-style properties and overlooks The Stray. The spacious, open-plan lobby has seating, a bar and the reception desk. Hidden downstairs is a cosy snug cellar. The French-influenced bistro offers high quality cooking and a great choice of wines. Bedrooms face front and back, and are smart and modern, with excellent 'deluge' showers.

Rooms 48 (4 GF) ⟟ **Facilities** Spa STV FTV Wi-fi ⟟ New Year **Conf** Class 20 Board 30 Thtr 60 Del from £135 to £200* **Services** Lift **Parking** 30 **Notes** Civ Wed 90

Nidd Hall Hotel

Warner Leisure Hotels
JUST FOR GROWN-UPS

★★★★ 78% ◉◉ COUNTRY HOUSE HOTEL

☎ 01423 771598
Nidd HG3 3BN
dir: A59 through Knaresborough, follow signs for Ripley. Hotel on right

This fine hotel is set in 45 acres of Victorian and Edwardian gardens. Bedrooms are spacious and appointed to a high standard, while public areas are delightful and retain many original features. Leisure and spa facilities are available along with a variety of outdoor activities. This is an adults-only (above 21 years old) hotel.

Rooms 183 (47 GF) ⟟ **S** fr £112; **D** fr £224 (incl. bkfst & dinner)* **Facilities** Spa FTV Wi-fi HL ⟟ supervised ⟟ Putt green Fishing ⟟ Gym ♪♪ Xmas New Year **Conf** Class 40 Board 30 Thtr 60 Del from £139* **Services** Lift **Parking** 200 **Notes** LB ⊗ No children 21yrs

The White Hart Hotel

★★★★ 78% ◉◉ HOTEL

☎ 01423 505681
2 Cold Bath Rd HG2 0NF
e-mail: reception@whitehart.net
web: www.whitehart.net
dir: A59 to Harrogate. A661 3rd exit on rdbt to Harrogate. Left at rdbt onto A6040 for 1m. Right onto A61. Bear left down Montpellier Hill

The White Hart Hotel has an excellent location in Harrogate and has been welcoming guests for over 200 years. The bedrooms, including executive rooms with four-posters and views over the Montpellier Quarter, are attractively designed. The Tea Rooms serve from early morning until late afternoon, and the hotel has introduced a pub concept called the Fat Badger, with real ales, an extensive wine list and high quality food. Alfresco eating and drinking are possible in good weather. Secure parking is available and there is Wi-fi throughout.

Rooms 53 (1 fmly) ⟟ **Facilities** FTV Wi-fi ⟟ Gym Xmas New Year **Conf** Class 40 Board 30 Thtr 80 **Services** Lift **Parking** 80 **Notes** ⊗ Civ Wed 80

H

H

HARROGATE *continued*

Studley Hotel

★★★★ 76% ⚜ ⚜ HOTEL

☎ 01423 560425
Swan Rd HG1 2SE
e-mail: info@studleyhotel.co.uk
web: www.studleyhotel.co.uk
dir: Adjacent to Valley Gardens, opposite Mercer Gallery

This friendly, well-established hotel, close to the town centre and Valley Gardens, is well known for its Orchid Restaurant, which provides a dynamic and authentic approach to Pacific Rim and Asian cuisine. Bedrooms are modern and come in a variety of styles and sizes, while the stylish bar lounge provides an excellent place for relaxing. A PC is available for guests' use.

Rooms 28 (1 fmly) ⚑ **S** fr £99; **D** fr £119 (incl. bkfst) **Facilities** STV Wi-fi ⚑ Free use of facilities at local Health Club **Conf** Class 15 Board 12 Thtr 15 **Services** Lift **Parking** 15 **Notes** LB ⊗ Closed 22-30 Dec

The Majestic Hotel

★★★★ 76% HOTEL

PUMA HOTELS
COLLECTION

☎ 01423 700300
Ripon Rd HG1 2HU
e-mail: majestic@pumahotels.co.uk
web: www.pumahotels.co.uk
dir: M1 onto A1(M) at Wetherby. Take A661 to Harrogate. Hotel in town centre adjacent to Royal Hall

Popular for conferences and functions, this grand Victorian hotel is set in 12 acres of landscaped grounds that is within walking distance of the town centre. It benefits from spacious public areas, and the comfortable bedrooms, including some spacious suites, come in a variety of sizes.

Rooms 174 (8 fmly) **Facilities** Spa STV Wi-fi ⚑ supervised ⚑ Gym Golf practice net Xmas New Year **Conf** Class 260 Board 70 Thtr 500 **Services** Lift **Parking** 250 **Notes** Civ Wed 200

Old Swan Hotel

★★★★ 76% HOTEL

CLASSIC LODGES
the sign of a great hotel

☎ 01423 500055
Swan Rd HG1 2SR
e-mail: info.theoldswan@classiclodges.co.uk
dir: From A1, A59 Ripon, left Empress rdbt, keep left, right at Prince of Wales rdbt. Straight across lights, left into Swan Rd

In the heart of Harrogate and within walking distance of the Harrogate International Centre and Valley Gardens, this hotel is famed as being Agatha Christie's hiding place during her disappearance in 1926. The bedrooms are stylishly furnished, and the public areas include the Library Restaurant, the Wedgwood Room and the lounge bar. Extensive conference and banqueting facilities are available.

Rooms 136 **Facilities** STV Wi-fi ⚑ Xmas New Year **Conf** Class 130 Board 100 Thtr 450 **Services** Lift **Parking** 175 **Notes** ⊗ Civ Wed 300

BEST WESTERN Cedar Court Hotel

Best Western

★★★★ 71% HOTEL

☎ 01423 858585 & 858595 (Res)
Queens Buildings, Park Pde HG1 5AH
e-mail: cedarcourt@bestwestern.co.uk
web: www.cedarcourthotels.co.uk
dir: From A1(M) follow signs to Harrogate on A661 past Sainsburys. At rdbt left onto A6040. Hotel right after church

This Grade II listed building was Harrogate's first hotel and enjoys a peaceful location in landscaped grounds, close to the town centre. It provides spacious, well-equipped accommodation. Public areas include a brasserie-style restaurant, a small gym and an open-plan lounge and bar. Functions and conferences are particularly well catered for.

Rooms 100 (8 fmly) (7 GF) **Facilities** FTV Wi-fi ⚑ Gym Xmas New Year **Conf** Class 80 Board 70 Thtr 320 **Services** Lift **Parking** 150 **Notes** ⊗ Civ Wed 320

Cairn Hotel

★★★ 68% HOTEL

☎ 01423 504005
Ripon Rd HG1 2JD
e-mail: salescairn@strathmorehotels.com

This large Victorian hotel is just a short walk from the town centre and also benefits from free on-site parking. Many of the original features have been retained and the spacious foyer lounge and bar areas are perfect for relaxing. Bedrooms are comfortable, with Club Rooms offering extra accessories and luxury touches. Complimentary Wi-fi is also provided in public areas and there is a fitness room with a mini gym.

Rooms 135 (7 fmly) ⚑ **S** £55-£135; **D** £65-£155 (incl. bkfst) **Facilities** Wi-fi Gym Xmas New Year **Conf** Class 170 Board 100 Thtr 400 Del from £125 to £160 **Services** Lift **Parking** 150 **Notes** LB Civ Wed

See advert on page 501

Premier Inn Harrogate

Premier Inn

BUDGET HOTEL

☎ 0871 527 8490
Hornbeam Park Av HG2 8RA
web: www.premierinn.com
dir: A1(M) junct 46 W, A661 to Harrogate. In 2m left at The Woodlands lights. 1.5m left into Hornbeam Park Ave

High quality, budget accommodation ideal for both families and business travellers. Spacious, en suite bedrooms feature tea and coffee making facilities, and Freeview TV in most hotels. Internet access and Wi-fi are available for a small fee. The adjacent family restaurant features a wide and varied menu. See also the Hotel Groups pages.

Rooms 50

Save on hotels. Book at **theAA.com/hotel**

HAR 197 **ENGLAND**

HARROW
Greater London

BEST WESTERN Cumberland Hotel

★★★ 72% METRO HOTEL PLAN 1 C5

☎ 020 8863 4111
1 St Johns Rd HA1 2EF
e-mail: reservations@cumberlandhotel.co.uk
web: www.cumberlandhotel.co.uk
dir: Into Harrow via Station or Sheepcote Rd, into Gayton Rd, then Lyon Rd which becomes St Johns Rd

Situated within walking distance of the town centre, this hotel is ideally located for all local attractions and amenities. Bedrooms provide good levels of comfort and are practically equipped to meet the requirements of all travellers. The public areas comprise a well-stocked pub-style bar, which serves homemade food. Parking is located at the rear of the building.

Rooms 85 (54 annexe) (6 fmly) (15 GF) **Facilities** FTV Wi-fi Xmas New Year **Conf** Class 70 Board 62 Thtr 130 **Parking** 67 **Notes** ⊗ Civ Wed 150

HARROW WEALD
Greater London

Grim's Dyke Hotel

★★★★ 82% ⊛ ⊛ HOTEL PLAN 1 B5

☎ 020 8385 3100 & 8954 4227
Old Redding HA3 6SH
e-mail: reservations@grimsdyke.com
web: www.grimsdyke.com
dir: A410 onto A409 north towards Bushey, at top of hill at lights turn left into Old Redding, opposite 'The Viewpoint'

Once home to Sir William Gilbert, this Grade II mansion contains many references to the well-known Gilbert and Sullivan productions. The house is set in over 40 acres of beautiful parkland and gardens. Bedrooms in the main house are elegant and traditional, while those in the adjacent lodge are aimed more at the business guest.

Rooms 46 (37 annexe) (4 fmly) (17 GF) S fr £65; D fr £75 (incl. bkfst)* **Facilities** STV FTV Wi-fi Gilbert & Sullivan opera dinner Murder mystery & Sabrage evenings ♬ Xmas New Year **Conf** Class 60 Board 32 Thtr 90 Del from £140* **Parking** 97 **Notes** RS 24-31 Dec Civ Wed 90

HARTLEPOOL
Co Durham   Map 19 NZ53

BEST WESTERN Grand Hotel

★★★ 77% HOTEL

☎ 01429 266345
Swainson St TS24 8AA
e-mail: grandhotel@tavistockleisure.com
dir: A689 into town centre. Left onto Victoria Rd, hotel on right

This hotel retains many original features and the public areas include a grand ballroom and a lively open-plan lounge bar. The modern, vibrant, basement restaurant is called Parmo's and serves freshly made Italian food. The bedrooms are modern in design and have high spec fixtures and fittings. The staff provide attentive and friendly service.

Rooms 48 (1 fmly) S £63-£92; D £74-£102 (incl. bkfst)* **Facilities** STV FTV Wi-fi Affiliation with local gym Beauty treatment room ♬ New Year **Conf** Class 200 Board 60 Thtr 250 Del from £105 to £125* **Services** Lift **Parking** 50 **Notes** LB ⊗ Civ Wed 200

Premier Inn Hartlepool Marina

BUDGET HOTEL

☎ 0871 527 8492
Maritime Av, Hartlepool Marina TS24 0XZ
web: www.premierinn.com
dir: Approx 1m from A689/A179 junct. On marina

High quality, budget accommodation ideal for both families and business travellers. Spacious, en suite bedrooms feature tea and coffee making facilities, and Freeview TV in most hotels. Internet access and Wi-fi are available for a small fee. The adjacent family restaurant features a wide and varied menu. See also the Hotel Groups pages.

Rooms 60

HARTLEY WINTNEY
Hampshire   Map 5 SU75

The Elvetham Hotel

★★★ 80% HOTEL

☎ 01252 844871
RG27 8AR
e-mail: enq@elvethamhotel.co.uk
web: www.elvethamhotel.co.uk
dir: M3 junct 4A W, junct 5 E (or M4 junct 11, A33, B3011). Hotel signed from A323 between Hartley Wintney & Fleet

The Elvetham Hotel is a spectacular 19th-century mansion set in 35 acres of grounds with an arboretum. All bedrooms are individually styled and many have views of the manicured gardens. A popular venue for weddings and conferences, the hotel lends itself to team building events and outdoor pursuits.

Rooms 72 (29 annexe) (10 fmly) (7 GF) **Facilities** STV FTV Wi-fi ⌕ Putt green Gym Badminton Boules Volleyball New Year **Conf** Class 80 Board 48 Thtr 110 **Parking** 200 **Notes** Closed 24-27 Dec Civ Wed 200

HARTSHEAD MOOR MOTORWAY SERVICE AREA (M62)
West Yorkshire   Map 19 SE12

Days Inn Bradford - M62

BUDGET HOTEL

☎ 01274 851706
Hartshead Moor Service Area, Clifton HD6 4JX
e-mail: hartshead.hotel@welcomebreak.co.uk
web: www.welcomebreak.co.uk
dir: M62 between junct 25 & 26

This modern building offers accommodation in smart, spacious and well-equipped bedrooms, suitable for families and business travellers, and all with en suite bathrooms. Continental breakfast is available and other refreshments may be taken at the nearby family restaurant. See also the Hotel Groups pages.

Rooms 38 (33 fmly) (17 GF) **Conf** Board 10

H

H

The Pier at Harwich

★★★★ 79% ◉◉ SMALL HOTEL

☎ 01255 241212
The Quay CO12 3HH
e-mail: pier@milsomhotels.com
web: www.milsomhotels.com
dir: From A12 take A120 to Quay. Hotel opposite lifeboat station

The Pier is situated on the quay, overlooking the ports of Harwich and Felixstowe. The bedrooms are tastefully decorated, thoughtfully equipped, and furnished in a contemporary style; many rooms have superb sea views. The public rooms include the informal Ha'Penny Bistro, the first-floor Harbourside Restaurant, a smart lounge bar and a plush residents' lounge.

Rooms 14 (7 annexe) (5 fmly) (1 GF) ⬧ **D** £115-£225 (incl. bkfst)* **Facilities** STV Wi-fi Day cruises on yachts Golf breaks arranged with nearby course Sea bass fishing Xmas **Conf** Board 16 Del from £155* **Parking** 12 **Notes** LB Civ Wed 50

Tower Hotel

★★★ 77% HOTEL

☎ 01255 504952
Dovercourt CO12 3PJ
e-mail: reception@tower-hotel-harwich.co.uk
web: www.tower-hotel-harwich.co.uk
dir: Follow main road into Harwich. Past BP garage on left

The Tower Hotel is an impressive late 17th-century Italian-style building, with a wealth of ornamental ceiling cornices, beautiful architraves and an impressive balustrade. Bedrooms, many named after prominent people from Harwich's past, are spacious

and furnished to a very high standard. Evening meals and breakfast are served in the decorative dining rooms, and Rigby's bar offers tempting meals and a wide range of refreshments.

Rooms 13 (2 fmly) (2 GF) **Facilities** Wi-fi **Conf** Class 30 Board 30 Thtr 30 **Parking** 30 **Notes** ⊗ Civ Wed 40

Cliff Hotel

★★ 67% HOTEL

☎ 01255 503345 & 507373
Marine Pde, Dovercourt CO12 3RE
e-mail: reception@cliffhotelharwich.fsnet.co.uk
web: www.thecliffhotelharwich.co.uk
dir: From A120 at rdbt into Parkeston Rd. At mini rdbt left onto B1325 signed Harwich. At lights in Dovercourt right into Kingsway, to seafront. Right into Marine Parade

The Cliff Hotel is conveniently situated on the seafront close to the railway station and ferry terminal. Public rooms are smartly appointed and include the Shade Bar, a comfortable lounge, a restaurant, and the Marine Bar with views of Dovercourt Bay. The pleasantly decorated bedrooms have co-ordinated soft furnishings and modern facilities; many have sea views.

Rooms 26 (3 fmly) **Facilities** STV Wi-fi New Year **Conf** Class 150 Board 40 Thtr 200 **Parking** 50 **Notes** ⊗ RS Xmas & New Year

Premier Inn Harwich

BUDGET HOTEL

☎ 0871 527 8494
Parkstone Rd, Dovercourt CO12 4NX
web: www.premierinn.com
dir: A120 to Harwich, hotel opposite Morrisons. Right at rdbt. Hotel entrance through Lidl car park

High quality, budget accommodation ideal for both families and business travellers. Spacious, en suite bedrooms feature tea and coffee making facilities, and Freeview TV in most hotels. Internet access and Wi-fi are available for a small fee. The adjacent family restaurant features a wide and varied menu. See also the Hotel Groups pages.

Rooms 45

Lythe Hill Hotel & Spa

★★★★ 75% ◉◉ HOTEL

☎ 01428 651251
Petworth Rd GU27 3BQ
e-mail: lythe@lythehill.co.uk
web: www.lythehill.co.uk
dir: From High St onto B2131. Hotel 1.25m on right

This privately-owned hotel sits in 22 acres of attractive parkland. The hotel has been described as a hamlet of character buildings, each furnished in a style that complements the age of the property; the oldest one dating back to 1475. The Restaurant offers interesting, quality dishes, and is also the venue for breakfast and afternoon tea. The bedrooms are split between a number of 15th-century buildings, and vary in size. The stylish Armana spa includes a 16-metre swimming pool, as well as various ESPA treatments and therapies, spa bath, sauna and a fully equipped gym.

Rooms 42 (9 fmly) (19 GF) ⬧ **Facilities** Spa FTV Wi-fi ⊛ ⊰ Fishing 🎣 Gym Boules Giant chess 🎵 Xmas New Year **Conf** Class 40 Board 30 Thtr 128 **Parking** 120 **Notes** Civ Wed 128

Bannatyne Spa Hotel Hastings

★★★★ 80% HOTEL

☎ 01424 851222
Battle Rd TN38 8EA
e-mail: enquiries.hastingshotel@bannatyne.co.uk
dir: M25 junct 5, A21 (Hastings). At 5th rdbt 2nd exit (Hastings/Filmwell). After 2 rdbts right (Folkestone/A259/Battle/A2100). Left at A2100/The Ridge Way. At 2nd rdbt right to hotel

This hotel offers a range of facilities that will appeal to both leisure and business travellers. The well-appointed accommodation is available in a range of types and sizes from small doubles to superior rooms, while the public areas are a tasteful blend of contemporary design and period features. The Conservatory Restaurant has attractive views over the formal garden. There is a spa and health club plus meeting facilities. Free Wi-fi is available.

Rooms 38 (7 fmly) (4 GF) ↙ **D** £100-£200 (incl. bkfst)* **Facilities** Spa FTV Wi-fi ↘ ⊗ supervised ⌇ Gym Xmas New Year **Conf** Class 300 Board 50 Thtr 500 Del from £149 to £189* **Services** Lift **Parking** 150 **Notes** LB ⊗ Civ Wed 300

BEST WESTERN Royal Victoria Hotel

★★★ 74% HOTEL

☎ 01424 445544
Marina, St Leonards-on-Sea TN38 0BD
e-mail: reception@royalvichotel.co.uk
web: www.royalvichotel.co.uk
dir: On A259 (seafront road) 1m W of Hastings pier

This imposing 18th-century property is situated in a prominent position overlooking the sea. A superb marble staircase leads up from the lobby to the main public areas on the first floor which has panoramic views of the sea. The spacious bedrooms are pleasantly decorated and well equipped, and include duplex and family suites.

Rooms 50 (15 fmly) **Facilities** STV Wi-fi ↘ Xmas New Year **Conf** Class 40 Board 40 Thtr 100 **Services** Lift **Parking** 6 **Notes** Civ Wed 50

The Chatsworth Hotel

★★★ 72% ⊛ HOTEL

☎ 01424 720188
Carlisle Pde TN34 1JG
e-mail: info@chatsworthhotel.com
dir: A21 to town centre. At seafront turn right before next lights

Enjoying a central position on the seafront, close to the pier, this hotel is a short walk from the old town and within easy reach of the county's many attractions. Bedrooms are smartly decorated, equipped with a range of extras, and many rooms enjoy splendid sea views. Guests can also enjoy an exciting Indian meal in the contemporary restaurant.

Rooms 52 (5 fmly) ↙ **S** £45-£75; **D** £55-£100* **Facilities** FTV Wi-fi Xmas New Year **Conf** Class 20 Board 20 Thtr 40 Del from £75 to £110 **Services** Lift **Parking** 8 **Notes** ⊗

Premier Inn Hastings

BUDGET HOTEL

☎ 0871 527 8496
1 John Macadam Way, St Leonards on Sea TN37 7DB
web: www.premierinn.com
dir: A21 into Hastings. Hotel on right after junct with A2100 (Battle road)

High quality, budget accommodation ideal for both families and business travellers. Spacious, en suite bedrooms feature tea and coffee making facilities, and Freeview TV in most hotels. Internet access and Wi-fi are available for a small fee. The adjacent family restaurant features a wide and varied menu. See also the Hotel Groups pages.

Rooms 44

HATFIELD
Hertfordshire   Map 6 TL20

Beales Hotel

★★★★ 79% ⊛ ⊛ HOTEL

☎ 01707 288500
Comet Way AL10 9NG
e-mail: hatfield@bealeshotels.co.uk
web: www.bealeshotels.co.uk
dir: On A1001 opposite Galleria Shopping Mall - follow signs for Galleria

Beales Hotel is a stunning contemporary property. Within easy access of the M25, its striking exterior incorporates giant glass panels and cedar wood slats. Bedrooms have luxurious beds, flat-screen TVs and smart bathrooms. Public areas include a small bar and attractive restaurant, which opens throughout the day. The hotel is fully air-conditioned and free wired broadband is available in bedrooms, conference and banqueting rooms.

Rooms 53 (3 fmly) (21 GF) ↙ **S** £70-£150; **D** £80-£160 (incl. bkfst)* **Facilities** STV Wi-fi Free use of nearby leisure club Xmas New Year **Conf** Class 124 Board 64 Thtr 300 Del from £155 to £195* **Services** Lift Air con **Parking** 126 **Notes** LB ⊗ RS 27-30 Dec Civ Wed 300

Ramada Hatfield

★★★ 75% HOTEL

☎ 01707 252400
St Albans Road West AL10 9RH
e-mail: enquiries@ramadahatfieldhotel.co.uk
web: www.ramadahatfieldhotel.co.uk
dir: A1(M) junct 3, take 2nd exit at rdbt signed Hatfield. Hotel on left

Conveniently located close to the business and shopping districts and only a short drive from the

M25, this Ramada is perfectly situated for both business and leisure guests. The bedrooms are spacious and well equipped, and complimentary Wi-fi is available throughout the hotel. The open-plan, art deco inspired public areas include a stylish bar.

Rooms 128 (5 fmly) (53 GF) ↙ **Facilities** STV FTV Wi-fi ↘ **Conf** Class 40 Board 45 Thtr 120 **Parking** 165 **Notes** ⊗ Civ Wed 100

Mercure Hatfield Oak Hotel

★★★ 73% HOTEL

☎ 01707 275701
Roehyde Way AL10 9AF
e-mail: enquiries@hotels-hatfield.com
web: www.hotels-hatfield.com
dir: M25 junct 23 between juncts 2 & 3 of A1(M). Roehyde Way runs parallel to A1(M)

The hotel enjoys an enviable location for both leisure and business guests, it is within easy reach of major roads and central London. In addition, the University of Hertfordshire is situated nearby. The accommodation has been appointed to a good standard with flat-screen TVs and Wi-fi, among other facilities. The hotel also caters for conference and banqueting.

Rooms 76 (5 fmly) (36 GF) ↙ **Facilities** FTV Wi-fi ↘ **Conf** Class 50 Board 50 Thtr 100 **Parking** 85 **Notes** ⊗ Civ Wed 120

Premier Inn Hatfield

BUDGET HOTEL

☎ 0871 527 8498
Lemsford Rd AL10 0DZ
web: www.premierinn.com
dir: From A1(M) junct 4, A1001 towards Hatfield. At rbt take 2nd exit, 1st right

High quality, budget accommodation ideal for both families and business travellers. Spacious, en suite bedrooms feature tea and coffee making facilities, and Freeview TV in most hotels. Internet access and Wi-fi are available for a small fee. The adjacent family restaurant features a wide and varied menu. See also the Hotel Groups pages.

Rooms 40

H

HATHERSAGE
Derbyshire   Map 16 SK28

George Hotel

★★★ 84% ◉◉ HOTEL

☎ 01433 650436
Main Rd S32 1BB
e-mail: info@george-hotel.net
web: www.george-hotel.net
dir: In village centre on A6187, SW of Sheffield

The George is a relaxing 500-year-old hostelry in the heart of this picturesque town. The beamed bar lounge has great character and traditional comfort, and the restaurant is light, modern and spacious with original artworks. Upstairs the decor is simpler with lots of light hues; the split-level and four-poster rooms are especially appealing. The quality cooking is a key feature of the hotel.

Rooms 24 (2 fmly) (5 GF) 🐾 **S** £70-£174; **D** £80-£198 (incl. bkfst)* **Facilities** FTV Wi-fi Xmas New Year **Conf** Class 20 Board 36 Thtr 80 Del from £148 to £168* **Parking** 40 **Notes** LB ⊗ Civ Wed 70

HAVANT
Hampshire   Map 5 SU70

Premier Inn Portsmouth (Havant)

BUDGET HOTEL

☎ 0871 527 8900
65 Bedhampton Hill, Bedhampton PO9 3JN
web: www.premierinn.com
dir: At rdbt just off A3(M) junct 5 towards Bedhampton

High quality, budget accommodation ideal for both families and business travellers. Spacious, en suite bedrooms feature tea and coffee making facilities, and Freeview TV in most hotels. Internet access and Wi-fi are available for a small fee. The adjacent family restaurant features a wide and varied menu. See also the Hotel Groups pages.

Rooms 37

HAVERHILL
Suffolk   Map 12 TL64

Days Inn Haverhill

BUDGET HOTEL

☎ 01440 716950
Phoenix Road & Bumpstead Rd, Haverhill Business Park CB9 7AE
e-mail: reservations@daysinnhaverhill.co.uk
web: www.haverhilldaysinn.co.uk
dir: A1017 (Haverhill bypass). Hotel on 5th rdbt

This modern building offers accommodation in smart, spacious and well-equipped bedrooms, suitable for families and business travellers, and all with en suite bathrooms. Continental breakfast is available and other refreshments may be taken at the nearby family restaurant. See also the Hotel Groups pages.

Rooms 80 (8 fmly) (14 GF) **Conf** Class 28 Board 24 Thtr 60

HAWES
North Yorkshire   Map 18 SD88

Simonstone Hall Hotel

★★★ 77% HOTEL

☎ 01969 667255
Simonstone DL8 3LY
e-mail: enquiries@simonstonehall.com
web: www.simonstonehall.com
dir: 1.5m N of Hawes on road signed Muker & Buttertubs

This former hunting lodge provides professional, friendly service and a relaxed atmosphere. There is an inviting drawing room, stylish fine dining restaurant, a bar and a conservatory. The generally spacious bedrooms are elegantly designed to reflect the style of the house, and many offer spectacular views of the countryside.

Rooms 18 (10 fmly) (2 GF) 🐾 **Facilities** FTV Wi-fi Xmas New Year **Conf** Class 20 Board 20 Thtr 50 **Parking** 40 **Notes** Civ Wed 70

HAYDOCK
Merseyside   Map 15 SJ59

Thistle Haydock

thistle

★★★★ 75% HOTEL

☎ 0871 376 9044 & 01942 292001
Penny Ln WA11 9SG
e-mail: haydock@thistle.co.uk
web: www.thistle.com/haydock
dir: M6 junct 23, follow Haydock Racecourse signs (A49) N towards Ashton-in-Makerfield, 1st left, after bridge 1st turn left

Thistle Haydock is a smart, purpose-built hotel which offers an excellent standard of thoughtfully equipped accommodation. It is conveniently situated between Liverpool and Manchester, just off the M6. The wide range of leisure and meeting facilities prove popular with guests.

Rooms 137 (10 fmly) (65 GF) 🐾 **Facilities** Spa STV FTV Wi-fi HL ⊗ supervised Gym Children's play area Sauna Steam room **Conf** Class 140 Board 40 Thtr 300 Del from £99 to £150 **Parking** 210 **Notes** Civ Wed 220

Premier Inn Haydock

BUDGET HOTEL

☎ 0871 527 8500
Yew Tree Way, Golbourne WA3 3JD
web: www.premierinn.com
dir: M6 junct 23, A580 towards Manchester. Approx 2m. Straight on at major rdbt. Hotel on left

High quality, budget accommodation ideal for both families and business travellers. Spacious, en suite bedrooms feature tea and coffee making facilities, and Freeview TV in most hotels. Internet access and Wi-fi are available for a small fee. The adjacent family restaurant features a wide and varied menu. See also the Hotel Groups pages.

Rooms 60

HAYLE
Cornwall   Map 2 SW53

Premier Inn Hayle

BUDGET HOTEL

☎ 0871 527 8506
Carwin Rise, Loggans TR27 4PN
web: www.premierinn.com
dir: On A30 at Loggans Moor rdbt exit into Carwin Rise. Hotel on right

High quality, budget accommodation ideal for both families and business travellers. Spacious, en suite

Save on hotels. Book at **theAA.com/hotel**

HAT – HEA 201 ENGLAND

bedrooms feature tea and coffee making facilities, and Freeview TV in most hotels. Internet access and Wi-fi are available for a small fee. The adjacent family restaurant features a wide and varied menu. See also the Hotel Groups pages.

Rooms 56

Rosewarne Manor

◉◉ RESTAURANT WITH ROOMS

☎ 01209 610414 & 07966 090341
20 Gwinear Rd TR27 5JQ
e-mail: enquiries@rosewarnemanor.co.uk
dir: A30 Camborne West towards Connor Downs, left into Gwinear Rd. 0.75m to Rosewarne Manor

Rosewarne Manor offers a flexible suite, which can be booked for Bed & Breakfast or Self Catering. The suite is well appointed and well equipped. The award-winning restaurant uses local, fresh produce, which is served in the attractive restaurant overlooking the garden. The Manor can also be booked for a range of functions. Parking is available.

Rooms 1 (1 annexe)

| HAYLING ISLAND | Map 5 SU70 |
| Hampshire | |

Langstone Hotel

★★★★ 73% ◉◉ HOTEL

☎ 023 9246 5011
Northney Rd PO11 0NQ
e-mail: info@langstonehotel.co.uk
web: www.langstonehotel.co.uk
dir: From A27 take A3023 signed Havant/Hayling Island. Over bridge onto Hayling Island, sharp left after bridge

This hotel is located on the north shore of Hayling Island, yet is only minutes from the M27 with easy access to Fareham, Havant and Chichester. All the smartly designed, air-conditioned bedrooms, including 45 superior rooms, have views over Langstone harbour. The Brasserie offers a good choice of dishes and overlooks the harbour. A gym, indoor pool, sauna, steam, beauty salon and fitness club are also available.

Rooms 148 (40 fmly) (60 GF) (5 smoking) ☇
Facilities Spa STV FTV Wi-fi ☇ HL ☇ supervised Gym Sauna Steam room Fitness classes Xmas New Year **Conf** Class 80 Board 50 Thtr 180 Del from £120 to £160* **Services** Lift Air con **Parking** 150 **Notes** Civ Wed 150

Sinah Warren Hotel

Warner Leisure Hotels JUST FOR GROWN-UPS

★★★ 79% HOTEL

☎ 023 9246 6421
Ferry Rd PO11 0BZ
e-mail: sinahwarren2@bourne-leisure.co.uk
dir: A27 at Havant junct, take A3023 to Hayling Island, 2nd exit at rdbt towards Manor Rd, 3rd exit at next rdbt into Ferry Rd. Hotel 1.5m on right

Located in a beautiful part of Hampshire, this hotel offers a great range of leisure facilities and numerous daily in-house and external activities catering for all. The accommodation is spacious, and some rooms have sea views. The packages range from a minimum two-night, half board stay. Please note that this is an adults-only (over 21 years) hotel.

Rooms 280 (34 annexe) (116 GF) ☇ **Facilities** Spa FTV Wi-fi HL ☇ ☇ supervised ☇ ☇ Gym ♫ Xmas New Year **Conf** Class 300 Board 250 Thtr 500 **Services** Lift **Parking** 260 **Notes** ⊗ No children 21yrs

Lakeside Coastal Village

Warner Leisure Hotels JUST FOR GROWN-UPS

AA Advertised

☎ 023 9246 3976
Fishery Ln PO11 9NR
dir: Take A27 towards Havant. At Havant rdbt onto A3023 towards Hayling Island for approx 4m, then mini rdbt. Take 1st exit into Church Rd, continue until Mengham, left into Selsmore Rd, follow right into Rails Ln, left into Fishery Ln

Surrounded by water, with cosy chalets and a nearby beach, this friendly holiday village is the perfect base for exploring Hayling Island and the South Coast. All breaks are half-board and include live nightly entertainment and a range of daytime activities.

Rooms 226 (206 GF) ☇ **Facilities** FTV Wi-fi ☇ ☇ Gym **Parking** 200

| HAYWARDS HEATH | Map 6 TQ32 |
| West Sussex | |

BEST WESTERN The Birch Hotel

★★★ 78% HOTEL

☎ 01444 451565
Lewes Rd RH17 7SF
e-mail: info@birchhotel.co.uk
dir: On A272 opposite Princess Royal Hospital & behind Shell Garage

Originally the home of an eminent Harley Street surgeon, this attractive Victorian property has been extended to combine modern facilities with the charm of its original period. Public rooms include the conservatory-style Pavilion Restaurant, along with an open-plan lounge and brasserie-style bar serving a range of light meals.

Rooms 51 (3 fmly) (12 GF) **Facilities** STV Wi-fi **Conf** Class 30 Board 26 Thtr 60 **Parking** 60 **Notes** Civ Wed 60

| HEACHAM | Map 12 TF63 |
| Norfolk | |

Heacham Manor Hotel

★★★ 85% ◉ HOTEL

☎ 01485 536030 & 579800
Hunstanton Rd PE31 7JX
e-mail: info@heacham-manor.co.uk
dir: On A149 between Heacham & Hunstanton. Near Hunstanton rdbt with water tower

This delightful 16th-century, Grade II listed house has been beautifully restored. The property is approached via a winding driveway through landscaped grounds to the front of the hotel. Public areas include a smart dining room, a sunny conservatory and a cosy bar which leads out onto a terrace. The bedrooms are very stylish and have modern facilities.

Rooms 45 (32 annexe) (10 fmly) (12 GF) **Facilities** FTV Wi-fi ☇ 18 Swimming pools & leisure facilities available at sister resort Xmas New Year **Conf** Class 35 Board 20 Thtr 40 **Parking** 55 **Notes** ⊗ Civ Wed 100

H

See also Slough & Staines-upon-Thames

Sheraton Skyline Hotel

★★★★ 81% HOTEL PLAN 1 A3

☎ 020 8759 2535
Bath Rd UB3 5BP
e-mail: res268_skyline@sheraton.com
dir: M4 junct 4 for Heathrow, follow Terminal 1, 2 & 3 signs. Before airport entrance take slip road to left for 0.25m signed A4/Central London

Within easy reach of all terminals this hotel offers well appointed and comfortable bedrooms with air conditioning. The extensive, contemporary public areas are light and spacious, and include a wide range of eating and drinking options, function rooms, club lounge and a gym.

Rooms 350 (59 fmly) ⚲ **Facilities** STV FTV Wi-fi ⮿ ⓢ supervised Gym 24hr Fitness centre Xmas New Year **Conf** Class 320 Board 100 Thtr 500 **Services** Lift Air con **Parking** 336 **Notes** Civ Wed 100

London Heathrow Marriott Hotel

Marriott.

★★★★ 77% ⊛ HOTEL PLAN 1 A3

☎ 020 8990 1100 & 8990 1119
Bath Rd UB3 5AN
e-mail: mhrs.lhrhr.ays@marriott.com
web: www.londonheathrowmarriott.co.uk
dir: M4 junct 4, follow signs for Heathrow Terminals 1, 2 & 3. Left at rdbt onto A4 towards central London. Hotel 0.5m on left

This smart, modern hotel, with its striking design, meets all the expectations of a successful airport hotel. The light and airy atrium offers several eating and drinking options, each with a different theme. Spacious bedrooms are appointed to a good standard with an excellent range of facilities, and there is a leisure club and business centre.

Rooms 393 (139 fmly) (30 smoking) ⚲ **S** £125-£219; **D** £125-£219* **Facilities** STV Wi-fi ⮿ ⓢ supervised Gym Steam room Sauna Spa pool **Conf** Class 300 Board 65 Thtr 480 Del from £240 to £297* **Services** Lift Air con **Parking** 280 **Notes** LB ⊗ Civ Wed 414

Crowne Plaza London - Heathrow

★★★★ 77% HOTEL PLAN 1 A3

☎ 0871 942 9140
Stockley Rd UB7 9NA
e-mail: lonha.reservations@ihg.com
web: www.cpheathrowairporthotel.co.uk
dir: M4 junct 4 follow signs to Uxbridge on A408, hotel 400yds on left

This smart hotel is conveniently located for access to Heathrow Airport and the motorway network. Excellent facilities include versatile conference and meeting rooms, a spa and a leisure complex. Guests have the choice of two bars, both serving food, plus two restaurants. Air-conditioned bedrooms are furnished and decorated to a high standard and feature a comprehensive range of extra facilities.

Rooms 465 (204 fmly) (37 GF) ⚲ **Facilities** STV Wi-fi ⮿ HL ⓢ supervised ⓛ 9 Putt green Gym Steam room Sauna Physiotherapy **Conf** Class 120 Board 75 Thtr 200 **Services** Lift Air con **Parking** 800 **Notes** ⊗

Heathrow/Windsor Marriott

Marriott.

★★★★ 77% HOTEL

☎ 01753 544244
Ditton Rd SL3 8PT
e-mail: mhrs.lhrsl.ays@marriotthotels.com
web: www.heathrowwindsormarriott.co.uk
dir: M4 junct 5, follow 'Langley' signs, left at lights into Ditton Rd

Ideally located for access to Heathrow and the M4, this smart hotel offers a wide range of facilities. There is a well-appointed leisure centre, extensive conference facilities, a bar offering 24-hour snacks and light meals, and a restaurant with a wide-ranging cuisine. Spacious bedrooms are well equipped for both leisure and business guests.

Rooms 382 (120 fmly) (96 GF) (20 smoking) **S** £59-£199; **Facilities** STV FTV Wi-fi ⮿ ⓢ supervised ⓢ Gym Sauna Steam room **Conf** Class 220 Board 42 Thtr 400 Del from £179 to £205* **Services** Lift Air con **Parking** 482 **Notes** ⊗ Civ Wed 300

BEST WESTERN PLUS Park Grand London Heathrow

★★★★ 74% HOTEL PLAN 1 B3

☎ 020 7479 2255 & 3118 9600
449 Great West Rd TW5 0BY
e-mail: john@montcalm.co.uk

This is a brand new hotel in a convenient location just five miles from London Heathrow Airport and with easy access to Central London. The hotel is modern in style with spacious open-plan public areas including a stylish bar and restaurant. Bedrooms are also modern in style and are very comfortable, all fully air-conditioned and benefit from digital TV and complimentary Wi-fi. Parking is available on site.

Rooms 116 (14 fmly) ⚲ **Facilities** STV Wi-fi ⮿ HL Gym **Conf** Class 120 Board 65 Thtr 100 Del from £99 to £249 **Services** Lift Air con **Parking** 30 **Notes** ⊗ Civ Wed 200

DoubleTree by Hilton London Heathrow Airport

★★★★ 74% HOTEL PLAN 1 A3

☎ 0208 564 4450
Bath Rd, Cranford TW5 9QE
dir: M4 junct 3 follow signs to Heathrow Terminals 1, 2 & 3. Hotel on right of A4 Bath Rd

This well presented hotel is conveniently situated just three miles from Heathrow Airport. Bedrooms are located in a smart block and all are well appointed for both business and leisure guests; each has a flat-screen TV, climate control and good lighting. Arts Bar and Brasserie lead from a contemporary open-plan reception area. Chargeable car park on site.

Rooms 200 (18 fmly) (37 GF) ⚲ **Facilities** FTV Wi-fi ⮿ **Conf** Class 45 Board 40 Thtr 70 **Services** Lift Air con **Parking** 60 **Notes** ⊗ Civ Wed 65

Holiday Inn London - Heathrow

Holiday Inn

★★★★ 74% HOTEL PLAN 1 A3

☎ 020 8990 0000
Bath Rd, Corner Sipson Way UB7 0DP
e-mail: enquiries@hiheathrow.co.uk
web: www.holidayinnheathrow.co.uk
dir: Exit airport via main tunnel, at end left towards A4/Other Routes, follow signs for A4. At main lights (hotel visable) turn right, 1st left into Sipson Way

A property close to the terminals, with a frequent bus service to the airport. Public areas include a large brasserie-style restaurant and bar plus shop, mini gym and parking. Bedrooms are spacious and air conditioned, with facilities to suit the business traveller; there are a number of executive rooms available.

Rooms 230 (15 fmly) (58 GF) (23 smoking) 🐾
S £59-£299; **D** £59-£299* **Facilities** FTV Wi-fi ⌦ HL
Gym New Year **Conf** Class 50 Board 50 Thtr 130
Del from £99 to £299* **Services** Lift Air con
Parking 60 **Notes** LB Civ Wed 80

Holiday Inn London Heathrow M4 Jct 4

★★★★ 74% HOTEL PLAN 1 A3

☎ 0871 942 9095
Sipson Rd UB7 0JU
e-mail: reservations-heathrowm4@ihg.com
web: www.holidayinn.co.uk
dir: M4 junct 4, keep left, 1st left into Holloway Lane,
left at mini rdbt then left. For detailed directions
contact hotel

This landmark hotel can be seen for miles when
travelling on the M4 and is situated close to Heathrow
Airport; it is an ideal base for the airport and for
families visiting local attractions. The bedrooms are
air conditioned and well equipped. There are two
restaurants, a small gym and ample parking.

Rooms 616 (120 fmly) (25 smoking) 🐾 **S** £104-£325;
D £104-£325* **Facilities** STV Wi-fi ⌦ HL Gym Xmas
New Year **Conf** Class 80 Board 80 Thtr 180
Del from £129 to £200* **Services** Lift Air con
Parking 450 **Notes** LB ⊗

Novotel London Heathrow

★★★★ 72% HOTEL PLAN 1 A3

☎ 01895 431431
Cherry Ln UB7 9HB
e-mail: H1551-gm@accor.com
web: www.novotel.co.uk
dir: M4 junct 4, follow Uxbridge signs on A408. Keep
left, take 2nd exit off traffic island into Cherry Ln
signed West Drayton. Hotel on left

Conveniently located for Heathrow Airport and the
motorway network, this modern hotel provides
comfortable accommodation. The large, airy indoor
atrium creates a sense of space in the public areas,
which include an all-day restaurant and bar, meeting
rooms, fitness centre and swimming pool. Ample
secure parking is available.

Rooms 178 (178 fmly) (10 GF) **Facilities** STV Wi-fi ⌦
HL ⊗ Gym **Conf** Class 100 Board 90 Thtr 250
Services Lift Air con **Parking** 100 **Notes** Civ Wed 160

Park Inn Heathrow

★★★★ 72% HOTEL PLAN 1 A3

☎ 020 8759 6611
Bath Rd UB7 0DU
e-mail: info.heathrow@rezidorparkinn.com
dir: M4 junct 4, follow signs for T1 & 3. Hotel on left,
take exit on left up ramp

Ideally located for Heathrow Airports and central
London, this hotel is spacious, purpose-built and
offers a range of well-appointed bedrooms,
conference rooms, a choice of bars and a fully-
equipped health club. The restaurant offers varied
dining ideal for a transient market, and there is
plenty of parking available.

Rooms 895 (121 fmly) (95 GF) (95 smoking) 🐾
S £65-£139; **D** £65-£139 **Facilities** STV Wi-fi ⌦ ⊗
Gym Xmas New Year **Conf** Class 360 Board 120
Thtr 700 **Services** Lift Air con **Parking** 475 **Notes** ⊗
Civ Wed 500

The Continental Hotel

★★★ 81% ● HOTEL PLAN 1 B2

☎ 020 8572 3131 & 8538 5883
29-31 Lampton Rd TW3 1JA
e-mail: reservations@thecontinental-hotel.com
dir: A4, right onto A3006, left onto A3005 then left
onto Lampton Rd

This hotel enjoys a prime location just a few minutes
walk from Hounslow Central Line; central London can
be reached in 40 minutes. The bedrooms are air
conditioned, and complimentary broadband is
available. The bedroom en suites are marble-clad wet
rooms with power showers. The on-site Golds Gym has
a 21-metre indoor pool, a state-of-the-art fitness
centre and beauty treatment rooms.

Rooms 70 (8 fmly) 🐾 **Facilities** Spa STV FTV Wi-fi ⊗
Gym ♬ Xmas New Year **Services** Lift Air con
Parking 70 **Notes** LB ⊗

Holiday Inn London Heathrow Ariel

★★★ 77% HOTEL PLAN 1 A3

☎ 0871 942 9040
118 Bath Rd UB3 5AJ
e-mail: reservations-heathrow@ihg.com
web: www.holidayinn.co.uk
dir: M4 junct 4, take spur road to Heathrow Airport,
1st left onto A4 Bath Rd, through 3 sets of lights.
Hotel on left

Located close to Heathrow Airport with good public
transport links to all terminals, this well sited hotel is
suitable for both the business and leisure traveller.
Public areas benefit from a spacious lounge bar area,
brasserie-style restaurant and extensive conference
facilities. Ample secure parking is an additional plus.

Rooms 184 (18 smoking) **Facilities** STV Wi-fi Xmas
Conf Class 35 Board 25 Thtr 50 **Services** Lift Air con
Parking 100 **Notes** ⊗ Civ Wed 50

Thistle London Heathrow

★★★ 75% HOTEL PLAN 1 A3

☎ 0871 376 9021
Bath Rd, Longford UB7 0EQ
e-mail: londonheathrow@thistle.co.uk
web: www.thistlehotels.com/londonheathrow
dir: M25 junct 14 signed Terminal 4 & Cargo Area.
Right at 1st rdbt signed Heathrow. Left at lights onto
A3044 signed Colnbrook & Longford

Located adjacent to the airport, with the benefit of
secure parking and regular coach transfers, this long
established hotel provides a range of well equipped
bedrooms for both the business and leisure guest.
Imaginative food is available in an attractive
restaurant and comprehensive breakfasts are served
in a separate first-floor dining room.

Rooms 264 (3 fmly) (132 GF) **S** £58.80-£180;
D £58.80-£180* **Facilities** FTV Wi-fi HL Use of nearby
health club Xmas New Year **Conf** Class 300 Board 25
Thtr 700 Del from £99 to £180* **Services** Air con
Parking 450 **Notes** ⊗ Civ Wed 540

Days Hotel Hounslow

★★★ 72% HOTEL PLAN 1 B2

☎ 020 8538 1230
8-10 Lampton Rd TW3 1JL
e-mail: gm@dhhounslow.com
dir: A4 (Bath Rd), A3006, into Lampton Rd (A3005)

A purpose-built hotel situated in the centre of
Hounslow, within walking distance of the tube station
and with easy access to the motorway network. The
accommodation is comfortable and offers a range of
amenities. The public areas are light and airy, and
parking is available.

Rooms 96 (11 fmly) (4 GF) **S** £79-£109; **D** £89-£149
(incl. bkfst)* **Facilities** FTV Wi-fi ♬ Xmas New Year
Conf Class 50 Board 60 Thtr 100 Del from £129 to
£159* **Services** Lift Air con **Parking** 20 **Notes** LB ⊗

H

H

HEATHROW AIRPORT (LONDON) *continued*

Comfort Hotel Heathrow

★★★ 71% HOTEL PLAN 1 A3

☎ 020 8573 6162
Shepiston Ln UB3 1LP
e-mail: info@comfortheathrow.com
web: www.comfortheathrow.com
dir: M4 junct 4, follow signs to Hayes & Shepiston Lane, hotel approx 1m, adjacent to fire station

This hotel is a short drive from the airport, and guests may prefer its quieter location. There is a frequent bus service, which runs to and from the hotel throughout the day. Bedrooms are thoughtfully equipped and many benefit from air conditioning.

Rooms 184 (7 fmly) (50 GF) ↖ **S** £37-£129; **D** £37-£139* **Facilities** FTV Wi-fi ⏰ Gym **Conf** Class 72 Board 90 Thtr 150 Del from £85 to £145 **Services** Lift **Parking** 120 **Notes** LB ⊗ Civ Wed 90

Ibis London Heathrow Airport

BUDGET HOTEL PLAN 1 A3

☎ 020 8759 4888
112/114 Bath Rd UB3 5AL
e-mail: HO794@accor.com
web: www.ibishotel.com/heathrow
dir: Follow Heathrow Terminals 1, 2 & 3 signs, then onto spur road, exit at sign for A4/Central London. Hotel 0.5m on left

Modern, budget hotel offering comfortable accommodation in bright and practical bedrooms. Breakfast is self-service and dinner is available in the restaurant. See also the Hotel Groups pages.

Rooms 351 (24 fmly) (39 GF) **Conf** Class 16 Board 16 Thtr 20

Premier Inn Hayes Heathrow

BUDGET HOTEL PLAN 1 A4

☎ 0871 527 8504
362 Uxbridge Rd UB4 0HF
web: www.premierinn.com
dir: M4 junct 3, A312 N straight across next rdbt onto dual carriageway, at A4020 junct turn left, hotel 100yds on right

High quality, budget accommodation ideal for both families and business travellers. Spacious, en suite bedrooms feature tea and coffee making facilities, and Freeview TV in most hotels. Internet access and Wi-fi are available for a small fee. The adjacent family restaurant features a wide and varied menu. See also the Hotel Groups pages.

Rooms 62

Premier Inn Heathrow Airport (Bath Road)

BUDGET HOTEL PLAN 1 A3

☎ 0871 527 8508
15 Bath Rd TW6 2AB
web: www.premierinn.com
dir: M4 junct 4, follow signs for Heathrow Terminals 1, 2 & 3. Left onto Bath Rd signed A4/London. Hotel on right after 0.5m

Rooms 590

Premier Inn Heathrow Airport (M4 Jct 4)

BUDGET HOTEL PLAN 1 A3

☎ 0871 527 8510
Shepiston Ln, Heathrow Airport UB3 1RW
web: www.premierinn.com
dir: M4 junct 4 take 3rd exit off rdbt. Hotel on right

Rooms 134

Premier Inn Heathrow Airport Terminal 5

BUDGET HOTEL

☎ 0871 527 8508
Heathrow Longford T5, 420 Bath Rd, Longford UB7 0RF
dir: M25 junct 14, follow A3113/Heathrow T4 & Cargo signs. At rdbt 1st left onto A3044, at next rdbt 3rd exit signed Longford. Hotel approx 250yds on left

Rooms 400

Renaissance London Heathrow Hotel

AA Advertised

☎ 020 8897 6363
Bath Rd TW6 2AQ
e-mail: re3@renaissanceheathrow.co.uk
web: www.renaissancelondonheathrow.co.uk
dir: M4 junct 4 take spur road towards airport, then 2nd left. At rdbt, 2nd exit signed 'Renaissance Hotel'. Hotel adjacent to Customs House

This spacious hotel is located on the perimeter of Heathrow Airport with spectacular views of the main runway, and is within easy reach of Windsor and motorway and rail networks to London. The hotel has excellent conference and leisure facilities.

Rooms 649 (56 GF) (30 smoking) ↖ **S** £72.25-£189; **D** £72.25-£189 **Facilities** STV Wi-fi ⏰ Gym Steam room Solarium Fitness studio Beauty & massage treatment Personal trainer Xmas **Conf** Class 300 Board 80 Thtr 450 Del from £169 to £229 **Services** Lift Air con **Parking** 700 **Notes** ⊗ Civ Wed 150

Sofitel London Heathrow

AA Advertised

☎ 020 8757 7777 & 020 8757 7725
Terminal 5, Wentworth Dr, London Heathrow Airport TW6 2GD
e-mail: H6214@sofitel.com
web: www.sofitelheathrow.com
dir: M25, junct 14

This is the only Heathrow Airport hotel with direct access to Terminal 5 via a covered walkway and Terminals 1, 2, 3 and 4 via courtesy of the Heathrow Express/Connect rail connection. It is only 21 minutes from Central London by train. Sofitel London Heathrow boasts 605 non-smoking bedrooms including 27 suites, 45 meeting rooms, 2 restaurants, 2 bars and a tea salon as well as private dining options. The hotel also offers a hair salon, a state-of-the-art health spa and gym as well as on-site car park.

Rooms 605 (38 GF) ↖ **Facilities** Spa STV FTV Wi-fi Gym **Conf** Class 820 Board 80 Thtr 1200 **Services** Lift Air con **Parking** 360 **Notes** ⊗ Civ Wed 220

HEDDON-ON-THE-WALL   Map 21 NZ16
Northumberland

INSPECTORS' CHOICE

Close House
★★★★ ◉◉ HOTEL

☎ 01661 852255
NE15 0HT
e-mail: reservations@closehouse.co.uk
web: www.closehouse.co.uk
dir: A1 N, A69 W. Follow B6528 at junct turn left, hotel signed

Dating back to 1779, this is a magnificent country house set in 300 acres of woodland and parkland in the secluded and beautiful Tyne Valley. It is just 20 minutes from Newcastle. The hotel provides accommodation designed to make a stay relaxing and special. All the bedrooms are equipped with high-tech mod cons. There is a magnificent restaurant and bar, and 24-hour room service is also available. There is a golf course in the grounds.

Rooms 31 (12 annexe) (6 GF) ✆ **Facilities** STV FTV Wi-fi ⊳ ⌁ 36 Putt green Driving range Xmas New Year **Conf** Class 30 Board 30 Thtr 140 **Services** Air con **Parking** 87 **Notes** LB Civ Wed 100

HELLIDON   Map 11 SP55
Northamptonshire

Hellidon Lakes Golf & Spa Hotel   QHOTELS
★★★★ 75% HOTEL

☎ 01327 262550
NN11 6GG
e-mail: hellidonlakes@qhotels.co.uk
web: www.qhotels.co.uk
dir: Off A361 between Daventry & Banbury, signed

Some 220 acres of beautiful countryside, which include 27 holes of golf and 12 lakes, combine to form a rather spectacular backdrop to this impressive hotel. Bedroom styles vary, from ultra smart, modern rooms through to those in the original wing that offer

superb views. There is an extensive range of facilities available, from meeting rooms to a swimming pool, gym and ten-pin bowling. Golfers of all levels can try some of the world's most challenging courses on the indoor golf simulator.

Rooms 110 (5 fmly) ✆ **S** £75-£179; **D** £85-£189 (incl. bkfst)* **Facilities** Spa FTV Wi-fi ⊳ ⌚ ⌁ 27 ⌣ Putt green Fishing ⤵ Gym Beauty therapist Indoor smart golf 10-pin bowling Steam room Coarse fishing lake Xmas New Year **Conf** Class 150 Board 80 Thtr 300 Del from £110 to £175 **Services** Lift **Parking** 200 **Notes** LB Civ Wed 220

HELMSLEY   Map 19 SE68
North Yorkshire

INSPECTORS' CHOICE

Feversham Arms Hotel & Verbena Spa
★★★★ HOTEL

☎ 01439 770766
1 High St YO62 5AG
e-mail: info@fevershamarmshotel.com
web: www.fevershamarmshotel.com
dir: A168 (signed Thirsk) A1, A170 or A64 (signed York) from A1 to York North, B1363 to Helmsley. Hotel 125mtrs from Market Place

This long established hotel lies just round the corner from the main square, and under caring ownership proves to be a refined operation, yet without airs and graces. There are several lounge areas and a high-ceilinged conservatory restaurant. The bedrooms, including four air-conditioned poolside suites (some with wood-burners) and spa suites with balconies or French balconies, all have their own individual character and decor. Expect Egyptian cotton sheets, duck down duvets and Bang and Olufsen TVs with DVD and CD player. The spa offers a comprehensive range of pampering treatments. The AA Rosette award for the Feversham Arms is currently suspended due to a change of chef. AA Rosettes may be awarded once

the inspectors have assessed the food created by the new kitchen regime.

Rooms 33 (9 fmly) (8 GF) **Facilities** Spa STV FTV Wi-fi ⌁ Sauna Saunarium Xmas New Year **Conf** Class 20 Board 24 Thtr 35 **Services** Lift **Parking** 50 **Notes** Civ Wed 50

Black Swan Hotel
★★★★ 77% ◉◉ HOTEL

☎ 01439 770466
Market Place YO62 5BJ
e-mail: enquiries@blackswan-helmsley.co.uk
web: www.blackswan-helmsley.co.uk
dir: A1 junct 49, A168, A170 east, hotel 14m from Thirsk

People have been visiting this establishment for over 200 years and it has become a landmark that dominates the market square. The hotel is renowned for its hospitality and friendliness; many of the staff are long-serving and dedicated. The bedrooms are stylish and include a junior suite and feature rooms. Dinner in the award-winning restaurant is the highlight of any stay. The hotel has a Tearoom and Patisserie that is open daily.

Rooms 45 (4 fmly) ✆ **S** £150-£222; **D** £198-£270 (incl. bkfst & dinner)* **Facilities** STV FTV Wi-fi Xmas New Year **Conf** Class 30 Board 26 Thtr 50 Del from £165* **Parking** 50 **Notes** Civ Wed 130

H

HELSTON   Map 2 SW62
Cornwall

Premier Inn Helston

BUDGET HOTEL

☎ 0871 527 8512
Clodgey Ln TR13 8FZ
web: www.premierinn.com
dir: A39 towards Falmouth. Right onto A394 towards
Helston, 8m. At rdbt 1st exit (Helston bypass) signed
Penzance (A394)/Lizard. Hotel at next rdbt on left (NB
for Sat Nav use TR13 0QD)

High quality, budget accommodation ideal for both
families and business travellers. Spacious, en suite
bedrooms feature tea and coffee making facilities,
and Freeview TV in most hotels. Internet access and
Wi-fi are available for a small fee. The adjacent
family restaurant features a wide and varied menu.
See also the Hotel Groups pages.

Rooms 50

HEMEL HEMPSTEAD   Map 6 TL00
Hertfordshire

Holiday Inn Hemel Hempstead

★★★ 79% HOTEL

☎ 0871 942 9041
Breakspear Way HP2 4UA
e-mail: reservations-hemelhempsteadm1@ihg.com
web: www.holidayinn.co.uk/hemelhempstead
dir: M1 junct 8, over rdbt, 1st left after BP garage

A modern, purpose-built hotel that is convenient for
the motorway networks. Bedrooms are spacious and
well suited to the business traveller. Executive rooms
and public areas are particularly well styled. Other
facilities include a leisure club and a range of
meeting rooms.

Rooms 144 (43 fmly) (42 GF) **S** £59-£155;
D £59-£155* **Facilities** Spa STV Wi-fi ↕ ⌾
supervised Gym Beauty treaments & physiotherapy by
appointment **Conf** Class 22 Board 30 Thtr 80
Services Lift Air con **Parking** 200 **Notes** LB ⊗
Civ Wed 60

BEST WESTERN The Watermill

★★★ 74% HOTEL

☎ 01442 349955
London Rd, Bourne End HP1 2RJ
e-mail: info@hotelwatermill.co.uk
web: www.hotelwatermill.co.uk
dir: From M25 & M1 follow signs to Aylesbury on A41,
A4251 to Bourne End. Hotel 0.25m on right

In the heart of the county this modern hotel has been
built around an old flour mill on the banks of the
River Bulbourne with water meadows adjacent. The
thoughtfully equipped, contemporary bedrooms are
located in three annexes situated around the complex.
A good range of air-conditioned conference and
meeting rooms complement the lounge bar and
restaurant.

Rooms 71 (71 annexe) (10 fmly) (35 GF) (8 smoking)
↾ **S** £54.95-£94.95; **D** £59.95-£99.95 (incl. bkfst)*
Facilities STV FTV Wi-fi Fishing Xmas New Year
Conf Class 150 Board 125 Thtr 200 Del from £135 to
£150* **Parking** 100 **Notes** ⊗ Civ Wed 180

The Bobsleigh Hotel

★★★ 74% HOTEL

☎ 0844 879 9033
Hempstead Rd, Bovingdon HP3 0DS
e-mail: bobsleigh@macdonald-hotels.co.uk
web: www.macdonald-hotels.co.uk
dir: M1 junct 8, A414 signed Hemel Hempstead. At
Plough Rdbt follow railway station signs. Pass rail
station on left, straight on at rdbt, under 2 bridges.
Left onto B4505 (Box Lane) signed Chesham. Hotel
1.5m on left

Located just outside the town, the hotel enjoys a
pleasant rural setting, yet is within easy reach of
local transport links and the motorway network.
Bedrooms vary in size; all are modern in style. There
is an open-plan lobby, a bar area and an attractive
dining room with views over the garden. Macdonald
Hotels is the AA Hotel Group of the Year 2013-14.

Rooms 46 (14 annexe) (6 fmly) (30 GF) ↾
Facilities FTV Wi-fi New Year **Conf** Class 50 Board 40
Thtr 150 **Parking** 60 **Notes** Civ Wed 100

Premier Inn Hemel Hempstead Central

BUDGET HOTEL

☎ 0871 527 8514
Moor End Rd HP1 1DL
web: www.premierinn.com
dir: M1 junct 8, A414, follow town centre signs. Right
at 1st mini rdbt, right at 2nd mini rdbt into Seldon
Hill Rd, follow Riverside car park sings (footbridge to
hotel from floor 3). (NB for Sat Nav use HP1 1BT)

High quality, budget accommodation ideal for both
families and business travellers. Spacious, en suite
bedrooms feature tea and coffee making facilities,
and Freeview TV in most hotels. Internet access and
Wi-fi are available for a small fee. The adjacent
family restaurant features a wide and varied menu.
See also the Hotel Groups pages.

Rooms 113

Premier Inn Hemel Hempstead West

BUDGET HOTEL

☎ 0871 527 8516
A41 Service Area, Bourne End HP1 2SB
web: www.premierinn.com
dir: M25 junct 20, A41 exit at services. Or from M1
junct 8, A414, A41, exit at services

Rooms 61

HENLEY-ON-THAMES
Oxfordshire
Map 5 SU78

Hotel du Vin Henley-on-Thames

★★★★ 76% ◎ ◎　TOWN HOUSE HOTEL

☎ 01491 848400
New St RG9 2BP
e-mail: info.henley@hotelduvin.com
web: www.hotelduvin.com
dir: M4 junct 8/9 signed High Wycombe, 2nd exit onto A404 in 2m. A4130 to Henley, over bridge, through lights, into Hart St, right into Bell St, right into New St, hotel on right

Situated just 50 yards from the water's edge, this hotel retains the character and much of the architecture of its former life as a brewery. Food, and naturally wine, take on a strong focus here and guests will find an interesting mix of dishes to choose from; there are three private dining rooms where the fermentation room and old malt house once were; alfresco dining is popular when the weather permits. Bedrooms provide comfort, style and a good range of facilities including power showers. Parking is available and there is a drop-off point in the courtyard.

Rooms 43 (4 fmly) (4 GF) 🐾 **Facilities** STV FTV Wi-fi ↘ Xmas New Year **Conf** Class 20 Board 36 Thtr 56 **Services** Air con **Parking** 46 **Notes** Civ Wed 60

Milsoms Henley-on-Thames

RESTAURANT WITH ROOMS

☎ 01491 845780 & 845789
20 Market Place RG9 2AH
e-mail: henley@milsomshotel.co.uk
dir: In centre of town, close to town hall

The seven en suite bedrooms are located in a listed building above the Loch Fyne Restaurant in Henley's Market Place. Each bedroom is individually appointed and equipped to meet the needs of the modern traveller; particular care has been taken to incorporate original features into the contemporary design. The restaurant has a commitment to offer ethically sourced seafood.

Rooms 7 (2 fmly)

HEREFORD
Herefordshire
Map 10 SO54

See also **Leominster**

Holme Lacy House Hotel

Warner Leisure Hotels
JUST FOR GROWN-UPS

★★★★ 72% ◎ ◎　COUNTRY HOUSE HOTEL

☎ 01432 870870
Holme Lacy HR2 6LP
web: www.holmelacyhouse.co.uk
dir: B4399 at Holme Lacy, take lane opposite college. Hotel 500mtrs on right

This is a grand Grade I listed mansion with a rich history, just a short drive from Hereford and in a peaceful location, set in twenty acres of superb parkland in the heart of the Wye Valley. The well-appointed bedrooms are comfortable and vary in size and style. There's plenty to do here, with a full daily entertainment programmes, an indoor pool, and health and beauty treatments. The three restaurants provide carefully selected menus of quality cuisine. Exclusively for adults (above 21 years old).

Rooms 180 (150 annexe) (53 GF) 🐾 **Facilities** Spa FTV Wi-fi ❄ ♨ Putt green Fishing 🏌 Gym Archery Rifle shooting Aquafit Yoga Fencing ♫ Xmas New Year **Services** Lift **Parking** 200 **Notes** ⊗ No children 21yrs

H

Castle
HOUSE

AA ◎ ◎

Tucked away in an elegant quarter of Hereford, just a two minute walk from the magnificent Cathedral, Castle House is an unique, family-owned boutique hotel. The most luxurious hotel in Hereford.

A Grade II listed building, once frequented by Elgar, Castle House has 24 individually designed suites and bedrooms, eight of which are in Number 25, a Georgian townhouse just yards from the hotel. The Castle Restaurant and Bistro offer the best dining in Herefordshire; they are the domain of one of England's premier chefs Claire Nicholls, who sources her ingredients from local producers in and around Herefordshire, as well as the hotel's nearby farm at Ballingham.

With its civil licence, Castle House is the perfect place for a wedding or a special event. It is an ideal base from which to explore this part of England. From here you can visit the historical city of Hereford with its world-famous Mappa Mundi and Chained Library and the natural beauty of the Herefordshire and Wye Valley countryside beyond.

Castle House, Castle Street, Hereford, England HR1 2NW
Tel:+44 (0)1432 356321　　Fax:+44 (0)1432 365909
info@castlehse.co.uk　　www.castlehse.co.uk

Follow us...　Like us...

H

HEREFORD *continued*

Castle House

★★★ 86% ◉◉ HOTEL

☎ 01432 356321
Castle St HR1 2NW
e-mail: info@castlehse.co.uk
web: www.castlehse.co.uk
dir: Follow signs to City Centre East. At junct of Commercial Rd & Union St follow hotel signs

Enjoying a prime city centre location, with a terraced garden leading to the castle moat, this delightful Grade II-listed Georgian mansion is the epitome of elegance and sophistication. The character bedrooms are equipped with every luxury to ensure a memorable stay and are complemented perfectly by the well-proportioned and restful lounge and bar, together with the elegant topiary-themed restaurant where award-winning modern British cuisine is served.

Rooms 24 (8 annexe) (4 GF) ☇ **Facilities** STV FTV Wi-fi ☇ Free membership at local spa Xmas New Year **Services** Lift **Parking** 12 **Notes** ⊗ Civ Wed 50

See advert on page 207

Three Counties Hotel

★★★ 78% HOTEL

☎ 01432 299955
Belmont Rd HR2 7BP
e-mail: enquiries@threecountieshotel.co.uk
web: www.threecountieshotel.co.uk
dir: On A465 (Abergavenny road)

Just a mile west of the city centre, this large, privately owned, modern complex has well-equipped, spacious bedrooms; many are located in separate single-storey buildings around the extensive car park. There is a spacious, comfortable lounge, a traditional bar and an attractive restaurant.

Rooms 60 (32 annexe) (4 fmly) (46 GF) **S** £68-£78; **D** £84-£92.50 (incl. bkfst)* **Facilities** STV FTV Wi-fi **Conf** Class 200 Board 120 Thtr 450 Del from £95 to £110* **Parking** 250 **Notes** LB Civ Wed 350

Premier Inn Hereford

BUDGET HOTEL

☎ 0871 527 8518
Holmer Rd, Holmer HR4 9RS
web: www.premierinn.com
dir: From N: M5 junct 7, A4103 to Worcester. M50 junct 4, A49 (Leominster road). Hotel 800yds on left

High quality, budget accommodation ideal for both families and business travellers. Spacious, en suite bedrooms feature tea and coffee making facilities, and Freeview TV in most hotels. Internet access and Wi-fi are available for a small fee. The adjacent family restaurant features a wide and varied menu. See also the Hotel Groups pages.

Rooms 81

HERNE BAY   Map 7 TR16
Kent

Premier Inn Canterbury North/Herne Bay

BUDGET HOTEL

☎ 0871 527 8520
Blacksole Farm, Margate Rd CT6 6LA
web: www.premierinn.com
dir: From M2 junct 7 follow Canterbury signs, A299 signed Ramsgate/Margate. Exit at Broomfield & Beltinge. Hotel just off rdbt

High quality, budget accommodation ideal for both families and business travellers. Spacious, en suite bedrooms feature tea and coffee making facilities, and Freeview TV in most hotels. Internet access and Wi-fi are available for a small fee. The adjacent family restaurant features a wide and varied menu. See also the Hotel Groups pages.

Rooms 50

HERTFORD   Map 6 TL31
Hertfordshire

White Horse Hotel

★★★ 78% HOTEL

☎ 01992 586791
Hertingfordbury Rd, Hertingfordbury SG14 2LB
e-mail: bgray@aquariushotels.co.uk
dir: From A10 follow A414 signs. From Hertford under rail bridge, over rdbt, left at next rdbt, hotel 300yds on right

The Georgian façade of this former coaching inn belies a much older interior with oak beams dating back 400 years. Many of the spacious bedrooms overlook the picturesque gardens. Public rooms include a beamed bar with its open fireplace and a spacious conservatory restaurant.

Rooms 42 (4 fmly) **Facilities** FTV Wi-fi Xmas New Year **Conf** Class 30 Board 26 Thtr 60 **Services** Air con **Parking** 50 **Notes** ⊗ Civ Wed 75

HESWALL   Map 15 SJ28
Merseyside

Premier Inn Wirral (Heswall)

BUDGET HOTEL

☎ 0871 527 9178
Chester Rd, Gayton CH60 3SD
web: www.premierinn.com
dir: M53 junct 4, A5137 signed Heswall. In 3m left at next rdbt, hotel on left

High quality, budget accommodation ideal for both families and business travellers. Spacious, en suite bedrooms feature tea and coffee making facilities, and Freeview TV in most hotels. Internet access and Wi-fi are available for a small fee. The adjacent family restaurant features a wide and varied menu. See also the Hotel Groups pages.

Rooms 37

Save on hotels. Book at **theAA.com/hotel**

HER – HEX 209 ENGLAND

HETHERSETT
Norfolk   Map 13 TG10

Park Farm Hotel
★★★★ 77% ◉ HOTEL

☎ 01603 810264
NR9 3DL
e-mail: enq@parkfarm-hotel.co.uk
web: www.parkfarm-hotel.co.uk
dir: 5m S of Norwich, exit A11 onto B1172

An elegant Georgian farmhouse set in landscaped grounds surrounded by open countryside. The property has been owned and run by the Gowing family since 1958. Bedrooms are pleasantly decorated and tastefully furnished; some rooms have patio doors with a sun terrace. Public rooms include a stylish conservatory, a lounge bar, a smart restaurant and superb leisure facilities.

Rooms 53 (16 annexe) (15 fmly) (26 GF) ⬆
Facilities Spa FTV Wi-fi ☜ supervised Gym Beauty salon Hairdressing Xmas New Year **Conf** Class 50 Board 50 Thtr 120 **Parking** 150 **Notes** LB ⊗ Civ Wed 100

HETTON
North Yorkshire   Map 18 SD95

INSPECTORS' CHOICE

The Angel Inn
◉ ◉ ◉ RESTAURANT WITH ROOMS

☎ 01756 730263
BD23 6LT
e-mail: info@angelhetton.co.uk
dir: B6265 from Skipton towards Grassington. At Rylstone turn left by pond, follow signs to Hetton

This roadside inn is steeped in history; parts of the building go back over 500 years. The restaurant and bar are in the main building which has ivy and green canopies at the front. Food is a highlight of any stay, offering excellent ingredients skilfully prepared and carefully presented. The large and stylish bedrooms are across the road in a converted barn which has great views of the Dales, its own wine cave and private parking.

Rooms 9

HEXHAM
Northumberland   Map 21 NY96

Langley Castle Hotel
★★★★ 81% ◉ ◉ HOTEL

☎ 01434 688888
Langley NE47 5LU
e-mail: manager@langleycastle.com
web: www.langleycastle.com
dir: From A69 S on A686 for 2m. Hotel on right

Langley is a magnificent 14th-century fortified castle, with its own chapel, set in ten acres of parkland. There is an award-winning restaurant, a comfortable drawing room and a cosy bar. Bedrooms are furnished with period pieces and most feature window seats. Restored buildings in the grounds have been converted into very stylish Castle View bedrooms.

Rooms 27 (18 annexe) (8 fmly) (9 GF) ⬆
S £119.50-£209.50; **D** £155-£277 (incl. bkfst)*
Facilities STV Wi-fi ↕ HL Xmas **Conf** Class 60 Board 40 Thtr 120 Del from £185 to £220*
Services Air con **Parking** 70 **Notes** LB ⊗ Civ Wed 120

De Vere Slaley Hall
★★★★ 80% ◉ HOTEL

☎ 0871 222 4688
Slaley NE47 0BX
e-mail: slaley.hall@devere-hotels.com
web: www.devere.co.uk
dir: A1 from S to A68 link road follow signs for Slaley Hall

One thousand acres of Northumbrian forest and parkland, two championship golf courses and indoor leisure facilities can all be found here. Spacious bedrooms are fully air conditioned, equipped with a range of extras and the deluxe rooms offer excellent standards. Public rooms feature a number of lounges and dining options, including the fine-dining Dukes Grill, informal Claret Jug and the impressive main restaurant that overlooks the golf course.

Rooms 142 (18 fmly) (37 GF) ⬆ **Facilities** Spa FTV Wi-fi ☜ supervised ♨ 36 Putt green Gym Quad bikes Archery Clay pigeon shooting 4x4 driving Xmas New Year **Conf** Class 220 Board 150 Thtr 300 **Services** Lift Air con **Parking** 500 **Notes** Civ Wed 250

BEST WESTERN Beaumont Hotel
★★★ 83% HOTEL

☎ 01434 602331
Beaumont St NE46 3LT
e-mail: reservations@beaumonthotelhexham.co.uk
dir: A69 towards town centre

In a region steeped in history, this family-run hotel is located in the centre of Hexham, overlooking the park and 7th-century abbey. The hotel has two bars, a comfortable reception lounge and a first-floor restaurant. Bedrooms are a mix of traditional and contemporary; the South Wing rooms are spacious with a more contemporary feel and have flat-screen TVs.

Rooms 34 (3 fmly) **S** £90-£100; **D** £130-£150 (incl. bkfst)* **Facilities** FTV Wi-fi ↕ Xmas **Conf** Class 60 Board 40 Thtr 100 **Services** Lift **Parking** 16 **Notes** LB ⊗ Closed 25-26 Dec Civ Wed 50

H

H

HICKSTEAD
West Sussex
Map 6 TQ22

The Hickstead Hotel
★★★ 78% COUNTRY HOUSE HOTEL

CLASSIC LODGES
the sign of a great hotel

☎ 01444 248023
Jobs Ln, Bolney RH17 5NZ
e-mail: info.hickstead@classiclodges.co.uk
web: www.classiclodges.co.uk
dir: M23, A23, becomes A2300. Follow Burgess Hill/
Hickstead signs. Left at top of slip road. Follow brown
hotel sign on left

This hotel is located in seven acres of grounds not far
from the main London to Brighton road. The smart
bedrooms have satellite TV, free Wi-fi and power
showers. Guests can choose to eat in the Oak Tree
Bistro or in the Grange Bar. The indoor leisure centre
is very popular. The hotel is close to a business park
and within easy striking distance of the south coast.

Rooms 52 (5 fmly) (26 GF) **S** £80-£120; **D** £90-£140
(incl. bkfst) **Facilities** STV FTV Wi-fi Xmas New Year
Conf Class 60 Board 55 Thtr 150 Del from £125 to
£155 **Parking** 100 **Notes** LB ⊗ Civ Wed 80

HIGHAM
Derbyshire
Map 16 SK35

Santo's Higham Farm Hotel
★★★ 79% ⊛ HOTEL

☎ 01773 833812
Main Rd DE55 6EH
e-mail: reception@santoshighamfarm.co.uk
web: www.santoshighamfarm.co.uk
dir: M1 junct 28, A38 towards Derby, then A61
towards Chesterfield. Onto B6013 towards Belper,
hotel 300yds on right

With panoramic views across the rolling Amber Valley,
this 15th-century crook barn and farmhouse has been
expertly restored and extended. There's an Italian
wing and an international wing of themed bedrooms

and mini suites. Freshly prepared dishes, especially
fish, are available in Guiseppe's restaurant. This
hotel makes an ideal romantic hideaway.

Rooms 29 (2 fmly) (7 GF) ↟ **S** £82-£225;
D £123-£266 (incl. bkfst)* **Facilities** FTV Wi-fi Xmas
New Year **Conf** Class 40 Board 34 Thtr 100 Del £105*
Parking 100 **Notes** LB ⊗ Civ Wed 100

HIGHCLIFFE
Dorset
Map 5 SZ29

Premier Inn Christchurch/ Highcliffe
BUDGET HOTEL

Premier Inn

☎ 0871 527 9276
266 Lymington Rd BH23 5ET
web: www.premierinn.com
dir: From A35 (Christchurch rdbt) onto A337 towards
New Milton & Lymington. Approx 2m hotel on left

High quality, budget accommodation ideal for both
families and business travellers. Spacious, en suite
bedrooms feature tea and coffee making facilities,
and Freeview TV in most hotels. Internet access and
Wi-fi are available for a small fee. The adjacent
family restaurant features a wide and varied menu.
See also the Hotel Groups pages.

Rooms 62

HIGH WYCOMBE
Buckinghamshire
Map 5 SU89

Holiday Inn High Wycombe
★★★ 78% HOTEL

Holiday Inn

☎ 0871 942 9042
Handy Cross HP11 1TL
e-mail: reception-highwycombe@ihg.com
web: www.hihighwycombehotel.co.uk
dir: M40 junct 4, take A4010 towards Aylesbury

A modern, purpose-built hotel, convenient for the
motorway networks. Bedrooms are spacious and well-
equipped for the business traveller and feature a
comprehensive range of extra facilities. Public rooms
are particularly stylish, while the Academy offers a
full range of meeting and conference services.

Rooms 112 (7 fmly) (57 GF) **S** £69-£229;
D £79-£239* **Facilities** FTV Wi-fi HL **Conf** Class 72
Board 50 Thtr 140 Del from £110 to £210*
Services Air con **Parking** 200 **Notes** LB ⊗
Civ Wed 120

Fox Country Inn
★★★ 68% HOTEL

☎ 0845 643 9933
Ibstone HP14 3XT
e-mail: info@foxcountryinn.co.uk
dir: M40 junct 5 follow signs to Ibstone, hotel 1.5m on
left

This stylish modern hotel enjoys a peaceful rural
location on the outskirts of High Wycombe. The
modern bedrooms are all attractively presented and
have a host of thoughtful little extras. Free Wi-fi is
available throughout the hotel. The bar and
restaurant have a contemporary open-plan style and
food is served throughout the day in the bar and on
the terrace.

Rooms 18 (2 fmly) (10 GF) **Facilities** FTV Wi-fi ♫
Xmas New Year **Conf** Class 40 Board 35 Thtr 45
Parking 45 **Notes** Civ Wed 200

Premier Inn High Wycombe
BUDGET HOTEL

Premier Inn

☎ 0871 527 8522
Thanstead Farm, London Rd, Loudwater HP10 9YL
web: www.premierinn.com
dir: M40 junct 3, A40 towards High Wycombe

High quality, budget accommodation ideal for both
families and business travellers. Spacious, en suite
bedrooms feature tea and coffee making facilities,
and Freeview TV in most hotels. Internet access and
Wi-fi are available for a small fee. The adjacent
family restaurant features a wide and varied menu.
See also the Hotel Groups pages.

Rooms 108

Premier Inn High Wycombe Central

BUDGET HOTEL

☎ 0871 527 9326
Arch Way HP13 5HL
dir: M4, junct 8/9, A404M signed Marlow & Wycombe.
Exit for High Wycombe, right at rdbt (town centre) via
Marlow Hill. Left at 1st mini rdbt, right at next rdbt,
left signed Dovecot. Right at next junct into Arch Way,
(Sainsburys on left) 1st left, left to hotel (NB for Sat
Nav use HP11 2DN)

Rooms 120

HINCKLEY　　　　　　　　　　　Map 11 SP49
Leicestershire

Sketchley Grange Hotel

★★★★　81%　◎◎　HOTEL　

☎ 01455 251133
Sketchley Ln, Burbage LE10 3HU
e-mail: info@sketchleygrange.co.uk
web: www.sketchleygrange.co.uk
dir: M69 junct 1, B4109 towards Hinkley. Left at 2nd
rdbt. Into Sketchley Ln, 1st right (also Sketchley Ln)

Close to motorway connections, this hotel is
peacefully set in its own grounds, and enjoys open
country views. Extensive leisure facilities include a
stylish health and leisure spa. Modern meeting
facilities, a choice of bars, and two dining options,
together with comfortable bedrooms furnished with
many extras, make this a special hotel.

Rooms 95 (9 fmly) (6 GF) ✆ **S** £150; **D** £150*
Facilities Spa STV FTV Wi-fi ⟳ ⟲ Gym Steam room
Sauna Xmas New Year **Conf** Class 150 Board 30
Thtr 300 Del £135* **Services** Lift **Parking** 270
Notes Civ Wed 120

Puma Hinckley Island Hotel

★★★★　76%　HOTEL

☎ 01455 631122
Watling Street (A5) LE10 3JA
e-mail: hinckleyisland@pumahotels.co.uk
web: www.pumahotels.co.uk
dir: On A5, S of junct 1 on M69

Puma Hinckley Island Hotel is a large, constantly
improving establishment offering good facilities for
both leisure and business guests. Bedrooms are well
equipped, with the Club Floors providing high levels
of comfort and good workspace. A choice of dining
styles is available in the Brasserie or Conservatory
restaurants, and the Triumph Bar is a must for motor
cycle enthusiasts. The modern leisure club also offers
a range of spa treatments.

Rooms 362 (14 GF) **Facilities** STV Wi-fi ⟳ supervised
Gym Steam room **Conf** Class 240 Board 40 Thtr 400
Services Lift Air con **Parking** 600 **Notes** ⊗
Civ Wed 350

Premier Inn Hinckley

BUDGET HOTEL

☎ 0871 527 8524
Coventry Rd LE10 0NB
web: www.premierinn.com
dir: M69 junct 1, A5 towards Nuneaton. In 2.5m right
at rdbt onto B4666 signed Hinckley Town Centre.
Hotel on right (entrance via Total petrol station)

High quality, budget accommodation ideal for both
families and business travellers. Spacious, en suite
bedrooms feature tea and coffee making facilities,
and Freeview TV in most hotels. Internet access and
Wi-fi are available for a small fee. The adjacent
family restaurant features a wide and varied menu.
See also the Hotel Groups pages.

Rooms 53

HINTLESHAM　　　　　　　　Map 13 TM04
Suffolk

INSPECTORS' CHOICE

Hintlesham Hall Hotel

★★★★　◎◎　HOTEL

☎ 01473 652334
George St IP8 3NS
e-mail: reservations@hintleshamhall.com
web: www.hintleshamhall.com
dir: 4m W of Ipswich on A1071 to Hadleigh &
Sudbury

Hospitality and service are key features at this
imposing Grade I listed country-house hotel,
situated in 175 acres of grounds and landscaped
gardens. Originally a manor house dating from the
Elizabethan era, the building was extended in the
17th and 18th centuries. It was a Red Cross
hospital in World War II and has been a hotel for
nearly forty years. Individually decorated bedrooms
offer a high degree of comfort; each one is
tastefully furnished and equipped with many
thoughtful touches. The spacious public rooms
include a series of comfortable lounges, and an
elegant restaurant which serves fine classical
cuisine based on top-notch ingredients. Wi-fi is
available throughout.

Rooms 33 (10 GF) ✆ **S** £90–£300; **D** £90–£550
(incl. bkfst) **Facilities** FTV Wi-fi ⤓ 18 Putt green ⛳
Health & Beauty services Clay pigeon shooting ♫
Xmas New Year **Conf** Class 50 Board 32 Thtr 80
Del from £165 to £199* **Parking** 60 **Notes** LB
Civ Wed 110

HINTON CHARTERHOUSE — Somerset — Map 4 ST75

Homewood Park Hotel & Spa

★★★★ 81% ◉◉ HOTEL

☎ 01225 723731
BA2 7TB
e-mail: info@homewoodpark.co.uk
web: www.homewoodpark.co.uk
dir: 6m SE of Bath on A36, left at 2nd sign for Freshford

This hotel has a delightful location in attractive parkland, close to Bath and the Longleat estate. Bedrooms are stylishly and comfortably appointed, and many enjoy splendid countryside views. The spa and leisure facilities are notable and a meal in the restaurant should not be missed.

Rooms 21 (2 annexe) (3 fmly) (2 GF) ➤ **Facilities** Spa FTV Wi-fi ↝ ⍭ Sauna Steam room Xmas New Year **Conf** Class 30 Board 25 Thtr 40 **Parking** 30 **Notes** Civ Wed 100

HITCHIN — Hertfordshire — Map 12 TL12

Redcoats Farmhouse Hotel

★★★ 73% ◉ SMALL HOTEL

☎ 01438 729500
Redcoats Green SG4 7JR
e-mail: sales@redcoats.co.uk
web: www.redcoats.co.uk
dir: A602 to Wymondley. Turn left to Redcoats Green. At top of hill straight over at junct

This delightful 15th-century property is situated in four acres of landscaped grounds only a short drive from the A1(M). Bedrooms in the main house and courtyard annexe are well appointed and spacious. Breakfast and dinner are served in the conservatory which overlooks the garden, and a series of intimate dining rooms is also available.

Rooms 13 (9 annexe) (1 fmly) (9 GF) ➤ **Facilities** FTV Wi-fi ⍭ New Year **Conf** Board 15 Thtr 30 **Parking** 50 **Notes** Closed BH & Xmas-7 Jan Civ Wed 75

HOCKLEY HEATH — West Midlands — Map 10 SP17

Nuthurst Grange Hotel

★★★★ 79% ◉◉ HOTEL

☎ 01564 783972
Nuthurst Grange Ln B94 5NL
e-mail: info@nuthurst-grange.co.uk
web: www.nuthurst-grange.co.uk
dir: Exit A3400, 0.5m south of Hockley Heath. Turn at sign into Nuthurst Grange Lane

A stunning avenue is the approach to this country-house hotel, set amid several acres of well-tended gardens and mature grounds, with views over rolling countryside. The spacious bedrooms and bathrooms offer considerable luxury and comfort, and public areas include restful lounges, meeting rooms and a sunny restaurant. The kitchen brigade produces highly imaginative British and French cuisine, complemented by very attentive, professional restaurant service.

Rooms 19 (7 fmly) (2 GF) ➤ S £132; D £143 (incl. bkfst)* **Facilities** STV FTV Wi-fi ⍭ **Conf** Class 50 Board 35 Thtr 100 Del £205* **Parking** 80 **Notes** ⊗ RS 24-26 Dec Civ Wed 100

HOLLINGBOURNE — Kent — Map 7 TQ85

Mercure Maidstone, Great Danes Hotel

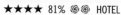

★★★★ HOTEL

☎ 0844 815 9045
ME17 1RE
e-mail: info@mercuremaidstone.co.uk
web: www.jupiterhotels.co.uk
dir: M20 junct 8, follow Leeds Castle signs, at 3rd rdbt turn right

Currently the rating for this establishment is not confirmed. This may be due to a change of ownership or because it has only recently joined the AA rating scheme.

Rooms 126 **Conf** Class 220 Board 60 Thtr 650

HOLT — Norfolk — Map 13 TG03

The Lawns Wine Bar

◉ RESTAURANT WITH ROOMS

☎ 01263 713390
26 Station Rd NR25 6BS
e-mail: info@lawnshotelholt.co.uk
dir: A148 (Cromer road). 0.25m from Holt rdbt, turn left, 400yds along Station Rd

The Lawns is a superb Georgian house situated in the centre of this delightful north Norfolk market town. The open-plan public areas include a large wine bar, a conservatory and a smart restaurant. The spacious bedrooms are tastefully appointed with co-ordinated soft furnishings and have many thoughtful touches.

Rooms 10 (2 annexe)

HONITON — Devon — Map 4 ST10

Monkton Court

◉◉ RESTAURANT WITH ROOMS

☎ 01404 42309 & 07761 281156
Monkton EX14 9QH
e-mail: enquiries@monktoncourthotel.co.uk
dir: 2m E A30 from Honiton

Located on the A30 near Honiton and on the edge of the ancient Blackdown Hills, Monkton Court is a former vicarage steeped in history. There is a range of well-equipped and comfortably furnished bedrooms and bathrooms, in addition to a relaxing lounge and spacious restaurant. Dinner should not be missed, with a range of skilful and flavoursome dishes showcasing local produce and creativity.

Rooms 7 (1 fmly)

HOOK
Hampshire   Map 5 SU75

Raven Hotel
★★★ 67% HOTEL   OldEngl sh

☎ 01256 762541
Station Rd RG27 9HS
e-mail: raven.hook@greeneking.co.uk

This former coaching inn, conveniently located close
to Hook railway station and a short distance from the
M3, has been tastefully converted into a hotel.
Bedrooms are comfortable and well appointed and
have free Wi-fi. The popular restaurant offers an
inviting menu of freshly prepared dishes plus daily-
changing specials. Function rooms are available as is
parking.

Rooms 41 (2 fmly) (5 GF) **Facilities** FTV Wi-fi New
Year **Conf** Class 60 Board 70 Thtr 100 **Parking** 60
Notes Civ Wed 120

HOPE
Derbyshire   Map 16 SK18

Losehill House Hotel & Spa
★★★★ 78% ◉ ◉ HOTEL

☎ 01433 621219
Lose Hill Ln, Edale Rd S33 6AF
e-mail: info@losehillhouse.co.uk
web: www.losehillhouse.co.uk
dir: A6187 into Hope. Into Edale Rd opposite church.
1m, left & follow signs to hotel

Situated down a quiet leafy lane, this hotel occupies
a secluded spot in the Peak District National Park.
Bedrooms are comfortable and beautifully
appointed. The outdoor hot tub, with stunning views
over the valley, is a real indulgence; a heated
swimming pool, sauna and spa treatments are also
on offer. The views from the Orangery Restaurant are
a real delight.

Rooms 24 (3 annexe) (4 fmly) (3 GF) S £90–£160;
D £160–£260 (incl. bkfst) **Facilities** Spa FTV Wi-fi
♫ Xmas New Year **Conf** Class 20 Board 15 Thtr 30
Del from £145 **Services** Lift **Parking** 25 **Notes** LB
Civ Wed 100

HORLEY
Hotels are listed under Gatwick Airport

HORNCASTLE
Lincolnshire   Map 17 TF26

BEST WESTERN Admiral Rodney Hotel
★★★ 78% HOTEL   Best Western

☎ 01507 523131
North St LN9 5DX
e-mail: reception@admiralrodney.com
web: www.admiralrodney.com

The Admiral Rodney, a former coaching inn, is located
in the picturesque town of Horncastle. Public areas
are mostly open plan with a large lounge and bar
area to relax in. The spacious bedrooms are well
appointed and include up-to-date technology; free
Wi-fi is also available throughout the hotel. A
brasserie-style menu is served throughout the day
and evening, and guests can eat in either the
Courtyard Restaurant or alfresco when the weather's
warmer. Large function rooms and extensive parking
are all available. The staff are very welcoming.

Rooms 31 (4 fmly) (7 GF) **Facilities** STV FTV Wi-fi
HL Xmas **Conf** Class 60 Board 40 Thtr 140
Del from £100 to £120* **Services** Lift **Parking** 60
Notes Civ Wed 100

HORSHAM
West Sussex   Map 6 TQ13

Premier Inn Horsham
BUDGET HOTEL   Premier Inn

☎ 0871 527 8526
57 North St RH12 1RB
web: www.premierinn.com
dir: Opposite railway station, 5m from M23 junct 11

High quality, budget accommodation ideal for both
families and business travellers. Spacious, en suite
bedrooms feature tea and coffee making facilities,
and Freeview TV in most hotels. Internet access and
Wi-fi are available for a small fee. The adjacent
family restaurant features a wide and varied menu.
See also the Hotel Groups pages.

Rooms 40

HORSLEY
Derbyshire   Map 11 SK34

Horsley Lodge Hotel & Golf Club
★★★ 81% HOTEL

☎ 01332 780838
Smalley Mill Rd DE21 5BL
e-mail: reception@horsleylodge.co.uk
web: www.horsleylodge.co.uk
dir: A61 N, A38 signed 'Ripley'. Right at Coxbench.
Follow to end, turn right, hotel 1m on left

This family-run hotel is full of character. Situated
equidistant from Derby and Nottingham, it is ideal for
exploring the Peak District. Bedrooms and bathrooms
have stylish decor, beautiful fabrics and quality
furnishings. Barn Cottage offers even greater luxury
and is tucked away not far from the main building.
The Brasserie overlooks the 18-hole golf course.

Rooms 12 (1 annexe) (2 fmly) S £49–£90; D £79–£130
(incl. bkfst) **Facilities** STV FTV Wi-fi ♪ ♫ 18 Putt
green Fishing Golf driving range Xmas New Year
Conf Class 70 Board 50 Thtr 100 Del from £100 to
£175 **Parking** 100 **Notes** LB Civ Wed 100

HOUGHTON-LE-SPRING
Tyne & Wear   Map 19 NZ34

Chilton Country Pub & Hotel
★★ 76% HOTEL

☎ 0191 385 2694
Black Boy Rd, Chilton Moor, Fencehouses DH4 6PY
e-mail: reception@chiltoncountrypub.co.uk
web: www.chiltoncountrypubandhotel.co.uk
dir: A1(M) junct 62, onto A690 towards Sunderland.
Left at Rainton Bridge & Fencehouses sign, right at
rdbt, next rdbt straight over, next left. At next
junct left, hotel on right

This country pub and hotel has been extended from
the original farm cottages. Bedrooms are modern and
comfortable and some rooms are particularly
spacious. This hotel is popular for weddings and
functions; there is also a well stocked bar, and a wide
range of dishes is served in the Orangery and
restaurant.

Rooms 25 (7 fmly) (11 GF) **Facilities** STV Wi-fi ♫
Xmas **Conf** Class 50 Board 30 Thtr 150 **Parking** 100
Notes

H

HOVE

***See* Brighton & Hove**

HOWTOWN
(NEAR POOLEY BRIDGE)
Cumbria

Map 18 NY41

INSPECTORS' CHOICE

Sharrow Bay Country House Hotel

★★★ ❀❀ COUNTRY HOUSE HOTEL

☎ 017684 86301
Sharrow Bay CA10 2LZ
e-mail: info@sharrowbay.co.uk
web: www.sharrowbay.co.uk
dir: M6 junct 40. From Pooley Bridge right fork by
church towards Howtown. Right at x-rds right,
follow lakeside road for 2m

Enjoying breathtaking views and an idyllic location
on the shores of Lake Ullswater, Sharrow Bay is
often described as the first country-house hotel.
Individually styled bedrooms, all with a host of
thoughtful extras, are situated either in the main
house, in delightful buildings in the grounds or at
Bank House - an Elizabethan farmhouse complete
with lounges and breakfast room. Opulently
furnished public areas include a choice of inviting
lounges and two elegant dining rooms.

Rooms 17 (10 annexe) (7 GF) 🛋 **Facilities** FTV Wi-fi
Xmas New Year **Conf** Class 15 Board 20 Thtr 30
Parking 35 **Notes** ❀ No children 10yrs Civ Wed 30

HUCKNALL
Nottinghamshire

Map 16 SK54

Premier Inn Nottingham North West (Hucknall)

BUDGET HOTEL

☎ 0871 527 8852
Nottingham Rd NG15 7PY
web: www.premierinn.com
dir: A611, A6002, straight on at 2 rdbts. Hotel 500yds
on right

High quality, budget accommodation ideal for both
families and business travellers. Spacious, en suite
bedrooms feature tea and coffee making facilities,
and Freeview TV in most hotels. Internet access and
Wi-fi are available for a small fee. The adjacent
family restaurant features a wide and varied menu.
See also the Hotel Groups pages.

Rooms 35

HUDDERSFIELD
West Yorkshire

Map 16 SE11

Cedar Court Hotel

★★★★ 71% HOTEL

☎ 01422 375431 & 314001
Ainley Top HD3 3RH
e-mail: sales@cedar-court-huddersfield.co.uk
web: www.cedarcourthotels.co.uk
dir: 500yds from M62 junct 24

Sitting adjacent to the M62, this hotel is an ideal
location for business travellers and for those touring
the West Yorkshire area. Bedrooms are comfortably
appointed; there is a busy lounge with snacks
available all day, as well as a modern restaurant and
a fully equipped leisure centre. In addition, the hotel
has extensive meeting and banqueting facilities.

Rooms 113 (6 fmly) (9 GF) **S** £49-£99; **D** £59-£99*
Facilities STV FTV Wi-fi ♨ 🎾 supervised Gym Steam
room Sauna Xmas New Year **Conf** Class 150
Board 100 Thtr 500 **Services** Lift **Parking** 250
Notes LB Civ Wed 400

Bagden Hall

★★★ 76% HOTEL

☎ 01484 865330
Wakefield Rd, Scissett HD8 9LE
e-mail: info.bagdenhall@classiclodges.co.uk
web: www.classiclodges.co.uk/Bagdenhall
dir: On A636, between Scissett & Denby Dale

Bagden Hall is an elegant mansion house that enjoys
wonderful views over the valley. Comfortable

bedrooms include classical feature rooms in the main
house and contemporary rooms in a separate
building. Guests can dine in the all-day Nortons
Bistro or the more formal elegant restaurant. The airy,
stylish conference suite and beautiful grounds make
this a popular wedding destination.

Rooms 36 (3 fmly) (15 GF) **Facilities** STV Wi-fi
Conf Class 120 Board 50 Thtr 180 **Parking** 96
Notes RS 25-26 Dec Civ Wed 150

The Huddersfield Central Lodge

★★★ 74% METRO HOTEL

☎ 01484 515551
11/15 Beast Market HD1 1QF
e-mail: angela@centrallodge.com
web: www.centrallodge.com
dir: In town centre off Lord St. Follow Beast Market
signs from ring road
This friendly, family-run Metro Hotel offers smart,
spacious bedrooms, all en-suite. Across a private
courtyard from the main building are more rooms,
many with kitchenettes. Public rooms include a fully
licensed bar and lounge, a 40 square metre
conservatory, and an outdoor covered and heated
smoking area. Large screen plasma TVs are in the
lounge and conservatory. Many recommended
restaurants with a wide variety of cuisine are within a
5 to 10 minute walk from the Central Lodge. On-site
secure free parking is available to all guests, along
with free Wi-fi throughout.

Rooms 22 (13 annexe) (2 fmly) (6 smoking) **Facilities**
FTV Wi-fi ♨ **Parking** 50

Premier Inn Huddersfield Central

BUDGET HOTEL

☎ 0871 527 8528
St Andrews Way HD1 3AQ
web: www.premierinn.com
dir: Telephone or see website for detailed directions

High quality, budget accommodation ideal for both
families and business travellers. Spacious, en suite
bedrooms feature tea and coffee making facilities,
and Freeview TV in most hotels. Internet access and
Wi-fi are available for a small fee. The adjacent
family restaurant features a wide and varied menu.
See also the Hotel Groups pages.

Rooms 52

Premier Inn Huddersfield West

BUDGET HOTEL

☎ 0871 527 8532
New Hey Rd, Ainley Top HD2 2EA
web: www.premierinn.com
dir: Just off M62 junct 24. From M62 take Brighouse exit from rdbt (A643). 1st left into Grimescar Rd, right into New Hey Rd

Rooms 42

315 Bar and Restaurant

◉ RESTAURANT WITH ROOMS

☎ 01484 602613
315 Wakefield Rd, Lepton HD8 0LX
e-mail: info@315barandrestaurant.co.uk
dir: M1 junct 38, A637 towards Huddersfield. At rdbt take A642 towards Huddersfield. Establishment on right in Lepton

In a wonderful setting 315 Bar and Restaurant is very well presented and benefits from countryside views from the well-appointed dining room and conservatory areas. The interior is modern with open fires that add character and ambiance, while the chef's table gives a real insight into the working of the kitchen. Bedrooms are well-appointed and modern, and most have feature bathrooms. Staff are friendly and attentive, and there are excellent parking facilities.

Rooms 10 (3 fmly)

HUNGERFORD   Map 5 SU36
Berkshire

Littlecote House Hotel   *Warner Leisure Hotels* <small>JUST FOR GROWN-UPS</small>

★★★★ 78% ◉◉ COUNTRY HOUSE HOTEL

☎ 01488 682509
RG17 0SU
e-mail: marie.jones@bourne-leisure.co.uk
dir: M4 junct 14, A338, right onto A4, right onto B4192, left into Littlecote Road, hotel 0.5m on right at top of hill

This hotel provides comfortable, spacious accommodation and is located in stunning grounds close to the Cotswolds, only a 10-minute drive from Hungerford. There are traditional-style bedrooms in the ornate Grade I listed Tudor building and more contemporary rooms in the main building. Facilities include a regular programme of entertainment, beauty treatments and a choice of dining locations in either Oliver's Bistro or Pophams Restaurant. This is an adults-only (over 21 years) hotel.

Rooms 201 (12 annexe) (55 GF) 🐾 **Facilities** Spa FTV Wi-fi HL 🅂 🏊 Putt green ⛳ Gym ♫ Xmas New Year **Conf** Class 70 Board 30 Thtr 70 Del from £150 to £250* **Services** Lift **Parking** 520 **Notes** No children 21yrs Civ Wed 120

The Bear Hotel

★★★ 80% ◉ HOTEL

☎ 01488 682512
41 Charnham St RG17 0EL
e-mail: info@thebearhotelhungerford.co.uk
web: www.thebearhotelhungerford.co.uk
dir: M4 junct 14, A338 to Hungerford for 3m, left at T-junct onto A4, hotel on left

Situated five miles south of the M4 this hotel dates back as far as the early 13th century and was once owned by King Henry VIII. It now has a contemporary feel throughout. Bedrooms are split between the main house, the courtyard and Bear Island. The award-winning restaurant is open for lunch and dinner, and lighter snacks are available in the bar and lounge. Guests can enjoy the sun terrace in the summer and log fires in the winter.

Rooms 39 (26 annexe) (2 fmly) (24 GF) **Facilities** FTV Wi-fi Xmas New Year **Conf** Class 35 Board 34 Thtr 80 **Parking** 68 **Notes** LB Civ Wed 80

Three Swans Hotel

★★★ 71% HOTEL

☎ 01488 682721
117 High St RG17 0LZ
e-mail: info@threeswans.net
web: www.threeswans.net
dir: M4 junct 14 follow signs to Hungerford. Hotel in High St on left

Centrally located in the bustling market town of Hungerford this charming former inn, dating back some 700 years, has been renovated in a fresh and airy style. Visitors will still see the original arch under which the horse-drawn carriages once passed. There is a wood panelled bar, a spacious lounge and attractive rear garden to relax in. The informal restaurant is decorated with artwork by local artists. Bedrooms are well appointed and comfortable.

Rooms 26 (10 annexe) (2 fmly) (5 GF) (3 smoking) 🐾 **S** £60-£95; **D** £70-£99 (incl. bkfst)* **Facilities** FTV Wi-fi Access to local private gym Xmas New Year **Conf** Class 40 Board 30 Thtr 55 **Parking** 30 **Notes** LB

HUNSTANTON   Map 12 TF64
Norfolk

BEST WESTERN Le Strange Arms Hotel

★★★★ 75% HOTEL

☎ 01485 534411
Golf Course Rd, Old Hunstanton PE36 6JJ
e-mail: reception@lestrangearms.co.uk
web: www.abacushotels.co.uk
dir: Off A149 1m N of Hunstanton. Left at sharp right bend by pitch & putt course

An impressive hotel with superb views from the wide lawns down to the sandy beach and across The Wash. Bedrooms in the main house have period furnishings whereas the rooms in the wing are more contemporary in style. Public rooms include a comfortable lounge bar and a conference and banqueting suite, plus a choice of dining options - Le Strange Restaurant and the Ancient Mariner.

Rooms 43 (7 annexe) (2 fmly) 🐾 **S** £55-£110; **D** £75-£130 (incl. bkfst)* **Facilities** STV Wi-fi 🐾 Xmas New Year **Conf** Class 150 Board 50 Thtr 180 **Services** Lift **Parking** 80 **Notes** LB ⊗ Civ Wed 70

H

HUNSTANTON *continued*

Caley Hall Hotel

★★★ 85% @ HOTEL

☎ 01485 533486
Old Hunstanton Rd PE36 6HH
e-mail: mail@caleyhallhotel.co.uk
web: www.caleyhallhotel.co.uk
dir: 1m from Hunstanton, on A149

Situated within easy walking distance of the seafront, Caley Hall Hotel offers tastefully decorated bedrooms in a series of converted outbuildings. Each is smartly furnished and thoughtfully equipped. Public rooms feature a large open-plan lounge/bar with plush leather seating, and a restaurant offering an interesting choice of dishes.

Rooms 39 (20 fmly) (30 GF) ⚡ **S** £60-£110;
D £80-£145 (incl. bkfst)* **Facilities** STV FTV Wi-fi New Year Child facilities **Parking** 50 **Notes** Closed 23-27 Dec

The Neptune Restaurant with Rooms

@ @ @ RESTAURANT WITH ROOMS

☎ 01485 532122
85 Old Hunstanton Rd, Old Hunstanton PE36 6HZ
e-mail: reservations@theneptune.co.uk
web: www.theneptune.co.uk
dir: On A149, past Hunstanton, 200mtrs on left after post office

This charming 18th-century coaching inn, now a restaurant with rooms, is ideally situated for touring the Norfolk coastline. The smartly appointed bedrooms are brightly finished with co-ordinated fabrics and hand-made New England furniture. Public rooms feature white clapboard walls, polished dark wood floors, fresh flowers and Lloyd Loom furniture. The food is very much a draw here with the carefully prepared, award-winning cuisine utilising excellent local produce, from oysters and mussels from Thornham to quinces grown on a neighbouring farm.

Rooms 6

HUNTINGDON　　　　　Map 12 TL27
Cambridgeshire

Huntingdon Marriott Hotel

Marriott.

★★★★ 78% HOTEL

☎ 01480 446000
Kingfisher Way, Hinchingbrooke Business Park PE29 6FL
e-mail:
mhrs.cbghd.front.office@marriotthotels.com
web: www.huntingdonmarriott.co.uk
dir: On A14, 1m from Huntington centre near Brampton racecourse

With its excellent road links, this modern, purpose-built hotel is a popular venue for conferences and business meetings, and is convenient for Huntingdon, Cambridge and racing at Brampton and Newmarket. Bedrooms are spacious and offer every modern comfort, including air conditioning. The leisure facilities are also impressive.

Rooms 150 (5 fmly) (45 GF) (2 smoking)
Facilities FTV Wi-fi ⓒ ⓒ supervised Gym Sauna Steam room Xmas New Year **Conf** Class 150 Board 100 Thtr 300 **Services** Lift Air con **Parking** 300 **Notes** ⊗ Civ Wed 300

The Old Bridge Hotel

★★★ 87% @ @ HOTEL

☎ 01480 424300
1 High St PE29 3TQ
e-mail: oldbridge@huntsbridge.co.uk
web: www.huntsbridge.com
dir: From A14 or A1 follow Huntingdon signs. Hotel visible from inner ring road

The Old Bridge Hotel is an imposing 18th-century building situated close to shops and amenities. On offer is superb accommodation in stylish and individually decorated bedrooms that include many useful extras. Guests can choose from the same menu whether dining in the open-plan terrace, or the more formal restaurant with its bold colour scheme. There is also an excellent business centre.

Rooms 24 (2 fmly) (2 GF) ⚡ **S** £99-£130;
D £160-£240 (incl. bkfst) **Facilities** STV FTV Wi-fi ⓒ Fishing Private mooring for boats Xmas New Year **Conf** Class 50 Board 30 Thtr 60 Del from £165 **Services** Air con **Parking** 50 **Notes** LB Civ Wed 100

The George

★★★ 73% HOTEL

OldEngl sh

☎ 01480 432444
George St PE29 3AB
e-mail: george.huntingdon@oldenglishinns.co.uk
web: www.oldenglish.co.uk
dir: Exit A14 for Huntingdon racecourse. 3m to junct with ring road. Hotel opposite

This former coaching inn is ideally situated in the centre of town and was once the home of Oliver Cromwell's grandfather. The public rooms include a spacious lounge bar with plush seating, and a smart brasserie offering an interesting choice of dishes. Bedrooms are pleasantly decorated and equipped with modern facilities.

Rooms 24 (3 fmly) **Facilities** Wi-fi ⚡ Xmas **Conf** Class 60 Board 60 Thtr 80 **Parking** 55 **Notes** Civ Wed 120

Premier Inn Huntingdon (A1/A14)

BUDGET HOTEL

☎ 0871 527 8540
Great North Rd, Brampton PE28 4NQ
web: www.premierinn.com
dir: At junct of A1 & A14. (NB from N do not use junct 14. Take exit for Huntingdon & Brampton). Access to hotel via Services

High quality, budget accommodation ideal for both families and business travellers. Spacious, en suite bedrooms feature tea and coffee making facilities, and Freeview TV in most hotels. Internet access and Wi-fi are available for a small fee. The adjacent family restaurant features a wide and varied menu. See also the Hotel Groups pages.

Rooms 80

HURLEY　　　　　Map 5 SU88
Berkshire

Black Boys Inn

@ @ RESTAURANT WITH ROOMS

☎ 01628 824212
Henley Rd SL6 5NQ
e-mail: info@blackboysinn.co.uk
web: www.blackboysinn.co.uk
dir: 1m W of Hurley on A4130

Just a short drive from Henley, the traditional exterior of this friendly establishment is a contrast to the smart modernity within. Popular with locals, the restaurant is the stage for Simon Bonwick's imaginative cuisine, and has a definite buzz. The well-appointed bedrooms are situated in converted barns close by.

Rooms 8 (8 annexe)

H

Save on hotels. Book at **theAA.com/hotel**

HUN – ILF 217 ENGLAND

HYDE
Greater Manchester Map 16 SJ99

Premier Inn Manchester (Hyde)

BUDGET HOTEL

☎ 0871 527 8712
Stockport Rd, Mottram SK14 3AU
web: www.premierinn.com
dir: At end of M67 between A57 & A560

High quality, budget accommodation ideal for both families and business travellers. Spacious, en suite bedrooms feature tea and coffee making facilities, and Freeview TV in most hotels. Internet access and Wi-fi are available for a small fee. The adjacent family restaurant features a wide and varied menu. See also the Hotel Groups pages.

Rooms 83

HYTHE
Kent Map 7 TR13

Mercure Hythe Imperial

★★★★ 68% HOTEL

☎ 01303 267441
Princes Pde CT21 6AE
e-mail: h6862@accor.com
web: www.mercure.com
dir: M20, junct 11 onto A261. In Hythe follow Folkestone signs. Right into Twiss Rd to hotel

This imposing seafront hotel is enhanced by impressive grounds including a 13-green golf course, tennis court and extensive gardens. Bedrooms are varied in style but all offer modern facilities, and many enjoy stunning sea views. The elegant restaurant, bar and lounges are traditional in style and retain many original features. The leisure club includes a gym, a squash court, an indoor pool, and a spa offering a range of luxury treatments.

Rooms 100 (11 fmly) (6 GF) ⚓ **Facilities** Spa FTV Wi-fi ⌑ ☒ ⅃ 13 ⚐ Putt green Gym Squash Snooker & pool table Aerobic studio Table tennis Sauna Steam room ♫ Xmas New Year **Conf** Class 120 Board 80 Thtr 220 **Services** Lift **Parking** 207 **Notes** Civ Wed 120

BEST WESTERN Stade Court

★★★ 75% HOTEL

☎ 01303 268263
Stade St, West Pde CT21 6DT
e-mail: stadecourt@bestwestern.co.uk
dir: M20 junct 11 follow signs for Hythe town centre. Follow brown tourist sign for hotel

This hotel is situated right on the seafront with many bedrooms having the benefit of uninterrupted views of the English Channel. The comfortable bedrooms are tastefully decorated and provide free Wi-fi and in-room beverage-making facilities. Guests can enjoy traditional English or Indian cuisine in the sea-facing restaurant.

Rooms 42 (5 fmly) ⚓ **S** £40-£60; **D** £50-£90 (incl. bkfst)* **Facilities** FTV Wi-fi Fishing ♫ Xmas New Year **Conf** Class 20 Board 30 Thtr 40 Del from £70 to £105* **Services** Lift **Parking** 11 **Notes** Civ Wed 60

ILFORD
Greater London

Premier Inn Ilford

BUDGET HOTEL PLAN 1 H5

☎ 0871 527 8542
Redbridge Lane East IG4 5BG
web: www.premierinn.com
dir: At end of M11 follow London East, A12 & Chelmsford signs onto A12, hotel on left at bottom of slip road

High quality, budget accommodation ideal for both families and business travellers. Spacious, en suite bedrooms feature tea and coffee making facilities, and Freeview TV in most hotels. Internet access and Wi-fi are available for a small fee. The adjacent family restaurant features a wide and varied menu. See also the Hotel Groups pages.

Rooms 44

ILFRACOMBE
Devon Map 3 SS54

Sandy Cove Hotel

★★★ 77% ● HOTEL

☎ 01271 882 243
Old Coast Rd, Combe Martin Bay, Berrynarbor EX34 9SR
e-mail: info@sandycove-hotel.co.uk
dir: A339 to Combe Martin, through village towards Ilfracombe for approx 1m. Turn right just over brow of hill marked Sandy Cove

This hotel enjoys a truly spectacular position, with front-facing bedrooms that benefit from uninterrupted views of the north Devon coastline. In addition, guests can relax on the sea decks or in the terraced garden, and really appreciate the peace and tranquillity. Locally sourced produce is a feature of the menus offered in the dining room, which makes the perfect setting for a romantic dinner or a family gathering.

Rooms 36 (15 fmly) (7 GF) ⚓ **Facilities** Wi-fi ⌑ ☒ ⅃ Sauna Steam room Heated relaxation loungers Xmas New Year **Conf** Class 20 Board 30 Thtr 30 Del from £110 to £190* **Parking** 45 **Notes** Civ Wed 150

Darnley Hotel

★★ 78% HOTEL

☎ 01271 863955
3 Belmont Rd EX34 8DR
e-mail: darnleyhotel@yahoo.co.uk
web: www.darnleyhotel.co.uk
dir: A361 to Barnstaple & Ilfracombe. Left at Church Hill, 1st left into Belmont Rd. 3rd entrance on left under walled arch

Standing in award-winning, mature gardens, with a wooded path to the High Street and the beach (about a five minute stroll away), this former Victorian gentleman's residence offers friendly, informal service. The individually furnished and decorated bedrooms vary in size. Dinners feature honest home cooking, with 'old fashioned puddings' always proving popular.

Rooms 10 (2 fmly) (2 GF) ⚓ **S** £40-£46; **D** fr £65 (incl. bkfst)* **Facilities** FTV Wi-fi Xmas New Year **Parking** 10 **Notes** No children 3yrs

Imperial Hotel

Leisureplex

★★ 69% HOTEL

☎ 01271 862536
Wilder Rd EX34 9AL
e-mail: imperial.ilfracombe@alfatravel.co.uk
web: www.leisureplex.co.uk
dir: Opposite Landmark Theatre

This popular hotel is just a short walk from the shops and harbour, overlooking gardens and the sea. Public areas include the spacious sun lounge, where guests can relax and enjoy the excellent views. Comfortable bedrooms are well equipped, with several having the added bonus of sea views.

Rooms 104 (6 fmly) ⚓ **Facilities** FTV Wi-fi ♫ Xmas New Year **Services** Lift **Parking** 7 **Notes** ⊗ Closed Dec-Feb (ex Xmas) RS Mar & Nov

I

ILKLEY
West Yorkshire   Map 19 SE14

BEST WESTERN Rombalds Hotel & Restaurant

★★★ 82% HOTEL

☎ 01943 603201
11 West View, Wells Rd LS29 9JG
e-mail: reception@rombalds.demon.co.uk
web: www.rombalds.co.uk
dir: A65 from Leeds. Left at 3rd main lights, follow
Ilkley Moor signs. Right at HSBC Bank onto Wells Rd.
Hotel 600yds on left

This elegantly furnished Georgian townhouse is
located in a peaceful terrace between the town and
the moors. Delightful day rooms include a choice of
comfortable lounges and an attractive restaurant
that provides a relaxed venue in which to sample the
skilfully prepared, imaginative meals. The bedrooms
are tastefully furnished, well equipped and include
several spacious suites.

Rooms 15 (2 fmly) 🛋 **S** £62.50-£105; **D** fr £90*
Facilities FTV Wi-fi ⌇ Xmas Child facilities
Conf Class 40 Board 25 Thtr 70 Del from £110 to
£155* **Parking** 28 **Notes** LB Closed 28 Dec-2 Jan
Civ Wed 70

The Craiglands Hotel

★★★ 68% HOTEL

☎ 01943 430001 & 886450
Cowpasture Rd LS29 8RQ
e-mail: reservations@craiglands.co.uk
web: www.craiglands.co.uk
dir: A65 into Ilkley. Left at T-junct. Past rail station,
fork right into Cowpasture Rd. Hotel opposite school

This grand Victorian hotel is situated close to the
town centre. Spacious public areas and a good range
of services are ideal for business or leisure. Extensive
conference facilities are available along with an
elegant restaurant and traditionally styled bar and
lounge. Bedrooms, varying in size and style, are
comfortably furnished and well equipped.

Rooms 62 (4 fmly) 🛋 **Facilities** FTV Wi-fi ⌇ Xmas
New Year **Conf** Class 200 Board 100 Thtr 500
Services Lift **Parking** 200 **Notes** ⊗ Civ Wed 500

ILSINGTON
Devon   Map 3 SX77

Ilsington Country House Hotel

★★★ 86% ◉◉ COUNTRY HOUSE HOTEL

☎ 01364 661452
Ilsington Village TQ13 9RR
e-mail: hotel@ilsington.co.uk
web: www.ilsington.co.uk
dir: M5 onto A38 to Plymouth. Exit at Bovey Tracey.
3rd exit from rdbt to 'Ilsington', then 1st right. Hotel
in 5m by Post Office

This friendly, family owned hotel, offers tranquillity
and far-reaching views from its elevated position on
the southern slopes of Dartmoor. The stylish suites
and bedrooms, some on the ground floor, are
individually furnished. The restaurant provides a
stunning backdrop for the innovative, daily changing
menus which feature local fish, meat and game.
Additional facilities include an indoor pool and the
Blue Tiger Inn, where a pint, a bite to eat and
convivial banter can all be enjoyed.

Rooms 25 (4 fmly) (6 GF) 🛋 **S** £90; **D** £100-£215
(incl. bkfst)* **Facilities** FTV Wi-fi 🏊 supervised ⌁
Gym Steam room Sauna Beauty treatments Xmas New
Year **Conf** Class 60 Board 40 Thtr 100 Del from £135
to £180* **Services** Lift **Parking** 100 **Notes** LB
Civ Wed 120

INSTOW
Devon   Map 3 SS43

Commodore Hotel

★★★ 82% HOTEL

☎ 01271 860347
Marine Pde EX39 4JN
e-mail: admin@commodore-instow.co.uk
web: www.commodore-instow.co.uk
dir: M5 junct 27 follow N Devon link road to Bideford.
Right before bridge, hotel in 3m

Maintaining its links with the local maritime and
rural communities, The Commodore provides an
interesting place to stay. Situated at the mouth of the
Taw and Torridge rivers and overlooking a sandy
beach, it offers well-equipped bedrooms, many with
balconies. There are five ground-floor suites. Eating
options include the restaurant, the Quarterdeck bar,
or the terrace in the warmer months.

Rooms 25 (1 fmly) (5 GF) 🛋 **S** £69-£99; **D** £150-£220
(incl. bkfst) **Facilities** FTV Wi-fi ⌇ Xmas New Year
Parking 200 **Notes** LB ⊗ No children 3yrs

IPSWICH
Suffolk   Map 13 TM14

INSPECTORS' CHOICE

Hintlesham Hall Hotel

★★★★ ◉◉ HOTEL

☎ 01473 652334
George St IP8 3NS
e-mail: reservations@hintleshamhall.com
web: www.hintleshamhall.com

(For full entry see Hintlesham)

INSPECTORS' CHOICE

Salthouse Harbour Hotel

★★★★ ◉◉ TOWN HOUSE HOTEL

☎ 01473 226789
No 1 Neptune Quay IP4 1AX
e-mail: staying@salthouseharbour.co.uk
dir: From A14 junct 56 follow signs for town centre,
then Salthouse signs

Situated just a short walk from the town centre,
this waterfront warehouse conversion is a clever
mix of contemporary styles and original features.
The hotel is stylishly designed throughout with
modern art, sculptures, interesting artefacts and
striking colours. The spacious bedrooms provide
luxurious comfort; some have feature bathrooms
and some have balconies. Two air-conditioned
penthouse suites, with stunning views, have extras
such as state-of-the-art sound systems and
telescopes. Award-winning food is served in the
busy, ground-floor brasserie, and alfresco eating is
possible in warmer weather.

Rooms 70 (6 fmly) 🛋 **Facilities** FTV Wi-fi
Services Lift **Parking** 30

milsoms Kesgrave Hall

★★★★ 77% ⚙ HOTEL

☎ 01473 333741
Hall Rd, Kesgrave IP5 2PU
e-mail: reception@kesgravehall.com
web: www.milsomshotels.com
dir: A12 N of Ipswich, left at Ipswich/Woodbridge rdbt
onto A1214. Right after 0.5m into Hall Rd. Hotel
200yds on left

A superb 18th-century, Grade II listed Georgian
mansion set amidst 38 acres of mature grounds.
Appointed in a contemporary style, the large open-
plan public areas include a smart bar, a lounge with
plush sofas, and a restaurant where guests can
watch the chefs in action. Bedrooms are tastefully
appointed and thoughtfully equipped.

Rooms 23 (8 annexe) (3 fmly) (8 GF) 🐾 **D** £125–£300
(incl. bkfst)* **Facilities** STV FTV Wi-fi ⓑ ⚑ Xmas
Conf Class 200 Board 24 Thtr 300 **Parking** 100
Notes LB

Novotel Ipswich Centre

★★★★ 72% HOTEL

☎ 01473 232400
Greyfriars Rd IP1 1UP
e-mail: h0995@accor.com
web: www.novotel.com
dir: From A14 towards Felixstowe. Left onto A137, 2m
into town centre. Hotel on double rdbt by Stoke Bridge

This modern, red brick hotel is perfectly placed in the
centre of town close to shops, bars and restaurants.

The open-plan public areas include a Mediterranean-
style restaurant and a bar with a small games area.
The bedrooms are smartly appointed and have many
thoughtful touches; three rooms are suitable for less
mobile guests.

Rooms 101 (8 fmly) 🐾 **S** £65–£175; **D** £65–£175*
Facilities STV Wi-fi ⓑ HL Gym Xmas New Year
Conf Class 100 Board 45 Thtr 180 **Services** Lift
Air con **Parking** 53 **Notes** Civ Wed 150

BEST WESTERN Claydon Country House Hotel

★★★ 83% ⚙ HOTEL

☎ 01473 830382
16-18 Ipswich Rd, Claydon IP6 0AR
e-mail: reception@hotelsipswich.com
dir: From A14, NW of Ipswich. After 4m take Great
Blakenham Rd (B1113) to Claydon, hotel on left

A delightful hotel situated just off the A14, within
easy driving distance of the town centre. The
pleasantly decorated bedrooms are thoughtfully
equipped and one room has a lovely four-poster bed.
An interesting choice of freshly prepared dishes is
available in the smart restaurant, and guests have
the use of a relaxing lounge bar.

Rooms 36 (5 fmly) (13 GF) 🐾 **S** £69–£89; **D** £79–£99*
Facilities STV Wi-fi ⓑ Xmas New Year **Conf** Class 60
Board 55 Thtr 120 Del from £120 to £150
Services Air con **Parking** 85 **Notes** LB ⊗
Civ Wed 100

BEST WESTERN Gatehouse Hotel

★★★ 80% ⚙ HOTEL

☎ 01473 741897
799 Old Norwich Rd IP1 6LH
dir: A14 junct 53, A1156 signed Ipswich, left at lights
into Norwich Rd, hotel on left

A Regency-style property set amidst three acres of
landscaped grounds, on the outskirts of town in a
quiet road just a short drive from the A14. The
spacious bedrooms have co-ordinated soft
furnishings and many thoughtful touches. Public
rooms include a smart lounge bar, an intimate
restaurant and a cosy drawing room with plush
leather sofas.

Rooms 15 (4 annexe) (3 fmly) (6 GF) 🐾 **S** £69–£89;
D £79–£99 **Facilities** STV FTV Wi-fi ⓑ Xmas
Parking 25 **Notes** LB ⊗

Ramada Encore Ipswich

★★★ 78% HOTEL

☎ 01473 694600
Ranelagh Rd IP2 0AD
e-mail: reservations@encoreipswich.co.uk
web: www.encoreipswich.co.uk
dir: A14/A1214. Hotel 0.3m from Ipswich rail station

A modern purpose-built hotel situated close to the
railway station and within easy walking distance of
Ipswich Town FC. The contemporary open-plan public
areas feature a smart lounge bar which leads through
to the bright and airy restaurant. The smart bedrooms
are very well equipped and have interactive flat-
screen TVs with internet access. The hotel also has a
small gym.

Rooms 126 (9 fmly) (16 GF) 🐾 **S** £39–£109;
D £39–£109* **Facilities** Wi-fi HL Gym **Conf** Class 16
Board 20 Thtr 35 Del £160* **Services** Lift Air con
Parking 24 **Notes** LB ⊗

Holiday Inn Ipswich

★★★ 77% HOTEL
                                  Holiday Inn

☎ 0871 942 9045
London Rd IP2 0UA
e-mail: reservations-ipswich@ihg.com
web: www.hiipswichhotel.co.uk
dir: From A14 & A12 junct take A1214 to West
Ipswich. Over 1st rdbt. Hotel on left on A1071

A modern, purpose built hotel conveniently situated
just off the A12/A14 junction to the west of the town
centre. Public areas include a popular bar, the
Junction Restaurant and a large open-plan lounge.
Bedrooms come in a variety of styles and are suited to
the needs of both the business and leisure guest
alike.

Rooms 108 (40 fmly) (48 GF) **Facilities** STV FTV Wi-fi
ⓑ supervised Gym Sauna **Conf** Class 50 Board 40
Thtr 120 **Services** Lift Air con **Parking** 200 **Notes** ⊗
Civ Wed 80

I

IPSWICH *continued*

Premier Inn Ipswich (Chantry Park)

BUDGET HOTEL

☎ 0871 527 8548
Old Hadleigh Rd IP8 3AR
web: www.premierinn.com
dir: From A12/A14 junct take A1214 to Ipswich town centre. Left at lights by Holiday Inn, left onto A1071. At mini rdbt turn right. Hotel on right

High quality, budget accommodation ideal for both families and business travellers. Spacious, en suite bedrooms feature tea and coffee making facilities, and Freeview TV in most hotels. Internet access and Wi-fi are available for a small fee. The adjacent family restaurant features a wide and varied menu. See also the Hotel Groups pages.

Rooms 49

Premier Inn Ipswich North

BUDGET HOTEL

☎ 0871 527 8550
Paper Mill Ln, Claydon IP6 0BE
web: www.premierinn.com
dir: A14 junct 52. At rdbt exit onto Paper Mill Lane. Hotel 1st left

Rooms 59

Premier Inn Ipswich South

BUDGET HOTEL

☎ 0871 527 8552
Bourne Hill, Wherstead IP2 8ND
web: www.premierinn.com
dir: From A14 follow Ipswich Central A137 signs, then Ipswich Central & Docks signs. At bottom of hill at rdbt 2nd exit. Hotel on right

Rooms 40

Premier Inn Ipswich South East

BUDGET HOTEL

☎ 0871 527 8554
Augusta Close, Ransomes Euro Park IP3 9SS
web: www.premierinn.com
dir: A14 junct 57, stay in right lane. At rdbt 2nd exit, then 1st left. Hotel adjacent to Swallow Restaurant

Rooms 20

IREBY — Map 18 NY23
Cumbria

Overwater Hall

★★★ 86% ◉◉ COUNTRY HOUSE HOTEL

☎ 017687 76566
CA7 1HH
e-mail: welcome@overwaterhall.co.uk
dir: From A591 take turn to Ireby at Castle Inn. Hotel signed after 2m on right

This privately owned country house dates back to 1811 and is set in lovely gardens surrounded by woodland. The owners have lovingly restored this Georgian property over the years paying great attention to the authenticity of the original design; guests will receive warm hospitality and attentive service in a relaxed manner. The elegant and well appointed bedrooms include the more spacious Superior Rooms and the Garden Room; all bedrooms have Wi-fi. Creative dishes are served in the traditional-style dining room.

Rooms 11 (2 fmly) (1 GF) S £100-£175; D £200-£290 (incl. bkfst & dinner)* **Facilities** FTV Wi-fi Xmas New Year **Parking** 20 **Notes** LB Civ Wed 30

KEGWORTH
See East Midlands Airport

KEIGHLEY — Map 19 SE04
West Yorkshire

Dalesgate Hotel

★★ 70% HOTEL

☎ 01535 664930
406 Skipton Rd, Utley BD20 6HP
e-mail: stephen.e.atha@btinternet.com
dir: In town centre follow A629 over rdbt onto B6265. Right after 0.75m into St. John's Rd. 1st right into hotel car park

Originally the residence of a local chapel minister, this modern, well-established hotel provides well-equipped, comfortable bedrooms. It also boasts a cosy bar and pleasant restaurant, serving an imaginative range of dishes. A large car park is provided to the rear.

Rooms 20 (2 fmly) (3 GF) **Parking** 25 **Notes** RS 22 Dec-4 Jan

---

Premier Inn Bradford North (Bingley)

BUDGET HOTEL

☎ 0871 527 8134
502 Bradford Rd, Sandbeds BD20 5NG
web: www.premierinn.com
dir: M62 juncts 26 or 27 follow A650/Keighley & Skipton signs. From Bingley Bypass (A650 Cottingley) right at 1st rdbt signed Crossflatts & Micklethwaite. Hotel 50yds on left. (NB for Sat Nav use BD20 5NH)

High quality, budget accommodation ideal for both families and business travellers. Spacious, en suite bedrooms feature tea and coffee making facilities, and Freeview TV in most hotels. Internet access and Wi-fi are available for a small fee. The adjacent family restaurant features a wide and varied menu. See also the Hotel Groups pages.

Rooms 40

KENDAL — Map 18 SD59
Cumbria

See also Crooklands

BEST WESTERN Castle Green Hotel in Kendal

★★★★ 77% ◉◉ HOTEL

☎ 01539 734000
LA9 6RG
e-mail: reception@castlegreen.co.uk
web: www.castlegreen.co.uk
dir: M6 junct 37, A684 towards Kendal. Hotel on right in 5m

This smart, modern hotel enjoys a peaceful location and is conveniently situated for access to both the town centre and the M6. Stylish bedrooms are thoughtfully equipped for both the business and leisure guest. The Greenhouse Restaurant provides imaginative dishes and boasts a theatre kitchen; alternatively Alexander's Pub serves food all day. The hotel has a fully equipped business centre and leisure club.

Rooms 99 (3 fmly) (25 GF) S £83-£113; D £79-£156 (incl. bkfst)* **Facilities** Spa FTV Wi-fi Gym Steam room Aerobics Yoga Beauty salon

Save on hotels. Book at **theAA.com/hotel**

IPS – KES 221 ENGLAND

Xmas New Year **Conf** Class 120 Board 100 Thtr 300 Del from £125 to £155* **Services** Lift **Parking** 200 **Notes** LB ⊗ Civ Wed 250

Riverside Hotel Kendal

★★★ 79% HOTEL

☎ 01539 734861
Beezon Rd, Stramongate Bridge LA9 6EL
e-mail: info@riversidekendal.co.uk
web: www.bestlakesbreaks.co.uk
dir: M6 junct 36 Sedburgh, Kendal 7m, left at end of Ann St, 1st right onto Beezon Rd, hotel on left

Centrally located in this market town, and enjoying a peaceful riverside location, this 17th-century former tannery provides a suitable base for both business travellers and tourists. The comfortable bedrooms are well equipped, and open-plan day rooms include the attractive restaurant and bar. Conference facilities are available, and the state-of-the-art leisure club has a heated pool, sauna, steam room, solarium and gym.

Rooms 50 (18 fmly) (10 GF) ⇗ **S** £79-£99; **D** £108-£158 (incl. bkfst)* **Facilities** STV Wi-fi ⇘ ⊗ supervised Gym Sauna Steam room Spa bath Xmas New Year **Conf** Class 200 Board 90 Thtr 200 Del from £115 to £135* **Services** Lift **Parking** 60 **Notes** LB Civ Wed 250

Stonecross Manor Hotel

★★★ 75% HOTEL

☎ 01539 733559
Milnthorpe Rd LA9 5HP
e-mail: info@stonecrossmanor.co.uk
web: www.stonecrossmanor.co.uk
dir: M6 junct 36, A590, follow signs to Windermere, take exit for Kendal South. Hotel just past 30mph sign on left

Located on the edge of Kendal, this smart hotel offers a good combination of traditional style and modern facilities. Bedrooms are comfortable, well equipped and some feature four-poster beds. Guests can relax in the lounges or bar and enjoy an extensive choice of home cooked meals in the pleasant restaurant. Facilities also include a swimming pool.

Rooms 30 (4 fmly) **S** £95-£158; **D** £106-£169 (incl. bkfst)* **Facilities** FTV Wi-fi ⇘ HL ⊗ Xmas New Year **Conf** Class 80 Board 40 Thtr 140 Del from £95 to £120* **Services** Lift **Parking** 55 **Notes** Civ Wed 130

Premier Inn Kendal Central

BUDGET HOTEL

☎ 0871 527 8562
Maude St LA9 4QD
web: www.premierinn.com
dir: M6 junct 36, A591 to Kendal. (NB ignore exit for Kendal South). At Plumbgarm Rdbt take 3rd exit, 0.5m to Kendal. Hotel on right

High quality, budget accommodation ideal for both families and business travellers. Spacious, en suite bedrooms feature tea and coffee making facilities, and Freeview TV in most hotels. Internet access and Wi-fi are available for a small fee. The adjacent family restaurant features a wide and varied menu. See also the Hotel Groups pages.

Rooms 55

KENILWORTH Map 10 SP27
Warwickshire

Chesford Grange

★★★★ 77% HOTEL

☎ 01926 859331
Chesford Bridge CV8 2LD
e-mail: chesfordreservations@qhotels.co.uk
web: www.qhotels.co.uk
dir: 0.5m SE of junct A46/A452. At rdbt turn right signed Leamington Spa, follow signs to hotel

This much-extended hotel set in 17 acres of private grounds is well situated for Birmingham International Airport, the NEC and major routes. Bedrooms range from traditional style to contemporary rooms featuring state-of-the-art technology. Public areas include a leisure club and extensive conference and banqueting facilities.

Rooms 205 (20 fmly) (43 GF) ⇗ **S** £65-£185; **D** £75-£195 (incl. bkfst)* **Facilities** Spa STV Wi-fi ⇘ ⊗ supervised Gym Steam room Solarium Xmas New Year **Conf** Class 350 Board 50 Thtr 710 Del from £100 to £165* **Services** Lift **Parking** 650 **Notes** LB Civ Wed 700

KENTON
Greater London

Premier Inn London Harrow

BUDGET HOTEL PLAN 1 C5

☎ 0871 527 8664
Kenton Rd HA3 8AT
web: www.premierinn.com
dir: M1 junct 5, follow Harrow & Kenton signs. Hotel between Harrow & Wembley on A4006 opposite Kenton railway station

High quality, budget accommodation ideal for both families and business travellers. Spacious, en suite bedrooms feature tea and coffee making facilities, and Freeview TV in most hotels. Internet access and Wi-fi are available for a small fee. The adjacent family restaurant features a wide and varied menu. See also the Hotel Groups pages.

Rooms 101

KESWICK Map 18 NY22
Cumbria

K

Skiddaw Hotel

★★★ 80% HOTEL

LAKE DISTRICT HOTELS

☎ 017687 72071
Main St CA12 5BN
e-mail: info@skiddawhotel.co.uk
web: www.lakedistricthotels.net/skiddawhotel
dir: A66 to Keswick, follow town centre signs. Hotel in market square

Occupying a central position overlooking the market square, this hotel provides smartly furnished bedrooms that include several family suites and a room with a four-poster bed. In addition to the restaurant, food is served all day in the bar and in the conservatory. There is also a quiet residents' lounge and two conference rooms.

Rooms 43 (7 fmly) ⇗ **Facilities** STV Wi-fi Use of leisure facilities at sister hotels (3m) ⊓ Xmas New Year **Conf** Class 60 Board 40 Thtr 70 Del from £115 to £130 **Services** Lift **Parking** 35 **Notes** Civ Wed 90

KESWICK *continued*

Dale Head Hall Lakeside Hotel

★★★ 79% ☺ COUNTRY HOUSE HOTEL

☎ 017687 72478
Lake Thirlmere CA12 4TN
e-mail: onthelakeside@daleheadhall.co.uk
web: www.daleheadhall.co.uk
dir: Between Keswick & Grasmere. Exit A591 onto
private drive

Set in attractive, tranquil grounds on the shores of
Lake Thirlmere, this historic lakeside residence dates
from the 16th century. Comfortable and inviting
public areas include a choice of lounges and a
traditionally furnished restaurant featuring a daily-
changing menu. Most bedrooms are spacious and
have views of the lake or surrounding mountains.

Rooms 12 (1 fmly) (2 GF) **Facilities** STV Wi-fi ⛲
Fishing ⛲ Fishing permits Boating Xmas New Year
Conf Class 20 Board 20 Thtr 20 **Parking** 34 **Notes** ⊗
Closed 3-30 Jan Civ Wed 50

Highfield Hotel

★★★ 79% SMALL HOTEL

☎ 017687 72508
The Heads CA12 5ER
e-mail: info@highfieldkeswick.co.uk
web: www.highfieldkeswick.co.uk
dir: M6 junct 40, A66, 2nd exit at rdbt. Left to T-junct,
left again. Right at mini-rdbt. Take 4th right

This friendly hotel, close to the centre of town, offers
stunning views of Skiddaw, Cats Bells and
Derwentwater. Attractively furnished bedrooms, many
of them spacious, are thoughtfully equipped. Public
areas include a choice of comfortable lounges and an
elegant restaurant, where imaginative, modern
cuisine is served.

Rooms 18 (1 fmly) (2 GF) **S £95; D £170-£220
(incl. bkfst & dinner)* **Facilities** FTV Wi-fi ⛲
Parking 20 **Notes** ⊗ Closed Jan

Keswick Country House Hotel

★★★ 74% HOTEL

☎ 0844 811 5580
Station Rd CA12 4NQ
e-mail: reservations@choicehotels.co.uk
web: www.thekeswickhotel.co.uk
dir: M6 junct 40, A66, 1st slip road into Keswick, then
follow signs for leisure pool

This impressive Victorian hotel is set amid attractive
gardens close to the town centre. Eight superior
bedrooms are available in the Station Wing, which is
accessed through a conservatory. The attractively
appointed main house rooms are modern in style and

offer a good range of amenities. Public areas include
a well-stocked bar, a spacious and relaxing lounge,
and a restaurant serving interesting dinners.

Rooms 70 (6 fmly) (4 GF) **Facilities** FTV Wi-fi Putt
green ⛳ Xmas New Year **Conf** Class 70 Board 60
Thtr 110 Del from £95 to £125* **Services** Lift
Parking 70 **Notes** ⊗ Civ Wed 100

Kings Arms Hotel

LAKE DISTRICT ▪▪▪▪ HOTELS

★★★ 71% HOTEL

☎ 017687 72083
27 Main St CA12 5BL
e-mail: kingsarms@lakedistricthotels.net

Located in the heart of Keswick, the Kings Arms Hotel
offers modern, tastefully refurbished bedrooms and
en suites, alongside intimate public areas and a
choice of two restaurants. The bar offers some great
local real ales and changing guest beers. The small
hands-on team offer friendly and relaxed service.

Rooms 13

Swinside Lodge Country House Hotel

★★ 85% ☺☺ COUNTRY HOUSE HOTEL

☎ 017687 72948
Grange Rd, Newlands CA12 5UE
e-mail: info@swinsidelodge-hotel.co.uk
web: www.swinsidelodge-hotel.co.uk
dir: A66, left at Portinscale to Grange, 2m (NB ignore
signs to Swinside). Hotel on right

Surrounded by fells, this beautifully maintained
Georgian property is situated at the foot of Cat Bells
and is only a five-minute stroll from the shores of
Derwentwater. Guests are made to feel genuinely
welcome, with the friendly proprietors on hand to
provide attentive service. The elegantly furnished
lounges are an ideal place to relax before dinner. The
four-course set dinner menu is creative, featuring
high quality ingredients and beautifully presented
dishes.

Rooms 7 (7 fmly) **Facilities** Wi-fi **Parking** 12
Notes ⊗ No children 12yrs Closed 9 Dec-1 Feb

KETTERING   Map 11 SP87
Northamptonshire

INSPECTORS' CHOICE

Rushton Hall Hotel and Spa

★★★★ ☺☺☺
COUNTRY HOUSE HOTEL

☎ 01536 713001
NN14 1RR
e-mail: enquiries@rushtonhall.com
web: www.rushtonhall.com
dir: A14 junct 7, A43 to Corby then A6003 to
Rushton, turn after bridge

Ruston Hall is an elegant country house hotel set
amidst 30 acres of parkland and surrounded by
open countryside. The stylish public rooms include
a library, a superb open-plan lounge bar with a
magnificent vaulted ceiling and plush sofas, and
an oak-panelled dining hall, where Adam Coulthard
oversees a very high quality operation. The
tastefully appointed bedrooms have co-ordinated
fabrics and many thoughtful touches.

Rooms 45 (5 fmly) (3 GF) **Facilities** Spa FTV
Wi-fi ⛲ ⛲ ⛲ Gym Billiard table Sauna Steam
room Xmas New Year **Conf** Class 100 Board 40
Thtr 200 **Services** Lift **Parking** 140 **Notes** ⊗
Civ Wed 160

Kettering Park Hotel & Spa

shire

★★★★ 78% ☺ HOTEL

☎ 01536 416666
Kettering Parkway NN15 6XT
e-mail: kpark@shirehotels.com
web: www.ketteringparkhotel.com
dir: Exit A14 junct 9 (M1 to A1 link road), hotel in
Kettering Venture Park

Expect a warm welcome at this stylish hotel situated
just off the A14. The spacious, smartly decorated
bedrooms are well equipped and meticulously
maintained. Guests can choose from classical or
contemporary dishes in the restaurant and lighter
meals that are served in the bar. The extensive leisure
facilities are impressive.

Rooms 119 (29 fmly) (35 GF) **S** £90-£150;
D £90-£150* **Facilities** STV FTV Wi-fi ⃕ HL ⌚ Gym
Steam room Sauna Beauty treatment room Children's
splash pool Activity studio New Year **Conf** Class 120
Board 40 Thtr 260 Del from £145 to £185*
Services Lift Air con **Parking** 200 **Notes** LB ⊗
Civ Wed 120

BEST WESTERN Naseby Hotel

★★★ 72% HOTEL

☎ 01536 734736
Sheep St NN16 0AN
e-mail: reservations@thenasebyhotel.co.uk
dir: A14 junct 8, left at rdbt, follow road to set of
lights. At rdbt take middle lane, straight over & left at
lights. Hotel on left

Situated in the heart of Kettering, and originally built
in the 16th century, this hotel has recently undergone
major refurbishment and has a sleek modern interior
along with some lovely original features. There is a
good range of stylish, modern bedrooms. Secure
parking is available, as is free Wi-fi.

Rooms 41 (1 fmly) (3 GF) **Facilities** FTV Wi-fi Xmas
New Year **Conf** Class 100 Board 80 Thtr 200
Services Air con **Parking** 15 **Notes** ⊗

Premier Inn Kettering

BUDGET HOTEL

☎ 0871 527 8564
Rothwell Rd NN16 8XF
web: www.premierinn.com
dir: Off A14 junct 7

High quality, budget accommodation ideal for both
families and business travellers. Spacious, en suite
bedrooms feature tea and coffee making facilities,
and Freeview TV in most hotels. Internet access and
Wi-fi are available for a small fee. The adjacent
family restaurant features a wide and varied menu.
See also the Hotel Groups pages.

Rooms 59

KIDDERMINSTER
Worcestershire
Map 10 SO87

Stone Manor Hotel

★★★★ 76% ◉ HOTEL

☎ 01562 777555
Stone DY10 4PJ
e-mail: enquiries@stonemanorhotel.co.uk
web: www.stonemanorhotel.co.uk
dir: 2.5m from Kidderminster on A448, on right

This converted, much extended former manor house
stands in 25 acres of impressive grounds and
gardens. The well-equipped accommodation includes

rooms with four-poster beds and luxuriously
appointed annexe bedrooms. Quality furnishing and
decor styles throughout the public areas highlight the
intrinsic charm of the interior; the hotel is a popular
venue for wedding receptions.

Rooms 57 (5 annexe) (7 GF) **Facilities** STV ⃕ 🛟 🏊
Pool table Complimentary use of local leisure centre
Conf Class 48 Board 60 Thtr 150 **Parking** 400
Notes ⊗ Civ Wed 150

The Granary Hotel & Restaurant

★★★ 80% ◉◉ HOTEL

☎ 01562 777535
Heath Ln, Shenstone DY10 4BS
e-mail: info@granary-hotel.co.uk
web: www.granary-hotel.co.uk
dir: On A450 between Stourbridge & Worcester, 1m
from Kidderminster

This modern hotel offers spacious, well-equipped
accommodation with many rooms enjoying views
towards Great Witley and the Amberley Hills. Public
areas include a new bar and a residents' lounge. The
attractive, modern restaurant serves dishes created
from locally sourced produce that is cooked with flair
and imagination. There are also extensive conference
facilities, and the hotel is popular as a wedding
venue.

Rooms 18 (1 fmly) (18 GF) **S** £60-£90; **D** £85-£150
(incl. bkfst)* **Facilities** FTV Wi-fi **Conf** Class 80
Board 70 Thtr 200 Del from £135 to £140*
Parking 96 **Notes** LB Civ Wed 120

Gainsborough House Hotel

THE INDEPENDENTS
HOTEL ASSOCIATION

★★★ 78% HOTEL

☎ 01562 820041
Bewdley Hill DY11 6BS
e-mail:
reservations@gainsboroughhousehotel.com
web: www.gainsboroughhousehotel.com
dir: Follow A456 to Kidderminster (West Midlands
Safari Park), pass hospital, hotel 500yds on left

This listed Georgian hotel provides a wide range of
thoughtfully furnished bedrooms that have smart
modern bathrooms. The contemporary decor and
furnishing throughout the public areas highlights the
many retained period features. A large function suite
and several meeting rooms are available.

Rooms 42 (16 fmly) (12 GF) **S** £54-£93; **D** £54-£99*
Facilities STV FTV Wi-fi Xmas New Year
Conf Board 60 Thtr 250 Del from £95 to £120*
Services Air con **Parking** 90 **Notes** LB ⊗
Civ Wed 250

Premier Inn Kidderminster

BUDGET HOTEL

☎ 0871 527 9350
Slingfield Mill, Weavers Wharf DY10 1AA
dir: M5 junct 3 , A456 towards Kidderminster, 5.5m.
Straight on at 1st rdbt, left into Lower Mill St.
Straight on into Crown Ln

High quality, budget accommodation ideal for both
families and business travellers. Spacious, en suite
bedrooms feature tea and coffee making facilities,
and Freeview TV in most hotels. Internet access and
Wi-fi are available for a small fee. The adjacent
family restaurant features a wide and varied menu.
See also the Hotel Groups pages.

Rooms 56

KINGSBRIDGE
Devon
Map 3 SX74

Buckland-Tout-Saints

EDEN HOTEL COLLECTION

★★★ 81% ◉
COUNTRY HOUSE HOTEL

☎ 01548 853055
Goveton TQ7 2DS
e-mail: buckland@tout-saints.co.uk
dir: Turn off A381 to Goveton. Follow brown tourist
signs to St Peter's Church. Hotel 2nd right after
church

It is well worth navigating the winding country lanes
to dine at this delightful Queen Anne manor house
that has been host to many famous guests over the
years. Set in over four acres of gardens the hotel is a
peaceful retreat. Bedrooms are tastefully furnished
and attractively decorated; the majority are very
spacious. Local produce is used with care and
imagination to create the dishes offered. This is a
popular choice for weddings.

Rooms 16 **Conf** Class 40 Board 26 Thtr 80

K

KING'S LANGLEY
Hertfordshire
Map 6 TL00

Premier Inn King's Langley

BUDGET HOTEL

☎ 0871 527 8568
Hempstead Rd WD4 8BR
web: www.premierinn.com
dir: 1m from M25 junct 20 on A4251 after King's Langley

High quality, budget accommodation ideal for both families and business travellers. Spacious, en suite bedrooms feature tea and coffee making facilities, and Freeview TV in most hotels. Internet access and Wi-fi are available for a small fee. The adjacent family restaurant features a wide and varied menu. See also the Hotel Groups pages.

Rooms 60

KING'S LYNN
Norfolk
Map 12 TF62

The Duke's Head Hotel
LEGACY HOTELS
★★★★ 77% HOTEL

☎ 01553 774996
5-6 Tuesday Market Place PE30 1JS
e-mail: reception@dukesheadhotel.com

Occupying a central location and overlooking the market square, this hotel is a beautiful property, which has recently undergone a multi-million pound refurbishment. The bedrooms are smartly decorated, and include wide-screen TVs, free Wi-fi and bathrooms with walk-in showers. Parking is also available.

Rooms 81 (5 fmly) 🦃 **Facilities** FTV Wi-fi ⓑ HL Xmas New Year **Conf** Class 180 Board 150 Thtr 250 **Services** Lift Air con **Parking** 35 **Notes** Civ Wed

BEST WESTERN PLUS Knights Hill Hotel and Spa

Best Western PLUS
★★★★ 72% HOTEL

☎ 01553 675566
Knights Hill Village, South Wootton PE30 3HQ
e-mail: reception@knightshill.co.uk
web: www.abacushotels.co.uk
dir: At junct A148 & A149

This hotel village complex is set on a 16th-century site on the outskirts of town. The smartly decorated, well-equipped bedrooms are situated in extensions of the original hunting lodge. Public areas have a wealth of historic charm including the Garden Restaurant and the Farmers Arms pub. The hotel also has conference and leisure facilities, including the Imagine Spa.

Rooms 79 (12 annexe) (1 fmly) (38 GF) 🦃 **S** £50-£120; **D** £60-£130* **Facilities** Spa STV Wi-fi ⓑ ⓢ ⓢ ⓢ Gym Xmas New Year **Conf** Class 150 Board 30 Thtr 200 **Parking** 350 **Notes** LB ⊗ Civ Wed 90

INSPECTORS' CHOICE
Congham Hall Country House Hotel
★★★ ⓘ ⓘ COUNTRY HOUSE HOTEL

☎ 01485 600250
Lynn Rd PE32 1AH
e-mail: info@conghamhallhotel.co.uk

(For full entry see Grimston)

Bank House Hotel
★★★ 83% ⓘ HOTEL

☎ 01553 660492
King's Staithe Square PE30 1RD
e-mail: info@thebankhouse.co.uk
dir: In King's Lynn Old Town follow quay, through floodgates, hotel on right opposite Custom House

This Grade II listed, 18th-century town house is situated on the quay side in the heart of King's Lynn's historical quarter. Bedrooms are individually decorated and have high quality fabrics and furnishings along with a range of useful facilities.

Public rooms include the Counting House coffee shop, a wine bar and brasserie restaurant, as well as a residents' lounge.

Rooms 11 (5 fmly) **Facilities** FTV Wi-fi ⓑ Xmas New Year **Conf** Class 20 Board 15 Thtr 30 **Notes** ⊗

Stuart House Hotel
★★★ 72% HOTEL

☎ 01553 772169
35 Goodwins Rd PE30 5QX
e-mail: reception@stuarthousehotel.co.uk
web: www.stuarthousehotel.co.uk
dir: At A47/A10/A149 rdbt follow signs to town centre. Under Southgate Arch, right into Guanock Terrace, right into Goodwins Rd

This small privately-owned hotel is situated in a peaceful residential area just a short walk from the town centre. Bedrooms come in a variety of styles and sizes; all are pleasantly decorated and thoughtfully equipped. There is a choice of eating options with informal dining in the bar and a daily-changing menu in the elegant restaurant.

Rooms 18 (2 fmly) (3 GF) 🦃 **Facilities** FTV Wi-fi ⓑ **Conf** Class 30 Board 20 Thtr 50 **Parking** 30 **Notes** ⊗ RS 25-26 Dec & 1 Jan Civ Wed 60

Grange Hotel
★★ 72% HOTEL

☎ 01553 673777 & 671222
Willow Park, South Wootton Ln PE30 3BP
e-mail: info@thegrangehotelkingslynn.co.uk
dir: A148 towards King's Lynn for 1.5m. At lights left into Wootton Rd, 400yds, on right into South Wootton Ln. Hotel 1st on left

Expect a warm welcome at this Edwardian house which is situated in a quiet residential area in its own grounds. Public rooms include a smart lounge bar and a cosy restaurant. The spacious bedrooms are pleasantly decorated and equipped with many thoughtful touches; some are located in an adjacent wing.

Rooms 9 (4 annexe) (2 fmly) (4 GF) **Facilities** Xmas **Conf** Class 15 Board 12 Thtr 20 **Parking** 15

Premier Inn King's Lynn

BUDGET HOTEL

☎ 0871 527 8570
Clenchwarton Rd, West Lynn PE34 3LJ
web: www.premierinn.com
dir: At junct of A47 & A17

High quality, budget accommodation ideal for both families and business travellers. Spacious, en suite bedrooms feature tea and coffee making facilities, and Freeview TV in most hotels. Internet access and Wi-fi are available for a small fee. The adjacent family restaurant features a wide and varied menu. See also the Hotel Groups pages.

Rooms 61

KINGSTON BAGPUIZE   Map 5 SU49
Oxfordshire

Fallowfields Hotel and Restaurant

★★★ 80% ◎◎ HOTEL

☎ 01865 820416
Faringdon Rd OX13 5BH
e-mail: stay@fallowfields.com
web: www.fallowfields.com
dir: A34 (Oxford Ring Rd) take A420 towards Swindon. At junct with A415 left, 100yds, exit at mini rdbt. Hotel on left after 1m

Located in rural Oxfordshire just ten miles from Oxford city centre, this small family-run hotel offers the personal touch. The bedrooms are generous in size and some have delightful views over the croquet lawn. The grounds are home to several breeds of cattle, pigs and chickens along with the kitchen garden where much of the produce for the menus is sourced.

Rooms 10 (2 fmly) ➨ S £110-£125; D £155-£175 (incl. bkfst) **Facilities** FTV Wi-fi ⬆ Falconry Archery Xmas New Year Child facilities **Conf** Class 25 Board 20 Thtr 60 Del from £185 to £214.50* **Parking** 50 **Notes** Civ Wed 100

KINGSTON UPON HULL   Map 17 TA02
East Riding of Yorkshire

BEST WESTERN Willerby Manor Hotel

★★★ 83% ◎ HOTEL

☎ 01482 652616
Well Ln HU10 6ER
e-mail: willerbymanor@bestwestern.co.uk
web: www.willerbymanor.co.uk

(For full entry see Willerby)

Holiday Inn Hull Marina

★★★ 81% HOTEL

☎ 0871 942 9043 & 01482 386300
The Marina, Castle St HU1 2BX
e-mail: reservations-hull@ihg.com
web: www.holidayinn.co.uk
dir: M62 junct 38, A63 to Hull. Follow Marina & Ice Arena signs. Hotel on left adjacent to Ice Arena

Situated overlooking the marina just off the A63, Holiday Inn Hull Marina offers well-equipped

---

accommodation including executive rooms. Public areas are attractively designed and include meeting rooms and a leisure club. The Junction Restaurant serves contemporary cuisine, and guests can eat alfresco on the patio if the weather permits.

Rooms 100 (10 fmly) **Facilities** STV Wi-fi ⬇ ⬚ supervised Gym New Year **Conf** Class 70 Board 50 Thtr 120 **Services** Lift Air con **Parking** 151 **Notes** ⊗ Civ Wed 120

Mercure Hull Royal Hotel

★★★ 75% HOTEL

☎ 01482 325087
170 Ferensway HU1 3UF
e-mail: reservations@hotels-hull.co.uk
web: www.hotels-hull.com
dir: A63 to city centre. Follow signs to railway station, hotel adjacent

A railway hotel in Victorian times, this impressive building has been modernised in recent years. The stunning central lounge area is the focal point and there are extensive conference and banqueting facilities, with complimentary parking and Wi-fi access also provided. The contemporary bedrooms have bold colour schemes with good facilities including flat-screen TVs; many have air conditioning. There is a leisure club adjacent to the hotel.

Rooms 155 (29 fmly) (20 smoking) **Facilities** FTV Wi-fi Xmas New Year **Conf** Class 150 Board 70 Thtr 400 **Services** Lift **Parking** 84 **Notes** Civ Wed 400

Campanile Hull

BUDGET HOTEL

☎ 01482 325530
Beverley Rd, Freetown Way (City Centre) HU2 9AN
e-mail: hull@campanile.com
web: www.campanile.com
dir: M62 junct 38, A63 to Hull, pass Humber Bridge on right. Over flyover, follow railway station signs onto A1079. Hotel at bottom of Ferensway

This modern building offers accommodation in smart, well-equipped bedrooms, all with en suite bathrooms. Refreshments may be taken at the informal bistro. See also the Hotel Groups pages.

Rooms 48 (48 annexe) (24 GF) S £29-£60; D £29-£60* **Conf** Class 15 Board 15 Thtr 25

Ibis Hull

BUDGET HOTEL

☎ 01482 387500
Osborne St HU1 2NL
e-mail: h3479-gm@accor-hotels.com
web: www.ibishotel.com
dir: M62/A63 straight across at rdbt, follow signs for Princes Quay onto Myton St. Hotel on corner of Osborne St & Ferensway

Modern, budget hotel offering comfortable accommodation in bright and practical bedrooms. Breakfast is self-service and dinner is available in the restaurant. See also the Hotel Groups pages.

Rooms 106 (19 GF)

Premier Inn Hull City Centre

BUDGET HOTEL

☎ 0871 527 8534
Tower St HU9 1TQ
web: www.premierinn.com
dir: M62, A63 into Hull city centre. At rdbt left onto A1165 (Great Union St), left into Citadel Way. Hotel at end on right

High quality, budget accommodation ideal for both families and business travellers. Spacious, en suite bedrooms feature tea and coffee making facilities, and Freeview TV in most hotels. Internet access and Wi-fi are available for a small fee. The adjacent family restaurant features a wide and varied menu. See also the Hotel Groups pages.

Rooms 136

Premier Inn Hull North

BUDGET HOTEL

☎ 0871 527 8536
Ashcombe Rd, Kingswood Park HU7 3DD
web: www.premierinn.com
dir: A63 to town centre, take A1079 N for approx 5m. Right at rdbt onto A1033. Hotel at 2nd rdbt in New Kingswood Park

Rooms 42

Premier Inn Hull West

BUDGET HOTEL

☎ 0871 527 8538
Ferriby Rd, Hessle HU13 0JA
web: www.premierinn.com
dir: A63 onto A15 to Humber Bridge (Beverley & Hessle Viewpoint). Hotel at 1st rdbt

Rooms 61

K

KINGSWINFORD
West Midlands
Map 10 SO88

Premier Inn Dudley (Kingswinford)

BUDGET HOTEL

☎ 0871 527 8314
Dudley Rd DY6 8WT
web: www.premierinn.com
dir: A4123 to Dudley, A461 follow signs for Russell's Hall Hospital. On A4101 to Kingswinford, hotel opposite Pensnett Trading Estate

High quality, budget accommodation ideal for both families and business travellers. Spacious, en suite bedrooms feature tea and coffee making facilities, and Freeview TV in most hotels. Internet access and Wi-fi are available for a small fee. The adjacent family restaurant features a wide and varied menu. See also the Hotel Groups pages.

Rooms 45

KINGTON
Herefordshire
Map 9 SO25

Burton Hotel

★★★ 78% HOTEL

☎ 01544 230323
Mill St HR5 3BQ
e-mail: info@burtonhotel.co.uk
web: www.burtonhotel.co.uk
dir: At A44 & A411 rdbt junct follow Town Centre signs

Situated in the town centre, this friendly, privately-owned hotel offers spacious, pleasantly proportioned and well-equipped bedrooms. Smartly presented public areas include a lounge bar, and leisure facilities including a well-equipped gym, spa and swimming pool. Outside there is a small, flood-lit golf-putting area laid with astro turf. The attractive restaurant offers carefully prepared cuisine. There are function and meeting facilities in a purpose-built, modern wing. Well spaced parking is located to the rear of the hotel.

Rooms 16 (5 fmly) ↝ **Facilities** Spa FTV Wi-fi ↻ ↺ supervised Putt green Gym Steam room Therapy rooms Xmas New Year **Conf** Class 100 Board 20 Thtr 150 **Services** Lift **Parking** 50 **Notes** LB Civ Wed 120

KIRKBY FLEETHAM
North Yorkshire
Map 19 SE29

The Black Horse

◉ ◉ RESTAURANT WITH ROOMS

☎ 01609 749010 & 749011
Lumley Ln DL7 0SH
e-mail: gm@blackhorsekirkbyfleetham.com
web: www.blackhorsekirkbyfleetham.com
dir: A1 onto A648 towards Northallerton. Left into Ham Hall Ln, through Scruton. At T-junct left into Fleetham Ln. Through Great Fencote to Kirkby Fleetham, into Lumley Ln, inn on left past post office

Set in a small village, The Black Horse provides everything needed for a getaway break including award-winning food. The spacious bedrooms, named after famous racehorses, are beautifully designed in New England/French style with pastel colours, co-ordinating fabrics and excellent beds; many of the superb bathrooms feature slipper or roll-top baths. There is a large dining room and bar that attracts locals as well as visitors from further afield.

Rooms 7 (1 fmly)

KIRKBY LONSDALE
Cumbria
Map 18 SD67

The Whoop Hall

★★ 76% HOTEL

☎ 015242 71284
Burrow with Burrow LA6 2HP
e-mail: info@whoophall.co.uk
dir: On A65, 1m SE of Kirkby Lonsdale

This popular inn combines traditional charm with modern facilities, that include a very well-equipped leisure complex. Bedrooms, some with four-poster beds, and some housed in converted barns, are appointed to a smart, stylish standard. A fire warms the bar on chillier days, and an interesting choice of dishes is available in both the bar and galleried restaurant throughout the day and evening.

Rooms 24 (4 fmly) (2 GF) ↝ **S** £60-£75; **D** £80-£115 (incl. bkfst)* **Facilities** FTV Wi-fi ↻ supervised Gym Beauty treatment room Sauna ♫ Xmas New Year **Conf** Class 72 Board 56 Thtr 169 **Parking** 100 **Notes** ⊗ Civ Wed 120

INSPECTORS' CHOICE

Hipping Hall

◉ ◉ ◉ RESTAURANT WITH ROOMS

☎ 015242 71187
Cowan Bridge LA6 2JJ
e-mail: info@hippinghall.com
dir: M6 junct 36, A65 through Kirkby Lonsdale towards Skipton. On right after Cowan Bridge

Close to the market town of Kirkby Lonsdale, Hipping Hall offers spacious, feature bedrooms, designed in soft shades with sumptuous textures and fabrics; the bathrooms use natural stone, slate and limestone to great effect. There are also three spacious cottage suites that create a real hideaway experience. The sitting room, with large, comfortable sofas has a traditional feel. The restaurant is a 15th-century hall with tapestries and a minstrels' gallery that is as impressive as it is intimate.

Rooms 9 (3 annexe)

The Sun Inn

◉ RESTAURANT WITH ROOMS

☎ 015242 71965
6 Market St LA6 2AU
e-mail: email@sun-inn.info
web: www.sun-inn.info
dir: From A65 follow signs to town centre. Inn on main street

The Sun is a 17th-century inn situated in a historic market town, overlooking St Mary's Church. The atmospheric bar features stone walls, wooden beams and log fires with real ales available. Delicious meals are served in the bar or the more formal, modern restaurant. Traditional and modern styles are blended together in the beautifully appointed rooms with excellent en suites.

Rooms 11 (1 fmly)

KIRKHAM
Lancashire
Map 18 SD43

Premier Inn Blackpool Kirkham M55 Jct 3

BUDGET HOTEL

☎ 0871 527 8104
Fleetwood Rd, Greenhalgh PR4 3HE
web: www.premierinn.com
dir: M6 junct 32, M55 towards Blackpool. Hotel just off junct 3 towards Kirkham

High quality, budget accommodation ideal for both families and business travellers. Spacious, en suite

Save on hotels. Book at **theAA.com/hotel**

KIN – KNU 227 **ENGLAND**

bedrooms feature tea and coffee making facilities, and Freeview TV in most hotels. Internet access and Wi-fi are available for a small fee. The adjacent family restaurant features a wide and varied menu. See also the Hotel Groups pages.

Rooms 28

KNARESBOROUGH
North Yorkshire — Map 19 SE35

General Tarleton Inn

⊛ ⊛ RESTAURANT WITH ROOMS

☎ 01423 340284
Boroughbridge Rd, Ferrensby HG5 0PZ
e-mail: gti@generaltarleton.co.uk
dir: A1(M) junct 48 at Boroughbridge, take A6055 to Knaresborough. 4m on right

This beautiful 18th-century coaching inn has been stylishly renovated. Though the physical aspects are impressive, the emphasis here is on food with high quality, skilfully prepared dishes served in the smart bar/brasserie and in the Orangery. There is also a richly furnished cocktail lounge with a galleried private dining room above it. Bedrooms are very comfortable and business guests are also well catered for.

Rooms 13

KNIPTON
Leicestershire — Map 11 SK83

The Manners Arms

RESTAURANT WITH ROOMS

☎ 01476 879222
Croxton Rd NG32 1RH
e-mail: info@mannersarms.com
web: www.mannersarms.com
dir: From A607 follow signs to Knipton; from A52 follow signs to Belvoir Castle

Part of the Rutland Estate and built as a hunting lodge for the 6th Duke, The Manners Arms offers thoughtfully furnished bedrooms designed by the present Duchess. Public areas include the intimate Beater's Bar and attractive Red Coats Restaurant, popular for its imaginative menus.

Rooms 10 (1 fmly)

KNOWSLEY
Merseyside — Map 15 SJ49

Suites Hotel Knowsley   THE INDEPENDENTS

★★★★ 73% HOTEL

☎ 0151 549 2222
Ribblers Ln L34 9HA
e-mail: enquiries@suiteshotelgroup.com
web: www.suiteshotelgroup.com
dir: M57 junct 4. Telephone for detailed directions

Located a close to the M57, this hotel is just a 10-minute drive from Liverpool's city centre. It offers superior, well-equipped accommodation and there is a choice of lounges plus Handley's Restaurant. Guests have the use of the impressive leisure centre, and there are extensive conference facilities.

Rooms 101 (39 fmly) (20 GF) (6 smoking) 🐾
Facilities STV Wi-fi ⋕ HL ⑤ supervised Gym Xmas New Year **Conf** Class 60 Board 50 Thtr 240 **Services** Lift Air con **Parking** 200 **Notes** LB ⊗ Civ Wed 140

KNUTSFORD
Cheshire — Map 15 SJ77

The Mere Golf Resort & Spa

★★★★ 82% ⊛ HOTEL

☎ 01565 830155
WA16 6LJ

This hotel sits alongside Mere Lake and is close to the picturesque town of Knutsford; there are excellent transport links with Manchester International Airport being only ten minutes away. The resort's historic main Victorian building conveys the classic charm of that era, and offers stylish, luxury accommodation. The championship golf course designed by James Braid is both beautiful and challenging. The spa features an extensive range of treatments and facilities including a Thermal Zone. The staff are professional and very friendly, offering personal service.

Rooms 81 **Conf** Class 350 Board 40 Thtr 700

Cottons Hotel & Spa   shire

★★★★ 79% ⊛ HOTEL

☎ 01565 650333
Manchester Rd WA16 0SU
e-mail: cottons@shirehotels.com
web: www.cottonshotel.com
dir: On A50, 1m from M6 junct 19

The superb leisure facilities and quiet location are great attractions at this hotel, which is just a short distance from Manchester Airport. Bedrooms are smartly appointed in various styles, and executive

rooms have very good working areas. The hotel has spacious lounge areas and an excellent leisure centre.

Rooms 109 (14 fmly) (38 GF) 🐾 **S** £90-£150; **D** £90-£150* **Facilities** Spa STV Wi-fi ⓘ ⋕ ♨ Gym Steam room Activity studio for exercise classes Sauna Children's splash pool Xmas New Year **Conf** Class 100 Board 36 Thtr 200 **Del** from £145 to £185* **Services** Lift Air con **Parking** 180 **Notes** LB ⊗ Civ Wed 120

Mere Court Hotel & Conference Centre

★★★★ 77% ⊛ HOTEL

☎ 01565 831000
Warrington Rd, Mere WA16 0RW
e-mail: sales@merecourt.co.uk
web: www.merecourt.co.uk
dir: A50, 1m W of junct with A556, on right

This is a smart and attractive hotel, set in extensive, well-tended gardens. The elegant and spacious bedrooms are individually styled and offer a host of thoughtful extras. Conference facilities are particularly impressive and there is a large, self contained, conservatory function suite. Dining is available in the fine dining Arboreum Restaurant.

Rooms 34 (24 fmly) (12 GF) **S** £80-£110; **D** £90-£120 **Facilities** STV FTV Wi-fi Xmas New Year **Conf** Class 75 Board 50 Thtr 200 **Services** Lift **Parking** 150 **Notes** LB ⊗ Civ Wed 150

The Longview Hotel & Stuffed Olive Restaurant

★★ 82% HOTEL

☎ 01565 632119
55 Manchester Rd WA16 0LX
e-mail: enquiries@longviewhotel.com
web: www.longviewhotel.com
dir: M6 junct 19 take A556 W towards Chester. Left at lights onto A5033, 1.5m to rdbt then left. Hotel 200yds on right

This friendly Victorian hotel offers high standards of hospitality and service. Attractive public areas include a cellar bar and foyer lounge area. The restaurant has a traditional feel and offers an imaginative selection of dishes. Bedrooms, some located in a superb renovation of nearby houses, are individually styled and offer a good range of thoughtful amenities, including broadband internet access.

Rooms 32 (19 annexe) (1 fmly) (5 GF) **Facilities** FTV Wi-fi **Conf** Class 20 Board 20 **Parking** 20 **Notes** RS 21 Dec-6 Jan

K

KNUTSFORD *continued*

Premier Inn Knutsford (Bucklow Hill)

BUDGET HOTEL

☎ 0871 527 8572
Bucklow Hill WA16 6RD
web: www.premierinn.com
dir: M6 junct 19, A556 towards Manchester Airport & Stockport

High quality, budget accommodation ideal for both families and business travellers. Spacious, en suite bedrooms feature tea and coffee making facilities, and Freeview TV in most hotels. Internet access and Wi-fi are available for a small fee. The adjacent family restaurant features a wide and varied menu. See also the Hotel Groups pages.

Rooms 69

Premier Inn Knutsford (Mere)

BUDGET HOTEL

☎ 0871 527 8574
Warrington Rd, Hoo Green, Mere WA16 0PZ
web: www.premierinn.com
dir: M6 junct 19, A556, follow Manchester signs. At 1st lights left onto A50 towards Warrington. Hotel 1m on right

Rooms 28

LACEBY   Map 17 TA20
Lincolnshire

BEST WESTERN Oaklands Hall Hotel

★★★ 79% HOTEL

☎ 01472 872248
Barton St DN37 7LF
e-mail: reception@oaklandshallhotel.co.uk
dir: At junct of A46 & A18 at Laceby, on edge of Grimsby

This attractive 19th-century property is located on a private estate in five acres of parkland. It has been refurbished with a contemporary style while retaining beautiful period features. The Comfy Duck restaurant is stylish, and food is a highlight of any stay, with a strong emphasis on local produce. Bedrooms are comfortable and complimentary Wi-fi is provided.

Rooms 46 (4 fmly) (10 GF) 🐾 **D** £70-£130 (incl. bkfst) **Facilities** FTV Wi-fi ♨ Xmas New Year **Conf** Class 150 Board 50 Thtr 180 **Parking** 80 **Notes** LB ⊗ Civ Wed 200

LANCASTER   Map 18 SD46
Lancashire

Lancaster House

English Lakes
Hotels Resorts & Venues

★★★★ 77% HOTEL

☎ 01524 844822
Green Ln, Ellel LA1 4GJ
e-mail: lancasterhouse@englishlakes.co.uk
web: www.elh.co.uk/hotels/lancaster
dir: M6 junct 33 N towards Lancaster. Through Galgate into Green Ln. Hotel before university on right

This modern hotel enjoys a rural setting south of the city and close to the university. The attractive open-plan reception and lounge boast a roaring log fire in colder months. Bedrooms are spacious, and include 19 rooms that are particularly well equipped for business guests. There are leisure facilities with a hot tub and a function suite.

Rooms 99 (29 fmly) (44 GF) 🐾 **Facilities** Spa STV Wi-fi ♨ HL ⊛ supervised Gym Beauty salon Xmas New Year **Conf** Class 60 Board 48 Thtr 250 **Parking** 120 **Notes** Civ Wed 140

Holiday Inn Lancaster

Holiday Inn

★★★ 79% HOTEL

☎ 01524 840066 & 0871 942 9047
Waterside Park, Caton Rd LA1 3RA
e-mail: reservations-lancaster@ihg.com
web: www.hilancasterhotel.co.uk
dir: M6 junct 34 towards Lancaster. Hotel 1st on right

Close to the M6 and Lancaster, this modern hotel caters well for business and leisure guests, including families. The ground floor is open plan, with an informal atmosphere in the lounge-bar and Traders restaurant. The Spirit Health Club features a 15-metre pool, sauna, steam room, beauty treatment rooms and a well-equipped gym.

Rooms 156 (72 fmly) (25 GF) **D** £49-£124 (incl. bkfst) **Facilities** STV FTV Wi-fi ⊛ supervised Gym Fitness classes Beauty treatment room Xmas New Year **Conf** Class 60 Board 60 Thtr 120 Del from £90 to £150 **Services** Lift Air con **Parking** 200 **Notes** Civ Wed 110

Penny Street Bridge

THWAITES
Inns of character

★★★ 74% TOWN HOUSE HOTEL

☎ 01524 599900
Penny St LA1 1XT
e-mail: relax@pennystreetbridge.co.uk
dir: In city centre

Ideally situated in the heart of the city, Penny Street Bridge has been transformed from a typical Victorian property to one that is fresh and contemporary, yet retains all the elegance of its original era. Bedrooms are modern and very well equipped. The stylish Bar & Brasserie are popular with both guests and local residents, serving meals and light bites throughout the day.

Rooms 28 (2 fmly) **Facilities** FTV Wi-fi ♨ **Conf** Board 20 Thtr 20 **Services** Lift Air con **Parking** 4 **Notes** ⊗

Premier Inn Lancaster

Premier Inn

BUDGET HOTEL

☎ 0871 527 8576
Lancaster Business Park, Caton Rd LA1 3PE
web: www.premierinn.com
dir: M6 junct 34, A683 towards Lancaster. Hotel 0.25m on left at entrance to Business Park

High quality, budget accommodation ideal for both families and business travellers. Spacious, en suite bedrooms feature tea and coffee making facilities, and Freeview TV in most hotels. Internet access and Wi-fi are available for a small fee. The adjacent family restaurant features a wide and varied menu. See also the Hotel Groups pages.

Rooms 85

LAND'S END Map 2 SW32
Cornwall

The Land's End Hotel

★★★ 71% HOTEL

☎ 01736 871844
TR19 7AA
e-mail: reservations@landsendhotel.co.uk
web: www.landsendhotel.co.uk
dir: From Penzance take A30, follow Land's End signs. After Sennen 1m to Land's End

This famous location provides a memorable setting for The Land's End Hotel. Bedrooms, many with stunning views of the Atlantic, are pleasantly decorated and comfortable. Refurbished public areas provide plenty of style and comfort with a relaxing lounge and convivial bar. The restaurant is equally impressive with accomplished cuisine complementing the amazing views out to sea.

Rooms 30 (4 fmly) **S** £60-£80; **D** £80-£120 (incl. bkfst)* **Facilities** FTV Wi-fi Free entry to Land's End Visitor Centre & Attractions Xmas **Conf** Class 50 Board 30 Thtr 100 **Parking** 100 **Notes** ✪ Civ Wed 120

LANGAR Map 11 SK73
Nottinghamshire

Langar Hall

★★★ 81% ◉◉ HOTEL

☎ 01949 860559
NG13 9HG
e-mail: info@langarhall.co.uk
web: www.langarhall.com
dir: Via Bingham from A52 or Cropwell Bishop from A46, both signed. Hotel behind church

This delightful hotel enjoys a picturesque rural location, yet is only a short drive from Nottingham. Individually styled bedrooms are furnished with fine period pieces and benefit from some thoughtful extras. There is a choice of lounges, warmed by real fires, and a snug little bar. Imaginative food is served in the dining room, while the garden conservatory provides a lighter menu.

Rooms 12 (1 fmly) (1 GF) **S** £100-£140; **D** £125-£198 (incl. bkfst)* **Facilities** FTV Wi-fi Fishing ✿ Xmas New Year Child facilities **Conf** Class 16 Board 12 Thtr 16 Del £175* **Parking** 20 **Notes** LB Civ Wed 50

LANGHO Map 18 SD73
Lancashire

INSPECTORS' CHOICE

Northcote

★★★★ ◉◉◉◉ SMALL HOTEL

☎ 01254 240555
Northcote Rd BB6 8BE
e-mail: reception@northcote.com
web: www.northcote.com
dir: M6 junct 31, 9m to Northcote. Follow Clitheroe (A59) signs, Hotel on left before rdbt

This is a gastronomic haven where guests return to sample the delights of its famous kitchen. The outstanding cooking includes Lancashire's finest fare, and fruit and herbs from the hotel's own beautifully laid out organic gardens. Drinks can be enjoyed in the comfortable, elegantly furnished lounges and bar. Each of the luxury bedrooms has its own identity with sumptuous fabrics and soft furnishings, sophisticated lighting and ultra modern bathrooms; some have a garden patio.

Rooms 14 (2 fmly) (4 GF) ✿ **S** £220-£245; **D** £255-£280 (incl. bkfst)* **Facilities** STV FTV Wi-fi ✿ New Year **Conf** Class 10 Board 22 Thtr 36 **Parking** 50 **Notes** LB ✪ Closed 25 Dec Civ Wed 40

BEST WESTERN Mytton Fold Hotel and Golf Complex

★★★ Ⓐ HOTEL

☎ 01254 240662 & 245392
Whalley Rd BB6 8AB
e-mail: reception@myttonfold.co.uk
web: www.bw-myttonfoldhotel.co.uk
dir: At large rdbt on A59, follow signs for Whalley, exit into Whalley Road. Hotel on right

Set in pretty and well maintained grounds that are a riot of colour in the summer, this hotel has views over the golf course to Pendle Hill beyond. The bedrooms are smart and include two with four-posters. This is a popular wedding venue.

Rooms 43 (12 fmly) (10 GF) ✿ **S** £59-£70; **D** £90-£99 (incl. bkfst)* **Facilities** STV Wi-fi ⚓ 18 Putt green Xmas **Conf** Class 60 Board 40 Thtr 290 Del from £87.50 to £97.50* **Services** Lift **Parking** 300 **Notes** ✪ Closed 1 Jan Civ Wed 250

LASTINGHAM Map 19 SE79
North Yorkshire

Lastingham Grange Hotel

★★★ 81% HOTEL

☎ 01751 417345 & 417402
YO62 6TH
e-mail: reservations@lastinghamgrange.com
web: www.lastinghamgrange.com
dir: From A170 follow signs for Appleton-le-Moors, continue into Lastingham, pass church on left, right, then left up hill. Hotel on right

A warm welcome and sincere hospitality have been the hallmarks of this hotel for over 50 years. Antique furniture is plentiful, and the lounge and the dining room both look out onto the terrace and sunken rose garden below. There is a large play area for older children and the moorland views are breathtaking.

Rooms 12 (2 fmly) **S** £75-£135; **D** £150-£199 (incl. bkfst)* **Facilities** FTV Wi-fi ✿ Large adventure playground **Parking** 30 **Notes** LB Closed Dec-Feb

LAUNCESTON Map 3 SX38
Cornwall

See also Lifton

Eagle House Hotel

★★ 74% SMALL HOTEL

☎ 01566 772036 & 774488
Castle St PL15 8BA
e-mail: eaglehousehotel@aol.com
dir: From Launceston on Holsworthy Rd follow brown hotel signs

Next to the castle, this elegant Georgian house dates back to 1767 and is within walking distance of all the local amenities. Many of the bedrooms have wonderful views over the Cornish countryside. A short carte is served each evening in the restaurant.

Rooms 14 (1 fmly) **S** £47; **D** £72 (incl. bkfst)* **Facilities** Wi-fi **Conf** Class 170 Board 170 Thtr 170 **Parking** 80 **Notes** ✪ Civ Wed 170

L

LAVENHAM
Suffolk   Map 13 TL94

INSPECTORS' CHOICE

The Swan

★★★★ ◉◉ HOTEL   T|A HOTEL COLLECTION

☎ 01787 247477
High St CO10 9QA
e-mail: info@theswanatlavenham.co.uk
web: www.theswanatlavenham.co.uk
dir: From Bury St Edmunds take A134 (S), then A1141 to Lavenham

The Swan is a delightful collection of listed buildings, dating back to the 14th century, lovingly restored to retain their original charm. Public rooms include comfortable lounge areas, a charming rustic bar, an informal brasserie and a fine-dining restaurant. Bedrooms are tastefully furnished and equipped with many thoughtful touches. The friendly staff are helpful, attentive and offer professional service.

Rooms 45 (7 fmly) (9 GF) ☞ **S** £105; **D** £195-£350 (incl. bkfst)* **Facilities** FTV Wi-fi ⌇ Xmas New Year **Conf** Class 36 Board 30 Thtr 50 Del £198* **Parking** 30 **Notes** Civ Wed 100

INSPECTORS' CHOICE

Lavenham Great House 'Restaurant With Rooms'

◉◉ RESTAURANT WITH ROOMS

☎ 01787 247431
Market Place CO10 9QZ
e-mail: info@greathouse.co.uk
web: www.greathouse.co.uk
dir: Exit A1141 into Market Ln, behind cross on Market Place

The 18th-century frontage on Market Place conceals a 15th-century timber-framed building that is now a restaurant with rooms. The Great House remains a pocket of France offering high-quality rural cuisine served by French staff. The spacious bedrooms are individually decorated and thoughtfully equipped with many useful extras; some rooms have a separate lounge area.

Rooms 5 (1 fmly)

LEA MARSTON
Warwickshire   Map 10 SP29

Lea Marston Hotel & Spa

★★★★ 76% ◉◉ HOTEL   CLASSIC BRITISH HOTELS

☎ 01675 470468
Haunch Ln B76 0BY
e-mail: info@leamarstonhotel.co.uk
web: www.leamarstonhotel.co.uk
dir: M42 junct 9, A4097 to Kingsbury. Hotel signed 1.5m on right

Excellent access to the motorway network and a good range of sports facilities make this hotel a popular choice for conferences and leisure breaks. Bedrooms are mostly set around an attractive quadrangle and are generously equipped. Diners can choose between the popular Sportsman's Lounge Bar and the elegant Adderley Restaurant.

Rooms 88 (18 fmly) (49 GF) ☞ **Facilities** Spa FTV Wi-fi ⊗ ♨ 9 ⌇ Putt green Gym Golf driving range Golf simulator Sauna Steam room Rasul Hydrotherapy bath Xmas New Year **Conf** Class 50 Board 30 Thtr 140 Del from £135 to £175* **Services** Lift **Parking** 200 **Notes** ⊗ Civ Wed 100

LEAMINGTON SPA (ROYAL)
Warwickshire   Map 10 SP36

INSPECTORS' CHOICE

Mallory Court Hotel

★★★ ◉◉◉ HOTEL   EDEN HOTEL COLLECTION

☎ 01926 330214
Harbury Ln, Bishop's Tachbrook CV33 9QB
e-mail: reception@mallory.co.uk
web: www.mallory.co.uk
dir: M40 junct 13 N'bound left, left again towards Bishops Tachbrook, right into Harbury Ln after 0.5m. M40 junct 14 S'bound A452 to Leamington, at 2nd rdbt left into Harbury Ln

Mallory Court Hotel is part of the Eden Hotel Collection and with its tranquil rural setting, this elegant Lutyens-style country house is an idyllic retreat, set in ten acres of landscaped gardens with immaculate lawns and an orchard. Relaxation is easy in the two sumptuous lounges, drawing room or conservatory. Dining is a treat in either the elegant restaurant or the brasserie. Simon Haigh heads up a team of expert chefs producing dishes that continue to delight. Bedrooms in the main house are luxuriously decorated and most have wonderful views. Those in the Knights Suite are more contemporary and have their own access via a smart conference and banqueting facility.

Rooms 31 (11 annexe) (2 fmly) (5 GF) ☞ **S** £139-£395; **D** £159-£550 (incl. bkfst) **Facilities** FTV Wi-fi ♨ ♨ Use of nearby club facilities Xmas New Year **Conf** Class 160 Board 50 Thtr 200 Del from £189 to £240 **Services** Lift **Parking** 100 **Notes** LB ⊗ Civ Wed 160

Angel Hotel

★★★ 77% HOTEL

☎ 01926 881296
143 Regent St CV32 4NZ
e-mail: angelhotel143@hotmail.com
web: www.angelhotelleamington.co.uk
dir: In town centre at junct of Regent St & Holly Walk

This centrally located hotel is divided into two parts: the original inn, and a more modern extension. Public rooms include a comfortable foyer lounge area, a smart restaurant and an informal bar. Bedrooms are individual in style, and, whether modern or traditional, all have the expected facilities.

Rooms 48 (3 fmly) (3 GF) **S** £59-£85; **D** £79-£105 (incl. bkfst)* **Facilities** STV FTV Wi-fi **Conf** Class 40 Board 40 Thtr 70 Del from £110* **Services** Lift **Parking** 38 **Notes** LB ⊗

BEST WESTERN Falstaff Hotel

★★★ 73% HOTEL

☎ 01926 312044
16-20 Warwick New Rd CV32 5JQ
e-mail: sales@falstaffhotel.com
web: www.falstaffhotel.com
dir: M40 junct 13 or 14, follow Leamington Spa signs. Over 4 rdbts, under bridge. Left into Princes Dr, right at mini-rdbt

Bedrooms at this hotel come in a variety of sizes and styles and are well equipped, with many thoughtful extras. Snacks can be taken in the relaxing lounge bar, and an interesting selection of English and continental dishes is offered in the restaurant; 24-hour room service is also available. Conference and banqueting facilities are extensive.

Rooms 59 (3 fmly) (16 GF) ☈ **S** £65-£95; **D** £85-£105 (incl. bkfst) **Facilities** FTV Wi-fi ☖ Arrangement with local health club Xmas New Year **Conf** Class 30 Board 30 Thtr 70 Del from £125 to £145 **Parking** 40

Premier Inn Leamington Spa Town Centre

BUDGET HOTEL

☎ 0871 527 9380
Regency Arcade, The Parade CV32 4BQ
web: www.premierinn.com
dir: From N, M40 junct 15/A452. Through 4 rdbts. At next rdbt take 4th exit, at final rdbt, take 1st exit A452 (Adelaide Road). Right onto Dormer Place & left onto St Peters Road into St Peters car park. Follow directional signage to Premier Inn. From S, M40 junct 13 then follow directions as above

High quality, budget accommodation ideal for both families and business travellers. Spacious, en suite bedrooms feature tea and coffee making facilities, and Freeview TV in most hotels. Internet access and Wi-fi are available for a small fee. The adjacent family restaurant features a wide and varied menu. See also the Hotel Groups pages.

Rooms 82

LEDBURY
Herefordshire   **Map 10 SO73**

Feathers Hotel

★★★ 81% HOTEL

☎ 01531 635266 & 638950
High St HR8 1DS
e-mail: mary@feathers-ledbury.co.uk
web: www.feathers-ledbury.co.uk
dir: S from Worcester on A449, E from Hereford on A438, N from Gloucester on A417. Hotel in town centre

A wealth of authentic features can be found at this historic timber-framed hotel, situated in the middle of town. The comfortably equipped bedrooms are tastefully decorated; there is also Eve's Cottage, in the grounds, and Lanark House, a two-bedroom apartment that is ideal for families and self-catering use. Well-prepared meals can be taken in Fuggles Brasserie with its adjoining bar, and breakfast is served in Quills Restaurant.

Rooms 22 (3 annexe) (2 fmly) ☈ **S** £97.50-£132.50; **D** £145-£250 (incl. bkfst)* **Facilities** STV FTV Wi-fi ☖ ☺ Gym Steam room New Year **Conf** Class 80 Board 40 Thtr 140 Del £137.50* **Parking** 30 **Notes** Civ Wed 100

Leadon House Hotel

AA Advertised

☎ 01531 631199
Ross Rd HR8 2LP
e-mail: leadon.house@btconnect.com
web: www.leadonhouse.com
dir: M5 junct 8/M50/A417 exit Ledbury. Left at 1st rdbt then take A449. Hotel 400yds on right by Ledbury Rugby Club

Enjoy a relaxing break at this family-run hotel, which has been tastefully refurbished in an Edwardian style, offering an idyllic environment and a peaceful night's stay. Many interesting architectural features add to the unique charm and elegance. All rooms are en suite and finished to a high standard, with plenty of attention paid to detail. Also available is the Coach House two bedroom apartment.

Rooms 8 (2 annexe) (1 fmly) (1 GF) ☈ **S** £54-£60; **D** £70-£105 (incl. bkfst)* **Facilities** FTV Wi-fi **Parking** 10 **Notes** LB ⊗

LEEDS
West Yorkshire   **Map 19 SE23**

See also Gomersal, Shipley & Wakefield

The New Ellington

★★★★ 85% ☺☺ TOWN HOUSE HOTEL

☎ 0113 204 2150
23-25 York Place LS1 2EY
e-mail: info@thenewellington.com

Near the central railway station and the civic and business quarters, this hotel, with an art deco and a musical theme in part, offers guests modern amenities. Bedrooms are air-conditioned, offer free Wi-fi, high quality bed linen and Nespresso coffee machines; some have quiet balconies too. The ground floor atrium Gin Bar lounge leads to the lower ground floor restaurant that serves a range of international dishes. Limited on-site chargeable parking is available on a first-come first-served basis.

Rooms 34 (3 GF) ☈ **S** £75-£395; **D** £75-£395* **Facilities** FTV Wi-fi ☖ **Conf** Class 15 Board 16 Thtr 30 Del from £135 to £175* **Services** Lift Air con **Parking** 6 **Notes** LB ⊗ Closed 24-27 Dec

Thorpe Park Hotel & Spa

shire
hotels & spas

★★★★ 84% ☺ HOTEL

☎ 0113 264 1000
Century Way, Thorpe Park LS15 8ZB
e-mail: thorpepark@shirehotels.com
web: www.thorpeparkhotel.com
dir: M1 junct 46, follow signs for Thorpe Park

Conveniently close to the M1, this hotel offers bedrooms that are modern in both style and facilities. The terrace and courtyard offer all-day casual dining and refreshments, and the restaurant features a Mediterranean-themed menu. There is also a state-of-the-art spa and leisure facility.

Rooms 111 (3 fmly) (25 GF) ☈ **S** £90-£150; **D** £90-£150* **Facilities** Spa STV Wi-fi ☖ HL ☺ Gym Activity studio Steam room Sauna New Year **Conf** Class 100 Board 50 Thtr 200 Del from £145 to £185* **Services** Lift Air con **Parking** 200 **Notes** LB ⊗ Civ Wed 150

L

LEEDS *continued*

De Vere Oulton Hall

★★★★ 83% ❀❀ HOTEL

☎ 0113 282 1000
Rothwell Ln, Oulton LS26 8HN
e-mail: oulton.hall@devere-hotels.com
web: www.devere-hotels.co.uk
dir: 2m from M62 junct 30, follow Rothwell signs, then 'Oulton 1m' sign. 1st exit at next 2 rdbts. Hotel on left. Or 1m from M1 junct 44, follow Castleford & Pontefract sign on A639

Surrounded by the beautiful Yorkshire Dales, yet only 15 minutes from the city centre, this elegant 19th-century house offers the best of both worlds. Impressive features include stylish, opulent day rooms and delightful formal gardens, which have been restored to their original design. The hotel boasts a choice of dining options, and extensive leisure facilities. Golfers can book preferential tee times at the adjacent golf club.

Rooms 152 **Facilities** Spa STV FTV Wi-fi HL ③ ♨ 27 ♨ Gym Beauty therapy Aerobics Xmas New Year **Conf** Class 150 Board 40 Thtr 350 **Services** Lift Air con **Parking** 260 **Notes** ⊛ Civ Wed 200

The Queens

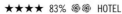

★★★★ 80% HOTEL

☎ 0113 243 1323
City Square LS1 1PJ
e-mail: queensreservations@qhotels.co.uk
web: www.qhotels.co.uk
dir: M621, M1 & M62 follow signs for city centre & rail station, along Neville St towards City Square. Under rail bridge, at lights left into slip road in front of hotel

A legacy from the golden age of railways and located in the heart of Leeds, overlooking City Square, this grand Victorian hotel retains much of its original splendour. Public rooms include the spacious lounge bar, a range of conference and function rooms along with the grand ballroom. Bedrooms vary in size but all are very well equipped, and there is a choice of suites available.

Rooms 215 (16 fmly) 🐾 **Facilities** STV Wi-fi ☇ Xmas New Year **Conf** Class 255 Board 80 Thtr 600 **Services** Lift Air con **Parking** 80 **Notes** ⊛ Civ Wed 600

Leeds Marriott Hotel

★★★★ 77% HOTEL

☎ 0113 236 6366
4 Trevelyan Square, Boar Ln LS1 6ET
e-mail:
london.regional.reservations@marriott.com
web: www.leedsmarriott.co.uk
dir: M621, M1 junct 3. Follow signs for city centre on A653. Stay in right lane. Energis building on left, turn right, follow signs to hotel

With a charming courtyard setting in the heart of the city, this modern, elegant hotel provides the perfect base for shopping and sightseeing. Air-conditioned bedrooms are tastefully decorated and offer good workspace. Public areas include a leisure club, an informal bar, lobby lounge area and a choice of restaurants including Georgetown which offers Colonial Malaysian cuisine. Valet parking is available.

Rooms 244 (29 fmly) (10 smoking) **Facilities** STV Wi-fi ☇ HL ③ supervised Gym Sauna Steam Room **Conf** Class 144 Board 80 Thtr 300 **Services** Lift Air con **Notes** ⊛ Civ Wed 300

Park Plaza Leeds

★★★★ 75% HOTEL

☎ 0113 380 4000
Boar Ln LS1 5NS
e-mail: pplinfo@pphe.com
web: www.parkplaza.com
dir: Follow signs for city centre

Chic, stylish, ultra modern, city-centre hotel located just opposite City Square. Chino Latino, located on the first floor, is a fusion Far East and modern Japanese restaurant with a Latino bar. Stylish, air-conditioned bedrooms are spacious and have a range of modern facilities, including high-speed internet connection.

Rooms 187 🐾 **Facilities** STV Wi-fi Gym Xmas New Year **Conf** Class 70 Board 60 Thtr 220 **Services** Lift Air con **Parking** 6 **Notes** Civ Wed 120

Radisson Blu Hotel Leeds

★★★★ 74% HOTEL

☎ 0113 236 6000
No 1 The Light, The Headrow LS1 8TL
e-mail: sarah.hawkin@radissonblu.com
web: www.radissonblu.co.uk
dir: Follow city centre 'loop' towards The Headrow/Light Complex. Hotel access on Cockeridge St off The Headrow

Situated in the shopping complex known as 'The Light', the hotel occupies a converted building that was formerly the headquarters of the Leeds Permanent Building Society. Three styles of bedrooms

are available but all have air conditioning and excellent business facilities. The lobby bar area serves substantial meals and is ideal for relaxation. Public parking is available, contact the hotel for details.

Rooms 147 (25 fmly) (3 smoking) 🐾 **Facilities** STV FTV Wi-fi ☇ HL ③ Gym Access to Virgin Active Xmas New Year **Conf** Class 30 Board 28 Thtr 60 Del from £165 to £185* **Services** Lift Air con **Notes** ⊛ Civ Wed

Crowne Plaza Hotel Leeds

★★★★ 73% HOTEL

☎ 0871 942 9170
Wellington St LS1 4DL
e-mail: sales.cpleeds@ihg.com
web: www.crowneplaza.co.uk
dir: From M1 follow signs to city centre. Left at City Sq into Wellington St

With easy access to the motorway and city centre, this modern hotel is an ideal choice for the business traveller. Bedrooms are of a good size with excellent facilities including air conditioning. There's a good sized pool and large gym - both are well worth a visit.

Rooms 135 (38 fmly) **Facilities** Spa STV Wi-fi ☇ HL ③ Gym Xmas New Year **Conf** Class 80 Board 60 Thtr 180 **Services** Lift Air con **Parking** 120 **Notes** ⊛ Civ Wed 180

The Met

★★★★ 73% HOTEL

☎ 0113 245 0841
King St LS1 2HQ
e-mail: metropole.sales@principal-hotels.com
web: www.principal-hotels.com
dir: From M1, M62 & M621 follow city centre signs. A65 into Wellington St. At 1st traffic island right into King St, hotel on right

Said to be the best example of this type of building in the city, this splendid terracotta-fronted hotel is centrally located and convenient for the railway station. All bedrooms are appointed to suit the business traveller, with hi-speed internet access and a working area. The Restaurant and the Tempest Bar make convenient dining options. There are also impressive conference and banqueting facilities. Some parking space is available.

Rooms 120 **Facilities** STV FTV Wi-fi ☇ **Conf** Class 100 Board 80 Thtr 250 **Services** Lift **Parking** 40 **Notes** ⊛ RS 24 Dec-1 Jan Civ Wed 200

Novotel Leeds Centre

★★★★ 73% HOTEL

☎ 0113 242 6446
4 Whitehall, Whitehall Quay LS1 4HR
e-mail: H3270@accor.com
web: www.novotel.com
dir: M621 junct 3, follow signs to rail station. Into Aire St & left at lights

With a minimalist style, this contemporary hotel provides a quality, value-for-money experience close to the city centre. Spacious, climate-controlled bedrooms are provided, whilst public areas offer deep leather sofas and an eye-catching water feature in reception. Light snacks are provided in the airy bar, and the restaurant doubles as a bistro. Staff are committed to guest care and nothing is too much trouble.

Rooms 196 (50 fmly) ⦰ **Facilities** STV FTV Wi-fi ⦰ HL Gym Steam room Sauna Xmas **Conf** Class 50 Board 50 Thtr 100 **Services** Lift **Parking** 80

Malmaison Leeds

★★★ 85% ⑳ HOTEL

☎ 0113 398 1000
1 Swingate LS1 4AG
e-mail: leeds@malmaison.com
web: www.malmaison.com
dir: M621/M1 junct 3, follow city centre signs. At KPMG building, right into Sovereign Street. Hotel at end on right

Close to the waterfront, this stylish property offers striking bedrooms with CD players and air conditioning. The popular bar and brasserie feature vaulted ceilings, intimate lighting and offer a choice of a full three-course meal or a substantial snack. Service is both willing and friendly. A small fitness centre and impressive meeting rooms complete the package.

Rooms 100 (4 fmly) ⦰ **Facilities** STV Wi-fi ⦰ Gym Xmas New Year **Conf** Class 30 Board 30 Thtr 80 **Services** Lift Air con **Notes** Civ Wed 70

BEST WESTERN PLUS Milford Hotel

★★★ 83% HOTEL

☎ 01977 681800
A1 Great North Rd, Peckfield LS25 5LQ
e-mail: enquiries@mlh.co.uk
web: www.mlh.co.uk

(For full entry see Garforth)

The Cosmopolitan

★★★ 81% HOTEL

☎ 0113 243 6454
2 Lower Briggate LS1 4AE
e-mail: info@cosmopolitan-hotel-leeds.com
web: www.cosmopolitan-hotel-leeds.com
dir: M621 junct 3. Keep in right lane. Follow until road splits into 4 lanes. Keep right, right at lights. (ASDA House on left). Left at lights. Over bridge, left, hotel opposite. Parking in 150mtrs

This smartly presented, Victorian building is located on the south side of the city. The well-equipped bedrooms offer a choice of standard or executive grades. Staff are friendly and helpful ensuring a warm and welcoming atmosphere. Discounted overnight parking is provided in the adjacent 24-hour car park.

Rooms 89 (5 fmly) (14 smoking) ⦰ **Facilities** STV FTV Wi-fi ⦰ Xmas New Year **Conf** Class 45 Board 40 Thtr 120 **Services** Lift

Chevin Country Park Hotel & Spa

★★★ 77% ⑳ HOTEL

☎ 01943 467818
Yorkgate LS21 3NU
e-mail: chevin@crerarhotels.com

(For full entry see Otley)

Bewleys Hotel Leeds

★★★ 77% HOTEL

☎ 0113 234 2340
City Walk, Sweet St LS11 9AT
e-mail: leeds@bewleyshotels.com
web: www.bewleyshotels.com
dir: M621 junct 3, at 2nd lights left into Sweet St, right & right again

Located on the edge of the city centre, this hotel has the added advantage of secure underground parking. Bedrooms are spacious and comfortable with an extensive room service menu. Downstairs, the light and airy bar lounge leads into a brasserie where a wide selection of popular dishes is offered. High quality meeting rooms are also available.

Rooms 334 (99 fmly) (27 smoking) ⦰ **S** £53-£99; **D** £53-£99* **Facilities** Wi-fi New Year **Conf** Class 44 Board 30 Thtr 70 Del £139* **Services** Lift **Parking** 160 **Notes** LB ⊗ Closed 24-29 Dec Civ Wed 60

Mercure Leeds Parkway Hotel

★★★ HOTEL

☎ 0844 815 9020
Otley Rd LS16 8AG
e-mail: info@mercureleeds.co.uk
web: www.jupiterhotels.co.uk
dir: From A1 take A58 towards Leeds, then right onto A6120. At A660 turn right towards Airport/Skipton. Hotel 2m on right

Currently the rating for this establishment is not confirmed. This may be due to a change of ownership or because it has only recently joined the AA rating scheme.

Rooms 118 **Conf** Class 120 Board 40 Thtr 300

Holiday Inn Express Leeds City Centre Armouries

BUDGET HOTEL

☎ 0113 380 4400
Armouries Dr LS10 1LT
e-mail: leeds@holidayinnexpress.org.uk
web: www.hiexpress.com/leeds
dir: M1 junct 43, follow brown Royal Armouries signs, M621 junct 4 follow Leeds City Centre signs to A61

A modern hotel ideal for families and business travellers. Fresh and uncomplicated, the spacious rooms include Sky TV, power shower and tea and coffee-making facilities. Continental buffet breakfast is included in the room rate; other meals may be taken at the nearby family pub or restaurant. See also the Hotel Groups pages.

Rooms 130 (72 fmly) (19 smoking) **Conf** Class 18 Board 20 Thtr 30

Holiday Inn Express Leeds - East

BUDGET HOTEL

☎ 0845 112 6039 & 0113 288 0574
Aberford Rd, Oulton LS26 8EJ
e-mail: reservations@hiexpressleedseast.co.uk
web: www.hiexpressleedseast.co.uk
dir: M62 junct 29, E towards Pontefract. Exit at junct 30, A642 signed Rothwell. Hotel opposite at 1st rdbt

Rooms 77 (50 fmly) (32 GF) ⦰ **S** £39-£69; **D** £39-£69 (incl. bkfst)* **Conf** Class 20 Board 20 Thtr 25

L

LEEDS continued

Ibis Leeds Centre

BUDGET HOTEL

☎ 0113 396 9000
Marlborough St LS1 4PB
e-mail: H3652@accor.com
web: www.ibis.com
dir: M1 junct 43 or M62 junct 2 take A643 & follow city centre signs. Left on slip road opposite Yorkshire Post. Hotel opposite

Modern, budget hotel offering comfortable accommodation in bright and practical bedrooms. Breakfast is self-service and dinner is available in the restaurant See also the Hotel Groups pages.

Rooms 168 (14 fmly) ✿ **S** £50-£95; **D** £50-£95*

Premier Inn Leeds/ Bradford Airport

BUDGET HOTEL

☎ 0871 527 8578
Victoria Av, Yeadon LS19 7AW
web: www.premierinn.com
dir: On A658, near Leeds/Bradford Airport

High quality, budget accommodation ideal for both families and business travellers. Spacious, en suite bedrooms feature tea and coffee making facilities, and Freeview TV in most hotels. Internet access and Wi-fi are available for a small fee. The adjacent family restaurant features a wide and varied menu. See also the Hotel Groups pages.

Rooms 60

Premier Inn Leeds/Bradford (South)

BUDGET HOTEL

☎ 0871 527 8580
Wakefield Rd, Drighlington BD11 1EA
web: www.premierinn.com
dir: On Drighlington bypass, adjacent to M62 junct 27. Take A650, right to Drighlington, right, hotel on left

Rooms 42

Premier Inn Leeds City Centre

BUDGET HOTEL

☎ 0871 527 8582
Citygate, Wellington St LS3 1LW
web: www.premierinn.com
dir: At A65 & A58 junct

Rooms 140

Premier Inn Leeds City West

BUDGET HOTEL

☎ 0871 527 8584
City West One Office Park, Gelderd Rd LS12 6LX
web: www.premierinn.com
dir: M621 junct 1 take ring road towards Leeds. At 1st lights right into Gelderd Rd, right at rdbt

Rooms 126

Premier Inn Leeds East

BUDGET HOTEL

☎ 0871 527 8586
Selby Rd, Whitkirk LS15 7AY
web: www.premierinn.com
dir: M1 junct 46 towards Leeds. At 2nd rdbt follow Temple Newsam signs. Hotel 500mtrs on right

Rooms 87

LEEK   Map 16 SJ95
Staffordshire

Three Horseshoes Inn & Country Hotel

★★★ 79% ◉◉ HOTEL

☎ 01538 300296
Buxton Rd, Blackshaw Moor ST13 8TW
e-mail: enquires@threeshoesinn.co.uk
web: www.threeshoesinn.co.uk
dir: 2m N of Leek on A53

This traditional, family-owned hostelry provides stylish, individually designed, modern bedrooms, including several four-poster rooms. The smart brasserie, with an open kitchen and countryside views, offers modern English and Thai dishes, and there is also a pub and carvery; the award-winning gardens and grounds are ideal for alfresco dining. The staff are attentive and friendly.

Rooms 26 (2 fmly) (10 GF) ✿ **S** £79.25-£116; **D** £88.50-£162 (incl. bkfst) **Facilities** FTV **Conf** Class 50 Board 25 Thtr 60 Del from £140* **Services** Lift **Parking** 80 **Notes** LB ⊗ Closed 24 Dec-1 Jan Civ Wed 120

LEICESTER   Map 11 SK50
Leicestershire

See also **Rothley**

Leicester Marriott

★★★★ 79% HOTEL

☎ 0116 282 0100
Smith Way, Grove Park, Enderby LE19 1SW
e-mail:
mhrs.emalm.frontoffice@marriotthotels.com
web: www.leicestermarriott.co.uk
dir: M1 junct 21/A563 signed Leicester. At rdbt take 1st left onto A563. Into right lane, at 2nd slip road turn right. At rdbt take last exit, hotel straight ahead

This purpose-built hotel offers stylish bedrooms, some of which are executive rooms with access to the executive lounge. There is a popular brasserie, cocktail bar, atrium lounge, indoor heated pool, gym, sauna and steam room. 18 meeting rooms provide conference facilities for up to 500 delegates and parking is extensive.

Rooms 227 (91 fmly) ✿ **Facilities** STV Wi-fi ↕ ⊛ supervised Gym **Conf** Class 180 Board 52 Thtr 500 **Services** Lift Air con **Parking** 280 **Notes** ⊗ Civ Wed 300

Mercure Leicester City Hotel

Mercure

★★★★ HOTEL

☎ 0844 815 9012
Granby St LE1 6ES
e-mail: info@mercureleicester.co.uk
dir: A5460 into city. Follow Leicester Central Station signs. Granby Street is left off St. Georges Way, A594

Currently the rating for this establishment is not confirmed. This may be due to a change of ownership or because it has only recently joined the AA rating scheme.

Rooms 104 **Conf** Class 200 Board 35 Thtr 450

Hotel Maiyango

★★★★ 75% ⊛ SMALL HOTEL

☎ 0116 251 8898
13-21 St Nicholas Place LE1 4LD
e-mail: reservations@maiyango.com
dir: B4114 (Narborough Rd) to city centre, right onto A47 (Hinkley Rd), keep right into St Nicholas Place

Hotel Maiyango is a boutique hotel offering a warm welcome and professional service. Access to the public areas is via a discreet foyer adjacent to a Middle Eastern-themed restaurant (under the same ownership), where imaginative food is sure to be a memorable experience. Spacious bedrooms, decorated in minimalist style are enhanced by quality modern art, fine furnishings and superb bathrooms. Parking is available close by.

Rooms 14 ⟡ **D** £99–£170 (incl. bkfst)* **Facilities** FTV Wi-fi ↳ ♫ Xmas New Year **Conf** Class 50 Board 30 Thtr 70 **Services** Lift Air con **Notes** ⊗ Closed 25 Dec & 1 Jan

Belmont Hotel

★★★ 81% HOTEL

☎ 0116 254 4773
De Montfort St LE1 7GR
e-mail: info@belmonthotel.co.uk
web: www.belmonthotel.co.uk
dir: From A6 take 1st right after rail station. Hotel 200yds on left

This well-established hotel, under the same family ownership, has been welcoming guests for over 70 years. It is conveniently situated within easy walking distance of the railway station and city centre though it sits in a quiet leafy residential area. Extensive public rooms are smartly appointed and include the informal Bowie's Bistro, Jamie's Bar with its relaxed atmosphere, and the more formal Cherry Restaurant.

Rooms 75 (7 fmly) (9 GF) (2 smoking) **Facilities** FTV Wi-fi ↳ Gym **Conf** Class 75 Board 65 Thtr 175 **Services** Lift **Parking** 70 **Notes** Closed 25-26 Dec Civ Wed 150

Holiday Inn Leicester

★★★ 79% HOTEL

☎ 0871 942 9048
St Nicholas Circle LE1 5LX
e-mail: leistercity.reservations@ihg.com
web: www.holidayinn.co.uk
dir: From S: M1 junct 21, A5460 towards city centre. Approx 3m follow Castle Gardens signs. Hotel at next rdbt. From N: M1 junct 22, A50 to city centre. Into Vaughan Way follow signs for A47 (avoid underpass). Hotel at rdbt

This purpose-built city centre hotel offers impressive accommodation suitable for both business and leisure guests. The smartly appointed bar and restaurant are open throughout the day and there is a well-equipped leisure club. Overnight guests are offered free parking at the adjacent multi-storey car park.

Rooms 188 (81 fmly) **Facilities** FTV Wi-fi HL ⊠ supervised Gym **Conf** Class 140 Board 90 Thtr 260 Del from £99 to £175* **Services** Lift Air con **Notes** Civ Wed 200

Campanile Leicester

BUDGET HOTEL

☎ 0116 261 6600
St Matthew's Way, 1 Bedford Street North LE1 3JE
e-mail: leicester@campanile.com
web: www.campanile.com
dir: A5460. Right at end of road, left at rdbt on A594. Follow Vaughan Way, Burleys Way then St. Matthew's Way. Hotel on left

This modern building offers accommodation in smart, well-equipped bedrooms, all with en suite bathrooms. Refreshments may be taken at the informal bistro. See also the Hotel Groups pages.

Rooms 93 **Conf** Class 30 Board 30 Thtr 40

Ibis Leicester

ibis

BUDGET HOTEL

☎ 0116 248 7200
St Georges Way, Constitution Hill LE1 1PL
e-mail: H3061@accor.com
web: www.ibishotel.com
dir: From M1/M69 junct 21, follow town centre signs, central ring road (A594)/railway station, hotel opposite Leicester Mercury

Modern, budget hotel offering comfortable accommodation in bright and practical bedrooms. Breakfast is self-service and dinner is available in the restaurant. See also the Hotel Groups pages.

Rooms 94 (15 fmly)

Premier Inn Leicester (Braunstone)

BUDGET HOTEL

☎ 0871 527 8590
Meridian Business Park, Thorpe Astley, Braunstone LE19 1LU
web: www.premierinn.com
dir: M1 junct 21, follow A563 (outer ring road) signs W to Thorpe Astley. At slip road after Texaco garage. Hotel on left

High quality, budget accommodation ideal for both families and business travellers. Spacious, en suite bedrooms feature tea and coffee making facilities, and Freeview TV in most hotels. Internet access and Wi-fi are available for a small fee. The adjacent family restaurant features a wide and varied menu. See also the Hotel Groups pages.

Rooms 51

Premier Inn Leicester (Braunstone South)

BUDGET HOTEL

☎ 0871 527 8588
Braunstone Lane East LE3 2FW
web: www.premierinn.com
dir: M1 junct 21, at M69 junct take A5460 towards city. After 1m right at lights to hotel

Rooms 170

Premier Inn Leicester Central (A50)

BUDGET HOTEL

☎ 0871 527 8594
Heathley Park, Groby Rd LE3 9QE
web: www.premierinn.com
dir: Off A50, city centre side of County Hall & Glenfield General Hospital

Rooms 76

Premier Inn Leicester City Centre

BUDGET HOTEL

☎ 0871 527 8596
1 St Georges Way LE1 1AA
web: www.premierinn.com
dir: Telephone for detailed directions

Rooms 135

L

LEICESTER *continued*

Premier Inn Leicester (Forest East)

BUDGET HOTEL

☎ 0871 527 8592
Hinckley Rd, Leicester Forest East LE3 3GD
web: www.premierinn.com
dir: M1 junct 21, A5460. At major junct (Holiday Inn
on right), left into Braunstone Lane. In 2m left onto
A47 towards Hinkley. Hotel 400yds on left

Rooms 40

Premier Inn Leicester North West

BUDGET HOTEL

☎ 0871 527 8598
Leicester Rd, Glenfield LE3 8HB
web: www.premierinn.com
dir: M1 junct 21a N'bound, A46. Onto A50 for
Glenfield & County Hall. Or M1 junct 22 S'bound onto
A50 towards Glenfield. Into County Hall. Hotel on left
adjacent to Gynsills

Rooms 43

Premier Inn Leicester South (Oadby)

BUDGET HOTEL

☎ 0871 527 8600
Glen Rise, Oadby LE2 4RG
web: www.premierinn.com
dir: M1 junct 21, A563 signed South. Right at
Leicester racecourse. Follow Market Harborough
signs. Dual carriageway, straight on at rdbt. Into
single lane, hotel on right

Rooms 30

**LEICESTER FOREST
MOTORWAY SERVICE AREA (M1)**   Map 11 SK50
Leicestershire

Days Inn Leicester Forest East - M1

BUDGET HOTEL

☎ 0116 239 0534
Leicester Forest East, M1 Junct 21 LE3 3GB
e-mail: leicester.hotel@welcomebreak.co.uk
web: www.welcomebreak.co.uk
dir: On M1 N'bound between junct 21 & 21A

This modern building offers accommodation in smart,
spacious and well-equipped bedrooms, suitable for
families and business travellers, and all with en suite
bathrooms. Continental breakfast is available, and
other refreshments may be taken at the nearby family
restaurant. See also the Hotel Groups pages.

Rooms 86 (71 fmly) (10 smoking) **Conf** Board 10

LEIGH   Map 15 SJ69
Greater Manchester

Park Inn by Radisson Leigh

park inn *by Radisson*

★★★ 75% HOTEL

☎ 01942 366334 & 687111
Altherleigh Way WN7 4JZ
e-mail: info.leigh@rezidorparkinn.com
dir: M6 junct 23, A580, 3.1m follow signs to Leigh
Sports Village

A stylish modern hotel, adjacent to Leigh Sports
Village, that is conveniently located close to the
motorway network and a short drive from Manchester
Airport and Warrington. The contemporary bedrooms
are equipped with the latest facilities including air
conditioning, flat-screen TVs and Wi-fi. The hotel has
a fitness suite, sauna and steam room along with
modern meeting rooms and a business centre.

Rooms 135 (10 fmly) (3 smoking) ➔ **D** £65-£125
Facilities FTV Wi-fi Gym Sauna Steam room Xmas
New Year **Conf** Class 72 Board 40 Thtr 150
Del from £99 to £125 **Services** Lift Air con **Parking** 50
Notes Civ Wed 100

LEINTWARDINE   Map 9 SO47
Herefordshire

The Lion

◎ RESTAURANT WITH ROOMS

☎ 01547 540203 & 540747
High St SY7 0JZ
e-mail: enquiries@thelionleintwardine.co.uk
web: www.thelionleintwardine.co.uk
dir: Beside bridge on A4113 (Ludlow to Knighton
road) in Leintwardine

This quiet country inn in the picturesque village of
Leintwardine, set beside the River Teme, is just a
short distance from Ludlow and Craven Arms. The
interior has been totally renovated and all the
contemporary bedrooms are en suite. Dining is taken
seriously here and the modern, imaginative food uses
the freshest local ingredients. The well-stocked bar
offers a selection of real ales and lagers and there is
a separate drinkers' bar too. The inn is particularly
popular with families as the garden has a secure
children's play area, and in warmer months guests
can eat alfresco. The friendly staff help to make any
visit memorable.

Rooms 8 (1 fmly)

LENHAM   Map 7 TQ85
Kent

Chilston Park Hotel

★★★★ ◎◎ HOTEL

☎ 01622 859803
Sandway ME17 2BE
e-mail: chilstonpark@handpicked.co.uk
web: www.handpickedhotels.co.uk/chilstonpark
dir: Exit A20 to Lenham, right into High St, pass
station on right, 1st left, over x-roads, hotel 0.25m
on left

This elegant Grade I listed country house is set in
23 acres of immaculately landscaped gardens and
parkland. An impressive collection of original
paintings and antiques creates a unique
environment. The sunken Venetian-style restaurant
serves modern British food with French influences.
Bedrooms are individual in design, some have four-
poster beds and many have garden views.

Rooms 53 (23 annexe) (2 fmly) (3 GF) ➔
S £89-£318; **D** £99-£328 (incl. bkfst) **Facilities** STV
FTV Wi-fi ➔ HL Fishing ➔ Xmas New Year
Conf Class 60 Board 50 Thtr 100 Del from £135 to
£190 **Services** Lift **Parking** 100 **Notes** LB ⊗
Civ Wed 90

LEOMINSTER   Map 10 SO45
Herefordshire

BEST WESTERN Talbot Hotel

★★★ 75% HOTEL

☎ 01568 616347
West St HR6 8EP
e-mail: talbot@bestwestern.co.uk
dir: From A49, A44 or A4112, hotel in town centre

This charming former coaching inn is located in the
town centre and makes an ideal base for exploring a
delightful area. Public areas feature original beams
and antique furniture, and include an atmospheric
bar and elegant restaurant. The bedrooms vary in
size, but all are comfortably furnished and equipped.

Facilities are available for private functions and conferences.

Rooms 28 (3 fmly) (2 GF) **Facilities** FTV Wi-fi
Conf Class 60 Board 30 Thtr 130 Del £95 **Parking** 26
Notes ⊗

LEWDOWN   Map 3 SX48
Devon

INSPECTORS' CHOICE

Lewtrenchard Manor

★★★ HOTEL

☎ 01566 783222
EX20 4PN
e-mail: info@lewtrenchard.co.uk
dir: A30 from Exeter to Plymouth/Tavistock road. At T-junct turn right, then left onto old A30 (Lewdown road). Left in 6m signed Lewtrenchard

This Jacobean mansion was built in the 1600s, has many interesting architectural features, and is surrounded by its own idyllic grounds in a quiet valley close to the northern edge of Dartmoor. Public rooms include a fine gallery, as well as magnificent carvings and oak panelling. Imaginative and carefully prepared dishes are created using the best Devon produce, much of it coming from the hotel's kitchen garden, and served either in the dining room or at the chef's table, the Purple Carrot. Head Chef John Hooker and his team, prepare meals in the kitchen, while the action is captured on camera to be viewed on large TV screens. Bedrooms, varying in style and including courtyard suites, are comfortably furnished and spacious. There are a variety of leisure activities including falconry, horse riding, fishing, cycling and clay pigeon shooting on offer.

Rooms 14 (2 fmly) (3 GF) ☞ **S** £100-£190;
D £135-£235 (incl. bkfst)* **Facilities** FTV Wi-fi ⌂
Fishing ⌁ Clay pigeon shooting Falconry Beauty therapies Xmas New Year **Conf** Class 40 Board 30
Thtr 60 Del from £185* **Parking** 50 **Notes** LB
Civ Wed 100

LEYLAND   Map 15 SD52
Lancashire

BEST WESTERN PREMIER
Leyland Hotel

★★★★ 76% HOTEL

☎ 01772 422922
Leyland Way PR25 4JX
e-mail: leylandhotel@feathers.uk.com
web: www.feathers.uk.com
dir: M6 junct 28, left at end of slip road, hotel 100mtrs on left

This purpose-built hotel enjoys a convenient location, just off the M6, within easy reach of Preston and Blackpool. Spacious public areas include extensive conference and banqueting facilities as well as a smart leisure club.

Rooms 93 (4 fmly) (31 GF) ☞ **S** £49-£179;
D £49-£179* **Facilities** FTV Wi-fi ⌂ HL ⌁ supervised
Gym Xmas New Year **Conf** Class 100 Board 40
Thtr 220 Del from £119 to £149* **Parking** 150
Notes LB ⊗ Civ Wed 200

Farington Lodge Hotel

★★★★ 74% HOTEL

☎ 01772 421321
Stanifield Ln, Farington PR25 4QR
e-mail: info.farington@classiclodges.co.uk
web: www.classiclodges.co.uk
dir: Left at rdbt at end of M65, left at next rdbt. Entrance 1m on right after lights

This Grade II listed Georgian house, ideally located close to the M6, M61 and M65, is set in three acres of quiet, mature gardens and offers a romantic getaway. The choice of bedroom styles range from classic and traditional rooms in the original house to the contemporary, purpose-built executive rooms; all are stylishly decorated to a very high standard. This hotel is a popular venue for weddings, private dining and other special occasions.

Rooms 27 (3 fmly) (6 GF) ☞ **S** £75-£119; **D** £85-£149
(incl. bkfst)* **Facilities** FTV Wi-fi ⌂ Xmas New Year
Conf Class 80 Board 60 Thtr 180 **Parking** 90
Notes LB ⊗ Civ Wed 150

LICHFIELD   Map 10 SK10
Staffordshire

INSPECTORS' CHOICE

Swinfen Hall Hotel

★★★★ ◉◉ HOTEL

☎ 01543 481494
Swinfen WS14 9RE
e-mail: info@swinfenhallhotel.co.uk
web: www.swinfenhallhotel.co.uk
dir: Set back from A38, 2.5m outside Lichfield, towards Birmingham

Dating from 1757, this lavishly decorated mansion has been painstakingly restored by the present owners. It is set in 100 acres of parkland which includes a deer park. Public rooms are particularly stylish, with intricately carved ceilings and impressive oil portraits. Bedrooms on the first floor boast period features and tall sash windows; those on the second floor (the former servants' quarters) are smaller and more contemporary by comparison. Service in the award-winning restaurant is both professional and attentive.

Rooms 17 (5 fmly) ☞ **S** £155; **D** £165-£335 (incl. bkfst)* **Facilities** STV FTV Wi-fi ⌂ ⌁ Fishing ⌁ Jogging trail 100 acre park New Year **Conf** Class 50 Board 50 Thtr 160 Del from £160 to £180* **Parking** 80 **Notes** LB ⊗ Civ Wed 120

L

LICHFIELD *continued*

BEST WESTERN The George Hotel

★★★ 81% HOTEL

☎ 01543 414822
12-14 Bird St WS13 6PR
e-mail: mail@thegeorgelichfield.co.uk
web: www.thegeorgelichfield.co.uk
dir: From Bowling Green Island on A461 take Lichfield exit. Left at next island into Swan Rd, as road bears left, turn right into Bird St for hotel car park

Situated in the city centre, this privately owned hotel provides good quality, well-equipped accommodation which includes a room with a four-poster bed. Facilities here include a large ballroom, plus several other rooms for meetings and functions.

Rooms 45 (5 fmly) **S** £45-£105; **D** £60-£125 (incl. bkfst) **Facilities** FTV Wi-fi ➜ HL Gym **Conf** Class 60 Board 40 Thtr 110 Del from £120 to £140 **Services** Lift **Parking** 45 **Notes** LB ❀ Civ Wed 110

Cathedral Lodge Hotel

★★★ 73% HOTEL

☎ 01543 414500
62 Beacon St WS13 7AR
e-mail: enquiries@cathedrallodgehotel.com
dir: From Birmingham, A38 to Lichfield. Hotel in city centre

This hotel is within easy walking distance of the famous cathedral and just a short drive from the NEC, Belfry Golf Course and many other attractions. The accommodation is modern, spacious and comfortable, and each room has a large, flat-screen TV with Sky. There is a large function suite together with conference facilities.

Rooms 36 (2 fmly) (6 smoking) **Facilities** STV FTV Wi-fi Xmas New Year **Conf** Class 80 Board 70 Thtr 80 **Notes** ❀

Premier Inn Lichfield

BUDGET HOTEL

☎ 0871 527 8602
Fine Ln, Fradley WS13 8RD
web: www.premierinn.com
dir: On A38, 3 NE of Lichfield

High quality, budget accommodation ideal for both families and business travellers. Spacious, en suite bedrooms feature tea and coffee making facilities, and Freeview TV in most hotels. Internet access and Wi-fi are available for a small fee. The adjacent family restaurant features a wide and varied menu. See also the Hotel Groups pages.

Rooms 30

Arundell Arms

★★★ 80% ◉◉ HOTEL

☎ 01566 784666
PL16 0AA
e-mail: reservations@arundellarms.co.uk
dir: 1m off A30, 3m E of Launceston

This former coaching inn, boasting a long history, sits in the heart of a quiet Devon village, and is internationally famous for its country pursuits such as winter shooting and angling. The bedrooms offer individual style and comfort. Public areas are full of character with a relaxed atmosphere, particularly around the open log fire during colder evenings. Award-winning cuisine is a celebration of local produce.

Rooms 24 (3 annexe) (3 fmly) (4 GF) **S** £98-£118; **D** £179-£199 (incl. bkfst)* **Facilities** FTV Wi-fi ➜ Fishing Skittle alley Game shooting (in winter) Fly fishing school New Year **Conf** Class 30 Board 40 Thtr 100 Del from £177 to £197* **Parking** 70 **Notes** LB RS 24-26 Dec Civ Wed 80

Tinhay Mill Guest House and Restaurant

◉ RESTAURANT WITH ROOMS

☎ 01566 784201
Tinhay PL16 0AJ
e-mail: tinhay.mill@talk21.com
web: www.tinhaymillrestaurant.co.uk
dir: A30/A388 approach Lifton, establishment at bottom of village on right

These former mill cottages are now a delightful restaurant with charming rooms. Beams and open fireplaces set the scene, and everything is geared to ensure a relaxed and comfortable stay. Bedrooms are spacious and well equipped, with many thoughtful extras. Cuisine is taken seriously here, using the best of local produce.

Rooms 6

BEST WESTERN PLUS Bentley Hotel & Spa

★★★★ 85% HOTEL

☎ 01522 878000
Newark Rd, South Hykeham LN6 9NH
e-mail: info@bentleyhotellincoln.co.uk
web: www.bentleyhotellincoln.co.uk
dir: A1 onto A46 E towards Lincoln for 10m. Over 1st rdbt on Lincoln Bypass to hotel 50yds on left

This modern hotel is on a ring road, so it is conveniently located for all local attractions. Attractive bedrooms, most with air conditioning, are well equipped and spacious. The hotel has a leisure suite with gym and large pool (with a hoist for the less able). Spa facilities include a hairdresser, treatment rooms and thermal suite. Extensive conference facilities are available.

Rooms 80 (5 fmly) (26 GF) ➚ **S** £96-£106; **D** £111-£121 (incl. bkfst)* **Facilities** Spa STV FTV Wi-fi ➜ HL ⊙ Gym Steam room Sauna New Year **Conf** Class 150 Board 30 Thtr 300 **Services** Lift Air con **Parking** 170 **Notes** LB ❀ Civ Wed 120

The Lincoln Hotel

★★★ 80% ◉ HOTEL

☎ 01522 520348
Eastgate LN2 1PN
e-mail: reservations@thelincolnhotel.com
web: www.thelincolnhotel.com
dir: Adjacent to cathedral

This privately owned modern hotel enjoys superb uninterrupted views of Lincoln Cathedral. There are ruins of the Roman wall and Eastgate in the grounds. Bedrooms are contemporary with up-to-the-minute facilities. An airy restaurant and bar, a cellar bar, plus a comfortable lounge are provided. There are substantial conference and meeting facilities.

Rooms 71 (4 fmly) (8 GF) **Facilities** FTV Wi-fi Gym **Conf** Class 50 Board 40 Thtr 120 **Services** Lift **Parking** 120 **Notes** ⊗ Civ Wed 150

Washingborough Hall Hotel

★★★ 79% ◉ COUNTRY HOUSE HOTEL

☎ 01522 790340
Church Hill, Washingborough LN4 1BE
e-mail: enquiries@washingboroughhall.com
dir: B1190 into Washingborough. Right at rdbt, hotel 500yds on left

This Georgian manor stands on the edge of the quiet village of Washingborough and is set in attractive gardens. Public rooms are pleasantly furnished and comfortable, while the restaurant offers interesting menus. Bedrooms are individually designed and most have views out over the grounds to the countryside beyond.

Rooms 12 (3 fmly) ⟟ **Facilities** FTV Wi-fi ♺ ⊌ Bicycles for hire New Year **Conf** Class 30 Board 26 Thtr 50 **Parking** 40 **Notes** Civ Wed 70

Branston Hall Hotel

★★★ 75% ◉◉ COUNTRY HOUSE HOTEL

☎ 01522 793305
Branston Park, Branston LN4 1PD
e-mail: info@branstonhall.com
web: www.branstonhall.com
dir: On B1188, 3m SE of Lincoln

Dating back to 1885 this country house sits in 88 acres of beautiful grounds complete with a lake. There is an elegant restaurant, a spacious bar and a beautiful lounge in addition to impressive conference and leisure facilities. Individually styled bedrooms vary in size and include several with four-poster beds. The hotel is a popular wedding venue.

Rooms 50 (7 annexe) (3 fmly) (4 GF) **Facilities** Spa STV FTV Wi-fi ♺ Gym Jogging circuit Xmas New Year **Conf** Class 54 Board 40 Thtr 200 **Services** Lift **Parking** 100 **Notes** ⊗ Civ Wed 160

The White Hart

★★★ 75% HOTEL

☎ 01522 526222 & 563293
Bailgate LN1 3AR
e-mail: info@whitehart-lincoln.co.uk
web: www.whitehart-lincoln.co.uk
dir: A46 onto B1226, through Newport Arch. Hotel 0.5m on left as road bends left

Lying in the shadow of Lincoln's magnificent cathedral, this hotel is perfectly positioned for exploring the shops and sights of this medieval city. The attractive bedrooms are furnished and decorated in a traditional style and many have views of the cathedral. Given the hotel's central location, parking is a real benefit.

Rooms 50 (3 fmly) **Facilities** FTV Wi-fi ♺ **Conf** Class 80 Board 103 Thtr 160 **Services** Lift **Parking** 50 **Notes** Civ Wed 120

Tower Hotel

★★★ 71% ◉ HOTEL

☎ 01522 529999
38 Westgate LN1 3BD
e-mail: tower.hotel@btclick.com
web: www.lincolntowerhotel.com
dir: From A46 follow signs to Lincoln N then to Bailgate area. Through arch, 2nd right

This hotel faces the Norman castle wall and is in a very convenient location for the city. The relaxed and friendly atmosphere is very noticeable here. There's a modern conservatory bar and a stylish restaurant where contemporary dishes are available throughout the day.

Rooms 15 (1 fmly) ⟟ **S** £70; **D** £95-£105 (incl. bkfst)* **Facilities** STV FTV Wi-fi **Conf** Class 24 Board 16 Thtr 24 **Notes** Closed 24-27 Dec & 1 Jan

Ibis Lincoln

BUDGET HOTEL

ibis

☎ 01522 698333
Runcorn Rd (A46), off Whisby Rd LN6 3QZ
e-mail: H3161@accor-hotels.com
web: www.ibishotel.com
dir: Exit A46 (ring road) into Whisby Rd. 1st left

Modern, budget hotel offering comfortable accommodation in bright and practical bedrooms. Breakfast is self-service and dinner is available in the restaurant See also the Hotel Groups pages.

Rooms 86 (19 fmly) (8 GF) ⟟ **S** £30-£80; **D** £30-£80* **Conf** Class 12 Board 20 Thtr 35 Del from £55 to £110*

L

LINCOLN *continued*

Premier Inn Lincoln

BUDGET HOTEL

☎ 0871 527 8604
Lincoln Rd, Canwick Hill LN4 2RF
web: www.premierinn.com
dir: Approx 1m S of city centre at junction of B1188 & B1131

High quality, budget accommodation ideal for both families and business travellers. Spacious, en suite bedrooms feature tea and coffee making facilities, and Freeview TV in most hotels. Internet access and Wi-fi are available for a small fee. The adjacent family restaurant features a wide and varied menu. See also the Hotel Groups pages.

Rooms 60

The Old Bakery

◉◉ RESTAURANT WITH ROOMS

☎ 01522 576057 & 07949 035554
26/28 Burton Rd LN1 3LB
e-mail: enquiries@theold-bakery.co.uk
dir: Exit A46 at Lincoln North follow signs for cathedral. 3rd exit at 1st rdbt, 1st exit at next rdbt

Situated close to the castle at the top of the town, this converted bakery offers well-equipped bedrooms and a delightful dining operation. The cooking is international and uses much local produce. Expect good friendly service from the dedicated staff.

Rooms 4 (1 fmly)

Old Thorns Manor Hotel Golf & Country Estate

★★★★ 72% HOTEL

☎ 01428 724555 & 725883
Griggs Green GU30 7PE
e-mail: reservations@oldthorns.com
web: www.oldthorns.com
dir: At Griggs Green exit A3, hotel 0.5m

Old Thorns is a modern relaxed and welcoming hotel, set in 400 acres of the peaceful Hampshire countryside, which includes a championship golf course. The bedrooms are spacious and stylish and offer high levels of comfort. The leisure facilities are extensive and include a health club, wellness centre and spa; in addition there is also a sports bar, champagne and cocktail bar, Kings Restaurant and all-day dining is also available.

Rooms 86 (2 fmly) (39 GF) ✆ **Facilities** Spa STV FTV Wi-fi ⬖ ☂ supervised ⚜ 18 Putt green Gym Xmas New Year **Conf** Class 100 Board 30 Thtr 300 **Services** Lift **Parking** 278 **Notes** ⊗ Civ Wed 250

Premier Inn Liskeard

BUDGET HOTEL

☎ 0871 527 8608
Liskeard Retail Park, Haviland Rd PL14 3FG
web: www.premierinn.com
dir: Off A38, on A390 SW of Liskeard

High quality, budget accommodation ideal for both families and business travellers. Spacious, en suite bedrooms feature tea and coffee making facilities, and Freeview TV in most hotels. Internet access and Wi-fi are available for a small fee. The adjacent family restaurant features a wide and varied menu. See also the Hotel Groups pages.

Rooms 51

Premier Inn Littlehampton

BUDGET HOTEL

☎ 0871 527 8610
Roundstone Ln, East Preston BN16 1EB
web: www.premierinn.com
dir: A27 onto A280 signed Littlehampton/Rustington & Angmering. At next rdbt follow Littlehampton, Rustington/A259 signs. At next rdbt 1st exit signed East Preston. Hotel on left

High quality, budget accommodation ideal for both families and business travellers. Spacious, en suite bedrooms feature tea and coffee making facilities, and Freeview TV in most hotels. Internet access and Wi-fi are available for a small fee. The adjacent family restaurant features a wide and varied menu. See also the Hotel Groups pages.

Rooms 20

Thornton Hall Hotel and Spa

★★★★ 79% ◉◉◉ HOTEL

☎ 0151 336 3938 & 353 3717
Neston Rd CH63 1JF
e-mail: reservations@thorntonhallhotel.com
web: www.thorntonhallhotel.com

(For full entry see Thornton Hough)

Save on hotels. Book at theAA.com/hotel

LIN – LIV **241** ENGLAND

Hope Street Hotel

★★★★ 78% ◎◎ HOTEL

☎ 0151 709 3000
40 Hope St L1 9DA
e-mail: sleep@hopestreethotel.co.uk
dir: Follow Cathedral & University signs on entering city. Telephone for detailed directions

This stylish property is located within easy walking distance of the city's cathedrals, theatres, major shops and attractions. Stylish bedrooms and suites are appointed with flat-screen TVs, DVD players, internet access and comfy beds with Egyptian cotton sheets; the bathrooms have rain showers and deep tubs. The London Carriage Works Restaurant specialises in local, seasonal produce and the adjacent lounge bar offers lighter all-day dining and wonderful cocktails.

Rooms 89 (16 fmly) (5 GF) ↟ **S** £79-£190; **D** £79-£190* **Facilities** STV FTV Wi-fi Gym Massage & beauty therapists Xmas New Year **Conf** Class 40 Board 30 Thtr 70 Del from £160 to £200* **Services** Lift Air con **Parking** 14 **Notes** LB Civ Wed 70

Liverpool Marriott Hotel City Centre

★★★★ 75% METRO HOTEL

☎ 0151 476 8000
1 Queen Square L1 1RH
e-mail: liverpool.city@marriotthotels.com
web: www.liverpoolmarriottcitycentre.co.uk
dir: End of M62 follow city centre signs, A5047, Edge Lane. From city centre follow signs for Queens Square parking

This impressive modern hotel is located in the heart of the city, surrounded by theatres and restaurants. The elegant public rooms include a ground-floor café bar and a cocktail bar. The hotel also boasts a well-equipped, indoor leisure health club with pool. Bedrooms are stylishly appointed and benefit from a host of extra facilities.

Rooms 146 (29 fmly) (12 smoking) **Facilities** STV Wi-fi Gym **Conf** Class 90 Board 30 Thtr 300 **Services** Lift Air con **Parking** 137 **Notes** ⊗ Civ Wed 300

Novotel Liverpool

★★★★ 75% HOTEL

☎ 0151 702 5100
40 Hanover St L1 4LY
e-mail: h6495@accor.com

This attractive and stylish city centre hotel is convenient for Liverpool Echo Arena, Liverpool One shopping centre and the Albert Dock; it is adjacent to a town centre car park. The hotel has a range of conference and leisure facilities which include an indoor heated pool and fitness suite. The restaurant offers a contemporary style menu. The bedrooms are comfortable and stylishly designed.

Rooms 209 (127 fmly) ↟ **Facilities** STV Wi-fi Gym Steam room **Conf** Class 60 Board 50 Thtr 90 **Services** Lift

Atlantic Tower, Liverpool

thistle

★★★★ 73% HOTEL

☎ 0871 376 9025
Chapel St L3 9RE
e-mail: atlantictower@thistle.co.uk
web: www.thistle.com/atlantictower
dir: M6 onto M62, follow signs for Albert Dock, right at Liver Building. Stay in lane marked Chapel St, hotel on left

Designed to include the shape of a ship's prow, this notable hotel commands a prominent position overlooking Pier Head and the Liver Building. There's a choice of junior suites, executive and standard rooms, and although many are compact, all are of good quality and benefit from full air conditioning. Public areas include a choice of lounges and The Vu Bar which adjoins an attractive patio garden with superb river views.

Rooms 225 ↟ **Facilities** STV FTV Wi-fi HL **Conf** Class 40 Board 30 Thtr 120 **Services** Lift Air con **Parking** 50 **Notes** ⊗ Civ Wed 120

Radisson Blu Hotel Liverpool

Radisson

★★★★ 72% HOTEL

☎ 0151 966 1500
107 Old Hall St L3 9LQ
e-mail: info.liverpool@radissonblu.com
dir: M62 W to end, follow signs to Albert Dock. Left onto Old Hall St from main Leeds St dual carriageway

This smart hotel is centrally located close to the city. Spacious public areas include the White Bar, an airy

restaurant and an impressive lobby. Bedrooms are well equipped and include a number of business class rooms and suites. A good range of conference and meeting rooms is available, as well as a good range of leisure facilities.

Rooms 194 ↟ **Facilities** STV FTV Wi-fi Gym Steam room Sauna **Conf** Class 120 Board 44 Thtr 180 **Services** Lift Air con **Parking** 25 **Notes** Civ Wed 180

Malmaison Liverpool

Malmaison

★★★ 83% ◎ HOTEL

☎ 0151 229 5000
7 William Jessop Way, Princes Dock L3 1QZ
e-mail: liverpool@malmaison.com
dir: A5080 follow signs for Pier Head/Southport/Bootle. Into Baln St to rdbt, 1st exit at rdbt, immediately left onto William Jessop Way

This is a purpose-built hotel with cutting edge and contemporary style. 'Mal' Liverpool, as its known, has a stunning location, alongside the river and docks, and in the heart of the city's regeneration. Bedrooms are stylish and comfortable and are provided with lots of extra facilities. The public areas are packed with fun and style, and there is a number of meeting rooms as well as private dining, including a chef's table.

Rooms 130 ↟ **Facilities** STV Wi-fi Gym **Conf** Class 28 Board 22 Thtr 50 **Services** Lift Air con

BEST WESTERN Alicia Hotel

★★★ 78% HOTEL

☎ 0151 727 4411
3 Aigburth Dr, Sefton Park L17 3AA
e-mail: aliciahotel@feathers.uk.com
web: www.feathers.uk.com
dir: From end of M62 take A5058 to Sefton Park, then left, follow park around

This stylish and friendly hotel overlooks Sefton Park and is just a few minutes' drive from both the city centre and John Lennon Airport. Bedrooms are well equipped and comfortable. Day rooms include a striking modern restaurant and bar. Extensive, stylish function facilities make this a popular wedding venue.

Rooms 41 (8 fmly) ↟ **Facilities** STV Wi-fi HL Xmas New Year **Conf** Class 80 Board 40 Thtr 120 **Services** Lift **Parking** 40 **Notes** ⊗ Civ Wed 120

L

LIVERPOOL *continued*

Jurys Inn Liverpool

★★★ 75% HOTEL

☎ 0151 244 3777
No 31 Keel Wharf L3 4FN
e-mail: jurysinnliverpool@jurysinns.com
dir: Follow City Centre & Albert Dock signs. Hotel at Kings Waterfront adjacent to Albert Dock, opposite BT Convention Centre & Echo Arena

Located on the Kings Waterfront adjacent to the BT Convention Centre, Echo Arena, Albert Dock complex and a short walk from the very popular shopping district of Liverpool One, this hotel offers contemporary and spacious bedrooms. Guests have a choice of dining options - the Innfusion restaurant and the Inntro bar. There are ten dedicated meeting rooms and Wi-fi is available throughout. There is ample secure parking nearby.

Rooms 310 (58 fmly) **Facilities** FTV Wi-fi ⌂
Conf Class 50 Board 40 Thtr 100 **Services** Lift Air con
Notes ⊗ Civ Wed 100

Campanile Liverpool

Campanile

BUDGET HOTEL

☎ 0151 709 8104
Chaloner St, Queens Dock L3 4AJ
e-mail: liverpool@campanile.com
web: www.campanile.com
dir: Follow tourist signs marked Albert Dock. Hotel on waterfront

This modern building offers accommodation in smart, well-equipped bedrooms, all with en suite bathrooms. Refreshments may be taken at the informal bistro. See also the Hotel Groups pages.

Rooms 100 (4 fmly) (33 GF) **D** £39-£160*
Conf Class 18 Board 24 Thtr 35

Ibis Liverpool Centre Albert Dock

ibis

BUDGET HOTEL

☎ 0151 706 9800
27 Wapping L1 8LY
e-mail: H3140@accor.com
web: www.ibishotel.com
dir: From M62 follow Albert Dock signs. Opposite Dock entrance

Modern, budget hotel offering comfortable accommodation in bright and practical bedrooms. Breakfast is self-service and dinner is available in the restaurant. See also the Hotel Groups pages.

Rooms 127 (15 fmly) (23 GF) 🐾

Premier Inn Liverpool (Aintree)

BUDGET HOTEL

☎ 0871 527 8612
Ormskirk Rd, Aintree L9 5AS
web: www.premierinn.com
dir: M58, A57, A59 towards Liverpool. Pass Aintree Retail Park, left at lights into Aintree Racecourse. Hotel on left

High quality, budget accommodation ideal for both families and business travellers. Spacious, en suite bedrooms feature tea and coffee making facilities, and Freeview TV in most hotels. Internet access and Wi-fi are available for a small fee. The adjacent family restaurant features a wide and varied menu. See also the Hotel Groups pages.

Rooms 40

Premier Inn Liverpool Airport

BUDGET HOTEL

☎ 0871 527 8626
57 Speke Hall Av L24 1YQ
web: www.premierinn.com
dir: A561 towards Liverpool follow 'Liverpool John Lennon Airport' signs into Seake Hall Ave, at 1st rdbt take 2nd left. Hotel 300mtrs on left

Rooms 10

Premier Inn Liverpool Albert Dock

BUDGET HOTEL

☎ 0871 527 8622
East Britannia Building, Albert Dock L3 4AD
web: www.premierinn.com
dir: Follow signs for Liverpool City Centre & Albert Dock

Rooms 130

Premier Inn Liverpool City Centre (Liverpool One)

BUDGET HOTEL

☎ 0871 527 9382
48 Hanover St L1 4AF
web: www.premierinn.com
dir: A5047 follow signs for city centre. At lights left onto A5048, at next lights right onto A5047. Head for A5038 signed Toxteth, Airport. Right into Renshaw Street & right onto Ranelagh Street. Premier Inn on left opposite BBC Radio Merseyside

Rooms 183

Premier Inn Liverpool City Centre (Moorfields)

BUDGET HOTEL

☎ 0871 527 8624
Vernon St L2 2AY
web: www.premierinn.com
dir: From M62 follow Liverpool City Centre &
Birkenhead Tunnel signs. At rdbt 3rd exit into Dale St,
right into Vernon St. Hotel on left

Rooms 165

Premier Inn Liverpool North

BUDGET HOTEL

☎ 0871 527 8628
Northern Perimeter Rd L30 7PT
web: www.premierinn.com
dir: 0.25m from end of M58/M5, on A5207

Rooms 63

Premier Inn Liverpool (Roby)

BUDGET HOTEL

☎ 0871 527 8616
Roby Rd, Huyton L36 4HD
web: www.premierinn.com
dir: Just off M62 junct 5 on A5080

Rooms 53

Premier Inn Liverpool (Tarbock)

BUDGET HOTEL

☎ 0871 527 8618
Wilson Rd, Tarbock L36 6AD
web: www.premierinn.com
dir: At M62 & M57 junct. M62 junct 6, take A5080
(Huyton).1st right into Wilson Rd

Rooms 41

Premier Inn Liverpool (West Derby)

BUDGET HOTEL

☎ 0871 527 8620
Queens Dr, West Derby L13 0DL
web: www.premierinn.com
dir: At end of M62 right under flyover onto A5058
(follow football stadium signs). Hotel 1.5m on left,
just past Esso garage

Rooms 84

LIVERSEDGE   Map 16 SE12
West Yorkshire

Healds Hall Hotel & Restaurant

THE INDEPENDENTS
HOTEL ASSOCIATION

★★★ 77% ® HOTEL

☎ 01924 409112
Leeds Rd WF15 6JA
e-mail: enquire@healdshall.co.uk
web: www.healdshall.co.uk
dir: On A62 between Leeds & Huddersfield. 50yds on
left after lights at Swan Pub

This 18th-century house, in the heart of West
Yorkshire, provides comfortable and well-equipped
accommodation and excellent hospitality. The hotel
has earned a good local reputation for the quality of
its food and offers a choice of casual or more formal
dining styles, from a wide range of dishes on the
various menus.

Rooms 24 (3 fmly) (3 GF) ↖ **S** £50-£95; **D** £65-£110
(incl. bkfst) **Facilities** FTV Wi-fi ♨ **Conf** Class 60
Board 45 Thtr 100 Del from £100 to £135 **Parking** 90
Notes LB Closed 1 Jan & BH Mon RS Sun eve
Civ Wed 100

LIZARD   Map 2 SW71
Cornwall

Housel Bay Hotel

★★★ 72% ® HOTEL

☎ 01326 290417 & 290917
Housel Cove TR12 7PG
e-mail: info@houselbay.com
dir: A39 or A394 to Helston, then A3083. At Lizard
sign turn left, left at school, down lane to hotel

This long-established hotel has stunning views
across the Western Approaches, equally enjoyable
from the lounge and many of the bedrooms. Good
cuisine is available in the stylish dining room, from
where guests might enjoy a stroll to the end of the
garden, which leads directly onto the Cornwall
coastal path.

Rooms 20 (1 fmly) ↖ **S** £65-£70; **D** £90-£175 (incl.
bkfst)* **Facilities** FTV Wi-fi ♨ Xmas New Year
Services Lift **Parking** 35 **Notes** LB ⊗

L

London

Trafalgar Square

Index of London Hotels

Page	Hotel name	District	Plan number	& grid
283	45 Park Lane	W1	4	G6
274	51 Buckingham Gate, Taj Suites and Residences	SW1	4	J4
	A			
270	All Seasons London Southwark Rose Hotel	SE1	5	F6
294	Ambassadors Bloomsbury Hotel	WC1	3	A5
265	ANdAZ Liverpool Street	EC2	3	H3
266	Apex City of London Hotel	EC3	3	H1
265	Apex London Wall Hotel	EC2	3	G2
266	Apex Temple Court	EC4	3	D2
284	Athenaeum Hotel & Apartments	W1	4	H6
	B			
280	Baglioni Hotel	SW7	4	C5
278	Beaufort, The	SW3	4	F4
293	Bedford Hotel	WC1	3	B3
271	Berkeley, The	SW1	4	G5
270	Bermondsey Square Hotel	SE1	5	H4
280	BEST WESTERN Burns Hotel	SW5	4	B3
294	Bloomsbury Park A Thistle Associate Hotel	WC1	3	B3
284	Brown's Hotel	W1	2	J1
281	Bulgari Hotel & Residences	SW7	4	F5
	C			
282	Cannizaro House	SW19	1	D2
277	Capital, The	SW3	4	F5
276	Cavendish London	SW1	4	J6
266	Chamberlain Hotel, The	EC3	3	J2
294	Charing Cross Hotel	WC2	3	B1
287	Chesterfield Mayfair, The	W1	4	H6
291	Chiswick Moran Hotel	W4	1	C3
285	Claridge's	W1	2	H1
283	Connaught, The	W1	2	G1
292	Copthorne Tara Hotel London Kensington	W8	4	B4
275	Corinthia Hotel London	SW1	5	B6
267	Crown Moran Hotel	NW2	1	D5
266	Crowne Plaza London - The City	EC4	3	E1
264	Crowne Plaza London - Docklands	E16	7	B1
291	Crowne Plaza London - Ealing	W5	1	C4
281	Crowne Plaze London - Kensington	SW7	4	C3
288	Cumberland, The	W1	2	F2
	D			
278	Days Hotel London Waterloo	SE1	5	D4
294	Dorchester, The	W1	4	G6
288	DoubleTree by Hilton Hotel, Marble Arch	W1	2	F2
277	Draycott Hotel, The	SW3	4	F3
272	DUKES London	SW1	4	J6

Page	Hotel name	District	Plan number	& grid
	E			
277	Egerton House Hotel, The	SW3	4	E4
	F			
287	Flemings Mayfair	W1	4	H6
263	Four Seasons Hotel London at Canary Wharf	E14	6	A3
285	Four Seasons Hotel London at Park Lane	W1	4	G6
	G			
274	Goring, The	SW1	4	H4
276	Grosvenor, The	SW1	4	H4
286	Grosvenor House, A JW Marriott Hotel	W1	2	G1
	H			
269	H10 London Waterloo Hotel	SE1	5	E5
272	Halkin by Como, The	SW1	4	G5
281	Harrington Hall Hotel	SW7	4	C3
268	Hendon Hall Hotel	NW4	1	D5
271	Holiday Inn Express London - Greenwich	SE10	1	H3
282	Holiday Inn Express Wimbledon South	SW19	1	E1
293	Holiday Inn London Bloomsbury	WC1	3	B4
268	Holiday Inn London - Brent Cross	NW2	1	D5
293	Holiday Inn London Kings Cross/Bloomsbury	WC1	3	C5
281	Holiday Inn London - Kensington Forum	SW7	4	C3
288	Holiday Inn London - Mayfair	W1	2	H1
289	Holiday Inn London - Regents Park	W1	2	H4
290	Hotel Indigo	W2	2	D2
293	Hotel Russell	WC1	3	B4
286	Hyatt Regency London - The Churchill	W1	2	F2
	I			
270	Ibis London Blackfriars	SE1	5	E6
263	Ibis London City	E1	3	J2
264	Ibis London Docklands	E14	6	D4
280	Ibis London Earls Court	SW6	4	A1
267	Ibis London Euston St Pancras	NW1	2	J5
265	Ibis London ExCeL Docklands	E16	7	B1
271	Ibis London Greenwich	SE10	8	B3
293	Ibis London Shepherd's Bush	W14	1	D3
264	Ibis London Stratford	E15	9	D3
	J			
273	Jumeirah Carlton Tower	SW1	4	F4
277	Jumeirah Lowndes Hotel	SW1	4	F4
	K			
280	K + K Hotel George	SW5	4	A3
293	Kingsley by Thistle, The	WC1	3	B3
292	K West Hotel & Spa	W14	1	D3

Index of London Hotels

Page	Hotel name	District	Plan number	& grid
	L			
290	Lancaster Gate Hotel	W2	2	C1
290	Lancaster London	W2	2	D1
267	Landmark London, The	NW1	2	F3
273	Lanesborough, The	SW1	4	G5
285	Langham London, The	W1	2	H3
286	Le Meridien Piccadilly	W1	2	J1
278	Levin, The	SW3	4	F4
269	London Bridge Hotel	SE1	5	G6
286	London Hilton on Park Lane	W1	4	G6
268	London Marriott Hotel County Hall	SE1	5	C5
287	London Marriott Hotel Grosvenor Square	W1	2	G1
287	London Marriott Hotel Marble Arch	W1	2	F2
285	London Marriott Hotel Park Lane	W1	2	F1
268	London Marriott Hotel Regents Park	NW3	1	E4
278	London Marriott Kensington	SW5	4	B3
268	London Marriott Maida Vale	NW6	1	E4
264	London Marriott West India Quay	E14	6	B4
	M			
265	Malmaison Charterhouse Square	EC1	3	E3
273	Mandarin Oriental Hyde Park, London	SW1	4	F5
287	Mandeville Hotel, The	W1	2	G2
267	Meliá White House	NW1	2	H4
269	Mercure London City Bankside	SE1	5	E6
285	Metropolitan London	W1	4	G6
292	Milestone Hotel, The	W8	4	B5
280	Millennium & Copthorne Hotels at Chelsea FC	SW6	1	E3
281	Millennium Bailey's Hotel London Kensington	SW7	4	C3
281	Millennium Gloucester Hotel London Kensington	SW7	4	C3
277	Millennium Hotel London Knightsbridge	SW1	4	F4
287	Millennium Hotel London Mayfair	W1	2	G1
290	Mitre House Hotel	W2	2	D2
293	Montague on the Gardens, The	WC1	3	B3
286	Montcalm, The	W1	2	F2
265	Montcalm London City at The Brewery, The	EC1	3	F3
	N			
275	No 41	SW1	4	H4
270	Novotel London Blackfriars	SE1	5	E6
270	Novotel London City South	SE1	5	F6
264	Novotel London ExCeL	E16	7	C1
271	Novotel London Greenwich	SE10	8	A2
290	Novotel London Paddington	W2	2	C3
266	Novotel London Tower Bridge	EC3	3	J1
270	Novotel London Waterloo	SE1	5	C3
291	Novotel London West	W6	1	D3
	P			
282	Park International Hotel	SW7	4	D3
269	Park Plaza County Hall	SE1	5	C5
270	Park Plaza Riverbank London	SE1	5	C3
288	Park Plaza Sherlock Holmes	W1	2	F3
276	Park Plaza Victoria London	SW1	4	J3
269	Park Plaza Westminster Bridge	SE1	5	C5
275	Park Tower Knightsbridge, The	SW1	4	F5
269	Plaza on the River - Club & Residence	SE1	5	B2
263	Premier Inn London Beckton	E6	1	H4

Page	Hotel name	District	Plan number	& grid
266	Premier Inn London Blackfriars (Fleet Street)	EC4	3	E2
263	Premier Inn London City (Tower Hill)	E1	3	J1
271	Premier Inn London County Hall	SE1	5	C5
265	Premier Inn London Docklands (ExCeL)	E16	7	D1
291	Premier Inn London Ealing	W5	1	C3
294	Premier Inn London Euston	WC1	3	A5
271	Premier Inn London Greenwich	SE10	8	A1
291	Premier Inn London Hammersmith	W6	1	D3
268	Premier Inn London Hampstead	NW3	1	E4
291	Premier Inn London Hanger Lane	W5	1	C4
280	Premier Inn London Kensington	SW5	4	B3
280	Premier Inn London Kensington (Olympia)	SW5	4	A3
267	Premier Inn London King's Cross St Pancras	N1	3	B6
294	Premier Inn London Leicester Square	WC2	3	A1
280	Premier Inn London Putney Bridge	SW6	1	D3
271	Premier Inn London Southwark	SE1	5	F6
271	Premier Inn London Southwark (Tate Modern)	SE1	5	E6
264	Premier Inn London - Stratford	E15	9	B3
271	Premier Inn London Tower Bridge	SE1	5	H5
277	Premier Inn London Victoria	SW1	4	J3
282	Premier Inn London Wimbledon South	SW19	1	E1
267	Pullman London St Pancras	NW1	3	A5
	R			
289	Radisson Blu Portman Hotel	W1	2	F2
291	Ramada Encore London West	W3	1	D4
264	Ramada Hotel & Suites London Docklands	E16	7	E1
281	Rembrandt Hotel, The	SW7	4	E4
284	Ritz London, The	W1	4	J6
292	Royal Garden Hotel	W8	4	B5
275	Royal Horseguards, The	SW1	5	B6
294	Royal Trafalgar London, The	WC2	3	A1
276	Rubens at the Palace, The	SW1	4	H4
	S			
276	St Ermins Hotel	SW1	4	K4
276	St James' Court - A Taj Hotel	SW1	4	J4
272	St James's Hotel and Club	SW1	4	J6
294	Savoy, The	WC2	3	C1
275	Sofitel London St James	SW1	4	K6
274	Stafford London by Kempinski, The	SW1	4	J6
	T			
265	Thistle City Barbican	EC1	3	F5
267	Thistle Euston	NW1	2	J5
290	Thistle Hyde Park	W2	2	C1
288	Thistle Marble Arch	W1	2	G2
290	Thistle Kensington Gardens	W2	2	C1
288	Thistle Piccadilly	W1	3	A1
263	Tower, The	E1	5	J6
278	Twenty Nevern Square Hotel	SW5	4	A3
	W			
288	Washington Mayfair Hotel, The	W1	4	H6
286	Westbury Hotel, The	W1	2	H1
282	Wyndham Grand London Chelsea Harbour	SW10	1	E3
	Z			
265	Zetter Hotel, The	EC1	3	E4

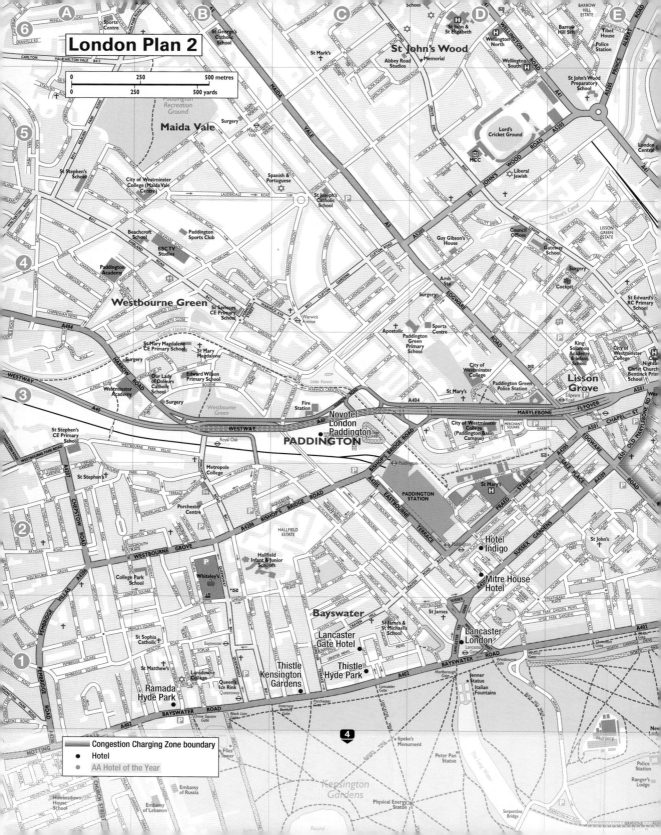

London Plan 4

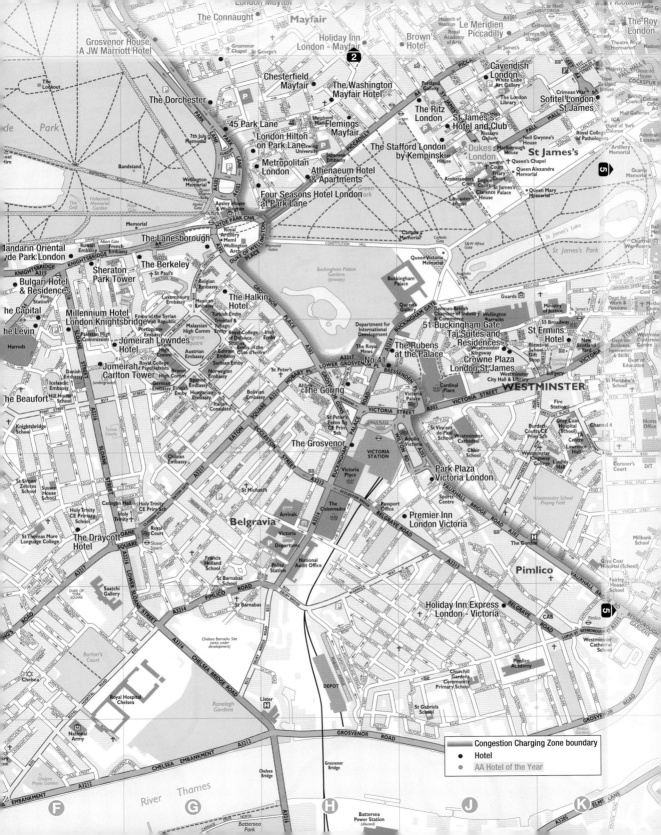

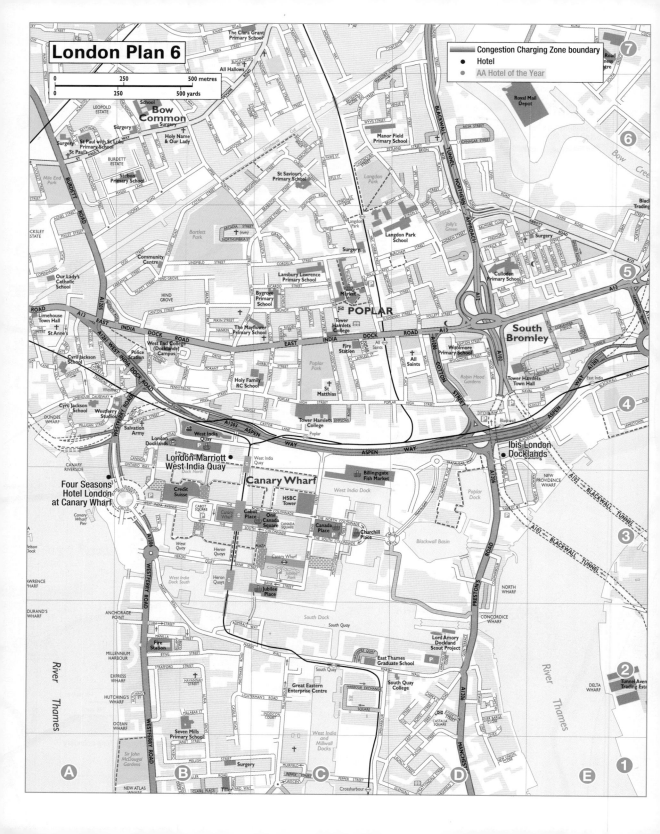

London Plan 6

Congestion Charging Zone boundary
● Hotel
● AA Hotel of the Year

0 — 250 — 500 metres
0 — 250 — 500 yards

7

6

Royal Mail Depot

The Clara Grant Primary School

All Hallows

School

Bow Common
Surgery

Holy Name & Our Lady

LEOPOLD ESTATE

Surgery
St Paul with St Luke Primary School
St Paul's
Surgery

BURDETT ESTATE

St John Primary School

Manor Field Primary School

Ailsa Street

Langdon Park

St Saviour's Primary School

Langdon Park School

Surgery

Culloden Primary School

Our Lady's Catholic School

Bartlett Park

Arcadia Street
(ruin)
Northumbria St

Community Centre

LINDFIELD STREET

Langdon Park

Jolly's Green

HIND GROVE

Lansbury Lawrence Primary School

Surgery

Bygrove Primary School

Market

POPLAR

Tower Hamlets College

5

South Bromley

Limehouse Town Hall
St Anne's

The Mayflower Primary School

West End College (Docklands) Campus

Police Station

EAST INDIA DOCK ROAD

Fire Station
All Saints
All Saints

Woolmore Primary School

Cyril Jackson School

Holy Family RC School

Poplar Park

St Matthias

Robin Hood Gardens

Tower Hamlets Town Hall

Cyril Jackson School
Westferry Studios

Salvation Army

Tower Hamlets College

4

Westferry

London Docklands
West India Quay

West India Quay

Ibis London Docklands

CANARY RIVERSIDE

London Marriott West India Quay

Billingsgate Fish Market

West India Dock

NEW PROVIDENCE WHARF

Four Seasons Hotel London at Canary Wharf

Credit Suisse

Canary Wharf

HSBC Tower

Poplar Dock

3

Canary Wharf Pier

CABOT SQUARE

One Canada Square

Canada Place

Churchill Place

Blackwall Basin

BLACKWALL TUNNEL

West Quay

Heron Quays

Canary Wharf
Jubilee Park

Blackwall Basin

NORTH WHARF

DURAND'S WHARF

Heron Quays

West India Dock South

Jubilee Place

CONCORDICE WHARF

ANCHORAGE POINT

MILLENNIUM HARBOUR

Fire Station

South Dock

South Quay

Lord Amory Dockland Scout Project

2

EXPRESS WHARF

HUTCHING'S WHARF

Great Eastern Enterprise Centre

East Thames Graduate School

South Quay College

DELTA WHARF

Tunnel Avenue Trading Estate

River Thames

OCEAN WHARF

Seven Mills Primary School

Surgery

Harbour Exchange

River Thames

Sir John McDougall Gardens

West India and Millwall Docks

Crossharbour

NEW ATLAS WHARF

A **B** **C** **D** **E**

1

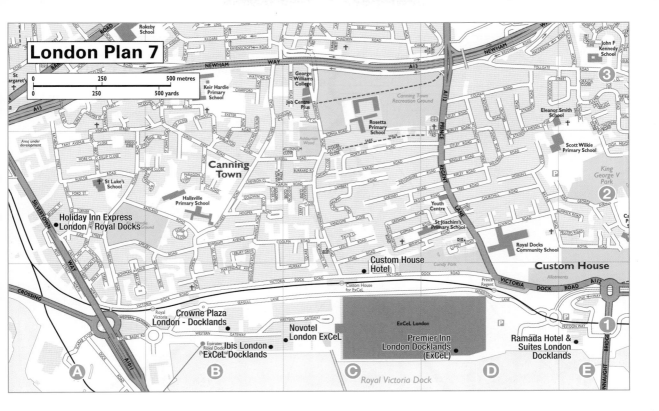

London Plan 7

0   250   500 metres
0   250   500 yards

Rokeby School
St argaret's
Keir Hardie Primary School
George Williams College
Job Centre Plus
NEWHAM WAY
A13
NEWHAM
John F Kennedy School
3
Eleanor Smith School
Rosetta Primary School
Ashburton Wood
Scott Wilkie Primary School
Area under development
Canning Town
Canning Town Recreation Ground
King George V Park
2
St Luke's School
Hallsville Primary School
Youth Centre
St Joachim's Primary School
Holiday Inn Express London - Royal Docks
Royal Docks Community School
Custom House Hotel
Custom House
Custom House
Custom House for ExCeL
VICTORIA DOCK ROAD
A112
CROSSING
1
Royal Victoria Dock
Crowne Plaza London - Docklands
Novotel London ExCeL
ExCeL London
Premier Inn London Docklands (ExCeL)
Ramada Hotel & Suites London Docklands
Ibis London ExCeL Docklands
NNAUGHT BRIDGE
A   B   C   D   E
Royal Victoria Dock

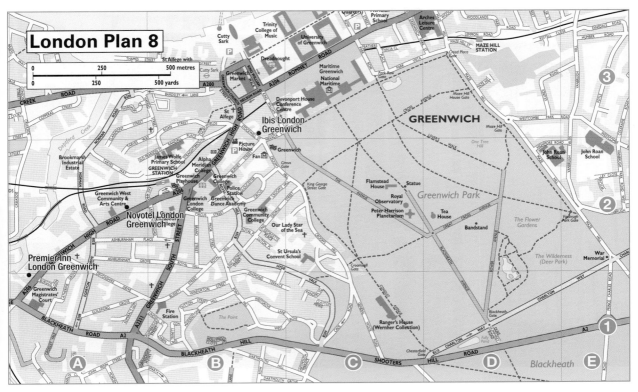

London Plan 8

0   250   500 metres
0   250   500 yards

Cutty Sark
Trinity College of Music
University of Greenwich
Primary School
Arches Leisure Centre
WOODLANDS
MAZE HILL STATION
3
CREEK ROAD
St Alfege with
Greenwich Market
Dreadnought
Maritime Greenwich
National Maritime
A200
Cutty Sark
A206 ROMNEY ROAD
Devonport House Conference Centre
GREENWICH
Maze Hill House Gate
Ibis London Greenwich
St Alfege
Picture House
Greenwich
One Tree Hill
Maze Hill Gate
WESTCOMBE PARK ROAD
John Roan School
John Roan School
Brookmarsh Industrial Estate
James Wolfe Primary School
GREENWICH STATION
Alpha Meridian College
Greenwich Playhouse
Greenwich College
Police Station
Circus Gate
King George Street Gate
Flamstead House
Statue
Royal Observatory
Greenwich Park
2
Greenwich West Community & Arts Centre
Greenwich London College
Greenwich Dance Academy
Peter Harrison Planetarium
Tea House
Vanbrugh Park Gate
The Flower Gardens
Novotel London Greenwich
Greenwich Community College
Our Lady Star of the Sea
Bandstand
Premier Inn London Greenwich
St Ursula's Convent School
The Wilderness (Deer Park)
War Memorial
Greenwich Magistrates' Court
Fire Station
The Point
Ranger's House (Wernher Collection)
Blackheath Gate
1
BLACKHEATH ROAD
A2
BLACKHEATH HILL
SHOOTERS HILL ROAD
CHARLTON ROAD
A2
Blackheath
A   B   C   D   E

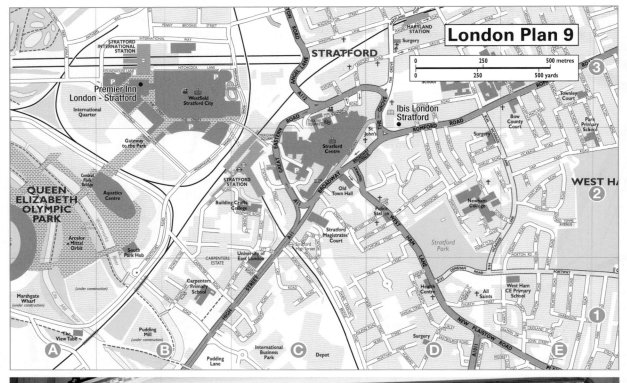

London Plan 9

STRATFORD

QUEEN ELIZABETH OLYMPIC PARK

WEST HAM

THEATRE ROYAL HAYMARKET

Save on hotels. Book at **theAA.com/hotel**

E1 – E14 263 **ENGLAND**

LONDON

Greater London Plans 1–9, pages 250–262. (Small scale maps 6 & 7 at back of book.) Hotels are listed below in postal district order, commencing East, then North, South and West, with a brief indication of the area covered. Detailed plans 2–9 show the locations of AA-appointed hotels within the Central London postal districts. If you do not know the postal district of the hotel you want, please refer to the index preceding the street plans for the entry and map pages. The plan reference for each AA-appointed hotel also appears within its directory entry.

E1 STEPNEY AND EAST OF THE TOWER OF LONDON

The Tower

★★★★ 74% HOTEL PLAN 5 J6

☎ 0870 333 9106
St Katherine's Way E1W 1LD
e-mail: tower@guoman.com
dir: Follow signs for Tower Bridge, left into St Katharine's Way. Car park (via control barrier)

This extensive modern hotel enjoys superb views over the Thames, Tower Bridge and St Katherine's Docks. Public areas include several lounges, a modern, contemporary bar and a choice of restaurants. Bedrooms are traditionally furnished and include a selection of impressive suites.

Rooms 801 (19 fmly) 🐾 **Facilities** STV Wi-fi HL Gym Xmas New Year **Conf** Class 320 Board 45 Thtr 500 **Services** Lift Air con **Parking** 100 **Notes** Civ Wed 500

Ibis London City

BUDGET HOTEL PLAN 3 J2   ibis

☎ 020 7422 8400
5 Commercial St E1 6BF
e-mail: H5011@accor.com
dir: M25 junct 30, A13, follow The City signs, then Aldgate signs

Modern, budget hotel offering comfortable accommodation in bright and practical bedrooms. Breakfast is self-service and dinner is available in the restaurant. See also the Hotel Groups pages.

Rooms 348 🐾

Premier Inn London City (Tower Hill)

BUDGET HOTEL PLAN 3 J1

☎ 0871 527 8646
22-24 Prescott St, Tower Hill E1 8BB
web: www.premierinn.com
dir: Nearest tube: Tower Hill. 3 mins walk from Docklands Light Rail (DLR)

High quality, budget accommodation ideal for both families and business travellers. Spacious, en suite bedrooms feature tea and coffee making facilities, and Freeview TV in most hotels. Internet access and Wi-fi are available for a small fee. The adjacent family restaurant features a wide and varied menu. See also the Hotel Groups pages.

Rooms 165

E6 EAST HAM

Premier Inn London Beckton

BUDGET HOTEL PLAN 1 H4

☎ 0871 527 8644
1 Woolwich Manor Way, Beckton E6 5NT
web: www.premierinn.com
dir: A13 onto A117 (Woolwich Manor Way) towards City Airport, hotel on left after 1st rdbt

High quality, budget accommodation ideal for both families and business travellers. Spacious, en suite bedrooms feature tea and coffee making facilities, and Freeview TV in most hotels. Internet access and Wi-fi are available for a small fee. The adjacent family restaurant features a wide and varied menu. See also the Hotel Groups pages.

Rooms 90

E14 CANARY WHARF & LIMEHOUSE

INSPECTORS' CHOICE

Four Seasons Hotel London at Canary Wharf

★★★★★ ◉ HOTEL PLAN 6 A3

☎ 020 7510 1999
Westferry Circus, Canary Wharf E14 8RS
e-mail: reservations.caw@fourseasons.com
web: www.fourseasons.com/canarywharf
dir: From A13 follow Canary Wharf, Isle of Dogs & Westferry Circus signs. Hotel off 3rd exit of Westferry Circus rdbt

With superb views over the London skyline and the Thames, this stylish modern hotel enjoys a delightful riverside location. Spacious contemporary bedrooms are particularly thoughtfully equipped. Public areas include the Italian Quadrato Bar and Restaurant, an impressive business centre and a gym. Guests also have complimentary use of the impressive Virgin Active Health Club adjacent to the hotel. Welcoming staff provide exemplary levels of service and hospitality.

Rooms 142 🐾 **S** £220-£400; **D** £220-£400 **Facilities** STV FTV Wi-fi ⌲ ⊛ supervised ⌖ Gym Fitness centre Beauty treatment room Xmas New Year **Conf** Class 120 Board 56 Thtr 200 **Services** Lift Air con **Parking** 31 **Notes** LB Civ Wed 200

LONDON

E14 CANARY WHARF & LIMEHOUSE *continued*

London Marriott West India Quay

★★★★★ 80% HOTEL PLAN 6 B4

☎ 020 7093 1000
22 Hertsmere Rd, Canary Wharf E14 4ED
e-mail: mhrs.loncw.ays@marriotthotels.com
web: www.londonmarriottwestindiaquay.co.uk
dir: Exit Aspen Way at Hertsmere Rd. Hotel opposite, adjacent to Canary Wharf

This spectacular skyscraper with curved glass façade is located at the heart of the docklands, adjacent to Canary Wharf and overlooking the water. The hotel is modern, but not pretentiously trendy; eye-catching floral displays add warmth to the public areas. Bedrooms, many of which overlook the quay, provide every modern convenience, including broadband and air conditioning. Curve Restaurant offers good quality cooking focusing on fresh fish.

Rooms 301 (22 fmly) 🐾 **Facilities** STV Wi-fi ↷ Gym Xmas New Year **Conf** Class 132 Board 27 Thtr 290 **Services** Lift Air con **Notes** ⊗ Civ Wed 290

Ibis London Docklands

BUDGET HOTEL PLAN 6 D4

☎ 020 7517 1100
1 Baffin Way E14 9PE
e-mail: H2177@accor.com
web: www.ibishotel.com
dir: From Tower Bridge follow City Airport and Royal Docks signs, exit for 'Isle of Dogs'. Hotel on 1st left opposite McDonalds

Modern, budget hotel offering comfortable accommodation in bright and practical bedrooms. Breakfast is self-service and dinner is available in the restaurant. See also the Hotel Groups pages.

Rooms 87 (15 GF)

E15 STRATFORD

Ibis London Stratford

BUDGET HOTEL PLAN 9 D3

☎ 020 8536 3700
1A Romford Rd, Stratford E15 4LJ
e-mail: h3099@accor.com
web: www.ibishotel.com

Modern, budget hotel offering comfortable accommodation in bright and practical bedrooms. Breakfast is self-service and dinner is available in the restaurant. See also the Hotel Groups pages.

Rooms 108 🐾 **D** £49-£199*

Premier Inn London - Stratford

BUDGET HOTEL PLAN 9 B3

☎ 0871 527 9286
International Square, Westfield Stratfield City, Montfichet Road, Olympic Park E15 1AZ
web: www.premierinn.com
dir: From A11 or A12 follow signs for Westfield Shopping City & Stratford International & Car Park A

High quality, budget accommodation ideal for both families and business travellers. Spacious, en suite bedrooms feature tea and coffee making facilities, and Freeview TV in most hotels. Internet access and Wi-fi are available for a small fee. The adjacent family restaurant features a wide and varied menu. See also the Hotel Groups pages.

Rooms 267

E16 SILVERTOWN

Novotel London ExCeL

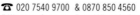

★★★★ 79% HOTEL PLAN 7 C1

☎ 020 7540 9700 & 0870 850 4560
7 Western Gateway, Royal Victoria Docks E16 1AA
e-mail: H3656@accor.com
web: www.novotel.com/3656
dir: M25 junct 30, A13 follow City signs, exit at Canning Town. Follow ExCeL West signs. Hotel adjacent

This hotel is situated adjacent to the ExCeL exhibition centre and overlooks the Royal Victoria Dock. Design throughout the hotel is contemporary and stylish. Public rooms include a range of meeting rooms, a modern coffee station, indoor leisure facilities and a smart bar and restaurant, both with a terrace overlooking the dock. Bedrooms feature modern decor, a bathroom with separate bath and shower, and an extensive range of extras.

Rooms 257 (176 fmly) 🐾 **Facilities** STV FTV Wi-fi ↷ Gym Sauna Steam room Relaxation room with massage bed **Conf** Class 55 Board 30 Thtr 70 **Services** Lift Air con **Parking** 160 **Notes** Civ Wed 50

Crowne Plaza London - Docklands

★★★★ 77% HOTEL PLAN 7 B1

☎ 020 7055 2000
Royal Victoria Dock, Western Gateway E16 1AL
e-mail: sales@crowneplazadocklands.co.uk
web: www.cpdocklands.co.uk
dir: A1020 towards ExCeL. Follow signs for ExCeL West. Hotel on left 400mtrs before ExCeL

Ideally located for the ExCel exhibition centre, Canary Wharf and London City airport, this unique, contemporary hotel overlooking Royal Victoria Dock, offers accommodation suitable for both the leisure and business travellers. Rooms are spacious and equipped with all modern facilities. The hotel has a busy bar, a contemporary restaurant and health and fitness facilities with an indoor pool, jacuzzi and sauna.

Rooms 210 (10 fmly) (4 smoking) 🐾 **Facilities** STV Wi-fi ↷ HL 🕑 supervised Gym Beauty treatment room Sauna Steam room Xmas New Year **Conf** Class 140 Board 62 Thtr 250 **Services** Lift Air con **Parking** 75 **Notes** ⊗ Civ Wed 275

Ramada Hotel & Suites London Docklands

★★★★ 72% HOTEL PLAN 7 E1

☎ 020 7540 4820
Excel 2 Festoon Way, Royal Victoria Dock E16 1RH
e-mail: reservations@ramadadocklands.co.uk
dir: Follow signs for ExCeL East & London City Airport. Over Connaught Bridge then immediately left at rdbt

This hotel benefits from a stunning waterfront location and is close to the events venue, ExCeL, the O2 Arena, Canary Wharf and London City Airport. The accommodation comprises a mix of spacious bedrooms and suites. The relaxed public areas consist of a modern restaurant and informal lounge area. Parking, a fitness room and meeting rooms are available on site. Free Wi-fi is available.

Rooms 224 (71 fmly) (23 smoking) 🐾 **Facilities** FTV Wi-fi Gym Xmas **Conf** Class 20 Board 25 Thtr 30 Del £300 **Services** Lift Air con **Parking** 60 **Notes** Civ Wed 120

Ibis London ExCeL Docklands

BUDGET HOTEL PLAN 7 B1

☎ 020 7055 2300
9 Western Gateway, Royal Victoria Docks E16 1AB
e-mail: H3655@accor.com
web: www.ibishotel.com
dir: M25, A13 to London, City Airport, ExCeL East

Modern, budget hotel offering comfortable accommodation in bright and practical bedrooms. Breakfast is self-service and dinner is available in the restaurant See also the Hotel Groups pages.

Rooms 278 (33 fmly) 🐾 **S** £49–£239; **D** £49–£239*

Premier Inn London Docklands (ExCeL)

BUDGET HOTEL PLAN 7 D1

☎ 0871 527 8650
Excel East, Royal Victoria Dock E16 1SL
web: www.premierinn.com
dir: A13 onto A1020. At Connaught rdbt take 2nd exit into Connaught Rd. Hotel on right

High quality, budget accommodation ideal for both families and business travellers. Spacious, en suite bedrooms feature tea and coffee making facilities, and Freeview TV in most hotels. Internet access and Wi-fi are available for a small fee. The adjacent family restaurant features a wide and varied menu. See also the Hotel Groups pages.

Rooms 202

EC1 CITY OF LONDON

The Zetter Hotel

★★★★ 80% ◉◉ HOTEL PLAN 3 E4

☎ 020 7324 4444 & 7324 4567
St John's Square, 86-88 Clerkenwell Rd EC1M 5RJ
e-mail: info@thezetter.com
dir: From West A401, Clerkenwell Rd A5201. Hotel 200mtrs on left

This iconic hotel offers individually styled bedrooms with an impressive array of amenities, including the latest in-room entertainment. The Roof Top Studio rooms, some with a private patio, have amazing views over London's historic Clerkenwell and beyond. The Bistrot Bruno Loubet offers award-winning, imaginative and modern French cuisine, and the Atrium Bar and Lounge is the place to meet for coffee, have a light lunch or enjoy a drink. Two stylish rooms are available for private events.

Rooms 59 🐾 **Facilities** STV Wi-fi Complimentary use of local gym **Conf** Class 28 Board 32 Thtr 50 **Services** Lift Air con **Parking** 1 **Notes** ⊗

Malmaison Charterhouse Square

★★★ 88% ◉◉ HOTEL PLAN 3 E3

☎ 020 7012 3700
18-21 Charterhouse Square, Clerkenwell EC1M 6AH
e-mail: london@malmaison.com
web: www.malmaison.com
dir: Exit Barbican Station turn left, take 1st left. Hotel on far left corner of Charterhouse Square

Situated in a leafy and peaceful square, Malmaison Charterhouse maintains the same focus on quality service and food as the other hotels in the group. The bedrooms, stylishly decorated in calming tones, have all the expected facilities including power showers, CD players and free internet access. The brasserie and bar at the hotel's centre has a buzzing atmosphere and offers traditional French cuisine.

Rooms 97 (5 GF) **Facilities** STV Wi-fi ⇗ Gym
Conf Class 18 Board 16 Thtr 30 **Services** Lift Air con

Thistle City Barbican   thistle

★★★ 76% HOTEL PLAN 3 F5

☎ 0871 376 9004
Central St, Clerkenwell EC1V 8DS
e-mail: citybarbican@thistle.co.uk
web: www.thistlehotels.com/citybarbican
dir: From Kings Cross E, follow Pentonville Rd, right into Goswell Rd. At lights left into Lever St. Hotel at junct of Lever St & Central St

Situated on the edge of The City, this modern hotel offers a complimentary shuttle bus to Barbican, Liverpool Street and Moorgate tube stations at peak times. Bedrooms are well equipped and include some smart executive and superior rooms; public areas include a bar, a coffee shop and restaurant along with a smart Otium leisure club.

Rooms 463 (166 annexe) (13 fmly) **S** £69–£169; **D** £89–£209* **Facilities** Spa STV FTV Wi-fi HL 🖫 supervised Gym Sauna Steam room Xmas New Year **Conf** Class 75 Board 35 Thtr 175 Del from £199 to £305 **Services** Lift **Parking** 10 **Notes** LB ⊗

See advert on page 289

The Montcalm London City at The Brewery

Ⓤ PLAN 3 F3

☎ 020 7614 0100
52 Chiswell St EC1Y 4SB

Currently the rating for this establishment is not confirmed. This may be due to a change of ownership or because it has only recently joined the AA rating scheme. For further details please see the AA website: theAA.com

Rooms 235 **Conf** Class 40 Board 40 Thtr 60

EC2

ANdAZ Liverpool Street

★★★★★ 86% ◉◉◉ HOTEL PLAN 3 H3

☎ 020 7961 1234
40 Liverpool St EC2M 7QN
e-mail: guestservices.londonliv@andaz.com
dir: On corner of Liverpool St & Bishopsgate, attached to Liverpool St station

ANdAZ is an exciting and contemporary place to stay - no reception desk here so guests are checked-in by staff with laptops. Bedrooms are stylish, and designed very much with the executive in mind, with iPods and Wi-fi as well as a mini bar stocked with healthy choices. The dining options are varied and many - 1 Rosette Miyako restaurant for Japanese cuisine, 3 Rosette 1901 Restaurant and Wine Bar, St Georges pub, 1 Rosétte Catch and Champagne bar, and the Eastway brasserie. There are also rooms for private dining and other events.

Rooms 267 🐾 **Facilities** STV FTV Wi-fi ⇗ Gym Steam room Beauty treatment rooms ♫ New Year **Conf** Class 120 Board 60 Thtr 250 **Services** Lift Air con **Notes** ⊗ Civ Wed 230

Apex London Wall Hotel

★★★★ 80% HOTEL PLAN 3 G2

☎ 0845 365 0000 & 020 7562 3030
7-9 Copthall Av EC2R 7NJ
e-mail: london.reservations@apexhotels.co.uk
dir: Near Moorgate & Bank stations

A sister property to the nearby City of London Hotel. This hotel is situated in the heart of London's financial district and is close to many places of interest. This 'boutique' property offers contemporary accommodation for both business and leisure travellers. Bedrooms and bathrooms have been fitted to a very high standard and feature some great guest comforts. Off the Wall restaurant offers informal dining with a modern British menu.

Rooms 89 🐾 **Facilities** FTV Wi-fi ⇗ Gym Xmas New Year **Services** Lift Air con **Notes** ⊗ No children

Apex City of London Hotel

★★★★ 81% @ HOTEL PLAN 3 H1

☎ 0845 365 0000 & 020 7702 2020
1 Seething Ln EC3N 4AX
e-mail: london.reservations@apexhotels.co.uk
web: www.apexhotels.co.uk
dir: Opposite Tower of London

Situated close to Tower Bridge, this hotel is in the heart of the business district. Bedrooms are appointed to a high standard and have walk-in power showers in the en suites. The gym has the most up-to-date equipment, and there is a sauna room. The Addendum Restaurant offers a good dining option.

Rooms 179 (5 GF) (6 smoking) ⚑ **Facilities** STV FTV Wi-fi ⅍ Gym **Conf** Class 36 Board 30 Thtr 80 **Services** Lift Air con **Notes** ⊗

The Chamberlain Hotel

★★★★ 78% HOTEL PLAN 3 J2

☎ 020 7680 1500
130-135 Minories EC3N 1NU
e-mail: thechamberlain@fullers.co.uk
web: www.thechamberlainhotel.com
dir: M25 junct 30, A13 W towards London. Follow into Aldgate, left after bus station. Hotel halfway down Minories

This smart hotel is ideally situated for the City, Tower Bridge, plus both Aldgate and Tower underground stations. The impressive bedrooms are stylish, well equipped and comfortable, and the modern bathrooms are fitted with TVs to watch from the bath. Informal day rooms include a popular pub, a lounge and an attractive restaurant.

Rooms 64 ⚑ **S** £95-£325; **D** £95-£325*
Facilities STV Wi-fi ⅍ **Conf** Class 20 Board 22 Thtr 40 Del from £175 to £285* **Services** Lift Air con **Notes** LB ⊗ Closed 24-28 Dec

Novotel London Tower Bridge

★★★★ 74% HOTEL PLAN 3 J1

☎ 020 7265 6000 & 7265 6002
10 Pepys St EC3N 2NR
e-mail: H3107@accor.com
web: www.novotel.com

Located near the Tower of London, this smart hotel is convenient for Docklands, the City, Heathrow and London City airports. Air-conditioned bedrooms are spacious, modern, and offer a great range of facilities. There is a smart bar and restaurant, a small gym, children's play area and extensive meeting and conference facilities.

Rooms 203 (130 fmly) ⚑ **Facilities** STV FTV Wi-fi ⅍ Gym Steam room Sauna Fitness room Xmas New Year **Conf** Class 56 Board 25 Thtr 100 Del from £180 to £525 **Services** Lift

Crowne Plaza London - The City

★★★★ 80% @ HOTEL PLAN 3 E1

☎ 0871 942 9190
19 New Bridge St EC4V 6DB
e-mail: loncy.info@ihg.com
web: www.cplondoncityhotel.co.uk
dir: Opposite Blackfriars station

This hotel has a 1919 façade, but is modern and bright inside; it is situated close to the north bank of the River Thames and also to Blackfriars station. Bedrooms are modern and well equipped. There is a small gym and valet parking is available. Booking for dinner is required.

Rooms 203 (60 fmly) (7 smoking) **Facilities** STV Wi-fi ⅍ HL Gym Xmas New Year **Conf** Class 100 Board 50 Thtr 160 Del from £225 to £350 **Services** Lift Air con **Notes** ⊗ Civ Wed 160

Apex Temple Court Hotel

★★★★ 78% HOTEL PLAN 3 D2

☎ 0845 365 0000 & 020 7353 4113
1-2 Serjeants' Inn, Fleet St EC4Y 1LL
e-mail: london.reservations@apexhotels.co.uk
dir: Within Inner Temple, off Fleet St

This property, located just off Fleet Street and a moment's walk from the Inner Temple, has undergone a complete transformation - the interior is now contemporary yet from the outside its appearance remains traditional. Bedrooms, incorporating up-to-date technology, are stylish and furnished with guest comfort in mind; some benefit from city skyline views. The cuisine is a highlight with brasserie-style dining in Chambers Restaurant and Bar, plus there are excellent breakfasts to look forward to. The hotel has a gym.

Rooms 184 ⚑ **Facilities** STV FTV Wi-fi ⅍ HL Gym Xmas New Year **Services** Lift Air con **Notes** ⊗

Premier Inn London Blackfriars (Fleet Street)

BUDGET HOTEL PLAN 3 E2

☎ 0871 527 9362
1-2 Dorset Rise EC4Y 8EN
web: www.premierinn.com
dir: Please telephone for detailed directions

High quality, budget accommodation ideal for both families and business travellers. Spacious, en suite bedrooms feature tea and coffee making facilities, and Freeview TV in most hotels. Internet access and Wi-fi are available for a small fee. The adjacent family restaurant features a wide and varied menu. See also the Hotel Groups pages.

Rooms 256

See **LONDON plan 1 F4**

Premier Inn London Angel Islington

BUDGET HOTEL

☎ 0871 527 8558
Parkfield St, Islington N1 0PS
dir: From A1 (Islington High St) into Berners Rd bear left into Parkfield St. N1 car park opposite hotel

High quality, budget accommodation ideal for both families and business travellers. Spacious, en suite bedrooms feature tea and coffee making facilities, and Freeview TV in most hotels. Internet access and Wi-fi are available for a small fee. The adjacent family restaurant features a wide and varied menu. See also the Hotel Groups pages.

Rooms 95

Premier Inn London City (Old Street)

BUDGET HOTEL

☎ 0871 527 9312
1 Silicon Way N1 6AT
dir: From Old Street tube station exit 1 (on foot) onto A501 (City Rd). Right into East St. 2nd right into Brunswick Place (Three Crowns pub on corner), 1st left into Corsham St

Rooms 251

Save on hotels. Book at **theAA.com/hotel**

EC3 – NW2 267 ENGLAND

Premier Inn London King's Cross St Pancras

BUDGET HOTEL PLAN 3 B6

☎ 0871 527 8672
26-30 York Way, Kings Cross N1 9AA
web: www.premierinn.com
dir: M25 junct 16 onto M40 (becomes A40). Follow City signs, exit at Euston Rd, follow one-way system to York Way

Rooms 276

INSPECTORS' CHOICE

The Landmark London

★★★★★ ◉◉ HOTEL PLAN 2 F3

☎ 020 7631 8000
222 Marylebone Rd NW1 6JQ
e-mail: reservations@thelandmark.co.uk
web: www.landmarklondon.co.uk
dir: Adjacent to Marylebone Station. Hotel on Marylebone Rd

Once one of the last truly grand railway hotels, The Landmark boasts a number of stunning features, the most spectacular being the naturally lit central atrium forming the hotel's focal point. When it comes to eating and drinking there are a number of choices, including the Cellars bar for cocktails and upmarket bar meals, the Mirror Bar, and The Gazebo - ideal for a business meeting or a quick snack. The Winter Garden Restaurant has the centre stage in the atrium and is a great place to watch the world go by; and the twotwentytwo restaurant and bar is a relaxing place to meet, eat and drink. The air-conditioned bedrooms are luxurious and have large, stylish bathrooms. The health club offers a complete wellbeing experience.

Rooms 300 (71 fmly) (52 smoking) 🐾
Facilities Spa STV FTV Wi-fi ⇘ 🐾 Gym Beauty treatments & massages 🎵 Xmas New Year
Conf Class 364 Board 50 Thtr 568 **Services** Lift Air con **Parking** 80 **Notes** ⊗ Civ Wed 300

Thistle Euston

thistle

★★★★ 81% HOTEL PLAN 2 J5

☎ 0871 376 9017
Cardington St NW1 2LP
e-mail: euston@thistle.co.uk
web: www.thistlehotels.com/euston
dir: From M40 continue to end of A40, follow Marylebone Rd, take Euston Rd to Melton St & into Cardington St

This smart, modern hotel is ideally located a short walk from Euston Station. Spacious public areas include a bar/lounge, extensive meeting and function rooms and a bright basement restaurant. Bedrooms include a large number of deluxe and executive rooms that are spacious, comfortable and well equipped. The hotel also has limited on-site parking.

Rooms 362 (32 fmly) (42 GF) 🐾 **S** £129-£230;
D £159-£250* **Facilities** STV FTV Wi-fi HL
Conf Class 45 Board 35 Thtr 90 **Services** Lift Air con
Notes LB ⊗

See advert on page 289

Meliá White House

★★★★ 80% ◉◉ HOTEL PLAN 2 H4

☎ 020 7391 3000
Albany St, Regents Park NW1 3UP
e-mail: melia.white.house@solmelia.com
dir: Opposite Gt Portland St underground station & next to Regents Park/Warren Street underground

Owned by the Spanish Solmelia company, this impressive art deco property is located opposite Great Portland Street tube station. Spacious public areas offer a high degree of comfort and include an elegant cocktail bar, a fine dining restaurant and a more informal brasserie. Stylish bedrooms come in a variety of sizes, but all offer high levels of comfort and are thoughtfully equipped.

Rooms 581 (7 fmly) 🐾 **Facilities** STV FTV Wi-fi ⇘ HL
Gym 🎵 Xmas New Year **Conf** Class 80 Board 60
Thtr 140 **Services** Lift Air con **Notes** ⊗ Civ Wed 140

Pullman London St Pancras

pullman

★★★★ 78% ◉ HOTEL PLAN 3 A5

☎ 020 7666 9000 & 7666 9010
100-110 Euston Rd NW1 2AJ
e-mail: H5309@accor.com
web: www.accorhotels.com/5309
dir: Between St Pancras & Euston stations, entrance opposite British Library

This hotel enjoys a central location adjacent to the British Library and close to some of London's main transport hubs. The style is modern and contemporary

throughout. Bedrooms vary in size but are all very well equipped and many have views over the city. Open-plan public areas include a leisure suite and extensive conference facilities including the Shaw Theatre. Free Wi-fi is available.

Rooms 312 (41 fmly) 🐾 **Facilities** Wi-fi ⇘ HL Gym
Steam room Sauna Xmas **Conf** Class 220 Board 80
Thtr 446 **Services** Lift Air con **Notes** ⊗

Ibis London Euston St Pancras

ibis

BUDGET HOTEL PLAN 2 J5

☎ 020 7388 7777
3 Cardington St NW1 2LW
e-mail: H0921@accor-hotels.com
web: www.ibishotel.com
dir: From Euston Rd or station, right to Melton St & into Cardington St

Modern, budget hotel offering comfortable accommodation in bright and practical bedrooms. Breakfast is self-service and dinner is available in the restaurant. See also the Hotel Groups pages.

Rooms 380 🐾 **Conf** Class 40 Board 40 Thtr 100

Crown Moran Hotel

MORAN HOTELS

★★★★ 74% HOTEL PLAN 1 D5

☎ 020 8452 4175
142-152 Cricklewood Broadway, Cricklewood NW2 3ED
e-mail: crownres@moranhotels.com
web: www.moranhotels.com
dir: M1 junct 1 follow signs onto North Circular (W) A406. Junct with A5 (Staples Corner). At rdbt take 1st exit onto A5 to Cricklewood

This striking hotel is connected by an impressive glass atrium to the popular Crown Pub. Features include excellent function and conference facilities, a leisure club, a choice of stylish lounges and bars and a contemporary restaurant. The air-conditioned bedrooms are appointed to a high standard and include a number of trendy suites.

Rooms 152 (82 fmly) (35 GF) 🐾 **S** £105-£190;
D £115-£480 **Facilities** STV Wi-fi ⇘ 🐾 Gym 🎵 Xmas
New Year **Conf** Class 150 Board 80 Thtr 300
Del from £190 to £250 **Services** Lift Air con
Parking 39 **Notes** ⊗ Civ Wed 300

NW2 BRENT CROSS & CRICKLEWOOD *continued*

Holiday Inn London - Brent Cross

★★★ 78% HOTEL PLAN 1 D5

☎ 0871 942 9112 & 020 8967 6359
Tilling Rd, Brent Cross NW2 1LP
web: www.holidayinn.co.uk
dir: At M1 junct 1. At rdbt after bridge turn left into Tilling Rd

Ideally located beside the M1 on the A406 North Circular, just a few minutes' walk from Brent Cross Shopping Centre and four miles from Wembley Stadium. The hotel offers well-appointed bedrooms with air conditioning and high-speed internet access; Wi-fi is available in the public areas. Conference rooms and a contemporary restaurant are available, plus there is ample parking.

Rooms 154 (87 fmly) (16 smoking) **Facilities** STV FTV Wi-fi New Year **Conf** Class 40 Board 32 Thtr 80 **Services** Lift Air con **Parking** 150 **Notes** ⊗

NW3 HAMPSTEAD AND SWISS COTTAGE

London Marriott Hotel Regents Park

★★★★ 76% HOTEL PLAN 1 E4

☎ 020 7722 7711 & 0800 221222
128 King Henry's Rd NW3 3ST
e-mail: london.regional.reservations@marriott.com
web: www.londonmarriottregentspark.co.uk
dir: 200yds off Finchley Rd on A41

Situated in a quieter part of town and close to the tube station, this hotel offers guests comfortably appointed, air-conditioned accommodation; all rooms boast balconies and are particularly well equipped to meet the needs of today's business traveller. The open-plan ground floor is spacious and airy and includes a well-equipped leisure centre with indoor pool. Secure parking is a bonus.

Rooms 304 (148 fmly) **Facilities** STV Wi-fi ⓫ ⓩ supervised Gym Hair & beauty salon Steam room Sauna **Conf** Class 150 Board 120 Thtr 300 **Services** Lift Air con **Parking** 110 **Notes** ⊗ Civ Wed 300

Premier Inn London Hampstead

BUDGET HOTEL PLAN 1 E4

☎ 0871 527 8662
215 Haverstock Hill, Hampstead NW3 4RB
web: www.premierinn.com
dir: A41 to Swiss Cottage. Before junct take feeder road left into Buckland Cresent into Belsize Ave. Left into Haverstock Hill

High quality, budget accommodation ideal for both families and business travellers. Spacious, en suite bedrooms feature tea and coffee making facilities, and Freeview TV in most hotels. Internet access and Wi-fi are available for a small fee. The adjacent family restaurant features a wide and varied menu. See also the Hotel Groups pages.

Rooms 143

NW4 HENDON

Hendon Hall Hotel

★★★★ 76% ◉◉ HOTEL

PLAN 1 D5

☎ 020 8203 3341
Ashley Ln, Hendon NW4 1HF
e-mail: hendonhall@handpicked.co.uk
web: www.handpickedhotels.co.uk/hendonhall
dir: M1 junct 2 follow A406. Right at lights into Parson St, right into Ashley Ln. Hotel on right

This impressive property was originally built in the 16th century when it was known as Hendon Manor, and is now a stylish hotel boasting smart, well-equipped, comfortable bedrooms with luxury toiletries, free Wi-fi and well-appointed en suites. Public areas include meeting and conference facilities, a contemporary cocktail bar and a richly decorated restaurant that opens onto a garden terrace. Staff are friendly and attentive.

Rooms 57 ⓫ **S** £99-£144; **D** £109-£154*
Facilities STV FTV Wi-fi ⓫ Xmas New Year
Conf Class 130 Board 76 Thtr 350 Del from £151 to £180* **Services** Lift Air con **Parking** 70 **Notes** ⊗ Civ Wed 120

NW6 MAIDA VALE

London Marriott Maida Vale

★★★★ 75% HOTEL PLAN 1 E4

☎ 020 7543 6000
Plaza Pde, Maida Vale NW6 5RP
e-mail: reservations.london.england.maidavale@marriotthotels.com
web: www.londonmarriottmaidavale.co.uk
dir: From M1 take A5 S'bound for 3m. Hotel on left. From Marble Arch take A5 N'bound. Hotel on right

This smart, modern hotel is conveniently located just north of central London. Air-conditioned bedrooms are tastefully decorated and provide a range of extras. The hotel also boasts extensive function facilities as well as an indoor leisure centre which has a swimming pool, gym and health and beauty salon.

Rooms 237 (40 fmly) **Facilities** STV Wi-fi ⓫ ⓩ Gym Hair & beauty salon Beauty treatment rooms Exercise studio & classes Xmas **Conf** Class 70 Board 30 Thtr 200 **Services** Lift Air con **Parking** 28 **Notes** ⊗ Civ Wed 100

SE1 SOUTHWARK AND WATERLOO

London Marriott Hotel County Hall

★★★★★ 84% ◉◉ HOTEL PLAN 5 C5

☎ 020 7928 5200
Westminster Bridge Rd, County Hall SE1 7PB
e-mail: sales.countyhall@marriott.com
web: www.londonmarriottcountyhall.co.uk
dir: On Thames South Bank, between Westminster Bridge & London Eye

This impressive building, appointed to a very high standard, enjoys an enviable position on the south bank of the Thames, adjacent to the London Eye. Public areas have a traditional elegance and the crescent-shaped restaurant offers fine views of Westminster. All bedrooms are smartly laid out and thoughtfully equipped especially with the business traveller in mind.

Rooms 200 (58 fmly) **S** fr £235; **D** fr £235*
Facilities Spa STV Wi-fi ⓫ HL ⓩ Gym Sauna Steam room Pilates classes Dance studio Xmas New Year **Conf** Class 40 Board 30 Thtr 80 **Services** Lift Air con **Parking** 70 **Notes** LB ⊗ Civ Wed 80

Save on hotels. Book at **theAA.com/hotel**

NW2 – SE1 269 ENGLAND

LONDON

Plaza on the River - Club & Residence

★★★★★ 81% TOWN HOUSE HOTEL PLAN 5 B2

☎ 020 7769 2525
18 Albert Embankment SE1 7TJ
e-mail: guestrelations@plazaontheriver.co.uk
dir: From Houses of Parliament turn into Millbank, at rdbt left into Lambeth Bridge. At rdbt 3rd exit into Albert Embankment

This is a superb modern townhouse overlooking London from the south bank of the Thames, with outstanding views of the capital's landmarks. The bedrooms are large and many are full suites with state-of-the-art technology and kitchen facilities; all are decorated in an elegant modern style. Service includes a full range of in-room dining options; additionally, the bar and restaurant in the adjacent Park Plaza are available to guests.

Rooms 65 (65 fmly) (65 smoking) **Facilities** STV FTV Wi-fi HL Gym Xmas New Year **Conf** Class 450 Board 40 Thtr 650 **Services** Lift Air con **Notes** Civ Wed 600

H10 London Waterloo Hotel

★★★★ 82% HOTEL PLAN 5 E5

☎ 020 7928 4062
284-302 Waterloo Rd SE1 8RQ
e-mail: h10.london.waterloo@h10hotels.com
dir: 450mtrs from Waterloo Station

This hotel, conveniently situated for the South Bank and Waterloo Station, has a host of features. Bedrooms are stylish and designed with the international traveller in mind. The bar provides a useful internet facility and the stylish restaurant offers fresh and interesting dishes. The staff are friendly and efficient.

Rooms 177 **Facilities** STV FTV Wi-fi Gym Beauty treatment room Xmas New Year **Conf** Class 45 Board 24 Thtr 70 **Services** Lift Air con **Notes** ⊗

Park Plaza Westminster Bridge

★★★★ 81% HOTEL PLAN 5 C5

☎ 020 7620 7200
SE1 7UT
e-mail: ppwlres@pphe.com

A very smart hotel located in the city, close to Waterloo Station, featuring eye-catching, contemporary decor, a state-of-the-art indoor leisure facility and extensive conference and banqueting facilities. There is the awarding wining Joel brasserie as well as Ichi, the popular sushi bar. The bedrooms are also up-to-the-minute in style and feature a host

of extras including a mini bar, a safe and modem points.

Rooms 1019 (420 fmly) **Facilities** Spa STV FTV Wi-fi HL Gym Xmas New Year **Conf** Class 800 Board 50 Thtr 1400 **Services** Lift Air con **Notes** ⊗ Civ Wed

London Bridge Hotel

★★★★ 81% HOTEL PLAN 5 G6

☎ 020 7855 2200
8-18 London Bridge St SE1 9SG
e-mail: sales@londonbridgehotel.com
web: www.londonbridgehotel.com
dir: Access through London Bridge Station (bus/taxi yard), into London Bridge St (one-way). Hotel on left, 50yds from station

This elegant, independently owned hotel enjoys a prime location on the edge of the city, adjacent to London Bridge station. Smartly appointed, well-equipped bedrooms include a number of spacious deluxe rooms and suites. Free Wi-fi is available throughout. The Quarter Bar & Lounge is the ideal place for light bites, old favourites and cocktails. The Londinium restaurant offers a seasonal British menu.

Rooms 138 (10 fmly) (5 smoking) **Facilities** STV FTV Wi-fi Gym **Conf** Class 36 Board 36 Thtr 80 **Services** Lift Air con **Notes** ⊗

Park Plaza County Hall

★★★★ 78% HOTEL PLAN 5 C5

☎ 020 7021 1800
1 Addington St SE1 7RY
e-mail: ppchinfo@pphe.com
web: www.parkplazacountyhall.com
dir: From Houses of Parliament cross Westminster Bridge (A302). At rdbt turn left. 1st right into Addington St. Hotel on left

This hotel is located just south of Westminster Bridge near Waterloo international rail station. This contemporary design-led, air-conditioned establishment features studios and suites, most with kitchenettes and seating areas with a flat-screen TV. There are six meeting rooms, an executive lounge, a restaurant and bar plus a fully-equipped gym with sauna and steam room. Wi-fi is available.

Rooms 398 (303 fmly) **Facilities** STV FTV Wi-fi Gym Sauna Steam room Beauty therapy room Xmas New Year **Conf** Class 60 Board 40 Thtr 100 **Services** Lift Air con **Notes** ⊗

Mercure London City Bankside

★★★★ 78% HOTEL PLAN 5 E6

☎ 020 7902 0800
71-79 Southwark St SE1 0JA
e-mail: H2814@accor.com
web: www.mercure.com
dir: A200 to London Bridge. Left into Southwark St

This smart, contemporary hotel forms part of the rejuvenation of the South Bank. With the City of London just over the river and a number of tourist attractions within easy reach, the hotel is well located for business and leisure visitors alike. Facilities include spacious air-cooled bedrooms, a modern bar and the stylish Loft Restaurant.

Rooms 144 (15 fmly) (5 GF) **Facilities** STV Wi-fi HL Gym Xmas **Conf** Class 40 Board 30 Thtr 60 **Services** Lift Air con

SE1 SOUTHWARK AND WATERLOO *continued*

Park Plaza Riverbank London

★★★★ 77% ◉ ◉ HOTEL PLAN 5 C3

☎ 020 7958 8000
18 Albert Embankment SE1 7SP
e-mail: rppres@pphe.com
web: www.parkplazariverbank.com
dir: From Houses of Parliament turn onto Millbank, at rdbt left onto Lambeth Bridge. At rdbt take 3rd exit onto Albert Embankment

Situated on the south side of the River Thames, this hotel offers guests the convenience of a central London location and high levels of comfort. Contemporary design coupled with a host of up-to-date facilities, the hotel is home to the Chino Latino brasserie. The air-conditioned bedrooms have flat-screen TVs and large work desks; some rooms and suites have stunning views of the Houses of Parliament. Other facilities include Wi-fi throughout, high-tech conference rooms, a business centre, and a fitness centre with cardiovascular equipment.

Rooms 394 🐾 **Facilities** STV FTV Wi-fi ☼ HL Gym **Conf** Class 405 Board 40 Thtr 700 **Services** Lift Air con **Notes** ⊗ Civ Wed 150

Novotel London City South

★★★★ 77% HOTEL PLAN 5 F6

☎ 020 7089 0400
Southwark Bridge Rd SE1 9HH
e-mail: H3269@accor.com
web: www.novotel.com
dir: At junct at Thrale St, off Southwark St

Conveniently located for both business and leisure guests, with The City just across the Thames; other major attractions are also easily accessible. The hotel is contemporary in design with smart, modern bedrooms and spacious public rooms. There is a gym, sauna and steam room on the 6th floor, and limited parking is available at the rear of the hotel.

Rooms 182 (139 fmly) 🐾 **Facilities** STV FTV Wi-fi ☼ Gym Steam room Sauna **Conf** Class 45 Board 40 Thtr 100 **Services** Lift Air con **Parking** 50

Novotel London Blackfriars

★★★★ 74% HOTEL PLAN 5 E6

☎ 020 7660 0834
46 Blackfriars Rd SE1 8NZ
e-mail: H7942@accor.com

This latest generation Novotel is just south of the Thames and was opened in late 2012, utilising the latest in hotel and bedroom technology. There are media hubs in each bedroom, as well as air

conditioning and glass walls to the bathroom that "steam-over" in an instant for privacy if desired. There are also a swimming pool, gym and sauna in the basement, and a bar and restaurant on the ground floor.

Rooms 182 (39 fmly) **S** £109-£280; **D** £119-£290* **Facilities** FTV Wi-fi ☼ Gym Saunarium **Conf** Class 50 Board 40 Thtr 90 Del from £185 to £225* **Services** Lift Air con **Notes** LB

Novotel London Waterloo

★★★★ 74% HOTEL PLAN 5 C3

☎ 020 7793 1010
113 Lambeth Rd SE1 7LS
e-mail: h1785@accor.com
web: www.novotel.com/1785
dir: Opposite Houses of Parliament on S bank of River Thames

This hotel is in an excellent location, with Lambeth Palace, the Houses of Parliament and Waterloo Station all within a short walk. The bedrooms are spacious and benefit from air conditioning. The open-plan public areas include the Elements bar and restaurant, and also a children's play area. There are also a fitness room, well-equipped conference facilities and secure parking.

Rooms 187 (80 fmly) **Facilities** STV Wi-fi ☼ HL Gym Steam room Sauna **Conf** Class 24 Board 24 Thtr 40 **Services** Lift Air con **Parking** 40

Bermondsey Square Hotel

★★★★ 73% ◉ HOTEL PLAN 5 H4

☎ 020 7378 2465 & 7378 2450
Bermondsey Square, Tower Bridge Rd, Southward SE1 3UN
e-mail: gm@bermondseysquarehotel.co.uk
dir: From London Bridge Station exit towards Guys Hospital, left into Saint Thomas St, 200mtrs then right into Bermondsey St, 400mtrs cross Abbey St into Bermondsey Square

This establishment offers a perfect haven for a variety of visitors including local residents, leisure and business guests. Alfie's provides a buzzing environment and a great range of freshly prepared food. A members and residents' club is available on the first floor providing a more exclusive area in which to relax and unwind. Accommodation is extremely stylish and comfortable with a range of individually designed, luxurious, rooftop rooms that have stunning views of London. Health and beauty treatments are available.

Rooms 79 (10 fmly) **Facilities** Spa STV FTV Wi-fi Access to local gym Xmas New Year **Conf** Class 48 Board 40 Thtr 77 **Services** Lift Air con **Notes** Civ Wed 80

All Seasons London Southwark Rose Hotel

BUDGET HOTEL PLAN 5 F6

☎ 020 7015 1480 & 7015 1491
Southwark Rose, 47 Southwark Bridge Rd SE1 9HH
e-mail: h7465@accor.com
dir: From Westminster Bridge, into Stamford Rd, continue to Southwark St, left into Southwark Bridge Rd

Conveniently located just south of the River Thames on Southwark Bridge, this modern hotel offers well equipped air-conditioned bedrooms, internet and ample work space. There is a pleasant restaurant, bar lounge and business area on the 6th floor offering breakfast and dinner. The staff are friendly and welcoming. A limited amount of parking is available at the rear of the hotel. See also the Hotel Groups pages.

Rooms 84 (6 fmly) **Conf** Class 35 Board 26 Thtr 60

Days Hotel London Waterloo

BUDGET HOTEL PLAN 5 D4

☎ 020 7922 1331
54 Kennington Rd SE1 7BJ
e-mail: book@hotelwaterloo.com
web: www.daysinn.com
dir: On corner of Kennington Rd & Lambeth Rd. Opposite Imperial War Museum

This modern building offers accommodation in smart, spacious and well-equipped bedrooms, suitable for families and business travellers, and all with en suite bathrooms. Continental breakfast is available and other refreshments may be taken at the nearby family restaurant. See also the Hotel Groups pages.

Rooms 162 (15 fmly) (13 GF) 🐾

Ibis London Blackfriars

BUDGET HOTEL PLAN 5 E6

☎ 020 7633 2720
49 Blackfriars Rd SE1 8NZ
e-mail: H7943@accor.com
dir: Next to Southwark and Blackfriars underground stations

Modern, budget hotel offering comfortable accommodation in bright and practical bedrooms. Breakfast is self-service and dinner is available in the restaurant. See also the Hotel Groups pages.

Rooms 297 (10 fmly) 🐾 **S** £97-£197; **D** £97-£197*

LONDON

Premier Inn London County Hall

BUDGET HOTEL PLAN 5 C5

☎ 0871 527 8648
Belvedere Rd, Westminster SE1 7PB
web: www.premierinn.com
dir: In County Hall building. Nearest tube: Waterloo

High quality, budget accommodation ideal for both families and business travellers. Spacious, en suite bedrooms feature tea and coffee making facilities, and Freeview TV in most hotels. Internet access and Wi-fi are available for a small fee. The adjacent family restaurant features a wide and varied menu. See also the Hotel Groups pages.

Rooms 313

Premier Inn London Greenwich

BUDGET HOTEL PLAN 8 A1

☎ 0871 527 9208
43-81 Greenwich High Rd, Greenwich SE10 8JL
web: www.premierinn.com
dir: Telephone for detailed directions

Rooms 150

Premier Inn London Southwark

BUDGET HOTEL PLAN 5 F6

☎ 0871 527 8676
Bankside, 34 Park St SE1 9EF
web: www.premierinn.com
dir: A3200 onto A300 (Southwark Bridge Rd), 1st left into Sumner St, right into Park St. From S: M3, A3 follow Central London signs

Rooms 59

Premier Inn London Southwark (Tate Modern)

BUDGET HOTEL PLAN 5 E6

☎ 0871 527 9332
15A Great Suffolk St, Southwark SE1 0FL
web: www.premierinn.com
dir: Please telephone for detailed directions

Rooms 122

Premier Inn London Tower Bridge

BUDGET HOTEL PLAN 5 H5

☎ 0871 527 8678
159 Tower Bridge Rd SE1 3LP
web: www.premierinn.com
dir: S of Tower Bridge on A100

Rooms 196

SE10 GREENWICH

Novotel London Greenwich

★★★★ 74% HOTEL PLAN 8 A2

☎ 020 8312 6800
173-185 Greenwich High Rd, Greenwich SE10 8JA
e-mail: H3476@accor.com
web: www.novotel.com
dir: Adjacent to Greenwich Station

This purpose-built hotel is conveniently located for rail and DLR stations, as well as major attractions such as the Royal Maritime Museum and the Royal Observatory. Air-conditioned bedrooms are spacious and equipped with a host of extras, and public areas include a small gym, contemporary lounge bar and restaurant.

Rooms 151 (34 fmly) 🐾 **S** £89-£270; **D** £89-£270*
Facilities STV FTV Wi-fi ⬇ HL Gym Steam room Xmas
Conf Class 40 Board 32 Thtr 92 Del from £175 to £215* **Services** Lift Air con **Parking** 30 **Notes** LB

Holiday Inn Express London - Greenwich

BUDGET HOTEL PLAN 1 H3

☎ 020 8269 5000
162 Bugsby Park, Greenwich SE10 0DQ
e-mail: greenwich@expressholidayinn.co.uk
web: www.hiexpress.com/greenwicha102m
dir: From A102 follow Woolwich A206 signs onto A1020 (Peartee Way). Left at rdbt into Bugby's Way (signed A102 Blackwall Tunnel), pass Odeon, hotel on left

A modern hotel ideal for families and business travellers. Fresh and uncomplicated, the spacious rooms include Sky TV, power shower and tea and coffee-making facilities. Continental buffet breakfast is included in the room rate; other meals may be taken at the nearby family pub or restaurant. See also the Hotel Groups pages.

Rooms 162 **Conf** Class 55 Board 35 Thtr 80

Ibis London Greenwich

BUDGET HOTEL PLAN 8 B3

☎ 020 8305 1177
30 Stockwell St, Greenwich SE10 9JN
e-mail: H0975@accor.com
web: www.ibishotel.com
dir: From Waterloo Bridge, Elephant & Castle, A2 to Greenwich

Modern, budget hotel offering comfortable accommodation in bright and practical bedrooms. Breakfast is self-service and dinner is available in the restaurant. See also the Hotel Groups pages.

Rooms 82 (10 fmly) (12 GF)

SW1 WESTMINSTER

INSPECTORS' CHOICE

The Berkeley

MAYBOURNE HOTEL GROUP

★★★★★ 🏵🏵🏵🏵 HOTEL PLAN 4 G5

☎ 020 7235 6000
Wilton Place, Knightsbridge SW1X 7RL
e-mail: info@the-berkeley.co.uk
dir: 300mtrs from Hyde Park Corner along Knightsbridge

This stylish hotel, just off Knightsbridge, boasts an excellent range of bedrooms, each furnished with care and a host of thoughtful extras. Newer rooms feature trendy, spacious glass and marble bathrooms and some of the private suites have their own roof terrace. The striking Blue Bar enhances the reception rooms, all of which are adorned with magnificent flower arrangements. Various eating options include the Caramel Room for breakfast, an all-day menu from 11am, and afternoon tea. Marcus Wareing at The Berkeley has attained 5 AA Rosettes for stunning French cuisine, and here guests can also book the chef's table. The health spa offers a range of treatment rooms and includes a stunning open-air, roof-top pool.

Rooms 210 🐾 **Facilities** Spa STV FTV Wi-fi ⬇ ⓢ Gym Beauty/therapy treatments Xmas
Conf Class 80 Board 54 Thtr 180 **Services** Lift Air con **Notes** ⊗ Civ Wed 160

LONDON

SW1 WESTMINSTER *continued*

INSPECTORS' CHOICE

St James's Hotel and Club

★★★★★ @ @ @ @ TOWN HOUSE HOTEL

PLAN 4 J6

☎ 020 7316 1600
7-8 Park Place SW1A 1LP
e-mail: info@stjameshotelandclub.com
web: www.stjameshotelandclub.com
dir: On A4 near Picadilly Circus & St James's St

Dating back to 1857, this elegant property with its distinctive neo-Gothic exterior is discreetly set in the heart of St James. Inside there is impressive decor created by interior designer Anne Maria Jagdfeld. Air-conditioned bedrooms are appointed to a very high standard and feature luxurious beds and a range of modern facilities. Stylish open-plan public areas offer a smart bar/lounge and the fine dining restaurant, Seven Park Place by William Drabble, which serves modern French dishes based on primarily British ingredients.

Rooms 60 (8 fmly) (15 GF) ⚓ **S** £260-£3000;
D £260-£3000* **Facilities** STV FTV Wi-fi
Conf Class 30 Board 25 Thtr 40 **Services** Lift
Air con **Notes** ⊗ Civ Wed 40

INSPECTORS' CHOICE

AA HOTEL OF THE YEAR FOR LONDON

DUKES London

★★★★★ @ @ @ HOTEL

PLAN 4 J6

☎ 020 7491 4840
35 St James's Place SW1A 1NY
e-mail: bookings@dukeshotel.com
web: www.dukeshotel.com
dir: From Pall Mall into St James's St. 2nd left into St James's Place. Hotel in courtyard on left

Discreetly tucked away in St James's, Dukes is over 100 years old. Its style is understated, with smart, well-equipped bedrooms and public areas. The Penthouse Suite has its own balcony with views over Green Park. Facilities include a gym, marble steam room and body-care treatments. The award-winning restaurant, Thirty Six by Nigel Mendham, offers British cuisine based on the very best ingredients. A smart lounge and a sophisticated and buzzing cocktail bar add to guests' enjoyment, and Martinis are a must! Dukes is the AA Hotel of the Year for London 2013-2014.

Rooms 90 (40 fmly) (4 GF) ⚓ **Facilities** STV FTV
Wi-fi ⅃ Gym Steam room Health club Personal training Xmas New Year **Conf** Class 30 Board 30
Thtr 70 **Services** Lift Air con **Notes** ⊗ Civ Wed 60

INSPECTORS' CHOICE

The Halkin by Como

★★★★★ @ @ @
TOWN HOUSE HOTEL   PLAN 4 G5

☎ 020 7333 1000
Halkin St, Belgravia SW1X 7DJ
e-mail: res.thehalkin@comohotel.com
dir: Between Belgrave Sq & Grosvenor Place. Via Chapel St into Headfort Place, left into Halkin St

This smart, contemporary hotel has an enviable and peaceful position just a short stroll from both Hyde Park and the designer shops of Knightsbridge. Service is attentive, friendly and very personalised. The stylish bedrooms and suites are equipped to the highest standard with white marble bathrooms and every conceivable extra. Each floor is discreetly designed following the themes of water, air, fire, earth and sky. There is the airy Halkin Bar that offers all-day eating including an afternoon tea menu, and a stylish restaurant serving award-winning dishes.

Rooms 41 ⚓ **Facilities** STV FTV Wi-fi
Complimentary use of gym & spa at sister hotel
Conf Class 20 Board 26 Thtr 40 **Services** Lift
Air con **Notes** ⊗

INSPECTORS' CHOICE
Jumeirah Carlton Tower
★★★★★ ◎◎◎ HOTEL PLAN 4 F4

☎ 020 7235 1234
Cadogan Place SW1X 9PY
e-mail: jctinfo@jumeirah.com
web: www.jumeirahcarltontower.com
dir: A4 towards Knightsbridge, right onto Sloane St. Hotel on left before Cadogan Place

This impressive hotel enjoys an enviable position in the heart of Knightsbridge, overlooking Cadogan Gardens. The stunningly designed bedrooms, including a number of suites, vary in size and style, and many have wonderful city views. Leisure facilities include a glass-roofed swimming pool, a well-equipped gym and a number of treatment rooms. The renowned Rib Room provides excellent dining, together with the other options of the Club Room, the Chinoiserie and the GILT Cocktail Lounge.

Rooms 220 (59 fmly) (70 smoking) **Facilities** Spa STV FTV Wi-fi ⊗ supervised ♨ Gym Golf simulator (50 courses) ♫ Xmas New Year **Conf** Class 250 Board 30 Thtr 400 **Services** Lift Air con **Parking** 170 **Notes** ⊗ Civ Wed 320

INSPECTORS' CHOICE
The Lanesborough
★★★★★ ◎◎◎ HOTEL PLAN 4 G5

☎ 020 7259 5599
Hyde Park Corner SW1X 7TA
e-mail: pmccolgan@lanesborough.com
dir: At Hyde Park corner

Occupying an enviable position on Hyde Park Corner, this elegant hotel offers the highest international standards of comfort, quality and security, much appreciated by a loyal clientele. The stylish bedrooms and suites reflect the historic nature of the property, offering high levels of comfort and a superb range of complimentary facilities including laptops and high speed internet access. Service is equally impressive with personal butlers ensuring individual attention. Apsleys offers award-winning, modern Italian cuisine and afternoon tea is offered.

Rooms 93 (7 fmly) (6 GF) (38 smoking) ✎
Facilities Spa STV FTV Wi-fi ♭ Gym ♫
Conf Class 48 Board 52 Thtr 100 **Services** Lift Air con **Parking** 48 **Notes** Civ Wed 100

INSPECTORS' CHOICE
Mandarin Oriental Hyde Park, London
★★★★★ ◎◎◎ HOTEL PLAN 4 F5

☎ 020 7235 2000
66 Knightsbridge SW1X 7LA
e-mail: molon-reservations@mohg.com
web: www.mandarinoriental.com/london
dir: Harrods 400mtrs on right & Harvey Nichols directly opposite hotel

Situated in fashionable Knightsbridge and overlooking Hyde Park, this iconic venue is a popular destination for highfliers, celebrities and the young and fashionable. Bedrooms, many with park views, are appointed to the highest standards with luxurious features such as the finest Irish linen and goose down pillows. Guests have a choice of dining options - Bar Boulud (with 2 AA Rosettes) offering a contemporary bistro menu of seasonal, rustic French dishes; and Dinner by Heston Blumenthal where the dishes are based on recipes dating as far back as the 14th century, but with Heston's legendary modern twist. The Mandarin Bar serves light snacks and cocktails. The stylish spa is a destination in its own right and offers a range of innovative treatments.

Rooms 198 ✎ **Facilities** Spa STV FTV Wi-fi ♭ Gym Sanarium Steam room Vitality pool Zen colour therapy Relaxation area ♫ Xmas New Year **Conf** Class 120 Board 60 Thtr 250 **Services** Lift Air con **Notes** ⊗ Civ Wed 250

LONDON

SW1 WESTMINSTER *continued*

INSPECTORS' CHOICE

The Goring

★★★★★ ◎ ◎ HOTEL PLAN 4 H4

☎ 020 7396 9000
Beeston Place SW1W 0JW
e-mail: reception@thegoring.com
web: www.thegoring.com
dir: Off Lower Grosvenor Place, just prior to Royal Mews

This icon of British hospitality for over 100 years is centrally located and within walking distance of the Royal Parks and principal shopping areas. Spacious bedrooms and suites, - some contemporary in style with state-of-the-art technology and others more classically furnished - all boast high levels of comfort and quality. The Duchess of Cambridge stayed in the newly created Royal Suite on the night before her wedding in 2011. Elegant day rooms include the Garden Bar and the drawing room, both popular for afternoon tea and cocktails. The stylish airy restaurant offers a popular menu of contemporary British cuisine, and delightful private dining rooms are available. Guests will experience a personalised service from the attentive and friendly team.

Rooms 69 (9 fmly) ↟ **S** £540; **D** £625*
Facilities STV Wi-fi ↳ Free membership of nearby health club Xmas New Year **Conf** Class 30 Board 25 Thtr 50 **Services** Lift Air con **Parking** 16 **Notes** ⊗ Civ Wed 50

INSPECTORS' CHOICE

The Stafford London by Kempinski

★★★★★ ◎ HOTEL PLAN 4 J6

☎ 020 7493 0111 & 518 1119
16-18 St James's Place SW1A 1NJ
e-mail: reservation.london@kempinski.com
web: www.kempinski.com/en/london
dir: Exit Pall Mall into St James's St. 2nd left into St James's Place

Tucked away in a quiet corner of St James's, this classically styled boutique hotel retains an air of understated luxury. The American Bar is a fabulous venue in its own right, festooned with an eccentric array of celebrity photos, caps and ties. Also, afternoon tea is a long established tradition here. From the pristine, tastefully decorated and air-conditioned bedrooms, to the highly professional, yet friendly service, this exclusive hotel maintains the highest standards. 26 stunning mews suites are available.

Rooms 105 (38 annexe) (8 GF) (2 smoking) ↟
S £278-£440; **D** £305-£660* **Facilities** STV Wi-fi ↳ Gym Use of fitness club nearby Xmas New Year **Conf** Class 20 Board 24 Thtr 60 **Services** Lift Air con **Notes** LB ⊗ Civ Wed 44

INSPECTORS' CHOICE

51 Buckingham Gate, Taj Suites and Residences

★★★★★ TOWN HOUSE HOTEL PLAN 4 J4

☎ 020 7769 7766
SW1E 6AF
e-mail: info@51-buckinghamgate.co.uk
dir: From Buckingham Palace onto Buckingham Gate, 100mtrs, hotel on right

This all-suites hotel is a favourite with those who desire a quiet, sophisticated environment. Each of the suites has its own butler on hand plus a kitchen, and most have large lounge areas furnished in a contemporary style with modern accessories. There are one, two, three and four bedroom suites to choose from, which include the stunning Jaguar Suite and the spectacular brand new Cinema Suite. The hotel has a spa and a well-equipped gym.

Rooms 86 (86 fmly) (4 GF) ↟ **Facilities** Spa STV Wi-fi ↳ HL Gym Sauna Steam room Xmas New Year **Conf** Class 90 Board 60 Thtr 180 **Services** Lift Air con **Notes** LB ⊗ Civ Wed 150

INSPECTORS' CHOICE

No 41

★★★★★ TOWN HOUSE HOTEL PLAN 4 H4

☎ 020 7300 0041
41 Buckingham Palace Rd SW1W 0PS
e-mail: book41@rchmail.com
web: www.41hotel.com
dir: Opposite Buckingham Palace Mews entrance

Small, intimate and very private, this stunning town house is located opposite the Royal Mews. Decorated in stylish black and white, bedrooms successfully combine comfort with state-of-the-art technology such as iPod docking stations, interactive TV and free high-speed internet access. Thoughtful touches such as fresh fruit, flowers and scented candles add to the very welcoming atmosphere. The large lounge is the focal point; food and drinks are available as are magazines and newspapers from around the world plus internet access. Attentive personal service and a host of thoughtful extra touches make No 41 really special. Red Carnation Hotels is the AA Small Hotel Group of the Year 2013-14.

Rooms 30 (2 fmly) ↖ **D** £323-£443* **Facilities** STV Wi-fi ↺ Local health club Beauty treatments In-room spa Xmas New Year **Conf** Board 8 Del from £400 to £500* **Services** Lift Air con **Notes** LB

The Park Tower Knightsbridge

★★★★★ 87% ❀❀❀
HOTEL PLAN 4 F5

☎ 020 7235 8050
101 Knightsbridge SW1X 7RN
e-mail: theparktowerknightsbridge@reservestarwood.com
web: www.theparktowerknightsbridge.com
dir: Adjacent to Harvey Nichols

Celebrating 40 years in the heart of one of London's most alluring locales, The Park Tower Knightsbridge is just a short walk away from leafy Hyde Park, and encapsulates the spirit of its refined location. Combining timeless elegance with bespoke contemporary design, the hotel lobby and reception have recently been renovated, now offering an even more exceptional arrival experience. All guest rooms and suites feature handcrafted pieces and marble bathrooms, and thanks to the hotel's iconic circular shape, provide views over Knightsbridge or neighbouring Hyde Park, while the suites offer breathtaking views over London's skyline, as well as the distinguished service of the Park Tower Butler. The Head Concierge and his team help to uncover hidden gems of the area to help visitors to get the most from their stay. The Knightsbridge Lounge is an idyllic tea parlour where afternoon tea is served under a canopy of magnolia blossoms. Taking influences from British members clubs, the Bar offers whiskies and cigars in an intimate and refined setting. Well regarded among local diners, Pascal Proyart's One-O-One restaurant is widely acclaimed as an excellent fish restaurant.

Rooms 280 (280 fmly) (62 smoking) ↖ **Facilities** STV Wi-fi ↺ Gym Fitness room ♨ **Conf** Class 60 Board 26 Thtr 120 **Services** Lift Air con **Notes** ⊗ Civ Wed 100

Corinthia Hotel London

★★★★★ 87% ❀❀ HOTEL PLAN 5 B6

☎ 020 7930 8181
Whitehall Place SW1A 2BD
e-mail: london@corinthia.com
dir: M4 onto A4, follow Central London signs. Pass Green Park, right into Coventry St, 1st right into Haymarket, left into Pall Mall East, right into Trafalgar Sq, 3rd exit into Whitehall Place

This refurbished hotel is steeped in history and is reputed to be one of London's earliest hotels having opened in 1885. After a very high quality refurbishment, the hotel has emerged with exceptional style. The team are welcoming and friendly and all requests are met with aplomb. Bedrooms, including suites and penthouses, are equipped to very high standards and offer all modern amenities. The eating options are The Northall with British cuisine and The Massimo Restaurant offering

Mediterranean seafood. The Bassoon Bar is the place for cocktails and its worth noting the counter which is actually an elongated piano. The Espa Spa offers world class facilities. Valet parking is available.

Rooms 294 (10 fmly) (46 smoking) ↖ **S** £700-£820; **D** £700-£820* **Facilities** Spa STV Wi-fi ↺ ⊙ Gym Vitality pool Nail studio Hair salon Relaxation sleep pod Xmas New Year **Conf** Class 120 Board 50 Thtr 250 **Services** Lift Air con **Notes** ⊗ Civ Wed 250

Sofitel London St James

★★★★★ 87% ❀ HOTEL PLAN 4 K6

☎ 020 7747 2200
6 Waterloo Place SW1Y 4AN
e-mail: H3144@sofitel.com
dir: 3 mins' walk from Piccadilly Circus & Trafalgar Square

Located in the exclusive area of St James's, this Grade II listed, former bank is convenient for most of the city's attractions, theatres and the financial district. The modern bedrooms are equipped to a high standard and feature luxurious beds, while more traditional public areas, including the French restaurant, provide a taste of classical charm.

Rooms 183 (102 fmly) ↖ **S** £200-£600; **D** £200-£600* **Facilities** Spa STV Wi-fi ↺ Gym So FIT, So SPA & Live entertainment Xmas New Year **Conf** Class 120 Board 44 Thtr 170 **Services** Lift Air con **Notes** Civ Wed 140

The Royal Horseguards

★★★★★ 83% ❀❀ HOTEL PLAN 5 B6

☎ 0871 376 9033
2 Whitehall Court SW1A 2EJ
e-mail: royalhorseguards@guoman.co.uk
web: www.theroyalhorseguards.com
dir: Trafalgar Sq to Whitehall, left to Whitehall Pl, turn right

This majestic hotel in the heart of Whitehall sits beside the Thames and enjoys unrivalled views of the London Eye and the city skyline. Bedrooms, appointed to a high standard, are well equipped and some of the luxurious bathrooms are finished in marble. Impressive public areas and outstanding meeting facilities are also available.

Rooms 282 (7 fmly) ↖ **Facilities** STV Wi-fi Gym ♨ Xmas New Year **Conf** Class 180 Board 84 Thtr 240 **Services** Lift Air con **Notes** ⊗ Civ Wed 228

LONDON

SW1 WESTMINSTER *continued*

The Rubens at the Palace

THE
RED CARNATION
HOTEL COLLECTION

★★★★ 83% ◉◉ HOTEL PLAN 4 H4

☎ 020 7834 6600
39 Buckingham Palace Rd SW1W 0PS
e-mail: bookrb@rchmail.com
web: www.rubenshotel.com
dir: Opposite Royal Mews, 100mtrs from Buckingham Palace

This hotel enjoys an enviable location close to Buckingham Palace. Stylish, air-conditioned bedrooms include the pinstripe-walled Savile Row rooms, which follow a tailoring theme, and the opulent Royal rooms, named after different monarchs. Public rooms include The Library fine dining restaurant, and a comfortable stylish cocktail bar and lounge. The team here pride themselves on their warmth and friendliness. Red Carnation Hotels is the AA Small Hotel Group of the Year 2013-14.

Rooms 161 (13 fmly) ☞ **S** £191-£323; **D** £203-£335* **Facilities** STV Wi-fi ↻ Health club & beauty treatment available nearby ♫ Xmas New Year **Conf** Class 50 Board 30 Thtr 90 Del from £250 to £380* **Services** Lift Air con **Notes** LB Civ Wed 80

St Ermins Hotel

★★★★ 82% ◉◉ HOTEL PLAN 4 K4

☎ 020 7222 7888 & 0800 635 0438
2 Caxton St, St James Park, Westminster SW1H 0QW
e-mail: reservations@sterminshotel.co.uk
dir: Just off Victoria St, directly opposite New Scotland Yard

Located in an enviable London location, the delightful courtyard offers a sanctuary from the hustle and bustle of the city. Following an impressive refurbishment the property boasts day rooms with quality finishes - no detail has been overlooked. The results are fresh, modern and innovative, with a respectful nod to the hotel's former character. Award-winning cuisine is served in the popular Caxton Grill. Limited valet parking is available by arrangement.

Rooms 331 (18 fmly) (12 GF) ☞ **S** £199-£459; **D** £199-£459* **Facilities** STV FTV Wi-fi ↻ Gym Xmas New Year **Conf** Class 80 Board 60 Thtr 160 Del from £259 to £499* **Services** Lift Air con **Notes** LB Civ Wed 160

Cavendish London

★★★★ 82% ◉ HOTEL PLAN 4 J6

☎ 020 7930 2111
81 Jermyn St SW1Y 6JF
e-mail: info@thecavendishlondon.com
web: www.thecavendishlondon.com
dir: From Piccadilly, pass The Ritz, 1st right into Dukes St before Fortnum & Mason

This smart, stylish hotel enjoys an enviable location in the prestigious St James's area, just a short walk from Green Park and Piccadilly. Bedrooms have a fresh, contemporary feel, and there are a number of spacious executive rooms, studios and suites. Elegant public areas include a spacious first-floor lounge and well-appointed conference and function facilities. The popular Petrichor restaurant is committed to sourcing sustainable ingredients, especially from British producers. A good value, pre-theatre menu is available.

Rooms 230 (12 fmly) ☞ **Facilities** STV Wi-fi HL **Conf** Class 50 Board 40 Thtr 80 **Services** Lift Air con **Parking** 50 **Notes** ⊗

St James' Court - A Taj Hotel

★★★★ 77% HOTEL PLAN 4 J4

☎ 020 7834 6655 & 7963 8308
Buckingham Gate SW1E 6AF
e-mail: sjc.london@tajhotels.com
web: www.tajhotels.com/stjamescourt
dir: With Buckingham Palace facing, turn left to Buckingham Gate. After 100mtrs hotel on right

Enjoying a prestigious location, this elegant Victorian hotel is a few minutes' walk from Buckingham Palace. Air-conditioned bedrooms are smartly appointed and superbly equipped. Public areas include a choice of three restaurants - Bank, Bistro 51 and Quilon, - two bars, conference and business facilities and a fitness club with Sodashi Spa. Service is attentive and friendly.

Rooms 338 (17 smoking) ☞ **S** £165-£495; **D** £165-£495* **Facilities** Spa STV FTV Wi-fi ↻ HL Gym Steam room Sauna ♫ Xmas New Year **Conf** Class 90 Board 60 Thtr 180 **Services** Lift Air con **Notes** LB ⊗ Civ Wed 180

Park Plaza Victoria London

Park Plaza
Hotels & Resorts

★★★★ 76% ◉ HOTEL PLAN 4 J3

☎ 020 7769 9999 & 7769 9800
239 Vauxhall Bridge Rd SW1V 1EQ
e-mail: info@victoriaparkplaza.com
web: www.parkplaza.com
dir: Turn right from Victoria Station

This smart modern hotel close to Victoria station is well located for all of central London's major attractions. Air-conditioned bedrooms are tastefully appointed and thoughtfully equipped for both business and leisure guests. Airy, stylish public areas include an elegant bar and restaurant, a popular coffee bar and extensive conference facilities complete with a business centre.

Rooms 299 ☞ **Facilities** Spa STV FTV Wi-fi ↻ Gym Sauna Steam room Xmas **Conf** Class 240 Board 45 Thtr 550 **Services** Lift Air con **Parking** 36 **Notes** ⊗ Civ Wed 500

The Grosvenor

GUOMAN
HOTELS

★★★★ 76% HOTEL PLAN 4 H4

☎ 0871 376 9038 & 020 7834 9494
101 Buckingham Palace Rd SW1W 0SJ
e-mail: grosvenor@guoman.co.uk
web: www.guoman.com
dir: Part of Victoria Station complex

In the last few years The Grosvenor, a listed building, has been sympathetically restored to its former Victorian splendour, yet it offers guests all the comforts of a 21st-century hotel. Just a short stroll from Buckingham Palace, it is well positioned for Victoria station. The quiet, air-conditioned bedrooms have Bose iPod docking stations, plasma-screen TVs, surround sound and Wi-fi, plus bathrooms with rainfall showers. The bar and brasserie is open all day, Cantonese cuisine is available in the Grand Imperial London, champagne and cocktails can be found in Reunion, and afternoon tea is served in the traditional lounge. A gym is located on the 7th floor.

Rooms 345 **Facilities** STV FTV Wi-fi ↻ HL Gym ♫ Xmas New Year **Conf** Class 80 Board 50 Thtr 110 **Services** Lift Air con **Notes** LB ⊗ Civ Wed 80

Millennium Hotel London Knightsbridge

★★★★ 75% ◎ HOTEL PLAN 4 F4

☎ 020 7235 4377
17 Sloane St, Knightsbridge SW1X 9NU
e-mail: reservations.knightsbridge@
millenniumhotels.co.uk
web: www.millenniumhotels.co.uk
dir: From Knightsbridge tube station towards Sloane
St. Hotel 70mtrs on right

This fashionable hotel boasts an enviable location in
Knightsbridge's chic shopping district. Air-
conditioned, thoughtfully equipped bedrooms are
complemented by a popular lobby lounge and MU
Restaurant and Lounge where the cuisine is French
with Asian influences. Valet parking is available if
pre-booked.

Rooms 222 (41 fmly) (38 smoking) **Facilities** STV FTV
Wi-fi ⓘ HL Xmas New Year **Conf** Class 80 Board 50
Thtr 120 **Services** Lift Air con **Parking** 11 **Notes** ⊗

Jumeirah Lowndes Hotel

Ⓤ PLAN 4 F4

☎ 020 7823 1234
21 Lowndes St SW1X 9ES
e-mail: jlhinfo@jumeirah.com
web: www.jumeirahlowndeshotel.com
dir: M4 onto A4 into London. Left from Brompton Rd
into Sloane St. Left into Pont St, Lowndes St next left.
Hotel on right

This hotel is a smart modern townhouse set in the
Belgravia area of Knightsbridge. Public areas are
limited in scale but an all-day bar and restaurant
with an outside terrace overlook the leafy side street.
The bedrooms vary in size, but all have a very modern
style and high spec facilities such as air-conditioning
and iPod speakers. Guests can also enjoy the
extensive facilities at the nearby Jumeirah Carlton
Hotel. For further details please see the AA website:
theAA.com

Rooms 87 (14 fmly) ⓘ **Facilities** Spa STV FTV Wi-fi ⓘ
Conf Class 12 Board 18 Thtr 25 **Services** Lift Air con
Notes ⊗

Premier Inn London Victoria

BUDGET HOTEL PLAN 4 J3

☎ 0871 527 8680
82-83 Eccleston Square, Victoria SW1V 1PS
web: www.premierinn.com
dir: From Victoria Station, right into Wilton Rd, 3rd
right into Gillingham St, hotel 150mtrs

High quality, budget accommodation ideal for both
families and business travellers. Spacious, en suite
bedrooms feature tea and coffee making facilities,
and Freeview TV in most hotels. Internet access and
Wi-fi are available for a small fee. The adjacent
family restaurant features a wide and varied menu.
See also the Hotel Groups pages.

Rooms 110

SW3 CHELSEA, BROMPTON

INSPECTORS' CHOICE

The Capital

★★★★★ ◎◎◎
TOWN HOUSE HOTEL PLAN 4 F5

☎ 020 7589 5171
Basil St, Knightsbridge SW3 1AT
e-mail: reservations@capitalhotel.co.uk
web: www.capitalhotel.co.uk
dir: 20yds from Harrods, & Knightsbridge tube
station

Personal service is assured at this small, family-
owned hotel set in the heart of Knightsbridge.
Beautifully designed bedrooms come in a number
of styles, but all rooms feature antique furniture, a
marble bathroom and a thoughtful range of extras.
Cocktails are a speciality in the delightful, stylish
bar, whilst afternoon tea in the elegant, bijou
lounge is a must. Excellent dining is guaranteed at
Outlaw's at The Capital, specialising in seafood
caught off the coast of Cornwall, and overseen by
eponymous chef Nathan Outlaw.

Rooms 49 **S** £270-£336; **D** £300-£420*
Facilities STV FTV Wi-fi ⓘ Xmas New Year
Conf Class 24 Board 24 Thtr 30 **Services** Lift
Air con **Parking** 12 **Notes** LB ⊗

The Egerton House Hotel

RED CARNATION
HOTEL COLLECTION

★★★★★ 84%
TOWN HOUSE HOTEL PLAN 4 E4

☎ 020 7589 2412
17 Egerton Ter, Knightsbridge SW3 2BX
e-mail: bookeg@rchmail.com
web: www.egertonhousehotel.com
dir: Just off Brompton Rd, between Harrods & Victoria
& Albert Museum, opposite Brompton Oratory

This delightful town house enjoys a prestigious
Knightsbridge location, a short walk from Harrods
and close to the Victoria & Albert Museum. Air-
conditioned bedrooms and public rooms are
appointed to the highest standards, with luxurious
furnishings and quality antique pieces; an
exceptional range of facilities include iPods, safes,
mini bars and flat-screen TVs. Staff offer the highest
levels of personalised, attentive service. Red
Carnation Hotels is the AA Small Hotel Group of the
Year 2013-14.

Rooms 28 (5 fmly) (2 GF) ⓘ **S** £300-£1200;
D £300-£1200* **Facilities** STV Wi-fi Xmas New Year
Conf Class 12 Board 10 Thtr 14 **Services** Lift Air con
Notes LB

The Draycott Hotel

★★★★★ 83% TOWN HOUSE HOTEL PLAN 4 F3

☎ 020 7730 6466
26 Cadogan Gardens SW3 2RP
e-mail: reservations@draycotthotel.com
web: www.draycotthotel.com
dir: From Sloane Sq station towards Peter Jones, keep
to left. At Kings Rd take 1st right into Cadogan Gdns,
2nd right, hotel on left corner

Enjoying a prime location just yards from Sloane
Square, this town house provides an ideal base in one
of the most fashionable areas of London. Many
regular guests regard this as their London residence
and staff pride themselves on their hospitality.
Beautifully appointed bedrooms include a number of
very spacious suites and all are equipped to a high
standard. Attractive day rooms, furnished with
antique and period pieces, include a choice of
lounges, one with access to a lovely sheltered garden.

continued

LONDON

SW3 CHELSEA, BROMPTON *continued*

Rooms 35 (9 fmly) (2 GF) ⌁ **S** £114–£198;
D £210–£306* **Facilities** STV FTV Wi-fi Beauty
treatments Massage **Services** Lift Air con **Notes** LB

INSPECTORS' CHOICE

The Levin

★★★★ TOWN HOUSE HOTEL
PLAN 4 F4

☎ 020 7589 6286
28 Basil St, Knightsbridge SW3 1AS
e-mail: reservations@thelevinhotel.co.uk
web: www.thelevinhotel.co.uk
dir: 20yds from Harrods, & Knightsbridge tube
station

This sophisticated town house is the sister property
to the adjacent Capital Hotel and enjoys a prime
location on the doorstep of Knightsbridge's stylish
department and designer stores. Bedrooms and en
suites offer stylish elegance alongside a host of up-
to-date modern comforts; extra touches include
champagne bars and state-of-the-art audio-visual
systems. Guests can enjoy all-day dining in the
stylish, popular, lower ground-floor Metro
Restaurant.

Rooms 12 (1 GF) **S** £244–£310; **D** £265–£360 (incl.
bkfst)* **Facilities** STV FTV Wi-fi ⌁ Xmas New Year
Services Lift Air con **Parking** 8 **Notes** ⊗

The Beaufort

★★★★ 80% TOWN HOUSE HOTEL PLAN 4 F4

☎ 020 7584 5252
33 Beaufort Gardens SW3 1PP
e-mail: reservations@thebeaufort.co.uk
web: www.thebeaufort.co.uk
dir: 100yds past Harrods on left of Brompton Rd

This friendly, attractive town house enjoys a peaceful
location in a tree-lined cul-de-sac just a few minutes'
walk from Knightsbridge. Air-conditioned bedrooms
are thoughtfully furnished and equipped with CD
players, movie channel access, safe and free Wi-fi.
Guests are offered complimentary drinks and
afternoon cream tea with home-made scones and
clotted cream. A good continental breakfast is served
in bedrooms.

Rooms 29 (3 GF) **S** £168–£228; **D** £228–£312*
Facilities STV FTV Wi-fi **Conf** Thtr 10 **Services** Lift
Air con **Notes** ⊗

SW5 EARL'S COURT

London Marriott Kensington

Marriott

★★★★ 82% HOTEL PLAN 4 B3

☎ 020 7973 1000
Cromwell Rd SW5 0TH
e-mail: kensington.marriott@marriotthotels.com
web: www.londonmarriottkensington.co.uk
dir: On A4, opposite Cromwell Rd Hospital

This stylish contemporary hotel features a stunning
glass exterior and a seven-storey atrium lobby. Fully
air-conditioned throughout, the hotel has elegant
design combined with a great range of facilities,
including indoor leisure, a range of conference rooms,
and parking. Smart bedrooms offer a host of extras
including the very latest communications technology.

Rooms 216 (20 fmly) ⌁ **S** £145–£195; **D** £145–£195*
Facilities STV FTV Wi-fi Gym **Conf** Class 80 Board 60
Thtr 150 Del from £210 to £290* **Services** Lift Air con
Parking 20 **Notes** ⊗

Twenty Nevern Square Hotel

★★★★ 71% TOWN HOUSE HOTEL PLAN 4 A3

☎ 020 7565 9555 & 7370 4934
20 Nevern Square, Earls Court SW5 9PD
e-mail: hotel@twentynevernsquare.co.uk
web: www.twentynevernsquare.co.uk
dir: From station take Warwick Rd exit, right, 2nd
right into Nevern Sq. Hotel 30yds on right

This smart boutique-style town house hotel is
discreetly located in Nevern Square and is ideally
situated for both Earls Court and Olympia. The
stylish, individually furnished bedrooms, which vary
in shape and size, are appointed to a high standard
and are well equipped. Public areas include a
delightful lounge and Café Twenty where breakfast
and light meals are served.

Rooms 20 (3 GF) **D** £70–£180 (incl. bkfst)*
Facilities FTV Wi-fi **Conf** Class 20 Board 20 Thtr 20
Services Lift **Parking** 4 **Notes** LB ⊗

See advert on opposite page

Save on hotels. Book at **theAA.com/hotel**

SW3 – SW5 279 ENGLAND

LONDON

TWENTY
NEVERN
SQUARE

Twenty Nevern Square Hotel

hotel@twentynevernsquare.co.uk
www.mayflowercollection.com

A distinctive, unique and elegantly stylish hotel that
overlooks a tranquil garden square, providing a
luxurious haven for travellers on business or
pleasure...

'Unrivalled attention to detail...' Conde Nast

LONDON

SW5 EARL'S COURT *continued*

K + K Hotel George

★★★ 83% HOTEL PLAN 4 A3

☎ 020 7598 8700 & 7598 8707
1-15 Templeton Place, Earl's Court SW5 9NB
e-mail: hotelgeorge@kkhotels.co.uk
web: www.kkhotels.com/george
dir: Earls Court Rd (A3220), right into Trebovir Rd, right into Templeton Place

This smart hotel enjoys a central location, just a few minutes' walk from Earls Court and with easy access to London's central attractions. Stylish public areas include a bar/bistro, an executive lounge and meeting facilities, and a restaurant that overlooks the attractive rear garden. Bedrooms are particularly well equipped with a host of useful extras including free, high-speed internet access.

Rooms 154 (38 fmly) (8 GF) (7 smoking)
S £150-£250; D £150-£300 (incl. bkfst) **Facilities** STV FTV Wi-fi ♿ HL Gym Wellness area with exercise machines Sauna **Conf** Class 14 Board 18 Thtr 35 Del from £200 to £300 **Services** Lift Air con **Parking** 20 **Notes** LB

BEST WESTERN Burns Hotel

★★★ 72% METRO HOTEL PLAN 4 B3

☎ 020 7373 3151
18-26 Barkston Gardens, Kensington SW5 0EN
e-mail: burnshotel@vienna-group.co.uk
dir: From A4, right to Earls Court Rd (A3220), 2nd left

This friendly Victorian hotel overlooks a leafy garden in a quiet residential area not far from the Earls Court exhibition centre and tube station. Bedrooms are attractively appointed, with modern facilities. Public areas, although not extensive, are stylish.

Rooms 105 (10 fmly) **Services** Lift **Notes** ⊗

Premier Inn London Kensington

BUDGET HOTEL PLAN 4 B3

☎ 0871 527 8666
11 Knaresborough Place, Kensington SW5 0TJ
web: www.premierinn.com
dir: Just off A4 (Cromwell Rd). Nearest tube: Earls Court

High quality, budget accommodation ideal for both families and business travellers. Spacious, en suite bedrooms feature tea and coffee making facilities, and Freeview TV in most hotels. Internet access and Wi-fi are available for a small fee. The adjacent family restaurant features a wide and varied menu. See also the Hotel Groups pages.

Rooms 184

Premier Inn London Kensington (Olympia)

BUDGET HOTEL PLAN 4 A3

☎ 0871 527 8668
22-32 West Cromwell Rd, Kensington SW5 9QJ
web: www.premierinn.com
dir: On N side of West Cromwell Rd, between juncts of Cromwell Rd, Earls Court Rd & Warwick Rd

Rooms 86

SW6 FULHAM

Millennium & Copthorne Hotels at Chelsea FC

★★★★ 76% HOTEL PLAN 1 E3

☎ 020 7565 1400
Stamford Bridge, Fulham Rd SW6 1HS
e-mail: reservations@chelseafc.com
web: www.millenniumhotels.co.uk
dir: 4 mins walk from Fulham Broadway tube station

A unique destination in a fashionable area of the city. Situated at Chelsea's famous Stamford Bridge ground, the accommodation offered here is very up-to-the-minute. Bedroom facilities include flat-screen LCD TVs, video on demand, broadband, Wi-fi and good-sized desk space; larger Club rooms have additional features. For eating there's a brasserie, the Bridge Bar and sports bar, and for corporate guests a flexible arrangement of meeting and event rooms is available.

Rooms 281 (64 fmly) **Facilities** STV FTV Wi-fi ♿ Stadium tours **Conf** Class 600 Board 30 Thtr 950 **Services** Lift Air con **Notes** ⊗ Civ Wed 50

Ibis London Earls Court

ibis

★★★ 70% HOTEL PLAN 4 A1

☎ 020 7610 0880
47 Lillie Rd SW6 1UD
e-mail: h5623@accor.com
web: www.ibishotel.com
dir: From Hammersmith flyover towards London, keep in right lane, right at Kings pub on Talgarth Rd to join North End Rd. At mini-rdbt turn right. Hotel on left

Situated opposite the Earls Court Exhibition Centre, this large, modern hotel is popular with business and leisure guests. Bedrooms are comfortable and well equipped. There is a café bar open all day, and a restaurant that serves evening meals. There are also extensive conference facilities and an underground car park.

Rooms 504 (20 fmly) **Facilities** FTV Wi-fi ♿
Conf Class 750 Board 25 Thtr 1200 **Services** Lift **Parking** 130

Premier Inn London Putney Bridge

BUDGET HOTEL PLAN 1 D3

☎ 0871 527 8674
3 Putney Bridge Approach SW6 3JD
web: www.premierinn.com
dir: Nearest tube: Putney Bridge. Hotel on A219, N of River Thames

High quality, budget accommodation ideal for both families and business travellers. Spacious, en suite bedrooms feature tea and coffee making facilities, and Freeview TV in most hotels. Internet access and Wi-fi are available for a small fee. The adjacent family restaurant features a wide and varied menu. See also the Hotel Groups pages.

Rooms 154

SW7 SOUTH KENSINGTON

INSPECTORS' CHOICE

Bulgari Hotel & Residences

★★★★★ ◉◉ HOTEL PLAN 4 F5

☎ 020 7151 1010 & 7151 1082
171 Knightsbridge SW7 1DW
e-mail: london-info@bulgarihouse.com

This striking, contemporary hotel is in the heart of Knightsbridge and becomes the third Bulgari property, after Milan and Bali. Luxury accommodation is stylish and deeply comfortable, complete with Bulgari trunks mini-bar and beverage facility. Bathrooms are equally lavish with deep baths and rain showers. Spacious public areas include a stunning spa complete with a 25m swimming pool, separate vitality pool and range of treatment rooms. A unique, hammered silver, oval bar provides the focal point of the bar with a sweeping staircase taking guests down to the restaurant which serves modern Italian food. Immaculately attired staff offer high standards of service and hospitality.

Rooms 85 (17 smoking) S £690-£890;
D £690-£890* **Facilities** Spa Wi-fi ♿ ⊗ Gym Xmas New Year **Conf** Class 80 Board 40 Thtr 100 **Services** Lift Air con

Save on hotels. Book at **theAA.com/hotel**

SW5 – SW7 281 ENGLAND

INSPECTORS' CHOICE

Baglioni Hotel

★★★★★ ⊛ HOTEL PLAN 4 C5

☎ 020 7368 5700
60 Hyde Park Gate, Kensington Rd, Kensington SW7 5BB
e-mail: info.london@baglionihotels.com
dir: On corner of Hyde Park Gate & De Vere Gardens

Located in the heart of Kensington and overlooking Hyde Park, this small hotel buzzes with Italian style and chic. Bedrooms, mostly suites, are generously sized and designed in bold dark colours; they have espresso machines, interactive plasma-screen TVs and a host of other excellent touches. Service is both professional and friendly, with personal butlers for the bedrooms. Public areas include the main open-plan space with bar, lounge and Brunello Restaurant, all merging together with great elan; there is a spa with four treatment rooms and a techno-gym, and a fashionable private club bar downstairs.

Rooms 67 (7 fmly) (30 smoking) ❧ **Facilities** Spa STV FTV Wi-fi ⇘ Gym Xmas New Year **Conf** Class 33 Board 34 Thtr 60 **Services** Lift Air con **Parking** 2 **Notes** Civ Wed 60

Millennium Bailey's Hotel London Kensington

★★★★ 76% ⊛ HOTEL PLAN 4 C3

☎ 020 7373 6000
140 Gloucester Rd SW7 4QH
e-mail:
reservations.baileys@millenniumhotels.co.uk
web: www.millenniumhotels.co.uk
dir: From A4, at Cromwell Hospital, into Knaresborough Place, to Courtfield Rd to corner of Gloucester Rd, hotel opposite tube station

This elegant hotel has a town house feel and enjoys a prime location. Air-conditioned bedrooms are smartly appointed and thoughtfully equipped, particularly the club rooms which benefit from DVD players. Public areas include a stylish contemporary restaurant and bar. Guests may also use the facilities at the larger sister hotel which is adjacent.

Rooms 211 (3 smoking) **Facilities** STV Wi-fi Gym **Conf** Class 12 Board 12 Thtr 12 **Services** Lift Air con **Parking** 110 **Notes** ⊗

Crowne Plaza London-Kensington

CROWNE PLAZA
HOTELS & RESORTS

★★★★ 76% HOTEL PLAN 4 C3

☎ 020 7373 2222
100 Cromwell Rd SW7 4ER
e-mail: info@cpkensington.co.uk
dir: Opposite Gloucester Road tube station. From M4 follow Central London signs. At Cromwell Rd hotel is visible on left

A boutique hotel with a grand Victorian townhouse façade and a one-acre landscaped garden, offering contemporary accommodation. Facilities include a state-of-the-art fitness suite, and sauna. The ground-floor Streetside Restaurant offers a relaxed atmosphere.

Rooms 162 (74 fmly) ❧ **Facilities** STV FTV Wi-fi ⇘ Gym **Conf** Class 60 Board 30 Thtr 100 **Services** Lift Air con **Notes** ⊗

Millennium Gloucester Hotel London Kensington

MILLENNIUM
HOTELS AND RESORTS
MILLENNIUM • COPTHORNE

★★★★ 76% HOTEL PLAN 4 C3

☎ 020 7373 6030
4-18 Harrington Gardens SW7 4LH
e-mail: reservations.gloucester@millenniumhotels.co.uk
web: www.millenniumhotels.co.uk
dir: Opposite Gloucester Rd tube station

This spacious, stylish hotel is centrally located, close to The Victoria & Albert Museum and Gloucester Road tube station. Air-conditioned bedrooms are furnished in a variety of contemporary styles and Clubrooms benefit from a dedicated club lounge with complimentary breakfast and snacks. A wide range of eating options includes Singaporean and Mediterranean cuisine.

Rooms 610 (8 fmly) (37 smoking) **Facilities** STV Wi-fi Gym **Conf** Class 300 Board 100 Thtr 500 **Services** Lift Air con **Parking** 110 **Notes** ⊗ Civ Wed 500

The Rembrandt Hotel

SAROVA
HOTELS

★★★★ 74% HOTEL PLAN 4 E4

☎ 020 7589 8100
11 Thurloe Place, Knightsbridge SW7 2RS
e-mail: rembrandt@sarova.co.uk
dir: M4 onto A4 (Cromwell Rd) into central London. Hotel opposite Victoria & Albert Museum

This attractive hotel is conveniently situated opposite the Victoria & Albert Museum, a stone's throw from Harrods. Smart, well-appointed bedrooms are thoughtfully equipped and public areas include a restaurant and an attractive bar lounge and conservatory. Guests also benefit from concessions at the adjacent Roman-styled health and leisure suite.

Rooms 193 ❧ **S** £370-£510; **D** £450-£510 (incl. bkfst)* **Facilities** Spa STV FTV Wi-fi ⇘ ⊛ Gym **Conf** Class 84 Board 80 Thtr 200 Del from £210 to £400* **Services** Lift **Notes** ⊗ Civ Wed 200

Harrington Hall Hotel

★★★★ 73% HOTEL PLAN 4 C3

☎ 020 7396 9696
5-25 Harrington Gardens SW7 4JW
e-mail: nhharringtonhall@nh-hotels.com
web: www.nh-hotels.com
dir: 2 mins walk from Gloucester Road tube station

This splendid period property is centrally located just a stone's throw from Gloucester Road tube station and is convenient for visiting the museums and for shopping in Knightsbridge. Spacious bedrooms are smartly appointed and boast a host of extra touches. The public areas include extensive meeting facilities, a lounge bar and a restaurant.

Rooms 200 (5 fmly) ❧ **Facilities** STV FTV Wi-fi ⇘ HL Gym Sauna Xmas New Year **Conf** Class 100 Board 50 Thtr 240 **Services** Lift Air con **Notes** ⊗ Civ Wed 200

Holiday Inn London - Kensington Forum

Holiday Inn

★★★★ 71% HOTEL PLAN 4 C3

☎ 0871 942 9100
97 Cromwell Rd SW7 4DN
e-mail: hikensingtonforum@ihg.com
web: www.holidayinn.co.uk
dir: From S Circular onto N Circular at Chiswick Flyover. Onto A4 (Cromwell Rd) to Gloucester Rd

This hotel is ideally situated within a few minutes' walk from the Gloucester Road underground station and close to many of London's attractions, such as the Natural History Museum, Science Museum, Kensington High Street and the West End. The bedrooms and bathrooms are well appointed and vary in size. The ground-floor areas include a gym and a stylish business lounge.

Rooms 906 (26 fmly) (46 smoking) **S** £120-£300; **D** £120-£300 **Facilities** STV FTV Wi-fi ⇘ Gym Fitness room Xmas New Year **Conf** Class 150 Board 50 Thtr 300 Del from £189 to £249 **Services** Lift Air con **Parking** 76 **Notes** ⊗ Civ Wed 250

SW7 SOUTH KENSINGTON *continued*

Park International Hotel

🅄 PLAN 4 D3

☎ 207 370 5711
117 - 129 Cromwell Rd SW7 4DT

Currently the rating for this establishment is not confirmed. This may be due to a change of ownership or because it has only recently joined the AA rating scheme. For further details please see the AA website: theAA.com

Rooms 172 **Conf** Class 20 Board 18 Thtr 30

SW10 WEST BROMPTON

Wyndham Grand London Chelsea Harbour

★★★★★ 82% ☻ HOTEL PLAN 1 E3

☎ 020 7823 3000
Chelsea Harbour SW10 0XG
e-mail: wyndhamlondon@wyndham.com
web: www.wyndhamgrandlondon.co.uk
dir: A4 to Earls Court Rd S towards river. Right into Kings Rd, left into Lots Rd

Against the picturesque backdrop of Chelsea Harbour's small marina, this modern hotel offers spacious, comfortable accommodation. All rooms are suites, which are superbly equipped; many enjoy splendid views of the marina. In addition, there are also several luxurious penthouse suites. Public areas include a modern bar and restaurant, excellent leisure facilities (including a spa) and extensive meeting and function rooms.

Rooms 158 (36 fmly) **Facilities** Spa STV FTV Wi-fi
Gym Sauna Steam room Xmas New Year
Conf Class 115 Board 40 Thtr 600 **Services** Lift
Air con **Parking** 2000 **Notes** ⊗ Civ Wed 450

SW19 WIMBLEDON

Cannizaro House

★★★★ 80% ☻☻ COUNTRY HOUSE HOTEL
PLAN 1 D2

☎ 020 8879 1464
West Side, Wimbledon Common SW19 4UE
e-mail: info@cannizarohouse.com
web: www.cannizarohouse.com
dir: From A3 follow A219 signed Wimbledon into Parkside, right into Cannizaro Rd, sharp right into West Side

This unique, elegant 18th-century house has a long tradition of hosting the rich and famous of London society. A few miles from the city centre, the landscaped grounds provide a peaceful escape and a country-house ambience; fine art, murals and stunning fireplaces feature throughout. Spacious bedrooms are individually furnished and equipped to a high standard. The award-winning restaurant menus proudly herald locally sourced, organic ingredients.

Rooms 46 (10 fmly) (5 GF) 🐾 **S** £155-£500;
D £155-£500 (incl. bkfst)* **Facilities** STV FTV Wi-fi
Conf Class 50 Board 40 Thtr 120 Del from £245 to £325 **Services** Lift **Parking** 95 **Notes** LB Civ Wed 100

Holiday Inn Express Wimbledon South

BUDGET HOTEL PLAN 1 E1

☎ 020 8545 7300
Miller's Meadhouse, 200 High St, Colliers Wood SW19 2BH
e-mail: reservations@exhiwimbledon.co.uk
web: www.exhiwimbledon.co.uk
dir: A238 Kingston Road, at lights into Merton High St, signed Colliers Wood. Hotel directly opposite Colliers Wood underground station

A modern hotel ideal for families and business travellers. Fresh and uncomplicated, the spacious rooms include Sky TV, power shower and tea and coffee-making facilities. Continental buffet breakfast is included in the room rate; other meals may be taken at the nearby family pub or restaurant. See also the Hotel Groups pages.

Rooms 139 (92 fmly) (12 GF) **S** £80-£120;
D £80-£120 (incl. bkfst) **Conf** Class 16 Board 25 Thtr 45

Premier Inn London Wimbledon South

BUDGET HOTEL PLAN 1 E1

☎ 0871 527 8684
27 Chapter Way, Off Merantun Way, Wimbledon SW19 2RF
web: www.premierinn.com
dir: M25 junct 10, A3 towards London. Exit A298 (Wimbledon) onto A238. Right onto A219, left onto A24 (Merantun Way). At rdbt 3rd exit signed Merton Abbey Mills

High quality, budget accommodation ideal for both families and business travellers. Spacious, en suite bedrooms feature tea and coffee making facilities, and Freeview TV in most hotels. Internet access and Wi-fi are available for a small fee. The adjacent family restaurant features a wide and varied menu. See also the Hotel Groups pages.

Rooms 132

LONDON

W1 WEST END

INSPECTORS' CHOICE

The Connaught

MAYBOURNE
HOTEL GROUP

★★★★★ ◎◎◎◎ HOTEL PLAN 2 G1

☎ 020 7499 7070
Carlos Place W1K 2AL
e-mail: info@the-connaught.co.uk
dir: Between Grosvenor Sq & Berkeley Sq

This iconic hotel is truly spectacular, with stunning interior design. There are sumptuous day rooms and stylish bedrooms with state-of-the-art facilities and marble en suites with deep tubs, TV screens and power showers. Butlers are available at the touch of a button and guests are pampered by friendly, attentive staff offering intuitive service. There is a choice of bars and restaurants including the Espelette bistro, and the award-winning cuisine of Hélène Darroze which is imaginative, inspired and truly memorable. The excellent Aman Spa at the hotel offers health and beauty treatments, a swimming pool and fitness centre.

Rooms 123 (17 smoking) ⟨ **Facilities** Spa STV FTV Wi-fi ⟨ Gym **Conf** Class 70 Board 60 Thtr 120 **Services** Lift Air con **Notes** ⊗ Civ Wed 200

INSPECTORS' CHOICE

The Dorchester

★★★★★ ◎◎◎◎ HOTEL PLAN 4 G6

☎ 020 7629 8888
Park Ln W1K 1QA
e-mail: info@thedorchester.com
dir: Halfway along Park Ln between Hyde Park Corner & Marble Arch

One of London's finest, The Dorchester remains one of the best-loved hotels in the country and always delivers. The spacious bedrooms and suites are beautifully appointed and feature fabulous marble bathrooms. Leading off from the foyer, The Promenade is the perfect setting for afternoon tea or drinks. In the evening guests can relax to the sound of live jazz, while enjoying a cocktail in the stylish bar. Dining options include the sophisticated Chinese restaurant, China Tang (2 AA Rosettes); Alain Ducasse at The Dorchester from the world renowned French chef of the same name (4 AA Rosettes); and of course, The Grill (2 AA Rosettes).

Rooms 250 ⟨ **S** £294-£738; **D** £354-£894*
Facilities Spa STV FTV Wi-fi ⟨ HL Gym Steam rooms Fitness suite ♫ Xmas New Year **Conf** Class 300 Board 42 Thtr 500 **Services** Lift Air con **Parking** 20 **Notes** ⊗ Civ Wed 500

INSPECTORS' CHOICE

45 Park Lane

★★★★★ ◎◎◎ HOTEL PLAN 4 G6

☎ 0207 493 4545
45 Park Ln W1K 1BJ
e-mail:
info45parklane@dorchestercollection.com

This hotel offers luxurious and contemporary interiors. The bedrooms, including ten suites, all have a view of Hyde Park; the Penthouse Suite has its own roof terrace. A striking central staircase leads to a mezzanine featuring Bar 45, a library and a private media room. Other public areas include a lounge area and CUT at 45 Park Lane, a modern American steak restaurant.

Rooms 45

LONDON

W1 WEST END *continued*

INSPECTORS' CHOICE

The Ritz London

★★★★★ ◎◎◎ HOTEL PLAN 4 J6

☎ 020 7493 8181
150 Piccadilly W1J 9BR
e-mail: enquire@theritzlondon.com
web: www.theritzlondon.com
dir: From Hyde Park Corner E on Piccadilly. Hotel on right after Green Park

This renowned, stylish hotel offers guests the ultimate in sophistication while still managing to retain all its former historic glory. Bedrooms and suites are exquisitely furnished in Louis XVI style, with fine marble bathrooms and every imaginable comfort. Elegant reception rooms include the Palm Court with its legendary afternoon teas, the beautiful fashionable Rivoli Bar and the sumptuous Ritz Restaurant, complete with gold chandeliers and extraordinary trompe-l'oeil decoration.

Rooms 133 (65 fmly) (23 smoking)
S £315–£1860; **D** £315–£1860* **Facilities** STV FTV Wi-fi Gym The Ritz Club & Casino The Ritz Salon ♬ Xmas New Year **Conf** Class 40 Board 30 Thtr 60 **Services** Lift Air con **Parking** 10 **Notes** LB ⊗ Civ Wed 60

INSPECTORS' CHOICE

Athenaeum Hotel & Apartments

★★★★★ ◎◎ HOTEL PLAN 4 H6

☎ 020 7499 3464
116 Piccadilly W1J 7BJ
e-mail: info@athenaeumhotel.com
web: www.athenaeumhotel.com
dir: On Piccadilly, overlooking Green Park

With a discreet address in Mayfair, this well-loved hotel offers bedrooms appointed to the highest levels of comfort; all include Bose iPod speakers, a pillow menu and Wi-fi, and several boast views over Green Park. The hotel also has suites, and for the ultimate luxury there's a roof-top suite with a private balcony. The hotel has a whisky bar, the Garden Lounge for award-winning afternoon teas, and even a pudding parlour open in the evenings. The stylish restaurant serves British cuisine which will appeals to all ages. A range of spacious and well-appointed apartments can be found in a row of Edwardian townhouses adjacent to the hotel. There is an extensive range of beauty treatments available along with conference and meeting facilities.

Rooms 156 (8 smoking) **Facilities** STV Wi-fi Gym Steam rooms Sauna Hairdressing salon Xmas New Year **Conf** Class 35 Board 36 Thtr 55 **Services** Lift Air con **Notes** ⊗ Civ Wed 80

INSPECTORS' CHOICE

Brown's Hotel

★★★★★ ◎◎ HOTEL
PLAN 2 J1

☎ 020 7493 6020
Albemarle St, Mayfair W1S 4BP
e-mail:
reservations.browns@roccofortehotels.com
web: www.roccofortehotels.com
dir: A short walk from Green Park, Bond St, Piccadilly & Buckingham Palace

Brown's is a London hospitality icon that maintains its charm through the successful balance of traditional and contemporary. Bedrooms are luxurious, furnished to the highest standard and come with all the modern comforts expected of such a grand Mayfair hotel. The hotel has 29 suites including two Royal Suites and two Presidential Suites. The elegant, yet informal, HIX at the Albemarle serves a traditional selection of popular British dishes that are created with great skill, and it is also home to a collection of works by leading British artists. The English Tea Room proves a great meeting place for afternoon tea.

Rooms 117 (12 smoking) **S** £275–£750; **D** £315–£1090* **Facilities** Spa STV Wi-fi Gym ♬ Xmas New Year **Conf** Class 30 Board 30 Thtr 70 **Services** Lift Air con **Notes** ⊗ Civ Wed 70

LONDON

Save on hotels. Book at **theAA.com/hotel**

W1 285 **ENGLAND**

Four Seasons Hotel London at Park Lane

★★★★★ ◉◉ HOTEL PLAN 4 G6

☎ 020 7499 0888
Hamilton Place, Park Ln W1J 7DR
e-mail: reservations@fourseasons.com
dir: From Piccadilly into Old Park Ln, into Hamilton Place

This long-established popular hotel is discreetly located near Hyde Park Corner, in the heart of Mayfair. It successfully combines modern efficiencies with traditional luxury. Guest care is consistently of the highest order, even down to the smallest detail of the personalised wake-up call. The bedrooms are elegant and spacious, and the unique conservatory rooms are particularly special. Spacious public areas include extensive conference and banqueting facilities, Lane's bar and fine-dining restaurant and an elegant lounge where wonderful afternoon teas are served.

Rooms 193 (49 smoking) ✿ **S** £420-£800; **D** £420-£800* **Facilities** Spa STV FTV Wi-fi ♜ Gym Fitness Centre ♫ Xmas New Year **Conf** Class 174 Board 108 Thtr 375 **Services** Lift Air con **Parking** 10 **Notes** Civ Wed 350

Claridge's

MAYBOURNE
HOTEL GROUP

★★★★★ HOTEL PLAN 2 H1

☎ 020 7629 8860
Brook St W1K 4HR
e-mail: info@claridges.co.uk
dir: 1st turn after Green Park tube station to Berkeley Sq & 4th exit into Davies St. 3rd right into Brook St

Once renowned as the resort of kings and princes, Claridge's today continues to set the standards by which other hotels are judged. The sumptuous, air-conditioned bedrooms are elegantly themed to reflect the Victorian or art deco architecture of the building. The stylish cocktail bar is a hit with residents and non-residents alike. Service throughout is punctilious and thoroughly professional. At the time of going to press, we were waiting to hear about a new direction for the dining concept at this hotel.

Rooms 203 (144 fmly) ✿ **D** £780-£8280* **Facilities** Spa STV Wi-fi Gym Beauty & health treatments Use of sister hotel's swimming pool ♫ Xmas New Year **Conf** Class 130 Board 60 Thtr 250 **Services** Lift Air con **Notes** LB ⊗ Civ Wed 200

The Langham, London

★★★★★ 86% ◉◉ HOTEL PLAN 2 H3

☎ 020 7636 1000
Portland Place W1B 1JA
e-mail: lon.info@langhamhotels.com
dir: N of Regent St, left opposite All Soul's Church

This hotel has a grand entrance which leads into restored interior elegance. Dating back to 1865 the building displays a contemporary, luxurious style. Situated near Regent Street it is ideally located for both theatreland and the principal shopping areas. Bedrooms are delightfully appointed and many have excellent views. The Landau restaurant and Artesian bar offer high standards of service, delivered by a friendly team. Palm Court is a great place for afternoon tea or a glass of champagne. There is also an extensive health club complete with a 16-metre pool.

Rooms 378 (9 fmly) (15 smoking) **Facilities** Spa STV Wi-fi ♜ ⊗ supervised Gym Health club Sauna Steam room ♫ Xmas New Year **Conf** Class 148 Board 80 Thtr 300 **Services** Lift Air con **Notes** ⊗ Civ Wed 280

Metropolitan London

★★★★★ 85% ◉◉ HOTEL PLAN 4 G6

☎ 020 7447 1000
Old Park Ln W1K 1LB
e-mail: res.met.lon@comohotels.com
dir: On corner of Old Park Ln & Hertford St

Overlooking Hyde Park this hotel is located within easy reach of the fashionable stores of Knightsbridge and Mayfair. The hotel's contemporary style allows freedom and space to relax. Understated luxury is the key here with bedrooms enjoying great natural light. There is also a Shambhala Spa, steam room and fully equipped gym. For those seeking a culinary experience, Nobu offers innovative Japanese cuisine with an upbeat atmosphere.

Rooms 144 (23 smoking) ✿ **D** £239-£409* **Facilities** Spa STV FTV Wi-fi ♜ Gym Steam rooms ♫ **Conf** Class 25 Board 30 Thtr 80 **Services** Lift Air con **Parking** 8 **Notes** Civ Wed 80

London Marriott Hotel Park Lane

ℳarriott.

★★★★★ 84% ◉◉ HOTEL PLAN 2 F1

☎ 020 7493 7000
140 Park Ln W1K 7AA
e-mail: mhrs.parklane@marriotthotels.com
web: www.londonmarriottparklane.co.uk
dir: From Hyde Park Corner left on Park Ln onto A4202, 0.8m. At Marble Arch onto Park Ln. Take 1st left into North Row. Hotel on left

This modern and stylish hotel is situated in a prominent position in the heart of central London. Bedrooms are superbly appointed and air conditioned. Public rooms include a popular lounge/bar, and there are excellent leisure facilities and an executive lounge.

Rooms 157 (11 smoking) ✿ **Facilities** STV Wi-fi ♜ ⊗ Gym Steam room Xmas New Year **Conf** Class 33 Board 42 Thtr 72 **Services** Lift Air con **Notes** ⊗

LONDON

W1 WEST END *continued*

Hyatt Regency London – The Churchill

★★★★★ 83% ◉◉◉ HOTEL PLAN 2 F2

☎ 020 7486 5800
30 Portman Square W1H 7BH
e-mail: london.churchill@hyatt.com
dir: From Marble Arch rdbt, follow signs for Oxford Circus into Oxford St. Left after 2nd lights into Portman St. Hotel on left

This smart hotel enjoys a central location overlooking Portman Square. Excellent conference and in-room facilities, plus a fitness room make this the ideal choice for both corporate and leisure guests. To set the style, guests are greeted by stunning floral displays in the sophisticated lobby. The Montagu restaurant offers contemporary dining, plus the option to sit at the Chef's Table for a front row seat to watch all the action in the kitchen.

Rooms 434 (66 smoking) ◄ **S** £200–£420; **D** £200–£420* **Facilities** STV FTV Wi-fi ⬐ 🏊 Gym Jogging track ♬ Xmas New Year **Conf** Class 160 Board 68 Thtr 250 Del from £305 to £525* **Services** Lift Air con **Parking** 48 **Notes** ⊗ Civ Wed 250

Grosvenor House, A JW Marriott Hotel

★★★★★ 82% ◉ HOTEL PLAN 2 G1

☎ 020 7499 6363 & 7399 8400
Park Ln W1K 7TN
e-mail: grosvenor.house@marriotthotels.com
web: www.londongrosvenorhouse.co.uk
dir: Centrally located on Park Ln, between Hyde Park Corner & Oxford St

This quintessentially British hotel, overlooking Hyde Park offers luxurious accommodation, warm hospitality and exemplary service that epitomises the fine hotel culture of London. The property boasts the largest ballroom in Europe, and there is a steakhouse and a cocktail bar. The Park Room and The Library make perfect settings for afternoon tea.

Rooms 494 (111 smoking) **Facilities** STV Wi-fi ⬐ Gym Fitness centre Xmas New Year **Conf** Class 800 Board 140 Thtr 1500 **Services** Lift Air con **Parking** 48 **Notes** ⊗ Civ Wed 1500

Le Meridien Piccadilly

★★★★★ 82% ◉ HOTEL PLAN 2 J1

☎ 020 7734 8000
21 Piccadilly W1J 0BH
e-mail: reservations.piccadilly@lemeridien.com
dir: 100mtrs from Piccadilly Circus

Situated in heart of Piccadilly, this well established hotel is ideally located for both the West End and Theatreland. The well-equipped, air-conditioned bedrooms, varying in shape and size, are modern and contemporary in style. Public areas include extensive leisure facilities, with a state-of-the-art gym, pool and sauna; the trendy Longitude 0° 8' cocktail bar, and the popular Terrace Restaurant which overlooks Piccadilly.

Rooms 280 ◄ **Facilities** Spa STV Wi-fi ⬐ ⊛ supervised Gym Squash **Conf** Class 160 Board 80 Thtr 250 **Services** Lift Air con **Notes** ⊗ Civ Wed 200

The Westbury Hotel

★★★★★ 81% ◉◉◉ HOTEL PLAN 2 H1

☎ 020 7629 7755
Bond St W1S 2YF
e-mail: reservations@westburymayfair.com
dir: From Oxford Circus S down Regent St, right onto Conduit St, hotel at junct of Conduit St & Bond St

A well-known favourite with an international clientele, The Westbury is located at the heart of London's finest shopping district and provides a calm atmosphere away from the hubbub. The standards of accommodation are high throughout and bedrooms have panoramic views; the options include a variety of suites and a two-bedroom penthouse suite. Reception rooms offer a good choice for both relaxing and eating and include the stylish Polo Bar, The Westbury lounge, the Tsukiji Sushi Restaurant and the fine-dining option in award-winning Alyn Williams at the Westbury. Private dining is also available.

Rooms 246 (80 fmly) ◄ **Facilities** STV FTV Wi-fi ⬐ Gym Fitness centre Steam room Sauna Xmas New Year **Conf** Class 100 Board 40 Thtr 200 **Services** Lift Air con **Notes** ⊗ Civ Wed 80

London Hilton on Park Lane

★★★★★ 81% HOTEL PLAN 4 G6

☎ 020 7493 8000
22 Park Ln W1K 1BE
e-mail: reservations.parklane@hilton.com
dir: From N: M1/A41 towards central London & West End. W along Oxford St, into Park Lane. From S: A23 for central London & West End, cross Vauxhall Bridge (A202) & into Park Lane

Located in the heart of Park Lane, this landmark hotel offers a luxury environment overlooking Hyde Park and the city. A dedicated team of staff is available to meet their guests' every need. Having undergone a full refurbishment, the bedrooms are designed with quality appointments and luxury fabrics. Several eating options are available - from the renowned Galvin at Windows to the all-day dining of Podium, which also serves a splendid afternoon tea. For guests arriving by car, valet parking is offered.

Rooms 453 (52 smoking) **Facilities** Spa STV FTV Wi-fi ⬐ Gym ♬ Xmas New Year **Conf** Class 600 Board 60 Thtr 1100 **Services** Lift Air con **Parking** 242 **Notes** ⊗ Civ Wed 1000

The Montcalm

★★★★★ 81% HOTEL PLAN 2 F2

☎ 020 7402 4288
Great Cumberland Place W1H 7TW
e-mail: reservations@montcalm.co.uk
dir: 2 mins' walk N from Marble Arch station

The Montcalm is ideally situated in the heart of London, just a short walk from Marble Arch, Oxford Street, Park Lane, Mayfair, Hyde Park and Theatreland. The elegantly decorated bedrooms are tastefully appointed and have many thoughtful touches. Public areas include a contemporary lounge bar and The Crescent restaurant which serves modern European cuisine. The hotel has a range of private rooms and conference suites, as well as spa, sauna, steam room, gym and exercise pool.

Rooms 143 (17 fmly) (7 GF) ◄ **Facilities** Spa STV Wi-fi ⊛ Gym **Conf** Class 250 Board 250 Thtr 500 Del from £400 to £600* **Services** Lift Air con **Notes** ⊗ Civ Wed 60

The Chesterfield Mayfair

THE RED CARNATION HOTEL COLLECTION

★★★★ ◉◉ HOTEL PLAN 4 H6

☎ 020 7491 2622
35 Charles St, Mayfair W1J 5EB
e-mail: bookch@rchmail.com
web: www.chesterfieldmayfair.com
dir: Hyde Park Corner along Piccadilly, left into Half Moon St. At end left & 1st right into Queens St, then right into Charles St

Quiet elegance and an atmosphere of exclusivity characterise this stylish Mayfair hotel where attentive, friendly service is paramount. The bedrooms, each with a marble-clad bathroom, have contemporary styles - perhaps with floral fabric walls, an African theme or with Savile Row stripes. In addition to these deluxe bedrooms there are 13 individually designed suites; some with four-poster beds and some with jacuzzis. The Butler's Restaurant is the fine dining option, and The Conservatory, with views over the garden, is just the place for cocktails, light lunches and afternoon teas. The hotel is air-conditioned throughout. Red Carnation Hotels is the AA Small Hotel Group of the Year 2013-14.

Rooms 107 ☏ **S** £180-£375; **D** £205-£1455*
Facilities STV Wi-fi ☍ ♫ **Conf** Class 45 Board 45 Thtr 100 Del from £335 to £645* **Services** Lift Air con **Notes** LB Civ Wed 120

London Marriott Hotel Grosvenor Square

★★★★ 84% ◉◉ HOTEL PLAN 2 G1

☎ 020 7493 1232
Grosvenor Square W1K 6JP
e-mail: dann.davies@marriotthotels.com
web: www.londonmarriottgrosvenorsquare.co.uk
dir: M4 E to Cromwell Rd through Knightsbridge to Hyde Park Corner. Into Park Lane, right at Brook Gate into Upper Brook St to Grosvenor Sq

Situated adjacent to Grosvenor Square in the heart of Mayfair, this hotel boasts convenient access to the

city, West End and some of London's most exclusive shops. Bedrooms and public areas are furnished and decorated to a high standard and retain the traditional elegance for which the area is known. The hotel's eating options include Maze Grill which has two AA Rosettes.

Rooms 237 (26 fmly) **Facilities** Wi-fi Gym Exercise & fitness centre Xmas **Conf** Class 500 Board 120 Thtr 900 **Services** Lift Air con **Notes** ⊗ Civ Wed 600

The Mandeville Hotel

★★★★ 80% ◉ HOTEL PLAN 2 G2

☎ 020 7935 5599
Mandeville Place W1U 2BE
e-mail: sales@mandeville.co.uk
web: www.mandeville.co.uk
dir: 3 mins walk from Bond St tube station

This is a stylish and attractive boutique-style hotel with a very contemporary feel. Bedrooms are high in quality, are air conditioned and large, and have very comfortable beds. One of the suites, The Penthouse, has a patio with views over London. The Reform Social & Grill Restaurant offers award-winning modern British cuisine, and the cocktail bar is always popular.

Rooms 142 (6 fmly) ☏ **Facilities** STV FTV Wi-fi ☍ Xmas New Year **Conf** Class 20 Board 20 Thtr 40 **Services** Lift Air con **Notes** ⊗

London Marriott Hotel Marble Arch

Marriott

★★★★ 80% HOTEL PLAN 2 F2

☎ 020 7723 1277
134 George St W1H 5DN
e-mail: mhrs.lonma.sales.marketing.coordinator@ marriotthotels.com
web: www.londonmarriottmarblearch.co.uk
dir: From Marble Arch turn into Edgware Rd, then 4th right into George St. Left into Dorset St for entrance

Situated just off the Edgware Road and close to the Oxford Street shops, this friendly hotel offers smart, well-equipped, air-conditioned bedrooms. Public areas are stylish, and include a smart indoor leisure club and an Italian-themed restaurant. Secure underground parking is available.

Rooms 240 (100 fmly) (7 smoking) ☏ **Facilities** STV FTV Wi-fi HL ☍ supervised Gym Xmas New Year **Conf** Class 100 Board 60 Thtr 150 Del from £294 to £344* **Services** Lift Air con **Parking** 83 **Notes** ⊗ Civ Wed 150

Millennium Hotel London Mayfair

MILLENNIUM HOTELS AND RESORTS
MILLENNIUM • COPTHORNE

★★★★ 79% ◉◉ HOTEL PLAN 2 G1

☎ 020 7629 9400
Grosvenor Square W1K 2HP
e-mail: reservations@millenniumhotels.co.uk
web: www.millenniumhotels.co.uk
dir: S side of Grosvenor Square, 5 mins walk from Oxford St & Bond St stations

This hotel benefits from a prestigious location in the heart of Mayfair, close to Bond Street. Smart bedrooms are generally spacious and club-floor rooms have exclusive use of their own lounge with complimentary refreshments. A choice of bars and dining options is available along with conference facilities and a fitness room.

Rooms 336 ☏ **S** £210-£580; **D** £228-£660 **Facilities** STV FTV Wi-fi ☍ HL Gym Fitness suite ♫ Xmas New Year **Conf** Class 250 Board 70 Thtr 500 Del from £275 to £400 **Services** Lift Air con **Notes** ⊗ Civ Wed 250

Flemings Mayfair

★★★★ 78% ◉ HOTEL PLAN 4 H6

☎ 020 7499 0000
Half Moon St, Mayfair W1J 7BH
e-mail: guest@flemings.co.uk
web: www.flemings-mayfair.co.uk
dir: On quiet residential street off Piccadilly, 3 mins walk from Green Park

The second oldest hotel in London offers modern décor with a cosy atmosphere and friendly, personal service. While public areas are compact, high quality is apparent with chandeliers and feature fireplaces. Bedrooms vary in size but have recently been upgraded and are equipped with an excellent range of facilities.

Rooms 129 (17 fmly) (24 GF) ☏ **S** £140-£255; **D** £155-£355 **Facilities** STV FTV Wi-fi ☍ Gym Xmas New Year **Conf** Board 22 Del from £350 **Services** Lift Air con **Notes** LB

LONDON

W1 WEST END *continued*

DoubleTree by Hilton Hotel, Marble Arch

★★★★ 77% @@@ HOTEL PLAN 2 F2

☎ 020 7935 2361
4 Bryanston St W1H 7BY
e-mail: janry.korpuz@hilton.com
web: www.doubletree.com
dir: Nearest tube stations: Marble Arch & Bond St

This hotel is a well located, historic property. The bedrooms, including executive and deluxe club floor rooms, vary in size but all are smartly equipped, boast bright trendy soft furnishings and are air conditioned; the en suites are equally modern and stylish. The public areas include a cocktail bar/lounge, Fire & Spice all-day dining concept, and the acclaimed Texture Restaurant which delivers impressive, modern cooking. The hotel offers free Wi-fi throughout.

Rooms 121 (15 fmly) (9 GF) **Facilities** Spa STV FTV Wi-fi ॐ Gym ♬ Xmas **Conf** Class 70 Board 50 Thtr 130 **Services** Lift Air con **Notes** ⊗

Thistle Piccadilly   thistle

★★★★ 77% HOTEL PLAN 3 A1

☎ 0871 376 9031
39 Coventry St W1D 6BZ
e-mail: piccadilly@thistle.co.uk
web: www.thistlehotels.com/piccadilly
dir: From Kings Cross follow signs for West End & Piccadilly

This popular hotel is centrally located between Leicester Square and Piccadilly Circus, ideal for all of the West End's attractions. All of the bedrooms have been completely refurbished offering high quality modern accommodations. Public areas are comfortably appointed with Costa Coffee in place open daily. The House Lounge Bar & Restaurant offers a stylish and quiet space in which to enjoy a relaxing drink and evening meal yet without missing out on any Leicester Square action with a live video feed in place.

Rooms 82 (2 fmly) **S** £109-£469; **D** £109-£469* **Facilities** STV FTV Wi-fi ॐ HL **Services** Lift Air con **Notes** ⊗

See advert on page 289

Park Plaza Sherlock Holmes

★★★★ 76% @ HOTEL PLAN 2 F3

☎ 020 7486 6161
108 Baker St W1U 6LJ
e-mail: info@sherlockholmeshotel.com
web: www.sherlockholmeshotel.com
dir: From Marylebone Flyover into Marylebone Rd. At Baker St turn right for hotel on left

Chic and modern, this boutique-style hotel is near a number of London underground and rail stations. Public rooms include a popular bar, sited just inside the main entrance, and Sherlock's Grill, where the mesquite-wood burning stove is a feature of the cooking. The hotel also features an indoor health suite and a relaxing lounge.

Rooms 119 (20 fmly) 🖰 **S** £100-£300; **D** £100-£300 **Facilities** STV Wi-fi Gym Beauty treatment room ♬ Xmas **Conf** Class 35 Board 30 Thtr 80 **Services** Lift Air con **Notes** LB ⊗ Civ Wed 80

Holiday Inn London - Mayfair

★★★★ 75% HOTEL PLAN 2 H1

☎ 0871 942 9110
3 Berkeley St W1J 8NE
e-mail: himayfair-reservations@ihg.com
web: www.hilondonmayfairhotel.co.uk
dir: At corner of Berkeley St & Piccadilly

Located in the heart of Mayfair and just minutes from Green Park tube station, this busy hotel has the benefit of well-proportioned, attractive bedrooms and elegant public areas. Options for dining include the graceful Nightingales Restaurant or choices from a substantial snack menu in the lounge bar.

Rooms 195 (63 fmly) **Facilities** STV Wi-fi ॐ Xmas New Year **Conf** Class 32 Board 32 Thtr 65 **Services** Lift Air con **Parking** 18 **Notes** ⊗

Thistle Marble Arch   thistle

★★★★ 75% HOTEL PLAN 2 G2

☎ 0871 971 1753 & 020 7629 8040
Bryanston St W1A 4UR
e-mail: marblearch@thistle.co.uk
web: www.thistlehotels.com/marblearch
dir: From Marble Arch monument into Oxford St. 1st left into Portman St, 1st left into Bryanston St. Hotel entrance on left

This centrally located hotel, adjacent to a car park, is ideal for the attractions of Oxford Street and Knightsbridge. The spacious bedrooms come in a range of size and price options, but all are very well equipped and have air conditioning. The public areas include a fast food service, Co-Motion, and a more

leisurely carvery restaurant, which also offers a carte menu. There is also a gym, a range of meeting rooms and an executive lounge.

Rooms 692 (60 fmly) 🖰 **S** £200-£250; **D** £210-£260 (incl. dinner)* **Facilities** STV FTV Wi-fi Gym ♬ Xmas New Year **Conf** Class 180 Board 94 Thtr 380 Del from £250 to £289* **Services** Lift Air con **Notes** LB ⊗ Civ Wed 300

See advert on opposite page

The Washington Mayfair Hotel

★★★★ 75% HOTEL PLAN 4 H6

☎ 020 7499 7000
5-7 Curzon St, Mayfair W1J 5HE
e-mail: sales@washington-mayfair.co.uk
web: www.washington-mayfair.co.uk
dir: From Green Park station take Piccadilly exit & turn right. 4th right into Curzon St

Situated in the heart of Mayfair, this stylish, independently owned hotel offers a very high standard of accommodation. The personalised, friendly service is noteworthy. Bedrooms are attractively furnished and provide high levels of comfort. The hotel is also a popular venue for afternoon tea and refreshments, served in the marbled and wood-panelled lounge.

Rooms 171 (32 smoking) 🖰 **S** £186-£400; **D** £186-£800 **Facilities** FTV Wi-fi ॐ Gym Xmas New Year **Conf** Class 40 Board 36 Thtr 110 **Services** Lift Air con **Notes** LB ⊗

The Cumberland

★★★★ 73% @ HOTEL PLAN 2 F2

☎ 0871 376 9014
Great Cumberland Place W1A 4RF
e-mail: enquiries@thecumberland.co.uk
dir: Behind Marble Arch monument, at top of Park Lane & Oxford St

This landmark hotel, occupying a prime position at Marble Arch, has a striking, airy lobby that is its focal point. There is a choice of bars, and two eating options - The Brasserie at the Cumberland, and a change of chef and new menus for the W1 restaurant. The facilities include extensive conference and meeting facilities - just some of what's on offer here. The bedrooms have a stylish contemporary feel and boast an excellent range of facilities.

Rooms 1019 (119 annexe) (8 fmly) (9 GF) 🖰 **S** £419; **D** £450* **Facilities** STV Wi-fi HL Gym ♬ Xmas New Year **Conf** Class 170 Board 85 Thtr 350 Del £469* **Services** Lift Air con **Notes** ⊗ Civ Wed 300

Save on hotels. Book at **theAA.com/hotel**

W1 289 ENGLAND

Radisson Blu Portman Hotel

★★★★ 73% HOTEL PLAN 2 F2

☎ 020 7208 6000
22 Portman Square W1H 7BG
e-mail: reservations.london@radissonblu.com
web: www.radissonblu.co.uk
dir: 100mtrs N of Oxford St; 300mtrs E of Edgware Rd

This smart, popular hotel enjoys a prime location a short stroll from Oxford Street and close to all the city's major attractions. The spacious, well-equipped bedrooms are themed, ranging from Oriental through to classical and contemporary Italian decor. Public areas include extensive conference facilities, a bar and the modern European Portman Restaurant.

Rooms 272 (93 fmly) (14 smoking) **Facilities** FTV Wi-fi ⟲ Gym Beauty treatment room Xmas **Conf** Class 280 Board 65 Thtr 600 **Services** Lift Air con **Parking** 400 **Notes** ⊗ Civ Wed 200

Holiday Inn London - Regents Park

★★★★ 71% HOTEL PLAN 2 H4

☎ 0871 942 9111 & 020 7388 2302
Carburton St, Regents Park W1W 5EE
e-mail: reservations-londonregentspark@ihg.com
web: www.hilondonregentsparkhotel.co.uk
dir: From E: from King's Cross, A50, left into Bolsover St. From W: A40 onto A501(Regent's Park Station on right). Left into Albany St, 1st right to cross Euston Rd. Pass Gt Portland St tube station to Bolsover St. Hotel on left

Well located and with the benefit of an adjacent public car park, this popular modern hotel provides a range of comfortable bedrooms equipped for both business and leisure guests. The attractive Junction Restaurant is the setting for brasserie-style eating and a comprehensive buffet breakfast provides a good start to the day. The hotel also provides excellent conference facilities within The Academy Centre.

Rooms 332 (4 smoking) **Facilities** STV FTV Wi-fi ⟳ HL **Conf** Class 200 Board 50 Thtr 350 **Services** Lift Air con **Notes** ⊗

The London Edition

Ⓤ

☎ 020 7781 0000
Berners St W1T 3NP

London's newest lifestyle hotel, this imposing historic building has been renovated and refurbished to the highest of standards incorporating high level design and comfort. The property is set to combine a personal and individualised lodging experience. At the time of going to print this establishment was completing its extensive refurbishment and development, for further information please see theAA.com.

Rooms 173

LONDON

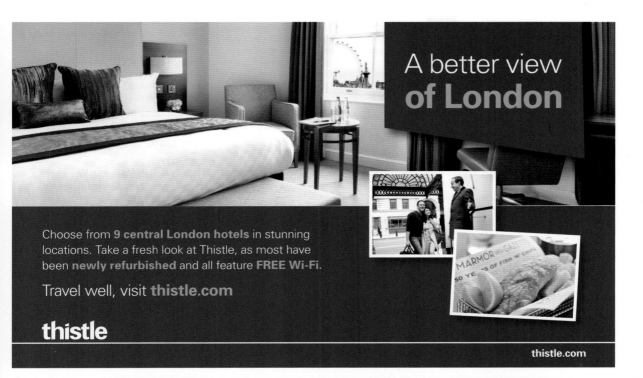

W2 BAYSWATER, PADDINGTON

Lancaster London

★★★★ 85% ◉◉ HOTEL PLAN 2 D1

☎ 020 7262 6737
Lancaster Ter W2 2TY
e-mail: book@lancasterlondon.com
web: www.lancasterlondon.com
dir: Adjacent to Lancaster Gate tube station

Located adjacent to Hyde Park, this large hotel offers a wide range of facilities. There are many room types; higher floors have excellent panoramic views of the city and park, and the suites are truly impressive. The hotel also offers two contrasting award-winning restaurants - the contemporary Island Restaurant & Bar, and Nipa restaurant with authentic Thai cuisine. There are spacious state-of-the-art, flexible conference and banqueting facilities, a 24-hour business centre and secure parking. This is an environmentally conscious hotel which has instigated many initiatives including a honey farm on the roof.

Rooms 416 (40 fmly) (28 smoking) **S** £170-£725; **D** £170-£725 **Facilities** STV Wi-fi Gym Xmas New Year **Conf** Class 550 Board 46 Thtr 1000 Del from £236 **Services** Lift Air con **Parking** 40 **Notes** ⊗ Civ Wed 1000

Novotel London Paddington

★★★★ 78% HOTEL PLAN 2 C3

☎ 020 7266 6000
3 Kingdom St, Paddington W2 6BD
e-mail: h6455@accor.com
dir: Easy access from Westway (A40) & Bishops Bridge Rd (A4206)

Located in the Paddington Central area, this hotel is easily accessible by road, and is only a few minutes walk from Paddington Station. Ideal for business or leisure guests. The facilities include the Elements Restaurant, a bar, conference facilities, a swimming pool, sauna, plus steam and fitness rooms. An NCP car park is a 5-minute walk away.

Rooms 206 (24 fmly) **Facilities** STV Wi-fi ↳ ⊛ Gym Steam room Sauna **Conf** Class 70 Board 40 Thtr 150 **Services** Lift

Thistle Kensington Gardens　　thistle

★★★★ 75% HOTEL PLAN 2 C1

☎ 0871 376 9024
104 Bayswater Rd W2 3HL
e-mail: kensingtongardens@thistle.co.uk
web: www.thistle.com/kensingtongardens

Located alongside Hyde Park, this modern hotel provides contemporary comforts in comfortable surroundings. The bedrooms and bathrooms are of a high standard and are suitable for both the leisure and business traveller. The informal Brasserie and Bar provide a good range of dishes. Parking is available on site, and the property is convenient for several tube stations.

Rooms 175 (13 fmly) ⟋ **Facilities** FTV Wi-fi **Conf** Class 30 Board 30 Thtr 45 **Services** Lift Air con **Parking** 62 **Notes** ⊗

See advert on page 289

Thistle Hyde Park　　thistle

★★★★ 74% HOTEL PLAN 2 C1

☎ 0871 376 9022
90-92 Lancaster Gate W2 3NR
e-mail: hydepark@thistle.co.uk
web: www.thistlehotels.com/hydepark
dir: From Marble Arch rdbt take A404 (Bayswater Rd)

The Thistle Hyde Park is a delightful building ideally situated overlooking Hyde Park and just a short walk from Kensington Gardens. The stylish public areas include a piano bar, a lounge and a smart restaurant. Bedrooms are tastefully appointed and equipped with many thoughtful touches; some rooms have views of the park.

Rooms 54 (12 fmly) **Facilities** STV FTV Wi-fi ↳ **Conf** Class 20 Board 20 Thtr 35 **Services** Lift Air con **Parking** 20 **Notes** ⊗

See advert on page 289

Hotel Indigo

★★★★ 72% HOTEL PLAN 2 D2

☎ 020 7706 4444
16 London St, Paddington W2 1HL
e-mail: malcolm@lth-hotels.com

This smart hotel is located within a stone's throw of Paddington Station. Contemporary and stylish, bedrooms are equipped with all modern extras; they boast high quality comfy beds ensuring a great night's sleep and en suites with power showers and quality toiletries. Delightful public areas include a restaurant, bar and a coffee shop offering tempting cakes.

Rooms 64 ⟋ **Facilities** STV FTV Wi-fi HL Gym **Services** Lift Air con **Notes** ⊗

Lancaster Gate Hotel

★★★ 74% HOTEL PLAN 2 C1

☎ 020 7479 2500 & 7262 5090
66 Lancaster Gate W2 3NA
e-mail: info@lghhydepark.co.uk
dir: Just off Bayswater Rd

This hotel offers a convenient location between Oxford Street and Knightsbridge and is also close to Hyde Park and Kensington Gardens. Bedrooms are well equipped with broadband and safes, as well as a range of TV channels. There is a comfortable bar and stylish restaurant, and the hotel also has a range of meeting rooms.

Rooms 188 (3 fmly) (13 GF) (4 smoking) **Facilities** STV FTV Wi-fi Off site leisure facilities available **Conf** Class 14 Board 14 Thtr 30 **Services** Lift Air con

Mitre House Hotel

★★ 72% METRO HOTEL PLAN 2 D2

☎ 020 7723 8040 & 7402 5695
178-184 Sussex Gardens, Hyde Park W2 1TU
e-mail: reservations@mitrehousehotel.com
web: www.mitrehousehotel.com
dir: Parallel to Bayswater Rd & one block from Paddington Station

This family-run hotel continues to offers a warm welcome and attentive service. It is ideally located, close to Paddington station and near the West End and major attractions. Bedrooms include a number of family suites and there is a lounge bar. Limited parking is available.

Rooms 69 (7 fmly) (7 GF) (69 smoking) **S** £80-£85; **D** £95-£100 **Facilities** STV Wi-fi **Services** Lift **Parking** 20 **Notes** ⊗

Save on hotels. Book at **theAA.com/hotel**

W2 – W6 291 **ENGLAND**

LONDON

W3 ACTON

Ramada Encore London West

★★★ 76% HOTEL PLAN 1 D4

☎ 020 8753 0800
4 Portal Way, Gypsy Corner, A40 Western Av W3 6RT
e-mail: reservations@encorelondonwest.co.uk
web: www.encorelondonwest.co.uk

Conveniently situated on the A40, this modern, purpose-built glass-fronted hotel offers smartly appointed accommodation with en suite power shower rooms and air conditioning. Open-plan public areas include a popular Asian and European restaurant, Wok Around the World, and a 2go café and sandwich bar. Secure parking and a range of meeting rooms complete the picture.

Rooms 150 (35 fmly) (15 smoking) ⌨ **Facilities** STV FTV Wi-fi ↻ Gym **Conf** Class 28 Board 26 Thtr 50 **Services** Lift Air con **Parking** 72 **Notes** ⊗

W4 CHISWICK

Chiswick Moran Hotel

★★★★ 75% HOTEL PLAN 1 C3

☎ 020 8996 5200
626 Chiswick High Rd W4 5RY
e-mail: chiswickres@moranhotels.com
web: www.moranhotels.com
dir: 200yds from M4 junct 2

This stylish, modern hotel is conveniently located for Heathrow and central London, with Gunnersby tube station just a few minutes' walk away. Airy, spacious public areas include a modern restaurant, a popular bar and excellent meeting facilities. Fully air-conditioned bedrooms are stylish and extremely well appointed with broadband, laptop safes and flat-screen TVs. All boast spacious, modern bathrooms, many with walk-in rain showers.

Rooms 123 (6 fmly) ⌨ **S** £79-£310; **D** £89-£320 (incl. bkfst)* **Facilities** STV FTV Wi-fi ↻ Gym Xmas New Year **Conf** Class 45 Board 40 Thtr 90 Del from £160 to £390* **Services** Lift Air con **Parking** 40 **Notes** LB ⊗ Civ Wed 80

W5 EALING

Crowne Plaza London - Ealing

★★★★ 77% ◉ HOTEL PLAN 1 C4

☎ 0871 942 9114 & 020 8233 3200
Western Av, Hanger Ln, Ealing W5 1HG
e-mail: info@cp-londonealing.co.uk
web: www.cp-londonealing.co.uk
dir: A40 from central London towards M40. Exit at Ealing & North Circular A406 sign. At rdbt take 2nd exit signed A40. Hotel on left

Appointed to a high standard, this hotel occupies a prime position on the A40 and North Circular at Hangar Lane; Wembley Stadium is easily accessible. Modern, well-equipped, air-conditioned and sound-proofed bedrooms offer good facilities. There is a smart gym, a steam room together with meeting facilities and the West 5 Brasserie. On-site parking is available.

Rooms 131 (17 GF) (15 smoking) **Facilities** FTV Wi-fi Gym Steam room Xmas New Year **Conf** Class 48 Board 35 Thtr 80 **Services** Lift Air con **Parking** 85 **Notes** ⊗

Premier Inn London Ealing

BUDGET HOTEL PLAN 1 C3

☎ 0871 527 9368
22-24 Uxbridge Rd, Ealing W5 2SR
web: www.premierinn.com
dir: M4 junct 1, A406 (signed North Circular & M1). Left onto A4020 (signed Ealing & Southall). Hotel on right after Ealing Broadway tube station

High quality, budget accommodation ideal for both families and business travellers. Spacious, en suite bedrooms feature tea and coffee making facilities, and Freeview TV in most hotels. Internet access and Wi-fi are available for a small fee. The adjacent family restaurant features a wide and varied menu. See also the Hotel Groups pages.

Rooms 165

Premier Inn London Hanger Lane

BUDGET HOTEL PLAN 1 C4

☎ 0871 527 8346
1-6 Ritz Pde, Ealing W5 3RA
web: www.premierinn.com
dir: M4 junct 2, A4 follow North Circular/A406 signs, for 0.5m. Take A406 for approx 2.5m. Right into Ashbourne Rd, immediately left into Ashbourne Parade, right into Ritz Parade. Hotel on right

Rooms 59

W6 HAMMERSMITH

Novotel London West

★★★★ 74% ◉ HOTEL PLAN 1 D3

☎ 020 8741 1555
1 Shortlands W6 8DR
e-mail: H0737@accor.com
web: www.novotellondonwest.co.uk
dir: M4 (A4) & A316 junct at Hogarth rdbt. Along Great West Rd, left for Hammersmith before flyover. On Hammersmith Bridge Rd to rdbt, take 5th exit. 1st left into Shortlands, 1st left to hotel main entrance

A Hammersmith landmark, this substantial hotel is a popular base for both business and leisure travellers. Spacious, air-conditioned bedrooms have a good range of extras and many have additional beds, making them suitable for families. The hotel also has its own car park, business centre and shop, and boasts one of the largest convention centres in Europe.

Rooms 630 (148 fmly) **Facilities** STV Wi-fi Gym **Conf** Class 700 Board 200 Thtr 1700 **Services** Lift Air con **Parking** 240 **Notes** Civ Wed 1400

Premier Inn London Hammersmith

BUDGET HOTEL PLAN 1 D3

☎ 0871 527 8660
255 King St, Hammersmith W6 9LU
web: www.premierinn.com
dir: From central London on A4 to Hammersmith, follow A315 towards Chiswick

High quality, budget accommodation ideal for both families and business travellers. Spacious, en suite bedrooms feature tea and coffee making facilities, and Freeview TV in most hotels. Internet access and Wi-fi are available for a small fee. The adjacent family restaurant features a wide and varied menu. See also the Hotel Groups pages.

Rooms 106

W8 KENSINGTON

INSPECTORS' CHOICE

Royal Garden Hotel

★★★★★ ⚛⚛⚛ HOTEL PLAN 4 B5

☎ 020 7937 8000
2-24 Kensington High St W8 4PT
e-mail: reservations@royalgardenhotel.co.uk
web: www.royalgardenhotel.co.uk
dir: Adjacent to Kensington Palace

This landmark hotel, just a short walk from the Royal Albert Hall, has airy, stylish public rooms that include the Park Terrace Restaurant, Lounge and Bar, Bertie's cocktail bar and the contemporary 10th-floor Min Jiang Restaurant, an exciting elegant restaurant offering authentic Chinese cuisine and enjoying breathtaking views of the city. The stylish and contemporary bedrooms are equipped with up-to-date facilities and include a number of spacious, air-conditioned rooms and suites with super views over Kensington Gardens. All rooms have iPod docking stations, flat-screen TVs and triple-glazed windows as standard. Guests have complimentary use of the Soma Spa gym, sauna and steam room.

Rooms 394 (41 fmly) (45 smoking) 🐾
S £200-£440; **D** £250-£490* **Facilities** Spa STV FTV Wi-fi ⅄ HL Gym Health club Sauna Steam room 🎵 Xmas New Year **Conf** Class 320 Board 100 Thtr 550 Del £450 **Services** Lift Air con **Parking** 200 **Notes** LB ⊗ Civ Wed 400

INSPECTORS' CHOICE

The Milestone Hotel

★★★★★ ⚛⚛ HOTEL
PLAN 4 B5

☎ 020 7917 1000
1 Kensington Court W8 5DL
e-mail: bookms@rchmail.com
web: www.milestonehotel.com
dir: From Warwick Rd right into Kensington High St. Hotel 400yds past Kensington tube station. Adjacent to Kensington Palace

This delightful town house enjoys a wonderful location opposite Kensington Palace and is near the elegant shops. The individually themed bedrooms include a selection of stunning suites that are equipped with every conceivable extra - fruit, cookies, chocolates, complimentary newspapers and even the next day's weather forecast. Up-to-the-minute technology includes high speed Wi-fi and interactive TV. Public areas include the luxurious Park Lounge where afternoon tea is served, the delightful split-level Stables Bar, a conservatory, the sumptuous Cheneston's restaurant and a fully equipped small gym, resistance pool and a spa treatment room. Red Carnation Hotels is the AA Small Hotel Group of the Year 2013-14.

Rooms 62 (6 fmly) (1 GF) (5 smoking) 🐾
S £354-£450; **D** £414-£510* **Facilities** STV FTV Wi-fi ⅄ HL ⓢ Gym Health club Beauty treatment room 🎵 Xmas New Year Child facilities **Conf** Class 20 Board 20 Thtr 50 Del from £469 to £575* **Services** Lift Air con **Parking** 1 **Notes** LB Civ Wed 30

Copthorne Tara Hotel
London Kensington

★★★★ 75% HOTEL PLAN 4 B4

☎ 020 7937 7211 ☎ 7872 2000
Scarsdale Place, Wrights Ln W8 5SR
e-mail: reservations.tara@millenniumhotels.co.uk
web: www.millenniumhotels.co.uk
dir: From Kensington High St into Wrights Ln (NB for Sat Nav use W8 5SY)

This expansive hotel is ideally placed for Kensington High Street shops and tube station. Smart public areas include a trendy coffee shop, a gym, a stylish brasserie and bar, plus extensive conference facilities. Bedrooms include several well-equipped rooms for less mobile guests, in addition to a number of Connoisseur rooms that have the use of a club lounge as one of its many complimentary facilities.

Rooms 833 (3 fmly) 🐾 **Facilities** FTV Wi-fi ⅄ HL Fitness room Xmas New Year **Conf** Class 160 Board 90 Thtr 280 Del from £145 to £300* **Services** Lift Air con **Parking** 91 **Notes** ⊗ Civ Wed 280

W14 WEST KENSINGTON

K West Hotel & Spa

★★★★ 80% HOTEL PLAN 1 D3

☎ 020 8008 6600
Richmond Way W14 0AX
e-mail: info@k-west.co.uk
web: www.k-west.co.uk
dir: From A40(M) take Shepherd's Bush exit. At Holland Park rdbt 3rd exit. 1st left & left again. Hotel straight ahead

This stylish, contemporary hotel is conveniently located for Notting Hill, the exhibition halls and the BBC; Bond Street is only a 10-minute tube journey away. Funky, minimalist public areas include a trendy lobby bar and mezzanine-style restaurant. Spacious bedrooms and suites are extremely well appointed and offer luxurious bedding and a host of thoughtful extras such as CD and DVD players. Wi-fi is available throughout. The spa offers a comprehensive range of health, beauty and relaxation treatments.

Rooms 220 (31 GF) 🐾 **Facilities** Spa STV FTV Wi-fi ⅄ Gym Hydrotherapy pool Sauna Steam room Snow room Solarium 🎵 New Year **Conf** Class 20 Board 25 Thtr 55 **Services** Lift Air con **Parking** 100 **Notes** ⊗

Save on hotels. Book at **theAA.com/hotel**

W8 – WC1 293 ENGLAND

Ibis London Shepherd's Bush

BUDGET HOTEL PLAN 1 D3

☎ 020 7348 2020
3-5 Rockley Rd W14 0DJ
e-mail: H7813@accor.com
dir: Walking distance from Shepherd's Bush Market & Shepherd's Bush Central Tube Station

Modern, budget hotel offering comfortable accommodation in bright and practical bedrooms. Breakfast is self-service and dinner is available in the restaurant. See also the Hotel Groups pages.

Rooms 128 ✎

WC1 BLOOMSBURY, HOLBORN

The Montague on the Gardens

★★★★ 85% ☺ HOTEL PLAN 3 B3

☎ 020 7637 1001
15 Montague St, Bloomsbury WC1B 5BJ
e-mail: bookmt@rchmail.com
web: www.montaguehotel.com
dir: Just off Russell Square, adjacent to British Museum

This stylish hotel is situated right next to the British Museum. A special feature is the alfresco terrace overlooking a delightful garden. Other public rooms include the Blue Door Bistro and Chef's Table, a bar, a lounge and a conservatory where traditional afternoon teas are served. The bedrooms are beautifully appointed and range from split-level suites to more compact rooms. Red Carnation Hotels is the AA Small Hotel Group of the Year 2013-14.

Rooms 100 (10 fmly) (19 GF) ✎ S £174-£330; D £192-£348* **Facilities** STV Wi-fi ↻ HL Gym ♫ Xmas New Year **Conf** Class 50 Board 50 Thtr 120 Del from £246 to £427* **Services** Lift Air con **Notes** LB Civ Wed 90

The Kingsley by Thistle

thistle

★★★★ 77% HOTEL PLAN 3 B3

☎ 0871 376 9006
Bloomsbury Way WC1A 2SD
e-mail: thekingsley@thistle.co.uk
web: www.thistlehotels.com/thekingsley
dir: A40(M) to A501 (Marylebone Rd), take sliproad before underpass to Holburn. Into Gower St, Bloomsbury St (A400). Left into Oxford St, then Bloomsbury Way

Well situated for theatregoers, this hotel enjoys a convenient central location. The well-equipped rooms are generally spacious with good quality fabrics and furnishings, with both family rooms and executive suites available. The ground-floor bar and lounge

areas are well appointed. There is a public car park nearby.

Rooms 129 ✎ **Facilities** STV FTV Wi-fi HL **Conf** Class 50 Board 30 Thtr 100 **Services** Lift Air con **Notes** ⊗

See advert on page 289

Hotel Russell

★★★★ 76% HOTEL PLAN 3 B4

☎ 020 7837 6470
Russell Square WC1B 5BE
e-mail: russell.reservations@principal-hayley.com
web: www.principal-hayley.com
dir: From A501 into Woburn Place. Hotel 500mtrs on left

This landmark Grade II, Victorian hotel is located on Russell Square, within walking distance of the West End and theatre district. Many bedrooms are stylish and state-of-the-art in design, while others are more traditional. Spacious public areas include the impressive foyer with a restored mosaic floor, a choice of lounges and an elegant restaurant.

Rooms 373 (2 fmly) ✎ **Facilities** STV FTV Wi-fi **Conf** Class 200 Board 75 Thtr 450 Del from £155 to £225* **Services** Lift Air con **Notes** ⊗ Civ Wed 300

Holiday Inn London Kings Cross/Bloomsbury

Holiday Inn

★★★★ 69% HOTEL PLAN 3 C5

☎ 020 7833 3900
1 Kings Cross Rd WC1X 9HX
e-mail: sales@holidayinnlondon.com
web: www.holidayinn.co.uk
dir: On corner of King Cross Rd & Calthorpe St

Conveniently located for Kings Cross station and The City, this modern hotel offers smart, spacious air-conditioned accommodation with a wide range of facilities. There are versatile meeting rooms, a bar, a well-equipped fitness centre and a choice of restaurants including one serving Indian cuisine.

Rooms 405 (163 fmly) (126 smoking) ✎ **Facilities** STV FTV Wi-fi HL ↻ Gym Beauty treatment room **Conf** Class 120 Board 30 Thtr 220 Del from £160 to £250* **Services** Lift Air con **Parking** 14 **Notes** ⊗

Holiday Inn London Bloomsbury

★★★ 82% HOTEL PLAN 3 B4

☎ 0871 942 9222
Coram St WC1N 1HT
e-mail: bloomsbury@ihg.com
web: www.holidayinn.co.uk
dir: Off Upper Woburn Place

Centrally located, this modern and stylish hotel is within easy reach of many of London's tourist attractions and close to St Pancras International Rail Station. The bedrooms boast a pillow menu, air-conditioning and high-speed internet access. The Junction restaurant offers a modern menu, while Callaghans is a traditional Irish pub featuring the best Irish beers. The meeting rooms can cater for many different events.

Rooms 314 (30 fmly) **Facilities** STV Wi-fi ↻ HL ♫ **Conf** Class 180 Board 80 Thtr 350 **Services** Lift Air con **Notes** ⊗

Bedford Hotel

★★★ 73% HOTEL PLAN 3 B3

☎ 020 7636 7822 & 7692 3620
83-93 Southampton Row WC1B 4HD
e-mail: info@imperialhotels.co.uk
web: www.imperialhotels.co.uk

Just off Russell Square, this intimate hotel is ideal for visits to the British Museum and Covent Garden. The bedrooms are well equipped with all the expected facilities including modem points if requested. The ground floor has a lounge, a bar and restaurant plus there's a delightful secret rear garden. The underground car park is a bonus.

Rooms 184 (1 fmly) S £90; (incl. bkfst)* **Facilities** FTV Wi-fi Xmas New Year **Conf** Board 12 Del £165* **Services** Lift **Parking** 50 **Notes** LB ⊗

LONDON

WC1 BLOOMSBURY, HOLBORN *continued*

Bloomsbury Park A Thistle Associate Hotel

thistle

★★★ 73% HOTEL PLAN 3 B3

☎ 0871 376 9007
126 Southampton Row WC1B 5AD
e-mail: bloomsburypark@thistle.co.uk
dir: 0.6m from Holburn Underground Station on Southampton Row

This Edwardian townhouse hotel has been refurbished to a high standard in a contemporary style, yet still retains some of the original features. Located a short stroll from key London attractions such as Oxford Street and Covent Garden, and just a moment away from the Tube network. Bedrooms and bathrooms are tastefully appointed, and enhanced with useful amenities for both business and leisure travellers. The popular Bloomsbury Bar & Restaurant offers meals and light snacks throughout the day and evening.

Rooms 95 (4 fmly) (7 GF) **S** £70–£160; **D** £80–£210 (incl. bkfst)* **Facilities** FTV Wi-fi ↳ HL Xmas New Year **Conf** Class 12 Board 20 Thtr 25 Del from £120 to £190 **Services** Lift **Notes** LB ⊗

See advert on page 289

Ambassadors Bloomsbury Hotel

⊔ PLAN 3 A5

☎ 020 7693 5400 & 7693 5410
12 Upper Woburn Place WC1H 0HX
e-mail: dutymanager@ambassadors.co.uk

Currently the rating for this establishment is not confirmed. This may be due to a change of ownership or because it has only recently joined the AA rating scheme. For further details please see the AA website: theAA.com

Rooms 100 **Facilities** STV Wi-fi ↳ Gym **Conf** Class 110 Board 50 Thtr 250 **Services** Lift Air con **Notes** ⊗

Premier Inn London Euston

BUDGET HOTEL PLAN 3 A5

☎ 0871 527 8656
1 Duke's Rd, Euston WC1H 9PJ
web: www.premierinn.com
dir: On corner of Euston Road & Duke's Road, between Kings Cross/St Pancras & Euston stations

High quality, budget accommodation ideal for both families and business travellers. Spacious, en suite bedrooms feature tea and coffee making facilities, and Freeview TV in most hotels. Internet access and Wi-fi are available for a small fee. The adjacent

---

family restaurant features a wide and varied menu. See also the Hotel Groups pages.

Rooms 220

WC2 SOHO, STRAND

INSPECTORS' CHOICE

The Savoy

★★★★★ ⍟⍟ HOTEL PLAN 3 C1

☎ 020 7836 4343
Strand WC2R 0EU
e-mail: savoy@fairmont.com
dir: Halfway along The Strand between Trafalgar Sq & Aldwych

The Savoy Hotel has been at the forefront of the London hotel scene since it opened in 1889. The hotel has been lovingly restored in recent years, with much of its art deco and Edwardian heritage kept intact. The bedrooms, including an extensive range of stunning suites, vary in style and size, and many overlook the River Thames. The famous River Restaurant, Savoy Grill and American Bar remain as well-loved favourites; the Thames Foyer is well known for its afternoon teas; and the Beaufort Bar offers a comprehensive range of champagnes. Immaculately presented staff offer excellent standards of hospitality and service.

Rooms 268 (5 fmly) (10 smoking) ♠ **Facilities** Spa STV FTV Wi-fi ⍟ supervised Gym Fitness gallery Health & beauty treatments Personal training ♫ Xmas New Year **Conf** Class 200 Board 32 Thtr 500 **Services** Lift Air con **Parking** 65 **Notes** Civ Wed 400

Charing Cross Hotel

★★★★ 80% HOTEL PLAN 3 B1

☎ 0871 376 9012
The Strand WC2N 5HX
e-mail: charingcross@guoman.co.uk
web: www.guoman.com
dir: E on The Strand towards Trafalgar Square, right into station forecourt

This centrally located and historic landmark hotel provides a friendly welcome. Spacious in design, the

---

original grand architecture blends nicely with the modern style of interior appointments, particularly in the bedrooms and bathrooms. There is a choice of dining options including the relaxed Brasserie, which has splendid views of London especially at night. The gym is exclusively for guests.

Rooms 239 (83 annexe) (12 fmly) **Facilities** STV Wi-fi Gym Xmas New Year **Conf** Class 96 Board 46 Thtr 140 **Services** Lift Air con **Notes** Civ Wed 140

The Royal Trafalgar, London

thistle

★★★★ 75% HOTEL PLAN 3 A1

☎ 0871 376 9037
Whitcomb St WC2H 7HG
e-mail: theroyaltrafalgar@thistle.co.uk
web: www.thistle.com/theroyaltrafalgar
dir: 100mtrs from Trafalgar Sq adjacent to Sainsbury Wing of National Gallery

Quietly located, this handily placed hotel is just a short walk from Trafalgar Square and Theatreland. This property has undergone refurbishment, with bedrooms and bathrooms, in a variety of sizes, offering very good levels of comfort and modern amenities. Dining options include Squares Restaurant serving a wide selection, and Gravity Lounge and Bar where light meals can be taken.

Rooms 108 (12 fmly) **S** £109–£469; **D** £109–£469* **Facilities** STV FTV Wi-fi ↳ **Conf** Class 20 Board 18 Thtr 30 **Services** Lift Air con **Notes** ⊗

Premier Inn London Leicester Square

Premier Inn

BUDGET HOTEL PLAN 3 A1

☎ 0871 527 9334
1 Leicester Place, Leicester Square WC2H 7BP
web: www.premierinn.com
dir: Nearest tube station: Leicester Sq. From Cranbourne St into Leicester Sq. Hotel on right (Leicester Pl). (Car parks: China Town & Witcombe St, approx 10 mins walk)

High quality, budget accommodation ideal for both families and business travellers. Spacious, en suite bedrooms feature tea and coffee making facilities, and Freeview TV in most hotels. Internet access and Wi-fi are available for a small fee. The adjacent family restaurant features a wide and varied menu. See also the Hotel Groups pages.

Rooms 83

Save on hotels. Book at **theAA.com/hotel**

WC1 – LOO 295 ENGLAND

LONDON GATEWAY MOTORWAY SERVICE AREA (M1)
Map 6 TQ19

Days Hotel London North - M1
★★★ 72% HOTEL

☎ 020 8906 7000
Welcome Break Service Area NW7 3HU
e-mail: lgw.hotel@welcomebreak.co.uk
web: www.welcomebreak.co.uk
dir: On M1 between junct 2/4 N'bound & S'bound

This modern building offers accommodation in smart, spacious and well-equipped bedrooms, suitable for families and business travellers, and all with en suite bathrooms. Continental breakfast is available and other refreshments may be taken at the nearby family restaurant.

Rooms 200 (190 fmly) (80 GF) (20 smoking)
Facilities FTV Wi-fi ↺ **Conf** Class 30 Board 50 Thtr 70
Services Lift Air con **Parking** 160 **Notes** Civ Wed 80

LONG EATON
Derbyshire
Map 11 SK43

Novotel Nottingham East Midlands
★★★ 71% HOTEL

☎ 0115 946 5111
Bostock Ln NG10 4EP
e-mail: H0507@accor.com
web: www.novotel.com
dir: M1 junct 25 onto B6002 to Long Eaton. Hotel 400yds on left

In close proximity to the M1, this purpose-built hotel has much to offer. All bedrooms are spacious, have sofa beds and provide exceptional desk space. Public rooms include a bright brasserie, which is open all day and provides extended dining until midnight. There is a comprehensive range of meeting rooms.

Rooms 108 (40 fmly) (20 GF) **S** £35-£105;
D £35-£105* **Facilities** Wi-fi ↺ HL ⤵ **Conf** Class 130 Board 100 Thtr 250 Del from £105 to £152*
Services Lift **Parking** 220 **Notes** LB

LONGHORSLEY
Northumberland
Map 21 NZ19

Macdonald Linden Hall, Golf & Country Club
★★★★ 80% ◉◉ HOTEL

☎ 01670 500000 & 0844 879 9084
NE65 8XF
e-mail: lindenhall@macdonald-hotels.co.uk
web: www.macdonaldhotels.co.uk
dir: N'bound on A1 take A697 towards Coldstream. Hotel 1m N of Longhorsley

This impressive Georgian mansion lies in 400 acres of parkland and offers extensive indoor and outdoor leisure facilities including a golf course. The Dobson Restaurant provides a fine dining experience, or guests can eat in the more informal Linden Tree pub. The good-sized bedrooms have a restrained modern style. The team of staff are enthusiastic and professional. Macdonald Hotels is the AA Hotel Group of the Year 2013-14.

Rooms 50 (3 fmly) (16 GF) **Facilities** Spa STV FTV Wi-fi ↺ ⓢ supervised ⚓ 18 ⛳ Putt green ⚑ Gym Steam room Sauna Xmas New Year **Conf** Class 120 Board 50 Thtr 300 **Services** Lift **Parking** 300 **Notes** Civ Wed 120

LONG MELFORD
Suffolk
Map 13 TL84

The Black Lion Hotel
★★★ 85% ◉◉ HOTEL

☎ 01787 312356
Church Walk, The Green CO10 9DN
e-mail: enquiries@blacklionhotel.net
web: www.blacklionhotel.net
dir: At junct of A134 & A1092

This charming 15th-century hotel is situated on the edge of this bustling town overlooking the green. Bedrooms are generally spacious and each is attractively decorated, tastefully furnished and equipped with useful extras. An interesting range of dishes is served in the lounge bar or guests may choose to dine from the same innovative menu in the more formal restaurant.

Rooms 10 (1 fmly) **Facilities** Wi-fi Xmas New Year
Conf Class 28 Board 28 Thtr 50 **Parking** 10
Notes Civ Wed 50

The Bull
★★★ 74% HOTEL

☎ 01787 378494
Hall St CO10 9JG
e-mail: bull.longmelford@greeneking.co.uk
web: www.bull-hotel.com
dir: 3m N of Sudbury on A134

The public areas of this delightful 14th-century property feature a wealth of charm and character, including exposed beams, carvings, heraldic markings and huge open fireplaces. Bedrooms are smartly decorated, thoughtfully equipped and retain many original features. Snacks or light lunches are served in the bar, or guests can choose to dine in the more formal restaurant.

Rooms 25 (4 fmly) ⤳ **S** £70-£80; **D** £90-£110 (incl. bkfst)* **Facilities** FTV Wi-fi Xmas New Year
Conf Class 40 Board 30 Thtr 100 Del from £99 to £135 **Parking** 35 **Notes** ⊗ Civ Wed 100

LOOE
Cornwall
Map 2 SX25

Trelaske Hotel & Restaurant
★★★ 79% ◉◉ HOTEL

☎ 01503 262159
Polperro Rd PL13 2JS
e-mail: info@trelaske.co.uk
dir: B252 signed Looe. Over Looe bridge signed Polperro. 1.9m, hotel signed on left, turn right

This small and welcoming hotel offers comfortable accommodation, professional and friendly service plus award-winning food. Set in its own very well-tended and pretty grounds, it is only two miles from Polperro and Looe.

Rooms 7 (4 annexe) (2 fmly) (2 GF) ⤳ **S** £90-£99;
D £100-£110 (incl. bkfst)* **Facilities** FTV Wi-fi
Conf Class 30 Board 40 Thtr 100 **Parking** 50

L

LOOE continued

Hannafore Point Hotel

THE INDEPENDENTS
HOTEL ASSOCIATION

★★★ 72% HOTEL

☎ 01503 263273
Marine Dr, West Looe PL13 2DG
e-mail: stay@hannaforepointhotel.com
dir: A38, left onto A385 to Looe. Over bridge turn left. Hotel 0.5m on left

With panoramic coastal views of St George's Island around to Rame Head, this popular hotel provides a warm welcome. The wonderful view is certainly a feature of the spacious restaurant and bar, creating a scenic backdrop for both dinners and breakfasts. Additional facilities include a heated indoor pool and a gym.

Rooms 37 (5 fmly) **Facilities** STV Wi-fi ⓦ Gym Spa pool Steam room Sauna ♫ Xmas New Year **Conf** Class 80 Board 40 Thtr 120 **Services** Lift **Parking** 32 **Notes** Civ Wed 150

LOSTWITHIEL
Cornwall
Map 2 SX15

BEST WESTERN Restormel Lodge Hotel

Best Western

★★★ 75% HOTEL

☎ 01208 872223
Castle Hill PL22 0DD
e-mail: bookings@restormellodgehotel.co.uk
web: www.bw-restormellodgehotel.co.uk
dir: On A390 in Lostwithiel town centre

A short drive from the Eden Project, this popular hotel offers a friendly welcome to all visitors and is ideally situated for exploring the area. The older building houses the bar, restaurant and lounges, with original features adding to the character. Bedrooms are comfortably furnished, with a number overlooking the secluded outdoor pool.

Rooms 36 (12 annexe) (2 fmly) (9 GF) 🐾 S £29-£79; D £49-£119 (incl. bkfst)* **Facilities** FTV Wi-fi ♪ ✦ Xmas New Year **Conf** Class 12 Board 12 Thtr 12 Del from £79.95 to £99.95 **Parking** 60 **Notes** LB

LOUGHBOROUGH
Leicestershire
Map 11 SK51

Quorn Country Hotel

PRIMA
HOTELS

★★★★ 77% ⊛ HOTEL

☎ 01509 415050 & 415061
Charnwood House, 66 Leicester Rd LE12 8BB
e-mail: reservations@quorncountryhotel.co.uk
web: www.quorncountryhotel.co.uk

(For full entry see Quorn)

Premier Inn Loughborough

Premier Inn

BUDGET HOTEL

☎ 0871 527 9314
Southfields Rd LE11 9SA
dir: M1 junct 23, A512 towards Loughborough. Left into Greenclose Ln. Right onto A6, Right into Southfield Rd, hotel on left

High quality, budget accommodation ideal for both families and business travellers. Spacious, en suite bedrooms feature tea and coffee making facilities, and Freeview TV in most hotels. Internet access and Wi-fi are available for a small fee. The adjacent family restaurant features a wide and varied menu. See also the Hotel Groups pages.

Rooms 112

LOUTH
Lincolnshire
Map 17 TF38

Brackenborough Hotel

★★★ 88% ⊛ HOTEL

☎ 01507 609169
Cordeaux Corner, Brackenborough LN11 0SZ
e-mail: reception@brackenborough.co.uk
web: www.oakridgehotels.co.uk
dir: On A16 (Louth to Grimsby road), 1m from Louth

In an idyllic setting amid well-tended gardens, this hotel offers attractive bedrooms, each individually decorated with co-ordinated furnishings and many extras. The award-winning bistro offers informal dining and the menu is based on locally sourced produce. The hotel specialises in weddings, events and private functions and has excellent conference facilities. Free Wi-fi is available. Guests have free access to state-of-the-art leisure facilities (less than half a mile away) that includes a swimming pool, tennis courts and a gym.

Rooms 24 (2 fmly) (6 GF) 🐾 S £87-£125; D £102-£160 (incl. bkfst)* **Facilities** FTV Wi-fi ♪ Gym ♫ Xmas New Year **Conf** Class 150 Board 50 Thtr 300 Del £114.95* **Services** Air con **Parking** 90 **Notes** LB ⊗ Civ Wed 220

BEST WESTERN Kenwick Park Hotel

Best Western

★★★ 77% HOTEL

☎ 01507 608806
Kenwick Park Estate LN11 8NR
e-mail: enquiries@kenwick-park.co.uk
web: www.kenwick-park.co.uk
dir: A16 from Grimsby, then A157 Mablethorpe/Manby Rd. Hotel 400mtrs down hill on right

This elegant Georgian house is situated on the 320-acre Kenwick Park estate, overlooking its own golf course. Bedrooms are spacious, comfortable and provide modern facilities. Public areas include a restaurant and a conservatory bar that overlook the grounds. There is also an extensive leisure centre and state-of-the-art conference and banqueting facilities.

Rooms 34 (5 annexe) (10 fmly) **Facilities** Spa Wi-fi ⓦ supervised ⚓ 18 ⛳ Putt green Gym Squash Health & beauty centre Xmas New Year **Conf** Class 40 Board 90 Thtr 250 **Parking** 100 **Notes** Civ Wed 200

LOWER BARTLE
Lancashire
Map 18 SD43

Bartle Hall Hotel

★★★★ 71% HOTEL

☎ 01772 690506
Lea Ln PR4 0HA
e-mail: recp@bartlehall.co.uk
dir: M6 junct 32 into Tom Benson Way, follow signs for Woodplumpton

Ideally situated between Preston and Blackpool, Bartle Hall is within easy access of the M6 and the Lake District. Set in its own extensive grounds the hotel offers comfortable, well-equipped and renovated accommodation. The restaurant cuisine uses local produce and there is a large comfortable bar and lounge. There are also extensive conference facilities, and this hotel is a popular wedding venue.

Rooms 15 (2 annexe) (2 fmly) (2 GF) 🐾 **Facilities** FTV Wi-fi ♪ HL New Year **Conf** Class 50 Board 40 Thtr 200 **Parking** 150 **Notes** Closed 25-26 Dec Civ Wed 130

LOWER BEEDING
West Sussex　　　　　　　　　Map 6 TQ22

South Lodge Hotel

★★★★★ 84% ◉◉◉◉
COUNTRY HOUSE HOTEL

☎ 01403 891711
Brighton Rd RH13 6PS
e-mail: enquiries@southlodgehotel.co.uk
web: www.southlodgehotel.co.uk
dir: A23, onto B2110. Right, through Handcross to A281 junct. Left, hotel on right

This impeccably presented 19th-century lodge with stunning views of the rolling South Downs is an ideal retreat. There is the traditional and elegant Camellia Restaurant, offering memorable, seasonal dishes, and The Pass Restaurant, which is an innovative take on the chef's table concept - a mini-restaurant within the kitchen itself. Guests can take a tour of the restored Victorian wine cellar, either with a sommelier or on their own. The elegant lounge is popular for afternoon teas. Bedrooms are individually designed with character and quality throughout. The conference facilities are impressive.

Rooms 89 (11 fmly) (19 GF) ↖ **D** £150-£711 (incl. bkfst)* **Facilities** STV Wi-fi ⌕ ⚓ 36 ⛳ Putt green Fishing ⚓ Gym Mountain biking Archery Clay pigeon shooting Xmas New Year **Conf** Class 100 Board 50 Thtr 170 Del £390* **Services** Lift **Parking** 200 **Notes** LB Civ Wed 130

LOWER SLAUGHTER
Gloucestershire　　　　　　　Map 10 SP12

INSPECTORS' CHOICE

Lower Slaughter Manor
★★★ ◉◉ COUNTRY HOUSE HOTEL

☎ 01451 820456
GL54 2HP
e-mail: info@lowerslaughter.co.uk
web: www.lowerslaughter.co.uk
dir: Exit A429 signed 'The Slaughters'. Manor 0.5m on right on entering village

There is a timeless elegance about this wonderful manor, which dates back to the 17th century. Its imposing presence makes it very much the centrepiece of this famous Cotswold village. Inside, the levels of comfort and quality are immediately evident, with crackling log fires warming the many sumptuous lounges. Spacious and tastefully furnished bedrooms are either in the main building or in the adjacent coach house. Fine dining at the hotel is in the award-winning Sixteen58 Restaurant where the menus are based on local, seasonal produce; special dietary needs can be catered for.

Rooms 19 (8 annexe) (5 fmly) (4 GF) ↖ **S** £330-£875; **D** £350-£895 (incl. bkfst)* **Facilities** STV FTV Wi-fi ⌕ ⚓ ⚓ Xmas New Year **Conf** Class 40 Board 30 Thtr 70 Del from £280* **Parking** 20 **Notes** LB Civ Wed 74

LOWESTOFT
Suffolk　　　　　　　　　　Map 13 TM59

Ivy House Country Hotel
★★★ 85% ◉◉ HOTEL

☎ 01502 501353 & 588144
Ivy Ln, Beccles Rd, Oulton Broad NR33 8HY
e-mail: aa@ivyhousecountryhotel.co.uk
web: www.ivyhousecountryhotel.co.uk
dir: On A146 SW of Oulton Broad turn into Ivy Ln beside Esso petrol station. Over railway bridge, follow private drive

A peacefully located, family-run hotel set in three acres of mature landscaped grounds and just a short walk from Oulton Broad. Public rooms include an 18th-century thatched barn restaurant where an interesting choice of dishes is served. The attractively decorated bedrooms are housed in garden wings, and many have lovely views of the grounds to the countryside beyond.

Rooms 20 (20 annexe) (1 fmly) (17 GF) ↖ **S** £99-£119; **D** £140-£250 (incl. bkfst)* **Facilities** FTV Wi-fi **Conf** Board 22 Thtr 55 Del from £135 to £170* **Parking** 50 **Notes** LB Closed 15 Dec-4 Jan Civ Wed 80

Premier Inn Lowestoft

BUDGET HOTEL

☎ 0871 527 8688
249 Yarmouth Rd NR32 4AA
web: www.premierinn.com
dir: On A12, 2m N of Lowestoft

High quality, budget accommodation ideal for both families and business travellers. Spacious, en suite bedrooms feature tea and coffee making facilities, and Freeview TV in most hotels. Internet access and Wi-fi are available for a small fee. The adjacent family restaurant features a wide and varied menu. See also the Hotel Groups pages.

Rooms 60

Corton Coastal Village　Warner Leisure Hotels
AA Advertised

☎ 01502 730 226
The Street, Corton NR32 5HR
dir: From A1(M)/M1, follow A47 towards Great Yarmouth. Take A12 south approx 8m. At end of dual carriage way left into Corton Long Lane. At end of Corton Long Lane left into The Street, Corton on right

Deckchairs, dancing and seaside fun is what Corton is all about. All breaks at this popular cliff top chalet resort include breakfast and dinner, a range of daytime activities and nightly entertainment.

Rooms 182 (112 GF) ↖ **Facilities** STV FTV Wi-fi ⟳ Putt green Gym Snooker Wii Table Tennis Shuffleboard Archery Rifle shooting ♫ Xmas New Year **Services** Air con **Parking** 180 **Notes** ⊗ No children 21yrs

L

LOWESTOFT *continued*

Gunton Hall Coastal Village

Warner Leisure Hotels
JUST FOR GROWN-UPS

AA Advertised

☎ 01502 730288
Gunton Av NR32 5DF
dir: From A1(M)/M1, follow A47 towards Great Yarmouth. Take A12, heading south approx 8m. At end of dual carriageway take 2nd left into Gunton Avenue. Gunton Hall located at very end

Just a short drive from the beach, this friendly coastal village is set in 50 acres of gardens and secluded woodland. Every break includes breakfast, 3 course dinners a host of daytime activities and fabulous nightly entertainment.

Rooms 202 ♠ **Facilities** Spa FTV Wi-fi Fishing Gym Shuffleboard Rifle shooting Pitch & putt Indoor bowls Archery Shooting **Parking** 120

LUDLOW
Shropshire
Map 10 SO57

INSPECTORS' CHOICE

Fishmore Hall

★★★ ◉◉◉ SMALL HOTEL

☎ 01584 875148
Fishmore Rd SY8 3DP
e-mail: reception@fishmorehall.co.uk
web: www.fishmorehall.co.uk
dir: A49 into Henley Rd. 1st right, Weyman Rd, at bottom of hill right into Fishmore Rd

Located in a rural area within easy reach of the town centre, this Palladian-style Georgian house has been sympathetically renovated and extended to provide high standards of comfort and facilities. The contemporary interior highlights many period features, and public areas include a comfortable lounge and restaurant, the setting for award-winning imaginative cooking.

Rooms 15 (1 GF) ♠ **Facilities** FTV Wi-fi ⛳ 🏊 In room beauty treatments & massage Xmas New Year **Conf** Class 60 Board 40 Thtr 130 **Services** Lift **Parking** 48 **Notes** LB Civ Wed 130

Overton Grange Hotel and Restaurant

★★★ 86% ◉◉ HOTEL

☎ 01584 873500 & 0845 476 1000
Old Hereford Rd SY8 4AD
e-mail: info@overtongrangehotel.com
dir: A49, B4361 to Ludlow. Hotel 200yds on left

This is a traditional country-house hotel with stylish, comfortable bedrooms, and high standards of guest care. Food is an important part of what the hotel has to offer and the restaurant serves classically based, French-style cuisine, using locally sourced produce whenever possible. Meeting and conference rooms are available.

Rooms 14 ♠ **Facilities** Spa FTV Wi-fi ⛳ Xmas **Conf** Class 50 Board 30 Thtr 100 Del £139.50* **Parking** 45 **Notes** ⊗ No children 7yrs Civ Wed 100

Dinham Hall Hotel

★★★ 80% ◉◉ HOTEL

☎ 01584 876464
By The Castle SY8 1EJ
e-mail: info@dinhamhall.com
dir: In town centre, opposite castle

Built in 1792, this lovely house stands in attractive gardens immediately opposite Ludlow Castle, and it has a well-deserved reputation for warm hospitality. The well-equipped bedrooms include two in a converted cottage, and some rooms have four-poster beds. The comfortable public rooms are elegantly appointed. Dishes served in the brasserie-style restaurant are based on good, seasonal produce.

Rooms 13 (2 annexe) (2 fmly) (2 GF) **Facilities** FTV Wi-fi Xmas New Year **Conf** Class 20 Board 26 Thtr 40 **Parking** 16 **Notes** No children 7yrs

The Feathers Hotel

★★★ 80% ◉ HOTEL

☎ 01584 875261
The Bull Ring SY8 1AA
e-mail: enquiries@feathersatludlow.co.uk
web: www.feathersatludlow.co.uk
dir: From A49 follow town centre signs to centre. Hotel on left

Famous for the carved woodwork outside and in, this picture-postcard 17th-century hotel is one of the town's best-known landmarks and is in an excellent location. Bedrooms are traditional both in style and decor. The public areas have retained much of the traditional charm, and the first-floor lounge is particularly stunning. Modern British menus are offered in the smart restaurant which has wooden beams and exposed brickwork.

Rooms 40 (3 fmly) **S** £85-£95; **D** £110-£205 (incl. bkfst)* **Facilities** STV FTV Wi-fi Xmas New Year **Conf** Class 40 Board 40 Thtr 80 Del £139* **Services** Lift **Parking** 33 **Notes** LB Civ Wed 80

Save on hotels. Book at **theAA.com/hotel**

LOW – LUT 299 ENGLAND

Cliffe Hotel

★★ 81% SMALL HOTEL

☎ 01584 872063
Dinham SY8 2JE
e-mail: thecliffehotel@hotmail.com
web: www.thecliffehotel.co.uk
dir: From town centre, left at castle gates to Dinham, over bridge. Right fork, hotel 200yds on left

Built in the 19th century and standing in extensive grounds and gardens, this privately owned and personally run hotel is quietly located close to the castle and the river. It provides well-equipped accommodation, and facilities include a lounge bar, a pleasant restaurant and a patio overlooking the garden.

Rooms 9 (2 fmly) ❦ **S** £53-£68; **D** £68-£100 (incl. bkfst) **Facilities** FTV Wi-fi **Parking** 22 **Notes** RS 24-26 Dec

The Clive Bar & Restaurant with Rooms

◉ ◉ RESTAURANT WITH ROOMS

☎ 01584 856565 & 856665
Bromfield SY8 2JR
e-mail: info@theclive.co.uk
web: www.theclive.co.uk
dir: 2m N of Ludlow on A49 in Bromfield

The Clive is just two miles from the busy town of Ludlow and is a convenient base for visiting the local attractions or for business. The bedrooms, located outside the main restaurant area, are spacious and very well equipped; some are suitable for families and many are on the ground-floor level. Meals are available in the well-known Clive Restaurant or in the bar areas. The property also has a small meeting room.

Rooms 15 (15 annexe) (9 fmly)

Luton Hoo Hotel, Golf and Spa

★★★★★ 83% ◉ ◉ HOTEL

☎ 01582 734437 & 698888
The Mansion House LU1 3TQ
e-mail: reservations@lutonhoo.com
dir: M1 junct 10a, 3rd exit onto A1081 towards Harpenden & St Albans. Hotel approx 1m on left

A luxury hotel in more than 1,000 acres of 'Capability' Brown designed parkland and formal gardens, with an 18-hole, par 73 golf course and the River Lea meandering through. The centrepiece is the Grade I listed Mansion House that has architectural influences by many famous architects including Robert Adams. There are three sumptuous lounges where guests can enjoy afternoon tea and pre-dinner drinks, and two eating options - The Wernher Restaurant and the Adams Brasserie. The spacious bedrooms and impressive suites combine historic character with modern amenities. The Robert Adams Club House is the perfect place for relaxation, with the brasserie, a spa, golf, pool and gym together with two bars, and Warren Weir, at the foot of the estate, on the river bank is an exclusive retreat for weddings and meetings.

Rooms 228 (50 fmly) (65 GF) ❦ **D** £280-£1100 (incl. bkfst) **Facilities** Spa FTV Wi-fi ⊙ ⅃ 18 ⚐ Putt green Fishing ⚐ Gym Bird watching Clay pigeon shooting Archery Falconry Cycling Snooker ♫ Xmas New Year **Conf** Class 220 Board 60 Thtr 388 **Services** Lift **Parking** 316 **Notes** LB Civ Wed 380

Menzies Hotels London Luton - Strathmore

MenziesHotels

★★★★ 77% ◉ HOTEL

☎ 01582 734199
Arndale Centre LU1 2TR
e-mail: strathmore@menzieshotels.co.uk
web: www.menzieshotels.co.uk
dir: Exit M1 junct 10a towards town centre, hotel adjacent to Arndale Centre car park

Situated in the centre of town with adjacent parking, this hotel is convenient for the shopping areas, and many guests stay here prior to catching flights at the nearby airport. The bedrooms are comfortable and well equipped with good facilities. Public areas include a spacious lounge bar and a contemporary brasserie-style restaurant. The Waves Health and Leisure Club offers guests beauty and message therapies plus a pool, sauna and steam room.

Rooms 152 (6 fmly) (21 smoking) ❦ **Facilities** Spa FTV Wi-fi ⅃ HL ⊙ supervised Gym Beauty salon Xmas New Year **Conf** Class 150 Board 60 Thtr 300 **Services** Lift **Parking** 5 **Notes** ⊗ Civ Wed 200

Icon Hotel

★★★ 81% HOTEL

☎ 01582 722123
15 Stuart St LU1 2SA
e-mail: reservations@iconhotelluton.com
dir: M1 junct 10 & 10A, A1081 signed Luton, left follow Luton Retail Park & station signs. Left at next rdbt, left at next rdbt onto A505 (Park Viaduct). Straight on at next rdbt, left into Hastings St

This modern, purpose-built hotel occupies a prominent position close to the town centre and is a short drive from the international airport. The contemporary, open-plan bar is very comfortable and Capello's Restaurant offers a modern Mediterranean menu. The bedrooms are attractively presented and feature the latest technology along with large LCD TVs and complimentary Wi-fi. There is a range of business suites and a well-equipped gym.

Rooms 60 (7 fmly) (5 GF) ❦ **S** £49-£179; **D** £49-£189* **Facilities** FTV Wi-fi ⅃ Gym Therapy treatments by prior arrangement ♫ Xmas New Year **Conf** Class 30 Board 25 Thtr 60 Del from £120 to £165* **Services** Lift Air con **Parking** 18 **Notes** LB ⊗

L

Ibis London Luton Airport

BUDGET HOTEL

☎ 01582 424488
Spittlesea Rd LU2 9NH
e-mail: H1040@accor.com
web: www.ibishotel.com
dir: M1 junct 10, follow signs to Luton Airport. Hotel 600mtrs from airport

Modern, budget hotel offering comfortable accommodation in bright and practical bedrooms. Breakfast is self-service and dinner is available in the restaurant. See also the Hotel Groups pages.

Rooms 162 (8 fmly) ☎ **Conf** Class 18 Board 30 Thtr 60

Premier Inn Luton Airport

BUDGET HOTEL

☎ 0871 527 8690
Osborne Rd LU1 3HJ
web: www.premierinn.com
dir: M1 junct 10, A1081 follow signs for Luton, at 3rd rdbt left into Gypsy Lane, left at next rdbt

High quality, budget accommodation ideal for both families and business travellers. Spacious, en suite bedrooms feature tea and coffee making facilities, and Freeview TV in most hotels. Internet access and Wi-fi are available for a small fee. The adjacent family restaurant features a wide and varied menu. See also the Hotel Groups pages.

Rooms 129

Royal Lion Hotel

★★★ 73% HOTEL

☎ 01297 445622
Broad St DT7 3QF
e-mail: enquiries@royallionhotel.com
web: www.royallionhotel.com
dir: From W on A35 take A3052, or from E take B3165 to Lyme Regis. Hotel in town centre, opposite The Fossil Shop

This 17th-century, former coaching inn is full of character and charm, and is situated a short walk from the seafront. Bedrooms vary in size; those in the newer wing are more spacious and some have balconies, sea views or a private terrace. In addition to the elegant dining room and guest lounges, a heated pool, jacuzzi, sauna and small gym are available. A good selection of enjoyable, well-

prepared dishes is offered in either the bar or main restaurant. There is a car park at the rear.

Rooms 33 (8 fmly) (4 GF) ☎ **S** £75-£80; **D** £110-£120 (incl. bkfst)* **Facilities** FTV Wi-fi ❄ Sauna Games room Snooker tables Table tennis Xmas New Year **Conf** Class 20 Board 20 Thtr 50 **Parking** 33 **Notes** LB

Swallows Eaves Hotel

★★ 85% SMALL HOTEL

☎ 01297 553184
Swan Hill Rd EX24 6QJ
e-mail: info@swallowseaves.co.uk
web: www.swallowseaves.co.uk

(For full entry see Colyford)

Stanwell House Hotel

★★★ 88% ❀❀ HOTEL

☎ 01590 677123
14-15 High St SO41 9AA
e-mail: enquiries@stanwellhouse.com
dir: M27 junct 1, follow signs to Lyndhurst then Lymington

Stanwell House Hotel is a privately owned Georgian building situated on the wide high street only a few minutes from the marina, and a short drive from the New Forest. Styling itself as a boutique hotel, the bedrooms are individually designed; there are Terrace rooms with garden access, four-poster rooms, and Georgian rooms in the older part of the building. The four suites include two with their own roof terrace. Dining options include the informal bistro and the intimate Seafood Restaurant. Service is friendly and attentive. A meeting room is available.

Rooms 29 (7 fmly) (5 GF) ☎ **Facilities** FTV Wi-fi Xmas New Year **Conf** Class 35 Board 30 Thtr 70 Del from £125 to £140* **Parking** 12 **Notes** Civ Wed 100

Macdonald Elmers Court Hotel & Resort

★★★ 82% HOTEL

☎ 0844 879 9060
South Baddesley Rd SO41 5ZB
e-mail: elmerscourt@macdonald-hotels.co.uk
web: www.macdonaldhotels.co.uk
dir: M27 junct 1, through Lyndhurst, Brockenhurst to Lymington, hotel 200yds right after Lymington ferry terminal

Originally known as The Elms, this Tudor manor house dates back to the 1820s. Ideally located at the edge of the New Forest and overlooking The Solent with

views towards the Isle of Wight, the hotel offers suites and self-catering accommodation in the grounds, along with a host of leisure facilities. Macdonald Hotels is the AA Hotel Group of the Year 2013-14.

Rooms 42 (42 annexe) (8 fmly) (22 GF) ☎ **Facilities** Spa FTV Wi-fi ❄ ⳼ supervised ⛳ Putt green ⛳ Gym Squash Steam room Aerobics classes Sauna Table tennis Xmas New Year **Conf** Class 70 Board 40 Thtr 120 **Parking** 100 **Notes** ⊗ Civ Wed 120

Premier Inn Lymington (New Forest Hordle)

BUDGET HOTEL

☎ 0871 527 8692
Silver St, Hordle SO41 0FN
web: www.premierinn.com
dir: M27 junct 1, A337. 3.5m, left into High St (A35) right into Gosport Ln. Left into Clay Hill (A337). Right into Grigg Ln (B3055). Approx 8m, left into Barrows Ln, right into Silver St

High quality, budget accommodation ideal for both families and business travellers. Spacious, en suite bedrooms feature tea and coffee making facilities, and Freeview TV in most hotels. Internet access and Wi-fi are available for a small fee. The adjacent family restaurant features a wide and varied menu. See also the Hotel Groups pages.

Rooms 20

The Lymm Hotel

★★★ 74% HOTEL

☎ 01925 752233
Whitbarrow Rd WA13 9AQ
e-mail: general.lymm@macdonald-hotels.co.uk
web: www.macdonaldhotels.co.uk/lymm
dir: M6 junct 20, B5158 to Lymm. Left at junct, 1st right, left at mini-rdbt, into Brookfield Rd, 3rd left into Whitbarrow Rd

In a peaceful residential area, this hotel benefits from both a quiet setting and convenient access to local motorway networks. It offers comfortable bedrooms equipped for both the business and leisure guest. Public areas include an attractive bar and an elegant restaurant. There is also extensive parking. Macdonald Hotels is the AA Hotel Group of the Year 2013-14.

Rooms 62 (38 annexe) (5 fmly) (11 GF) ☎ **S** £57-£97; **D** £57-£97* **Facilities** STV Wi-fi Xmas New Year **Conf** Class 60 Board 40 Thtr 120 Del from £99 to £120* **Parking** 75 **Notes** Civ Wed 100

Save on hotels. Book at **theAA.com/hotel**

LUT – LYN 301 **ENGLAND**

LYNDHURST
Hampshire
Map 5 SU30

INSPECTORS' CHOICE

Lime Wood

★★★★★ ◉◉◉

COUNTRY HOUSE HOTEL

☎ 023 8028 7177
Beaulieu Rd SO43 7FZ
e-mail: info@limewood.co.uk
dir: Exit A35 onto B3056 towards Beaulieu, hotel 1m on right

This meticulously restored country house situated deep in the New Forest, provides a wealth of facilities and much opulence. The hotel prides itself on its relaxed, friendly and attentive service, and has lots to interest and captivate. The luxurious bedrooms are notable; some are in the pavilion and some in the main house. Recent changes have seen the end of The Dining Room and The Scullery and the creation of a single restaurant, Hartnett Holder & Co which will be headed up by current head Chef Luke Holder, and Angela Hartnett. The Herb House spa offers a hydro therapy pool and many other excellent facilities along with a gym and steam room.

Rooms 32 (16 annexe) (5 fmly) (4 GF) ⌂
D £195-£315* **Facilities** Spa STV FTV Wi-fi ⌂ ☒
Gym Xmas New Year **Conf** Board 30 Thtr 50
Del from £325 to £365* **Services** Lift **Parking** 60
Notes LB Civ Wed 80

BEST WESTERN Forest Lodge Hotel

NEW FOREST HOTELS

★★★ 83% ◉◉ HOTEL

☎ 023 8028 3677 & 0800 444 441
Pikes Hill, Romsey Rd SO43 7AS
e-mail: forest@newforesthotels.co.uk
web: www.newforesthotels.co.uk
dir: M27 junct 1, A337 towards Lyndhurst. In village, with police station & courts on right, take 1st right into Pikes Hill

Situated on the edge of Lyndhurst, this hotel is set well back from the main road. The smart,

contemporary bedrooms include four-poster rooms and family rooms; children are very welcome here. The eating options are the Forest Restaurant and the fine-dining Glasshouse Restaurant. There is an indoor swimming pool and Nordic sauna.

Rooms 36 (11 fmly) (10 GF) ⌂ **S** £119; **D** £197 (incl. bkfst)* **Facilities** FTV Wi-fi ⌂ ☒ Xmas New Year
Conf Class 70 Board 60 Thtr 120 Del £141.60
Parking 50 **Notes** LB Civ Wed 60

The Bell Inn

★★★ 82% ◉ HOTEL

☎ 023 8081 2214
SO43 7HE
e-mail: bell@bramshaw.co.uk
web: www.bellinnbramshaw.co.uk

(For full entry see Brook (Near Cadnam))

The Crown Manor House Hotel

★★★ 77% HOTEL

☎ 023 8028 2922
9 High St SO43 7NF
e-mail: stay@crownhotel-lyndhurst.co.uk
dir: 4m from M27 junct 1. Turn off at Stoney Cross after Lyndurst exit, pass Rufus Stone Services & take Emery Down exit. Hotel opposite church

Occupying a prime spot on the high street stands this Edwardian styled country house, with its stone mullioned windows, wood panelled rooms and period features. Bedrooms are generally spacious and offer a well-chosen range of facilities. Public rooms are versatile and include meeting and function rooms. There is also a pleasant garden and terrace.

Rooms 50 (7 fmly) ⌂ **D** £72-£255 (incl. bkfst)*
Facilities FTV Wi-fi ⌂ Xmas New Year **Conf** Class 80
Board 40 Thtr 120 **Services** Lift Air con **Parking** 60
Notes Civ Wed 120

Penny Farthing Hotel

★★★ 74% METRO HOTEL

☎ 023 8028 4422
Romsey Rd SO43 7AA
e-mail: stay@pennyfarthinghotel.co.uk
dir: M27 junct 1, A337 to Lyndhurst. Hotel on left after White Rabbit Inn

This friendly, well-appointed establishment on the edge of town is suitable for business or for exploring the New Forest area. The attractive bedrooms are well-equipped, and some are located in an adjacent cottage. There is a spacious breakfast room, a comfortable lounge bar and a cycle store.

Rooms 20 (4 annexe) (1 fmly) (1 GF) ⌂
S £52.50-£78; **D** £78-£118 (incl. bkfst)*
Facilities FTV Wi-fi ⌂ **Parking** 26 **Notes** ☒ Closed Xmas week

Ormonde House Hotel

★★★ 70% METRO HOTEL

☎ 023 8028 2806
Southampton Rd SO43 7BT
e-mail: enquiries@ormondehouse.co.uk
web: www.ormondehouse.co.uk
dir: M27/M271/A35 E through Ashurst, hotel on right on entering Lyndhurst

Ormonde House is located on the edge of Lyndhurst village in the heart of the New Forest, and provides comfortable en suite accommodation, with breakfast served in the dining room and conservatory. It is dog friendly with ample off-street parking. The ideal location for all New Forest activities and attractions.

Rooms 22 (4 annexe) (2 fmly) (7 GF) ⌂ **S** £65-£85;
D £79-£139 (incl. bkfst)* **Facilities** FTV Wi-fi New Year **Parking** 22 **Notes** LB Closed 13-27 Dec

LYNMOUTH
Devon
Map 3 SS74

Tors Hotel

★★★ 79% ◉ HOTEL

☎ 01598 753236
EX35 6NA
e-mail: info@torshotellynmouth.co.uk
dir: Adjacent to A39 on Countisbury Hill just before entering Lynmouth from Minehead

In an elevated position overlooking Lynmouth Bay, this friendly hotel is set in five acres of woodland and has recently undergone a transformation. Stylish public areas showcase an eclectic collection of objets d'art and antiques, interspersed with lovely comfy sofas. The hotel even has its own cinema and superb outdoor terraces with unrivalled views of the bay. The majority of the bedrooms also benefit from the wonderful outlook with a variety of options available. In the AA rosette restaurant you will find a relaxed atmosphere with superb quality food, an excellent wine list and probably the best views in the village. The whole family will find a warm welcome in the restaurant and as much care will be taken with your little one's ice cream as with your carefully prepared main meal.

Rooms 28 (5 fmly) **S** £85-£210; **D** £130-£260 (incl. bkfst)* **Facilities** STV FTV Wi-fi Xmas New Year
Conf Class 40 Board 25 Thtr 60 **Services** Lift
Parking 40 **Notes** LB Closed 7 Nov-7 Dec Civ Wed 70

L

LYNMOUTH *continued*

Rising Sun Hotel

★★ 80% ● HOTEL

☎ 01598 753223
Harbourside EX35 6EG
e-mail: reception@risingsunlynmouth.co.uk
web: www.risingsunlynmouth.co.uk
dir: M5 junct 23, A39 to Minehead. Hotel on harbour

This delightful thatched establishment, once a smugglers' inn, sits on the harbour front. Popular with locals and guests alike, there is the option of eating in either the convivial bar or the restaurant; a comfortable, quiet lounge is also available. Bedrooms, located in the inn and adjoining cottages, are individually designed and have modern facilities.

Rooms 14 (1 fmly) (1 GF) **Facilities** Xmas

Bath Hotel

★★ 72% HOTEL

☎ 01598 752238
Sea Front EX35 6EL
e-mail: info@bathhotellynmouth.co.uk
dir: M5 junct 25, A39 to Lynmouth

This well established, friendly hotel, situated near the harbour, offers lovely views from the attractive, sea-facing bedrooms and is an excellent starting point for scenic walks. There are two lounges and a sun lounge. The restaurant menu is extensive, and features daily-changing specials that make good use of fresh produce and local fish.

Rooms 22 (9 fmly) **S** £45-£55; **D** £75-£120 (incl. bkfst)* **Facilities** FTV Wi-fi **Parking** 12 **Notes** Closed Dec & Jan RS Nov & Feb

LYTHAM ST ANNES   Map 18 SD32
Lancashire

Clifton Arms Hotel

★★★★ 76% ● HOTEL

☎ 01253 739898
West Beach, Lytham FY8 5QJ
e-mail: welcome@cliftonarms-lytham.com
web: www.cliftonarms-lytham.com
dir: On A584 along seafront

This well established hotel occupies a prime position overlooking Lytham Green and the Ribble Estuary beyond. Bedrooms vary in size and are appointed to a high standard; front-facing rooms are particularly spacious and enjoy splendid views. There is an elegant restaurant, a stylish open-plan lounge and cocktail bar, as well as function and conference facilities.

Rooms 48 (2 fmly) ✦ **S** £75-£105; **D** £120-£200 (incl. bkfst)* **Facilities** STV FTV Wi-fi Xmas New Year **Conf** Class 100 Board 60 Thtr 200 **Services** Lift **Parking** 40 **Notes** LB ⊗ Civ Wed 100

Bedford Hotel

★★★ 82% ● HOTEL

☎ 01253 724636
307-313 Clifton Drive South FY8 1HN
e-mail: reservations@bedford-hotel.com
web: www.bedford-hotel.com
dir: From M55 follow signs for airport to last lights. Left through 2 sets of lights. Hotel 300yds on left

This popular family-run hotel is close to the town centre and the seafront. Bedrooms vary in size and style and include superior and club class rooms. The newer bedrooms are particularly elegant and tastefully appointed. Spacious public areas include a choice of lounges, a coffee shop, fitness facilities and an impressive function suite.

Rooms 45 (6 GF) ✦ **S** £55-£75; **D** £90-£120 (incl. bkfst)* **Facilities** FTV Wi-fi ⌨ Gym Hydrotherapy spa bath Beauty treatment room Xmas New Year **Conf** Class 140 Board 60 Thtr 200 **Services** Lift **Parking** 25 **Notes** LB ⊗ Civ Wed 150

BEST WESTERN Glendower Promenade Hotel

★★★ 80% HOTEL

☎ 01253 723241
North Promenade FY8 2NQ
e-mail: recp@theglendowerhotel.co.uk
web: www.theglendowerhotel.co.uk
dir: M55 follow airport signs. Left at Promenade to St Annes. Hotel 500yds from pier

Located on the seafront and with easy access to the town centre, this popular, friendly hotel offers comfortably furnished, well-equipped accommodation. Bedrooms vary in size and style, and include four-poster rooms and very popular family suites. Public areas feature a choice of smart, comfortable lounges, a bright, modern leisure club and function facilities.

Rooms 60 (17 fmly) **Facilities** FTV Wi-fi ⌨ Gym Nintendo Wii play area Snooker table ♫ Xmas New Year **Conf** Class 120 Board 50 Thtr 150 **Services** Lift **Parking** 45 **Notes** Civ Wed 150

Chadwick Hotel

★★★ 75% HOTEL

☎ 01253 720061
South Promenade FY8 1NP
e-mail: info@thechadwickhotel.com
web: www.thechadwickhotel.com
dir: M6 junct 32, M55 to Blackpool, A5230 to South Shore. Follow signs for St Annes, hotel on Promenade's south end

This popular, comfortable and traditional hotel enjoys a seafront location. Bedrooms vary in size and style, but all are very thoughtfully equipped; those at the front boast panoramic sea views. Public rooms are spacious and comfortably furnished and the smart bar is stocked with some 200 malt whiskies. The hotel has a well-equipped, air-conditioned gym and indoor pool.

Rooms 73 (28 fmly) (13 GF) ✦ **S** £58-£85; **D** £96-£150 (incl. bkfst & dinner) **Facilities** FTV Wi-fi ⌨ Gym Turkish bath Games room Soft play adventure area Wii room Sauna ♫ Xmas New Year Child facilities **Conf** Class 24 Board 28 Thtr 70 Del from £120 to £135 **Services** Lift **Parking** 40 **Notes** ⊗

MACCLESFIELD   Map 16 SJ97
Cheshire

Shrigley Hall Hotel, Golf & Country Club

★★★★ 78% ● HOTEL

☎ 01625 575757
Shrigley Park, Pott Shrigley SK10 5SB
e-mail: shrigleyhall@pumahotels.co.uk
web: www.pumahotels.co.uk
dir: Exit A523 at Legh Arms towards Pott Shrigley. Hotel 2m on left before village

Originally built in 1825, Shrigley Hall is an impressive hotel set in 262 acres of mature parkland, commanding stunning views of the countryside. Features include a championship golf course. There is a wide choice of bedroom sizes and styles. The public areas are spacious, combining traditional and contemporary decor, and include a well-equipped gym.

Save on hotels. Book at **theAA.com/hotel**

LYN – MAI 303 ENGLAND

Rooms 148 (11 fmly) **Facilities** Spa STV Wi-fi 🕲 supervised ⅃ 18 🏌 Putt green Fishing Gym Beauty salon Hydro centre ♫ Xmas New Year **Conf** Class 110 Board 42 Thtr 180 **Services** Lift **Parking** 300 **Notes** Civ Wed 150

Hollin Hall Country House Hotel & Restaurant

★★★ 75% HOTEL

☎ 08444 119072 & 0330 333 2872
Jackson Ln, Kerridge, Bollington SK10 5BG
e-mail: events@hollinhallhotel.com
dir: From Macclesfield A523 (The Silk Road) towards Bollington, at rdbt right onto B5090 signed Bollington. 1st right signed Kerridge. 2.5m, hotel entrance on left

Within easy reach of the Peak District and visitor attractions, this elegant Victorian hotel offers a combination of traditional and contemporary design. Beautifully maintained period features are complemented by stylish, smartly presented decor and furnishings. Bedrooms are well equipped and cater well for both leisure and business guests; complimentary Wi-fi is provided.

Rooms 58 (5 fmly) (16 GF) 🐾 **S** £50-£90; **D** £59-£100* **Facilities** FTV Wi-fi ☙ Gym Xmas New Year **Conf** Class 50 Board 50 Thtr 120 Del from £109 to £159* **Services** Lift **Parking** 75 **Notes** LB Civ Wed 120

Premier Inn Macclesfield North

BUDGET HOTEL

☎ 0871 527 8694
Tytherington Business Park, Springwood Way, Tytherington SK10 2XA
web: www.premierinn.com
dir: On A523 in Tytherington Business Park

High quality, budget accommodation ideal for both families and business travellers. Spacious, en suite bedrooms feature tea and coffee making facilities, and Freeview TV in most hotels. Internet access and Wi-fi are available for a small fee. The adjacent family restaurant features a wide and varied menu. See also the Hotel Groups pages.

Rooms 41

Premier Inn Macclesfield South West

BUDGET HOTEL

☎ 0871 527 8696
Congleton Rd, Gawsworth SK11 7XD
web: www.premierinn.com
dir: M6 junct 17, A534 towards Congleton, A536 towards Macclesfield to Gawsworth. Hotel on left

Rooms 28

MAIDENCOMBE

See **Torquay**

MAIDENHEAD
Berkshire
Map 6 SU88

Fredrick's Hotel Restaurant Spa

★★★★ 81% ⊛⊛ HOTEL

☎ 01628 581000
Shoppenhangers Rd SL6 2PZ
e-mail: reservations@fredricks-hotel.co.uk
web: www.fredricks-hotel.co.uk
dir: M4 junct 8/9 onto A404(M) to Maidenhead West & Henley. 1st exit 9a to White Waltham. Left into Shoppenhangers Rd to Maidenhead, hotel on right

Just half an hour from London, this delightful hotel enjoys a peaceful location yet is within easy reach of the M4 and a short drive from Wentworth and Sunningdale golf courses. The spacious bedrooms are comfortably furnished and very well equipped. An enthusiastic team of staff ensure friendly and efficient service. The imaginative cuisine is a highlight, as is the luxurious spa that offers the ultimate in relaxation and wellbeing.

Rooms 34 (11 GF) **Facilities** Spa FTV Wi-fi ☙ 🕲 supervised ↖ supervised Gym Rasul suite Oriental steam Dead Sea floatation room **Conf** Class 80 Board 60 Thtr 120 Del from £199 to £245* **Services** Air con **Parking** 90 **Notes** ⊛ Closed 24 Dec-3 Jan Civ Wed 120

Holiday Inn Maidenhead/ Windsor

★★★★ 73% HOTEL

☎ 0871 942 9053 & 01628 506000
Manor Ln SL6 2RA
e-mail: reservations-maidenhead@ihg.com
web: www.himaidenheadhotel.co.uk
dir: A404 towards High Wycombe. Exit at junct 9A. Left at mini rdbt. Hotel on right

Located close to Maidenhead town centre with transport links to Windsor and the M4, this well sited hotel is suitable for both the business and leisure

traveller. Public areas include a spacious lounge bar, brasserie-style restaurant and extensive conference facilities. The popular leisure club includes swimming pool and a full gym.

Rooms 197 (23 fmly) (56 GF) 🐾 **S** £49-£149; **D** £49-£149* **Facilities** STV Wi-fi ☙ HL 🕲 supervised Gym Steam room Sauna New Year **Conf** Class 200 Board 100 Thtr 400 Del from £99 to £169* **Services** Lift Air con **Parking** 250 **Notes** LB ⊛ Civ Wed 400

MAIDSTONE
Kent
Map 7 TQ75

Tudor Park, A Marriott Hotel & Country Club

★★★★ 78% HOTEL

☎ 01622 734334 & 632004
Ashford Rd, Bearsted ME14 4NQ
e-mail: mhrs.tdmgs.frontdesk@marriotthotels.com
web: www.marriotttudorpark.co.uk
dir: M20 junct 8 to Lenham. At rdbt follow Bearsted & Maidstone signs on A20. Hotel 1m on left

Located on the outskirts of Maidstone in a wooded valley below Leeds Castle, this fine country hotel is set in 220 acres of parkland. Spacious bedrooms provide good levels of comfort and a comprehensive range of extras. Facilities include a championship golf course, a fully equipped gym and two dining options.

Rooms 120 (48 fmly) (60 GF) **S** fr £89; **D** fr £99 (incl. bkfst)* **Facilities** Spa Wi-fi 🕲 ⅃ 18 🏌 Putt green Gym Driving range Beauty salon Steam room Xmas New Year **Conf** Class 100 Board 60 Thtr 250 Del from £130* **Services** Lift **Parking** 250 **Notes** ⊛ Civ Wed 160

Grange Moor Hotel

★★★ 🅰

☎ 01622 677623
4-8 St Michael's Rd ME16 8BS
e-mail: reservations@grangemoor.co.uk
dir: From town centre towards A26 (Tonbridge road). Hotel 0.25m on left, just after church

This establishment is easily recognised by the colourful hanging baskets in summer. It offers 50 well-appointed bedrooms that have TV, radio alarm clock, hairdryer, and tea- and coffee-making facilities. There is a guest lounge area and a Tudor-style bar and restaurant.

Rooms 50 (11 annexe) (5 fmly) (7 GF) 🐾 **S** £48.45-£61; **D** £58.65-£75 (incl. bkfst)* **Facilities** FTV Wi-fi **Conf** Class 60 Board 40 Thtr 100 **Parking** 60 **Notes** LB ⊛ Closed 23-30 Dec Civ Wed

M

MAIDSTONE *continued*

Premier Inn Maidstone (A26/Wateringbury)

BUDGET HOTEL

☎ 0871 527 8706
103 Tonbridge Rd, Wateringbury ME18 5NS
web: www.premierinn.com
dir: M25 junct 3 onto M20. Exit at junct 4 onto A228
towards West Malling. A26 towards Maidstone, approx
3m

High quality, budget accommodation ideal for both
families and business travellers. Spacious, en suite
bedrooms feature tea and coffee making facilities,
and Freeview TV in most hotels. Internet access and
Wi-fi are available for a small fee. The adjacent
family restaurant features a wide and varied menu.
See also the Hotel Groups pages.

Rooms 40

Premier Inn Maidstone (Allington)

BUDGET HOTEL

☎ 0871 527 8698
London Rd ME16 0HG
web: www.premierinn.com
dir: M20 junct 5, 0.5m on London Rd towards
Maidstone

Rooms 40

Premier Inn Maidstone (Leybourne)

BUDGET HOTEL

☎ 0871 527 8702
Castle Way, Leybourne, West Malling ME19 5TR
web: www.premierinn.com
dir: M20 junct 4, A228, hotel on left

Rooms 40

Premier Inn Maidstone (Sandling)

BUDGET HOTEL

☎ 0871 527 8704
Allington Lock, Sandling ME14 3AS
web: www.premierinn.com
dir: M20 junct 6, follow Museum of Kent Life signs

Rooms 40

MALMESBURY   Map 4 ST98
Wiltshire

INSPECTORS' CHOICE

Whatley Manor Hotel and Spa

★★★★★ ◎◎◎◎ HOTEL

☎ 01666 822888
Easton Grey SN16 0RB
e-mail: reservations@whatleymanor.com
web: www.whatleymanor.com
dir: M4 junct 17, follow signs to Malmesbury,
continue over 2 rdbts. Follow B4040 & signs for
Sherston, hotel 2m on left

Sitting in 12 acres of beautiful countryside, this
impressive country house provides the most
luxurious surroundings. Spacious bedrooms, most
with views over the attractive gardens, are
individually decorated with splendid features such
as Bang & Olufsen sound and vision systems and
unique works of art. Several eating options are
available: Le Mazot, a Swiss-style brasserie, The
Dining Room that serves classical French cuisine
with a contemporary twist via carte and tasting
menus, plus the Kitchen Garden Terrace for alfresco
breakfasts, lunches and dinners. Guests might
even like to take a hamper and a picnic rug and
find a quiet spot in the grounds. The old Loggia
Barn is ideal for wedding ceremonies, and the
Aquarius Spa is magnificent.

Rooms 23 (4 GF) ✺ **S** £305-£865; **D** £305-£865
(incl. bkfst)* **Facilities** Spa STV Wi-fi ⓧ Fishing
Gym Cinema Hydro pool (indoor/outdoor) Xmas New
Year **Conf** Class 20 Board 24 Thtr 60 Del £325*
Services Lift **Parking** 100 **Notes** LB No children
12yrs Civ Wed 120

Old Bell Hotel

★★★ 81% ◎◎ HOTEL

☎ 01666 822344
Abbey Row SN16 0BW
e-mail: info@oldbellhotel.com
web: www.oldbellhotel.com
dir: M4 junct 17, A429 N. Left at 1st rdbt. Left at
T-junct. Hotel adjacent to Abbey

Dating back to 1220, the wisteria-clad Old Bell is
reputed to be the oldest purpose-built hotel in
England. Bedrooms vary in size and style; those in the
main house tend to be more spacious and are
traditionally furnished with antiques, while the newer
bedrooms in the coach house have a contemporary
feel. Guests have a choice of comfortable sitting
areas and dining options, including the main
restaurant where the award-winning cuisine is based
on high quality ingredients.

Rooms 33 (15 annexe) (7 GF) ✺ **S** £89.50;
D £115-£275 (incl. bkfst)* **Facilities** FTV Wi-fi Xmas
New Year **Conf** Class 32 Board 32 Thtr 60
Del from £175 to £225* **Parking** 33 **Notes** LB
Civ Wed 90

BEST WESTERN Mayfield House Hotel

★★★ 74% ◎ HOTEL

☎ 01666 577409
Crudwell SN16 9EW
e-mail: reception@mayfieldhousehotel.co.uk
web: www.mayfieldhousehotel.co.uk
dir: M4 junct 17, A429 to Cirencester. 2m N of
Malmesbury on left in Crudwell village

This popular hotel is in an ideal location for exploring
the many attractions that Wiltshire and The
Cotswolds have to offer. Bedrooms come in a range of
shapes and sizes, and include some on the ground-
floor level in a cottage adjacent to the main building.
In addition to outdoor seating, guests can relax with a
drink in the comfortable lounge area where orders are
taken for the carefully prepared dinner to follow.

Rooms 28 (8 annexe) (4 fmly) (8 GF) ✺ **S** £68-£78;
D £88-£108 (incl. bkfst)* **Facilities** FTV Wi-fi ⓧ ⬧
Xmas New Year **Conf** Class 30 Board 25 Thtr 40
Del from £95 to £125 **Parking** 50 **Notes** LB

Save on hotels. Book at **theAA.com/hotel**

MAI – MAL 305 **ENGLAND**

MALTON
North Yorkshire   Map 19 SE77

The Talbot Hotel

★★★★ 85% ⊛⊛ HOTEL

☎ 01653 639096
Yorkersgate YO17 7AJ
e-mail: info@talbotmalton.co.uk
dir: From York take A64, exit at Malton sign. Hotel on right

This hotel is owned by the Fitzwilliam Estate and is set in its own beautifully landscaped grounds close to the historic market town. The newly designed interior features individually decorated bedrooms, including two luxurious suites. Each of the guest rooms has been given a distinct personality. The restaurant has elegant furniture, crisp white linen and fine silver cutlery, and with James Martin as executive chef the best of Yorkshire produce is sure to be on offer. Elegant public areas can be found throughout this stunning hotel.

Rooms 26 (3 GF) ☾ **S** £85-£190; **D** £99-£295 (incl. bkfst) **Facilities** FTV Wi-fi HL Xmas New Year **Conf** Class 30 Board 24 Thtr 60 **Parking** 35 **Notes** LB Civ Wed

MALVERN
Worcestershire   Map 10 SO74

The Malvern

★★★★ 75% ⊛ HOTEL

☎ 01684 898290
Grovewood Rd WR14 1GD
e-mail: enquiries@themalvernspa.com
dir: A4440 to Malvern. Over 2 rdbts, at 3rd rdbt turn left. 6m, left at rdbt, over 1st rdbt, hotel on right

This modern, friendly hotel is set on the outskirts of the famous spa town. The bedrooms are contemporary with sumptuous beds, and many guest extras are provided; the bathrooms have quality fixtures and fittings. There is a brasserie restaurant which offers quality seasonal menus that include healthy options and vegetarian dishes. The Malvern Spa, designed exclusively for adults, includes a hydrotherapy pool which goes from inside to outside, heat experiences, a range of saunas, crystal steam room, salt grotto, adventure showers along with a host of treatments. There is also a 50-station gym with state-of-the-art equipment. There is ample parking around the hotel.

Rooms 32 ☾ **S** £85-£145; **D** £99-£159 (incl. bkfst)*
Facilities Spa FTV Wi-fi ⊗ ⊀ Gym Exercise classes Xmas New Year **Conf** Class 40 Board 20 Thtr 80 Del from £145 to £165* **Services** Lift Air con **Parking** 82 **Notes** ⊗ No children 18yrs

The Abbey Hotel

★★★★ 74% HOTEL   SAROVA HOTELS

☎ 01684 892332 & 897897
Abbey Rd WR14 3ET
e-mail: abbey@sarova.co.uk
dir: In Great Malvern town centre, opposite theatres

This large, impressive, ivy-clad hotel stands in the centre of Great Malvern, at the foot of the Malvern Hills, next to the Abbey and close to the theatre. It provides well-equipped modern accommodation equally suitable for business guests and tourists. Facilities include a good range of function rooms making the hotel a popular venue for meetings and events.

Rooms 103 (11 fmly) (23 GF) **S** £80-£170; **D** £90-£180 (incl. bkfst)* **Facilities** STV FTV Wi-fi ⊗ Xmas New Year **Conf** Class 120 Board 40 Thtr 300 Del from £99 to £140* **Services** Lift **Parking** 85 **Notes** LB Civ Wed 300

The Cottage in the Wood Hotel

★★★ 86% ⊛⊛ HOTEL

☎ 01684 588860
Holywell Rd, Malvern Wells WR14 4LG
e-mail: reception@cottageinthewood.co.uk
web: www.cottageinthewood.co.uk
dir: 3m S of Great Malvern off A449, 500yds N of B4209, on opposite side of road

Sitting high up on a wooded hillside, this delightful, family-run hotel boasts stunning views over the Severn Valley. The bedrooms are divided between the main house, Beech Cottage and the Pinnacles. The public areas are very stylishly decorated, and imaginative food is served in an elegant dining room, overlooking the immaculate grounds.

The Cottage in the Wood Hotel

Rooms 30 (23 annexe) (9 GF) ☾ **S** £79-£121; **D** £99-£198 (incl. bkfst)* **Facilities** FTV Wi-fi Xmas New Year **Conf** Board 14 Thtr 20 Del £159* **Parking** 40 **Notes** LB

Colwall Park Hotel

★★★ 82% ⊛⊛ HOTEL

☎ 01684 540000
Walwyn Rd, Colwall WR13 6QG
e-mail: hotel@colwall.com
web: www.colwall.co.uk
dir: Between Malvern & Ledbury in centre of Colwall on B4218

Standing in extensive gardens, this hotel was purpose built in the early 20th century to serve the local racetrack. Today the proprietors and loyal staff provide high levels of hospitality and service. The Seasons Restaurant has a well-deserved reputation for its cuisine. Bedrooms are tastefully appointed and public areas help to create a fine country-house atmosphere.

Rooms 22 (1 fmly) ☾ **S** £79-£95; **D** £100-£175 (incl. bkfst)* **Facilities** FTV Wi-fi ⊗ ⊛ Boules Xmas New Year **Conf** Class 80 Board 50 Thtr 150 Del from £130 to £150* **Parking** 40 **Notes** LB ⊗

M

MALVERN *continued*

The Cotford Hotel & L'Amuse Bouche Restaurant

★★★ 80% ◉◉ HOTEL

☎ 01684 572427
51 Graham Rd WR14 2HU
e-mail: reservations@cotfordhotel.co.uk
web: www.cotfordhotel.co.uk
dir: From Worcester follow signs to Malvern on A449.
Left into Graham Rd signed town centre, hotel on
right

This delightful house, built in 1851, reputedly for the
Bishop of Worcester, stands in attractive gardens
with stunning views of The Malverns. Bedrooms have
been authentically renovated, retaining many of the
original features and with a good selection of
welcome extras. Food, service and hospitality are all
major strengths.

Rooms 15 (3 fmly) (1 GF) ⚲ **S** £67.50-£85;
D £120-£135 (incl. bkfst) **Facilities** STV FTV Wi-fi ⓑ
⚬ **Conf** Class 26 Board 12 Thtr 26 **Parking** 15
Notes LB

See advert on opposite page

The Malvern Hills Hotel

★★★ 80% HOTEL

☎ 01684 540690
Wynds Point WR13 6DW
web: www.malvernhillshotel.co.uk
dir: 4m S, at junct of A449 & B4232

This 19th-century hostelry is situated to the west of
Malvern, opposite the British Camp, which was
fortified and occupied by the Ancient Britons. The
bedrooms are well equipped and benefit from smart

modern bathrooms. Public areas include a choice of
bars, retaining original features, modern conference
facilities and an attractive restaurant.

Rooms 15 (2 fmly) (3 GF) ⚲ **S** £80-£85; **D** £115-£140
(incl. bkfst)* **Facilities** FTV Wi-fi Xmas New Year
Conf Class 24 Board 30 Thtr 40 **Parking** 45

Mount Pleasant Hotel

★★★ 70% HOTEL

☎ 01684 561837
Belle Vue Ter WR14 4PZ
e-mail: reception@mountpleasanthotel.co.uk
web: www.mountpleasanthotel.co.uk
dir: On A449, in town centre opposite Priory Church

Mount Pleasant is an attractive Georgian house in the
town centre that occupies an elevated position, and
overlooks Priory Church and the picturesque Severn
Plain. This family-run hotel, with a relaxed
atmosphere, offers spacious, fully equipped
bedrooms, and the Spring Bar and Restaurant serves
home-made classic British cuisine as well as tea,
coffee, cakes and biscuits. In winter guests can sit
beside real log fires, and in warmer months the
garden makes a delightful place to relax.

Rooms 14 (1 fmly) ⚲ **S** £74; **D** £105-£125 (incl.
bkfst)* **Facilities** FTV Wi-fi Hair salon Complementary
therapists Xmas New Year **Conf** Class 40 Board 50
Thtr 90 **Parking** 20 **Notes** LB ⊗

Holdfast Cottage Hotel

★★ 81% HOTEL

☎ 01684 310288
Marlbank Rd, Welland WR13 6NA
e-mail: enquiries@holdfast-cottage.co.uk
web: www.holdfast-cottage.co.uk
dir: M50 junct 1, follow Upton Three Counties/A38
signs, onto A4104 to Welland

At the base of the Malvern Hills this delightful
wisteria-covered hotel sits in attractive manicured
grounds. Charming public areas include an intimate
bar, a log fire enhanced lounge and an elegant dining
room. Bedrooms vary in size but all are comfortable
and well appointed. Fresh local and seasonal produce
are the basis for the cuisine.

Rooms 8 (1 fmly) **S** fr £55; **D** fr £99 (incl. bkfst)
Facilities FTV Wi-fi ⓑ Xmas New Year **Conf** Class 30
Board 30 Thtr 26 Del from £180 to £250 **Parking** 16
Notes Civ Wed 50

The Great Malvern Hotel

★★ 72% HOTEL

☎ 01684 563411
Graham Rd WR14 2HN
e-mail: sutton@great-malvern-hotel.co.uk
dir: From Worcester on A449, left after fire station into
Graham Rd. Hotel at end on right

Close to the town centre this privately owned and
managed hotel is ideally situated for many of
Malvern's attractions. The accommodation is
spacious and well equipped. Public areas include
quiet lounge areas, and a cosy bar which is popular
with locals.

Rooms 13 (1 fmly) **S** £55-£65; **D** £70-£85 (incl.
bkfst)* **Facilities** STV FTV Wi-fi ⓑ ♫ **Conf** Class 20
Board 20 Thtr 20 **Services** Lift **Parking** 9 **Notes** LB

MANCHESTER	Map 16 SJ89
Greater Manchester	

See also **Manchester Airport & Sale**

The Lowry Hotel

★★★★★ 84% ◉◉ HOTEL

THE ROCCO FORTE COLLECTION

☎ 0161 827 4000
50 Dearmans Place, Chapel Wharf, Salford M3 5LH
e-mail: enquiries.lowry@roccofortehotels.com
web: www.roccofortehotels.com
dir: M6 junct 19, A556/M56/A5103 for 4.5m. At rdbt
take A57(M) to lights, right onto Water St. Left to New
Quay St/Trinity Way. At 1st lights right into Chapel St
for hotel

This modern, contemporary hotel, set beside the River
Irwell in the centre of the city, offers spacious
bedrooms equipped to meet the needs of business
and leisure visitors alike. Many of the rooms look out
over the river, as do the sumptuous suites. The River
Room restaurant produces good brasserie cooking.
Extensive business and function facilities are
available, together with a spa to provide extra
pampering.

Rooms 165 (7 fmly) ⚲ **S** £129-£589; **D** £129-£589*
Facilities Spa STV FTV Wi-fi ⓑ HL Gym Swimming
facilities available nearby ♫ Xmas New Year
Conf Class 250 Board 60 Thtr 400 **Services** Lift
Air con **Parking** 100 **Notes** LB Civ Wed 400

Save on hotels. Book at **theAA.com/hotel**

MAL – MAN 307 ENGLAND

The Midland

★★★★ 86% ◉◉◉ HOTEL

☎ 0161 236 3333
Peter St M60 2DS
e-mail: midlandsales@qhotels.co.uk
web: www.qhotels.co.uk
dir: M602 junct 3, follow Manchester Central
Convention Complex signs, hotel opposite

This much loved, centrally located, well-established
Edwardian-style hotel (Grade II listed) offers stylish,
thoughtfully equipped bedrooms that have a
contemporary feel. Elegant public areas are equally
impressive and facilities include extensive function
and meeting rooms. Eating options include the
award-winning French by Simon Rogan, the Octogan
Lounge and the Wyvern Restaurant.

Rooms 312 (13 fmly) 🐾 **Facilities** STV Wi-fi ॽ HL ⟳
Gym Squash Hair & beauty salon ♫ **Conf** Class 300
Board 120 Thtr 600 **Services** Lift Air con **Notes** ⊗
Civ Wed 600

Worsley Park, A Marriott Hotel & Country Club

★★★★ 80% ◉ HOTEL

☎ 0161 975 2000
Worsley Park, Worsley M28 2QT
e-mail:
uk.pennines.sales.office@marriotthotels.com
web: www.marriottworsleypark.co.uk
dir: M60 junct 13, over 1st rdbt take A575. Hotel
400yds on left

This smart, modern hotel is set in impressive grounds
with a championship golf course. Bedrooms are
comfortably appointed and well equipped for both
leisure and business guests. Public areas include
extensive leisure and conference facilities, and an
elegant restaurant offering imaginative cuisine.

Rooms 158 (33 fmly) (49 GF) **Facilities** Spa STV Wi-fi
ॽ HL ⟳ ♨ 18 Putt green Gym Fitness suite Sauna
Steam room Health & beauty salon Aerobics studio
Conf Class 150 Board 100 Thtr 250 Del from £145 to
£153* **Services** Lift **Parking** 400 **Notes** ⊗
Civ Wed 200

Macdonald Manchester Hotel

★★★★ 78% ◉ HOTEL

☎ 0844 879 9088 & 0161 272 3200
London Rd M1 2PG
e-mail:
general.manchester@macdonald-hotels.co.uk
web: www.macdonald-hotels.co.uk
dir: Opposite Piccadilly Station

Ideally situated just a short walk from Piccadilly
Station, this hotel provides a handy location for both
business and leisure travellers. Stylish, modern rooms
have plasma TVs and iPod docking stations and the
bathrooms offer walk-in power showers and luxury
baths. The first-floor restaurant serves skilfully
prepared dinners and hearty breakfasts. Staff
throughout are cheerful and keen to please.
Macdonald Hotels is the AA Hotel Group of the Year
2013-14.

Rooms 338 (14 fmly) 🐾 **Facilities** Spa FTV Wi-fi ॽ HL
Gym Sauna New Year **Conf** Class 150 Board 80
Thtr 250 **Services** Lift Air con **Parking** 85 **Notes** ⊗
Civ Wed 200

Holiday Inn Manchester - MediaCityUK

★★★★ 77% HOTEL

☎ 0161 813 1040
Media City UK, Salford M50 2HT
dir: M602 junct 2 onto A576 to Salford Quays signed
MediaCityUK

Located in the heart of the exciting media district on
Salford Quays, this hotel is adjacent to the main
production studios and only minutes from Old
Trafford and The Lowry Centre. The stylish Hub Bar
features TV-themed murals and the attractive Green
Room Restaurant is on the mezzanine floor. Bedrooms
are well equipped with safes and mini-bars, and
many have views of the Manchester Shipping Canal.
There's complimentary Wi-fi throughout, and a mini-
gym is available to guests.

Rooms 218 (10 fmly) 🐾 **S** £79-£149; **D** £79-£149*
Facilities STV FTV Wi-fi ॽ HL Gym Xmas New Year
Conf Class 25 Board 30 Thtr 44 Del from £99 to
£199* **Services** Lift Air con **Parking** 5000 **Notes** LB
⊗

M

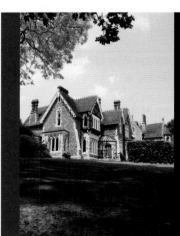

MANCHESTER *continued*

Marriott Manchester Victoria & Albert Hotel

★★★★ 77% HOTEL

☎ 0161 832 1188
Water St M3 4JQ
e-mail:
london.regional.reservations@marriott.com
web:
www.manchestermarriottvictoriaandalbert.co.uk
dir: M602 to A57 through lights on Regent Rd. Pass
Sainsbury's, left at lights onto ring road, right at
lights into Water St

This uniquely converted warehouse, with an interior
featuring exposed brickwork and iron pillars, is
located on the banks of the River Irwell, just a short
stroll from the city centre. There are stylish,
comfortable and well-equipped bedrooms together
with attractive public areas. A large bar lounge leads
onto an intimate restaurant, and extensive conference
facilities are available.

Rooms 148 (30 fmly) (7 smoking) **Facilities** FTV Wi-fi
↨ HL Complimentary use of Bannatyne's Health Club
New Year **Conf** Class 120 Board 72 Thtr 250
Services Lift Air con **Parking** 100 **Notes** ⊗
Civ Wed 200

Copthorne Hotel Manchester

★★★★ 76% HOTEL

☎ 0161 873 7321
Clippers Quay, Salford Quays M50 3SN
e-mail:
reservations.manchester@millenniumhotels.co.uk
web: www.millenniumhotels.co.uk
dir: From M602 follow signs for Salford Quays &
Trafford Park on A5063. Hotel 0.75m on right

This smart hotel enjoys a convenient location on the
redeveloped Salford Quays close to Old Trafford, The
Lowry Centre and The Imperial War Museum.
Bedrooms are carefully appointed and well
equipped for both business and leisure guests. The
informal Clippers Restaurant serves a wide range of
modern dishes.

Rooms 166 (6 fmly) (23 GF) ⋔ **S** £54-£265;
D £54-£265* **Facilities** STV Wi-fi ↨ HL **Conf** Class 80
Board 70 Thtr 160 Del from £99 to £155*
Services Lift **Parking** 120 **Notes** ⊗ Civ Wed 160

Crowne Plaza Manchester City Centre

★★★★ 75% HOTEL

☎ 0161 828 8600
70 Shudehill M4 4AF
e-mail: reception@cpmanchester.com
web: www.cpmanchester.com
dir: In city centre, Northern Quarter

A stylish hotel located in the heart of Manchester in
the trendy Northern Quarter, with Victoria and
Piccadilly Stations and Shudehill Tram and Bus
Interchange all within walking distance. Bedrooms,
including Club Rooms with a Club Lounge, have one
or two queen or king sized beds. The contemporary
bathrooms feature separate bath and shower.
Complimentary internet access is provided and a mini
gym is available 24 hours a day.

Rooms 228 ⋔ **Facilities** STV FTV Wi-fi ↨ HL Gym ♫
Xmas New Year **Conf** Class 100 Board 80 Thtr 200
Services Lift Air con **Notes** ⊗ Civ Wed 200

Macdonald Townhouse Manchester

★★★★ 74% TOWN HOUSE HOTEL

☎ 0161 236 5122
101 Portland St M1 6DF
e-mail: gm.townhouse@macdonald-hotels.co.uk
dir: From Piccadilly Station, along Piccadilly. Left into
Portland St, hotel at junct with Princess St

This hotel, a former cotton warehouse and now a
Grade II listed building, is ideally located for exploring
the City of Manchester. There are comfortable and
well-appointed bedrooms, a stylish bar and a lounge
with a restaurant that is open for pre-theatre meals.
Macdonald Hotels is the AA Hotel Group of the Year
2013-14.

Rooms 85 (24 fmly) **Facilities** FTV Wi-fi ♫
Conf Class 26 Board 30 Thtr 48 **Services** Lift Air con

Novotel Manchester Centre

★★★★ 74% HOTEL

☎ 0161 235 2200
21 Dickinson St M1 4LX
e-mail: H3145@accor.com
web: www.novotel.com
dir: From Oxford St into Portland St, left into
Dickinson St. Hotel on right

This smart, modern property enjoys a central location
convenient for theatres, shops, China Town and
Manchester's business district. Spacious bedrooms
are thoughtfully equipped and brightly decorated.
Open-plan, contemporary public areas include an all-

day restaurant and a stylish bar. Extensive conference
and meeting facilities are available.

Rooms 164 (15 fmly) ⋔ **S** £81-£189; **D** £81-£189*
Facilities STV FTV Wi-fi ↨ HL Gym Steam room Sauna
Aromatherapy **Conf** Class 50 Board 36 Thtr 90
Services Lift Air con **Notes** LB

The Palace Hotel

★★★★ 74% HOTEL

☎ 0161 288 1111
Oxford St M60 7HA
e-mail: richard.grove@principal-hayley.com
web: www.principal-hayley.com
dir: Opposite Manchester Oxford Road rail station

Formerly the offices of the Refuge Life Assurance
Company, this impressive neo-Gothic building
occupies a central location. There is a vast lobby,
spacious open-plan bar lounge and restaurant, and
extensive conference and function facilities.
Bedrooms vary in size and style but are all spacious
and well equipped.

Rooms 275 (59 fmly) ⋔ **Facilities** STV Wi-fi
Conf Class 650 Board 200 Thtr 1000 **Services** Lift
Notes ⊗ Civ Wed 600

Park Inn by Radisson Manchester Victoria
park inn

★★★★ 72% HOTEL

☎ 0161 832 6565
Cheetham Hill Rd M4 4EW
e-mail: info.manchester-victoria@rezidorparkinn.com

This modern hotel is ideally located for the Arena and
Manchesters' many shops centres. The hotel offers
comfortable accommodation, relaxing bar and lounge
with full spa facilities including; pool, gym and
treatment rooms. Food can be taken throughout the
day in rbg's restaurant.

Rooms 252

Malmaison Manchester
Malmaison

★★★ 86% ⊛ HOTEL

☎ 0161 278 1000 & 0844 6930657
Piccadilly M1 3AQ
e-mail: manchester@malmaison.com
web: www.malmaison.com
dir: Follow city centre signs, then signs to Piccadilly
station. Hotel at bottom of station approach

Stylish and chic, Malmaison Manchester offers the
best of contemporary hotel-keeping in a relaxed and
comfortable environment. Converted from a former
warehouse, it offers a range of bright meeting rooms,
a gym and treatment rooms. The new Smoak Bar &
Grill is impressive and understandably popular. Air-

conditioned suites combine comfort with stunning design. Expect the unusual in some of the rooms, for instance the Cinema Suites have a private screening room with 52" screen and surround-sound.

Rooms 167 🐾 **S** £79-£230; **D** £79-£230* **Facilities** STV Wi-fi 🏊 HL Gym Sauna Spa Relaxation area Solarium Massage chairs Xmas New Year **Conf** Class 48 Board 30 Thtr 100 Del from £170 to £300* **Services** Lift Air con **Notes** LB Civ Wed 100

The Portland by Thistle, Manchester   *thistle*

★★★ 81% HOTEL

☎ 0871 376 9026
3/5 Portland St, Piccadilly Gardens M1 6DP
e-mail: reservations.manchester@thistle.co.uk
web: www.thistle.com/manchester
dir: M6 junct 19 onto M56, A5103 signed city centre, straight on at rdbt, right at 2nd lights, straight at next lights into Portland St, hotel on right

The hotel is located close to the Piccadilly Gardens and five minutes' walk from the central and financial districts. Bedrooms are compact and well equipped, and the Portland Bar and Restaurant offers a wide selection of meals, drinks and wines. There is also an Otium Leisure Centre, and conference facilities are available.

Rooms 204 (1 fmly) 🐾 **Facilities** STV Wi-fi HL 🕃 supervised Gym Steam room Sauna Plunge pool Xmas New Year **Conf** Class 140 Board 50 Thtr 300 **Services** Lift Air con **Notes** ⊗ Civ Wed 220

Mercure Manchester Piccadilly Hotel

★★★ HOTEL

☎ 0844 815 9024
Portland St M1 4PH
e-mail: info@mercuremanchester.co.uk
web: www.jupiterhotels.co.uk
dir: Opposite Piccadilly Gardens

Currently the rating for this establishment is not confirmed. This may be due to a change of ownership or because it has only recently joined the AA rating scheme.

Rooms 280 **Conf** Class 420 Board 30 Thtr 800

BEST WESTERN Willow Bank Hotel

★★★ 78% HOTEL

☎ 0161 224 0461
340-342 Wilmslow Rd, Fallowfield M14 6AF
e-mail: gm-willowbank@feathers.uk.com
web: www.feathers.uk.com
dir: M60 junct 5, A5103, left onto B5093. Hotel 2.5m on left

This popular hotel is conveniently located three miles from the city centre, close to the universities. Bedrooms vary in size and style but all are appointed to impressively high standards; they are well equipped and many rooms benefit from CD players and PlayStations. Spacious, elegant public areas include a bar, a restaurant and meeting rooms.

Rooms 116 (4 fmly) **S** £54-£154; **D** £69-£169 (incl. bkfst)* **Facilities** FTV Wi-fi Xmas New Year **Conf** Class 60 Board 70 Thtr 125 **Parking** 100 **Notes** Civ Wed 125

Jurys Inn Manchester

★★★ 78% HOTEL

☎ 0161 953 8888
56 Great Bridgewater St M1 5LE
e-mail: manchester_inn@jurysinns.com
web: www.jurysinns.com
dir: In city centre adjacent to Manchester Central & Bridgewater Hall

Enjoying a prime city centre location, this hotel offers good value, air-conditioned accommodation, ideal for both business travellers and families. Public areas include a smart, spacious lobby, the Inn Pub and the Infusion Restaurant. There are several conveniently located car parks with special rates available.

Rooms 265 (11 fmly) (16 GF) **S** £49-£299; **D** £49-£299 **Facilities** FTV Wi-fi 🏊 **Conf** Class 25 Board 25 Thtr 50 **Services** Lift Air con **Notes** ⊗

Novotel Manchester West

★★★ 73% HOTEL

☎ 0161 799 3535
Worsley Brow M28 2YA
e-mail: H0907@accor.com
web: www.novotel.com

(For full entry see Worsley)

Chancellors Hotel & Conference Centre

★★★ 72% HOTEL

☎ 0161 907 7414
Moseley Rd, Fallowfield M14 6NN
e-mail: chancellors@manchester.ac.uk
dir: Telephone for detailed directions

A Grade II listed manor house set in five acres of landscaped gardens hidden in the heart of Fallowfield, well located for the city's shopping, business and commercial centres. Bedrooms offer modern facilities and the cuisine is enjoyable. Wi-fi and secure parking are available.

Rooms 70 (4 fmly) (16 GF) 🐾 **S** £40-£60; **D** £50-£99 (incl. bkfst)* **Facilities** FTV Wi-fi 🏊 **Conf** Class 100 Board 50 Thtr 125 Del from £95 to £125* **Services** Lift **Parking** 70 **Notes** ⊗ Civ Wed 125

Diamond Lodge

★★ 71% HOTEL

☎ 0161 231 0770
Hyde Rd, Belle Vue M18 7BA
web: www.diamondlodge.co.uk
dir: On A57, 2.5m W of M60 junct 24 (Manchester Orbital) into city

Offering very good value, this modern lodge, near the city centre, motorway networks and football stadiums, provides comfortable accommodation. The ground floor features a bright open-plan lounge and informal dining room where complimentary tea and coffee are provided; a wide choice of evening meals are served. Wi-fi is available throughout the hotel.

Rooms 85 (13 fmly) (16 GF) (13 smoking) 🐾 **Facilities** FTV Wi-fi 🏊 **Parking** 90 **Notes** ⊗ Closed 24-26 Dec RS 31 Dec

Arora Hotel

Ⓤ

☎ 0161 236 8999
18-24 Princess St M1 4LY
e-mail: manchesterreservations@arorahotels.com
dir: Telephone for detailed directions

Currently the rating for this establishment is not confirmed. This may be due to a change of ownership or because it has only recently joined the AA rating scheme. For further details please see the AA website: theAA.com

Rooms 141 (32 fmly) (15 GF) **D** £69.75-£249.75 (incl. bkfst)* **Facilities** FTV Wi-fi Gym **Conf** Class 40 Board 45 Thtr 100 Del from £129.75 to £309.75* **Services** Lift **Notes** ⊗ Civ Wed 60

M

MANCHESTER *continued*

Campanile Manchester

BUDGET HOTEL

☎ 0161 833 1845
55 Ordsall Ln, Regent Rd, Salford M5 4RS
e-mail: manchester@campanile.com
web: www.campanile.com
dir: M602 to Manchester, then A57. After large rdbt
with Sainsbury's on left, left at next lights. Hotel on
right

This modern building offers accommodation in smart,
well-equipped bedrooms, all with en suite bathrooms.
Refreshments may be taken at the informal bistro.
See also the Hotel Groups pages.

Rooms 104 (25 GF) **Conf** Class 40 Board 30 Thtr 50

Holiday Inn Express Manchester - Oxford Road

BUDGET HOTEL

☎ 0843 208 3005
Oxford Road 2 M1 5QA
e-mail: info@hiemanchester.co.uk
dir: From A57(M) follow signs for Peters Fields &
A5103, into Cambridge St. 2nd right into Hulme St,
ahead onto Charles St

A modern hotel ideal for families and business
travellers. Fresh and uncomplicated, the spacious
rooms include Sky TV, power shower and tea and
coffee-making facilities. Continental buffet breakfast
is included in the room rate; other meals may be
taken at the nearby family pub or restaurant. See also
the Hotel Groups pages.

Rooms 147 (80 fmly) ⤢ **S** £59-£149; **D** £59-£149
(incl. bkfst)* **Conf** Class 20 Board 20 Thtr 20

Ibis Manchester Centre Portland Street

BUDGET HOTEL

☎ 0161 6199 000
96 Portland St M1 4GY
e-mail: H3142@accor.com
web: www.ibishotel.com
dir: In city centre, between Princess St & Oxford St

Modern, budget hotel offering comfortable
accommodation in bright and practical bedrooms.
Breakfast is self-service and dinner is available in
the restaurant. See also the Hotel Groups pages.

Rooms 127 (16 fmly) ⤢ **S** £50-£199; **D** £50-£199*

Ibis Manchester Princess Street

BUDGET HOTEL

☎ 0161 272 5000
Charles St, Princess St M1 7DL
e-mail: H3143@accor.com
web: www.ibishotel.com
dir: M62, M602 towards Manchester Centre, follow
signs for UMIST(A34)

Rooms 126 ⤢ **S** £39-£169;

Premier Inn Manchester Central

BUDGET HOTEL

☎ 0871 527 8742
Bishopsgate, 7-11 Lower Mosley St M2 3DW
web: www.premierinn.com
dir: M56 to end, A5103 towards city. Right at 2nd
lights. At next lights left into Oxford Rd, left at
junct of St Peters Sq. Hotel on left

High quality, budget accommodation ideal for both
families and business travellers. Spacious, en suite
bedrooms feature tea and coffee making facilities,
and Freeview TV in most hotels. Internet access and
Wi-fi are available for a small fee. The adjacent
family restaurant features a wide and varied menu.
See also the Hotel Groups pages.

Rooms 147

Premier Inn Manchester City Centre

BUDGET HOTEL

☎ 0871 527 9390
72 Dale St M1 2HR
web: www.premierinn.com
dir: Please telephone for detailed directions

Rooms 193 (14 fmly)

Premier Inn Manchester City Centre (Deansgate)

BUDGET HOTEL

☎ 0871 527 8740
Medlock St M15 5FJ
web: www.premierinn.com
dir: M60 junct 24, A57(M) (Mancunian Way) towards
city centre. Hotel adjacent, on A5103 (Medlock St)

Rooms 200

Premier Inn Manchester City Centre (Portland Street)

BUDGET HOTEL

☎ 0871 527 8746
The Circus, 112-114 Portland St M1 4WB
web: www.premierinn.com
dir: M6 junct 19, A556. M56, exit junct 3 onto A5103
to Medlock St, right into Whitworth St, left into Oxford
St, right into Portland St

Rooms 225

Premier Inn Manchester City MEN/ Printworks

BUDGET HOTEL

☎ 0871 527 8744
North Tower, Victoria Bridge St, Salford M3 5AS
web: www.premierinn.com
dir: M602 to city centre, A57(M) towards GMEX. 2nd
exit follow A56 city centre signs. Left before MEN
arena onto A6, 1st left

Rooms 170

Premier Inn Manchester (Denton)

BUDGET HOTEL

☎ 0871 527 8708
**Alphagate Dr, Manchester Rd South, Denton
M34 3SH**
web: www.premierinn.com
dir: M60 junct 24, A57 signed Denton. 1st right at
lights, right at next lights, hotel on left

Rooms 40

Premier Inn Manchester (Heaton Park)

BUDGET HOTEL

☎ 0871 527 8710
Middleton Rd, Crumpsall M8 4NB
web: www.premierinn.com
dir: M60 junct 19, A576 towards Manchester, through
2 sets of lights. Hotel on left

Rooms 45

M

Premier Inn Manchester North (Middleton)

BUDGET HOTEL

☎ 0871 527 8748
818 Manchester Old Rd, Rhodes, Middleton M24 4RF
web: www.premierinn.com
dir: M60/M62 junct 18 follow Manchester/Middleton
signs. M60 junct 19 take A576 towards Middleton

Rooms 42

Premier Inn Manchester Old Trafford

BUDGET HOTEL

☎ 0871 527 8750
Waters Reach, Trafford Park M17 1WS
web: www.premierinn.com
dir: M6 junct 19, A556 towards Altrincham. Follow
Stretford & Manchester City Centre signs (road
becomes A56). Follow Manchester United Football
Stadium signs. At stadium left at lights. Into Sir Matt
Busby Way, after 1st lights hotel on right

Rooms 160

Premier Inn Manchester (Salford Quays)

BUDGET HOTEL

☎ 0871 527 8718
11 The Quays, Salford Quays, Salford M50 3SQ
web: www.premierinn.com
dir: M602 junct 3, A5063, on Salford Quays

Rooms 52

Premier Inn Manchester Trafford Centre North

BUDGET HOTEL

☎ 0871 527 8752
18-20 Trafford Boulevard,, Urmston M41 7JE
web: www.premierinn.com
dir: M6, onto M62 at junct 21a, towards Manchester.
M62 junct 1, M60 towards south. M60 junct 10, take
B5214. Hotel on left just before Ellesmere Circle

Rooms 42

Premier Inn Manchester Trafford Centre South

BUDGET HOTEL

☎ 0871 527 8754
Wilderspool Wood, Trafford Centre M17 8WW
web: www.premierinn.com
dir: M6 onto M62 junct 21a towards Manchester. Or
M62 junct 1 onto M60 S. Or M60 junct 10, B5124
towards Trafford Park. At 1st rdbt take last exit for
Trafford Centre parking. At 2nd rdbt straight on. Hotel
on left

Rooms 59

Premier Inn Manchester Trafford Centre West

BUDGET HOTEL

☎ 0871 527 8756
Old Park Ln M17 8PG
web: www.premierinn.com
dir: M60 junct 10 towards The Trafford Centre

Rooms 161

Premier Inn Manchester (West Didsbury)

BUDGET HOTEL

☎ 0871 527 8722
Christies Field Office Park, Derwent Ave, Didsbury M21 7QS
web: www.premierinn.com
dir: M60 junct 5, A5103 (Princess Parkway) towards
Manchester on A5103. Hotel approx 1m

Rooms 80

MANCHESTER AIRPORT　　Map 15 SJ88
Greater Manchester

See also Altrincham

Stanneylands Hotel

★★★★　80%　◉◉　HOTEL

☎ 01625 525225
Stanneylands Rd SK9 4EY
e-mail: reservations@stanneylandshotel.co.uk
web: www.stanneylandshotel.co.uk
dir: From M56 at airport exit, follow signs to
Wilmslow. Left towards Handforth. Left at lights into
Stanneylands Rd, hotel on left

This traditional country house hotel, just three miles
from Manchester Airport, offers well-equipped
bedrooms that include suites, prestige and executive
rooms together with delightful, comfortable day
rooms. The cuisine in the restaurant is of a high
standard, and ranges from traditional favourites to
more imaginative contemporary dishes. There is also
the contemporary Calico café bar in a conservatory
setting offering all-day menus, including afternoon
tea, and live music played on the baby grand piano.
The hotel makes an ideal wedding venue and is
licensed to hold civil weddings. The staff throughout
are friendly and obliging.

Rooms 56 (2 fmly) (10 GF) ✎ **S** £69-£100;
D £69-£100* **Facilities** STV FTV Wi-fi ⚲ ♫ Xmas New
Year **Conf** Class 50 Board 40 Thtr 120 Del from £110
to £140* **Services** Lift **Parking** 108 **Notes** LB ⊗
Civ Wed 100

M

MANCHESTER AIRPORT *continued*

Manchester Airport Marriott Hotel

★★★★ 80% HOTEL

☎ 0161 904 0301

Hale Rd, Hale Barns WA15 8XW

e-mail: london.regional.reservations@marriott.com

web: www.manchesterairportmarriott.co.uk

dir: M56 junct 6, in left lane (Hale, Altrincham). Left at lights, on approach to bridge into right lane. At rdbt 3rd exit into hotel car park

With good airport links and convenient access to the city, this sprawling modern hotel is a popular destination. The hotel offers extensive leisure and business facilities, a choice of eating and drinking options and ample parking. Bedrooms are situated around courtyards and have a comprehensive range of facilities.

Rooms 215 (22 fmly) (43 GF) (16 smoking) **S** £95-£119; **D** £95-£119* **Facilities** Spa STV Wi-fi HL ⓣ supervised Gym **Conf** Class 70 Board 50 Thtr 160 Del from £135 to £145* **Services** Lift Air con **Parking** 400 **Notes** LB ⊗ Civ Wed 110

Radisson Blu Hotel Manchester Airport

★★★★ 78% HOTEL

☎ 0161 490 5000

Chicago Av M90 3RA

e-mail: sales.manchester@radissonblu.com

web: www.radissonblu.co.uk/hotel-manchesterairport

dir: M56 junct 5, follow signs for Terminal 2. At rdbt 2nd left & follow signs for railway station. Hotel next to station

All the airport terminals are quickly accessed by covered, moving walkways from this modern hotel. There is an excellent and well-equipped leisure club complete with indoor pool, and extensive conference and banqueting facilities are available. Air-conditioned bedrooms are thoughtfully equipped and come in a variety of decorative themes. Super views of the runway can be enjoyed in the Phileas Fogg Restaurant that offers international cuisine; there's also an all-day brasserie.

Rooms 360 (2 fmly) (25 smoking) ⓡ **Facilities** Spa STV Wi-fi ⓣ Gym Sauna Steam room Xmas New Year **Conf** Class 150 Board 60 Thtr 350 **Services** Lift Air con **Parking** 222 **Notes** ⊗ Civ Wed 350

Hallmark Hotel Manchester

★★★★ 77% HOTEL

☎ 0161 437 0511

Stanley Rd SK9 3LD

e-mail: linda.gregory@hallmarkhotels.co.uk

dir: M60 junct 3/A34 signed Cheadle/Wilmslow. Right at 3rd rdbt into Stanley Rd (B5094). Hotel on left

Ideally located for Manchester Airport and just a few miles from both the Trafford Centre and the city's many shops, the Hallmark Hotel offers well appointed bedrooms. Guests can relax and unwind in the hotel's 20-metre pool, jacuzzi and steam rooms. The brasserie is open for both lunch and dinner, and offers a range of international dishes.

Rooms 88 (12 fmly) (12 GF) **Facilities** Spa FTV Wi-fi ⓣ Gym Steam room Sauna Hair salon New Year **Conf** Class 300 Board 150 Thtr 500 **Services** Lift **Notes** ⊗ Civ Wed

Crowne Plaza Manchester Airport

★★★★ 76% HOTEL

☎ 0871 942 9055

Ringway Rd M90 3NS

e-mail: reservations-manchesterairport@ihg.com

web: www.crowneplaza.co.uk

dir: M56 junct 5 signed Manchester Airport. At airport, follow signs to Terminal 1 & 3. Hotel adjacent to Terminal 3. Long stay car park on left

Located by Terminal 3 this smart, modern hotel offers well-equipped, comfortable bedrooms, all with air-conditioning and effective double-glazing. A choice of dining options and bars is available, and the hotel has spacious leisure facilities and ample on-site parking. The hospitality is friendly, with several long-serving staff members who greet regular customers as friends.

Rooms 294 (100 fmly) (51 GF) **Facilities** STV Wi-fi ⓣ HL Gym Saunas **Conf** Class 25 Board 20 Thtr 30 **Services** Lift Air con **Parking** 300 **Notes** ⊗

Etrop Grange Hotel

★★★★ 75% ⓢⓢ HOTEL

☎ 0844 855 9118

Thorley Ln M90 4EG

e-mail: gm@etrophotel.co.uk

dir: M56 junct 5 follow signs for Terminal 2, on slip road to rdbt take 1st exit. Immediately left, hotel 400yds

This Georgian country-house style hotel is close to Terminal 2 but one would never know once inside. Stylish, comfortable bedrooms provide modern comforts and good business facilities. Elegant day rooms include the Coach House Restaurant that serves creative dishes. Complimentary chauffeured transport to the airport is available for guests using the airport.

Rooms 64 (4 fmly) (9 GF) **Facilities** STV Wi-fi Xmas New Year **Conf** Class 50 Board 40 Thtr 100 Del from £99 to £165 **Parking** 80 **Notes** Civ Wed 90

BEST WESTERN PLUS Pinewood on Wilmslow

★★★★ 73% HOTEL

☎ 01625 529211

180 Wilmslow Rd SK9 3LG

e-mail: pinewood.res@pinewood-hotel.co.uk

dir: Telephone for detailed directions

This stylish hotel is conveniently situated for the M60, Trafford Park, Trafford Centre and Manchester Airport. Bedrooms provide very good quality accommodation, comfortable beds, and a wealth of extras for the modern traveller. Well cooked meals and hearty breakfasts are served overlooking the gardens.

Rooms 58 (2 fmly) **S** £60-£70; **D** £60-£80* **Facilities** FTV Wi-fi Use of nearby Total Fitness Club Xmas New Year **Conf** Class 60 Board 60 Thtr 120 Del from £115 to £130* **Services** Lift **Parking** 120 **Notes** LB ⊗ Civ Wed 120

Bewleys Hotel Manchester Airport

★★★ 78% HOTEL

☎ 0161 498 0333 & 498 1310

Outwood Ln M90 4HL

e-mail: man@bewleyshotels.com

web: www.bewleyshotels.com

dir: At Manchester Airport. Follow signs to Manchester Airport Terminal 3. Hotel on left on Terminal 3 rdbt

Located adjacent to the airport this modern, stylish hotel provides an ideal stop-off for air travellers and

Save on hotels. Book at **theAA.com/hotel**

MAN – MAR 313 ENGLAND

business guests alike. All bedrooms are spacious and well equipped and include a wing of superior rooms. Spacious, open-plan day rooms are stylishly appointed and include a large bar and restaurant along with a good range of meeting and conference facilities.

Rooms 365 (111 fmly) (24 GF) 🐾 **S** fr £60; **D** fr £60* **Facilities** Wi-fi 🏌 Gym **Conf** Class 40 Board 30 Thtr 100 Del from £125* **Services** Lift **Parking** 300 **Notes** ⊗

Premier Inn Manchester Airport

BUDGET HOTEL

☎ 0871 527 8726
Runger Ln, Wilmslow Rd M90 5DL
web: www.premierinn.com
dir: M56 junct 6, follow Wilmslow & Hale signs. Merge onto M56 signed Warrington, Macclesfield & Hale. Left into Runger Ln (signed Freight Terminal)

High quality, budget accommodation ideal for both families and business travellers. Spacious, en suite bedrooms feature tea and coffee making facilities, and Freeview TV in most hotels. Internet access and Wi-fi are available for a small fee. The adjacent family restaurant features a wide and varied menu. See also the Hotel Groups pages.

Rooms 195

Premier Inn Manchester Airport (FT)

BUDGET HOTEL

☎ 0871 527 8730
Runger Ln, Wilmslow Rd M90 5DL
web: www.premierinn.com
dir: M56 junct 6, follow Airport signs. 2nd exit at rdbt. Hotel on left. Through Travelodge car park. Hotel on right

Rooms 166

Premier Inn Manchester (Handforth)

BUDGET HOTEL

☎ 0871 527 8732
30 Wilmslow Rd SK9 3EW
web: www.premierinn.com
dir: M56 junct 6, A538 towards Wilmslow. At main junct into town centre bear left. In 2m hotel at top of hill on right just after Wilmslow Garden Centre

Rooms 35

Premier Inn Manchester (Wilmslow)

BUDGET HOTEL

☎ 0871 527 8736
Racecourse Rd, Wilmslow SK9 5LR
web: www.premierinn.com
dir: M6 junct 19 to Knutsford, follow Wilmslow signs. Left at 1st & 2nd lights towards Wilmslow. Through Mobberley, left just before Bird in Hand pub. At T-junct, right. Hotel 150yds on right

Rooms 37

MARAZION   Map 2 SW53
Cornwall

Mount Haven Hotel & Restaurant

★★★ 83% ֍ ֍ HOTEL

☎ 01736 710249
Turnpike Rd TR17 0DQ
e-mail: reception@mounthaven.co.uk
web: www.mounthaven.co.uk
dir: From A30 towards Penzance. At rdbt take exit for Helston onto A394. Next rdbt right into Marazion, hotel on left

This hotel enjoys spectacular views across the sea towards St Michaels Mount. All rooms have spacious balconies from where the views can be enjoyed - sunrises and sunsets can be spectacular. Bedrooms are contemporarily styled and have comfortable beds and exotic fabrics. Dining is a highlight with the freshest local seafood and fish used to create interesting menus. A range of holistic therapies is available, and the attentive and friendly service helps make a relaxing and enchanting environment throughout.

Rooms 18 (1 fmly) (6 GF) 🐾 **S** £90–£200; **D** £130–£230* **Facilities** FTV Wi-fi Aromatherapy Reflexology Massage Reiki Hot rocks Beauty treatment room Xmas New Year **Parking** 30 **Notes** ⊗

Marazion Hotel

★★ 75% SMALL HOTEL

☎ 01736 710334
The Square TR17 0AP
e-mail: enquiries@marazionhotel.co.uk
web: www.marazionhotel.co.uk
dir: A30 to Penzance, at rdbt follow St Michael's Mount signs. Hotel on left

Within 50 yards of one of Cornwall's safest beaches, this family-run hotel offers a relaxed atmosphere with friendly service. The individually furnished and decorated bedrooms are comfortable, and many have the benefit of stunning views across to St Michael's Mount. The hotel incorporates the Cutty Sark public bar and restaurant where a wide range of meals is offered to suit all palates and budgets.

Rooms 10 (3 fmly) 🐾 **S** £72–£109; **D** £88–£134 (incl. bkfst)* **Facilities** FTV Wi-fi 🏌 Xmas **Parking** 20 **Notes** LB ⊗

MARCH   Map 12 TL49
Cambridgeshire

Oliver Cromwell Hotel

★★★ 70% HOTEL

☎ 01354 602890
High St PE15 9LH
e-mail: reception@olivercromwellhotel.co.uk
dir: In village centre

This purpose built hotel is ideally situated for touring the Cambridgeshire countryside, and within easy reach of Ely and Wisbech. The spacious bedrooms are pleasantly decorated and thoughtfully equipped. Public rooms include a smart lounge bar and a dining room as well as conference and banqueting facilities.

Rooms 42 (2 fmly) (8 GF) **Facilities** FTV Wi-fi 🏌 Gym Sauna Steam room **Conf** Class 80 Board 40 Thtr 120 **Services** Lift Air con **Parking** 60 **Notes** ⊗ Civ Wed 100

M

MARGATE
Kent   Map 7 TR37

Premier Inn Margate

BUDGET HOTEL

☎ 0871 527 8762
Station Green, Station Rd CT9 5AF
web: www.premierinn.com
dir: M2, A299, A28 to Margate seafront. Hotel adjacent to Margate station

High quality, budget accommodation ideal for both families and business travellers. Spacious, en suite bedrooms feature tea and coffee making facilities, and Freeview TV in most hotels. Internet access and Wi-fi are available for a small fee. The adjacent family restaurant features a wide and varied menu. See also the Hotel Groups pages.

Rooms 44

MARKET DRAYTON
Shropshire   Map 15 SJ63

Goldstone Hall

★★★ 87% ◉◉ HOTEL

☎ 01630 661202
Goldstone TF9 2NA
e-mail: enquiries@goldstonehall.com
dir: 4m S of Market Drayton, 4m N of Newport. Hotel signed from A529 & A41

Situated in extensive grounds, this sympathetically refurbished period property is a family-run hotel. It provides traditionally furnished, well-equipped accommodation with outstanding en suite bathrooms and lots of thoughtful extras. Public rooms are extensive and include a choice of lounges, a snooker room and a conservatory. The kitchen has a well deserved reputation for good food that utilises home-grown produce, and a warm welcome is assured.

Rooms 12 (2 GF) ⟆ **S** fr £85; **D** fr £130 **Facilities** STV FTV Wi-fi ⟆ Snooker table New Year **Conf** Class 30 Board 30 Thtr 50 Del from £130 **Parking** 60 **Notes** LB ⊗ Civ Wed 100

Ternhill Farm House & The Cottage Restaurant

◉◉ RESTAURANT WITH ROOMS

☎ 01630 638984 & 638752
Ternhill TF9 3PX
e-mail: info@ternhillfarm.co.uk
web: www.ternhillfarm.co.uk
dir: On junct A53 & A41, archway off A53 to back of property

This elegant Grade II listed Georgian farmhouse stands in a large pleasant garden and has been modernised to provide quality accommodation. There is a choice of comfortable lounges, and The Cottage Restaurant features imaginative dishes using local produce. Secure parking is an additional benefit.

Rooms 7 (2 fmly)

MARKET HARBOROUGH
Leicestershire   Map 11 SP78

BEST WESTERN Three Swans Hotel

★★★ 77% HOTEL

☎ 01858 466644
21 High St LE16 7NJ
e-mail: sales@threeswans.co.uk
web: www.bw-threeswanshotel.co.uk
dir: M1 junct 20, A304 to Market Harborough. Through town centre on A6 from Leicester, hotel on right

Public areas in this former coaching inn include an elegant fine dining restaurant and cocktail bar, a smart foyer lounge and popular public bar areas. Bedroom styles and sizes vary, but are very well appointed and equipped. Those in the wing are particularly impressive, offering high quality and spacious accommodation.

Rooms 61 (48 annexe) (8 fmly) (20 GF) ⟆ **S** £55.50-£60.50; **D** £68-£73 (incl. bkfst)

Facilities STV FTV Wi-fi ⟆ Xmas New Year **Conf** Class 90 Board 50 Thtr 250 Del from £115 to £145 **Services** Lift **Parking** 100 **Notes** LB Civ Wed 140

Premier Inn Market Harborough

BUDGET HOTEL

☎ 0871 527 8764
Melton Rd, East Langton LE16 7TG
web: www.premierinn.com
dir: On A6, N of Market Harborough. Hotel on rdbt junct of A6 & B6047

High quality, budget accommodation ideal for both families and business travellers. Spacious, en suite bedrooms feature tea and coffee making facilities, and Freeview TV in most hotels. Internet access and Wi-fi are available for a small fee. The adjacent family restaurant features a wide and varied menu. See also the Hotel Groups pages.

Rooms 40

MARKET RASEN
Lincolnshire   Map 17 TF18

The Advocate Arms

◉ RESTAURANT WITH ROOMS

☎ 01673 842364
2 Queen St LN8 3EH
e-mail: info@advocatearms.co.uk
dir: In town centre

Appointed to a high standard this 18th-century property is located in the heart of Market Rasen and combines historic character and contemporary design. The operation centres around the stylish restaurant where service is friendly yet professional and the food is a highlight. The attractive bedrooms are very well equipped and feature luxury bathrooms.

Rooms 10 (2 fmly)

MARKFIELD
Leicestershire　　　　　Map 11 SK40

Field Head Hotel

★★★ 66% HOTEL　　

☎ 01530 245454
Markfield Ln LE6 9PS
e-mail: 9160@greeneking.co.uk
web: www.oldenglish.co.uk
dir: M1 junct 22, towards Leicester. At rdbt turn left, then right

This conveniently situated hotel dates back to the 17th century when it was a farmhouse; it has been considerably extended over the years. Within the public areas, the bar and lounge are the focal point for residents and non-residents alike, while meals can be taken either in the bar or the dining room. Bedrooms are modern and well furnished, and offer good all-round comforts and facilities. Four large feature bedrooms are available.

Rooms 28 (1 fmly) (13 GF) **Facilities** FTV Wi-fi ⌨ ♫ Xmas New Year **Conf** Class 30 Board 36 Thtr 60 Del from £99 to £119* **Parking** 65 **Notes** Civ Wed 54

MARLBOROUGH
Wiltshire　　　　　Map 5 SU16

The Castle & Ball

★★★ 74% HOTEL　　

☎ 01672 515201
High St SN8 1LZ
e-mail: castleandball
marlboroughreservations
@greeneking.co.uk
web: www.oldenglish.co.uk
dir: From either A4 or A346 into town centre

This traditional coaching inn in the town centre offers contemporary and very well equipped bedrooms. Open-plan public areas include a comfortable bar/lounge area and a smartly appointed restaurant, which serves food all day. Meeting rooms are also available.

Rooms 37 (3 annexe) (5 fmly) (3 GF) ⌨
Facilities Wi-fi Xmas New Year **Parking** 48

MARLOW
Buckinghamshire　　　　　Map 5 SU88

Macdonald Compleat Angler

★★★★ ◉◉◉ HOTEL

☎ 0844 879 9128
Marlow Bridge SL7 1RG
e-mail:
compleatangler@macdonald-hotels.co.uk
web:
www.macdonaldhotels.co.uk/compleatangler
dir: M4 junct 8/9 or M40 junct 4, A404(M) to rdbt, Bisham exit, 1m to Marlow Bridge, hotel on right

This well-established hotel enjoys an idyllic location overlooking the River Thames and the delightful Marlow weir. The bedrooms, which differ in size and style, are all individually decorated and are equipped with flat-screen satellite TVs, high-speed internet and air-conditioning. Some rooms have balconies with views of the weir and some have four-posters. Aubergine has three AA rosettes and offers modern French cuisine; Bowaters Restaurant serves British dishes and has gained two AA rosettes. In summer guests can use two boats that the hotel has moored on the river and fishing is, of course, a popular activity - a ghillie can accompany guests if arranged in advance. Staff throughout are keen to please and nothing is too much trouble. Macdonald Hotels is the AA Hotel Group of the Year 2013-14.

Rooms 64 (6 fmly) (6 GF) **D** £130-£270 (incl. bkfst)* **Facilities** FTV Wi-fi ⌨ HL Fly & coarse fishing River trips (Apr-Sep) Xmas New Year **Conf** Class 65 Board 36 Thtr 150 Del from £230 to £290* **Services** Lift **Parking** 100 **Notes** LB Civ Wed 120

Danesfield House Hotel & Spa

★★★★ 83% ◉◉◉◉ HOTEL

☎ 01628 891010
Henley Rd SL7 2EY
e-mail: reservations@danesfieldhouse.co.uk
web: www.danesfieldhouse.co.uk
dir: 2m from Marlow on A4155 towards Henley

Set in 65 acres of elevated grounds just 45 minutes from central London and 30 minutes from Heathrow, this hotel enjoys spectacular views across the River Thames. Impressive public rooms include the cathedral-like Great Hall, an impressive spa, and The Orangery for informal dining. The beautiful restaurant, Adam Simmonds at Danesfield House, is an ideal setting to enjoy superb, imaginative fine dining. Some bedrooms have balconies and stunning views. Nothing is too much trouble for the team of committed staff.

Rooms 78 (3 fmly) (27 GF) ⌨ **S** £139-£204; **D** £154-£284 (incl. bkfst)* **Facilities** Spa STV Wi-fi ⌨ ⊛ ♨ Putt green ⛳ Gym Jogging trail Steam room Hydrotherapy room Sauna Xmas New Year **Conf** Class 60 Board 50 Thtr 100 Del from £260 to £370* **Services** Lift **Parking** 100 **Notes** ⊗ Civ Wed 100

See advert on page 316

M

MARLOW *continued*

Crowne Plaza Marlow

★★★★ 80% ◎◎ HOTEL

☎ 01628 496800
Field House Ln SL7 1GJ
e-mail: enquiries@cpmarlow.co.uk
web: www.cpmarlow.co.uk
dir: A404 exit to Marlow, left at mini rdbt, left into Field House Lane

This hotel is in the Thames Valley not far from Windsor, Henley-on-Thames and the motorway. The public areas are air conditioned and include the Agua Café and Bar and Glaze Restaurant. Leisure facilities include an up-to-the-minute gym and large pool. The bedrooms, including six contemporary suites, enjoy plenty of natural light and have excellent workstations; the Club Rooms have European and US power points

Rooms 168 (47 fmly) (56 GF) (11 smoking) ◖
Facilities Spa STV FTV Wi-fi HL ⊗ ⤳ Gym Sauna Steam room Dance studio Xmas New Year
Conf Class 180 Board 30 Thtr 450 **Services** Lift Air con **Parking** 300 **Notes** ⊗ Civ Wed 400

Premier Inn Marlow

BUDGET HOTEL

☎ 0871 527 8766
The Causeway SL7 2AA
web: www.premierinn.com
dir: M40 junct 4, A404 signed Marlow/Maidenhead. Left, follow A4155 signs to Marlow. At 3rd rdbt 1st exit into High St, signed Bisham. Straight on at mini rdbt. Hotel on left

High quality, budget accommodation ideal for both families and business travellers. Spacious, en suite bedrooms feature tea and coffee making facilities, and Freeview TV in most hotels. Internet access and Wi-fi are available for a small fee. The adjacent family restaurant features a wide and varied menu. See also the Hotel Groups pages.

Rooms 17 (6 fmly)

MARSTON
Lincolnshire   Map 11 SK84

The Olde Barn Hotel

★★★ 70% HOTEL

☎ 01400 250909
Toll Bar Rd NG32 2HT
e-mail: reservations@theoldebarnhotel.co.uk
dir: From A1 N: left to Marston adjacent to petrol station. From A1 S: 1st right after Allington/Belton exit

Located in the countryside one mile from the A1, this sympathetically renovated and extended former period barn provides a range of thoughtfully furnished bedrooms, ideal for both business and leisure customers. Imaginative food is offered in the attractive beamed restaurant, and extensive leisure facilities include a swimming pool, sauna, steam room and a well-equipped gym.

Rooms 101 (11 fmly) (51 GF) ◖ **S** £60-£100;
D £80-£140* **Facilities** Spa STV FTV Wi-fi ↳ ⊗ Gym Xmas New Year **Conf** Class 180 Board 100 Thtr 300 Del from £110 to £150 **Services** Lift **Parking** 280 **Notes** LB Civ Wed 250

M

M

MASHAM
North Yorkshire   Map 19 SE28

INSPECTORS' CHOICE

Swinton Park
★★★★ ◉◉◉ HOTEL

☎ 01765 680900
HG4 4JH
e-mail: reservations@swintonpark.com
web: www.swintonpark.com
dir: Please telephone for detailed directions

Although extended during the Victorian and Edwardian eras, the original part of this welcoming castle dates from the 17th century. Bedrooms are luxuriously furnished and come with a host of thoughtful extras. Samuel's restaurant (built by the current owner's great-great-great grandfather) is very elegant and serves imaginative dishes using local produce. The majority of the food is sourced from the 20,000-acre Swinton Estate, as the hotel, winner of several green awards, is committed to keeping the 'food miles' to a minimum. The gardens, including a four-acre walled garden, have been gradually restored. The Deerhouse is the venue for the hotel's alfresco food festivals, summer BBQs and weddings.

Swinton Park

Rooms 31 (6 fmly) ⚡ **S** fr £185; **D** £185-£380 (incl. bkfst)* **Facilities** Spa FTV Wi-fi ⏬ ⌘ 9 Putt green Fishing ⛳ Gym Shooting Falconry Pony trekking Cookery school Off-road driving Xmas New Year Child facilities **Conf** Class 60 Board 40 Thtr 110 Del from £150* **Services** Lift **Parking** 50 **Notes** LB Civ Wed 120

MATFEN
Northumberland   Map 21 NZ07

Matfen Hall
★★★★ 81% ◉◉ HOTEL

PRIMA

☎ 01661 886500 & 855708
NE20 0RH
e-mail: info@matfenhall.com
web: www.matfenhall.com
dir: A69 onto B6318. Hotel just before village

This fine mansion lies in landscaped parkland overlooking its own golf course. Bedrooms are a blend of contemporary and traditional, but all are very comfortable and well equipped. Impressive public rooms include a splendid drawing room and the elegant Library and Print Room Restaurant, as well as a conservatory bar and very stylish spa, leisure and conference facilities.

Rooms 53 (11 fmly) ⚡ **S** £79-£180; **D** £89-£320 (incl. bkfst)* **Facilities** Spa STV FTV Wi-fi ⏬ HL ⓢ supervised ⚓ 27 Putt green Gym Sauna Steam room Salt grotto Ice fountain Aerobics Driving range Golf academy Xmas New Year **Conf** Class 46 Board 40 Thtr 120 Del from £145 to £180* **Services** Lift **Parking** 150 **Notes** LB Civ Wed 120

MAWGAN PORTH
Cornwall   Map 2 SW86

The Scarlet Hotel
★★★★ 80% ◉◉ HOTEL

☎ 01637 861800
Tredragon Rd TR8 4DQ
e-mail: stay@scarlethotel.co.uk
dir: A39, A30 towards Truro. At Trekenning rdbt take A3059, follow Newquay Airport signs. Right after garage signed St Mawgan & Airport. Right after airport, at T-junct signed Padstow (B3276). At Mawgan Porth left. Hotel 250yds

Built as an eco hotel, this strikingly modern property has a stunning cliff-top location with magnificent views and offers something a little different. The very stylish and well-equipped bedrooms are categorised in five types: Just Right, Generous, Unique, Spacious and Indulgent. The Ayurvedic spa is exceptional and encompasses the rejuvenation of the whole body and mind; relaxation is the key here. Cuisine is equally important, and in tune with the hotel's environment policies, daily-changing menus feature fresh, seasonal and local produce. The team of 'hosts' offer a high level of hospitality and service.

Rooms 37 (5 GF) ⚡ **S** £175-£440; **D** £195-£460 (incl. bkfst)* **Facilities** Spa FTV Wi-fi ⏬ ⓢ ⌘ Yoga ♫ Xmas New Year **Conf** Board 16 **Services** Lift **Parking** 37 **Notes** LB No children 16yrs Closed 2-31 Jan Civ Wed 74

Bedruthan Steps Hotel
★★★★ 77% HOTEL

☎ 01637 861200 & 860860
TR8 4BU
e-mail: stay@bedruthan.com
dir: From A39 or A30 follow signs to Newquay Airport. Pass airport, right at T-junct to Mawgan Porth. Hotel at top of hill on left

With stunning views over Mawgan Porth Bay from the public rooms and the majority of the bedrooms, this is a child-friendly hotel. Children's clubs for various ages are provided in addition to children's dining areas and appropriate meals and times. A homage to architecture of the 1970s, with a comfortable, contemporary feel, this hotel also has conference facilities. A choice of dining options is available with the relaxed vibe of the Wild Café, or alternatively The Herring which offers a creative and innovative menu, utilising excellent Cornish produce.

continued

MAWGAN PORTH *continued*

Rooms 101 (60 fmly) (1 GF) ⁿ **Facilities** Spa FTV
Wi-fi ⌨ ⚲ ↖ ⚘ Gym Jungle tumble ball pool Sauna
Steam room Hydro pool Pool table Snooker room ♫
New Year Child facilities **Conf** Class 60 Board 40
Thtr 180 **Services** Lift **Parking** 100 **Notes** Closed
22-28 Dec Civ Wed 150

Budock Vean - The Hotel on the River

★★★★ 79% ⊛ COUNTRY HOUSE HOTEL

☎ 01326 252100 & 0800 833927
TR11 5LG
e-mail: relax@budockvean.co.uk
web: www.budockvean.co.uk
dir: From A39 follow tourist signs to Trebah Gardens.
0.5m to hotel

Set in 65 acres of attractive, well-tended grounds,
this peaceful hotel offers an impressive range of
facilities. It is convenient for visiting the Helford River
estuary and many local gardens, or simply as a
tranquil venue for a leisure break. The bedrooms are
spacious and come in a choice of styles; some
overlook the grounds and the golf course.

Rooms 57 (2 fmly) ⁿ **S** £74-£143; **D** £148-£286
(incl. bkfst & dinner)* **Facilities** Spa FTV Wi-fi ⌨ ⚲ ⚖
9 ⚘ Putt green ⚑ Private river boat & foreshore ♫
Xmas New Year **Conf** Class 40 Board 30 Thtr 60
Del from £121.50 to £178.50* **Services** Lift
Parking 100 **Notes** LB Closed 3 wks Jan Civ Wed 65

Meudon Hotel

★★★ 85% COUNTRY HOUSE HOTEL

☎ 01326 250541
TR11 5HT
e-mail: wecare@meudon.co.uk
web: www.meudon.co.uk
dir: From Truro A39 towards Falmouth at Hillhead
(Anchor & Cannons) rdbt, follow signs to Maenporth
Beach. Hotel on left in 1m

This charming late Victorian mansion is a relaxing
place to stay, with friendly hospitality and attentive
service. It sits in impressive 9-acre gardens that lead
down to a private beach. The spacious and
comfortable bedrooms are situated in a more modern
building. The cuisine features the best of local
Cornish produce and is served in the conservatory
restaurant.

Rooms 29 (2 fmly) (15 GF) **Facilities** FTV Wi-fi ⌨
Fishing Private beach Hair salon Yacht for skippered
charter Xmas **Conf** Class 20 Board 15 Thtr 30
Services Lift **Parking** 50 **Notes** LB Closed 28 Dec-Jan

Trelawne Hotel

★★★ 77% HOTEL

☎ 01326 250226
TR11 5HS
e-mail: info@trelawnehotel.co.uk
web: www.trelawnehotel.co.uk
dir: A39 to Falmouth, right at Hillhead rdbt signed
Maenporth. Past beach, up hill, hotel on left

This hotel is surrounded by attractive lawns and
gardens, and enjoys superb coastal views. An
informal atmosphere prevails, and many guests
return year after year. Bedrooms, many with sea
views, are of varying sizes, but all are well equipped.
Dinner features quality local produce used in
imaginative dishes.

Rooms 14 (2 fmly) (4 GF) ⁿ **S** £42-£90; **D** £80-£200
(incl. bkfst)* **Facilities** FTV Wi-fi Xmas **Parking** 20
Notes LB

Shaw Country Hotel

★★ 76% SMALL HOTEL

☎ 01225 702836 & 790321
Bath Rd, Shaw SN12 8EF
e-mail: info@shawcountryhotel.com
web: www.shawcountryhotel.com
dir: 1m from Melksham, 9m from Bath on A365

Located within easy reach of both Bath and the M4,
this relaxed and friendly hotel sits in its own gardens
and includes a patio area ideal for enjoying a drink
during the summer months. The house boasts very
well-appointed bedrooms, a comfortable lounge and
bar, and the Mulberry Restaurant, where a wide
selection of innovative dishes make up both carte and
set menus. A spacious function room is a useful
addition.

Rooms 13 (2 fmly) ⁿ **S** £63; **D** £88-£108 (incl.
bkfst)* **Facilities** FTV Wi-fi **Conf** Class 40 Board 20
Thtr 60 **Parking** 30 **Notes** LB RS 26-27 Dec & 1 Jan
Civ Wed 90

INSPECTORS' CHOICE

Stapleford Park

★★★★ ⊛⊛ COUNTRY HOUSE HOTEL

☎ 01572 787000
Stapleford LE14 2EF
e-mail: reservations@stapleford.co.uk
web: www.staplefordpark.com
dir: 1m SW of B676, 4m E of Melton Mowbray & 9m
W of Colsterworth

This stunning mansion, dating back to the 14th
century, sits in over 500 acres of beautiful grounds.
Spacious, sumptuous public rooms include a choice
of lounges and an elegant restaurant. An additional
brasserie-style restaurant is located in the golf
complex. The hotel also boasts a spa with health
and beauty treatments and gym, plus horse riding
and many other country pursuits. Bedrooms are
individually styled and furnished to a high
standard. Attentive service is delivered with a
relaxed yet professional style. Dinner, in the
impressive dining room, is a highlight of any stay.

Rooms 55 (7 annexe) (10 fmly) ⁿ **Facilities** Spa
STV FTV Wi-fi ⌨ ⚖ 18 ⚘ Putt green Fishing ⚑
Gym Archery Croquet Falconry Horse riding
Petanque Shooting Billiards Xmas New Year
Conf Class 140 Board 80 Thtr 200 **Services** Lift
Parking 120 **Notes** Civ Wed 150

Sysonby Knoll Hotel

★★★ 79% HOTEL

☎ 01664 563563
Asfordby Rd LE13 0HP
e-mail: reception@sysonby.com
web: www.sysonby.com
dir: 0.5m from town centre on A6006

This well established hotel sits on the edge of Melton
Mowbray and is set in attractive gardens with ample
parking. The hotel has been run by the same family
since 1965 and continues to provide friendly,
attentive service. The lounges are comfortable and
Wi-fi is available throughout. Freshly prepared dishes

M

are served in the restaurant which overlooks the attractive gardens. The bedrooms are spacious and of a high quality and include four-poster rooms in the main building and executive rooms in an annexe.

Rooms 30 (7 annexe) (1 fmly) (7 GF) 🟥 **Facilities** FTV Wi-fi ➷ Fishing ➷ **Conf** Class 25 Board 34 Thtr 50 **Parking** 48 **Notes** Closed 25 Dec-1 Jan

Quorn Lodge Hotel

★★★ 71% HOTEL

☎ 01664 566660
46 Asfordby Rd LE13 0HR
e-mail: quornlodge@aol.com
dir: From town centre take A6006. Hotel 300yds from junct of A606/A607 on right

Centrally located, this smart privately owned and managed hotel offers a comfortable and welcoming atmosphere. Bedrooms are individually decorated and thoughtfully designed. The public rooms consist of a bright restaurant overlooking the garden, a cosy lounge bar and a modern function suite. High standards are maintained throughout and parking is a bonus.

Rooms 21 (4 fmly) (3 GF) 🟥 **Facilities** STV FTV Wi-fi ➷ Gym **Conf** Class 70 Board 80 Thtr 100 **Parking** 38 **Notes** ⊗ Civ Wed 80

Scalford Hall

★★★ 71% HOTEL

☎ 01664 444654
Scalford Rd LE14 4UB
e-mail: sales@scalfordhall.co.uk
dir: A6006 towards Melton Mowbray. Left at 2nd lights into Scalford Rd, hotel 3m on left

Set in extensive grounds, Scalford Hall is just three miles north of Melton Mowbray. The bedrooms are tastefully furnished, and well equipped for business and leisure guests; many have views over the gardens. Public rooms include a spacious lounge area and a small bar.

Rooms 88 (21 annexe) (6 fmly) (19 GF) 🟥 **Facilities** FTV Wi-fi Putt green ➷ Gym New Year **Conf** Class 36 Board 40 Thtr 150 **Parking** 120 **Notes** ⊗ Civ Wed 100

MEMBURY MOTORWAY SERVICE AREA (M4)   Map 5 SU37
Berkshire

Days Inn Membury - M4

BUDGET HOTEL

☎ 01488 72336
Membury Service Area RG17 7TZ
e-mail: membury.hotel@welcomebreak.co.uk
web: www.welcomebreak.co.uk
dir: M4 between junct 14 & 15

This modern building offers accommodation in smart, spacious and well-equipped bedrooms, suitable for families and business travellers, and all with en suite bathrooms. Continental breakfast is available and other refreshments may be taken at the nearby family restaurant. See also the Hotel Groups pages.

Rooms 38 (32 fmly) (17 GF) (5 smoking)
Conf Board 10

MERIDEN   Map 10 SP28
West Midlands

Forest of Arden, A Marriott Hotel & Country Club

★★★★ 82% ◉ HOTEL

☎ 01676 522335
Maxstoke Ln CV7 7HR
web: www.marriottforestofarden.co.uk
dir: M42 junct 6 onto A45 towards Coventry, over Stonebridge flyover. After 0.75m left into Shepherds Ln. Left at t-junct. Hotel 1.5m on left

The ancient oaks, rolling hills and natural lakes of the 10,000 acre Forest of Arden estate provide an idyllic backdrop for this modern hotel and country club. The hotel boasts an excellent range of leisure facilities and is regarded as one of the finest golfing destinations in the UK. Bedrooms provide every modern convenience and a full range of facilities.

Rooms 214 (65 GF) (5 smoking) 🟥 **Facilities** Spa Wi-fi 🏊 ✤ 18 ⛳ Putt green Fishing ➷ Gym Floodlit golf academy New Year **Conf** Class 180 Board 40 Thtr 300 **Services** Lift **Parking** 300 **Notes** ⊗ Civ Wed 250

BEST WESTERN PLUS Manor NEC Birmingham

★★★★ 75% ◉◉ HOTEL

☎ 01676 522735
Main Rd CV7 7NH
e-mail: reservations@manorhotelmeriden.co.uk
web: www.manorhotelmeriden.co.uk
dir: M42 junct 6, A45 towards Coventry then A452 signed Leamington. At rdbt take B4102 signed Meriden, hotel on left

This sympathetically extended Georgian manor in the heart of a sleepy village is just a few minutes away from the M6, M42 and National Exhibition Centre. The Regency Restaurant offers modern dishes, while Houston's serves lighter meals and snacks. The bedrooms are smart and well equipped.

Rooms 112 (15 fmly) (20 GF) **S** £55-£180; **D** £55-£180* **Facilities** FTV Wi-fi ➷ Xmas New Year **Conf** Class 150 Board 60 Thtr 250 Del from £100 to £270* **Services** Lift **Parking** 190 **Notes** LB Civ Wed 200

MEVAGISSEY   Map 2 SX04
Cornwall

Trevalsa Court Hotel

★★★ 78% HOTEL

☎ 01726 842468
School Hill, Polstreath PL26 6TH
e-mail: stay@trevalsa-hotel.co.uk
web: www.trevalsa-hotel.co.uk
dir: From St Austell take B3273 to Mevagissey. Pass sign to Pentewan. At top of hill left at x-rds. Hotel signed

Very well located above the town of Mevagissey, with easy access to nearby attractions, this establishment is an Arts & Crafts style property appointed to a high standard throughout with lots of original features. Bedrooms, many with sea views, are comfortable and well presented; there is also a stylish guests' sitting room with views across the bay.

Rooms 14 (1 annexe) (1 fmly) (4 GF) 🟥 **Facilities** FTV Wi-fi **Parking** 20 **Notes** Closed Dec & Jan

M

MEVAGISSEY *continued*

Tremarne Hotel

★★ 84% HOTEL

☎ 01726 842213
Polkirt PL26 6UY
e-mail: info@tremarne-hotel.co.uk
dir: From A390 at St Austell take B3273 to
Mevagissey. Follow Portmellon signs through
Mevagissey. At top of Polkirt Hill 1st right into
Higherwell Park. Hotel drive facing

A very popular hotel, set in landscaped gardens with
a swimming pool, that has superb views towards
Mevagissey. The friendliness of Michael, Fitz and the
team cannot be bettered. The hotel offers
comfortable, individually styled bedrooms that either
have views of the sea or the countryside. Guests can
expect good service and freshly-cooked food on a
daily-changing menu.

Rooms 13 (2 fmly) 🐾 **S** £82-£88; **D** £96-£174 (incl.
bkfst)* **Facilities** FTV Wi-fi 🏌 New Year **Parking** 14
Notes LB ⊗ No children 6yrs Closed Jan

BEST WESTERN Pastures Hotel

★★★ 82% HOTEL

☎ 01709 577707
Pastures Rd S64 0JJ
e-mail: info@pastureshotel.co.uk
web: www.pastureshotel.co.uk
dir: 0.5m from town centre on A6023, left by CLS Mot,
signed Denaby Ings & Cadeby. Hotel on right

This private hotel is in a rural setting beside a
working canal with view of Conisbro Castle in the
distance, and is convenient for Doncaster or the
Dearne Valley with its nature reserves and leisure
centre. Guests can dine in the Pastures Lodge pub
and family restaurant situated opposite the hotel, or
in Reeds fine dining restaurant in the hotel (open
Tuesday-Saturday). Bedrooms, in a modern, purpose-
built block, are quiet, comfortable and equipped with
many modern facilities.

Rooms 60 (5 fmly) (28 GF) 🐾 **S** £60; **D** £70 (incl.
bkfst)* **Facilities** STV Wi-fi 🏌 Xmas New Year
Conf Class 170 Board 100 Thtr 250 Del £118.80*
Services Lift **Parking** 179 **Notes** ⊗ Civ Wed 200

Days Inn Michaelwood - M5

BUDGET HOTEL

☎ 01454 261513
Michaelwood Service Area, Lower Wick GL11 6DD
e-mail: michaelwood.hotel@welcomebreak.co.uk
web: www.welcomebreak.co.uk
dir: M5 N'bound between junct 13 & 14

This modern building offers accommodation in smart,
spacious and well-equipped bedrooms, suitable for
families and business travellers, and all with en suite
bathrooms. Continental breakfast is available and
other refreshments may be taken at the nearby family
restaurant. See also the Hotel Groups pages.

Rooms 38 (15 fmly) (7 smoking) **Conf** Board 10

Thistle Hotel Middlesbrough   thistle

★★★★ 74% HOTEL

☎ 0871 376 9028 & 01642 232000
Fry St TS1 1JH
e-mail: middlesbrough@thistle.co.uk
web: www.thistlehotels.com/middlesbrough
dir: A19 onto A66 signed Middlesbrough. A66 after
Zetland car park. 3rd exit at 1st rdbt, 2nd exit at 2nd
rdbt

The staff here are committed to guest care and
nothing is too much trouble. Located close to the town
centre and football ground this establishment offers
bedrooms of varying sizes, that are well furnished
and comfortably equipped. The contemporary first-
floor CoMotion café bar leads into the open-plan
Gengis restaurant featuring an interesting range of
globally inspired dishes. Guests have full use of the
hotel's Otium health club.

Rooms 132 (8 fmly) 🐾 **Facilities** Spa STV FTV Wi-fi ⇨
HL 🏌 Gym Steam room Sauna Hair & beauty salon
New Year **Conf** Class 144 Board 100 Thtr 400
Del from £99 to £179* **Services** Lift **Parking** 66
Notes Civ Wed 400

Premier Inn Middlesbrough Central South

BUDGET HOTEL

☎ 0871 527 8770
Marton Way TS4 3BS
web: www.premierinn.com
dir: Off A172 opposite South Cleveland Hospital
complex

High quality, budget accommodation ideal for both
families and business travellers. Spacious, en suite
bedrooms feature tea and coffee making facilities,
and Freeview TV in most hotels. Internet access and
Wi-fi are available for a small fee. The adjacent
family restaurant features a wide and varied menu.
See also the Hotel Groups pages.

Rooms 74

The Teesdale Hotel

★★ 71% HOTEL

☎ 01833 640264
Market Place DL12 0QG
e-mail: enquiries@teesdalehotel.co.uk
web: www.teesdalehotel.co.uk
dir: From Barnard Castle take B6278, follow signs for
Middleton-in-Teesdale & Highforce. Hotel in town
centre

Located in the heart of this popular village, The
Teesdale Hotel is a family-run establishment that
offers a relaxed and friendly atmosphere. Bedrooms
and bathrooms are well equipped and offer a good
standard of quality and comfort. Public areas include
a residents' lounge on the first floor, a spacious
restaurant and a lounge bar which is popular with
locals.

Rooms 14 (1 fmly) 🐾 **S** £35-£50; **D** £65-£95 (incl.
bkfst)* **Facilities** Wi-fi **Conf** Class 20 Board 20
Thtr 40 **Parking** 20

BEST WESTERN Jersey Arms

★★ 76% HOTEL

☎ 01869 343234 & 343270
OX25 4AD
e-mail: jerseyarms@bestwestern.co.uk
web: www.jerseyarms.co.uk
dir: 3m from A34, on B430, 10m N of Oxford, between
junct 9 & 10 of M40

With a history dating back to the 13th century, the
Jersey Arms combines old-fashioned charm with
contemporary style and elegance. The individually

Save on hotels. Book at **theAA.com/hotel**

MEV – MIL 321 ENGLAND

designed bedrooms are well equipped and comfortable. The lounge has an open fire, and the smart and spacious restaurant provides a calm atmosphere in which to enjoy the popular cuisine.

Rooms 20 (14 annexe) (3 fmly) (9 GF) **S** £75–£79; **D** £85–£110 (incl. bkfst)* **Facilities** FTV Wi-fi ⓭ Xmas New Year **Conf** Class 20 Board 20 Thtr 20 Del from £120 to £145* **Parking** 55 **Notes** ⊗

MILDENHALL
Suffolk

Map 12 TL77

The Bull Inn
★★★ 85% ⊛ HOTEL

☎ 01638 711001
The Street, Barton Mills IP28 6AA
e-mail: reception@bullinn-bartonmills.com
web: www.bullinn-bartonmills.com
dir: A11 between Newmarket & Mildenhall, signed Barton Mills. Hotel by Five Ways rdbt

This delightful 16th-century coaching inn is lovingly cared for by the owners. Public rooms offer a choice of bars, a brasserie-style restaurant and a further lounge area. The contemporary bedrooms are tastefully appointed with co-ordinated soft furnishings and many thoughtful touches.

Rooms 15 (2 annexe) (2 fmly) (2 GF) 🐾 **S** £85–£135; **D** £95–£175 (incl. bkfst)* **Facilities** STV FTV Wi-fi **Conf** Class 20 Board 20 Thtr 30 **Parking** 60 **Notes** ⊗ RS 25 Dec

See advert on page 333

MILTON COMMON
Oxfordshire

Map 5 SP60

The Oxfordshire
★★★★ 81% ⊛ HOTEL

☎ 01844 278300
Rycote Ln OX9 2PU
e-mail: gm@theoxfordshire.com
dir: M40 junct 7 N'bound (junct 8 S'bound), A329 towards Thame

Located within easy reach of the M40, this hotel is at the championship golf course, The Oxfordshire, in the heart of the beautiful Chilterns. The accommodation offers impressive levels of comfort and quality, and all rooms are air-conditioned and have access onto a balcony. The Tempus Spa includes a 15-metre pool, modern gym and three treatment rooms. This resort makes an ideal location for a relaxing break, especially for golf enthusiasts.

Rooms 50 (18 GF) **Facilities** Spa FTV Wi-fi ⓭ ⓧ ⬙ 18 Putt green Gym Sauna Steam room New Year **Conf** Class 66 Board 54 Thtr 180 **Services** Lift Air con **Parking** 150 **Notes** ⊗ Civ Wed

The Oxford Belfry

★★★★ 79% HOTEL

☎ 01844 279381
OX9 2JW
e-mail: oxfordbelfry@qhotels.co.uk
web: www.qhotels.co.uk
dir: M40 junct 7 onto A329 to Thame. Left onto A40, hotel 300yds on right

This modern hotel has a relatively rural location and enjoys lovely views of the countryside to the rear. The hotel is built around two very attractive courtyards and has a number of lounges and conference rooms, as well as indoor leisure facilities and outdoor tennis courts. Bedrooms are large and feature a range of extras.

Rooms 154 (20 fmly) (66 GF) 🐾 **S** £79–£165; **D** £89–£175 (incl. bkfst) **Facilities** Spa FTV Wi-fi ⓭ HL ⓧ ⬙ ⬙ Gym Steam room Sauna Aerobics studio Xmas New Year **Conf** Class 180 Board 100 Thtr 450 Del from £130 to £179 **Services** Lift **Parking** 350 **Notes** LB Civ Wed 300

MILTON KEYNES
Buckinghamshire

Map 11 SP83

See also Aspley Guise

Mercure Milton Keynes Parkside Hotel

★★★★ 73% ⊛ HOTEL

☎ 01908 661919
Newport Rd, Woughton on the Green MK6 3LR
e-mail: H6627-gm@accor.com
web: www.mercure.com
dir: M1 junct 14, A509 towards Milton Keynes. 2nd exit on H6 follow signs to Woughton on the Green

Situated in five acres of landscaped grounds in a peaceful village setting, this hotel is only five minutes' drive from the hustle and bustle of the town centre. Bedrooms are divided between executive rooms in the main house and standard rooms in the adjacent coach house. Public rooms include a range of meeting rooms, and Strollers bar. The Lanes Restaurant provides a relaxing venue where eclectic modern dishes are offered.

Rooms 49 (1 fmly) (19 GF) **Facilities** STV Wi-fi Free entry to health & fitness club (approx 2m) Xmas New Year **Conf** Class 60 Board 50 Thtr 150 **Parking** 75 **Notes** Civ Wed 120

Holiday Inn Milton Keynes

★★★★ 73% HOTEL

☎ 01908 698541
500 Saxon Gate West MK9 2HQ
e-mail: reservations-miltonkeynes@ihg.com
web: www.holidayinn.co.uk/miltonkeynes
dir: M1 junct 14. Straight on at 7 rdbts. At 8th (Saxon South) turn right. Hotel after lights on left

Ideally located to explore central England, with both Oxford and Cambridge within an hour's drive, and central London just 40 minutes away by train. The hotel is a spacious, purpose-built, city-centre property offering a range of well-appointed bedrooms, conference rooms and a fully-equipped health club. The Junction restaurant offers a contemporary dining experience in a relaxing environment.

Rooms 166 (17 fmly) 🐾 **Facilities** STV Wi-fi HL ⓧ supervised Gym Sauna Beauty room Xmas New Year **Conf** Class 50 Board 50 Thtr 130 **Services** Lift Air con **Parking** 85 **Notes** ⊗ Civ Wed 70

M

MILTON KEYNES *continued*

Novotel Milton Keynes

★★★ 75% HOTEL

☎ 01908 322212
Saxon St, Layburn Court, Heelands MK13 7RA
e-mail: H3272@accor.com
web: www.novotel.com
dir: M1 junct 14, follow Childsway signs towards city centre. Right into Saxon Way, straight across all rdbts, hotel on left

Contemporary in style, this purpose-built hotel is situated on the outskirts of the town, just a few minutes' drive from the centre and mainline railway station. Bedrooms provide ample workspace and a good range of facilities for the modern traveller, and public rooms include a children's play area and indoor leisure centre.

Rooms 124 (40 fmly) (33 GF) ⌇ **S** £55-£149; **D** £55-£149* **Facilities** FTV Wi-fi ⌇ ⌇ Gym Steam room Sauna **Conf** Class 75 Board 40 Thtr 120 **Services** Lift **Parking** 130 **Notes** Civ Wed 100

Ramada Encore Milton Keynes

★★★ 75% HOTEL

☎ 01908 545500
312 Midsummer Boulevard MK9 2EA
e-mail: enquiries@encoremiltonkeynes.co.uk
web: www.encoremiltonkeynes.co.uk

This hotel is located in the heart of the town centre, close to the central railway station. The accommodation is stylish, contemporary and has all the modern comforts such as air conditioning and Wi-fi. There are two meeting rooms as well as an attractive bar and restaurant. Limited on-site parking is available, charged at a daily rate.

Rooms 159 (28 fmly) (16 smoking) **Facilities** STV Wi-fi Xmas New Year **Conf** Class 30 Board 30 Thtr 64 **Services** Lift Air con **Parking** 50 **Notes** ⊗

Broughton Hotel

BUDGET HOTEL

☎ 01908 667726
Broughton MK10 9AA
e-mail: 6418@greeneking.co.uk
web: www.hungryhorse.co.uk
dir: M1 junct 14, at 1st rdbt A5130 signed Woburn, 600yds. Right for Broughton, hotel on left

This hotel is within easy reach of road networks and offers modern accommodation. Day rooms are dominated by an open-plan lounge bar and the Hungry Horse food concept, which proves particularly popular with young families. See also the Hotel Groups pages.

Rooms 30 (2 fmly) (14 GF) **Conf** Class 30 Board 30 Thtr 80

Campanile Milton Keynes   Campanile

BUDGET HOTEL

☎ 01908 649819
40 Penn Road (off Watling St), Fenny Stratford, Bletchley MK2 2AU
e-mail: miltonkeynes@campanile.com
web: www.campanile.com
dir: M1 junct 14, A4146 to A5. S'bound on A5. 4th exit at 1st rdbt to Fenny Stratford. Hotel 500yds on left

This modern building offers accommodation in smart, well-equipped bedrooms, all with en suite bathrooms. Refreshments may be taken at the informal bistro. See also the Hotel Groups pages.

Rooms 80 (26 GF) **Conf** Class 30 Board 30 Thtr 40

Premier Inn Milton Keynes Central

BUDGET HOTEL

☎ 0871 527 8774
Secklow Gate West MK9 3BZ
web: www.premierinn.com
dir: M1 junct 14 follow H6 route over 6 rdbts, at 7th (South Secklow) turn right, hotel on left

High quality, budget accommodation ideal for both families and business travellers. Spacious, en suite bedrooms feature tea and coffee making facilities, and Freeview TV in most hotels. Internet access and Wi-fi are available for a small fee. The adjacent family restaurant features a wide and varied menu. See also the Hotel Groups pages.

Rooms 38

Premier Inn Milton Keynes East (Willen Lake)

BUDGET HOTEL

☎ 0871 527 8778
Brickhill St, Willen Lake MK15 9HQ
web: www.premierinn.com
dir: M1 junct 14 , H6 (Childsway). Right at 3rd rdbt into Brickhill St. Right at 1st mini rdbt, hotel 1st left

Rooms 41

Premier Inn Milton Keynes South

BUDGET HOTEL

☎ 0871 527 8780
Lakeside Grove, Bletcham Way, Caldecotte MK7 8HP
web: www.premierinn.com
dir: M1 junct 14, towards Milton Keynes on H6 (Childs Way). Straight on at 2 rdbts. Left at 3rd onto V10 (Brickhill St). Straight on at 5 rdbts, at 6th right onto H10 (Bletcham Way)

Rooms 41

Premier Inn Milton Keynes South West (Furzton Lake)

BUDGET HOTEL

☎ 0871 527 8776
Shirwell Crescent, Furzton MK4 1GA
web: www.premierinn.com
dir: M1 junct 14, A509 to Milton Keynes. Straight on at 8 rdbts, at 9th rdbt (North Grafton) left onto V6. Right at next onto H7. Over The Bowl rdbt, hotel on left

Rooms 120

MINEHEAD	Map 3 SS94
Somerset	

Channel House Hotel

★★★ 80% SMALL HOTEL

☎ 01643 703229
Church Path TA24 5QG
e-mail: channelhouse@btconnect.com
dir: From A39 right at rdbt to seafront, left onto promenade. 1st right, 1st left into Blenheim Gdns,1st right into Northfield Rd

This family-run hotel offers relaxing surroundings, yet is only a short walk from the town centre. The South West Coastal Path starts from the hotel's two-acre gardens. Many of the exceptionally well-equipped bedrooms benefit from wonderful views. Imaginative menus are created from the best local produce. The hotel is totally non-smoking.

Rooms 8 ⌇ **D** £166-£202 (incl. bkfst & dinner)* **Facilities** FTV Wi-fi **Services** Air con **Parking** 10 **Notes** ⊗ No children 15yrs Closed Nov & 29 Dec-15 Mar

Northfield Hotel

★★★ 77% HOTEL

☎ 01643 705155
Northfield Rd TA24 5PU
e-mail: res@nfhotel.co.uk
web: www.northfield-hotel.co.uk
dir: M5 junct 23, follow A38 to Bridgwater then A39 to Minehead

Dating back to the Edwardian era, this hotel was originally a private house. From its elevated position, it enjoys lovely views out over the town and the Bristol Channel. The peaceful setting makes it an ideal location for exploring both locally and further afield, with the stunning expanse of Exmoor just a short drive away. Bedrooms offer good levels of comfort and quality, likewise the spacious and elegant public areas with a choice of lounges available. The attractive wood-panelled dining room is the venue for enjoyable cuisine with a range of dishes to suit all tastes. Additional facilities include a lovely garden and indoor swimming pool.

Rooms 30 (4 fmly) (4 GF) ⚑ **S** £60-£70; **D** £116-£136 (incl. bkfst)* **Facilities** FTV Wi-fi ⊕ Putt green Gym Xmas New Year **Conf** Class 30 Board 20 Thtr 40 Del from £110 to £130* **Services** Lift **Parking** 30 **Notes** LB

MINSTER
Kent   Map 7 TR36

Premier Inn Ramsgate

BUDGET HOTEL

☎ 0871 527 9270
Tothill St CT12 4HY
web: www.premierinn.com
dir: M25 onto A2 (signed Dover) merge onto M2 (signed Canterbury). Onto A299 (signed Margate/Ramsgate). Hotel at Minister rdbt

High quality, budget accommodation ideal for both families and business travellers. Spacious, en suite bedrooms feature tea and coffee making facilities, and Freeview TV in most hotels. Internet access and Wi-fi are available for a small fee. The adjacent family restaurant features a wide and varied menu. See also the Hotel Groups pages.

Rooms 71

MONK FRYSTON
North Yorkshire   Map 16 SE52

Monk Fryston Hall Hotel

★★★ 81% COUNTRY HOUSE HOTEL

☎ 01977 682369
LS25 5DU
e-mail: reception@monkfrystonhallhotel.co.uk
web: www.monkfrystonhallhotel.co.uk
dir: A1(M) junct 42, A63 towards Selby. Monk Fryston 2m, hotel on left

This delightful 16th-century mansion house enjoys a peaceful location in 30 acres of grounds, yet is only minutes' drive from the A1. Many original features have been retained and the public rooms are furnished with antique and period pieces. Bedrooms are individually styled and thoughtfully equipped for both business and leisure guests.

Rooms 29 (2 fmly) (5 GF) ⚑ **S** £65-£85; **D** £120-£135 (incl. bkfst)* **Facilities** STV FTV Wi-fi ⤙ Xmas New Year **Conf** Class 30 Board 25 Thtr 70 Del from £125 to £140* **Parking** 80 **Notes** LB Civ Wed 72

MORECAMBE
Lancashire   Map 18 SD46

The Midland   English Lakes
                                       Hotels Resorts & Venues

★★★★ 75% HOTEL

☎ 01524 424000
Marine Road West LA4 4BU
e-mail: themidland@englishlakes.co.uk
dir: A589 towards Morecambe, follow seafront signs, left on B5321 (Lancaster Rd) then Easton Rd, left into Central Drive. Right at rdbt on seafront. Left to hotel entrance

This art deco hotel sits on the seafront and commands stunning views across Morecambe Bay to the mountains of the Lake District. Stylish and modern accommodation is provided in the well-appointed bedrooms. Spa facilities are available on site, and guests can use the leisure club at the nearby sister hotel.

Rooms 44 ⚑ **S** £77-£204; **D** £94-£348 (incl. bkfst)* **Facilities** FTV Wi-fi ⇕ Xmas New Year **Conf** Class 30 Board 48 Thtr 140 **Services** Lift **Parking** 70 **Notes** Civ Wed 140

Clarendon Hotel

★★★ 71% HOTEL

☎ 01524 410180
76 Marine Road West, West End Promenade LA4 4EP
e-mail: clarendon@mitchellshotels.co.uk
dir: M6 junct 34 follow Morecambe signs. At rdbt (with 'Toby Carvery' on corner) 1st exit to Westgate, follow to seafront. Right at lights, hotel 3rd block

This traditional seafront hotel offers views over Morecambe Bay, modern facilities and convenient parking. An extensive fish and grill menu is offered in the contemporary Waterfront Restaurant and guests can relax in the comfortable lounge bar. Davy Jones Locker in the basement has a more traditional pub atmosphere and offers cask ales and regular live entertainment.

Rooms 29 (3 fmly) ⚑ **S** £45-£60; **D** £70-£90 (incl. bkfst)* **Facilities** STV Wi-fi HL Xmas New Year **Conf** Class 40 Board 40 Thtr 90 **Services** Lift **Parking** 22 **Notes** LB Civ Wed 60

Lothersdale Hotel

★★★ 🅰 HOTEL

☎ 01524 416404
320-323 Marine Rd LA4 5AA
e-mail: mail@bfhotels.com
web: www.bfhotels.com
dir: M6 junct 34 follow signs for Morecambe & Heysham. Straight over 3 rdbts following sign for Promenade. At seafront turn left, hotel 0.5m on left

The Lothersdale Hotel is on the Promenade with breathtaking views of Morecambe Bay and the Lakeland Fells, and these same views are enjoyed by the Superior bedrooms. The Bury family and their staff are keenly interested in the comfort of their visitors. The hotel is close to the start of the 'Way of the Roses', and is an ideal base for those venturing across country on this popular route. The lounge and bar are attractively furnished and decorated, and there is a weekly program of entertainment.

Rooms 45 (1 fmly) (6 GF) ⚑ **S** £30-£50; **D** £50-£110 (incl. bkfst)* **Facilities** FTV Wi-fi ⇕ ♫ Xmas New Year **Conf** Class 100 Board 50 Thtr 150 Del from £85 to £110* **Services** Lift **Parking** 21 **Notes** LB ⊗ Civ Wed 45

M

MORETONHAMPSTEAD — Map 3 SX78
Devon

The White Hart Hotel
★★★ 79% HOTEL

☎ 01647 440500
The Square TQ13 8NQ
e-mail: enquiries@whitehartdartmoor.co.uk
web: www.whitehartdartmoor.co.uk
dir: A30 towards Okehampton. At Whiddon Down take A382 for Moretonhampstead

Dating back to the 1700s, this former coaching inn is located on the edge of Dartmoor. A relaxed and friendly atmosphere prevails, with the staff providing attentive service. Comfortable bedrooms have a blend of traditional and contemporary styles with thoughtful extras provided. Dining is in either the brasserie restaurant or more informally in the bar, where quality cuisine is served.

Rooms 28 (8 annexe) (3 fmly) (4 GF) ➧ **Facilities** FTV Wi-fi ↕ Xmas New Year **Conf** Class 30 Board 20 Thtr 50 **Notes** LB Civ Wed 60

MORETON-IN-MARSH — Map 10 SP23
Gloucestershire

Manor House Hotel
★★★★ 79% ⚬⚬ HOTEL

☎ 01608 650501
High St GL56 0LJ
e-mail: info@manorhousehotel.info
web: www.cotswold-inns-hotels.co.uk/manor
dir: Off A429 at south end of town. Take East St off High St, hotel car park 3rd right

Dating back to the 16th century, this charming Cotswold coaching inn retains much of its original character with stone walls, impressive fireplaces and a relaxed, country-house atmosphere. Bedrooms vary in size and reflect the individuality of the building; all are well equipped and some are particularly opulent. Comfortable public areas include a popular bar, a brasserie and the stylish Mulberry Restaurant where the chance to enjoy an evening meal should not be missed.

Rooms 35 (1 annexe) (3 fmly) (1 GF) ➧ **S** £120-£160; **D** £158-£350 (incl. bkfst)* **Facilities** FTV Wi-fi Xmas New Year **Conf** Class 48 Board 54 Thtr 120 **Services** Lift **Parking** 24 **Notes** Civ Wed 120

White Hart Royal Hotel
★★★ 79% ⚬ HOTEL

☎ 01608 650731
High St GL56 0BA
e-mail: whr@bpcmail.co.uk
web: www.whitehartroyal.co.uk
dir: On High St at junct with Oxford Rd

This historic hotel has been providing accommodation for hundreds of years and today offers high standards of quality and comfort. Public areas are full of character, and the bedrooms, in a wide range of shapes and sizes, include several very spacious and luxurious rooms situated adjacent to the main building. A varied range of well prepared dishes is available throughout the day and evening in the main bar and the relaxing restaurant.

Rooms 28 (8 annexe) (2 fmly) (9 GF) ➧ **Facilities** FTV Wi-fi ↕ HL Xmas New Year **Conf** Class 40 Board 20 Thtr 55 **Parking** 6

Redesdale Arms
★★★ 77% ⚬ HOTEL

☎ 01608 650308
High St GL56 0AW
e-mail: info@redesdalearms.com
dir: On A429, 0.5m from rail station

This fine old inn has played a central role in the town for centuries. Traditional features combine successfully with contemporary comforts; bedrooms are located in the main building and in an annexe. Guests can choose from an imaginative menu in either in the stylish restaurant or the conservatory.

Rooms 34 (26 annexe) (4 fmly) (16 GF) ➧ **S** £69-£110; **D** £89-£189 (incl. bkfst)* **Facilities** STV FTV Wi-fi ↕ Xmas New Year **Parking** 17 **Notes** LB ⊗

MORLEY — Map 11 SK34
Derbyshire

The Morley Hayes Hotel
★★★★ 78% ⚬⚬ HOTEL

☎ 01332 780480
Main Rd DE7 6DG
e-mail: hotel@morleyhayes.com
web: www.morleyhayes.com
dir: 4m N of Derby on A608

Located in rolling countryside this modern golfing destination provides extremely comfortable, stylish bedrooms with wide-ranging facilities, plasma TVs, and state-of-the-art bathrooms; the plush suites are particularly eye-catching. Creative cuisine is offered in the Dovecote Restaurant, and both Roosters and the Spikes sports bar provide informal eating options.

Rooms 32 (4 fmly) (15 GF) ➧ **S** £80-£130; **D** £120-£150 (incl. bkfst)* **Facilities** STV Wi-fi ↕ HL ⌗ 27 Putt green Golf driving range **Conf** Class 50 Board 40 Thtr 120 Del from £139.95 to £147* **Services** Lift Air con **Parking** 245 **Notes** LB ⊗ Civ Wed 90

MOTTRAM ST ANDREW — Map 16 SJ87
Cheshire

De Vere Mottram Hall
★★★★ 81% HOTEL

☎ 01625 828135
Wilmslow Rd SK10 4QT
e-mail: dmh.sales@devere-hotels.com
web: www.devere.co.uk
dir: M6 junct 18 from S, M6 junct 20 from N, M56 junct 6, A538 Prestbury

Set in 272 acres of some of Cheshire's most beautiful parkland, this 18th-century Georgian country house is certainly an idyllic retreat. The hotel boasts extensive leisure facilities, including a championship golf course, swimming pool, gym and spa. Bedrooms are well equipped and elegantly furnished, and include a number of four-poster rooms and suites.

Rooms 120 (44 GF) ➧ **S** £95-£195; **D** £95-£195 (incl. bkfst) **Facilities** Spa STV Wi-fi ↕ ⌗ supervised ⌗ 18 ⌗ Putt green Fishing Gym FA approved football pitch Xmas New Year **Conf** Class 120 Board 60 Thtr 180 Del from £130 to £230 **Services** Lift **Parking** 300 **Notes** LB ⊗ Civ Wed 160

MOUSEHOLE — Map 2 SW42
Cornwall

The Cornish Range Restaurant with Rooms
⚬ RESTAURANT WITH ROOMS

☎ 01736 731488
6 Chapel St TR19 6BD
e-mail: info@cornishrange.co.uk
dir: From Penzance take B3315, through Newlyn to Mousehole. Along harbour, past Ship Inn, sharp right, left, establishment on right

This is a memorable place to eat and stay. Stylish rooms, with delightful Cornish home-made furnishings, and attentive, friendly service create a relaxing environment. Interesting and accurate cuisine relies heavily on freshly-landed, local fish and shellfish, as well as local meat and poultry, and the freshest fruit and vegetables.

Rooms 3

Save on hotels. Book at **theAA.com/hotel**

MOR – MUL 325 **ENGLAND**

Raven Hotel

★★★ 78% ◉◉ HOTEL

☎ 01952 727251
30 Barrow St TF13 6EN
e-mail: enquiry@ravenhotel.com
web: www.ravenhotel.com
dir: M54 junct 4 or 5, take A442 S, then A4169 to Much Wenlock

This town-centre hotel spreads across several historic buildings with a 17th-century coaching inn at its centre. The accommodation is well furnished and equipped to offer modern comfort; some ground-floor rooms are available. Public areas feature an interesting collection of prints and memorabilia connected with the modern-day Olympic Games - an idea which was, interestingly, born in Much Wenlock.

Rooms 20 (13 annexe) (5 GF) **S** £105-£115; **D** £120-£130 (incl. bkfst)* **Facilities** FTV Wi-fi ⬧ New Year **Conf** Board 16 Thtr 16 **Parking** 30 **Notes** LB ⊗ Closed 25-26 Dec

Gaskell Arms

★★★ 75% SMALL HOTEL

☎ 01952 727212
Bourton Rd TF13 6AQ
e-mail: maxine@gaskellarms.co.uk
web: www.gaskellarms.co.uk
dir: M6 junct 10A onto M54, exit at junct 4, follow signs for Ironbridge/Much Wenlock & A4169

This 17th-century former coaching inn has exposed beams and log fires in the public areas, and much original charm and character is retained throughout.

In addition to the lounge bar and restaurant offering a wide range of meals and snacks, there is a small bar which is popular with locals. Well-equipped bedrooms, some located in stylishly renovated stables, provide good standards of comfort.

Rooms 16 (3 fmly) (5 GF) **S** £70-£85; **D** £95-£120 (incl. bkfst)* **Facilities** FTV Wi-fi ⬧ **Conf** Class 30 Board 20 Thtr 30 **Parking** 40 **Notes** LB ⊗

See **Christchurch**

Mullion Cove Hotel

★★★ 80% ◉ HOTEL

☎ 01326 240328
TR12 7EP
e-mail: enquiries@mullion-cove.co.uk
web: www.mullion-cove.co.uk
dir: A3083 towards The Lizard. Through Mullion towards Mullion Cove. Hotel in approx 1m

Built at the turn of the last century and set high above the working harbour of Mullion, this hotel has spectacular views of the rugged coastline; seaward facing rooms are always popular. The elegant restaurant offers some carefully prepared dishes using local produce, while an alternative option is to eat less formally in the stylish bistro. After dinner, guests might like to relax in one of the elegant lounges.

Mullion Cove Hotel

Rooms 30 (3 fmly) (3 GF) ⬧ **S** £85-£305; **D** £100-£320 (incl. bkfst)* **Facilities** FTV Wi-fi ⬧ Xmas New Year **Conf** Class 20 Board 30 Thtr 50 Del from £120 to £320* **Services** Lift **Parking** 60 **Notes** LB

See advert below

M

NAILSWORTH
Gloucestershire
Map 4 ST89

Wild Garlic Restaurant and Rooms

◉◉ RESTAURANT WITH ROOMS

☎ 01453 832615
3 Cossack Square GL6 ODB
e-mail: info@wild-garlic.co.uk
dir: M4 junct 18, A46 towards Stroud. Enter Nailsworth, left at rdbt, immediately left. Establishment opposite Britannia pub

Situated in a quiet corner of this charming Cotswold town, this restaurant with rooms offers a delightful combination of welcoming, relaxed hospitality and high quality cuisine. The spacious and well-equipped bedrooms are situated above the restaurant. The small and friendly team of staff ensure guests are very well looked after throughout their stay.

Rooms 3 (2 fmly)

NANTWICH
Cheshire
Map 15 SJ65

INSPECTORS' CHOICE

Rookery Hall Hotel & Spa

Hand PICKED HOTELS
BUILT FOR PLEASURE

★★★★ ◉◉ HOTEL

☎ 01270 610016 & 0845 072 7533
Main Rd, Worleston CW5 6DQ
e-mail: rookeryhall@handpicked.co.uk
web: www.handpickedhotels.co.uk/rookeryhall
dir: From A51 N of Nantwich take B5074(Winsford) signed Rookery Hall. Hotel 1.5m on right

This fine 19th-century mansion is set in 38 acres of gardens, pasture and parkland. Bedrooms are spacious and appointed to a high standard with wide-screen plasma TVs and DVD players; many rooms have separate walk-in showers as well as deep tubs. Public areas are delightful and retain many original features. There is an extensive, state-of-the art spa and leisure complex.

Rooms 70 (39 annexe) (6 fmly) (23 GF) ♥
Facilities Spa STV FTV Wi-fi ↕ HL ⟳ ⤵ Gym Sauna

Crystal steam room Hydrotherapy pool ♫ Xmas New Year **Conf** Class 90 Board 46 Thtr 200 **Services** Lift **Parking** 120 **Notes** ⊗ Civ Wed 140

Alvaston Hall Hotel

Warner Leisure Hotels
JUST FOR GROWN-UPS

★★★ 77% HOTEL

☎ 01270 624341
Middlewich Rd CW5 6PD

A Grade-II listed Victorian property located in the delightful Cheshire countryside and set in extensive grounds. Bedrooms vary in size and style; some have spacious seating areas and some have outdoor terraces. Outdoor and indoor leisure facilities include a 9-hole golf course, hair and beauty treatments, and a great range of entertainment and activities. Please note that this is an adults-only (over 21) hotel.

Rooms 168 (52 annexe) (96 GF) ♥ **S** £83-£161; **D** £166-£322 (incl. bkfst & dinner)* **Facilities** Spa FTV Wi-fi ⟳ supervised ⚡ 9 Putt green ⤵ Gym Archery Bowling green Floodlit driving range ♫ Xmas New Year **Conf** Class 24 Board 16 Thtr 30 **Services** Lift **Parking** 108 **Notes** LB ⊗ No children 21yrs

The Crown Hotel & Casa Brasserie

★★ 75% HOTEL

☎ 01270 625283
High St CW5 5AS
e-mail: info@crownhotelnantwich.com
web: www.crownhotelnantwich.com
dir: A52 to Nantwich, hotel in town centre

Ideally set in the heart of this historic and delightful market town, The Crown has been offering hospitality for centuries. It has an abundance of original features and the well-equipped bedrooms retain an old world charm. The atmospheric bar offers real ales and the lively brasserie is an ideal venue for relaxed dining. Complimentary Wi-fi is available.

Rooms 18 (2 fmly) (1 smoking) ♥ **S** £60-£76; **D** £70-£88* **Facilities** FTV Wi-fi ♫ **Conf** Class 150 Board 70 Thtr 200 Del from £110 to £130* **Parking** 18 **Notes** LB Closed 25 Dec Civ Wed 140

Premier Inn Crewe/ Nantwich

Premier Inn

BUDGET HOTEL

☎ 0871 527 8782
221 Crewe Rd CW5 6NE
web: www.premierinn.com
dir: M6 junct 16, A500 towards Chester, A534 towards Nantwich. Hotel approx 100yds on right

High quality, budget accommodation ideal for both families and business travellers. Spacious, en suite

bedrooms feature tea and coffee making facilities, and Freeview TV in most hotels. Internet access and Wi-fi are available for a small fee. The adjacent family restaurant features a wide and varied menu. See also the Hotel Groups pages.

Rooms 37

NETHER STOWEY
Somerset
Map 4 ST13

Apple Tree Hotel

★★★ 71% HOTEL

☎ 01278 733238
Keenthorne TA5 1HZ
e-mail: reservations@appletreehotel.com
web: www.appletreehotel.com
dir: A39 from Bridgwater towards Minehead. Hotel on left, 2m past Cannington

Once a farm cottage, dating back over 300 years, this popular hotel now provides a perfect base from which to explore the many and varied places of interest in the locale, including the unspoilt beauty of the Quantock Hills. Whether choosing to stay for business or leisure, the warmth of welcome is always the same with the owners very much hands-on and ensuring guests are well looked after. Bedrooms provide all the expected contemporary comforts with rooms offered in both the main building and adjacent garden rooms. Dinner is served in the conservatory restaurant, perhaps preceded with a relaxing drink in the convivial bar or library lounge.

Rooms 16 (2 fmly) (7 GF) ♥ **S** £73-£79; **D** £99-£109 (incl. bkfst)* **Facilities** FTV Wi-fi ⟳ **Conf** Class 12 Board 12 Thtr 20 **Parking** 30 **Notes** ⊗

NEWARK-ON-TRENT
Nottinghamshire
Map 17 SK75

Premier Inn Newark

Premier Inn

BUDGET HOTEL

☎ 0871 527 8784
Lincoln Rd NG24 2DB
web: www.premierinn.com
dir: At junct of A1 & A46 & A17, follow B6166 signs

High quality, budget accommodation ideal for both families and business travellers. Spacious, en suite bedrooms feature tea and coffee making facilities, and Freeview TV in most hotels. Internet access and Wi-fi are available for a small fee. The adjacent family restaurant features a wide and varied menu. See also the Hotel Groups pages.

Rooms 40

N

NEWBURY
Berkshire   Map 5 SU46

See also Andover

INSPECTORS' CHOICE

The Vineyard

★★★★★ ◉◉◉ HOTEL

☎ 01635 528770
Stockcross RG20 8JU
e-mail: general@the-vineyard.co.uk
web: www.the-vineyard.co.uk
dir: From M4 junct 13, A34 towards Newbury, exit at 3rd junct for Speen. Right at rdbt then right again at 2nd rdbt

A haven of style in the Berkshire countryside, this hotel prides itself on a superb art collection, which can be seen throughout the building. Bedrooms come in a variety of styles, including many split-level suites that are exceptionally well equipped. Comfortable lounges lead into the stylish restaurant, which serves the imaginative and precise contemporary French cuisine created by Daniel Galmiche, complemented by an equally impressive selection of wines from California and around the world; the cellar holds over 30,000 wines including bottles from the award-winning estate of owner Sir Peter Michael. The welcome throughout the hotel is warm and sincere, the service professional yet relaxed.

Rooms 49 (18 GF) ☏ **S** £190-£335; **D** £285-£385*
Facilities Spa STV Wi-fi ↕ ⊗ Gym ♫ Xmas New Year **Conf** Class 70 Board 30 Thtr 140
Del from £295 to £395 **Services** Lift Air con **Parking** 100 **Notes** LB ⊗ Civ Wed 100

Donnington Valley Hotel & Spa
CLASSIC BRITISH HOTELS

★★★★ 86% ◉◉ HOTEL

☎ 01635 551199
Old Oxford Rd, Donnington RG14 3AG
e-mail: general@donningtonvalley.co.uk
web: www.donningtonvalley.co.uk
dir: M4 junct 13, A34 signed Newbury. Take exit signed Donnington/Services, at rdbt 2nd exit signed Donnington. Left at next rdbt. Hotel 2m on right

In its own grounds complete with an 18-hole golf course, this stylish hotel boasts excellent facilities for both corporate and leisure guests; from the state-of-the-art spa offering excellent treatments, to an extensive range of meeting and function rooms. Air-conditioned bedrooms are stylish, spacious and particularly well equipped with fridges, lap-top safes and internet access. The Wine Press restaurant offers imaginative food complemented by a superb wine list.

Rooms 111 (3 fmly) (36 GF) ☏ **S** £114-£237;
D £129-£252 (incl. bkfst)* **Facilities** Spa STV Wi-fi ↕ ⊗ ♨ 18 Putt green Gym Aromatherapy Sauna Steam room Studio Xmas New Year **Conf** Class 50 Board 65 Thtr 160 Del £285 **Services** Lift Air con **Parking** 150 **Notes** LB ⊗ Civ Wed 85

Regency Park Hotel

★★★★ 75% ◉ HOTEL

☎ 01635 871555
Bowling Green Rd, Thatcham RG18 3RP
e-mail: info@regencyparkhotel.co.uk
web: www.regencyparkhotel.co.uk
dir: From Newbury take A4 signed Thatcham & Reading. 2nd rdbt exit signed Cold Ash. Hotel 1m on left

This smart, stylish hotel is ideal for both business and leisure guests. Spacious, well-equipped bedrooms include a number of contemporary, tasteful executive rooms. Smart, airy public areas include a state-of-the-art spa and leisure club, plus the Watermark Restaurant which offers appealing cuisine.

Rooms 108 (10 fmly) (9 GF) **S** £88-£185; **D** £98-£195 (incl. bkfst)* **Facilities** Spa STV FTV Wi-fi ↕ ⊗ Gym Beauty treatments Sauna Steam room New Year **Conf** Class 80 Board 70 Thtr 200 **Services** Lift **Parking** 200 **Notes** LB ⊗ Civ Wed 100

BEST WESTERN West Grange Hotel
Best Western

★★★★ 71% HOTEL

☎ 01635 273074
Cox's Ln, Bath Rd, Midgham RG7 5UP
e-mail: reservations@westgrangehotel.co.uk
dir: M4 junct 12, A4 (Bath Rd), follow Newbury signs. Through Woolhampton, hotel on right in approx 2m

Conveniently situated between Reading and Newbury this modern hotel has well-appointed, spacious bedrooms; executive rooms are beautifully presented and have a host of additional features. The contemporary open-plan lounge and restaurant area serves an extensive choice of British cuisine. There is a range of business suites along with a larger conference room. Gardens are a real feature and the central courtyard is popular with guests.

Rooms 62 **Conf** Class 25 Board 30 Thtr 50

N

NEWBURY *continued*

Mercure Newbury Elcot Park

★★★★ 71% HOTEL

☎ 0844 815 9060
Elcot RG20 8NJ
e-mail: gm.mercurenewburyelcotpark@jupiterhotels.co.uk
web: www.jupiterhotels.co.uk
dir: M4 junct 13, A338 to Hungerford, A4 to Newbury. Hotel 4m from Hungerford

Enjoying a peaceful location yet within easy reach of both the A4 and M4, this country-house hotel is set in 16 acres of gardens and woodland. Bedrooms are comfortably appointed and include some located in an adjacent mews. Public areas include the Orangery Restaurant which enjoys views over the Kennet Valley, a leisure club and a range of conference rooms.

Rooms 73 (17 annexe) (4 fmly) (25 GF) (5 smoking) **Facilities** FTV Wi-fi ⌨ ☺ ♨ Gym New Year **Conf** Class 45 Board 35 Thtr 110 **Services** Lift **Parking** 130 **Notes** Civ Wed 120

Newbury Manor Hotel

★★★ 77% ◉ HOTEL

☎ 01635 528838
London Rd RG14 2BY
e-mail: enquiries@newbury-manor-hotel.co.uk
dir: On A4 between Newbury & Thatcham

This former Georgian watermill, which still features the original millrace, is situated beside the River Kennet in well tended grounds. The character bedrooms vary in style and size and offer many accessories. Guests can dine in the award-winning River Bar Restaurant.

Rooms 34 (4 fmly) (11 GF) ⌨ **S** £59-£149; **D** £59-£180 (incl. bkfst)* **Facilities** FTV Wi-fi ⌨ Fishing Xmas New Year Child facilities **Conf** Class 90 Board 50 Thtr 190 Del from £125 to £145* **Parking** 100 **Notes** LB ⊗ Civ Wed 180

The Chequers Hotel

★★★ 72% HOTEL

☎ 01635 38000
6-8 Oxford St RG14 1JB
e-mail: info@chequershotelnewbury.co.uk
web: www.chequershotelnewbury.co.uk
dir: M4 junct 13, A34 S, A339 to Newbury. At 2nd rdbt right to town centre. At clock tower rdbt right, hotel on right

Situated just at the top of the main shopping street in Newbury and convenient for fast road connections, this 18th-century former coaching inn retains original features along with contemporary touches. The bedrooms come in a range of sizes and JP's Bistro is a popular eaterie. The hotel has ample parking which is a definite advantage in this town.

Rooms 56 (2 fmly) (6 GF) **Facilities** FTV Wi-fi ⌨ **Conf** Class 36 Board 40 Thtr 160 **Parking** 60 **Notes** ⊗ Civ Wed 120

Premier Inn Newbury/Thatcham

BUDGET HOTEL

☎ 0871 527 8786
Bath Rd, Midgham RG7 5UX
web: www.premierinn.com
dir: M4 junct 12, A4 towards Newbury. Hotel 7m on right

High quality, budget accommodation ideal for both families and business travellers. Spacious, en suite bedrooms feature tea and coffee making facilities, and Freeview TV in most hotels. Internet access and Wi-fi are available for a small fee. The adjacent family restaurant features a wide and varied menu. See also the Hotel Groups pages.

Rooms 49

Lakeside Hotel Lake Windermere

★★★★ 88% ◉◉ HOTEL

☎ 015395 30001
Lakeside LA12 8AT
e-mail: sales@lakesidehotel.co.uk
web: www.lakesidehotel.co.uk
dir: M6 junct 36, A590 to Barrow, follow signs to Newby Bridge. Right over bridge, hotel 1m on right

This impressive hotel enjoys an enviable location on the southern edge of Lake Windermere and has easy access to the Lakeside & Haverthwaite Steam Railway, and the ferry terminal. Bedrooms are individually styled, and many enjoy delightful lake views. Spacious lounges and a choice of restaurants are available. The state-of-the-art spa is exclusive to residents and provides a range of treatment suites. Staff throughout are friendly and nothing is too much trouble.

Rooms 75 (8 fmly) (8 GF) ⌨ **S** £99-£310; **D** £139-£349 (incl. bkfst)* **Facilities** Spa STV Wi-fi ⌨ Fishing Gym Private jetty Rowing boats ♫ Xmas New Year **Conf** Class 50 Board 40 Thtr 100 Del from £120* **Services** Lift **Parking** 200 **Notes** LB ⊗ Civ Wed 70

The Swan Hotel & Spa

★★★★ 81% HOTEL

☎ 015395 31681
LA12 8NB
e-mail: enquiries@swanhotel.com
web: www.swanhotel.com
dir: M6 junct 36, A591, merge onto A590. At rdbts follow A590, left at Newby Bridge rdbt, 1st right for hotel

Set in idyllic surroundings, this hotel offers something to suit every taste, from a gym and spa therapies for adults to a dedicated children's lounge. The well-equipped bedrooms are thoroughly modern, but each has a vintage touch. Good quality meals are served in the River Room; in good weather guests can eat on the riverside terrace.

Rooms 51 (8 fmly) (14 GF) ⌨ **S** £99-£190; **D** £99-£190 (incl. bkfst)* **Facilities** Spa FTV Wi-fi ⌨ Gym Sauna Steam room Xmas New Year Child facilities **Conf** Class 60 Board 40 Thtr 100 Del £175* **Services** Lift Air con **Parking** 100 **Notes** ⊗ Civ Wed 100

Whitewater Hotel

★★★★ 72% ◉ HOTEL

☎ 015395 31133
The Lakeland Village LA12 8PX
e-mail: enquiries@whitewater-hotel.co.uk
web: www.whitewater-hotel.co.uk
dir: M6 junct 36, follow signs for A590 (Barrow), 1m, through Newby Bridge. Right at sign for Lakeland Village, hotel on left

This tasteful conversion of an old mill on the River Leven is close to the southern end of Lake Windermere. Bedrooms, many with lovely river views, are spacious and comfortable. Public areas include a luxurious, well-equipped spa, squash courts, and a choice of comfortable lounges. The Dolly Blue bar overlooks the river and is a vibrant informal alternative to the fine dining restaurant.

Rooms 38 (10 fmly) (2 GF) ⌨ **Facilities** Spa STV FTV Wi-fi ⌨ supervised ♨ Gym Squash Table tennis Xmas New Year **Conf** Class 32 Board 40 Thtr 80 **Services** Lift **Parking** 50 **Notes** ⊗ Civ Wed 110

N

NEWCASTLE-UNDER-LYME   Map 10 SJ84
Staffordshire

Holiday Inn Stoke-on-Trent

★★★ 75% HOTEL

☎ 01782 557000 & 557018
Clayton Rd, Clayton ST5 4DL
e-mail: reservations-stoke@ihg.com
web: www.histokeontrenthotel.co.uk
dir: M6 junct 15. Follow Clayton Rd signs towards
Newcastle-under-Lyme. Hotel 200yds on left

Stylish and contemporary, this modern hotel is well
located just minutes from the motorway junction.
Bedrooms are comfortable and boast an excellent
range of facilities. Guests have the use of the leisure
club.

Rooms 118 (38 fmly) **Facilities** STV Wi-fi ⓦ HL ⓢ
supervised Gym Beauty treatment room New Year
Conf Class 30 Board 22 Thtr 70 **Services** Air con
Parking 150 **Notes** ⊗

Premier Inn Newcastle-under-Lyme

BUDGET HOTEL

☎ 0871 527 8808
Talke Rd, Chesterton ST5 7AL
web: www.premierinn.com
dir: M6 junct 12, A500, A34 to Newcastle-under-
Lyme. Hotel 0.5m on right

High quality, budget accommodation ideal for both
families and business travellers. Spacious, en suite
bedrooms feature tea and coffee making facilities,
and Freeview TV in most hotels. Internet access and
Wi-fi are available for a small fee. The adjacent
family restaurant features a wide and varied menu.
See also the Hotel Groups pages.

Rooms 83

NEWCASTLE UPON TYNE   Map 21 NZ26
Tyne & Wear

INSPECTORS' CHOICE

Jesmond Dene House
★★★★ ◉◉◉ HOTEL

☎ 0191 212 3000
Jesmond Dene Rd NE2 2EY
e-mail: info@jesmonddenehouse.co.uk
web: www.jesmonddenehouse.co.uk
dir: A167 N to A184. Right, right again into
Jesmond Dene Rd, hotel on left

This grand house, overlooking the wooded valley of
Jesmond Dene, yet just five minutes from the centre
of town, has been sympathetically converted into a
stylish, contemporary hotel destination. The
bedrooms are beautifully designed and boast flat-
screen TVs, sumptuous beds with Egyptian cotton
linen, digital radios, well-stocked mini bars, free
broadband, desk space and safes. Equally eye-
catching bathrooms with underfloor heating are
equipped with high quality bespoke amenities. The
stylish restaurant is the venue for innovative
cooking which will prove a highlight of any stay.

Rooms 40 (8 annexe) (1 fmly) (4 GF) ⌂
S £110-£240; **D** £120-£400* **Facilities** STV Wi-fi ⓦ
HL **Conf** Class 80 Board 44 Thtr 125 Del from £185
to £220* **Services** Lift **Parking** 64 **Notes** LB ⊗
Civ Wed 100

Hotel du Vin Newcastle

★★★★ 79% ◉◉
TOWN HOUSE HOTEL

☎ 0191 229 2200
Allan House, City Rd NE1 2BE
e-mail: reception.newcastle@hotelduvin.com
dir: A1 junct 65 onto A184 Gateshead/Newcastle,
Quayside to City Rd

The former maintenance depot of the Tyne Tees
Shipping Company, this is a landmark building on the
Tyne. It has been transformed into a modern and
stylish hotel. Bedrooms are well equipped and deeply
comfortable with all the Hotel du Vin trademark items
such as Egyptian cotton sheets, plasma TVs, DVD
players and monsoon showers. Guests can dine in the
bistro or alfresco if the weather allows in the courtyard.

Rooms 42 (6 GF) ⌂ **S** £160-£400; **D** £160-£400 (incl.
bkfst)* **Facilities** STV Wi-fi **Conf** Board 20 Thtr 26
Del from £200 to £225* **Services** Lift Air con
Parking 10 **Notes** LB Civ Wed 40

Newcastle Gateshead Marriott Hotel MetroCentre

★★★★ 76% HOTEL

☎ 0191 493 2233
MetroCentre NE11 9XF
e-mail: reservations.newcastle.england.
metrocentre@marriotthotels.co.uk
web: www.newcastlemarriottmetrocentre.co.uk

(For full entry see Gateshead)

Newcastle Marriott Hotel Gosforth Park
★★★★ 76% HOTEL

☎ 0191 236 4111
High Gosforth Park, Gosforth NE3 5HN
web: www.newcastlemarriottgosforthpark.co.uk
dir: Onto A1056 to Killingworth & Wideopen. 3rd exit
to Gosforth Park, hotel ahead

Set within its own grounds, this modern hotel offers
extensive conference and banqueting facilities, along
with indoor and outdoor leisure. There is a choice of
dining in the more formal Plate Restaurant or the
relaxed Chat's lounge bar. Many of the air-
conditioned bedrooms have views over the park. The
hotel is conveniently located for the bypass, airport
and racecourse.

Rooms 178 (17 smoking) **Facilities** Spa STV Wi-fi ⓢ
supervised ⌁ Gym Squash Jogging trail ♫ New Year
Conf Class 280 Board 60 Thtr 800 Del from £140 to
£150* **Services** Lift Air con **Parking** 340
Notes Civ Wed 300

N

NEWCASTLE UPON TYNE *continued*

Holiday Inn Newcastle Jesmond

★★★★ 75% HOTEL

☎ 0191 281 5511
Jesmond Rd NE2 1PR

Holiday Inn Newcastle Jesmond is located next to the Metro Station and benefits from off-road parking. The interior is modern, and there is a vibrant restaurant and bar operation. This is a great location to enjoy the café culture of Jesmond or the upbeat pace of the city centre.

Rooms 116 **Conf** Class 160 Board 46 Thtr 250

Copthorne Hotel Newcastle

★★★★ 74% HOTEL

☎ 0191 222 0333
The Close, Quayside NE1 3RT
e-mail: sales.newcastle@millenniumhotels.co.uk
web: www.millenniumhotels.co.uk
dir: Follow signs to Newcastle city centre. Take B1600 Quayside exit, hotel on right

Set on the banks of the River Tyne close to the city centre, this stylish purpose-built hotel provides modern amenities including a leisure centre, conference facilities and a choice of restaurants for dinner. Bedrooms overlook the river, and there is a floor of 'Connoisseur' rooms that have their own dedicated exclusive lounge and business support services.

Rooms 156 (4 fmly) **Facilities** STV Wi-fi ⊗ supervised Gym Steam room Xmas New Year **Conf** Class 90 Board 60 Thtr 220 **Services** Lift **Parking** 180 **Notes** ⊗ Civ Wed 150

Malmaison Newcastle

★★★ 88% ⊚ HOTEL

☎ 0191 245 5000
Quayside NE1 3DX
e-mail: newcastle@malmaison.com
dir: Follow signs for city centre, then for Quayside/Law Courts. Hotel 100yds past Law Courts

Overlooking the river and the Millennium Bridge, the hotel has a prime position in the very popular quayside district. Bedrooms have striking decor, CD/DVD players, mini-bars and a number of individual touches. Food and drink are an integral part of the operation here, with a stylish brasserie-style restaurant and café bar, plus the Café Mal, a deli-style café next door to the main entrance.

Rooms 122 (10 fmly) **Facilities** Spa STV Wi-fi Gym **Conf** Board 18 Thtr 30 **Services** Lift Air con **Parking** 50

Eslington Villa Hotel

★★★ 82% ⊚ HOTEL

☎ 0191 487 6017 & 420 0666
8 Station Rd, Low Fell NE9 6DR
e-mail: home@eslingtonvilla.co.uk

(For full entry see Gateshead)

County Hotel, Newcastle   **thistle**

★★★ 82% HOTEL

☎ 0871 376 9029 & 0191 2322 471
Neville St NE1 5DF
e-mail: newcastle@thistle.co.uk
web: www.thistlehotels.com/newcastle
dir: A1 onto A184. Cross Redheugh Bridge, right at 2nd lights, right after cathedral, left at pedestrian zone

A 19th-century listed building, the hotel enjoys a central location opposite the city's Central Station, which also has links to the Metro system. Bedrooms are comfortably appointed for both business and leisure guests. Limited free parking is available.

Rooms 114 ⊮ S £45-£270; D £59-£320 **Facilities** FTV Wi-fi HL Complimentary use of nearby gym New Year **Conf** Class 100 Board 100 Thtr 250 Del from £99 to £214 **Services** Lift **Parking** 19 **Notes** LB ⊗ Civ Wed 100

Mercure Newcastle George Washington Hotel

★★★ 81% HOTEL

☎ 0191 402 9988
Stone Cellar Rd, High Usworth NE37 1PH
e-mail: reservations@georgewashington.co.uk
web: www.georgewashington.co.uk

(For full entry see Washington)

Horton Grange Country House Hotel

★★★ 78% HOTEL

☎ 01661 860686
Berwick Hill, Ponteland NE13 6BU
e-mail: info@hortongrange.co.uk
web: www.hortongrange.co.uk
dir: A1/A19 junct at Seaton Burn take 1st exit at 1st rdbt, after 1m, left signed Ponteland/Dinnington. Hotel on right approx 2m

A Grade II listed building set in its own grounds just a short distance from Newcastle Airport and Ponteland. The main house has traditionally styled executive bedrooms, and in addition there are four contemporary garden rooms that are elegant and spacious. All bedrooms have flat-screen TVs, digital radios and broadband access. Food is served in the light and airy restaurant and the lounge that both overlook the gardens.

Rooms 9 (4 annexe) (1 fmly) (4 GF) **Facilities** FTV Wi-fi Xmas New Year **Conf** Class 40 Board 30 Thtr 120 **Parking** 50 **Notes** LB ⊗ Civ Wed 120

The Caledonian Hotel, Newcastle

PEEL HOTELS PLC

★★★ 77% HOTEL

☎ 0191 281 7881
64 Osborne Rd, Jesmond NE2 2AT
e-mail: info@caledonian-hotel-newcastle.com
web: www.peelhotels.co.uk
dir: From A1 follow signs to Newcastle City, cross Tyne Bridge to Tynemouth. Left at lights at Osborne Rd, hotel on right

This hotel is located in the Jesmond area of the city, and offers comfortable bedrooms that are well equipped. The public areas include the trendy Billabong Bar and Bistro which serves food all day, and the terrace where a cosmopolitan atmosphere prevails. Alfresco dining is available.

Rooms 90 (6 fmly) (7 GF) (7 smoking) ⊮ **Facilities** Wi-fi Xmas New Year **Conf** Class 50 Board 50 Thtr 100 **Services** Lift **Parking** 35 **Notes** ⊗ Civ Wed 70

BEST WESTERN New Kent Hotel

★★★ 73% HOTEL

☎ 0191 281 7711
127 Osborne Rd NE2 2TB
e-mail: reservations@newkenthotel.co.uk
web: www.newkenthotel.co.uk
dir: On B1600, opposite St Georges Church

This popular business hotel offers relaxed service and typical Geordie hospitality. The bright modern bedrooms are well equipped and the modern bar is an ideal meeting place. A range of generous, good value dishes is served in the restaurant, which doubles as a wedding venue.

Rooms 32 (4 fmly) **Facilities** STV FTV Wi-fi Xmas New Year **Conf** Class 30 Board 40 Thtr 60 **Parking** 22 **Notes** Civ Wed 90

Newgate Hotel

fOCUShotels

★★★ 66% METRO HOTEL

☎ 0191 232 6570
Newgate St NE1 5SX
e-mail: enquiries@hotels-newcastle.com
dir: A184, A189 over bridge, right at 2nd lights, left at lights into Clayton St. 1st right to Fenkle St, 1st left to car park at end

Ideally located right in the heart of Newcastle, this hotel makes the perfect base for exploring the city. Bedrooms offer comfortable beds and free Wi-fi. Breakfast is served in the sixth-floor restaurant that has great views of the city.

Rooms 93 (8 fmly) **Facilities** STV Wi-fi **Conf** Board 12 Thtr 14 **Services** Lift **Parking** 120 **Notes** Closed 24-27 Dec

Premier Inn Newcastle Central

BUDGET HOTEL

☎ 0871 527 8802
New Bridge Street West NE1 8BS
web: www.premierinn.com
dir: Follow Gateshead & Newcastle signs on A167(M), over Tyne Bridge. A193 signed Wallsend & city centre, left to Carliol Square, hotel on corner

High quality, budget accommodation ideal for both families and business travellers. Spacious, en suite bedrooms feature tea and coffee making facilities, and Freeview TV in most hotels. Internet access and Wi-fi are available for a small fee. The adjacent family restaurant features a wide and varied menu. See also the Hotel Groups pages.

Rooms 172

Premier Inn Newcastle City Centre (Millennium Bridge)

BUDGET HOTEL

☎ 0871 527 8800
City Rd, Quayside NE1 2AN
web: www.premierinn.com
dir: At corner of City Rd (A186) & Crawhall Rd

Rooms 81

Premier Inn Newcastle (Holystone)

BUDGET HOTEL

☎ 0871 527 8790
The Stonebrook, Edmund Rd, Holystone NE27 0UN
web: www.premierinn.com
dir: 3m N of Tyne Tunnel. From A19 take A191 signed Gosforth. Hotel on left

Rooms 40

Premier Inn Newcastle Quayside

BUDGET HOTEL

☎ 0871 527 8804
The Quayside NE1 3AE
web: www.premierinn.com
dir: S'bound: A1, A167(M), A186 signed Walker & Wallsend follow B1600 Quayside signs. N'bound: A1, A184, A189 (cross river). 1st exit, follow B1600 Quayside signs. Hotel at foot of Tyne Bridge in Exchange building

Rooms 152

Novotel Newcastle Airport

★★★ 79% HOTEL

☎ 0191 214 0303
Ponteland Rd, Kenton NE3 3HZ
e-mail: H1118@accor-hotels.com
web: www.novotel.com
dir: A1(M) airport junct onto A696, take Kingston Park exit

This modern, well-proportioned hotel lies just off the bypass and is a five minute drive from the airport. The hotel has a scheduled shuttle service and flight information screens for air passengers. Bedrooms are spacious with a range of extras. The Elements Restaurant offers a flexible dining option and is open until late. There is a contemporary lounge bar and also a small leisure centre for the more energetic guests. Secure parking is available.

Rooms 126 (36 fmly) **Facilities** Wi-fi ⊛ Gym **Conf** Class 90 Board 40 Thtr 200 **Services** Lift **Parking** 260 **Notes** Civ Wed 200

Premier Inn Newcastle Airport

BUDGET HOTEL

☎ 0871 527 8796
Newcastle Int Airport, Ponteland Rd, Prestwick NE20 9DB
web: www.premierinn.com
dir: A1 onto A696, follow Airport signs. At rdbt take turn immediately after airport exit

High quality, budget accommodation ideal for both families and business travellers. Spacious, en suite bedrooms feature tea and coffee making facilities, and Freeview TV in most hotels. Internet access and Wi-fi are available for a small fee. The adjacent family restaurant features a wide and varied menu. See also the Hotel Groups pages.

Rooms 88

Premier Inn Newcastle Airport (South)

BUDGET HOTEL

☎ 0871 527 8798
Callerton Lane Ends, Woolsington NE13 8DF
web: www.premierinn.com
dir: Just off A696 on B6918, 0.3m from airport

Rooms 53

N

NEWENT
Gloucestershire
Map 10 SO72

Three Choirs Vineyards

◉ RESTAURANT WITH ROOMS

☎ 01531 890223
GL18 1LS
e-mail: info@threechoirs.com
web: www.threechoirs.com
dir: On B4215 N of Newent, follow brown tourist signs

This thriving vineyard continues to go from strength to strength and provides a wonderfully different place to stay. The restaurant, which overlooks the 100-acre estate, enjoys a popular following thanks to well-executed dishes that make good use of local produce. Spacious, high quality bedrooms are equipped with many extras, and each opens onto a private patio area which has wonderful views.

Rooms 11 (11 annexe) (1 fmly)

NEWHAVEN
East Sussex
Map 6 TQ40

Premier Inn Newhaven

BUDGET HOTEL

☎ 0871 527 8810
Avis Rd BN9 0AG
web: www.premierinn.com
dir: From A26 (New Rd) through Drove Industrial Estate, left after underpass. Hotel in same complex as Sainsbury's

High quality, budget accommodation ideal for both families and business travellers. Spacious, en suite bedrooms feature tea and coffee making facilities, and Freeview TV in most hotels. Internet access and Wi-fi are available for a small fee. The adjacent family restaurant features a wide and varied menu. See also the Hotel Groups pages.

Rooms 70

NEWICK
East Sussex
Map 6 TQ42

INSPECTORS' CHOICE

Newick Park Hotel & Country Estate

★★★ ◉◉ HOTEL

☎ 01825 723633
BN8 4SB
e-mail: bookings@newickpark.co.uk
web: www.newickpark.co.uk
dir: Exit A272 at Newick Green, 1m, pass church & pub. Turn left, hotel 0.25m on right

Newick Park is a delightful Grade II listed Georgian country house set amid 250 acres of Sussex parkland and landscaped gardens. The spacious, individually decorated bedrooms are tastefully furnished, thoughtfully equipped and have superb views of the grounds; many rooms have huge American king-size beds. The comfortable public rooms include a study, a sitting room, lounge bar and an elegant restaurant.

Rooms 16 (3 annexe) (5 fmly) (1 GF) ☍
S £125-£245; **D** £165-£285 (incl. bkfst)*
Facilities FTV Wi-fi ⚲ Fishing ⚓ Clay pigeon shooting Helicopter rides Quad biking Tank driving Laser quest Xmas **Conf** Class 40 Board 40 Thtr 80 Del from £185* **Parking** 52 **Notes** No children 3yrs Closed 31 Dec & 1 Jan Civ Wed 110

NEWMARKET
Suffolk
Map 12 TL66

Tuddenham Mill

★★★★ 81% ◉◉◉ HOTEL

☎ 01638 713552
High St, Tuddenham St Mary IP28 6SQ
e-mail: info@tuddenhammill.co.uk
dir: M11 junct 9, merge A14. Left lane junct 38 towards Thetford/Norwich. Signed Tuddenham

A beautifully converted old watermill set amidst landscaped grounds between Newmarket and Bury St Edmunds. The contemporary style bedrooms are situated in separate buildings adjacent to the main building, and each one is tastefully appointed with co-ordinated fabrics and soft furnishings. The public areas have a wealth of original features such as the water wheel and exposed beams; they include a lounge bar, a smart restaurant, a meeting room and choice of terraces.

Rooms 15 (12 annexe) (8 GF) ☍ **D** £130-£395 (incl. bkfst) **Facilities** STV FTV Wi-fi ⚲ Xmas New Year **Conf** Class 16 Board 16 Thtr 40 Del £150* **Parking** 40 **Notes** LB Civ Wed 60

Bedford Lodge Hotel

★★★★ 80% ◉◉ HOTEL

☎ 01638 663175
Bury Rd CB8 7BX
e-mail: info@bedfordlodgehotel.co.uk
web: www.bedfordlodgehotel.co.uk
dir: From town centre take A1304 towards Bury St Edmunds, hotel 0.5m on left

Bedford Lodge Hotel is an imposing 18th-century Georgian hunting lodge with more modern additions, set in three acres of secluded landscaped gardens. Public rooms feature the newly refurbished and re-named Squires restaurant, Roxana Bar and a small lounge. The hotel also features superb leisure facilities including the Eden Health and Fitness Club, as well as self-contained conference and banqueting suites. Contemporary bedrooms have a light, airy feel, and each is tastefully furnished and well equipped.

Rooms 77 (6 fmly) (21 GF) (3 smoking) ☍
S £89-£240; **D** £99-£240 (incl. bkfst) **Facilities** Spa FTV Wi-fi ⚲ ⚐ Gym Steam room Sauna Spa bath Hydrotherapy pool Rasul Dry floatation Xmas New Year **Conf** Class 80 Board 60 Thtr 200 Del from £140 to £195* **Services** Lift Air con **Parking** 120 **Notes** LB ⊗ RS Sat lunch Civ Wed 150

N

The Rutland Arms Hotel

★★★ 79% @ HOTEL

☎ 01638 664251

High St CB8 8NB

e-mail:
reservations.rutlandarms@bespokehotels.com
web: www.bespokehotels.com/rutlandarms
dir: A14 junct 37 onto A142, or M11 junct 9 onto A11
then A1304 - follow signs for town centre

Expect a warm welcome at this former coaching inn situated in the heart of town. The property is built around a 17th-century cobbled courtyard and still retains many original features. The public rooms include a large lounge bar and Carriages, a contemporary restaurant and wine bar. Bedrooms are smartly appointed and well equipped.

Rooms 46 (1 fmly) **Facilities** FTV Wi-fi ♫
Conf Class 40 Board 30 Thtr 70 **Parking** 40 **Notes** ⊗

Premier Inn Newmarket

BUDGET HOTEL

☎ 0871 527 9296

Fred Archer Way CB8 7XN

web: www.premierinn.com
dir: A14 junct 37, A142 (Fordham Rd). 2.3m, straight on at 2 rdbts. At end of Fordham Rd, into right lane, turn right. Hotel on right

High quality, budget accommodation ideal for both families and business travellers. Spacious, en suite bedrooms feature tea and coffee making facilities, and Freeview TV in most hotels. Internet access and Wi-fi are available for a small fee. The adjacent family restaurant features a wide and varied menu. See also the Hotel Groups pages.

Rooms 75

Premier Inn Newport / Telford

BUDGET HOTEL

☎ 0871 527 8808

Stafford Rd TF10 9BY

web: www.premierinn.com
dir: From A41 E of Newport take A518 towards Stafford. Hotel on right adjacent to Mere Park Garden Centre

High quality, budget accommodation ideal for both families and business travellers. Spacious, en suite bedrooms feature tea and coffee making facilities, and Freeview TV in most hotels. Internet access and Wi-fi are available for a small fee. The adjacent family restaurant features a wide and varied menu. See also the Hotel Groups pages.

Rooms 50

Premier Inn Isle of Wight (Newport)

BUDGET HOTEL

☎ 0871 527 8556

Seaclose, Fairlee Rd PO30 2DN

web: www.premierinn.com
dir: From Newport take A3054 signed Ryde. In 0.75m at Seaclose lights, turn left. Hotel adjacent to council offices

High quality, budget accommodation ideal for both families and business travellers. Spacious, en suite bedrooms feature tea and coffee making facilities, and Freeview TV in most hotels. Internet access and Wi-fi are available for a small fee. The adjacent family restaurant features a wide and varied menu. See also the Hotel Groups pages.

Rooms 68

N

NEW MILTON — Hampshire — Map 5 SZ29

INSPECTORS' CHOICE

Chewton Glen Hotel & Spa

★★★★★ ⚜⚜⚜
COUNTRY HOUSE HOTEL

☎ 01425 275341
Christchurch Rd BH25 6QS
e-mail: reservations@chewtonglen.com
web: www.chewtonglen.com
dir: A35 from Lyndhurst for 10m, left at staggered junct. Follow tourist sign for hotel through Walkford, take 2nd left

Chewton has had a revitalisation over recent months; the eco-friendly tree-houses are a new venture, which sets the hotel in a fresh and exciting direction. Developments in the extensive grounds, which already boast so much, including golf and croquet, now see a walled garden, which provides for the hotel kitchen, but is a feature in its own right. Bedrooms are luxurious and delightfully appointed, while public areas are stylish and comfortable, the perfect place for traditional afternoon tea. Cuisine as ever, is at the forefront, and the Vetiver restaurant has something for every diner.

Rooms 70 (12 annexe) (11 GF) ⚑ **D** £325-£1580*
Facilities Spa STV FTV Wi-fi 🏊 ⚡ ↲ 9 ⛳ Putt
green 🏌 Gym Hydrotherapy spa Dance studio
Cycling & jogging trail Clay shooting Archery 🎵
Xmas New Year Child facilities **Conf** Class 70
Board 40 Thtr 150 Del from £295 to £395*
Services Air con **Parking** 150 **Notes** LB ⊗
Civ Wed 140

NEWQUAY — Cornwall — Map 2 SW86

Headland Hotel

★★★★ 81% HOTEL

☎ 01637 872211
Fistral Beach TR7 1EW
e-mail: reception@headlandhotel.co.uk
web: www.headlandhotel.co.uk
dir: A30 onto A392 at Indian Queens, approaching Newquay follow signs for Fistral Beach, hotel adjacent

This Victorian hotel enjoys a stunning location overlooking the sea on three sides, so views can be enjoyed from most of the windows. Bedrooms are comfortable and spacious. The grand public areas, with impressive floral displays, include various lounges and as a complement to the formal dining room, Sands Brasserie offers a relaxed alternative. Recent additions include the 'Wellness Area', comprising of spa pool, steam room, aromatherapy showers and sauna. Self-catering cottages are available, and guests staying in these are welcome to use the hotel facilities.

Rooms 96 (40 fmly) ⚑ **S** £59-£139; **D** £79-£389
(incl. bkfst)* **Facilities** Spa STV FTV Wi-fi 🏊 ⚡ ↲ 9
⛳ Putt green 🏌 Gym Boules Outdoor activities Surf
school 🎵 Xmas New Year Child facilities
Conf Class 120 Board 40 Thtr 250 **Services** Lift
Parking 300 **Notes** LB Civ Wed 250

Atlantic Hotel

★★★★ 75% HOTEL

☎ 01637 872244
Dane Rd TR7 1EN
e-mail: info@atlantichotelnewquay.co.uk
web: www.atlantichotelnewquay.co.uk

Located on a cliff top with stunning views of Newquay and the Atlantic seascape, this imposing property dominates the skyline and offers traditional hotel keeping with modern comforts. All bedrooms are appointed to a high standard and offer ample modern comforts; balcony suites are available. Silks restaurant is popular with locals and residents alike.

Atlantic Hotel

Rooms 55 (10 fmly) ⚑ **Facilities** STV FTV W-fi 🏊 ⚡
Xmas New Year **Conf** Class 350 Board 150 Thtr 350
Services Lift **Parking** 55 **Notes** ⊗ Civ Wed 360

See advert on opposite page

Porth Veor Manor

★★★ 78% HOTEL

☎ 01637 873274 & 839542
Porth Way, Porth TR7 3LW
e-mail: enquiries@porthveormanor.com
web: www.porthveormanor.com
dir: From A3058 at main rdbt onto B3276, hotel 0.5m on left

Overlooking Porth Beach and in a quiet location, this pleasant mid 19th-century manor house offers a relaxed and friendly atmosphere. The spacious bedrooms have satellite TVs, and many have views of the beach; superior rooms are available. The hotel has a fine dining restaurant, a lounge/bar, and an outdoor heated pool. There is direct access via a private path from the hotel grounds to the beach, and the coastal paths are just a short walk away.

Rooms 18 (6 fmly) **Facilities** STV FTV Wi-fi 🏊 ⚡ Putt
green 🏌 Xmas New Year **Parking** 36 **Notes** ⊗ No
children 5yrs Civ Wed 80

Save on hotels. Book at **theAA.com/hotel**

NEW 335 **ENGLAND**

BEST WESTERN Hotel Bristol

★★★ 77% HOTEL

☎ 01637 875181

Narrowcliff TR7 2PQ
e-mail: info@hotelbristol.co.uk
web: www.hotelbristol.co.uk
dir: A30 onto A392, then A3058. Hotel 2.5m on left

This hotel is conveniently situated, and many of the bedrooms enjoy fine sea views. Staff are friendly and provide a professional and attentive service. There is a range of comfortable lounges, ideal for relaxing prior to eating in the elegant dining room. There are also leisure and conference facilities.

Rooms 74 (23 fmly) **Facilities** FTV Wi-fi ⓣ Table tennis New Year **Conf** Class 80 Board 30 Thtr 200 **Services** Lift **Parking** 105 **Notes** Closed 23-27 Dec & 4-18 Jan

Hotel Victoria

★★★ 77% HOTEL

☎ 01637 872255

East St TR7 1DB
e-mail: bookings@hotel-victoria.co.uk
web: www.hotel-victoria.co.uk
dir: A30 towards Bodmin following signs to Newquay. Hotel next to Newquay's main post office

Standing on the cliffs, overlooking Newquay Bay, the hotel is situated at the centre of this vibrant town. The spacious lounges and bar areas all benefit from glorious views. Varied menus, using the best of local produce, are offered in the restaurant. Bedrooms vary from spacious superior rooms and suites to standard inland-facing rooms. Berties pub, a nightclub, and indoor leisure facilities are also available.

Hotel Victoria

Rooms 71 (23 fmly) (1 GF) (5 smoking) 🐾 **Facilities** FTV Wi-fi ⓣ Gym Beauty room New Year **Conf** Class 130 Board 50 Thtr 200 **Services** Lift **Parking** 50 **Notes** Civ Wed 90

See advert on page 336

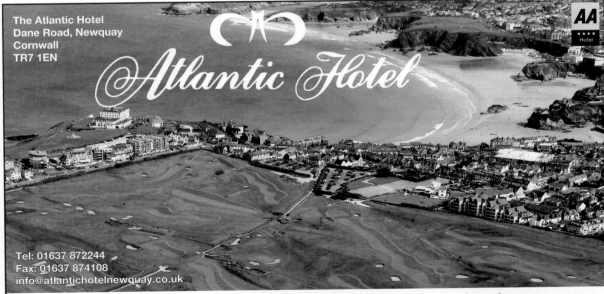

N

NEWQUAY *continued*

Trebarwith Hotel

★★★ 75% HOTEL

☎ 01637 872288 & 0800 387520
Trebarwith Crescent TR7 1BZ
e-mail: trebahotel@aol.com
web: www.trebarwith-hotel.co.uk
dir: From A3058 into Mount Wise Rd. 3rd right into
Marcus Hill, across East St into Trebarwith Cres. Hotel
at end

With breathtaking views of the rugged coastline and
a path leading to the beach, this friendly, family-run
hotel is set in its own grounds close to the town
centre. The public rooms include a lounge, ballroom,
restaurant and cinema. The comfortable bedrooms
include four-poster and family rooms, and many
benefit from the sea views.

Rooms 41 (8 fmly) (1 GF) 🐾 **S** £40-£60; **D** £80-£150
(incl. bkfst)* **Facilities** FTV Wi-fi ⌕ Fishing Video
theatre Games room Surf school Padi/SSI scuba
diving centre ♫ Child facilities **Conf** Class 30
Board 18 Thtr 45 **Parking** 41 **Notes** LB ⊗ Closed
Nov-5 Apr

Hotel California

★★★ 68% HOTEL

☎ 01637 879292 & 872798
Pentire Crescent TR7 1PU
e-mail: info@hotel-california.co.uk
web: www.hotel-california.co.uk
dir: A392 to Newquay, follow signs for Pentire Hotels
& Guest Houses

This hotel is tucked away in a delightful location,
close to Fistral Beach and adjacent to the River
Gannel. Many bedrooms have views across the river
towards the sea, and some have balconies. There is
an impressive range of leisure facilities, including
ten-pin bowling and both indoor and outdoor pools.
The cuisine is enjoyable and menus offer a range of
interesting dishes.

Rooms 70 (27 fmly) (13 GF) **Facilities** FTV Wi-fi HL ⌕
⚹ Squash 4-lane American bowling alley Hairdresser
Snooker & pool room Sauna Solarium ♫ Xmas New
Year **Conf** Class 100 Board 30 Thtr 100 **Services** Lift
Parking 66 **Notes** Closed 3-25 Jan Civ Wed 150

Kilbirnie Hotel

★★★ 68% HOTEL

☎ 01637 875155
Narrowcliff TR7 2RS
e-mail: info@kilbirniehotel.co.uk
web: www.kilbirniehotel.co.uk
dir: On A392

With delightful views over the open space known as
The Barrowfields and beyond to the sea, this
privately-run hotel offers an impressive range of
facilities. The reception rooms are spacious and
comfortable, and during summer months become the
venue for a programme of entertainment. Bedrooms
vary in size and style, and some enjoy fine sea views.

Rooms 66 (6 fmly) (8 GF) 🐾 **Facilities** Wi-fi ⌕ ⚹
Gym Fitness room Hair salon Xmas New Year
Conf Class 50 Board 25 Thtr 100 **Services** Lift Air con
Parking 58 **Notes** ⊗ Closed 2-31 Jan

Priory Lodge Hotel

★★ 75% HOTEL

☎ 01637 874111
30 Mount Wise TR7 2BN
e-mail: fionapocklington@tiscali.co.uk
dir: From lights in town centre onto Berry Rd, right
onto B3282 (Mount Wise), 0.5m on right

This hotel enjoys a central location close to the town
centre, the harbour and the local beaches. Secure
parking is available at the hotel along with a range of
leisure facilities including a heated pool, sauna,
games room and hot tub. Attractively decorated
bedrooms vary in size and style - many have sea
views over Towan Beach.

Rooms 28 (6 annexe) (13 fmly) (1 GF) **S** £35-£45;
D £50-£90 (incl. bkfst) **Facilities** FTV Wi-fi ⌕ ⚹ ♫
Parking 30 **Notes** ⊗ Closed Dec-end Mar

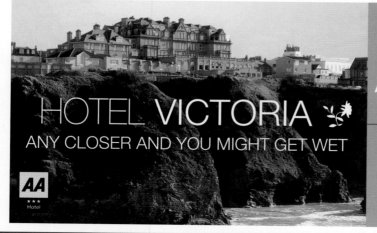

Eliot Hotel

★★ 72% HOTEL

☎ 01637 878177
Edgcumbe Av TR7 2NH
e-mail: eliot.newquay@alfatravel.co.uk
web: www.leisureplex.co.uk
dir: A30 onto A392 towards Quintrell Downs. Right at rdbt onto A3058. 4m to Newquay, left at amusements onto Edgcumbe Ave. Hotel on left

Located in a quiet residential area just a short walk from the beaches and the varied attractions of the town, this long-established hotel offers comfortable accommodation. Entertainment is provided most nights throughout the season and guests can relax in the spacious public areas.

Rooms 76 (10 fmly) ✎ **S** £35-£46; **D** £56-£78 (incl. bkfst)* **Facilities** FTV ✎ Pool table Table tennis ♫ Xmas New Year **Services** Lift **Parking** 20 **Notes** ⊗ Closed Dec-Jan (ex Xmas) RS Feb-Mar

Premier Inn Quintrell Downs

BUDGET HOTEL

☎ 0871 527 8818
Quintrell Downs TR8 4LE
web: www.premierinn.com
dir: From A30 take A39. At rdbt 2nd exit signed Newquay A392. 4m, in Quintrell Downs take 1st exit at rdbt. Hotel on left

High quality, budget accommodation ideal for both families and business travellers. Spacious, en suite bedrooms feature tea and coffee making facilities, and Freeview TV in most hotels. Internet access and Wi-fi are available for a small fee. The adjacent family restaurant features a wide and varied menu. See also the Hotel Groups pages.

Rooms 75

Lewinnick Lodge

RESTAURANT WITH ROOMS

☎ 01637 878117
Pentire Headland TR7 1QD
e-mail: thelodge@hospitalitycornwall.com
dir: From A392, at rdbt exit into Pentire Rd then Pentire Ave. Turn right to Lewinnick Lodge

Set above the cliffs of Pentire Headland, looking out across the mighty Atlantic, these are guaranteed amazing coastal views. There are ten bedrooms that were designed by Guy Bostock. They are modern, spacious, and offer many thoughtful extras, some with open-plan bathrooms. Modern British food with an emphasis on fresh fish is served all day.

Rooms 10

NEW ROMNEY
Kent

The Ship Hotel

AA Advertised

☎ 01797 362776
83 High St TN28 8AZ
e-mail: theshiphotelandrestaurant@gmail.com

Built from ship timbers in the 15th century at the heart of Romney Marsh and extensively reworked over the centuries, The Ship Hotel offers a large restaurant with a conservatory, indoor and outdoor bars, and a fully heated patio garden, as well as ten en suite bedrooms. All rooms have Wi-fi, tea and coffee-making facilities, and flat-screen TV with Freeview. Functions are catered for, and Friday night is disco night, with live music once a month.

Rooms 10 (1 fmly) ✎ **S** £50-£55; **D** £70-£75 (incl. bkfst)* **Facilities** FTV Wi-fi ♫ Xmas New Year **Conf** Board 20 **Parking** 20

NEWTON ABBOT   Map 3 SX87
Devon

See also Ilsington

BEST WESTERN Passage House Hotel

★★★ 73% HOTEL

☎ 01626 355515
Hackney Ln, Kingsteignton TQ12 3QH
e-mail: hotel@passagehousegroup.co.uk
dir: A380 onto A381, follow racecourse signs

With memorable views of the Teign Estuary, this popular hotel provides spacious, well-equipped bedrooms. An impressive range of leisure and meeting facilities is offered and a conservatory provides a pleasant extension to the bar and lounge. A choice of eating options is available, either in the main restaurant, or the adjacent Passage House Inn for less formal dining.

Rooms 90 (52 annexe) (64 fmly) (26 GF) **Facilities** Spa STV Wi-fi ⊛ supervised Gym **Conf** Class 50 Board 40 Thtr 120 Del from £115 to £125 **Services** Lift **Parking** 300 **Notes** ⊗ RS 24-27 Dec Civ Wed 75

BEST WESTERN Queens Hotel

★★★ 70% METRO HOTEL

☎ 01626 363133
Queen St TQ12 2EZ
e-mail: reservations@queenshotel-southwest.co.uk
dir: A380. At Penn Inn turn right towards town, hotel opposite station

Pleasantly and conveniently located close to the railway station and racecourse, this hotel continues to be a popular venue for both business visitors and tourists. Bedrooms are comfortable and spacious. Light snacks and sandwiches are available in the café/bar and lounge.

Rooms 24 (3 fmly) ✎ **Facilities** FTV Wi-fi **Conf** Class 20 Board 20 Thtr 40 **Parking** 6 **Notes** ⊗ RS 24 Dec-2 Jan

Premier Inn Newton Abbot

BUDGET HOTEL

☎ 0871 527 9300
Newton Abbott Racecourse, Newton Rd TQ12 3AF
web: www.premierinn.com
dir: A380 exit at Ware Barton signed A383/Ashburton, follow brown signs for Newton Abbot Racecourse through Kingsteignton. Then follow Officials Entrance sign to hotel

High quality, budget accommodation ideal for both families and business travellers. Spacious, en suite bedrooms feature tea and coffee making facilities, and Freeview TV in most hotels. Internet access and Wi-fi are available for a small fee. The adjacent family restaurant features a wide and varied menu. See also the Hotel Groups pages.

Rooms 60

NEWTON AYCLIFFE   Map 19 NZ22
Co Durham

Premier Inn Durham (Newton Aycliffe)

BUDGET HOTEL

☎ 0871 527 8336
Ricknall Ln, Great North Rd DL5 6JG
web: www.premierinn.com
dir: On A167 E of Newton Aycliffe, 3m from A1(M)

High quality, budget accommodation ideal for both families and business travellers. Spacious, en suite bedrooms feature tea and coffee making facilities, and Freeview TV in most hotels. Internet access and Wi-fi are available for a small fee. The adjacent family restaurant features a wide and varied menu. See also the Hotel Groups pages.

Rooms 44

N

NEWTON-LE-WILLOWS   Map 15 SJ59
Merseyside

Holiday Inn Haydock M6 Jct 23

★★★ 79% HOTEL

☎ 0871 942 9039
Lodge Ln WA12 0JG
e-mail: haydock@ihg.com
web: www.holidayinn.co.uk
dir: M6 junct 23, A49 to Ashton-in-Makerfield. Hotel 0.25m on right by racecourse

This hotel has an ideal location adjacent to Haydock Racecourse and within easy reach of north-west cities and attractions. A variety of bedrooms is available and public areas include extensive meeting and conference facilities, a smart Spirit health and leisure club and a spacious bar and restaurant.

Rooms 136 (12 fmly) (23 GF) (12 smoking)
Facilities STV Wi-fi HL ⓘ Gym Xmas New Year
Conf Class 70 Board 60 Thtr 180 **Services** Lift Air con **Parking** 204 **Notes** Civ Wed 120

NORMAN CROSS   Map 12 TL19
Cambridgeshire

Premier Inn Peterborough A1(M) Jct 16

BUDGET HOTEL

☎ 0871 527 8870
Norman Cross, A1(M) Junction 16 PE7 3TB
web: www.premierinn.com
dir: A1(M) junct 16, A15 towards Yaxley, hotel in 100yds

High quality, budget accommodation ideal for both families and business travellers. Spacious, en suite bedrooms feature tea and coffee making facilities, and Freeview TV in most hotels. Internet access and Wi-fi are available for a small fee. The adjacent family restaurant features a wide and varied menu. See also the Hotel Groups pages.

Rooms 95

NORMANTON   Map 11 SK90
Rutland

BEST WESTERN Normanton Park Hotel

★★★ 70% HOTEL

☎ 01780 720315
Oakham LE15 8RP
e-mail: info@normantonpark.co.uk
web: www.bw-normantonparkhotel.co.uk
dir: From A1 follow A606 towards Oakham, 5m. Turn left, 1.5m. Hotel on right

This hotel offers some of Rutland Water's best views over the south shore. The comfortable bedrooms are located in the main house and the courtyard. Public rooms include a conservatory dining room overlooking the water, and a cosy lounge is available for guests to relax in.

Rooms 30 (7 annexe) (6 fmly) (11 GF) ⌁
S £52.50-£89; **D** £65-£150 (incl. bkfst) **Facilities** FTV Wi-fi Xmas New Year **Conf** Class 60 Board 80 Thtr 200 **Parking** 100 **Notes** LB Civ Wed 100

NORTHAMPTON   Map 11 SP76
Northamptonshire

Northampton Marriott Hotel

★★★★ 75% HOTEL

☎ 01604 768700
Eagle Dr NN4 7HW
e-mail: mhrs.ormnh.salesadmin@marriotthotels.com
web: www.northamptonmarriott.co.uk
dir: M1 junct 15, follow signs to Delapre Golf Course, hotel on right

Located on the outskirts of town, close to major road networks, this modern hotel caters to a cross section of guests. A self-contained management centre makes this a popular conference venue, and its spacious and well-designed bedrooms will suit business travellers particularly well. This is a good base for exploring the attractions the area has to offer.

Rooms 120 (10 fmly) (52 GF) (5 smoking) ⌁
Facilities STV Wi-fi ⌁ ⓘ supervised Gym Steam room Beauty treatment room Sauna Xmas New Year **Conf** Class 72 Board 30 Thtr 250 **Services** Air con **Parking** 200 **Notes** ⊗ Civ Wed 180

Park Inn by Radisson Northampton

★★★ 73% HOTEL

☎ 01604 739988
Silver St NN1 2TA
e-mail: reservations.northampton@rezidorparkinn.com
web: www.northampton.parkinn.co.uk
dir: In town centre

Ideally located within the city centre, the hotel is a spacious, purpose-built property offering a range of well-appointed bedrooms, conference rooms and a fully-equipped health club. The popular restaurant offers an open-plan contemporary dining experience in a relaxing environment.

Rooms 146 ⌁ **Facilities** Spa FTV Wi-fi ⌁ ⓘ Gym New Year **Conf** Class 300 Board 100 Thtr 600 Del from £90 to £145* **Services** Lift Air con **Parking** 160 **Notes** ⊗ Civ Wed 600

Westone Manor Hotel   fОCUShotels

★★★ 71% HOTEL

☎ 01604 739955
Ashley Way, Weston Favell NN3 3EA
e-mail: enquiries@hotels-northampton.com
dir: M1 junct 15 towards Wellingborough/ Northampton. Follow Kettering signs for 0.5m. A4500 (Town Centre/Weston Favell). Take left A4500, 1st right over small rdbt, hotel on left

Ideally located with easy access from the motorway and city centre, Westone Manor Hotel offers a range of accommodation to suit the needs of both the business and leisure traveller. Many of the original features have been retained in the public areas. There is ample parking, and there are banqueting facilities that can cater for anything from small business meetings to a wedding reception.

Rooms 69 (30 annexe) (1 fmly) (15 GF) **Facilities** FTV Wi-fi **Conf** Class 50 Board 50 Thtr 140 **Services** Lift **Parking** 65 **Notes** Civ Wed 100

Campanile Northampton   Campanile

★★★ 70% HOTEL

☎ 01604 662599
Cheaney Dr, Grange Park NN4 5FB
e-mail: northampton@campanile.com
web: www.campanile.com
dir: M1 junct 15, A508 towards Northampton. 2nd exit at 1st rdbt, 2nd exit at 2nd rdbt into Grange Park

This modern building offers accommodation in smart, well-equipped bedrooms, all with en suite bathrooms. Refreshments may be taken at the informal bistro.

Save on hotels. Book at **theAA.com/hotel**

NEW – NOR 339 ENGLAND

Rooms 87 (18 fmly) **Facilities** STV FTV Wi-fi Xmas New Year **Conf** Class 60 Board 60 Thtr 150 **Services** Lift Air con **Parking** 100

Ibis Northampton Centre

BUDGET HOTEL

☎ 01604 608900
Sol Central, Marefair NN1 1SR
e-mail: H3657@accor.com
web: www.ibishotel.com
dir: M1 junct 15/15a & city centre towards railway station

Modern, budget hotel offering comfortable accommodation in bright and practical bedrooms. Breakfast is self-service and dinner is available in the restaurant. See also the Hotel Groups pages.

Rooms 151 (14 fmly) 🐾 **Conf** Board 10

Premier Inn Northampton Bedford Road/A428

BUDGET HOTEL

☎ 0871 527 8822
The Lakes, Bedford Rd NN4 7YD
web: www.premierinn.com
dir: M1 junct 15, follow A508 (A45) signs to Northampton. A428 at rdbt take 4th exit (signed Bedford). Left at next rdbt. Hotel on right

High quality, budget accommodation ideal for both families and business travellers. Spacious, en suite bedrooms feature tea and coffee making facilities, and Freeview TV in most hotels. Internet access and Wi-fi are available for a small fee. The adjacent family restaurant features a wide and varied menu. See also the Hotel Groups pages.

Rooms 44

Premier Inn Northampton Great Billing/A45

BUDGET HOTEL

☎ 0871 527 8824
Crow Ln, Great Billing NN3 9DA
web: www.premierinn.com
dir: M1 junct 15, A508, A45 follow Billing Aquadrome signs

Rooms 60

Premier Inn Northampton South (Wootton)

BUDGET HOTEL

☎ 0871 527 8826
Newport Pagnell Road West, Wootton NN4 7JJ
web: www.premierinn.com
dir: M1 junct 15, A508 towards Northampton, exit at junct with A45. At rdbt take B526. Hotel on right

Rooms 45

Premier Inn Northampton West (Harpole)

BUDGET HOTEL

☎ 0871 527 8828
Harpole Turn, Weedon Rd, Harpole NN7 4DD
web: www.premierinn.com
dir: M1 junct 16, A45 towards Northampton. In 1m left into Harpole Turn. Hotel on left

Rooms 51

NORTH FERRIBY
East Riding of Yorkshire — Map 17 SE92

Hallmark Hotel Hull

★★★★ 71% HOTEL

☎ 01482 645212
Ferriby High Rd HU14 3LG
dir: M62 onto A63 towards Hull. Exit at Humber Bridge signage. Follow North Ferriby signs, hotel 0.5m on left

This property is situated just outside Hull city centre, with breathtaking views of the Humber Bridge. Service is attentive with a friendly atmosphere. The comfortable bedrooms are tastefully appointed and are suitable for both business and leisure guests. The restaurant and bar serve a good choice of dishes. Conference facilities are available along with free Wi-fi and private parking.

Rooms 95 (3 fmly) (16 GF) 🐾 **Facilities** STV FTV Wi-fi 🐾 Xmas New Year **Conf** Class 85 Board 86 Thtr 200 **Parking** 150 **Notes** Civ Wed 200

NORTH KILWORTH
Leicestershire — Map 11 SP68

INSPECTORS' CHOICE

Kilworth House Hotel & Theatre

★★★★ ◉◉ HOTEL

☎ 01858 880058
Lutterworth Rd LE17 6JE
e-mail: info@kilworthhouse.co.uk
web: www.kilworthhouse.co.uk
dir: A4304 towards Market Harborough, after Walcote, hotel 1.5m on right

A restored Victorian country house located in 38 acres of private grounds offering state-of-the-art conference rooms. The gracious public areas feature many period pieces and original art works. The bedrooms are very comfortable and well equipped, and the large Orangery is now used for informal dining, while the opulent Wordsworth Restaurant has a more formal air. Close to the lake an open-air theatre which seats 540 has been built; professional productions take place here, and picnics can be arranged, or dinner back at the hotel is also an option.

Rooms 44 (2 fmly) (13 GF) 🐾 **D** £110-£300 (incl. bkfst)* **Facilities** FTV Wi-fi 🐾 Fishing 🏊 Gym Beauty therapy rooms Xmas **Conf** Class 30 Board 30 Thtr 80 Del from £159 to £260* **Services** Lift **Parking** 140 **Notes** LB ⊗ Civ Wed 130

N

NORTH SHIELDS
Tyne & Wear   Map 21 NZ36

Premier Inn North Shields

BUDGET HOTEL

☎ 0871 527 8818
Coble Dene Rd NE29 6DL
web: www.premierinn.com
dir: From all directions follow signs for Royal Quays (Outlet Centre) & International Ferry Terminal. From A187 take Coble Dene Rd. At 3rd rdbt right, 1st right at mini rdbt

High quality, budget accommodation ideal for both families and business travellers. Spacious, en suite bedrooms feature tea and coffee making facilities, and Freeview TV in most hotels. Internet access and Wi-fi are available for a small fee. The adjacent family restaurant features a wide and varied menu. See also the Hotel Groups pages.

Rooms 50

NORTH WALSHAM
Norfolk   Map 13 TG23

INSPECTORS' CHOICE

Beechwood Hotel
★★★ ◉◉ HOTEL

☎ 01692 403231
Cromer Rd NR28 0HD
e-mail: info@beechwood-hotel.co.uk
web: www.beechwood-hotel.co.uk
dir: B1150 from Norwich. At North Walsham left at 1st lights, then right at next

Expect a warm welcome at this elegant 18th-century house, situated just a short walk from the town centre. The individually styled bedrooms are tastefully furnished with well chosen antique pieces, attractive co-ordinated soft fabrics and many thoughtful touches. The spacious public areas include a lounge bar with plush furnishings, a further lounge and a smartly appointed restaurant.

Rooms 17 (4 GF) ✿ **S** fr £88; **D** £100-£160 (incl. bkfst) **Facilities** FTV Wi-fi ✤ New Year **Conf** Class 20 Board 20 Thtr 20 Del from £140 to £160 **Parking** 20 **Notes** LB No children 10yrs

NORTH WALTHAM
Hampshire   Map 5 SU54

Premier Inn Basingstoke South

BUDGET HOTEL

☎ 0871 527 8064
RG25 2BB
web: www.premierinn.com
dir: M3 junct 7, A30 follow signs for Kingsworthy and crematorium. Hotel 2m on right, adjacent to Wheatsheaf

High quality, budget accommodation ideal for both families and business travellers. Spacious, en suite bedrooms feature tea and coffee making facilities, and Freeview TV in most hotels. Internet access and Wi-fi are available for a small fee. The adjacent

family restaurant features a wide and varied menu. See also the Hotel Groups pages.

Rooms 28

NORTHWICH
Cheshire   Map 15 SJ67

Premier Inn Northwich (Sandiway)

BUDGET HOTEL

☎ 0871 527 8830
520 Chester Rd, Sandiway CW8 2DN
web: www.premierinn.com
dir: M6 junct 19, A556 towards Chester. Hotel in 11m

High quality, budget accommodation ideal for both families and business travellers. Spacious, en suite bedrooms feature tea and coffee making facilities, and Freeview TV in most hotels. Internet access and Wi-fi are available for a small fee. The adjacent family restaurant features a wide and varied menu. See also the Hotel Groups pages.

Rooms 42

Premier Inn Northwich South

BUDGET HOTEL

☎ 0871 527 8832
London Rd, Leftwich CW9 8EG
web: www.premierinn.com
dir: Just off M6 junct 19. Follow A556 towards Chester. Right at sign for Northwich & Davenham

Rooms 33

NORWICH
Norfolk   Map 13 TG20

Sprowston Manor, A Marriott Hotel & Country Club

★★★★ 82% ◉ HOTEL

☎ 01603 410871
Sprowston Park, Wroxham Rd, Sprowston NR7 8RP
e-mail: mhrs.nwigs.frontdesk@marriotthotels.com
web: www.marriottsprowstonmanor.co.uk
dir: NE of Norwich take A1151 (Wroxham road). 2m, follow signs to Sprowston Park

Surrounded by open parkland, this imposing property is set in attractively landscaped grounds and is just a short drive from the city centre. Bedrooms are spacious and feature a variety of decorative styles. The hotel also has extensive conference, banqueting and leisure facilities. Other public rooms include an array of seating areas and the elegant Manor Restaurant.

Rooms 94 (31 fmly) (5 GF) (8 smoking) **S** £115-£145; **D** £125-£155 (incl. bkfst)* **Facilities** Spa FTV Wi-fi ⊗ ⅃ 18 Putt green Gym Steam room Sauna Xmas New Year **Conf** Class 100 Board 80 Thtr 500 Del from £145 to £155* **Services** Lift **Parking** 150 **Notes** LB ⊗ Civ Wed 300

St Giles House Hotel

★★★★ 81% ◎◎ HOTEL

☎ 01603 275180
41-45 St Giles St NR2 1JR
e-mail: reception@stgileshousehotel.com
web: www.stgileshousehotel.com
dir: A11 into central Norwich. Left at rdbt (Chapelfield Shopping Centre). 3rd exit at next rdbt. Left onto St Giles St. Hotel on left

A stylish 19th-century, Grade II listed building situated in the heart of the city. The property has a wealth of magnificent original features such as wood-panelling, ornamental plasterwork and marble floors. Public areas include an open-plan lounge bar/restaurant, a smart lounge with plush sofas and a Parisian-style terrace. The spacious, contemporary bedrooms are individually designed and have many thoughtful touches.

Rooms 24 (3 GF) ↖ **S** fr £120; **D** fr £130* **Facilities** Spa FTV Wi-fi Xmas New Year **Conf** Class 20 Board 24 Thtr 45 **Services** Lift **Parking** 30 **Notes** ⊗ Civ Wed 60

Barnham Broom Hotel, Golf & Restaurant

★★★★ 78% ◎◎ HOTEL

☎ 01603 759393
NR9 4DD
web: www.barnham-broom.co.uk

(For full entry see Barnham Broom)

Mercure Norwich Hotel

★★★★ HOTEL

☎ 0844 815 9036
121-131 Boundary Rd NR3 2BA
e-mail: info@mercurenorwich.co.uk
web: www.jupiterhotels.co.uk
dir: Approx 2m from airport on A140 (Norwich ring road)

Currently the rating for this establishment is not confirmed. This may be due to a change of ownership or because it has only recently joined the AA rating scheme.

Rooms 107 **Conf** Class 150 Board 80 Thtr 300

Park Farm Hotel

★★★★ 77% ◎ HOTEL

☎ 01603 810264
NR9 3DL
e-mail: enq@parkfarm-hotel.co.uk
web: www.parkfarm-hotel.co.uk

(For full entry see Hethersett)

De Vere Dunston Hall

★★★★ 77% HOTEL

☎ 01508 470444
Ipswich Rd NR14 8PQ
e-mail: dhreception@devere-hotels.com
web: www.devere.co.uk
dir: From A47 take A140 (Ipswich road). 0.25m, hotel on left

An imposing Grade II listed building set amidst 170 acres of landscaped grounds just a short drive from the city centre. The spacious bedrooms are smartly decorated, tastefully furnished and equipped to a high standard. The attractively appointed public rooms offer a wide choice of areas in which to relax, and the hotel also boasts a superb range of leisure facilities including an 18-hole PGA golf course, floodlit tennis courts and a football pitch.

Rooms 169 (16 fmly) (16 GF) (2 smoking) **Facilities** Spa Wi-fi ⊗ ⅃ 18 Putt green Gym Floodlit driving range Xmas New Year **Conf** Class 140 Board 80 Thtr 300 **Services** Lift **Parking** 500 **Notes** Civ Wed 90

The Maids Head Hotel

★★★★ 75% ◎ HOTEL

☎ 0844 855 9120
Tombland NR3 1LB
e-mail: gm@maidsheadhotel.co.uk
web: www.maidsheadhotel.co.uk
dir: In city centre. Telephone or see website for detailed directions

The Maids Head Hotel is an impressive 13th-century building situated close to the impressive Norman cathedral, the Anglian TV studios, and within easy walking distance of the city centre. The bedrooms are pleasantly decorated and thoughtfully equipped; some rooms have original oak beams. The spacious public rooms include a Jacobean bar, a range of seating areas and the Courtyard Restaurant.

Rooms 84 (10 fmly) (10 GF) **Facilities** FTV Wi-fi ⊗ Beauty treatment room Use of nearby gym Xmas New Year **Conf** Class 30 Board 50 Thtr 100 **Services** Lift **Parking** 83 **Notes** ⊗ Civ Wed 100

BEST WESTERN Annesley House Hotel

★★★ 88% ◎◎ HOTEL

☎ 01603 624553
6 Newmarket Rd NR2 2LA
e-mail: annesleyhouse@bestwestern.co.uk
dir: On A11, 0.5m before city centre

Delightful Georgian property set in three acres of landscaped gardens close to the city centre. Bedrooms are split between three separate houses, two of which are linked by a glass walkway. Each is attractively decorated, tastefully furnished and thoughtfully equipped. Public rooms include a comfortable lounge/bar and a smart conservatory restaurant which overlooks the gardens.

Rooms 30 (12 annexe) (1 fmly) (9 GF) ↖ **S** £70-£85; **D** £90-£115 (incl. bkfst)* **Facilities** FTV Wi-fi ↘ **Parking** 28 **Notes** LB ⊗ Closed 24 Dec-2 Jan

Stower Grange

★★★ 80% ◎ COUNTRY HOUSE HOTEL

☎ 01603 860210
School Rd, Drayton NR8 6EF
e-mail: enquiries@stowergrange.co.uk
web: www.stowergrange.co.uk
dir: Norwich ring road N to Asda supermarket. Take A1067 (Fakenham road) at Drayton, right at lights into School Rd. Hotel 150yds on right

Expect a warm welcome at this 17th-century, ivy-clad property situated in a peaceful residential area close to the city centre and airport. The individually decorated bedrooms are generally quite spacious; each is tastefully furnished and equipped with many thoughtful touches. Public rooms include a smart open-plan lounge bar and an elegant restaurant.

Rooms 11 (1 fmly) ↖ **S** £80; **D** £100-£150 (incl. bkfst)* **Facilities** FTV Wi-fi ↘ New Year **Conf** Class 45 Board 30 Thtr 100 Del from £125 to £150* **Parking** 40 **Notes** LB Civ Wed 100

N

NORWICH *continued*

Holiday Inn Norwich

★★★ 80% HOTEL

Holiday Inn

☎ 0871 942 9060 & 0800 405060
Ipswich Rd NR4 6EP
e-mail: reservations-norwich@ihg.com
web: www.holidayinn.co.uk
dir: A47 (Great Yarmouth) then A140 (Norwich). 1m, hotel on right

A modern, purpose-built hotel situated just off the A140 which is a short drive from the city centre. Public areas include a popular bar, the Junction Restaurant and a large open-plan lounge. Bedrooms come in a variety of styles and are suited to the needs of both the business and leisure guest alike.

Rooms 119 (41 fmly) (39 GF) **S** £49-£165;
D £49-£165* **Facilities** STV FTV Wi-fi ⓑ HL ⊙
supervised Gym Sauna Steam room Xmas New Year
Conf Class 48 Board 40 Thtr 150 Del from £99 to
£145* **Services** Air con **Parking** 250 **Notes** LB ⊗
Civ Wed 120

BEST WESTERN George Hotel

★★★ 75% ◉ HOTEL

Best
Western

☎ 01603 617841
10 Arlington Ln, Newmarket Rd NR2 2DA
e-mail: reservations@georgehotel.co.uk
web: www.arlingtonhotelgroup.co.uk
dir: From A11 follow city centre signs, becomes Newmarket Rd. Hotel on left

Within just 10 minutes' walk of the town centre, this friendly, family-run hotel is well placed for guests wishing to explore the many sights of this historic city. The hotel occupies three adjacent buildings; the restaurant, bar and most bedrooms are located in the main building, while the adjacent cottages have been converted into comfortable and modern guest bedrooms.

Rooms 43 (5 annexe) (4 fmly) (19 GF) **Facilities** FTV
Wi-fi Beauty therapist Holistic treatments Xmas New
Year **Conf** Class 30 Board 30 Thtr 70 **Parking** 40
Notes LB ⊗

BEST WESTERN Brook Hotel Norwich

★★★ 72% HOTEL

Best
Western

☎ 01603 741161
2 Barnard Rd, Bowthorpe NR5 9JB
e-mail: welcome@brookhotelnorwich.com
web: www.brookhotelnorwich.com
dir: A47 towards Swaffham then A1074. Over double rdbt, to next rdbt, hotel on last exit

A modern, purpose-built hotel situated to the west of the city centre, just off the A47. The open-plan public areas include a lounge bar with TV, a foyer with plush sofas and a large dining room. The spacious bedrooms are equipped for both leisure and business guest alike.

Rooms 81 (13 fmly) (40 GF) **Facilities** FTV Wi-fi Gym
Xmas New Year **Conf** Class 90 Board 60 Thtr 200
Services Air con **Parking** 100 **Notes** Civ Wed 200

INSPECTORS' CHOICE

The Old Rectory

★★ ◉◉ SMALL HOTEL

☎ 01603 700772
103 Yarmouth Rd, Thorpe St Andrew NR7 0HF
e-mail: enquiries@oldrectorynorwich.com
web: www.oldrectorynorwich.com
dir: From A47 southern bypass onto A1042 towards Norwich N & E. Left at mini rdbt onto A1242. After 0.3m through lights. Hotel 100mtrs on right

This delightful Grade II listed Georgian property is ideally located in a peaceful area overlooking the River Yare, just a few minutes' drive from the city centre. Spacious bedrooms are individually designed with carefully chosen soft fabrics, plush furniture and many thoughtful touches; many of the rooms overlook the swimming pool and landscaped gardens. Accomplished cooking is offered via an interesting daily-changing menu, which features skilfully prepared local produce.

Rooms 8 (3 annexe) ⓡ **S** £99-£125; **D** £130-£165
(incl. bkfst)* **Facilities** FTV Wi-fi ⓑ ⟍
Conf Class 18 Board 16 Thtr 25 **Parking** 15
Notes LB ⊗ Closed 23 Dec-3 Jan

Premier Inn Norwich Airport

BUDGET HOTEL

Premier Inn

☎ 0871 527 8836
Delft Way NR6 6BB
web: www.premierinn.com
dir: From Norwich take A140 signed Cromer & Airport. Right at lights into Amsterdam Way. At mini-rdbt turn right. Hotel on right

High quality, budget accommodation ideal for both families and business travellers. Spacious, en suite bedrooms feature tea and coffee making facilities, and Freeview TV in most hotels. Internet access and Wi-fi are available for a small fee. The adjacent family restaurant features a wide and varied menu. See also the Hotel Groups pages.

Rooms 40

Premier Inn Norwich Central South

BUDGET HOTEL

☎ 0871 527 8838
**Broadlands Business Park, Old Chapel Way
NR7 0WG**
web: www.premierinn.com
dir: A47 onto A1042, 3m E of city centre

Rooms 92

Premier Inn Norwich City Centre (Duke Street)

BUDGET HOTEL

☎ 0871 527 8840
Duke St NR3 3AP
web: www.premierinn.com
dir: From A1074, straight on at lights (Toys'R'Us) into St Benedict's St (or from A147 (A140, A11) right at lights. At next lights into Duke St (car park in St Andrews multi-storey on right - free to guests)

Rooms 117

Premier Inn Norwich Nelson City Centre

BUDGET HOTEL

☎ 0871 527 8842
Prince of Wales Rd NR1 1DX
web: www.premierinn.com
dir: Follow city centre, football ground & railway station signs. Hotel opposite station

Rooms 160

Premier Inn Norwich (Showground A47)

BUDGET HOTEL

☎ 0871 527 8834
Longwater Interchange, Dereham Rd, New Costessey NR5 0TP
web: www.premierinn.com
dir: A47 towards Dereham, take A1074 to City Centre. At rdbt 2nd exit, hotel on right. From N: A47 through Dereham. Straight on at 1st rdbt, at 2nd rdbt take 3rd exit. Hotel on left

Rooms 40

INSPECTORS' CHOICE

Brasteds

◉ ◉ RESTAURANT WITH ROOMS

☎ 01508 491112
Manor Farm Barns, Framingham Pigot NR14 7PZ
e-mail: enquiries@brasteds.co.uk
web: www.brasteds.co.uk
dir: A11 onto A47 towards Great Yarmouth, then A146. 0.5m, right into Fox Rd, 0.5m on left

Brasteds is a lovely detached property set in 20 acres of mature, landscaped parkland on the outskirts of Norwich. The tastefully appointed bedrooms have beautiful soft furnishings and fabrics along with comfortable seating and many thoughtful touches. Public rooms include a cosy snug with plush sofas, and a smart dining room where breakfast is served. Dinner is available in Brasteds Restaurant, which can be found in an adjacent building.

Rooms 6 (1 fmly)

See also Langar

Hart's Hotel

★★★★ 82% ◉ ◉ HOTEL

☎ 0115 988 1900
Standard Hill, Park Row NG1 6FN
e-mail: reception@hartsnottingham.co.uk
web: www.hartsnottingham.co.uk
dir: At junct of Park Row & Ropewalk

This outstanding modern building stands on the site of the ramparts of the medieval castle, overlooking the city. Many of the bedrooms enjoy splendid views; all are well appointed and stylish. The Park Bar is the focal point of the public areas. Service is professional and caring and fine dining is offered at nearby Hart's Restaurant. Secure parking and private gardens are an added bonus.

Rooms 32 (1 fmly) (7 GF) ➦ **D** £125-£265*
Facilities STV FTV Wi-fi ➲ Small unsupervised exercise room Beauty treatments Xmas New Year **Conf** Class 75 Board 30 Thtr 100 Del from £190*
Services Lift **Parking** 16 **Notes** LB Civ Wed 100

The Nottingham Belfry

★★★★ 79% HOTEL

QHOTELS

☎ 0115 973 9393
Mellor's Way, Off Woodhouse Way NG8 6PY
e-mail: nottinghambelfry@qhotels.co.uk
web: www.qhotels.co.uk
dir: From M1 junct 26 take A610 towards Nottingham. A6002 to Stapleford/Strelley. 0.75m, last exit at rdbt, hotel on right

Set conveniently close to the motorway links, yet not far from the city centre attractions, this modern hotel has a stylish and impressive interior. Bedrooms and bathrooms are spaciously appointed and very comfortable. There are two restaurants and two bars that offer interesting and satisfying cuisine. Staff are friendly and helpful.

Rooms 120 (20 fmly) (36 GF) ➦ **Facilities** Spa STV FTV Wi-fi ➲ ⊘ Gym Sauna Steam room Aerobic studio Xmas New Year **Conf** Class 360 Board 60 Thtr 700 **Services** Lift **Parking** 250 **Notes** Civ Wed 150

Park Plaza Nottingham

★★★★ 73% ◉ HOTEL

Park Plaza
Hotels & Resorts

☎ 0115 947 7200
41 Maid Marian Way NG1 6GD
e-mail: ppnsales@pphe.com
web: www.parkplaza.com/nottinghamuk
dir: A6200 (Derby Rd) into Wollaton St. 2nd exit into Maid Marian Way. Hotel on left

This modern hotel is located in the centre of the city within walking distance of retail, commercial and tourist attractions. Bedrooms are spacious and comfortable, with many extras, including laptop safes and air conditioning. Service is discreetly attentive in the foyer lounge and the Chino Latino restaurant, where Pan-Asian cooking is a feature.

Rooms 178 (10 fmly) (16 smoking) **S** £49-£170; **D** £49-£170* **Facilities** STV FTV Wi-fi ➲ Gym Complimentary fitness suite **Conf** Class 100 Board 54 Thtr 200 Del from £99 to £250* **Services** Lift Air con **Notes** LB ⊗ Civ Wed 180

Park Inn by Radisson Nottingham

park inn
by Radisson

★★★ 75% HOTEL

☎ 0115 935 9988
Mansfield Rd NG5 2BT
e-mail: reservations.nottingham@rezidorparkinn.com
dir: Approx 1m from city centre on A60 (Mansfield Rd), at large rdbt, straight on at lights. Hotel on right

Ideally located to explore the city centre, the hotel is a spacious, purpose-built property offering a range of well-appointed bedrooms, conference rooms and a fully-equipped leisure club. The popular restaurant offers a contemporary dining experience in an airy environment.

Rooms 172 (8 fmly) **Facilities** STV FTV Wi-fi ⊘ supervised Gym Beauty treatment room Sauna Steam room Spa bath New Year **Conf** Class 45 Board 40 Thtr 180 **Services** Lift Air con **Parking** 410 **Notes** ⊗ Civ Wed 200

N

NOTTINGHAM *continued*

BEST WESTERN Bestwood Lodge

★★★ 71% HOTEL

☎ 0115 920 3011
Bestwood Country Park, Arnold NG5 8NE
e-mail: enquiries@bestwoodlodgehotel.co.uk
web: www.bw-bestwoodlodge.co.uk
dir: From Nottingham take A60, left at lights into
Oxclose Ln, right at next lights into Queens Bower Rd.
1st right. Keep right at fork in road

Set in 700 acres of parkland this Victorian building,
once a hunting lodge, has stunning architecture that
includes Gothic features and high vaulted ceilings.
Bedrooms include all the modern comforts, suitable
for both business and leisure guests, and the popular
restaurant serves an extensive menu.

Rooms 39 (5 fmly) **Facilities** FTV Wi-fi ♨ Guided
walks Xmas **Conf** Class 65 Board 50 Thtr 200
Parking 120 **Notes** RS 25 Dec & 1 Jan Civ Wed 80

The Strathdon

PEEL HOTELS PLC

★★ 71% HOTEL

☎ 0115 941 8501
Derby Rd NG1 5FT
e-mail: info@strathdon-hotel-nottingham.com
web: www.strathdon-hotel-nottingham.com
dir: From M1 follow city centre signs. At Canning
Circus into one-way system into Wollaton St, keep
right, next right to hotel

This city-centre hotel has modern facilities and is
very convenient for all city attractions. A popular
themed bar has a large-screen TV and serves an
extensive range of popular fresh food, while more
formal dining is available in Bobbins Restaurant on
certain evenings.

Rooms 68 (4 fmly) (16 smoking) **Facilities** FTV Wi-fi ⌨
Xmas New Year **Conf** Class 60 Board 40 Thtr 150
Services Lift **Notes** Civ Wed 85

Ibis Nottingham Centre

BUDGET HOTEL

☎ 0115 985 3600
16 Fletcher Gate NG1 2FS
e-mail: h6160@accor.com
dir: In Lace Market area of city centre

Modern, budget hotel offering comfortable
accommodation in bright and practical bedrooms.
Breakfast is self-service and dinner is available in
the restaurant. See also the Hotel Groups pages.

Rooms 142 (33 fmly) 🐾 **S** £55-£119; **D** £55-£119*

Premier Inn Nottingham Arena (London Rd)

BUDGET HOTEL

☎ 0871 527 8848
Island Site, London Rd NG2 4UU
web: www.premierinn.com
dir: M1 junct 25, A52 into city centre. Follow signs for
A60 to Loughborough. Hotel adjacent to BBC building

High quality, budget accommodation ideal for both
families and business travellers. Spacious, en suite
bedrooms feature tea and coffee making facilities,
and Freeview TV in most hotels. Internet access and
Wi-fi are available for a small fee. The adjacent
family restaurant features a wide and varied menu.
See also the Hotel Groups pages.

Rooms 87

Premier Inn Nottingham Castle Marina

BUDGET HOTEL

☎ 0871 527 8844
Castle Marina Park, Castle Bridge Rd NG7 1GX
web: www.premierinn.com
dir: M1 junct 24, A453. Follow ring road & signs for
Queen's Drive Industrial Estate. After Homebase left
into Castle Bridge Rd, opposite Pizza Hut restaurant.
Hotel adjacent to Boathouse Beefeater

Rooms 39

Premier Inn Nottingham City Centre (Goldsmith Street)

BUDGET HOTEL

☎ 0871 527 8846
Goldsmith St NG1 5LT
web: www.premierinn.com
dir: A610 to city centre. Follow signs for Nottingham
Trent University into Talbot St. 1st left into Clarendon
St. Right at lights. Hotel on right

Rooms 161

Premier Inn Nottingham North (Daybrook)

BUDGET HOTEL

☎ 0871 527 8850
101 Mansfield Rd, Daybrook NG5 6BH
web: www.premierinn.com
dir: M1 junct 26, A610 towards Nottingham. Left onto
A6514. Left onto A60 towards Mansfield. Hotel 0.25m
on left

Rooms 64

Premier Inn Nottingham South

BUDGET HOTEL

☎ 0871 527 8854
Loughborough Rd, Ruddington NG11 6LS
web: www.premierinn.com
dir: M1 junct 24, follow A453 signs to Nottingham,
A52 to Grantham. Hotel at 1st rdbt on left

Rooms 42

Premier Inn Nottingham West

BUDGET HOTEL

☎ 0871 527 8856
The Phoenix Centre, Millennium Way West NG8 6AS
web: www.premierinn.com
dir: M1 junct 26, 1m on A610 towards Nottingham

Rooms 86

Restaurant Sat Bains with Rooms

@@@@ RESTAURANT WITH ROOMS

☎ 0115 986 6566
Trentside, Lenton Ln NG7 2SA
e-mail: info@restaurantsatbains.net
dir: M1 junct 24, A453 Nottingham S. Over River
Trent into central lane to rdbt. Left, left again
towards river. Establishment on left after bend

This charming restaurant with rooms, a stylish
conversion of Victorian farm buildings, is situated on
the river and close to the industrial area of
Nottingham. The bedrooms create a warm
atmosphere by using quality soft furnishings together
with antique and period furniture; suites and four-
poster rooms are available. Public areas are chic and
cosy, and the delightful restaurant complements the
truly outstanding, much acclaimed cuisine.

Rooms 8 (4 annexe)

Cockliffe Country House

@@ RESTAURANT WITH ROOMS

☎ 0115 968 0179
**Burntstump Country Park, Burntstump Hill, Arnold
NG5 8PQ**
e-mail: enquiries@cockliffehouse.co.uk

Expect a warm welcome at this delightful property
situated in a peaceful rural location amidst neat
landscaped grounds, close to Sherwood Forest. Public
areas include a smart breakfast room, a tastefully
appointed restaurant and a cosy lounge bar. The
individually decorated bedrooms have co-ordinated
soft furnishings and many thoughtful touches.

Rooms 11 (4 annexe)

Save on hotels. Book at **theAA.com/hotel**

NOT – OAK 345 ENGLAND

BEST WESTERN Weston Hall Hotel

★★★ 74% HOTEL

☎ 024 7631 2989
Weston Ln, Bulkington CV12 9RU
e-mail: info@westonhallhotel.co.uk
dir: M6 junct 2, B4065 through Ansty. Left in Shilton, from Bulkington follow Nuneaton signs, into Weston Ln at 30mph sign

This Grade II listed hotel, with origins dating back to the reign of Elizabeth I, sits within seven acres of peaceful grounds. The original three-gabled building retains many original features, such as the carved wooden fireplace in the library. Friendly service is provided; and the bedrooms, that vary in size, are thoughtfully equipped.

Rooms 40 (1 fmly) (14 GF) **Facilities** FTV Wi-fi ⛲
New Year **Conf** Class 100 Board 60 Thtr 200
Parking 300 **Notes** Civ Wed 200

Premier Inn Nuneaton/ Coventry

BUDGET HOTEL

☎ 0871 527 8858
Coventry Rd CV10 7PJ
web: www.premierinn.com
dir: M6 junct 3, A444 towards Nuneaton. Hotel on B4113 on right, just off Griff Rdbt towards Bedworth

High quality, budget accommodation ideal for both families and business travellers. Spacious, en suite bedrooms feature tea and coffee making facilities, and Freeview TV in most hotels. Internet access and Wi-fi are available for a small fee. The adjacent family restaurant features a wide and varied menu. See also the Hotel Groups pages.

Rooms 48

INSPECTORS' CHOICE

Hambleton Hall

★★★★ ◉ ◉ ◉ ◉
COUNTRY HOUSE HOTEL

☎ 01572 756991
Hambleton LE15 8TH
e-mail: hotel@hambletonhall.com
web: www.hambletonhall.com
dir: 3m E off A606

Established over 30 years ago by Tim and Stefa Hart this delightful country house enjoys tranquil and spectacular views over Rutland Water. The beautifully manicured grounds are a delight to walk in. The bedrooms in the main house are stylish, individually decorated, and equipped with a range of thoughtful extras. A two-bedroom folly, with its own sitting and breakfast room, is only a short walk away. Day rooms include a cosy bar and a sumptuous drawing room, both featuring open fires. The elegant restaurant serves very accomplished, award-winning cuisine with menus highlighting locally sourced, seasonal produce - some of which is grown in the hotel's own grounds.

Rooms 17 (2 annexe) ⛳ **S** £195-£220;
D £255-£550 (incl. bkfst)* **Facilities** STV FTV Wi-fi
⛄ ⛳ ⛲ ⛵ Private access to lake Xmas New Year
Conf Board 24 Thtr 40 Del from £300 to £330*
Services Lift **Parking** 40 **Notes** LB Civ Wed 64

Barnsdale Lodge Hotel

★★★ 78% ◉ HOTEL

☎ 01572 724678
The Avenue, Rutland Water, North Shore LE15 8AH
e-mail: enquiries@barnsdalelodge.co.uk
web: www.barnsdalelodge.co.uk
dir: A1 onto A606. Hotel 5m on right, 2m E of Oakham

A popular and interesting hotel converted from a farmstead overlooking Rutland Water. The public areas are dominated by a successful food operation with a good range of appealing meals on offer for either formal or informal dining. Bedrooms are comfortably appointed with excellent beds enhanced by contemporary soft furnishings and thoughtful extras.

Rooms 45 (2 fmly) (16 GF) ⛳ **S** £80-£95; **D** £95-£150
(incl. bkfst)* **Facilities** FTV Wi-fi ⛄ Fishing ⛲ Archery
Beauty treatment room Golf Sailing Shooting Xmas
New Year **Conf** Class 120 Board 76 Thtr 330
Del from £99* **Parking** 200 **Notes** LB Civ Wed 200

O

Ashbury Hotel

★★ 72% HOTEL

☎ 01837 55453
Higher Maddaford, Southcott EX20 4NL
dir: Exit A30 at Sourton Cross onto A386. Left onto A3079 to Bude at Fowley Cross. After 1m right to Ashbury. Hotel 0.5m on right

With no less than five courses and a clubhouse with lounge, bar and dining facilities, The Ashbury is a golfers' paradise. The majority of the well-equipped bedrooms are located in the farmhouse and the courtyard-style development around the putting green. Guests can enjoy the many on-site leisure facilities or join the activities available at the nearby sister hotel.

Rooms 186 (79 fmly) (77 GF) ⚑ **Facilities** Spa FTV Wi-fi ⊗ ♨ 99 ☘ Putt green Fishing Gym Badminton Shooting ranges Ten-pin bowling Indoor bowls 5-a-side New Year **Conf** Thtr 250 **Parking** 200 **Notes** ⊗

Manor House Hotel

★★ 72% HOTEL

☎ 01837 53053
Fowley Cross EX20 4NA
e-mail: reception@manorhousehotel.co.uk
web: www.manorhousehotel.co.uk
dir: Exit A30 at Sourton Cross flyover, right onto A386. Hotel 1.5m on right

Enjoying views to Dartmoor in the distance, this hotel specialises in short breaks and is set in 17 acres of grounds, close to the A30. The superb range of sporting and craft facilities has been enhanced by an impressive swimming pool; golf is also offered at the adjacent sister hotel. Bedrooms, many located on the ground floor, are comfortable and well equipped.

Rooms 200 (91 fmly) (90 GF) ⚑ **Facilities** Spa FTV Wi-fi ⊗ ♨ 99 ☘ Putt green Fishing ⚓ Gym Squash Craft centre Indoor bowls Shooting ranges Indoor tennis Exercise classes Xmas New Year **Parking** 200 **Notes** ⊗

White Hart Hotel

★★ 72% HOTEL

☎ 01837 52730 & 54514
Fore St EX20 1HD
e-mail: enquiry@thewhitehart-hotel.com
web: www.thewhitehart-hotel.com
dir: In town centre, adjacent to lights, car park at rear of hotel

Dating back to the 17th century and situated on the edge of the Dartmoor National Park, the White Hart offers modern facilities. Bedrooms are well equipped and spacious. Locally sourced, home-cooked food is on offer in the bars and the Courtney Restaurant; or guests can choose to eat in Vines Pizzeria. Wi-fi is available in public areas.

Rooms 19 (2 fmly) **Facilities** FTV Wi-fi ⊗ Xmas **Conf** Class 30 Board 40 Thtr 100 **Parking** 20

Premier Inn Birmingham Oldbury M5 Jct 2

BUDGET HOTEL

☎ 0871 527 8090
Wolverhampton Rd B69 2BH
web: www.premierinn.com
dir: M5 junct 2, A4123 (Wolverhampton Rd) N towards Dudley

High quality, budget accommodation ideal for both families and business travellers. Spacious, en suite bedrooms feature tea and coffee making facilities, and Freeview TV in most hotels. Internet access and Wi-fi are available for a small fee. The adjacent family restaurant features a wide and varied menu. See also the Hotel Groups pages.

Rooms 60

BEST WESTERN Hotel Smokies Park

★★★ 80% HOTEL

☎ 0161 785 5000
Ashton Rd, Bardsley OL8 3HX
e-mail: sales@smokies.co.uk
web: www.smokies.co.uk
dir: On A627 between Oldham & Ashton-under-Lyne

This modern, stylish hotel offers smart, comfortable bedrooms and suites. A wide range of Italian and English dishes is offered in the Mediterranean-style restaurant and there is a welcoming lounge bar with live entertainment at weekends. Also available are a small yet well equipped, residents-only fitness centre and extensive function facilities.

Rooms 73 (2 fmly) (22 GF) ⚑ **S** £50-£90; **D** £50-£90* **Facilities** FTV Wi-fi ⊗ Xmas New Year **Conf** Class 100 Board 40 Thtr 400 Del from £135* **Services** Lift **Parking** 120 **Notes** ⊗ RS 25 Dec-3 Jan Civ Wed 400

Premier Inn Oldham (Broadway)

BUDGET HOTEL

☎ 0871 527 8860
Broadway/Hollinwood Av, Chadderton OL9 8DW
web: www.premierinn.com
dir: M60 (anti-clockwise) junct 21, signed Manchester city centre. Take A663, hotel 400yds on left

High quality, budget accommodation ideal for both families and business travellers. Spacious, en suite bedrooms feature tea and coffee making facilities, and Freeview TV in most hotels. Internet access and Wi-fi are available for a small fee. The adjacent family restaurant features a wide and varied menu. See also the Hotel Groups pages.

Rooms 40

Premier Inn Oldham Central

BUDGET HOTEL

☎ 0871 527 8862
Westwood Park, Chadderton Way, Chadderton OL1 2NA
web: www.premierinn.com
dir: M62 junct 20, A627(M) to Oldham. Take A627 (Chadderton Way). Hotel on left opposite B&Q Depot

Rooms 40

OLD HARLOW
Essex
Map 6 TL41

Premier Inn Harlow
BUDGET HOTEL

☎ 0871 527 8488
Cambridge Rd CM20 2EP
web: www.premierinn.com
dir: M11 junct 7, A414, A1184 (Sawbridgeworth to Bishop's Stortford road)

High quality, budget accommodation ideal for both families and business travellers. Spacious, en suite bedrooms feature tea and coffee making facilities, and Freeview TV in most hotels. Internet access and Wi-fi are available for a small fee. The adjacent family restaurant features a wide and varied menu. See also the Hotel Groups pages.

Rooms 61

OLDSTEAD
North Yorkshire
Map 19 SE57

INSPECTORS' CHOICE

The Black Swan at Oldstead
◉ ◉ ◉ RESTAURANT WITH ROOMS

☎ 01347 868387
YO61 4BL
e-mail: enquiries@blackswanoldstead.co.uk
dir: Exit A19, 3m S Thirsk for Coxwold, left in Coxwold, left at Byland Abbey for Oldstead

The Black Swan is set amidst the stunning scenery of the North Yorkshire National Park, and parts of the building date back to the 16th century. Well appointed, very comfortable bedrooms and bathrooms provide the perfect get-away-from-it-all. Open fires, a traditional bar and a restaurant, serving award-winning food, is the icing on the cake for this little gem of a property.

Rooms 4

OLLERTON
Nottinghamshire
Map 16 SK66

Thoresby Hall Hotel
Warner Leisure Hotels
JUST FOR GROWN-UPS

★★★★ 81% ◉ ◉ COUNTRY HOUSE HOTEL

☎ 01623 821000 & 821033
Thoresby Park NG22 9WH
e-mail: reception.thoresbyhall@bourne-leisure.co.uk

This hotel is set in acres of rolling parklands on the edge of Sherwood Forest. Thoresby Hall is a magnificent Grade I Victorian country house. Guests can choose to relax in the spa, stroll around the beautiful gardens or just sit and relax in the Great Hall. Bedrooms vary in style and size. This is an adults only (over 21 years) hotel.

Rooms 221 (168 annexe) (72 GF) **Facilities** Spa Wi-fi HL ⓣ supervised ⌁ Putt green Fishing ⚓ Gym Rifle shooting Archery Outdoor bowls Fencing Laser clay Yoga Tai chi ♫ Xmas New Year **Conf** Class 200 Board 30 Thtr 400 **Services** Lift **Parking** 140 **Notes** ⊗ No children 21yrs Civ Wed 92

ORFORD
Suffolk
Map 13 TM45

The Crown & Castle
★★★ 87% ◉ ◉ HOTEL

☎ 01394 450205
IP12 2LJ
e-mail: info@crownandcastle.co.uk
web: www.crownandcastle.co.uk
dir: Turn right from B1084 on entering village, towards castle

The Crown & Castle is a delightful inn situated adjacent to the Norman castle keep. Contemporary style bedrooms are spilt between the main house and the garden wing; the latter are more spacious and have patios with access to the garden. The restaurant has an informal atmosphere with polished tables and local artwork; the menu features quality, locally sourced produce.

Rooms 21 (14 annexe) (2 fmly) (13 GF) ⌕
S £115-£170; **D** £130-£190 (incl. bkfst)*
Facilities FTV Wi-fi ↕ HL Xmas New Year **Parking** 17
Notes LB No children 8yrs

ORMSKIRK
Lancashire
Map 15 SD40

Premier Inn Southport (Ormskirk)
BUDGET HOTEL

☎ 0871 527 9010
544 Southport Rd, Scarisbrick L40 9RG
web: www.premierinn.com
dir: From Southport follow Ormskirk/A570 signs. Hotel on right of A570 (Southport Rd) at 1st lights (entrance just after lights)

High quality, budget accommodation ideal for both families and business travellers. Spacious, en suite bedrooms feature tea and coffee making facilities, and Freeview TV in most hotels. Internet access and Wi-fi are available for a small fee. The adjacent family restaurant features a wide and varied menu. See also the Hotel Groups pages.

Rooms 20

ORSETT
Essex
Map 6 TQ68

Orsett Hall Banqueting & Conference Centre
★★★★ 77% ◉ ◉ COUNTRY HOUSE HOTEL

☎ 01375 891402
Prince Charles Av RM16 3HS
dir: M25 junct 29, A127 Southend, A128 Hotel 3m on right

This beautiful country house hotel, conveniently located for the M25, is set in 12 acres of landscaped gardens, and has individually designed, luxurious bedrooms. The award-winning Garden restaurant is a fabulous dining venue and the stylish modern bar is popular with guests for afternoon tea. Orsett Hall has a first rate Spa, a very well equipped Gym along with a range of business suites, and free Wi-fi is available throughout.

Rooms 38 (2 annexe) (3 fmly) ⌕ **S** £134-£164;
D £144-£184* **Facilities** Spa FTV Wi-fi Gym Xmas New Year **Conf** Class 200 Board 50 Thtr 450 Del from £155 to £175* **Services** Lift Air con **Parking** 250 **Notes** LB Civ Wed 120

O

OSWESTRY
Map 15 SJ22
Shropshire

Wynnstay Hotel

★★★★ 77% ®® HOTEL

☎ 01691 655261
Church St SY11 2SZ
e-mail: info@wynnstayhotel.com
web: www.wynnstayhotel.com
dir: B4083 to town, fork left at Honda Garage, right at lights. Hotel opposite church

This Georgian property was once a coaching inn and posting house and surrounds a unique 200-year-old Crown Bowling Green. Elegant public areas include a health, leisure and beauty centre, which is housed in a former coach house. Well-equipped bedrooms are individually styled and include several suites, four-poster rooms and a self-catering apartment. The Four Seasons Restaurant has a well deserved reputation for its food, and the adjacent Wilsons café/bar is a stylish, informal alternative.

Rooms 34 (5 fmly) ☼ **S** £50-£75; **D** £70-£95*
Facilities Spa FTV Wi-fi ⓢ supervised Gym Crown bowling green Beauty suite ♫ New Year
Conf Class 150 Board 50 Thtr 290 **Parking** 80
Notes LB ⊗ Civ Wed 90

Lion Quays Waterside Resort

★★★★ 77% HOTEL

☎ 01691 684300
Moreton, Weston Rhyn SY11 3EN
e-mail: reservations@lionquays.com
dir: On A5, 3m N of Oswestry

This resort is situated beside the Llangollen Canal which is in a convenient location for visiting Chester to the north and the Snowdonia region to the west. The comfortable bedrooms have views over the countryside or the magnificent grounds and gardens. Guests can dine either in the Waterside Bar or the Country Club which has a stunning 25-metre

swimming pool, a state-of-the-art gym plus spa facilities. Extensive conference and meeting facilities are also available.

Rooms 82 (3 fmly) (25 GF) ☼ **Facilities** Spa FTV Wi-fi ⓢ supervised ❦ Gym Sauna Steam room Xmas New Year **Conf** Class 200 Board 150 Thtr 600
Del from £120 to £135* **Services** Lift **Parking** 250
Notes ⊗ Civ Wed 600

Pen-y-Dyffryn Country Hotel

★★★ 85% ®® COUNTRY HOUSE HOTEL

☎ 01691 653700
Rhydycroesau SY10 7JD
e-mail: stay@peny.co.uk
web: www.peny.co.uk
dir: A5 into town centre. Follow signs to Llansilin on B4580, hotel 3m W of Oswestry before Rhydycroesau

Peacefully situated in five acres of grounds, this charming old house dates back to around 1840, when it was built as a rectory. The tastefully appointed public rooms have real fires, lit in colder weather, and the accommodation includes several mini-cottages, each with its own patio. Many guests are attracted to this hotel for the excellent food and attentive, friendly service.

Rooms 12 (4 annexe) (1 fmly) (1 GF) ☼ **S** £75-£92; **D** £126-£180 (incl. bkfst)* **Facilities** STV FTV Wi-fi ⓢ Guided walks New Year **Parking** 18 **Notes** LB No children 3yrs Closed 18 Dec-19 Jan

Premier Inn Oswestry

BUDGET HOTEL

☎ 0871 527 8864
SY10 8NN
web: www.premierinn.com
dir: From rdbt junct of A483 & A5 (SE of Oswestry) take A5 signed Oswestry B4579. Hotel 500yds

High quality, budget accommodation ideal for both families and business travellers. Spacious, en suite bedrooms feature tea and coffee making facilities, and Freeview TV in most hotels. Internet access and Wi-fi are available for a small fee. The adjacent family restaurant features a wide and varied menu. See also the Hotel Groups pages.

Rooms 59

Sebastians

®® RESTAURANT WITH ROOMS

☎ 01691 655444
45 Willow St SY11 1AQ
e-mail: sebastians.rest@virgin.net
web: www.sebastians-hotel.co.uk
dir: From town centre, take turn signed Selattyn into Willow St. 400yds from junct on left opposite Willow Street Gallery

Sebastians is an intrinsic part of the leisure scene in Oswestry and has built up a loyal local following. Meals feature French influences, with a multi-choice set menu as well as a simpler Market menu. Rooms are set around the pretty terrace courtyard, and provide very comfortable accommodation with all the comforts of home.

Rooms 5 (4 annexe) (4 fmly)

OTLEY
Map 19 SE24
West Yorkshire

Chevin Country Park Hotel & Spa

★★★ 77% ® HOTEL

☎ 01943 467818
Yorkgate LS21 3NU
e-mail: chevin@crerarhotels.com
dir: From Leeds/Bradford Airport rdbt take A658 N towards Harrogate, 0.75m to lights. Left, 2nd left into Yorkgate. Hotel 0.5m on left

Peacefully located in its own woodland yet convenient for major road links and the airport. Bedrooms are split between the original main building and chalet-style accommodation in the extensive grounds. Public areas include a bar and several lounges. The Lakeside Restaurant provides views over the small lake, and good leisure facilities are available.

Rooms 49 (30 annexe) (7 fmly) (45 GF) **Facilities** Spa FTV Wi-fi ⓢ ❦ Fishing Gym Steam room Xmas New Year **Conf** Class 90 Board 50 Thtr 120 **Parking** 100
Notes Civ Wed 100

O

Save on hotels. Book at **theAA.com/hotel**

OSW – OXF 349 ENGLAND

OTTERSHAW
Surrey   Map 6 TQ06

Foxhills Club and Resort

★★★★ 84% ⊛ HOTEL

☎ 01932 872050 & 704500
Stonehill Rd KT16 0EL
e-mail: reservations@foxhills.co.uk
web: www.foxhills.co.uk
dir: M25 junct 11, A320 to Woking. 2nd rdbt last exit into Chobham Rd. Right into Foxhills Rd, left into Stonehill Rd

This 19th-century mansion hotel enjoys a peaceful setting in extensive grounds, not far from the M25 and Heathrow. Spacious well-appointed bedrooms are provided in a choice of annexes situated a short walk from the main house. Golf, tennis, three pools and impressive indoor leisure facilities are available. There is a superb spa offering a range of treatments and therapies plus a health club with all the latest fitness equipment. The eating options are the Manor Restaurant, in the former music room, and the Summerhouse Brasserie.

Rooms 70 (8 fmly) (39 GF) ↖ **S** £120-£205; **D** £145-£245 (incl. bkfst)* **Facilities** Spa STV FTV Wi-fi ⤵ ⊛ ⤵ ⚡ 45 ⚐ Putt green ≋ Gym Squash Children's adventure playground Country pursuits Off-road course Hairdresser ♫ Xmas New Year Child facilities **Conf** Class 62 Board 56 Thtr 100 Del from £205 to £305* **Parking** 500 **Notes** LB ⊗ Civ Wed 75

OTTERY ST MARY
Devon   Map 3 SY19

Tumbling Weir Hotel

★★ 79% SMALL HOTEL

☎ 01404 812752
Canaan Way EX11 1AQ
e-mail: reception@tumblingweirhotel.com
web: www.tumblingweirhotel.co.uk
dir: A30 onto B3177 into Ottery St Mary, hotel signed from Mill St, access through old mill

Quietly located between the River Otter and its millstream, and set in well-tended gardens, this family-run hotel offers friendly and attentive service. Bedrooms are attractively presented and equipped with modern comforts. In the dining room, where a selection of carefully prepared dishes makes up the carte menu, beams and subtle lighting help to create an intimate atmosphere.

Rooms 10 (1 fmly) ↖ **S** £55-£65; **D** £90-£110 (incl. bkfst)* **Facilities** FTV Wi-fi ⤵ ⚐ **Conf** Class 60 Board 50 Thtr 90 Del from £90 to £105* **Parking** 10 **Notes** ⊗ Closed 22 Dec-7 Jan Civ Wed 80

OUNDLE
Northamptonshire   Map 11 TL08

The Talbot Hotel

★★★ 77% ⊛ HOTEL

☎ 01832 273621
New St PE8 4EA
e-mail: talbot@bpcmail.co.uk
dir: A605 Northampton/Oundle at rdbt exit Oundle A427 - Station Road turn onto New Street

This Grade I listed property is steeped in history and is reputed to house the staircase that Mary Queen of Scots walked down to her execution in 1587. Following extensive refurbishment, the hotel offers an open-plan eatery and coffee shop for relaxed dining. Accommodation offers a mix of traditional and contemporary, but all provide up-to-date amenities for guest comfort.

Rooms 34 (2 fmly) (12 GF) ↖ **S** £69-£99; **D** £75-£125 (incl. bkfst)* **Facilities** FTV Wi-fi Xmas New Year **Conf** Class 50 Board 30 Thtr 100 Del from £100 to £150 **Parking** 30 **Notes** LB Civ Wed 80

OXFORD
Oxfordshire   Map 5 SP50

INSPECTORS' CHOICE

Le Manoir Aux Quat' Saisons

★★★★★ ⊛⊛⊛⊛⊛ HOTEL

☎ 01844 278881
Church Rd OX44 7PD
e-mail: lemanoir@blanc.co.uk
web: www.manoir.com

(For full entry see Great Milton)

Macdonald Randolph Hotel

 MACDONALD
HOTELS & RESORTS

★★★★★ 82% ⊛⊛ HOTEL

☎ 01865 256400
Beaumont St OX1 2LN
e-mail: randolph@macdonald-hotels.co.uk
web: www.macdonaldhotels.co.uk
dir: M40 junct 8, A40 signed Oxford/Cheltenham, 5m, at lights to ring road rdbt. Right signed Kidlington/ North Oxford. At next rdbt left towards city centre (A4165/ Banbury Rd). Through Summertown to lights at end of St Giles. Hotel on right

Superbly located near the city centre, The Randolph boasts impressive neo-Gothic architecture and tasteful decor. The spacious and traditional restaurant, complete with picture windows, is the ideal place to watch the world go by while enjoying freshly prepared, modern dishes. Bedrooms include a

mix of classical and contemporary wing rooms, which have been appointed to a high standard. Parking is a real bonus. Macdonald Hotels is the AA Hotel Group of the Year 2013-14.

Rooms 151 ↖ **S** £159-£299; **D** £189-£309* **Facilities** Spa STV FTV Wi-fi Gym Beauty treatment rooms Thermal suite Mini gym ♫ Xmas New Year **Conf** Class 130 Board 60 Thtr 300 **Services** Lift **Parking** 60 **Notes** LB Civ Wed 120

The Old Bank Hotel

★★★★ 79% TOWN HOUSE HOTEL

☎ 01865 799599
92-94 High St OX1 4BN
e-mail: reception@oldbank-hotel.co.uk
web: www.oldbank-hotel.co.uk
dir: From Magdalen Bridge onto High St, hotel 50yds on left

Located close to the city centre and the colleges, this former bank benefits from an excellent location. An eclectic collection of modern pictures and photographs, many by well-known artists, are on display. Bedrooms are smart with excellent business facilities plus the benefit of air conditioning. Public areas include the vibrant all-day Quod Bar and Restaurant. The hotel has its own car park - a definite advantage in this busy city.

Rooms 42 (4 fmly) (1 GF) ↖ **Facilities** STV FTV Wi-fi ⤵ Beauty treatment room Bicycles Free use of nearby gym Walking tours ♫ Xmas **Conf** Board 30 Thtr 50 **Services** Lift Air con **Parking** 40 **Notes** ⊗

The Oxford Hotel

★★★★ 76% ⊛ HOTEL   ⓅP PUMA HOTELS COLLECTION

☎ 01865 489988
Godstow Rd, Wolvercote Roundabout OX2 8AL
e-mail: oxford@pumahotels.co.uk
web: www.pumahotels.co.uk
dir: Adjacent to A34/A40, 2m from city centre

Conveniently located on the northern edge of the city centre, this purpose-built hotel offers bedrooms that are bright, modern and well equipped. Guests can eat in the Medio Restaurant or try the Cappuccino Lounge menu. There is also the option to eat alfresco on the Patio Terrace when the weather is fine. The hotel offers impressive conference, business and leisure facilities.

Rooms 168 (11 fmly) (89 GF) **Facilities** Spa STV Wi-fi ⊛ supervised Gym Squash Steam room Beauty treatments New Year **Conf** Class 130 Board 110 Thtr 320 **Parking** 250 **Notes** Civ Wed 250

O

OXFORD *continued*

Old Parsonage Hotel

★★★★ 76% TOWN HOUSE HOTEL

☎ 01865 310210
1 Banbury Rd OX2 6NN
e-mail: reception@oldparsonage-hotel.co.uk
web: www.oldparsonage-hotel.co.uk
dir: From Oxford ring road to city centre via
Summertown. Hotel last building on right before
entering St Giles

Dating back in parts to the 16th century, this stylish
hotel offers great character and charm and is
conveniently located at the northern edge of the city
centre. The focal point of the operation is the busy
all-day bar and restaurant which has a clubby,
bohemian atmosphere; the small garden areas and
terraces prove popular in summer months. The Pike
Room is available for private lunches and dinners,
weddings and meetings. Liveried bicycles are
available for guests to explore the city.

Rooms 30 (4 fmly) (10 GF) **Facilities** STV FTV Wi-fi ⟲
In room beauty treatments Use of nearby fitness club
House bikes Walking tours Xmas New Year
Conf Class 8 Board 12 Thtr 20 **Services** Air con
Parking 14 **Notes** Closed 4 Nov 2013 - Jun 2014 for
refurbishment Civ Wed 60

Oxford Spires Four Pillars Hotel

★★★★ 76% HOTEL

☎ 0800 374692 & 01865 324324
Abingdon Rd OX1 4PS
e-mail: spires@four-pillars.co.uk
web: www.four-pillars.co.uk/spires
dir: M40 junct 8 towards Oxford. Left towards Cowley.
At 3rd rdbt follow city centre signs. Hotel in 1m

This purpose-built hotel is surrounded by extensive
parkland, yet is only a short walk from the city centre.
Bedrooms are attractively furnished, well equipped
and include several apartments. Public areas include
a spacious restaurant, open-plan bar/lounge, leisure
club and extensive conference facilities.

Rooms 174 (10 annexe) (1 fmly) (54 GF) 🌙
S £125-£250; **D** £125-£250 **Facilities** FTV Wi-fi ⟲ 🏊
Gym Beauty treatments Steam room Sauna Xmas New

Year **Conf** Class 96 Board 76 Thtr 266 Del from £130
to £199 **Services** Lift **Parking** 95 **Notes** LB ⊗
Civ Wed 200

Oxford Thames Four Pillars Hotel

★★★★ 76% HOTEL

☎ 0800 374692 & 01865 334444
Henley Rd, Sandford-on-Thames OX4 4GX
e-mail: thames@four-pillars.co.uk
web: www.four-pillars.co.uk/thames
dir: M40 junct 8 towards Oxford, follow ring road. Left
at rdbt towards Cowley. At rdbt with lights turn left to
Littlemore, hotel approx 1m on right

Set in 30 acres of beautiful grounds beside the river,
this mellow stone property provides a quiet retreat,
yet is close to the city. The spacious and traditional
River Room Restaurant has superb views of the
hotel's own boat moored on the river. The gardens can
be enjoyed from the patios or balconies in the newer
bedroom wings. Public rooms include a beamed bar
and lounge area with minstrels' gallery, and Jerome's
Leisure Club. The hotel is popular as a wedding
venue.

Rooms 84 (5 fmly) (37 GF) 🌙 **S** £125-£250;
D £125-£250 **Facilities** FTV Wi-fi ⟲ 🏊 Gym Steam
room Sauna Beauty treatment room Xmas New Year
Conf Class 80 Board 40 Thtr 120 Del from £130 to
£199 **Parking** 130 **Notes** LB ⊗ Civ Wed 100

Cotswold Lodge Hotel

★★★★ 75% HOTEL

CLASSIC
BRITISH HOTELS

☎ 01865 512121
66a Banbury Rd OX2 6JP
e-mail: info@cotswoldlodgehotel.co.uk
web: www.cotswoldlodgehotel.co.uk
dir: A40 (Oxford ring road) onto A4165 (Banbury road)
signed city centre/Summertown. Hotel 2m on left

This Victorian property is located close to the centre
of Oxford and offers smart, comfortable
accommodation. Stylish bedrooms and suites are
attractively presented and some have balconies. The
public areas have an elegant country-house feel. The
hotel is popular with business guests and caters for
conferences and banquets.

Rooms 49 (14 GF) 🌙 **S** £65-£165; **D** £115-£220 (incl.
bkfst)* **Facilities** STV FTV Wi-fi ⟲ Xmas New Year
Conf Class 45 Board 40 Thtr 100 Del from £130 to
£195 **Parking** 40 **Notes** ⊗ Civ Wed 100

Malmaison Oxford

★★★ 83% ⊛ HOTEL

Malmaison

☎ 01865 268400 & 0844 6930 659
3 Oxford Castle, New Rd OX1 1AY
e-mail: csteadman@malmaison.com
web: www.malmaison.com
dir: M40 junct 9, A34 N to Botley interchange. Follow
city centre & rail station signs. At rail station straight
ahead to 2nd lights. Turn right, at next lights left into
Park End St. Straight on at next lights, hotel 2nd left

Once the city's prison, this is definitely a hotel with a
difference. Many of the rooms are actually converted
from the old cells. Not to worry though there have
been many improvements since the prisoners left!
Exceedingly comfortable beds and luxury bathrooms
are just two of the changes. The hotel has a popular
brasserie with quality and value much in evidence.
Limited parking space is available.

Rooms 95 (5 GF) 🌙 **Facilities** STV Wi-fi Gym Xmas
New Year **Conf** Class 40 Board 40 Thtr 80
Services Lift **Parking** 30 **Notes** Civ Wed 80

Mercure Oxford Eastgate Hotel

Mercure

★★★ 82% ⊛ HOTEL

☎ 01865 248332
73 High St OX1 4BE
e-mail: h6668@accor.com
web: www.mercure.com
dir: A40 follow signs to Headington & Oxford city
centre, over Magdalen Bridge, stay in left lane,
through lights, left into Merton St, entrance to car
park on left

Just a short stroll from the city centre, this hotel, as
its name suggests, occupies the site of the city's
medieval East Gate and boasts its own car park.
Bedrooms are appointed and equipped to a high
standard. Stylish public areas include the all-day
Town House Brasserie and Bar.

Rooms 64 (3 fmly) (4 GF) 🌙 **Facilities** Wi-fi Xmas
New Year **Services** Lift Air con **Parking** 40 **Notes** ⊗

Save on hotels. Book at **theAA.com/hotel**

OXF 351 ENGLAND

Holiday Inn Oxford

★★★ 79% HOTEL

☎ 0870 942 9086 & 01865 888 467
Peartree Roundabout, Woodstock Rd OX2 8JD
e-mail: oxford@ihg.com
web: www.hioxfordhotel.co.uk
dir: A34 at Peartree Interchange signed Oxford & Services. Hotel on left

Located at The Peartree Roundabout, this purpose-built, modern hotel is ideal for business and leisure guests visiting Oxford. Bedrooms are spacious, well equipped and have air cooling. There is a smart bar and restaurant plus a well-equipped gym and large swimming pool. There are meeting facilities and ample free parking.

Rooms 154 (33 fmly) (23 GF) (6 smoking)
S £89–£180; **D** £89–£180 (incl. bkfst)* **Facilities** Spa STV FTV Wi-fi ↕ HL ☒ supervised Gym Sauna Steam room **Conf** Class 65 Board 40 Thtr 150 Del from £120 to £167* **Services** Lift Air con **Parking** 184 **Notes** LB ☒ Civ Wed 100

Hawkwell House

★★★ 78% HOTEL

☎ 01865 749988
Church Way, Iffley Village OX4 4DZ
e-mail: reservations@hawkwellhouse.co.uk
web: www.hawkwellhouse.co.uk
dir: A34 follow signs to Cowley. At Littlemore rdbt A4158 exit into Iffley Rd. After lights left to Iffley

Set in a peaceful residential location, Hawkwell House is just a few minutes' drive from the Oxford ring road. The spacious rooms are modern, attractively decorated and well equipped. Public areas are tastefully appointed and the conservatory-style restaurant offers an interesting choice of dishes. The hotel also has a range of conference and function facilities.

Rooms 66 (10 fmly) (4 GF) ⋔ **Facilities** FTV Wi-fi ⮇ Xmas New Year **Conf** Class 100 Board 80 Thtr 200 **Services** Lift **Parking** 120 **Notes** LB ☒ Civ Wed 150

Manor House Hotel

★★ 72% METRO HOTEL

☎ 01865 727627
250 Iffley Rd OX4 1SE
e-mail: manorhousehotel@hotmail.com
dir: On A4158, 1m from city centre

This family run establishment is easily accessible from the city centre and all major road links. The hotel provides informal but friendly and attentive service. The comfortably furnished bedrooms are well equipped. The hotel has a bar but there is a selection of restaurants and popular pubs within easy walking distance. Limited private parking is available.

Rooms 8 (2 fmly) **Facilities** STV FTV Wi-fi ↕ **Parking** 6 **Notes** ☒ Closed 20 Dec–20 Jan

Bath Place Hotel

★★ 68% METRO HOTEL

☎ 01865 791812
4-5 Bath Place, Holywell St OX1 3SU
e-mail: info@bathplace.co.uk
dir: On S side of Holywell St (parallel to High St)

The hotel has been created from a group of 17th-century cottages originally built by Flemish weavers who were permitted to settle outside the city walls. This lovely hotel is very much at the heart of the city today and offers individually designed bedrooms, including some with four-posters.

Rooms 16 (3 fmly) (5 GF) ⋔ **S** £90–£105; **D** £115–£145 (incl. bkfst)* **Facilities** FTV Wi-fi **Parking** 16

The Balkan Lodge Hotel

★★ 67% METRO HOTEL

☎ 01865 244524
315 Iffley Rd OX4 4AG
e-mail: info@balkanlodgeoxford.co.uk
web: www.balkanlodgeoxford.co.uk
dir: From M40, A40 take eastern bypass, into city on A4158

Conveniently located for the city centre and the ring road, this family operated metro hotel offers a comfortable stay. Bedrooms are attractive and well equipped. Public areas include a lounge and bar. A secure private car park is located to the rear of the building.

Rooms 12 **Facilities** Wi-fi **Parking** 12 **Notes** ☒

Vanbrugh House Hotel

Ⓤ

☎ 01865 244622
20-24 St Michael's St OX1 2EB
e-mail: colin@sojournhotels.co.uk

Currently the rating for this establishment is not confirmed. This may be due to a change of ownership or because it has only recently joined the AA rating scheme. For further details please see the AA website: theAA.com

Rooms 22

Premier Inn Oxford

BUDGET HOTEL

☎ 0871 527 8866
Oxford Business Park, Garsington Rd OX4 2JZ
web: www.premierinn.com
dir: On Oxford Business Park, just off A4142 & B480 junct

High quality, budget accommodation ideal for both families and business travellers. Spacious, en suite bedrooms feature tea and coffee making facilities, and Freeview TV in most hotels. Internet access and Wi-fi are available for a small fee. The adjacent family restaurant features a wide and varied menu. See also the Hotel Groups pages.

Rooms 121

OXFORD	Map 5 SP60
MOTORWAY SERVICE AREA (M40)	
Oxfordshire	

Days Inn Oxford - M40

BUDGET HOTEL

☎ 01865 877000
M40 junction 8A, Waterstock OX33 1LJ
e-mail: oxford.hotel@welcomebreak.co.uk
web: www.welcomebreak.co.uk
dir: M40 junct 8a, at Welcome Break service area

This modern building offers accommodation in smart, spacious and well-equipped bedrooms, suitable for families and business travellers, and all with en suite bathrooms. Continental breakfast is available and other refreshments may be taken at the nearby family restaurant. See also the Hotel Groups pages.

Rooms 59 (56 fmly) (25 GF) (10 smoking)

O

PADSTOW
Cornwall   Map 2 SW97

The Metropole

★★★★ 74% ⚜ HOTEL

RICHARDSON HOTELS
Where Memories are Made

☎ 01841 532486
Station Rd PL28 8DB
e-mail: reservations@the-metropole.co.uk
web: www.the-metropole.co.uk
dir: M5/A30 pass Launceston, follow Wadebridge & N
Cornwall signs. Take A39, follow Padstow signs

This long-established hotel first opened its doors to
guests back in 1904, and it still retains an air of the
sophistication and elegance of a bygone age.
Bedrooms are soundly appointed and well equipped;
dining options include the informal Met Café Bar, and
the main restaurant with its enjoyable cuisine and
wonderful views over the Camel estuary.

Rooms 58 (3 fmly) (2 GF) ⚲ **Facilities** Spa FTV Wi-fi
⚲ Swimming pool open Jul & Aug only Xmas New
Year **Conf** Class 20 Board 20 Thtr 40 **Services** Lift
Parking 36 **Notes** Civ Wed 110

St Petroc's Hotel and Bistro

★★ 85% ⚜ SMALL HOTEL

☎ 01841 532700
4 New St PL28 8EA
e-mail: reservations@rickstein.com
dir: A39 onto A389, follow signs to town centre. Follow
one-way system, hotel on right on leaving town

One of the oldest buildings in town, this charming
establishment is just up the hill from the picturesque
harbour. Style, comfort and individuality are all great
strengths here, particularly so in the impressively
equipped bedrooms. Breakfast, lunch and dinner all
reflect a serious approach to cuisine, and the popular
restaurant has a relaxed, bistro style. Comfortable
lounges, a reading room and lovely gardens complete
the picture.

Rooms 14 (4 annexe) (3 fmly) (3 GF) ⚲ **D** £150-£290
(incl. bkfst)* **Facilities** FTV Wi-fi Cookery school New
Year **Conf** Board 12 **Parking** 12 **Notes** LB Closed
1 May & 25-26 Dec RS 24 Dec eve

The Old Ship Hotel

★★ 78% HOTEL

☎ 01841 532357
Mill Square PL28 8AE
e-mail: stay@oldshiphotel-padstow.co.uk
web: www.oldshiphotel-padstow.co.uk
dir: From M5 take A30 to Bodmin then A389 to
Padstow, follow brown tourist signs to car park

This attractive inn is situated in the heart of the old
town's quaint and winding streets, just a short walk
from the harbour. A warm welcome is assured,
accommodation is pleasant and comfortable, and
public areas offer plenty of character. Freshly caught
fish features on both the bar and restaurant menus.
On site parking is a bonus.

Rooms 14 (4 fmly) **S** £60-£65; **D** £80-£120 (incl.
bkfst)* **Facilities** STV FTV Wi-fi ♫ Xmas New Year
Parking 20 **Notes** LB RS 15-30 Dec

INSPECTORS' CHOICE

The Seafood Restaurant

⚜ ⚜ ⚜ RESTAURANT WITH ROOMS

☎ 01841 532700
Riverside PL28 8BY
e-mail: reservations@rickstein.com
dir: Into town centre down hill, follow round sharp
bend, restaurant on left

Food lovers continue to beat a well-trodden path to
this legendary establishment. Situated on the edge
of the harbour, just a stone's throw from the shops,
The Seafood Restaurant offers stylish and
comfortable bedrooms that boast numerous
thoughtful extras; some have views of the estuary
and a couple have stunning private balconies.
Service is relaxed and friendly; booking is essential
for both accommodation and a table in the
restaurant.

Rooms 20 (6 annexe) (6 fmly)

PAIGNTON
Devon   Map 3 SX86

Redcliffe Hotel

★★★ 78% HOTEL

☎ 01803 526397
Marine Dr TQ3 2NL
e-mail: redclfe@aol.com
dir: On seafront at Torquay end of Paignton Green

Set at the water's edge in three acres of well-tended
grounds, this popular hotel enjoys uninterrupted
views across Tor Bay. On offer is a diverse range of
facilities including a leisure complex, beauty
treatments and lots of outdoor family activities in the
summer. Bedrooms are pleasantly appointed and
comfortably furnished, while public areas offer ample
space for rest and relaxation.

Rooms 68 (8 fmly) (3 GF) ⚲ **S** £62-£67; **D** £124-£134
(incl. bkfst)* **Facilities** Spa FTV Wi-fi ⚲ supervised
⚲ Putt green Fishing Gym Table tennis Carpet bowls
Xmas New Year **Conf** Class 50 Board 50 Thtr 150
Del from £78 to £88* **Services** Lift **Parking** 80
Notes LB ⊗ Civ Wed 150

Premier Inn (Goodrington Sands)

BUDGET HOTEL

☎ 0871 527 9206
Tanners Rd, Goodrington TQ4 6LP
web: www.premierinn.com
dir: From Newton Abbot take A380 S. Left into A3022
(Totnes Rd), right at Hayes Rd into Penwill Way, right
at B3199 into Dartmouth Rd, at lights left into
Tanners Rd

High quality, budget accommodation ideal for both
families and business travellers. Spacious, en suite
bedrooms feature tea and coffee making facilities,
and Freeview TV in most hotels. Internet access and
Wi-fi are available for a small fee. The adjacent
family restaurant features a wide and varied menu.
See also the Hotel Groups pages.

Rooms 33

P

Premier Inn Paignton South (Brixham Road)

BUDGET HOTEL

☎ 0871 527 9324
White Rock, Long Road South TQ4 7AZ
web: www.premierinn.com
dir: From A3022 (Brixham Rd) between Tweenaway &
GAlmpton Warborough, right into Long Rd

Rooms 61

PAINSWICK   Map 4 SO80
Gloucestershire

INSPECTORS' CHOICE

Cotswolds88Hotel

★★★★ ◎ ◎ ◎   SMALL HOTEL

☎ 01452 813688
Kemps Ln GL6 6YB
e-mail: reservations@cotswolds88hotel.com
web: www.cotswolds88hotel.com
dir: From Stroud towards Cheltenham on A46, in
Painswick centre right at St Marys Church into
Victoria St. Left into St Marys St, right into Tibbiwell
St, right into Kemps Lane

In the heart of a pretty village, this 18th-century
house offers a range of beautifully presented and
individually styled bedrooms. Most of the rooms
have stunning countryside views and all are
equipped to the highest standard. Residents have
access to the private lounge with balcony and the
cosy library. The modern award-winning restaurant
has a well deserved reputation, and the dishes
feature the finest locally sourced and organic
produce.

Rooms 17 (8 annexe) (2 fmly) ⁿ **D** £99-£450 (incl.
bkfst)* **Facilities** STV FTV Wi-fi ♨ HL Beauty
treatment room Xmas New Year **Conf** Class 34
Board 30 Thtr 60 Del from £145 to £188*
Parking 17 **Notes** Closed 1-14 Jan Civ Wed 120

PALTERTON   Map 16 SK46
Derbyshire

Twin Oaks Hotel

★★★ 75% HOTEL

☎ 01246 855455
Church Ln S44 6UZ
e-mail: book@twinoakshotel.co.uk
web: www.twinoakshotel.co.uk
dir: M1 junct 29, take Palterton turn, hotel 100mtrs
down road on left

This hotel began life as a picturesque row of colliery
cottages, but it has been meticulously redesigned
and configured to meet the expectations of the
modern business and leisure traveller. The bedrooms
provide contemporary accommodation and the
attractive public areas include a brasserie and bistro
providing a range of dining options. The hotel is a
popular wedding destination and enjoys very good
transport links as it is near the M1.

Rooms 26 (4 annexe) (4 fmly) (14 GF) **Facilities** FTV
Wi-fi ♨ **Conf** Class 25 Board 25 Thtr 40 **Parking** 80
Notes ⊗ Civ Wed 80

PANGBOURNE   Map 5 SU67
Berkshire

The Elephant at Pangbourne

★★★ 79% ◎ HOTEL

☎ 0118 984 2244
Church Rd RG8 7AR
e-mail: matt@elephanthotel.co.uk
web: www.elephanthotel.co.uk
dir: M4 junct 12, A4 signed Theale/Newbury, right at
2nd rdbt signed Pangbourne. Hotel in village centre
on left

Centrally located in this bustling village, just a short
drive from Reading. Bedrooms are individual in style
but identical in the attention to detail, with
handcrafted Indian furniture and rich oriental rugs.
Guests can enjoy award-winning cuisine in the
restaurant, or there is bistro-style dining in the bar
area.

Rooms 22 (8 annexe) (2 fmly) (4 GF) **Facilities** FTV
Wi-fi ♨ Xmas New Year **Conf** Class 40 Board 30
Thtr 60 **Parking** 10 **Notes** Civ Wed 70

PATTERDALE   Map 18 NY31
Cumbria

Patterdale Hotel

★★ 71% HOTEL

☎ 0844 811 5580 & 017684 82231
CA11 0NN
e-mail: reservations@choice-hotels.co.uk
dir: M6 junct 40, A592 towards Ullswater. 10m to
Patterdale

Patterdale is a real tourist destination and this hotel
makes a good base for those taking part in the many
activity pursuits available in this area. The hotel
enjoys delightful views of the valley and fells, being
located at the southern end of Ullswater. The modern
bedrooms vary in style. In busier periods
accommodation is let for a minimum period of two
nights.

Rooms 57 (15 fmly) (6 GF) ⁿ **Facilities** FTV Wi-fi ♨
Free bike hire Xmas New Year **Services** Lift
Parking 30 **Notes** ⊗

PATTINGHAM   Map 10 SO89
Staffordshire

Patshull Park Hotel Golf & Country Club

★★★ 80% HOTEL

☎ 01902 700100
Patshull Park WV6 7HR
e-mail: sales@patshull-park.co.uk
web: www.patshull-park.co.uk
dir: 1.5m W of Pattingham, at church into Patshull
Rd, hotel 1.5m on right

Dating from the 1730s and sitting in 280 acres of
parkland, with good golf and fishing, this comfortably
appointed hotel has a range of modern leisure and
conference facilities. Public rooms include a lounge
bar, Earl's Brasserie and the Lakeside Restaurant
with delightful views over the lake. Bedrooms are well
appointed and thoughtfully equipped; most have good
views of either the golf course or lake.

Rooms 49 (15 fmly) (16 GF) **S** £59-£109; **D** £79-£129
(incl. bkfst)* **Facilities** STV FTV Wi-fi ⊛ ♨ 18 Putt
green Fishing Gym Beauty therapist Cardio suite
Steam rooms Saunas Xmas New Year **Conf** Class 75
Board 44 Thtr 160 Del from £115 to £125*
Parking 200 **Notes** LB Civ Wed 120

P

PECKFORTON
Cheshire   Map 15 SJ55

Peckforton Castle
★★★★ 85% ◉◉◉ HOTEL

☎ 01829 260930
Stone House Ln CW6 9TN
e-mail: info@peckfortoncastle.co.uk
web: www.peckfortoncastle.co.uk
dir: A49. At Beeston Castle pub right signed
Peckforton Castle. Approx 2m, entrance on right

Built in the mid-19th century by parliamentarian and
landowner Lord John Tollemache, and now lovingly
cared for by The Naylor Family, this Grade I medieval-
style castle has been sympathetically renovated to
provide high standards of comfort without losing
original charm and character. Bedrooms and public
areas retain many period features, and dining in the
1851 Restaurant is a memorable experience. Head
Chef Mark Ellis is passionate about using only the
finest ingredients, sourced locally where possible.
There is a falconry centre at the castle.

Rooms 48 (7 fmly) (2 GF) **Facilities** FTV Wi-fi HL
Falconry Outdoor pursuits Land Rover experience
Abseiling Beauty salon Xmas New Year **Conf** Class 80
Board 40 Thtr 180 **Services** Lift **Parking** 400
Notes ⊗ Civ Wed 165

PENDLEBURY
Greater Manchester   Map 15 SD70

Premier Inn Manchester (Swinton)

BUDGET HOTEL

☎ 0871 527 8720
219 Bolton Rd M27 8TG
web: www.premierinn.com
dir: M60 junct 13 towards A572, at rdbt take 3rd exit
towards Swinton. At next rdbt take A572. In 2m right
onto A580. After 2nd lights A666 Kearsley, 1st left at
rdbt. Pass fire station on right, 1st right

High quality, budget accommodation ideal for both
families and business travellers. Spacious, en suite
bedrooms feature tea and coffee making facilities,
and Freeview TV in most hotels. Internet access and
Wi-fi are available for a small fee. The adjacent
family restaurant features a wide and varied menu.
See also the Hotel Groups pages.

Rooms 31

PENKRIDGE
Staffordshire   Map 10 SJ91

Mercure Stafford South Hatherton House Hotel
Mercure
★★★ 70% HOTEL

☎ 01785 712459
Pinfold Ln ST19 5QP
e-mail: enquiries@hotels-stafford.com
web: www.hotels-stafford.com
dir: A449 to Wolverhampton. In Penkridge turn right
into Pinfold Ln. Hotel on left in 300yds

The hotel offers comfortable accommodation to both
leisure and business guests. The leisure facilities
consist of a pool, steam room and jacuzzi with a well-
equipped gym and two squash courts. Conference
facilities are also available. There is free parking and
easy access to the city and countryside.

Rooms 51 (4 fmly) (18 GF) **S** £65-£99; **D** £75-£115*
Facilities FTV Wi-fi ⓢ Gym Squash Sauna Steam
room Xmas New Year **Conf** Class 160 Board 120
Thtr 260 Del from £89 to £138* **Parking** 200
Notes LB Civ Wed 200

PENRITH
Cumbria   Map 18 NY53

See also Glenridding and Shap

North Lakes Hotel & Spa
shire
★★★★ 78% ◉ HOTEL

☎ 01768 868111
Ullswater Rd CA11 8QT
e-mail: nlakes@shirehotels.com
web: www.northlakeshotel.com
dir: M6 junct 40 at junct with A66

With a great location, it's no wonder that this modern
hotel is perpetually busy. Amenities include a good
range of meeting and function rooms and excellent
health and leisure facilities including a full spa.
Themed public areas have a contemporary,
Scandinavian country style and offer plenty of space
and comfort. High standards of service are provided
by a friendly team of staff.

Rooms 84 (6 fmly) (22 GF) **S** £90-£150; **D** £90-£150*
Facilities Spa STV Wi-fi ⓢ Gym Children's splash
pool Steam room Activity & wellness studios Sauna
New Year **Conf** Class 140 Board 30 Thtr 200
Del from £145 to £185* **Services** Lift **Parking** 150
Notes LB ⊗ Civ Wed 200

Temple Sowerby House Hotel & Restaurant
★★★ 88% ◉◉ COUNTRY HOUSE HOTEL

☎ 017683 61578
CA10 1RZ
e-mail: stay@templesowerby.com
web: www.templesowerby.com

(For full entry see Temple Sowerby)

Westmorland Hotel
★★★ 83% ◉ HOTEL

☎ 015396 24351
Westmorland Place, Orton CA10 3SB
e-mail: reservations@westmorlandhotel.com
web: www.westmorlandhotel.com

(For full entry see Tebay)

The George Hotel
LAKE DISTRICT HOTELS
★★★ 80% HOTEL

☎ 01768 862696 & 0800 840 1242
Devonshire St CA11 7SU
e-mail: georgehotel@lakedistricthotels.net
dir: M6 junct 40, 1m to town centre. From A6/A66 to
Penrith

This inviting and popular hotel was once visited by
'Bonnie' Prince Charlie. Extended over the years, it
currently offers well equipped bedrooms, and
spacious public areas that retain a timeless charm.
There is a choice of lounge areas that make ideal
places for morning coffee and afternoon tea.

Rooms 35 (4 fmly) **S** £78-£116; **D** £140-£214 (incl.
bkfst)* **Facilities** FTV Wi-fi ⓢ Xmas New Year
Conf Class 80 Board 50 Thtr 120 Del from £115 to
£145 **Parking** 40 **Notes** LB Civ Wed 120

PENZANCE   Map 2 SW43
Cornwall

Hotel Penzance
★★★ 86% ◉◉ HOTEL

☎ 01736 363117
Britons Hill TR18 3AE
e-mail: reception@hotelpenzance.com
web: www.hotelpenzance.com
dir: From A30 into Penzance, left at last rdbt for town
centre. 3rd right onto Britons Hill. Hotel on right

This Edwardian house has been tastefully redesigned,
particularly in the contemporary Bay Restaurant. The
focus on style is not only limited to the decor, but is
also apparent in the award-winning cuisine that is
based on fresh Cornish produce. Bedrooms have been
appointed to modern standards and are particularly
well equipped; many have views across Mounts Bay.

Rooms 25 (2 GF) 🐾 **S** £85-£91; **D** £135-£205 (incl.
bkfst)* **Facilities** FTV Wi-fi ⚡ Xmas New Year
Conf Class 50 Board 25 Thtr 80 Del from £149 to
£188* **Parking** 12 **Notes** LB Civ Wed 80

Queens Hotel
★★★ 74% HOTEL

☎ 01736 362371
The Promenade TR18 4HG
e-mail: enquiries@queens-hotel.com
web: www.queens-hotel.com
dir: A30 to Penzance, follow signs for seafront pass
harbour onto promenade, hotel on right

With views across Mount's Bay towards Newlyn, this
impressive Victorian hotel has a long and
distinguished history. Comfortable public areas are
filled with interesting pictures and artefacts, and in
the dining room guests can choose from the daily-
changing menu. Bedrooms, many with sea views, vary
in style and size.

Rooms 70 (10 fmly) 🐾 **S** £65-£95; **D** £130-£190
(incl. bkfst)* **Facilities** FTV Wi-fi ⚡ Xmas New Year
Conf Class 200 Board 120 Thtr 200 Del from £100 to
£150 **Services** Lift **Parking** 50 **Notes** LB Civ Wed 250

PETERBOROUGH   Map 12 TL19
Cambridgeshire

Bull Hotel
★★★★ 76% ◉ HOTEL   PEEL HOTELS PLC

☎ 01733 561364
Westgate PE1 1RB
e-mail: rooms@bull-hotel-peterborough.com
web: www.peelhotels.co.uk
dir: From A1 follow city centre signs. Hotel opposite
Queensgate shopping centre. Car park on Broadway
adjacent to library

This pleasant city-centre hotel offers well-equipped,
modern accommodation, which includes several
wings of deluxe bedrooms. Public rooms include a
popular bar and a brasserie-style restaurant serving
a flexible range of dishes, with further informal dining
available in the lounge. There is a good range of
meeting rooms and conference facilities.

Rooms 118 (2 fmly) (5 GF) (4 smoking) 🐾
S £120-£135; **D** £130-£150* **Facilities** STV Wi-fi
Xmas New Year **Conf** Class 120 Board 40 Thtr 200
Parking 100 **Notes** ⊗ Civ Wed 200

BEST WESTERN PLUS Orton Hall Hotel
 Best Western PLUS
★★★★ 71% ◉ HOTEL

☎ 01733 391111
Orton Longueville PE2 7DN
e-mail: reception@ortonhall.co.uk
web: www.abacushotels.co.uk
dir: Off A605 E, opposite Orton Mere

An impressive country-house hotel set in 20 acres of
woodland on the outskirts of town and with easy
access to the A1. The spacious and relaxing public
areas include the baronial Great Room and the Orton
Suite for banqueting and for meetings, and the oak-
panelled, award-winning Huntly Restaurant. The on-
site pub, Ramblewood Inn, is an alternative, informal
dining option.

Rooms 70 (2 fmly) (15 GF) 🐾 **S** £70-£170;
D £80-£180* **Facilities** Spa FTV Wi-fi ⚡ ⚡ Gym
Sauna Steam room Xmas New Year **Conf** Class 70
Board 60 Thtr 160 Del from £120 to £180*
Parking 200 **Notes** LB Civ Wed 150

Bell Inn Hotel
★★★ 81% ◉ HOTEL

☎ 01733 241066
Great North Rd PE7 3RA
e-mail: reception@thebellstilton.co.uk
web: www.thebellstilton.co.uk

(For full entry see Stilton)

Queensgate Hotel
★★★ 81% HOTEL

☎ 01733 562572
5-7 Fletton Av PE2 8AX
e-mail: reservations@thequeensgatehotel.co.uk
dir: In town centre

This hotel is ideally situated close to the centre of
town with its range of shops and amenities.
Bedrooms are contemporary in style, and ideally
equipped for both business and leisure guests. The
modern public rooms include a lounge bar, two dining
areas and a beauty therapy suite.

Rooms 40 (2 fmly) (10 GF) 🐾 **Facilities** FTV Wi-fi
Beauty clinic Xmas New Year **Conf** Class 35 Board 26
Thtr 72 **Notes** ⊗

Park Inn by Radisson Peterborough   park inn by Radisson
★★★ 80% HOTEL

☎ 01733 353750
Wentworth St PE1 1BA
e-mail: info.peterborough@rezidorparkinn.com
dir: Off A15, 4 mins walk from station

Situated adjacent to Queensgate Shopping Centre,
and within easy walking distance of the main train
station. The spacious bedrooms are modern and
equipped to a very good standard. Public rooms
feature the open-plan Red Bar Grill, a cosy lounge
and a range of meeting rooms.

Rooms 115 (9 fmly) 🐾 **S** £65-£119; **D** £75-£129*
Facilities FTV Wi-fi Beauty treatment room Use of gym
facilities (1m) & swimming pool (0.5m) **Conf** Class 80
Board 40 Thtr 140 Del from £89 to £149*
Services Lift Air con **Parking** 45 **Notes** LB ⊗
Civ Wed 30

P

PETERBOROUGH *continued*

Days Inn Peterborough - A1

BUDGET HOTEL

☎ 01733 371540
Peterborough Extra Services, A1 Junction 17, Great North Road, Haddon PE7 3UQ
e-mail: peterborough.hotel@welcomebreak.co.uk
dir: A1(M) junct 17

This modern, purpose-built accommodation offers smartly appointed, particularly well-equipped bedrooms with good power showers. There is a choice of adjacent food outlets where guests can enjoy breakfast, snacks and meals. See also the Hotel Groups pages.

Rooms 82 (16 fmly) (40 GF) (11 smoking) ⊁

Premier Inn Peterborough (Ferry Meadows)

BUDGET HOTEL

☎ 0871 527 8872
Ham Ln, Orton Meadows, Nene Park PE2 5UU
web: www.premierinn.com
dir: A1(M) S junct 16, A15 through Yaxley, left at rdbt. A1(M) N junct 17, A1139 junct 3 right to Yaxley, right at 2nd rdbt

High quality, budget accommodation ideal for both families and business travellers. Spacious, en suite bedrooms feature tea and coffee making facilities, and Freeview TV in most hotels. Internet access and Wi-fi are available for a small fee. The adjacent family restaurant features a wide and varied menu. See also the Hotel Groups pages.

Rooms 40

Premier Inn Peterborough (Hampton)

BUDGET HOTEL

☎ 0871 527 8874
Ashbourne Rd, off London Rd, Hampton PE7 8BT
web: www.premierinn.com
dir: A1(M) S junct 16, A15 through Yaxley, hotel on left at 1st rdbt. Or A1(M) N junct 17, A1139, 2nd exit junct 3 follow Yaxley signs. Hotel on right at 2nd rdbt

Rooms 83

Premier Inn Peterborough North

BUDGET HOTEL

☎ 0871 527 8876
1023 Lincoln Rd, Walton PE4 6AH
web: www.premierinn.com
dir: A1, A47 towards Peterborough. In 7m exit at junct 17 signed city centre. At rdbt (bottom of slip road) straight on signed city centre. At next rdbt left onto dual carriageway. At next rdbt double back, follow signs for city centre. Hotel in 200mtrs

Rooms 40

| PETERSFIELD | Map 5 SU72 |
| Hampshire | |

Langrish House

★★★ 77% ◉◉ HOTEL

☎ 01730 266941
Langrish GU32 1RN
e-mail: frontdesk@langrishhouse.co.uk
web: www.langrishhouse.co.uk
dir: A3 onto A272 towards Winchester. Hotel signed, 2.5m on left

Langrish House has been in the same family for seven generations. It is located in an extremely peaceful area just a few minutes' drive from Petersfield, halfway between Guildford and Portsmouth. Bedrooms are comfortable and well equipped with stunning views across the gardens to the hills. Guests can eat in the intimate Frederick's Restaurant with views over the lawn, or in the Old Vaults which have an interesting history dating back to 1644. The hotel is licensed for civil ceremonies and various themed events take place throughout the year.

Rooms 13 (1 fmly) (3 GF) ⊁ **Facilities** FTV Wi-fi ⓢ Xmas New Year **Conf** Class 18 Board 25 Thtr 60 **Parking** 80 **Notes** Closed Early Jan Civ Wed 80

Premier Inn Petersfield

BUDGET HOTEL

☎ 0871 527 8878
Winchester Rd GU32 3BS
web: www.premierinn.com
dir: At junct of A3 & A272 W'bound signed Services

High quality, budget accommodation ideal for both families and business travellers. Spacious, en suite bedrooms feature tea and coffee making facilities, and Freeview TV in most hotels. Internet access and Wi-fi are available for a small fee. The adjacent family restaurant features a wide and varied menu. See also the Hotel Groups pages.

Rooms 51

| PICKERING | Map 19 SE78 |
| North Yorkshire | |

The White Swan Inn

★★★ 80% ◉◉ HOTEL

☎ 01751 472288
Market Place YO18 7AA
e-mail: welcome@white-swan.co.uk
web: www.white-swan.co.uk
dir: In town, between church & steam railway station

This 16th-century coaching inn offers well-equipped, comfortable bedrooms, including suites, either of a more traditional style in the main building or modern in the annexe. Service is friendly and attentive. Good food is served in the attractive restaurant, in the cosy bar and the lounge, where a log fire burns in cooler months. A comprehensive wine list focuses on many fine vintages. A private dining room is also available.

Rooms 21 (9 annexe) (3 fmly) (8 GF) ⊁ **S** £119-£209; **D** £149-£239 (incl. bkfst)* **Facilities** FTV Wi-fi Xmas New Year **Conf** Class 18 Board 25 Thtr 35 Del from £180 to £210* **Parking** 45 **Notes** LB

BEST WESTERN Forest & Vale Hotel

★★★ 80% HOTEL

☎ 01751 472722
Malton Rd YO18 7DL
e-mail: forestvale@bestwestern.co.uk
dir: On A169 towards York at rdbt on outskirts of Pickering

This lovely 18th-century manor house hotel makes an excellent base from which to explore the east coast resorts and the North Yorkshire Moors National Park, one of England's most beautiful areas. A dedicated approach to upgrading means that the hotel is particularly well maintained, inside and out. In addition to standard bedrooms there are more spacious deluxe, superior and executive rooms; they are more traditional in the main house while the ones in the wing are contemporary; one has a four-poster bed.

Rooms 22 (5 annexe) (7 fmly) (5 GF) **Facilities** FTV Wi-fi ⓠ **Conf** Class 40 Board 30 Thtr 100 **Parking** 40 **Notes** ⊗ Closed 24-26 Dec Civ Wed 90

Save on hotels. Book at **theAA.com/hotel**

PET – PLY 357 ENGLAND

The Old Manse

★★ 76% HOTEL

☎ 01751 476484
19 Middleton Rd YO18 8AL
e-mail: info@oldmansepickering.com
web: www.oldmansepickering.co.uk
dir: A169, left at rdbt, through lights, 1st right into
Potter Hill. Follow road to left. From A170 left at 'local
traffic only' sign

A peacefully located house standing in mature
grounds close to the town centre. It offers a combined
dining room and lounge area, and comfortable
bedrooms that are well equipped. Expect good
hospitality from the resident owners.

Rooms 10 (2 fmly) (2 GF) **Facilities** Wi-fi New Year
Conf Class 12 Board 10 Thtr 20 **Parking** 12
Notes Closed 24-27 Dec

| PIERCEBRIDGE | Map 19 NZ21 |
| Co Durham | |

George Hotel

★★★ 77% HOTEL

☎ 01325 374576
DL2 3SW
e-mail: george@bpcmail.co.uk
dir: A1 junct 56, left at rdbt, 5m down B2675

This well appointed and attractive hotel, once a
coaching inn, is located in the rural village of
Piercebridge and backing onto the River Tees; it has
great countryside views. The hotel has well-
appointed, traditionally styled bedrooms, inviting,
spacious public areas with roaring fires in winter, and
extensive function rooms. Guests can enjoy an
evening meal in the restaurant that overlooks the
river, and choose to relax outside for lunch, afternoon
tea or just a drink. The riverside ballroom makes an
ideal venue for wedding receptions. Off-street parking
is also available.

Rooms 29 (7 fmly) (13 GF) ♠ **S** £39-£49; **D** £39-£99*
Facilities FTV Wi-fi ♘ Fishing Xmas New Year
Conf Class 120 Board 180 Thtr 200 Del from £95 to
£120* **Parking** 100 **Notes** Civ Wed 200

| PLYMOUTH | Map 3 SX45 |
| Devon | |

Duke of Cornwall Hotel

★★★ 78% ⊛ HOTEL

☎ 01752 275850 & 275855
Millbay Rd PL1 3LG
e-mail: enquiries@thedukeofcornwall.co.uk
web: www.thedukeofcornwall.co.uk
dir: Follow city centre, then Plymouth Pavilions
Conference & Leisure Centre signs. Hotel opposite
Plymouth Pavilions

A historic landmark, this city centre hotel is
conveniently located. The spacious public areas
include a popular bar, comfortable lounge and multi-
functional ballroom. Bedrooms, many with far-
reaching views, are individually styled and
comfortably appointed. The range of dining options
includes meals in the bar, or the elegant dining room
for a more formal atmosphere.

Rooms 71 (4 fmly) (20 smoking) ♠ **Facilities** STV FTV
Wi-fi ♘ Xmas New Year **Conf** Class 125 Board 84
Thtr 300 **Services** Lift **Parking** 25 **Notes** Civ Wed 300

Invicta Hotel

★★★ 78% HOTEL

☎ 01752 664997
11-12 Osborne Place, Lockyer St, The Hoe PL1 2PU
e-mail: info@invictahotel.co.uk
web: www.invictahotel.co.uk
dir: A38 to Plymouth, follow city centre signs, then
signs to The Hoe & Barbican. Hotel opposite Hoe Park
on Lockyer St at junct with Citadel Rd

Just a short stroll from the city centre, this elegant
Victorian establishment stands opposite the famous
bowling green. The atmosphere is relaxed and friendly
and bedrooms are neatly presented, well-equipped
and attractively decorated. Eating options include
meals in the bar or in the more formal setting of the
dining room.

Rooms 23 (4 fmly) (1 GF) **Facilities** FTV Wi-fi Xmas
Conf Class 30 Board 45 Thtr 45 **Parking** 14 **Notes** ⊗

New Continental Hotel

★★★ 77% HOTEL

☎ 01752 220782 & 276798
Millbay Rd PL1 3LD
e-mail: reservations@newcontinental.co.uk
web: www.newcontinental.co.uk
dir: A38, follow city centre signs for Continental
Ferryport. Hotel before ferryport, adjacent to Plymouth
Pavilions Conference Centre

Within easy reach of the city centre and The Hoe, this
privately owned hotel continues to offer high

standards of service and hospitality. A variety of
bedroom sizes and styles is available, all with the
same levels of equipment and comfort. The hotel is a
popular choice for conferences and functions.

Rooms 99 (20 fmly) **Facilities** FTV Wi-fi ⊙
supervised Gym Sauna Steam room **Conf** Class 100
Board 70 Thtr 350 Del from £140* **Services** Lift
Parking 100 **Notes** ⊗ Closed 24 Dec-2 Jan
Civ Wed 140

Copthorne Hotel Plymouth

★★★ 75% HOTEL

☎ 01752 224161
Armada Way PL1 1AR
e-mail: sales.plymouth@millenniumhotels.co.uk
web: www.millenniumhotels.co.uk
dir: From M5 follow A38 to Plymouth city centre.
Follow ferryport signs over 2 rdbts. Hotel on 1st exit
left before 4th rdbt

This hotel is conveniently located near the city's main
attractions and the business area, and is also well
situated for the theatre and The Hoe. The bedrooms
offer a good range of facilities and are available in a
range of sizes. The restaurant provides enjoyable
dining and there is an all-day lounge and bar service.
The secure parking is an asset.

Rooms 135 **Facilities** STV Wi-fi HL Gym New Year
Conf Class 60 Board 60 Thtr 140 Del from £99 to
£140* **Services** Lift **Parking** 50 **Notes** ⊗
Civ Wed 100

Ibis Hotel Plymouth

BUDGET HOTEL

☎ 01752 601087
Marsh Mills, Longbridge Rd, Forder Valley PL6 8LD
e-mail: H2093@accor.com
web: www.ibishotel.com
dir: A38 to Plymouth, 1st exit after flyover towards
Estover, Leigham & Parkway Industrial Est. At rdbt,
hotel at 4th exit

Modern, budget hotel offering comfortable
accommodation in bright and practical bedrooms.
Breakfast is self-service and dinner is available in
the restaurant. See also the Hotel Groups pages.

Rooms 52 (1 fmly) (26 GF) ♠

P

PLYMOUTH *continued*

Premier Inn Plymouth Centre (Sutton Harbour)

BUDGET HOTEL

☎ 0871 527 8882
Sutton Rd, Shepherds Wharf PL4 0HX
web: www.premierinn.com
dir: A38, A374 towards Plymouth. Follow Coxside & National Marine Aquarium signs. Right at lights after leisure park. Hotel adjacent to Lockyers Quay (NB there are 2 Premier Inns on this site, this hotel is the larger)

High quality, budget accommodation ideal for both families and business travellers. Spacious, en suite bedrooms feature tea and coffee making facilities, and Freeview TV in most hotels. Internet access and Wi-fi are available for a small fee. The adjacent family restaurant features a wide and varied menu. See also the Hotel Groups pages.

Rooms 107

Premier Inn Plymouth City Centre (Lockyers Quay)

BUDGET HOTEL

☎ 0871 527 8880
1 Lockyers Quay, Coxside PL4 0DX
web: www.premierinn.com
dir: From A38 (Marsh Mills rdbt) take A374 into Plymouth. Follow Coxside & National Marine Aquarium signs

Rooms 62

Premier Inn Plymouth East

BUDGET HOTEL

☎ 0871 527 8884
300 Plymouth Rd, Crabtree PL3 6RW
web: www.premierinn.com
dir: From E: Exit A38 at Marsh Mill junct. Straight on at rdbt, exit slip road 100mtrs on left. From W: Exit A38 at Plympton junct, at rdbt exit slip road adjacent to A38

Rooms 41

POCKLINGTON   Map 17 SE84
East Riding of Yorkshire

Feathers Hotel

★★ 71% HOTEL

☎ 01759 303155
56 Market Place YO42 2AH
e-mail: info@thefeathers-hotel.co.uk
dir: From York, B1246 signed Pocklington. Hotel just off A1079

This busy, traditional inn provides comfortable, well-equipped and spacious accommodation. Public areas are smartly presented. Enjoyable meals are served in the bar and the conservatory restaurant; the wide choice of dishes makes excellent use of local and seasonal produce.

Rooms 16 (10 annexe) (1 fmly) (10 GF) ☏ S £50-£52; D £55-£65 (incl. bkfst)* **Facilities** FTV Wi-fi **Parking** 25 **Notes** ⊗

POLPERRO   Map 2 SX25
Cornwall

Talland Bay Hotel

★★★ 87% ⊛⊛ COUNTRY HOUSE HOTEL

☎ 01503 272667
Porthallow PL13 2JB
e-mail: info@tallandbayhotel.co.uk
web: www.tallandbayhotel.co.uk
dir: From Looe over bridge towards Polperro on A387, 2nd turn to hotel

This hotel has the benefit of a wonderful location with far-reaching views, situated in its own extensive gardens that run down almost to the cliff edge. A warm and friendly atmosphere prevails. The bedrooms come in a range of styles - classic twins and doubles, and rooms and suites with sea views. There is also cottage accommodation, and one is particularly suitable for families or those with dogs. The public areas of the hotel are impressive and stylish. Eating options include a Brasserie and the Terrace Restaurant, where guests will find accomplished cooking, with an emphasis on carefully prepared local produce.

Rooms 20 (2 fmly) (5 GF) ☏ S £90-£240; D £120-£260 (incl. bkfst)* **Facilities** FTV Wi-fi ⌕ ⌣ Xmas New Year **Conf** Class 20 Board 20 Thtr 20 **Parking** 20 **Notes** LB Civ Wed 65

PONTEFRACT   Map 16 SE42
West Yorkshire

Wentbridge House Hotel

★★★★ 78% ⊛⊛ HOTEL

☎ 01977 620444
Wentbridge WF8 3JJ
e-mail: info@wentbridgehouse.co.uk
web: www.wentbridgehouse.co.uk
dir: M62 junct 33 onto A1 S, hotel in 4m

This well-established hotel sits in 20 acres of landscaped gardens, offering spacious, well-equipped bedrooms and a choice of dining styles. Service in the Fleur de Lys restaurant is polished and friendly, and a varied menu offers a good choice of interesting dishes. The Brasserie has a more relaxed style of modern dining.

Rooms 41 (4 annexe) (4 fmly) (4 GF) ☏ S £110-£190; D £140-£220 (incl. bkfst)* **Facilities** FTV Wi-fi Xmas New Year **Conf** Class 100 Board 60 Thtr 130 **Services** Lift **Parking** 100 **Notes** LB ⊗ Civ Wed 130

Premier Inn Pontefract North

BUDGET HOTEL

☎ 0871 527 8886
Pontefract Rd, Knottingley WF11 0BU
web: www.premierinn.com
dir: M62 junct 33 onto A1 N. Exit at Pontefract junct (A645) to T-junct, right towards Pontefract. Hotel on right

High quality, budget accommodation ideal for both families and business travellers. Spacious, en suite bedrooms feature tea and coffee making facilities, and Freeview TV in most hotels. Internet access and Wi-fi are available for a small fee. The adjacent family restaurant features a wide and varied menu. See also the Hotel Groups pages.

Rooms 41

Save on hotels. Book at **theAA.com/hotel**

PLY – POO 359 ENGLAND

Premier Inn Pontefract South

BUDGET HOTEL

☎ 0871 527 8888
Great North Rd, Darrington WF8 3BL
web: www.premierinn.com
dir: Just off A1, 2m S of M62 junct 33

Rooms 28

POOLE	Map 4 SZ09
Dorset	

Harbour Heights Hotel

★★★★ 76% ◉◉ HOTEL

☎ 01202 707272 & 0845 337 1550
73 Haven Rd, Sandbanks BH13 7LW
e-mail: reservations@fjbhotels.co.uk
web: www.fjbcollection.net
dir: Follow signs for Sandbanks, hotel on left after
Canford Cliffs

The unassuming appearance of this 'boutique' hotel
belies a wealth of innovation, quality and style. The
very stylish, contemporary bedrooms, many with sea
views, combine state-of-the-art facilities with
traditional comforts; all have spa baths. The smart
public areas include the award-winning Harbar
Bistro, popular bars and sitting areas where picture
windows accentuate panoramic views of Poole
Harbour. The south-facing sun deck is the perfect
setting for watching the cross-channel ferries come
and go.

Rooms 38 (2 fmly) **Facilities** STV Wi-fi Spa bath in all
rooms ♫ Xmas New Year **Conf** Class 36 Board 22
Thtr 70 **Services** Lift Air con **Parking** 50 **Notes** ⊗
Civ Wed 100

Hotel du Vin Poole

★★★★ 76% ◉ HOTEL

☎ 0844 748 9265
Thames St BH15 1JN
e-mail: info.poole@hotelduvin.com
web: www.hotelduvin.com
dir: A31 to Poole, follow channel ferry signs. Left at
Poole bridge onto Poole Quay, 1st left into Thames St.
Hotel opposite St James Church

Offering a fresh approach to the well-established
company style, this property boasts some delightful
rooms packed with comfort and all the expected Hotel
du Vin features. Situated near the harbour the hotel
offers nautically-themed bedrooms and suites that
have plasma TVs, DVD players and bathrooms with
power showers. The public rooms are light, open
spaces, and as with the other hotels in this group, the
bar and restaurant form centre stage.

Rooms 38 (4 GF) ↖ **D** £109-£169* **Facilities** STV
Wi-fi Xmas New Year **Conf** Class 20 Board 20 Thtr 60
Services Air con **Parking** 50 **Notes** LB Civ Wed 100

The Haven

★★★★ 75% ◉◉ HOTEL

☎ 01202 707333 & 0845 337 1550
Banks Rd, Sandbanks BH13 7QL
e-mail: reservations@fjbhotels.co.uk
web: www.fjbcollection.co.uk
dir: B3965 towards Poole Bay, left onto the Peninsula.
Hotel 1.5m on left adjacent to Swanage Toll Ferry

Enjoying an enviable location at the water's edge with
views of Poole Bay, this well established hotel was
once the home of radio pioneer, Guglielmo Marconi. A
friendly team of staff provide good levels of customer
care. Bedrooms vary in size and style; many have
balconies and wonderful sea or harbour views. The
leisure facilities are noteworthy - the Harmony at the
Haven is where guests can find spa treatments, a
fully equipped gym, indoor and outdoor heated pools
and an all-weather tennis court. The hotel is a
popular venue for conferences and weddings.

Rooms 88 (4 fmly) **Facilities** Spa STV Wi-fi ⊛ ℞
supervised ⟍ supervised ⟳ Gym Dance studio
Health & Beauty suite Sauna Steam room ♫ Xmas
New Year **Conf** Class 70 Board 50 Thtr 160
Services Lift **Parking** 160 **Notes** ⊗ Civ Wed 40

The Sandbanks

★★★★ 74% ◉ HOTEL

☎ 01202 707377 & 0845 337 1550
15 Banks Rd, Sandbanks BH13 7PS
e-mail: reservations@fjbhotels.co.uk
web: www.fjbcollection.co.uk
dir: A338 from Bournemouth onto Wessex Way, to
Liverpool Victoria rdbt. Left, then 2nd exit onto B3965.
Follow beach signs. Hotel on left

Set on the delightful Sandbanks Peninsula, this well
loved hotel has direct access to the seven-mile blue
flag beach and has stunning views across Poole
Harbour and the sea. Most of the spacious bedrooms
have sea views; some are air conditioned. There is an
extensive range of leisure facilities, including an on-
site watersports academy. A family friendly hotel.

Rooms 108 (31 fmly) **Facilities** STV FTV Wi-fi ℞
supervised Gym Sailing Mountain bikes Children's
play area Watersports academy ♫ Xmas New Year
Conf Class 50 Board 80 Thtr 150 **Services** Lift
Parking 120 **Notes** ⊗ Civ Wed 100

Thistle Poole

thistle

★★★ 80% HOTEL

☎ 0871 376 9032
The Quay BH15 1HD
e-mail: poole@thistle.co.uk
web: www.thistlehotels.com/poole
dir: On quay adjacent to Dolphin Marina

Situated on the quayside overlooking the harbour, this
modern hotel is situated close to the ferry terminal
and is also a good base for exploring the beautiful
Dorset countryside. Many of the bedrooms have views
of Poole harbour. There is a restaurant and two bars,
plus two meeting rooms are available.

Rooms 70 (22 GF) **Facilities** FTV Wi-fi ⅄ HL Xmas
New Year **Conf** Class 80 Board 60 Thtr 120
Services Lift **Parking** 120 **Notes** Civ Wed 120

Arndale Court Hotel

★★★ 70% HOTEL

☎ 01202 683746
62/66 Wimborne Rd BH15 2BY
e-mail: info@arndalecourthotel.com
web: www.arndalecourthotel.com
dir: On A349, opposite Poole Stadium

Ideally situated for the town centre and ferry terminal,
this is a small, privately owned hotel. Bedrooms are
well equipped, spacious and comfortable. Particularly
well suited to business guests, this hotel has a
pleasant range of stylish public areas and good
parking.

Rooms 39 (7 fmly) (14 GF) (8 smoking) **S** £83; **D** £110
(incl. bkfst)* **Facilities** STV FTV Wi-fi **Conf** Class 20
Board 30 Thtr 50 Del £130* **Parking** 40
Notes RS 23 Dec-2 Jan

Holiday Inn Express Poole

BUDGET HOTEL

☎ 01202 649222
Walking Field Ln, Seldown Bridge Site BH15 1TJ
e-mail: reservations@exhipoole.co.uk
web: www.hiexpress.com/pooleuk
dir: A350 to town centre, pass bus station. Right at
next rdbt, take slip road to left. Hotel adjacent to
Dolphin Swimming Pool

A modern hotel ideal for families and business
travellers. Fresh and uncomplicated, the spacious
rooms include Sky TV, power shower and tea and
coffee-making facilities. Continental buffet breakfast
is included in the room rate; evening meals are
available in the spacious café/bar. See also the Hotel
Groups pages.

Rooms 85 (42 fmly) (10 GF) (7 smoking) ↖
Conf Class 16 Board 18 Thtr 30

P

POOLE *continued*

Premier Inn Poole Centre (Holes Bay)

BUDGET HOTEL

☎ 0871 527 8892
Holes Bay Rd BH15 2BD
web: www.premierinn.com
dir: S of A35 & A349 on A350 (dual carriageway). Follow Poole Channel Ferry signs

High quality, budget accommodation ideal for both families and business travellers. Spacious, en suite bedrooms feature tea and coffee making facilities, and Freeview TV in most hotels. Internet access and Wi-fi are available for a small fee. The adjacent family restaurant features a wide and varied menu. See also the Hotel Groups pages.

Rooms 83

Premier Inn Poole North

BUDGET HOTEL

☎ 0871 527 8894
Cabot Ln BH17 7DA
web: www.premierinn.com
dir: Follow Poole/Channel Ferries signs. At Darby's Corner rdbt take 2nd exit. At 2nd lights right into Cabot Ln. Hotel on right

Rooms 126

Milsoms Poole

RESTAURANT WITH ROOMS

☎ 01202 609000
47 Haven Rd, Canford Cliffs BH13 7LH
e-mail: poole@milsomshotel.co.uk

Milsoms Poole is located in the Canford Cliffs area, moments from some of the country's best beaches and the picturesque Purbeck Hills. Comfortable and stylish en suite accommodation is situated above the popular seafood Loch Fyne Restaurant. The friendly and helpful team provide a warm welcome. Limited on-site parking is available.

Rooms 8

INSPECTORS' CHOICE

The Oaks Hotel

★★★ ◉ HOTEL

☎ 01643 862265
TA24 8ES
e-mail: info@oakshotel.co.uk
dir: From E of A39, enter village (road narrows to single track) then follow hotel sign. From W: down Porlock Hill, through village, hotel sign on right

A relaxing atmosphere is found at this charming Edwardian house, located near to the setting of R D Blackmore's novel, *Lorna Doone*. Quietly located and set in attractive grounds, the hotel enjoys elevated views across the village towards the sea. Bedrooms are thoughtfully furnished and comfortable, and the public rooms include a charming bar and a peaceful drawing room. In the dining room, guests can choose from the daily-changing menu, which features fresh, quality local produce.

Rooms 8 ☛ **D** £220-£250 (incl. bkfst & dinner) **Facilities** FTV Wi-fi ☕ Xmas New Year **Parking** 12 **Notes** LB ✖ No children 8yrs Closed Nov-Mar (ex Xmas & New Year)

Kota Restaurant with Rooms

◉ RESTAURANT WITH ROOMS

☎ 01326 562407
Harbour Head TR13 9JA
e-mail: kota@btconnect.com
dir: B3304 from Helston into Porthleven. Kota on harbour opposite slipway

Overlooking the water, this 300-year-old building is the home of Kota Restaurant (Kota being the Maori word for shellfish). The bedrooms are approached from a granite stairway to the side of the building. The family room is spacious and has the benefit of harbour views, while the smaller, double room is at

---

the rear of the property. The enthusiastic young owners ensure guests enjoy their stay here, and a meal in the restaurant should not be missed. Breakfast features the best local produce.

Rooms 2 (2 annexe) (1 fmly)

Premier Inn Portishead

BUDGET HOTEL

☎ 0871 527 8898
Wyndham Way BS20 7GA
web: www.premierinn.com
dir: M5 junct 19, A369 towards Portishead. Over 1st rdbt, hotel at next rdbt

High quality, budget accommodation ideal for both families and business travellers. Spacious, en suite bedrooms feature tea and coffee making facilities, and Freeview TV in most hotels. Internet access and Wi-fi are available for a small fee. The adjacent family restaurant features a wide and varied menu. See also the Hotel Groups pages.

Rooms 58

The Lugger Hotel

★★★ 85% ◉◉ HOTEL

☎ 01872 501322
TR2 5RD
e-mail: reservations.lugger@ohiml.com
web: www.oxfordhotelsandinns.com
dir: A390 to Truro, B3287 to Tregony, A3078 (St Mawes Rd), left for Veryan, left for Portloe

This delightful hotel enjoys a unique setting adjacent to the slipway of the harbour, where fishing boats still come and go. Bedrooms, some in adjacent buildings and cottages, are contemporary in style and well equipped. The sitting room, which reflects the original building's character, has beams and open fireplaces that create a cosy atmosphere. The modern restaurant enjoys superb views, and in warmer months a sun terrace overlooking the harbour proves a popular place to enjoy a meal.

Rooms 22 (17 annexe) (1 GF) **Facilities** FTV Wi-fi Xmas New Year **Parking** 26 **Notes** Civ Wed 50

Save on hotels. Book at **theAA.com/hotel**

POO – POR 361 **ENGLAND**

PORTSCATHO
Cornwall — Map 2 SW83

INSPECTORS' CHOICE

Driftwood

★★★ ◉◉◉ HOTEL

☎ 01872 580644
Rosevine TR2 5EW
e-mail: info@driftwoodhotel.co.uk
dir: A390 towards St Mawes. On A3078 turn left to Rosevine at Trewithian

Poised on the cliff side with panoramic views, this contemporary hotel has a peaceful and secluded location. A warm welcome is guaranteed here, where professional standards of service are provided in an effortless and relaxed manner. Cuisine is at the heart of any stay, with quality local produce used in a sympathetic and highly skilled manner. The extremely comfortable and elegant bedrooms are decorated in soft shades reminiscent of the seashore. There is a sheltered terraced garden that has a large deck for sunbathing.

Rooms 15 (1 annexe) (3 fmly) (1 GF) **Facilities** FTV Wi-fi ↻ Private beach Beauty treatments on request **Parking** 30 **Notes** ⊗ Closed 7 Dec–5 Feb RS Xmas & New Year

PORTSMOUTH & SOUTHSEA
Hampshire — Map 5 SU60

Portsmouth Marriott Hotel

★★★★ 79% ◉ HOTEL

☎ 0870 400 7285 & 023 9238 3151
Southampton Rd PO6 4SH
web: www.portsmouthmarriott.co.uk
dir: M27 junct 12, keep left off slip road, exit Cosham. Hotel on left at lights

Close to the motorway and ferry port, this hotel is well suited to the business trade. The comfortable and well laid-out bedrooms provide a comprehensive range of facilities including up-to-date workstations. The leisure club offers a pool, a gym, and a health and beauty salon.

Rooms 174 (77 fmly) (5 smoking) **Facilities** STV FTV Wi-fi ↻ HL ☜ supervised Gym Exercise studio Beauty salon & treatment room Xmas New Year **Conf** Class 180 Board 30 Thtr 350 Del from £140 to £165* **Services** Lift Air con **Parking** 196 **Notes** Civ Wed 350

BEST WESTERN Royal Beach Hotel

★★★ 79% HOTEL

☎ 023 9273 1281
South Pde, Southsea PO4 0RN
e-mail: enquiries@royalbeachhotel.co.uk
web: www.royalbeachhotel.co.uk
dir: M27 to M275, follow signs to seafront. Hotel on seafront

This former Victorian seafront hotel is a smart and comfortable venue suitable for leisure and business guests alike. Bedrooms and public areas are well presented and generally spacious, and the smart Coast Bar is an ideal venue for a relaxing drink.

Rooms 124 (12 fmly) ↻ **Facilities** STV FTV Wi-fi ↻ Xmas New Year **Conf** Class 180 Board 40 Thtr 280 Del from £112 to £132* **Services** Lift **Parking** 50 **Notes** Civ Wed 85

Holiday Inn Portsmouth

★★★ 79% HOTEL

☎ 0871 942 9065
Pembroke Rd PO1 2TA
e-mail: portsmouth@ihg.com
web: www.holidayinn.co.uk
dir: M275 into city centre, follow signs for seafront. Hotel on right after Kings Rd rdbt

This hotel occupies a great location close to Portsmouth seafront and near the Gunwharf Quays

Shopping Centre. Restricted, complimentary parking is available on a first-come-first-served basis at the hotel. Accommodation is comfortable and very well maintained; some rooms have magnificent sea views. On-site facilities include a swimming pool, fitness room, a stylish restaurant and meeting rooms.

Rooms 166 (12 fmly) (6 GF) **S** £100–£180; **D** £100–£180 (incl. bkfst) **Facilities** FTV Wi-fi HL ☜ supervised Gym Health club Steam room Sauna Xmas New Year **Conf** Class 70 Board 60 Thtr 160 Del from £120 to £200 **Services** Lift Air con **Parking** 60 **Notes** LB ⊗ Civ Wed 120

The Farmhouse & Innlodge Hotel

BUDGET HOTEL

☎ 023 9265 0510
Burrfields Rd PO3 5HH
e-mail: farmhouse.portsmouth@greeneking.co.uk
web: www.farmhouseinnlodge.com
dir: A3(M)/M27 onto A27. Take Southsea exit, follow A2030. 3rd lights right into Burrfields Rd. Hotel 2nd car park on left

Located on the eastern fringe of the city, this purpose-built hotel is conveniently located for all major routes. The spacious, modern bedrooms are well equipped and include ground floor and family rooms. The Farmhouse Hungry Horse Pub offers a wide range of eating options, and there is an ActionZone adventure area. See also the Hotel Groups pages.

Rooms 74 (6 fmly) (33 GF) **S** £50–£65; **D** £50–£70* **Conf** Class 64 Board 40 Thtr 150 Del £99*

Ibis Portsmouth Centre

BUDGET HOTEL

☎ 023 9264 0000
Winston Churchill Av PO1 2LX
e-mail: h1461@accor.com
web: www.ibishotel.com
dir: M27 junct 12 onto M275. Follow signs for city centre, Sealife Centre & Guildhall. Right at rdbt into Winston Churchill Ave

Modern, budget hotel offering comfortable accommodation in bright and practical bedrooms. Breakfast is self-service and dinner is available in the restaurant. See also the Hotel Groups pages.

Rooms 144 ↻ **S** £60–£150; **D** £60–£150* **Conf** Class 20 Board 20 Thtr 30

P

PORTSMOUTH & SOUTHSEA *continued*

Premier Inn Portsmouth (Horndean)

BUDGET HOTEL

☎ 0871 527 8902
2 Havant Rd PO8 0DT
web: www.premierinn.com
dir: A3(M) junct 2, take B2149 signed Emsworth, Horndean. At rdbt left onto B2149, follow Horndean signs. At next rdbt left onto A3 towards Waterlooville. Hotel on left (behind Red Lion)

High quality, budget accommodation ideal for both families and business travellers. Spacious, en suite bedrooms feature tea and coffee making facilities, and Freeview TV in most hotels. Internet access and Wi-fi are available for a small fee. The adjacent family restaurant features a wide and varied menu. See also the Hotel Groups pages.

Rooms 25

Premier Inn Portsmouth (Port Solent)

BUDGET HOTEL

☎ 0871 527 8906
Binnacle Way PO6 4FB
web: www.premierinn.com
dir: M27 junct 12, left at lights onto Southampton Rd. Left after 200mtrs at lights onto Compass Rd. At mini-rdbt right onto Binnacle Way, hotel on right

Rooms 108

Premier Inn Portsmouth (Port Solent East)

BUDGET HOTEL

☎ 0871 527 8904
1 Southampton Rd, North Harbour PO6 4SA
web: www.premierinn.com
dir: M27 junct 12, A3, left onto A27. Hotel on left

Rooms 64

Premier Inn Southsea

BUDGET HOTEL

☎ 0871 527 9014
Long Curtain Rd, Southsea PO5 3AA
web: www.premierinn.com
dir: M1 junct 24, A453. Follow ring road & Queen's Drive Industrial Estate signs. After Homebase left into Castle Bridge Rd, hotel opposite Pizza Hut restaurant

Rooms 40

PORT SUNLIGHT   Map 15 SJ38
Merseyside

Leverhulme Hotel

★★★★ 83% ◉◉ HOTEL

☎ 0151 644 6655 & 644 5555
Central Rd CH62 5EZ
e-mail: enquiries@leverhulmehotel.co.uk
web: www.leverhulmehotel.co.uk
dir: From Chester: M53 junct 5, A41 (Birkenhead) in approx 4m left into Bolton Rd, on at rdbt, 0.1m right into Church Drive. 0.2m hotel on right. From Liverpool: A41 (Chester), 2.7m, 3rd exit at 3rd rdbt into Bolton Rd (follow directions as above)

Built in 1907, this Grade II listed, former cottage hospital is set in the picturesque garden village of Port Sunlight, which was created by Lord Leverhulme for his soap-factory workers in the late 19th century. Following an extensive restoration project, this art deco hotel has stylish bedrooms, appointed to a very high standard; all have impressive facilities including bathrooms with separate showers and LCD TVs; the suites have roof-top terraces and hot tubs. The hotel also features a range of day rooms and an ultra-modern, award-winning restaurant.

Rooms 19 (4 annexe) (1 fmly) (4 GF) ✿ **S** £114–£490; **D** £125–£510 (incl. bkfst)* **Facilities** STV FTV Wi-fi ♿ HL Putt green ⛳ Gym Games room Children's play area Xmas New Year Child facilities **Conf** Class 140 Board 30 Thtr 300 Del £165* **Parking** 73 **Notes** LB ⊗ Civ Wed 240

PRESTON   Map 18 SD52
Lancashire

See also Garstang

Barton Grange Hotel

★★★★ 79% HOTEL

☎ 01772 862551
Garstang Rd PR3 5AA
e-mail: stay@bartongrangehotel.com
web: www.bartongrangehotel.co.uk

(For full entry see Barton)

Macdonald Tickled Trout

★★★★ 74% HOTEL

☎ 0844 8799053
Preston New Rd, Samlesbury PR5 0UJ
e-mail: general.tickledtrout@macdonald-hotels.co.uk
web: www.macdonald-hotels.co.uk
dir: M6 junct 31. A59 towards Preston

On the banks of the River Ribble, this hotel is conveniently located for the motorway, making it a popular venue for both business and leisure guests.

Smartly appointed bedrooms are all tastefully decorated and equipped with a thoughtful range of extras. The hotel boasts a stylish wing of meeting rooms. Macdonald Hotels is the AA Hotel Group of the Year 2013-14.

Rooms 98 (6 fmly) (10 GF) ✿ **Facilities** FTV Wi-fi ♿ Fishing ♫ Xmas New Year **Conf** Class 60 Board 50 Thtr 120 **Services** Lift **Parking** 180 **Notes** Civ Wed 90

The Pines Hotel

★★★ 81% ◉ HOTEL

☎ 01772 338551
570 Preston Rd, Clayton-Le-Woods, Chorley PR6 7EB
e-mail: mail@thepineshotel.co.uk
dir: Exit M6 junct 28 N'bound towards Blackburn for 2.5m to hotel. M6 junct 2 S'bound towards Chorley for 1m. On A6

This unique and stylish hotel sits in four acres of mature grounds just a short drive from the motorway. Elegant bedrooms are individually designed and offer high levels of comfort and facilities. Day rooms include a smart bar and the aptly named Rosette Restaurant, while extensive function rooms make this hotel a popular venue for weddings.

Rooms 35 (2 fmly) (14 GF) ✿ **S** £55–£150; **D** £65–£200 (incl. bkfst) **Facilities** FTV Wi-fi ♿ ♫ Xmas New Year **Conf** Class 250 Board 100 Thtr 400 Del from £85 to £120 **Parking** 120 **Notes** ⊗ Civ Wed 250

The Park Hotel

★★★ 78% SMALL HOTEL

☎ 01772 726250 & 728096
209 Tulketh Rd, Ashton-On-Ribble PR2 1ES
e-mail: info@parkhotelpreston.co.uk
dir: A59 then A5085 Blackpool Road 2.4m, left into Tulketh Road, A5072, hotel 200yds on right

This Edwardian Mansion House provides quality and comfort in keeping with its history. Original features including tall ceilings, tiled floors and stained glass windows are a real bonus. The main bedrooms and bathrooms are spacious and well equipped. Public areas include the homely bar for pre-dinner drinks and the well appointed dining room. Ample off-road car parking is available.

Rooms 18 (1 fmly) (8 GF) ⚅ **S** £50-£59; **D** £65-£110 (incl. bkfst)* **Facilities** FTV Wi-fi ⚅ **Conf** Class 15 Board 15 Thtr 20 Del from £105 to £130* **Notes** ⊗

The Legacy Preston International Hotel

★★★ 71% HOTEL

☎ 08444 119 028 & 0330 333 2828
Marsh Ln PR1 2YF
e-mail: res-prestoninternational@legacy-hotels.co.uk
dir: M6 junct 31 or 32, A59 (ring road). Hotel in approx 3.5m (on one way system)

This hotel is ideally located close to the town centre and the M6 making it a popular choice with both business and leisure guests. The contemporary bedrooms are very comfortable and well equipped, and free Wi-fi is available. The public areas include a light-filled lounge, and the menu in the restaurant offers a wide choice to suit most tastes. The hotel has secure parking.

Rooms 75 (12 fmly) ⚅ **Facilities** FTV Wi-fi ⚅ **Conf** Class 20 Board 20 Thtr 40 **Services** Lift **Parking** 40 **Notes** ⊗

Ibis Preston North

BUDGET HOTEL

☎ 01772 861800
Garstang Rd, Broughton PR3 5JE
e-mail: H3162@accor.com
web: www.ibishotel.com
dir: M6 junct 32, then M55 junct 1. Left lane onto A6. Left at slip road, left again at mini-rdbt. 2nd turn, hotel on right past pub

Modern, budget hotel offering comfortable accommodation in bright and practical bedrooms. Breakfast is self-service and dinner is available in the restaurant. See also the Hotel Groups pages.

Rooms 82 (27 fmly) (16 GF) (12 smoking)
Conf Class 20 Board 20 Thtr 30

Premier Inn Preston Central

BUDGET HOTEL

☎ 0871 527 8908
Fox St PR1 2AB
web: www.premierinn.com
dir: Off Ridgway (A59). Telephone for detailed directions

High quality, budget accommodation ideal for both families and business travellers. Spacious, en suite

bedrooms feature tea and coffee making facilities, and Freeview TV in most hotels. Internet access and Wi-fi are available for a small fee. The adjacent family restaurant features a wide and varied menu. See also the Hotel Groups pages.

Rooms 110

Premier Inn Preston East

BUDGET HOTEL

☎ 0871 527 8910
Bluebell Way, Preston East Link Rd, Fulwood PR2 5PZ
web: www.premierinn.com
dir: M6 junct 31a, follow ring road under motorway, hotel on left. (NB no exit for S'bound traffic - exit at M6 junct 31, join M6 N'bound, exit at junct 31a)

Rooms 65

Premier Inn Preston South (Craven Drive)

BUDGET HOTEL

☎ 0871 527 8914
Lostock Ln, Bamber Bridge PR5 6BZ
web: www.premierinn.com
dir: M6 junct 29, A582 (Lostock Ln). Straight on at 1st lights, into left lane, hotel on left adjacent to B&Q

Rooms 74

Premier Inn Preston South (Cuerden Way)

BUDGET HOTEL

☎ 0871 527 8916
Lostock Ln, Bamber Bridge PR5 6BA
web: www.premierinn.com
dir: Off M65 junct 1 (0.5m from M6 junct 29) close to rdbt junct of A582 & A6

Rooms 42

Premier Inn Preston West

BUDGET HOTEL

☎ 0871 527 8918
Blackpool Rd, Lea PR4 0XB
web: www.premierinn.com
dir: Off A583, opposite Texaco garage

Rooms 38

PRESTWICH   Map 15 SD80
Greater Manchester

Premier Inn Manchester (Prestwich)

BUDGET HOTEL

☎ 0871 527 8714
Bury New Rd M25 3AJ
web: www.premierinn.com
dir: M60 junct 17, A56 signed Mancehseter City Centre, Prestwich & Whitefield. Hotel on left

High quality, budget accommodation ideal for both families and business travellers. Spacious, en suite bedrooms feature tea and coffee making facilities, and Freeview TV in most hotels. Internet access and Wi-fi are available for a small fee. The adjacent family restaurant features a wide and varied menu. See also the Hotel Groups pages.

Rooms 60

PUDDINGTON   Map 15 SJ37
Cheshire

Macdonald Craxton Wood Hotel

★★★★ 77% ◉◉ HOTEL

☎ 0844 879 9038
Parkgate Rd, Ledsham CH66 9PB
e-mail: craxton@macdonald-hotels.co.uk
web: www.macdonald-hotels.co.uk
dir: From M6 take M56 towards N Wales, then A5117/A540 to Hoylake. Hotel on left 200yds past lights

Set in extensive grounds, this hotel offers a variety of bedroom styles; the modern rooms are particularly comfortable. The Aiden Byrne British Grill is a highlight, featuring stylish decor and classic dishes on the menu. Full leisure facilities and a choice of function suites complete the package. Macdonald Hotels is the AA Hotel Group of the Year 2013-14.

Rooms 72 (8 fmly) (30 GF) ⚅ **S** £82-£156; **D** £97-£171 (incl. bkfst)* **Facilities** Spa FTV Wi-fi HL ⚅ Gym Sauna Steam room Xmas New Year **Conf** Class 200 Board 160 Thtr 300 Del from £99 to £170* **Services** Lift **Parking** 220 **Notes** LB Civ Wed 350

P

PUDDINGTON *continued*

Premier Inn Wirral (Two Mills)

BUDGET HOTEL

☎ 0871 527 9180
Parkgate Rd, Two Mills CH66 9PD
web: www.premierinn.com
dir: 5m from M56 junct 16 & M53 junct 5. On x-rds of A550 & A540

High quality, budget accommodation ideal for both families and business travellers. Spacious, en suite bedrooms feature tea and coffee making facilities, and Freeview TV in most hotels. Internet access and Wi-fi are available for a small fee. The adjacent family restaurant features a wide and varied menu. See also the Hotel Groups pages.

Rooms 31

PURTON
Wiltshire   Map 5 SU08

The Pear Tree at Purton

★★★ 81% ◉◉ HOTEL

☎ 01793 772100
Church End SN5 4ED
e-mail: stay@peartreepurton.co.uk
dir: M4 junct 16 follow signs to Purton, at Hartford House Stores turn right. Hotel 0.25m on left

A charming 15th-century, former vicarage set amidst extensive landscaped gardens in a peaceful location in the Vale of the White Horse near the Saxon village of Purton. The resident proprietors and staff provide efficient, dedicated service and friendly hospitality. The spacious bedrooms are individually decorated and have a good range of thoughtful extras such as fresh fruit, sherry and shortbread. Fresh ingredients feature on the award-winning menus.

Rooms 17 (2 fmly) (6 GF) **S** £119-£149; **D** £119-£149 (incl. bkfst)* **Facilities** STV FTV Wi-fi ↕ ⊌ Outdoor giant chess Vineyard New Year **Conf** Class 30 Board 30 Thtr 60 Del £179.50* **Parking** 60 **Notes** LB Civ Wed 50

QUORN
Leicestershire   Map 11 SK51

Quorn Country Hotel

★★★★ 77% ◉ HOTEL

☎ 01509 415050 & 415061
Charnwood House, 66 Leicester Rd LE12 8BB
e-mail: reservations@quorncountryhotel.co.uk
web: www.quorncountryhotel.co.uk
dir: M1 junct 23 onto A512 into Loughborough. Follow A6 signs. At 1st rdbt towards Quorn, through lights, hotel 500yds from 2nd rdbt

Professional service is one of the key strengths of this pleasing hotel, which sits beside the river in four acres of landscaped gardens and grounds. The smart modern conference centre and function suites are popular for both corporate functions and weddings. Public rooms include a smart comfortable lounge and bar, and guests have the choice of two dining options: the formal Shires restaurant and the informal conservatory-style Orangery.

Rooms 36 (2 fmly) (11 GF) **D** £79-£169* **Facilities** STV Wi-fi ↕ Fishing New Year **Conf** Class 162 Board 40 Thtr 300 **Services** Lift **Parking** 100 **Notes** ⊗ Civ Wed 200

RADLETT
Hertfordshire   MAP 6 TL10

Premier Inn St Albans/ Bricket Wood

BUDGET HOTEL

☎ 0871 527 9016
Smug Oak Ln, Bricketwood AL2 3PN
web: www.premierinn.com
dir: M1 junct 6 (or M25 junct 21a) follow Watford signs, left at lights signed M1/Bricket Wood. 2nd left into Mount Pleasant Ln, straight on at 2 mini rdbts, right at The Gate pub. Hotel at end

High quality, budget accommodation ideal for both families and business travellers. Spacious, en suite bedrooms feature tea and coffee making facilities, and Freeview TV in most hotels. Internet access and Wi-fi are available for a small fee. The adjacent family restaurant features a wide and varied menu. See also the Hotel Groups pages.

Rooms 56

RAINHAM
Greater London   Map 6 TQ58

The Manor Hotel & Restaurant

★★★ 78% HOTEL

☎ 01708 555586
Berwick Pond Rd RM13 9EL
e-mail: info@themanoressex.co.uk
web: www.themanoressex.co.uk
dir: M25 junct 30/31, A13, 1st exit signed Wennington, right, at main lights right onto Upminster Rd North, left into Berwick Pond Rd

Located in countryside, the former Berwick Manor has been lovingly restored, and today offers well-appointed, contemporary accommodation. The rooms are equipped with a good range of amenities including complimentary Wi-fi. Lunch and dinner are served in the attractive restaurant whilst alfresco dining is possible on the terrace. Two function suites provide the ideal events venue.

Rooms 15 (1 fmly) ↖ **S** £69-£95; **D** £75-£115 (incl. bkfst) **Facilities** STV FTV Wi-fi Xmas New Year **Conf** Class 60 Board 40 Thtr 100 **Services** Lift **Parking** 60 **Notes** ⊗ Civ Wed 60

Premier Inn Rainham

BUDGET HOTEL

☎ 0871 527 8920
New Rd, Wennington RM13 9ED
web: www.premierinn.com
dir: M25 junct 30/31, A13 for Dagenham/Rainham,
A1306 towards Wennington, Aveley, & Rainham. Hotel
0.5m on right

High quality, budget accommodation ideal for both
families and business travellers. Spacious, en suite
bedrooms feature tea and coffee making facilities,
and Freeview TV in most rooms. Internet access and
Wi-fi are available for a small fee. The adjacent
family restaurant features a wide and varied menu.
See also the Hotel Groups pages.

Rooms 61

RAINHILL   Map 15 SJ49
Merseyside

Premier Inn Liverpool (Rainhill)

BUDGET HOTEL

☎ 0871 527 8614
804 Warrington Rd L35 6PE
web: www.premierinn.com
dir: Just off M62 junct 7, A57 towards Rainhill

High quality, budget accommodation ideal for both
families and business travellers. Spacious, en suite
bedrooms feature tea and coffee making facilities,
and Freeview TV in most hotels. Internet access and
Wi-fi are available for a small fee. The adjacent
family restaurant features a wide and varied menu.
See also the Hotel Groups pages.

Rooms 34

RAMSGATE   Map 7 TR36
Kent

The Pegwell Bay Hotel

★★★ 78% HOTEL

☎ 01843 599590
81 Pegwell Rd, Pegwell CT11 0NJ
e-mail: reception@pegwellbayhotel.co.uk
dir: Telephone for detailed directions

Boasting stunning views over The Channel, this
historic cliff-top hotel is suitable for guests staying
either on business or for leisure. Spacious,
comfortable bedrooms are well equipped and include
Wi-fi. A modern lounge, majestic dining room and
traditional pub offer a variety of options for eating
and for relaxation.

Rooms 42 (1 fmly) (6 GF) **Facilities** FTV Wi-fi Xmas
New Year **Conf** Class 65 Board 65 Thtr 100
Services Lift **Parking** 80 **Notes** ⊗ Civ Wed 70

Comfort Inn Ramsgate

★★★ 71% HOTEL

☎ 01843 592345
Victoria Pde, East Cliff CT11 8DT
e-mail: reservations@comfortinnramsgate.co.uk
dir: From M2 take A299 signed Ramsgate, B2054 to
Victoria Parade, follow sign to harbour

This Victorian hotel stands on the seafront, close to
the ferry terminal and the town. Bedrooms, some with
balconies, are generously sized and well equipped.
Guests can relax in the modern bar and lounge or be
pampered in the beauty treatment room. The popular
restaurant serves a particularly wide choice of dishes
ranging from traditional British cuisine to Indian
favourites.

Rooms 44 (8 fmly) ☛ **Facilities** STV FTV Wi-fi ♨
Beauty salon Xmas New Year **Conf** Class 30 Board 30
Thtr 50 **Services** Lift Air con **Parking** 10 **Notes** LB ⊗

The Oak Hotel

★★ 84% HOTEL

☎ 01843 583686 & 581582
66 Harbour Pde CT11 8LN
e-mail: reception@oakhotel.co.uk
dir: Follow road around harbour, right into Harbour
Parade

Located within easy reach of the railway station, ferry
terminal and the town centre's shops, this stylish
hotel enjoys spectacular views of the marina and
harbour. The comfortable bedrooms are attractively
presented and very well equipped. The Atlantis fish
restaurant, Caffe Roma and the contemporary bar
offer a variety of dining options.

Rooms 34 (9 fmly) (7 GF) **Facilities** STV FTV Wi-fi
Conf Class 60 Board 50 Thtr 100 **Notes** ⊗

Royal Harbour Hotel

★★ 79% METRO HOTEL

☎ 01843 591514
10-11 Nelson Crescent CT11 9JF
e-mail: info@royalharbourhotel.co.uk
dir: A253 to Ramsgate. Follow signs to seafront. At
Churchill Tavern, 1st left into Nelson Crescent

Dating back to 1799, this hotel is made up of
adjoining Georgian Grade II listed townhouses, and
occupies a prime position in the town's well known
historic garden crescent. Many of the bedrooms boast
magnificent views over the 'Royal Harbour', the yacht
marina and the English Channel. The atmosphere is
relaxed, the service is attentive and the breakfast is
superb.

Rooms 19 (3 fmly) (1 GF) ☛ **S** £70-£100; **D** £90-£200
(incl. bkfst) **Facilities** FTV Wi-fi **Conf** Class 30
Board 25 Thtr 30 Del from £150 to £200 **Parking** 4

RAVENGLASS   Map 18 SD09
Cumbria

The Pennington Hotel

★★★ 82% ◉ HOTEL

☎ 01229 717222 & 0845 450 6445
CA18 1SD
e-mail: info@penningtonhotels.com
dir: In village centre

This hotel has a very relaxed atmosphere throughout
and the public areas are open plan with high quality
fabrics and artwork. The bedrooms are modern in
design and have high spec fixtures and fittings in the
bathrooms. Honest cooking, based on local and fine
quality ingredients, is offered on the seasonal menus.
Staff show exceptional customer awareness and
provide very attentive and friendly service.

Rooms 21 (3 annexe) (6 fmly) (5 GF) ☛ **S** £90-£120;
D £90-£140 **Facilities** FTV Wi-fi ♨ Xmas New Year
Conf Class 40 Board 40 Thtr 80 Del £135*
Parking 53

R

RAVENSCAR — Map 19 NZ90
North Yorkshire

Raven Hall Country House Hotel

★★★ 79% HOTEL

☎ 01723 870353
YO13 0ET
e-mail: enquiries@ravenhall.co.uk
web: www.ravenhall.co.uk
dir: A171 towards Whitby. At Cloughton turn right onto unclassified road to Ravenscar

This impressive cliff top mansion enjoys breathtaking views over Robin Hood's Bay. Extensive well-kept grounds include tennis courts, putting green, swimming pools and historic battlements. The bedrooms vary in size but all are comfortably equipped, and many offer panoramic views. There are also eight environmentally-friendly Finnish lodges that have been furnished to a high standard.

Rooms 60 (8 annexe) (20 fmly) (5 GF) **Facilities** FTV Wi-fi 🕾 🏌 9 🐾 Putt green 🐾 Bowls Table tennis Xmas New Year **Conf** Class 80 Board 40 Thtr 100 Del from £95 to £125* **Services** Lift **Parking** 200 **Notes** Civ Wed 100

RAYLEIGH — Map 7 TQ89
Essex

Premier Inn Basildon (Rayleigh)

BUDGET HOTEL

☎ 0871 527 8058
Rayleigh Weir, Arterial Road (A127) SS6 7XJ
web: www.premierinn.com
dir: M25 junct 29, A127 towards Southend. Approx 13m exit at Rayleigh Weir junct onto A129 to Rayleigh. Straight on at 2 lights, 1st left (NB Sat Nav use code SS6 7XJ)

High quality, budget accommodation ideal for both families and business travellers. Spacious, en suite bedrooms feature tea and coffee making facilities, and Freeview TV in most hotels. Internet access and Wi-fi are available for a small fee. The adjacent family restaurant features a wide and varied menu. See also the Hotel Groups pages.

Rooms 49

READING — Map 5 SU77
Berkshire

The Forbury

★★★★★ 83% ◎◎ HOTEL

☎ 0118 952 7770
26 The Forbury RG1 3EJ
e-mail: reception@theforburyhotel.co.uk
dir: Telephone for detailed directions

The imposing exterior of this hotel belies the caring approach of the staff who provide helpful service with a smile. The up-to-the-minute bedrooms have very appealing designs and sensory appeal. For film buffs, a 30-seater cinema is also available, complete with refreshments! Cerise is the convivial and stylish venue for award-winning cuisine.

Rooms 23 🛏 **S** £174-£234; **D** £174-£234 (incl. bkfst) **Facilities** FTV Wi-fi 🕭 🎵 Xmas New Year **Conf** Class 24 Board 24 Thtr 35 Del from £240 to £264 **Services** Lift **Parking** 20 **Notes** LB ⊗ Civ Wed 50

Holiday Inn Reading M4 Jct 10

★★★★ 80% ◎◎ HOTEL

☎ 0118 944 0444
Wharfedale Rd, Winnersh Triangle RG41 5TS
e-mail: reservations@hireadinghotel.com
web: www.meridianleisurehotels.com/reading
dir: M4 junct 10/A329(M) towards Reading (E), 1st exit signed Winnersh/Woodley/A329, left at lights into Wharfedale Rd. Hotel on left

Situated in the Winnersh Triangle within close proximity of the M4, Reading, Bracknell and Wokingham, this hotel offers a range of air-conditioned, contemporary and stylish bedrooms, eight state-of-the-art meeting rooms and the Esprit Fitness and Spa with extensive leisure facilities including a 19-metre indoor pool and Dermalogica Spa. The Caprice Restaurant offers relaxed dining throughout the day. Complimentary underground parking is provided.

Rooms 174 (25 fmly) (8 smoking) 🛏 **S** £52-£159; **D** £52-£159 **Facilities** Spa FTV Wi-fi 🕭 HL 🕃 Gym Sauna Steam room 🎵 Xmas New Year **Conf** Class 160 Board 64 Thtr 260 Del from £120 to £209 **Services** Lift Air con **Parking** 120 **Notes** Civ Wed 260

Millennium Madejski Hotel Reading

★★★★ 79% ◎◎ HOTEL

☎ 0118 925 3500
Madejski Stadium RG2 0FL
e-mail: sales.reading@millenniumhotels.co.uk
web: www.millenniumhotels.co.uk
dir: M4 junct 11 onto A33, follow signs for Madejski Stadium Complex

A stylish hotel, that features an atrium lobby with specially commissioned water sculpture, is part of the Madejski stadium complex, home to both Reading FC and the London Irish rugby team. Bedrooms are appointed with spacious workstations and plenty of amenities; there is also a choice of suites and a club floor with its own lounge. The hotel also has a fine dining restaurant.

Rooms 201 (39 fmly) (19 smoking) **Facilities** Spa STV Wi-fi 🕭 🕃 supervised Gym **Conf** Class 36 Board 30 Thtr 66 **Services** Lift Air con **Parking** 250 **Notes** RS Xmas & New Year

Novotel Reading Centre

★★★★ 78% HOTEL

☎ 0118 952 2600
25b Friar St RG1 1DP
e-mail: h5432@accor.com
web: www.novotel.com
dir: M4 junct 11 or A33 towards Reading, left for Garrard St car park, at rdbt 3rd exit on Friar St

This attractive and stylish city centre hotel is convenient for Reading's business and shopping centre; it is adjacent to a town centre car park, and has a range of conference facilities and excellent leisure options. The restaurant offers a contemporary style menu and a good wine list too. Bedrooms are comfortable and stylishly designed.

Rooms 178 (15 fmly) **Facilities** STV FTV Wi-fi 🕃 Gym Steam room **Conf** Class 50 Board 36 Thtr 90 **Services** Lift Air con **Parking** 15

Malmaison Reading

★★★★ 74% ⚙ HOTEL

☎ 0844 693 0660 & 0118 956 2300
Great Western House, 18-20 Station Rd RG1 1JX
e-mail: reading@malmaison.com
web: www.malmaison.com
dir: Opposite rail station

This historic hotel has been transformed to a funky, Malmaison style which reflects its proximity and long-standing relationship with the railway. Public areas feature rail memorabilia and excellent pictures, and include a Café Mal and a meeting room. Bedrooms here have all the amenities a modern executive would expect, plus comfort and quality in abundance. Dining is interesting too, with a menu that features home-grown and local produce accompanied by an impressive wine list.

Rooms 75 (6 fmly) (4 GF) ☞ **S** £120-£250; **D** £120-£250* **Facilities** FTV Wi-fi ↳ HL Xmas New Year **Conf** Class 12 Board 16 Del from £180 to £310* **Services** Lift Air con **Notes** LB Civ Wed 30

The French Horn

★★★ 85% ⚙⚙ HOTEL

☎ 0118 969 2204
Sonning RG4 6TN
e-mail: info@thefrenchhorn.co.uk
dir: From A4 into Sonning, follow B478 through village over bridge, hotel on right, car park on left

This long established Thames-side establishment has a lovely village setting and retains the traditions of classic hotel keeping. The restaurant is a particular attraction and provides attentive service. Bedrooms, including four cottage suites, are spacious and comfortable; many offer stunning views over the river. A private boardroom is available for corporate guests.

Rooms 21 (8 annexe) (4 GF) (4 smoking) ☞ **S** £125-£170; **D** £160-£215 (incl. bkfst)* **Facilities** FTV Wi-fi Fishing Affiliation with Nirvana Spa (15 mins by car) **Conf** Board 14 Del from £255* **Services** Air con **Parking** 40 **Notes** LB ⊗

Holiday Inn Reading South M4 Jct 11

★★★ 78% HOTEL

☎ 0871 702 9067
Basingstoke Rd RG2 0SL
e-mail: reading@ihg.com
web: www.holidayinn.co.uk
dir: A33 to Reading. 1st rdbt right onto Imperial Way. Hotel on left

This bright hotel provides modern accommodation and the addition of leisure facilities which are a bonus at the end of a busy day. Meals are served in Traders restaurant, or snacks are available in the lounge. Callaghans, an Irish-style pub, offers live sports coverage. The business centre has a good range of conference and meeting rooms.

Rooms 202 (60 fmly) (99 GF) (10 smoking) **Facilities** FTV Wi-fi ↳ HL ⊛ supervised Gym Health & fitness centre New Year **Conf** Class 45 Board 50 Thtr 100 Del from £99 to £199 **Services** Air con **Parking** 300 **Notes** ⊗ Civ Wed 100

BEST WESTERN Calcot Hotel

★★★ 73% HOTEL

☎ 0118 941 6423
98 Bath Rd, Calcot RG31 7QN
e-mail: enquiries@calcothotel.net
web: www.calcothotel.co.uk
dir: M4 junct 12, A4 towards Reading, hotel in 0.5m

This hotel is conveniently located in a residential area just off the motorway. Bedrooms are well equipped with good business facilities, such as data ports and good workspace. There are attractive public rooms and function suites, and the informal restaurant offers enjoyable food in welcoming surroundings.

Rooms 79 (3 fmly) (6 GF) **Facilities** FTV Wi-fi ♫ New Year **Conf** Class 35 Board 35 Thtr 120 **Parking** 130 **Notes** Closed 25-31 Dec RS 2 Dec-6 Jan Civ Wed 200

Ibis Reading Centre

BUDGET HOTEL

☎ 0118 953 3500
25A Friar St RG1 1DP
e-mail: H5431@accor.com
web: www.ibishotel.com
dir: A329 into Friar St. Hotel near central railway station. Access by car in Garrard St

Modern, budget hotel offering comfortable accommodation in bright and practical bedrooms. Breakfast is self-service and dinner is available in the restaurant. See also the Hotel Groups pages.

Rooms 182 ☞ **D** fr £55*

Premier Inn Reading (Caversham Bridge)

BUDGET HOTEL

☎ 0871 527 8922
Richfield Av RG1 8EQ
web: www.premierinn.com
dir: M4 junct 11, A33 to Reading. A329 towards Caversham. Left at TGI Friday's. Left at Crowne Plaza. Hotel 200yds on right

High quality, budget accommodation ideal for both families and business travellers. Spacious, en suite bedrooms feature tea and coffee making facilities, and Freeview TV in most hotels. Internet access and Wi-fi are available for a small fee. The adjacent family restaurant features a wide and varied menu. See also the Hotel Groups pages.

Rooms 74

Premier Inn Reading Central

BUDGET HOTEL

☎ 0871 527 8924
Letcombe St RG1 2HN
web: www.premierinn.com
dir: M4 junct 11, A33 towards town centre, straight on at 3 rdbts (approx 3.5m). Right onto A329 signed The Oracle, Riverside Shopping Centre. Branch immediately left, hotel opposite The Oracle shopping centre

Rooms 151

Premier Inn Reading South

BUDGET HOTEL

☎ 0871 527 8926
Goring Ln, Grazeley Green RG7 1LS
web: www.premierinn.com
dir: M4 junct 11, A33 towards Basingstoke. At rdbt take exit towards Burghfield & Mortimer. 3rd right into Grazeley Green. Under rail bridge turn left. Hotel on left

Rooms 32

R

REDDITCH
Worcestershire
Map 10 SP06

Abbey Hotel Golf & Spa
★★★★ 78% HOTEL

☎ 01527 406600
Hither Green Ln, Dagnell End Rd, Bordesley B98 9BE
e-mail: info@theabbeyhotel.co.uk
web: www.theabbeyhotel.co.uk
dir: M42 junct 2, A441 to Redditch. End of carriageway turn left (A441), Dagnell End Rd on left. Hotel 600yds on right

With convenient access to the motorway and a proximity to many attractions, this modern hotel is popular with both business and leisure travellers. Bedrooms are well equipped and attractively decorated; the executive corner rooms are especially spacious. Facilities include an 18-hole golf course, pro shop, large indoor pool and extensive conference facilities.

Rooms 99 (20 fmly) (23 GF) ⋔ **Facilities** Spa FTV Wi-fi ↕ ☜ ⅃ 18 Putt green Fishing Gym Flood lit golf driving range Xmas New Year **Conf** Class 60 Board 30 Thtr 170 **Services** Lift **Parking** 200 **Notes** ⊗ Civ Wed 100

Holiday Inn Express Birmingham - Redditch
BUDGET HOTEL

☎ 01527 584658
2 Hewell Rd, Enfield B97 6AE
e-mail: reservations@express.gb.com
web: www.meridianleisurehotels.com/redditch
dir: M42 junct 2/A441 follow signs to rail station. Before station turn right into Hewell Rd, 1st left into Gloucester Close

This modern hotel, adjacent to the station, is ideal for families and business travellers. Fresh and uncomplicated, the spacious rooms include TVs with Freeview channels, and bathrooms with power showers. A complimentary hot buffet breakfast is included in the room rate; freshly prepared meals are served in the GR Restaurant daily from 6pm-10pm. There are two air-conditioned meeting rooms, with

natural light, available. See also the Hotel Groups pages.

Rooms 100 (75 fmly) (10 GF) (8 smoking) ⋔ **S** £40-£66.50; **D** £40-£66.50 (incl. bkfst) **Conf** Class 26 Board 20 Thtr 50 Del from £99 to £109

Premier Inn Redditch
BUDGET HOTEL

☎ 0871 527 8928
Birchfield Rd B97 6PX
web: www.premierinn.com
dir: M5 junct 4, A38 towards Bromsgrove. At rdbt take A448 to Redditch. 1st exit for Webheath. At next rdbt 3rd exit, 1st right into Birchfield Rd

High quality, budget accommodation ideal for both families and business travellers. Spacious, en suite bedrooms feature tea and coffee making facilities, and Freeview TV in most hotels. Internet access and Wi-fi are available for a small fee. The adjacent family restaurant features a wide and varied menu. See also the Hotel Groups pages.

Rooms 33

REDHILL
Surrey
Map 6 TQ25

Nutfield Priory Hotel & Spa
★★★★ 82% ⊛⊛ HOTEL

☎ 01737 824400 & 0845 072 7485
Nutfield RH1 4EL
e-mail: nutfieldpriory@handpicked.co.uk
web: www.handpickedhotels.co.uk/nutfieldpriory
dir: M25 junct 6, follow Redhill signs via Godstone on A25. Hotel 1m on left after Nutfield Village. Or M25 junct 8, A25 through Reigate & Redhill. Hotel on right 1.5m after rail bridge

This Victorian country house dates back to 1872 and is set in 40 acres of grounds with stunning views over the Surrey countryside. Bedrooms are individually decorated and equipped with an excellent range of facilities. Public areas include the impressive grand hall, Cloisters Restaurant, the library, and a cosy lounge bar area.

Rooms 60 (4 fmly) ⋔ **Facilities** Spa STV FTV Wi-fi ↕ HL ☜ Gym Squash Steam room Beauty therapy Aerobic & Step classes Saunas Xmas New Year **Conf** Class 45 Board 40 Thtr 80 **Services** Lift Air con **Parking** 130 **Notes** ⊗ Civ Wed 80

Premier Inn Redhill
BUDGET HOTEL

☎ 0871 527 8930
Brighton Rd, Salfords RH1 5BT
web: www.premierinn.com
dir: On A23, 2m S of Redhill; 3m N of Gatwick Airport

High quality, budget accommodation ideal for both families and business travellers. Spacious, en suite bedrooms feature tea and coffee making facilities, and Freeview TV in most hotels. Internet access and Wi-fi are available for a small fee. The adjacent family restaurant features a wide and varied menu. See also the Hotel Groups pages.

Rooms 48

REDRUTH
Cornwall
Map 2 SW64

Penventon Park Hotel
★★★ 79% HOTEL

☎ 01209 203000
TR15 1TE
e-mail: enquiries@penventon.com
web: www.penventon.co.uk
dir: Exit A30 at Redruth. Follow signs for Redruth West, hotel 1m S

Set in attractive parkland, this Georgian mansion is ideal for both business and leisure guests, and is well placed for visiting the glorious Cornish coastal areas. The smart bedrooms include 20 Garden Suites with patio doors that give access to a decking area and the garden beyond. The menus offer a wide choice of Cornish, British, Italian and French dishes. Leisure facilities include a pool, fitness suite, and health spa with beauty and holistic therapies, as well as function rooms and bars.

Rooms 63 (3 fmly) (24 GF) ⋔ **S** £69.50-£164.50; **D** £139-£219 (incl. bkfst)* **Facilities** Spa FTV Wi-fi ↕ ☜ supervised Gym Sauna Pool table Solarium Personal trainer ♫ Xmas New Year **Conf** Class 100 Board 60 Thtr 200 Del from £119.50 to £182.50* **Parking** 100 **Notes** LB Civ Wed 150

R

Save on hotels. Book at **theAA.com/hotel**

RED – RET 369 ENGLAND

REDWORTH
Co Durham
Map 19 NZ22

Redworth Hall Hotel

★★★★ 81% ⊛
COUNTRY HOUSE HOTEL

☎ 01388 770600
DL5 6NL
e-mail: redworthhall@pumahotels.co.uk
web: www.pumahotels.co.uk
dir: From A1(M) junct 58, A68 signed Corbridge.
Follow hotel signs

This imposing Georgian building includes a health
club with state-of-the-art equipment and impressive
conference facilities, making this hotel a popular
destination for business travellers. There are several
spacious lounges to relax in along with the
Conservatory Restaurant. Bedrooms are very
comfortable and well equipped.

Rooms 143 (12 fmly) **Facilities** STV Wi-fi ⓢ ♨ ♨
Gym Bodysense Health & Leisure Club ♬ Xmas New
Year **Conf** Class 144 Board 90 Thtr 300 **Services** Lift
Parking 300 **Notes** Civ Wed 240

REEPHAM
Norfolk
Map 13 TG12

Old Brewery House

★★★ 66% HOTEL

☎ 01603 870881
Market Place NR10 4JJ
e-mail: reservations.oldbreweryhouse@ohiml.com
web: www.oxfordhotelsandinns.com
dir: A1067, right at Bawdeswell onto B1145 into
Reepham, hotel on left in Market Place

This Grade II listed Georgian building is situated in
the heart of this bustling town centre. Public areas
include a cosy lounge, a bar, a conservatory and a
smart restaurant. Bedrooms come in a variety of
styles; each one is pleasantly decorated and equipped
with a good range of facilities.

Rooms 23 (2 fmly) (7 GF) **Facilities** ⓢ Gym Squash
Xmas **Conf** Class 80 Board 30 Thtr 200 **Parking** 40
Notes Civ Wed 45

REIGATE
Surrey
Map 6 TQ25

BEST WESTERN Reigate Manor Hotel

★★★ 73% HOTEL

☎ 01737 240125
Reigate Hill RH2 9PF
e-mail: hotel@reigatemanor.co.uk
web: www.reigatemanor.co.uk
dir: On A217, 1m S of M25 junct 8

On the slopes of Reigate Hill, the hotel is ideally
located for access to the town and for motorway links.
A range of public rooms is provided along with a
variety of function rooms. Bedrooms are either
traditional in style in the old house or of contemporary
design in the wing.

Rooms 50 (1 fmly) **S** fr £85; **D** fr £85* **Facilities** STV
Wi-fi **Conf** Class 80 Board 50 Thtr 200 Del £144*
Parking 130 **Notes** LB ⊗ Civ Wed 200

RENISHAW
Derbyshire
Map 16 SK47

Sitwell Arms Hotel

★★★ 73% HOTEL

☎ 01246 435226
Station Rd S21 3WF
e-mail: info@sitwellarms.com
dir: On A6135 to Sheffield, W of M1 junct 30

Parts of this attractive stone building date from the
18th century when it was a coaching inn. It has been
extended to provide spacious comfortable bedrooms
with modern facilities. A wide range of meals is
served in the Wild Boar Restaurant; there is also a
cocktail bar, informal lounge bar and a smart beer
garden with patio and children's play area. The hotel
has a gym and a hair and beauty salon.

Sitwell Arms Hotel

Rooms 31 (8 fmly) (9 GF) **S** £37.50-£39.50;
D £73.50-£110 (incl. bkfst)* **Facilities** FTV Wi-fi Gym
Fitness studio Hair & beauty salon Xmas New Year
Conf Class 60 Board 60 Thtr 160 Del from £87 to
£120 **Services** Lift **Parking** 150 **Notes** ⊗
Civ Wed 150

RETFORD
Nottinghamshire
Map 17 SK78

Ye Olde Bell Hotel & Restaurant

★★★★ 78% HOTEL

☎ 01777 705121
DN22 8QS
e-mail: enquiries@yeoldebell-hotel.co.uk
web: www.yeoldebell-hotel.co.uk

(For full entry see Barnby Moor)

BEST WESTERN PLUS West Retford Hotel

★★★ 79% HOTEL

☎ 01777 706333
24 North Rd DN22 7XG
e-mail: reservations@westretfordhotel.co.uk
dir: From A1 take A620 to Ranby/Retford. Left at rdbt
into North Rd (A638). Hotel on right

Stylishly appointed throughout, and set in very
attractive gardens close to the town centre, this 18th-
century manor house offers a good range of well-
equipped meeting rooms. The spacious, well-laid out
bedrooms and suites are located in separate
buildings and all offer modern facilities and
comforts.

Rooms 63 (15 fmly) (32 GF) ✆ **S** £72-£105;
D £79-£125 (incl. bkfst) **Facilities** FTV Wi-fi Xmas
New Year **Conf** Class 80 Board 40 Thtr 150
Del from £110 to £140 **Parking** 150
Notes Civ Wed 150

R

R

RICCALL
North Yorkshire
Map 16 SE63

Per Bracco at The Park View
RESTAURANT WITH ROOMS

☎ 01757 248458
20 Main St YO19 6PX
e-mail: gianlucasechi6@hotmail.co.uk
dir: A19 from Selby, left for Riccall by water tower, house 100yds on right

This spacious detached property is located in a quiet residential area and is convenient for York. The ground floor has been converted into an authentic Italian restaurant and there is a wide choice of fresh, homemade dishes and a friendly atmosphere. The restaurant is the main part of the business but there is also a range of comfortable en suite bedrooms. Ample parking is available.

Rooms 3

RICHMOND
North Yorkshire
Map 19 NZ10

The Frenchgate Restaurant and Hotel

★★★★ 75% ⦿⦿ TOWN HOUSE HOTEL

☎ 01748 822087 & 07921 136362
59-61 Frenchgate DL10 7AE
e-mail: info@thefrenchgate.co.uk
dir: From A1 (Scotch Corner) to Richmond on A6108. After lights, 1st left into Lile Close (leading to Flints Terr) for hotel car park. Or for front entrance continue to 1st rdbt, left into Dundas St. At T-junct left into Frenchgate.

This sympathetic conversion of an 18th-century town house building offers an impressive level of contemporary, quality accommodation. Modern artworks by local artists adorn the walls of the house. The intimate dining room serves award-winning evening meals and memorable breakfasts. Personal,

attentive and friendly staff are on hand to ensure a relaxing stay. Some off-road parking is available.

Rooms 9 (3 fmly) (1 GF) 🕿 **S** £88-£138; **D** £118-£250 (incl. bkfst)* **Facilities** FTV Wi-fi ☖ Xmas New Year **Conf** Class 24 Board 20 Thtr 20 Del from £118 to £148* **Parking** 12 **Notes** LB ⊗ Civ Wed 150

RICHMOND (UPON THAMES)
Greater London

The Petersham Hotel

★★★★ 79% ⦿⦿ HOTEL PLAN 1 C2

☎ 020 8940 7471 & 8939 1010
Nightingale Ln TW10 6UZ
e-mail: enq@petershamhotel.co.uk
web: www.petershamhotel.co.uk
dir: From Richmond Bridge rdbt A316 follow Ham & Petersham signs. Hotel in Nightingale Ln on left off Petersham Rd

Managed by the same family for over 25 years, this attractive hotel is located on a hill overlooking water meadows and a sweep of the River Thames. Bedrooms and suites are comfortably furnished, whilst public areas combine elegance and some fine architectural features. High quality produce features in dishes offered in the restaurant that looks out over the Thames below.

Rooms 60 (6 fmly) (3 GF) 🕿 **S** £95-£150; **D** £165-£215 (incl. bkfst) **Facilities** STV FTV Wi-fi ☖ Xmas New Year **Conf** Board 25 Thtr 35 Del from £235 to £299 **Services** Lift **Parking** 60 **Notes** LB ⊗ Civ Wed 40

The Richmond Hill Hotel

★★★★ 75% ⦿ HOTEL PLAN 1 C2

☎ 0208 940 2247
Richmond Hill TW10 6RW
e-mail: info.richmond@kewgreen.co.uk
dir: A316 for Richmond, hotel at top of Richmond Hill

This attractive Georgian manor is situated on Richmond Hill, enjoying elevated views over the Thames, and the town and the park are within walking distance. Bedrooms vary in size and style but all are comfortable and contemporary in style. There is a well-designed heath club, and extensive conference and banqueting facilities.

Rooms 149 (1 fmly) (15 GF) 🕿 **Facilities** Spa STV FTV Wi-fi ☖ Gym Steam room Health & beauty suite Sauna Xmas New Year **Conf** Class 80 Board 50 Thtr 180 **Services** Lift Air con **Parking** 97 **Notes** ⊗ Civ Wed 182

Bingham

★★★ ⦿⦿⦿ TOWN HOUSE HOTEL
PLAN 1 C2

☎ 020 8940 0902
61-63 Petersham Rd TW10 6UT
e-mail: info@thebingham.co.uk
web: www.thebingham.co.uk
dir: On A307

This Georgian building, dating back to 1740, overlooks the River Thames and is within easy reach of the town centre, Kew Gardens and Hampton Court. The contemporary bedrooms feature bespoke art deco style furniture and up-to-the-minute facilities such as Wi-fi, a digital music library, flat-screen TVs and 'rain dance' showers. Public rooms have views of the pretty garden and river. Guests can choose from a selection of meals that range from light snacks to two or three-course dinners.

Rooms 15 (2 fmly) 🕿 **S** £175; **D** £195-£290* **Facilities** FTV Wi-fi ☖ In room beauty treatments Xmas New Year **Conf** Class 70 Board 40 Thtr 100 Del from £255* **Services** Lift Air con **Parking** 8 **Notes** LB ⊗ Civ Wed 90

Premier Inn London Richmond

BUDGET HOTEL

☎ 0871 527 9346
136-138 Lower Mortlake Rd, Richmond TW9 2JZ
web: www.premierinn.com
dir: Please telephone for directions

High quality, budget accommodation ideal for both families and business travellers. Spacious, en suite bedrooms feature tea and coffee making facilities, and Freeview TV in most hotels. Internet access and Wi-fi are available for a small fee. The adjacent family restaurant features a wide and varied menu. See also the Hotel Groups pages.

Rooms 92

RICKMANSWORTH　　Map 6 TQ09
Hertfordshire

See also **Chenies**

INSPECTORS' CHOICE

The Grove

★★★★★ ◉◉◉ HOTEL

☎ 01923 807807
Chandler's Cross WD3 4TG
e-mail: marketing@thegrove.co.uk
web: www.thegrove.co.uk
dir: M25 junct 19, A411 towards Watford. Hotel on right

Set amid 300 acres of rolling countryside, much of which is golf course, the hotel combines historic features with cutting-edge, modern design. The spacious bedrooms have the latest in temperature control, lighting technology and flat-screen TVs; many have balconies. Suites in the original mansion are particularly stunning. Championship golf, a world-class spa and three dining options are just a few of the treasures to sample here. The hotel also has extensive crèche facilities. The hotel has three dining options - Collette's with 3 AA Rosettes that offers fine dining, and a more relaxed style in the Glasshouse and Stables restaurants. The walled garden is also well worth exploring.

Rooms 217 (69 fmly) (35 GF) ⚹ **S** £285-£975; **D** £310-£1000 (incl. bkfst)* **Facilities** Spa STV FTV Wi-fi ⬓ ⬓ ➘ supervised ⬩ 18 ⬩ Putt green ⬩ Gym Walking & cycling trails Giant chess Orchid house Golf driving range Xmas New Year Child facilities **Conf** Class 300 Board 78 Thtr 450 Del from £292* **Services** Lift Air con **Parking** 400 **Notes** LB ⊗ Civ Wed 450

Long Island Hotel
★★ 🅰 HOTEL　　

☎ 01923 779466
2 Victoria Close WD3 4EQ
e-mail: office@longisland.fsbusiness.co.uk
web: www.oldenglish.co.uk
dir: M25 junct 18, A404, 1.5m. Left at rdbt into Nightingale Rd, 1st left

Located opposite Rickmansworth train station and 25 minutes from both Heathrow and Luton airports, this modern hotel provides comfortable accommodation for business or leisure guests. Evening meals and breakfasts are served in the American-themed Exchange Bar & Grill.

Rooms 50 (3 fmly) (12 GF) **Facilities** ♫ **Conf** Class 15 Board 8 Thtr 12 **Parking** 120 **Notes** ⊗

RINGWOOD　　Map 5 SU10
Hampshire

Tyrrells Ford Country House Hotel
★★★ 72% SMALL HOTEL

☎ 01425 672646
Avon BH23 7BH
e-mail: info@tyrrellsford.co.uk
web: www.tyrrellsford.co.uk
dir: From A31 to Ringwood take B3347. Hotel 3m S on left

Set in the New Forest, this delightful family-run hotel has much to offer. Most bedrooms have views over the open country. Diners may eat in the formal restaurant, or sample the wide range of bar meals; all dishes are prepared using fresh local produce. The Gallery Lounge offers guests a peaceful area in which to relax.

Rooms 14 **Conf** Class 20 Board 20 Thtr 40 **Parking** 100 **Notes** ⊗ Civ Wed 60

RIPLEY　　Map 16 SK35
Derbyshire

Premier Inn Ripley
BUDGET HOTEL　　

☎ 0871 527 8935
Nottingham Rd DE5 3QP
web: www.premierinn.com
dir: From S: M1 junct 26, A610 towards Ripley. Hotel off rdbt adjacent to Butterley Park. From N: M1 junct 28, A38, A610 towards Nottingham. Hotel on right at rdbt

High quality, budget accommodation ideal for both families and business travellers. Spacious, en suite bedrooms feature tea and coffee making facilities, and Freeview TV in most hotels. Internet access and Wi-fi are available for a small fee. The adjacent family restaurant features a wide and varied menu. See also the Hotel Groups pages.

Rooms 60

RISLEY　　Map 11 SK43
Derbyshire

Risley Hall Hotel & Spa
★★★ 74% ◉ HOTEL　　"bespoke"

☎ 0115 939 9000 & 921 8523
Derby Rd DE72 3SS
e-mail: reservations.risleyhall@ohiml.com
web: www.oxfordhotelsandinns.com
dir: M1 junct 25, Sandiacre exit into Bostock Ln. Left at lights, hotel on left in 0.25m

Set in 17 acres of private landscaped grounds and attractive mature gardens, this 11th-century manor house offers a good range of comfortable accommodation and relaxing day rooms. The friendly and attentive service complements the imaginative cuisine in the fine dining restaurant. The spa and beauty treatment rooms prove particularly popular with members and leisure guests alike.

Rooms 35 (8 GF) **Facilities** Spa STV FTV ⬓ Xmas New Year **Conf** Class 22 Board 20 Thtr 100 **Services** Lift **Notes** ⊗ Civ Wed 100

ROCHDALE　　Map 16 SD81
Greater Manchester

Mercure Manchester Norton Grange Hotel & Spa
★★★★ 75% HOTEL　　Mercure

☎ 0870 1942119 & 01706 630788
Manchester Rd, Castleton OL11 2XZ
e-mail: h6631@accor.com
web: www.mercure.com
dir: M62 junct 20, follow A664/Castleton signs. Right at next 2 rdbts. Hotel 0.5m on left. (NB for Sat Nav use M24 2UB)

Standing in nine acres of grounds and mature gardens, this Victorian house provides comfort in elegant surroundings. The well-equipped bedrooms provide a host of extras for both the business and leisure guest. Public areas include the Pickwick bistro and smart Grange Restaurant, both offering a good choice of dishes. There is also an impressive leisure centre.

Rooms 81 (17 fmly) (10 GF) **Facilities** Spa Wi-fi ⬓ Gym Leisure centre Indoor/Outdoor hydrotherapy pool Thermal suite Rock sauna Xmas New Year **Conf** Class 120 Board 70 Thtr 220 **Services** Lift **Parking** 150 **Notes** Civ Wed 150

R

ROCHDALE *continued*

BEST WESTERN Broadfield Park Hotel

★★★ 77% HOTEL

☎ 01706 639000
Sparrow Hill OL16 1AF
e-mail: reception@broadfieldparkhotel.co.uk
web: www.broadfieldparkhotel.co.uk
dir: M60 junct 20, follow signs for Rochdale & town centre. A640 into Drake St, hotel signed 0.5m on left

Overlooking historic Broadfield Park and the town centre and only minutes away from the M60 and M62. Bedrooms are comfortably furnished and attractively decorated. The hotel offers a range of carefully prepared meals and snacks in either the formal restaurant, or the lounge bar. Service is friendly and attentive.

Rooms 29 (4 fmly) **Facilities** FTV Wi-fi Xmas New Year **Conf** Class 120 Board 80 Thtr 200 **Parking** 30 **Notes** Civ Wed 200

Premier Inn Rochdale

BUDGET HOTEL

☎ 0871 527 8936
Newhey Rd, Milnrow OL16 4JF
web: www.premierinn.com
dir: M62 junct 21, at rdbt right towards Shaw, under motorway bridge, & 1st left

High quality, budget accommodation ideal for both families and business travellers. Spacious, en suite bedrooms feature tea and coffee making facilities, and Freeview TV in most hotels. Internet access and Wi-fi are available for a small fee. The adjacent family restaurant features a wide and varied menu. See also the Hotel Groups pages.

Rooms 40

ROCHESTER
Kent
Map 6 TQ76

Premier Inn Rochester

BUDGET HOTEL

☎ 0871 527 8938
Medway Valley Leisure Park, Chariot Way, Strood ME2 2SS
web: www.premierinn.com
dir: M2 junct 2, follow Rochester & West Malling signs. At rdbt onto A228 signed Rochester & Strood. At next rdbt 2nd exit into Roman Way signed Medway Valley Park. At next rdbt 1st exit into Chariot Way, hotel in 100mtrs

High quality, budget accommodation ideal for both families and business travellers. Spacious, en suite bedrooms feature tea and coffee making facilities, and Freeview TV in most hotels. Internet access and Wi-fi are available for a small fee. The adjacent family restaurant features a wide and varied menu. See also the Hotel Groups pages.

Rooms 121

ROMALDKIRK
Co Durham
Map 19 NY92

INSPECTORS' CHOICE

The Rose & Crown

★★★ ◉◉ HOTEL

☎ 01833 650213
DL12 9EB
e-mail: hotel@rose-and-crown.co.uk
web: www.rose-and-crown.co.uk
dir: 6m NW from Barnard Castle on B6277

This charming 18th-century country inn is located in the heart of the village, overlooking fine dale scenery. The attractively furnished bedrooms, including suites, are split between the main house and the rear courtyard. Guests might like to have a drink in the cosy bar with its log fire, after returning from a long walk. Good local produce features extensively on the menus that can be enjoyed in the oak-panelled restaurant, or in the brasserie and bar. Service is both friendly and attentive.

Rooms 12 (5 annexe) (2 fmly) (5 GF) **S** £95-£125; **D** £150-£220 (incl. bkfst)*
Facilities FTV Wi-fi Spa & golf available at Headlam Hall New Year **Parking** 20 **Notes** LB

ROMFORD
Greater London
Map 6 TQ58

Premier Inn Romford Central

BUDGET HOTEL

☎ 0871 527 8940
Mercury Gardens RM1 3EN
web: www.premierinn.com
dir: M25 junct 28, A12 to Gallows Corner. Take A118 to next rdbt, turn left

High quality, budget accommodation ideal for both families and business travellers. Spacious, en suite bedrooms feature tea and coffee making facilities, and Freeview TV in most hotels. Internet access and Wi-fi are available for a small fee. The adjacent family restaurant features a wide and varied menu. See also the Hotel Groups pages.

Rooms 64

Premier Inn Romford West

BUDGET HOTEL

☎ 0871 527 8942
Whalebone Lane North, Chadwell Heath RM6 6QU
web: www.premierinn.com
dir: 6m from M25 junct 28 on A12 at junct with A1112

Rooms 42

R

R

The White Horse Hotel & Brasserie

★★★★ 75% ◉◉ HOTEL

☎ 01794 512431
19 Market Place SO51 8ZJ
e-mail: reservations@silkshotels.com
web: www.silkshotels.com
dir: M27 junct 3, follow signs for Romsey, right at
Broadlands. In Town centre

This family friendly hotel is located overlooking the
market square of this historic town. This traditional,
former coaching inn provides very comfortable and
very stylish, individually designed bedrooms,
including Loft Suites and a Penthouse. Public areas
boast relaxing day rooms and an elegant
contemporary bar. The Brasserie offers award-
winning cuisine, with alfresco dining a possibility
during the warmer summer months. Public car parks
can be found close by, although the property does
operate a valet parking service.

Rooms 31 (4 fmly) ✎ **S** £85-£95; **D** £115-£135*
Facilities FTV Wi-fi ☇ Xmas New Year **Conf** Class 40
Board 30 Thtr 30 Del from £135 to £165*
Notes Civ Wed 65

See advert on page 373

Potters Heron Hotel

★★★ 77% HOTEL

☎ 023 8027 7800
Winchester Rd, Ampfield SO51 9ZF
e-mail: thepottersheron@pebblehotels.com
dir: M3 junct 12 follow Chandler's Ford signs. 2nd
exit at 3rd rdbt follow Ampfield signs, over x-rds.
Hotel on left in 1m

This distinctive thatched hotel retains many original
features. In a convenient location with access to
Winchester, Southampton and the M3, Potters Heron
Hotel has modern accommodation and stylish,
spacious public areas. Most of the bedrooms have
their own balcony or terrace. The pub and restaurant
both offer an interesting range of dishes that will suit
a variety of tastes.

Rooms 54 (1 fmly) (29 GF) ✎ **S** £75-£125;
D £80-£125 (incl. bkfst)* **Facilities** Wi-fi ☇ Xmas
New Year **Conf** Class 40 Board 30 Thtr 100 Del £165*
Services Lift **Parking** 120 **Notes** LB ⊗ Civ Wed 100

Premier Inn Southampton West

BUDGET HOTEL

☎ 0871 527 9004
Romsey Rd, Ower SO51 6ZJ
web: www.premierinn.com
dir: Just off M27 junct 2. Take A36 towards Salisbury.
Follow brown tourist signs 'Vine Inn'

High quality, budget accommodation ideal for both
families and business travellers. Spacious, en suite
bedrooms feature tea and coffee making facilities,
and Freeview TV in most hotels. Internet access and
Wi-fi are available for a small fee. The adjacent
family restaurant features a wide and varied menu.
See also the Hotel Groups pages.

Rooms 67

The Cromwell Arms Country Pub With Rooms

RESTAURANT WITH ROOMS

☎ 01794 519515
Mainstone SO51 8HG
e-mail: info@thecromwellarms.com

This charming country pub has a popular restaurant
serving food all day and every day. In addition, there
are luxury bedrooms, which are spacious, beautifully
styled and come with a host of extras. Bathrooms are
modern and come with high quality towels and
toiletries. There is also ample parking, well kept
grounds and great access to major roads.

Rooms 10 (10 fmly)

BEST WESTERN PREMIER Mount Pleasant Hotel

★★★★ 80% ◉ HOTEL

☎ 01302 868696 & 868219
Great North Rd DN11 0HW
e-mail: reception@mountpleasant.co.uk
web: www.mountpleasant.co.uk
dir: On A638 (Great North Road) between Bawtry &
Doncaster

This charming 18th-century house stands in 100
acres of wooded parkland between Doncaster and
Bawtry, near Robin Hood Airport. Spacious public
areas include well furnished lounges and the elegant
Garden Restaurant. There are also a health and
wellbeing centre, modern conference facilities and
beautiful grounds, ideal for weddings. Bedrooms are
individually designed; some have four-poster beds
and the spa suites are even more impressive with
luxurious bathrooms.

Rooms 56 (18 fmly) (27 GF) ✎ **S** £79-£199;
D £99-£499 (incl. bkfst) **Facilities** Spa STV Wi-fi ☇
Beauty salon **Conf** Class 70 Board 70 Thtr 200
Services Lift **Parking** 140 **Notes** LB ⊗ Closed 25 Dec
RS 24 Dec Civ Wed 180

The Chase Hotel

★★★ 81% ◉ HOTEL

☎ 01989 763161 & 760644
Gloucester Rd HR9 5LH
e-mail: res@chasehotel.co.uk
web: www.chasehotel.co.uk
dir: M50 junct 4, 1st left exit towards rdbt, left at rdbt
towards A40. Right at 2nd rdbt towards town centre,
hotel 0.5m on left

This attractive Georgian mansion sits in its own
landscaped grounds and is only a short walk from the
town centre. Bedrooms, including two four-poster
rooms, vary in size and character; all rooms are
appointed to impressive standards. There is a light
and spacious bar, and also Harry's restaurant which
offers an excellent selection of enjoyable dishes.

Rooms 36 (1 fmly) ✎ **S** £55-£105; **D** £69-£210 (incl.
bkfst)* **Facilities** STV FTV Wi-fi ☇ New Year
Conf Class 100 Board 80 Thtr 300 Del from £99 to
£135 **Parking** 75 **Notes** LB ⊗ Closed 24-27 Dec
Civ Wed 150

R

Save on hotels. Book at **theAA.com/hotel**

ROM – ROS 375 ENGLAND

Glewstone Court Country House Hotel

★★★ 74% ◉ COUNTRY HOUSE HOTEL

☎ 01989 770367
Glewstone HR9 6AW
e-mail: info@glewstonecourt.com
web: www.glewstonecourt.com
dir: From Ross-on-Wye market place follow A40/A49 Monmouth/Hereford signs, over Wilton Bridge to rdbt, left onto A40 towards Monmouth, in 1m right for hotel

This charming hotel enjoys an elevated position with views over Ross-on-Wye, and is set in well-tended gardens. Informal service is delivered with great enthusiasm by Bill Reeve-Tucker, whilst the kitchen is the domain of Christine Reeve-Tucker who offers an extensive menu of well executed dishes. Bedrooms come in a variety of sizes and are tastefully furnished and well equipped.

Rooms 8 (2 fmly) (1 GF) **S** £85-£100; **D** £125-£150 (incl. bkfst)* **Facilities** FTV Wi-fi 🏊 New Year **Conf** Class 18 Board 12 Thtr 24 Del from £125 to £155* **Parking** 25 **Notes** LB Closed 25-27 Dec Civ Wed 72

King's Head Hotel

★★★ 72% HOTEL

☎ 01989 763174
8 High St HR9 5HL
e-mail: enquiries@kingshead.co.uk
web: www.kingshead.co.uk
dir: In town centre, past market building on right

This establishment dates back to the 14th century and has a wealth of charm and character. Bedrooms are well equipped and comfortable with thoughtful guest extras provided; both four-poster and family rooms are available. The restaurant offers menus and a specials board that reflect a varied selection of local produce including fresh fish, free range beef and lamb. There is also a well-stocked bar serving hand-pulled, real ales.

Rooms 15 (1 fmly) 🐾 **S** £56; **D** £80-£110 (incl. bkfst)* **Facilities** FTV Wi-fi **Parking** 15

Pengethley Manor

★★★ 72% HOTEL

☎ 01989 730211
Pengethley Park HR9 6LL
e-mail: reservations@pengethleymanor.co.uk
dir: 4m N on A49 (Hereford road), from Ross-on-Wye

Delightfully located with views in all directions over the countryside, this traditional manor-style hotel has plenty of character and comfort throughout. The bedrooms are divided between the main house and a more modern adjacent annexe. A good selection of dishes is offered both at lunch and dinner. A number of country walks start from the front door of the hotel.

Rooms 19 (8 annexe) (2 GF) 🐾 **Facilities** Wi-fi ♿ ⚓ 9 Putt green Xmas New Year **Parking** 30 **Notes** Civ Wed 80

The Royal Hotel

★★★ 68% HOTEL

 OldEnglish

☎ 01989 565105
Palace Pound HR9 5HZ
e-mail: 6504@greeneking.co.uk
web: www.oldenglish.co.uk
dir: At end of M50 take A40 signed Monmouth. At 3rd rdbt, left to Ross-on-Wye, over bridge, follow The Royal Hotel sign

Close to the town centre, this imposing hotel enjoys panoramic views from its prominent hilltop position. Reputedly visited by Charles Dickens in 1867, the establishment has been sympathetically furnished to combine the ambience of a bygone era with the comforts of today. In addition to the bar and dining areas, there are function rooms, an elegant restaurant and an attractive garden.

Rooms 42 (1 fmly) 🐾 **Facilities** FTV Wi-fi ♿ Xmas New Year **Conf** Class 20 Board 28 Thtr 85 **Parking** 38 **Notes** Civ Wed 75

Chasedale Hotel

★★ 74% SMALL HOTEL

☎ 01989 562423 & 565801
Walford Rd HR9 5PQ
e-mail: chasedale@supanet.com
web: www.chasedale.co.uk
dir: From town centre, S on B4234, hotel 0.5m on left

This large, mid-Victorian property is situated on the south-west outskirts of the town. Privately owned and personally run, it provides spacious, well-proportioned public areas and extensive grounds. The accommodation is well equipped and includes ground floor and family rooms, whilst the restaurant offers a wide selection of wholesome food.

Rooms 10 (2 fmly) (1 GF) **Facilities** FTV Wi-fi **Conf** Class 30 Board 25 Thtr 40 **Parking** 14 **Notes** LB

Premier Inn Ross-on-Wye

 Premier Inn

BUDGET HOTEL

☎ 0871 527 8944
Ledbury Rd HR9 7QJ
web: www.premierinn.com
dir: M50 junct 4, 1m from town centre

High quality, budget accommodation ideal for both families and business travellers. Spacious, en suite bedrooms feature tea and coffee making facilities, and Freeview TV in most hotels. Internet access and Wi-fi are available for a small fee. The adjacent family restaurant features a wide and varied menu. See also the Hotel Groups pages.

Rooms 43

Wilton Court Restaurant with Rooms

◉◉ RESTAURANT WITH ROOMS

☎ 01989 562569
Wilton Ln HR9 6AQ
e-mail: info@wiltoncourthotel.com
dir: M50 junct 4, A40 towards Monmouth at 3rd rdbt left signed Ross-on-Wye, 1st right, on right

Dating back to the 16th century, this establishment has great charm and a wealth of character. Standing on the banks of the River Wye and just a short walk from the town centre, there is a genuinely relaxed, friendly and unhurried atmosphere created by hosts Roger and Helen Wynn and their reliable team. Bedrooms are tastefully furnished and well equipped, while public areas include a comfortable lounge, traditional bar and pleasant restaurant with a conservatory extension overlooking the garden. High standards of food, using fresh, locally sourced ingredients, are offered.

Rooms 10 (1 fmly)

R

ROSTHWAITE
Cumbria   Map 18 NY21

See also Borrowdale

Scafell Hotel
★★★ 81% HOTEL

☎ 017687 77208
CA12 5XB
e-mail: info@scafell.co.uk
web: www.scafell.co.uk
dir: M6 junct 40 to Keswick on A66. Take B5289 to Rosthwaite

Scafell Hotel is a friendly establishment, which enjoys a peaceful location, and is popular with walkers. Bedrooms have been tastefully appointed in a warm country house style with a contemporary twist; some have traditional antique furniture. Public areas include a residents' cocktail bar, lounge and spacious restaurant as well as the popular Riverside Inn, offering all-day menus in summer months.

Rooms 23 (2 fmly) (8 GF) 🐾 **S** £50-£85; **D** £100-£170 (incl. bkfst)* **Facilities** FTV Wi-fi Guided walks Xmas New Year **Parking** 50 **Notes** LB Civ Wed 75

ROTHERHAM
South Yorkshire   Map 16 SK49

Hellaby Hall Hotel
★★★★ 73% HOTEL   PRIMA

☎ 01709 702701
Old Hellaby Ln, Hellaby S66 8SN
e-mail: reservations@hellabyhallhotel.co.uk
web: www.hellabyhallhotel.co.uk
dir: 0.5m off M18 junct 1, onto A631 towards Maltby. Hotel in Hellaby. (NB do not use postcode for Sat Nav)

This 17th-century house was built to a Flemish design with high, beamed ceilings, staircases which lead off to private meeting rooms and a series of oak-panelled lounges. Bedrooms are elegant and well equipped, and guests can dine in the formal Attic Restaurant. There are extensive leisure facilities and conference areas, and the hotel holds a licence for civil weddings.

Rooms 90 (6 fmly) (17 GF) **Facilities** Spa STV FTV Wi-fi ⇗ ⓒ supervised Gym Beauty salon Exercise studio Spinning bike studio Xmas New Year **Conf** Class 300 Board 150 Thtr 500 Del £150* **Services** Lift **Parking** 250 **Notes** Civ Wed 200

Carlton Park Hotel
★★★ 78% HOTEL

☎ 01709 849955
102/104 Moorgate Rd S60 2BG
e-mail: reservations@carltonparkhotel.com
web: www.carltonparkhotel.com
dir: M1 junct 33, onto A631, then A618. Hotel 800yds past District General Hospital

This modern hotel is situated in a pleasant residential area of the town, close to the hospital, yet within minutes of the M1. Bedrooms and bathrooms offer very modern facilities; three have separate sitting rooms. The restaurant and bar provide a lively atmosphere and there is a pool and leisure centre.

Rooms 80 (19 fmly) (16 GF) (7 smoking) **S** £49-£99; **D** £54-£104 (incl. bkfst) **Facilities** STV FTV Wi-fi ⓒ Gym ♫ Xmas New Year **Conf** Class 120 Board 60 Thtr 300 **Services** Lift **Parking** 120 **Notes** LB ⊗ Civ Wed 150

Ibis Rotherham East

BUDGET HOTEL

☎ 01709 730333
Moorhead Way, Bramley S66 1YY
e-mail: H3163@accor-hotels.com
web: www.ibishotel.com
dir: M18 junct 1, left at rdbt, left at 1st lights. Hotel adjacent to supermarket

Modern, budget hotel offering comfortable accommodation in bright and practical bedrooms. Breakfast is self-service and dinner is available in the restaurant. See also the Hotel Groups pages.

Rooms 86 (22 fmly) (8 GF) 🐾 **S** £29-£62; **D** £29-£62* **Conf** Class 20 Board 20 Thtr 30

Premier Inn Rotherham
BUDGET HOTEL

☎ 0871 527 8946
Bawtry Rd S65 3JB
web: www.premierinn.com
dir: On A631 towards Wickersley, between M18 junct 1 & M1 junct 33

High quality, budget accommodation ideal for both families and business travellers. Spacious, en suite bedrooms feature tea and coffee making facilities, and Freeview TV in most hotels. Internet access and Wi-fi are available for a small fee. The adjacent family restaurant features a wide and varied menu. See also the Hotel Groups pages.

Rooms 37

R

ROTHERWICK
Hampshire   Map 5 SU75

INSPECTORS' CHOICE

Tylney Hall Hotel
★★★★ ◎◎ HOTEL

☎ 01256 764881
RG27 9AZ
e-mail: sales@tylneyhall.com
web: www.tylneyhall.com
dir: M3 junct 5, A287 to Basingstoke, over
junct with A30, over rail bridge, towards Newnham.
Right at Newnham Green. Hotel 1m on left

A grand Victorian country house set in 66 acres of beautiful parkland. The hotel offers high standards of comfort in relaxed yet elegant surroundings, featuring magnificently restored water gardens, originally laid out by the famous gardener, Gertrude Jekyll. Spacious public rooms include Italian and Wedgwood styled drawing rooms and the panelled Oak Room Restaurant, filled with stunning flower arrangements and warmed by log fires, that offers cuisine based on locally sourced ingredients. The spacious bedrooms are traditionally furnished and offer individual style and high degrees of comfort. The excellent leisure facilities include indoor and outdoor swimming pools, tennis courts, jogging trails, croquet lawns and a spa.

Rooms 112 (77 annexe) (1 fmly) (40 GF) 🐾
S £220-£500; **D** £250-£530 (incl. bkfst)*
Facilities Spa STV FTV Wi-fi ⬅ 🎢 ⤴ ⛳ 🏌 Gym
Clay pigeon shooting Archery Falconry Balloon rides
Laser shooting Jogging trail Xmas New Year
Conf Class 70 Board 40 Thtr 120 **Parking** 120
Notes LB Civ Wed 120

ROTHLEY
Leicestershire   Map 11 SK51

Rothley Court
★★★ 73% HOTEL   OldEnglish

☎ 0116 237 4141
Westfield Ln LE7 7LG
e-mail: 6501@greeneking.co.uk
web: www.oldenglish.co.uk
dir: On B5328

Mentioned in the Domesday Book, and complete with its own chapel, this historic property sits in seven acres of well-tended grounds. Public areas retain much of their original character and include an oak-panelled restaurant and a choice of function and meeting rooms. Bedrooms, some located in an adjacent stable block, are individually styled.

Rooms 30 (18 annexe) (3 fmly) (6 GF) 🐾 **S** £75-£115;
D £80-£125 (incl. bkfst & dinner)* **Facilities** Wi-fi
Xmas **Conf** Class 35 Board 35 Thtr 100 Del £99*
Parking 100 **Notes** ⊗ Civ Wed 85

ROWDE
Wiltshire   Map 4 ST96

The George & Dragon
◎◎ RESTAURANT WITH ROOMS

☎ 01380 723053
High St SN10 2PN
e-mail: thegandd@tiscali.co.uk
dir: 1.5m from Devizes on A350 towards Chippenham

The George & Dragon dates back to the 14th century when it was a meeting house. Exposed beams, wooden floors, antique rugs and open fires create a warm atmosphere in the bar and restaurant. Bedrooms and bathrooms are very well decorated and equipped with some welcome extras. Dining in the bar or restaurant should not be missed, as local produce and fresh fish deliveries from Cornwall are offered on the daily-changing blackboard menu.

Rooms 3 (1 fmly)

ROWSLEY
Derbyshire   Map 16 SK26

INSPECTORS' CHOICE

East Lodge Country House Hotel
★★★ HOTEL

☎ 01629 734474
DE4 2EF
e-mail: info@eastlodge.com
web: www.eastlodge.com
dir: A6, 3m from Bakewell, 5m from Matlock

This hotel enjoys a romantic setting in ten acres of landscaped grounds and gardens. The stylish bedrooms are equipped with many extras such as TVs with DVD players, and most have lovely garden views. The popular restaurant serves much produce sourced from the area, and the conservatory lounge, overlooking the gardens, offers afternoon teas and light meals. The AA Rosette award for the East Lodge Country House Hotel is currently suspended due to a change of chef. AA Rosettes may be awarded once the inspectors have assessed the food created by the new kitchen regime.

Rooms 12 (2 fmly) (1 GF) 🐾 **Facilities** STV FTV
Wi-fi ⬅ HL Fishing ⛳ Xmas New Year
Conf Class 50 Board 25 Thtr 100 Del from £195 to
£225* **Parking** 40 **Notes** ⊗ No children 12yrs
Civ Wed 150

R

ROWSLEY *continued*

INSPECTORS' CHOICE

The Peacock at Rowsley

★★★ ◎◎◎ HOTEL

☎ 01629 733518
Bakewell Rd DE4 2EB
e-mail: reception@thepeacockatrowsley.com
web: www.thepeacockatrowsley.com
dir: A6, 3m before Bakewell, 6m from Matlock towards Bakewell

Owned by Lord Manners of Haddon Hall, this hotel combines stylish contemporary design by India Mahdavi with original period and antique features. Bedrooms are individually designed and boast DVD players, complimentary Wi-fi and smart marble bathrooms. Two rooms are particularly special - one with a four-poster and one with an antique bed originating from Belvoir Castle in Leicestershire. Imaginative cuisine, using local, seasonal produce, is a highlight. Guests are warmly welcomed and service is attentive. Fly fishing is popular in this area and the hotel has its own fishing rights on seven miles of the Rivers Wye and Derwent.

Rooms 15 (6 fmly) ♠ **S** £85-£130; **D** £155-£230 (incl. bkfst)* **Facilities** Wi-fi Fishing ⏴ Free use of Woodlands Fitness Centre Free membership to Bakewell Golf Club ♫ New Year **Conf** Class 8 Board 16 Del £200* **Parking** 25 **Notes** No children 10yrs Civ Wed 20

RUBERY
West Midlands   Map 10 SO97

Premier Inn Birmingham South (Rubery)

BUDGET HOTEL

☎ 0871 527 8094
Birmingham Great Park, Ashbrook Dr, Parkway B45 9FP
web: www.premierinn.com
dir: M5 junct 4, A38 towards Birmingham. Left at lights before Morrisons signed Great Park. Right at rdbt. Right at next rdbt, hotel on right

High quality, budget accommodation ideal for both families and business travellers. Spacious, en suite bedrooms feature tea and coffee making facilities, and Freeview TV in most hotels. Internet access and Wi-fi are available for a small fee. The adjacent family restaurant features a wide and varied menu. See also the Hotel Groups pages.

Rooms 62

RUGBY
Warwickshire   Map 11 SP57

Brownsover Hall Hotel

★★★ 78% HOTEL

CLASSIC
BRITISH HOTELS

☎ 01788 546100 & 555362
Brownsover Ln, Old Brownsover CV21 1HU
e-mail: reservations@brownsoverhall.co.uk
web: www.brownsoverhall.co.uk
dir: M6 junct 1, A426 to Rugby. After 0.5m at rdbt follow Brownsover signs, right into Brownover Rd, right again into Brownsover Ln. Hotel 250yds on left

Brownsover Hall is a Grade II listed, Victorian Gothic building designed by Sir Gilbert Scott, set in seven acres of wooded parkland. Bedrooms vary in size and style, including spacious and contemporary rooms in the converted stable block. The former chapel makes a stylish restaurant, and for a less formal meal or a relaxing drink, the Whittle Bar is popular.

Rooms 47 (20 annexe) (3 fmly) (11 GF) **S** £72-£139; **D** £82-£149 (incl. bkfst)* **Facilities** STV FTV Wi-fi ↳ Xmas New Year **Conf** Class 36 Board 40 Thtr 70 **Parking** 100 **Notes** LB ⊗ Civ Wed 56

The Golden Lion Hotel

★★★ 74% HOTEL

☎ 01788 833577 & 832265
Easenhall CV23 0JA
e-mail: reception@goldenlionhotel.org
web: www.goldenlionhotel.org
dir: From A426 at Avon Mill rdbt follow Newbold-upon-Avon B4112 signs, approx 2m left at Harborough Parva sign, follow brown tourist signs, opposite agricultural showroom, 1m to Easenhall

This friendly, family-run, 16th-century inn is situated between Rugby and Coventry, and is convenient for access to the M6. Bedrooms, some in a smart extension, are equipped with both practical and homely items; one features a stunning Chinese bed. The beamed bar and restaurant retain many original features and a warm welcome is assured.

Rooms 20 (2 fmly) (6 GF) **Facilities** FTV Wi-fi ↳ Xmas New Year **Conf** Class 30 Board 24 Thtr 80 **Parking** 80 **Notes** ⊗ Civ Wed 100

Premier Inn Rugby North M6 Jct 1

BUDGET HOTEL

☎ 0871 527 8948
Central Park Dr, Central Park CV23 0WE
web: www.premierinn.com
dir: M6 junct 1, S'bound onto A426. Hotel approx 1m on left at rdbt

High quality, budget accommodation ideal for both families and business travellers. Spacious, en suite bedrooms feature tea and coffee making facilities, and Freeview TV in most hotels. Internet access and Wi-fi are available for a small fee. The adjacent family restaurant features a wide and varied menu. See also the Hotel Groups pages.

Rooms 58

Premier Inn Rugby North (Newbold)

BUDGET HOTEL

☎ 0871 527 8950
Brownsover Rd CV21 1HL
web: www.premierinn.com
dir: M6 junct 1, A426 follow Rugby signs. Straight on at 2 rdbts. At 3rd rdbt, hotel on right. (NB for Sat Nav use CV21 1NX)

Rooms 49

R

RUGELEY
Staffordshire Map 10 SK01

Premier Inn Rugeley

BUDGET HOTEL

☎ 0871 527 9272
Tower Business Park WS15 2HJ
web: www.premierinn.com
dir: M6 junct 14, A5013 towards Stafford. At rdbt 2nd exit onto A34. Take A513 signed Rugeley. At rdbt take 2nd exit onto A51. Left into Wolsley Rd, left into Powerstation Rd. Hotel off rdbt. (NB for Sat Nav use WS15 1PR)

High quality, budget accommodation ideal for both families and business travellers. Spacious, en suite bedrooms feature tea and coffee making facilities, and Freeview TV in most hotels. Internet access and Wi-fi are available for a small fee. The adjacent family restaurant features a wide and varied menu. See also the Hotel Groups pages.

Rooms 50

RUISLIP
Greater London

The Barn Hotel

★★★ 78% ◉◉ HOTEL PLAN 1 A5

☎ 01895 636057
West End Rd HA4 6JB
e-mail: info@thebarnhotel.co.uk
web: www.thebarnhotel.co.uk
dir: A40 onto A4180 (Polish War Memorial) exit to Ruislip. 2m to hotel entrance at mini-rdbt before Ruislip tube station

A mix of old and new, with parts dating back to the 17th century, this impressive property sits in three acres of gardens. Bedrooms vary in style, from contemporary to traditional with oak-beams; all are comfortable and well appointed. The public areas provide a high level of quality and luxury.

Rooms 73 (3 fmly) (33 GF) (20 smoking)
Facilities FTV Wi-fi ⬚ Xmas New Year **Conf** Class 50 Board 30 Thtr 80 **Parking** 42 **Notes** ⊗ Civ Wed 74

Premier Inn Ruislip

BUDGET HOTEL PLAN 1 A5

☎ 0871 527 8952
Ickenham Rd HA4 7DR
web: www.premierinn.com
dir: From Ruislip High St into Ickenham Rd (B466). At mini rdbt 1st exit (The Orchard on left)

High quality, budget accommodation ideal for both families and business travellers. Spacious, en suite bedrooms feature tea and coffee making facilities,

and Freeview TV in most hotels. Internet access and Wi-fi are available for a small fee. The adjacent family restaurant features a wide and varied menu. See also the Hotel Groups pages.

Rooms 20

RUNCORN
Cheshire Map 15 SJ58

Holiday Inn Runcorn

★★★ 73% HOTEL *Holiday Inn*

☎ 0871 942 9070
Wood Ln, Beechwood WA7 3HA
e-mail: jonathan.huglin@ihg.com
web: www.holidayinn.co.uk
dir: M56 junct 12, left at rdbt, 100yds on left into Halton Station Rd under rail bridge, into Wood Ln

This modern hotel offers extensive conference, meeting and leisure facilities. The bedrooms are well equipped and the spacious restaurant is open for lunch and dinner with an all-day menu provided in the lounge and bar. There is also a well equipped leisure centre and extensive conference facilities available.

Rooms 153 (149 fmly) (31 GF) **Facilities** STV Wi-fi HL ⬚ supervised Gym Xmas New Year **Conf** Class 250 Board 60 Thtr 500 **Services** Lift Air con **Parking** 250 **Notes** Civ Wed 500

Campanile Runcorn

Campanile

BUDGET HOTEL

☎ 01928 581771
Lowlands Rd WA7 5TP
e-mail: runcorn@campanile.com
web: www.campanile.com
dir: M56 junct 12, A557, follow signs for Runcorn rail station/Runcorn College

This modern building offers accommodation in smart, well-equipped bedrooms, all with en suite bathrooms. Refreshments may be taken at the informal bistro. See also the Hotel Groups pages.

Rooms 53 (18 GF) **Conf** Class 24 Board 24 Thtr 35

Premier Inn Runcorn

BUDGET HOTEL

☎ 0871 527 8954
Chester Rd, Preston Brook WA7 3BB
web: www.premierinn.com
dir: 1m from M56 junct 11, at Preston Brook

High quality, budget accommodation ideal for both families and business travellers. Spacious, en suite bedrooms feature tea and coffee making facilities, and Freeview TV in most hotels. Internet access and Wi-fi are available for a small fee. The adjacent

family restaurant features a wide and varied menu. See also the Hotel Groups pages.

Rooms 43

RUSPER
West Sussex Map 6 TQ23

Ghyll Manor

★★★ 86% ◉ COUNTRY HOUSE HOTEL

☎ 0845 345 3426
High St RH12 4PX
e-mail: enquiries@ghyllmanor.co.uk
web: www.ghyllmanor.co.uk
dir: A24 onto A264. Exit at Faygate, follow signs for Rusper, 2m to village

Located in the quiet village of Rusper, this traditional mansion house is set in 45 acres of idyllic, peaceful grounds. Accommodation is in either the main house or a range of courtyard-style cottages. A pre-dinner drink can be taken beside the fire, followed by an imaginative meal in the charming restaurant.

Rooms 29 (20 annexe) (7 fmly) (18 GF) ⬚
Facilities STV FTV Wi-fi ⬚ ⬚ Gym Xmas New Year
Conf Class 60 Board 40 Thtr 120 **Parking** 50
Notes Civ Wed 120

RYDE
Isle of Wight Map 5 SZ59

Lakeside Park Hotel

★★★★ 75% HOTEL

☎ 01983 882266
High St PO33 4LJ
e-mail: reception@lakesideparkhotel.com
web: www.lakesideparkhotel.com
dir: A3054 towards Newport. Hotel on left after crossing Wotton Bridge

This hotel has picturesque views of the tidal lake and surrounding countryside. Bedrooms are well appointed with modern amenities and stylish design, with guest comfort in mind. Public areas feature a comfortable open-plan bar and lounge, and two restaurants that showcase the best of island produce. Sizable conference and banqueting facilities are available while the leisure area includes an indoor pool and spa therapy.

Rooms 44 (2 fmly) (16 GF) ⬚ **D** £120–£175 (incl. bkfst)* **Facilities** Spa FTV Wi-fi ⬚ Sauna Steam room Relaxation room **Conf** Class 60 Board 40 Thtr 150 **Services** Lift Air con **Parking** 140 **Notes** ⊗ Civ Wed 120

R

RYDE *continued*

Yelf's Hotel

★★★ 73% HOTEL

☎ 01983 564062
Union St PO33 2LG
e-mail: manager@yelfshotel.com
web: www.yelfshotel.com
dir: From Esplanade into Union St. Hotel on right

This former coaching inn has smart public areas including a busy bar, a separate lounge and an attractive dining room. Bedrooms are comfortably furnished and well equipped; some are located in an adjoining wing and some in an annexe. A conservatory lounge bar and stylish terrace are ideal for relaxing.

Rooms 40 (9 annexe) (5 fmly) (3 GF) (3 smoking) 🐾
Facilities STV FTV Wi-fi Spa & treatments at sister hotel nearby **Conf** Class 30 Board 50 Thtr 100 Del £130* **Services** Lift **Parking** 23 **Notes** ⊗ Civ Wed 100

Appley Manor Hotel

★★ 74% HOTEL

☎ 01983 564777
Appley Rd PO33 1PH
e-mail: appleymanor@live.co.uk
web: www.appley-manor.co.uk
dir: A3055 onto B3330. Hotel 0.25m on left

A Victorian manor house located only five minutes from the town and set in peaceful surroundings. The spacious bedrooms are well furnished and decorated. Dinner can be taken in the popular adjoining Manor Inn.

Rooms 12 (2 fmly) **S** £56; **D** £66* **Facilities** FTV Wi-fi **Conf** Class 40 Board 30 Thtr 40 **Parking** 60 **Notes** ⊗

RYE	
East Sussex	Map 7 TQ92

The George in Rye

★★★★ 78% ⚘ HOTEL

☎ 01797 222114
98 High St TN31 7JT
e-mail: stay@thegeorgeinrye.com
dir: M20 junct 10, A2070 to Brenzett, A259 to Rye

This attractive 16th-century property, situated in the heart of historic Rye, has been sympathetically styled to retain many original features including a stunning Georgian ballroom complete with a minstrels' gallery. The bedrooms are stylishly appointed and filled with an abundance of thoughtful touches. Contemporary public areas include a bar, lounge and dining room plus an excellent alfresco area for summer dining.

Rooms 34 (3 GF) 🐾 **D** £135-£295 (incl. bkfst)*
Facilities FTV Wi-fi Xmas New Year **Conf** Class 65 Board 40 Thtr 100 **Notes** ⊗ Civ Wed 100

Mermaid Inn

★★★ 82% ⚘⚘ HOTEL

☎ 01797 223065 & 223788
Mermaid St TN31 7EY
e-mail: info@mermaidinn.com
web: www.mermaidinn.com
dir: A259, follow signs to town centre, then into Mermaid St

Situated near the top of a cobbled side street, this famous smugglers' inn is steeped in history, dating back to 1450 with 12th-century cellars. The charming interior has many architectural features such as attractive stone work. The bedrooms vary in size and style but all are tastefully furnished; there are no less than eight four-posters, and the Elizabethan and Dr Syn's Bedchambers are particularly noteworthy. Delightful public rooms include a choice of lounges, cosy bar and smart restaurant.

Rooms 31 (5 fmly) **S** fr £75; **D** fr £150 (incl. bkfst)*
Facilities Wi-fi Xmas New Year **Conf** Class 40 Board 30 Thtr 50 Del £160* **Parking** 25 **Notes** LB ⊗

Rye Lodge Hotel

★★★ 79% METRO HOTEL

☎ 01797 223838 & 226688
Hilders Cliff TN31 7LD
e-mail: info@ryelodge.co.uk
web: www.ryelodge.co.uk
dir: On one-way system follow town centre signs, through Landgate arch, hotel 100yds on right

Standing in an elevated position, Rye Lodge has panoramic views across Romney Marshes and the Rother Estuary. Traditionally styled bedrooms come in a variety of sizes; they are attractively decorated and thoughtfully equipped. Public rooms feature indoor leisure facilities and the Terrace Room Restaurant where home-made dishes are offered. Lunch and afternoon tea are served on the flower-filled outdoor terrace in warmer months.

Rooms 19 (5 GF) 🐾 **S** £75-£125; **D** £85-£220*
Facilities STV FTV Wi-fi ♨ HL 🕥 Aromatherapy Steam cabinet Sauna Exercise machines **Parking** 20 **Notes** LB

The Hope Anchor Hotel

★★★ 78% SMALL HOTEL

☎ 01797 222216
Watchbell St TN31 7HA
e-mail: info@thehopeanchor.co.uk
web: www.thehopeanchor.co.uk
dir: From A268, Quayside, right into Wish Ward, into Mermaid St, right into West St, right into Watchbell St, hotel at end

This historic inn sits high above the town with enviable views out over the harbour and Romney Marsh, and is accessible via delightful cobbled streets. A relaxed and friendly atmosphere prevails within the cosy public rooms, while the attractively furnished bedrooms are well equipped and many enjoy good views over the marshes.

Rooms 16 (3 fmly) (1 GF) 🐾 **S** £75-£160; **D** £110-£180 (incl. bkfst)* **Facilities** FTV Wi-fi Xmas New Year **Conf** Class 30 Board 20 Thtr 40 Del from £125 to £160* **Parking** 12 **Notes** LB Civ Wed 40

The Riverhaven Hotel

★★★ 71% HOTEL

☎ 01797 227982
Quayside, Winchelsea Rd TN31 7EL
e-mail: info@riverhaven.co.uk

Located by the Strand Quay over looking the River Tillingham, this hotel is located in the historic town of Rye and just a couple of minutes walk into the town centre. Accommodation is traditional in style and very comfortable. There is a riverside restaurant where breakfast and dinner are served daily. There is plenty of parking available on site, which is a clear benefit for this area.

Rooms 22 **S** £55-£80; **D** £80-£100 (incl. bkfst)*
Notes Closed 24-27 Dec

White Vine House

RESTAURANT WITH ROOMS

☎ 01797 224748
24 High St TN31 7JF
e-mail: info@whitevinehouse.co.uk
dir: In town centre

Situated in the heart of the ancient Cinque Port town of Rye, this property's origins go back to the 13th century. The cellar is the oldest part, but the current building dates from 1560 and boasts an impressive Georgian frontage. The original timber framework is

R

visible in many areas, and certainly adds to the house's sense of history. The bedrooms have period furniture along with luxury bath or shower rooms; one bedroom has an antique four-poster.

Rooms 7 (1 fmly)

ST AGNES	Map 2 SW75
Cornwall	

Rose-in-Vale Country House Hotel

★★★★ 71% ⏝ COUNTRY HOUSE HOTEL

☎ 01872 552202
Mithian TR5 0QD
e-mail: reception@rose-in-vale-hotel.co.uk
web: www.rose-in-vale-hotel.co.uk
dir: A30 S towards Redruth. At Chiverton Cross at rdbt take B3277 signed St Agnes. In 500mtrs follow tourist sign for Rose-in-Vale. Into Mithian, right at Miners Arms, down hill. Hotel on left

Peacefully located in a wooded valley, this Georgian manor house has a wonderfully relaxed atmosphere and abundant charm. Guests are assured of a warm welcome. Accommodation varies in size and style; several rooms are situated on the ground floor. An imaginative fixed-price menu featuring local produce is served in the spacious restaurant.

Rooms 23 (3 annexe) (1 fmly) (6 GF) ⟟ **Facilities** FTV Wi-fi ▷ ⤳ ⥇ ♫ Xmas New Year **Conf** Class 50 Board 40 Thtr 75 **Services** Lift **Parking** 50 **Notes** No children 12yrs Civ Wed 80

Beacon Country House Hotel

★★★ 75% SMALL HOTEL

☎ 01872 552318
Goonvrea Rd TR5 0NW
e-mail: info@beaconhotel.co.uk
dir: A30 onto B3277 to St Agnes. At rdbt left into Goonvrea Rd. Hotel 0.75m on right

Set in a quiet and attractive area away from the busy village, this family-run, relaxed hotel has splendid views over the countryside and along the coast to St Ives. Hospitality and customer care are great strengths, with guests assured of a very warm and friendly stay. Bedrooms are comfortable and well equipped, and many benefit from glorious views.

Rooms 11 (2 fmly) (2 GF) ⟟ **Facilities** FTV Wi-fi ▷ Xmas New Year **Conf** Class 20 Board 20 **Parking** 12 **Notes** No children 8yrs Closed 4-31 Jan

Rosemundy House Hotel

★★★ 71% HOTEL

☎ 01872 552101
Rosemundy Hill TR5 0UF
e-mail: info@rosemundy.co.uk
dir: A30 to St Agnes, approx 3m. On entering village 1st right signed Rosemundy, hotel at foot of hill

This elegant Queen Anne house has been carefully restored and extended to provide comfortable bedrooms and spacious, inviting public areas. The hotel is set in well-maintained gardens complete with an outdoor pool which is available in warmer months. There is a choice of relaxing lounges and a cosy bar.

Rooms 46 (3 fmly) (9 GF) ⟟ **S** £48-£66; **D** £96-£132 (incl. bkfst)* **Facilities** FTV Wi-fi ⤳ Putt green ⥇ ♫ Xmas New Year **Conf** Board 80 **Parking** 50 **Notes** ⊗ No children 5yrs

ST ALBANS	Map 6 TL10
Hertfordshire	

St Michael's Manor

★★★★ 79% ⏝⏝ HOTEL

☎ 01727 864444
Fishpool St AL3 4RY
e-mail: reservations@stmichaelsmanor.com
web: www.stmichaelsmanor.com
dir: From St Albans Abbey follow Fishpool Street towards St Michael's village. Hotel 0.5m on left

Hidden from the street, adjacent to listed buildings, mills and ancient inns, this hotel, with a history dating back 500 years, is set in six acres of beautiful landscaped grounds. Inside there is a real sense of luxury, the high standard of decor and attentive service is complemented by award-winning food; the elegant restaurant overlooks the gardens and lake. The bedrooms are individually styled and have satellite TVs, DVDs and free internet access.

Rooms 30 (8 annexe) (3 fmly) (4 GF) (6 smoking) ⟟ **S** fr £145; (incl. bkfst)* **Facilities** STV FTV Wi-fi ▷ ⤳ Licenced fishing in season Guided tours New Year **Conf** Class 20 Board 27 Thtr 30 **Del** from £190 to £295* **Services** Air con **Parking** 60 **Notes** ⊗ Civ Wed 140

Sopwell House

★★★★ 79% ⏝ HOTEL

☎ 01707 864477
Cottonmill Ln, Sopwell AL1 2HQ
e-mail: enquiries@sopwellhouse.co.uk
web: www.sopwellhouse.co.uk
dir: M25 junct 21a, 1st exit rdbt to A405. A414 towards St Albans/Hatfield. Slip road Shenley, mini rdbt left

This fine country house hotel is situated in 12 acres of beautifully landscaped gardens and the house overlooks the hotel's golf course. Sopwell House Hotel was once the country home of Lord Mountbatten and has undergone major renovations in 2012. The bedrooms are all very well appointed and the leisure facilities are impressive. Afternoon teas are served in the comfortable lounges and there is a choice of restaurants for dinner. .

Rooms 129 (16 annexe) (28 fmly) (7 GF) **Facilities** Spa STV FTV Wi-fi ▷ ⥀ Gym Sauna Steam room Dance studio Xmas New Year **Conf** Class 160 Board 110 Thtr 380 **Del** from £200 to £280* **Services** Lift Air con **Parking** 250 **Notes** ⊗ Civ Wed 380

Thistle St Albans

thistle

★★★★ 72% HOTEL

☎ 0871 376 9034
Watford Rd AL2 3DS
e-mail: stalbans@thistle.co.uk
web: www.thistlehotels.com/stalbans
dir: M1 junct 6/M25 junct 21a, follow St. Albans signs, A405. Hotel 0.5m

Conveniently located for access to both the M1 and M25, this Victorian hotel lies within its own grounds and has secure parking. Bedrooms are neatly appointed in a traditional style. Public areas include a choice of restaurants, The Noke or the more informal Oak and Avocado, and there is also a small modern leisure club.

Rooms 110 (2 fmly) (56 GF) **Facilities** FTV Wi-fi ⥀ supervised Gym Sauna Steam room Beauty treatment room **Conf** Class 30 Board 30 Thtr 300 **Parking** 150 **Notes** ⊗ Civ Wed 100

S

ST ALBANS *continued*

Quality Hotel St Albans

★★★ 73% HOTEL

☎ 01727 857858
232-236 London Rd AL1 1JQ
e-mail: st.albans@quality-hotels.net
dir: M25 junct 22 follow A1081 to St Albans, after
2.5m hotel on left, before overhead bridge

This smartly presented property is conveniently
situated close to the major road networks and the
railway station. The contemporary style bedrooms
have co-ordinated fabrics and a good range of useful
facilities. Public rooms include an open-plan lounge
bar and brasserie restaurant. The hotel has a leisure
complex along with air-conditioned meeting rooms.

Rooms 81 (7 fmly) (14 GF) ✿ **S** £45-£90; **D** £65-£115
(incl. bkfst)* **Facilities** STV FTV Wi-fi ↻ 🏊 supervised
Gym Saunarium Sunbed Beauty treatments
Conf Class 40 Board 50 Thtr 200 Del from £82 to
£196* **Services** Lift **Parking** 80 **Notes** ⊗

Ardmore House Hotel

THE INDEPENDENTS
HOTEL ASSOCIATION

★★★ 🅰 HOTEL

☎ 01727 859313
54 Lemsford Rd AL1 3PR
e-mail: info@ardmorehousehotel.co.uk
web: www.ardmorehousehotel.co.uk
dir: A1081 signed St Albans, through 3 sets of lights
& 2 mini rdbts. Right at 3rd mini rdbt, through 2 sets
of lights. Hotel on right in 800yds

Located in immaculate surroundings close to the
town centre and cathedral, this extended Edwardian
house and annexe provides a range of facilities much
appreciated by a loyal commercial clientele. The
practically furnished bedrooms offer a good range of
facilities and the extensive public areas include a
spacious conservatory dining room.

Rooms 40 (4 annexe) (5 fmly) (5 GF)
S £67.50-£71.50; **D** £79.50-£145 (incl. bkfst)*
Facilities STV FTV Wi-fi ↻ **Conf** Class 50 Board 50
Thtr 130 Del from £140* **Parking** 40 **Notes** LB ⊗
Civ Wed 150

Premier Inn Luton South M1 Jct 9

BUDGET HOTEL

☎ 0871 527 8334
London Rd, Flamstead AL3 8HT
web: www.premierinn.com
dir: M1 junct 9, A5 towards Dunstable

High quality, budget accommodation ideal for both
families and business travellers. Spacious, en suite
bedrooms feature tea and coffee making facilities,

and Freeview TV in most hotels. Internet access and
Wi-fi are available for a small fee. The adjacent
family restaurant features a wide and varied menu.
See also the Hotel Groups pages.

Rooms 75

ST ANNES

See **Lytham St Annes**

ST AUSTELL
Cornwall

Map 2 SX05

Carlyon Bay Hotel

★★★★ 79% 🏵 HOTEL

☎ 01726 812304
Sea Rd, Carlyon Bay PL25 3RD
e-mail: reservations@carlyonbay.com
web: www.carlyonbay.com
dir: From St Austell, follow signs for Charlestown.
Carlyon Bay signed on left, hotel at end of Sea Rd

Built in the 1920s, this long-established hotel sits on
the cliff top in 250 acres of grounds which include
indoor and outdoor pools, a golf course and a spa.
Bedrooms are well maintained, and many have
marvellous views across St Austell Bay. A good choice
of comfortable lounges is available, while facilities
for families include kids' clubs and entertainment.

Rooms 86 (14 fmly) ✿ **S** £75-£145; **D** £130-£390*
Facilities Spa FTV Wi-fi ↻ 🏓 ⚓ ⅃ 18 🏌 Putt green
Gym Hydrotherapy spa pool Hot stone beds ♫ Xmas
New Year Child facilities **Conf** Thtr 150 **Services** Lift
Parking 100 **Notes** LB ⊗ Civ Wed 100

See advert on opposite page

The Cornwall Hotel, Spa & Estate

★★★★ 75% 🏵 COUNTRY HOUSE HOTEL

☎ 01726 874050
Pentewan Rd, Tregorrick PL26 7AB
e-mail: enquiries@thecornwall.com
dir: A391 to St Austell then B3273 towards
Mevagissey. Hotel approx 0.5m on right

Set in 43 acres of wooded parkland, this renovated
manor house offers guests a real retreat. The restored
White House has suites and traditionally styled
bedrooms, and adjoining are the contemporary
Woodland rooms ranging across standard, family,
accessible, and also deluxe which have private
balcony areas overlooking the Pentewan Valley. There
are superb leisure facilities including the spa with
luxury treatments, an infinity pool and state-of-the-
art fitness centre. There is a choice of eating options -
The Arboretum and the more informal Acorns plus the
Drawing Room and Parkland Terrace for afternoon tea
and cocktails. This is an ideal base for visiting The
Eden Project, The Lost Gardens of Heligan and south
Cornwall fishing villages.

Rooms 65 (4 fmly) **Facilities** Spa STV FTV Wi-fi ↻ ❄
🏊 💆 Gym Xmas New Year **Conf** Class 30 Board 14
Thtr 50 **Services** Lift **Parking** 200 **Notes** Civ Wed 60

Porth Avallen Hotel

★★★ 77% HOTEL

☎ 01726 812802
Sea Rd, Carlyon Bay PL25 3SG
e-mail: info@porthavallen.co.uk
web: www.porthavallen.co.uk
dir: A30 onto A391 to St Austell. Right onto A390. Left
at lights, follow brown signs, left at rdbt, right into
Sea Rd

This traditional hotel boasts panoramic views over
the rugged Cornish coastline. It offers smartly
appointed public areas and well-presented bedrooms,
many with sea views. There is an oak-panelled lounge
and conservatory; both are ideal for relaxation.
Extensive dining options, including the stylish
Reflections Restaurant, invite guests to choose from
fixed-price, carte and all-day brasserie menus. The
Olive Garden, inspired by the Mediterranean, is a
lovely place to eat alfresco.

Rooms 28 (3 fmly) (3 GF) ✿ **S** £50-£75; **D** £80-£115
(incl. bkfst)* **Facilities** FTV Wi-fi Xmas New Year
Conf Class 100 Board 80 Thtr 160 Del from £110 to
£140* **Parking** 60 **Notes** LB ⊗ Civ Wed 160

S

Save on hotels. Book at **theAA.com/hotel**

ST 383 ENGLAND

BEST WESTERN Cliff Head Hotel

★★★ 75% HOTEL

☎ 01726 812345
Sea Rd, Carlyon Bay PL25 3RB
e-mail: info@cliffheadhotel.com
web: www.cliffheadhotel.com
dir: 2m E off A390

Set in extensive grounds and conveniently located for visiting the Eden Project, this hotel faces south and enjoys views over Carlyon Bay. A choice of lounges is provided, together with a seasonal swimming pool and sauna. Bay Restaurant offers a range of menus, which feature an interesting selection of dishes.

Rooms 57 (4 fmly) (11 GF) ↑ **Facilities** FTV Wi-fi ↘ Xmas **Conf** Class 90 Board 50 Thtr 150 **Parking** 60 **Notes** Civ Wed 70

The Pier House

★★★ 75% HOTEL

☎ 01726 67955
Harbour Front, Charlestown PL25 3NJ
e-mail: pierhouse@btconnect.com
dir: A390 to St Austell, at Mt Charles rdbt left into Charlestown Rd

This genuinely friendly hotel boasts a wonderful harbour location. The unspoilt working port has been the setting for many film and television productions. Most bedrooms have sea views, and the hotel's convivial Harbourside Inn is popular with locals and tourists alike. Locally caught fish features on the varied and interesting restaurant menu.

Rooms 28 (2 annexe) (3 fmly) (2 GF) ↑ **S** £58-£68; **D** £110-£145 (incl. bkfst)* **Facilities** STV Wi-fi **Parking** 50 **Notes** ⊗ Closed 24-25 Dec

The White Hart Hotel

★★★ 75% HOTEL

☎ 01726 72100
Church St PL25 4AT
e-mail: info@whitehartstaustell.co.uk
dir: A30 then A391 towards St Austell. Follow signs to town centre

The White Hart Hotel retains the essence of an old coaching inn combined with up-to-date facilities and an enviable location. The bar offers award-winning St Austell Brewery Ales and a wide selection of wines and spirits while local and seasonal food is used on both menus. The accommodation is comfortable and offers all modern facilities. A large function room is the perfect setting for a range of events.

Rooms 17 (2 fmly) **S** £40-£80; **D** £55-£125 (incl. bkfst)* **Facilities** FTV Wi-fi **Conf** Class 35 Board 35 Thtr 50 **Parking** 15 **Notes** ⊗ Closed 25-26 Dec RS 24 Dec

Premier Inn St Austell

BUDGET HOTEL

☎ 0871 527 9018
St Austell Enterprise Park, Treverbyn Rd PL25 4EL
web: www.premierinn.com
dir: A30 onto A391 signed St Austell. Through Bugle. Continue on A391 at rdbt. Continue to follow St Austell signs. 1st exit at Carclaze rdbt. Hotel at St Austell Enterprise Park

High quality, budget accommodation ideal for both families and business travellers. Spacious, en suite bedrooms feature tea and coffee making facilities, and Freeview TV in most hotels. Internet access and Wi-fi are available for a small fee. The adjacent family restaurant features a wide and varied menu. See also the Hotel Groups pages.

Rooms 61

ST HELENS
Merseyside
Map 15 SJ59

Premier Inn St Helens (A580/East Lancs)

BUDGET HOTEL

☎ 0871 527 9020
Garswood Old Rd, East Lancs Rd WA11 7LX
web: www.premierinn.com
dir: 3m from M6 junct 23, on A580 towards Liverpool

High quality, budget accommodation ideal for both families and business travellers. Spacious, en suite bedrooms feature tea and coffee making facilities, and Freeview TV in most hotels. Internet access and Wi-fi are available for a small fee. The adjacent family restaurant features a wide and varied menu. See also the Hotel Groups pages.

Rooms 44

Premier Inn St Helens South

BUDGET HOTEL

☎ 0871 527 9022
Eurolink, Lea Green WA9 4TT
web: www.premierinn.com
dir: M62 junct 7, A570 towards St Helens

Rooms 40

ST IVES
Cambridgeshire
Map 12 TL37

Olivers Lodge Hotel

THE INDEPENDENTS
HOTEL ASSOCIATION

★★★ 74% HOTEL

☎ 01480 463252
Needingworth Rd PE27 5JP
e-mail: reception@oliverslodge.co.uk
web: www.oliverslodge.co.uk
dir: A14 towards Huntingdon/Cambridge, take B1040 to St Ives. Cross 1st rdbt, left at 2nd rdbt then 1st right. Hotel 500mtrs on right

A privately owned hotel situated in a peaceful residential area just a short walk from the town centre. Public rooms include a smart air-conditioned bar, a choice of lounges and a conservatory dining room. The pleasantly decorated bedrooms are equipped with modern facilities and have co-ordinated fabrics.

Rooms 20 (7 annexe) (3 fmly) (7 GF) **S** £62-£78; **D** £72-£90 (incl. bkfst)* **Facilities** FTV Wi-fi Free use of local leisure centre Xmas New Year **Conf** Class 30 Board 25 Thtr 65 Del from £120 to £150* **Parking** 25 **Notes** Civ Wed 65

The Dolphin Hotel

★★★ 70% HOTEL

☎ 01480 466966
London Rd PE27 5EP
e-mail: enquiries@dolphinhotelcambs.co.uk
dir: A14 between Huntingdon & Cambridge onto A1096 towards St Ives. Left at 1st rdbt & immediately right. Hotel on left after 0.5m

This modern hotel sits by delightful water meadows on the banks of the River Ouse. Open-plan public rooms include a choice of bars and a pleasant restaurant offering fine river views. The bedrooms are modern and varied in style; some are in the hotel while others occupy an adjacent wing; all are comfortable and spacious. Conference and function suites are available.

Rooms 67 (37 annexe) (4 fmly) (22 GF) (2 smoking) ♠ **Facilities** FTV ♭ Fishing Gym **Conf** Class 50 Board 50 Thtr 150 **Parking** 400 **Notes** ⊗ RS 24 Dec-2 Jan Civ Wed 60

ST IVES
Cornwall
Map 2 SW54

Carbis Bay Hotel

★★★ 81% ⊛ HOTEL

☎ 01736 795311
Carbis Bay TR26 2NP
e-mail: info@carbisbayhotel.co.uk
web: www.carbisbayhotel.co.uk
dir: A3074, through Lelant. 1m, at Carbis Bay 30yds before lights, right into Porthrepta Rd to hotel

In a peaceful location with access to its own white-sand beach, this hotel offers comfortable accommodation. The attractive public areas feature a smart bar and lounge, and a sun lounge overlooking the sea. Bedrooms, many with fine views, are well equipped. Interesting cuisine and particularly enjoyable breakfasts are offered. A small complex of luxury, self-catering apartments is available.

Rooms 47 (16 fmly) (3 GF) ♠ **Facilities** Spa Wi-fi ♭ Fishing Private beach ♫ Xmas New Year Child facilities **Conf** Class 80 Board 60 Thtr 120 Del £130 **Parking** 200 **Notes** ⊗ Civ Wed 150

Garrack Hotel & Restaurant

★★★ 78% ⊛ HOTEL

☎ 01736 796199
Burthallan Ln, Higher Ayr TR26 3AA
e-mail: aa@garrack.com
dir: Exit A30 for St Ives. From B3311 follow brown signs for Tate Gallery, then Garrack signs

Enjoying a peaceful, elevated position with splendid views across the harbour and Porthmeor Beach, the

Garrack sits in its own delightful grounds and gardens. Bedrooms are comfortable and many have sea views. Public areas include a small leisure suite, a choice of lounges and an attractive restaurant, where locally sourced ingredients are used in the enjoyable dishes.

Rooms 18 (2 annexe) (2 fmly) (3 GF) **Facilities** FTV Wi-fi ⊗ Gym New Year **Conf** Class 10 Board 10 Thtr 20 **Parking** 30

St Ives Harbour Hotel

★★★ 78% HOTEL

☎ 01736 795221
The Terrace TR26 2BN
e-mail: stives@harbourhotels.co.uk
web: www.stives-harbour-hotel.co.uk
dir: On A3074

This friendly hotel enjoys an enviable location with spectacular views of St Ives Bay. Extensive leisure facilities, a versatile function suite and a number of elegant and stylish lounges are available. The majority of bedrooms are appointed to a very high standard, and many rooms have spectacular sea views, as does the restaurant which looks out over the bay and golden sands below.

Rooms 46 (9 fmly) ♠ **Facilities** Spa FTV Wi-fi Gym Steam room Xmas New Year **Conf** Class 20 Board 35 Thtr 130 **Services** Lift **Parking** 60 **Notes** Civ Wed 160

Primrose Valley

★★★ 75% METRO HOTEL

☎ 01736 794939
Porthminster Beach TR26 2ED
e-mail: info@primroseonline.co.uk
web: www.primroseonline.co.uk
dir: A3074 to St Ives, 25yds after town sign right into Primrose Valley, left under bridge, along beach front, left back under bridge, property on left

St Ives is just a short walk from this stylish, friendly, family-run establishment close to Porthminster Beach. The property is light and airy, and modernisation has resulted in good levels of comfort; some bedrooms have balconies with stunning views. There is a lounge and bar area, and breakfast features local produce and home-made items.

Rooms 10 ♠ **S** £65-£100; **D** £75-£170 (incl. bkfst)* **Facilities** FTV Wi-fi ♨ **Parking** 11 **Notes** LB ⊗ No children 8yrs Closed 22-26 Dec

Save on hotels. Book at **theAA.com/hotel**

ST 385 ENGLAND

Tregenna Castle Hotel

★★★ 74% HOTEL

☎ 01736 795254
TR26 2DE
e-mail: hotel@tregenna-castle.co.uk
web: www.tregenna-castle.co.uk
dir: A30 from Exeter to Penzance, at Lelant take
A3074 to St Ives, through Carbis Bay, main entrance
signed on left

Sitting at the top of town in beautiful landscaped
sub-tropical gardens with woodland walks, this
popular hotel boasts spectacular views of St Ives.
Many leisure facilities are available, including indoor
and outdoor pools, a gym and a sauna. Families are
particularly welcome. The individually designed
bedrooms are in general, spacious. There are two
restaurants, the Trelawny Room and the Godrevy
Room, and a brasserie provides lighter options in a
less formal atmosphere.

Rooms 81 (37 fmly) (16 GF) ♠ **Facilities** Spa STV FTV
Wi-fi HL ⬚ ⚲ supervised ♨ 18 ♗ Putt green ⚑ Gym
Squash Steam room Badminton court ⊓ Xmas New
Year Child facilities **Conf** Class 150 Board 30
Thtr 250 **Services** Lift **Parking** 200 **Notes** ⊗
Civ Wed 160

Chy-an-Albany Hotel

★★★ 72% HOTEL

☎ 01736 796759
Albany Ter TR26 2BS
e-mail: info@chyanalbanyhotel.com
dir: A30 onto A3074 signed St Ives, hotel on left just
before junct

Conveniently located, this pleasant hotel enjoys
splendid sea views. The comfortable bedrooms come
in a variety of sizes; some featuring balconies for
enjoying those sea views. The friendly staff and the
relaxing environment mean that some guests return
on a regular basis. Freshly prepared and appetising
cuisine is served in the dining room and a bar menu
is also available.

Rooms 39 (9 fmly) ♠ **Facilities** FTV Wi-fi
Conf Class 30 Board 30 Thtr 50 **Services** Lift
Parking 33 **Notes** ⊗ Civ Wed 70

Cottage Hotel

★★ 71% HOTEL

 Leisureplex

☎ 01736 795252
Boskerris Rd, Carbis Bay TR26 2PE
e-mail: cottage.stives@alfatravel.co.uk
web: www.leisureplex.co.uk
dir: From A30 take A3074 to Carbis Bay. Right into
Porthreptor Rd. Just before rail bridge, left through
railway car park into hotel car park

Set in quiet, lush gardens, this pleasant hotel offers
friendly and attentive service. Smart bedrooms are
pleasantly spacious and many rooms enjoy splendid
views. Public areas are varied and include a snooker
room, a comfortable lounge and a spacious dining
room with sea views over the beach and Carbis Bay.

Rooms 80 (7 fmly) (2 GF) **Facilities** FTV ⚲ Snooker
⊓ Xmas New Year **Services** Lift **Parking** 20 **Notes** ⊗
Closed Dec-Feb (ex Xmas) RS Nov & Mar

ST LEONARDS-ON-SEA

See Hastings & St Leonards

ST MARY CHURCH

See Torquay

ST MARY'S
Cornwall (Isles of Scilly) Map 2 SV91

Tregarthen's Hotel

★★★ 80% HOTEL

☎ 01720 422540
Hugh Town TR21 0PP
e-mail: reception@tregarthens-hotel.co.uk
dir: 100yds from town & quay

Opened in 1848 by Captain Tregarthen, this well-
established hotel has impressive public areas that
provide wonderful views overlooking St Mary's
harbour and some of the many islands, including
Tresco and Bryher. Bedrooms are well equipped and
neatly furnished. Traditional cuisine is served in the
restaurant.

Rooms 33 (1 annexe) (8 fmly) ♠ S £140-£205; (incl.
bkfst & dinner)* **Facilities** FTV Wi-fi Spa & beauty
treatments available **Conf** Class 20 Board 15 Thtr 30
Notes LB ⊗ Closed late Oct-mid Mar

ST MELLION
Cornwall Map 3 SX36

St Mellion International Resort

★★★★ 81% ⚘⚘ HOTEL

☎ 01579 351351
PL12 6SD
e-mail: stmellion@crown-golf.co.uk
dir: From M5, A38 towards Plymouth & Saltash. St
Mellion off A38 on A388 towards Callington &
Launceston

Set in 450 acres of Cornish countryside, this
impressive golfing and leisure complex has much to
offer. A vast range of leisure facilities are provided,
including three pools, spa facilities and a health
club. In addition, the hotel also boasts a choice of
championship golf courses. The Jack Nicklaus
signature course has hosted many PGA tour events.
The bedrooms provide contemporary comforts and
many have views across the course. Public areas are
equally stylish with a choice of dining options
including An Boesti, a fine-dining restaurant
overlooking the 18th green.

Rooms 80 (20 fmly) (18 GF) **Facilities** Spa FTV Wi-fi ⬚
⬚ supervised ♨ 36 ♗ Putt green Gym Studio classes
Lawn bowls Xmas New Year **Conf** Class 200 Board 80
Thtr 400 **Services** Lift Air con **Parking** 450 **Notes** ⊗
Civ Wed 300

ST NEOTS
Cambridgeshire Map 12 TL16

The George Hotel & Brasserie

★★★ 88% ⚘⚘ HOTEL

☎ 01480 812300
High St, Buckden PE19 5XA
e-mail: mail@thegeorgebuckden.com
web: www.thegeorgebuckden.com
dir: 2m S of A1 & A14 junct at Buckden

Ideally situated in the heart of this historic town
centre and just a short drive from the A1. Public
rooms feature a bustling ground-floor brasserie,
which offers casual dining throughout the day and
evening; there is also an informal lounge bar with an
open fire and comfy seating. Bedrooms are stylish,
tastefully appointed and thoughtfully equipped.

Rooms 12 (1 fmly) ♠ S £95-£150; D £120-£150
(incl. bkfst)* **Facilities** STV Wi-fi ⬚ **Conf** Class 30
Board 30 Thtr 50 Del from £160 to £180*
Services Lift **Parking** 25 **Notes** LB Civ Wed 60

S

ST NEOTS *continued*

Abbotsley Golf Hotel

★★★ 64% HOTEL

☎ 01480 474000
Potton Rd, Eynesbury Hardwicke PE19 6XN
e-mail: manager@abbotsley.com
web: www.abbotsley.com

Situated in a rural location on the outskirts of St
Neots, this property is set in 250-acre grounds with
two golf courses, a golf school and leisure complex.
The well-equipped bedrooms are situated in a
courtyard and another adjacent block; some rooms
have views over the golf course. Public rooms include
two bars, a conservatory dining room and a choice of
lounges.

Rooms 42 (42 annexe) (2 fmly) (29 GF) **Facilities** FTV
Wi-fi ⅃ 45 Putt green Gym Squash ♫ Xmas New Year
Conf Class 60 Board 60 Thtr 80 **Parking** 200
Notes Civ Wed 90

Premier Inn St Neots (A1/ Wyboston)

BUDGET HOTEL

☎ 0871 527 9024
Great North Rd, Eaton Socon PE19 8EN
web: www.premierinn.com
dir: Just off A1 at rdbt of A428 & B1428 before St
Neots. 1m from St Neots rail station

High quality, budget accommodation ideal for both
families and business travellers. Spacious, en suite
bedrooms feature tea and coffee making facilities,
and Freeview TV in most hotels. Internet access and
Wi-fi are available for a small fee. The adjacent
family restaurant features a wide and varied menu.
See also the Hotel Groups pages.

Rooms 65

Premier Inn St Neots (Colmworth Park)

BUDGET HOTEL

☎ 0871 527 9026
2 Marlborough Rd, Colmworth Business Park
PE19 8YP
web: www.premierinn.com
dir: From A1 N'bound: A428 towards Cambridge. 2nd
exit at rdbt onto A4128 signed St Neots. Hotel on
right. From A1 S'bound: follow A428 Cambridge signs.
At rdbt 1st exit onto A4128 signed St Neots, hotel on
right

Rooms 41

SALCOMBE   Map 3 SX73
Devon

Thurlestone Hotel

★★★★ 83% ◉ HOTEL

☎ 01548 560382
TQ7 3NN
e-mail: enquiries@thurlestone.co.uk
web: www.thurlestone.co.uk

(For full entry see Thurlestone)

Soar Mill Cove Hotel

★★★★ 79% ◉◉ HOTEL

☎ 01548 561566
Soar Mill Cove, Malborough TQ7 3DS
e-mail: info@soarmillcove.co.uk
web: www.soarmillcove.co.uk
dir: 3m W of town off A381 at Malborough. Follow
Soar signs

Situated amid spectacular scenery with dramatic sea
views, this hotel is ideal for a relaxing stay. Family-
run, with a committed team, keen standards of
hospitality and service are upheld. Bedrooms are well
equipped and many have private terraces. There are
different seating areas where, if guests wish,
impressive cream teas can be enjoyed, and for the
more active, there's a choice of swimming pools.
Local produce and seafood are used to good effect in
the restaurant.

Rooms 22 (5 fmly) (21 GF) ♪ £115-£250;
D £140-£275* **Facilities** FTV Wi-fi ⓢ ⌇ Putt green
Gym Table tennis Games room Beauty treatment room
Leisure complex ♫ Xmas Child facilities
Conf Class 50 Board 50 Thtr 100 **Parking** 30
Notes LB Closed 2 Jan-8 Feb Civ Wed 150

Tides Reach Hotel

★★★ 83% ◉ HOTEL

☎ 01548 843466
South Sands TQ8 8LJ
e-mail: enquire@tidesreach.com
web: www.tidesreach.com
dir: Exit A38 at Buckfastleigh to Totnes. Then A381 to
Salcombe, follow signs to South Sands

Superbly situated at the water's edge, this personally
run, friendly hotel has splendid views of the estuary
and beach. Bedrooms, many with balconies, are
spacious and comfortable. In the bar and lounge,
attentive service can be enjoyed along with the view,
and the Garden Room restaurant serves appetising
and accomplished cuisine.

Rooms 32 (5 fmly) ♪ S £85-£150; D £150-£350
(incl. bkfst & dinner)* **Facilities** Spa STV FTV Wi-fi ⓢ
supervised Gym Squash Windsurfing Sailing Kayaking
Scuba diving Hair & beauty treatment **Services** Lift
Parking 100 **Notes** LB No children 8yrs Closed
Dec-early Feb

SALE   Map 15 SJ79
Greater Manchester

Premier Inn Manchester (Sale)

BUDGET HOTEL

☎ 0871 527 8716
Carrington Ln, Ashton-upon-Mersey M33 5BL
web: www.premierinn.com
dir: M60 junct 8, A6144(M) towards Carrington. Left
at 1st lights, hotel on left

High quality, budget accommodation ideal for both
families and business travellers. Spacious, en suite
bedrooms feature tea and coffee making facilities,
and Freeview TV in most hotels. Internet access and
Wi-fi are available for a small fee. The adjacent
family restaurant features a wide and varied menu.
See also the Hotel Groups pages.

Rooms 43

Save on hotels. Book at **theAA.com/hotel**

ST – SAL 387 ENGLAND

SALISBURY
Wiltshire
Map 5 SU12

Mercure Salisbury White Hart Hotel

★★★★ 74% HOTEL

☎ 0870 400 8125 & 01722 327476
St John St SP1 2SD
e-mail: H6616@accor.com
web: www.mercure.com
dir: M3 juncts 7/8, A303 to A343 for Salisbury then A30. Follow city centre signs on ring road, into Exeter St, leading into St John St. Car park at rear on Brown St

There has been a hotel on this site since the 16th century. Bedrooms vary - some are contemporary and some are decorated in more traditional style, but all boast a comprehensive range of facilities. The bar and lounge areas are popular with guests and locals alike for morning coffees and afternoon teas.

Rooms 68 (6 fmly) **Facilities** STV Wi-fi Xmas New Year **Conf** Class 40 Board 40 Thtr 100 **Parking** 60 **Notes** Civ Wed 100

Milford Hall Hotel

CLASSIC
BRITISH HOTELS

★★★★ 73% ⊛ HOTEL

☎ 01722 417411 & 424116
206 Castle St SP1 3TE
e-mail: reception@milfordhallhotel.com
web: www.milfordhallhotel.com
dir: Near junct of Castle St, A36 (ring road) & A345 (Amesbury road)

This hotel offers high standards of accommodation and is within easy walking distance of the city centre. There are two categories of bedroom - traditional rooms in the original Georgian house, and spacious, modern rooms in a purpose-built extension; all are extremely well equipped. Meals are served in the smart brasserie where a varied choice of dishes is provided.

Rooms 45 (2 fmly) (22 GF) ☂ **S** £79-£129; **D** £79-£198* **Facilities** STV FTV Wi-fi Xmas New Year **Conf** Class 90 Board 60 Thtr 200 **Parking** 60 **Notes** LB ⊗ Civ Wed 120

The Legacy Rose & Crown Hotel

 LEGACY HOTELS

★★★★ 72% HOTEL

☎ 08444 119046 & 0330 333 2846
Harnham Rd SP2 8JQ
e-mail: res-roseandcrown@legacy-hotels.co.uk
web: www.legacy-hotels.co.uk
dir: M3 junct 8, A303 & follow Salisbury Ring Road & A338 towards Harnham then Harnham Rd. Hotel on right

This 13th-century coaching inn, situated beside the river, enjoys picturesque views of Salisbury Cathedral, especially from the Pavilion Restaurant which provides a good range of dishes. Many original features are still retained in the heavy oak-beamed bars. All bedrooms and bathrooms are beautifully appointed. Excellent conference and banqueting facilities are available.

Rooms 29 (5 fmly) (3 GF) **Facilities** FTV Wi-fi Xmas New Year **Conf** Class 30 Board 26 Thtr 90 **Parking** 60 **Notes** ⊗ Civ Wed 120

BEST WESTERN Red Lion Hotel

 Best Western

★★★ 75% ⊛ HOTEL

☎ 01722 323334
Milford St SP1 2AN
e-mail: reception@the-redlion.co.uk
web: www.the-redlion.co.uk
dir: In city centre close to Guildhall Square

This 750-year-old hotel is full of character, with individually designed bedrooms that combine contemporary comforts with historic features; one room has a medieval fireplace dating back to 1220. The distinctive public areas include a bar, lounge and the elegant Vine Restaurant that serves an interesting mix of modern and traditional dishes.

Rooms 51 (1 fmly) **Facilities** Wi-fi Xmas New Year **Conf** Class 50 Board 40 Thtr 100 **Services** Lift **Notes** ⊗ Civ Wed 80

Grasmere House Hotel

THE INDEPENDENTS
HOTEL ASSOCIATION

★★★ 70% HOTEL

☎ 01722 338388
Harnham Rd SP2 8JN
e-mail: info@grasmerehotel.com
web: www.grasmerehotel.com
dir: On A3094 on S side of Salisbury adjacent to Harnham church

This popular hotel, dating from 1896, has gardens that overlook the water meadows and the cathedral. The attractive bedrooms vary in size, some offer excellent quality and comfort, and some rooms are specially equipped for less mobile guests. In summer

there is the option of dining on the pleasant outdoor terrace.

Rooms 38 (31 annexe) (16 fmly) (9 GF) ☂ **Facilities** STV FTV Wi-fi Fishing ⚓ Xmas New Year **Conf** Class 45 Board 45 Thtr 110 **Parking** 64 **Notes** Civ Wed 120

Premier Inn Salisbury

 Premier Inn

BUDGET HOTEL

☎ 0871 527 8956
Pearce Way, Bishopsdown SP1 3YU
web: www.premierinn.com
dir: From Salisbury take A30 towards Marlborough. 1m. Hotel off Hampton Park at rdbt

High quality, budget accommodation ideal for both families and business travellers. Spacious, en suite bedrooms feature tea and coffee making facilities, and Freeview TV in most hotels. Internet access and Wi-fi are available for a small fee. The adjacent family restaurant features a wide and varied menu. See also the Hotel Groups pages.

Rooms 62

SALTASH
Cornwall
Map 3 SX45

China Fleet Country Club

★★★ 79% HOTEL

☎ 01752 848668 & 854661
PL12 6LJ
e-mail: sales@china-fleet.co.uk
web: www.china-fleet.co.uk
dir: A38 towards Plymouth/Saltash. Cross Tamar Bridge, take slip road before tunnel. Right at lights, 1st right follow signs, 0.5m

Set in 180 acres of stunning Cornish countryside overlooking the beautiful Tamar estuary, this hotel has easy access to Plymouth and the countryside. It offers an extensive range of leisure facilities including an impressive golf course. The one and two-bedroom apartments are located in annexe buildings; each has a kitchen, lounge and flexible sleeping arrangements. The dining options include a brasserie, a coffee shop and the Farm House Restaurant.

Rooms 40 (39 fmly) (21 GF) ☂ **S** £71-£91; **D** £71-£101* **Facilities** Spa FTV Wi-fi ☒ ⊛ supervised ⛳ 18 ⚑ Putt green Gym Squash 28-bay floodlit driving range Health & beauty suite Hairdresser Xmas New Year **Conf** Class 80 Board 60 Thtr 300 Del from £119.95 to £124.95* **Services** Lift **Parking** 400 **Notes** ⊗ Civ Wed 300

S

S

SALTBURN-BY-THE-SEA Map 19 NZ62
North Yorkshire

Hunley Hotel & Golf Club

★★★ 77% HOTEL

☎ 01287 676216
Ings Ln, Brotton TS12 2FT
e-mail: enquiries@hunleyhotel.co.uk
dir: From A174 bypass left at rdbt with monument, left at T-junct, pass church, turn right. 50yds right, through housing estate, hotel approx 0.5m

Spectacularly situated, this hotel overlooks the 27-hole golf course and beyond to the coastline. The members' bar is licensed and serves snacks all day, and the restaurant offers a wide choice of interesting dishes. The bedrooms are very comfortably equipped and some are particularly spacious.

Rooms 26 (4 fmly) (16 GF) S £89-£150; D £99-£150 **Facilities** FTV Wi-fi ♨ ⚲ 27 Putt green Driving range Xmas New Year **Conf** Class 32 Board 28 Thtr 50 Del from £104 to £124* **Parking** 100 **Notes** Civ Wed 130

SANDBANKS

See Poole

SANDIACRE Map 11 SK43
Derbyshire

Holiday Inn Derby/ Nottingham

★★★ 73% HOTEL

☎ 0871 942 9062
Bostocks Ln NG10 5NJ
e-mail: reservations-derby-nottingham@ihg.com
web: www.hiderbyhotel.co.uk
dir: M1 junct 25 follow Sandiacre signs, hotel on right

This hotel is conveniently located by the M1, and ideal for exploring Derby and Nottingham. The bedrooms are modern and smart. The restaurant offers a wide range of dishes for breakfast, lunch and dinner. The lounge/bar area is a popular meeting place, with food served all day.

Rooms 92 (31 fmly) (53 GF) S £39-£145; D £49-£155* **Facilities** STV FTV Wi-fi ♨ HL Xmas New Year **Conf** Class 26 Board 30 Thtr 60 **Services** Air con **Parking** 200 **Notes** LB Civ Wed 50

SANDIWAY Map 15 SJ67
Cheshire

Nunsmere Hall Hotel

★★★★ ◎◎
COUNTRY HOUSE HOTEL

☎ 01606 889100
Tarporley Rd CW8 2ES
e-mail: reception@nunsmere.co.uk
web: www.nunsmere.co.uk
dir: M6 junct 18, A54 to Chester, at x-rds with A49 turn left towards Tarporley, hotel 2m on left

In an idyllic and peaceful setting of well-kept grounds, including a 60-acre lake, this delightful house dates back to 1900. Spacious bedrooms are individually styled, tastefully appointed to a very high standard and thoughtfully equipped. Guests can relax in the elegant lounges, the library or the oak-panelled bar. Dining in the Crystal Restaurant is a highlight and both a traditional carte and a gourmet menu are offered.

Rooms 36 (8 fmly) (2 GF) ⚲ **Facilities** FTV Wi-fi ♨ 🦢 Xmas New Year **Conf** Class 24 Board 30 Thtr 50 Del from £145 to £190* **Services** Lift **Parking** 80 **Notes** Civ Wed 120

SANDOWN Map 5 SZ58
Isle of Wight

The Wight Montrene Hotel

★★ 78% HOTEL

☎ 01983 403722
11 Avenue Rd PO36 8BN
e-mail: enquiries@wighthotel.co.uk
web: www.wighthotel.co.uk
dir: 100yds after mini-rdbt between High St & Avenue Rd

A family hotel, set in secluded grounds, that is only a short walk from Sandown's beach and high street shops. Bedrooms provide comfort and are either on the ground or first floor. Guests can relax in the heated swimming pool and enjoy the spa facility; there's also evening entertainment in the bar. The

dinner menu changes nightly, and a plentiful breakfast is served in the colourful dining room.

Rooms 41 (18 fmly) (21 GF) ⚲ **Facilities** Spa Wi-fi ✪ Gym Steam room Sauna Solarium Table tennis Full size snooker table 🎵 Xmas New Year **Conf** Thtr 80 **Parking** 40

Bayshore Hotel

Leisureplex

★★ 74% HOTEL

☎ 01983 403154
12-16 Pier St PO36 8JX
e-mail: bayshore.sandown@alfatravel.co.uk
web: www.leisureplex.co.uk
dir: From Broadway into Melville St, follow Tourist Information Office signs. Across High St, right opposite pier. Hotel on right

This large hotel is located on the seafront opposite the pier and offers extensive public rooms where live entertainment is provided in season. The bedrooms are well equipped and staff are very friendly and helpful.

Rooms 80 (18 fmly) (2 GF) ⚲ S £35-£51; D £56-£88 (incl. bkfst)* **Facilities** FTV Wi-fi 🎵 Xmas New Year **Services** Lift **Notes** LB ⊗ Closed Dec-Feb (ex Xmas) RS Mar & Nov

Sandringham Hotel

★★ 74% HOTEL

☎ 01983 406655
Esplanade PO36 8AH
e-mail: info@sandringhamhotel.co.uk

With a prime seafront location and splendid views, this is one of the largest hotels on the island. Comfortable public areas include a spacious lounge and a heated indoor swimming pool and jacuzzi. Bedrooms vary in size and many sea-facing rooms have a balcony. Regular entertainment is provided in the ballroom.

Rooms 110 (39 fmly) (6 GF) **Facilities** ✪ 🎵 Xmas **Services** Lift **Parking** 82 **Notes** ⊗

Riviera Hotel

★★ 71% HOTEL

☎ 01983 402518
2 Royal St PO36 8LP
e-mail: enquiries@rivierahotel.org.uk
web: www.rivierahotel.org.uk
dir: At top of High St, beyond Post Office

Guests return year after year to this friendly and welcoming family-run hotel. It is located near to the High Street and just a short stroll from the beach, pier and shops. Bedrooms, including several at ground floor level, are very well furnished and comfortably equipped. Enjoyable home-cooked meals are served in the spacious dining room.

Rooms 43 (6 fmly) (11 GF) ⬕ **Facilities** FTV ♫ Xmas New Year **Parking** 30

SANDWICH
Kent   Map 7 TR35

The Lodge at Princes
★★★ 83% ◉ ◉ HOTEL

☎ 01304 611118
Prince's Dr, Sandwich Bay CT13 9QB
e-mail: j.george@princesgolfclub.co.uk
web: www.princesgolfclub.co.uk
dir: M2 onto A299 Thanet Way to Manston Airport, A256 to Sandwich, follow sign to golf course

A newly built hotel in one of the most sought after locations of the South East Coast, The Lodge offers a choice of bedrooms within three adjoining Lodge Houses. Most rooms offer enviable views of the golf course or the Bay of Sandwich. All rooms have been carefully designed and offer a range of practical amenities including club storage. Award winning cuisine is served in The Brasserie on the Bay.

Rooms 38 (24 annexe) (1 fmly) (12 GF) ⬕ **S** £90-£95; **D** £90-£120 (incl. bkfst)* **Facilities** FTV Wi-fi ⬕ HL ⬕ 27 Putt green Gym Xmas New Year **Conf** Class 60 Board 50 Thtr 120 Del from £130 to £150* **Services** Lift **Parking** 50 **Notes** LB ⊗

SAUNTON
Devon   Map 3 SS43

Saunton Sands Hotel

★★★★ 79% ◉ HOTEL

☎ 01271 890212
EX33 1LQ
e-mail: reservations@sauntonsands.com
web: www.sauntonsands.com
dir: Exit A361 at Braunton, signed Croyde B3231, hotel 2m on left

Stunning sea views and direct access to five miles of sandy beach are just two of the highlights at this popular hotel. The majority of sea-facing rooms have balconies, and splendid views can be enjoyed from all of the public areas, which include comfortable lounges. In addition to the dining room, in summer an outside grill has tables on the terrace overlooking the sea. Alternatively, The Sands café/bar, an informal eating option, is a successful innovation located on the beach.

Saunton Sands Hotel

Rooms 92 (39 fmly) ⬕ **S** £75-£155; **D** £150-£540 (incl. bkfst)* **Facilities** Spa STV FTV Wi-fi ⬕ ⊛ ⬕ ⬕ Putt green Gym Squash Sauna Sun shower Beauty treatment room Snooker room ♫ Xmas New Year Child facilities **Conf** Class 180 Board 50 Thtr 200 Del from £126 to £147* **Services** Lift **Parking** 140 **Notes** LB ⊗ Civ Wed 200

See advert below

S

SAWBRIDGEWORTH
Hertfordshire
Map 6 TL41

Manor of Groves Hotel, Golf & Country Club

★★★ 77% HOTEL

☎ 01279 600777 & 0870 410 8833
High Wych CM21 0JU
e-mail: info@manorofgroves.co.uk
web: www.manorofgroves.com
dir: A1184 to Sawbridgeworth, left to High Wych, right at village green & hotel 200yds left

Delightful Georgian manor house set in 150 acres of secluded grounds and gardens, with its own 18-hole championship golf course and superb leisure facilities. Public rooms include an imposing open-plan glass atrium that features a bar, lounge area and modern restaurant. The spacious bedrooms are smartly decorated and equipped with modern facilities.

Rooms 80 (2 fmly) (17 GF) ↱ **Facilities** Spa FTV Wi-fi ↳ ⊛ supervised ⚓ 18 Putt green Gym Dance studio Beauty salon Sauna Steam rooms Xmas New Year **Conf** Class 250 Board 50 Thtr 500 **Services** Lift Parking 350 **Notes** ⊗ RS 24 Dec-2 Jan Civ Wed 300

SCARBOROUGH
North Yorkshire
Map 17 TA08

Crown Spa Hotel

★★★★ 78% HOTEL

☎ 01723 357400
Esplanade YO11 2AG
e-mail: info@crownspahotel.com
web: www.crownspahotel.com
dir: On A64 follow town centre signs to lights opposite railway station, turn right over Valley Bridge, 1st left, right into Belmont Rd to cliff top

This well-known hotel has an enviable position overlooking the harbour and South Bay, and most of the front-facing bedrooms have excellent views. All the bedrooms, including suites, are contemporary and have the latest amenities including feature bathrooms. An extensive range of treatments are available in the outstanding spa.

Crown Spa Hotel

Rooms 115 (42 fmly) ↱ **S** £53-£150; **D** £63-£250 **Facilities** Spa FTV Wi-fi ↳ HL ⊛ Gym Fitness classes Massage Sauna Steam room Xmas New Year **Conf** Class 100 Board 80 Thtr 260 Del from £115 to £215 **Services** Lift Parking 17 **Notes** LB ⊗ Civ Wed 260

See advert on opposite page

Ambassador Spa Hotel

★★★ 80% HOTEL

☎ 01723 362841
Centre of the Esplanade YO11 2AY
e-mail: ask@ambassadorspahotel.co.uk
web: www.ambassadorspahotel.co.uk
dir: A64, right at mini rdbt opposite B&Q, right at next mini rdbt, immediately left into Avenue Victoria to cliff top

Standing on the South Cliff with excellent views over the bay, this friendly hotel offers well-equipped bedrooms; some are executive rooms, some have sea views. A spa with pool and many rejuvenating and pampering facilities is available. Entertainment is provided during the summer season.

Rooms 58 (10 fmly) (1 GF) ↱ **Facilities** Spa FTV Wi-fi ↳ ⊛ Sauna Spa bath ♬ Xmas New Year **Conf** Class 60 Board 40 Thtr 120 **Services** Lift Air con **Notes** LB ⊗ Civ Wed 120

Palm Court Hotel

★★★ 80% HOTEL

☎ 01723 368161
St Nicholas Cliff YO11 2ES
e-mail: info@palmcourt-scarborough.co.uk
dir: Follow signs for town centre & town hall, hotel before town hall on right

The public rooms are spacious and comfortable at this modern, town centre hotel. Traditional cooking is provided in the attractive restaurant and staff are friendly and helpful. Bedrooms are quite delightfully furnished and well equipped. Extra facilities include a swimming pool and free, covered parking.

Rooms 40 (11 fmly) ↱ **S** £75; **D** £110-£155 (incl. bkfst)* **Facilities** FTV Wi-fi ⊛ Xmas New Year

Conf Class 70 Board 60 Thtr 80 Del from £114 to £120* **Services** Lift **Parking** 40 **Notes** LB ⊗ Civ Wed 80

Beiderbecke's Hotel

★★★ 75% ⊛ HOTEL

☎ 01723 365766
1-3 The Crescent YO11 2PW
e-mail: info@beiderbeckes.com
dir: In town centre, 200mtrs from railway station

Situated in a Georgian crescent this hotel is close to all the main attractions. Bedrooms are very smart, well equipped and offer plenty of space and comfort. Some rooms have views over the town to the sea. Marmalade's, the restaurant, offers international cuisine with a modern twist and hosts live music acts at weekends, including the resident jazz band.

Rooms 27 (4 fmly) **Facilities** STV FTV Wi-fi ♬ Xmas New Year **Conf** Class 40 Board 30 Thtr 80 **Services** Lift Parking 18 **Notes** LB ⊗

Esplanade Hotel

★★★ 70% HOTEL

☎ 01723 360382
Belmont Rd YO11 2AA
e-mail: enquiries@theesplanade.co.uk
dir: From town centre over Valley Bridge, left then immediately right into Belmont Rd, hotel 100mtrs on right

This large hotel enjoys a superb position overlooking South Bay and the harbour. Both the terrace, leading from the lounge bar, and the restaurant, with its striking oriel window, benefit from magnificent views. Bedrooms are comfortably furnished and are well equipped. Touring groups are also well catered for.

Rooms 70 (7 fmly) ↱ **S** £35-£70; **D** £60-£140 (incl. bkfst) **Facilities** FTV Wi-fi Xmas New Year **Conf** Class 100 Board 30 Thtr 120 Del from £40 to £80 **Services** Lift **Parking** 15 **Notes** LB Closed 2 Jan-9 Feb

Four star luxury

Crown Spa Hotel ★ ★ ★ ★

One of Scarborough's most prestigious landmarks, the hotel dominates the centre piece of a listed Victorian terrace which commands the finest cliff top location of any Yorkshire coast hotel. Looking south to Flamborough Head, north to the castle and harbour and vistas of the sea and South Bay beach. The vibrant town centre to the North is just a short walk along the quiet and exclusive South Cliff Esplanade.

In-house we have: Taste Restaurant & Cafe Bar offering fine dining. Conference, Meeting & Event Suites with dedicated Events Team. A fully equipped Health Club to help you tone up, and Crown Spa Treatments to help you wind down.

tel: 01723 357400
web: www.CrownSpaHotel.com
email: info@CrownSpaHotel.com

Crown Spa Hotel, The Esplanade, Scarborough, North Yorkshire, YO11 2AG

S

SCARBOROUGH *continued*

Red Lea Hotel

★★★ 70% HOTEL

☎ 01723 362431
Prince of Wales Ter YO11 2AJ
e-mail: info@redleahotel.co.uk
web: www.redleahotel.co.uk
dir: Follow South Cliff signs. Prince of Wales Terrace is off Esplanade opposite cliff lift

This friendly, family-run hotel is situated close to the cliff lift. Bedrooms are well equipped and comfortably furnished, and many at the front have picturesque views of the coast. There are two large lounges and a spacious dining room where good-value, traditional food is served.

Rooms 66 (7 fmly) 🐾 **S** £40-£75; **D** £50-£130 (incl. bkfst) **Facilities** FTV Wi-fi 🕸 Xmas New Year **Conf** Class 25 Board 25 Thtr 40 Del from £75 to £160 **Services** Lift **Notes** LB ⊗

The Mount Hotel

★★ 76% HOTEL

☎ 01723 360961
Cliff Bridge Ter, Saint Nicholas Cliff YO11 2HA
e-mail: info@mounthotel.com
dir: On one-way system. From A165 (Valley Bridge Rd) left into Somerset Terrace, straight on at lights, straight on at rdbt (Palm Court Hotel on right). Next right into St Nicholas Cliff. Hotel at end on right

Standing in a superb, elevated position and enjoying magnificent views of the South Bay, this elegant Regency hotel is operated to high standards. The richly furnished and comfortable public rooms are inviting, and the well-equipped bedrooms have been attractively decorated. The spacious deluxe rooms are mini-suites.

Rooms 50 (5 fmly) **Facilities** Xmas **Services** Lift **Notes** Closed Jan-mid Mar

Park Manor Hotel

★★ 75% HOTEL

☎ 01723 372090
Northstead Manor Dr YO12 6BB
e-mail: info@parkmanor.co.uk
web: www.parkmanor.co.uk
dir: Off A165, adjacent to Peasholm Park

Enjoying a peaceful residential setting with sea views, this smartly presented, friendly hotel provides the seaside tourist with a wide range of facilities. Bedrooms vary in size and style but all are smartly furnished and well equipped. There is a spacious lounge, smart restaurant, games room and indoor pool plus a steam room for relaxation.

Rooms 41 (6 fmly) (1 GF) 🐾 **S** £44-£54.50; **D** £88-£174.50 (incl. bkfst)* **Facilities** FTV Wi-fi 🕸 Pool table Spa bath Steam room Table tennis New Year **Conf** Class 20 Board 20 Thtr 30 Del from £75 to £85* **Services** Lift **Parking** 20 **Notes** LB ⊗ No children 3yrs

The Cumberland

★★ 74% HOTEL   **Leisureplex**

☎ 01723 361826
Belmont Rd YO11 2AB
e-mail: cumberland@alfatravel.co.uk
web: www.leisureplex.co.uk
dir: A64 onto B1437, left at A165 towards town centre. Right into Ramshill Rd, right into Belmont Rd

On the South Cliff, convenient for the spa complex, beach and town centre shops, this hotel offers comfortably appointed bedrooms; each floor can be accessed by lift. Entertainment is provided most evenings and the meals are carefully cooked.

Rooms 86 (6 fmly) 🐾 **S** £38-£48; (incl. bkfst)* **Facilities** FTV Wi-fi 🎵 Xmas New Year **Services** Lift **Notes** LB ⊗ Closed Jan RS Nov-Dec & Feb

Premier Inn Scarborough

BUDGET HOTEL   **Premier Inn**

☎ 0871 527 9292
Falconer Rd YO11 2EN
web: www.premierinn.com
dir: From A64 into Seamer Rd, follow rail station signs. Right into Valley Bridge Rd. At 1st lights follow Town Hall signs into Somerset St (towards Brunswick shopping centre). At lights follow Town Hall signs into Falconers Rd

High quality, budget accommodation ideal for both families and business travellers. Spacious, en suite bedrooms feature tea and coffee making facilities, and Freeview TV in most hotels. Internet access and Wi-fi are available for a small fee. The adjacent family restaurant features a wide and varied menu. See also the Hotel Groups pages.

Rooms 74

SCUNTHORPE   Map 17 SE81
Lincolnshire

Forest Pines Hotel & Golf Resort

★★★★ 79% ⊛ HOTEL

☎ 01652 650770
Ermine St, Broughton DN20 0AQ
e-mail: forestpines@qhotels.co.uk
web: www.qhotels.co.uk
dir: 200yds from M180 junct 4, on Brigg-Scunthorpe rdbt

This smart hotel provides a comprehensive range of leisure facilities. Extensive conference rooms, a modern health and beauty spa, and a championship golf course ensure that it is a popular choice with both corporate and leisure guests. The well-equipped bedrooms are modern, spacious, and appointed to a good standard. Extensive public areas include a choice of dining options, with fine dining available in The Eighteen57 fish restaurant, and more informal eating in the Grill Bar.

Rooms 188 (66 fmly) (67 GF) **Facilities** Spa STV FTV Wi-fi 🕸 supervised ♨ 27 Putt green Gym Mountain bikes Jogging track Xmas New Year **Conf** Class 170 Board 96 Thtr 370 **Services** Lift **Parking** 400 **Notes** Civ Wed 250

Premier Inn Scunthorpe

BUDGET HOTEL   **Premier Inn**

☎ 0871 527 8960
Lakeside Retail Park, Lakeside Parkway DN16 3UA
web: www.premierinn.com
dir: M180 junct 4, A18 towards Scunthorpe. At Morrisons rdbt left onto Lakeside Retail Park, hotel behind Morrisons petrol station

High quality, budget accommodation ideal for both families and business travellers. Spacious, en suite bedrooms feature tea and coffee making facilities, and Freeview TV in most hotels. Internet access and Wi-fi are available for a small fee. The adjacent family restaurant features a wide and varied menu. See also the Hotel Groups pages.

Rooms 60

S

Save on hotels. Book at **theAA.com/hotel**

SCA – SED 393 **ENGLAND**

SEAHAM
Co Durham — Map 19 NZ44

Seaham Hall Hotel

U

☎ 0191 516 1400
Lord Byron's Walk SR7 7AG
e-mail: info@seaham-hall.com
web: www.seaham-hall.com
dir: From A19 take B1404 to Seaham. At lights straight over level crossing. Hotel approx 0.25m on right

Currently the rating for this establishment is not confirmed. We are working with the management / owners whilst works and changes take place to achieve an AA star rating. For further details please see the AA website: theAA.com

Rooms 20 (4 GF) ⌁ **D** £295-£695 (incl. bkfst)***Facilities** Spa STV Wi-fi ⬠ ⊗ Gym Putt green Croquet lawn LB Xmas New Year **Conf** Class 48 Board 40 Thtr 100 **Services** Lift Air con Hearing loop **Parking** 122 **Notes** ⊗ Civ Wed 100

SEAHOUSES
Northumberland — Map 21 NU23

The Links Hotel

★★ 79% SMALL HOTEL

☎ 01665 720062
8 King St NE68 7XP
e-mail: linkshotel@hotmail.com
dir: Off A1 at Browleside & follow signs along country road

This family-owned small hotel is in the heart of Seahouses. The restaurant is popular with residents and locals alike, offering relaxed and informal dining with quality home cooking and generous portions. Bedrooms are well presented and equipped and some off-road parking is available.

Rooms 11 (2 fmly) (2 GF) ⌁ **S** £41-£49; **D** £62-£78 (incl. bkfst)* **Facilities** STV FTV Wi-fi ⬠ **Parking** 11

SEASCALE
Cumbria — Map 18 NY00

Sella Park House Hotel

★★★★ 77% ⊛ COUNTRY HOUSE HOTEL

☎ 0845 450 6445 & 01946 841601
Calderbridge CA20 1DW
e-mail: info@penningtonhotels.com
dir: From A595 at Calderbridge, follow sign for North Gate. Hotel 0.5m on left

This property, which some believe dates back to the 13th century, is set in six acres of mature grounds which lead down to the River Calder. The individually

designed bedrooms are very well appointed and have many extras; public areas are comfortable and welcoming. Food in the Priory Restaurant is a highlight with local produce at the heart of each menu selection.

Rooms 16 (5 annexe) (2 GF) ⌁ **S** £80-£140; **D** £100-£160 (incl. bkfst)* **Facilities** FTV Wi-fi ⬠ HL Fishing Xmas New Year **Conf** Class 80 Board 80 Thtr 300 **Parking** 30 **Notes** LB Civ Wed 150

SEAVIEW
Isle of Wight — Map 5 SZ69

The Seaview Hotel & Restaurant

★★★ 82% ⊛ HOTEL

☎ 01983 612711
High St PO34 5EX
e-mail: reception@seaviewhotel.co.uk
web: www.seaviewhotel.co.uk
dir: From B3330 (Ryde-Seaview road), turn left via Puckpool along seafront

Located in the quiet and tranquil area of Seaview, the hotel is just a short walk from the seafront, and there are views from the front terrace, especially enjoyable in the summer months. Bedrooms are split between three main areas yet all offer modern and stylish accommodation; all have free broadband, DVD TVs plus slippers and robes. There is a modern restaurant where guests can enjoy breakfast, lunch and dinner, and there is also The Pump Bar with very traditional decor which is popular with both residents and locals alike.

Rooms 29 (4 fmly) (5 GF) ⌁ **S** £95-£160; **D** £125-£180 (incl. bkfst)* **Facilities** FTV Wi-fi ⬠ Use of nearby sports club New Year **Conf** Class 20 Board 20 Thtr 20 **Parking** 10 **Notes** LB Closed 22-26 Dec

Priory Bay Hotel

★★★ 80% ⊛ HOTEL

☎ 01983 613146
Priory Dr PO34 5BU
e-mail: enquiries@priorybay.co.uk
web: www.priorybay.co.uk
dir: B3330 towards Seaview, through Nettlestone. (NB do not follow Seaview turn, but continue 0.5m to hotel sign)

This peacefully located hotel has much to offer and comes complete with its own stretch of private beach and 6-hole golf course. Bedrooms are a wonderful mix of styles, all of which provide much comfort and character. Public areas are equally impressive with a choice of enticing lounges to relax and unwind. The kitchen creates interesting and imaginative dishes, using the excellent island produce as much as possible.

Rooms 22 (4 annexe) (6 fmly) (2 GF) ⌁ **S** £90-£225; **D** £160-£300 (incl. bkfst)* **Facilities** FTV Wi-fi ⬠ ⅃ 6 ⬠ ⬠ Private beach Xmas New Year Child facilities **Conf** Class 60 Board 40 Thtr 80 Del from £99 to £199* **Parking** 100 **Notes** LB ⊗ Civ Wed 300

SEDGEFIELD
Co Durham — Map 19 NZ32

BEST WESTERN Hardwick Hall Hotel

★★★★ 79% ⊛ HOTEL

☎ 01740 620253
TS21 2EH
e-mail: info@hardwickhallhotel.co.uk
dir: Exit A1(M) junct 60 towards Sedgefield, left at 1st rdbt, hotel 400mtrs on left

Set in extensive parkland, this 18th-century house suits both leisure and corporate guests. It is a top conference and function venue offering an impressive meeting and banqueting complex. Luxurious accommodation includes contemporary rooms, and some with antique furnishings. All are appointed to the same high standard, many have feature bathrooms, and some have stunning views over the lake. Both the modern lounge bar and cellar bistro have a relaxed atmosphere.

Rooms 51 (6 fmly) (12 GF) ⌁ **S** £69-£190; **D** £85-£210 (incl. bkfst)* **Facilities** STV FTV Wi-fi ⬠ Xmas New Year **Conf** Class 100 Board 80 Thtr 700 Del from £130 to £160* **Services** Lift **Parking** 300 **Notes** ⊗ Civ Wed 450

SEDGEMOOR
MOTORWAY SERVICE AREA (M5)
Somerset — Map 4 ST35

Days Inn Sedgemoor - M5

BUDGET HOTEL

☎ 01934 750831
Sedgemoor BS24 0JL
e-mail: sedgemoor.hotel@welcomebreak.co.uk
web: www.welcomebreak.co.uk
dir: M5 northbound junct 21/22

This modern building offers accommodation in smart, spacious and well-equipped bedrooms, suitable for families and business travellers, and all with en suite bathrooms. Continental breakfast is available and other refreshments may be taken at the nearby family restaurant. See also the Hotel Groups pages.

Rooms 40 (22 fmly) (19 GF) (8 smoking)

S

BEST WESTERN Royal Chase Hotel

★★★ 71% ⚛ HOTEL

☎ 01747 853355
Royal Chase Roundabout SP7 8DB
e-mail: reception@theroyalchasehotel.co.uk
web: www.theroyalchasehotel.co.uk
dir: A303 to A350 signed Blandford Forum. Avoid town centre, follow road to 3rd rdbt

Equally suitable for both leisure and business guests, this well-known local landmark is situated close to the famous Gold Hill. Both Standard and Crown bedrooms offer good levels of comfort and quality. In addition to the fixed-price menu in the Byzant Restaurant, guests have the option of eating more informally in the convivial bar.

Rooms 33 (13 fmly) (6 GF) ✎ **S** £60-£85; **D** £90-£130 (incl. bkfst)* **Facilities** FTV Wi-fi ↻ ⛲ Turkish steam room Spa pool Xmas New Year **Conf** Class 90 Board 50 Thtr 180 Del from £125 to £140* **Parking** 100 **Notes** LB Civ Wed 76

La Fleur de Lys Restaurant with Rooms

⚛ ⚛   RESTAURANT WITH ROOMS

☎ 01747 853717
Bleke St SP7 8AW
e-mail: info@lafleurdelys.co.uk
web: www.lafleurdelys.co.uk
dir: From junct of A30 & A350, 0.25m towards town centre

Located just a few minutes' walk from the famous Gold Hill, this light and airy restaurant with rooms combines efficient service in a relaxed and friendly atmosphere. Bedrooms, which are suitable for both business and leisure guests, vary in size but all are well equipped, comfortable and tastefully furnished. A relaxing guest lounge and courtyard are available for afternoon tea or pre-dinner drinks.

Rooms 7 (2 fmly)

Channel View Hotel

★★★ 78% HOTEL

☎ 01983 862309
Hope Rd PO37 6EH
e-mail: enquiries@channelviewhotel.co.uk
web: www.channelviewhotel.co.uk
dir: Exit A3055 at Esplanade & Beach sign. Hotel 250mtrs on left

With an elevated cliff-top location overlooking Shanklin Bay, several rooms at this hotel enjoy pleasant views and all are very well decorated and furnished. The hotel is family run, and guests can enjoy efficient service, regular evening entertainment, a heated indoor swimming pool and holistic therapy.

Rooms 56 (15 fmly) ✎ **S** £42-£61; **D** £84-£122 (incl. bkfst) **Facilities** FTV Wi-fi ↻ ⛲ Holistic therapies Aromatherapy 🎵 **Services** Lift **Parking** 32 **Notes** Closed Jan-Feb

Melbourne Ardenlea Hotel

★★ 78% HOTEL

☎ 01983 862596
4-6 Queens Rd PO37 6AP
e-mail: reservations@mahotel.co.uk
web: www.mahotel.co.uk
dir: A3055 to Shanklin. Then follow signs to Ventnor via A3055 (Queens Rd). Hotel just before end of road on right

This quietly located hotel is within easy walking distance of the town centre and the lift down to the promenade. Bedrooms are traditionally furnished and guests can enjoy the various spacious public areas including a welcoming bar and a large heated indoor swimming pool.

Rooms 54 (5 fmly) (6 GF) ✎ **Facilities** FTV Wi-fi ⛲ Sauna 🎵 Xmas New Year **Conf** Class 24 Board 20 Thtr 80 **Services** Lift **Parking** 26 **Notes** Closed 1-15 Jan

Auckland Hotel

★★ 72% HOTEL

☎ 01983 862960
10 Queens Rd PO37 6AN
e-mail: aucklandhotel@tiscali.co.uk

This family run hotel is located in the heart of Shanklin. Bedrooms are traditional in style yet spacious and all front rooms benefit from balconies with views of Sandown Beach. There is a spacious bar often providing evening entertainment and a restaurant where both dinner and breakfast daily. This hotel has ample off road parking and is within just a short walk to the Cliff Lift providing easy access to the seafront.

Rooms 30 **S** £45-£55; **D** £65-£85 (incl. bkfst)* **Notes** Closed Mar-Nov

Malton House Hotel

★★ 69% HOTEL

☎ 01983 865007
8 Park Rd PO37 6AY
e-mail: couvoussis@maltonhouse.freeserve.co.uk
web: www.maltonhouse.co.uk
dir: Up hill from Hope Rd lights then 3rd left

A well-kept Victorian hotel set in its own gardens in a quiet area, conveniently located for cliff-top walks and the public lift down to the promenade. The bedrooms are comfortable and public rooms include a small lounge, a separate bar and a dining room where traditional homemade meals are served.

Rooms 12 (3 fmly) (2 GF) **S** £34-£39; **D** £60-£70 (incl. bkfst)* **Facilities** Wi-fi **Parking** 12 **Notes** ⊗ No children 3yrs Closed Oct-Apr

BEST WESTERN Shap Wells Hotel

★★★ 77% HOTEL

☎ 01931 716628
CA10 3QU
e-mail: reservations@shapwellshotel.com
dir: Between A6 & B6261, 4m S of Shap

This hotel occupies a wonderful secluded position amid trees and waterfalls. Extensive public areas include function and meeting rooms, a well-stocked bar, a choice of lounges and a spacious restaurant. Bedrooms vary in size and style but all are equipped with the expected facilities.

Rooms 100 (9 annexe) (10 fmly) (10 GF) ✎ **Facilities** FTV Wi-fi ↻ Games room Cardiovascular gym ♫ Xmas New Year **Conf** Class 80 Board 40 Thtr 170 Del from £90 to £120 **Services** Lift **Parking** 200 **Notes** Closed 2-24 Jan Civ Wed 150

SHEDFIELD
Hampshire   Map 5 SU51

Meon Valley, A Marriott Hotel & Country Club

★★★★ 78% ❀ HOTEL

☎ 01329 833455
Sandy Ln SO32 2HQ
web: www.marriottmeonvalley.co.uk
dir: M27 junct 7 take A334 towards Wickham & Botley. Sandy Ln on left 2m from Botley

This modern, smartly appointed hotel and country club has extensive indoor and outdoor leisure facilities, including two golf courses. Bedrooms are spacious and well equipped, and guests have a choice of eating and drinking options. It is ideally suited for easy access to both Portsmouth and Southampton.

Rooms 113 (43 fmly) (29 GF) (10 smoking) **Facilities** Spa FTV Wi-fi ↝ ❍ ♨ 27 ♨ Putt green Gym Cardiovascular aerobics Health & beauty salon Xmas New Year **Conf** Class 50 Board 32 Thtr 100 **Services** Lift **Parking** 360 **Notes** ⊗ Civ Wed 90

SHEFFIELD
South Yorkshire   Map 16 SK49

Copthorne Hotel Sheffield

MILLENNIUM
HOTELS AND RESORTS
MILLENNIUM • COPTHORNE

★★★★ 79% ❀ HOTEL

☎ 0114 252 5480
Sheffield United Football Club, Bramhall Ln S2 4SU
e-mail: reservations.sheffield@millenniumhotels.co.uk
dir: M1 junct 33/A57. At Park Square rdbt follow A61 (Chesterfield Rd). Follow brown signs for Bramall Lane

This modern and stylish hotel is situated in the centre of Sheffield. Located next to the home of Sheffield United FC it offers contemporary public areas and an award-winning restaurant on the ground floor. A well-equipped gym is situated on the first floor. Bedrooms are spacious and comfortable. Ample parking is a plus in this central location.

Rooms 158 (23 fmly) ↟ **Facilities** STV FTV Wi-fi ↝ Fitness room **Conf** Class 150 Board 40 Thtr 400 Del from £110 to £140 **Services** Lift Air con **Parking** 250 **Notes** ⊗

Whitley Hall Hotel

CLASSIC
BRITISH HOTELS

★★★★ 78% ❀❀ HOTEL

☎ 0114 245 4444 & 246 0456
Elliott Ln, Grenoside S35 8NR
e-mail: reservations@whitleyhall.com
web: www.whitleyhall.com
dir: A61 past football ground, 2m, right just before Norfolk Arms, left at bottom of hill. Hotel on left

This 16th-century house stands in 20 acres of landscaped grounds and gardens. Public rooms are full of character and interesting architectural features, and command the best views of the gardens. The individually styled bedrooms are furnished in keeping with the country house setting, as are the oak-panelled restaurant and bar. The hotel is a popular wedding venue.

Rooms 32 (3 annexe) (2 fmly) (8 GF) ↟ S £82.50-£102.50; D £82.50-£102.50* **Facilities** STV FTV Wi-fi ↝ **Conf** Class 50 Board 34 Thtr 70 Del £155* **Services** Lift **Parking** 100 **Notes** ⊗ Civ Wed 100

Mercure Sheffied St Paul's Hotel & Spa

Mercure

★★★★ 77% HOTEL

☎ 0114 278 2000
119 Norfolk St S1 2JE
e-mail: h6628@accor.com
web: www.mercure.com
dir: M1 junct 33, 4th exit at rdbt, left at 1st lights, right at 2nd in front of Crucible Theatre

This modern, luxury hotel enjoys a central location close to key attractions in the city. Open-plan public areas are situated in a steel and glass atrium and include a popular Champagne bar, the Yard Restaurant and Zucca, an Italian Bistro. Bedrooms are superbly presented and richly furnished. The Vital health and beauty treatment centre provides a fabulous thermal suite.

Rooms 163 (40 fmly) **Facilities** Spa Wi-fi ↝ Sauna Steam room Snail shower Ice fountain Fitness classes Xmas New Year **Conf** Class 400 Board 30 Thtr 600 **Services** Lift Air con **Notes** ⊗ Civ Wed 350

Kenwood Hall

principal hayley

★★★★ 75% HOTEL

☎ 0114 258 3811
Kenwood Rd S7 1NQ
dir: A61 (Barnsley ring road) into St Mary's Rd. Straight over rdbt, left into London Rd, right at lights. 2nd exit at 2nd rdbt, hotel ahead

A smart, modern hotel peacefully located in a residential suburb a few miles from the city centre. The stylishly decorated bedrooms are spacious, quiet and well equipped. The hotel also has an extensive range of leisure and meeting facilities, and secure parking is located in extensive landscaped gardens.

Rooms 114 (8 fmly) **Facilities** STV Wi-fi ↝ Fishing Gym Steam room Sauna Solarium Beauty treatment rooms New Year **Conf** Class 100 Board 60 Thtr 250 **Services** Lift **Parking** 150 **Notes** Civ Wed 260

Novotel Sheffield Centre

NOVOTEL

★★★★ 72% HOTEL

☎ 0114 278 1781
50 Arundel Gate S1 2PR
e-mail: h1348@accor.com
web: www.novotel.com
dir: Between Registry Office & Crucible/Lyceum Theatres, follow signs to Town Hall/Theatres & Hallam University

In the heart of the city centre, this hotel has stylish public areas including a very modern restaurant, indoor swimming pool and a range of meeting rooms. Spacious bedrooms are suitable for family occupation, and the Novation rooms are ideal for business users.

Rooms 144 (136 fmly) ↟ **Facilities** STV FTV Wi-fi ↝ Gym Steam room Xmas New Year **Conf** Class 180 Board 100 Thtr 220 **Services** Lift Air con **Parking** 60 **Notes** Civ Wed 180

S

SHEFFIELD *continued*

BEST WESTERN PLUS Mosborough Hall Hotel

★★★ 82% HOTEL

☎ 0114 248 4353
High St, Mosborough S20 5EA
e-mail: hotel@mosboroughhall.co.uk
web: www.mosboroughhall.co.uk
dir: M1 junct 30, A6135 towards Sheffield. Follow Eckington/Mosborough signs 2m. Sharp bend at top of hill, hotel on right

This 16th-century, Grade II listed manor house is set in gardens not far from the M1 and is convenient for the city centre. The bedrooms offer very high quality and good amenities; some are very spacious. There is a galleried lounge and conservatory bar, and freshly prepared dishes are served in the traditional style dining room.

Rooms 44 (17 GF) ✿ **S** £66-£175; **D** £66-£175 (incl. bkfst)* **Facilities** FTV Wi-fi ♨ Spa & beauty treatments Xmas New Year **Conf** Class 125 Board 70 Thtr 220 Del from £125 to £165 **Parking** 100 **Notes** LB Civ Wed 250

Staindrop Lodge Hotel

★★★ 80% ◉ HOTEL

☎ 0114 284 3111
Lane End, Chapeltown S35 3UH
e-mail: info@staindroplodge.co.uk
dir: M1 junct 35, A629 for 1m, straight over 1st rdbt, right at 2nd rdbt, hotel approx 0.5m on right

This hotel, bar and brasserie offers smart modern public areas and accommodation. An art deco theme continues throughout the open-plan public rooms and the comfortably appointed, spacious bedrooms. Service is relaxed and friendly, and all-day menus are available.

Rooms 37 (5 annexe) (1 fmly) (3 GF) ✿ **Facilities** STV FTV Wi-fi ♨ **Conf** Class 60 Board 40 Thtr 80 **Parking** 80 **Notes** ❀ Civ Wed 80

BEST WESTERN PLUS Aston Hall Hotel

★★★ 79% HOTEL

☎ 0114 287 2309
Worksop Rd, Aston S26 2EE
e-mail: reservations@astonhallhotel.co.uk
web: www.astonhallhotel.co.uk
dir: M1 junct 31, follow A57 to Sheffield & follow signs to hotel

Originally built as a manor house and set in spacious grounds with open views across the countryside to the south of the city, this hotel is well located for the M1, Meadowhall, the city or touring. Extensive conference, banqueting facilities and picturesque grounds make it an ideal wedding venue. Bedrooms are comfortable and well equipped.

Rooms 52 (9 GF) ✿ **Facilities** FTV Wi-fi ♨ Gym Xmas New Year **Conf** Class 200 Board 60 Thtr 300 **Services** Lift **Parking** 90 **Notes** ❀ Civ Wed 300

BEST WESTERN Cutlers Hotel

★★★ 72% HOTEL

☎ 0114 273 9939
Theatreland George St S1 2PF
e-mail: enquiries@cutlershotel.co.uk
dir: M1 junct 33. At Park Sq follow signs to City Centre & Theatres. At top of Commercial St, left into Arundel Gate. Into right lane, at lights right into Norfolk St, 2nd right into George St. Hotel 50mtrs on left

Situated in the heart of the city, near the theatres and only minutes from the bus and railway stations. Each of the bedrooms has a flat-screen TV, iPod docking station, free Wi-fi and broadband access. Mariano's Restaurant & Bar on the upper mezzanine level offers a relaxed atmosphere. A function room is also available. Discounted overnight parking is provided in the nearby public car park.

Rooms 45 (2 fmly) **Facilities** STV FTV Wi-fi Beauty treatment rooms Xmas New Year **Conf** Class 20 Board 25 Thtr 80 **Services** Lift **Notes** ❀ Civ Wed 60

Ibis Sheffield City Centre

BUDGET HOTEL

☎ 0114 241 9600
Shude Hill S1 2AR
e-mail: H2891@accor.com
web: www.ibishotel.com
dir: M1 junct 33, follow signs to Sheffield City Centre (A630/A57), at rdbt take 5th exit, signed Ponds Forge, for hotel

Modern, budget hotel offering comfortable accommodation in bright and practical bedrooms. Breakfast is self-service and dinner is available in the restaurant. See also the Hotel Groups pages.

Rooms 95 (15 fmly) (3 GF) ✿

Premier Inn Sheffield (Arena)

BUDGET HOTEL

☎ 0871 527 8964
Attercliffe Common Rd S9 2LU
web: www.premierinn.com
dir: M1 junct 34, follow signs to city centre. Hotel opposite Arena

High quality, budget accommodation ideal for both families and business travellers. Spacious, en suite bedrooms feature tea and coffee making facilities, and Freeview TV in most hotels. Internet access and Wi-fi are available for a small fee. The adjacent family restaurant features a wide and varied menu. See also the Hotel Groups pages.

Rooms 61

Premier Inn Sheffield City Centre

BUDGET HOTEL

☎ 0871 527 8972
Young St, St Marys Gate S1 4LA
web: www.premierinn.com
dir: M1 junct 33, A630, A57 follow Sheffield City Centre signs. At Park Square rdbt 3rd exit signed A61/Chesterfield. At Granville Square right onto A61 signed Ring Rd. Keep in left lane. At rdbt 3rd exit signed A621. Left into Cumberland St. Left into South Lane. Right into Young St

Rooms 122

S

Premier Inn Sheffield City Centre Angel St

BUDGET HOTEL

☎ 0871 527 8970
Angel St, (Corner of Bank Street) S3 8LN
web: www.premierinn.com
dir: M1 junct 33, follow city centre, A630, A57 signs.
At Park Square rdbt 4th exit (A61 Barnsley). Left at
4th lights into Snig Hill, right at lights into Bank St

Rooms 160

Premier Inn Sheffield (Meadowhall)

BUDGET HOTEL

☎ 0871 527 8966
Sheffield Rd, Meadowhall S9 2YL
web: www.premierinn.com
dir: On A6178 approx 6m from city centre

Rooms 103

SHEPPERTON
Surrey

Harrisons Hotel

★★★ 64% HOTEL PLAN 1 A1

☎ 01932 227320
Rusell Rd TW17 9HX
dir: M25 junct 11, then A320 Chertsey, A317, B387,
B375. Hotel on left

Being located on the banks of the Thames, close to a
number of visitor attractions and major transport
networks makes this hotel suitable for both the
leisure and business traveller. The tastefully
appointed bedrooms and bathrooms are appointed to
a high standard and have guest comfort very much in
mind. The Bar and Bistro offers contemporary dining
with popular favourites available for all tastes.
Parking with CCTV is located nearby.

Rooms 32 ☏ **Facilities** FTV Wi-fi New Year
Conf Class 45 Board 30 Thtr 100 **Parking** 40
Notes ⊗

SHEPTON MALLET   Map 4 ST64
Somerset

Charlton House Spa Hotel

★★★★ 76% ◉◉ HOTEL

☎ 01749 342008
Charlton Rd BA4 4PR
e-mail: gm.charltonhousehotel@bannatyne.co.uk
web: www.bannatyne.co.uk
dir: On A361 towards Frome, 1m from town centre

A peaceful location with grounds and relaxing spa
facilities are just part of the charm of this interesting
hotel. Individually designed bedrooms include larger
suites and a luxurious lodge in the garden. Guests
can relax in the 'shabby chic' lounges or bar area, or
in the warmer months there's plenty of outdoor
seating. Dinner in the stylish restaurant offers a
selection of carefully prepared, high quality dishes.
The spa offers a wide range of facilities including
treatment rooms, hydrotherapy pool, crystal room,
sauna and a fitness studio to name but a few. The
hotel is a popular wedding venue.

Rooms 28 (6 annexe) (3 fmly) (12 GF) ☏ **D** £95–£400
(incl. bkfst)* **Facilities** Spa FTV Wi-fi ⊗ ♨ ☞ Gym
Sauna Steam room Laconium Experience showers
Xmas New Year **Conf** Class 50 Board 30 Thtr 90
Del from £170 to £189* **Parking** 70 **Notes** LB ⊗
Civ Wed 120

SHERBORNE   Map 4 ST61
Dorset

BEST WESTERN The Grange at Oborne

★★★ 80% ◉◉ HOTEL

☎ 01935 813463
Oborne DT9 4LA
e-mail: reception@thegrange.co.uk
web: www.thegrangeatoborne.co.uk
dir: Exit A30, follow signs through village

Set in beautiful gardens in a quiet hamlet, this
200-year-old, family run, country-house hotel has a
wealth of charm and character. It offers friendly
hospitality together with attentive service. Bedrooms
are comfortable and tastefully appointed. Public
areas are elegantly furnished and the popular
restaurant offers a good selection of dishes.

Rooms 18 (3 fmly) (2 GF) ☏ **S** £88–£169;
D £107–£188 (incl. bkfst)* **Facilities** STV Wi-fi ⊗
Xmas New Year **Conf** Class 40 Board 30 Thtr 80
Del from £146.95 to £155.95* **Parking** 45 **Notes** LB
⊗ Civ Wed 120

Eastbury Hotel

★★★ 79% ◉◉ HOTEL

☎ 01935 813131
Long St DT9 3BY
e-mail: enquiries@theeastburyhotel.co.uk
web: www.theeastburyhotel.co.uk
dir: From A30 W'bound, left into North Rd, then St
Swithin's, left at bottom, hotel 800yds on right

Much of the original Georgian charm and elegance is
maintained at this smart, comfortable hotel. Just five
minutes' stroll from the abbey and close to the town
centre, the Eastbury's friendly and attentive staff
ensure a relaxed and enjoyable stay. Award-winning
cuisine is served in the attractive dining room,
overlooking the walled garden, with an alfresco bistro
option also available.

Rooms 23 (1 fmly) (3 GF) ☏ **S** £66–£70; **D** £106–£189
(incl. bkfst)* **Facilities** FTV Wi-fi ⊗ ☞ New Year
Conf Class 40 Board 28 Thtr 80 Del £121*
Parking 30 **Notes** LB Civ Wed 80

The Sherborne Hotel

★★★ 67% HOTEL

☎ 01935 813191
Horsecastles Ln DT9 6BB
e-mail: info@sherbornehotel.co.uk
dir: At junct of A30 & A352

This hotel is in a quiet location with attractive
grounds yet is only just off the main road. The
bedrooms are spacious and well equipped, the open-
plan lounge and bar area are comfortable, and
satellite TV is provided. There is a good range of
dishes to choose from and the dining room looks out
to the garden.

Rooms 60 (24 GF) ☏ **S** £39–£59; **D** £59–£79 (incl.
bkfst)* **Facilities** FTV Wi-fi HL ☞ Concessionary
swimming rates at leisure centre opposite ♫ Xmas
New Year **Conf** Class 35 Board 30 Thtr 80
Del from £65 to £95* **Parking** 90 **Notes** LB ⊗

S

SHERINGHAM — Norfolk   Map 13 TG14

Dales Country House Hotel

★★★★ 83% ◉◉ HOTEL

☎ 01263 824555

Lodge Hill, Upper Sheringham NR26 8TJ
e-mail: dales@mackenziehotels.com
dir: From Sheringham take B1157 to Upper Sheringham. Through village, hotel on left

Superb Grade II listed building situated in extensive landscaped grounds on the edge of Sheringham Park. The attractive public rooms are full of original character; they include a choice of lounges as well as an intimate restaurant and a cosy lounge bar. The spacious bedrooms are individually decorated with co-ordinated soft furnishings and many thoughtful touches.

Rooms 21 (5 GF) 🐾 **Facilities** Wi-fi 🏊 🎾 Giant garden games (chess & Jenga) Xmas New Year **Conf** Class 20 Board 27 Thtr 40 **Services** Lift **Parking** 50 **Notes** No children 14yrs

Beaumaris Hotel

★★ 79% HOTEL

☎ 01263 822370

South St NR26 8LL
e-mail: beauhotel@aol.com
web: www.thebeaumarishotel.co.uk
dir: Exit A148, left at rdbt, 1st right over rail bridge, 1st left by church, 1st left into South St

The Beaumaris Hotel is situated in a peaceful side road just a short walk from the beach, town centre and golf course. This friendly hotel has been owned and run by the same family for over 60 years and continues to provide comfortable, thoughtfully equipped accommodation throughout. Public rooms feature a smart dining room, a cosy bar and two quiet lounges.

Rooms 21 (5 fmly) (2 GF) 🐾 **S** £55-£68; **D** £110-£136 (incl. bkfst)* **Facilities** FTV Wi-fi **Parking** 25 **Notes** LB 🐾 Closed mid Dec-1 Mar

SHIFNAL — Shropshire   Map 10 SJ70

Park House Hotel

★★★★ 76% ◉ HOTEL

☎ 01952 460128

Park St TF11 9BA
e-mail: reception@parkhousehotel.net
dir: M54 junct 4, A464 (Wolverhampton road) for approx 2m, under railway bridge, hotel 100yds on left

Park House Hotel was created from what were originally two country houses of very different architectural styles. Located on the edge of this historic market town, it offers guests easy access to motorway networks, a choice of banqueting and meeting rooms, plus leisure facilities. Butlers Bar and Restaurant is the setting for imaginative food. Service is friendly and attentive.

Rooms 54 (16 annexe) (4 fmly) (8 GF) (4 smoking) 🐾 **Facilities** STV FTV Wi-fi 🚲 🎾 Gym Steam room Sauna Xmas New Year **Conf** Class 80 Board 40 Thtr 160 **Services** Lift **Parking** 90 **Notes** Civ Wed 200

SHIPLEY — West Yorkshire   Map 19 SE13

Hollins Hall, A Marriott Hotel & Country Club

★★★★ 76% HOTEL

☎ 01274 530053

Hollins Hill, Baildon BD17 7QW
e-mail: mhrs.lbags.frontdesk@marriotthotels.com
web: www.marriotthollinshall.co.uk
dir: From A650 follow signs to Salt Mill. At lights in Shipley take A6038. Hotel 3m on left

The hotel is located close to Leeds and Bradford and is easily accessible from motorway networks. Built in the 19th-century, this Elizabethan-style building is set within 200 acres of grounds and offers extensive leisure facilities, including a golf course and gym. Bedrooms are attractively decorated and have a range of additional facilities.

Rooms 122 (50 fmly) (25 GF) **S** fr £85; **D** fr £95 (incl. bkfst)* **Facilities** Spa STV FTV Wi-fi 🚲 HL 🎾 🏌 18 Putt green Gym Dance studio Swimming lessons **Conf** Class 90 Board 80 Thtr 200 Del from £129 to £145* **Services** Lift **Parking** 260 **Notes** LB 🐾 Civ Wed 70

Ibis Bradford Shipley

ibis

BUDGET HOTEL

☎ 01274 589333

Quayside, Salts Mill Rd BD18 3ST
e-mail: H3158@accor.com
web: www.ibis.com
dir: Follow tourist signs for Salts Mill. Follow A650 signs through Bradford for approx 5m to Shipley

Modern, budget hotel offering comfortable accommodation in bright and practical bedrooms. Breakfast is self-service and dinner is available in the restaurant. See also the Hotel Groups pages.

Rooms 78 (20 fmly) (22 GF) **S** £33-£59; **D** £33-£59* **Conf** Class 16 Board 18 Thtr 20

SHREWSBURY — Shropshire   Map 15 SJ41

Albright Hussey Manor Hotel & Restaurant

★★★★ 77% ◉◉ HOTEL

☎ 01939 290571 & 290523

Ellesmere Rd SY4 3AF
e-mail: info@albrighthussey.co.uk
web: www.albrighthussey.co.uk
dir: 2.5m N of Shrewsbury on A528, follow signs for Ellesmere

The estate was mentioned in the Domesday Book, but the current manor house is Tudor, dating from around 1524, and is approached over a moat. This Grade II listed, partly black-and-white timbered building maintains an abundance of original features including huge open fireplaces, oak-panelling and beams. The bedrooms, including four-poster rooms, are situated in either the sumptuously appointed main house or in the more modern wing. There's an intimate, award-winning restaurant and a comfortable cocktail bar and lounge.

Rooms 26 (4 fmly) (8 GF) 🐾 **S** £79-£130; **D** £95-£190 (incl. bkfst)* **Facilities** FTV Wi-fi 🎾 Xmas New Year **Conf** Class 180 Board 80 Thtr 250 **Parking** 100 **Notes** LB Civ Wed 180

Mercure Shrewsbury Albrighton Hall Hotel & Spa

★★★★ 75% COUNTRY HOUSE HOTEL

☎ 01939 291000
Albrighton SY4 3AG
e-mail: H6629@accor.com
web: www.mercure.com
dir: From S: M6 junct 10a to M54 to end. From N: M6 junct 12 to M5 then M54. Follow signs Harlescott & Ellesmere to A528

Dating back to 1630, this former ancestral home is set in 15 acres of attractive gardens. The bedrooms are generally spacious and the stable rooms are particularly popular. Elegant public rooms have rich oak panelling and there is a modern, well-equipped health and fitness centre.

Rooms 87 (16 annexe) (6 fmly) (21 GF) **Facilities** Spa STV Wi-fi ⓢ ⓢ Gym Squash Thermal suite Relax room Spray tan Aerobics Xmas New Year **Conf** Class 150 Board 80 Thtr 300 **Services** Lift **Parking** 200 **Notes** ⓧ Civ Wed 250

Rowton Castle Hotel

★★★ 88% HOTEL

☎ 01743 884044
Halfway House SY5 9EP
e-mail: post@rowtoncastle.com
web: www.rowtoncastle.com
dir: From A5 near Shrewsbury take A458 to Welshpool. Hotel 4m on right

Standing in 17 acres of grounds where a castle has stood for nearly 800 years, this Grade II listed building dates in parts back to 1696. Many original features remain, including the oak panelling in the restaurant and a magnificent carved oak fireplace. Most bedrooms are spacious and all have modern facilities; some have four-poster beds. The hotel has a well deserved reputation for its food and is a popular venue for weddings.

Rooms 19 (3 fmly) **Facilities** Wi-fi ⓢ **Conf** Class 30 Board 30 Thtr 80 **Parking** 100 **Notes** ⓧ Civ Wed 110

Prince Rupert Hotel

★★★ 85% HOTEL

☎ 01743 499955
Butcher Row SY1 1UQ
e-mail: reservations@prince-rupert-hotel.co.uk
web: www.prince-rupert-hotel.co.uk
dir: Follow town centre signs, over English Bridge & Wyle Cop Hill. Right into Fish St, hotel 200yds

Parts of this popular town centre hotel date back to medieval times and many bedrooms have exposed beams and other original features. Luxury suites, family rooms and rooms with four-poster beds are all available. As an alternative to the main Royalist Restaurant, diners have a less formal option in Chambers, a popular brasserie. The Camellias Tea Rooms are adjacent, providing snacks and afternoon teas. The hotel's valet parking service is also commendable.

Rooms 70 (2 fmly) ⓡ S £70-£85; D £115-£175 (incl. bkfst) **Facilities** FTV Wi-fi ⓡ Gym Weight training Steam shower Sauna Snooker room Hair salon Beauty treatment room Xmas New Year **Conf** Class 80 Board 40 Thtr 120 Del from £120 to £140 **Services** Lift **Parking** 70 **Notes** LB ⓧ

Lion & Pheasant Hotel

★★★ 78% ⓢⓢ TOWN HOUSE HOTEL

☎ 01743 770345
49-50 Wyle Cop SY1 1XJ
e-mail: info@lionandpheasant.co.uk
web: www.lionandpheasant.co.uk
dir: From S & E: pass abbey, cross river on English Bridge to Wyle Cop, hotel on left. From N & W : follow Town Centre signs on one-way system to Wyle Cop. Hotel at bottom of hill on right

This 16th-century property stands on Wyle Cop, part of the historic centre of Shrewsbury. The interior décor is minimalist and uses natural materials such as limed oak, linens and silks. The bedrooms are of a high standard and include twin, double and family rooms. Award-winning food is offered in the first-floor restaurant and also in the ground-floor bar area.

Rooms 22 (2 fmly) ⓡ **Facilities** FTV Wi-fi ⓡ **Conf** Class 30 Board 30 Thtr 30 **Parking** 15 **Notes** ⓧ

Mytton & Mermaid Hotel

★★★ 77% ⓢⓢ HOTEL

☎ 01743 761220
Atcham SY5 6QG
e-mail: reception@myttonandmermaid.co.uk
web: www.myttonandmermaid.co.uk
dir: From Shrewsbury over old bridge in Atcham. Hotel opposite main entrance to Attingham Park on B4380

Convenient for Shrewsbury, this former coaching inn enjoys a pleasant location beside the River Severn. Some bedrooms, including family suites, are in a converted stable block adjacent to the hotel. There is a large lounge bar, a comfortable lounge, and a brasserie that has gained a well-deserved local reputation for the quality of its food.

Rooms 18 (7 annexe) (1 fmly) (6 GF) S £85-£95; D £110-£175 (incl. bkfst)* **Facilities** Wi-fi Fishing ⓡ New Year **Conf** Class 24 Board 28 Thtr 70 **Parking** 50 **Notes** LB ⓧ Closed 25 Dec Civ Wed 80

Lord Hill Hotel

★★★ 75% HOTEL

☎ 01743 232601
Abbey Foregate SY2 6AX
e-mail: reception@thelordhill.co.uk
web: www.thelordhill.co.uk
dir: From M54 take A5, left at 1st rdbt , at 2nd rdbt 4th exit into London Rd. At next rdbt (Lord Hill Column) take 3rd exit, hotel 300yds on left

This pleasant, attractively appointed hotel is located close to the town centre. Most of the modern bedrooms are set in a separate purpose-built property, but those in the main building include one with a four-poster, as well as full suites. Public areas include a conservatory restaurant and spacious function suites.

Rooms 35 (24 annexe) (2 fmly) (8 GF) ⓡ S £60-£64.50; D £70-£75 (incl. bkfst)* **Facilities** FTV Wi-fi ⓡ Xmas New Year **Conf** Class 180 Board 180 Thtr 250 **Parking** 110 **Notes** Civ Wed 250

S

SHREWSBURY *continued*

Abbots Mead Hotel

★★ 74% METRO HOTEL

☎ 01743 235281
9 St Julian's Friars SY1 1XL
e-mail: res@abbotsmeadhotel.co.uk
dir: From S into town, 2nd left after English Bridge

This well maintained Georgian town house is located in a quiet cul-de-sac, near the English Bridge and close to both the River Severn and town centre with its many restaurants. Bedrooms are compact, neatly decorated and well equipped. Two lounges are available in addition to an attractive dining room, the setting for breakfasts, and dinner parties by prior arrangement.

Rooms 16 (2 fmly) **S** £55-£65; **D** £70-£80 (incl. bkfst)* **Facilities** Wi-fi **Parking** 10 **Notes** Closed certain days at Xmas

Premier Inn Shrewsbury (Harmers Hill)

BUDGET HOTEL

☎ 0871 527 8974
Wem Rd, Harmer Hill SY4 3DS
web: www.premierinn.com
dir: M54 junct 7, A5 signed Telford for approx 7m, at rdbt take A49, approx 3m. At next 2 rdbts 2nd exit, at next rdbt 4th exit signed Ellesmere & A528. In approx 3m hotel on left

High quality, budget accommodation ideal for both families and business travellers. Spacious, en suite bedrooms feature tea and coffee making facilities, and Freeview TV in most hotels. Internet access and Wi-fi are available for a small fee. The adjacent family restaurant features a wide and varied menu. See also the Hotel Groups pages.

Rooms 20

Drapers Hall

◉◉ RESTAURANT WITH ROOMS

☎ 01743 344679
10 Saint Mary's Place SY1 1DZ
e-mail: goodfood@drapershallrestaurant.co.uk
dir: From A5191 (Saint Mary's St) on one-way system into St Mary's Place

This 16th-century, timber-framed property is situated in the heart of the market town of Shrewsbury. It provides high quality accommodation, including two suites, with modern facilities. Careful renovation of the original beams and wood panels, together with beautiful wooden furniture, has created a harmony between the past and present. Accomplished dining, headed up by Nigel Huxley, can be enjoyed in the main restaurant, Huxleys at Drapers Hall.

Rooms 4 (2 fmly)

Mad Jack's Restaurant & Bar

◉ RESTAURANT WITH ROOMS

☎ 01743 358870 & 761220
15 Saint Mary's St SY1 1EQ
e-mail: info@madjacks.uk.com
dir: Follow one-way system around town, opposite St Mary's church

This fine property is located in the heart of the town. Its name comes from a eccentric squire in the 18th century who squandered a fortune and then landed in jail for his drunken and riotous behaviour. The four individually designed bedrooms, including a suite, are very comfortable and have spacious and contemporary bathrooms. Downstairs the award-winning, vibrant bar and restaurant specialises in British food with a classic twist. Breakfast offers a quality range of dishes. Secure parking is available in a nearby public car park.

Rooms 4 (1 fmly)

SIDLESHAM	Map 5 SZ89
West Sussex	

The Crab & Lobster

◉◉ RESTAURANT WITH ROOMS

☎ 01243 641233
Mill Ln PO20 7NB
e-mail: enquiries@crab-lobster.co.uk
dir: A27 onto B2145 signed Selsey. 1st left after garage at Sidlesham into Rookery Ln to Crab & Lobster

Hidden away on the south coast near Pagham Harbour and only a short drive from Chichester is the stylish Crab & Lobster. Bedrooms are superbly appointed, and bathrooms are a feature with luxury toiletries and powerful 'raindrop' showers. Guests can enjoy lunch or dinner in the smart restaurant where the menu offers a range of locally caught fresh fish amongst other regionally-sourced, seasonal produce.

Rooms 4

SIDMOUTH	Map 3 SY18
Devon	

The Victoria Hotel

★★★★ 83% ◉ HOTEL

☎ 01395 512651
The Esplanade EX10 8RY
e-mail: reservations@victoriahotel.co.uk
web: www.victoriahotel.co.uk
dir: On seafront

This imposing building, with manicured gardens, is situated overlooking the town. Wonderful sea views can be enjoyed from many of the comfortable bedrooms and elegant lounges. With indoor and outdoor leisure facilities, the hotel caters to a year-round clientele. Carefully prepared meals are served in the refined atmosphere of the restaurant. The staff provide a professional and friendly service.

Save on hotels. Book at **theAA.com/hotel**

SHR – SID 401 ENGLAND

The Victoria Hotel

Rooms 62 (6 fmly) ☎ **S** £140-£160; **D** £185-£370*
Facilities FTV Wi-fi ⓦ ⓢ ⌇ ⚘ Putt green Hot stone
relaxation beds Spa bath Sauna Beauty treatment
room Games room ♫ Xmas New Year Child facilities
Conf Thtr 60 **Services** Lift **Parking** 100 **Notes** LB ⊗

See advert on page 403

Hotel Riviera

★★★★ 82% ❀ HOTEL

☎ 01395 515201
The Esplanade EX10 8AY
e-mail: enquiries@hotelriviera.co.uk
web: www.hotelriviera.co.uk
dir: M5 junct 30 & follow A3052

Overlooking the sea and close to the town centre, the
Riviera is a fine example of Regency architecture. The
large number of guests that become regular visitors
here are testament to the high standards of service
and hospitality offered. The front-facing bedrooms
benefit from wonderful sea views, and the daily-
changing menu places an emphasis on fresh, local
produce.

Hotel Riviera

Rooms 26 (6 fmly) ☎ **S** £109-£199; **D** £198-£378
(incl. bkfst & dinner)* **Facilities** FTV Wi-fi ⓦ ♫ Xmas
New Year **Conf** Class 60 Board 30 Thtr 85
Services Lift **Parking** 26 **Notes** LB

See advert below

S

SIDMOUTH *continued*

The Belmont Hotel

★★★★ 76% HOTEL

☎ 01395 512555
The Esplanade EX10 8RX
e-mail: reservations@belmont-hotel.co.uk
web: www.belmont-hotel.co.uk
dir: On seafront

Prominently positioned on the seafront just a few minutes' walk from the town centre, this traditional hotel has many returning guests. A choice of comfortable lounges provides ample space for relaxation, and the air-conditioned restaurant has a pianist playing most evenings. Bedrooms are attractively furnished and many have fine views over the esplanade. Leisure facilities are available at the adjacent sister hotel, The Victoria.

Rooms 50 (1 fmly) (2 GF) ♦ **S** £130-£170; **D** £160-£245* **Facilities** STV Wi-fi ⌀ Putt green Leisure facilities available at sister hotel ♫ Xmas New Year Child facilities **Conf** Thtr 50 **Services** Lift **Parking** 45 **Notes** LB ⊗ Civ Wed 110

See advert on opposite page

Kingswood & Devoran Hotel

★★★ 85% HOTEL

☎ 01395 516367 & 08000 481731
The Esplanade EX10 8AX
e-mail:
kingswoodanddevoran@hotels-sidmouth.co.uk
web: www.hotels-sidmouth.co.uk
dir: M5 junct 30, A3052 signed Sidmouth on right, follow Station Rd down to Esplanade

This seafront hotel continues to offer friendly hospitality and service. Many bedrooms enjoy the sea views; all are well appointed and have smart bathrooms. Cuisine is pleasant and offers enjoyable dining featuring freshly prepared dishes.

Rooms 49 (8 fmly) (1 GF) ♦ **S** £63-£88; **D** £126-£176 (incl. bkfst & dinner)* **Facilities** FTV Wi-fi Xmas **Conf** Class 30 Board 40 Thtr 60 **Services** Lift **Parking** 23 **Notes** LB Closed 27 Dec-10 Feb

Westcliff Hotel

★★★ 79% HOTEL

☎ 01395 513252
Manor Rd EX10 8RU
e-mail: stay@westcliffhotel.co.uk
web: www.westcliffhotel.co.uk
dir: Exit A3052 to Sidmouth then to seafront & esplanade, turn right, hotel directly ahead

This charming hotel is ideally located within walking distance of Sidmouth's elegant promenade and beaches. The spacious lounges and the cocktail bar open onto a terrace which leads to the pool and croquet lawn. Bedrooms, several with balconies and glorious sea views, are spacious and comfortable, whilst the restaurant offers a choice of well-prepared dishes.

Rooms 40 (1 fmly) (5 GF) ♦ **S** £60-£130; **D** £95-£250 (incl. bkfst)* **Facilities** FTV Wi-fi ⌀ Putt green Xmas New Year **Conf** Class 20 Board 15 Thtr 30 **Services** Lift **Parking** 40 **Notes** Civ Wed 80

Bedford Hotel

★★★ 75% HOTEL

☎ 01395 513047 & 0797 394 0671
Esplanade EX10 8NR
e-mail: info@bedfordhotelsidmouth.co.uk
web: www.bedfordhotelsidmouth.co.uk
dir: M5 junct 30, A3052 & to Sidmouth. Hotel at centre of Esplanade

Situated on the seafront, this long established, family-run hotel provides a warm welcome and relaxing atmosphere. Bedrooms are well appointed and many have the added bonus of wonderful sea views. Public areas combine character and comfort with a choice of lounges in which to relax. In addition to the hotel dining room, Pyne's bar and restaurant offers an interesting range of dishes in a convivial environment.

Rooms 37 (1 GF) **Facilities** Xmas **Services** Lift **Parking** 6

S

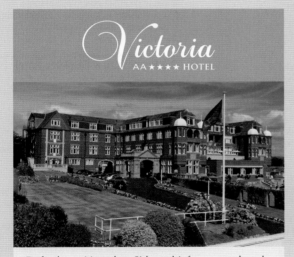
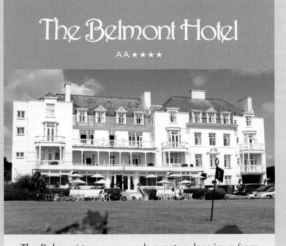

SIDMOUTH *continued*

Hotel Elizabeth

★★★ 75% HOTEL

☎ 01395 513503 & 08000 481731
The Esplanade EX10 8AT
e-mail: elizabeth@hotels-sidmouth.co.uk
web: www.hotels-sidmouth.co.uk
dir: M5 junct 30, A3052 to Sidmouth. 1st exit on right to Sidmouth, left onto esplanade

Occupying a prime location on the Esplanade, this elegant hotel attracts many loyal guests who return to enjoy the relaxed atmosphere and attentive service. Bedrooms are both comfortable and smartly appointed; all have sea views and some have balconies. The spacious lounge and sunny patio, with wonderful views across the bay, are perfect places to sit and just watch the world go by.

Rooms 28 (3 fmly) (1 GF) ⬧ **S** £65-£73; **D** £130-£176 (incl. bkfst & dinner)* **Facilities** FTV Wi-fi Xmas **Services** Lift **Parking** 16 **Notes** LB ⊗ Closed 28 Dec-10 Feb

Royal Glen Hotel

★★★ 75% HOTEL

☎ 01395 513221 & 513456
Glen Rd EX10 8RW
e-mail: info@royalglenhotel.co.uk
dir: A303 to Honiton, A375 to Sidford, follow seafront signs, right onto esplanade, right at end into Glen Rd

This historic 17th-century, Grade I listed hotel has been owned by the same family for several generations. The comfortable bedrooms are furnished in period style. Guests may use the well-maintained gardens and a heated indoor pool, and can enjoy well-prepared food in the elegant dining room.

Rooms 32 (3 fmly) (3 GF) ⬧ **S** £48-£73; **D** £96-£146 (incl. bkfst)* **Facilities** FTV Wi-fi ⬧ Gym **Services** Lift **Parking** 22 **Notes** LB Closed Dec-21 Feb

Hunters Moon Hotel

★★ 82% HOTEL

☎ 01395 513380
Sid Rd EX10 9AA
e-mail: huntersmoon.hotel@virgin.net
dir: From Exeter on A3052 to Sidford, right at lights into Sidmouth, 1.5m, at cinema turn left. Hotel in 0.25m

Set in three acres of attractive and well-tended grounds, this friendly, family-run hotel is located in a quiet area within walking distance of the town and esplanade. The light and airy bedrooms, some at ground floor level, are comfortable and well equipped. There is a lounge and a cosy bar. The restaurant provides a choice of imaginative dishes, and weather permitting, tea may be taken on the lawn.

Rooms 33 (4 fmly) (11 GF) ⬧ **S** £62-£65; **D** £118-£122 (incl. bkfst) **Facilities** FTV Wi-fi Putt green Xmas **Parking** 33 **Notes** LB No children 3yrs Closed Jan-9 Feb RS Dec & Feb

Mount Pleasant Hotel

★★ 82% HOTEL

☎ 01395 514694
Salcombe Rd EX10 8JA
dir: Exit A3052 at Sidford x-rds, in 1.25m turn left into Salcombe Rd, opposite Radway Cinema. Hotel on right after bridge

Quietly located within almost an acre of gardens, this modernised Georgian hotel is minutes from the town centre and seafront. Bedrooms and public areas provide good levels of comfort and high quality furnishings. Guests return on a regular basis, especially to experience the friendly, relaxed atmosphere. The light and airy restaurant overlooks the pleasant garden and offers a daily-changing menu of imaginative, yet traditional home-cooked dishes.

Rooms 17 (1 fmly) (3 GF) **S** £59.50-£74.50; **D** £119-£149 (incl. bkfst & dinner)* **Facilities** Putt green **Parking** 20 **Notes** ⊗ No children 8yrs Closed Dec-Feb

The Royal York & Faulkner Hotel

★★ 80% HOTEL

☎ 01395 513043 & 0800 220714
The Esplanade EX10 8AZ
e-mail: stay@royalyorkhotel.co.uk
web: www.royalyorkhotel.co.uk
dir: M5 junct 30 take A3052, 10m to Sidmouth, hotel in centre of Esplanade

This seafront hotel, owned and run by the same family for over 60 years, maintains its Regency charm and grandeur. The attractive bedrooms vary in size, and many have balconies and sea views. Public rooms are spacious, and traditional dining is offered, alongside Blinis Café-Bar, which is more contemporary in style and offers coffees, lunch and afternoon tea. The spa facilities include a hydrotherapy pool, steam room, sauna and a variety of treatments.

Rooms 70 (2 annexe) (8 fmly) (5 GF) ⬧ **S** £59.50-£95; **D** £119-£211 (incl. bkfst & dinner)* **Facilities** Spa FTV Wi-fi ⬧ HL Hydrotherapy pool Steam Room Sauna Complimentary use of pool (200yds from hotel) ♫ Xmas New Year **Services** Lift **Parking** 20 **Notes** LB Closed Jan

S

The Woodlands Hotel

★★ 74% HOTEL

☎ 01395 513120
Cotmaton Cross EX10 8HG
e-mail: info@woodlands-hotel.com
web: www.woodlands-hotel.com
dir: Follow signs for Sidmouth

Located in the heart of the town and ideally situated for exploring Devon and Dorset, this listed property has numerous character features. There is a spacious bar and a lounge where guests may relax. Freshly prepared dinners can be enjoyed in the smart dining room. Families with children are made very welcome and may dine early.

Rooms 20 (4 fmly) (8 GF) ⚡ **Facilities** FTV Wi-fi ↘
Parking 20 **Notes** LB Closed 20 Dec–15 Jan

The Salty Monk

◉ ◉ RESTAURANT WITH ROOMS

☎ 01395 513174
Church St, Sidford EX10 9QP
e-mail: saltymonk@btconnect.com
web: www.saltymonk.co.uk
dir: On A3052 opposite church in Sidford

Set in the village of Sidford, this attractive property dates from the 16th century. There's oodles of style and appeal here and each bedroom has a unique identity. Bathrooms are equally special with multi-jet showers, spa baths and cosseting robes and towels. The output from the kitchen is impressive with excellent local produce very much in evidence, served in the elegant surroundings of the restaurant. A mini spa facility is available.

Rooms 6 (1 annexe)

SILLOTH   Map 18 NY15
Cumbria

The Golf Hotel

★★ 75% HOTEL

☎ 016973 31438
Criffel St CA7 4AB
e-mail: info@golfhotelsilloth.co.uk

A friendly welcome waits at this hotel which occupies a prime position in the centre of the historic market town, and is a popular meeting place for the local community. Bedrooms are mostly well proportioned and are comfortably equipped. The lounge bar is a popular venue for dining, with a wide range of dishes on offer.

Rooms 22 (4 fmly) ⚡ **S** £50–£65; **D** £45–£75 (incl. bkfst)* **Facilities** FTV Wi-fi ↘ Xmas New Year **Conf** Class 50 Board 30 Thtr 100 Del from £65 to £90* **Notes** LB Civ Wed 100

SILVERSTONE   Map 11 SP64
Northamptonshire

Premier Inn Silverstone

BUDGET HOTEL

☎ 0871 527 8976
Brackley Hatch, Syresham NN13 5TX
web: www.premierinn.com
dir: On A43 near Silverstone

High quality, budget accommodation ideal for both families and business travellers. Spacious, en suite bedrooms feature tea and coffee making facilities, and Freeview TV in most hotels. Internet access and Wi-fi are available for a small fee. The adjacent family restaurant features a wide and varied menu. See also the Hotel Groups pages.

Rooms 41

SITTINGBOURNE   Map 7 TQ96
Kent

Hempstead House Country Hotel

★★★ 86% ◉ HOTEL

☎ 01795 428020
London Rd, Bapchild ME9 9PP
e-mail: info@hempsteadhouse.co.uk
web: www.hempsteadhouse.co.uk
dir: 1.5m from town centre on A2 towards Canterbury

Expect a warm welcome at this charming detached Victorian property, situated amidst four acres of mature landscaped gardens. Bedrooms are attractively decorated with lovely co-ordinated fabrics, tastefully furnished and equipped with many thoughtful touches. Public rooms feature a choice of elegant lounges as well as a superb conservatory dining room. In summer guests can eat on the terraces. There is a spa and fitness studio.

Rooms 34 (7 fmly) (1 GF) ⚡ **S** £85–£115; **D** £110–£160 (incl. bkfst)* **Facilities** Spa STV FTV Wi-fi 🕙 ⛳ Gym Fitness studio Steam room Sauna Hydrotherapy pool Xmas New Year **Conf** Class 150 Board 100 Thtr 150 Del from £152.50* **Services** Lift **Parking** 200 **Notes** LB Civ Wed 150

Premier Inn Sittingbourne

BUDGET HOTEL

☎ 9871 527 8978
Bobbing Corner, Sheppy Way, Bobbing ME9 8RZ
web: www.premierinn.com
dir: M2 junct 5, A249 towards Sheerness, approx 2m. Take 1st slip road after A2 underpass. At rdbt take 1st exit, hotel on left

High quality, budget accommodation ideal for both families and business travellers. Spacious, en suite bedrooms feature tea and coffee making facilities, and Freeview TV in most hotels. Internet access and Wi-fi are available for a small fee. The adjacent family restaurant features a wide and varied menu. See also the Hotel Groups pages.

Rooms 40

S

SKEGNESS
Lincolnshire   **Map 17 TF56**

BEST WESTERN The Vine Hotel

★★★ 77% HOTEL

☎ 01754 763018 & 610611
Vine Rd, Seacroft PE25 3DB
e-mail: info@thevinehotel.com
dir: A52 to Skegness, S towards Gibraltar Point, right into Drummond Rd, 0.5m, right into Vine Rd

With its long history this traditional hotel is something of a local landmark. The smartly decorated bedrooms are well equipped and comfortably appointed. Public areas include two character bars that serve excellent local beers. Freshly prepared dishes are offered in the bar and the restaurant; service is both friendly and helpful.

Rooms 25 (3 fmly) **S** £70-£90; **D** £90-£110 (incl. bkfst)* **Facilities** FTV Wi-fi Xmas New Year **Conf** Class 25 Board 30 Thtr 100 **Parking** 50 **Notes** LB ⊗ Civ Wed 100

BEST WESTERN North Shore Hotel & Golf Course
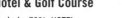
★★★ 72% HOTEL

☎ 01754 763298
North Shore Rd PE25 1DN
e-mail: info@northshorehotel.co.uk
web: www.northshorehotel.co.uk
dir: 1m N of town centre on A52, turn right into North Shore Rd (opposite Fenland laundry)

This hotel enjoys an enviable position on the beachfront, adjacent to its own championship golf course and only ten minutes from the town centre. Spacious public areas include a terrace bar serving informal meals and real ales, a formal restaurant and impressive function rooms. Bedrooms are smartly decorated and thoughtfully equipped.

Best Western North Shore Hotel & Golf Course

Rooms 34 (3 annexe) (4 fmly) (3 GF) ⌇ **S** £35-£55; **D** £50-£75 **Facilities** FTV Wi-fi ⌿ 18 Putt green Xmas New Year **Conf** Class 60 Board 60 Thtr 220 Del from £80 to £110 **Parking** 100 **Notes** LB ⊗ Civ Wed 180

See advert on opposite page

SKIPTON
North Yorkshire   **Map 18 SD95**

The Coniston Hotel & Country Estate
★★★★ 77% HOTEL

☎ 01756 748080
Coniston Cold BD23 4EA
e-mail: info@theconistonhotel.com
web: www.theconistonhotel.com
dir: On A65, 6m NW of Skipton

This privately owned hotel set in 1,400 acres of prime country estate is a haven for both leisure and corporate guests. All bedrooms and bathrooms are appointed to a very high standard; the bedroom wing offers large rooms with balconies. The reception, bar and restaurant have style and elegance, and the stunning spa adds to the impressive list of activities for guests.

Rooms 71 (13 fmly) (35 GF) ⌇ **S** £81-£108; **D** £81-£108 **Facilities** STV FTV Wi-fi Clay pigeon shooting Falconry centre The Land Rover Experience Fly fishing Xmas New Year **Conf** Class 80 Board 50 Thtr 200 Del from £135 **Services** Lift **Parking** 170 **Notes** LB Civ Wed 120

Herriots Hotel
★★★ 80% HOTEL

☎ 01756 792781
Broughton Rd BD23 1RT
e-mail: info@herriotsforleisure.co.uk
web: www.herriotsforleisure.co.uk
dir: 2m from A59 at entrance to town; 50yds from railway station

This friendly hotel is situated in the centre of the delightful market town of Skipton and is just a short walk from the canal; the nearby railway has links to Leeds and the Settle to Carlisle route with its breathtaking scenery. The well-equipped bedrooms are contemporary in style yet maintain the character of this Victorian listed building; some rooms have French doors that overlook the canal; the largest rooms have four-posters and spas, and can be converted to accommodate families. Rhubarb restaurant offers British cuisine with a Yorkshire 'twist' that is based on local, seasonal produce.

Rooms 23 (3 fmly) ⌇ **S** £45-£70; **D** £69-£110 (incl. bkfst)* **Facilities** FTV Wi-fi ⌿ Private access onto Leeds Liverpool Canal Xmas New Year **Conf** Class 50 Board 52 Thtr 100 Del from £115 to £145* **Services** Lift **Parking** 26 **Notes** LB ⊗ Civ Wed 80

Premier Inn Skipton North (Gargrave)

BUDGET HOTEL

☎ 0871 527 8980
Hellifield Rd, Gargrave BD23 3NB
web: www.premierinn.com
dir: NW of Skipton at rdbt junct of A59 & A65, take A65 signed Kendal, Settle & Gargrave. 3.5m. Through Gargrave. Hotel on left

High quality, budget accommodation ideal for both families and business travellers. Spacious, en suite bedrooms feature tea and coffee making facilities, and Freeview TV in most hotels. Internet access and Wi-fi are available for a small fee. The adjacent family restaurant features a wide and varied menu. See also the Hotel Groups pages.

Rooms 21

Save on hotels. Book at **theAA.com/hotel**

SKE – SLO 407 ENGLAND

SLEAFORD
Lincolnshire   Map 12 TF04

The Carre Arms Hotel & Conference Centre

★★★ 68% SMALL HOTEL

☎ 01529 303156
1 Mareham Ln NG34 7JP
e-mail: enquiries@carrearmshotel.co.uk
web: www.carrearmshotel.co.uk
dir: Take A153 to Sleaford, hotel on right at level crossing

This friendly, family run hotel is located close to the station and offers suitably appointed accommodation. Public areas include a smart brasserie and two spacious bars where a good selection of meals is offered. There is also a conservatory and a former stable that houses the spacious function room.

Rooms 13 (2 fmly) 🐾 **S** fr £68.40; **D** fr £104.40 (incl. bkfst)* **Facilities** FTV Wi-fi **Conf** Class 70 Board 40 Thtr 120 Del from £82.50* **Parking** 80 **Notes** ⊗ Civ Wed 80

SLOUGH
Berkshire   Map 6 SU97

Copthorne Hotel Slough-Windsor

 MILLENNIUM
HOTELS AND RESORTS
MILLENNIUM • COPTHORNE

★★★★ 75% HOTEL

☎ 01753 516222
400 Cippenham Ln SL1 2YE
e-mail: sales.slough@millenniumhotels.co.uk
web: www.millenniumhotels.co.uk
dir: M4 junct 6, A355 towards Slough. At next rdbt left & left again for hotel entrance

Conveniently located for the motorway and for Heathrow Airport, this modern hotel of striking design offers visitors a wide range of indoor leisure facilities; Bugis Street Brasserie offers menus of Chinese, Malaysian and Singaporean dishes. Bedrooms provide a useful range of extras including climate control and satellite TV. The hotel offers a discounted entrance fee to some of the attractions in the area.

Rooms 219 (47 fmly) (6 smoking) 🐾 **D** £54–£148 **Facilities** STV FTV Wi-fi Gym Steam room Sauna **Conf** Class 160 Board 60 Thtr 280 **Services** Lift **Parking** 303 **Notes** LB Civ Wed 280

The Pinewood Hotel

"bespoke"

★★★★ 72% HOTEL

☎ 01753 896400
Wexham Park Ln, George Green SL3 6AP
e-mail: info@pinewoodhotel.co.uk
web: www.pinewoodhotel.co.uk
dir: A4 N from Slough, A412 towards Uxbridge. Hotel 3m on left

This is a small luxury hotel on the outskirts of Slough. Excellent design is at the forefront throughout, together with good levels of comfort. The Eden brasserie specialises in quality produce, carefully prepared, including dishes cooked on the wood-burning stove. Service is friendly and attentive.

Rooms 49 (16 annexe) (4 fmly) (12 GF) 🐾 **Facilities** FTV Wi-fi Free use of nearby leisure facilities New Year **Conf** Class 46 Board 40 Thtr 120 Del from £145 to £225* **Services** Lift Air con **Parking** 40 **Notes** ⊗ Closed 24-28 Dec Civ Wed 130

Holiday Inn Express London Heathrow T5

Holiday Inn Express

BUDGET HOTEL

☎ 01753 684001
London Rd SL3 8QB
e-mail: info@hiexheathrowt5.co.uk
web: www.hiexheathrowt5.co.uk
dir: M4 junct 5, follow signs for Colnbrook. Hotel 0.5m on right

A modern hotel ideal for families and business travellers. Fresh and uncomplicated, the spacious rooms include Sky TV, power shower and tea and coffee-making facilities. Continental buffet breakfast is included in the room rate; other meals may be taken at the nearby family pub or restaurant. See also the Hotel Groups pages.

Rooms 300 (300 fmly) 🐾 **Conf** Class 50 Board 40 Thtr 120

S

SLOUGH *continued*

Premier Inn Slough

BUDGET HOTEL

☎ 0871 527 8982
76 Uxbridge Rd SL1 1SU
web: www.premierinn.com
dir: 2m from M4 junct 5, 3m from junct 6. Just off A4

High quality, budget accommodation ideal for both families and business travellers. Spacious, en suite bedrooms feature tea and coffee making facilities, and Freeview TV in most hotels. Internet access and Wi-fi are available for a small fee. The adjacent family restaurant features a wide and varied menu. See also the Hotel Groups pages.

Rooms 84

| SNAINTON | Map 17 SE98 |
| North Yorkshire | |

The Coachman Inn

⊚ RESTAURANT WITH ROOMS

☎ 01723 859231
Pickering Road West YO13 9PL
e-mail: info@coachmaninn.co.uk
web: www.coachmaninn.co.uk
dir: From A170 between Pickering & Scarborough onto B1258 (High St) in Snainton

This Grade II listed property was built in 1776 as a coaching inn and stands just on the outskirts of Snainton. It now offers comfortable, double, en suite rooms, fine dining in a wonderful large dining room, a locals' bar, a quiet lounge for residents, and ample parking.

Rooms 6 (1 fmly)

| SNETTISHAM | Map 12 TF63 |
| Norfolk | |

The Rose & Crown

★★ 81% ⊚ HOTEL

☎ 01485 541382
Old Church Rd PE31 7LX
e-mail: info@roseandcrownsnettisham.co.uk
dir: A149 towards Hunstanton. In village centre into Old Church Rd, hotel 100yds on left

This lovely village inn provides comfortable, well-equipped bedrooms. A range of quality meals is served in the many dining areas, complemented by a good variety of real ales and wines. Service is friendly and a delightful atmosphere prevails. A walled garden is available on sunny days, as is a children's play area.

Rooms 16 (5 fmly) (2 GF) ⚓ Facilities FTV Wi-fi ♨ ☻ ⚓ Xmas New Year Conf Class 40 Board 40 Thtr 60 Parking 70

| SOLIHULL | Map 10 SP17 |
| West Midlands | |

See also Dorridge

The St Johns Hotel

P// | principal hayley

★★★★ 75% HOTEL

☎ 0121 711 3000 & 712 7601
651 Warwick Rd B91 1AT
e-mail: enquiriesstjohns@principal-hayley.com
dir: M42 junct 5, A41 (Solihull Bypass) signed Solihull. At lights left into Load Ln (signed Solihull Town Centre). At next rdbt 3rd exit onto B425 (Warwick Rd). Hotel on right

With its town centre location, this modern hotel is conveniently situated for the NEC, Birmingham and many local attractions. Bedrooms are air conditioned, attractively decorated and equipped with a comprehensive range of extras. The hotel provides extensive conference facilities, an indoor leisure facility and extensive parking.

Rooms 180 (1 fmly) (9 GF) ⚓ Facilities STV FTV Wi-fi HL ☺ Gym Sauna Steam room Xmas New Year Conf Class 350 Board 40 Thtr 700 Services Lift Air con Parking 300 Notes Civ Wed 350

Premier Inn Solihull (Hockley Heath)

BUDGET HOTEL

☎ 0871 527 8984
Stratford Rd, Hockley Heath B94 6NX
web: www.premierinn.com
dir: On A3400, 2m S of M42 junct 4

High quality, budget accommodation ideal for both families and business travellers. Spacious, en suite bedrooms feature tea and coffee making facilities, and Freeview TV in most hotels. Internet access and Wi-fi are available for a small fee. The adjacent family restaurant features a wide and varied menu. See also the Hotel Groups pages.

Rooms 55

Premier Inn Solihull North

BUDGET HOTEL

☎ 0871 527 8988
Stratford Rd, Shirley B90 3AG
web: www.premierinn.com
dir: M42 junct 4 follow signs for Birmingham. Hotel in Shirley town centre on A34

Rooms 43

Premier Inn Solihull (Shirley)

BUDGET HOTEL

☎ 0871 527 8986
Stratford Rd, Shirley B90 4EP
web: www.premierinn.com
dir: M42 junct 4, A34N. Hotel in 1m

Rooms 51

Premier Inn Solihull Town Centre

BUDGET HOTEL

☎ 0871 527 9366
Station Rd B91 3RX
web: www.premierinn.com
dir: M42 junct 5. At rdbt, take 3rd exit onto A41. At lights, turn left onto Lode Lane. At rdbt, take 2nd exit & continue down Lode Lane. At rdbt take 1st exit onto Station Road

Rooms 115

| SOURTON | Map 3 SX59 |
| Devon | |

Collaven Manor Hotel

★★ 79% COUNTRY HOUSE HOTEL

☎ 01837 861522
EX20 4HH
e-mail: collavenmanor@supanet.com
dir: A30 onto A386 to Tavistock, hotel 2m on right

This delightful 15th-century manor house is quietly located in five acres of well-tended grounds. The friendly proprietors provide attentive service and ensure a relaxing environment. Charming public rooms have old oak beams and granite fireplaces, provide a range of comfortable lounges, and include a well stocked bar. In the restaurant, a daily-changing menu offers interesting dishes.

Rooms 9 (1 fmly) Facilities FTV Wi-fi ☻ Bowls Conf Class 20 Board 16 Thtr 30 Parking 50 Notes Closed Dec-Jan Civ Wed 50

SOUTHAMPTON
Hampshire   Map 5 SU41

See also Botley

Botleigh Grange Hotel
★★★★ 75% ◉ HOTEL

☎ 01489 787700 & 776969
Grange Rd, Hedge End SO30 2GA
e-mail: info@botleighgrangehotel.net
web: www.botleighgrangehotel.net
dir: M27 junct 7, A334 to Botley, hotel 1m on left

This impressive mansion, situated close to the M27, displays good quality throughout. The bedrooms are spacious with a good range of facilities. Public areas include a large conference room and a pleasant terrace with views overlooking the gardens and lake. The restaurant offers interesting menus using fresh, local produce.

Rooms 56 (7 fmly) (9 GF) S £90-£160; D £125-£175 (incl. bkfst)* Facilities Spa FTV Wi-fi ♥ ☜ supervised Putt green Fishing Gym Sauna Steam room Relaxation room Monsoon showers Xmas New Year
Conf Class 105 Board 40 Thtr 500 Del from £130 to £170* Services Lift Notes LB Civ Wed 275

Novotel Southampton
★★★★ 72% HOTEL

☎ 023 8033 0550
1 West Quay Rd SO15 1RA
e-mail: H1073@accor.com
web: www.novotel.com
dir: M27 junct 3, follow city centre/A33 signs. In 1m take right lane for West Quay & Dock Gates 4-10. Hotel entrance on left. Turn at lights by McDonalds, left at rdbt, hotel straight ahead

A modern, purpose-built hotel situated close to the city centre, railway station, ferry terminal and major road networks. The brightly decorated bedrooms are ideal for families and business guests; four rooms have facilities for the less mobile. The open-plan public areas include the Garden Brasserie, a bar and a leisure complex.

Rooms 121 (50 fmly) ☜ S £84-£220; D £84-£220* Facilities STV FTV Wi-fi ♥ ☜ Gym Sauna New Year Conf Class 250 Board 150 Thtr 450 Del from £125 to £225* Services Lift Parking 300 Notes Civ Wed 300

Mercure Southampton Centre Dolphin Hotel

★★★★ 70% ◉ HOTEL

☎ 023 8038 6460
34-35 High St SO14 2HN
e-mail: H7876@accor.com
web: www.mercure.com
dir: From A33 follow signs for Docks, Old Town & Isle of Wight ferry. At ferry terminal right into High Street, hotel 400yds on left

Originally a coaching inn, this hotel enjoys a central location set almost in the heart of the town, yet close to the ferry terminals. The bedrooms are appointed to a high standard, and public areas include a traditional bar, popular restaurant and two meeting rooms. Parking at the rear of the hotel is an added bonus.

Rooms 99 (9 annexe) (6 fmly) (27 GF) ☜ Facilities FTV Wi-fi Xmas New Year Conf Class 50 Board 40 Thtr 120 Services Lift Parking 80 Notes Civ Wed 120

BEST WESTERN Chilworth Manor

★★★ 79% HOTEL

☎ 023 8076 7333
Chilworth SO16 7PT
e-mail: sales@chilworth-manor.co.uk
web: www.bw-chilworthmanor.co.uk
dir: 1m from M3/M27 junct on A27 (Romsey road) N from Southampton. Pass Chilworth Arms on left, in 200mtrs turn left at Southampton Science Park sign. Hotel immediately right

Set in 12 acres of delightful grounds, this attractive Edwardian manor house is conveniently located for Southampton and also the New Forest National Park. Bedrooms are located in both the main house and an adjoining wing. The hotel is particularly popular as both a conference and a wedding venue.

Rooms 95 (6 fmly) (23 GF) Facilities Spa FTV Wi-fi ♥ ☜ Gym Trail walking Giant chess Petanque New Year Conf Class 50 Board 50 Thtr 130 Services Lift Parking 200 Notes ⊗ Civ Wed 105

Holiday Inn Southampton
★★★ 75% HOTEL

☎ 0871 942 9073
Herbert Walker Av SO15 1HJ
e-mail: southamptonhi@ihg.com
web: www.holidayinn.co.uk
dir: M27 junct 3 follow 'Dockgate 1-10 & Southampton Waterfront' signs. Hotel adjacent to Dock Gate 8

Convenient for both the port and town centre, this modern hotel is popular with both business and leisure guests. The well-equipped bedrooms are comfortably furnished. Public areas include an informal lounge bar and a contemporary restaurant offering an extensive range of popular dishes. Conference and leisure facilities are also available.

Rooms 130 (6 fmly) (15 smoking) Facilities STV Wi-fi ☜ supervised Gym New Year Conf Class 75 Board 60 Thtr 180 Services Lift Air con Parking 140 Notes ⊗ Civ Wed

The Elizabeth House Hotel
★★ 80% HOTEL

☎ 023 8022 4327
42-44 The Avenue SO17 1XP
e-mail: mail@elizabethhousehotel.com
web: www.elizabethhousehotel.com
dir: On A33, hotel on left after Southampton Common, before main lights

This hotel is conveniently situated close to the city centre, so provides an ideal base for both business and leisure guests. The bedrooms are well equipped and are attractively furnished with comfort in mind. There is also a cosy and atmospheric bistro in the cellar where evening meals are served.

Rooms 27 (7 annexe) (9 fmly) (8 GF) ☜ S £65-£72.50; D £75-£84.50 (incl. bkfst)* Facilities FTV Wi-fi ♥ Conf Class 24 Board 24 Thtr 40 Del £112.50* Parking 31

S

SOUTHAMPTON *continued*

Holiday Inn Express Southampton M27 Jct 7

BUDGET HOTEL

☎ 023 8060 6060
Botley Rd, West End SO30 3XA
e-mail: reservations@expressbyholidayinn.uk.net
web: www.meridianleisurehotels.com/southampton
dir: M27 junct 7, follow brown Ageas Bowl signs.
Hotel 1m from junct 7 at entrance to The Ageas Bowl
on corner Marshall Drive & Botley Rd

Set in landscaped gardens this hotel, adjacent to the
Ageas Bowl, is conveniently located for Southampton
Airport, Cruise Terminal and Docks and has ample
free parking. There is an air-conditioned restaurant
serving conference lunches, evening meals and
complimentary hot breakfast, a fully licensed bar and
lounge area with a 42" plasma TV with Freeview
channels. The hotel offers high speed Wi-fi
throughout. Leisure facilities are available at the
adjacent Virgin Active Leisure Centre for an
additional fee. See also the Hotel Groups pages.

Rooms 176 (129 fmly) (38 GF) (9 smoking)
S £50-£74.95; **D** £50-£74.95 (incl. bkfst)
Conf Class 26 Board 20 Thtr 52 Del from £99 to £109

Ibis Southampton Centre

BUDGET HOTEL

☎ 023 8063 4463
West Quay Rd, Western Esplanade SO15 1RA
e-mail: H1039@accor.com
web: www.ibishotel.com
dir: M27 junct 3, M271, left to city centre (A35),
follow Old Town Waterfront to 4th lights, left, left
again, hotel opposite station

Modern, budget hotel offering comfortable
accommodation in bright and practical bedrooms.
Breakfast is self-service and dinner is available in
the restaurant. See also the Hotel Groups pages.

Rooms 93 **Conf** Class 50 Board 40 Thtr 80
Del from £99 to £298*

Premier Inn Southampton Airport

BUDGET HOTEL

☎ 0871 527 8998
Mitchell Way SO18 2XU
web: www.premierinn.com
dir: M27 junct 5, A335 towards Eastleigh. Right at
rdbt into Wide Lane. 1st exit at next rdbt into Mitchell
Way

High quality, budget accommodation ideal for both
families and business travellers. Spacious, en suite
bedrooms feature tea and coffee making facilities,
and Freeview TV in most hotels. Internet access and
Wi-fi are available for a small fee. The adjacent
family restaurant features a wide and varied menu.
See also the Hotel Groups pages.

Rooms 121

Premier Inn Southampton City Centre

BUDGET HOTEL

☎ 0871 527 9266
6 Dials, New Rd SO14 0YN
web: www.premierinn.com
dir: M27 junct 5, A335 signed City Centre. At
Charlotte Place rdbt take 3rd exit into East Park
Terrace, 1st left into New Rd. Hotel on right

Rooms 172

Premier Inn Southampton North

BUDGET HOTEL

☎ 0871 527 9002
Romsey Rd, Nursling SO16 0XJ
web: www.premierinn.com
dir: M27 junct 3, M271 towards Romsey. At next rdbt
take 3rd exit towards Southampton (A3057). Hotel
1.5m on right

Rooms 32

Premier Inn Southampton West Quay

BUDGET HOTEL

☎ 0871 527 9298
Harbour Pde SO15 1ST
web: www.premierinn.com
dir: M27 junct 3, follow M271(S)/Southampton/The
Docks signs, onto M271, at Redbridge rdbt onto A35
follow Southampton/The Docks/A3024 signs. Merge
onto A35 (Redbridge Rd), continue onto Millbrook
Flyover/A3024, right at West Quay Rd/A3057, left
after Ikea into Harbour Parade

Rooms 155

Ennio's Restaurant & Boutique Rooms

RESTAURANT WITH ROOMS

☎ 023 8022 1159 & 07748 966113
Town Quay Rd SO14 3AS
e-mail: info@ennios.co.uk
dir: Opposite Red Funnel Ferry terminal

Formerly the Geddes Warehouse, this fine boutique
hotel offers guests luxurious accommodation on
Southampton's Waterfront. All rooms are en suite and
are furnished to a very high standard including mini-
bars and over-sized showers. Downstairs there is the
popular Ennio's Restaurant and bar, which is the idea
setting to dine. There is also limited parking available
at the rear.

Rooms 10

SOUTH CAVE   Map 17 SE93
East Riding of Yorkshire

Cave Castle Hotel & Country Club

★★★ 77% HOTEL

☎ 01430 422245
Church Hill HU15 2EU
e-mail: info@cavecastlehotel.com
web: www.cavecastlehotel.com
dir: In village, opposite school

This beautiful Victorian manor retains original
turrets, stone features and much charm, together
with modern comforts and style. It stands in 150
acres of meadow and parkland that provide a
peaceful setting. Bedrooms are a careful mix of
traditional and contemporary styles. Public areas
include a well-equipped leisure complex and pool.

Rooms 70 (14 GF) **S** £80-£105; **D** £110-£130 (incl.
bkfst) **Facilities** Spa Wi-fi ⊛ supervised ⌁ 18 Putt
green Fishing Gym New Year **Conf** Class 150
Board 100 Thtr 250 Del from £110 to £132
Services Lift **Parking** 100 **Notes** LB ⊗ Civ Wed 150

Save on hotels. Book at theAA.com/hotel

SOU 411 ENGLAND

SOUTH CERNEY
Gloucestershire — Map 5 SU09

Cotswold Water Park Four Pillars Hotel

★★★★ 79% HOTEL

☎ 0800 374692 & 01285 864000
Lake 6 Spine Road East GL7 5FP
e-mail: waterpark@four-pillars.co.uk
web: www.cotswoldwaterparkhotel.co.uk
dir: Off A419, 3m from Cirencester (NB for Sav Nav use GL7 5TL)

This impressive hotel has well-appointed bedrooms and suites, conference facilities for up to 800 delegates, a spa with an 11-metre pool, a gym, a hydro pool and treatment rooms. An excellent range of dining options is available, and a large car park is provided.

Rooms 328 (61 fmly) (126 GF) ↰ **Facilities** Spa FTV Wi-fi ↳ ⊛ Fishing Gym Beauty treatment rooms & therapies Steam room Sauna Xmas New Year **Conf** Class 204 Board 68 Thtr 370 **Services** Lift **Parking** 200 **Notes** ⊗ Civ Wed 370

SOUTHEND-ON-SEA
Essex — Map 7 TQ88

The Roslin Beach Hotel

★★★★ 77% ⊛ HOTEL

☎ 01702 586375
Thorpe Esplanade, Thorpe Bay SS1 3BG
e-mail: info@roslinhotel.com
web: www.roslinhotel.com
dir: A127, follow Southend-on-Sea signs. Hotel between Walton Rd & Clieveden Rd on seafront

This friendly hotel is situated at the quiet end of the esplanade, overlooking the beach and sea. The spacious bedrooms are pleasantly decorated and thoughtfully equipped; some rooms have superb sea views. Public rooms include a large lounge bar, the Mulberry Restaurant and a smart conservatory which overlooks the sea.

Rooms 62 (5 fmly) (11 GF) ↰ **S** £65-£95; **D** £80-£145 (incl. bkfst)* **Facilities** Spa FTV Wi-fi Gym Xmas New Year **Conf** Class 65 Board 45 Thtr 90 Del from £136* **Parking** 48 **Notes** LB Civ Wed 100

Park Inn by Radisson Palace

★★★ 78% HOTEL

☎ 01702 455100
Church Rd SS1 2AL
e-mail: info.southend-on-sea@rezidorparkinn.com
dir: From N: via A1, M11, M25, A27. Take M25 junct 29 for 32km, then follow signs for Southend. From S: via M25, Dartford Tunnel, A13. Take M25 junct 30 for 40km, then follow signs for Southend

This hotel, in the centre of the town's tourist area, offers comfortable and modern rooms to meet the needs of both leisure and business travellers; the front facing bedrooms have breathtaking sea views. The public areas include the all-day dining RBG Bar & Grill, both overlooking the mouth of the River Thames. There is a range of meeting rooms to cater for all occasions.

Rooms 137 (22 fmly) ↰ **Facilities** STV FTV Wi-fi ↳ Gym Xmas New Year **Conf** Class 90 Board 70 Thtr 280 **Services** Lift Air con **Notes** ⊗ Civ Wed 280

Westcliff Hotel

★★★ 77% HOTEL

☎ 01702 345247
Westcliff Pde, Westcliff-on-Sea SS0 7QW
e-mail: westcliff@zolahotels.com
dir: M25 junct 29, A127 towards Southend, follow signs for Cliffs Pavillion when approaching town centre

This impressive Grade II listed Victorian building is situated in an elevated position overlooking gardens and cliffs with views to the sea beyond. The spacious bedrooms are tastefully decorated and thoughtfully equipped; many have lovely sea views. Public rooms include a smart conservatory-style restaurant, a spacious lounge and a range of function rooms.

Rooms 55 (2 fmly) ↰ **S** £79; **D** £109 (incl. bkfst) **Facilities** FTV Wi-fi ♫ Xmas New Year **Conf** Class 90 Board 64 Thtr 225 **Services** Lift **Notes** LB ⊗ Civ Wed 120

Camelia Hotel

★★★ 🅰 HOTEL

☎ 01702 587917
176-178 Eastern Esplanade, Thorpe Bay SS1 3AA
e-mail: enquiries@cameliahotel.com
web: www.cameliahotel.com
dir: From A13 or A127 follow signs to Southend seafront; on seafront left, hotel 1m E of pier

Situated on the seafront with views of the Thames Estuary, this hotel has individually designed bedrooms including four-poster rooms and a honeymoon suite. There is a smart, air-conditioned restaurant offering both set and carte menus, and in summer a patio overlooking the sea for enjoying a relaxing drink.

Rooms 28 (8 annexe) (3 fmly) (8 GF) ↰ **S** £55-£95; **D** £76-£130 (incl. bkfst)* **Facilities** FTV Wi-fi ↳ **Parking** 100 **Notes** LB ⊗

Premier Inn Southend Airport

BUDGET HOTEL

☎ 0871 527 9008
Thanet Grange SS2 6GB
web: www.premierinn.com
dir: At A127 & B1013 junct

High quality, budget accommodation ideal for both families and business travellers. Spacious, en suite bedrooms feature tea and coffee making facilities, and Freeview TV in most hotels. Internet access and Wi-fi are available for a small fee. The adjacent family restaurant features a wide and varied menu. See also the Hotel Groups pages.

Rooms 80

Premier Inn Southend-on-Sea (Thorpe Bay)

BUDGET HOTEL

☎ 0871 527 9006
213 Eastern Esplanade SS1 3AD
web: www.premierinn.com
dir: Follow signs for A1159 (A13) Shoebury onto dual carriageway. At rdbt, follow signs for Thorpe Bay & seafront, at seafront turn right. Hotel on right

Rooms 43

S

Days Inn South Mimms - M25

BUDGET HOTEL

☎ 01707 665440
Bignells Corner, Potters Bar EN6 3QQ
e-mail: south.mimms@welcomebreak.co.uk
web: www.welcomebreak.co.uk
dir: M25 junct 23, at rdbt follow signs

This modern building offers accommodation in smart, spacious and well-equipped bedrooms, suitable for families and business travellers, and all with en suite bathrooms. Continental breakfast is available and other refreshments may be taken at the nearby family restaurant. See also the Hotel Groups pages.

Rooms 75 (19 fmly) (23 GF) (10 smoking)

Premier Inn South Mimms/ Potters Bar

BUDGET HOTEL

☎ 0871 527 8990
Swanland Rd EN6 3NH
web: www.premierinn.com
dir: M25 junct 23 & A1 take services exit off main rdbt then 1st left & follow hotel signs

High quality, budget accommodation ideal for both families and business travellers. Spacious, en suite bedrooms feature tea and coffee making facilities, and Freeview TV in most hotels. Internet access and Wi-fi are available for a small fee. The adjacent family restaurant features a wide and varied menu. See also the Hotel Groups pages.

Rooms 142

The George Hotel

★★ 78% HOTEL

☎ 01769 572514
1 Broad St EX36 3AB
e-mail: info@georgehotelsouthmolton.co.uk
web: www.georgehotelsouthmolton.co.uk
dir: Exit A361 at rdbt signed South Molton, 1.5m to centre

Retaining many of its original features, this charming 17th-century hotel is situated in the centre of town. Providing comfortable accommodation, complemented by informal and friendly service, this hotel is an ideal base for touring the area. Regularly changing menus, featuring local produce, are offered

in both the restaurant and the bar, which also serves real ales.

Rooms 10 (1 fmly) ⚑ **S** £55-£65; **D** £85-£100 (incl. bkfst)* **Facilities** FTV Wi-fi ♫ **Conf** Class 30 Board 30 Thtr 100 **Parking** 12 **Notes** LB ⊗ RS 1st wk Jan

The Derbyshire Hotel

★★★★ 74% HOTEL

☎ 01773 812000
Carter Lane East DE55 2EH
e-mail: reservations.derbyshire@principal-hayley.com
dir: M1 junct 28, E on A38 to Mansfield

Conveniently located by the motorway, this hotel offers comfortable accommodation and a relaxed informal atmosphere through the lounge bar and restaurant. The conference and meeting rooms are appointed to a smart modern standard; delegates also have use of on-site sauna, jacuzzi and steam room in the spa.

Rooms 157 (10 fmly) (61 GF) **Facilities** Spa STV Wi-fi ⌂ ⌕ Gym Steam room Sauna New Year **Conf** Class 120 Board 25 Thtr 250 **Parking** 220 **Notes** ⊗ Civ Wed 150

Premier Inn Mansfield

BUDGET HOTEL

☎ 0871 527 8758
Carter Lane East DE55 2EH
web: www.premierinn.com
dir: M1 junct 28, A38 signed Mansfield. Entrance 200yds on left

High quality, budget accommodation ideal for both families and business travellers. Spacious, en suite bedrooms feature tea and coffee making facilities, and Freeview TV in most hotels. Internet access and Wi-fi are available for a small fee. The adjacent family restaurant features a wide and varied menu. See also the Hotel Groups pages.

Rooms 82

Vincent Hotel

★★★★ 82% ⊛⊛ TOWN HOUSE HOTEL

☎ 01704 883800
98 Lord St PR8 1JR
e-mail: manager@thevincenthotel.com
dir: M58 junct 3, follow signs to Ormskirk & Southport

This stylish, boutique property occupies a prime location on Southport's famous boulevard. Bedrooms, some with views of the beach, are appointed to a high standard with oversized beds, extremely well stocked mini-bars and stylish en suites with deep tubs. Public areas include a trendy cocktail bar, and an all-day dining concept. The friendly staff offer a professional and personalised service.

Rooms 59 (2 fmly) ⚑ **D** £88-£151* **Facilities** Spa STV FTV Wi-fi ⌂ Gym **Conf** Class 96 Board 50 Thtr 196 Del from £125 to £165* **Services** Lift Air con **Parking** 50 **Notes** LB ⊗ Civ Wed 150

BEST WESTERN Royal Clifton Hotel & Spa

★★★ 74% HOTEL

☎ 01704 533771
Promenade PR8 1RB
e-mail: sales@royalclifton.co.uk
dir: Adjacent to Marine Lake

This grand, traditional hotel benefits from a prime location on the promenade. Bedrooms range in size and style, but all are comfortable and thoughtfully equipped. Public areas include the lively Bar C, the elegant Pavilion Restaurant and a modern, well-equipped leisure club. Extensive conference and banqueting facilities make this hotel a popular function venue.

Rooms 120 (23 fmly) (6 GF) **Facilities** Spa STV Wi-fi ⌕ supervised Gym Hair & beauty Steam room Aromatherapy ♫ Xmas New Year **Conf** Class 100 Board 65 Thtr 250 **Services** Lift **Parking** 60 **Notes** ⊗ Civ Wed 150

Balmoral Lodge Hotel

★★ 74% HOTEL

☎ 01704 544298
41 Queens Rd PR9 9EX
e-mail: balmorallg@aol.com
dir: On edge of town on A565 (Preston road). E at rdbt at North Lord St, left at lights, hotel 200yds on left

Situated in a quiet residential area, this popular friendly hotel is ideally situated just 50 yards from Lord Street. Bedrooms are comfortably appointed and family rooms are available. In addition to the

S

restaurant which offers freshly prepared dishes, there is a choice of lounges including a comfortable lounge bar.

Rooms 15 (4 annexe) (3 fmly) (4 GF) **S** £25-£39; **D** £35-£80 (incl. bkfst) **Facilities** STV FTV Wi-fi ⮧ **Conf** Class 30 Board 30 Thtr 30 Del from £40 to £60 **Parking** 12 **Notes** LB

Premier Inn Southport Central

BUDGET HOTEL

☎ 0871 527 9012
Marine Dr PR8 1RY
web: www.premierinn.com
dir: From Southport follow Promenade & Marine Drive signs. Hotel at junct of Marine Parade & Marine Drive

High quality, budget accommodation ideal for both families and business travellers. Spacious, en suite bedrooms feature tea and coffee making facilities, and Freeview TV in most hotels. Internet access and Wi-fi are available for a small fee. The adjacent family restaurant features a wide and varied menu. See also the Hotel Groups pages.

Rooms 59

SOUTHSEA

See **Portsmouth & Southsea**

SOUTH SHIELDS   Map 21 NZ36
Tyne & Wear

BEST WESTERN The Sea Hotel

★★★ 77% HOTEL

☎ 0191 427 0999
Sea Rd NE33 2LD
e-mail: info@seahotel.co.uk
dir: A1(M), past Washington Services onto A194. Then A183 through town centre along Ocean Rd. Hotel on seafront

Dating from the 1930s, this long-established business hotel overlooks the boating lake and the Tyne estuary. Bedrooms are generally spacious and well equipped and include five annexe rooms with wheelchair access. A range of generously portioned meals is served in both the bar and restaurant.

Rooms 37 (5 annexe) (5 fmly) (5 GF) ⮧ **Facilities** STV Wi-fi ⮧ New Year **Conf** Class 100 Board 50 Thtr 200 **Parking** 70 **Notes** RS 26 Dec

Premier Inn South Shields (Port of Tyne)

BUDGET HOTEL

☎ 0871 527 8992
Hobson Av, Newcastle Rd NE34 9PQ
web: www.premierinn.com
dir: A1(M) onto A194(M). 2nd exit at rdbt into Leam Lane (A194). At next rdbt 2nd exit, next rdbt 3rd exit, next rdbt 2nd exit (A194), next rdbt 2nd exit. Hotel on left adjacent to Taybarns

High quality, budget accommodation ideal for both families and business travellers. Spacious, en suite bedrooms feature tea and coffee making facilities, and Freeview TV in most hotels. Internet access and Wi-fi are available for a small fee. The adjacent family restaurant features a wide and varied menu. See also the Hotel Groups pages.

Rooms 66

SOUTHWOLD   Map 13 TM57
Suffolk

Swan Hotel

★★★★ 78% HOTEL

☎ 01502 722186
Market Place IP18 6EG
e-mail: swan.hotel@adnams.co.uk
dir: A1095 to Southwold. Hotel in town centre. Parking via archway to left of building

The Swan Hotel is a charming 17th-century coaching inn situated in the heart of this bustling town centre overlooking the market place. Public rooms feature an elegant restaurant, a comfortable drawing room, a cosy bar and a lounge where guests can enjoy afternoon tea. The spacious bedrooms are attractively decorated, tastefully furnished and thoughtfully equipped.

Rooms 42 (17 annexe) (11 fmly) (17 GF) ⮧ **D** £99-£300* **Facilities** STV FTV Wi-fi HL Beauty treatment room Xmas New Year **Conf** Class 40 Board 30 Thtr 80 **Services** Lift **Parking** 42 **Notes** Civ Wed 60

The Blyth Hotel

★★ 85% ◉ SMALL HOTEL

☎ 01502 722632 & 0845 348 6867
Station Rd IP18 6AY
e-mail: reception@blythhotel.com
dir: A12 onto A1095 signed Southwold

Expect a warm welcome at this delightful family run hotel which is situated just a short walk from the town centre. The spacious public rooms include a smart residents' lounge, an open-plan bar and a large restaurant. Bedrooms are tastefully appointed with co-ordinated fabrics and have many thoughtful touches.

Rooms 13 ⮧ **Facilities** FTV Wi-fi Xmas New Year **Conf** Class 20 Board 12 Thtr 20 **Parking** 8 **Notes** LB

The Crown

★★★ 80% ◉◉ HOTEL

☎ 01502 722275
90 High St IP18 6DP
e-mail: crown.hotel@adnams.co.uk
web: www.adnams.co.uk
dir: A12 onto A1095 to Southwold. Hotel on left in High Street

The Crown is a delightful old posting inn situated in the heart of this bustling town. The property combines a pub, wine bar and restaurant with superb accommodation. The tastefully decorated bedrooms have attractive co-ordinated soft furnishings and many thoughtful touches. Public rooms feature an elegant lounge and a back room bar serving traditional Adnams ales.

Rooms 14 (2 fmly) **Facilities** FTV Wi-fi Xmas New Year **Conf** Board 8 **Parking** 23 **Notes** ⊗

Sutherland House

◉◉ RESTAURANT WITH ROOMS

☎ 01502 724544
56 High St IP18 6DN
e-mail: enquiries@sutherlandhouse.co.uk
web: www.sutherlandhouse.co.uk
dir: A1095 into Southwold, on High St on left after Victoria St

A delightful 16th-century house situated in the heart of the bustling town centre with a wealth of character, Sutherland House has oak beams, exposed brickwork, open fireplaces and two superb ornate plasterwork ceilings. The stylish bedrooms are tastefully decorated, have co-ordinated fabrics and many thoughtful touches. Public rooms feature a large open-plan contemporary restaurant with plush furniture.

Rooms 4 (1 fmly)

S

SPALDING
Lincolnshire   Map 12 TF22

Woodlands Hotel

★★★ 73% SMALL HOTEL

☎ 01775 769933
80 Pinchbeck Rd PE11 1QF
e-mail:
reservations@woodlandshotelspalding.com
web: www.woodlandshotelspalding.com
dir: 10mins walk from City Centre

A delightful Victorian house ideally situated just a short walk from the town centre. The public areas have many original features; they include the Oakleaf dining room, the Silver Birch meeting room and the Willows bar. The smartly decorated bedrooms have lovely co-ordinated soft furnishings and many thoughtful touches.

Rooms 17 (5 GF) **S** £52-£65; **D** £62-£85 (incl. bkfst) **Facilities** FTV Wi-fi ॐ **Conf** Class 30 Board 30 Thtr 60 Del from £99 to £120 **Parking** 30 **Notes** ⊗ Civ Wed 65

STAFFORD
Staffordshire   Map 10 SJ92

The Moat House

★★★★ 82% ◉◉ HOTEL

☎ 01785 712217
Lower Penkridge Rd, Acton Trussell ST17 0RJ
e-mail: info@moathouse.co.uk
web: www.moathouse.co.uk
dir: M6 junct 13 onto A449 through Acton Trussell. Hotel on right on exiting village

This 17th-century timbered building, with an idyllic canal-side setting, has been skilfully extended. Bedrooms are stylishly furnished, well equipped and comfortable. The bar offers a range of snacks and the restaurant boasts a popular fine dining option where the head chef displays his skills using top quality produce.

Rooms 41 (4 fmly) (15 GF) **Facilities** Wi-fi New Year **Conf** Class 60 Board 50 Thtr 200 **Services** Lift **Parking** 200 **Notes** ⊗ Closed 25 Dec Civ Wed 150

Tillington Hall Hotel

★★★ 73% HOTEL

☎ 01785 253531
Eccleshall Rd ST16 1JJ
e-mail: reservations@tillingtonhall.co.uk
web: www.tillingtonhall.co.uk
dir: M6 junct 14, A5013 towards Stafford. Hotel 0.5m on left

Located close to the M6, this modern hotel is ideal for both business and leisure guests. There is a spacious restaurant, relaxing coffee lounge and smart bar. There is a range of function rooms for meetings and events, including the new Garden Suite. Complimentary Wi-fi access is available.

Rooms 91 (4 fmly) (25 GF) ✎ **S** £60-£80; **D** £70-£100 (incl. bkfst)* **Facilities** FTV Wi-fi HL Xmas New Year **Conf** Class 150 Board 75 Thtr 300 Del from £110 to £135* **Services** Lift **Parking** 200 **Notes** LB ⊗ Civ Wed 300

Premier Inn Stafford North (Hurricane)

BUDGET HOTEL

☎ 0871 527 9030
1 Hurrican Close ST16 1GZ
web: www.premierinn.com
dir: M6 junct 14, A34 towards Stafford. Hotel approx 2m NW of town centre

High quality, budget accommodation ideal for both families and business travellers. Spacious, en suite bedrooms feature tea and coffee making facilities, and Freeview TV in most hotels. Internet access and Wi-fi are available for a small fee. The adjacent family restaurant features a wide and varied menu. See also the Hotel Groups pages.

Rooms 96

Premier Inn Stafford North (Spitfire)

BUDGET HOTEL

☎ 0871 527 9032
1 Spitfire Close ST16 1GX
web: www.premierinn.com
dir: M6 junct 14, A34 N. Hotel approx 1m on left

Rooms 60

STAINES-UPON-THAMES
Surrey   Map 6 TQ07

Mercure London Staines Thames Lodge

★★★ 77% HOTEL

☎ 01784 464433
Thames St TW18 4SJ
e-mail: h6620@accor.com
web: www.mercure.com
dir: M25 junct 13. Follow A30/town centre signs (bus station on right). Hotel straight ahead

Located on the banks of the River Thames in a bustling town, this hotel is well positioned for both business and leisure travellers. Meals are served in the Riverside Restaurant, and snacks are available in the spacious lounge/bar; weather permitting the terrace provides a good place for a drink on a summer evening. On-site parking is an additional bonus.

Rooms 88 (17 fmly) (31 GF) **Facilities** STV FTV Wi-fi Moorings Xmas New Year **Conf** Class 40 Board 20 Thtr 40 **Parking** 40

STAMFORD
Lincolnshire   Map 11 TF00

The William Cecil

★★★★ 81% ◉ HOTEL

☎ 01780 750070
High St PE9 2LG
e-mail: enquiries@thewilliamcecil.co.uk
dir: Exit A1 signed Stamford & Burghley Park. Hotel 1st building on right on entering town

This lovely refurbished property is situated on the edge of town within the Burghley Estate. The stylish bedrooms are spacious, individually decorated and have lots of extra little touches. The public rooms include a lounge bar with plush seating and a panelled restaurant. A smart terrace is available for alfresco dining when the weather permits.

Rooms 27 (2 fmly) (5 GF) ✎ **S** £90-£180; **D** £100-£190 (incl. bkfst)* **Facilities** FTV Wi-fi ॐ Xmas New Year **Conf** Class 60 Board 40 Thtr 120 Del from £130 to £185* **Parking** 80 **Notes** LB Civ Wed 120

S

The George of Stamford

★★★★ 78% ◉ HOTEL

☎ 01780 750750 & 750700 (res)
71 St Martins PE9 2LB
e-mail: reservations@georgehotelofstamford.com
web: www.georgehotelofstamford.com
dir: A1, 15m N of Peterborough onto B1081, hotel 1m on left

Steeped in hundreds of years of history, this delightful coaching inn provides spacious public areas that include a choice of dining options, inviting lounges, a business centre and a range of quality shops. A highlight is afternoon tea, taken in the colourful courtyard when the weather permits. Bedrooms are stylishly appointed and range from traditional to contemporary in design.

Rooms 47 (24 fmly) **S** £95-£110; **D** £160-£290 (incl. bkfst)* **Facilities** STV Wi-fi ᐅ ⤴ Complimentary membership to local gym Xmas New Year **Conf** Class 25 Board 25 Thtr 50 Del from £150 to £180* **Parking** 110 **Notes** LB Civ Wed 50

Crown Hotel

★★★ 81% HOTEL

☎ 01780 763136
All Saints Place PE9 2AG
e-mail:
reservations@thecrownhotelstamford.co.uk
web: www.thecrownhotelstamford.co.uk
dir: A1 onto A43, through town to Red Lion Sq, hotel behind All Saints Church

This small, privately owned hotel where hospitality is spontaneous and sincere, is ideally situated in the town centre. Unpretentious British food is served in the modern dining areas and the spacious bar is popular with locals. Bedrooms are appointed to a very high standard being quite contemporary in style and very well equipped; some have four-poster beds. Additional 'superior' rooms are located in a renovated Georgian town house just a short walk up the street.

Rooms 28 (10 annexe) (1 fmly) (1 GF) ⬧ **S** £70-£140; **D** £70-£165 (incl. bkfst)* **Facilities** FTV Wi-fi ᐅ Use of local health/gym club Xmas New Year **Conf** Class 12 Board 12 Thtr 20 Del from £140 to £180* **Parking** 21 **Notes** LB ⊗

Candlesticks

RESTAURANT WITH ROOMS

☎ 01780 764033
1 Church Ln PE9 2JU
e-mail: info@candlestickshotel.co.uk
dir: B1081 into Stamford. Left onto A43. Right into Worthorpe Rd, right into Church Ln

Candlesticks is a 17th-century property situated in a quiet lane in the oldest part of Stamford just a short walk from the centre of town. The bedrooms are pleasantly decorated and equipped with a good range of useful extras. Public rooms feature Candlesticks restaurant, a small lounge and a cosy bar.

Rooms 8

STANDISH Map 15 SD51
Greater Manchester

Premier Inn Wigan North

BUDGET HOTEL

☎ 0871 527 9166
Almond Brook Rd WN6 0SS
web: www.premierinn.com
dir: M6 junct 27 follow signs for Standish. Left at T-junct, then 1st right

High quality, budget accommodation ideal for both families and business travellers. Spacious, en suite bedrooms feature tea and coffee making facilities, and Freeview TV in most hotels. Internet access and Wi-fi are available for a small fee. The adjacent family restaurant features a wide and varied menu. See also the Hotel Groups pages.

Rooms 36

STANLEY Map 19 NZ15
Co Durham

BEST WESTERN Beamish Hall Hotel

★★★★ 73% COUNTRY HOUSE HOTEL

☎ 01207 233733
Beamish DH9 0YB
e-mail: info@beamish-hall.co.uk
dir: A693 to Stanley. Follow signs for hotel & Beamish Museum. Left at museum entrance. Hotel on left 0.2m after golf club

This hotel is set in 24 acres of impeccably maintained grounds and can trace its history back many centuries. The public areas are elegant, with leather suites and wooden floors. The beautifully decorated dining room has a real feeling of grandeur, with high ceilings and wonderful views of the gardens. All the bedrooms are stylishly designed and well equipped, and include larger rooms that have jacuzzi baths and

separate showers; some of the premier rooms are interconnecting, and there is also a two bedroom apartment with its own kitchen and family room.

Rooms 42 (18 fmly) (4 GF) **Facilities** STV FTV Wi-fi ᐅ Xmas New Year **Conf** Class 160 Board 160 Thtr 300 Del from £115 to £145* **Services** Lift **Parking** 300 **Notes** ⊗ Civ Wed 200

STANSTED AIRPORT Map 6 TL52
Essex

See also Birchanger Green Motorway Service Area (M11)

Radisson Blu Hotel London Stansted Airport

★★★★ 79% HOTEL

☎ 01279 661012
Waltham Close, Stansted Airport CM24 1PP
e-mail: info.stansted@radissonblu.com
web: www.radissonblu.co.uk/hotel-stanstedairport
dir: M11 junct 8 onto A120. Follow London Stansted Airport signs

This modern glass-fronted hotel, linked to the airport terminal by a covered walkway, is particularly well appointed. Facilities include a wide choice of restaurants, a smart leisure club and spa, extensive conference and meeting rooms, and the much talked about wine tower, complete with wine angels. Bedrooms follow a contemporary theme and include a host of thoughtful extras.

Rooms 500 (42 fmly) (51 smoking) **Facilities** Spa STV FTV Wi-fi ᐅ ❄ Gym Steam room Sauna Solarium ♬ Xmas New Year **Conf** Class 180 Board 36 Thtr 400 **Services** Lift Air con **Parking** 220 **Notes** ⊗

Premier Inn Stansted Airport

BUDGET HOTEL

☎ 0871 527 9352
Thremhall Av, Stansted Airport CM24 1PY
web: www.premierinn.com
dir: M11 junct 8/8a, follow signs Stanstead Airport Terminal. Main rdbt 3rd exit follow signs mid-stay car park. Adjacent BP Petrol Station

High quality, budget accommodation ideal for both families and business travellers. Spacious, en suite bedrooms feature tea and coffee making facilities, and Freeview TV in most hotels. Internet access and Wi-fi are available for a small fee. The adjacent family restaurant features a wide and varied menu. See also the Hotel Groups pages.

Rooms 303 (22 fmly)

S

STANTON ST QUINTIN   Map 4 ST97
Wiltshire

Stanton Manor Hotel
★★★ 79% ◉ HOTEL

☎ 01666 837552
SN14 6DQ
e-mail: reception@stantonmanor.co.uk
web: www.stantonmanor.co.uk
dir: M4 junct 17, A429 Malmesbury/Cirencester, 200yds, 1st left signed Stanton St Quintin, hotel entrance on left after church

Set in five acres of lovely gardens that includes a short golf course, this charming manor house, mentioned in the Domesday Book, has easy access to the M4. Public areas are a delight offering both character and comfort. The restaurant offers a short carte of imaginative dishes and an interesting wine selection.

Rooms 23 (4 fmly) (8 GF) 🐾 **Facilities** Wi-fi ⛵ Xmas New Year **Conf** Class 40 Board 32 Thtr 80 Del from £140 to £170* **Parking** 60 **Notes** Civ Wed 120

STEEPLE ASTON   Map 11 SP42
Oxfordshire

The Holt Hotel
★★★ 73% HOTEL

☎ 01869 340259
Oxford Rd OX25 5QQ
e-mail: info@holthotel.co.uk
web: www.holthotel.co.uk
dir: At junct of B4030 & A4260

This attractive former coaching inn has given hospitality to many over the centuries, not least to Claude Duval, a notorious 17th-century highwayman. Today guests are offered well-equipped, modern bedrooms and attractive public areas, which include a relaxing bar, restaurant and a well-appointed lounge. A selection of meeting rooms is available.

Rooms 86 (19 fmly) (20 GF) (8 smoking)
S £58.80-£82.80; **D** £70.80-£106.80 (incl. bkfst)*
Facilities FTV Wi-fi Xmas New Year **Conf** Class 57 Board 32 Thtr 140 Del from £120 to £140*
Parking 200 **Notes** Civ Wed 120

STEVENAGE   Map 12 TL22
Hertfordshire

Holiday Inn Stevenage
★★★★ 75% HOTEL

☎ 01438 722727 & 346060
St George's Way SG1 1HS
e-mail: reservations@histevenage.com
dir: A1(M) junct 7 take A602 to Stevenage, across 1st rdbt, 1st exit at 2nd rdbt, 2nd exit at next rdbt along St George's Way. Hotel 100yds on right

Situated in the heart of the town centre and just 25 minutes from central London by train. Bedrooms are air conditioned and well equipped; ideal for business and leisure travellers. Public areas are smart, capacious and stylish, and as well as a comfortable bar and restaurant, there is a mini gym. Parking is limited.

Rooms 140 (8 fmly) 🐾 **Facilities** STV FTV Wi-fi ⌁ HL Gym Xmas New Year **Conf** Class 180 Board 190 Thtr 400 **Services** Lift Air con **Parking** 23 **Notes** Civ Wed 400

Novotel Stevenage
★★★ 79% HOTEL

☎ 01438 346100
Knebworth Park SG1 2AX
e-mail: H0992@accor.com
web: www.novotel.com
dir: A1(M) junct 7, at entrance to Knebworth Park

Ideally situated just off the A1(M) is this purpose built hotel, which is a popular business and conference venue. Bedrooms are pleasantly decorated and equipped with a good range of useful extras. Public rooms include a large open plan lounge bar serving a range of snacks, and a smartly appointed restaurant.

Rooms 101 (20 fmly) (30 GF) **Facilities** STV Wi-fi ⌁ Use of local health club New Year **Conf** Class 80 Board 70 Thtr 150 **Services** Lift **Parking** 120 **Notes** Civ Wed 120

BEST WESTERN Roebuck Inn
★★★ 73% HOTEL

☎ 01438 365445 & 365653
London Rd, Broadwater SG2 8DS
e-mail: hotel@roebuckinn.com
dir: A1(M) junct 7, right towards Stevenage. At 2nd rdbt take 2nd exit signed Roebuck-London/Knebworth/B197. Hotel in 1.5m

Suitable for both the business and leisure traveller, this hotel provides spacious contemporary accommodation in well-equipped bedrooms. The older part of the building, where there is a restaurant and a cosy public bar with log fire and real ales, dates back to the 15th century.

Rooms 26 (8 fmly) (13 GF) 🐾 **Facilities** STV FTV Wi-fi ⌁ Xmas New Year **Conf** Class 20 Board 30 Thtr 50 Del from £130 to £150* **Parking** 50 **Notes** ⊗

Holiday Inn Express Stevenage
BUDGET HOTEL

☎ 01438 344300
Danestreet SG1 1XB
e-mail: gsm@hiexpressstevenage.co.uk
web: www.hiexpressstevenage.co.uk
dir: A1(M) junct 7, A72, bear left, 3rd exit onto A1070, then 2nd exit to Danestrete

A modern hotel ideal for families and business travellers. Fresh and uncomplicated, the spacious rooms include Sky TV, power shower and tea and coffee-making facilities. Continental buffet breakfast is included in the room rate; other meals may be taken at the nearby family pub or restaurant. See also the Hotel Groups pages.

Rooms 129 (100 fmly) (5 GF) (23 smoking) 🐾 **Conf** Class 30 Board 20 Thtr 40

S

Ibis Stevenage Centre

BUDGET HOTEL

☎ 01438 779955

Danestrete SG1 1EJ

e-mail: H2794@accor.com

web: www.ibishotel.com

dir: In town centre adjacent to Tesco & Westgate multi storey car park

Modern, budget hotel offering comfortable accommodation in bright and practical bedrooms. Breakfast is self-service and dinner is available in the restaurant. See also the Hotel Groups pages.

Rooms 98 🐾 **S** £35-£180; **D** £35-£180*

Premier Inn Stevenage Central

BUDGET HOTEL

☎ 0871 527 9034

Six Hills Way, Horizon Technology Park SG1 2DD

web: www.premierinn.com

dir: A1(M) junct 7, follow Stevenage signs. Left into Gunnels Wood Rd. (NB do not use underpass). Left at next rdbt. Hotel in Horizon Technology Park on left

High quality, budget accommodation ideal for both families and business travellers. Spacious, en suite bedrooms feature tea and coffee making facilities, and Freeview TV in most hotels. Internet access and Wi-fi are available for a small fee. The adjacent family restaurant features a wide and varied menu. See also the Hotel Groups pages.

Rooms 115

Premier Inn Stevenage North

BUDGET HOTEL

☎ 0871 527 9036

Corey's Mill Ln SG1 4AA

web: www.premierinn.com

dir: A1(M) junct 8, at intersection with A602 (Hitchin Rd & Corey's Mill Lane)

Rooms 41

STEYNING   Map 6 TQ11
West Sussex

BEST WESTERN Old Tollgate Hotel & Restaurant

★★★ 78% HOTEL

☎ 01903 879494

The Street, Bramber BN44 3WE

e-mail: info@oldtollgatehotel.com

web: www.oldtollgatehotel.com

dir: From A283 at Steyning rdbt to Bramber. Hotel 200yds on right

As its name suggests, this well-presented hotel is built on the site of the old toll house. The spacious bedrooms are smartly designed and are furnished to a high standard; eight rooms are air conditioned and have smart power showers. Open for both lunch and dinner, the popular carvery-style restaurant offers an extensive choice of dishes.

Rooms 38 (28 annexe) (5 fmly) (14 GF) 🐾 **D** fr £60* **Facilities** STV Wi-fi ⌕ HL New Year **Conf** Class 32 Board 24 Thtr 50 Del £144* **Services** Lift **Parking** 60 **Notes** LB ⊗ Civ Wed 70

STILTON   Map 12 TL18
Cambridgeshire

Bell Inn Hotel

★★★ 81% ◉ HOTEL

☎ 01733 241066

Great North Rd PE7 3RA

e-mail: reception@thebellstilton.co.uk

web: www.thebellstilton.co.uk

dir: A1(M) junct 16, follow Stilton signs. Hotel in village centre

This delightful inn is steeped in history and retains many original features, with imaginative food served in both the character village bar/brasserie and the elegant beamed first floor restaurant; refreshments can be enjoyed in the attractive courtyard and rear gardens when weather permits. Individually designed bedrooms are stylish and equipped to a high standard.

Rooms 22 (3 annexe) (1 fmly) (3 GF) 🐾 **S** £80-£120; **D** £108-£140 (incl. bkfst) **Facilities** STV FTV Wi-fi **Conf** Class 46 Board 50 Thtr 130 Del from £125 to £143* **Parking** 30 **Notes** LB ⊗ Closed 25 Dec (pm) RS 26 Dec (pm) & 1 Jan (pm) Civ Wed 130

STOCK   Map 6 TQ69
Essex

Greenwoods Hotel Spa & Retreat

★★★★ 78% HOTEL

☎ 01277 829990 & 829205

Stock Rd CM4 9BE

e-mail: info@greenwoodshotel.co.uk

web: www.greenwoodshotel.co.uk

dir: A12 junct 16 take B1007 signed Billericay. Hotel on right on entering village

Greenwoods is a beautiful 17th-century, Grade II listed manor house set in extensive landscaped gardens. All bedrooms are tastefully appointed, have marble bathrooms and a wide range of extras; the premier rooms have spa baths and antique beds. The spa facilities are impressive offering the latest beauty treatments, together with saunas, a jacuzzi, steam rooms, a monsoon shower and a 20-metre pool.

Rooms 39 (6 GF) 🐾 **S** £149-£165; **D** £229-£250* **Facilities** Spa STV FTV Wi-fi ⌕ Gym Steam room Sauna Monsoon shower New Year **Conf** Class 70 Board 52 Thtr 110 Del from £193 to £229* **Services** Lift **Parking** 100 **Notes** LB ⊗ No children 16yrs Closed 26 Dec & 1 Jan Civ Wed 110

S

STOCKPORT
Greater Manchester

Map 16 SJ89

See also Manchester Airport

Bredbury Hall Hotel & Country Club

★★★ 80% HOTEL

☎ 0161 430 7421
Goyt Valley, Bredbury SK6 2DH
e-mail: reservations@bredburyhallhotel.com
dir: M60 junct 25 signed Bredbury, right at lights, left
onto Osbourne St, hotel 500mtrs on right

With views over open countryside, this large, modern
hotel is conveniently located for the M60. The well-
equipped bedrooms are spacious and comfortable,
and the restaurant serves a very wide range of freshly
prepared dishes. Additional facilities include a fitness
suite, complimentary Wi-fi and conference rooms
accommodating up to 200 delegates.

Rooms 148 (2 fmly) (50 GF) 🐾 **Facilities** STV FTV
Wi-fi ⌗ Fishing Gym Night club (Fri & Sat eve) 🎵
Xmas New Year **Conf** Class 120 Board 60 Thtr 200
Services Lift **Parking** 450 **Notes** ⊗ Civ Wed 80

Alma Lodge Hotel

★★★ 75% HOTEL

☎ 0161 483 4431
149 Buxton Rd SK2 6EL
e-mail: reception@almalodgehotel.com
web: www.almalodgehotel.com
dir: M60 junct 1 at rdbt take 2nd exit under rail
viaduct at lights opposite. At Debenhams turn right
onto A6. Hotel approx 1.5m on left

A large hotel located on the main road close to the
town, offering modern and well-equipped bedrooms.
It is family-owned and run and serves a good range of
quality Italian cooking in Luigi's restaurant. Good
function rooms and free internet access are also
available.

Rooms 52 (32 annexe) (2 fmly) **S** £45-£55; **D** £62-£70
(incl. bkfst) **Facilities** FTV Wi-fi **Conf** Class 100
Board 60 Thtr 250 Del from £95 to £135 **Parking** 120
Notes ⊗ RS BHs Civ Wed 200

The Wycliffe Hotel

★★★ 74% HOTEL

☎ 0161 477 5395
74 Edgeley Rd, Edgeley SK3 9NQ
e-mail: reception@wycliffe-hotel.com
web: www.wycliffe-hotel.com
dir: M60 junct 2, follow A560 Stockport signs, right at
1st lights, hotel 0.5m on left

The Wycliffe is a family-run hotel close to the town
centre and convenient for Manchester airport. The
contemporary bedrooms are very well maintained and
equipped, with LCD TVs and data ports provided.
There is a well-stocked bar and a popular restaurant
where the menu has an Italian bias. There is also a
large car park.

Rooms 14 (3 fmly) (2 GF) **S** £67.50-£75;
D £75.50-£89 (incl. bkfst)* **Facilities** FTV Wi-fi
Conf Class 20 Board 20 Thtr 30 Del £99* **Parking** 46
Notes ⊗ Closed 25-27 Dec RS BHs

Premier Inn Manchester Airport Heald Green

BUDGET HOTEL

☎ 0871 527 8734
Finney Ln, Heald Green SK8 3QH
web: www.premierinn.com
dir: M56 junct 5 follow signs to Terminal 1, at rdbt
take 2nd exit, at next rdbt follow Cheadle signs. Left
at lights, right at next lights

High quality, budget accommodation ideal for both
families and business travellers. Spacious, en suite
bedrooms feature tea and coffee making facilities,
and Freeview TV in most hotels. Internet access and
Wi-fi are available for a small fee. The adjacent
family restaurant features a wide and varied menu.
See also the Hotel Groups pages.

Rooms 66

Premier Inn Stockport Central

BUDGET HOTEL

☎ 0871 527 9040
Churchgate SK1 1YG
web: www.premierinn.com
dir: M60 junct 27, A626 towards Marple. Right at
Spring Gardens

Rooms 46

Premier Inn Stockport South

BUDGET HOTEL

☎ 0871 527 9042
Buxton Rd, Heaviley SK2 6NB
web: www.premierinn.com
dir: On A6, 1.5m from town centre

Rooms 40

STOCKTON-ON-TEES
Co Durham

Map 19 NZ41

BEST WESTERN Parkmore Hotel & Leisure Club

★★★ 80% HOTEL

☎ 01642 786815
636 Yarm Rd, Eaglescliffe TS16 0DH
e-mail: enquiries@parkmorehotel.co.uk
dir: Exit A19 at Crathorne, A67 to Yarm. Through
Yarm right onto A135 to Stockton. Hotel 1m on left

Set in its own gardens, this smart hotel has grown
from its Victorian house origins to provide stylish
public areas, as well as extensive leisure and beauty
facilities including a hydrotherapy pool. There are
also conference facilities. The well-equipped
bedrooms include junior suites. The restaurant known
as J's@636 has a reputation for creative meals, and
service is friendly and obliging.

Rooms 55 (8 fmly) (9 GF) **Facilities** Spa STV Wi-fi ☺
supervised Gym Beauty salon Badminton Aerobics
studio Hydrotherapy Xmas New Year **Conf** Class 40
Board 40 Thtr 130 **Parking** 90 **Notes** Civ Wed 130

Premier Inn Stockton-on-Tees/Hartlepool

BUDGET HOTEL

☎ 0871 527 9044
Coal Ln, Wolviston TS22 5PZ
web: www.premierinn.com
dir: A1(M) junct 60, A689, follow Teeside then
Hartlepool signs. Hotel on left at A89 & A19 junct

High quality, budget accommodation ideal for both
families and business travellers. Spacious, en suite
bedrooms feature tea and coffee making facilities,
and Freeview TV in most hotels. Internet access and
Wi-fi are available for a small fee. The adjacent
family restaurant features a wide and varied menu.
See also the Hotel Groups pages.

Rooms 49

Premier Inn Stockton-on-Tees/ Middlesbrough

BUDGET HOTEL

☎ 0871 527 9048
Whitewater Way, Thornaby TS17 6QB
web: www.premierinn.com
dir: A19, A66 towards Stockton & Darlington. Take 1st exit signed Teeside Park/Teesdale. Right at lights over viaduct bridge rdbt & Tees Barrage

Rooms 62

Premier Inn Stockton-on-Tees West

BUDGET HOTEL

☎ 0871 527 9046
Yarm Rd TS18 3RT
web: www.premierinn.com
dir: A1(M) junct 60, A689 towards Teeside. Follow Hartlepool signs. Hotel on left at A689 & A19 interchange

Rooms 40

STOKE-BY-NAYLAND Map 13 TL93
Suffolk

The Crown

★★★ 86% ◉◉ SMALL HOTEL

☎ 01206 262001 & 262346
CO6 4SE
e-mail: reservations@crowninn.net
web: www.crowninn.net
dir: Follow Stoke-by-Nayland signs from A12 & A134. Hotel in village off B1068 towards Higham

Situated in a picturesque village this establishment, with an award-winning restaurant, has a reputation for making everyone feel welcome. It offers quiet, individually decorated rooms that look out over the countryside. Ground floor rooms, including three with a terrace, are of a contemporary design while upstairs rooms are in a country-house style; each room has Wi-fi, DVDs and luxury toiletries.

Rooms 11 (1 fmly) (8 GF) ⦁ **Facilities** FTV Wi-fi ⊿ New Year **Conf** Board 10 **Parking** 49 **Notes** ⊗

STOKE D'ABERNON Map 6 TQ15
Surrey

Woodlands Park Hotel

★★★★ 81% ◉◉ HOTEL

☎ 01372 843933 & 0845 072 7581
Woodlands Ln KT11 3QB
e-mail: woodlandspark@handpicked.co.uk
web: www.handpickedhotels.co.uk/woodlandspark
dir: A3 exit at Cobham. Through town centre & Stoke D'Abernon, left at garden centre into Woodlands Lane, hotel 0.5m on right

Originally built for the Bryant family, of the matchmaking firm Bryant & May, this lovely Victorian mansion enjoys an attractive parkland setting in ten and a half acres of Surrey countryside. Bedrooms in the wing are contemporary in style while those in the main house are more traditionally decorated. The hotel boasts two dining options, Benson's Brasserie and the Oak Room Restaurant.

Rooms 57 (4 fmly) ⦁ **Facilities** STV Wi-fi ⊿ HL ◔ ⦁ Xmas New Year **Conf** Class 20 Board 50 Thtr 150 **Services** Lift Air con **Parking** 150 **Notes** ⊗ Civ Wed 200

STOKE-ON-TRENT Map 10 SJ84
Staffordshire

BEST WESTERN PLUS Stoke-on-Trent Moat House

★★★★ 73% HOTEL

☎ 01782 609988
Etruria Hall, Festival Way, Festival Park ST1 5BQ
e-mail: reservations.stoke@qmh-hotels.com
web:
dir: M6 junct 15 (or junct 16), A500, follow A53 & Festival Park signs. Keep in left lane, take 1st slip road on left. Left at island, hotel opposite at next island

This large, modern hotel is located in Stoke's Festival Park, which adjoins Etruria Hall, the former home of Josiah Wedgwood. Bedrooms are spacious and well equipped, and include family rooms, suites and executive rooms. Public areas include a spacious lounge bar and restaurant as well as a business centre, extensive conference facilities and a leisure club.

Rooms 147 **Conf** Class 400 Board 40 Thtr 650

Quality Hotel Stoke

★★★ 74% HOTEL

☎ 01782 202361
66 Trinity St, Hanley ST1 5NB
e-mail: enquiries@qualityhotelsstoke.co.uk
dir: M6 junct 15(S)/16(N) then A500 to city centre & Festival Park. A53 to Leek, keep in left lane, 3rd exit at rdbt for Hanley/City Centre/Cultural Quarter. Hotel on left at top of hill

This large city centre hotel provides a range of bedrooms and extensive public areas including a choice of popular bars. A well lit spacious car park and modern leisure facilities are additional benefits.

Rooms 136 (8 annexe) (54 fmly) (5 GF) ⦁ **S** £42-£72; **D** £55-£85* **Facilities** Wi-fi ⊿ ◔ supervised Gym Sports massage ♪ Xmas New Year **Conf** Class 125 Board 60 Thtr 300 Del from £89 to £129* **Services** Lift **Parking** 150 **Notes** LB Civ Wed 250

Premier Inn Stoke (Trentham Gardens)

BUDGET HOTEL

☎ 9871 527 9050
Stone Rd, Trentham ST4 8JG
web: www.premierinn.com
dir: M6 junct 15, A500, follow Trentham signs. At rdbt 3rd exit onto A34, 2m to hotel on right in Trentham Gardens

High quality, budget accommodation ideal for both families and business travellers. Spacious, en suite bedrooms feature tea and coffee making facilities, and Freeview TV in most hotels. Internet access and Wi-fi are available for a small fee. The adjacent family restaurant features a wide and varied menu. See also the Hotel Groups pages.

Rooms 119

Weathervane

OldEngl∤sh

BUDGET HOTEL

☎ 01782 388799
Lysander Rd ST3 7WA
e-mail: 5305@greenking.co.uk
web: www.oldenglish.co.uk

A few minutes from the A50 and convenient for both the city and industrial areas, this popular, modern pub and restaurant, under the 'Hungry Horse' brand, provides hearty, well-cooked food at reasonable prices. Adjacent bedrooms are furnished for both commercial and leisure customers. See also the Hotel Groups pages.

Rooms 39 (8 fmly) (18 GF) **Conf** Class 20 Board 20 Thtr 20

S

STOKE POGES — Map 6 SU98
Buckinghamshire

Stoke Park

★★★★★ ◉◉◉ HOTEL

☎ 01753 717171
Park Rd SL2 4PG
e-mail: info@stokepark.com
dir: M4 junct 6, A355 towards Slough, B416 (Park Rd). Hotel 1.25m on right

Located within 300 acres of beautiful parkland created by 'Capability' Brown and Humphry Repton, this hotel offers outstanding leisure and sporting facilities. Inside the stunning mansion house, designed by George III's architect, the public areas display lavish opulence throughout and the bedrooms have a luxurious and classic feel. In contrast, the Pavilion features more contemporary bedrooms and public areas; as well as extensive state-of-the-art health and beauty facilities. The hotel has a championship golf course, tennis courts, and three restaurants, including the award-winning Humphry's and the more informal Italian brasserie, San Marco. There are bars, lounges and meeting rooms as well.

Rooms 49 (28 annexe) (6 fmly) ♠ **D** £285-£1500* **Facilities** Spa STV FTV Wi-fi ⬡ ♨ 27 ♣ Putt green Fishing ⚓ Gym Indoor golf swing studio Creche Games room New Year Child facilities **Conf** Class 30 Board 34 Thtr 80 Del £444* **Services** Lift **Parking** 460 **Notes** ⊗ Closed 24-26 Dec Civ Wed 120

Stoke Place

★★★★ 76% ◉◉◉ HOTEL

☎ 01753 534790
Stoke Green SL2 4HT
e-mail: enquiries@stokeplace.co.uk
dir: A355, right at 1st lights to A4 Bath Rd. At 1st rdbt take 2nd exit onto Stoke Rd. B416 to Stoke Green. Hotel 200mtrs on right

Originally built in 1690 and set in 26 acres of 'Capability' Brown designed gardens, this is a delightful William and Mary style manor house. It offers a range of stylish modern bedrooms that are equipped to a very high standard; rear-facing rooms have fantastic view of the garden. Guests can relax in the peaceful lounge and enjoy afternoon tea if they wish. The award-winning Garden Restaurant serves imaginative dishes and the tranquil bar area is ideal for post-dinner drinks.

Rooms 39 (15 annexe) (14 GF) ♠ **S** £105-£185; **D** £120-£195 (incl. bkfst)* **Facilities** STV FTV Wi-fi ⬡ Fishing ⚓ Gym Outdoor jogging track Bicycles Boule pitch Giant kids games Xmas New Year **Conf** Class 100 Board 60 Thtr 200 Del from £195 to £325* **Parking** 120 **Notes** LB Civ Wed 150

STON EASTON — Map 4 ST65
Somerset

Ston Easton Park Hotel

★★★★ ◉◉ COUNTRY HOUSE HOTEL

☎ 01761 241631
BA3 4DF
e-mail: info@stoneaston.co.uk
web: www.stoneaston.co.uk
dir: On A37

Surrounded by The Mendips, this outstanding Palladian mansion lies in extensive parklands that were landscaped by Humphrey Repton. The architecture and decorative features are stunning. The state rooms include one of England's earliest surviving Print Rooms, and the Palladian Saloon is considered one of Somerset's finest rooms. There is even an Edwardian kitchen that guests might like to take a look at. The helpful and attentive team provide a very efficient service, and the award-winning cuisine uses organic produce from the hotel's own kitchen garden. The bedrooms and bathrooms are all appointed to an excellent standard.

Rooms 22 (3 annexe) (2 fmly) ♠ **Facilities** FTV Wi-fi ⬡ ♣ Fishing ⚓ Archery Clay pigeon shooting Quad bikes Hot air ballooning Xmas New Year **Conf** Class 60 Board 30 Thtr 100 **Parking** 120 **Notes** Civ Wed 120

STOURPORT-ON-SEVERN — Map 10 SO87
Worcestershire

Menzies Hotels Birmingham - Stourport Manor

★★★★ 77% HOTEL

☎ 01299 289955
35 Hartlebury Rd DY13 9JA
e-mail: stourport@menzieshotels.co.uk
web: www.menzieshotels.co.uk
dir: M5 junct 6, A449 towards Kidderminster, B4193 towards Stourport. Hotel on right

Once the home of Prime Minister Sir Stanley Baldwin, this much extended country house is set in attractive grounds. A number of bedrooms and suites are located in the original building, although the majority are in a more modern, purpose-built section. Spacious public areas include a range of lounges, a popular restaurant, a leisure club and conference facilities.

Rooms 68 (17 fmly) (31 GF) (10 smoking) ♠ **Facilities** FTV Wi-fi ⬡ ⊕ ♨ Putt green Gym Squash Xmas New Year **Conf** Class 110 Board 100 Thtr 400 **Parking** 300 **Notes** Civ Wed 300

STOWMARKET — Map 13 TM05
Suffolk

Cedars Hotel

★★★ 75% HOTEL

☎ 01449 612668
Needham Rd IP14 2AJ
e-mail: info@cedarshotel.co.uk
dir: A14 junct 15, A1120 towards Stowmarket. At junct with A1113 turn right. Hotel on right

Expect a friendly welcome at this privately owned hotel, which is situated just off the A14 within easy reach of the town centre. Public rooms are full of charm and character with features such as exposed beams and open fireplaces. Bedrooms are pleasantly decorated and thoughtfully equipped with modern facilities.

Rooms 25 (3 fmly) (9 GF) ♠ **Facilities** Wi-fi **Conf** Class 60 Board 40 Thtr 150 **Parking** 75 **Notes** Closed 25 Dec-1 Jan

Save on hotels. Book at **theAA.com/hotel**

STO – STR 421 **ENGLAND**

STOW-ON-THE-WOLD Map 10 SP12
Gloucestershire

Number Four at Stow Hotel & Restaurant

★★★★ 77% ◉◉ SMALL HOTEL

☎ 01451 830297
Fosseway GL54 1JX
e-mail: reservations@hotelnumberfour.co.uk
dir: A424 - Burford to Stow Road

This hotel is situated in one of the most picturesque areas of the Cotswolds. Service is relaxed and friendly, and the bedrooms are very stylish and beautifully presented. The award-winning Cutler's Restaurant serves imaginative dishes using the finest in local produce. Public areas include a contemporary lounge area and a well-equipped business suite.

Rooms 18 (5 fmly) (12 GF) **S** £95-£130; **D** £110-£150 (incl. bkfst)* **Facilities** FTV Wi-fi **Conf** Class 15 Board 28 Thtr 50 Del £180* **Services** Air con **Parking** 50 **Notes** ⊗ Closed 23-29 Dec

Wyck Hill House Hotel & Spa

★★★★ 76% ◉◉ HOTEL

☎ 01451 831936
Burford Rd GL54 1HY
e-mail: info.wyckhillhouse@bespokehotels.com
dir: Exit A429. Hotel 1m on right

This charming 18th-century house enjoys superb views across the Windrush Valley and is ideally positioned for a relaxing weekend exploring the Cotswolds. The spacious and thoughtfully equipped bedrooms provide high standards of comfort and quality, located both in the main house and also the original coach house. Elegant public rooms include a cosy bar, library and the magnificent front hall with crackling log fire. The imaginative cuisine makes extensive use of local produce.

Rooms 60 (4 GF) 🐾 **S** £135-£405; **D** £165-£405 (incl. bkfst)* **Facilities** Spa FTV Wi-fi Sauna Steam room Xmas New Year **Conf** Class 50 Board 50 Thtr 150 Del from £145 to £185* **Services** Lift **Parking** 100 **Notes** LB ⊗ Civ Wed 120

Fosse Manor

★★★ 80% ◉◉ HOTEL

CLASSIC BRITISH HOTELS

☎ 01451 830354
GL54 1JX
e-mail: enquiries@fossemanor.co.uk
web: www.fossemanor.co.uk
dir: 1m S on A429, 300yds past junct with A424

Deriving its name from the historic Roman-built Fosse Way, this popular hotel is ideally situated for exploring the many delights of this picturesque area. Bedrooms, located both in the main building and the adjacent coach house, offer high standards of comfort and quality. Public areas include a small lounge, spacious bar and light and airy restaurant. Classy cuisine is on offer, and quality produce is used to create imaginative dishes.

Rooms 19 (8 annexe) (3 fmly) (5 GF) 🐾 **Facilities** FTV Wi-fi 🛥 Xmas New Year **Conf** Class 40 Board 40 Thtr 100 **Parking** 30 **Notes** ⊗ Civ Wed 70

Stow Lodge Hotel

★★★ 77% SMALL HOTEL

☎ 01451 830485
The Square GL54 1AB
e-mail: enquiries@stowlodge.com
web: www.stowlodge.com
dir: In town centre

Situated in smart grounds, this family-run hotel has direct access to the market square and provides high standards of customer care. Bedrooms are offered both within the main building and in the converted coach house, all of which provide similar standards of homely comfort. Extensive menus and an interesting wine list make for an enjoyable dining experience.

Rooms 21 (10 annexe) (1 fmly) 🐾 **S** £70-£115; **D** £90-£170 (incl. bkfst) **Facilities** Wi-fi **Parking** 30 **Notes** LB ⊗ No children 5yrs Closed Xmas-end Jan

Old Stocks Hotel

★★ 72% SMALL HOTEL

☎ 01451 830666
The Square GL54 1AF
e-mail: aa@oldstockshotel.co.uk
web: www.oldstockshotel.co.uk
dir: Exit A429 to town centre. Hotel facing village green

Overlooking the old market square, this Grade II listed, mellow Cotswold-stone building is a comfortable and friendly base from which to explore this picturesque area. There's lots of character throughout, and the bedrooms offer individuality and charm. Facilities include a guest lounge, restaurant and bar, whilst outside, the patio is a popular summer venue for refreshing drinks and good food.

Rooms 18 (3 annexe) (5 fmly) (4 GF) 🐾 **S** £36-£56; **D** £72-£132 (incl. bkfst)* **Facilities** FTV Wi-fi New Year **Parking** 10

STRATFORD-UPON-AVON Map 10 SP25
Warwickshire

INSPECTORS' CHOICE

Ettington Park Hotel

HandPICKED HOTELS
BUILT FOR PLEASURE

★★★★ ◉◉
COUNTRY HOUSE HOTEL

☎ 01789 450123 & 0845 072 7454
CV37 8BU
e-mail: ettingtonpark@handpicked.co.uk
web: www.handpickedhotels.co.uk/ettingtonpark

(For full entry see Alderminster)

S

STRATFORD-UPON-AVON *continued*

Menzies Welcombe Hotel Spa & Golf Club

★★★★ 85% ◉◉ HOTEL

☎ 01789 295252
Warwick Rd CV37 0NR
e-mail: welcombe@menzieshotels.co.uk
web: www.menzieshotels.co.uk
dir: M40 junct 15, A46 towards Stratford-upon-Avon, at rdbt follow signs for A439. Hotel 3m on right

This Jacobean manor house is set in 157 acres of landscaped parkland. Public rooms are impressive, especially the lounge with its wood panelling and ornate marble fireplace, and the gentleman's club-style bar. Bedrooms in the original building are stylish and gracefully proportioned; those in the garden wing are comfortable and thoughtfully equipped. The spa development incorporates advanced, luxurious facilities and treatments.

Rooms 78 (12 fmly) (11 GF) (6 smoking) ⚞
Facilities Spa STV FTV Wi-fi ⚞ ⚞ ⚞ 18 ⚞ Putt green Gym Xmas New Year **Conf** Class 65 Board 40 Thtr 200 **Parking** 200 **Notes** ⊗ Civ Wed 120

The Arden Hotel

★★★★ 82% ◉◉ HOTEL

☎ 01789 298682
Waterside CV37 6BA
e-mail: enquiries@theardenhotelstratford.com
web: www.theardenhotelstratford.com
dir: M40 junct 15 follow signs to town centre. At Barclays Bank rdbt left onto High St, 2nd left onto Chapel Lane (Nash's House on left). Hotel car park on right in 40yds

This property is on the same road as the world famous Royal Shakespeare and Swan theatres, and just a short walk from the town centre. The bedrooms and bathrooms have been tastefully designed and have quality fixtures and fittings. The dedicated team provide polite and professional service. Award-winning cuisine is served in the popular restaurant. Ample secure parking is available.

Rooms 45 (6 fmly) (17 GF) **Facilities** FTV Wi-fi Xmas New Year **Conf** Class 18 Board 28 Thtr 50 **Parking** 50 **Notes** ⊗ Civ Wed 50

Billesley Manor Hotel

PUMA HOTELS COLLECTION

★★★★ 79% ◉◉ HOTEL

☎ 01789 279955
Billesley, Alcester B49 6NF
e-mail: billesleymanor@pumahotels.co.uk
web: www.pumahotels.co.uk
dir: A46 towards Evesham. Over 3 rdbts, right for Billesley after 2m

This 16th-century manor is set in peaceful grounds and parkland with a delightful yew topiary garden and fountain. The spacious bedrooms and suites, most in traditional country-house style, are thoughtfully designed and well equipped. Conference facilities and some of the bedrooms are found in the cedar barns. Public areas retain many original features, such as oak panelling, fireplaces and exposed stone.

Rooms 72 (29 annexe) (5 GF) **Facilities** Spa ⚞ supervised ⚞ ⚞ Gym Steam room Beauty treatments Yoga studio Xmas New Year **Conf** Class 60 Board 50 Thtr 100 **Parking** 100 **Notes** Civ Wed 75

Macdonald Alveston Manor

MACDONALD HOTELS & RESORTS

★★★★ 79% ◉ HOTEL

☎ 0844 879 9138
Clopton Bridge CV37 7HP
e-mail:
sales.alvestonmanor@macdonald-hotels.co.uk
web: www.macdonald-hotels.co.uk
dir: On rdbt south of Clopton Bridge

A striking red-brick and timbered façade, well-tended grounds, and a giant cedar tree all contribute to the charm of this well-established hotel, just five minutes from Stratford. The bedrooms vary in size and character, and the coach house conversion offers an impressive mix of full and junior suites. The superb leisure complex offers a 20-metre swimming pool, steam room, sauna, a high-tech gym and a host of beauty treatments. Macdonald Hotels is the AA Hotel Group of the Year 2013-14.

Rooms 113 (8 fmly) (45 GF) **Facilities** Spa FTV Wi-fi ⚞ supervised Gym Techno-gym Beauty treatments Sauna Steam room Xmas New Year **Conf** Class 80 Board 40 Thtr 140 **Del from** £130 to £180* **Services** Air con **Parking** 150 **Notes** Civ Wed 110

The Stratford

QHOTELS

★★★★ 79% HOTEL

☎ 01789 271000 & 271007
Arden St CV37 6QQ
e-mail: thestratfordreservations@qhotels.co.uk
web: www.qhotels.co.uk
dir: A439 into Stratford. In town follow A3400/ Birmingham, at lights left into Arden St, hotel 150yds on right

Situated adjacent to the hospital, this eye-catching modern hotel with its red-brick façade is within walking distance of the town centre. The hotel offers modern, well-equipped and spacious bedrooms. The open-plan public areas include a comfortable lounge, a small, atmospheric bar and a spacious restaurant with exposed beams.

Rooms 102 (7 fmly) (14 GF) ⚞ **Facilities** STV Wi-fi ⚞ Gym Free use of Stratford Manor's leisure facilities Xmas New Year **Conf** Class 66 Board 54 Thtr 132 **Services** Lift Air con **Parking** 92 **Notes** ⊗ Civ Wed 132

Stratford Manor

QHOTELS

★★★★ 77% HOTEL

☎ 01789 731173
Warwick Rd CV37 0PY
e-mail: stratfordmanor@qhotels.co.uk
web: www.qhotels.co.uk
dir: M40 junct 15, A46 signed Stratford. At 2nd rdbt take A439 signed Stratford Town Centre. Hotel 1m on left. Or from Stratford centre take A439 signed Warwick & M40. Hotel 3m on right

Just outside Stratford, this hotel is set against a rural backdrop with lovely gardens and ample parking. Public areas include a stylish lounge bar and a contemporary restaurant. Service is both professional and helpful. Bedrooms are smartly appointed, spacious and have generously sized beds and a range of useful facilities. The leisure centre boasts a large indoor pool.

Rooms 104 (8 fmly) (24 GF) ⚞ **Facilities** Spa Wi-fi ⚞ HL ⚞ ⚞ Gym Sauna Steam room Xmas New Year **Conf** Class 120 Board 100 Thtr 350 **Services** Lift **Parking** 220 **Notes** Civ Wed 150

S

Save on hotels. Book at **theAA.com/hotel**

STR 423 ENGLAND

The Legacy Falcon Hotel

★★★★ 74% ⊛ HOTEL

☎ 08444 119005 & 0330 333 2805
Chapel St CV37 6HA
e-mail: res-falcon@legacy-hotels.co.uk
web: www.legacy-hotels.co.uk
dir: M40 junct 15, A46, A349, A3400 towards
Stratford. Into one-way system into right lane marked
Town Centre. At rdbt (Barclays Bank facing) left into
High St. 2nd right into Scholars Lane

Situated in the heart of the town just a short walk
from all the Shakespeare properties, this hotel dates
back to 1500. In the 17th century an extra storey was
added. Bedrooms provide contemporary
accommodation and the public areas are cosy.
Service is provided by a friendly team. The restaurant
provides good quality cuisine using fresh, local
ingredients.

Rooms 83 (11 annexe) (6 fmly) (3 GF) 🐾
Facilities STV Wi-fi ₷ Xmas New Year **Conf** Class 80
Board 50 Thtr 150 **Services** Lift **Parking** 120
Notes Civ Wed 150

Holiday Inn Stratford-upon-Avon

★★★★ 74% HOTEL

☎ 0871 942 9270 & 01789 279988
Bridgefoot CV37 6YR
e-mail: histratford@qmh-hotels.com
web: www.holidayinn.co.uk
dir: A439 to Stratford-upon-Avon. On entering town
bear left, hotel 200mtrs on left

This large modern hotel sits beside the River Avon in
landscaped grounds and has ample parking.
Bedrooms have a light contemporary feel and are
equipped with a good range of facilities that include
air conditioning and Wi-fi. Day rooms include a
terrace lounge and bar, a carvery restaurant and the
Club Moativation health and fitness facility that
proves popular with both corporate and leisure
guests.

Rooms 259 (8 fmly) **Facilities** STV Wi-fi ⊗
supervised Gym Sauna Steam room Solarium Beauty
Salon Xmas New Year **Conf** Class 340 Board 42
Thtr 550 **Services** Lift Air con **Parking** 350 **Notes** ⊗

Macdonald Swan's Nest Hotel

★★★★ 74% HOTEL

☎ 0844 879 9140
Bridgefoot CV37 7LT
e-mail:
sales.swansnest@macdonald-hotels.co.uk
web: www.macdonald-hotels.co.uk/swansnest
dir: A439 towards Stratford, follow one-way system,
left over bridge (A3400), hotel on right

Dating back to the 17th century, this hotel is said to
be one of the earliest brick-built houses in Stratford.
It occupies a prime position on the banks of the River
Avon and is ideally situated for exploring the town.
Bedrooms and bathrooms are appointed to a high
standard with some thoughtful guest extras provided.
Macdonald Hotels is the AA Hotel Group of the Year
2013-14.

Rooms 68 (2 fmly) (25 GF) **Facilities** FTV Wi-fi Use of
facilities at Macdonald Alveston Manor New Year
Conf Class 100 Board 60 Thtr 150 **Parking** 80
Notes Civ Wed 150

Mercure Stratford-upon-Avon Shakespeare Hotel

★★★★ 72% ⊛ HOTEL

☎ 01789 294997
Chapel St CV37 6ER
e-mail: h6630@accor.com
web: www.mercure.com
dir: M40 junct 15. Follow signs for Stratford town
centre on A439. Follow one-way system into Bridge St.
Left at rdbt, hotel 200yds on left opposite HSBC bank

Dating back to the early 17th century, The
Shakespeare is one of the oldest hotels in this historic
town. The hotel name represents one of the earliest
exploitations of Stratford as the birthplace of one of
the world's leading playwrights. With exposed beams
and open fires, the public rooms retain an ambience
reminiscent of this era. Bedrooms are appointed to a
good standard and remain in keeping with the style of
the property.

Rooms 78 (11 annexe) (3 GF) **Facilities** Wi-fi Xmas
New Year **Conf** Class 45 Board 40 Thtr 90
Services Lift **Parking** 31 **Notes** Civ Wed 100

BEST WESTERN Grosvenor Hotel

★★★ 78% HOTEL

☎ 01789 269213
Warwick Rd CV37 6YT
e-mail: res@bwgh.co.uk
web: www.bwgh.co.uk
dir: M40 junct 15, follow Stratford signs to A439
(Warwick Rd). Hotel 7m, on one-way system

This hotel is a short distance from the town centre
and many historic attractions. Bedroom styles and
sizes vary, and the friendly staff offer an efficient
service. Refreshments are served in the lounge all
day, and room service is available. The Garden Room
restaurant offers a choice of dishes from set price
and carte menus.

Rooms 73 (16 fmly) (25 GF) **Facilities** STV FTV Wi-fi ₷
Xmas New Year **Conf** Class 45 Board 50 Thtr 100
Parking 46 **Notes** ⊗ Civ Wed 100

Premier Inn Stratford-upon-Avon Central

BUDGET HOTEL

☎ 0871 527 9282
Payton Rd CV37 6UQ
web: www.premierinn.com
dir: A439, A4300 signed Stratford-upon-Avon. Hotel
on left

High quality, budget accommodation ideal for both
families and business travellers. Spacious, en suite
bedrooms feature tea and coffee making facilities,
and Freeview TV in most hotels. Internet access and
Wi-fi are available for a small fee. The adjacent
family restaurant features a wide and varied menu.
See also the Hotel Groups pages.

Rooms 87

Premier Inn Stratford-upon-Avon Waterways

BUDGET HOTEL

☎ 0871 527 9316
The Waterways, Birmingham Rd CV37 0AZ
dir: A3400 (Birmingham Rd) towards town centre,
pass large retail park on left. Straight over mini rdbt,
approx 150yds. Hotel on right

Rooms 130

S

STREET
Somerset
Map 4 ST43

Wessex Hotel

★★★ 64% HOTEL

☎ 01458 443383
High St BA16 0EF
e-mail: info@wessexhotel.com
dir: From A303, onto B3151 to Somerton. Then 7m, pass lights by Millfield School. Left at mini-rdbt

The Wessex Hotel is centrally located in this popular town, with easy access to all the shops and attractions. The bedrooms and bathrooms vary slightly in size but most rooms provide good levels of quality and comfort. A wide range of snacks and refreshments is available throughout the day, including a regular carvery at dinner. Entertainment is often offered in the main season.

Rooms 51 (9 fmly) **Facilities** FTV Wi-fi ♫ Xmas New Year **Conf** Class 120 Board 80 Thtr 400 **Services** Lift **Parking** 70 **Notes** ⊗

STROUD
Gloucestershire
Map 4 SO80

The Bear of Rodborough

COTSWOLD
INNS & HOTELS

★★★ 82% HOTEL

☎ 01453 878522
Rodborough Common GL5 5DE
e-mail: info@bearofrodborough.info
web: www.cotswold-inns-hotels.co.uk/bear
dir: M5 junct 13, A419 to Stroud. Follow signs to Rodborough. Up hill, left at top at T-junct. Hotel on right

This popular 17th-century coaching inn is situated high above Stroud in acres of National Trust parkland. Character abounds in the lounges and cocktail bar, and in the Box Tree Restaurant where the cuisine utilises fresh local produce. Bedrooms offer equal measures of comfort and style with plenty of extra touches. There is also a traditional and well-patronised public bar.

Rooms 46 (2 fmly) **S** £85-£95; **D** £140-£250 (incl. bkfst)* **Facilities** FTV Wi-fi Xmas New Year **Conf** Class 35 Board 30 Thtr 60 **Parking** 70 **Notes** Civ Wed 70

Burleigh Court Hotel

★★★ 79% ⊛⊛ HOTEL

☎ 01453 883804
Burleigh, Minchinhampton GL5 2PF
e-mail: burleighcourt@aol.com
web: www.burleighcourthotel.co.uk
dir: From Stroud A419 towards Cirencester. Right after 2.5m signed Burleigh & Minchinhampton. Left after 500yds signed Burleigh Court. Hotel 300yds on right

Dating back to the 18th century, this former gentleman's manor house is in a secluded and elevated, though accessible, position with some wonderful countryside views. Public rooms are elegantly styled and include an oak-panelled bar for pre-dinner drinks beside a crackling fire. Combining comfort and quality, no two bedrooms are alike; some are in an adjoining coach house.

Rooms 18 (7 annexe) (2 fmly) (3 GF) ♠ **S** £95-£120; **D** £150-£210 (incl. bkfst)* **Facilities** Wi-fi ⚘ ⚘ New Year **Conf** Class 30 Board 30 Thtr 50 Del £180* **Parking** 40 **Notes** LB Closed 24-26 Dec Civ Wed 50

Premier Inn Stroud

Premier Inn

BUDGET HOTEL

☎ 0871 527 9052
Stratford Lodge, Stratford Rd GL5 4AF
web: www.premierinn.com
dir: M5 junct 13, A419 to town centre, follow Leisure Centre signs. Hotel adjacent to Tesco superstore

High quality, budget accommodation ideal for both families and business travellers. Spacious, en suite bedrooms feature tea and coffee making facilities, and Freeview TV in most hotels. Internet access and Wi-fi are available for a small fee. The adjacent family restaurant features a wide and varied menu. See also the Hotel Groups pages.

Rooms 32

STUDLEY
Warwickshire
Map 10 SP06

BEST WESTERN Studley Castle

Best Western

★★★ 74% HOTEL

☎ 01527 853111 & 855200
Castle Rd B80 7AJ
e-mail: bookings@studleycastle.com
dir: A435 S into Studley, left at castle sign, hotel 1m on right

This hotel has a delightful parkland location close to Stratford. Specialising in providing meeting room venues, the hotel has an impressive range of public areas. The restaurant also offers a relaxing environment and lovely views across the countryside. Bedrooms are available in a range of sizes and all are well equipped.

Rooms 57 (2 fmly) ♠ **Facilities** STV Wi-fi Putt green Gym Sauna Xmas New Year **Conf** Class 66 Board 20 Thtr 150 Del from £110 to £140 **Services** Lift **Parking** 150 **Notes** Civ Wed 150

SUDBURY
Derbyshire
Map 10 SK13

The Boars Head Hotel

★★★ 75% HOTEL

☎ 01283 820344
Lichfield Rd DE6 5GX
e-mail: enquiries@boars-head-hotel.co.uk
web: www.boars-head-hotel.co.uk
dir: A50 onto A515 towards Lichfield, hotel 1m on right

This popular hotel offers comfortable accommodation in well-equipped bedrooms. There is a relaxed atmosphere in the public rooms, which consist of several bars and dining options. The beamed lounge bar provides informal dining thanks to a popular carvery, while the restaurant and cocktail bar offer a more formal environment.

Rooms 23 (1 annexe) (14 GF) **Facilities** STV Wi-fi Beauty salon Xmas New Year **Parking** 85

SUDBURY
Suffolk

The Case Restaurant with Rooms

◉ RESTAURANT WITH ROOMS

☎ 01787 210483
Further St, Assington CO10 5LD
e-mail:
restaurant@thecaserestaurantwithrooms.co.uk
dir: Exit A12 at Colchester onto A134 to Sudbury. 7m,
establishment on left

The Case Restaurant with Rooms offers dining in
comfortable surroundings, along with luxurious
accommodation in bedrooms that all enjoy
independent access. Some bathrooms come complete
with corner jacuzzi, while internet access comes as
standard. In the restaurant, local produce is used in
all dishes, and fresh bread and desserts are made
every day.

Rooms 7 (2 fmly)

SUNBURY
Surrey

See LONDON SECTION plan 1 A1

Premier Inn Sunbury (Kempton Park)

BUDGET HOTEL

☎ 0871 527 9054
Staines Road West, Sunbury Cross TW16 7AT
web: www.premierinn.com
dir: M25 junct 12, onto M3 signed London &
Richmond. Exit at junct 1, take 1st exit at rdbt into
Staines Road West (A308). 1st left into Crossways.
Hotel on right

High quality, budget accommodation ideal for both
families and business travellers. Spacious, en suite
bedrooms feature tea and coffee making facilities,
and Freeview TV in most hotels. Internet access and
Wi-fi are available for a small fee. The adjacent
family restaurant features a wide and varied menu.
See also the Hotel Groups pages.

Rooms 109

SUNDERLAND
Tyne & Wear   Map 19 NZ35

Sunderland Marriott Hotel

★★★★ 72% HOTEL

☎ 0191 529 2041
Queen's Pde, Seaburn SR6 8DB
e-mail: mhrs.nclsl.frontoffice@marriotthotels.com
web: www.sunderlandmarriott.co.uk
dir: A19, A184 (Boldon/Sunderland North), 3m. At
rdbt left, then right. At rdbt left, follow to coast. Turn
right, hotel on right

Comfortable and spacious accommodation, some
with fabulous views of the North Sea and vast
expanses of sandy beach, is provided at this seafront
hotel. Public rooms are bright and modern and a
number of meeting rooms are available. The hotel is
conveniently located for access to the local visitor
attractions.

Rooms 82 (6 fmly) **Facilities** STV Wi-fi ⌕ ⌖ Gym
Xmas New Year **Conf** Class 120 Board 70 Thtr 300
Services Lift **Parking** 110 **Notes** ⊗ Civ Wed 160

BEST WESTERN Roker Hotel

★★★ 78% HOTEL

☎ 0191 567 1786
Roker Ter, Roker SR6 9ND
e-mail: info@rokerhotel.co.uk

This modern hotel offers stunning views of the
coastline. Well-equipped bedrooms come in a variety
of sizes, and several have feature bathrooms.
Functions, conferences and weddings are all well
catered for. A choice of dining options is available
including Restaurant Italia and Restaurant China, as
well as an impressive range of bar meals in the
R-bar.

Rooms 43 (8 fmly) (3 GF) ⌕ **Facilities** STV FTV Wi-fi
⌕ ♫ Xmas New Year **Conf** Class 150 Board 100
Thtr 300 Del from £85 to £155* **Services** Lift Air con
Parking 150 **Notes** ⊗ Civ Wed 350

Premier Inn Sunderland A19/A1231

BUDGET HOTEL

☎ 0871 527 9058
Wessington Way, Castletown SR5 3HR
web: www.premierinn.com
dir: From A19 take A1231 towards Sunderland. Hotel
100yds

High quality, budget accommodation ideal for both
families and business travellers. Spacious, en suite
bedrooms feature tea and coffee making facilities,
and Freeview TV in most hotels. Internet access and
Wi-fi are available for a small fee. The adjacent
family restaurant features a wide and varied menu.
See also the Hotel Groups pages.

Rooms 61

Premier Inn Sunderland North West

BUDGET HOTEL

☎ 0871 527 9056
**Timber Beach Rd, off Wessington Way, Castletown
SR5 3XG**
web: www.premierinn.com
dir: A1(M) junct 65, A1231 towards Sunderland,
(cross over A19)

Rooms 63

SURBITON
Greater London

Holiday Inn London - Kingston South

★★★★ 78% HOTEL PLAN 1 C1

☎ 020 8786 6565 & 8786 6500
Kingston Tower, Portsmouth Rd KT6 5QQ
e-mail: enquiries@hikingston.co.uk
dir: M25 junct 10, A3, left onto A243, 3rd exit at rdbt.
At lights left onto A307

This hotel occupies a convenient location overlooking
the River Thames just outside Kingston-upon-Thames
and close to Surbiton. Many front-facing bedrooms
have beautiful river views; all are comfortable and
stylish. The public areas include a small yet well-
equipped fitness room. Complimentary parking and
Wi-fi are also available.

Rooms 116 (2 fmly) ⌕ **S** £79-£250; **D** £89-£260
(incl. bkfst) **Facilities** STV FTV Wi-fi ⌕ HL Gym
Conf Class 125 Board 60 Thtr 250 Del from £159 to
£250 **Services** Lift Air con **Parking** 120 **Notes** LB
Civ Wed 300

S

SUTTON
Greater London
Map 6 TQ26

Holiday Inn London - Sutton
★★★ 77% HOTEL

☎ 020 8234 1100 & 8234 1104
Gibson Rd SM1 2RF
e-mail: sales-sutton@ihg.com
web: www.hilondonsuttonhotel.co.uk
dir: M25 junct 8, A217, B2230. Pass rail station, follow one-way system in right lane. At lights, right then immediately left, left into Gibson Rd

Well located for many famous attractions such as Chessington World of Adventure, the All England Tennis Club at Wimbledon, and Epsom Racecourse. This hotel offers air-conditioned bedrooms ranging from standard to executive, a variety of conference rooms, and leisure facilities with a swimming pool.

Rooms 119 (4 fmly) **Facilities** Spa STV FTV Wi-fi ⚡ HL 🕭 supervised Gym Xmas New Year **Conf** Class 100 Board 70 Thtr 180 **Services** Lift Air con **Parking** 115 **Notes** ⊗ Civ Wed 160

SUTTON COLDFIELD
West Midlands
Map 10 SP19

New Hall Hotel & Spa
★★★★ 82% ⊛⊛ HOTEL

☎ 0845 072 7577 & 0121 378 2442
Walmley Rd B76 1QX
e-mail: newhall@handpicked.co.uk
web: www.handpickedhotels.co.uk/newhall
dir: M42 junct 9, A4097, 2m to rdbt, take 2nd exit signed Walmley. Take 2nd exit from next 5 rdbts follow Sutton Coldfield signs. At 6th rdbt take 3rd exit follow Sutton Coldfield signs. Hotel on left

Situated in 26 acres of beautiful grounds this hotel is reputed to be the oldest inhabited, moated house in the country. The house's medieval charm and character combine well with 21st-century guest facilities. Executive and luxury suites are available. Public areas, with their fine panelling and mullioned stained-glass windows include the magnificent Great Chamber.

Rooms 60 (14 fmly) (25 GF) 🕭 **S** £99-£141; **D** £109-£151 (incl. bkfst)* **Facilities** Spa STV FTV Wi-fi 🕭 supervised ♨ 9 ♨ Fishing ♨ Gym Steam room Pitch & putt Xmas New Year **Conf** Class 75 Board 35 Thtr 150 Del from £151 to £168* **Parking** 80 **Notes** LB ⊗ Civ Wed 75

BEST WESTERN PREMIER
Moor Hall Hotel & Spa

★★★★ 77% HOTEL

☎ 0121 308 3751
Moor Hall Dr, Four Oaks B75 6LN
e-mail: mail@moorhallhotel.co.uk
web: www.moorhallhotel.co.uk
dir: A38 onto A453 towards Sutton Coldfield, right at lights into Weeford Rd. Hotel 150yds on left

Although only a short distance from the city centre this hotel enjoys a peaceful setting, overlooking extensive grounds and an adjacent golf course. Bedrooms are well equipped and executive rooms are particularly spacious. Public rooms include the formal Oak Room Restaurant, and the informal Country Kitchen which offers a carvery and blackboard specials. The hotel also has a well-equipped spa with pool, sauna, steam room, jacuzzi and treatment rooms.

Rooms 82 (5 fmly) (33 GF) 🕭 **S** £55-£149; **D** £88-£169 (incl. bkfst) **Facilities** Spa FTV Wi-fi ⚡ HL 🕭 Gym Aerobics studio Sauna Steam room **Conf** Class 120 Board 45 Thtr 250 Del from £135 to £155 **Services** Lift **Parking** 170 **Notes** LB ⊗ Civ Wed 180

Ramada Birmingham, Sutton Coldfield
★★★ 74% HOTEL

☎ 0121 351 3111
Penns Ln, Walmley B76 1LH
e-mail: enquiries@ramadasuttonhotel.co.uk
web: www.ramadasuttonhotel.co.uk
dir: From S: M6 junct 5 A452, 3rd rdbt right into Eachelhurst Rd, left at lights into Penns Lane. From N/W: M6 junct 6, Sutton Coldfield A5127, follow signs, 2m on at lights (Macdonalds) 4th right into Penns Lane

This hotel offers comfortable bedrooms which are fully equipped with a range of thoughtful accessories. The public areas provide a leisure facility with a well-equipped gym, alongside a smart lounge bar and function rooms.

Rooms 170 (23 annexe) (26 fmly) (48 GF) 🕭 **Facilities** Spa STV FTV Wi-fi 🕭 Fishing Gym Squash Sauna Steam room Studio Hair salon New Year **Conf** Class 200 Board 80 Thtr 600 **Services** Lift **Parking** 500 **Notes** Civ Wed 200

Premier Inn Birmingham North (Sutton Coldfield)

BUDGET HOTEL

☎ 0871 527 8088
Whitehouse Common Rd B75 6HD
web: www.premierinn.com
dir: M42 junct 9, A446 towards Lichfield, then A453 to Sutton Coldfield. Left into Whitehouse Common Rd, hotel on left

High quality, budget accommodation ideal for both families and business travellers. Spacious, en suite bedrooms feature tea and coffee making facilities, and Freeview TV in most hotels. Internet access and Wi-fi are available for a small fee. The adjacent family restaurant features a wide and varied menu. See also the Hotel Groups pages.

Rooms 42

SUTTON ON SEA
Lincolnshire
Map 17 TF58

The Grange & Links Hotel
★★★ 73% HOTEL

☎ 01507 441334
Sea Ln, Sandilands LN12 2RA
e-mail: grangeandlinkshotel@btconnect.com
web: www.grangeandlinkshotel.co.uk
dir: A1111 to Sutton-on-Sea, follow signs to Sandilands

This friendly, family-run hotel sits in five acres of grounds, close to both the beach and its own 18-hole links golf course. Bedrooms are pleasantly appointed and are well equipped for both business and leisure guests. Public rooms include ample lounge areas, a formal restaurant and a traditional bar, serving a wide range of meals and snacks.

Rooms 23 (10 fmly) (3 GF) **Facilities** Wi-fi ♨ 18 ♨ Putt green ♨ Gym Xmas New Year **Conf** Class 200 Board 100 Thtr 200 **Parking** 60 **Notes** Civ Wed 150

SUTTON SCOTNEY
Hampshire   Map 5 SU43

Norton Park
★★★★ 78% HOTEL

☎ 0845 074 0055 & 01962 763000
SO21 3NB
e-mail: nortonpark@qhotels.co.uk
web: www.qhotels.co.uk
dir: From A303 & A34 junct follow signs to Sutton
Scotney. Hotel on Micheldever Station Rd (old A30),
1m from Sutton Scotney

Set in 54 acres of beautiful parkland in the heart of
Hampshire, Norton Park offers both business and
leisure guests a great range of amenities. Dating
from the 16th century, the hotel is complemented by
extensive buildings housing the bedrooms, and public
areas which include a superb leisure club and
numerous conference facilities. Ample parking is
available.

Rooms 175 (11 fmly) (80 GF) **Facilities** Spa Wi-fi
supervised Gym Steam room Sauna Experience
shower Ice fountain Xmas New Year **Conf** Class 250
Board 80 Thtr 340 **Services** Lift **Parking** 220
Notes Civ Wed 340

SWANAGE
Dorset   Map 5 SZ07

The Pines Hotel
★★★ 79% HOTEL

☎ 01929 425211
Burlington Rd BH19 1LT
e-mail: reservations@pineshotel.co.uk
web: www.pineshotel.co.uk
dir: A351 to seafront, left then 2nd right. Hotel at end
of road

Enjoying a peaceful location with spectacular views
over the cliffs and sea, The Pines is a pleasant place
to stay. Many of the comfortable bedrooms have sea
views. Guests can take tea in the lounge, enjoy
appetising bar snacks in the attractive bar, and dine
on interesting cuisine in the restaurant.

The Pines Hotel

Rooms 41 (26 fmly) (6 GF) **S** £70; **D** £140-£190
(incl. bkfst)* **Facilities** FTV Wi-fi Xmas New Year
Conf Class 80 Board 80 Thtr 80 Del from £90 to
£110.60* **Services** Lift **Parking** 60 **Notes** LB

See advert below

SWANAGE *continued*

Grand Hotel

★★★ 68% HOTEL

☎ 01929 423353
Burlington Rd BH19 1LU
e-mail: reservations@grandhotelswanage.co.uk
web: www.grandhotelswanage.co.uk

Dating back to 1898, this hotel is located on the Isle of Purbeck and has spectacular views across Swanage Bay and Peveril Point. Bedrooms are individually decorated and well equipped; public rooms offer a number of choices from relaxing lounges to extensive leisure facilities. The hotel also has its own private beach.

Rooms 30 (2 fmly) **Facilities** FTV Wi-fi ⊗ supervised Fishing Gym Table tennis Beauty treatment room Sauna Solarium Xmas New Year **Conf** Class 40 Board 40 Thtr 120 **Services** Lift **Parking** 15

Premier Inn Swanley

BUDGET HOTEL

☎ 0871 527 9288
London Rd BR8 7QD
web: www.premierinn.com
dir: M25 junct 3, B2173 towards Swanley. At rdbt 2nd exit onto B258 (High St). At next rdbt 4th exit into Swanley Ln, 1st exit into Bartholomew Way, at next rdbt 3rd exit into London Rd

High quality, budget accommodation ideal for both families and business travellers. Spacious, en suite bedrooms feature tea and coffee making facilities, and Freeview TV in most hotels. Internet access and Wi-fi are available for a small fee. The adjacent family restaurant features a wide and varied menu. See also the Hotel Groups pages.

Rooms 61

Sway Manor Restaurant & Hotel

★★★ 77% HOTEL

☎ 01590 682754
Station Rd SO41 6BA
e-mail: info@swaymanor.com
web: www.swaymanor.com
dir: Exit B3055 (Brockenhurst/New Milton road) into village centre

Built at the turn of the 20th century, this attractive mansion is set in its own grounds, and is conveniently located in the village centre. Bedrooms are well appointed and generously equipped; most have views over the gardens and pool. The bar and conservatory restaurant, both with views over the gardens, are popular with locals.

Rooms 15 (3 fmly) **S** £39-£79; **D** £59-£129* **Facilities** FTV Wi-fi ⊗ ⊰ ♫ Xmas New Year **Conf** Class 20 Board 15 **Services** Lift **Parking** 40 **Notes** LB Civ Wed 80

Swindon Marriott Hotel

★★★★ 74% HOTEL

☎ 01793 512121
Pipers Way SN3 1SH
e-mail: mhrs.swidt.frontdesk@marriotthotels.com
web: www.swindonmarriott.co.uk
dir: M4 junct 15, A419, A4259 to Coate rdbt & B4006 signed 'Old Town'

With convenient access to the motorway, this hotel is a good venue for meetings, and an ideal base from which to explore Wiltshire and the Cotswolds. The hotel offers a good range of public rooms, including a well-equipped leisure centre, Chats café bar and an informal, brasserie-style Mediterrano restaurant.

Rooms 156 (42 fmly) **Facilities** Spa STV FTV Wi-fi ⊗ ⊗ ⊰ Gym Aerobics studio Hairdresser Health & beauty salon Sauna Steam room **Conf** Class 100 Board 40 Thtr 280 **Services** Lift Air con **Parking** 300 **Notes** ⊗ Civ Wed 280

Menzies Swindon

★★★★ 73% HOTEL

☎ 01793 528282
Fleming Way SN1 1TN
e-mail: swindon@menzieshotels.co.uk
web: www.menzieshotels.co.uk
dir: M4 junct 15/16, follow town centre signs

This modern hotel is conveniently located in the centre of the town with the added advantage of nearby parking. The hotel offers bedrooms and bathrooms that are well equipped with plenty of useful extras. The brasserie serves an exciting selection of dishes. There are also various conference and event facilities available.

Rooms 95 (2 fmly) ⋔ **Facilities** FTV Wi-fi ⊗ Xmas New Year **Conf** Class 80 Board 60 Thtr 200 **Services** Lift **Notes** ⊗ Civ Wed 200

BEST WESTERN PLUS Blunsdon House Hotel

★★★★ 72% HOTEL

☎ 01793 721701
Blunsdon SN26 7AS
e-mail: reservations@blunsdonhouse.co.uk
web: www.blunsdonhouse.co.uk
dir: M4 junct 15, A419 towards Cirencester. Exit at Turnpike junct, right, follow brown hotel signs

Located just to the north of Swindon, Blunsdon House is set in 30 acres of well-kept grounds, and offers extensive leisure facilities and spacious day rooms. The hotel has a choice of eating and drinking options in three bars and two restaurants; the lively and informal Christopher's, and Nichols for fine dining. Bedrooms are comfortably furnished, and include family rooms with bunk beds and the contemporary spacious Pavilion rooms.

Rooms 108 (17 fmly) (27 GF) ⋔ **S** £79-£149; **D** £79-£149 **Facilities** Spa STV FTV Wi-fi ⊗ HL ⊗ ↟ 9 ⊰ Putt green Gym Squash Beauty therapy Woodland walk Xmas New Year Child facilities **Conf** Class 200 Board 55 Thtr 300 Del from £129 to £169 **Services** Lift **Parking** 300 **Notes** LB ⊗ Civ Wed 200

The Pear Tree at Purton

★★★ 81% ⊛⊛ HOTEL

☎ 01793 772100
Church End SN5 4ED
e-mail: stay@peartreepurton.co.uk

(For full entry see Purton)

Save on hotels. Book at theAA.com/hotel

SWA – SWI 429 ENGLAND

Stanton House Hotel

★★★ 78% HOTEL

☎ 0843 507 1388
The Avenue, Stanton Fitzwarren SN6 7SD
e-mail: reception@stantonhouse.co.uk
web: www.stantonhouse.co.uk
dir: A419 onto A361 towards Highworth, left towards
Stanton Fitzwarren about 600yds past business park,
hotel on left

Extensive grounds and superb gardens surround this
Cotswold-stone manor house: the park and Stanton
Lake are accessible to guests and provide great
walks. Smart, well-maintained bedrooms have been
equipped with modern comforts. Public areas include
a conservatory, a bar and two eating options - The
Rosemary Restaurant offering a wide choice of
Japanese and European dishes, and the Mt Fuji
Restaurant specialising in authentic Japanese food in
traditional surroundings. The friendly, multi-lingual
staff create a relaxing atmosphere for their guests.

Rooms 78 (27 GF) **Facilities** STV Wi-fi Xmas New
Year **Conf** Class 70 Board 40 Thtr 110 Del from £104*
Services Lift **Parking** 110 **Notes** ⊗ Civ Wed 110

Holiday Inn Swindon

★★★ 77% HOTEL

☎ 01793 817000 & 0871 942 9079
Marlborough Rd SN3 6AQ
e-mail: swindon@ihg.com
web: www.holidayinn.co.uk
dir: M4 junct 15, A419 towards Swindon. Take A4259
for 1m. Hotel on right opposite Sun Inn

With convenient access to both the M4 and Swindon's
centre, this hotel provides an ideal base for business
or leisure guests. Bedrooms are well decorated and
have a good range of useful extras. Guests can enjoy
the facilities of The Spirit Health and Fitness Club
and then relax in the comfortable bar. A good
selection of dishes is available whether by way of
room service, lounge snacks or the welcoming,
informal restaurant.

Rooms 99 (25 fmly) (48 GF) (4 smoking)
Facilities STV FTV Wi-fi 🕭 🕭 supervised Gym
Conf Class 30 Board 30 Thtr 60 **Services** Air con
Parking 120 **Notes** ⊗ Civ Wed 80

Chiseldon House Hotel

★★★ 75% ⊛ HOTEL

☎ 01793 741010
New Rd, Chiseldon SN4 0NE
e-mail: welcome@chiseldonhouse.com
web: www.chiseldonhouse.com
dir: M4 junct 15, A346 signed Marlborough. In 0.5m
right onto B4500, 0.25m, hotel on right

Conveniently located for access to the M4, Chiseldon
House is in a quiet location and has a relaxed
ambience. Bedrooms include a number of larger
rooms but all are comfortably furnished. The award-
winning restaurant offers a selection of carefully
prepared dishes utilising high quality produce.
Guests are welcome to enjoy the pleasant garden with
outdoor seating.

Rooms 21 (4 fmly) **Facilities** FTV Wi-fi 🕭
Conf Class 20 Board 32 Thtr 65 **Parking** 50 **Notes** ⊗
Civ Wed 85

Mercure Swindon South Marston Hotel & Spa

★★★ 72% HOTEL

☎ 01793 833700
Old Vicarage Ln, South Marston SN3 4SH
e-mail: info@southmarstonhotel.com
web: www.southmarstonhotel.com
dir: M4 junct 15, A419 N to Cirencester. Exit 2nd
junct signed A420 Oxford, left to South Marston. Hotel
past pub on left

Located just outside Swindon, this hotel offers smart,
modern, well-appointed bedrooms and spacious
public areas. Leisure facilities include a spa with
health and beauty treatments, a well-equipped gym
and a 23-metre pool. The light and airy restaurant
serves modern British cuisine. Free Wi-fi is available
throughout.

Rooms 60 (7 fmly) (30 GF) **Facilities** Spa FTV Wi-fi 🕭
🕭 Gym Squash Sauna Steam room Fitness studio
Spinning room Xmas New Year **Conf** Class 75
Board 60 Thtr 150 **Parking** 200 **Notes** ⊗
Civ Wed 120

Marsh Farm Hotel

★★★ 70% HOTEL

☎ 01793 842800 & 848044
Coped Hall, Royal Wootton Bassett SN4 8ER
e-mail: info@marshfarmhotel.co.uk
web: www.marshfarmhotel.co.uk
dir: M4 junct 16 onto A3102, straight on at 1st rdbt,
right at 2nd rdbt. Hotel 200yds on left

The well decorated and comfortably furnished
bedrooms at this hotel are situated in converted

barns and extensions around the original farmhouse,
which is set in its own grounds less than a mile from
the M4. A relaxed and welcoming atmosphere prevails
especially at dinner, when an extensive range of
dishes to suit all tastes, is offered in the conservatory
restaurant.

Rooms 50 (39 annexe) (1 fmly) (16 GF) 🕭
S £58-£105; **D** £68-£135 (incl. bkfst)* **Facilities** FTV
Wi-fi Putt green Beauty salon Use of nearby leisure
centre New Year **Conf** Class 60 Board 50 Thtr 120
Parking 100 **Notes** ⊗ Closed 26-30 Dec RS 25 Dec
Civ Wed 100

Campanile Swindon

Campanile

BUDGET HOTEL

☎ 01793 514777
Delta Business Park, Great Western Way SN5 7XG
e-mail: swindon@campanile.com
web: www.campanile-swindon.co.uk
dir: M4 junct 16, A3102 towards Swindon. After 2nd
rdbt, 2nd exit onto Welton Rd (Delta Business Park),
1st left

This modern building offers accommodation in smart,
well-equipped bedrooms, all with en suite bathrooms.
Refreshments may be taken at the informal bistro.
See also the Hotel Groups pages.

Rooms 120 (6 fmly) (22 GF) 🕭 **Conf** Class 40
Board 40 Thtr 70

Premier Inn Swindon Central

Premier Inn

BUDGET HOTEL

☎ 0871 527 9064
Kembrey Business Park, Kembrey St SN2 8YS
web: www.premierinn.com
dir: M4 junct 15, A419 (Swindon bypass) towards
Cirencester. In 6m at Turnpike Rdbt 1st left. Hotel on
left in 2m

High quality, budget accommodation ideal for both
families and business travellers. Spacious, en suite
bedrooms feature tea and coffee making facilities,
and Freeview TV in most hotels. Internet access and
Wi-fi are available for a small fee. The adjacent
family restaurant features a wide and varied menu.
See also the Hotel Groups pages.

Rooms 50

S

SWINDON *continued*

Premier Inn Swindon North

BUDGET HOTEL

☎ 0871 527 9066
Broad Bush, Blunsdon SN26 8DJ
web: www.premierinn.com
dir: N of Swindon. 5m from M4 junct 15. At junct of A419 & B4019

Rooms 62

Premier Inn Swindon West

BUDGET HOTEL

☎ 0871 527 9068
Great Western Way SN5 8UY
web: www.premierinn.com
dir: M4 junct 16, A3102 to Lydiard Fields. Past Hilton, entrance on left. (NB for Sat Nav use SN5 8UB

Rooms 63

SWINTON	Map 15 SD70
Greater Manchester	

Premier Inn Manchester (Worsley East/A580)

BUDGET HOTEL

☎ 0871 527 8724
East Lancs Rd M27 0AA
web: www.premierinn.com
dir: M60 junct 13 (Swinton/Leigh), A580

High quality, budget accommodation ideal for both families and business travellers. Spacious, en suite bedrooms feature tea and coffee making facilities, and Freeview TV in most hotels. Internet access and Wi-fi are available for a small fee. The adjacent family restaurant features a wide and varied menu. See also the Hotel Groups pages.

Rooms 27

TADWORTH	Map 6 TQ25
Surrey	

Premier Inn Epsom South

BUDGET HOTEL

☎ 0871 527 8382
Brighton Rd, Burgh Heath KT20 6BW
web: www.premierinn.com
dir: Just off M25 junct 8 on A217 towards Sutton

High quality, budget accommodation ideal for both families and business travellers. Spacious, en suite bedrooms feature tea and coffee making facilities, and Freeview TV in most hotels. Internet access and Wi-fi are available for a small fee. The adjacent

family restaurant features a wide and varied menu. See also the Hotel Groups pages.

Rooms 76

TAMWORTH	Map 10 SK20
Staffordshire	

Drayton Court Hotel

★★ 83% HOTEL

☎ 01827 285805
65 Coleshill St, Fazeley B78 3RG
e-mail: draytoncthotel@yahoo.co.uk
web: www.draytoncourthotel.co.uk
dir: M42 junct 9, A446 to Lichfield, at next rdbt right onto A4091. 2m, Drayton Manor Theme Park on left. Hotel on right

Conveniently located close to the M42, this lovingly restored hotel offers bedrooms that are elegant and have been thoughtfully equipped to suit both business and leisure guests. Beds are particularly comfortable, and one room has a four-poster. Public areas include a panelled bar, a relaxing lounge and an attractive restaurant.

Rooms 19 (3 fmly) S £72.50-£92.50;
D £72.50-£92.50* Facilities Wi-fi ↳ Conf Board 12 Parking 23 Notes ⊛ Closed 22 Dec-1 Jan

Premier Inn Tamworth Central

BUDGET HOTEL

☎ 0871 527 9070
Bonehill Rd, Bitterscote B78 3HQ
web: www.premierinn.com
dir: M42 junct 10, A5 towards Tamworth. Left in 3m onto A51 signed Tamworth. Straight on at 1st rdbt. At next rdbt 3rd exit. Hotel adjacent to Ladybridge Beefeater

High quality, budget accommodation ideal for both families and business travellers. Spacious, en suite bedrooms feature tea and coffee making facilities, and Freeview TV in most hotels. Internet access and Wi-fi are available for a small fee. The adjacent family restaurant features a wide and varied menu. See also the Hotel Groups pages.

Rooms 58

Premier Inn Tamworth South

BUDGET HOTEL

☎ 0871 527 9072
Watling St, Wilnecote B77 5PN
web: www.premierinn.com
dir: M42 junct 10, A5 towards Tamworth. Left in 200yds signed Wilnecote/B5404. Left at next rdbt, hotel on left

Rooms 58

TANKERSLEY	Map 16 SK39
South Yorkshire	

Tankersley Manor

★★★★ 77% HOTEL

☎ 01226 744700
Church Ln S75 3DQ
e-mail: tankersleymanor@qhotels.co.uk
web: www.qhotels.co.uk
dir: M1 junct 36, A61 (Sheffield road)

High on the moors with views over the countryside, this 17th-century residence is well located for major cities, tourist attractions and motorway links. Where appropriate, bedrooms retain original features such as exposed beams and Yorkshire-stone window sills. The hotel has a newly refurbished bar and brasserie which has old beams and open fires. A well-equipped leisure centre is also available.

Rooms 98 (10 fmly) (16 GF) ↟ S £75-£135;
D £85-£145 (incl. bkfst)* Facilities Spa STV FTV Wi-fi ↳ ✈ Gym Swimming lessons Beauty treatments Xmas New Year Conf Class 200 Board 100 Thtr 400 Services Lift Parking 350 Notes Civ Wed 250

Premier Inn Sheffield/ Barnsley M1 Jct 36

BUDGET HOTEL

☎ 0871 527 8968
Maple Rd S75 3DL
web: www.premierinn.com
dir: M1 junct 35A (N'bound exit only), A616 for 2m. From M1 junct 36, A61 towards Sheffield

High quality, budget accommodation ideal for both families and business travellers. Spacious, en suite bedrooms feature tea and coffee making facilities, and Freeview TV in most hotels. Internet access and Wi-fi are available for a small fee. The adjacent family restaurant features a wide and varied menu. See also the Hotel Groups pages.

Rooms 62

Save on hotels. Book at **theAA.com/hotel**

SWI – TAU 431 ENGLAND

TAPLOW
Buckinghamshire
Map 6 SU98

INSPECTORS' CHOICE

Cliveden

★★★★★ ◉◉ COUNTRY HOUSE HOTEL

☎ 01628 668561
SL6 0JF
e-mail: info@clivedenhouse.co.uk
web: www.clivedenhouse.co.uk
dir: M4 junct 7, A4 towards Maidenhead, 1.5m, onto B476 towards Taplow, 2.5m, hotel on left

This wonderful stately home stands at the top of a gravelled boulevard. Visitors are treated as house-guests and staff recapture the tradition of fine hospitality. Bedrooms have individual quality and style, and reception rooms retain a timeless elegance. Exceptional leisure facilities include cruises along Cliveden Reach and massages in the Pavilion. The Terrace Restaurant with its delightful views has been awarded two AA Rosettes.

Rooms 39 (1 annexe) (16 fmly) (10 GF) 🐾 **S** £252-£1572; **D** £252-£1572 (incl. bkfst)* **Facilities** Spa STV FTV Wi-fi ⊗ 🏊 ♨ ⚒ Gym Squash Full range of beauty treatments 3 vintage boats 🎵 Xmas New Year **Conf** Class 48 Board 40 Thtr 120 Del from £295* **Services** Lift **Parking** 60 **Notes** LB Civ Wed 150

Taplow House Hotel

★★★★ 75% ◉◉ HOTEL

☎ 01628 670056
Berry Hill SL6 0DA
e-mail: reception@taplowhouse.com
dir: Exit A4 onto Berry Hill, hotel 0.5m on right

This elegant Georgian manor is set amid beautiful gardens and has been skilfully restored. Character public rooms are pleasing and include a number of air-conditioned conference rooms and an elegant restaurant. Comfortable bedrooms are individually decorated and furnished to a high standard.

Rooms 32 (4 fmly) (2 GF) 🐾 **Facilities** STV FTV Wi-fi ♨ Complimentary use of private leisure facilities (1m) Xmas New Year **Conf** Class 50 Board 50 Thtr 120 **Services** Air con **Parking** 100 **Notes** ⊗ Civ Wed 100

TARPORLEY
Cheshire
Map 15 SJ56

Macdonald Portal Hotel Golf & Spa

★★★★ 79% ◉ HOTEL

☎ 0844 879 9082
Cobblers Cross Ln CW6 0DJ
e-mail: general.portal@macdonaldhotels.co.uk
dir: M6 junct 18, A54 towards Middlewich/Winsford. Left onto A49, through Cotebrook. In approx 1m follow signs for hotel

This hotel is located in beautiful rolling countryside and provides a luxury base for both the leisure and business guest. The spacious and well-equipped bedrooms have bathrooms with baths and power showers. Extensive leisure facilities include a superb spa, state-of-the-art fitness equipment, three golf courses and a golf academy. The Ranulf Restaurant delivers skilfully prepared, innovative cooking, as well as an excellent breakfast. Staff throughout are very friendly and nothing is too much trouble. Macdonald Hotels is the AA Hotel Group of the Year 2013-14.

Rooms 85 (29 GF) 🐾 **S** £80-£236; **D** £80-£236 **Facilities** Spa STV FTV Wi-fi ♨ HL ⊗ ⚒ 45 Putt green Gym Golf academy Outdoor pursuits New Year **Conf** Class 180 Board 60 Thtr 250 **Services** Lift **Parking** 250 **Notes** LB Civ Wed 250

TAUNTON
Somerset
Map 4 ST22

The Mount Somerset Hotel & Spa

★★★★ 77% ◉◉ COUNTRY HOUSE HOTEL

☎ 01823 442500
Lower Henlade TA3 5NB
e-mail: info@mountsomersethotel.co.uk
dir: M5 junct 25, A358 towards Chard/Ilminster, at Henlade right into Stoke Rd, left at T-junct at end, then right into drive

From its elevated and rural position, this impressive Regency house has wonderful views over Taunton Vale. There are impressive quality and comfort levels throughout in the stylish bedrooms and bathrooms. The elegant public rooms combine elegance and flair with an engaging and intimate atmosphere. In addition to the daily-changing, fixed-price menu, a carefully selected seasonal carte is available in the restaurant.

Rooms 19 (1 fmly) 🐾 **S** £100-£205; **D** £145-£275 (incl. bkfst)* **Facilities** Spa FTV Wi-fi ♨ Gym Hydrotherapy pool Sauna Steam room Experience showers Xmas New Year **Conf** Class 60 Board 35 Thtr 70 Del from £145 to £164* **Services** Lift **Parking** 100 **Notes** LB ⊗ Civ Wed 80

Holiday Inn Taunton M5 Jct 25

★★★ 74% HOTEL

☎ 0871 942 9080 & 01823 281600
Deane Gate Av TA1 2UA
web: www.hitauntonhotelm5.co.uk
dir: Adjacent to M5 junct 25, hotel before Harvester on right at entrance to business park

Handily located close to the M5, this is a popular choice for both business and leisure travellers. The open-plan public areas have a light and airy feel and include extensive leisure facilities. Bedrooms are well equipped and contemporary, with executive rooms also available. A choice of menus, with daily specials, is served in the relaxed restaurant.

Rooms 99 (68 fmly) (48 GF) (8 smoking) **Facilities** Wi-fi ⊗ Gym Xmas New Year **Conf** Class 100 Board 30 Thtr 280 **Services** Lift Air con **Parking** 300 **Notes** ⊗ Civ Wed 200

T

TAUNTON *continued*

Salisbury House Hotel

★★★ 73% METRO HOTEL

☎ 01823 272083
14 Billetfield TA1 3NN
e-mail: res@salisburyhousehotel.co.uk
web: www.salisburyhousehotel.co.uk

Centrally and conveniently located, this elegant
establishment dates back to the 1850s and retains
many original features such as stained-glass
windows and a wonderful oak staircase. Bedrooms
provide impressive levels of comfort and quality with
well-equipped, modern bathrooms. Public areas
reflect the same high standards that are a hallmark
throughout this hotel.

Rooms 17 (4 fmly) (6 GF) (2 smoking) ❧ S £65–£85;
D £75–£95 (incl. bkfst)* **Facilities** FTV Wi-fi ☟
Parking 17 **Notes** ⊗

Corner House Hotel

★★★ 71% HOTEL

☎ 01823 284683
Park St TA1 4DQ
e-mail: res@corner-house.co.uk
web: www.corner-house.co.uk
dir: 0.3m from town centre. Hotel on junct of Park St
& A38 (Wellington Rd)

The unusual Victorian façade of the Corner House,
with its turrets and stained-glass windows, belies the
wealth of innovation, quality and style to be found
inside. The contemporary bedrooms have state-of-
the-art facilities including flat-screen TVs, ample
working space, and fridges with complimentary water
and fresh milk. The smart public areas include the
convivial bar and the relaxed and enjoyable 'Wine &
Sausage' eating rooms. Free Wi-fi is available
throughout the hotel.

Rooms 44 (9 annexe) (4 fmly) (5 GF) **Facilities** FTV
Wi-fi **Conf** Class 30 Board 28 Thtr 50 **Parking** 30
Notes ⊗

Castle Hotel

🆄

☎ 01823 272671
Castle Green TA1 1NF
e-mail: reception@the-castle-hotel.com

Currently the rating for this establishment is not
confirmed. This may be due to a change of ownership
or because it has only recently joined the AA rating
scheme. For further details please see the AA website:
theAA.com

Rooms 44 S £80–£99; D £155–£200*

Premier Inn Taunton Central (North)

BUDGET HOTEL

☎ 0871 527 9076
Massingham Park, Priorswood Rd TA2 7RX
web: www.premierinn.com
dir: M5 junct 25, A358 into Taunton, at 2nd rdbt right
onto Obridge Viaduct. Hotel at next rdbt

High quality, budget accommodation ideal for both
families and business travellers. Spacious, en suite
bedrooms feature tea and coffee making facilities,
and Freeview TV in most hotels. Internet access and
Wi-fi are available for a small fee. The adjacent
family restaurant features a wide and varied menu.
See also the Hotel Groups pages.

Rooms 40

Premier Inn Taunton East

BUDGET HOTEL

☎ 0871 527 9080
81 Bridgwater Rd TA1 2DU
web: www.premierinn.com
dir: M5 junct 25 follow signs to Taunton. Straight on
at 1st rdbt, keep left at Creech Castle lights, hotel
200yds on right

Rooms 40

Premier Inn Taunton (Ruishton)

BUDGET HOTEL

☎ 0871 527 9074
Ruishton Ln, Ruishton TA3 5LU
web: www.premierinn.com
dir: Just off M5 junct 25 on A38

Rooms 38

TAVISTOCK
Devon   Map 3 SX47

The Horn of Plenty

★★★ 85% ❀❀ HOTEL

☎ 01822 832528
Gulworthy PL19 8JD
e-mail: enquiries@thehornofplenty.co.uk
web: www.thehornofplenty.co.uk
dir: From Tavistock take A390 W for 3m. Right at
Gulworthy Cross. In 400yds turn left, hotel in 400yds
on right

With stunning views over the Tamar Valley, The Horn
of Plenty maintains its reputation as one of Britain's
best country-house hotels. Bedrooms are well
equipped and have many thoughtful extras. The
garden rooms offer impressive levels of both quality

and comfort, while award-winning cuisine is served
with accomplished skill and a passion for local
produce.

Rooms 10 (6 annexe) (3 fmly) (4 GF) ❧ S £85–£215;
D £95–£225 (incl. bkfst)* **Facilities** FTV Wi-fi ☟ HL
Xmas New Year **Conf** Class 22 Board 14 Thtr 22
Parking 25 **Notes** LB Civ Wed 80

Bedford Hotel

★★★ 76% ❀ HOTEL

☎ 01822 613221
1 Plymouth Rd PL19 8BB
e-mail: enquiries@bedford-hotel.co.uk
web: www.bedford-hotel.co.uk
dir: M5 junct 31, A30 (Launceston/Okehampton).
Then A386 to Tavistock, follow town centre signs.
Hotel opposite church

Built on the site of a Benedictine abbey, this
impressive castellated building has been welcoming
visitors for over 200 years. Very much a local
landmark, the hotel offers comfortable and relaxing
public areas, all reflecting charm and character
throughout. Bedrooms are traditionally styled with
contemporary comforts, whilst the Woburn Restaurant
provides a refined setting for enjoyable cuisine.

Rooms 31 (2 fmly) (5 GF) S £49.50–£70; D £70–£140
(incl. bkfst)* **Facilities** FTV Wi-fi ☟ Xmas New Year
Conf Class 100 Board 60 Thtr 160 Del from £99 to
£125* **Parking** 45 **Notes** LB Civ Wed 120

TEBAY
Cumbria   Map 18 NY60

Westmorland Hotel

★★★ 83% HOTEL

☎ 015396 24351
Westmorland Place, Orton CA10 3SB
e-mail: reservations@westmorlandhotel.com
web: www.westmorlandhotel.com
dir: Signed from Tebay Services M6 between junct 38
& 39 N'bound & S'bound

With fine views over rugged moorland, this modern
and friendly hotel is ideal for conferences and
meetings. Bedrooms are spacious and comfortable,
with executive rooms being particularly well
equipped. Open-plan public areas provide a Tyrolean
touch and include a split-level restaurant.

Rooms 51 (5 fmly) (12 GF) ❧ **Facilities** FTV Wi-fi HL
Xmas New Year **Conf** Class 24 Board 30 Thtr 120
Del from £99* **Services** Lift **Parking** 60
Notes Civ Wed 120

TEIGNMOUTH
Devon   Map 3 SX97

Cliffden Hotel

★★★ 74% HOTEL

☎ 01626 770052
Dawlish Rd TQ14 8TE
e-mail: cliffden.hotel@visionhotels.co.uk
dir: M5 junct 31, A380, B3192 to Teignmouth. Down hill on Exeter Rd to lights, left to rdbt (station on left). Left, follow Dawlish signs. Up hill. Hotel next right

While this hotel mainly caters for visually impaired guests, their families, friends and guide dogs, it offers a warm welcome to all. This establishment is a listed Victorian building set in six acres of delightful gardens overlooking a small valley. Bedrooms are comfortable, very spacious and thoughtfully equipped. There are also leisure facilities and, of course, special provision for guide dogs.

Rooms 47 (8 fmly) (10 GF) ⌇ **Facilities** FTV Wi-fi ⊗ supervised ♫ Xmas New Year **Conf Class** 30 **Board** 30 **Thtr** 50 **Services** Lift **Parking** 25 **Notes** Civ Wed 60

TELFORD
Shropshire   Map 10 SJ60

Telford Hotel & Golf Resort

★★★★ 79% HOTEL

☎ 01952 429977
Great Hay Dr, Sutton Heights TF7 4DT
e-mail: telford@qhotels.co.uk
web: www.qhotels.co.uk
dir: M54 junct 4, A442. Follow signs for Telford Golf Club

Set on the edge of Telford with panoramic views of the famous Ironbridge Gorge, this hotel offers excellent standards. Smart bedrooms are complemented by spacious public areas, large conference facilities, a spa with treatment rooms, a golf course and a driving range. Ample parking is available.

Rooms 114 (8 fmly) (50 GF) ⌇ **S** £69-£169; **D** £79-£179 (incl. bkfst)* **Facilities** Spa STV Wi-fi ⊗ ♪ ⌇ 18 Putt green Gym Xmas New Year **Conf Class** 220 **Board** 100 **Thtr** 350 **Del from** £125 to £155* **Services** Lift **Parking** 200 **Notes** LB Civ Wed 250

BEST WESTERN Valley Hotel

★★★ 82% ◉◉ HOTEL

☎ 01952 432247
Ironbridge TF8 7DW
e-mail: info@thevalleyhotel.co.uk
dir: M6, M54 junct 6 onto A5223 to Ironbridge

This privately owned hotel is situated in attractive gardens, close to the famous Iron Bridge. It was once the home of the Maws family who manufactured ceramic tiles, and fine examples of their craft are found throughout the house. Bedrooms vary in size and are split between the main house and a mews development; imaginative meals are served in the attractive Chez Maws restaurant.

Rooms 44 (3 fmly) (6 GF) ⌇ **Facilities** FTV Wi-fi ⊗ **Conf Class** 80 **Board** 60 **Thtr** 150 **Services** Lift **Parking** 80 **Notes** ⊗ Closed 24 Dec-2 Jan RS 25 Dec Civ Wed 150

Mercure Telford Madeley Court Hotel

Mercure

★★★ 77% HOTEL

☎ 01952 680068
Castlefields Way, Madeley TF7 5DW
e-mail: enquiries@hotels-telford.com
web: www.hotels-telford.com
dir: A464 to Telford then A442, A4169 to Castlefields rdbt, 1st exit onto B4373. Hotel 200yds on left

This beautifully restored 16th-century manor house is set in extensive grounds and gardens. Bedrooms vary between character rooms and the newer annexe rooms. Public areas consist of two wood-panelled lounges, a lakeside bar and at the centre of the original manor house, The Priory restaurant. The 16th-century Grade I listed mill house makes a lovely location for wedding receptions.

Rooms 49 (49 annexe) (4 fmly) (21 GF) **Facilities** FTV Wi-fi Xmas New Year **Conf Class** 150 **Board** 50 **Thtr** 175 **Parking** 150 **Notes** LB Civ Wed 175

Park Inn by Radisson, Telford

★★★ 70% HOTEL

☎ 01952 429988
Forgegate TF3 4NA
e-mail: info.telford@rezidorparkinn.com
dir: M54 junct 5

In a convenient location just off the motorway this is a comfortable place to stay. The facilities include a spa, indoor swimming pool, and conference rooms. There is also an on-site car valet service as well as secure parking. The restaurant provides a relaxing setting with lots of natural daylight. Bedrooms are comfortably appointed.

Rooms 153 (1 fmly) (17 GF) ⌇ **S** £55-£165; **D** £65-£175* **Facilities** FTV Wi-fi ⊗ ⊘ Gym Weights room Xmas New Year **Conf Class** 200 **Board** 100 **Thtr** 400 **Del from** £120 to £165* **Services** Lift **Parking** 300 **Notes** Civ Wed 400

Premier Inn Telford Central

Premier Inn

BUDGET HOTEL

☎ 0871 527 9082
Euston Way TF3 4LY
web: www.premierinn.com
dir: M54 junct 5 follow Central Railway Station signs. Hotel at 2nd exit off rdbt signed railway station

High quality, budget accommodation ideal for both families and business travellers. Spacious, en suite bedrooms feature tea and coffee making facilities, and Freeview TV in most hotels. Internet access and Wi-fi are available for a small fee. The adjacent family restaurant features a wide and varied menu. See also the Hotel Groups pages.

Rooms 62

Premier Inn Telford North (Donnington)

BUDGET HOTEL

☎ 0871 527 9084
Donnington Wood Way, Donnington TF2 8LE
web: www.premierinn.com
dir: From Telford M54 junct 4, B5060 (Redhill Way) signed Donnington. At rdbt straight on (becomes Donnington Wood Way then School Rd). At mini rdbt take 1st left into Wellington Rd (hotel adjacent to McDonalds & Shell garage)

Rooms 20

T

TELFORD SERVICE AREA (M54) Map 10 SJ70
Shropshire

Days Inn Telford - M54

BUDGET HOTEL

☎ 01952 238400
Telford Services, Priorslee Rd TF11 8TG
e-mail: telford.hotel@welcomebreak.co.uk
web: www.welcomebreak.co.uk
dir: At M54 junct 4

This modern building offers accommodation in smart, spacious and well-equipped bedrooms, suitable for families and business travellers, and all with en suite bathrooms. Continental breakfast is available, and other refreshments may be taken at the nearby family restaurant. See also the Hotel Groups pages.

Rooms 48 (45 fmly) (21 GF) (8 smoking) **Conf** Board 8

TEMPLE CLOUD Map 4 ST65
Somerset

Cameley Lodge
★★★ 75% SMALL HOTEL

☎ 01761 452790
Cameley BS39 5AH
e-mail: john@cameleylodge.co.uk
dir: A37 at Temple Cloud, 1m, hotel signed

A peacefully located property with views over a lake and surrounded by pleasant countryside. Being a small hotel, friendly and personal service is delivered by the resident proprietors and their staff. The bedrooms and bathrooms have been appointed to provide very good levels of quality and comfort. The modern and stylish restaurant offers a good selection of carefully prepared dishes, and the conference and wedding facilities are popular.

Rooms 9 (2 fmly) **Facilities** Wi-fi Fishing Clay pigeon shooting **Conf** Class 64 Board 24 Thtr 80 **Services** Lift **Parking** 48 **Notes** ⊗ Civ Wed 100

TEMPLE SOWERBY Map 18 NY62
Cumbria

Temple Sowerby House Hotel & Restaurant
★★★ 88% ◉◉ COUNTRY HOUSE HOTEL

☎ 017683 61578
CA10 1RZ
e-mail: stay@templesowerby.com
web: www.templesowerby.com
dir: 7m from M6 junct 40, midway between Penrith & Appleby, in village centre

The hotel is set in the heart of the Eden Valley, ideal for exploring the northern Lake District and Pennine Fells. Bedrooms are comfortable and stylish, most feature ultra-modern bathrooms, and there is a choice of pleasant lounges. The restaurant, with picture windows overlooking the beautiful walled garden, is a splendid place to enjoy the award-winning cuisine. Staff throughout are friendly and keen to please.

Rooms 12 (4 annexe) (2 GF) ✸ **S** £95-£110; **D** £135-£160 (incl. bkfst)* **Facilities** FTV Wi-fi ⛴ New Year **Conf** Class 20 Board 20 Thtr 30 Del from £170 to £185* **Parking** 15 **Notes** LB ⊗ No children 12yrs Closed 20-29 Dec Civ Wed 40

TENBURY WELLS Map 10 SO56
Worcestershire

Cadmore Lodge Hotel & Country Club
★★ 74% ◉ HOTEL

☎ 01584 810044
Berrington Green, St Michaels WR15 8TQ
e-mail: reception.cadmore@cadmorelodge.com
web: www.cadmorelodge.com
dir: From A4112 (Leominster-Tenbury Wells road), follow signs for Berrington

Cadmore Lodge is situated in an idyllic rural location overlooking a private lake. The 70-acre private estate features a 9-hole golf course and two fishing lakes. The traditionally styled bedrooms have modern amenities, and a large function room with lake views is popular for weddings and special occasions. The hotel has a well deserved reputation for its food.

Rooms 15 (1 fmly) **Facilities** ⊗ ⌗ 9 Fishing Gym Bowling green Steam room Nature reserve Xmas New Year **Conf** Class 40 Board 20 Thtr 100 **Parking** 100 **Notes** ⊗ Civ Wed 160

TENTERDEN Map 7 TQ83
Kent

Little Silver Country Hotel
★★★ 80% HOTEL

☎ 01233 850321 & 0845 166 2516
Ashford Rd, St Michael's TN30 6SP
e-mail: enquiries@little-silver.co.uk
web: www.little-silver.co.uk
dir: M20 junct 8, A274 signed Tenterden

Located just outside the charming town of Tenterden and within easy reach of many local Kent attractions, this charming hotel is ideal for leisure and business guests as well as being a popular wedding venue. Bedrooms are spaciously appointed and well equipped; many boast spa baths. There are a spacious lounge, small bar and a modern restaurant that overlooks beautifully tended gardens.

Rooms 16 (2 fmly) (6 GF) ✸ **S** £65-£85; **D** £99-£199 (incl. bkfst)* **Facilities** FTV Wi-fi ⅃ Xmas **Conf** Class 50 Board 25 Thtr 75 Del £123.50* **Parking** 70 **Notes** LB ⊗ Civ Wed 120

London Beach Country Hotel, Spa & Golf Club
★★★ 71% HOTEL

☎ 01580 766279
Ashford Rd TN30 6HX
e-mail: enquiries@londonbeach.com
web: www.londonbeach.com
dir: M20 junct 9, A28 follow signs to Tenterden (10m). Hotel on right 1m before Tenterden

A modern purpose-built hotel situated in mature grounds on the outskirts of Tenterden. The spacious bedrooms are smartly decorated, have co-ordinated soft furnishings and most rooms have balconies with superb views over the golf course. The open-plan public rooms feature a brasserie-style restaurant, where a good choice of dishes is served.

Rooms 26 (2 fmly) (3 smoking) **Facilities** Spa Wi-fi ⊗ ⌗ 9 Putt green Fishing Driving range Health club Xmas New Year **Conf** Class 75 Board 40 Thtr 100 **Services** Lift **Parking** 100 **Notes** ⊗ Civ Wed 100

Save on hotels. Book at theAA.com/hotel

TEL – TET 435 ENGLAND

TETBURY
Gloucestershire
Map 4 ST89

INSPECTORS' CHOICE

Calcot Manor
★★★★ ◎◎ HOTEL

☎ 01666 890391
Calcot GL8 8YJ
e-mail: reception@calcotmanor.co.uk
web: www.calcotmanor.co.uk
dir: 3m W of Tetbury at A4135 & A46 junct

Cistercian monks built the ancient barns and stables around which this lovely English farmhouse is set. No two rooms are identical, and each is beautifully decorated in a variety of styles and equipped with contemporary comforts. Sumptuous sitting rooms, with crackling log fires in the winter, look out over immaculate gardens. There are two dining options: the elegant conservatory restaurant and the informal Gumstool Inn. There are also ample function rooms. The superb health and leisure spa includes an indoor pool, high-tech gym, massage tables, complementary therapies and much more. For children, a supervised crèche and 'playzone' are a great attraction.

Rooms 35 (23 annexe) (13 fmly) (17 GF) 🐾
S £252-£530; **D** £280-£580 (incl. bkfst)*
Facilities Spa STV Wi-fi ⇄ ⊗ ⤳ ♨ ⬥ Gym Clay pigeon shooting Archery Cycling Running track Xmas New Year Child facilities **Conf** Class 40 Board 35 Thtr 120 Del £300* **Parking** 150 **Notes** ⊗ Civ Wed 100

Hare & Hounds Hotel
★★★★ 78% ◎◎ HOTEL

Cotswold Inns & Hotels

☎ 01666 881000
Westonbirt GL8 8QL
e-mail: reception@hareandhoundshotel.com
web: www.hareandhoundshotel.com
dir: 2.5m SW of Tetbury on A433

This popular hotel, set in extensive grounds, is situated close to Westonbirt Arboretum and has remained under the same ownership for over 50 years. The stylish bedrooms are individually designed; those in the main house are more traditional and the cottage rooms are contemporary. The public rooms include an informal bar and light, airy lounges - one with a log fire lit in colder months. Guests can eat either in the bar or the attractive Beaufort Restaurant.

Rooms 42 (21 annexe) (8 fmly) (13 GF) 🐾
S £99-£109; **D** £158-£350 (incl. bkfst)* **Facilities** FTV Wi-fi ⤳ ⬥ Beauty treatment room Xmas New Year **Conf** Class 80 Board 40 Thtr 120 **Parking** 85 **Notes** Civ Wed 200

The Priory Inn
★★★ 77% SMALL HOTEL

☎ 01666 502251
London Rd GL8 8JJ
e-mail: info@theprioryinn.co.uk
web: www.theprioryinn.co.uk
dir: On A433 (Cirencester to Tetbury road). Hotel 200yds from Market Square

A warm welcome is assured at this attractive inn where friendly service is a high priority. Public areas and bedrooms have a contemporary style that mixes well with more traditional features, such as an open fireplace in the cosy bar dining room. Cuisine, using locally sourced produce, is offered on a menu that should suit all tastes.

Rooms 14 (1 fmly) (4 GF) **D** £99-£135* **Facilities** FTV Wi-fi ♫ **Conf** Class 28 Board 28 Thtr 30 Del £125* **Parking** 35 **Notes** LB ⊗

Snooty Fox
★★★ 74% SMALL HOTEL

☎ 01666 502436
Market Place GL8 8DD
e-mail: res@snooty-fox.co.uk
web: www.snooty-fox.co.uk
dir: In town centre

Centrally situated, this 16th-century coaching inn retains original features and is a popular venue for weekend breaks. The relaxed and friendly atmosphere, the high standard of accommodation, and the food offered in the bar and restaurant, are all very good reasons why many guests return here time and again.

Rooms 12 **S** £60-£130; **D** £70-£210 (incl. bkfst)*
Facilities FTV Wi-fi ⇄ Xmas New Year **Conf** Class 12 Board 16 Thtr 24 Del from £90 to £150*

The Ormond at Tetbury
★★★ 70% HOTEL

☎ 01666 505690
23 Long St GL8 8AA
e-mail: info@theormond.co.uk
dir: Exit A433 from Cirencester into Long St. Hotel approx 100yds on left

Located on the main street of this charming town, The Ormond provides a choice of individually styled and comfortably furnished bedrooms in a variety of shapes and sizes. The ambience is relaxed and friendly, and guests may choose to dine in either the popular bar area or in the adjoining restaurant. In warmer weather, outdoor seating is available in the courtyard.

Rooms 15 (3 fmly) **Facilities** FTV Wi-fi Xmas New Year **Conf** Class 20 Board 20 Thtr 40 **Notes** Civ Wed 80

T

TEWKESBURY
Gloucestershire   Map 10 SO83

Premier Inn Tewkesbury Central

BUDGET HOTEL

☎ 0871 527 9088
Shannon Way, Ashchurch GL20 8ND
web: www.premierinn.com
dir: M5 junct 9, A438 towards Tewkesbury, hotel
400yds on right

High quality, budget accommodation ideal for both
families and business travellers. Spacious, en suite
bedrooms feature tea and coffee making facilities,
and Freeview TV in most hotels. Internet access and
Wi-fi are available for a small fee. The adjacent
family restaurant features a wide and varied menu.
See also the Hotel Groups pages.

Rooms 40

THETFORD
Norfolk   Map 13 TL88

Premier Inn Thetford

BUDGET HOTEL

☎ 0871 527 9090
Lynn Wood, Maine St IP24 3PG
web: www.premierinn.com
dir: From A11 N follow Thetford signs. At 3rd rdbt 1st
exit for town centre into Brandon Rd. 1st exit into
Maine St

High quality, budget accommodation ideal for both
families and business travellers. Spacious, en suite
bedrooms feature tea and coffee making facilities,
and Freeview TV in most hotels. Internet access and
Wi-fi are available for a small fee. The adjacent
family restaurant features a wide and varied menu.
See also the Hotel Groups pages.

Rooms 40

THIRSK
North Yorkshire   Map 19 SE48

White Horse Lodge Hotel

★★★ 72% HOTEL

☎ 01845 522293
Sutton Rd YO7 2ER
e-mail: enquiries@whitehorselodgehotel.co.uk
dir: A1 or A19 to Thirsk, A170 signed Helmsley/
Scarborough. Hotel approx 1.3m on left

This hotel is located just a short drive from Thirsk's
centre and the racecourse, as well as being only 20
minutes from York. Now refurbished, the hotel is
smart with well-appointed bedrooms; all have the
modern facilities including free Wi-fi. Real ales are

served in the large, modern bar and the restaurant
serves home-cooked food, based on produce from
local suppliers. The lodge has attractive gardens, and
ample parking is provided.

Rooms 14 (1 fmly) (4 GF) 🐾 **D** £48-£99 (incl. bkfst)*
Facilities FTV Wi-fi **Conf** Class 40 Board 30 Thtr 60
Del from £60 to £110* **Parking** 30 **Notes** LB Closed
mid Dec-early Jan

THORNBURY
Gloucestershire   Map 4 ST69

INSPECTORS' CHOICE

Thornbury Castle

★★★ ◉◉ COUNTRY HOUSE HOTEL

☎ 01454 281182
Castle St BS35 1HH
e-mail: info@thornburycastle.co.uk
web: www.thornburycastle.co.uk
dir: On A38 N'bound from Bristol take 1st turn to
Thornbury. At end of High St left into Castle St,
follow brown sign, entrance to Castle on left behind
St Mary's Church

Henry VIII ordered the first owner of this castle to be
beheaded! Guests today have the opportunity of
sleeping in historical surroundings fitted out with
all the modern amenities. Most rooms have four-
poster or coronet beds and real fires, and guests
can even choose to sleep in the Duke's Bedchamber
where King Henry and Anne Boleyn once slept, or in
the Tower Suite that has reputedly the widest four-
poster bed in England. Tranquil lounges enjoy views
over the wonderful gardens, while elegant, wood-
panelled dining rooms make memorable settings
for a leisurely award-winning meal. Activities
include falconry and archery and there is a
500-year-old vineyard. The castle is, of course, a
popular wedding venue.

Rooms 27 (3 fmly) (4 GF) 🐾 **S** £90-£120;
D £90-£550 (incl. bkfst)* **Facilities** STV FTV Wi-fi ↘
🏊 Archery Helicopter rides Clay pigeon shooting
Massage treatment Xmas New Year **Conf** Class 40
Board 30 Thtr 70 **Parking** 50 **Notes** LB Civ Wed 70

THORNTON HOUGH
Merseyside   Map 15 SJ38

Thornton Hall Hotel and Spa

★★★★ 79% ◉◉◉ HOTEL

☎ 0151 336 3938 & 353 3717
Neston Rd CH63 1JF
e-mail: reservations@thorntonhallhotel.com
web: www.thorntonhallhotel.com
dir: M53 junct 4, B5151/Neston onto B5136 to
Thornton Hough (signed)

Dating back to the mid 1800s, this country-house
hotel has been carefully extended and restored. Public
areas include an impressive leisure spa boasting
excellent facilities, a choice of restaurants and a
spacious bar. Bedrooms vary in style and include
feature rooms in the main house and more
contemporary rooms in the garden wing. Delightful
grounds and gardens, and impressive function
facilities make this a popular wedding venue.

Rooms 63 (6 fmly) (28 GF) 🐾 **Facilities** Spa STV FTV
Wi-fi ↘ 🐾 🏊 Gym Outdoor spa pools **Conf** Class 225
Board 80 Thtr 650 **Parking** 250 **Notes** ⊗
Civ Wed 500

THORPENESS
Suffolk   Map 13 TM45

Thorpeness Hotel

★★★ 83% ◉ HOTEL   T|A HOTEL COLLECTION

☎ 01728 452176
Lakeside Av IP16 4NH
e-mail: info@thorpeness.co.uk
web: www.thorpeness.co.uk
dir: A1094 towards Aldeburgh, take coast road N for
2m

Ideally situated in an unspoilt, tranquil setting close
to Aldeburgh and Snape Maltings. The extensive
public rooms include a choice of lounges, a
restaurant, a smart bar, a snooker room and
clubhouse. The spacious bedrooms are pleasantly
decorated, tastefully furnished and equipped with
modern facilities. An 18-hole golf course and tennis
courts are also available.

Rooms 36 (36 annexe) (10 fmly) (10 GF)
Facilities Wi-fi ⚓ 18 ⚑ Putt green Fishing Cycle hire

Rowing boat hire Birdwatching Xmas New Year
Conf Class 30 Board 24 Thtr 130 **Parking** 80
Notes Civ Wed 130

THURLASTON	Map 11 SP47
Warwickshire	

Draycote Hotel

★★★ 72% HOTEL

☎ 01788 521800
London Rd CV23 9LF
e-mail: mail@draycotehotel.co.uk
web: www.draycotehotel.co.uk
dir: M1 junct 17 onto M45, A45. Hotel 500mtrs on left

Located in the picturesque Warwickshire countryside
and within easy reach of motorway networks, this
hotel offers modern, comfortable and well-equipped
accommodation with a relaxed and friendly welcome.
The hotel has a challenging golf course.

Rooms 49 (24 fmly) (24 GF) **S** £59-£95; **D** £59-£95
Facilities FTV Wi-fi ↻ ♨ 18 Putt green Golf driving
range Chipping green New Year **Conf** Class 78
Board 30 Thtr 250 Del £110 **Parking** 150 **Notes** LB ⊗
Civ Wed 180

THURLESTONE	Map 3 SX64
Devon	

Thurlestone Hotel

★★★★ 83% ◉ HOTEL

☎ 01548 560382
TQ7 3NN
e-mail: enquiries@thurlestone.co.uk
web: www.thurlestone.co.uk
dir: A38, A384 into Totnes, A381 towards Kingsbridge,
A379 towards Churchstow, onto B3197. Into lane
signed to Thurlestone

This perennially popular hotel has been in the same
family-ownership since 1896 and continues to go
from strength to strength. A vast range of facilities is
available for all the family including indoor and
outdoor pools, a golf course and a beauty salon.
Bedrooms are equipped to ensure a comfortable stay
with many having wonderful views of the south Devon
coast. The range of eating options includes the
elegant and stylish restaurant with its stunning
views.

Rooms 65 (23 fmly) ♠ **S** £95-£260; **D** £190-£520
(incl. bkfst)* **Facilities** STV Wi-fi ↻ ♨ ♨ supervised
♨ 9 ♨ Putt green ⤳ Gym Squash Badminton Games
room Toddler room Snooker room Beauty treatment
room ♫ Xmas New Year Child facilities
Conf Class 100 Board 40 Thtr 150 Del from £195 to
£300* **Services** Lift **Parking** 121 **Notes** LB Closed
1-2 wks Jan Civ Wed 160

THURSFORD	Map 13 TF93
Norfolk	

The Old Forge Seafood Restaurant

◉ RESTAURANT WITH ROOMS

☎ 01328 878345
Fakenham Rd NR21 0BD
e-mail: sarah.goldspink@btconnect.com
dir: On A148 (Fakenham to Holt road)

Expect a warm welcome at this delightful relaxed
restaurant with rooms. The open-plan public areas
include a lounge bar area with comfy sofas, and an
intimate restaurant with pine tables. Bedrooms are
pleasantly decorated and equipped with a good range
of useful facilities.

Rooms 3

TICEHURST	Map 6 TQ63
East Sussex	

Dale Hill Hotel & Golf Club

★★★★ 80% ◉ HOTEL

☎ 01580 200112
TN5 7DQ
e-mail: info@dalehill.co.uk
web: www.dalehill.co.uk
dir: M25 junct 5, A21. 5m after Lamberhurst right at
lights onto B2087 to Flimwell. Hotel 1m on left

This modern hotel is situated just a short drive from
the village. Extensive public rooms include a lounge
bar, a conservatory brasserie, a formal restaurant
and the Spike Bar, which is mainly frequented by golf
club members and has a lively atmosphere. The hotel
also has two superb 18-hole golf courses, a
swimming pool and gym.

Rooms 35 (8 fmly) (23 GF) **Facilities** STV Wi-fi ↻ ♨
36 Putt green Gym Covered driving range Pool table
Xmas New Year **Conf** Class 50 Board 50 Thtr 120
Services Lift **Parking** 220 **Notes** ⊗ Civ Wed 150

TINTAGEL	Map 2 SX08
Cornwall	

Atlantic View Hotel

★★ 78% SMALL HOTEL

☎ 01840 770221
Treknow PL34 0EJ
e-mail: atlantic-view@eclipse.co.uk
web: www.holidayscornwall.com
dir: B3263 to Tregatta, turn left into Treknow, hotel on
road to Trebarwith Strand Beach

Conveniently located for all the attractions of
Tintagel, this family-run hotel has a wonderfully
relaxed and welcoming atmosphere. Public areas
include a bar, comfortable lounge, TV/games room

and heated swimming pool. Bedrooms are generally
spacious and some have the added advantage of
distant sea views.

Rooms 9 (1 fmly) ♠ **S** fr £70; **D** fr £96 (incl. bkfst)*
Facilities FTV Wi-fi ↻ Pool table **Parking** 10
Notes LB ⊗ Closed Nov-Feb RS Mar

TITCHWELL	Map 13 TF74
Norfolk	

Titchwell Manor Hotel

★★★ 86% ◉◉◉ HOTEL

☎ 01485 210221
PE31 8BB
e-mail: margaret@titchwellmanor.com
web: www.titchwellmanor.com
dir: On A149 (coast road) between Brancaster &
Thornham

Friendly family-run hotel ideally placed for touring the
north Norfolk coastline. The tastefully appointed
bedrooms are very comfortable; some in the adjacent
annexe offer ground floor access. Smart public rooms
include a lounge area, relaxed informal bar and the
delightful Conservatory Restaurant, overlooking the
walled garden. Head Chef Eric Snaith produces
imaginative menus that feature quality local produce
and fresh fish.

Rooms 26 (18 annexe) (4 fmly) (16 GF) ♠
S £55-£200; **D** £95-£250 (incl. bkfst)* **Facilities** FTV
Wi-fi Xmas New Year Child facilities **Conf** Class 50
Board 30 Thtr 30 Del from £150 to £250* **Parking** 50
Notes LB Civ Wed 80

T

TOLLESHUNT KNIGHTS — Map 7 TL91
Essex

Crowne Plaza Resort Colchester - Five Lakes

★★★★ 78% ◉ HOTEL

☎ 01621 868888
Colchester Rd CM9 8HX
e-mail: enquiries@cpcolchester.co.uk
web: www.cpcolchester.co.uk
dir: Exit A12 at Kelvedon, follow brown signs through Tiptree to hotel

This hotel is set amidst 320 acres of open countryside, featuring two golf courses. The spacious bedrooms are furnished to a high standard and have excellent facilities. The public rooms offer a high degree of comfort and include five bars, two restaurants and a large lounge. The property also boasts extensive leisure facilities.

Rooms 194 (80 annexe) (4 fmly) (40 GF) 🐾
Facilities Spa STV FTV Wi-fi ⓢ ♨ 36 ♨ Putt green Gym Squash Sauna Steam room Health & beauty spa Badminton Aerobics Studio Hairdresser ♬ Xmas New Year **Conf** Class 700 Board 60 Thtr 2000 **Services** Lift **Parking** 550 **Notes** ⊗ Civ Wed 250

TONBRIDGE — Map 6 TQ54
Kent

BEST WESTERN Rose & Crown Hotel

★★★ 78% HOTEL

☎ 01732 357966
125 High St TN9 1DD
e-mail: rose.crown@bestwestern.co.uk

A 15th-century coaching inn situated in the heart of this bustling town centre. The public areas are light and airy yet still retain much original character such as oak beams and Jacobean panelling. Food is served throughout the day in the Oak Room Bar & Grill. Bedrooms are stylishly decorated, spacious and well presented; amenities include free Wi-fi.

Rooms 56 (3 fmly) (10 GF) 🐾 **Facilities** FTV Wi-fi ⌕
Conf Class 60 Board 60 Thtr 125 **Parking** 43
Notes ⊗ Civ Wed 60

Premier Inn Tonbridge

BUDGET HOTEL

☎ 0871 527 9096
Pembury Rd TN11 0NA
web: www.premierinn.com
dir: 11m from M25 junct 5. Follow A21 towards Hastings, pass A26 (Tunbridge Wells) junct. Exit at next junct, 1st exit at rdbt

High quality, budget accommodation ideal for both families and business travellers. Spacious, en suite bedrooms feature tea and coffee making facilities, and Freeview TV in most hotels. Internet access and Wi-fi are available for a small fee. The adjacent family restaurant features a wide and varied menu. See also the Hotel Groups pages.

Rooms 40

Premier Inn Tonbridge North

BUDGET HOTEL

☎ 0871 527 9098
Hilden Manor, London Rd TN10 3AN
web: www.premierinn.com
dir: From A21 follow Seven Oaks & Hildenborough signs. At rdbt take 2nd exit onto B245 signed Hildenborough. In 2m hotel on right

Rooms 41

TORBAY

See Brixham, Paignton & Torquay

TORQUAY — Map 3 SX96
Devon

The Imperial Hotel

PUMA HOTELS COLLECTION

★★★★ 81% ◉ HOTEL

☎ 01803 294301
Park Hill Rd TQ1 2DG
e-mail: imperialtorquay@pumahotels.co.uk
web: www.pumahotels.co.uk
dir: A380 towards seafront. Turn left to harbour, right at clocktower. Hotel 300yds on right

This hotel has an enviable location with extensive views of the coastline. Traditional in style, the public areas are elegant and offer a choice of dining options including the Regatta Restaurant, with its stunning views over the bay. Bedrooms are spacious, most with private balconies, and the hotel has an extensive range of indoor and outdoor leisure facilities.

Rooms 152 (14 fmly) **Facilities** Spa STV Wi-fi ⓢ ♨ supervised ♨ Gym Squash Beauty salon Hairdresser Steam room ♬ Xmas New Year **Conf** Class 200 Board 30 Thtr 350 **Services** Lift **Parking** 140 **Notes** Civ Wed 250

T

Save on hotels. Book at **theAA.com/hotel**

TOL – TOR 439 **ENGLAND**

Grand Hotel

★★★★ 77% ⊛ HOTEL

RICHARDSON HOTELS
Where Memories are Made

☎ 01803 296677
Sea Front TQ2 6NT
e-mail: reservations@grandtorquay.co.uk
web: www.grandtorquay.co.uk
dir: A380 to Torquay. At seafront turn right, then 1st right. Hotel on corner, entrance 1st on left

Within level walking distance of the town, this large Edwardian hotel overlooks the bay and offers modern facilities. Many of the bedrooms, some with balconies, enjoy the best of the views, but all are very well equipped. The Compass Bar also benefits from the stunning views, and offers an informal alternative to the Gainsborough Restaurant.

Rooms 132 (32 fmly) (3 GF) ⚡ **Facilities** FTV Wi-fi ⌕ ⊛ ⚲ supervised ⚲ Gym Beauty clinic Car valeting ♪ Xmas New Year **Conf** Class 150 Board 60 Thtr 250 Del from £99 to £140* **Services** Lift **Parking** 57 **Notes** Civ Wed 250

Palace Hotel

★★★★ 72% HOTEL

☎ 01803 200200
Babbacombe Rd TQ1 3TG
e-mail: info@palacetorquay.co.uk
web: www.palacetorquay.co.uk
dir: Towards harbour, left by clocktower into Babbacombe Rd, hotel on right after 1m

Set in 25 acres of stunning, beautifully tended wooded grounds, the Palace offers a tranquil environment. Suitable for business and leisure, the hotel boasts a huge range of well-presented indoor and outdoor facilities. Much of the original charm and grandeur is still in evidence, particularly in the dining room. Many of the bedrooms enjoy views of the magnificent gardens.

Rooms 141 (7 fmly) **Facilities** Wi-fi ⊛ ⚲ ↓ 9 ⚲ Putt green ⚲ Gym Squash Table tennis Snooker Childrens' play area Xmas New Year **Conf** Class 800 Board 40 Thtr 1000 **Services** Lift **Parking** 140 **Notes** ⊛

BEST WESTERN Hotel Gleneagles

★★★ 80% HOTEL

Best Western

☎ 01803 293637
Asheldon Rd, Wellswood TQ1 2QS
e-mail: enquiries@hotel-gleneagles.com
dir: A380 onto A3022 to A379, follow to St Mathias Church, turn right into Asheldon Rd

From its hillside location, looking out over Anstey's Cove towards Lyme Bay, this peacefully located hotel

is appointed to an impressive standard. Stylish public areas combine comfort, flair and quality with ample space in which to find a quiet spot and unwind. Bedrooms also have a contemporary feel; many have balconies or patios. The pool area has a real Riviera feel, with elegant Lloyd Loom sun loungers and palm trees.

Rooms 41 (2 fmly) (5 GF) ⚡ **S** £29.50-£80; **D** £59-£160 (incl. bkfst) **Facilities** FTV Wi-fi ⌕ ⚲ Xmas New Year **Conf** Class 20 Board 25 Thtr 40 Del from £55 to £95 **Services** Lift **Parking** 21 **Notes** LB Civ Wed

The Headland Hotel

★★★ 80% HOTEL

☎ 01803 295666
Daddyhole Rd TQ1 2EF
e-mail: info@headlandtorquay.com
dir: A380 to Torquay sea front, left then far side of harbour, up hill, 500mtrs & turn right

This hotel has a delightful location set apart from the bustle of town, but within easy walking distance of the numerous attractions. Having some splendid grounds and an elevated view of the bay, the hotel has an enviable position. Bedrooms are very comfortably appointed, many with sea views. Cuisine is a highlight, and the friendly team offer attentive service.

Rooms 78 (16 fmly) (7 GF) ⚡ **S** £31-£80; **D** £62-£160 (incl. bkfst)* **Facilities** FTV Wi-fi ⚲ ⚲ Gym ♪ Xmas New Year **Conf** Class 50 Board 40 Thtr 150 Del from £50 to £100* **Services** Lift **Parking** 20 **Notes** LB ⊛ Civ Wed 150

Corbyn Head Hotel

★★★ 78% HOTEL

☎ 01803 213611
Torbay Rd, Sea Front TQ2 6RH
e-mail: info@corbynhead.com
web: www.corbynhead.com
dir: Follow signs to Torquay seafront, turn right on seafront. Hotel on right with green canopies

This hotel occupies a prime position overlooking Torbay, and offers well-equipped bedrooms, many with sea views and some with balconies. The staff are

friendly and welcoming, and a well-stocked bar and comfortable lounge are available. Guests can enjoy fine dining in the Harbour View Restaurant, with attentive service assured.

Rooms 45 (4 fmly) (9 GF) **Facilities** FTV Wi-fi ⚲ Gym Squash ♪ Xmas New Year **Conf** Class 30 Board 30 Thtr 50 **Parking** 50 **Notes** Civ Wed 85

Livermead House Hotel

★★★ 74% HOTEL

☎ 01803 294361 & 294363
Torbay Rd TQ2 6QJ
e-mail: info@livermead.com
web: www.livermead.com
dir: From seafront turn right, follow A379 towards Paignton & Livermead, hotel opposite Institute Beach

Having a splendid waterfront location, this hotel dates back to the 1820s, and is where Charles Kingsley is said to have written *The Water Babies*. Bedrooms vary in size and style, excellent public rooms are popular for private parties and meetings, and a range of leisure facilities is provided. Enjoyable cuisine is served in the impressive restaurant.

Rooms 67 (6 fmly) (2 GF) **Facilities** ⚲ Gym Squash ♪ Xmas **Conf** Class 175 Board 80 Thtr 320 **Services** Lift **Parking** 131

T

TORQUAY *continued*

BEST WESTERN Livermead Cliff Hotel

★★★ 71% HOTEL

☎ 01803 299666
Torbay Rd TQ2 6RQ
e-mail: info@livermeadcliff.co.uk
web: www.livermeadcliff.co.uk
dir: A379, A3022 to Torquay, towards seafront, turn right towards Paignton. Hotel 600yds on seaward side

Situated at the water's edge, this long-established hotel offers friendly service and traditional hospitality. The splendid views can be enjoyed from the lounge, bar and dining room. Alternatively, guests can take advantage of refreshment on the wonderful terrace and enjoy one of the best outlooks in the bay. Bedrooms, many with sea views and some with balconies, are comfortable and well equipped; a range of room sizes is available.

Rooms 65 (17 fmly) ➔ S £60-£90; D £120-£180 (incl. bkfst)* **Facilities** FTV Wi-fi Fishing Use of facilities at sister hotel Xmas New Year **Conf** Class 60 Board 40 Thtr 120 Del from £79.95 to £99.95* **Services** Lift **Parking** 80 **Notes** LB Civ Wed 200

Abbey Lawn Hotel

★★★ 67% HOTEL

☎ 01803 299199 & 203181
Scarborough Rd TQ2 5UQ
e-mail: nicky@holdsworthhotels.freeserve.co.uk

Conveniently located for both the seafront and town centre, this is an ideal base for visiting the attractions of the 'English Riviera'. Many of the bedrooms, including the four-poster suite, benefit from lovely sea views. Facilities include a health club with extensive leisure activities, plus indoor and outdoor pools. Traditional cuisine is served in the elegant restaurant, and evening entertainment is a regular feature in the ballroom.

Rooms 57 (3 fmly) **Facilities** ⊛ supervised ➔ supervised Gym Steam room ♫ Xmas New Year **Services** Lift **Parking** 20 **Notes** ⊗ Closed Jan

Anchorage Hotel

★★ 74% HOTEL

☎ 01803 326175
Cary Park, Aveland Rd, Babbacombe TQ1 3PT
e-mail: enquiries@anchoragehotel.co.uk

Quietly located in a residential area and providing a friendly welcome, this family-run establishment enjoys a great deal of repeat business. Bedrooms come in a range of sizes but all rooms are neatly presented. Evening entertainment is provided regularly in the large and comfortable lounge.

Rooms 56 (5 fmly) (17 GF) **Facilities** FTV Wi-fi ➔ ♫ Xmas New Year **Services** Lift **Parking** 26

Regina Hotel

★★ 71% HOTEL

☎ 01803 292904
Victoria Pde TQ1 2BE
e-mail: regina.torquay@alfatravel.co.uk
web: www.leisureplex.co.uk
dir: Into Torquay, follow harbour signs, hotel on outer corner of harbour

This hotel enjoys a pleasant and convenient location right on the harbourside, a short stroll from the town's attractions. Bedrooms, some with harbour views, vary in size. Entertainment is provided on most nights and there is a choice of bars.

Rooms 68 (5 fmly) **Facilities** FTV ♫ Xmas New Year **Services** Lift **Parking** 6 **Notes** ⊗ Closed Jan & part Feb RS Nov-Dec (ex Xmas) & Feb-Mar

The Heritage Hotel

★★ 68% HOTEL

☎ 01803 299332
Seafront, Shedden Hill TQ2 5TY
e-mail: enquiries@heritagehoteltorquay.co.uk
web: www.heritagehoteltorquay.co.uk
dir: A380 to Torquay follow signs to seafront. Hotel on left

In an elevated position overlooking Tor Abbey Sands, this hotel is a short walk from both the harbour and the shops. The bedrooms are traditionally furnished and come in various sizes; all have sea views except one. There is a variety of eating options based on American food themes and a large sun deck for relaxation in summer.

Rooms 24 (24 fmly) (4 GF) ➔ S £40-£50; D £80-£100 (incl. bkfst)* **Facilities** STV FTV Wi-fi ⊛ **Services** Lift **Parking** 40 **Notes** LB ⊗

Maycliffe Hotel

★★ 68% HOTEL

☎ 01803 294964
St Lukes Road North TQ2 5PD
e-mail: bob.west1@virgin.net
web: www.maycliffehotel.co.uk
dir: Left from Kings Dr, along seafront keep in left lane, at next lights (Belgrave Rd) up Shedden Hill, 2nd right into St Lukes Rd then 1st left

Set in a quiet and elevated position which is convenient for the town centre and attractions, the Maycliffe is a popular choice for leisure breaks. The bedrooms are individually decorated and equipped with modern facilities; there are two rooms on the ground floor suitable for less able guests. There is a quiet lounge for relaxation, and the bar hosts a cabaret on certain nights during the season.

Rooms 28 (1 fmly) (2 GF) **Facilities** ♫ Xmas **Services** Lift **Parking** 10 **Notes** ⊗ No children 4yrs Closed 2 Jan-12 Feb

Shelley Court Hotel

★★ 67% HOTEL

☎ 01803 295642
29 Croft Rd TQ2 5UD
e-mail: shelleycourthotel@hotmail.com
dir: From B3199 up Shedden Hill Rd, 1st left into Croft Rd

This hotel, popular with groups, is located in a pleasant, quiet area that overlooks the town towards Torbay. With a friendly team of staff, many guests return here time and again. Entertainment is provided most evenings in the season. Bedrooms come in a range of sizes and there is a large and comfortable lounge bar.

Rooms 27 (3 fmly) (6 GF) **Facilities** FTV ⤴ Pool table Indoor skittle alley ♫ Xmas New Year **Parking** 20 **Notes** Closed 4 Jan-10 Feb

Save on hotels. Book at **theAA.com/hotel**

TOR – TRU 441 ENGLAND

Ashley Court Hotel

★★ 64% HOTEL

☎ 01803 292417
107 Abbey Rd TQ2 5NP
e-mail: reception@ashleycourt.co.uk
web: www.ashleycourt.co.uk
dir: A380 to seafront, left to Shedden Hill to lights, hotel opposite

Located close to the town centre and within easy strolling distance of the seafront, this hotel offers a warm welcome to guests. Bedrooms are pleasantly appointed and some have sea views. The outdoor pool and patio are popular with guests wishing to soak up some sunshine. Live entertainment is provided every night throughout the season.

Rooms 83 (12 fmly) (8 GF) (14 smoking) 🐾
Facilities 🎣 Games room 🎵 Xmas New Year
Services Lift **Parking** 51 **Notes** ⊗ Closed
3 Jan-1 Feb

Premier Inn Torquay

BUDGET HOTEL

☎ 0871 527 9102
Seafront, Belgrave Rd TQ2 5HE
web: www.premierinn.com
dir: On A380 into Torquay, continue to lights (Torre Station on right). Right into Avenue Road to Kings Drive. Left at seafront, hotel at lights

High quality, budget accommodation ideal for both families and business travellers. Spacious, en suite bedrooms feature tea and coffee making facilities, and Freeview TV in most hotels. Internet access and Wi-fi are available for a small fee. The adjacent family restaurant features a wide and varied menu. See also the Hotel Groups pages.

Rooms 83

Orestone Manor

◉◉ RESTAURANT WITH ROOMS

☎ 01803 328098
Rockhouse Ln, Maidencombe TQ1 4SX
e-mail: info@orestonemanor.com
dir: N of Torquay on A379, on sharp bend in village of Maidencombe

Set in a super location overlooking the bay, Orestone has a long history of fine food and very comfortable accommodation, coupled with friendly, attentive service. Log fires burn in cooler months, and there are a conservatory, a bar and a sitting room for guests to enjoy, along with an outdoor pool.

Rooms 10 (1 annexe) (6 fmly)

Pendley Manor Hotel

★★★★ 77% ◉◉ HOTEL

☎ 01442 891891
Cow Ln HP23 5QY
e-mail: info@pendley-manor.co.uk
web: www.pendley-manor.co.uk
dir: M25 junct 20, A41 (Tring exit). At rdbt follow Berkhamsted/London signs. 1st left signed Tring Station & Pendley Manor

Pendley Manor Hotel is an impressive Victorian mansion set in extensive and mature landscaped grounds where peacocks roam. The spacious bedrooms are situated in both the manor house and the wing, and offer a useful range of facilities. Public areas include a cosy bar, a conservatory lounge and an intimate restaurant as well as a leisure centre.

Rooms 73 (17 fmly) (17 GF) **Facilities** Spa FTV Wi-fi 🔁
🔁 💆 Gym Steam room Dance Studio Sauna Snooker room **Conf** Class 80 Board 80 Thtr 250 Del from £150 to £230* **Services** Lift **Parking** 150 **Notes** ⊗
Civ Wed 160

Premier Inn Tring

BUDGET HOTEL

☎ 0871 527 9104
Tring Hill HP23 4LD
web: www.premierinn.com
dir: M25 junct 20, A41 towards Aylesbury, at end of Hemel Hempstead/Tring bypass straight on at rdbt, hotel approx 100yds on right

High quality, budget accommodation ideal for both families and business travellers. Spacious, en suite bedrooms feature tea and coffee making facilities, and Freeview TV in most hotels. Internet access and Wi-fi are available for a small fee. The adjacent

family restaurant features a wide and varied menu. See also the Hotel Groups pages.

Rooms 30

Fieldways Hotel & Health Club

★★ 69% SMALL HOTEL

☎ 01225 768336
Hilperton Rd BA14 7JP
e-mail: fieldwayshotel@yahoo.co.uk
dir: A361 from Trowbridge towards Melksham, Chippenham, Devizes. Hotel last property on left

Originally part of a Victorian mansion this hotel is quietly set in well-kept grounds and provides a pleasant combination of spacious, comfortably furnished bedrooms. There are two splendid wood-panelled dining rooms, one of which is impressively finished in oak, pine, rosewood and mahogany. The indoor leisure facilities include a gym, a pool and treatment rooms; 'Top to Toe' days are especially popular.

Rooms 13 (5 annexe) (2 fmly) (2 GF) **S** £60; **D** £80 (incl. bkfst)* **Facilities** Spa Wi-fi 🔁 Gym Range of beauty treatments/massage Pampering days
Conf Class 40 Board 20 Thtr 40 **Parking** 70

Mannings Hotel

★★★ 85% HOTEL

☎ 01872 270345
Lemon St TR1 2QB
e-mail: reception@manningshotels.co.uk
web: www.manningshotels.co.uk
dir: A30 to Carland Cross then Truro. Follow brown signs to hotel in city centre

This popular hotel is located in the heart of Truro and offers an engaging blend of traditional and contemporary. Public areas have a stylish atmosphere with the bar and restaurant proving popular with locals and residents alike. A wide choice of appetising dishes is available, including ethnic, classic and vegetarian as well as daily specials. Bedrooms are pleasantly appointed.

Rooms 43 (9 annexe) (4 fmly) (3 GF) 🐾 **Facilities** FTV
Wi-fi **Parking** 43 **Notes** ⊗ Closed 25-26 Dec

T

TRURO *continued*

Merchant House

★★ 76% METRO HOTEL

☎ 01872 272450
49 Falmouth Rd TR1 2HL
e-mail: reception@merchant-house.co.uk
dir: A39 Truro, on approaching centre proceed across
1st & 2nd rdbts onto bypass. At top of hill turn right
at twin mini rdbt into Falmouth Rd. Hotel is 100mtrs
on right

Just a short stroll from the City centre, this is an ideal
location for guests looking to access local amenities
or explore the nearby coast and countryside. The
friendly team are committed to ensuring a relaxing
and rewarding stay with a flexible and helpful
approach to guest welfare. A range of bedrooms are
offered, some of which have benefited from the
ongoing refurbishment programme, all offering good
levels of comfort. Public areas are smartly appointed
with period features retained where possible. The
convivial bar provides an engaging venue for a
refreshing glass of something, perhaps accompanied
by a tasty dish from the bar menu.

Rooms 29 (3 fmly) (4 GF) ☞ **S** £35-£55; **D** £50-£90
(incl. bkfst)* **Facilities** FTV Wi-fi ⚑ HL **Conf** Class 48
Board 36 Thtr 64 **Parking** 40 **Notes** LB Closed
24-28 Dec

The Alverton Hotel

Ⓤ

☎ 01872 276633
Tregolls Rd TR1 1ZQ
e-mail: stay@thealverton.co.uk
web: www.thealverton.co.uk
dir: From A30 at Carland Cross take A39 to Truro. At
lights right onto A39 (Tregolls Rd) signed Truro/
Falmouth

Currently the rating for this establishment is not
confirmed. This may be due to a change of ownership
or because it has only recently joined the AA rating
scheme. For further details please see the AA website:
theAA.com

Rooms 33 (4 fmly) (3 GF) **Facilities** FTV Wi-fi ⚑ Xmas
New Year **Conf** Class 50 Board 30 Thtr 140
Del from £108.50 to £170* **Parking** 71
Notes Civ Wed 90

Premier Inn Truro

BUDGET HOTEL

☎ 0871 527 9106
Old Carnon Hill, Carnon Downs TR3 6JT
web: www.premierinn.com
dir: On A39 (Truro to Falmouth road), 3m SW of Truro

High quality, budget accommodation ideal for both
families and business travellers. Spacious, en suite
bedrooms feature tea and coffee making facilities,
and Freeview TV in most hotels. Internet access and
Wi-fi are available for a small fee. The adjacent
family restaurant features a wide and varied menu.
See also the Hotel Groups pages.

Rooms 62

TUNBRIDGE WELLS (ROYAL)   Map 6 TQ53
Kent

The Spa Hotel

★★★★ 81% ⚛ HOTEL

☎ 01892 520331
Mount Ephraim TN4 8XJ
e-mail: reservations@spahotel.co.uk
web: www.spahotel.co.uk
dir: A21 to A26, follow A264 East Grinstead signs,
hotel on right

Set in 14 acres of beautifully tended grounds, this
imposing 18th-century mansion offers spacious,
modern bedrooms that are stylishly decorated and
thoughtfully equipped. The public rooms include the
Chandelier Restaurant, a champagne bar and the
Orangery which complements the traditional lounge.
There are extensive meeting and health club
facilities, and a spa offering treatment rooms. It is
also licensed for civil wedding ceremonies.

Rooms 70 (4 fmly) (1 GF) **S** £110-£230; **Facilities** Spa
STV FTV Wi-fi ⚛ ⚒ ⚓ Gym ♫ Xmas New Year
Conf Class 90 Board 90 Thtr 300 **Services** Lift
Parking 150 **Notes** LB ⊗ Civ Wed 150

Hotel du Vin Tunbridge Wells

★★★★ 74% ⚛
TOWN HOUSE HOTEL

☎ 01892 526455
Crescent Rd TN1 2LY
e-mail: reception.tunbridgewells@hotelduvin.com
web: www.hotelduvin.com
dir: Follow town centre, to main junct of Mount
Pleasant Rd & Crescent Rd/Church Rd. Hotel 150yds
on right just past Phillips House

This impressive Grade II listed building dates from
1762, and as a princess, Queen Victoria often stayed
here. The spacious bedrooms are available in a range
of sizes, beautifully and individually appointed, and
equipped with a host of thoughtful extras. Public
rooms include a bistro-style restaurant, two elegant
lounges and a small bar.

Rooms 34 ☞ **Facilities** STV Wi-fi Boules court in
garden **Conf** Class 40 Board 25 Thtr 60 **Services** Lift
Parking 30 **Notes** Civ Wed 84

Mercure Tunbridge Wells

★★★★ 72% HOTEL

☎ 0844 815 9074
8 Tonbridge Rd, Pembury TN2 4QL
e-mail: sales.mercuretunbridgewells@jupiterhotels.
co.uk
web: www.jupiterhotels.co.uk
dir: M25 junct 5, A21 S. Left at 1st rdbt signed
Pembury Hospital. Hotel on left, 400yds past hospital

Built in the style of a traditional Kentish oast house,
this well presented hotel is conveniently located just
off the A21 with easy access to the M25. Bedrooms
are comfortably appointed for both business and
leisure guests. Public areas include a leisure club
and a range of meeting rooms.

Rooms 84 (8 fmly) (40 GF) ☞ **Facilities** STV FTV Wi-fi
⚑ HL ⚛ Steam room Sauna Xmas New Year
Conf Class 80 Board 50 Thtr 150 **Parking** 200
Notes Civ Wed 150

Russell Hotel

★★ 65% METRO HOTEL

☎ 01892 544833
80 London Rd TN1 1DZ
e-mail: sales@russell-hotel.com
web: www.russell-hotel.com
dir: From Tunbridge Wells A26 junct with Lime Hill Road turn (no through road)

This detached Victorian property is situated just a short walk from the centre of town. The generously proportioned bedrooms in the main house are pleasantly decorated and well equipped. In addition, there are several smartly appointed self-contained suites in an adjacent building. The public rooms include a lounge and cosy bar.

Rooms 26 (5 annexe) (5 fmly) (1 GF) **S** £45-£75; **D** £60-£98 (incl. bkfst) **Facilities** FTV Wi-fi **Conf** Class 10 Board 10 Thtr 10 **Parking** 14 **Notes** ⊗

TURNERS HILL   Map 6 TQ33
West Sussex

Alexander House Hotel & Utopia Spa

★★★★★ 86% ❀❀❀ HOTEL

☎ 01342 714914
East St RH10 4QD
e-mail: info@alexanderhouse.co.uk
web: www.alexanderhouse.co.uk
dir: 6m from M23 junct 10, on B2110 between Turners Hill & East Grinstead

Set in 175 acres of parkland and landscaped gardens, this delightful country house hotel dates back to the 17th century. Most of the bedrooms are very spacious and all have luxurious bathrooms; the rooms in the most recent wing are particularly stunning. There are two options for dining - the AG's Grill which has been awarded AA Rosettes, or the lively Reflections which is set around an open courtyard, ideal for eating alfresco. The Utopia Spa has a state-of-the-art pool and gym, as well as specialised treatments.

Rooms 38 (12 fmly) (1 GF) ⋒ **S** £119-£275; **D** £150-£305* **Facilities** Spa STV FTV Wi-fi ⊗ ☕ ⛳ Gym Clay shooting Archery Mountain bikes Pony trekking Xmas New Year **Conf** Class 70 Board 40 Thtr 150 **Services** Lift **Parking** 100 **Notes** LB ⊗ Civ Wed 100

TWICKENHAM
Greater London

London Marriott Hotel Twickenham

★★★★ 78% HOTEL PLAN 1 C2

☎ 020 8891 8200
198 Whitton Rd TW2 7BA
dir: A316, exit Whitton Rd rdbt towards stadium. Hotel within South Stand of stadium

This purpose-built hotel occupies an area of the South Stand of the Twickenham Rugby Club Stadium. The bedrooms have the latest Marriott innovations including flat-screen LCD TVs and state-of-the-art technology; six suites even overlook the pitch. There is a popular Twenty Two South restaurant, the Side Step sports bar and a café lounge. Guests can use the health club and there's a wide range of meeting rooms and conference facilities. Hampton Court Palace, Kew Gardens and the River Thames are all close by.

Rooms 156 (76 fmly) ⋒ **Facilities** STV FTV Wi-fi ⊗ HL ⊗ Gym Sauna Steam room Soft climbing wall **Conf** Class 100 Board 30 Thtr 240 **Services** Lift Air con **Parking** 250 **Notes** ⊗

Premier Inn Twickenham East

BUDGET HOTEL PLAN 1 B2

☎ 0871 527 9108
Corner Sixth Cross, Staines Rd TW2 5PE
web: www.premierinn.com
dir: M25 junct 12 onto M3, follow Central London signs, at end of M3 becomes A316. Straight on at 1st rdbt. Hotel 500yds on left

High quality, budget accommodation ideal for both families and business travellers. Spacious, en suite bedrooms feature tea and coffee making facilities, and Freeview TV in most hotels. Internet access and Wi-fi are available for a small fee. The adjacent family restaurant features a wide and varied menu. See also the Hotel Groups pages.

Rooms 17

Premier Inn Twickenham Stadium

BUDGET HOTEL PLAN 1 B2

☎ 0871 527 9110
Chertsey Rd, Whitton TW2 6LS
web: www.premierinn.com
dir: From M3 onto A316, then A305 signed Twickenham. At Hospital Bridge Rdbt 3rd exit into Hospital Bridge Rd. Take B358 signed Teddington. Becomes Sixth Cross Rd. Hotel on left

Rooms 31

TWO BRIDGES   Map 3 SX67
Devon

Two Bridges Hotel

★★★ 78% ❀ HOTEL

☎ 01822 892300
PL20 6SW
e-mail: enquiries@twobridges.co.uk
web: www.twobridges.co.uk
dir: At junct of B3212 & B3357

This wonderfully relaxing hotel is set in the heart of the Dartmoor National Park, in a beautiful riverside location. Three standards of comfortable rooms provide every modern convenience, and include four-poster rooms. There is a choice of lounges, and fine dining is available in the restaurant, where menus feature local game and other seasonal produce.

Rooms 33 (2 fmly) (6 GF) ⋒ **Facilities** STV Wi-fi Fishing Xmas New Year **Conf** Class 60 Board 40 Thtr 130 **Parking** 100 **Notes** Civ Wed 130

TYNEMOUTH   Map 21 NZ36
Tyne & Wear

Grand Hotel

★★★ 82% HOTEL

☎ 0191 293 6666
Grand Pde NE30 4ER
e-mail: reservations@grandhotel-uk.com
web: www.grandhotel-uk.com
dir: A1058 for Tynemouth. At coast rdbt turn right. Hotel on right approx 0.5m

This grand Victorian building offers stunning views of the coast. Bedrooms come in a variety of styles and are well equipped, tastefully decorated and have impressive bathrooms. In addition to the restaurant there are two bars. The elegant and imposing staircase is a focal point, and is a favourite spot for the bride and groom to have their photograph taken after their wedding here.

Rooms 45 (5 annexe) (11 fmly) **S** £75-£165; **D** £90-£175 (incl. bkfst)* **Facilities** FTV Wi-fi Xmas New Year **Conf** Class 40 Board 40 Thtr 130 Del from £165 to £275* **Services** Lift **Parking** 16 **Notes** LB ⊗ RS Sun evening Civ Wed 120

T

UCKFIELD
East Sussex   Map 6 TQ42

INSPECTORS' CHOICE

Buxted Park Hotel

HandPICKED
HOTELS
BUILT FOR PLEASURE

★★★★ ◎◎ HOTEL

☎ 01825 733333 & 0845 458 0901
Buxted TN22 4AY
e-mail: buxtedpark@handpicked.co.uk
web: www.handpickedhotels.co.uk/buxtedpark
dir: From A26 (Uckfield bypass) take A272 signed Buxted. Through lights, hotel 1m on right

An attractive Grade II listed Georgian mansion dating back to the 17th century. The property is set amidst 300 acres of beautiful countryside and landscaped gardens. The stylish, thoughtfully equipped bedrooms are split between the main house and the modern Garden Wing. An interesting choice of dishes is served in the restaurant.

Rooms 44 (7 fmly) (16 GF) ⚓ **S** £89.10-£368; **D** £99-£378 (incl. bkfst)* **Facilities** FTV Wi-fi Ⓡ HL Fishing ⚐ Gym Orienteering Walking trail Snooker room Xmas New Year **Conf** Class 80 Board 42 Thtr 180 Del from £145 to £175* **Services** Lift **Parking** 100 **Notes** LB ⊗ Civ Wed 120

East Sussex National Golf Resort & Spa

★★★★ 77% ◎ HOTEL

☎ 01825 880088
Little Horsted TN22 5ES
e-mail: reception@eastsussexnational.co.uk
dir: M25 junct 6, A22 signed East Grinstead & Eastbourne. Straight on at rdbt junct of A22 & A26 (Little Horsted). At next rdbt right to hotel

This modern hotel is located in a lovely country location and offers a super range of facilities with two golf courses and an impressive leisure suite. In addition there are also conference and meeting facilities. The bedrooms are spacious and have good facilities; all have delightful views across the golf course to the countryside beyond. The cuisine is enjoyable; particularly at breakfast, which is served in the restaurant that overlooks the course.

Rooms 104 (3 fmly) (36 GF) ⚓ **S** £100-£170; **D** £110-£180 (incl. bkfst)* **Facilities** Spa STV FTV Wi-fi ⓇⓈ ⚐ 36 ⚐ Putt green ⚐ Gym Academy of Golf Xmas New Year **Conf** Class 200 Board 50 Thtr 450 Del from £150* **Services** Lift Air con **Parking** 500 **Notes** LB ⊗ Civ Wed 250

INSPECTORS' CHOICE

Horsted Place

★★★ ◎◎ HOTEL

☎ 01825 750581
Little Horsted TN22 5TS
e-mail: hotel@horstedplace.co.uk
dir: From Uckfield 2m S on A26 towards Lewes

This property is one of Britain's finest examples of Gothic revivalist architecture, and much of the 1850s building was designed by Augustus Pugin. The hotel is situated in extensive landscaped grounds, with a tennis court and croquet lawn, and is adjacent to the East Sussex National Golf Club. The spacious bedrooms, in a range of both sizes and designs, are attractively decorated, tastefully furnished, and equipped with many thoughtful touches such as flowers and books. Most bedrooms also have a separate sitting area. Formal dining can be enjoyed in the elegant dining room (no children after 7pm) where the menus are based on quality seasonal produce. Pre-dinner drinks and after-dinner coffees can be enjoyed either in the Drawing Room or on the terrace overlooking the garden.

Rooms 20 (3 annexe) (5 fmly) (2 GF) ⚓ **S** £145-£360; **D** £145-£360 (incl. bkfst)* **Facilities** STV FTV Wi-fi ⚐ 36 ⚐ ⚐ Free use of gym & indoor pool at nearby hotel ♫ Xmas New Year **Conf** Class 50 Board 40 Thtr 80 Del from £170* **Services** Lift **Parking** 32 **Notes** LB ⊗ No children 7yrs Civ Wed 100

ULLESTHORPE
Leicestershire   Map 11 SP58

BEST WESTERN PLUS
Ullesthorpe Court Hotel & Golf Club

Best Western
PLUS

★★★★ 75% HOTEL

☎ 01455 209023
Frolesworth Rd LE17 5BZ
e-mail: bookings@ullesthorpecourt.co.uk
web: www.bw-ullesthorpecourt.co.uk
dir: M1 junct 20 towards Lutterworth. Follow brown tourist signs

Complete with its own golf club, this impressively equipped hotel is within easy reach of the motorway network, NEC and Birmingham airport. Public areas include both formal and informal eating options and extensive conference and leisure facilities. Spacious bedrooms are thoughtfully equipped for both the business and leisure guests, and a four-poster room is available.

Rooms 72 (3 fmly) (16 GF) ⚓ **Facilities** Spa STV Wi-fi ⓇⓈ supervised ⚐ 18 ⚐ Putt green Gym Beauty room Steam room Sauna Snooker room New Year **Conf** Class 48 Board 30 Thtr 80 Del from £120 to £145* **Services** Lift **Parking** 280 **Notes** ⊗ RS 25-26 Dec Civ Wed 120

ULLSWATER

See **Glenridding & Patterdale**

U

Save on hotels. Book at **theAA.com/hotel**

UCK – VEN 445 ENGLAND

UPPER SLAUGHTER
Gloucestershire
Map 10 SP12

INSPECTORS' CHOICE

Lords of the Manor

★★★★ 圇圇圇

COUNTRY HOUSE HOTEL

☎ 01451 820243

GL54 2JD

e-mail: reservations@lordsofthemanor.com

web: www.lordsofthemanor.com

dir: 2m W of A429. Exit A40 onto A429, take 'The Slaughters' turn. Through Lower Slaughter for 1m to Upper Slaughter. Hotel on right

This wonderfully welcoming 17th-century manor house hotel sits in eight acres of gardens and parkland surrounded by Cotswold countryside. A relaxed atmosphere, underpinned by professional and attentive service is the hallmark here, so that guests are often reluctant to leave. The hotel has elegant public rooms that overlook the immaculate lawns, and the restaurant is the venue for consistently impressive cuisine. Bedrooms have much character and charm, combined with the extra touches expected of a hotel of this stature.

Rooms 26 (4 fmly) (9 GF) ✿ **D** £199-£495 (incl. bkfst)* **Facilities** FTV Wi-fi Fishing ⚓ Xmas New Year **Conf** Class 20 Board 20 Thtr 30 Del £270* **Parking** 40 **Notes** Civ Wed 80

UPPINGHAM
Rutland
Map 11 SP89

The Lake Isle

圇圇 RESTAURANT WITH ROOMS

☎ 01572 822951

16 High Street East LE15 9PZ

e-mail: info@lakeisle.co.uk

web: www.lakeisle.co.uk

dir: From A47, turn left at 2nd lights, 100yds on right

This attractive townhouse centres round a delightful restaurant and small elegant bar. There is also an inviting first-floor guest lounge, and the bedrooms are extremely well appointed and thoughtfully equipped;

spacious split-level cottage suites situated in a quiet courtyard are also available. The imaginative cooking and an extremely impressive wine list are highlights.

Rooms 12 (3 annexe) (1 fmly)

UPTON UPON SEVERN
Worcestershire
Map 10 SO84

White Lion Hotel

★★★ 74% 圇 HOTEL

☎ 01684 592551

21 High St WR8 0HJ

e-mail: reservations@whitelionhotel.biz

dir: A422, A38 towards Tewkesbury. In 8m take B4104, after 1m cross bridge, turn left to hotel, past bend on left

Famed for being the inn depicted in Henry Fielding's novel *The History of Tom Jones, a Foundling*, this 16th-century hotel is a reminder of 'Old England' with features such as exposed beams and wall timbers still remaining. The quality furnishing and the decor throughout enhance its character; the bedrooms are smart and include one four-poster room.

Rooms 13 (2 annexe) (2 fmly) (2 GF) ✿ **S** £70-£95; **D** £99-£125 (incl. bkfst) **Facilities** FTV Wi-fi **Parking** 14 **Notes** LB Closed 1 Jan RS 25 Dec

---

UTTOXETER
Staffordshire
Map 10 SK03

Premier Inn Uttoxeter

BUDGET HOTEL

☎ 0871 527 9112

Derby Rd ST14 5AA

web: www.premierinn.com

dir: At junct of A50 & B5030 on outskirts of Uttoxeter, 7m S of Alton Towers Theme Park

High quality, budget accommodation ideal for both families and business travellers. Spacious, en suite bedrooms feature tea and coffee making facilities, and Freeview TV in most hotels. Internet access and Wi-fi are available for a small fee. The adjacent family restaurant features a wide and varied menu. See also the Hotel Groups pages.

Rooms 41

UXBRIDGE

***See* Ruislip**

VENTNOR
Isle of Wight
Map 5 SZ57

The Royal Hotel

★★★★ 79% 圇圇 HOTEL

☎ 01983 852186

Belgrave Rd PO38 1JJ

e-mail: enquiries@royalhoteliow.co.uk

web: www.royalhoteliow.co.uk

dir: A3055 into Ventnor follow one-way system, after lights left into Belgrave Rd. Hotel on right

This smart hotel enjoys a central yet peaceful location in its own gardens, complete with an outdoor pool. Spacious, elegant public areas include a bright conservatory, bar and lounge. Bedrooms, appointed to a high standard, vary in size and style. Staff are friendly and efficient, particularly in the smart restaurant, where modern British cuisine is offered.

Rooms 53 (9 fmly) **S** £105-£140; **D** £175-£275 (incl. bkfst)* **Facilities** FTV Wi-fi ⚲ Xmas New Year **Conf** Class 40 Board 24 Thtr 100 Del from £150 to £260* **Services** Lift **Parking** 50 **Notes** LB ⊗ Closed 1st 2 wks Jan Civ Wed 120

Eversley Hotel

★★★ 74% HOTEL

☎ 01983 852244 & 852462

Park Av PO38 1LB

e-mail: eversleyhotel@yahoo.co.uk

web: www.eversleyhotel.uk.com

dir: On A3055 W of Ventnor, next to Ventnor Park

Located west of Ventnor, this hotel enjoys a quiet location and has some rooms with garden and pool views. The spacious restaurant is sometimes used for local functions, and there are a bar, television room, lounge area, and card room as well as a jacuzzi and gym. Bedrooms are generally a good size.

Rooms 28 (6 fmly) (2 GF) ✿ **S** £39-£75; **D** £69-£115 (incl. bkfst) **Facilities** STV FTV Wi-fi ⚲ Gym Xmas New Year **Conf** Class 40 Board 20 **Parking** 23 **Notes** LB Closed 30 Nov-22 Dec & 2 Jan-8 Feb

V

VENTNOR *continued*

Ventnor Towers Hotel

★★★ 70% HOTEL

☎ 01983 852277
54 Madeira Rd PO38 1QT
e-mail: reservations@ventnortowers.com
web: www.ventnortowers.com
dir: From E, 1st left off A3055 just before pelican crossing

This mid-Victorian hotel, set in spacious grounds with a path that leads down to the shore, is high above the bay and enjoys splendid sea views. Many potted plants and fresh flowers grace the day rooms, which include two lounges and a spacious bar. Bedrooms include two four-poster rooms and some that have their own balconies.

Rooms 25 (4 fmly) (6 GF) **Facilities** Wi-fi ૨ ↨ 9 ♨ Putt green Xmas New Year **Conf** Class 60 Board 44 Thtr 100 **Parking** 20 **Notes** Civ Wed 150

The Wellington Hotel

★★★ 🅰 HOTEL

☎ 01983 856600
Belgrave Rd PO38 1JH
e-mail: enquiries@thewellingtonhotel.net
web: www.thewellingtonhotel.net

This hotel, a commanding white building with ornate balconies, has amazing sea views. Double, twin and deluxe bedrooms are on offer and very nearly all have uninterrupted views of the sea. Each has an understate decor in calming colour schemes.

Rooms 28 (5 fmly) (7 GF) **S** £82-£102; **D** £112-£132 (incl. bkfst)* **Facilities** FTV Wi-fi ↨ **Parking** 10 **Notes** LB ⊗ Civ Wed 60

The Hambrough

RESTAURANT WITH ROOMS

☎ 01983 856333
Hambrough Rd PO38 1SQ
e-mail: reservations@robert-thompson.com
dir: Telephone for directions

A former Victorian villa set on the hillside above Ventnor and with memorable views out to sea, The Hambrough has a modern, stylish interior with well equipped and boutique-style accommodation. The kitchen team's passion for food is clearly evident in the superb cuisine served in the minimalistic styled restaurant.

Rooms 7 (3 fmly)

VERYAN Map 2 SW93
Cornwall

The Nare

★★★★ ◉
COUNTRY HOUSE HOTEL

☎ 01872 501111
Carne Beach TR2 5PF
e-mail: stay@narehotel.co.uk
web: www.narehotel.co.uk
dir: A3078 from Tregony, approx 1.5m. Left at Veryan sign, through village towards sea & hotel

The Nare offers a relaxed, country-house atmosphere in a spectacular coastal setting. The elegantly designed bedrooms, many with balconies, have fresh flowers, carefully chosen artwork and antiques that contribute to their engaging individuality. A choice of dining options is available, from light snacks to superb local seafood.

Rooms 37 (7 fmly) (7 GF) 🐾 **S** £140-£268; **D** £270-£768 (incl. bkfst)* **Facilities** Spa FTV Wi-fi 🔄 ૨ ♨ ⚜ Gym Health & beauty clinic Sauna Steam room Hotel sailing boat Shooting Xmas New Year **Services** Lift **Parking** 80 **Notes** LB

WADDESDON Map 11 SP71
Buckinghamshire

The Five Arrows

◎ ◎ RESTAURANT WITH ROOMS

☎ 01296 651727
High St HP18 0JE
e-mail: five.arrows@nationaltrust.org.uk
dir: On A41 in Waddesdon. Into Baker St for car park

This Grade II listed building with elaborate Elizabethan chimney stacks, stands at the gates of Waddesdon Manor and was named after the Rothschild family emblem. Individually styled en suite bedrooms are comfortable and well appointed. Friendly staff are on hand to offer a warm welcome. Alfresco dining is possible in the warmer months.

Rooms 11

WAKEFIELD Map 16 SE32
West Yorkshire

See also **Liversedge**

Waterton Park Hotel

★★★★ 78% ◉ HOTEL

CLASSIC
BRITISH HOTELS

☎ 01924 257911 & 249800
Walton Hall, The Balk, Walton WF2 6PW
e-mail: info@watertonparkhotel.co.uk
web: www.watertonparkhotel.co.uk
dir: 3m SE off B6378. Exit M1 junct 39 towards Wakefield. At 3rd rdbt right for Crofton. At 2nd lights right & follow signs

This Georgian mansion, built on an island in the centre of a 26-acre lake is in a truly idyllic setting. The main house contains many feature bedrooms, and the annexe houses more spacious rooms, all equally well equipped with modern facilities; most of the bedrooms have views over the lake or the 18-hole golf course. The delightful beamed restaurant, two bars and leisure club are located in the old hall, and there is a licence for civil weddings.

Rooms 65 (43 annexe) (5 fmly) (23 GF) 🐾 **S** £69-£110; **D** £80-£195 (incl. bkfst)* **Facilities** STV FTV Wi-fi ↨ ⌕ supervised Fishing Gym Steam room Sauna New Year **Conf** Class 80 Board 80 Thtr 150 Del from £125 to £155* **Services** Lift **Parking** 200 **Notes** LB ⊗ Civ Wed 130

V

Cedar Court Hotel Wakefield

THE INDEPENDENTS
HOTEL ASSOCIATION

★★★★ 73% HOTEL

☎ 01924 276310
Denby Dale Rd WF4 3QZ
e-mail: sales@cedarcourthotels.co.uk
web: www.cedarcourthotels.co.uk
dir: Adjacent to M1 junct 39

This hotel enjoys a convenient location just off the M1. Traditionally styled bedrooms offer a good range of facilities while open-plan public areas include a busy bar and restaurant operation. Conferences and functions are extremely well catered for and a modern leisure club completes the picture.

Rooms 149 (2 fmly) (74 GF) 🐾 **Facilities** FTV Wi-fi ↕ 🕭 supervised Gym Sauna Steam room Beauty treatment room Xmas New Year **Conf** Class 140 Board 80 Thtr 400 **Services** Lift **Parking** 350 **Notes** Civ Wed 250

Holiday Inn Leeds - Wakefield

Holiday Inn

★★★ 75% HOTEL

☎ 0871 942 9082
Queen's Dr, Ossett WF5 9BE
e-mail: reception-wakefield@ihg.com
web: www.holidayinn.co.uk/wakefield
dir: M1 junct 40 follow signs for Wakefield. Hotel on right in 200yds

Situated close to major motorway networks, this modern hotel offers well-equipped and comfortable bedrooms. Public areas include the popular Traders restaurant and a comfortable lounge where a menu is available throughout the day. Conference facilities are also available.

Rooms 104 (32 fmly) (35 GF) (4 smoking) **Facilities** STV Wi-fi ↕ Xmas New Year **Conf** Class 80 Board 80 Thtr 160 **Services** Lift Air con **Parking** 180 **Notes** Civ Wed 160

Campanile Wakefield

Campanile
HOTEL RESTAURANT

BUDGET HOTEL

☎ 01924 201054
Monckton Rd WF2 7AL
e-mail: wakefield@campanile.com
web: www.campanile.com
dir: M1 junct 39, A636, 1m towards Wakefield, left into Monckton Rd, hotel on left

This modern building offers accommodation in smart, well-equipped bedrooms, all with en suite bathrooms. Refreshments may be taken at the informal bistro. See also the Hotel Groups pages.

Rooms 76 (76 annexe) (4 fmly) (25 GF) **Conf** Class 15 Board 15 Thtr 25

Premier Inn Wakefield Central

Premier Inn

BUDGET HOTEL

☎ 0871 527 9114
Thornes Park, Denby Dale Rd WF2 8DY
web: www.premierinn.com
dir: M1 junct 41, A650 towards Wakefield. Approx 1.5m. Hotel on right

High quality, budget accommodation ideal for both families and business travellers. Spacious, en suite bedrooms feature tea and coffee making facilities, and Freeview TV in most hotels. Internet access and Wi-fi are available for a small fee. The adjacent family restaurant features a wide and varied menu. See also the Hotel Groups pages.

Rooms 42

Premier Inn Wakefield City North

BUDGET HOTEL

☎ 0871 527 9116
Paragon Business Park, Herriot Way WF1 2UJ
web: www.premierinn.com
dir: M1 junct 41, A650 (Bradford Rd) for approx 1.5m towards Wakefield centre. Hotel on right adjacent to Bannatynes Health Club

Rooms 47

Premier Inn Wakefield South M1 Jct 39

BUDGET HOTEL

☎ 0871 527 9118
Calder Park, Denby Dale Rd WF4 3BB
web: www.premierinn.com
dir: M1 junct 39, A636 towards Wakefield. At 1st rdbt 1st exit into Calder Park. Hotel on right

Rooms 74

WALLASEY   Map 15 SJ29
Merseyside

Grove House Hotel

★★★ 82% HOTEL

☎ 0151 639 3947 & 630 4558
Grove Rd CH45 3HF
e-mail: reception@thegrovehouse.co.uk
web: www.thegrovehouse.co.uk
dir: M53 junct 1, A554 (Wallasey New Brighton), right after church into Harrison Drive, left after Windsors Garage into Grove Rd

Ideally situated for Liverpool and the M53, this friendly hotel offers attractive and comfortable bedrooms, which come with a wealth of extras. Well-cooked meals are served in the elegant panelled dining room. Weddings and conferences also catered for.

Rooms 14 (7 fmly) 🐾 **S** £59; **D** £79-£130* **Facilities** FTV Wi-fi **Conf** Class 30 Board 50 Thtr 50 Del £120.90* **Parking** 28 **Notes** ⊗ RS BHs Civ Wed 50

W

The Springs Hotel & Golf Club

★★★ 81% ◎ HOTEL

☎ 01491 836687
Wallingford Rd, North Stoke OX10 6BE
e-mail: reception@thespringshotel.com
web: www.thespringshotel.com
dir: A4074 (Oxford-Reading road) onto B4009
(Goring). Hotel approx 1m on right

Set on its own 18-hole, par 72 golf course, this
Victorian mansion has a timeless and peaceful
atmosphere. The generously equipped, individually
styled bedrooms vary in size but many are spacious.
Some bedrooms overlook the pool and grounds while
others have views of the spring-fed lake, as does the
elegant restaurant. There is also a comfortable
lounge, with original features, to relax in.

Rooms 31 (3 fmly) (10 GF) **Facilities** FTV Wi-fi ↕ ⤳ ♨
18 Putt green Fishing ⤵ Boat trips on Thames Xmas
New Year **Conf** Class 16 Board 26 Thtr 60
Parking 150 **Notes** Civ Wed 150

The George

★★★ 77% HOTEL   PEEL HOTELS PLC

☎ 01491 836665
High St OX10 0BS
e-mail: info@george-hotel-wallingford.com
web: www.peelhotels.co.uk
dir: E side of A329, N end of Wallingford

Old world charm and modern facilities merge
seamlessly in this former coaching inn. Bedrooms in
the main house have character in abundance. Those
in the wing have a more contemporary style, but all
are well equipped and attractively decorated. Diners

can choose between the restaurant and bistro, or
relax in the cosy bar.

Rooms 39 (1 fmly) (9 GF) **S** £100-£150; **D** £118-£175
(incl. bkfst)* **Facilities** STV Wi-fi Xmas New Year
Conf Class 60 Board 50 Thtr 150 Del from £125 to
£148* **Parking** 60 **Notes** LB ⊗ Civ Wed 100

Fairlawns Hotel & Spa

★★★ 86% ◎◎ HOTEL   CLASSIC BRITISH HOTELS

☎ 01922 455122
178 Little Aston Rd WS9 0NU
e-mail: reception@fairlawns.co.uk
web: www.fairlawns.co.uk
dir: Exit A452 towards Aldridge at x-roads with A454.
Hotel 600yds on right

In a rural location with immaculate landscaped
grounds, this constantly improving hotel offers a wide
range of facilities and modern, comfortable
bedrooms. Family rooms, one with a four-poster bed,
and suites are also available. The Fairlawns
Restaurant serves a wide range of award-winning
seasonal dishes. The extensive, comprehensively
equipped leisure complex is mainly for adult use as
there is restricted availability to young people.

Rooms 58 (8 fmly) (1 GF) (3 smoking) ⤳
Facilities Spa STV FTV Wi-fi ↕ ⓢ supervised ⤴ ⤵
Gym Dance studio Beauty salon Bathing suite
Floatation suite Sauna Aromatherapy room New Year
Conf Class 40 Board 30 Thtr 80 **Services** Lift
Parking 150 **Notes** RS 24 Dec-2 Jan Civ Wed 100

Beverley Hotel

★★★ 73% HOTEL

☎ 01922 622999
58 Lichfield Rd WS4 2DJ
e-mail: info@beverley-hotel.com
dir: 1m N of town centre on A461 to Lichfield

This privately owned hotel dates back to 1880.
Bedrooms are comfortably appointed, and the
tastefully decorated public areas include a spacious
bar combined with a conservatory. The restaurant
offers guests a choice of carefully prepared,
appetising dishes.

Rooms 31 (2 fmly) (4 GF) ⤳ **S** £49.50-£75;
D £59.50-£85 (incl. bkfst) **Facilities** FTV Wi-fi ↕ New
Year **Conf** Class 30 Board 30 Thtr 80 Del £99
Parking 68 **Notes** LB Civ Wed 80

Holiday Inn Express Walsall M6 Jct 10

BUDGET HOTEL

☎ 01922 705250
Tempus Ten, Tempus Dr WS2 8TJ
e-mail: admin@hiexwalsall.com
web: www.hiexpress.co.uk
dir: M6 junct 10/A454 to Walsall. Right at 1st lights,
hotel 200mtrs on right

A modern hotel ideal for families and business
travellers. Fresh and uncomplicated, the spacious
rooms include Sky TV, power shower and tea and
coffee-making facilities. Continental buffet breakfast
is included in the room rate; other meals may be
taken at the nearby family pub or restaurant. See also
the Hotel Groups pages.

Rooms 120 (77 fmly) (30 GF) ⤳ **S** fr £40; **D** fr £40
(incl. bkfst)* **Conf** Class 45 Board 36 Thtr 60

Premier Inn Walsall M6 Jct 10

BUDGET HOTEL

☎ 0871 527 9120
Bentley Green, Bentley Road North WS2 0WB
web: www.premierinn.com
dir: M6 junct 10, A454 signed Wolverhampton. 2nd
exit (Ansons junct). Left at rdbt, 1st left at next rdbt,
hotel on right

High quality, budget accommodation ideal for both
families and business travellers. Spacious, en suite
bedrooms feature tea and coffee making facilities,
and Freeview TV in most hotels. Internet access and
Wi-fi are available for a small fee. The adjacent
family restaurant features a wide and varied menu.
See also the Hotel Groups pages.

Rooms 40

Premier Inn Walsall Town Centre

BUDGET HOTEL

☎ 0871 527 9374
Waterfront, Wolverhampton St WS2 8LR
web: www.premierinn.com
dir: M6 junct 10/A454 Wolverhampton Road to
Walsall. Continue on A454. Follow signs for Crown
Wharf Shopping Centre. Premier Inn situated on right
on Wolverhampton Street

Rooms 100 (75 fmly)

W

WALTHAM ABBEY
Essex   Map 6 TL30

Premier Inn Waltham Abbey

BUDGET HOTEL

☎ 0871 527 9122
Sewardstone Rd EN9 3QF
web: www.premierinn.com
dir: M25 junct 26, A121 towards Waltham Abbey. Left onto A112, hotel 0.5m on left

High quality, budget accommodation ideal for both families and business travellers. Spacious, en suite bedrooms feature tea and coffee making facilities, and Freeview TV in most hotels. Internet access and Wi-fi are available for a small fee. The adjacent family restaurant features a wide and varied menu. See also the Hotel Groups pages.

Rooms 93

WANSFORD
Cambridgeshire   Map 12 TL09

The Haycock Hotel
★★★ 86% ◉ HOTEL

☎ 01780 782223 & 781124
PE8 6JA
e-mail: sales@thehaycock.co.uk
dir: A1 junct to A47 Leicester

A charming 17th-century coaching inn set in attractive landscaped grounds in a peaceful village location. The smartly decorated bedrooms are tastefully furnished and thoughtfully equipped. Public rooms include a choice of restaurants, a lounge bar, a cocktail bar and a stylish lounge. The hotel has a staffed business centre, and banqueting facilities are also available. Macdonald Hotels is the AA Hotel Group of the Year 2013-14.

Rooms 48 (1 fmly) (14 GF) ⬟ **Facilities** FTV Wi-fi ⬟ Beauty treatment room New Year **Conf** Class 100 Board 45 Thtr 300 Del from £130 to £155* **Parking** 300 **Notes** Civ Wed 200

WANTAGE
Oxfordshire   Map 5 SU38

La Fontana Restaurant with Accommodation

RESTAURANT WITH ROOMS

☎ 01235 868287
Oxford Rd, East Hanney OX12 0HP
e-mail: anna@la-fontana.co.uk
dir: A338 from Wantage towards Oxford. Restaurant on right in East Hanney

Guests are guaranteed a warm welcome at this family-run Italian restaurant which is located on the outskirts of the busy town of Wantage. The stylish bedrooms are individually designed, well equipped and very comfortable. Dinner should not to be missed - the menu features a wide range of regional Italian specialities.

Rooms 15 (7 annexe) (2 fmly)

WARE
Hertfordshire   Map 6 TL31

Hanbury Manor, A Marriott Hotel & Country Club
★★★★★ 81% ◉◉

COUNTRY HOUSE HOTEL

☎ 01920 487722 & 0870 400 7222
SG12 0SD
e-mail:
mhrs.stngs.guestrelations@marriotthotels.com
web: www.marriotthanburymanor.co.uk
dir: M25 junct 25, A10 N for 12m, take A1170, right at rdbt, hotel on left

Set in 200 acres of landscaped grounds, this impressive Jacobean-style mansion boasts an enviable range of leisure facilities, including an excellent health club and championship golf course. Bedrooms are traditionally and comfortably furnished in the country-house style and have lovely marbled bathrooms. There are a number of food and drink options, including the renowned Zodiac and Oakes restaurants.

Rooms 161 (27 annexe) (60 fmly) ⬟ **Facilities** Spa STV FTV Wi-fi ⬟ supervised ⬟ 18 ⬟ Putt green ⬟ Gym Health & beauty treatments Aerobics Yoga Dance class Xmas New Year **Conf** Class 86 Board 36 Thtr 150 **Services** Lift **Parking** 200 **Notes** Civ Wed 120

WARMINSTER
Wiltshire   Map 4 ST84

The Bishopstrow Hotel & Spa
★★★★ 76% ◉ HOTEL

☎ 01985 212312
Borenam Rd BA12 9HH
dir: From rdbt on A36 take B3414 towards Warminster. Follow brown hotel signs

The Bishopstrow Hotel is set in 27 acres of delightful grounds which include modern spa facilities, tennis courts and country walks. Bedrooms are comfortable and stylish, and all are well appointed. Public areas offer several day rooms, and retain the style of the original house. Cuisine is a feature here, and menus offer fresh and local produce.

Rooms 32 (2 annexe) (16 fmly) (9 GF) ⬟ S £99-£175; D £145-£480 (incl. bkfst)* **Facilities** Spa STV FTV Wi-fi ⬟ ⬟ ⬟ Fishing Gym Thermal rooms Relaxation room Xmas New Year **Conf** Class 40 Board 36 Thtr 60 Del from £168 to £216* **Parking** 70 **Notes** Civ Wed 82

WARRINGTON
Cheshire   Map 15 SJ68

The Park Royal
★★★★ 78% HOTEL

☎ 01925 730706
Stretton Rd, Stretton WA4 4NS
e-mail: parkroyalreservations@qhotels.co.uk
web: www.qhotels.co.uk
dir: M56 junct 10, A49 to Warrington, at lights turn right to Appleton Thorn, 1st right into Spark Hall Close, hotel on left

This modern hotel enjoys a peaceful setting, yet is conveniently located just minutes from the M56. The bedrooms are contemporary, well furnished and attractively co-ordinated. Spacious, stylish public areas include extensive conference and function facilities and a comprehensive leisure centre complete with outdoor tennis courts and a spa. Complimentary Wi-fi is also provided.

Rooms 146 (32 fmly) (34 GF) ⬟ **Facilities** Spa FTV Wi-fi ⬟ ⬟ Gym Dance studio Sauna Xmas New Year **Conf** Class 180 Board 90 Thtr 400 Del from £109 to £199 **Services** Lift **Parking** 400 **Notes** Civ Wed 300

W

WARRINGTON *continued*

BEST WESTERN Fir Grove Hotel

★★★ 78% HOTEL

☎ 01925 267471
Knutsford Old Rd WA4 2LD
e-mail: firgrove@bestwestern.co.uk
web: www.bw-firgrovehotel.co.uk
dir: M6 junct 20, follow signs for A50 to Warrington for 2.4m, before swing bridge over canal, turn right & right again

Situated in a quiet residential area, this hotel is convenient for both the town centre and the motorway network. Comfortable, smart bedrooms, including spacious executive rooms, offer some excellent extra facilities such as iPod docking stations. Public areas include a smart lounge/bar, a neatly appointed restaurant, and excellent function and meeting facilities.

Rooms 52 (3 fmly) (20 GF) **Facilities** STV FTV Wi-fi Xmas New Year **Conf** Class 150 Board 50 Thtr 200 **Parking** 100 **Notes** Civ Wed 200

Holiday Inn Warrington

Holiday Inn

★★★ 77% HOTEL

☎ 0871 942 9087
Woolston Grange Av, Woolston WA1 4PX
e-mail: paul.ellison@ihg.com
web: www.hiwarringtonhotel.co.uk
dir: M6 junct 21, follow signs for Birchwood

Ideally located within the M62 and M56 interchange, this hotel provides the ideal base for all areas of the north-west region for both corporate and leisure guests. Rooms are spacious and well equipped, and a wide choice of meals is available in the comfortable restaurant and cosy bar. Meeting and conference facilities are also available.

Rooms 96 (40 fmly) (9 GF) **Facilities** STV FTV Wi-fi HL Xmas New Year **Conf** Board 20 Thtr 30 **Services** Lift Air con **Parking** 101

Ramada Encore Warrington

★★★ 71% HOTEL

☎ 01925 847050
Aston Avene, Birchwood Business Park WA3 6ZN
e-mail: gm@encorewarrington.co.uk
web: www.encorewarrington.co.uk
dir: M6 junct 21a, M62 junct 11. Follow signs for Birchwood Park on A574

This purpose-built hotel makes a good base for both business and leisure guests. The bedrooms are spacious and bright with en suite power-shower

rooms. Public areas include a restaurant, bar and lounge. Secure parking is available on site.

Rooms 103 (16 fmly) (7 GF) **Facilities** FTV Wi-fi **Conf** Class 30 Board 18 Thtr 40 **Services** Lift Air con **Parking** 94 **Notes** ⊗

Villaggio

★★ 63% HOTEL

☎ 01925 630106
5-9 Folly Ln WA5 0LZ
e-mail: villaggiowarrington@hotmail.co.uk
dir: M62 junct 9, A49, through 2 rdbts to x-rds. Left at McDonalds, through lights, hotel on left

Conveniently located close to northwest motorway networks and only half a mile from the town centre. Bedrooms are simply furnished in a contemporary style with good quality accessories such as flat-screen TVs and complimentary Wi-fi. An extensive choice of meals is served in the spacious restaurant. Off-road parking is available.

Rooms 19 (2 fmly) **Facilities** FTV Wi-fi Xmas New Year **Conf** Class 180 Board 100 Thtr 230 Del from £80 to £120* **Parking** 30

Premier Inn Warrington A49/M62 Jct 9

BUDGET HOTEL

☎ 0871 527 9128
Winwick Rd WA2 8RN
web: www.premierinn.com
dir: M62 junct 9 towards Warrington, hotel 100yds

High quality, budget accommodation ideal for both families and business travellers. Spacious, en suite bedrooms feature tea and coffee making facilities, and Freeview TV in most hotels. Internet access and Wi-fi are available for a small fee. The adjacent family restaurant features a wide and varied menu. See also the Hotel Groups pages.

Rooms 74

Premier Inn Warrington Centre

BUDGET HOTEL

☎ 0871 527 9126
1430 Centre Park, Park Boulevard WA1 1PR
web: www.premierinn.com
dir: Take A49 to Brian Beven Island Rdbt, into Park Boulevard (Centre Park). Over bridge. Hotel on right

Rooms 42

Premier Inn Warrington (M6 Jct 21)

BUDGET HOTEL

☎ 0871 527 9124
Manchester Rd, Woolston WA1 4GB
web: www.premierinn.com
dir: Just off M6 junct 21 on A57 to Warrington

Rooms 105

Premier Inn Warrington North

BUDGET HOTEL

☎ 0871 527 9128
Winwick Rd WA2 8RN
web: www.premierinn.com
dir: M62 junct 9, A49 signed Warrington. At next rdbt follow Town Centre signs. Straight on at next rdbt, left into Warrington Collegiate Camp

Rooms 74

Premier Inn Warrington North East

BUDGET HOTEL

☎ 0871 527 9130
Golborne Rd, Winwick WA2 8LF
web: www.premierinn.com
dir: M6 junct 22, A573 towards Newton-le-Willows. Dual carriageway to end, take 3rd exit at rdbt. Hotel adjacent to church

Rooms 42

Premier Inn Warrington South

BUDGET HOTEL

☎ 0871 527 9134
Tarporley Rd, Stretton WA4 4NB
web: www.premierinn.com
dir: Just off M56 junct 10. Follow A49 to Warrington, left at 1st lights

Rooms 29

WARWICK   Map 10 SP26
Warwickshire

See also Leamington Spa (Royal) & Wroxall

Ardencote Manor Hotel, Country Club & Spa

★★★★ 80% ◉◉ HOTEL

☎ 01926 843111
The Cumsey, Lye Green Rd, Claverdon CV35 8LT
e-mail: hotel@ardencote.com
web: www.ardencote.com

(For full entry see Claverdon)

W

Chesford Grange

★★★★ 77% HOTEL

☎ 01926 859331
Chesford Bridge CV8 2LD
e-mail: chesfordreservations@qhotels.co.uk
web: www.qhotels.co.uk

(For full entry see Kenilworth)

Premier Inn Warwick

BUDGET HOTEL

☎ 0871 527 9320
Opus 40, Birmingham Rd CV34 5JL
web: www.premierinn.com
dir: M40 junct 15, A46 (Warick bypass) towards Warwick. Follow A425 signs. From A425 1st left into industrial estate (Opus 40). Hotel 200yds, opposite IBM office

High quality, budget accommodation ideal for both families and business travellers. Spacious, en suite bedrooms feature tea and coffee making facilities, and Freeview TV in most hotels. Internet access and Wi-fi are available for a small fee. The adjacent family restaurant features a wide and varied menu. See also the Hotel Groups pages.

Rooms 124

> **WARWICK** Map 10 SP35
> **MOTORWAY SERVICE AREA (M40)**
> Warwickshire

Days Inn Warwick North - M40

BUDGET HOTEL

☎ 01926 651681
Warwick Services, M40 Northbound Junction 12-13, Banbury Rd CV35 0AA
e-mail: warwick.north.hotel@welcomebreak.co.uk
web: www.welcomebreak.co.uk
dir: M40 northbound between junct 12 & 13

This modern building offers accommodation in smart, spacious and well-equipped bedrooms, suitable for families and business travellers, and all with en suite bathrooms. Continental breakfast is available and other refreshments may be taken at the nearby family restaurant. See also the Hotel Groups pages.

Rooms 54 (45 fmly) (8 smoking) **Conf** Board 30

Days Inn Warwick South - M40

BUDGET HOTEL

☎ 01926 650168
Warwick Services, M40 Southbound, Banbury Rd CV35 0AA
e-mail: warwick.south.hotel@welcomebreak.co.uk
web: www.welcomebreak.co.uk
dir: M40 southbound between junct 14 & 12

Rooms 40 (38 fmly) (5 smoking)

> **WASHINGTON** Map 19 NZ35
> Tyne & Wear

Mercure Newcastle George Washington Hotel

★★★ 81% HOTEL

☎ 0191 402 9988
Stone Cellar Rd, High Usworth NE37 1PH
e-mail: reservations@georgewashington.co.uk
web: www.georgewashington.co.uk
dir: A1(M) junct 65 onto A194(M). Take A195 signed Washington North. Take last exit from rdbt for Washington then right at mini-rdbt. Hotel 0.5m on right

Popular with business and leisure guests, this purpose-built hotel boasts two golf courses and a driving range. Bedrooms are stylish and modern, generally spacious and comfortably equipped. Public areas include extensive conference facilities, a business centre and fitness club.

Rooms 103 (9 fmly) (41 GF) **S** £40-£135; **D** £40-£135* **Facilities** Spa STV FTV Wi-fi 🕙 🏌 18 Putt green Gym Golf driving range Beauty salon Xmas New Year **Conf** Class 80 Board 80 Thtr 200 Del from £99 to £150* **Parking** 180 **Notes** LB ⊗ Civ Wed 180

Holiday Inn Washington

★★★ 79% HOTEL

☎ 0871 942 9084
Emerson District 5 NE37 1LB
e-mail: washingtonhi@ihg.com
web: www.hiwashingtonhotel.co.uk
dir: Just off A1(M) junct 64. Left at rdbt, hotel on left

This is an ideally located hotel, just off the A1(M), and near to historic Durham, Sunderland and Newcastle's city centre. It is a well established hotel noted for its friendly staff. Bedrooms are air conditioned, and executive rooms are available. The eating options are Traders Restaurant and the lounge bar area.

Rooms 136 (6 GF) (4 smoking) **Facilities** STV FTV Wi-fi 🕙 Xmas New Year **Conf** Class 60 Board 50 Thtr 100 **Services** Lift Air con **Parking** 200 **Notes** Civ Wed 150

Campanile Washington

Campanile

BUDGET HOTEL

☎ 0191 416 5010
Emerson Rd, District 5 NE37 1LE
e-mail: washington@campanile.com
web: www.campanile.com
dir: A1(M) junct 64, A195 to Washington, 1st left at rdbt into Emerson Rd. Hotel 800yds on left

This modern building offers accommodation in smart, well-equipped bedrooms, all with en suite bathrooms. Refreshments may be taken at the informal bistro. See also the Hotel Groups pages.

Rooms 79 (79 annexe) (1 fmly) (28 GF) **S** £39-£120; **D** £39-£120* **Conf** Class 15 Board 25 Thtr 40 Del from £60 to £145*

W

WASHINGTON *continued*

Premier Inn Newcastle (Washington)

BUDGET HOTEL

☎ 0871 527 9136
Emerson Rd NE37 1LB
web: www.premierinn.com
dir: A1(M) junct 64, A195, follow Emerson signs. Left at rdbt, hotel 250yds left

High quality, budget accommodation ideal for both families and business travellers. Spacious, en suite bedrooms feature tea and coffee making facilities, and Freeview TV in most hotels. Internet access and Wi-fi are available for a small fee. The adjacent family restaurant features a wide and varied menu. See also the Hotel Groups pages.

Rooms 74

| WATERMILLOCK | Map 18 NY42 |
| Cumbria | |

INSPECTORS' CHOICE

Rampsbeck Country House Hotel

★★★★ ◉◉ HOTEL

☎ 017684 86442
CA11 0LP
e-mail: enquiries@rampsbeck.co.uk
web: www.rampsbeck.co.uk
dir: M6 junct 40, A592 to Ullswater, at T-junct (with lake opposite) turn right, hotel 1.5m

This fine country house lies in 18 acres of parkland on the shores of Lake Ullswater, and is furnished with many period and antique pieces. There are three delightful lounges, an elegant restaurant and a traditional bar. Bedrooms come in three grades; the most spacious of which are spectacular and overlook the lake. Service is attentive and the award-winning cuisine a real highlight.

Rooms 19 (1 fmly) (1 GF) ↟ **Facilities** STV FTV Wi-fi Putt green ↯ Private boat trips on Lake Ullswater Xmas New Year **Conf** Class 10 Board 15 Thtr 15 **Parking** 25 **Notes** Civ Wed 60

Macdonald Leeming House

★★★★ 76% ◉ HOTEL

☎ 0844 879 9142
CA11 0JJ
e-mail: sales/oldengland@macdonald-hotels.co.uk
web: www.macdonald-hotels.co.uk
dir: M6 junct 40, A66 to Keswick. At rdbt take A592 (Ullswater). 5m to T-junct, right (A592). Hotel on left in 3m

This hotel enjoys a superb location, being set in 20 acres of mature wooded gardens in the Lake District National Park, and overlooking Ullswater and the towering fells. Many rooms offer views of the lake and the rugged mountains beyond, with more than half having their own balcony. Public rooms include three sumptuous lounges, a cosy bar and library. Macdonald Hotels is the AA Hotel Group of the Year 2013-14.

Rooms 41 (1 fmly) (10 GF) **Facilities** Wi-fi Fishing ↯ Xmas New Year **Conf** Class 40 Board 30 Thtr 80 **Parking** 50 **Notes** Civ Wed 80

| WATFORD | Map 6 TQ19 |
| Hertfordshire | |

Mercure London Watford Hotel

★★★ HOTEL

☎ 0844 815 9056
A41, Watford Bypass WD25 8JH
e-mail: info@mercurewatford.co.uk
web: www.jupiterhotels.co.uk
dir: M1 junct 5, A41 S to London. Straight on at island, hotel 1m on left

Currently the rating for this establishment is not confirmed. This may be due to a change of ownership or because it has only recently joined the AA rating scheme.

Rooms 218 **Conf** Class 120 Board 60 Thtr 200

BEST WESTERN White House

★★★ 74% HOTEL

☎ 01923 237316
Upton Rd WD18 0JF
e-mail: info@whitehousehotel.co.uk
web: www.bw-whitehousehotel.co.uk
dir: From centre ring road into Exchange Rd, exit left into Upton Rd, hotel on left

This popular commercial hotel is situated within easy walking distance of the town centre. Bedrooms are pleasantly decorated and offer a good range of facilities that include interactive TV with internet. The public areas are open plan; they include a comfortable lounge/bar, cosy snug and an attractive conservatory restaurant with a sunny open terrace for summer dining. Functions suites are also available.

Rooms 57 (8 GF) **Facilities** STV FTV Wi-fi HL **Conf** Class 80 Board 50 Thtr 150 Del £135* **Services** Lift **Parking** 50 **Notes** ◉ RS 25 Dec-2 Jan Civ Wed 120

Park Inn London Watford

★★★ 68% HOTEL

☎ 01923 429988 & 429900
30-40 St Albans Rd WD17 1RN
e-mail: info.watford@rezidorparkinn.com
web: www.watford.parkinn.co.uk
dir: On A412 between Town Hall & Watford Junction Station

Located within walking distance of Watford Junction main station, which has easy connections to London, this modern hotel has contemporary bedrooms and bathrooms providing comfortable accommodation for both the leisure or business guest. The larger bedroom range is particularly suitable for visiting executives and for families. The restaurant and lounge areas offer a substantial menu. A number of up-to-date conference rooms are available, and secure parking is an asset.

Rooms 100 (6 fmly) ↟ **Facilities** FTV Wi-fi Gym Xmas New Year **Conf** Class 90 Board 40 Thtr 180 **Services** Lift Air con **Parking** 92 **Notes** Civ Wed 180

W

Save on hotels. Book at **theAA.com/hotel**

WAS – WEL 453 ENGLAND

Premier Inn Watford Centre

BUDGET HOTEL

☎ 0871 527 9140
Timms Meadow, Water Ln WD17 2NJ
web: www.premierinn.com
dir: M1 junct 5, A41 into town centre. At rdbt take 3rd exit, stay in left lane through lights. Take 1st left into Water Ln. Hotel on left

High quality, budget accommodation ideal for both families and business travellers. Spacious, en suite bedrooms feature tea and coffee making facilities, and Freeview TV in most hotels. Internet access and Wi-fi are available for a small fee. The adjacent family restaurant features a wide and varied menu. See also the Hotel Groups pages.

Rooms 105

Premier Inn Watford (Croxley Green)

BUDGET HOTEL

☎ 0871 527 9138
2 Ascot Rd WD18 8AD
web: www.premierinn.com
dir: M25 junct 18, A404 signed Watford/Rickmansworth, left at 1st rdbt signed A412 Watford. Follow Croxley Green Business Park/Watford signs, at 4th rdbt, 3rd exit. M1 junct 5, A41 towards Watford, follow Watford West & Rickmansworth A412 signs. Then Croxley Green Business Park signs

Rooms 121

Premier Inn Watford North

BUDGET HOTEL

☎ 0871 527 9142
859 St Albans Rd, Garston WD25 0LH
web: www.premierinn.com
dir: M1 junct 6, A405 towards Watford. At 2nd lights onto A412 (St Albans Rd). Into TGI Friday's car park. Hotel directly behind

Rooms 45

WATTON   Map 13 TF90
Norfolk

Broom Hall Country Hotel

★★★ 77% COUNTRY HOUSE HOTEL

☎ 01953 882125
Richmond Rd, Saham Toney IP25 7EX
e-mail: enquiries@broomhallhotel.co.uk
web: www.broomhallhotel.co.uk
dir: From A11 at Thetford onto A1075 to Watton (12m), B1108 towards Swaffham, in 0.5m at rdbt turn right to Saham Toney, hotel 0.5m on left. From A47 take A1075, left onto B1108

A delightful Victorian country house situated down a private drive and set in mature landscaped gardens surrounded by parkland. The well-equipped bedrooms are split between the main house and an adjacent building. Public rooms include a relaxing lounge, a brasserie restaurant, a lounge bar, a conservatory and a smart restaurant. There is an indoor swimming pool.

Rooms 15 (5 annexe) (3 fmly) (5 GF) ↝ **S** £70-£95; **D** £85-£150 (incl. bkfst) **Facilities** FTV Wi-fi ⇗ ⊛ Massage Beauty treatments **Conf** Class 30 Board 22 Thtr 80 Del from £120 to £150 **Parking** 30 **Notes** LB Closed 24 Dec-4 Jan Civ Wed 70

WELLESBOURNE   Map 10 SP25
Warwickshire

Walton Hall

★★★★ 81% ⊛ ⊛ HOTEL

☎ 01789 842424
Walton CV35 9HU
e-mail: waltonhall.mande@pumahotels.co.uk
dir: A429 through Barford towards Wellesbourne, right after watermill, follow signs to hotel

Sitting in 65 acres of beautiful countryside, this hotel is just 10 minutes from the M40. It has a fascinating history, with parts dating back to the 1500s. The property has been appointed in a style that combines both the traditional and the modern. The individually designed bedrooms, many with stunning views over the lake and garden, have plasma screen TVs, DVD players and safes big enough for a laptop. Premium rooms and suites are available. The award-winning Moncreiffe Restaurant is situated in the hall and has views over the lovely gardens.

Rooms 56 (19 annexe) (11 GF) **Facilities** Spa STV FTV Wi-fi ⇗ supervised Gym Dance studio Beauty salon Xmas New Year **Conf** Class 60 Board 36 Thtr 240 **Services** Air con **Parking** 240 **Notes** ⊗ Civ Wed 240

Walton Hotel

PUMA HOTELS COLLECTION

Ⓤ

☎ 01789 842424
Walton CV35 9HU
e-mail: waltonhotel@pumahotels.co.uk

Currently the rating for this establishment is not confirmed. This may be due to a change of ownership or because it has only recently joined the AA rating scheme. For further details please see the AA website: theAA.com

Rooms 130

WELLINGBOROUGH   Map 11 SP86
Northamptonshire

Ibis Wellingborough

ibis

BUDGET HOTEL

☎ 01933 228333
Enstone Court NN8 2DR
e-mail: H3164@accor.com
web: www.ibishotel.com
dir: At junct of A45 & A509 towards Kettering, SW outskirts of Wellingborough

Modern, budget hotel offering comfortable accommodation in bright and practical bedrooms. Breakfast is self-service and dinner is available in the restaurant. See also the Hotel Groups pages.

Rooms 78 (19 fmly) (22 GF) ↝ **Conf** Thtr 20

Premier Inn Wellingborough

BUDGET HOTEL

☎ 0871 527 9144
London Rd NN8 2DP
web: www.premierinn.com
dir: 0.5m from town centre on A5193, near Dennington Industrial Estate

High quality, budget accommodation ideal for both families and business travellers. Spacious, en suite bedrooms feature tea and coffee making facilities, and Freeview TV in most hotels. Internet access and Wi-fi are available for a small fee. The adjacent family restaurant features a wide and varied menu. See also the Hotel Groups pages.

Rooms 40

W

BEST WESTERN PLUS Swan Hotel

★★★ 86% ◉◉ HOTEL

☎ 01749 836300
Sadler St BA5 2RX
e-mail: info@swanhotelwells.co.uk
web: www.swanhotelwells.co.uk
dir: A39, A371, on entering Wells follow signs for Hotels & Deliveries. Hotel on right opposite cathedral

Situated in the shadow of Wells Cathedral, this privately-owned hotel enjoys a truly stunning location and extends a genuinely friendly welcome. Full of character and with a rich history, the hotel has been restored and extended to provide high levels of quality and comfort. Guests can choose between the larger, period bedrooms in the main building or the more contemporary coach house rooms. Dinner in the oak-panelled restaurant should not be missed.

Rooms 51 (3 fmly) (4 GF) ⌁ **D** £124-£157 (incl. bkfst)* **Facilities** FTV Wi-fi Gym Xmas New Year **Conf** Class 45 Board 40 Thtr 120 Del £135* **Parking** 25 **Notes** LB ⊗ Civ Wed 90

White Hart Hotel

THE INDEPENDENTS
HOTEL ASSOCIATION

★★ 78% HOTEL

☎ 01749 672056
Sadler St BA5 2RR
e-mail: info@whitehart-wells.co.uk
web: www.whitehart-wells.co.uk
dir: Sadler St at start of one-way system. Hotel opposite cathedral

A former coaching inn dating back to the 15th century, this hotel offers comfortable, modern accommodation. Some bedrooms are in an adjoining former stable block and some are at ground-floor level. Public areas include a guest lounge, a bar and the popular restaurant, Brufani's, where delicious steaks and gourmet burgers are in high demand.

Rooms 15 (3 fmly) (2 GF) **S** £90-£95; **D** £110-£115 (incl. bkfst)* **Facilities** Wi-fi Xmas New Year **Conf** Class 50 Board 35 Thtr 150 Del £120* **Parking** 17 **Notes** LB Civ Wed 100

Ancient Gate House Hotel

★★ 71% ◉ HOTEL

☎ 01749 672029
20 Sadler St BA5 2SE
e-mail: info@ancientgatehouse.co.uk
web: www.ancientgatehouse.co.uk
dir: 1st hotel on left on cathedral green

Guests are treated to good old-fashioned hospitality and a friendly informal atmosphere at this charming hotel which is full of character. Bedrooms, many with unrivalled cathedral views and four-poster beds, are smartly appointed and stylishly co-ordinated. The Rugantino Restaurant remains popular, offering a mix of traditional and contemporary Italian dishes.

Rooms 9 **S** £90-£95; **D** £110-£130 (incl. bkfst)* **Facilities** FTV Wi-fi Xmas New Year **Notes** LB Closed 27-29 Dec

Coxley Vineyard Hotel

★★ 67% HOTEL

☎ 01749 670285
Coxley BA5 1RQ
e-mail: max@orofino.freeserve.co.uk
dir: A39 from Wells signed Coxley. Village halfway between Wells & Glastonbury. Hotel at end of village

This privately owned and personally run hotel was built on the site of an old cider farm. It was later part of a commercial vineyard and some of the vines are still in evidence. It provides well equipped, modern bedrooms, and most are situated on the ground floor. There is a comfortable bar and a spacious restaurant with an impressive lantern ceiling. The hotel is a popular venue for conferences and other functions.

Rooms 9 (5 fmly) (8 GF) **Facilities** FTV Wi-fi ⬧ ⬧ Xmas **Conf** Class 50 Board 40 Thtr 90 **Parking** 50

The White Hart Hotel

★★★ 75% ◉ HOTEL

☎ 01438 715353
2 Prospect Place AL6 9EN
e-mail: bookings@thewhiteharthotel.net
web: www.thewhiteharthotel.net
dir: A1(M) junct 6. From N: take 3rd exit at rdbt, follow road under motorway bridge, keep left passing fire station, hotel on right at T-junct. From S: 1st exit, 1st right after BP petrol station, hotel 0.25m ahead

Enjoying a prominent position in the heart of the pretty village of Welwyn, this 17th-century coaching inn offers a very good choice of well-appointed bedrooms. The very popular bar serves a good choice of Cask Marque traditional real ales. The bar is used

for casual dining and the restaurant has a warm, welcoming atmosphere.

Rooms 13 (4 annexe) (4 GF) ⌁ **S** £75-£165; **D** £85-£175 (incl. bkfst)* **Facilities** STV FTV Wi-fi ⬧ Discounts available at local gym, spa & golf course Xmas New Year **Conf** Class 22 Board 18 Thtr 48 Del from £145 to £215* **Parking** 22 **Notes** ⊗ RS 25-26 Dec & 1 Jan

Tewin Bury Farm Hotel

★★★★ 77% ◉◉ HOTEL

☎ 01438 717793
Hertford Road (B1000) AL6 0JB
e-mail: reservations@tewinbury.co.uk
dir: From N: A1(M) junct 6, 1st exit signed A1000, at next rdbt 1st exit towards Digswell. 0.1m straight on at rdbt. 1m on B100. Hotel on left

Situated not far from the A1(M) and within easy reach of Stevenage and Knebworth House, this delightful country-house hotel is part of a thriving farm. Stylish, well-equipped bedrooms of varying sizes are perfectly suited for both leisure and business guests. An award-winning restaurant and meeting rooms are all part of this family-run establishment.

Rooms 29 (20 annexe) (6 fmly) (21 GF) ⌁ **S** £124-£144; **D** £139-£159 (incl. bkfst)* **Facilities** FTV Wi-fi ⬧ Fishing Cycling Xmas New Year **Conf** Class 300 Board 40 Thtr 500 Del from £170 to £225 **Services** Lift **Parking** 400 **Notes** LB ⊗ Civ Wed 300

BEST WESTERN Homestead Court Hotel

★★★ 77% HOTEL

☎ 01707 324336
Homestead Ln AL7 4LX
e-mail: enquiries@homesteadcourt.co.uk
web: www.bwhomesteadcourt.co.uk
dir: Exit A1000, left at lights at Bushall Hotel. Right at rdbt into Howlands, 2nd left at Hollybush public house into Hollybush Lane. 2nd right at War Memorial into Homestead Lane

This family run hotel enjoys a quiet location and is a short drive from the centre of Welwyn Garden City and the major road network. Bedrooms are all attractively presented and very well equipped. Free Wi-fi is available throughout the hotel and there is an extensive choice on the restaurant menu. Ample secure parking is provided and the cosy lounge is a popular casual dining venue.

W

Rooms 74 (8 annexe) (6 fmly) (2 GF) (2 smoking)
Facilities STV Wi-fi ↕ **Conf** Class 60 Board 60
Thtr 200 **Services** Lift **Parking** 70 **Notes** ⊗
Civ Wed 110

Premier Inn Welwyn Garden City

BUDGET HOTEL

☎ 0871 527 9146
Stanborough Rd AL8 6DQ
web: www.premierinn.com
dir: A1(M) junct 4, A6129

High quality, budget accommodation ideal for both
families and business travellers. Spacious, en suite
bedrooms feature tea and coffee making facilities,
and Freeview TV in most hotels. Internet access and
Wi-fi are available for a small fee. The adjacent
family restaurant features a wide and varied menu.
See also the Hotel Groups pages.

Rooms 90

WEMBLEY
Greater London

Quality Hotel Wembley London & Conference Centre

★★★ 72% HOTEL PLAN 1 C5

☎ 020 8733 9000
Empire Way HA9 0NH
e-mail: sales@hotels-wembley.com
dir: M1 junct 6, A406, right onto A404. Right onto
Empire Way, after rdbt at lights. Hotel on right

Conveniently situated within walking distance of both
the Arena and conference centres this modern hotel
offers smart, comfortable, spacious bedrooms; many
are air conditioned. All rooms offer an excellent range
of amenities. Air-conditioned public areas include a
large restaurant serving a wide range of
contemporary dishes.

Rooms 165 (70 fmly) (3 GF) (48 smoking)
S £60-£295; **D** £65-£315 (incl. bkfst)* **Facilities** STV
FTV Wi-fi ↕ **Conf** Class 90 Board 90 Thtr 150
Del from £125 to £135* **Services** Lift Air con
Parking 65 **Notes** ⊗

Ibis London Wembley

BUDGET HOTEL PLAN 1 C4

☎ 020 8453 5100
Southway HA9 6BA
e-mail: H3141@accor.com
web: www.ibishotel.com
dir: From Hanger Lane on A40, take A406 N, exit at
Wembley. A404 to lights junct with Wembley Hill Rd,
right, 1st right into Southway. Hotel 75mtrs on left

Modern, budget hotel offering comfortable
accommodation in bright and practical bedrooms.
Breakfast is self-service and dinner is available in
the restaurant. See also the Hotel Groups pages.

Rooms 210 (44 fmly)

Premier Inn London Wembley Stadium

BUDGET HOTEL PLAN 1 C5

☎ 0871 527 8682
151 Wembley Park Dr HA9 8HQ
web: www.premierinn.com
dir: A406 (North Circular) take A404 towards
Wembley. 2m right into Wembley Hill Rd, keep right
into Empire Way (B4565), pass Wembley Arena on
right, keep right around petrol station. Hotel 200yds
on left

High quality, budget accommodation ideal for both
families and business travellers. Spacious, en suite
bedrooms feature tea and coffee making facilities,
and Freeview TV in most hotels. Internet access and
Wi-fi are available for a small fee. The adjacent
family restaurant features a wide and varied menu.
See also the Hotel Groups pages.

Rooms 154

WEST AUCKLAND   Map 19 NZ12
Co Durham

The Manor House Hotel

★★★ 78% HOTEL

☎ 01388 834834
The Green DL14 9HW
e-mail: enquiries@manorhousehotelcountydurham.
co.uk
web: www.manorhousehotelcountydurham.co.uk
dir: A1(M) junct 58, A68 to West Auckland. At T-junct
left, hotel 150yds on right

This historic manor house, dating back to the 14th
century, is full of character. Welcoming log fires await
guests on cooler evenings. Comfortable bedrooms are
individual in style, tastefully furnished and well
equipped. The brasserie and Juniper's restaurant both
offer an interesting selection of freshly prepared
dishes. Well-equipped leisure facilities are available.

Rooms 35 (11 annexe) (6 fmly) (3 GF) ✎
Facilities FTV Wi-fi ☯ Gym Steam room Sauna Xmas
New Year Child facilities **Conf** Class 80 Board 50
Thtr 100 Del from £100 to £150 **Parking** 150
Notes Civ Wed 120

WEST BAY

See Bridport

WEST BROMWICH   Map 10 SP09
West Midlands

Park Inn by Radisson Birmingham West

★★★ 78% HOTEL

☎ 0121 609 9988 & 609 9931
Birmingham Rd B70 6RS
e-mail: info.birminghamwest@rezidorparkinn.com
dir: Birmingham Rd towards town centre, 1st right
into Beechs Rd, 2nd right into Europa Ave. Hotel on
right

Convenient for the M5, M42 and M6, this large,
purpose-built hotel provides versatile and well-
equipped contemporary accommodation. Facilities
include a spacious restaurant, comfortable lounge
areas, a bar and secure parking, as well as meeting
rooms and function suites. There is also a modern
leisure complex.

Rooms 168 (16 fmly) (33 GF) (9 smoking) ✎
S £49-£120; **D** £49-£120* **Facilities** STV FTV Wi-fi ↕
☯ supervised Gym Beauty treatment room Sauna
Dance studio **Conf** Class 80 Board 60 Thtr 180
Del from £99 to £140 **Services** Lift Air con
Parking 300

Premier Inn West Bromwich

BUDGET HOTEL

☎ 0871 527 9148
New Gas St B70 0NP
web: www.premierinn.com
dir: M5 junct 1, A41 (Expressway) towards
Wolverhampton. At 3rd rdbt, hotel on right

High quality, budget accommodation ideal for both
families and business travellers. Spacious, en suite
bedrooms feature tea and coffee making facilities,
and Freeview TV in most hotels. Internet access and
Wi-fi are available for a small fee. The adjacent
family restaurant features a wide and varied menu.
See also the Hotel Groups pages.

Rooms 40

W

WEST BROMICH *continued*

Premier Inn West Bromwich Central

BUDGET HOTEL

☎ 0871 527 9150
144 High St B70 6JJ
web: www.premierinn.com
dir: M5 junct 1 towards town centre, hotel 2m

Rooms 85

WEST DRAYTON

Hotels are listed under Heathrow Airport

WEST THURROCK   Map 6 TQ57
Essex

Ibis London Thurrock

BUDGET HOTEL

☎ 01708 686000
Weston Av RM20 3JQ
e-mail: H2176@accor.com
web: www.ibishotel.com
dir: M25 junct 31 to West Thurrock Services, right at 1st & 2nd rdbts, left at 3rd rdbt. Hotel on right in 500yds

Modern, budget hotel offering comfortable accommodation in bright and practical bedrooms. Breakfast is self-service and dinner is available in the restaurant. See also the Hotel Groups pages.

Rooms 102 (18 GF) 🐾

Premier Inn Thurrock East

BUDGET HOTEL

☎ 0871 527 9092
Fleming Rd, Unicorn Estate, Chafford Hundred RM16 6YJ
web: www.premierinn.com
dir: From A13 follow Lakeside Shopping Centre signs. Right at 1st rdbt, straight on at next rdbt, then 1st slip road. Left at next rdbt

High quality, budget accommodation ideal for both families and business travellers. Spacious, en suite bedrooms feature tea and coffee making facilities, and Freeview TV in most hotels. Internet access and Wi-fi are available for a small fee. The adjacent family restaurant features a wide and varied menu. See also the Hotel Groups pages.

Rooms 62

Premier Inn Thurrock West

BUDGET HOTEL

☎ 0871 527 9094
Stonehouse Ln RM19 1NS
web: www.premierinn.com
dir: From N: M25 junct 31, A1090 to Purfleet. (NB do not cross Dartford Bridge or follow signs for Lakeside). From S: M25 junct 31. On approach to Dartford Tunnel, bear far left signed Dagenham. After tunnel, hotel at top of slip road

Rooms 161

WEST WITTON   Map 19 SE08
North Yorkshire

INSPECTORS' CHOICE

The Wensleydale Heifer

◉ RESTAURANT WITH ROOMS

☎ 01969 622322
Main St DL8 4LS
e-mail: info@wensleydaleheifer.co.uk
web: www.wensleydaleheifer.co.uk
dir: A1 to Leeming Bar junct, A684 towards Bedale for approx 10m to Leyburn, then towards Hawes 3.5m to West Witton

Describing itself as 'boutique style', this 17th-century former coaching inn is very much in the 21st century. The bedrooms, with Egyptian cotton linen and Molton Brown toiletries as standard, are each designed with a unique and interesting theme - for example, Black Sheep, Night at the Movies, True Romantics and Shooters, and for chocolate lovers there's a bedroom where they can eat as much chocolate as they like! The food is very much the focus here in both the informal fish bar and the contemporary style restaurant. The kitchen prides itself on sourcing the freshest fish and locally reared meats.

Rooms 13 (4 annexe) (2 fmly)

WESTLETON   Map 13 TM46
Suffolk

The Westleton Crown

★★★ 79% ◉◉ HOTEL

☎ 01728 648777
The Street IP17 3AD
e-mail: info@westletoncrown.co.uk
web: www.westletoncrown.co.uk
dir: A12 N, turn right for Westleton just after Yoxford. Hotel opposite on entering Westleton

The Westleton Crown is a charming coaching inn situated in a peaceful village location just a few

minutes from the A12. Public rooms include a smart, award-winning restaurant, comfortable lounge, and busy bar with exposed beams and open fireplaces. The stylish bedrooms are tastefully decorated and equipped with many thoughtful little extras.

Rooms 34 (22 annexe) (5 fmly) (13 GF) 🐾
S £90-£100; D £95-£215 (incl. bkfst)* **Facilities** FTV Wi-fi ⌇ Xmas New Year **Conf** Class 40 Board 30 Thtr 60 **Parking** 34 **Notes** Civ Wed 90

WESTON-SUPER-MARE   Map 4 ST36
Somerset

The Royal Hotel

★★★ 77% HOTEL

☎ 01934 423100
1 South Pde BS23 1JP
e-mail: reservations@royalhotelweston.com
web: www.royalhotelweston.com
dir: M5 junct 21, follow signs to seafront. Hotel next to Winter Gardens Pavillion

The Royal, which opened in 1810, was the first hotel in Weston and occupies a prime seafront position. It is a grand building and many of the bedrooms, including some with sea views, are spacious and comfortable; family apartments are also available. Public areas include a choice of bars and a restaurant which offers a range of dishes to meet all tastes. Entertainment is provided during the season.

Rooms 44 (3 annexe) (8 fmly) 🐾 S £73-£93; D £105-£169 (incl. bkfst)* **Facilities** FTV Wi-fi HL Beauty treatment room Hair salon ♬ **Conf** Class 100 Board 60 Thtr 200 Del from £115* **Services** Lift **Parking** 152 **Notes** LB ⊗ Civ Wed 200

See advert on opposite page

W

Save on hotels. Book at **theAA.com/hotel**

WES 457 ENGLAND

Welcome
to Excellence

The Royal Hotel

Weston–super–Mare

Telephone: 01934 423100

This charismatic historic & luxuriously appointed Georgian Hotel is centrally located in a unique location enjoying both a wonderful sea view and close proximity to the promenade, Grand Pier, Shopping Centre & high Street.

- 3 Star Seafront Hotel
- Shopping Centre 200 Metres
- Themed Luxury Rooms
- Ala Carte Restaurant
- Late Licence Bar & Bar Menu
- Entertainment Friday Nights
- Live Jazz Band Sunday Lunchtime
- Special Offers & Breaks
- Beauty Room & Hair Salon
- Electric Car Charging Station

VisitBritain Gold Highly Commended.

BREAKFAST AWARD

Green Tourism SILVER

EV

www.royalhotelweston.com

Download our Free App!

W

WESTON-SUPER-MARE *continued*

Beachlands Hotel

★★★ 71% HOTEL

☎ 01934 621401

17 Uphill Road North BS23 4NG

e-mail: info@beachlandshotel.com

web: www.beachlandshotel.com

dir: M5 junct 21, follow signs for hospital. At hospital rdbt follow signs for beach, hotel 300yds before beach

This popular hotel is very close to the 18-hole links course and a short walk from the seafront. Elegant public areas include a bar, a choice of lounges and a bright dining room. Bedrooms vary slightly in size, but all are well equipped for both the business and leisure guest. There is the added bonus of a 10-metre indoor pool and a sauna.

Rooms 21 (6 fmly) (11 GF) ⬧ **S** £65-£95; **D** £99-£140 (incl. bkfst)* **Facilities** FTV Wi-fi ⬧ Sauna Beauty treatment room New Year **Conf** Class 20 Board 30 Thtr 60 Del from £92.25 to £108.25 **Parking** 28 **Notes** LB ⬧ Closed 23-29 Dec Civ Wed 110

Lauriston Hotel

★★★ 70% HOTEL

☎ 01934 620758

6-12 Knightstone Rd BS23 2AN

e-mail: lauriston.hotel@actionforblindpeople.org.uk

dir: 1st right after Winter Gardens, hotel entrance opposite Cabot Court Hotel

A friendly welcome is assured at this pleasant hotel, located right on the seafront, just a few minutes' stroll from the pier. The hotel welcomes everyone but caters especially for the visually impaired, their families, friends and guide dogs. There are comfortable and well-appointed bedrooms; special facilities for the guide dogs are, of course, available.

Rooms 37 (2 fmly) (8 GF) ⬧ **Facilities** FTV Wi-fi HL ♫ Xmas New Year **Conf** Class 12 Board 10 Thtr 18 **Services** Lift **Parking** 16

Anchor Head Hotel

★★ 67% HOTEL

☎ 01934 620880

19 Claremont Crescent, Birnbeck Rd BS23 2EE

e-mail: anchor.weston@alfatravel.co.uk

web: www.leisureplex.co.uk

dir: M5 junct 21, A370 to seafront, right, past Grand Pier towards Brimbeck Pier. Hotel at end of terrace on left

Enjoying a very pleasant location with views across the bay, the Anchor Head offers a varied choice of comfortable lounges and a relaxing outdoor patio area. Bedrooms and bathrooms are traditionally furnished and include several ground-floor rooms. Dinner and breakfast are served in the spacious dining room that also benefits from sea views.

Rooms 52 (1 fmly) (5 GF) **Facilities** FTV ♫ Xmas New Year **Services** Lift **Notes** ⬧ Closed Dec-Feb (ex Xmas) RS Mar & Nov

Premier Inn Weston-Super-Mare East

BUDGET HOTEL

☎ 0871 527 9156

Hutton Moor Rd BS22 8LY

web: www.premierinn.com

dir: M5 junct 21, A370 towards Weston-Super-Mare. After 3rd rbt right at lights into Hutton Moor Leisure Centre. Left, into car park

High quality, budget accommodation ideal for both families and business travellers. Spacious, en suite bedrooms feature tea and coffee making facilities, and Freeview TV in most hotels. Internet access and Wi-fi are available for a small fee. The adjacent family restaurant features a wide and varied menu. See also the Hotel Groups pages.

Rooms 88

WESTON-UNDER-REDCASTLE Map 15 SJ52
Shropshire

Hawkstone Park Hotel

★★★ 77% HOTEL

☎ 01948 841700

SY4 5UY

e-mail: enquiries@hawkstone.co.uk

dir: 1m E of A49 between Shrewsbury & Whitchurch

Built in the 1700s, this splendid former coaching inn is set in 400 acres of lovely scenery which includes two championship golf courses and the much remarked upon 18th-century follies. The bedrooms are comfortably appointed and well equipped for both leisure and business guests, and the public areas include conference facilities and a pleasant dining room.

Rooms 67 (19 annexe) (2 fmly) (26 GF) ⬧ **S** £42-£92; **D** £72-£122* **Facilities** STV Wi-fi ⬧ HL ♪ 42 Putt green ♪ Xmas New Year **Conf** Class 90 Board 50 Thtr 200 Del from £99 to £139* **Parking** 200 **Notes** LB Civ Wed 200

WETHERBY Map 16 SE44
West Yorkshire

INSPECTORS' CHOICE

Wood Hall Hotel & Spa

★★★★ ◉◉ HOTEL

☎ 01937 587271

Trip Ln, Linton LS22 4JA

e-mail: woodhall@handpicked.co.uk

web: www.handpickedhotels.co.uk/woodhall

dir: From Wetherby take Harrogate road N (A661) for 0.5m, left to Sicklinghall & Linton. Cross bridge, left to Linton & Wood Hall. Turn right opposite Windmill Inn, 1.25m to hotel

A long sweeping drive leads to this delightful Georgian house situated in 100 acres of parkland. Spacious bedrooms are appointed to an impressive standard and feature comprehensive facilities, including large plasma-screen TVs. Public rooms reflect the same elegance and include a smart drawing room and dining room, both with fantastic views.

Rooms 44 (30 annexe) (5 fmly) ⬧ **Facilities** Spa STV FTV Wi-fi ⬧ HL ⬧ Fishing Gym Beauty spa Xmas New Year **Conf** Class 70 Board 40 Thtr 100 Del from £130 to £180* **Services** Lift **Parking** 200 **Notes** ⬧ Civ Wed 100

The Bridge Hotel & Spa

★★★★ 77% HOTEL

☎ 01937 580115

Walshford LS22 5HS

e-mail: info@bridgewetherby.co.uk

web: www.bridgewetherby.co.uk

dir: From N exit A1(M) at junct 47 (York) or S junct 46 (Wetherby Race Centre), 1st left Walshford, follow brown tourist signs

A very conveniently located hotel close to the A1 with spacious public areas and a good range of services make this an ideal venue for business or leisure. The stylish bedrooms are comfortable and well equipped. The Bridge offers a choice of bars and a large open-plan restaurant. Conference and banqueting suites are also available.

W

Save on hotels. Book at **theAA.com/hotel**

WES – WEY 459 ENGLAND

Rooms 30 (2 fmly) (10 GF) S £70-£100; D £95-£140 (incl. bkfst) **Facilities** Spa FTV Wi-fi ☇ Gym Xmas New Year **Conf** Class 50 Board 50 Thtr 200 **Parking** 150 **Notes** LB Civ Wed 150

Mercure Wetherby Hotel
★★★ HOTEL

☎ 0844 815 9067
Leeds Rd LS22 5HE
e-mail: info@mercurewetherby.co.uk
web: www.jupiterhotels.co.uk
dir: A1/A659, then follow A168. Hotel on rdbt

Currently the rating for this establishment is not confirmed. This may be due to a change of ownership or because it has only recently joined the AA rating scheme.

Rooms 103 **Conf** Class 50 Board 50 Thtr 150

Days Inn Wetherby
BUDGET HOTEL

☎ 01937 547557
Junction 46 A1(M), Kirk Deighton LS22 5GT
e-mail: reservations@daysinnwetherby.co.uk
dir: A1(M) junct 46 at Moto Service Area

This modern building offers accommodation in smart, spacious and well-equipped bedrooms, suitable for families and business travellers, and all with en suite bathrooms. Continental breakfast is available and other refreshments may be taken at the nearby family restaurant. See also the Hotel Groups pages.

Rooms 129 (33 fmly) (35 GF) ⚡ S £49-£89; D £49-£89 **Conf** Class 20 Board 20 Thtr 30

WEYBRIDGE Map 6 TQ06
Surrey

Brooklands Hotel
★★★★ 80% ◉ HOTEL

☎ 01932 335700
Brooklands Dr KT13 0SL
e-mail: info@brooklandshotelsurrey.com
dir: Telephone for detailed directions

Overlooking the historic motoring racing circuit, this hotel has stunning design that reflects the art deco style and that of the Mercedes Benz racetrack's heyday in the 1920 and 30s. The bedrooms are notably spacious and very comfortable with many contemporary facilities; all have floor-to-ceiling windows, and many come with balconies overlooking the racetrack. There is a wealth of public areas including leisure and meeting rooms as well as a spa. The contemporary 1907 Restaurant, Bar and Grill offers imaginative menus.

Rooms 120 (16 fmly) ⚡ **Facilities** Spa STV FTV Wi-fi ☇ Gym New Year **Conf** Class 86 Board 90 Thtr 174 **Services** Lift Air con **Parking** 120 **Notes** ⊗ Civ Wed 174

Oatlands Park Hotel
★★★★ 77% ◉ HOTEL

☎ 01932 847242
146 Oatlands Dr KT13 9HB
e-mail: info@oatlandsparkhotel.com
web: www.oatlandsparkhotel.com
dir: Through High Street to Monument Hill mini rdbt. Left into Oatlands Drive. Hotel 500yds on left

Once a palace for Henry VIII, this impressive building sits in extensive grounds encompassing tennis courts, a gym and a 9-hole golf course. The spacious lounge and bar create a wonderful first impression with tall marble pillars and plush comfortable seating. Most of the bedrooms are very spacious, and all are well equipped.

Rooms 144 (24 fmly) (30 GF) S £100-£190; D £120-£220 **Facilities** STV Wi-fi ☇ HL ⚴ 9 ⚑ Putt green ⚑ Gym Jogging course Fitness suite Xmas New Year **Conf** Class 150 Board 80 Thtr 300 Del from £165 to £210 **Services** Lift Air con **Parking** 180 **Notes** Civ Wed 220

BEST WESTERN Ship Hotel
★★★ 78% HOTEL

☎ 01932 848364
Monument Green KT13 8BQ
e-mail: reservations@desboroughhotels.com
dir: M25 junct 11, at 3rd rdbt left into High St. Hotel 300yds on left

This former coaching inn has retained much of its period charm and is now a spacious and comfortable hotel. Bedrooms, some overlooking a delightful courtyard, are spacious and cheerfully decorated. Public areas include a lounge and cocktail bar, restaurant and a popular pub. The high street location and private parking are a bonus.

Rooms 76 (2 fmly) ⚡ S £105-£135; D £120-£150 (incl. bkfst)* **Facilities** FTV Wi-fi ☇ Xmas New Year **Conf** Class 70 Board 60 Thtr 180 Del from £140* **Services** Lift **Parking** 65 **Notes** LB ⊗

WEYMOUTH Map 4 SY67
Dorset

Hotel Prince Regent
★★★ 73% HOTEL

☎ 01305 771313
139 The Esplanade DT4 7NR
e-mail: info@princeregentweymouth.co.uk
web: www.princeregentweymouth.co.uk
dir: From A354 follow seafront signs. Left at Jubilee Clock, 25mtrs on seafront

Dating back to 1855, this welcoming resort hotel boasts splendid views over Weymouth Bay from the majority of public rooms and front-facing bedrooms. It is conveniently close to the town centre and harbour, and is opposite the beach. The restaurant offers a choice of menus, and entertainment is regularly provided in the ballroom during the season.

Rooms 70 (12 fmly) (5 GF) ⚡ S £45-£89; D £65-£109 (incl. bkfst)* **Facilities** Wi-fi Xmas New Year **Conf** Class 150 Board 150 Thtr 180 Del from £95 to £105* **Services** Lift **Parking** 10 **Notes** LB ⊗ Civ Wed 200

BEST WESTERN Hotel Rembrandt
★★★ 72% HOTEL

☎ 01305 764000
12-18 Dorchester Rd DT4 7JU
e-mail: reception@hotelrembrandt.co.uk
web: www.hotelrembrandt.co.uk
dir: On A354 from Dorchester, turn left at Manor rdbt & proceed for 0.75m

Only a short distance from the seafront and the town centre, this hotel is ideal for visiting local attractions. Facilities include indoor leisure facilities, a bar and extensive meeting rooms. The restaurant offers an impressive carvery and carte menu, which proves popular with locals and residents alike.

Rooms 78 (27 fmly) (5 GF) ⚡ S £67.71-£112.50; D £89.14-£145 (incl. bkfst)* **Facilities** STV FTV Wi-fi ☇ ⚴ Gym Steam room Sauna Beautician Beauty treatment room **Conf** Class 100 Board 60 Thtr 200 Del from £105 to £125* **Services** Lift **Parking** 80 **Notes** LB ⊗ Civ Wed 100

W

WEYMOUTH *continued*

Hotel Rex

★★★ 71% HOTEL

☎ 01305 760400
29 The Esplanade DT4 8DN
e-mail: rex@kingshotels.co.uk
web: www.kingshotels.co.uk
dir: On seafront opposite Alexandra Gardens

Originally built as the summer residence for the Duke of Clarence, this hotel benefits from a seafront location with stunning views across Weymouth Bay. Bedrooms, including several sea-facing rooms, are well equipped. A wide range of imaginative dishes is served in the popular and attractive restaurant.

Rooms 31 (2 fmly) ↣ **S** £50-£88.50; **D** £80-£153 (incl. bkfst)* **Facilities** FTV Wi-fi New Year **Conf** Class 30 Board 25 Thtr 40 **Services** Lift **Parking** 10 **Notes** LB ⊗ Closed Xmas

Crown Hotel

★★ 75% HOTEL

☎ 01305 760800
51-53 St Thomas St DT4 8EQ
e-mail: crown@kingshotels.co.uk
web: www.kingshotels.co.uk
dir: From Dorchester, A354 to Weymouth. Follow Back Water on left & cross 2nd bridge

This popular hotel is conveniently located adjacent to the old harbour and is ideal for shopping, local attractions and transportation links, including the ferry. Public areas include an extensive bar, ballroom and comfortable residents' lounge on the first floor. Themed events, such as mock cruises, are a speciality.

Rooms 86 (15 fmly) **Facilities** 🎵 New Year **Services** Lift **Parking** 14 **Notes** ⊗ Closed Xmas

Hotel Central

★★ 71% HOTEL

☎ 01305 760700
17-19 Maiden St DT4 8BB
e-mail: central@kingshotels.co.uk
dir: In town centre

Well located for the town, the beach and the ferries to the Channel Islands, and with off-road parking, this privately owned hotel has friendly staff. The bedrooms are comfortable, and three are designed for guests with limited mobility. The pleasant dining room offers a varied menu. Live entertainment is provided during the season.

Rooms 28 (5 fmly) (4 GF) (9 smoking) **Facilities** 🎵 **Services** Lift **Parking** 16 **Notes** ⊗ Closed mid Dec-1 Mar

Fairhaven Hotel

★★ 69% HOTEL

☎ 01305 760200
37 The Esplanade DT4 8DH
e-mail: fairhaven@kingshotels.co.uk
dir: On right just before Alexandra Gardens

A popular sea-facing, family-run hotel which has a friendly young team of staff. Bedrooms are comfortable and well maintained, and the hotel boasts two bars, one with panoramic views of the bay. Entertainment is provided most nights during the season.

Rooms 82 (23 fmly) (1 GF) (60 smoking) **Facilities** 🎵 **Services** Lift **Parking** 16 **Notes** ⊗ Closed Nov-1 Mar

Premier Inn Weymouth

BUDGET HOTEL

☎ 0871 527 9158
Lodmoor Country Park, Preston Beach Rd, Green Hill DT4 7SX
web: www.premierinn.com
dir: Follow signs to Weymouth then brown route signs to Lodmoor Country Park (height restriction 9' 4" at barrier). Hotel adjacent to Lodmoor Brewers Fayre (NB for Sat Nav use DT4 7SL)

High quality, budget accommodation ideal for both families and business travellers. Spacious, en suite bedrooms feature tea and coffee making facilities, and Freeview TV in most hotels. Internet access and Wi-fi are available for a small fee. The adjacent family restaurant features a wide and varied menu. See also the Hotel Groups pages.

Rooms 64

| WHITBY | Map 19 NZ81 |
| North Yorkshire | |

Dunsley Hall

★★★ 82% ⊛ COUNTRY HOUSE HOTEL

☎ 01947 893437
Dunsley YO21 3TL
e-mail: reception@dunsleyhall.com
web: www.dunsleyhall.com
dir: 3m N of Whitby, signed off A171

Friendly service is found at this fine country mansion set in a quiet hamlet with coastal views north of Whitby. The house has Gothic overtones and boasts fine woodwork and panelling, particularly in the magnificent lounge. Two lovely dining rooms offer imaginative dishes and there is also a cosy bar.

Rooms 26 (2 fmly) (10 GF) ↣ **S** £75-£105; **D** £99-£208 (incl. bkfst)* **Facilities** FTV Wi-fi 🏌 Putt green Xmas New Year **Conf** Class 50 Board 40 Thtr 95 Del from £180* **Parking** 30 **Notes** LB ⊗ Civ Wed 100

The Cliffemount Hotel

★★★ 80% ⊛⊛ SMALL HOTEL

☎ 01947 840103
Bank Top Ln, Runswick Bay TS13 5HU
e-mail: info@cliffemounthotel.co.uk
dir: Exit A174, 8m N of Whitby, 1m to end

Overlooking Runswick Bay this property offers a relaxed and romantic atmosphere with open fires and individual, carefully designed bedrooms; some have a private balcony overlooking the bay. Dining is recommended; the food is modern British in style and uses locally sourced fresh seafood, and game from nearby estates.

Rooms 20 (4 fmly) (5 GF) **S** £75-£180; **D** £115-£180 (incl. bkfst)* **Facilities** FTV Wi-fi Xmas New Year **Conf** Class 25 Board 16 Thtr 25 Del from £125 to £230* **Parking** 25 **Notes** LB

Saxonville Hotel

★★★ 77% HOTEL

☎ 01947 602631
Ladysmith Av, Argyle Rd YO21 3HX
e-mail: newtons@saxonville.co.uk
web: www.saxonville.co.uk
dir: A174 to North Promenade. Turn inland at large four-towered building visible on West Cliff, into Argyle Rd, then 1st right

The friendly service is noteworthy at this long-established holiday hotel. Well maintained throughout, it offers comfortable bedrooms and inviting public areas that include a well-proportioned restaurant where quality dinners are served.

Rooms 23 (2 fmly) (1 GF) **S** £45-£65; **D** £90-£150 (incl. bkfst)* **Facilities** Wi-fi **Conf** Class 40 Board 40 Thtr 100 Del from £57.50 to £102.50* **Parking** 20 **Notes** ⊗ Closed Dec-Jan RS Feb-Mar

Estbek House

⊛⊛ RESTAURANT WITH ROOMS

☎ 01947 893424
East Row, Sandsend YO21 3SU
e-mail: info@estbekhouse.co.uk
dir: From Whitby take A174. In Sandsend, left into East Row

A speciality seafood restaurant on the first floor is the focus of this listed building in a small coastal village north west of Whitby. The seasonal menu is based on local fresh local ingredients, and is overseen by James the chef, who has guided his team to 2 AA

Rosette recognition. There is also a small bar and breakfast room, and four individually appointed bedrooms offering luxury and comfort.

Rooms 4

WHITCHURCH
Shropshire   Map 15 SJ54

Macdonald Hill Valley Spa, Hotel & Golf

★★★★ 78% HOTEL

☎ 0844 879 9049
Tarporley Rd SY13 4JH
e-mail:
general.hillvalley@macdonald-hotels.co.uk
web: www.macdonald-hotels.co.uk/hillvalley
dir: 2nd exit off A41 towards Whitchurch

Located in rural surroundings on the town's outskirts, this modern hotel is surrounded by two golf courses, and a very well equipped leisure spa is also available. Spacious bedrooms, with country views, are furnished in minimalist style and public areas include a choice of bar lounges and extensive conference facilities. Macdonald Hotels is the AA Hotel Group of the Year 2013-14.

Rooms 80 (15 fmly) (27 GF) ☛ **Facilities** Spa STV FTV Wi-fi ⬚ ⓣ ⚡ 36 Putt green Gym Mud Rasul Xmas New Year **Conf** Class 150 Board 150 Thtr 300 **Services** Lift **Parking** 300 **Notes** Civ Wed 300

WHITEHAVEN
Cumbria   Map 18 NX91

Premier Inn Whitehaven

BUDGET HOTEL

☎ 0871 527 9160
Howgate CA28 6PL
web: www.premierinn.com
dir: On A595 just outside Whitehaven

High quality, budget accommodation ideal for both families and business travellers. Spacious, en suite bedrooms feature tea and coffee making facilities, and Freeview TV in most hotels. Internet access and Wi-fi are available for a small fee. The adjacent family restaurant features a wide and varied menu. See also the Hotel Groups pages.

Rooms 47

WHITLEY BAY
Tyne & Wear   Map 21 NZ37

The Royal Hotel

★★★ 73% HOTEL

☎ 0191 252 4777
13-17 East Pde NE26 1AP
e-mail: info@royalhotelwhitleybay.co.uk
web: www.royalhotelwhitleybay.co.uk
dir: From Whitley Bay Metro station left onto Station Square, bear right onto Victoria Terrace, right onto North Parade then right & right again, then left

Overlooking the sea front, this recently refurbished hotel offers warm hospitality from the friendly team. Bedrooms are well appointed and dinner is served in the Davanti Italian restaurant. Limited off-road car parking is available to the front of the hotel.

Rooms 37 ☛ **Facilities** FTV Wi-fi ⬚ **Parking** 10 **Notes** ⊗ Closed 23 Dec-2 Jan

WHITSTABLE
Kent   Map 7 TR16

Premier Inn Whitstable

BUDGET HOTEL

☎ 0871 527 9162
Thanet Way CT5 3DB
web: www.premierinn.com
dir: 2m W of town centre on B2205

High quality, budget accommodation ideal for both families and business travellers. Spacious, en suite bedrooms feature tea and coffee making facilities, and Freeview TV in most hotels. Internet access and Wi-fi are available for a small fee. The adjacent family restaurant features a wide and varied menu. See also the Hotel Groups pages.

Rooms 41

WHITTLEBURY
Northamptonshire   Map 11 SP64

Whittlebury Hall

★★★★ 79% ⚜⚜ HOTEL

☎ 01327 857857
NN12 8QH
e-mail: reservations@whittleburyhall.co.uk
web: www.whittleburyhall.co.uk
dir: A43, A413 towards Buckingham, through Whittlebury, turn for hotel on right (signed)

A purpose-built, Georgian-style country house hotel with excellent spa and leisure facilities and pedestrian access to the Silverstone circuit. Grand public areas include F1 car racing memorabilia and the accommodation includes some lavishly appointed suites. Food is a strength, with a choice of various

dining options. Particularly noteworthy are the afternoon teas in the spacious, comfortable lounge and the fine dining in Murray's Restaurant.

Rooms 212 (4 fmly) (13 smoking) **Facilities** Spa FTV Wi-fi ⬚ ⓣ Gym Beauty treatments Relaxation room Hair studio Heat & Ice experience Leisure club ♫ Xmas New Year **Conf** Class 175 Board 40 Thtr 500 **Services** Lift **Parking** 450 **Notes** ⊗

WIDNES
Cheshire   Map 15 SJ58

Premier Inn Widnes

BUDGET HOTEL

☎ 0871 527 9306
Venture Fields WA8 0GY
web: www.premierinn.com
dir: M62 junct 7. At Rainhill Stoops rdbt 2nd exit onto A557 (Widnes). Left into Earle Rd (Widnes Waterfront), into Venture Field Leisure Entertainment complex. Hotel on left

High quality, budget accommodation ideal for both families and business travellers. Spacious, en suite bedrooms feature tea and coffee making facilities, and Freeview TV in most hotels. Internet access and Wi-fi are available for a small fee. The adjacent family restaurant features a wide and varied menu. See also the Hotel Groups pages.

Rooms 60

WIGAN
Greater Manchester   Map 15 SD50

Wrightington Hotel & Country Club

CLASSIC
BRITISH HOTELS

★★★★ 75% ⚜ HOTEL

☎ 01257 425803
Moss Ln, Wrightington WN6 9PB
e-mail: info@wrightingtonhotel.co.uk
dir: M6 junct 27, 0.25m W, hotel on right after church

Situated in open countryside close to the M6, this privately owned hotel offers friendly hospitality. Accommodation is well equipped and spacious, and public areas include an extensive leisure complex complete with hair salon, boutique and sports injury lab. Blazers Restaurant, two bars and air-conditioned banqueting facilities appeal to a broad market.

Rooms 73 (6 fmly) (36 GF) **Facilities** Spa STV FTV Wi-fi ⓣ Gym Squash Hairdressing salon Sports injury clinic New Year **Conf** Class 120 Board 40 Thtr 200 **Services** Lift **Parking** 240 **Notes** Civ Wed 100

W

WIGAN *continued*

Macdonald Kilhey Court Hotel

★★★★ 73% @ HOTEL

☎ 0844 879 9045 & 01257 472100
Chorley Rd, Standish WN1 2XN
e-mail: general.kilheycourt@macdonald-hotels.co.uk
web: www.macdonaldhotels.co.uk/kilheycourt
dir: M6 junct 27, A5209 Standish, over at lights, past church on right, left at rdbt (1st exit), hotel on right 350yds. M61 junct 6, signed Wigan & Haigh Hall. 3m & right at rdbt (2nd exit). Hotel 0.5m on right

Macdonald Kilhey Court Hotel is peacefully located in its own grounds yet is convenient for the motorway network. Bedrooms are divided between the Victorian house and the modern extension, while public areas have original features, and the split-level restaurant has views over the Worthington Lakes. There are eleven meeting rooms, ideal for exhibitions, and extensive landscaped grounds available for weddings. Facilities also include an indoor pool and spa. Macdonald Hotels is the AA Hotel Group of the Year 2013-14.

Rooms 62 (18 fmly) (8 GF) **Facilities** Spa STV FTV Wi-fi ↻ HL ⓣ Gym Aerobics classes Beauty treatments Xmas New Year **Conf** Class 180 Board 60 Thtr 400 **Services** Lift **Parking** 200 **Notes** Civ Wed 300

Mercure Wigan Oak Hotel

★★★ 77% HOTEL

☎ 01942 826888
Orchard St WN1 3SS
e-mail: enquiries@hotels-wigan.com
web: www.hotels-wigan.com
dir: From S: M6 junct 25, A49 signed Wigan then B5238, right after Grand Arcade Shopping. From N: M6 junct 27, A5209, right onto A49, left at lights, hotel opposite Tesco

This modern and stylish hotel is situated in the centre of Wigan; easily accessed from the M6 and M61 and well positioned for public transport. The bedrooms are both comfortable and well equipped and public rooms include the restaurant, conservatory and popular bar. There is free Wi-fi throughout, and conference and events facilities are available. Ample parking is a plus in this central location.

Rooms 88 (7 fmly) (16 GF) ⚑ **S** £55-£95; **D** £55-£95*
Facilities FTV Wi-fi ↻ New Year **Conf** Class 80 Board 40 Thtr 160 Del from £85 to £125*
Services Lift **Parking** 100 **Notes** LB Civ Wed 50

Premier Inn Haydock Park (Wigan South)

BUDGET HOTEL

☎ 0871 527 8502
53 Warrington Rd, Ashton-in-Makerfield WN4 9PJ
web: www.premierinn.com
dir: Just off M6 junct 23, A49 towards Wigan

High quality, budget accommodation ideal for both families and business travellers. Spacious, en suite bedrooms feature tea and coffee making facilities, and Freeview TV in most hotels. Internet access and Wi-fi are available for a small fee. The adjacent family restaurant features a wide and varied menu. See also the Hotel Groups pages.

Rooms 30

Premier Inn Wigan M6 Jct 25

BUDGET HOTEL

☎ 0871 527 9164
Warrington Rd, Marus Bridge WN3 6XB
web: www.premierinn.com
dir: M6 junct 25 (N'bound). At rdbt left, hotel on left

Rooms 40

Premier Inn Wigan West

BUDGET HOTEL

☎ 0871 527 9168
Orrell Rd, Orrell WN5 8HQ
web: www.premierinn.com
dir: M6 junct 26 follow signs for Upholland & Orrell. At 1st lights turn left. Hotel on right behind Priory Wood Beefeater

Rooms 40

The Beeches

RESTAURANT WITH ROOMS

☎ 01257 426432 & 421316
School Ln, Standish WN6 0TD
e-mail: mail@beecheshotel.co.uk
dir: M6 junct 27, A5209 into Standish & into School Ln

Located just a mile away from junction 27 of the M6, this privately owned, spacious Victorian property is set in pleasant gardens. Bedrooms are well equipped and offer modern facilities. A wide choice of food is offered in the brasserie. There are many seasonal and entertainment events throughout the year with tribute acts very popular. There is a self-contained function suite making this venue ideal for conferences, functions and special occasions. The beautifully presented Piano Lounge also offers live entertainment on Friday and Saturday evenings.

Rooms 10 (4 fmly)

WILLERBY   **Map 17 TA03**
East Riding of Yorkshire

BEST WESTERN Willerby Manor Hotel

★★★ 83% @ HOTEL

☎ 01482 652616
Well Ln HU10 6ER
e-mail: willerbymanor@bestwestern.co.uk
web: www.willerbymanor.co.uk
dir: Exit A63, signed Humber Bridge. Right at rdbt by Waitrose. At next rdbt hotel signed

Set in a quiet residential area, amid well-tended gardens, this hotel was originally a private mansion; it has now been thoughtfully extended to provide very comfortable bedrooms, equipped with many useful extras. There are extensive leisure facilities and a wide choice of meals offered in the contemporary Figs Brasserie which has an impressive heated outdoor area.

Rooms 63 (6 fmly) (20 GF) (1 smoking) ⚑
S £67-£100; **D** £107-£127 (incl. bkfst)* **Facilities** STV FTV Wi-fi HL ⓣ supervised ⚑ Gym Steam room Beauty treatment room Aerobic classes New Year **Conf** Class 200 Board 100 Thtr 500 Del £165*
Parking 300 **Notes** LB Closed 24-26 Dec Civ Wed 150

W

Save on hotels. Book at **theAA.com/hotel**

WIG – WIN 463 ENGLAND

Mercure Hull Grange Park Hotel

★★★ HOTEL

☎ 0844 815 9037
Grange Park Ln HU10 6EA
e-mail: info@mercurehull.co.uk
web: www.jupiterhotels.co.uk
dir: A164 to Beverley signed Willerby Shopping Park. Left at rdbt into Grange Park Lane, hotel at end

Currently the rating for this establishment is not confirmed. This may be due to a change of ownership or because it has only recently joined the AA rating scheme.

Rooms 100 **Conf** Class 250 Board 80 Thtr 550

WILMINGTON   Map 6 TQ50
East Sussex

Crossways

◉◉ RESTAURANT WITH ROOMS

☎ 01323 482455
Lewes Rd BN26 5SG
e-mail: stay@crosswayshotel.co.uk
web: www.crosswayshotel.co.uk
dir: On A27 between Lewes & Polegate, 2m E of Alfriston rdbt

Amidst stunning gardens and attractively tended grounds sits this well-established, popular restaurant. The well-presented bedrooms are tastefully decorated and provide an abundance of thoughtful amenities including free Wi-fi. Guest comfort is paramount and the naturally warm hospitality ensures guests often return.

Rooms 7

WILMSLOW

See Manchester Airport

WIMBORNE MINSTER   Map 5 SZ06
Dorset

Les Bouviers Restaurant with Rooms

◉◉ RESTAURANT WITH ROOMS

☎ 01202 889555
Arrowsmith Rd, Canford Magna BH21 3BD
e-mail: info@lesbouviers.co.uk
web: www.lesbouviers.co.uk
dir: A31 onto A349. Left in 0.6m. In approx 1m right into Arrowsmith Rd. Establishment approx 100yds on right

An excellent restaurant with rooms in a great location, set in five and a half acres of grounds. Food is a highlight of any stay here as is the friendly, attentive service. Chef patron James Coward's team turn out impressive cooking, which has been recognised with 2 AA Rosettes. Bedrooms are extremely well equipped and beds are supremely comfortable. Cream tea can be taken on the terrace.

Rooms 6 (4 fmly)

WINCANTON   Map 4 ST72
Somerset

Holbrook House

★★★ 82% ◉◉ COUNTRY HOUSE HOTEL

☎ 01963 824466 & 828844
Holbrook BA9 8BS
e-mail: enquiries@holbrookhouse.co.uk
web: www.holbrookhouse.co.uk
dir: From A303 at Wincanton left onto A371 towards Castle Cary & Shepton Mallet

This handsome country house offers a unique blend of quality and comfort combined with a friendly atmosphere. Set in 17 acres of peaceful gardens and wooded grounds, Holbrook House makes a perfect retreat. The restaurant provides a selection of innovative dishes prepared with enthusiasm and served by a team of caring staff.

Rooms 21 (5 annexe) (2 fmly) (5 GF) 🐾 **Facilities** Spa FTV Wi-fi ▷ ⊗ ♨ ⛲ Gym Exercise classes Sauna Steam room Fitness suite ♫ Xmas New Year **Conf** Class 50 Board 55 Thtr 200 **Parking** 100 **Notes** Civ Wed 250

WINCHCOMBE   Map 10 SP02
Gloucestershire

Wesley House

◉◉ RESTAURANT WITH ROOMS

☎ 01242 602366
High St GL54 5LJ
e-mail: enquiries@wesleyhouse.co.uk
web: www.wesleyhouse.co.uk
dir: In town centre

This 15th-century, half-timbered property is named after John Wesley, founder of the Methodist Church, who stayed here while preaching in the town. Bedrooms are small but full of character. In the rear dining room, a unique lighting system changes colour to suit the mood required, and also highlights the various floral creations by a world-renowned flower arranger. A glass atrium covers the outside terrace.

Rooms 5

WINCHESTER   Map 5 SU42
Hampshire

Lainston House Hotel

★★★★★ 85% ◉◉◉ HOTEL   LAINSTON HOUSE

☎ 01962 776088
Sparsholt SO21 2LT
e-mail: enquiries@lainstonhouse.com
web: www.lainstonhouse.com
dir: 2m NW off B3049 towards Stockbridge

This graceful example of a William and Mary House enjoys a countryside location amidst mature grounds and gardens. Staff provide good levels of courtesy and care with a polished, professional service. Bedrooms are tastefully appointed and include some spectacular, spacious rooms with stylish handmade beds and stunning bathrooms. Public rooms include a cocktail bar built entirely from a single cedar and stocked with an impressive range of rare drinks and cigars.

Rooms 49 (6 fmly) (18 GF) 🐾 **D** £165-£745* **Facilities** STV FTV Wi-fi ▷ ♨ Fishing ⛲ Gym Archery Clay pigeon shooting Cycling Hot air ballooning On-site falconer ♫ Xmas New Year **Conf** Class 80 Board 40 Thtr 166 Del £340* **Parking** 200 **Notes** LB Civ Wed 200

W

WINCHESTER *continued*

Holiday Inn Winchester

★★★★ 77% ⏺ HOTEL

Holiday Inn

☎ 01962 670700 & 0871 942 9188
Telegraph Way, Morn Hill SO21 1HZ
e-mail: info@hiwinchester.co.uk
dir: M3 junct 9, A31 signed Alton, A272 & Petersfield.
1st exit at rdbt onto A31, 1.6m, take 1st exit into
Alresford Rd, left into Telegraph Way

Located a few miles from the historic city of
Winchester and within easy reach of the south's
transport links, this modern, purpose-built property is
presented to a high standard. Bedrooms are spacious
and well-equipped for both the business and leisure
guest. Enjoyable cuisine is served in the restaurant
and there is a very good range of freshly prepared
dishes to choose from. Conference facilities and
ample parking are available.

Rooms 141 (7 fmly) (60 GF) ↖ **Facilities** STV FTV
Wi-fi HL Xmas New Year **Conf** Class 110 Board 120
Thtr 250 **Services** Lift Air con **Parking** 167 **Notes** ⊗
Civ Wed 200

The Winchester Hotel & Spa

★★★★ 76% ⏺ HOTEL

☎ 01962 709988
Worthy Ln SO23 7AB
e-mail: info@thewinchesterhotel.co.uk
web: www.thewinchesterhotel.co.uk
dir: A33 then A3047, hotel 1m on right

This hotel is just a few minutes' walk from the city
centre, is very smartly appointed throughout, and
includes a great leisure centre. The staff are
extremely friendly and helpful, and praiseworthy food
is served in the contemporary Hutton's Brasserie.

Rooms 96 (2 fmly) (6 GF) **S** £70-£170; **D** £80-£180*
Facilities Spa FTV Wi-fi ↕ ⑂ Gym Sauna Steam room
Xmas New Year **Conf** Class 100 Board 40 Thtr 200
Services Lift Air con **Parking** 60 **Notes** LB ⊗
Civ Wed 180

Hotel du Vin Winchester

★★★★ 74% ⏺⏺
TOWN HOUSE HOTEL

Hotel du Vin & Bistro

☎ 01962 841414
Southgate St SO23 9EF
e-mail: info@winchester.hotelduvin.com
web: www.hotelduvin.com
dir: M3 junct 11 towards Winchester, follow signs.
Hotel in approx 2m on left just past cinema

Continuing to set high standards, this inviting hotel
is best known for its high profile bistro. The
individually designed bedrooms have all the Hotel du

Vin signature touches including fine Egyptian cotton
linen, power showers and Wi-fi. The bistro serves
imaginative yet simply cooked dishes from a
seasonal, daily-changing menu.

Rooms 24 (4 annexe) (4 GF) ↖ **S** £165; **D** £165*
Facilities STV Wi-fi ↕ Xmas New Year **Conf** Class 30
Board 20 Thtr 40 **Services** Air con **Parking** 35
Notes Civ Wed 60

Mercure Winchester Wessex Hotel

★★★★ 71% HOTEL

Mercure

☎ 01962 861611
Paternoster Row SO23 9LQ
e-mail: H6619@accor.com
web: www.mercure.com
dir: M3 junct 10, 2nd exit at rdbt signed Winchester/
B3330. Right at lights, left at 2nd rdbt. Over small
bridge, straight on at next rdbt into Broadway. Past
Guildhall, 1st left into Colebrook St. Hotel 50yds on
right

Occupying an enviable location in the centre of this
historic city and adjacent to the spectacular
cathedral, Mercure Winchester Wessex Hotel is quietly
situated on a side street. Inside, the atmosphere is
restful and welcoming, with public areas and some
bedrooms enjoying unrivalled views of the hotel's
centuries-old neighbour.

Rooms 94 (6 fmly) **S** £75-£160; **D** £75-£160
Facilities STV Wi-fi Xmas New Year **Conf** Class 25
Board 40 Thtr 100 **Del from** £130 to £160
Services Lift **Parking** 30 **Notes** LB Civ Wed 120

Marwell Hotel

★★★ 81% ⏺⏺ HOTEL

☎ 01962 777681
Thompsons Ln, Colden Common, Marwell SO21 1JY
e-mail: info@marwellhotel.co.uk
web: www.marwellhotel.co.uk
dir: B3354 through Twyford. 1st exit at rdbt (B3354),
left onto B2177 signed Bishop Waltham. Left into
Thomsons Ln after 1m, hotel on left

Taking its theme from the adjacent zoo, this unusual
hotel is based on the famous TreeTops safari lodge in
Kenya. The well-equipped bedrooms, split between
four lodges, convey a safari style, while the smart
public areas include an airy lobby bar and an *Out of
Africa* themed restaurant. There is also a selection of
meeting and leisure facilities.

Rooms 68 (10 fmly) (38 GF) **Facilities** Wi-fi ↕ ⑂ ♨
36 Putt green Gym Sauna New Year **Child** facilities
Conf Class 60 Board 60 Thtr 175 **Parking** 120
Notes Civ Wed 150

WINDERMERE
Cumbria

Map 18 SD49

INSPECTORS' CHOICE

Gilpin Hotel & Lake House

★★★★ ⏺⏺⏺ HOTEL

RELAIS & CHATEAUX

☎ 015394 88818
Crook Rd LA23 3NE
e-mail: hotel@thegilpin.co.uk
web: www.thegilpin.co.uk
dir: M6 junct 36, A590, A591 to rdbt N of Kendal,
onto B5284, hotel 5m on right

This smart Victorian residence is set amidst
delightful gardens leading to the fells, and is just a
short drive from the lake. The individually designed
bedrooms are stylish and a number benefit from
private terraces; all are spacious and thoughtfully
equipped, and each has a private sitting room. In
addition there are luxury Garden Suites that lead
onto private gardens with cedar wood hot tubs. The
welcoming atmosphere is notable and the
attractive day rooms are perfect for relaxing,
perhaps beside a real fire. Eating in any of the
quartet of dining rooms is a must. The Lake House
situated a mile from the main hotel offers an
additional six suites, spa and stunning lakeside
views.

Rooms 26 (12 annexe) (1 fmly) (12 GF) ↖
S £225-£555; **D** £335-£595 (incl. bkfst & dinner)*
Facilities Wi-fi ☙ Free membership at local
leisure club Xmas New Year **Parking** 40 **Notes** LB
⊗ No children 7yrs

W

Save on hotels. Book at **theAA.com/hotel**

WIN 465 ENGLAND

INSPECTORS' CHOICE

Holbeck Ghyll Country House Hotel

★★★★ ◎◎◎ COUNTRY HOUSE HOTEL

☎ 015394 32375
Holbeck Ln LA23 1LU
e-mail: stay@holbeckghyll.com
dir: 3m N of Windermere on A591, right into Holbeck Lane (signed Troutbeck), hotel 0.5m on left

Holbeck Ghyll sits high up overlooking the majestic Lake Windermere surrounded by well maintained grounds. The original house was bought in 1888 by Lord Lonsdale, the first president of the AA, who used it as a hunting lodge. Guests today will find that this is a delightful place where the service is professional and attentive. There are beautifully designed, spacious bedrooms situated in the main house and also in lodges in the grounds; each has lake views and some have patios. There are also The Shieling and Miss Potter suites. Each bedroom has Egyptian cotton linens, fresh flowers, LCD satellite TV, CD/ DVD players, bathrobes and a decanter of damson gin. The restaurant impresses with its award-winning cuisine. The hotel also has a health spa, gym and boutique store.

Rooms 26 (13 annexe) (5 fmly) (11 GF)
S £145-£285; D £190-£470 (incl. bkfst)
Facilities Spa FTV Wi-fi ⊾ ⓢ ⥲ Sauna Steam room Beauty massage Xmas New Year **Conf** Class 40 Board 30 Thtr 60 Del £225* **Parking** 34 **Notes** LB Civ Wed 60

INSPECTORS' CHOICE

Linthwaite House Hotel & Restaurant

★★★★ ◎◎◎ COUNTRY HOUSE HOTEL

☎ 015394 88600
Crook Rd LA23 3JA
e-mail: stay@linthwaite.com
web: www.linthwaite.com
dir: A591 towards The Lakes for 8m to large rdbt, take 1st exit (B5284), 6m, hotel on left. 1m past Windermere golf club

Linthwaite House is set in 14 acres of hilltop grounds and enjoys stunning views over Lake Windermere. Inviting public rooms include an attractive conservatory and adjoining lounge, and an elegant restaurant which occupies three rooms and offers menus based on the finest local ingredients. Bedrooms, which are individually decorated, combine contemporary furnishings with classical styles; all are thoughtfully equipped and include CD players, radios and free Wi-fi. There is also a Garden Suite and the luxurious Loft Suite which even has a retractable roof and telescope for star gazing. Service and hospitality are attentive and friendly.

Rooms 30 (1 fmly) (7 GF) ⋔ S £185-£214;
D £290-£700 (incl. bkfst & dinner)* **Facilities** STV FTV Wi-fi � Putt green Fishing ⥲ Beauty treatments Massage Access to nearby spa with pool & gym Xmas New Year **Conf** Class 22 Board 25 Thtr 54 **Parking** 40 **Notes** Civ Wed 64

Macdonald Old England Hotel & Spa

★★★★ 84% ◎◎ HOTEL

☎ 0844 879 9144
Church St, Bowness LA23 3DF
e-mail:
sales.oldengland@macdonald-hotels.co.uk
web: www.macdonaldhotels.co.uk
dir: Through Windermere to Bowness, straight across at mini-rdbt. Hotel behind church on right

This hotel stands right on the shore of England's largest lake and boasts superb views, especially through the floor-to-ceiling windows in the Vinand Restaurant. There are several bedroom types; standard, executive and suites; some rooms have been designed for wheelchairs users. The spa has a 20-metre pool, a gym, sauna and steam room. Macdonald Hotels is the AA Hotel Group of the Year 2013-14.

Rooms 106 (6 fmly) (14 GF) ⋔ **Facilities** Spa STV Wi-fi ⓢ supervised Gym Private jetties Rock sauna Aromatherapy shower Steam room Ice room Xmas New Year **Conf** Class 60 Board 25 Thtr 150 **Services** Lift **Parking** 90 **Notes** ⊗ Civ Wed 100

Lindeth Howe Country House Hotel & Restaurant

★★★★ 79% ◎◎ COUNTRY HOUSE HOTEL

☎ 015394 45759
Lindeth Dr, Longtail Hill LA23 3JF
e-mail: hotel@lindeth-howe.co.uk
web: www.lindeth-howe.co.uk
dir: Exit A592, 1m S of Bowness onto B5284 (Longtail Hill) signed Kendal & Lancaster, hotel last driveway on right

Historic photographs commemorate the fact that this delightful house was once the family home of Beatrix Potter. Secluded in landscaped grounds, it enjoys views across the valley and Lake Windermere. Public rooms are plentiful and inviting, with the restaurant being the perfect setting for modern country-house cooking. Deluxe and superior bedrooms are spacious and smartly appointed.

Rooms 34 (3 fmly) (2 GF) ⋔ S £70-£95; D £170-£280 (incl. bkfst)* **Facilities** STV Wi-fi ⓢ Gym Sauna Fitness room Xmas New Year **Conf** Class 20 Board 18 Thtr 30 Del £180* **Parking** 50 **Notes** LB ⊗

W

WINDERMERE *continued*

Low Wood Bay

English Lakes
Hotels Resorts & Venues

★★★★ 77% HOTEL

☎ 015394 33338 & 0845 850 3502
LA23 1LP
e-mail: lowwoodbay@englishlakes.co.uk
dir: M6 junct 36, A590, A591 to Windermere, then 3m towards Ambleside, hotel on right

Benefiting from a lakeside location, this hotel offers an excellent range of leisure and conference facilities. Bedrooms, many with panoramic lake views, are attractively furnished, and include a number of larger executive rooms and suites. There is a choice of bars, a spacious restaurant and the more informal Café del Lago. The poolside bar offers internet access.

Rooms 111 (13 fmly) (21 GF) ✿ S £79-£160; **D** £98-£260 (incl. bkfst)* **Facilities** Spa FTV Wi-fi ⓑ supervised Fishing ⚓ Gym Squash Water skiing Canoeing Beauty salon Marina Xmas New Year **Conf** Class 180 Board 150 Thtr 340 Del from £99 to £143* **Services** Lift **Parking** 200 **Notes** LB Civ Wed 280

Storrs Hall Hotel

★★★★ 76% ◉◉ HOTEL

☎ 015394 47111
Storrs Park LA23 3LG
e-mail: enquiries@storrshall.com
web: www.storrshall.com
dir: On A592, 2m S of Bowness, on Newby Bridge road

Set in 17 acres of landscaped grounds by the lakeside, this imposing Georgian mansion is delightful. There are numerous lounges to relax in, furnished with fine art and antiques. Individually styled bedrooms are generally spacious and boast impressive bathrooms. Imaginative cuisine is served in the elegant restaurant, which offers fine views across the lawn to the lake and fells beyond.

Rooms 30 **Facilities** FTV Wi-fi Fishing ⚓ Use of nearby sports/beauty facilities Xmas New Year **Conf** Class 35 Board 24 Thtr 50 **Parking** 50 **Notes** No children 12yrs Civ Wed 94

Beech Hill Hotel

★★★★ 74% ◉ HOTEL

☎ 015394 42137
Newby Bridge Rd LA23 3LR
e-mail: reservations@beechhillhotel.co.uk
web: www.beechhillhotel.co.uk
dir: M6 junct 36, A591 to Windermere. Left onto A592 towards Newby Bridge. Hotel 4m from Bowness-on-Windermere

Located on the edge of Lake Windermere, the panoramic views across the lake to the Cumbrian fells beyond are impressive. The bedrooms are well appointed and some have balconies overlooking the lake. The open areas, for enjoying coffee or drinks, prove very popular in the summer, and there are cosy lounges with log fires, a fine restaurant, leisure facilities and landscaped gardens. High standards of service can be expected from the attentive, informative and very friendly staff.

Rooms 57 (5 fmly) (4 GF) ✿ S fr £69; **D** £125-£418 (incl. bkfst)* **Facilities** FTV Wi-fi ⓑ Fishing Solarium ♫ Xmas New Year **Parking** 70 **Notes** LB ⊗ Civ Wed 130

The Samling

★★★ ◉◉◉ HOTEL

☎ 015394 31922
Ambleside Rd LA23 1LR
e-mail: info@thesamlinghotel.co.uk
web: www.thesamlinghotel.co.uk
dir: M6 junct 36, A591 through Windermere towards Ambleside. 2m. 300yds past Low Wood Water Sports Centre just after sharp bend turn right into hotel entrance

This stylish house, built in the late 1700s, is situated in 67 acres of grounds and enjoys an elevated position overlooking Lake Windermere. The spacious, beautifully furnished bedrooms and suites, some in adjacent buildings, are thoughtfully equipped and all have superb bathrooms. Public rooms include a sumptuous drawing room, a small library and an elegant dining room where imaginative, skilfully prepared food is served.

Rooms 11 (6 annexe) (6 fmly) (6 GF) ✿ **Facilities** STV FTV Wi-fi ⓑ ⚓ Xmas New Year **Conf** Board 14 Thtr 30 **Parking** 20 **Notes** Civ Wed 50

Miller Howe Hotel

★★★ 86% ◉◉ COUNTRY HOUSE HOTEL

☎ 015394 42536
Rayrigg Rd LA23 1EY
e-mail: info@millerhowe.com
dir: M6 junct 36, A591 past Windermere, left at rdbt towards Bowness

This long established hotel enjoys a lakeside setting amidst delightful landscaped gardens. The bright and welcoming day rooms include sumptuous lounges, a conservatory and an opulently decorated restaurant. Imaginative dinners make use of fresh, local produce where possible and there is an extensive, well-balanced wine list. Stylish bedrooms, many with fabulous lake views, include well-equipped cottage rooms and a number with whirlpool baths.

Rooms 15 (3 annexe) (1 GF) ✿ **S** £80-£150; **D** £160-£300 (incl. bkfst) **Facilities** FTV Wi-fi ⓑ HL Xmas New Year **Parking** 35 **Notes** LB Civ Wed 75

W

Lindeth Fell Country House Hotel

★★★ 86% COUNTRY HOUSE HOTEL

☎ 015394 43286 & 44287
Lyth Valley Rd, Bowness-on-Windermere LA23 3JP
e-mail: kennedy@lindethfell.co.uk
web: www.lindethfell.co.uk
dir: 1m S of Bowness on A5074

Enjoying delightful views, this smart Edwardian residence stands in seven acres of glorious, landscaped gardens. Bedrooms, which vary in size and style, are comfortably equipped. Skilfully prepared dinners are served in the spacious dining room that commands fine views. The resident owners and their attentive, friendly staff provide high levels of hospitality and service.

Rooms 14 (2 fmly) (1 GF) ⬩ **S** £85; **D** £170–£210 (incl. bkfst)* **Facilities** FTV Wi-fi Putt green Fishing ⬩ Bowling Xmas New Year **Conf** Class 12 Board 12 **Parking** 20 **Notes** ⊗ Closed 3-7 Feb

Windermere Manor Hotel

★★★ 78% HOTEL

☎ 01539 445801
Rayrigg Rd LA23 1ES
e-mail: windermere@actionforblindpeople.org.uk
dir: A591 towards Ambleside. At mini-rdbt turn left, hotel 1st on left

Set above the shores of Lake Windermere in wooded landscaped gardens, this former manor house has been restored to its original splendour. The bedrooms and suites are smart and well appointed. The attractive dining room has an unusual barrel-vaulted wooden roof and serves delicious home cooking. The hotel extends a warm welcome to everyone but caters especially for the visually impaired, their families, friends and guide dogs. Special facilities for guide dogs are provided.

Rooms 35 (7 annexe) (2 fmly) (10 GF) ⬩ **Facilities** FTV Wi-fi HL ⬩ supervised Gym Xmas New Year **Conf** Class 30 Board 15 Thtr 40 **Services** Lift **Parking** 28 **Notes** Civ Wed 40

Craig Manor

★★★ 77% HOTEL

☎ 015394 88877
Lake Rd LA23 2JF
e-mail: info@craigmanor.co.uk
dir: A590, then A591 into Windermere, left at Windermere Hotel, through village, pass Magistrates' Court, hotel on left

Situated in the heart of the Lake District, Craig Manor has a relaxed and friendly atmosphere with professional staff providing attentive service. Bedrooms are comfortable and well equipped, and some rooms offer stunning views across the lake. The attractive and elegant lake-facing restaurant serves an excellent choice of quality dishes. The large car park is a further benefit in this popular tourist resort.

Rooms 16

Hillthwaite House Hotel

★★★ 75% HOTEL

☎ 015394 43636 & 46691
Thornbarrow Rd LA23 2DF
e-mail: reception@hillthwaite.com
dir: M6 junct 36, A591 Windermere, follow lane road through village (A5074), left opposite Goodley Dale School, approx 0.5m from A591

Located between the villages of Windermere and Bowness, this family-run hotel sits in an elevated position with excellent views of the lake and surrounding landscape. Service from the dedicated team is warm and friendly with nothing being too much trouble. Bedrooms and bathrooms are well equipped, some of the larger rooms have excellent views and feature bathrooms with a roll top bath and walk-in showers. Afternoon tea in the cosy lounge area is popular for guests and visitors alike while a daily changing dinner menu offers a very good range of well prepared local ingredients. Ample car parking is available.

Rooms 33 (4 fmly) (2 GF) **S** £69.50–£79.50; **D** £119–£249 (incl. bkfst & dinner)* **Facilities** FTV Wi-fi ⬩ Sauna Steam room New Year **Parking** 30 **Notes** LB

Cedar Manor Hotel & Restaurant

★★ 85% ⬩⬩ HOTEL

☎ 015394 43192 & 45970
Ambleside Rd LA23 1AX
e-mail: info@cedarmanor.co.uk
dir: From A591 follow signs to Windermere. Hotel on left just beyond St Mary's Church

Built in 1854 as a country retreat, this lovely old house enjoys a peaceful location that is within easy walking distance of the town centre. Bedrooms, some on the ground floor, are attractive and well equipped, with a luxurious annexe suite available for longer stays or romantic getaways. There is a comfortable lounge bar where guests can relax before enjoying dinner in the well-appointed dining room.

Rooms 10 (1 annexe) (1 fmly) (3 GF) ⬩ **S** £90–£350; **D** £100–£350 (incl. bkfst)* **Facilities** FTV Wi-fi New Year **Conf** Board 10 Del from £199 to £299* **Parking** 11 **Notes** LB ⊗ Closed 3-21 Jan

Jerichos

⬩⬩ RESTAURANT WITH ROOMS

☎ 015394 42522
College Rd LA23 1BX
e-mail: info@jerichos.co.uk
dir: A591 to Windermere, 2nd left into Elleray Rd then 1st right into College Rd

Dating back to around 1870, this centrally located property has been lovingly restored by its current owners. All the elegantly furnished bedrooms are en suite and the top floor rooms have views of the fells. Breakfast is served in the Restaurant Room, and the comfortable lounge has a real fire to relax by on chillier days. The chef/proprietor has established a strong reputation for his creative menus that use the best local and seasonal produce. The restaurant is always busy so booking is essential. Wi-fi is available.

Rooms 10

W

WINDSOR
Berkshire   Map 6 SU97

INSPECTORS' CHOICE

Macdonald Windsor Hotel

★★★★ ◉ HOTEL

☎ 0844 879 9101
23 High St SL4 1LH
e-mail: gm.windsor@macdonaldwindsor.co.uk
dir: M4 junct 6 A355, take A332, rdbt 1st exit signed towncentre. In 0.7m turn left into Bachelors Acre

Just across the street from Windsor Castle, this hotel is an ideal base for visiting the castle, and all the other famous attractions of the town. It has well-appointed contemporary, designer-led bedrooms, some overlooking the castle, that are decorated in soft shades to create a calm atmosphere, and include flat-screen TVs and Bose iPod docks. The Scottish Steak Club@ Caleys restaurant offers a relaxed and informal dining venue, and 24-hour room service is also available. There is complimentary Wi-fi in the bedrooms and the conference rooms. The hotel has excellent wedding facilities. Macdonald Hotels is the AA Hotel Group of the Year 2013-14.

Rooms 120 (4 fmly) 🐾 S £115-£350; D £115-£350* **Facilities** FTV Wi-fi ⌕ HL ♬ **Conf** Class 80 Board 35 Thtr 100 Del from £200 to £300* **Services** Lift Air con **Parking** 42 **Notes** LB Civ Wed 100

Oakley Court Hotel
PH principal hayley

★★★★ 81% ◉◉ HOTEL

☎ 01753 609988 & 609900
Windsor Rd, Water Oakley SL4 5UR
e-mail: reservations@theoakleycourthotel.com
web: www.theoakleycourthotel.com
dir: M4 junct 6, A355, then A332 towards Windsor, right onto A308 towards Maidenhead. Pass racecourse, hotel 2.5m on right

Built in 1859 this splendid Victorian Gothic mansion is enviably situated in extensive grounds that lead down to the Thames. All bedrooms are spacious, beautifully furnished and many enjoy river views. Extensive public areas include a range of comfortable lounges and the Oakleaf Restaurant. The comprehensive leisure facilities include a 9-hole golf course.

Rooms 118 (108 annexe) (6 fmly) (42 GF) S £86-£286; D £96-£296* **Facilities** Spa Wi-fi HL ⌕ ↨ 9 ⛳ Putt green ☘ Gym Boating Sauna Steam room Snooker Xmas New Year **Conf** Class 90 Board 50 Thtr 170 Del from £185 to £330* **Services** Air con **Parking** 200 **Notes** LB ⊗ Civ Wed 170

Mercure Windsor Castle Hotel
Mercure

★★★★ 77% ◉◉ HOTEL

☎ 01753 851577
18 High St SL4 1LJ
e-mail: h6618@accor.com
web: www.mercure.com
dir: M4 junct 6/M25 junct 15, follow signs to Windsor town centre & castle. Hotel at top of hill opposite Guildhall

This is one of the oldest hotels in Windsor, beginning life as a coaching inn in the 16th century. Located opposite Windsor Castle, it is an ideal base from which to explore the town and its royal connections. Stylish bedrooms are thoughtfully equipped and include four-poster and executive rooms. Public areas are spacious and tastefully decorated.

Rooms 108 (70 annexe) (18 fmly) (3 GF) 🐾 **Facilities** STV FTV Wi-fi Xmas New Year **Conf** Class 150 Board 50 Thtr 400 **Services** Lift Air con **Parking** 135 **Notes** ⊗ Civ Wed 300

Sir Christopher Wren Hotel and Spa

SAROVA HOTELS

★★★★ 76% ◉ HOTEL

☎ 01753 442400
Thames St SL4 1PX
e-mail: wrens@sarova.co.uk
dir: M4 junct 6, at 1st exit follow signs to Windsor, 1st major exit on left, left at lights

Located by the side of the Thames and close to the Eton Bridge stands this well presented hotel. Bedrooms vary - with both traditional and contemporary tastes catered for. There are comfortable lounges, a popular restaurant with great views of the river, and also a well-equipped leisure club. Limited parking is available.

Rooms 99 (42 annexe) (5 fmly) (10 GF) 🐾 S £95-£170; D £115-£240* **Facilities** Spa STV Wi-fi ⌕ Gym Sauna ♬ Xmas New Year **Conf** Class 50 Board 45 Thtr 100 Del from £199 to £290* **Parking** 14 **Notes** LB ⊗ Civ Wed 100

BEST WESTERN Royal Adelaide Hotel

Best Western

★★★★ 72% HOTEL

☎ 01753 863916 & 07710 473130
46 Kings Rd SL4 2AG
e-mail: info@theroyaladelaide.com
web: www.theroyaladelaide.com
dir: M4 junct 6, A322 to Windsor. 1st left at rdbt into Clarence Rd. At 4th lights right into Sheet St, then Kings Rd. Hotel on right

This attractive Georgian-style hotel enjoys a quiet location yet is only a short walk from the town centre. Bedrooms vary in size. Public areas are tastefully appointed and include a range of meeting rooms, a bar and an elegant restaurant. Off-street parking is available.

Rooms 42 (4 annexe) (6 fmly) (8 GF) (5 smoking) 🐾 **Facilities** STV FTV Wi-fi Xmas **Conf** Class 80 Board 50 Thtr 100 **Services** Air con **Parking** 16 **Notes** Civ Wed 110

Save on hotels. Book at **theAA.com/hotel**

WIN – WIT 469 ENGLAND

Christopher Hotel

★★★ 80% HOTEL

☎ 01753 852359
110 High St, Eton SL4 6AN
e-mail: reservations@thechristopher.co.uk
web: www.thechristopher.co.uk
dir: M4 junct 5 (Slough E), Colnbrook Datchet Eton
(B470). At rdbt 2nd exit for Datchet. Right at mini
rdbt (Eton), left into Eton Rd (3rd rdbt). Left, hotel on
right

This hotel benefits from an ideal location in Eton,
being only a short stroll across the pedestrian bridge
from historic Windsor Castle and the many other
attractions the town has to offer. The hotel has
comfortable and smartly decorated accommodation,
and a wide range of dishes is available in the
informal bar and grill. A stylish room is available for
private dining or for meetings.

Rooms 34 (23 annexe) (10 fmly) (22 GF) 🐾
S £100-£144; **D** £145-£200* **Facilities** FTV Wi-fi ⸖
Xmas New Year **Conf** Board 10 Thtr 30 Del £178*
Parking 19 **Notes** LB

WINTERINGHAM	Map 17 SE92
Lincolnshire	

INSPECTORS' CHOICE

Winteringham Fields

☺ ☺ ☺ RESTAURANT WITH ROOMS

☎ 01724 733096
DN15 9ND
e-mail: reception@winteringhamfields.co.uk
dir: In village centre at x-rds

This highly regarded restaurant with rooms, located
deep in the countryside in Winteringham village, is
six miles west of the Humber Bridge. Public rooms
and bedrooms, some of which are housed in
renovated barns and cottages, are delightfully
cosseting. There is an abundance of charm and
period features are combined with rich furnishings
and fabrics. The award winning food is a highlight
of any stay and guests can expect highly skilled
dishes, excellent quality and stunning presentation.

Rooms 11 (7 annexe) (2 fmly)

WISBECH	Map 12 TF40
Cambridgeshire	

Crown Lodge Hotel

THE INDEPENDENTS
HOTEL ASSOCIATION

★★★ 85% ☺ HOTEL

☎ 01945 773391 & 772206
Downham Rd, Outwell PE14 8SE
e-mail: office@thecrownlodgehotel.co.uk
web: www.thecrownlodgehotel.co.uk
dir: On A1122, approx 5m from Wisbech

A friendly, privately owned hotel situated in a
peaceful location on the banks of Well Creek a short
drive from Wisbech. The bedrooms are pleasantly
decorated, with co-ordinated fabrics and modern
facilities. The public areas are very stylish; they
include a lounge bar, brasserie restaurant and a
large seating area with plush leather sofas.

Rooms 10 (1 fmly) (10 GF) 🐾 **S** £79; **D** £99 (incl.
bkfst)* **Facilities** FTV Wi-fi ⸖ Squash **Conf** Class 60
Board 40 Thtr 80 **Services** Air con **Parking** 55
Notes LB Closed 25-26 Dec & 1 Jan

Elme Hall Hotel

★★★ 73% HOTEL

☎ 01945 475566
Elm High Rd PE14 0DQ
e-mail: elmehallhotel@btconnect.com
web: www.elmehall.co.uk
dir: A47 onto A1101 towards Wisbech. Hotel on right

An imposing, Georgian-style property conveniently
situated on the outskirts of the town centre just off
the A47. Individually decorated bedrooms are
tastefully furnished with quality reproduction pieces
and equipped to a high standard. Public rooms
include a choice of attractive lounges, as well as two
bars, meeting rooms and a banqueting suite.

Rooms 42 (34 annexe) (3 fmly) (21 GF) 🐾 **S** £73-£88;
D £78-£245 (incl. bkfst)* **Facilities** FTV Wi-fi ♫
Conf Class 200 Board 20 Thtr 350 **Parking** 200
Notes Civ Wed 350

WITNEY	Map 5 SP31
Oxfordshire	

Oxford Witney Four Pillars Hotel

FOUR PILLARS HOTELS

★★★★ 71% HOTEL

☎ 0800 374692 & 01993 779777
Ducklington Ln OX28 4TJ
e-mail: witney@four-pillars.co.uk
web: www.four-pillars.co.uk/witney
dir: M40 junct 9, A34 to A40, exit A415 Witney/
Abingdon. Hotel on left, 2nd exit for Witney

This attractive modern hotel is close to Oxford and
Burford and offers spacious, well-equipped
bedrooms. The cosy Spinners Bar has comfortable
seating areas and the popular Weavers Restaurant
offers a good range of dishes. Other amenities
include extensive function and leisure facilities,
complete with indoor swimming pool.

Rooms 87 (14 fmly) (21 GF) 🐾 **S** £80-£150;
D £80-£150 **Facilities** FTV Wi-fi ⸖ ⊗ Gym Steam
room Sauna Xmas New Year **Conf** Class 76 Board 44
Thtr 150 Del from £99 **Parking** 120 **Notes** LB ⊗
Civ Wed 150

W

The Inn at Woburn

★★★ 84% ◎◎ HOTEL

☎ 01525 290441
George St MK17 9PX
e-mail: inn@woburn.co.uk
web: www.woburn.co.uk/inn
dir: M1 junct 13, towards Woburn. In Woburn left at
T-junct, hotel in village

This inn provides a high standard of accommodation.
Bedrooms are divided between the original house, a
modern extension and some stunning cottage suites.
Public areas include the beamed, club-style Tavistock
Bar, a range of meeting rooms and an attractive
restaurant with interesting dishes on offer.

Rooms 55 (7 annexe) (4 fmly) (25 GF)
Facilities FTV Wi-fi 54 Putt green Concessionary
rate to access Woburn Safari Park & Woburn Abbey
Xmas New Year **Conf** Class 30 Board 35 Thtr 60
Del from £165 to £180* **Parking** 80 **Notes** ⊗
Civ Wed 60

Premier Inn Woking

BUDGET HOTEL

☎ 0871 527 9182
Bridge Barn Ln, Horsell GU21 6NL
web: www.premierinn.com
dir: From A324 at rdbt into Parley Drive. Left at next
rdbt into Goldsworth Rd

High quality, budget accommodation ideal for both
families and business travellers. Spacious, en suite
bedrooms feature tea and coffee making facilities,
and Freeview TV in most hotels. Internet access and
Wi-fi are available for a small fee. The adjacent
family restaurant features a wide and varied menu.
See also the Hotel Groups pages.

Rooms 34

See also **Pattingham**

Novotel Wolverhampton

★★★ 81% HOTEL

☎ 01902 871100
Union St WV1 3JN
e-mail: H1188@accor.com
web: www.novotel.com
dir: 6m from M6 junct 10. A454 to Wolverhampton.
Hotel on main ring road

This large, modern, purpose-built hotel stands close
to the town centre. It provides spacious, smartly
presented and well-equipped bedrooms, all of which
contain convertible bed settees for family occupancy.
In addition to the open-plan lounge and bar area,
there is an attractive brasserie-style restaurant,
which overlooks an attractive patio garden.

Rooms 132 (9 fmly) **S** £50-£129; **D** £50-£129*
Facilities FTV Wi-fi **Conf** Class 100 Board 80 Thtr 200
Del from £99 to £145* **Services** Lift **Parking** 120
Notes LB RS 23 Dec-4 Jan Civ Wed 170

Holiday Inn Wolverhampton

★★★ 75% HOTEL

☎ 01902 390004
Dunstall Park WV6 0PE
e-mail:
holidayinn@wolverhampton-racecourse.com
web: www.holidayinn.co.uk
dir: Off A449, 1.5m from city centre. Follow brown
sign for Dunstall Park

Located at Wolverhampton Racecourse, which is a
floodlit racecourse with afternoon and evening meets,
this modern hotel provides a range of well-equipped
bedrooms and an open-plan public area with bar,
lounge and brasserie-style restaurant.

Rooms 54 (18 fmly) **Facilities** STV Wi-fi **Services** Lift
Parking 1500

Mercure Wolverhampton Goldthorn Hotel

★★★ 74% HOTEL

☎ 01902 429216
126 Penn Rd WV3 0ER
e-mail: enquiries@hotels-wolverhampton.com
web: www.hotels-wolverhampton.com
dir: A454 then A449 signed Kidderminster. Hotel 1m
on right

This hotel is situated just on the outskirts of the old
town and offers easy access to major motorway
networks. The bedrooms are comfortable and well
equipped; free Wi-fi is available throughout the hotel.
The leisure facilities include a health club with a
swimming pool, gym, steam room and sauna. There is
also free on-site parking.

Rooms 74 (16 annexe) (12 fmly) (4 GF) **Facilities** FTV
Wi-fi Gym Sauna Steam room **Conf** Class 70
Board 40 Thtr 140 Del from £100 to £135*
Parking 100 **Notes** Civ Wed 100

W

Save on hotels. Book at theAA.com/hotel

WOB – WOO 471 ENGLAND

The Connaught Hotel

★★★ 70% HOTEL

☎ 01902 424433

Tettenhall Rd WV1 4SW
e-mail: info@theconnaughthotel.net
dir: A41 junct 3, 1st exit at rdbt. Follow signs for Tettenhall. In Tettenhall Rd, hotel on left

This hotel is located a short walk from the city centre and the railway station, with convenient access to the motorway networks. Bedrooms provide modern comfort with contemporary decor. Complimentary Wi-fi is available throughout the hotel. The Americano steakhouse and bar offers American-style dishes, with exotic meats a speciality. There are seven air-conditioned conference and banqueting suites.

Rooms 60 (3 fmly) **Facilities** STV FTV Wi-fi ⌂ Xmas New Year **Conf** Class 300 Board 60 Thtr 500 **Services** Lift **Parking** 120 **Notes** ⊗ Civ Wed 500

Premier Inn Wolverhampton City Centre

BUDGET HOTEL

☎ 0871 527 9186

Broad Gauge Way WV10 0BA
web: www.premierinn.com
dir: M6 junct 10, A454 signed Wolverhampton for approx 2m. Right into Neachalls Ln (signed Wednesfield). 0.75m. At rdbt 1st exit onto A4124 (Wednesfield Way). 1st exit at next rdbt. 2nd exit at 3rd rdbt. At 2nd lights left into Sun St. 1st right, hotel at end of road

High quality, budget accommodation ideal for both families and business travellers. Spacious, en suite bedrooms feature tea and coffee making facilities, and Freeview TV in most hotels. Internet access and Wi-fi are available for a small fee. The adjacent family restaurant features a wide and varied menu. See also the Hotel Groups pages.

Rooms 88

Premier Inn Wolverhampton North

BUDGET HOTEL

☎ 0871 527 9184

Greenfield Ln, Stafford Rd WV10 6TA
web: www.premierinn.com
dir: M54 junct 2. Hotel at lights in approx 100yds

Rooms 77

Premier Inn Barnsley (Dearne Valley)

BUDGET HOTEL

☎ 0871 527 8050

Meadow Gate, Dearne Valley S73 0UN
web: www.premierinn.com
dir: M1 junct 36 E'bound, A6195 towards Doncaster (5m). Hotel at rdbt adjacent to Meadows Brewers Fayre

High quality, budget accommodation ideal for both families and business travellers. Spacious, en suite bedrooms feature tea and coffee making facilities, and Freeview TV in most hotels. Internet access and Wi-fi are available for a small fee. The adjacent family restaurant features a wide and varied menu. See also the Hotel Groups pages.

Rooms 41

Chequers Inn

★★★ 79% ◉ ◉ HOTEL

☎ 01628 529575

Kiln Ln, Wooburn HP10 0JQ
e-mail: info@chequers-inn.com
web: www.chequers-inn.com
dir: M40 junct 2, A40 through Beaconsfield Old Town towards High Wycombe. 2m from town left into Broad Ln. Inn 2.5m

This 17th-century inn enjoys a peaceful, rural location beside the common. Bedrooms feature stripped-pine furniture, co-ordinated fabrics and an excellent range of extra facilities. The bar, with its massive oak post, beams and flagstone floor; and the restaurant, which overlooks a pretty patio, are very much focal points here.

Rooms 17 (8 GF) **S** £85-£99.50; **D** £90-£140*
Facilities FTV Wi-fi **Conf** Class 30 Board 20 Thtr 50 Del £155* **Parking** 60 **Notes** LB ⊗

Days Inn Sheffield - M1

BUDGET HOTEL

☎ 0114 248 7992

Woodall Service Area S26 7XR
e-mail: woodall.hotel@welcomebreak.co.uk
web: www.welcomebreak.co.uk
dir: M1, between juncts 30 & 31 S'bound, at Woodall Services

This modern building offers accommodation in smart, spacious and well-equipped bedrooms, suitable for families and business travellers, and all with en suite bathrooms. Continental breakfast is available and other refreshments may be taken at the nearby family restaurant. See also the Hotel Groups pages.

Rooms 38 (32 fmly) (16 GF) (6 smoking)
Conf Board 10

Seckford Hall Hotel

★★★★ 76% ◉ ◉ HOTEL

CLASSIC BRITISH HOTELS

☎ 01394 385678

IP13 6NU
e-mail: reception@seckford.co.uk
web: www.seckford.co.uk
dir: Signed on A12. (NB do not follow signs for town centre)

Seckford Hall is an elegant Tudor manor house set amid landscaped grounds just off the A12. It is reputed that Queen Elizabeth I visited this property, and it retains much of its original character. Public rooms include a superb panelled lounge, a cosy bar and an intimate restaurant. The spacious bedrooms are attractively decorated, tastefully furnished and thoughtfully equipped.

Rooms 32 (10 annexe) (4 fmly) (7 GF) **Facilities** Wi-fi ⌂ Putt green Fishing Gym Beauty salon & treatment room Xmas New Year **Conf** Class 46 Board 40 Thtr 100 **Parking** 100 **Notes** Civ Wed 120

W

WOODBRIDGE *continued*

The Crown at Woodbridge

T|A|HOTEL COLLECTION

★★★ 87% ◉◉ HOTEL

☎ 01394 384242
2 Thoro'fare IP12 1AD
e-mail: info@thecrownatwoodbridge.co.uk
dir: A12 follow signs for Woodbridge onto B1438.
1.25m from rdbt left into Quay St. Hotel on right
approx 100yds

This 17th-century property offers contemporary-style
accommodation throughout. The open-plan public
areas are tastefully appointed and include a large
lounge bar, a restaurant and a private dining room.
The stylish bedrooms are tastefully appointed and
equipped with modern facilities.

Rooms 10 (2 fmly) **S** £100-£140; **D** £120-£180 (incl.
bkfst) **Facilities** STV Wi-fi **Parking** 40 **Notes** LB ⊗

Ufford Park Hotel Golf & Spa

★★★ 83% HOTEL

☎ 01394 383555
Yarmouth Rd, Ufford IP12 1QW
e-mail: enquiries@uffordpark.co.uk
web: www.uffordpark.co.uk
dir: A12 N to A1152, in Melton left at lights, follow
B1438, hotel 1m on right

Ufford Park is a modern hotel set in open countryside
boasting superb leisure facilities including a
challenging golf course. The spacious public rooms
provide a wide choice of areas in which to relax and
include a busy lounge bar, a carvery restaurant and
the Vista Restaurant. Bedrooms are smartly
appointed and pleasantly decorated; each is
thoughtfully equipped and many overlook the golf
course.

Rooms 87 (20 fmly) (32 GF) ☞ **S** £79-£109;
D £89-£159 (incl. bkfst)* **Facilities** Spa FTV Wi-fi ⊗
⊗ supervised ⚓ 18 Putt green Fishing ⚑ Gym Golf
Academy with PGA tuition 2 storey floodlit driving
range Dance studio Xmas New Year **Conf** Class 120
Board 120 Thtr 300 Del from £109 to £119*
Services Lift **Parking** 250 **Notes** LB Civ Wed 120

Woodbury Park Hotel and Golf Club

★★★★ 76% ◉ HOTEL

☎ 01395 233382
Woodbury Castle EX5 1JJ
e-mail: enquiries@woodburypark.co.uk
web: www.woodburypark.co.uk
dir: M5 junct 30, A376 then A3052 towards Sidmouth,
onto B3180, hotel signed

Situated in 500 acres of beautiful and unspoilt
countryside, yet within easy reach of Exeter and the
M5, this hotel offers smart, well-equipped and
immaculately presented accommodation together
with a host of sporting and banqueting facilities.
There is a choice of golf courses, a Bodyzone beauty
centre and enjoyable dining in the Atrium Restaurant.

Rooms 60 (4 annexe) (4 fmly) (28 GF) **Facilities** Spa
STV FTV Wi-fi ⊗ ⊗ ⚓ 27 ⚐ Putt green Fishing Gym
Squash Beauty salon Football pitch Driving range
Fitness Studio Xmas New Year **Conf** Class 100
Board 40 Thtr 250 **Services** Lift **Parking** 400
Notes ⊗ Civ Wed 150

Menzies Hotels London Chigwell Prince Regent

MenziesHotels

★★★★ 75% HOTEL

☎ 020 8505 9966
Manor Rd IG8 8AE
e-mail: princeregent@menzieshotels.co.uk
web: www.menzieshotels.co.uk
dir: From A113 (Chigwell Rd) S of Chigwell into B173
(Manor Rd)

Situated on the edge of Woodford Bridge and
Chigwell, this hotel with delightful rear gardens,
offers easy access into London as well as to the M11
and M25. There is a good range of spacious, well-
equipped bedrooms. Extensive conference and
banqueting facilities are particularly well appointed,
and are very suitable for weddings or business
events.

Rooms 61 (4 fmly) (15 GF) (10 smoking) ☞
Facilities STV FTV Wi-fi ⊗ Xmas New Year
Conf Class 180 Board 80 Thtr 400 **Services** Lift
Parking 225 **Notes** Civ Wed 350

Petwood

★★★ 73% HOTEL

☎ 01526 352411
Stixwould Rd LN10 6QG
e-mail: reception@petwood.co.uk
web: www.petwood.co.uk
dir: From Sleaford take A153 (signed Skegness). At
Tattershall turn left on B1192. Hotel is signed from
village

This lovely Edwardian house, set in 30 acres of
gardens and woodlands, is adjacent to Woodhall Golf
Course. Built in 1905, the house was used by 617
Squadron, the famous Dambusters, as an officers'
mess during World War II. Bedrooms and public areas
are spacious and comfortable, and retain many
original features. Weddings and conferences are well
catered for in modern facilities.

Rooms 53 (3 GF) ☞ **Facilities** FTV Wi-fi HL Putt green
⚑ ♬ Xmas New Year **Conf** Class 100 Board 50
Thtr 250 **Services** Lift **Parking** 140
Notes Civ Wed 200

Golf Hotel

★★★ 72% HOTEL

☎ 01526 353535
The Broadway LN10 6SG
e-mail: reception@thegolf-hotel.com
web: www.thegolf-hotel.com
dir: From Lincoln take B1189 to Metheringham onto
B1191 towards Woodhall Spa. Hotel on left in approx
500yds from rdbt

Located near the centre of the village, this traditional
hotel is ideally situated to explore the Lincolnshire
countryside and coast. The adjacent golf course
makes this a popular venue for golfers, and the
hotel's hydrotherapy suite uses the original spa water
supplies. Bedrooms vary in size.

Rooms 50 (2 fmly) (8 GF) (3 smoking) **Facilities** Spa
FTV Wi-fi Xmas New Year **Conf** Class 50 Board 50
Thtr 150 **Services** Lift **Parking** 100
Notes Civ Wed 150

W

WOODLANDS   Map 5 SU31
Hampshire

Woodlands Lodge Hotel
★★★ 78% ◉ HOTEL

☎ 023 8029 2257
Bartley Rd, Woodlands SO40 7GN
e-mail: reception@woodlands-lodge.co.uk
web: www.woodlands-lodge.co.uk
dir: M27 junct 2, left at rdbt towards Fawley. 2nd rdbt right towards Cadnam. 1st left at White Horse pub onto Woodlands Rd, over cattle grid

An 18th-century former hunting lodge, this hotel is set in four acres of impressive and well-tended grounds on the edge of the New Forest. Well-equipped bedrooms come in varying sizes and styles and a number of bathrooms have a jacuzzi bath. Public areas include a pleasant lounge and intimate cocktail bar.

Rooms 17 (3 fmly) (3 GF) ⮰ **D** £59-£249 (incl. bkfst)* **Facilities** FTV Wi-fi Xmas New Year **Conf** Class 20 Board 20 Thtr 65 Del from £100 to £175* **Parking** 60 **Notes** Civ Wed 100

WOODSTOCK   Map 11 SP41
Oxfordshire

The Feathers Hotel
★★★★ 80% ◉ ◉
TOWN HOUSE HOTEL

☎ 01993 812291
Market St OX20 1SX
e-mail: reception@feathers.co.uk
dir: From A44 (Oxford to Woodstock), 1st left after lights. Hotel on left

This intimate and unique hotel enjoys a town centre location with easy access to nearby Blenheim Palace. Public areas are elegant and full of traditional character from the cosy drawing room to the atmospheric restaurant. Individually styled bedrooms are appointed to a high standard and are furnished with attractive period and reproduction furniture.

Rooms 21 (5 annexe) (4 fmly) (2 GF) ⮰ **S** £129-£229; **D** £199-£229 (incl. bkfst) **Facilities** FTV Wi-fi ⮰ Xmas New Year **Conf** Class 18 Board 20 Thtr 40 Del £216 **Notes** LB

Macdonald Bear Hotel

★★★★ 77% ◉ ◉ HOTEL

☎ 0844 879 9143
Park St OX20 1SZ
e-mail: gm.bear@macdonaldhotels.co.uk
web: www.macdonaldhotels.co.uk
dir: M40 junct 9 follow signs for Oxford & Blenheim Palace. A44 to town centre, hotel on left

With its ivy-clad façade, oak beams and open fireplaces, this 13th-century coaching inn exudes charm and cosiness. The bedrooms are decorated in a modern style that remains in keeping with the historic character of the building. Public rooms include a variety of function rooms, an intimate bar area and an attractive restaurant where attentive service and good food are offered. Macdonald Hotels is the AA Hotel Group of the Year 2013-14.

Rooms 54 (18 annexe) (1 fmly) (8 GF) ⮰ **Facilities** FTV Wi-fi Xmas New Year **Conf** Class 12 Board 24 Thtr 40 **Parking** 40

Kings Arms Hotel
★★★ 79% ◉ HOTEL

☎ 01993 813636
19 Market St OX20 1SU
e-mail: stay@kingshotelwoodstock.co.uk
web: www.kings-hotel-woodstock.co.uk
dir: In town centre, on corner of Market St & A44

This appealing and contemporary hotel is situated in the centre of town just a short walk from Blenheim Palace. Public areas include an attractive bistro-style restaurant and a smart bar. Bedrooms and bathrooms are comfortably furnished and well equipped, and appointed to a high standard.

Rooms 15 ⮰ **Facilities** FTV Wi-fi Xmas New Year **Notes** ⊗ No children 12yrs

Hope House Woodstock

AA Advertised

☎ 01993 815990 & 07587 775040
14 Oxford St OX20 1TS
e-mail: stay@hopehousewoodstock.co.uk
dir: M40 junct 8, A40 towards Oxford, A44 towards Woodstock. Left into Hewsington Rd on right after Punch Bowl pub

Built in the early 18th century for a local councillor and mayor, Hope House is one of a few grand houses in Woodstock built at the same time as Blenheim Palace, in the same architectural style, and to which it is seen as a sister property. The Money family owned and operated glove-making factories in Woodstock, and held a Royal Warrant to supply Queen Victoria with leather boots, saddles and gloves. The Moneys have lived here for centuries and it is still

owned and operated by a descendant of the family. There are three suites and an apartment, all of which are sumptuously decorated and equipped. Breakfast is very special, using locally sourced produce and home-made sausages.

Rooms 6 (1 annexe) (2 fmly) (1 GF) **S** £195-£495; **D** £250-£495 (incl. bkfst)* **Facilities** STV FTV Wi-fi ⮰ Fishing Beauty treatments **Services** Air con **Parking** 5 **Notes** ⊗

WOODY BAY   Map 3 SS64
Devon

Woody Bay Hotel
★★ 78% HOTEL

☎ 01598 763264 & 763563
EX31 4QX
e-mail: info@woodybayhotel.co.uk
dir: Signed from A39 between Blackmoor Gate & Lynton

Popular with walkers, this Victorian country style hotel is perfectly situated to enjoy sweeping views over Woody Bay. Bedrooms vary in style and size, but all boast truly magnificent views across dense woodland to the sea beyond. The same views can be enjoyed from the restaurant where local fish features prominently on the imaginative menus.

Rooms 7 (1 fmly) **Parking** 7 **Notes** ⊗ No children 5yrs Closed Dec-Jan RS Nov & Feb

WOOKEY HOLE   Map 4 ST54
Somerset

Wookey Hole Hotel
★★ 74% HOTEL

☎ 01749 672243
BA5 1BB
e-mail: witch@wookey.co.uk

This impressive, newly-built hotel is located in the heart of the pretty village, famous for its magnificent cave system and just a couple of miles from the historic cathedral city of Wells. The bedrooms are modern, spacious and comfortable with both family and connecting rooms available. Additional facilities include a bar and restaurant. There is ample parking provision.

Rooms 58 (37 fmly) (27 GF) **Facilities** FTV Wi-fi ⮰ 9 hole adventure golf course Xmas New Year **Conf** Class 200 Board 200 Thtr 450 Del from £50 to £200 **Services** Lift **Parking** 800 **Notes** ⊗ Civ Wed 250

W

WOOLACOMBE
Devon   Map 3 SS44

Watersmeet Hotel

★★★★ 76% ◉◉ HOTEL

☎ 01271 870333
Mortehoe EX34 7EB
e-mail: info@watersmeethotel.co.uk
web: www.watersmeethotel.co.uk
dir: B3343 into Woolacombe, right onto esplanade, hotel 0.75m on left

With magnificent views, and steps leading directly to the beach, this popular hotel offers guests attentive service and a relaxing atmosphere. Bedrooms benefit from the wonderful sea views and some have private balconies. Diners in the attractive tiered restaurant can admire the beautiful sunsets while enjoying an innovative range of dishes offered on the fixed-price menu. Both indoor and outdoor pools are available.

Rooms 25 (4 fmly) (3 GF) ⚫ **Facilities** FTV Wi-fi ♦ ⓧ ⚫ ⚫ Steam room ♫ Xmas New Year **Conf** Board 20 Thtr 20 **Services** Lift **Parking** 38 **Notes** ⊗ Civ Wed 60

The Woolacombe Bay Hotel

★★★★ 74% HOTEL

☎ 01271 870388
South St EX34 7BN
e-mail: enquiries@woolacombebayhotel.co.uk
web: www.woolacombebayhotel.com
dir: A361 onto B3343 to Woolacombe. Hotel in centre

This family-friendly hotel is adjacent to the beach and the village centre, and has a welcoming environment. The public areas are spacious and comfortable, and many of the well-equipped bedrooms have balconies with splendid views over the bay. In addition to the elegant surroundings of Doyle's Restaurant, The Bay Brasserie is available for an informal alternative. Extensive leisure facilities are also provided.

Rooms 69 (26 fmly) (2 GF) ⚫ **S** £105-£160; **D** £210-£320 (incl. bkfst)* **Facilities** Spa FTV Wi-fi ⓧ ⚫ ⚫ 9 ⚫ Gym Squash Paddling pool Table tennis Snooker Steam room Sauna Outdoor short mat bowls Xmas New Year Child facilities **Conf** Class 150 Board 150 Thtr 200 Del from £110 to £210* **Services** Lift **Parking** 150 **Notes** ⊗ Closed 2 Jan-14 Feb Civ Wed 150

Trimstone Manor Country House Hotel

★★★ ☒

☎ 01271 862841 & 868050
Trimstone EX34 8NR
e-mail: info@trimstone.co.uk
web: www.trimstone.co.uk
dir: M5 junct 27 towards Barnstaple, A361, through Braunton & Knowle. Left into Trimstone Lane after 1m, hotel 300yds on left.

With a history that goes back to the Domesday Book and parts of the building dating back 400 years, this manor house, in 44-acre landscaped grounds, is situated near the sandy beaches at Saunton Sands, Woolacombe and Croyde. The public areas include a lounge bar, Tyme Restaurant, a swimming pool, sauna, gym and games room; outside there is a terrace - perfect for enjoying a drink while enjoying the views.

Rooms 15 (2 fmly) (3 GF) ⚫ **Facilities** FTV Wi-fi ⓧ ⚫ Gym Sauna Games room Xmas New Year **Conf** Class 45 Board 40 Thtr 100 **Parking** 20 **Notes** Civ Wed 179

WORCESTER
Worcestershire   Map 10 SO85

Premier Inn Worcester

BUDGET HOTEL

☎ 0871 527 9188
Wainwright Way, Warndon WR4 9FA
web: www.premierinn.com
dir: M5 junct 6. At entrance of Warndon commercial development area

High quality, budget accommodation ideal for both families and business travellers. Spacious, en suite bedrooms feature tea and coffee making facilities, and Freeview TV in most hotels. Internet access and Wi-fi are available for a small fee. The adjacent family restaurant features a wide and varied menu. See also the Hotel Groups pages.

Rooms 60

WORKINGTON
Cumbria   Map 18 NY02

Washington Central Hotel

★★★★ 74% HOTEL

☎ 01900 65772
Washington St CA14 3AY
e-mail: kawildwchotel@aol.com
web: www.washingtoncentralhotelworkington.com
dir: M6 junct 40, A66 to Workington. Left at lights, hotel on right

Enjoying a prominent town centre location, this modern hotel boasts memorably hospitable staff. The well-maintained and comfortable bedrooms are equipped with a range of thoughtful extras. Public areas include numerous lounges, a spacious bar, Caesars leisure club, a smart restaurant and a popular coffee shop. The comprehensive conference facilities are ideal for meetings and weddings.

Rooms 46 (4 fmly) **S** £95-£115; **D** £140-£220 (incl. bkfst)* **Facilities** FTV Wi-fi ♦ ⓧ supervised Gym Sauna Steam room New Year **Conf** Class 200 Board 100 Thtr 300 Del £145* **Services** Lift **Parking** 25 **Notes** LB ⊗ Civ Wed 300

WORKSOP
Nottinghamshire   Map 16 SK57

BEST WESTERN Lion Hotel

★★★ 80% HOTEL

☎ 01909 477925
112 Bridge St S80 1HT
e-mail: reception@thelionworksop.co.uk
web: www.thelionworksop.co.uk
dir: A57 to town centre, turn right at Sainsburys, follow to Norfolk Arms, turn left

This former coaching inn lies on the edge of the main shopping precinct, with a car park to the rear. It has been extended to offer modern accommodation that includes excellent executive rooms. A wide range of interesting dishes is offered in both the restaurant and bar.

Rooms 46 (3 fmly) (7 GF) 🏠 **S** £61-£91; **D** £74-£104 (incl. bkfst)* **Facilities** STV FTV Wi-fi 🕽 Xmas New Year **Conf** Class 80 Board 70 Thtr 160 Del from £105 to £140* **Services** Lift **Parking** 50 **Notes** LB Civ Wed 150

WORSLEY
Map 15 SD70
Greater Manchester

Novotel Manchester West

★★★ 73% HOTEL

☎ 0161 799 3535
Worsley Brow M28 2YA
e-mail: H0907@accor.com
web: www.novotel.com
dir: Adjacent to M60 junct 13

Well placed for access to the Peak District and the Lake District, as well as Manchester, this modern hotel successfully caters for both families and business guests. The spacious bedrooms have sofa beds and a large work area; the hotel has an outdoor swimming pool, children's play area and secure parking.

Rooms 119 (10 fmly) (41 GF) 🏠 **Facilities** STV Wi-fi 🕽 Gym Xmas New Year **Conf** Class 130 Board 60 Thtr 220 **Services** Lift **Parking** 95 **Notes** Civ Wed 140

WORTHING
Map 6 TQ10
West Sussex

Ardington Hotel

★★★ 80% HOTEL

☎ 01903 230451
Steyne Gardens BN11 3DZ
e-mail: reservations@ardingtonhotel.co.uk
web: www.ardingtonhotel.co.uk
dir: A27 to Lancing, to seafront. Follow signs for Worthing. Left at church into Steyne Gardens

Overlooking Steyne Gardens adjacent to the seafront, this popular hotel offers well-appointed bedrooms with a good range of facilities. There's a stylishly modern lounge/bar with ample seating, where a light menu is available throughout the day. The popular restaurant offers local seafood and a choice of modern dishes. Wi-fi is available in lounge/bar.

Rooms 45 (4 fmly) (12 GF) **S** £65-£79; **D** £80-£170 (incl. bkfst)* **Facilities** STV FTV Wi-fi **Conf** Class 60 Board 35 Thtr 140 Del from £90 to £150* **Notes** LB Closed 25 Dec-4 Jan

Kingsway Hotel

★★ 74% HOTEL

☎ 01903 237542
Marine Pde BN11 3QQ
e-mail: accounts@kingswayhotel-worthing.co.uk
dir: A27 to Worthing seafront follow signs 'Hotel West'. Hotel 0.75m west of pier

Ideally located on the seafront and close to the town centre, this family-owned property extends a warm welcome to guests. Bedrooms vary in size, and some are very spacious with impressive sea views. Comfortable public areas include two modern lounges, a bright, stylish bar and well appointed restaurant.

Rooms 36 (7 annexe) (4 fmly) (3 GF) 🏠 **Facilities** FTV Wi-fi Xmas **Conf** Class 25 Board 25 Thtr 50 **Services** Lift **Parking** 9

WOTTON-UNDER-EDGE
Map 4 ST79
Gloucestershire

Tortworth Court Four Pillars Hotel

★★★★ 78% ⊛ HOTEL

☎ 0800 374 692 & 01454 263000
Tortworth GL12 8HH
e-mail: tortworth@four-pillars.co.uk
web: www.four-pillars.co.uk/tortworth
dir: M5 junct 14, B4509 towards Wotton. 1st right into Tortworth Rd next right, hotel 0.5m on right

Set within 30 acres of parkland, this Gothic mansion displays original features cleverly combined with contemporary additions. Elegant public rooms include a choice of dining options, one housed within the library, another in the atrium and the third in the orangery. Bedrooms are well equipped, and additional facilities include a host of conference rooms and a leisure centre.

Rooms 190 (25 fmly) (74 GF) **S** £79-£149; **D** £79-£149 **Facilities** Spa FTV Wi-fi 🕃 🏊 Gym Steam room Sauna Xmas New Year **Conf** Class 200 Board 80 Thtr 400 Del from £139 to £189 **Services** Lift **Parking** 200 **Notes** LB ⊗ Civ Wed 400

WREA GREEN
Map 18 SD33
Lancashire

The Spa Hotel at Ribby Hall Village

★★★★ 80% ⊛⊛ HOTEL

☎ 01772 671111 & 0800 085 1717
Ribby Hall Village, Ribby Rd PR4 2PR
e-mail: enquiries@ribbyhall.co.uk
dir: M55 junct 33 follow A585 towards Kirkham & brown tourist signs for Ribby Hall Village. Straight across 3 rdbts. Ribby Hall Village 200yds on left

Set in one hundred acres of rolling countryside, Ribby Hall is a tranquil and relaxing place to stay. The well appointed bedrooms are comfortable. The spa has a range of facilities including an outdoor pool and sauna. The hotel also has a gym and treatment rooms.

Rooms 42 (14 GF) 🏠 **S** £90-£190; **D** £180-£380 (incl. bkfst)* **Facilities** Spa STV FTV Wi-fi 🕽 🏊 Fishing Gym Squash **Services** Lift Air con **Parking** 124 **Notes** LB ⊗ No children 18yrs

WROTHAM
Map 6 TQ65
Kent

Holiday Inn Maidstone Sevenoaks

Holiday Inn

★★★ 77% HOTEL

☎ 0871 942 9054 & 01732 781510
London Rd, Wrotham Heath TN15 7RS
e-mail: reservations-maidstone@ihg.com
web: www.holidayinn.co.uk
dir: M26 junct 2A onto A20. Hotel on left

This purpose-built hotel is located within easy reach of the world-famous Brands Hatch racing circuit as well as historic Leeds and Hever Castles. Bedrooms are very spacious, and comfortably furnished with many accessories. A bar, restaurant and lounges are also available as well as a range of modern meeting rooms and a fully equipped leisure centre.

Rooms 105 (16 fmly) (6 GF) (10 smoking) **Facilities** STV Wi-fi 🕃 supervised Gym Steam room Sauna Beaty treatment room New Year **Conf** Class 35 Board 30 Thtr 100 **Services** Air con **Parking** 120 **Notes** ⊗ Civ Wed 100

W

WROTHAM *continued*

Premier Inn Sevenoaks/ Maidstone

BUDGET HOTEL

☎ 0871 527 8962
London Rd, Wrotham Heath TN15 7RX
web: www.premierinn.com
dir: M26 junct 2a, A20 S. At light left onto A20 towards West Malling. Hotel on right.

High quality, budget accommodation ideal for both families and business travellers. Spacious, en suite bedrooms feature tea and coffee making facilities, and Freeview TV in most hotels. Internet access and Wi-fi are available for a small fee. The adjacent family restaurant features a wide and varied menu. See also the Hotel Groups pages.

Rooms 40

WROXALL   Map 10 SP27
Warwickshire

Wroxall Abbey Estate

★★★★ 75% HOTEL

☎ 01926 484470 & 486730
Birmingham Rd CV35 7NB
e-mail: info@wroxall.com
dir: Between Solihull & Warwick on A4141

Situated in 27 acres of open parkland, yet only 10 miles from the NEC and Birmingham International Airport, this hotel is a magnificent Victorian mansion. Some of the individually designed bedrooms have traditional decor but there are some modern loft rooms as well; some rooms have four-posters. Sonnets Restaurant, with its impressive fireplace and oak panelling, makes the ideal setting for fine dining.

Rooms 70 (22 annexe) (10 GF) 🛏 **S** £89-£145;
D £99-£399* **Facilities** Spa STV Wi-fi 🕃 🏊 Fishing 🏌 Gym Ten-pin bowling Walking & jogging trail 🎵 Xmas New Year **Conf** Class 80 Board 60 Thtr 160 Del from £99* **Services** Lift **Parking** 200 **Notes** ⊗ No children 12yrs Civ Wed 200

WROXHAM   Map 13 TG31
Norfolk

Hotel Wroxham

★★ 71% HOTEL

☎ 01603 782061
The Bridge NR12 8AJ
e-mail: reservations@hotelwroxham.co.uk
web: www.arlingtonhotelgroup.co.uk
dir: From Norwich, A1151 signed Wroxham & The Broads, approx 7m. Over bridge at Wroxham, 1st right, sharp right. Hotel car park on right

Perfectly placed for touring the Norfolk Broads this hotel is in the heart of the bustling town centre. The bedrooms are pleasantly decorated and well equipped, and some have balconies with lovely views of the busy waterways. The open-plan public rooms include the lively riverside bar, lounge, large sun terrace and restaurant.

Rooms 18 (2 fmly) **S** £59.90-£69.50;
D £88.50-£98.50 (incl. bkfst)* **Facilities** FTV Wi-fi Fishing Boating facilities (by arrangement) **Conf** Class 50 Board 20 Thtr 200 Del from £100 to £125 **Parking** 45 **Notes** LB Civ Wed 40

WYBOSTON   Map 12 TL15
Bedfordshire

Wyboston Lakes Hotel

★★★ 80% ⍟ HOTEL

☎ 0333 700 7667 & 01480 479300
Wyboston Lakes, Great North Rd MK44 3BA
e-mail: reservations@wybostonlakes.co.uk
dir: From A1, A428, follow brown Cambridge signs. Wyboston Lakes & hotel on right, marked by flags

Ideally located adjacent to the A1 on the Cambridgeshire/Bedfordshire border, Wyboston Lakes is easily accessible. The hotel is located within an extensive conference and leisure complex that includes a brand new beauty and spa department and full golf facilities. Bedrooms are contemporary, and offer a range of amenities to suit both the business and leisure traveller. The dining room overlooks the idyllic lake.

Rooms 103 (39 annexe) (18 fmly) (50 GF)
S £72-£112; **D** £82-£122 (incl. bkfst)* **Facilities** Spa FTV Wi-fi 🕃 🏌 18 Putt green Fishing Gym Golf driving range **Conf** Class 56 Board 40 Thtr 130 Del from £99* **Services** Lift **Parking** 200 **Notes** LB ⊗ Closed 24-26 & 31 Dec & 1 Jan Civ Wed 100

YARM   Map 19 NZ41
North Yorkshire

Crathorne Hall Hotel

★★★★ ⍟⍟ HOTEL

☎ 01642 700398
Crathorne TS15 0AR
e-mail: crathornehall@handpicked.co.uk
web: www. handpickedhotels.co.uk/crathorne-hall
dir: From A19 take slip road signed Teesside Airport & Kirklevington, right signed Crathorne to hotel

This splendid Edwardian hall sits in its own landscaped grounds and enjoys fine views of the Leven Valley and rolling Cleveland Hills. The impressively equipped bedrooms and delightful public areas offer sumptuous levels of comfort, with elegant antique furnishings that complement the hotel's architectural style. All bedrooms and suites offer large flat-screen TVs and free broadband among their many facilities. The elegant Leven Restaurant is a traditional setting for fine dining; there's also the Drawing Room for lighter food options. Weather permitting, alfresco eating is available on the terrace, and afternoon tea is always popular. Conference and banqueting facilities are available.

Rooms 37 (10 fmly) 🛏 **S** £100-£130; **D** £130-£170 (incl. bkfst)* **Facilities** STV FTV Wi-fi 🕃 HL 🏊 Jogging track Clay pigeon shooting Xmas **Conf** Class 75 Board 60 Thtr 120 Del from £155 to £175* **Services** Lift **Parking** 88 **Notes** LB ⊗ Civ Wed 90

W

INSPECTORS' CHOICE

Judges Country House Hotel

★★★ ◉◉◉
COUNTRY HOUSE HOTEL

☎ 01642 789000
Kirklevington Hall TS15 9LW
e-mail: enquiries@judgeshotel.co.uk
web: www.judgeshotel.co.uk
dir: 1.5m from A19. At A67 junct, follow Yarm road, hotel on left

Formerly a lodging for local circuit judges, this gracious mansion lies in landscaped grounds through which a stream runs. Stylish bedrooms are individually decorated and come with plenty of extras; four-poster bedrooms and suites are available. The Conservatory restaurant serves award-winning cuisine, and private dining for a small number of guests is available in the wine cellar. Judges is a popular wedding venue. The genuinely caring and attentive service from the staff is truly memorable.

Rooms 21 (3 fmly) (5 GF) ✿ **S** £99-£180;
D £110-£210* **Facilities** FTV Wi-fi ↕ ⚓ Gym Mountain bikes Nature trails Beauty treatment room Xmas New Year **Conf** Class 120 Board 80 Thtr 200 Del from £210 to £240* **Parking** 102 **Notes** LB ⊗ Civ Wed 200

YARMOUTH	Map 5 SZ38
Isle of Wight	

INSPECTORS' CHOICE

The George Hotel

★★★ ◉◉ HOTEL

☎ 01983 760331
Quay St PO41 0PE
e-mail: res@thegeorge.co.uk
dir: Between castle & pier

This delightful 17th-century hotel enjoys a wonderful location at the water's edge, adjacent to the castle and the quay. Public areas include a bright brasserie where organic and local produce are utilised, a cosy bar and an inviting lounge. Individually styled bedrooms, with many thoughtful extras, are beautifully appointed; some benefit from spacious balconies. The hotel's motor yacht is available for guests to hire.

Rooms 19 (1 GF) **S** £99-£137.50; **D** £190-£287 (incl. bkfst)* **Facilities** STV Wi-fi Sailing from Yarmouth Mountain biking **Conf** Class 20 Board 20 Thtr 40 Del from £185* **Notes** LB ⊗ No children 10yrs

---

Norton Grange Coastal Village

Warner Leisure Hotels

AA Advertised

☎ 01983 760 323
PO41 0SD
dir: From Yarmouth Ferry Terminal leaving Yarmouth harbour, turn right at rdbt, follow road across Yarmouth bridge (A3054). After approx 0.5m hotel on right after bend

Sitting pretty in one of the UK's sunniest spots just five minutes from Yarmouth ferry port, with access to scenic coastal walks, this friendly chalet village is a favourite for sunseekers. A wide range of leisure activities is on offer, and there is nightly entertainment on the popular half-board breaks.

Rooms 208 **Notes** Closed Jan-Mar

YATELEY	Map 5 SU86
Hampshire	

Casa Hotel & Marco Pierre White Restaurant

★★★ 74% HOTEL

☎ 01252 873275
Handford Ln GU46 6BT
e-mail: reservations@casadeicesari.co.uk
dir: M3 junct 4a, follow signs for town centre. Hotel signed

This delightful hotel where a warm welcome is guaranteed is ideally located for transport networks. It boasts rooms with quality and comfort, and the Marco Pierre White Wheeler's of St James's Restaurant, which is very popular locally, serves an extensive traditional menu.

Rooms 63 (2 fmly) (15 GF) (33 smoking)
Facilities Wi-fi ↕ Xmas New Year **Conf** Class 60 Board 60 Thtr 150 **Services** Lift **Parking** 80 **Notes** ⊗ Civ Wed 150

YATTON	Map 4 ST46
Somerset	

Bridge Inn

BUDGET HOTEL

OldEnglish

☎ 01934 839100 & 839101
North End Rd BS49 4AU
e-mail: bridge.yatton@newbridgeinns.co.uk
web: www.oldenglish.co.uk
dir: M5 junct 20, B3133 to Yatton. 1st left at rdbt, 1st left at 2nd rdbt. Hotel 2.5m on right

This establishment offers spacious, well-equipped bedrooms, and the bar/restaurant serves a variety of dishes throughout the day in a relaxed and informal environment. Breakfast is a self-service buffet plus a full English breakfast served at the table. There is also a play zone area for children. See also the Hotel Groups pages.

Rooms 41 (4 fmly) (20 GF) ✿ **Conf** Class 30 Board 50 Thtr 100

Y

YAXLEY
Suffolk — Map 13 TM17

The Auberge
◎ ◎ RESTAURANT WITH ROOMS

☎ 01379 783604
Ipswich Rd IP23 8BZ
e-mail: aubmail@the-auberge.co.uk
web: www.the-auberge.co.uk
dir: On A140 between Norwich & Ipswich at x-rds with B1117

A warm welcome awaits at this charming 15th-century property, which has been lovingly converted by the present owners from a rural pub into a smart restaurant with rooms. The restaurant has gained AA Rosettes for the good use of fresh, quality produce. The public areas have a wealth of character, such as exposed brickwork and beams, and the grounds are particularly well-kept and attractive. The spacious bedrooms are tastefully appointed and have many thoughtful touches; one bedroom has a four-poster.

Rooms 11 (11 annexe) (2 fmly)

YELVERTON
Devon — Map 3 SX56

Moorland Garden Hotel
★★★ 79% HOTEL

☎ 01822 852245
Yelverton PL20 6DA
e-mail: stay@moorlandgardenhotel.co.uk
dir: A38 from Exeter to Plymouth, then A386 towards Tavistock. 5m onto open moorland, hotel 1m on left

This hotel has a great location for either the city or Dartmoor, and sits in delightful gardens, a convenient and peaceful location. Bedrooms are spacious, all with garden views and some have impressive balconies. There is a choice of dining as well as a range of meeting and function rooms. Pleasant Devon cream teas are served in the garden in warmer months.

Rooms 44 (5 fmly) (17 GF) ♚ **S** £89-£200; **D** £125-£225 (incl. bkfst)* **Facilities** FTV Wi-fi ♄ HL Xmas New Year **Conf** Class 60 Board 50 Thtr 170 Del from £125 to £150* **Parking** 75 **Notes** LB Civ Wed 160

YEOVIL
Somerset — Map 4 ST51

The Yeovil Court Hotel & Restaurant
★★★ 78% ◎ ◎ HOTEL

☎ 01935 863746
West Coker Rd BA20 2HE
e-mail: unwind@yeovilhotel.com
web: www.yeovilcourthotel.com
dir: 2.5m W of town centre on A30

This comfortable, family-run hotel offers a very relaxed and caring atmosphere. Bedrooms are well equipped and neatly presented; some are located in an adjacent building. Public areas consist of a smart lounge, a popular bar and an attractive restaurant. Menus combine an interesting selection that includes lighter options and dishes suited to special occasion dining.

Rooms 30 (12 annexe) (3 fmly) (11 GF) **Facilities** FTV Wi-fi ♄ **Conf** Class 18 Board 30 Thtr 50 **Parking** 65 **Notes** RS Sat lunch, 25 Dec eve & 26 Dec Civ Wed 70

Premier Inn Yeovil
BUDGET HOTEL

☎ 0871 527 9192
Alvington Ln, Brympton BA22 8UX
web: www.premierinn.com
dir: M5 junct 25, A358, A303 follow Yeovil signs. At rdbt onto A3088. At next rdbt 1st left, at next rdbt turn left. Hotel on left

High quality, budget accommodation ideal for both families and business travellers. Spacious, en suite bedrooms feature tea and coffee making facilities, and Freeview TV in most hotels. Internet access and Wi-fi are available for a small fee. The adjacent family restaurant features a wide and varied menu. See also the Hotel Groups pages.

Rooms 20

Little Barwick House
◎ ◎ ◎ RESTAURANT WITH ROOMS

☎ 01935 423902
Barwick Village BA22 9TD
e-mail: littlebarwick@hotmail.com
dir: From Yeovil A37 towards Dorchester, left at 1st rdbt, 1st left, 0.25m on left

Situated in a quiet hamlet in three and half acres of gardens and grounds, this listed Georgian dower house is an ideal retreat for those seeking peaceful surroundings and good food. Just one of the highlights of a stay here is a meal in the restaurant, where good use is made of local ingredients. Each of the bedrooms has its own character, and a range of thoughtful extras such as fresh flowers, bottled water and magazines is provided.

Rooms 6

YORK
North Yorkshire — Map 16 SE65

***See also** Aldwark & Escrick*

Cedar Court Grand Hotel & Spa
★★★★★ 86% ◎ ◎ HOTEL

☎ 01904 380038
Station Rise YO1 6HT
e-mail: info@cedarcourtgrand.co.uk
web: www.cedarcourtgrand.co.uk
dir: In city centre, near station

Located in the heart of the city, this majestic Edwardian building, originally built in 1908, has been transformed into a luxury hotel. Spacious, air-conditioned accommodation offers deeply comfortable rooms with luxurious bathrooms. Public areas are equally impressive with a range of delightful lounges, a modern spa in the former vaults, and excellent meeting rooms. The Grill offers a high standard of cooking with modern, classic dishes on the menus, plus afternoon tea. Valet parking is a great asset given the hotel's central location.

Rooms 107 (14 GF) ♚ **S** £130-£300; **D** £130-£300* **Facilities** Spa FTV Wi-fi ♄ ⓣ supervised Gym Sauna Steam room Xmas New Year **Conf** Class 60 Board 50 Thtr 120 **Services** Lift Air con **Notes** LB ⊗ Civ Wed 120

Save on hotels. Book at **theAA.com/hotel**

YAX – YOR 479 **ENGLAND**

INSPECTORS' CHOICE

Middlethorpe Hall & Spa

★★★★ ◉◉ HOTEL

☎ 01904 641241
Bishopthorpe Rd, Middlethorpe YO23 2GB
e-mail: info@middlethorpe.com
dir: A1/A64 follow York West (A1036) signs, then
Bishopthorpe, Middlethorpe racecourse signs

This fine house, dating from the reign of William
and Mary, sits in acres of beautifully landscaped
gardens. The bedrooms vary in size but all are
comfortably furnished; some are located in the
main house, and others are in a cottage and
converted courtyard stables. Public areas include a
small spa and a stately drawing room where
afternoon tea is quite an event. The delightful
panelled restaurant is a perfect setting for enjoying
the imaginative cuisine.

Rooms 29 (19 annexe) (2 fmly) (10 GF) ⋔
S £139-£149; **D** £199-£279 (incl. bkfst)*
Facilities Spa FTV Wi-fi ⋈ ⊗ ⋓ Gym Xmas New
Year **Conf** Class 30 Board 25 Thtr 56 Del from £180
to £195* **Services** Lift **Parking** 71 **Notes** LB No
children 6yrs RS 25 & 31 Dec Civ Wed 56

Hotel du Vin York

★★★★ 81% ◉ HOTEL   Hotel du Vin & Bistro

☎ 01904 557350
89 The Mount YO24 1AX
e-mail: info.york@hotelduvin.com
web: www.hotelduvin.com
dir: A1036 towards city centre, 6m. Hotel on right
through lights.

This Hotel du Vin offers luxury and quality that will
cosset even the most discerning guest. Bedrooms are
decadent in design and the bathrooms have huge
monsoon showers and feature baths. Dinner in the
bistro provides a memorable highlight thanks to
exciting menus and a superb wine list. Staff
throughout are naturally friendly, nothing is too much
trouble.

Rooms 44 (3 fmly) (14 GF) **Facilities** STV FTV Wi-fi
Conf Class 8 Board 22 Thtr 22 **Services** Lift Air con
Parking 18 **Notes** Civ Wed 50

The Grange Hotel

★★★★ 78% ◉◉ HOTEL

☎ 01904 644744
1 Clifton YO30 6AA
e-mail: info@grangehotel.co.uk
web: www.grangehotel.co.uk
dir: On A19 York/Thirsk road, approx 500yds from city
centre

This bustling Regency town house is just a few
minutes' walk from the centre of York. A professional
service is efficiently delivered by caring staff in a very
friendly and helpful manner. Public rooms are
comfortable and have been stylishly furnished; these
include two dining options, the popular and informal
Cellar Bar, and main hotel restaurant The Ivy
Brasserie, which offers fine dining in a lavishly
decorated environment. The individually designed
bedrooms are comfortably appointed and have been
thoughtfully equipped.

Rooms 36 (6 GF) **Facilities** STV FTV Wi-fi Use of
nearby health club (chargeable) Xmas New Year
Conf Class 24 Board 24 Thtr 50 **Parking** 26
Notes Civ Wed 90

York Marriott Hotel

★★★★ 78% HOTEL

☎ 01904 701000
Tadcaster Rd YO24 1QQ
e-mail: mhrs.qqyyk.dos@marriott.com
web: www.yorkmarriott.co.uk
dir: From A64 at York 'West' onto A1036, follow signs
to city centre. Approx 1.5m, hotel on right after church
and lights

Overlooking the racecourse and Knavesmire Parkland,
this hotel offers modern accommodation, including
family rooms, all with comfort cooling. Within the
hotel, guests enjoy the use of extensive leisure
facilities including indoor pool, putting green and
tennis court. For those wishing to explore the historic
and cultural attractions, the city is less than a mile
away.

Rooms 151 (45 fmly) (27 GF) ⋔ **Facilities** Spa STV
FTV Wi-fi ⋈ HL ⊗ ⊜ Gym Beauty treatment Xmas
New Year **Conf** Class 90 Board 40 Thtr 190
Del from £135 to £155* **Services** Lift Air con
Parking 140 **Notes** ⊗ Civ Wed 140

BEST WESTERN PLUS Dean Court Hotel

★★★★ 76% ◉ HOTEL

☎ 01904 625082
Duncombe Place YO1 7EF
e-mail: sales@deancourt-york.co.uk
web: www.deancourt-york.co.uk
dir: In city centre opposite York Minster

This smart hotel enjoys a central location overlooking
The Minster, and guests will find the service is
particularly friendly and efficient. Bedrooms are
stylishly appointed and vary in size. Public areas are
elegant in a contemporary style and include the
popular D.C.H. restaurant which enjoys wonderful
views of the cathedral, and The Court café-bistro and
bar where a more informal, all-day menu is offered.
Valet parking is available.

Rooms 37 (4 fmly) ⋔ **S** £85-£150; **D** £99-£245 (incl.
bkfst)* **Facilities** FTV Wi-fi ⋈ Xmas New Year
Conf Class 12 Board 32 Thtr 50 Del from £130 to
£190* **Services** Lift **Parking** 30 **Notes** LB ⊗
Civ Wed 50

Y

YORK *continued*

Novotel York Centre

★★★★ 75% HOTEL

☎ 01904 611660
Fishergate YO10 4FD
e-mail: H0949@accor.com
web: www.novotel.com
dir: A19 north to city centre, hotel set back on left

Set just outside the ancient city walls, this modern, family-friendly hotel is conveniently located for visitors to the city. Bedrooms feature bathrooms with a separate toilet room, plus excellent desk space and sofa beds. Four rooms are equipped for less able guests. The hotel's facilities include indoor and outdoor children's play areas and an indoor pool.

Rooms 124 (124 fmly) **S** £65-£189; **D** £65-£189*
Facilities STV Wi-fi ↘ HL ⓣ Xmas New Year
Conf Class 100 Board 120 Thtr 210 Del from £120 to £239* **Services** Lift **Parking** 140 **Notes** LB

The Royal York Hotel & Events Centre

★★★★ 75% HOTEL

☎ 01904 653681
Station Rd YO24 1AA
e-mail: royalyork.reservations@principal-hayley.com
web: www.principal-hayley.com
dir: Adjacent to railway station

Situated in three acres of landscaped grounds in the very heart of the city, this Victorian railway hotel has views over the city and York Minster. Contemporary bedrooms are divided between those in the main hotel and the air-conditioned garden mews. There is also a leisure complex and state-of-the-art conference centre.

Rooms 167 (8 fmly) **Facilities** Wi-fi ⓣ Gym Steam room Weights room Xmas New Year **Conf** Class 250 Board 80 Thtr 410 **Services** Lift **Parking** 80 **Notes** ⊗ Civ Wed 160

Marmadukes Hotel

★★★★ 74% TOWN HOUSE HOTEL

☎ 01904 640101
4-5 St Peters Grove, Bootham YO30 6AQ
e-mail: reservations@marmadukesyork.com
web: www.marmadukesyork.com
dir: A1036 signed York for approx 6m past train station then signed Inner Ring Rd. Over Lendal bridge, at lights left onto A19 (Bootham Bar) for 0.4m, right into St Peters Grove

Quietly situated just a short walk from the Minster, Marmadukes is a classically furnished, period property with all the expected modern amenities. Steeped in history and with a Roman burial ground underneath the lawn, it also has a sauna and spa bath in the grounds. The bedrooms have antique furniture and many of the bathrooms have roll-top baths. The public areas, including the conservatory-style breakfast room, are equally impressive with an air of spaciousness.

Rooms 21 (2 fmly) (2 GF) ⚓ **Facilities** FTV Wi-fi ↘ Sauna **Conf** Class 20 Board 16 Thtr 20 **Parking** 14 **Notes** ⊗ Civ Wed 50

Mercure York Fairfield Hotel

★★★★ 73% COUNTRY HOUSE HOTEL

☎ 0844 815 9038
Shipton Rd, Skelton YO30 1XW
e-mail: gm.mercureyorkfairfieldmanor@jupiterhotels.co.uk
web: www.jupiterhotels.co.uk
dir: Exit A1237 onto A19, hotel 0.5m on left

This stylish Georgian mansion stands in six acres of private grounds on the outskirts of the city. The contemporary bedrooms, styled in reds or blues, have broadband access and flat-screen TVs; some rooms have garden and courtyard views. The suites have either four-poster or king-size beds and a separate seating area. Kilby's Restaurant serves bistro food, and 24-hour room service is available. There are good conference facilities.

Rooms 89 (20 fmly) (24 GF) ⚓ **Facilities** Wi-fi ↘ HL Xmas New Year **Conf** Class 72 Board 60 Thtr 180 **Services** Lift **Parking** 130 **Notes** ⊗ Civ Wed 150

The Churchill Hotel

★★★ 82% ◉◉ HOTEL

☎ 01904 644456
65 Bootham YO30 7DQ
e-mail: info@churchillhotel.com
dir: On A19 (Bootham), W from York Minster, hotel 250yds on right

A late Georgian manor house set in its own grounds, just a short walk from the Minster and other attractions. Period features and interesting artefacts relating to Winston Churchill are incorporated into smart contemporary design and up-to-date technology. Public areas include the Piano Bar & Restaurant, where innovative menus feature high quality, local produce.

Rooms 32 (4 fmly) (5 GF) **Facilities** Wi-fi ♫ Xmas New Year **Conf** Class 50 Board 30 Thtr 100 **Services** Lift **Parking** 40 **Notes** Civ Wed 70

Mount Royale

★★★ 80% HOTEL

☎ 01904 628856
The Mount YO24 1GU
e-mail: reservations@mountroyale.co.uk
web: www.mountroyale.co.uk
dir: W on A1036, 0.5m after racecourse. Hotel on right after lights

This friendly hotel, a listed building from the 1830s, offers comfortable bedrooms in a variety of styles, several leading onto the delightful gardens. Public rooms include a lounge, a meeting room and a cosy bar; the hotel has an outdoor pool, a sauna and a hot tub plus a beauty therapist. There is a separate restaurant called The Burbridges Restaurant, and a cocktail lounge overlooking the gardens. Limited car parking is also available.

Rooms 24 (3 fmly) (6 GF) ⚓ **S** £95-£185; **D** £125-£265 (incl. bkfst)* **Facilities** Spa FTV Wi-fi ⚛ supervised Beauty treatment centre Sauna Steam room Xmas New Year **Conf** Board 25 Thtr 35 Del £155* **Parking** 27 **Notes** LB

The Parsonage Country House Hotel

★★★ 79% ◉ COUNTRY HOUSE HOTEL

☎ 01904 728111
York Rd YO19 6LF
e-mail: reservations@parsonagehotel.co.uk
web: www.parsonagehotel.co.uk

(For full entry see Escrick)

BEST WESTERN Kilima Hotel

★★★ 79% HOTEL

☎ 01904 625787
129 Holgate Rd YO24 4AZ
e-mail: sales@kilima.co.uk
web: www.kilima.co.uk
dir: On A59, 1m from York city ctr

This establishment, a former rectory, is conveniently situated within easy walking distance of the city centre. There is a relaxed and friendly atmosphere with professional, friendly staff providing attentive service. Bedrooms are comfortable and well equipped. There is an indoor pool, a fitness centre and a Turkish steam room.

Rooms 26 (4 fmly) (10 GF) **S** £60-£120; **D** £80-£200 (incl. bkfst)* **Facilities** FTV Wi-fi ⇗ 🕲 Gym Leisure complex Steam room Fitness suite Xmas New Year **Conf** Board 14 Del from £125 to £195 **Parking** 26 **Notes** LB ⊗

BEST WESTERN Monkbar Hotel

★★★ 78% HOTEL

☎ 01904 638086
Monkbar YO31 7JA
e-mail: sales@monkbarhotel.co.uk
web: www.monkbarhotel.co.uk
dir: A64 onto A1079 to city, turn right at city walls, take middle lane at lights. Hotel on right

This smart hotel enjoys a prominent position adjacent to the city walls, and is just a few minutes' walk from York Minster. Individually styled bedrooms are well equipped for both business and leisure guests. Spacious public areas include comfortable lounges, a traditional Yorkshire bar, an airy restaurant and impressive meeting and training facilities.

Rooms 99 (8 fmly) (2 GF) 🌤 **S** £73.80-£130; **D** £78.30-£155* **Facilities** FTV Wi-fi ⇗ HL Xmas New Year **Conf** Class 80 Board 50 Thtr 140 Del from £130 to £165* **Services** Lift **Parking** 66 **Notes** LB Civ Wed 80

BEST WESTERN York Pavilion Hotel

★★★ 78% HOTEL

☎ 01904 622099 & 239900
45 Main St, Fulford YO10 4PJ
e-mail: reservations@yorkpavilionhotel.com
web: www.yorkpavilionhotel.com
dir: Exit A64 (York ring road) at A19 junct towards York. Hotel 0.5m on right opposite Pavilion Court

An attractive Georgian hotel situated in its own grounds. All the bedrooms are individually designed to a high specification; some are in the old house and some in the converted stables set around a garden terrace. There is a comfortable lounge, a conference centre and an inviting brasserie-style restaurant with a regularly changing menu.

Rooms 57 (4 fmly) (11 GF) 🌤 **S** £75-£95; **D** £85-£150 (incl. bkfst)* **Facilities** FTV Wi-fi ⇗ Xmas New Year **Conf** Class 120 Board 68 Thtr 250 Del from £110 to £140 **Parking** 55 **Notes** LB Civ Wed 250

Holiday Inn York

★★★ 78% HOTEL

☎ 0871 942 9085
Tadcaster Rd YO24 1QF
e-mail: reservations-york@ihg.com
web: www.hiyorkhotel.co.uk
dir: From A1(M) take A64 towards York. In 7m take A1036 to York. Straight over at rdbt to city centre. Hotel 0.5m on right

Located in a suburban area close to the city centre and overlooking York race course, this modern hotel caters equally well for business and leisure guests. Public areas include the spacious family friendly Junction Restaurant, a lounge bar and the Cedar Tree Terrace. Seven function rooms are also available for meetings and social events.

Rooms 142 (50 fmly) (14 GF) **Facilities** STV Wi-fi ⇗ HL Xmas New Year **Conf** Class 45 Board 55 Thtr 100 **Services** Lift Air con **Parking** 160

Park Inn by Radisson York City Centre

★★★ 73% HOTEL

☎ 01904 459988 & 459900
North St YO1 6JF
e-mail: info.york@rezidorparkinn.com
dir: A64/A1063 follow signs for city centre, into North St, hotel 250yds on right

Boasting spectacular views over the River Ouse in the heart of York, this hotel is just minutes away from all the attractions of this historic, walled city. There are impressive conference rooms and leisure facilities, and the RBG Lounge Bar, overlooking the river, serves a wide-ranging menu throughout the day. Private parking is available.

Rooms 200 (8 fmly) **Facilities** FTV Wi-fi Gym Sauna Dance studio Exercise classes Beauty treatments Reflexology Sports therapy Xmas New Year **Conf** Class 150 Board 75 Thtr 400 **Services** Lift Air con **Parking** 60 **Notes** ⊗

Knavesmire Manor Hotel

★★ 74% SMALL HOTEL

☎ 01904 702941
302 Tadcaster Rd YO24 1HE
e-mail: enquire@knavesmire.co.uk
dir: A1036 into city centre. Hotel on right, overlooking racecourse

Commanding superb views across York's famous racecourse, this former manor house offers comfortable, well-equipped bedrooms, either in the main house or the garden rooms to the rear. Comfortable day rooms are stylishly furnished, while the heated indoor pool provides a popular addition.

Rooms 20 (9 annexe) (3 fmly) **Facilities** FTV Wi-fi ⇗ 🕲 New Year **Conf** Class 36 Board 30 Thtr 40 Del from £89 to £120* **Services** Lift **Parking** 28 **Notes** Closed 23-27 Dec

Y

YORK *continued*

Lady Anne Middleton's Hotel

★★ 72% HOTEL

☎ 01904 611570
Skeldergate YO1 6DS
e-mail: bookings@ladyannes.co.uk
web: www.ladyannes.co.uk
dir: From A64 (Leeds) A1036 towards city centre.
Right at City Walls lights, keep left, 1st left before
bridge, then 1st left into Cromwell Rd. Hotel on right.
(NB for Sat Nav use YO1 6DU)

This hotel has been created from several listed
buildings and is very well located in the centre of
York. Bedrooms are comfortably equipped. Among its
amenities is a bar-lounge and a dining room where a
satisfying range of food is served. An extensive
fitness club is also available along with private
parking.

Rooms 57 (20 annexe) (15 fmly) (17 GF) 🐾
Facilities FTV Wi-fi ⟳ Gym Fitness centre Beauty
treatments Massage **Conf** Class 36 Board 36 Thtr 60
Parking 40 **Notes** ⊗ Closed 24-28 Dec

Holiday Inn Express York

BUDGET HOTEL

☎ 01904 438660
Malton Rd YO32 9TE
web: www.hiexpressyorkeast.co.uk
dir: From A64 take A1036 towards York centre. Hotel
on left behind The Hopgrove Toby Carvery

A modern hotel ideal for families and business
travellers. Fresh and uncomplicated, the spacious
rooms include Sky TV, power shower and tea and
coffee-making facilities. Continental buffet breakfast
is included in the room rate; other meals may be
taken at the nearby family pub or restaurant. See also
the Hotel Groups pages.

Rooms 49 (20 fmly) (21 GF) 🐾

Ibis York Centre

BUDGET HOTEL

☎ 01904 658301
77 The Mount YO24 1BN
e-mail: H6390@accor.com
dir: A64/A1036 follow signs to city centre, hotel on
right

Modern, budget hotel offering comfortable
accommodation in bright and practical bedrooms.
Breakfast is self-service and dinner is available in
the restaurant. See also the Hotel Groups pages.

Rooms 91 (17 fmly) (3 GF) 🐾 **Conf** Class 16 Board 16
Thtr 24

Premier Inn York City (Blossom St North)

BUDGET HOTEL

☎ 0871 527 9196
20 Blossom St YO24 1AJ
web: www.premierinn.com
dir: 12m from A1 junct 47, off A59

High quality, budget accommodation ideal for both
families and business travellers. Spacious, en suite
bedrooms feature tea and coffee making facilities,
and Freeview TV in most hotels. Internet access and
Wi-fi are available for a small fee. The adjacent
family restaurant features a wide and varied menu.
See also the Hotel Groups pages.

Rooms 86

Premier Inn York City (Blossom St South)

BUDGET HOTEL

☎ 0871 527 9194
28-40 Blossom St YO24 1AJ
web: www.premierinn.com
dir: From S, E & W: A64, A1036 (signed York West).
From N: A1 (or A19), A59, follow city centre signs. At
lights left onto A1036. Hotel on left just after cinema.
(NB no drop-off point, parking at NCP, Queens St)

Rooms 91

Premier Inn York North

BUDGET HOTEL

☎ 0871 527 9198
Shipton Rd YO30 5PA
web: www.premierinn.com
dir: From A1237 (ring road), A19 (Shipton Road
South) signed York Centre. Hotel on right in Clifton
Park

Rooms 49

Premier Inn York North West

BUDGET HOTEL

☎ 0871 527 9200
**White Rose Close, York Business Park, Nether
Poppleton YO26 6RL**
web: www.premierinn.com
dir: On A1237 between A19 (Thirsk road) & A59
(Harrogate road)

Rooms 64

Premier Inn York South West

BUDGET HOTEL

☎ 0871 527 9202
Bilbrough Top, Colton YO23 3PP
web: www.premierinn.com
dir: On A64 between Tadcaster & York

Rooms 61

YOXFORD	Map 13 TM36
Suffolk	

Satis House Hotel

★★★ 88% ◉◉ COUNTRY HOUSE HOTEL

☎ 01728 668418
IP17 3EX
e-mail: enquiries@satishouse.co.uk
web: www.satishouse.co.uk
dir: Off A12 between Ipswich & Lowestoft. 9m E
Aldeburgh & Snape

Expect a warm welcome from the caring hosts at this
delightful 18th-century, Grade II listed property set in
three acres of parkland. The stylish public areas have
a really relaxed atmosphere; they include a choice of
dining rooms, a smart bar and a cosy lounge. The
individually decorated bedrooms are tastefully
appointed and thoughtfully equipped.

Rooms 12 (4 annexe) (1 fmly) (4 GF) 🐾 **Facilities** STV
FTV Wi-fi ♪ Xmas New Year **Conf** Class 40 Board 20
Thtr 40 **Parking** 30 **Notes** Closed 23-27 Dec
Civ Wed 50

ISLE OF MAN

DOUGLAS   MAP 24 SC37

Mount Murray Hotel and Country Club

★★★★ 70% HOTEL

☎ 01624 661111
Santon IM4 2HT
e-mail: hotel@mountmurray.com
web: www.mountmurray.com
dir: 4m from Douglas towards airport. Hotel signed at Santon

This large, modern hotel and country club offers a wide range of sporting and leisure facilities, and a superb health and beauty salon. The attractively appointed public areas provide a choice of bars and eating options, including the Mallards Restaurant. The spacious bedrooms are well equipped and many enjoy fine views over the 200-acre grounds and golf course. There is a very large conference suite.

Rooms 103 (4 fmly) (27 GF) **Facilities** FTV Wi-fi 18 Putt green Gym Squash Driving range New Year **Conf** Class 200 Board 100 Thtr 300 **Services** Lift **Parking** 400 **Notes** ⊗ Civ Wed 120

Admiral House Hotel

★★★ 78% ◉◉ HOTEL

☎ 01624 629551
12 Loch Promenade IM1 2LX
e-mail: enquiries@admiralhouse.com
dir: Located 2 mins from Douglas Ferry Terminal. 20 mins from airport

Admiral House Hotel is a grand Victorian building with stunning views over Douglas Bay. Spacious bedrooms and public areas combine period features with contemporary style. The restaurant, Natica by Malcolm Bartolo, is a highlight, offering excellent food, a stylish setting and professional service. There is also a modern champagne and cocktail bar, and IGI's Café serves snacks and light meals throughout the day. Complimentary Wi-fi is provided throughout.

Rooms 23 (3 fmly) **Facilities** FTV Wi-fi Xmas New Year **Services** Lift **Notes** ⊗

PORT ERIN   Map 24 SC16

Falcon's Nest

★★ 72% HOTEL

☎ 01624 834077
The Promenade IM9 6AF
e-mail: falconsnest@enterprise.net
web: www.falconsnesthotel.co.uk
dir: Follow coast road S from airport or ferry. Hotel on seafront, immediately after steam railway station

Situated overlooking the bay and harbour, this Victorian hotel offers generally spacious bedrooms. There is a choice of bars, one of which attracts many locals. Meals can be taken in the lounge bar, the conservatory or in the attractively decorated main restaurant.

Rooms 39 (7 fmly) (15 smoking) **S** £49; **D** £85 (incl. bkfst)* **Facilities** FTV Wi-fi Xmas New Year **Conf** Class 50 Board 50 Thtr 50 **Parking** 20

ISLE OF MAN

Channel Islands

Save on hotels. Book at **theAA.com/hotel**

ALDERNEY – ST (GUERNSEY) 485 ENGLAND

ALDERNEY

ALDERNEY   Map 24

Braye Beach Hotel

★★★★ 73% ◉ HOTEL

☎ 01481 824300
Braye St GY9 3XT
e-mail: reception@brayebeach.com
web: www.brayebeach.com
dir: Follow coast road from airport

Situated just a stone's throw from Braye's harbour and beach, this hotel provides comfortable yet stylish accommodation where many guest rooms have sea views; all bedrooms are well appointed and generously equipped. Public rooms include the popular bar and lounge, spacious terrace for the summer months and even a cinema. The well-appointed restaurant offers a varied seasonal menu often showcasing locally caught fish. Private dining can be catered for in the vaulted wine cellar.

Rooms 27 (2 fmly) ⁂ **Facilities** FTV Wi-fi ⇘ Cinema Xmas New Year **Conf** Class 12 Board 16 Thtr 19 **Services** Lift **Notes** ⊗ Civ Wed 80

GUERNSEY

CASTEL   Map 24

Cobo Bay Hotel

★★★ 87% ◉◉ HOTEL

☎ 01481 257102
Coast Rd, Cobo GY5 7HB
e-mail: reservations@cobobayhotel.com
web: www.cobobayhotel.com
dir: From airport turn right, follow road to W coast at L'Eree. Turn right onto coast road for 3m to Cobo Bay. Hotel on right

A popular hotel situated on the seafront overlooking Cobo Bay. The well-equipped bedrooms are pleasantly decorated; many of the front rooms have balconies and there is a secluded sun terrace to the rear. Public rooms include the Chesterfield Bar with its leather sofas and armchairs and a welcoming award-winning restaurant and terrace with stunning views of the bay.

Rooms 34 (4 fmly) ⁂ **S** £59-£99; **D** £95-£210 (incl. bkfst)* **Facilities** STV FTV Wi-fi ⇘ Sauna Steam room **Conf** Class 30 Board 30 Thtr 100 **Services** Lift **Parking** 60 **Notes** LB ⊗

FOREST   Map 24

Le Chene Hotel

★★ 69% HOTEL

☎ 01481 235566
Forest Rd GY8 0AH
e-mail: info@lechene.co.uk
web: www.lechene.co.uk
dir: Between airport & St Peter Port. From airport left to St Peter Port. Hotel on right after 1st lights

This Victorian manor house is well located for guests wishing to explore Guernsey's spectacular south coast. The building has been skilfully extended to house a range of well-equipped, modern bedrooms. There is a swimming pool, a cosy cellar bar and a varied range of enjoyable freshly cooked dishes at dinner.

Rooms 26 (2 fmly) (1 GF) (1 smoking) **Facilities** Wi-fi ⇘ Library Xmas New Year **Parking** 20 **Notes** ⊗

ST MARTIN   Map 24

INSPECTORS' CHOICE

Bella Luce Hotel, Restaurant & Spa

★★★★ SMALL HOTEL

☎ 01481 238764
La Fosse GY4 6EB
e-mail: wakeup@bellalucehotel.com
dir: From airport, turn left to St Martin. At 3rd set of lights continue 30yds, turn right, straight on to hotel

This delightful hotel has taken a dramatic jump in to the contemporary and luxurious; a recent refurbishment has brought stylish bedrooms with comfortable beds and designer furnishings, superb bathrooms and up-to-the-minute technology. Public rooms have many interesting features and lots of soft settees and nooks and crannies where guests can relax. The restaurant offers the best produce Guernsey can provide, and chef has a keen sense of adventure. Staff are friendly and attentive, and make sure guests feel welcome.

Rooms 23 (4 fmly) (2 GF) **S** £135-£165; **D** £135-£240 (incl. bkfst)* **Facilities** STV FTV Wi-fi ⇘ ⓛ 18 Fishing Gym Sauna **Conf** Class 18 Board 25 Thtr 40 **Parking** 33 **Notes** ⊗ Closed 1st 2 wks Jan

La Barbarie Hotel

★★★ 82% ◉ HOTEL

☎ 01481 235217
Saints Rd, Saints Bay GY4 6ES
e-mail: reservations@labarbariehotel.com
web: www.labarbariehotel.com

This former priory dates back to the 17th century and retains much charm and style. Staff help to create a very friendly and attentive atmosphere, and the modern facilities offer guests a relaxing stay. Excellent choices and fresh local ingredients form the basis of the interesting menus in the attractive restaurant and bar.

Rooms 30 (8 GF) **S** £79-£112; **D** £79-£148 (incl. bkfst)* **Facilities** STV Wi-fi ⇘ **Parking** 50 **Notes** LB ⊗ Closed Nov-11 Mar

Hotel Jerbourg

★★★ 79% ◉ HOTEL

☎ 01481 238826
Jerbourg Point GY4 6BJ
e-mail: stay@hoteljerbourg.com
dir: From airport turn left to St Martin, right at filter, straight on at lights, hotel at end of road on right

This hotel boasts excellent sea views from its cliff-top location. Public areas are smartly appointed and include an extensive bar/lounge and bright conservatory-style restaurant. In addition to the fairly extensive carte, a daily-changing menu is available. Bedrooms are well presented and comfortable, and the luxury bay rooms are generally more spacious.

Rooms 32 (4 fmly) (5 GF) **S** £74-£159; **D** £89-£169 (incl. bkfst)* **Facilities** FTV Wi-fi ⇘ Petanque Xmas New Year **Parking** 50 **Notes** ⊗ Closed 5 Jan-1 Mar

ST MARTIN *continued*

Saints Bay Hotel

★★★ 77% HOTEL

☎ 01481 238888
Icart Rd GY4 6JG
e-mail: info@saintsbayhotel.com
dir: From St Martin take Saints Rd into Icart Rd

Ideally situated in an elevated position near Icart
Point headland and above the fishing harbour at
Saints Bay, this hotel has superb views. The spacious
public rooms include a smart lounge bar, a first-floor
lounge and a smart conservatory restaurant that
overlooks the swimming pool. Bedrooms are
pleasantly decorated and thoughtfully equipped.

Rooms 35 (1 fmly) (13 GF) **Facilities** FTV Wi-fi ⚡
Xmas New Year **Parking** 15 **Notes** ⊗

La Villette Hotel & Leisure Suite

★★★ 77% HOTEL

☎ 01481 235292
GY4 6QG
e-mail: reservations@lavillettehotel.co.uk
dir: Turn left from airport. Follow road past La Trelade
Hotel. Take next right, hotel on left

Set in spacious grounds, this peacefully located,
family-run hotel has a friendly atmosphere. The well-
equipped bedrooms are spacious and comfortable.
Live music is a regular feature in the large bar, while
in the separate restaurant a fixed-price menu is
provided. Residents have use of the excellent indoor
leisure facilities, and there are also beauty
treatments and a hairdressing salon.

Rooms 35 (3 fmly) (14 GF) ⚡ S £53-£60; D £90-£103
(incl. bkfst)* **Facilities** FTV Wi-fi 🐾 supervised ⚡
Gym Steam room Leisure suite Beauty salon
Hairdresser Petanque Xmas New Year **Conf** Board 40
Thtr 80 **Services** Lift **Parking** 50 **Notes** ⊗

ST PETER PORT   Map 24

The Old Government House Hotel & Spa

THE RED CARNATION HOTEL COLLECTION

★★★★★ 83% ◎◎ HOTEL

☎ 01481 724921
St Ann's Place GY1 2NU
e-mail: ogh@theoghhotel.com
web: www.theoghhotel.com
dir: At junct of St Julian's Ave & St Anns Place

The affectionately known OGH is one of the island's
leading hotels. Located in the heart of St Peter Port, it
is the perfect base from which to explore Guernsey
and the other islands of the Bailiwick. Bedrooms vary
in size but all are comfortable, and offer high quality
accommodation. There is an indulgent health club
and spa, and the eating options are the OGH
Brasserie, and award-winning Governor's that offers
local produce with a French twist. Red Carnation
Hotels is the AA Small Hotel Group of the Year
2013-14.

Rooms 62 (3 annexe) (6 fmly) ⚡ S £173-£430;
D £173-£430 (incl. bkfst) **Facilities** Spa STV Wi-fi 🦶
HL ⚡ Gym Steam room Sauna Spa pools Relaxiation
room 🎵 Xmas New Year **Conf** Class 69 Board 66
Thtr 200 Del from £268 to £525 **Services** Lift Air con
Parking 20 **Notes** LB

Fermain Valley Hotel

★★★★ 79% ◎◎ HOTEL

☎ 0800 316 0314 & 01481 235666
Fermain Ln GY1 1ZZ
e-mail: info@fermainvalley.com
dir: Turn left from airport, follow Forest Rd, right into
Le Route de Sausmarez, right into Fermain Lane at
Fermain Tavern. Hotel 100mtrs on left

This hotel occupies an amazing location high above
Fermain Bay with far reaching views out to sea; there
are lovely walks along the cliff or down the lanes from
the hotel. The delightfully furnished bedrooms, some
with balconies, have either views of the sea, the
valley or the well tended gardens. Informal eating is
available in the stylish Rock Garden bar, and in
summer on the terrace; the Valley Restaurant is the
fine dining option. The leisure facilities include a
pool, a sauna and a private cinema. The well-trained
staff provide warm and friendly service.

Rooms 43 (11 annexe) (2 fmly) ⚡ S £85-£210;
D £100-£225 (incl. bkfst) **Facilities** FTV Wi-fi 🐾 3D
Cinema Sauna Xmas New Year **Conf** Class 70
Board 45 Thtr 100 **Services** Lift **Parking** 50 **Notes** LB
⊗

The Duke of Richmond Hotel

THE RED CARNATION HOTEL COLLECTION

★★★★ 79% ◎ HOTEL

☎ 01481 726221
Cambridge Park GY1 1UY
e-mail: manager@dukeofrichmond.com
web: www.dukeofrichmond.com
dir: On corner of Cambridge Park & L'Hyvreuse Ave,
opposite leisure centre

Peacefully located in a mainly residential area
overlooking Cambridge Park, this hotel has
comfortable, well-appointed bedrooms that vary in
size. Public areas include a spacious lounge, a
terrace and the unique Sausmarez Bar, with its
nautical theme. The smartly uniformed team of staff
provide professional standards of service. Red
Carnation Hotels is the AA Small Hotel Group of the
Year 2013-14.

Rooms 73 (11 fmly) ⚡ S £145-£340; D £145-£340
(incl. bkfst) **Facilities** STV Wi-fi 🦶 HL ⚡ Xmas New
Year **Conf** Class 80 Board 40 Thtr 300 Del from £230
to £425 **Services** Lift Air con **Parking** 5 **Notes** LB

La Frégate Hotel & Restaurant

★★★★ 75% SMALL HOTEL

☎ 01481 724624
Les Cotils GY1 1UT
e-mail: enquiries@lafregatehotel.com

This intimate hotel enjoys a fabulous location with
unobstructed views overlooking St Peter Port and is
just a few minutes walk from the centre of town.
Bedrooms are appointed to a high standard; all are
spacious and all have a sea view. Public areas are
cosy and the dining room menus feature good use of
local produce.

Rooms 22 (4 fmly) ⚡ S £99.50; D £180-£232 (incl.
bkfst)* **Facilities** STV FTV Wi-fi Xmas New Year
Conf Class 20 Board 20 Thtr 40 Del from £175 to
£250* **Services** Lift **Parking** 20 **Notes** LB ⊗

St Pierre Park Hotel

★★★★ 74% HOTEL

☎ 01481 728282
Rohais GY1 1FD
e-mail: reservations@stpierrepark.co.uk
web: www.stpierrepark.co.uk
dir: From harbour straight over rdbt, up hill through 3
sets of lights. Right at filter, to lights. Straight ahead,
hotel 100mtrs on left

Peacefully located on the outskirts of town amidst 45
acres of grounds, this well established hotel also
features a 9-hole golf course. Most of the bedrooms
overlook the pleasant gardens and have either a
balcony or a terrace. Public areas include a choice of
restaurants and a stylish bar which opens onto a
spacious terrace, overlooking an elegant water
feature.

Rooms 131 (5 fmly) (20 GF) **S** £89–£189;
D £105–£209 (incl. bkfst) **Facilities** Spa STV Wi-fi
⚑ ⚓ 9 Putt green Gym Bird watching
Children's playground Crazy golf Xmas New Year
Conf Class 120 Board 70 Thtr 200 **Services** Lift
Parking 150 **Notes** LB ⊗

BEST WESTERN Hotel de Havelet

★★★ 81% HOTEL

☎ 01481 722199
Havelet GY1 1BA
e-mail: havelet@sarniahotels.com
dir: From airport follow signs for St Peter Port through
St. Martins. At bottom of 'Val de Terres' hill turn left
at top of hill, hotel on right

This extended Georgian hotel looks over the harbour to
Castle Cornet. Many of the well-equipped bedrooms
are set around a pretty colonial-style courtyard. Day
rooms in the original building have period elegance;
the restaurant and bar are on the other side of the car
park in converted stables.

Rooms 34 (4 fmly) (8 GF) (10 smoking)
S £85–£125; **D** £98–£164 (incl. bkfst)* **Facilities** FTV
Wi-fi Sauna Steam room Xmas New Year
Conf Class 20 Board 18 Thtr 30 Del from £120 to
£180* **Parking** 40 **Notes** LB ⊗

Les Rocquettes Hotel

★★★ 80% HOTEL

☎ 01481 722146
Les Gravees GY1 1RN
e-mail: rocquettes@sarniahotels.com
dir: From ferry terminal take 2nd exit at rdbt, through
5 sets of lights. After 5th lights into Les Gravees.
Hotel on right opposite church

This late 18th-century country mansion is in a good
location close to St Peter Port and Beau Sejour.
Bedrooms come in three grades - Deluxe, Superior
and Standard, but all have plenty of useful facilities.
Guests can eat in Oaks restaurant and bar. The hotel
has attractive lounge areas on three levels; there is a
health suite with a gym and swimming pool with an
integrated children's pool.

Rooms 51 (5 fmly) **S** £67–£125; **D** £88–£154 (incl.
bkfst)* **Facilities** FTV Wi-fi supervised Gym
Beauty treatment room Sauna Steam room Whirlpool
New Year **Conf** Class 60 Board 60 Thtr 100
Services Lift **Parking** 60 **Notes** LB ⊗

BEST WESTERN Moores Hotel

★★★ 79% HOTEL

☎ 01481 724452
Pollet GY1 1WH
e-mail: moores@sarniahotels.com
dir: Left at airport, follow signs to St Peter Port. Fort
Road to seafront, straight on, turn left before rdbt, to
hotel

An elegant granite town house situated in the heart of
St Peter Port amidst the shops and amenities. Public
rooms feature a smart conservatory restaurant which
leads out onto a first-floor terrace for alfresco dining;
there is also a choice of lounges and bars as well as
a patisserie. Bedrooms are pleasantly decorated and
thoughtfully equipped.

Rooms 49 (3 annexe) (8 fmly) **S** £85–£130;
D £90–£240 (incl. bkfst)* **Facilities** FTV Wi-fi Gym
Sauna Xmas New Year **Conf** Class 20 Board 18
Thtr 40 Del from £120 to £160* **Services** Lift
Notes LB ⊗

Duke of Normandie Hotel

★★★ 79% HOTEL

☎ 01481 721431
Lefebvre St GY1 2JP
e-mail: enquiries@dukeofnormandie.com
web: www.dukeofnormandie.com
dir: From harbour rdbt St Julians Ave, 3rd left into
Anns Place, continue to right, up hill, then left into
Lefebvre St, archway entrance on right

An 18th-century hotel situated close to the high street
and just a short stroll from the harbour. Bedrooms
vary in style and include some that have their own
access from the courtyard. Public areas feature a
smart brasserie, a contemporary lounge/lobby area
and a busy bar with beams and an open fireplace.

Rooms 37 (17 annexe) (8 GF) **S** £49–£65;
D £100–£150 (incl. bkfst) **Facilities** STV Wi-fi
Conf Class 30 Board 20 Thtr 40 Del from £140 to
£180 **Parking** 15 **Notes** LB ⊗

CHANNEL ISLANDS

ST PETER PORT *continued*

Sunnycroft Hotel

★★ 72% METRO HOTEL

☎ 01481 723008 & 0800 316 0314
5 Constitution Steps GY1 2PN
e-mail: sunnycrofthotel@cwgsy.com
dir: In centre of town, past Salvation Army Building
on left down Constitution steps

This property is located in one of St Peter Port's
cobbled, stepped alleyways and has great views
overlooking the marina. The bedrooms are cosy and
provide a good level of comfort; many have sea views.
An honesty bar is available and breakfast is served in
the rooftop dining room. Access to the property is by
foot only and might be unsuitable for those who are
less steady on their feet.

Rooms 14 (7 GF) **S** £60-£80; **D** £75-£100 (incl. bkfst)
Facilities FTV Wi-fi

The Farmhouse Hotel

★★★★ 84% ⊛ SMALL HOTEL

☎ 01481 264181
Route Des Bas Courtils GY7 9YF
e-mail: enquiries@thefarmhouse.gg
web: www.thefarmhouse.gg
dir: From airport turn left. Approx 1m left at lights.
100mtrs, left, around airport runway perimeter. 1m,
left at staggered junct. Hotel in 100mtrs on right. For
directions from harbour please see hotel website or
contact hotel

This hotel provides spacious accommodation with
amazingly comfortable beds and state-of-the-art
bathrooms with under-floor heating. Guests can
choose from various stylish dining options including
alfresco eating in the warmer months. The outdoor
swimming pool is available to guests in the summer
and there are lots of countryside walks to enjoy.

The Farmhouse Hotel

Rooms 14 (7 fmly) 🐾 **S** £125-£295; **D** £125-£295
(incl. bkfst)* **Facilities** STV Wi-fi 🏋 🍴 🎵 Xmas New
Year **Conf** Class 130 Board 30 Thtr 150 Del £225*
Services Air con **Parking** 80 **Notes** LB ⊗

See advert below

Peninsula Hotel

★★★ 78% HOTEL

☎ 01481 248400
Les Dicqs GY6 8JP
e-mail: peninsula@guernsey.net
dir: On coast road at Grand Havre Bay

Adjacent to the sandy beach and set in five acres of
grounds, this modern hotel provides comfortable
accommodation. Bedrooms have an additional sofa
bed to suit families and good workspace for the
business traveller. Both fixed-price and carte menus
are served in the restaurant, or guests can eat
informally in the bar.

Rooms 99 (99 fmly) (25 GF) (5 smoking) 🐾
Facilities STV Wi-fi 🏋 Putt green Petanque
Children's playground Xmas New Year **Conf** Class 140
Board 105 Thtr 250 **Services** Lift **Parking** 120
Notes ⊗ Closed Jan

HERM

HERM   Map 24

White House Hotel
★★★ 83% ◉◉ HOTEL

☎ 01481 750075
GY1 3HR
e-mail: hotel@herm.com
web: www.herm.com
dir: Transport to island by catamaran ferry from St Peter Port, Guernsey

Enjoying a unique island setting, this attractive hotel is just 20 minutes from Guernsey by sea. Set in well-tended gardens, the hotel offers neatly decorated bedrooms, located in either the main house or adjacent cottages; the majority of rooms have sea views. Guests can relax in one of several lounges, enjoy a drink in one of two bars and choose from two dining options.

Rooms 40 (23 annexe) (23 fmly) (7 GF)
Facilities Wi-fi ⋌ ♨ ⛵ Fishing trips Yacht & motor boat charters **Conf** Board 10 Thtr 50 **Notes** ⊗ Closed Nov-Mar

JERSEY

GOREY   Map 24

The Moorings Hotel & Restaurant
★★★ 83% ◉◉ HOTEL

☎ 01534 853633
Gorey Pier JE3 6EW
e-mail: reservations@themooringshotel.com
web: www.themooringshotel.com
dir: At foot of Mont Orgueil Castle

Enjoying an enviable position by the harbour, the heart of this hotel is the restaurant where a selection of menus offers an extensive choice of dishes. Other public areas include a bar, coffee shop and a comfortable first-floor residents' lounge. Bedrooms at the front have a fine view of the harbour; three have access to a balcony. A small sun terrace at the back of the hotel is available to guests.

Rooms 15 ⋔ **S** £56.50-£77.50; **D** £113-£185.50 (incl. bkfst)* **Facilities** FTV Wi-fi ⅄ Xmas New Year **Conf** Class 20 Board 20 Thtr 20 Del £105.50* **Notes** LB ⊗

Old Court House Hotel
★★★ 72% HOTEL

☎ 01534 854444
JE3 9FS
e-mail: info@ochoteljersey.com
web: www.ochoteljersey.com

Situated on the east of the island, a short walk from the beach, this long established hotel continues to have a loyal following for its relaxed atmosphere and friendly staff. Bedrooms are of similar standard throughout and some have balconies overlooking the gardens. Spacious public areas include a comfortable, quiet lounge, a restaurant, and a large bar with a dance floor.

Rooms 58 (4 fmly) (9 GF) **S** £53-£80; **D** £106-£160 (incl. bkfst)* **Facilities** FTV Wi-fi ⋌ **Services** Lift **Parking** 40 **Notes** LB Closed Oct-Apr

The Dolphin Hotel and Restaurant
★★ 75% HOTEL

☎ 01534 853370
Gorey Pier JE3 6EW
e-mail: dolphinhotel@jerseymail.co.uk
dir: At foot of Mont Orgueil Castle

Located on the main harbour at Gorey, many bedrooms at this popular hotel enjoy views over the sea and beaches. The relaxed and friendly style is apparent from the moment of arrival, and the busy restaurant and bar are popular with locals and tourists alike. Outdoor seating is available in season, and fresh fish and seafood are included on the menu.

Rooms 16 **S** £43-£56; **D** £86-£112 (incl. bkfst)* **Facilities** STV Wi-fi ⅄ Xmas New Year **Conf** Class 20 Board 20 Thtr 20 Del from £150 to £190* **Notes** LB ⊗

Maison Gorey
★★ 69% HOTEL

☎ 01534 857775 & 07797 715051
Gorey Village Main Rd JE3 9EP
e-mail: maisongorey@jerseymail.co.uk
dir: Adjacent to Jersey Pottery

Located in the middle of Gorey, this small, relaxing hotel provides well-equipped bedrooms and bathrooms. In addition to a spacious bar, a small TV lounge is available for guests. Some off-street parking is available in front of the hotel.

Rooms 26 (26 annexe) (2 fmly) **Facilities** FTV Wi-fi ⅄ Xmas New Year **Parking** 6 **Notes** ⊗ No children 5yrs Civ Wed 85

GROUVILLE   Map 24

The Beausite Hotel
★★★ 72% HOTEL

☎ 01534 857577
Les Rue des Pres, Grouville Bay JE3 9DJ
e-mail: beausite@jerseymail.co.uk
web: www.southernhotels.com
dir: Opposite Royal Jersey Golf Course

This hotel is situated on the south-east side of the island; a short distance from the picturesque harbour at Gorey. With parts dating back to 1636, the public rooms retain original character and charm; bedrooms are generally spacious and modern in design. The indoor swimming pool, fitness room, saunas and spa bath are all added bonuses.

Rooms 75 (5 fmly) (18 GF) **S** £42-£64.50; **D** £84-£168 (incl. bkfst)* **Facilities** STV FTV Wi-fi ⓢ Gym **Parking** 60 **Notes** Closed Oct-Mar

ROZEL   Map 24

Château la Chaire
★★★★ 74% ◉◉ HOTEL

☎ 01534 863354
Rozel Bay JE3 6AJ
e-mail: res@chateau-la-chaire.co.uk
web: www.chateau-la-chaire.co.uk
dir: From St Helier on B38 turn left in village by Rozel Bay Inn, hotel 100yds on right

Built as a gentleman's residence in 1843, Château la Chaire is a haven of peace and tranquillity, set in a secluded wooded valley. Picturesque Rozel Harbour is within easy walking distance, and the house is surrounded by terraced gardens and woods. The helpful staff deliver high standards of guest care, and imaginative menus, making the best use of local produce, are served in the oak-panelled dining room, the conservatory, or on the terrace when the weather permits. Bedroom and suite styles and sizes vary, but all are beautifully appointed and include many nice touches such as towelling robes, slippers, flowers and DVD players. Free Wi-fi is available throughout the hotel.

Rooms 14 (2 fmly) (1 GF) ⬧ **S** £95-£130; **D** £105-£325 (incl. bkfst)* **Facilities** FTV Wi-fi ⬧ Xmas New Year **Conf** Class 20 Board 20 Thtr 20 Del from £145 to £175* **Parking** 30 **Notes** LB ⊗ No children 7yrs Civ Wed 60

ST BRELADE   Map 24

INSPECTORS' CHOICE

The Atlantic Hotel
★★★★ ◉◉◉◉ HOTEL

☎ 01534 744101
Le Mont de la Pulente JE3 8HE
e-mail: info@theatlantichotel.com
web: www.theatlantichotel.com
dir: From Petit Port turn right into Rue de la Sergente, right again, hotel signed

Adjoining the manicured fairways of La Moye championship golf course, this hotel enjoys a peaceful setting with breathtaking views over St Ouen's Bay. Stylish bedrooms look onto the course or the sea, and offer a blend of high quality and reassuring comfort. An air of understated luxury is apparent throughout, and the attentive service achieves the perfect balance of friendliness and professionalism. The Ocean restaurant's very talented chef, Mark Jordan, uses the best island produce to create outstanding and impeccably modern cuisine.

Rooms 50 (8 GF) ⬧ **S** £100-£200; **D** £150-£350 (incl. bkfst)* **Facilities** STV Wi-fi ⬧ ⬧ ⬧ Gym Saunas Xmas New Year **Conf** Class 40 Board 20 Thtr 60 Del from £200 to £250* **Services** Lift **Parking** 60 **Notes** LB ⊗ Closed 2 Jan-1 Feb Civ Wed 80

L'Horizon Hotel & Spa
HandPICKED HOTELS
BUILT FOR PLEASURE
★★★★ 85% ◉◉ HOTEL

☎ 01534 743101
St Brelade's Bay JE3 8EF
e-mail: lhorizon@handpicked.co.uk
web: www.handpickedhotels.co.uk/lhorizon
dir: From airport right at rdbt towards St Brelades & Red Houses. Through Red Houses, hotel 300mtrs on right in centre of bay

The combination of a truly wonderful setting on the golden sands of St Brelade's Bay, a relaxed atmosphere and excellent facilities prove a winning formula here. Bedrooms are stylish and have a real contemporary feel, all with plasma TVs and a host of extras; many have balconies or terraces and superb sea views. Spacious public areas include a spa and leisure club, a choice of dining options and relaxing lounges.

Rooms 105 (1 fmly) (15 GF) ⬧ **S** £85-£150; **D** £170-£300 (incl. bkfst)* **Facilities** Spa STV FTV Wi-fi ⬧ ⬧ ⬧ Gym Windsurfing Water skiing Sailing Sauna Steam room ♫ Xmas New Year **Conf** Class 100 Board 50 Thtr 250 Del from £145 to £195* **Services** Lift **Parking** 125 **Notes** ⊗ Civ Wed 240

St Brelade's Bay Hotel
★★★★ 81% HOTEL

☎ 01534 746141
JE3 8EF
web: www.stbreladesbayhotel.com
dir: SW corner of island

The hotel, set in five-acres of gardens, enjoys a fabulous location with unobstructed views overlooking St Brelade's Bay, and a sandy beach right on the doorstep. Bedrooms are beautifully presented and equipped to a very high standard. They include two-bedroom suites, family rooms and superb penthouse suites that have large balconies, and even telescopes. The relaxing public areas include a stylish, comfortable lounge along with a spacious bar. The gardens feature a pool area, terraces for relaxing and eating, and a tennis court. A superb new leisure and fitness centre with state-of-the-art equipment has been recently completed. Attentive friendly service is guaranteed in the elegant restaurant with its sea views.

Rooms 77 (8 fmly) 🐾 **Facilities** Spa FTV Wi-fi ⊕ ⋌ 🛎 Gym Beauty treatment rooms ♫ Xmas New Year **Conf** Class 30 Board 12 Thtr 60 **Services** Lift **Parking** 90 **Notes** ⊗ Civ Wed 70

Hotel La Place

★★★★ 73% ⚜ HOTEL

☎ 01534 744261
Route du Coin, La Haule JE3 8BT
e-mail: reservations@hotellaplacejersey.com
dir: Off main St Helier/St Aubin coast road at La Haule Manor (B25). Up hill, 2nd left (to Red Houses), 1st right. Hotel 100mtrs on right

Developed around a 17th-century farmhouse, this hotel is well placed for exploration of the island. Attentive, friendly service is very much part of the ethos here. Many of the bedrooms have benefited from an impressive refurbishment program and offer high levels of quality and comfort; some have private patios and direct access to the pool area. The cocktail bar is popular for pre-dinner drinks, and the stylish lounge is a perfect place to sit back and enjoy the tranquil delights of this peaceful setting. Cuisine is also an important feature here with the menu offering a good range of local, seasonal produce, served within the elegant restaurant.

Rooms 42 (1 fmly) (10 GF) **Facilities** STV Wi-fi ⋌ Discount at Les Ormes Country Club Xmas **Conf** Class 40 Board 40 Thtr 100 **Parking** 100 **Notes** Civ Wed 100

Beau Rivage Hotel

★★★ 77% HOTEL

☎ 01534 745983
St Brelade's Bay JE3 8EF
e-mail: beau@jerseyweb.demon.co.uk
web: www.jersey.co.uk/hotels/beau
dir: Sea side of coast road in centre of St Brelade's Bay, 1.5m S of airport

With direct access to one of Jersey's most popular beaches, residents and non-residents alike are welcome to this hotel's bar and terrace. All of the well-equipped bedrooms are now suites, most have wonderful sea views, and some have the bonus of balconies. Residents have a choice of lounges, plus a sun deck exclusively for their use. A range of dishes, featuring English and Continental cuisine, is available from a selection of menus in either the bar or the main bistro restaurant.

Rooms 12 (12 fmly) (12 smoking) **Facilities** STV FTV Wi-fi ⋌ Games room **Services** Lift **Parking** 16 **Notes** ⊗ RS Nov-Mar Civ Wed 80

Highlands Hotel

★★★ 72% HOTEL

☎ 01534 744288
Corbiere JE3 8HN
e-mail: enquiries@highlandshotel.com
dir: 3m from Jersey airport

This hotel has an enviable location, ideally suited to touring and walking the island and is close to the coast and beaches of St Brelade's Bay. There are several leisure facilities, including a swimming pool, and games room. The restaurant and many of the bedrooms have delightful views. Bedrooms and bathrooms are very pleasantly appointed in a bright and pleasant style.

Rooms 55

Hotel Miramar

★★ 72% HOTEL

☎ 01534 743831
Mont Gras d'Eau JE3 8ED
e-mail: reservations@miramarjersey.com
web: www.miramarjersey.com
dir: From airport take B36 at lights, turn left onto A13, 1st right into Mont Gras d'Eau

A friendly welcome awaits at this family-run hotel set in delightful sheltered gardens, overlooking the beautiful bay. Accommodation is comfortable with well-appointed bedrooms; some are on the ground floor, and there are two on the lower ground with their own terrace overlooking the outdoor heated pool. The restaurant offers a varied set menu.

Rooms 38 (2 fmly) (12 GF) 🐾 **Facilities** FTV Wi-fi ⋌ **Parking** 30 **Notes** Closed Oct-mid Apr

ST CLEMENT   Map 24

Pontac House Hotel

★★★ 74% HOTEL

☎ 01534 857771
St Clements Bay JE2 6SE
e-mail: info@pontachouse.com
web: www.pontachouse.com
dir: 10 mins from St Helier

Overlooking the sandy beach of St Clement's Bay, this hotel is located on the south eastern corner of Jersey. Many guests return on a regular basis to experience the friendly, relaxed style of service. The bedrooms, most with splendid views, are comfortable and well equipped. Varied menus, featuring local seafood, are on offer each evening.

Rooms 27 (1 fmly) (5 GF) 🐾 **Facilities** FTV Wi-fi ⋌ **Parking** 35 **Notes** Closed 18 Dec-1 Mar

The Samares Coast Hotel

★★★ 72% HOTEL

☎ 01534 723411 & 873006
St Clement's Coast Rd JE2 6SB
e-mail: admin@morvanhotels.com
dir: On main esplanade

This hotel is situated on the south coast in a prime seafront location with delightful views from the restaurant and many of the bedrooms. All the bedrooms are well appointed and the sea-facing; balcony rooms prove especially popular. Facilities include a leisure complex with swimming pool and gym, and there are pleasant gardens. Carefully prepared dishes are offered in the comfortable restaurant.

Rooms 52 (4 annexe) (5 fmly) (14 GF) **Facilities** STV FTV Wi-fi ⊕ ⋌ Gym Steam room **Services** Lift **Parking** 35 **Notes** ⊗ Closed Nov-Mar

ST HELIER   Map 24

Grand Jersey

★★★★★ 82% ⚜⚜⚜ HOTEL

☎ 01534 722301
The Esplanade JE2 3QA
e-mail: reservations@grandjersey.com
web: www.grandjersey.com

A local landmark, the Grand Hotel has pleasant views across St Aubin's Bay to the front, and the bustling streets of St Helier to the rear. The hotel is elegant and contemporary in design with a real touch of grandeur throughout. The air-conditioned bedrooms, including six suites, come in a variety of designs, but all have luxurious beds, ottomans and LCD TVs. The spacious public areas, many looking out onto the bay, include the very popular Champagne Lounge, Victorias brasserie, and the impressive and intimate Tassili fine-dining restaurant. There is a large terrace for alfresco eating in the summer months, and the spa offers an indoor pool, gym and treatment rooms.

Rooms 123 (18 fmly) (6 GF) 🐾 **S** £79-£125; **D** £99-£240 (incl. bkfst)* **Facilities** Spa STV FTV Wi-fi ⌕ ⊕ Gym ♫ Xmas New Year **Conf** Class 100 Board 50 Thtr 180 **Services** Lift Air con **Parking** 27 **Notes** LB ⊗ Civ Wed 180

CHANNEL ISLANDS

CHANNEL ISLANDS

ST HELIER *continued*

INSPECTORS' CHOICE

The Club Hotel & Spa

★★★★ ◉◉◉ TOWN HOUSE HOTEL

☎ 01534 876500
Green St JE2 4UH
e-mail: reservations@theclubjersey.com
web: www.theclubjersey.com
dir: 5 mins walk from main shopping centre

This swish, town house hotel is conveniently located close to the centre of town and features stylish, contemporary decor throughout. All the guest rooms and suites have power showers and state-of-the-art technology including wide-screen LCD TV, DVD and CD systems. The choice of restaurants includes Bohemia, a sophisticated eating option that continues to offer outstanding cuisine. For relaxation there is an elegant spa with a luxurious range of treatments.

Rooms 46 (4 fmly) (4 GF) **S** £99-£445; **D** £99-£445 (incl. bkfst)* **Facilities** Spa STV FTV Wi-fi 🕲 ⚲ Sauna Steam room Salt cabin Hydrothermal bench Rasul room New Year **Conf** Class 60 Board 34 Thtr 80 Del from £165 to £195* **Services** Lift Air con **Parking** 32 **Notes** LB ⊗ Closed 24-30 Dec Civ Wed 84

The Royal Yacht

★★★★ 84% ◉◉ HOTEL

☎ 01534 720511
The Weighbridge JE2 3NF
e-mail: reception@theroyalyacht.com
web: www.theroyalyacht.com
dir: In town centre, opposite marina & harbour

Overlooking the marina and steam clock, the Royal Yacht is thought to be the oldest established hotel on the island. Although it has a long history, it is very much a 21st-century hotel, with state-of-the-art technology in all the bedrooms and the two penthouse suites. There is a range of impressive dining options to suit all tastes, with Sirocco's Restaurant offering high quality local produce. In addition to a choice of bars and conference facilities guests can enjoy the luxury spa with an indoor pool and gym.

Rooms 110 🛏 **D** £145-£750 (incl. bkfst)* **Facilities** Spa STV Wi-fi ᕁ 🕲 Gym ♫ Xmas New Year **Conf** Class 150 Board 40 Thtr 280 **Services** Lift Air con **Notes** LB ⊗ Civ Wed 250

See advert on opposite page

Pomme d'Or Hotel

★★★★ 80% HOTEL

☎ 01534 880110
Liberation Square JE1 3UF
e-mail: enquiries@pommedorhotel.com
dir: Opposite harbour

This historic hotel overlooks Liberation Square and the marina and offers comfortably furnished, well-equipped bedrooms. Popular with the business fraternity, a range of conference facilities and meeting rooms are available. Dining options include The Harbour Room Carvery and the café bar.

Rooms 143 (3 fmly) 🛏 **Facilities** STV FTV Wi-fi ᕁ Free use of The Aquadome at The Merton Hotel Xmas New Year **Conf** Class 100 Board 50 Thtr 220 Del from £145 to £165* **Services** Lift Air con **Notes** ⊗ Civ Wed 100

Radisson Blu Waterfront Hotel, Jersey

★★★★ 80% HOTEL

☎ 01534 671100 & 671173
The Waterfront, La Rue de L'Etau JE2 3WF
e-mail: info.jersey@radissonblu.com
web: www.radissonblu.com/hotel-jersey
dir: Follow signs to St Helier. From A2 follow signs to harbour. At rdbt just before harbour take 2nd exit, continue to hotel

Most of the bedrooms at this purpose-built hotel have fabulous views of the coastline. Facilities include a popular brasserie, cocktail bar, lounges, indoor heated pool, gym, sauna and steam room. A wide range of meeting rooms provides conference facilities for delegates; parking is extensive.

Rooms 195 🛏 **S** £79-£290; **D** £79-£290* **Facilities** Spa STV Wi-fi ᕁ HL 🕲 Gym Sauna Steam room ♫ Xmas New Year **Conf** Class 184 Board 30 Thtr 400 Del from £129 to £199* **Services** Lift Air con **Parking** 70 **Notes** ⊗ Civ Wed 400

CHANNEL ISLANDS

ST HELIER *continued*

Hotel Savoy

★★★★ 75% ◉ HOTEL

☎ 01534 727521
37 Rouge Bouillon JE2 3ZA
e-mail: info@thesavoy.biz
web: www.thesavoy.biz
dir: From airport 1st exit at rdbt. At next rdbt 2nd exit right, down Beaumont Hill. At bottom left, along coast onto dual carriageway. At 3rd lights 1st left. Right at end. Remain in right lane, into left lane before hospital. Hotel on left opposite police station

This family-run hotel, a manor house dating from the 19th century, sits peacefully in its own grounds, just a short walk from the main shopping area in St Helier. It offers spacious, comfortable accommodation and smart public rooms. The Montana Restaurant serves carefully prepared, imaginative cuisine. A car park and leisure facilities are also available.

Rooms 56 (2 fmly) (10 GF) ⬩ **S** £80–£100; **D** £125–£150 (incl. bkfst)* **Facilities** STV FTV Wi-fi ⬩ ⬩ Gym ♫ **Conf** Class 70 Board 12 Thtr 120 Del from £125 to £175* **Services** Lift **Parking** 46 **Notes** LB ⊗ Civ Wed 80

BEST WESTERN Royal Hotel

★★★ 79% ◉ HOTEL

☎ 01534 726521 & 873006
David Place JE2 4TD
e-mail: enquiries@royalhoteljersey.com
web: www.royalhoteljersey.com
dir: From Airport: In St Helier on Victoria Ave, left by Grand Hotel into Peirson Rd. Follow one-way system into Cheapside. Left at filter, follow Ring Rd signs into Rouge Boullion (A14). At rdbt right, stay in right lane, right at lights into Midvale Rd. Through 2 lights, hotel on left

This long established hotel is located in the centre of town and is within walking distance of the business district and shops. Seasons Restaurant offers a modern approach to dining, and the adjoining bar provides a relaxed venue for residents and locals alike. The bedrooms are individually styled. Extensive conference facilities are available.

Rooms 89 (4 fmly) (9 smoking) **Facilities** Wi-fi Gym Xmas New Year **Conf** Class 120 Board 80 Thtr 300 **Services** Lift **Parking** 15 **Notes** ⊗ Civ Wed 30

The Monterey Hotel

★★★ 73% HOTEL

☎ 01534 724762 & 873006
St Saviour's Rd JE2 7LA
e-mail: admin@morvanhotels.com

Conveniently located for the town, this comfortable hotel has the added benefit of ample parking and a range of leisure facilities including an indoor pool. Bedrooms are well decorated and furnished, and include a number of superior rooms. The relaxing bar area is open all day, and a good range of freshly prepared dishes is offered each evening.

Rooms 73 (6 fmly) (9 GF) **Facilities** STV FTV Wi-fi ⬩ ⬩ Gym Xmas New Year **Conf** Class 12 Board 22 Thtr 40 **Services** Lift **Parking** 40 **Notes** ⊗

Hampshire Hotel

★★★ 71% HOTEL

☎ 01534 724115
53 Val Plaisant JE2 4TB
e-mail: info@hampshirehotel.je

Located a short walk from the town centre, this hotel features spacious public areas and comfortable bedrooms. There are premier, standard and family rooms, each with a flat-screen TV. The spacious restaurant features seasonal changing dinner menus of popular dishes; at breakfast a wide choice is offered. The outdoor swimming pool and sun terrace are popular in the summer months.

Rooms 42 (2 fmly) (5 GF) **S** £40–£65; **D** £69–£129 (incl. bkfst)* **Facilities** STV Wi-fi ⬩ ⬩ ♫ Xmas New Year **Services** Lift **Parking** 30 **Notes** ⊗

The Hotel Revere

★★★ 71% HOTEL

☎ 01534 611111
Kensington Place JE2 3PA
e-mail: reservations@revere.co.uk
web: www.revere.co.uk
dir: From Esplanade left after De Vere Grand Hotel

Situated on the west side of the town and convenient for the centre and harbour side, this hotel dates back to the 17th century and retains many period features. The style here is engagingly different, and bedrooms are individually decorated. There are three dining options and a small sun terrace.

Rooms 56 (2 fmly) (4 GF) ⬩ **S** £40–£60; **D** £80–£120 (incl. bkfst)* **Facilities** FTV Wi-fi ⬩ ♫ Xmas New Year **Notes** LB ⊗ Civ Wed 50

The Norfolk Lodge Hotel

★★★ 71% HOTEL

☎ 01534 722950 & 873006
Rouge Bouillon JE2 3ZB
e-mail: admin@morvanhotels.com

Centrally located and just a short walk to the main town, this popular hotel has a large number of regularly returning guests. Bedrooms are well decorated and equipped, and include some on the ground floor. In addition to an indoor swimming pool, the hotel offers regular evening entertainment during the main season. A range of well-prepared dishes is offered at dinner in the spacious restaurant

Rooms 101 (11 annexe) (8 fmly) (15 GF) ⬩ **S** £66–£92; **D** £81–£107 (incl. bkfst)* **Facilities** FTV Wi-fi ⬩ Children's pool ♫ Child facilities **Services** Lift **Parking** 40 **Notes** ⊗ Closed Nov-Mar

Apollo Hotel

★★★ 64% HOTEL

☎ 01534 725441
St Saviours Rd JE2 4GJ
e-mail: reservations@huggler.com
web: www.huggler.com
dir: On St Saviours Rd at junct with La Motte St

Centrally located, this popular hotel has a relaxed, informal atmosphere. Bedrooms are comfortably furnished and include useful extras. Many guests return regularly to enjoy the variety of leisure facilities including an outdoor pool with water slide and indoor pool with separate jacuzzi. The separate cocktail bar is an ideal place for a pre-dinner drink.

Rooms 85 (5 fmly) **S** £49–£99; **D** £59–£159 (incl. bkfst)* **Facilities** FTV Wi-fi ⬩ supervised ⬩ supervised Gym Xmas New Year **Conf** Class 100 Board 80 Thtr 150 Del from £79 to £189* **Services** Lift **Parking** 40 **Notes** ⊗

Save on hotels. Book at **theAA.com/hotel**

ST (JERSEY) 495 **ENGLAND**

Millbrook House Hotel

★★ 76% HOTEL

☎ 01534 733036
Rue De Trachy, Millbrook JE2 3JN
e-mail: millbrook.house@jerseymail.co.uk
web: www.millbrookhousehotel.com
dir: 1.5m W of town off A1

Peacefully located within its own grounds, this small, personally run hotel offers a friendly welcome and relaxing ambience. Bedrooms and bathrooms vary in size; many have pleasant, countryside views. In addition to outdoor seating in the warmer months, guests can relax in the library, maybe with a drink before dinner.

Rooms 24 (2 fmly) (6 GF) **S** £33-£42; **D** £57-£83*
Facilities Wi-fi Putt green **Services** Lift **Parking** 20
Notes Closed Oct-13 May

Westhill Country Hotel

★★ 74% COUNTRY HOUSE HOTEL

☎ 01534 723260
Mont-a-l'abbe JE2 3HB
e-mail: info@westhillhoteljersey.com
web: www.westhillhoteljersey.com
dir: Telephone for detailed directions

Set in its own beautifully landscaped gardens this hotel enjoys a prominent position just on the outskirts of St Helier. Service is attentive and guests are guaranteed a warm welcome and genuine hospitality throughout the hotel. The bedrooms are spacious and well equipped; several rooms have commanding views over the gardens to the countryside beyond. Public areas include a stylish lounge bar and popular restaurant. Free Wi-fi is available in the public areas and the swimming pool proves very popular with guests.

Rooms 90 (20 fmly) (16 GF) ☎ **S** £46-£63; **D** £92-£146 (incl. bkfst)* **Facilities** FTV Wi-fi ╲ ♫ **Parking** 75 **Notes** ⊗ Closed early Oct-early Apr Civ Wed 75

Sarum Hotel

★★ 64% METRO HOTEL

☎ 01534 731340
19/21 New St Johns Rd JE2 3LD
e-mail: sarum@jerseyweb.demon.co.uk
dir: On NW edge of St Helier, 0.5m from town centre

This hotel, just 600yds from the beach, offers self-catering bedrooms and a number of suites. The friendly staff provide a warm welcome, and there is a spacious recreational lounge with pool tables, plasma-screen TV and internet access. A garden and outdoor pool are also available. Local restaurants are just a short walk away, and bar snacks are available throughout the day.

Rooms 52 (5 annexe) (6 fmly) (2 GF) (52 smoking)
Facilities STV FTV Wi-fi Games room **Services** Lift **Parking** 10 **Notes** ⊗

ST MARY Map 24

West View Hotel

★★ 72% HOTEL

☎ 01534 481643
La Grande Rue JE3 3BD
e-mail: westview@jerseymail.co.uk
web: www.westviewhoteljersey.com
dir: At junct of B33 & C103

Located in the quiet parish of St Mary, this welcoming hotel is close to the delightful walks and cycle routes of the north coast. Bedrooms here are well equipped especially the larger, superior rooms. Entertainment is provided in the lounge bar during the summer months, when guests can also enjoy a swim in the heated outdoor pool.

Rooms 42 (3 fmly) (18 GF) **S** £38-£49; **D** £66-£96 (incl. bkfst)* **Facilities** FTV Wi-fi ╲ **Parking** 38 **Notes** ⊗ Closed Nov-Apr

ST PETER Map 24

Greenhills Country Hotel

★★★★ 76% ⊛ COUNTRY HOUSE HOTEL

☎ 01534 481042
Mont de L'Ecole JE3 7EL
e-mail: reserve@greenhillshotel.com
dir: Follow signs to St Peter's Village, the A11, turn into Le Mont de l'ecole, Hotel on left

Located in the rural centre of Jersey, this relaxing country-house hotel, with delightful gardens, has a lovely atmosphere. Bedrooms extend from the main building around the courtyard; all are modern and well equipped with satellite LED TVs, luxurious bathrobes, white duck down duvets and linen. A varied menu, based on fresh local produce, is served in the restaurant, and guests also have use of the Aquadome at the Merton Hotel.

Rooms 31 (2 fmly) (9 GF) **S** £45-£141; **D** £79-£235*
Facilities STV FTV Wi-fi ╲ Free use of Merton Hotel's Aquadome & Leisure Centre **Conf** Class 12 Board 16 Thtr 20 **Parking** 40 **Notes** ⊗ Closed mid Dec-early Feb Civ Wed 40

CHANNEL ISLANDS

ST SAVIOUR — Map 24

INSPECTORS' CHOICE

Longueville Manor Hotel

★★★★★ ◎◎◎ HOTEL

☎ 01534 725501
JE2 7WF
e-mail: info@longuevillemanor.com
web: www.longuevillemanor.com
dir: A3 E from St Helier towards Gorey. Hotel 1m on left

Dating back to the 13th century, there is something very special about Longueville Manor, which is why so many guests return time and again. It is set in 16 acres of grounds including woodland walks, a spectacular rose garden, Victorian kitchen garden and a lake. Bedrooms have great style and individuality boasting fresh flowers, fine embroidered bed linen and a host of extras. The very accomplished cuisine is also a highlight of any stay. In summer the pool and terrace are popular spots, plus there are also croquet and tennis courts. Families are particularly welcome, and there are extra activities arranged for children, including an adventure zone to explore. They also have their own menus and DVD library. The committed team of staff create a welcoming atmosphere and every effort is made to ensure a memorable stay.

Rooms 30 (1 annexe) (7 GF) 🐾 **S** £85-£285; **D** £170-£570 (incl. bkfst)* **Facilities** STV Wi-fi ◊ ◄ ◄ ➘ Xmas New Year **Conf** Class 30 Board 30 Thtr 45 **Services** Lift **Parking** 40 **Notes** LB Civ Wed 40

TRINITY — Map 24

Water's Edge Hotel

★★★ 75% ◎ HOTEL

☎ 01534 862777
Bouley Bay JE3 5AS
e-mail: admin@watersedgejersey.com
dir: On NE coast. 4m from St Helier & 7.4m from Jersey Airport

Set in the tranquil surroundings of Bouley Bay on the north coast, this hotel is situated exactly as its name conveys. The well-furnished bedrooms offer high standards of quality and comfort, and the vast majority enjoy delightful views of either the garden or over the bay towards France. A range of modern British dishes, including fresh seafood, is offered in the comfortable dining room which also benefits from the splendid views. Free Wi-fi is available.

Rooms 50 (6 fmly) **S** £42.50-£64.50; **D** £50-£124 (incl. bkfst)* **Facilities** FTV Wi-fi ◄ **Services** Lift **Parking** 20 **Notes** LB ⊗ Closed mid Oct-mid Apr

SARK

SARK — Map 24

Stocks Hotel

[U]

☎ 01481 832001
GY10 1SD
e-mail: reception@stockshotel.com

Currently the rating for this establishment is not confirmed. This may be due to a change of ownership or because it has only recently joined the AA rating scheme. For further details please see the AA website: theAA.com

Rooms 23 **S** £217-£279; **D** £232-£294 (incl. bkfst) **Notes** Closed Jan-1 Mar

Scotland

Forth Rail Bridge

ABERDEEN
City of Aberdeen

MAP 23 NJ90

See also Aberdeen Airport

Norwood Hall Hotel

★★★★ 81% ® HOTEL

☎ 01224 868951
Garthdee Rd, Cults AB15 9FX
e-mail: info@norwood-hall.co.uk
web: www.norwood-hall.co.uk
dir: Off A90, at 1st rdbt cross Bridge of Dee, left at rdbt onto Garthdee Rd (B&Q & Sainsburys on left) continue to hotel sign

This imposing Victorian mansion has retained many of its original features, most notably the fine oak staircase, stained glass and ornately decorated walls and ceilings. Accommodation varies in style from individually designed bedrooms in the main house to the newest contemporary bedrooms. The extensive grounds ensure the hotel is popular as a wedding venue.

Rooms 73 (14 GF) **Facilities** STV FTV Wi-fi ↻ Xmas New Year **Conf** Class 100 Board 70 Thtr 200 **Services** Lift **Parking** 140 **Notes** ⊗ Civ Wed 150

Holiday Inn Aberdeen West

★★★★ 76% HOTEL

☎ 01224 270300
Westhill Dr, Westhill AB32 6TT
e-mail: info@hiaberdeenwest.co.uk
web: www.holidayinn.co.uk/aberdeenwest
dir: On A944 in Westhill

In a good location at the west side of the city, this modern hotel caters well for the needs of both business and leisure guests. The nicely appointed bedrooms and bathrooms have a contemporary feel. Luigi's restaurant serves modern Italian food, and the popular lounge offers more informal dining. There is a separate pub operation with wide-screen TVs showing a range of sporting events.

Rooms 86 (30 fmly) ↻ **S** fr £59; **D** £59-£350 (incl. bkfst)* **Facilities** STV FTV Wi-fi ↻ Gym **Conf** Class 150 Board 80 Thtr 300 Del from £120 to £195* **Services** Lift Air con **Parking** 90 **Notes** LB Civ Wed 250

Mercure Aberdeen Ardoe House Hotel & Spa

★★★★ 74% ® HOTEL

☎ 01224 860600
South Deeside Rd, Blairs AB12 5YP
e-mail: h6626@accor.com
web: www.mercure.com
dir: 4m W of city off B9077

From its elevated position on the banks of the River Dee, this 19th-century baronial-style mansion commands excellent countryside views. Beautifully decorated, thoughtfully equipped bedrooms are located in the main house, and in the more modern extension. Public rooms include a spa and leisure club, a cosy lounge and whisky bar and impressive function facilities.

Rooms 119 **Facilities** Spa STV Wi-fi ↻ ☺ ♨ Gym Aerobics studio Xmas New Year **Conf** Class 200 Board 150 Thtr 600 Del from £175 to £195* **Services** Lift **Parking** 220 **Notes** ⊗ Civ Wed 250

The Caledonian, Aberdeen

thistle

★★★★ 73% HOTEL

☎ 0871 376 9003
10-14 Union Ter AB10 1WE
e-mail: aberdeencaledonian@thistle.co.uk
web: www.thistlehotels.com/thecaledonian
dir: Follow signs to city centre & Union St. Turn into Union Terrace. Hotel on left, parking behind hotel in Diamond St

Centrally located just off Union Street and overlooking Union Terrace Gardens, this traditional hotel offers modern, comfortable and well-appointed bedrooms, and attractive public areas. The upbeat Café Bar Caley serves a wide-ranging menu and offers a relaxing area to enjoy a drink. A small car park is available to the rear.

Rooms 83 (5 fmly) ↻ **Facilities** FTV Wi-fi ↻ HL Xmas New Year **Conf** Class 40 Board 30 Thtr 80 **Services** Lift **Parking** 22 **Notes** ⊗ Civ Wed 50

Copthorne Hotel Aberdeen

★★★★ 73% HOTEL

☎ 01224 630404
122 Huntly St AB10 1SU
e-mail:
reservations.aberdeen@millenniumhotels.co.uk
web: www.millenniumhotels.co.uk/aberdeen
dir: West end of city centre, off Union St, up Rose St, hotel 0.25m on right on corner with Huntly St

Situated just outside of the city centre, this hotel offers friendly, attentive service. The smart bedrooms are well proportioned and guests will appreciate the added quality of the Connoisseur rooms. The West End Bistro and Bar provides a relaxed atmosphere in which to enjoy a drink or a meal; a great traditional steak and grill selection is on offer.

Rooms 89 (15 fmly) ↻ **Facilities** STV FTV Wi-fi HL New Year **Conf** Class 100 Board 70 Thtr 200 **Services** Lift **Parking** 15 **Notes** RS 24-26 Dec Civ Wed 180

Maryculter House Hotel

★★★★ 71% ® HOTEL

☎ 01224 732124
South Deeside Rd, Maryculter AB12 5GB
e-mail: info@maryculterhousehotel.com
web: www.maryculterhousehotel.com
dir: Exit A90 S of Aberdeen onto B9077. Hotel 8m on right, 0.5m beyond Deeside Holiday Park

Set in grounds on the banks of the River Dee, this charming Scottish mansion dates back to medieval times and is now a popular wedding and conference venue. Exposed stonework and open fires feature in the oldest parts, which house the cocktail bar and Priory Restaurant. Lunch and breakfast are taken overlooking the river; bedrooms are equipped especially with business travellers in mind.

Rooms 39 (1 fmly) (16 GF) ↻ **Facilities** STV FTV Wi-fi ↻ Fishing Xmas New Year **Conf** Class 100 Board 50 Thtr 200 Del £190* **Parking** 120 **Notes** Civ Wed 220

Save on hotels. Book at **theAA.com/hotel**

ABE 501 SCOTLAND

A

A

ABERDEEN *continued*

Thistle Aberdeen Altens

thistle

★★★★ 71% HOTEL

☎ 0871 376 9002
Souter Head Rd, Altens AB12 3LF
e-mail: aberdeenaltens@thistle.co.uk
web: www.thistle.com/aberdeenaltens
dir: A90 onto A956 signed Aberdeen Harbour. Hotel just off rdbt

Popular with oil industry personnel, this large purpose-built hotel lies in the Altens area, south east of the city. It's worth asking for one of the executive bedrooms that provide excellent space. A wide choice of meals are available in the Restaurant or the Cairngorm Bar where there is a relaxed atmosphere.

Rooms 216 (96 fmly) (48 GF) ✱ **S** £55–£250;
D £65–£260 (incl. bkfst)* **Facilities** FTV Wi-fi ↕ HL ⊙ Gym Sauna Steam room Solarium Aerobic studio New Year **Conf** Class 144 Board 30 Thtr 400 Del from £150 to £300* **Services** Lift **Parking** 300 **Notes** LB ⊗ Civ Wed 150

Malmaison Aberdeen

★★★ 86% ⊛ HOTEL

☎ 01224 327370
49-53 Queens Rd AB15 4YP
e-mail: info.aberdeen@malmaison.com
dir: A90, 3rd exit into Queens Rd at 3rd rdbt, hotel on right

Popular with business travellers and as a function venue, this well-established hotel lies east of the city centre. Public areas include a reception lounge and an intimate restaurant, plus the extensive bar menu which remains a popular choice for many regulars. There are two styles of accommodation, with the superior rooms being particularly comfortable and well equipped.

Rooms 79 (8 fmly) (10 GF) **Facilities** Spa STV FTV Wi-fi Gym Steam room Xmas New Year **Conf** Class 30 Board 20 Thtr 40 **Services** Lift **Parking** 50

Park Inn by Radisson Aberdeen

★★★ 81% HOTEL

☎ 01224 592999
1 Juctice Mill Ln AB11 6EQ
e-mail: info.aberdeen@rezidorparkinn.com
dir: Off Union St

Conveniently located in the centre of the 'Granite City' and overlooking the historic harbour, this hotel is perfectly situated for both business and leisure guests. Stylish bedrooms include flat-screen TVs and free Wi-fi. The contemporary bar and RBG Bar & Grill are welcoming areas for guests to relax in and there is a range of dining options. A fitness centre and range of meeting rooms are also available.

Rooms 183 ✱ **Facilities** FTV Wi-fi ↕ Gym **Conf** Class 100 Board 60 Thtr 200 **Services** Lift Air con **Parking** 70 **Notes** Civ Wed 120

The Craighaar Hotel

★★★ 79% HOTEL

☎ 01224 712275
Waterton Rd, Bucksburn AB21 9HS
e-mail: info@craighaar.co.uk
dir: From A96 (Airport/Inverness) onto A947, hotel signed

Conveniently located for the airport, this welcoming hotel is a popular base for business people and tourists alike. Guests can make use of a quiet library lounge, and enjoy meals in the bar or restaurant. All bedrooms are well equipped, plus there is a wing of duplex suites that provide additional comfort.

Rooms 53 (6 fmly) (16 GF) ✱ **S** £49–£112;
D £69–£125 (incl. bkfst)* **Facilities** STV FTV Wi-fi Library **Conf** Class 33 Board 30 Thtr 90 Del £129.50* **Parking** 80 **Notes** ⊗ Closed 25-26 Dec Civ Wed 40

The Mariner Hotel

★★★ 79% HOTEL

☎ 01224 588901
349 Great Western Rd AB10 6NW
e-mail: info@themarinerhotel.co.uk
dir: E off Anderson Drive (A90) at Great Western Rd. Hotel on right on corner of Gray St

This well maintained, family-operated hotel is located west of the city centre. The smart, spacious bedrooms are well equipped and particularly comfortable, with executive suites available. The public rooms are restricted to the lounge bar, which is food driven, and the Atlantis Restaurant that showcases the region's wide choice of excellent seafood and meats.

Rooms 25 (8 annexe) (4 GF) ✱ **S** £55–£100;
D £85–£140 (incl. bkfst)* **Facilities** FTV Wi-fi New Year **Parking** 51 **Notes** ⊗

Holiday Inn Express Aberdeen City Centre

BUDGET HOTEL

☎ 01224 623500
Chapel St AB10 1SQ
e-mail: info@hieaberdeen.co.uk
web: www.hiexpress.com/exaberdeencc
dir: In west end of city, just off Union Street

A modern hotel ideal for families and business travellers. Fresh and uncomplicated, the spacious rooms include Sky TV, power shower and tea and coffee-making facilities. Continental buffet breakfast is included in the room rate; other meals may be taken at the nearby family pub or restaurant. See also the Hotel Groups pages.

Rooms 155 (50 fmly) ✱ **S** £55–£180; **D** £55–£180 (incl. bkfst)* **Conf** Class 18 Board 16 Thtr 35 Del from £110 to £210*

Ibis Aberdeen Centre Hotel

ibis

BUDGET HOTEL

☎ 01224 285820
15 Shiprow AB11 5BY
e-mail: H5170@accor.com

Situated in a convenient location in the heart of Aberdeen, the newly constructed hotel provides a comfortable place to stay in a modern environment. Attractive and spacious bedrooms are equipped with a host of features including flat-screen TVs and Wi-fi access. Snacks are available 24 hours of the day and breakfast is offered in the stylish restaurant. Parking is available adjacent to the hotel. See also the Hotel Groups pages.

Rooms 107 ✱ **S** £44–£149; **D** £44–£149*

Premier Inn Aberdeen Central West

BUDGET HOTEL

☎ 0871 527 8006
North Anderson Dr AB15 6DW
web: www.premierinn.com
dir: Into Aberdeen from S on A90 follow airport signs. Hotel 1st left after fire station. (NB for Sat Nav use AB15 6TP)

High quality, budget accommodation ideal for both families and business travellers. Spacious, en suite bedrooms feature tea and coffee making facilities, and Freeview TV in most hotels. Internet access and Wi-fi are available for a small fee. The adjacent family restaurant features a wide and varied menu. See also the Hotel Groups pages.

Rooms 62

Premier Inn Aberdeen City Centre

BUDGET HOTEL

☎ 0871 527 8008
Inverlair House, West North St AB24 5AS
web: www.premierinn.com
dir: A90 onto A9013 into city centre. Take A956 towards King St, 1st left into Meal Market St

Rooms 162

Premier Inn Aberdeen North (Murcar)

BUDGET HOTEL

☎ 0871 527 8010
Ellon Rd, Murcar, Bridge of Don AB23 8BP
web: www.premierinn.com
dir: From city centre take A90 N follow Peterhead signs. At rdbt 2m after Aberdeen Exhibition & Conference Centre, left onto B999. Hotel on right

Rooms 40

Premier Inn Aberdeen South

BUDGET HOTEL

☎ 0871 527 8012
Mains of Balquharn, Portlethen AB12 4QS
web: www.premierinn.com
dir: From A90 follow Portlethen & Badentoy Park signs. Hotel on right

Rooms 40

Premier Inn Aberdeen (Westhill)

BUDGET HOTEL

☎ 0871 527 8004
Straik Rd, Westhill AB32 6HF
web: www.premierinn.com
dir: On A944 towards Alford, hotel adjacent to Tesco

Rooms 61

ABERDEEN AIRPORT   **Map 23 NJ81**   A
City of Aberdeen

Aberdeen Marriott Hotel

★★★★ 76% HOTEL

☎ 01224 770011
Overton Circle, Dyce AB21 7AZ
e-mail: reservations.scotland@marriotthotels.com
web: www.aberdeenmarriott.co.uk
dir: Follow A96 to Bucksburn, right at rdbt onto A947. Hotel in 2m at 2nd rdbt

Close to the airport and conveniently located for the business district, this purpose-built hotel is a popular conference venue. The well-proportioned bedrooms come with many thoughtful extras. Public areas include an informal bar and lounge, a split-level restaurant and a leisure centre that can be accessed directly from a number of bedrooms.

Rooms 155 (81 fmly) (61 GF) **Facilities** STV Wi-fi HL ⊛ supervised Gym Saunas (male & female) Solarium Xmas New Year **Conf** Class 200 Board 60 Thtr 400 Del from £100 to £255 **Services** Air con **Parking** 220 **Notes** ⊗ Civ Wed 90

A

ABERDEEN AIRPORT *continued*

Thistle Aberdeen Airport   **thistle**

★★★★ 75% HOTEL

☎ 0871 376 9001
Aberdeen Airport, Argyll Rd AB21 0AF
e-mail: aberdeenairport@thistle.co.uk
web: www.thistle.com/aberdeenairport
dir: Adjacent to Aberdeen Airport

Ideally located at the entrance to the airport this hotel offers ample parking plus a courtesy bus service to the terminal. This is a well presented establishment that benefits from good-sized bedrooms and comfortable public areas. Just Gym offers a good variety of exercise equipment.

Rooms 147 (3 fmly) (74 GF) **Facilities** FTV Wi-fi ⇣ HL Gym **Conf** Class 350 Board 100 Thtr 600 Del from £188 to £205* **Parking** 300 **Notes** ⊗

Menzies Hotels Aberdeen
Airport Dyce   MenziesHotels

★★★ 77% HOTEL

☎ 01224 723101
Farburn Ter, Dyce AB21 7DW
e-mail: dyce@menzieshotels.co.uk
dir: A96/A947 airport E after 1m turn left at lights. Hotel in 250yds

This hotel is very convenient for air travellers and for those wishing to explore this lovely Highland area. The spacious, well-equipped bedrooms have all the expected up-to-date amenities. The public areas are welcoming and include a contemporary brasserie. Secure parking and Wi-fi are also provided.

Rooms 212 (212 annexe) (3 fmly) (107 GF) (54 smoking) **Facilities** STV FTV Wi-fi Xmas New Year **Conf** Class 160 Board 120 Thtr 400 **Parking** 150 **Notes** Civ Wed 220

ABERDOUR   Map 21 NT18
Fife

The Woodside Hotel

★★★ 🅰 HOTEL

☎ 01383 860328
High St KY3 0SW
e-mail: reception@thewoodsidehotel.co.uk
web: www.thewoodsidehotel.co.uk
dir: M90 junct 1, E on A291 for 5m, hotel on left on entering village

The Woodside Hotel is a 19th-century mansion in the Fife Hills that looks out over the Earl of Moray's estate to the lovely Firth of Fife beyond. Each of the bedrooms is named after a Scottish clan, and include a spacious family room and the Rennie Suite with a

---

four-poster bed. The hotel has facilities for conferences, weddings and banquets.

Rooms 20 (1 fmly) 🅒 **S** £72; **D** £72-£98 (incl. bkfst)* **Facilities** FTV Wi-fi **Conf** Class 80 Board 30 Thtr 60 Del from £120 to £180* **Parking** 22 **Notes** LB ⊗ Closed 25 Dec & 1 Jan

ABERFOYLE   Map 20 NN50
Stirling

Macdonald Forest Hills
Hotel & Resort   MACDONALD HOTELS & RESORTS

★★★★ 76% ⊛ HOTEL

☎ 0844 879 9057 & 01877 389500
Kinlochard FK8 3TL
e-mail: forest_hills@macdonald-hotels.co.uk
web: www.macdonald-hotels.co.uk/foresthills
dir: A84, A873, A81 to Aberfoyle onto B829

Situated in the heart of The Trossachs with wonderful views of Loch Ard, this popular hotel forms part of a resort complex offering a range of indoor and outdoor facilities. The main hotel has relaxing lounges and a restaurant that all overlook the landscaped gardens. A separate building houses the leisure centre, lounge bar and bistro. Macdonald Hotels is the AA Hotel Group of the Year 2013-14.

Rooms 55 (16 fmly) (12 GF) 🅒 **D** £107-£260 (incl. bkfst)* **Facilities** Spa STV FTV Wi-fi ⊗ ⅃ Gym Children's club Snooker Watersports Quad biking Archery Clay pigeon shooting ♫ Xmas New Year **Conf** Class 60 Board 45 Thtr 150 Del £165* **Services** Lift **Parking** 100 **Notes** LB Civ Wed 100

ABERLADY   Map 21 NT47
East Lothian

Ducks at Kilspindie

⊛⊛ RESTAURANT WITH ROOMS

☎ 01875 870682
Main St EH32 0RE
e-mail: kilspindie@ducks.co.uk
web: www.ducks.co.uk
dir: A1 (Bankton junct) take 1st exit to North Berwick. At next rdbt 3rd exit onto A198 signed Longniddry, left towards Aberlady. At T-junct, facing river, right to Aberlady

The name of this restaurant with rooms is referenced around the building - Ducks Restaurant for award-winning cuisine; Donald's Bistro and the Ducklings informal coffee shop. The warm and welcoming public areas include a great bar offering real ales and various objets d'art. The bedrooms are comfortable and well appointed with well-presented en suites. The team are informal, friendly and take the time to chat to their guests.

Rooms 23 (1 fmly)

ABINGTON   Map 21 NS92
MOTORWAY SERVICE AREA (M74)
South Lanarkshire

Days Inn Abington - M74
                              Welcome Break

BUDGET HOTEL

☎ 01864 502782
ML12 6RG
e-mail: abington.hotel@welcomebreak.co.uk
web: www.welcomebreak.co.uk
dir: M74 junct 13, accessible from N'bound and S'bound carriageways

This modern building offers accommodation in smart, spacious and well-equipped bedrooms, suitable for families and business travellers, and all with en suite bathrooms. Continental breakfast is available and other refreshments may be taken at the nearby family restaurant. See also the Hotel Groups pages.

Rooms 54 (50 fmly) (4 smoking) **Conf** Board 10

ARDUAINE   Map 20 NM71
Argyll & Bute

Loch Melfort Hotel

★★★ 83% ⊛⊛ HOTEL

☎ 01852 200233
PA34 4XG
e-mail: reception@lochmelfort.co.uk
web: www.lochmelfort.co.uk
dir: On A816, midway between Oban & Lochgilphead

Enjoying one of the finest locations on the West Coast, this popular, family-run hotel has outstanding views across Asknish Bay towards the Islands of Jura, Scarba and Shuna. Accommodation is provided in either the balconied rooms of the Cedar wing or the more traditional rooms in the main hotel. Dining options include the main restaurant with stunning views or the more informal bistro.

Rooms 25 (20 annexe) (2 fmly) (10 GF) 🅒 **S** £135-£183; **D** £210-£306 (incl. bkfst & dinner)* **Facilities** Wi-fi 4 moorings Childrens' play park Xmas New Year **Conf** Class 40 Board 20 Thtr 50 **Parking** 50 **Notes** Closed 2 wks mid Jan RS Winter Civ Wed 100

AUCHENCAIRN　　　　Map 21 NX75
Dumfries & Galloway

Balcary Bay Hotel
★★★ 87% ◉◉ HOTEL

☎ 01556 640217 & 640311
DG7 1QZ
e-mail: reservations@balcary-bay-hotel.co.uk
web: www.balcary-bay-hotel.co.uk
dir: On A711 between Dalbeattie & Kirkcudbright, hotel 2m from Auchencairn

Taking its name from the bay on which it lies, this hotel has lawns running down to the shore. The larger bedrooms enjoy stunning views over the bay, while others overlook the gardens. The comfortable public areas are very relaxing. Imaginative dishes feature at dinner, accompanied by a good wine list.

Rooms 20 (1 fmly) (3 GF) ☞ **S** £83; **D** £150-£180 (incl. bkfst) **Facilities** FTV Wi-fi **Parking** 50 **Notes** Closed 1st Sun Dec-1st Fri Feb

AUCHTERARDER　　　　Map 21 NN91
Perth & Kinross

INSPECTORS' CHOICE

The Gleneagles Hotel
★★★★★ ◉◉◉◉ HOTEL

☎ 01764 662231 & 0800 169 2984
PH3 1NF
e-mail: resort.sales@gleneagles.com
web: www.gleneagles.com
dir: Off A9 at exit for A823 follow signs for Gleneagles Hotel

With its international reputation for high standards, this grand hotel provides something for everyone. Set in 850 acres of glorious countryside, Gleneagles offers a peaceful retreat, as well as many sporting activities, including the famous championship golf courses. All bedrooms are appointed to a high standard and offer both traditional and contemporary styles. Stylish public areas include various dining options: the Deseo 'Mediterranean Food Market' eaterie; The Strathearn, with two AA Rosettes; as well as inspired cooking at Andrew Fairlie at Gleneagles, a restaurant with four AA Rosettes. There's also the Clubhouse and many bars. The award-winning EPSA spa offers the very latest treatments to restore both body and soul. Service is always professional - the staff are friendly and nothing is too much trouble.

Rooms 232 (115 fmly) (11 GF) **D** £335-£445 (incl. bkfst)* **Facilities** Spa STV FTV Wi-fi supervised supervised 54 Putt green Fishing Gym Falconry Off-road driving Golf Archery Clay shooting Gundog School Horse riding Xmas New Year **Conf** Class 240 Board 60 Thtr 360 **Services** Lift **Parking** 277 **Notes** LB Civ Wed 360

AVIEMORE　　　　Map 23 NH81
Highland

Macdonald Highlands Hotel
MACDONALD HOTELS & RESORTS

★★★★ 74% HOTEL

☎ 01479 815100
Aviemore Highland Resort PH22 1PN
e-mail: general@aviemorehighlandresort.com
web: www.aviemorehighlandresort.com
dir: From N: Exit A9 to Aviemore (B970). Right at T-junct, through village. Right (2nd exit) at 1st rdbt into Macdonald Aviemore Highland Resort, follow reception signs. From S: Exit A9 to Aviemore, left at T-junct. Immediately after Esso garage, turn left into Resort

This hotel is part of the Aviemore Highland Resort which boasts a wide range of activities including a championship golf course. The modern, well-equipped bedrooms suit business, leisure guests and families, and Aspects Restaurant is the fine dining option. In addition there is a state-of-the-art gym, spa treatments and a 25-metre pool with a wave machine and flume. Macdonald Hotels is the AA Hotel Group of the Year 2013-14.

Rooms 151 (10 fmly) (44 GF) **Facilities** Spa STV FTV Wi-fi supervised 18 Putt green Fishing Gym Steam room Sauna Children's indoor & outdoor playgrounds Xmas New Year **Conf** Class 610 Board 38 Thtr 1000 **Services** Lift **Parking** 500 **Notes** ⊗ Civ Wed 300

AYR　　　　Map 20 NS32
South Ayrshire

The Western House Hotel
★★★★ 82% ◉◉ HOTEL

☎ 0870 055 5510
2 Whitletts Rd KA8 0HA
e-mail: info@westernhousehotel.co.uk
web: www.westernhousehotel.co.uk
dir: From Glasgow M77 then A77 towards Ayr. At Whitletts rdbt take A719 towards town centre

This impressive hotel is located in its own attractive gardens on the edge of Ayr racecourse. Bedrooms in the main house are superbly appointed, and the courtyard rooms offer much comfort too. Nicely appointed day rooms include the light and airy restaurant with views across the course. The staff are attentive and welcoming.

Rooms 49 (39 annexe) (39 fmly) (16 GF) ☞ **Facilities** STV Wi-fi Xmas New Year **Conf** Class 300 Board 50 Thtr 1200 **Services** Lift **Parking** 250 **Notes** Civ Wed 200

A

AYR *continued*

Fairfield House Hotel

★★★★ 78% ◉◉ HOTEL

☎ 01292 267461
12 Fairfield Rd KA7 2AR
e-mail: reservations@fairfieldhotel.co.uk
dir: From A77 towards Ayr South (A30). Follow town centre signs, down Miller Rd, left, then right into Fairfield Rd

Situated in a leafy cul-de-sac close to the esplanade, this hotel enjoys stunning seascapes towards to the Isle of Arran. Bedrooms are in either modern or classical styles, the latter featuring impressive bathrooms. Public areas provide stylish, modern rooms in which to relax. Skilfully prepared meals are served in the casual brasserie or elegant restaurant.

Rooms 44 (4 annexe) (3 fmly) (9 GF) **S** £69-£109; **D** £79-£149* **Facilities** FTV Wi-fi ⓦ ⓣ supervised Gym Fitness room Sauna Steam room Xmas New Year **Conf** Class 80 Board 40 Thtr 120 Del from £120 to £140* **Services** Lift **Parking** 50 **Notes** LB ⊗ Civ Wed 150

Enterkine Country House

★★★★ 77% ◉◉ COUNTRY HOUSE HOTEL

☎ 01292 520580
Annbank KA6 5AL
e-mail: mail@enterkine.com
dir: 5m E of Ayr on B743

This luxurious art deco country mansion dates from the 1930s and retains many original features, notably some splendid bathroom suites. The focus is very much on dining, and in country house tradition there is no bar, drinks being served in the elegant lounge and library. The well-proportioned bedrooms are furnished and equipped to high standards, many with lovely countryside views.

Rooms 14 (8 annexe) (2 fmly) (3 GF) ⚡ **S** £50-£120; **D** £60-£195 (incl. bkfst) **Facilities** FTV Wi-fi Xmas New Year **Conf** Class 140 Board 140 Thtr 200 Del from £120 to £140 **Parking** 40 **Notes** LB Civ Wed 250

Mercure Ayr Hotel

★★★ HOTEL

☎ 0844 815 9005
Dalblair Rd KA7 1UG
e-mail: info@mercureayr.co.uk
web: www.jupiterhotels.co.uk
dir: M77 towards Prestwick Airport, then A77 Ayr, 1st rdbt 3rd exit, 2nd rdbt straight over, left at lights, then 2nd lights turn left, bottom of road turn right, hotel on left

Currently the rating for this establishment is not confirmed. This may be due to a change of ownership or because it has only recently joined the AA rating scheme.

Rooms 118 **Conf** Class 160 Board 200 Thtr 460

Premier Inn Ayr/Prestwick Airport

BUDGET HOTEL

☎ 0871 527 8038
Kilmarnock Rd, Monkton KA9 2RJ
web: www.premierinn.com
dir: At Dutch House Rdbt (at junct of A77 & A78) at Monkton

High quality, budget accommodation ideal for both families and business travellers. Spacious, en suite bedrooms feature tea and coffee making facilities, and Freeview TV in most hotels. Internet access and Wi-fi are available for a small fee. The adjacent family restaurant features a wide and varied menu. See also the Hotel Groups pages.

Rooms 64

BALLANTRAE Map 20 NX08
South Ayrshire

INSPECTORS' CHOICE

Glenapp Castle

★★★★★ ◉◉◉ HOTEL

☎ 01465 831212
KA26 0NZ
e-mail: enquiries@glenappcastle.com
web: www.glenappcastle.com
dir: S through Ballantrae, cross bridge over River Stinchar, 1st right, hotel gates 1m

Friendly hospitality and attentive service prevail at this stunning Victorian castle, set in extensive private grounds to the south of the village. Impeccably furnished bedrooms are graced with antiques and period pieces, and include two master rooms and a ground-floor family suite. Breathtaking views of Arran and Ailsa Craig can be enjoyed from the delightful, sumptuous day rooms and from many of the bedrooms. The outstanding cuisine is a real draw here; dinner is offered on a well crafted and imaginative fixed six-course menu. Much of the fruit, vegetables and herbs come from the hotel's own garden. Guests should make a point of walking round the wonderful 36-acre grounds, and take a look at the azalea pond, walled vegetable gardens and restored Victorian greenhouses.

Rooms 17 (2 fmly) (7 GF) ⚡ **S** £235-£440; **D** £370-£575 (incl. bkfst)* **Facilities** STV FTV Wi-fi ⓦ ⓢ ⓛ New Year **Conf** Class 12 Board 25 Thtr 25 Del from £250 to £405* **Services** Lift **Parking** 20 **Notes** LB Closed Jan-mid Mar & Xmas week Civ Wed 40

B

BALLATER
Aberdeenshire   Map 23 NO39

INSPECTORS' CHOICE

Darroch Learg Hotel

★★★ ◉ ◉ SMALL HOTEL

☎ 013397 55443
Braemar Rd AB35 5UX
e-mail: enquiries@darrochlearg.co.uk
web: www.darrochlearg.co.uk
dir: On A93, W of Ballater

Set high above the road in extensive wooded grounds, this long-established hotel offers superb views over the hills and countryside of Royal Deeside. Nigel and Fiona Franks are caring and attentive hosts who improve their hotel every year. Bedrooms, some with four-poster beds, are individually styled, bright and spacious. Food is a highlight of any visit, whether it is a freshly prepared breakfast or the fine cuisine served in the delightful conservatory restaurant.

Rooms 12 (1 GF) **S** £95-£160; **D** £140-£250 (incl. bkfst)* **Facilities** New Year **Conf** Board 12 Thtr 25 Del from £125 to £220* **Parking** 15 **Notes** LB Closed Xmas & Jan (ex New Year)

Loch Kinord Hotel

★★★ 78% ◉ HOTEL

☎ 013398 85229
Ballater Rd, Dinnet AB34 5JY
e-mail: stay@lochkinord.com
web: www.lochkinord.com
dir: Between Aboyne & Ballater, on A93, in Dinnet

Family-run, this roadside hotel is well located for leisure and sporting pursuits. It has lots of character and a friendly atmosphere. There are two bars, one outside and a cosy one inside, plus a dining room with a bold colour scheme. Bedrooms are stylish and have smart bathrooms.

Rooms 20 (3 fmly) (4 GF) ☎ **Facilities** FTV Wi-fi ☜ Xmas **Conf** Class 30 Board 30 Thtr 40 **Parking** 20 **Notes** Civ Wed 50

BALLOCH
West Dumbartonshire   Map 20 NS38

Cameron House on Loch Lomond

★★★★★ 85% ◉ ◉ HOTEL

☎ 01389 755565
G83 8QZ
e-mail: reservations@cameronhouse.co.uk
web: www.devere.co.uk
dir: M8 (W) junct 30 for Erskine Bridge. A82 for Crainlarich. 14m, at rdbt signed Luss, hotel on right

Enjoying an idyllic location on the banks of Loch Lomond in over 100 acres of wooded parkland, this stylish hotel offers an excellent range of leisure facilities. These include two golf courses, a world-class spa and a host of indoor and outdoor sporting activities. A choice of restaurants and bars cater for all tastes and include the Scottish-themed Cameron Grill and a fine dining operation, Martin Wishart at Loch Lomond. Bedrooms are stylish, well equipped and many boast wonderful loch views.

Rooms 132 (9 fmly) (18 GF) ☎ **S** £129-£195; **D** £159-£225 (incl. bkfst)* **Facilities** Spa STV Wi-fi ☜ HL ☜ supervised ♨ 9 ♒ Fishing ☜ Gym Squash Motor boat on Loch Lomond Hairdresser Sea plane Falconry Archery Segways Xmas New Year Child facilities **Conf** Class 180 Board 80 Thtr 300 Del from £195 to £325* **Services** Lift Air con **Parking** 200 **Notes** LB ⊗ Civ Wed 200

BANCHORY
Aberdeenshire   Map 23 NO69

Raemoir House Hotel

★★★ 85% ◉ ◉ COUNTRY HOUSE HOTEL

☎ 01330 824884
Raemoir AB31 4ED
e-mail: hotel@raemoir.com

A beautiful Georgian country house set in 11 acres of secluded, peaceful grounds, close to Aberdeen and perfectly situated for the Whisky, Castle and Golf trails. The current owners have recently refurbished the property, and the individually styled bedrooms feature all modern comforts including Wi-fi access. Cooking is a highlight with delicious meals served in the Oval Dining Room. The hotel has a helicopter pad.

Rooms 20 (6 annexe) (2 fmly) (3 GF) ☎ **S** £105-£125; **D** £120-£220 (incl. bkfst) **Facilities** FTV Wi-fi ☜ Xmas New Year **Conf** Class 50 Board 40 Thtr 80 Del from £165 to £175* **Parking** 30 **Notes** LB No children 12yrs Civ Wed 60

B

BANCHORY *continued*

BEST WESTERN Burnett Arms Hotel

★★★ 71% SMALL HOTEL

☎ 01330 824944
25 High St AB31 5TD
e-mail: theburnett@btconnect.com
web: www.bw-burnettarms.co.uk
dir: Town centre on N side of A93

This popular hotel is located in the heart of the town centre and gives easy access to the many attractions of Royal Deeside. Public areas include a choice of eating and drinking options, with food served in the restaurant, bar and foyer lounge. Bedrooms are thoughtfully equipped and comfortably modern.

Rooms 18 (1 fmly) ↱ **S** £70-£80; **D** £89-£99 (incl. bkfst)* **Facilities** STV FTV Wi-fi Xmas New Year **Conf** Class 50 Board 50 Thtr 100 Del from £110 to £130* **Parking** 23 **Notes** LB Civ Wed 100

See advert on page 503

See advert on page 503

BATHGATE — Map 21 NS96
West Lothian

Premier Inn Livingston (Bathgate)

BUDGET HOTEL

☎ 0871 527 8630
Starlaw Rd EH48 1LQ
web: www.premierinn.com
dir: M8 junct 3A. At 1st rdbt 1st exit (Bathgate). Over bridge, at 2nd rdbt take 1st exit. Hotel 200yds on left

High quality, budget accommodation ideal for both families and business travellers. Spacious, en suite bedrooms feature tea and coffee making facilities, and Freeview TV in most hotels. Internet access and Wi-fi are available for a small fee. The adjacent family restaurant features a wide and varied menu. See also the Hotel Groups pages.

Rooms 74

BEAULY — Map 23 NH54
Highland

Priory Hotel

★★★ 75% HOTEL

☎ 01463 782309
The Square IV4 7BX
e-mail: reservations@priory-hotel.com
web: www.priory-hotel.com
dir: Signed from A832, into Beauly, hotel in square on left

This popular hotel occupies a central location in the town square. Standard and executive rooms are on offer, both providing a good level of comfort and range of facilities. Food is served throughout the day in the open-plan public areas, with menus offering a first rate choice.

Rooms 38 (3 fmly) (1 GF) ↱ **S** £47.50-£67.50; **D** £75-£120 (incl. bkfst)* **Facilities** STV FTV Wi-fi Xmas New Year **Conf** Class 40 Board 30 Thtr 40 Del from £75 to £95* **Services** Lift **Parking** 20 **Notes** LB ⊗

The Lovat Arms

★★★ 71% HOTEL

☎ 01463 782313
IV4 7BS
e-mail: info@lovatarms.com
web: www.lovatarms.com
dir: From The Square past Royal Bank of Scotland, hotel on right

This fine, family-run hotel enjoys a prominent position in this charming town which is a short drive from Inverness. The bedrooms are comfortable and well appointed. The spacious foyer has a real fire and comfortable seating, while the Strubag lounge is ideal for informal dining.

Rooms 33 (12 annexe) (4 fmly) (6 GF) ↱ **Facilities** STV FTV Wi-fi ⇃ Xmas New Year **Conf** Class 26 Board 40 Thtr 80 **Parking** 25 **Notes** Civ Wed 60

BOAT OF GARTEN — Map 23 NH91
Highland

Boat Hotel

★★★ 78% ◉◉ HOTEL

☎ 01479 831258 & 831696
PH24 3BH
e-mail: info@boathotel.co.uk
dir: Exit A9 N of Aviemore onto A95, follow signs to Boat of Garten

A well established hotel situated in the heart of this pretty village. Public areas include a choice of comfortable lounges and The Osprey Bistro & Bar, which is inviting and relaxed, with appealing menus and a well deserved reputation for good food. Individually styled bedrooms reflect the unique character of the hotel; all are comfortable and well equipped.

Rooms 34 (8 fmly) ↱ **S** £46-£76; **D** £76-£117 (incl. bkfst) **Facilities** FTV Wi-fi Xmas New Year **Conf** Class 30 Board 25 Thtr 40 Del from £137 to £167 **Parking** 36 **Notes** Civ Wed 60

Save on hotels. Book at **theAA.com/hotel**

BAN – CLY 509 SCOTLAND

BOTHWELL
South Lanarkshire
Map 20 NS75

Bothwell Bridge Hotel

★★★ 78% HOTEL

☎ 01698 852246
89 Main St G71 8EU
e-mail: reception@bothwellbridge-hotel.com
web: www.bothwellbridge-hotel.com
dir: M74 junct 5 & follow signs to Uddingston, right at mini-rdbt. Hotel just past shops on left

This red-sandstone mansion house is a popular business, function and conference hotel and is conveniently placed for the motorway. Most bedrooms are spacious and all are well equipped. The conservatory is a bright and comfortable restaurant serving an interesting variety of Italian influenced dishes. The lounge bar offers a comfortable seating area that proves popular as a stop for coffee.

Rooms 90 (14 fmly) (13 GF) **Facilities** STV FTV Wi-fi ⊾ HL ♬ Xmas New Year **Conf** Class 80 Board 50 Thtr 200 **Services** Lift **Parking** 125 **Notes** ⊗ Civ Wed 250

BRORA
Highland
Map 23 NC90

Royal Marine Hotel, Restaurant & Spa

★★★★ 77% ⚜ HOTEL

☎ 01408 621252
Golf Rd KW9 6QS
e-mail: info@royalmarinebrora.com
web: www.royalmarinebrora.com
dir: Off A9 in village towards beach & golf course

A sympathetically extended, distinctive Edwardian residence, the Royal Marine attracts a mixed market. Its leisure centre is popular, and the restaurant, Hunters Lounge and café bar offer three contrasting eating options. A modern bedroom wing complements the original bedrooms, which retain their period style. There are also luxury apartments just a short walk away.

Rooms 21 (1 fmly) (2 GF) ⊅ **Facilities** FTV Wi-fi ⊾ ⊠ ⦆ Putt green Fishing ⥁ Gym Steam room Sauna Xmas New Year **Conf** Class 40 Board 40 Thtr 70 **Parking** 40 **Notes** Civ Wed 60

CALLANDER
Stirling
Map 20 NN60

INSPECTORS' CHOICE

Roman Camp Country House Hotel

★★★ ⚜⚜⚜ COUNTRY HOUSE HOTEL

☎ 01877 330003
FK17 8BG
e-mail: mail@romancamphotel.co.uk
web: www.romancamphotel.co.uk
dir: N on A84, left at east end of High Street. 300yds to hotel

Built in the 17th century and originally used as a shooting lodge, this charming country house has a rich history, and has been in the same ownership for over twenty years. Twenty acres of gardens and grounds lead down to the River Teith, and the town centre and its attractions are only a short walk away. Each bedroom is individually and elegantly designed, and offers much pampering comfort. Food is a highlight of any stay and menus are dominated by high-quality Scottish produce that is sensitively treated by the talented kitchen team. Real fires warm the atmospheric public areas and service is friendly yet professional.

Rooms 15 (4 fmly) (7 GF) ⊅ **S** £100-£110; **D** £155-£255 (incl. bkfst) **Facilities** STV FTV Wi-fi ⊾ Fishing Xmas New Year **Conf** Class 60 Board 30 Thtr 120 **Del** from £175 to £255 **Parking** 80 **Notes** LB Civ Wed 150

Callander Meadows

⚜ RESTAURANT WITH ROOMS

☎ 01877 330181
24 Main St FK17 8BB
e-mail: mail@callandermeadows.co.uk
web: www.callandermeadows.co.uk
dir: M9 junct 10, A84 to Callander, house on main street just past A81 junct

Located on the high street in Callander, this family-run business offers comfortable accommodation and a restaurant that has quickly become very popular with the locals. The bedrooms have been appointed to a high standard. Private parking is available to the rear.

Rooms 3

CARNOUSTIE
Angus
Map 21 NO53

C

Carnoustie Golf Hotel & Spa

★★★★ 73% ⚜ HOTEL

☎ 0843 178 7109
The Links DD7 7JE
e-mail: reservations.carnoustie@bespokehotels.com
web: www.bespokehotels.com
dir: Adjacent to Carnoustie Golf Links

This fine hotel enjoys an enviable location and is adjacent to the 1st and 18th green of the famous Championship Course of Carnoustie. All bedrooms are spacious and attractively presented; most overlook the magnificent course and enjoy breathtaking coastal views. Fine dining can be enjoyed in the restaurant with more informal meals served in the comfortable bar.

Rooms 85 (12 fmly) ⊅ **Facilities** Spa FTV Wi-fi ⊾ ⦆ Putt green Gym Xmas New Year **Conf** Class 200 Board 100 Thtr 350 **Services** Lift Air con **Parking** 100 **Notes** ⊗ Civ Wed 325

CLYDEBANK
West Dunbartonshire
Map 20 NS47

Beardmore Hotel

★★★★ 76% ⚜ HOTEL

☎ 0141 951 6000
Beardmore St G81 4SA
e-mail: info@beardmore.scot.nhs.uk
web: www.thebeardmore.com
dir: M8 junct 19, follow signs for Clydeside Expressway to Glasgow road, then A814 (Dumbarton road), then follow Clydebank Business Park signs. Hotel on left

Attracting much business and conference custom, this stylish modern hotel lies beside the River Clyde and shares an impressive site with a hospital (although the latter does not intrude). Spacious and imposing public areas include the stylish restaurant providing innovative contemporary Scottish cooking, and The BBar lounge which offers a more extensive choice of lighter dishes. The leisure facilities include a 15-metre swimming pool, sauna and steam room. All bedrooms come with iMac entertainment systems.

Rooms 166 **Facilities** STV Wi-fi ⦆ supervised Gym Sauna Steam room Whirlpool Xmas New Year **Conf** Class 84 Board 27 Thtr 240 **Services** Lift Air con **Parking** 300 **Notes** ⊗ Civ Wed 170

C

COMRIE
Perth & Kinross — Map 21 NN72

Royal Hotel

★★★ 82% ● HOTEL

☎ 01764 679200
Melville Square PH6 2DN
e-mail: reception@royalhotel.co.uk
web: www.royalhotel.co.uk
dir: A9 on A822 to Crieff, then B827 to Comrie. Hotel in main square on A85

The traditional façade gives little indication of the style and elegance to be found inside this long-established hotel located in the village centre. Public areas include a bar and library, a bright modern restaurant and a conservatory-style brasserie. The bedrooms are tastefully appointed and furnished with smart reproduction antiques.

Rooms 13 (2 annexe) **Facilities** STV Wi-fi Fishing Shooting arranged New Year **Conf** Class 10 Board 20 Thtr 20 **Parking** 22 **Notes** Closed 25-26 Dec

CONNEL
Argyll & Bute — Map 20 NM93

Falls of Lora Hotel

THE INDEPENDENTS
HOTEL ASSOCIATION

★★★ 73% HOTEL

☎ 01631 710483
PA37 1PB
e-mail: enquiries@fallsoflora.com
web: www.fallsoflora.com
dir: From Glasgow take A82, A85. Hotel 0.5m past Connel sign (5m before Oban)

Personally run and welcoming, this long-established and thriving holiday hotel enjoys inspiring views over Loch Etive. The spacious ground floor takes in a comfortable, traditional lounge and a cocktail bar with over a hundred whiskies and an open log fire. Guests can eat in the popular, informal bistro, which is open all day. Bedrooms come in a variety of styles, ranging from the cosy standard rooms to high quality luxury rooms.

Falls of Lora Hotel

Rooms 30 (4 fmly) (4 GF) (30 smoking) ⚑
S £49.50-£69.50; **D** £59-£159 (incl. bkfst)*
Facilities FTV Wi-fi Child facilities **Conf** Class 20 Board 15 Thtr 45 **Parking** 40 **Notes** LB Closed mid Dec & Jan

See advert on opposite page

CRAIGELLACHIE
Moray — Map 23 NJ24

Craigellachie Hotel

"bespoke"

★★★★ 73% ● HOTEL

☎ 01340 881204
AB38 9SR
e-mail: reservations.craigellachie@bespokehotels.com
web: www.bespokehotels.com/craigellachiehotel
dir: On A95 between Aberdeen & Inverness

This impressive and popular hotel is located in the heart of Speyside, so it's no surprise that malt whisky takes centre stage in the Quaich Bar with over 700 varieties featured. Bedrooms come in various sizes but all are tastefully decorated and bathrooms are of a high specification. Creative dinners showcase local ingredients in the traditionally styled Ben Aigen dining room or the more informal Bremners Lounge and Bar.

Rooms 26 (1 fmly) (6 GF) ⚑ **Facilities** FTV Wi-fi Xmas New Year **Conf** Class 35 Board 30 Thtr 60 **Parking** 30 **Notes** Civ Wed 60

CRIANLARICH
Stirling — Map 20 NN32

The Crianlarich Hotel

Best Western

★★★ 74% HOTEL

☎ 01838 300272
FK20 8RW
e-mail: info@crianlarich-hotel.co.uk
web: www.crianlarich-hotel.co.uk
dir: At junct of A85 & A82

Standing at what has been an important transport junction for many years, this hotel continues to cater to travellers' needs. The ground-floor areas are impressive, and the pleasant bedrooms are smartly appointed and offer all the usual amenities. Friendly relaxed service and high quality food makes this an enjoyable place to stay especially as it is close to Loch Lomond and the Trossachs National Park.

Rooms 36 (5 fmly) ⚑ **Facilities** FTV Wi-fi ⚑ ♫ Xmas New Year **Conf** Class 60 Board 40 Thtr 100 **Services** Lift **Parking** 30 **Notes** Civ Wed 100

CUMBERNAULD
North Lanarkshire — Map 21 NS77

The Westerwood Hotel & Golf Resort

★★★★ 81% ● HOTEL

☎ 01236 457171
1 St Andrews Dr, Westerwood G68 0EW
e-mail: westerwood@qhotels.co.uk
web: www.qhotels.co.uk

This stylish, contemporary hotel enjoys an elevated position within 400 acres at the foot of the Campsie Hills. Accommodation is provided in spacious, bright bedrooms, many with super bathrooms, and day rooms include sumptuous lounges and an airy restaurant; extensive golf, fitness and conference facilities are available.

Rooms 148 (15 fmly) (49 GF) **Facilities** Spa STV Wi-fi ⚑ ⚑ ⚑ 18 ⚑ Putt green Gym Beauty salon Relaxation room Sauna Steam room Xmas New Year **Conf** Class 120 Board 60 Thtr 400 **Services** Lift **Parking** 250 **Notes** Civ Wed 350

Premier Inn Glasgow (Cumbernauld)

BUDGET HOTEL

☎ 0871 527 8424
4 South Muirhead Rd G67 1AX
web: www.premierinn.com
dir: From A80, A8011 follow Cumbernauld & town centre signs. Hotel opposite Asda & McDonalds

High quality, budget accommodation ideal for both families and business travellers. Spacious, en suite bedrooms feature tea and coffee making facilities, and Freeview TV in most hotels. Internet access and Wi-fi are available for a small fee. The adjacent family restaurant features a wide and varied menu. See also the Hotel Groups pages.

Rooms 37

Save on hotels. Book at **theAA.com/hotel**

COM – DRY 511 SCOTLAND

DALKEITH
Midlothian Map 21 NT36

Premier Inn Edinburgh (Dalkeith)

BUDGET HOTEL

☎ 0871 527 9290
Melville Dykes Rd EH18 1AN
web: www.premierinn.com
dir: Exit A720 at Sheriffhall rdbt onto A7 signed Galashiels/Harwick/Carlisle. At 2nd rdbt take 3rd exit into Melville Dykes Rd (A768). Hotel on left

High quality, budget accommodation ideal for both families and business travellers. Spacious, en suite bedrooms feature tea and coffee making facilities, and Freeview TV in most hotels. Internet access and Wi-fi are available for a small fee. The adjacent family restaurant features a wide and varied menu. See also the Hotel Groups pages.

Rooms 40

DINGWALL
Highland Map 23 NH55

Tulloch Castle Hotel

"bespoke"

★★★★ 72% HOTEL

☎ 01349 861325
Tulloch Castle Dr IV15 9ND
e-mail: reservations.tulloch@ohiml.com
web: www.oxfordhotelsandinns.com
dir: A9 N, Tore rdbt 2nd left signed Dingwall. On to A862 at 3rd lights through Dingwall, left, hotel signed

Overlooking the town of Dingwall, this 12th-century castle is still the gathering place of the Clan

Davidson and boasts its own ghost in the shape of the Green Lady. The friendly team are very helpful and love to tell you about the history of the castle; the ghost tour after dinner is a must. The hotel has a self contained suite and a number of bedrooms with four-posters.

Rooms 20 (2 fmly) ➹ **Facilities** FTV Wi-fi Xmas New Year **Conf** Class 70 Board 70 Thtr 120 **Parking** 50 **Notes** Civ Wed 110

DORNOCH
Highland Map 23 NH78

Dornoch Castle Hotel

★★★ 75% ◉ HOTEL

☎ 01862 810216
Castle St IV25 3SD
e-mail: enquiries@dornochcastlehotel.com
web: www.dornochcastlehotel.com
dir: 2m N of Dornoch Bridge on A9, turn right to Dornoch. Hotel in village centre

Situated opposite the cathedral, this fully restored ancient castle has become a popular wedding venue. Within the original castle are some splendid themed bedrooms, and elsewhere the more modern bedrooms have all of the expected facilities. There is a character bar and a delightful conservatory restaurant overlooking the garden.

Rooms 23 (3 fmly) (4 GF) ➹ **Facilities** FTV Wi-fi New Year **Conf** Class 40 Board 30 Thtr 60 **Parking** 16 **Notes** ⊗ Closed 24-26 Dec & 2nd wk Jan

DRYMEN
Stirling Map 20 NS48

BEST WESTERN Buchanan Arms Hotel & Spa

★★★ 79% HOTEL

☎ 01360 660588
23 Main St G63 0BQ
e-mail: info@buchananarms.co.uk

This former coaching inn is located in the quiet conservation village of Drymen, and provides a perfect base for touring this area, with Loch Lomond just a few miles away. There are well-appointed bedrooms and welcoming public areas. Good leisure facilities are an added benefit.

Rooms 52 (9 fmly) (3 GF) **S** £60-£135; **D** £80-£155 (incl. bkfst) **Facilities** Spa FTV Wi-fi ⤸ ☒ supervised Gym Squash Steam room Sauna Spa bath Xmas New Year **Conf** Class 140 Board 60 Thtr 250 Del from £99 to £135 **Parking** 120 **Notes** ⊗ Civ Wed 160

D

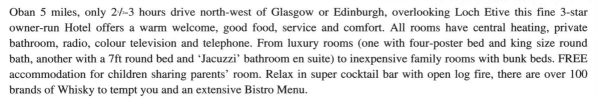

D

DRYMEN *continued*

Winnock Hotel

★★★ 74% HOTEL

☎ 01360 660245
The Square G63 0BL
e-mail: info@winnockhotel.com
web: www.winnockhotel.com
dir: From S: M74 onto M8 junct 16b through Glasgow.
Follow A809 to Aberfoyle

Occupying a prominent position overlooking the
village green, this popular hotel offers well-equipped
bedrooms of various sizes and styles. The public
rooms include a bar, a lounge and an attractive
formal dining room that serves dishes of good, locally
sourced food.

Rooms 73 (18 fmly) (19 GF) **Facilities** FTV Wi-fi ⌁
Xmas New Year **Conf** Class 60 Board 70 Thtr 140
Parking 60 **Notes** ⊗ Civ Wed 100

DUMBARTON   Map 20 NS37
East Dunbartonshire

Premier Inn Dumbarton

BUDGET HOTEL

☎ 0871 527 9274
Lomondgate Dr G82 2QU
web: www.premierinn.com
dir: From Glasgow follow A82 towards Crainlarich,
right at Lomondgate rdbt onto A813, hotel on right.
From N: A82 towards Glasgow, left at Lomondgate
rdbt onto A813, hotel on right

High quality, budget accommodation ideal for both
families and business travellers. Spacious, en suite
bedrooms feature tea and coffee making facilities,
and Freeview TV in most hotels. Internet access and
Wi-fi are available for a small fee. The adjacent
family restaurant features a wide and varied menu.
See also the Hotel Groups pages.

Rooms 60

DUMFRIES   Map 21 NX97
Dumfries & Galloway

See also **Kirkbean**

Cairndale Hotel & Leisure Club

★★★ 80% HOTEL

☎ 01387 254111
English St DG1 2DF
e-mail: sales@cairndalehotel.co.uk
web: www.cairndalehotel.co.uk
dir: From S on M6 take A75 to Dumfries, left at 1st
rdbt, cross rail bridge to lights, hotel 1st building on
left

Within walking distance of the town centre, this hotel
provides a wide range of amenities, including leisure
facilities and an impressive conference and
entertainment centre. Bedrooms range from stylish
suites to cosy singles. There's a choice of eating
options in the evening. The Reivers Restaurant is
smartly modern with food to match.

Rooms 91 (22 fmly) (5 GF) **Facilities** Wi-fi ⌁
supervised Gym Steam room Sauna ♫ Xmas New
Year **Conf** Class 150 Board 50 Thtr 300 **Services** Lift
Parking 100 **Notes** Civ Wed 200

BEST WESTERN Station Hotel

★★★ 79% HOTEL

☎ 01387 254316
49 Lovers Walk DG1 1LT
e-mail: info@stationhotel.co.uk
web: www.stationhoteldumfries.co.uk
dir: A75, follow signs to town centre, hotel opposite
railway station

This friendly Victorian hotel offers stylish, well-
equipped bedrooms that feature satellite TVs and free
Wi-fi; three rooms have four-poster beds and spa
baths. The Courtyard restaurant creates an informal
atmosphere where guests can enjoy a popular range
of dishes at dinner; in addition, good-value meals are
served at lunchtime in either the lounge bar or on the
patio in warmer weather. There is a delightful small
garden to relax in.

Rooms 32 ⌁ **Facilities** Wi-fi Use of local gym
Conf Class 35 Board 30 Thtr 80 **Services** Lift
Parking 34 **Notes** Closed 26 Dec & 2 Jan Civ Wed 50

Premier Inn Dumfries

BUDGET HOTEL

☎ 0871 527 8316
Annan Rd, Collin DG1 3JX
web: www.premierinn.com
dir: At rdbt junct of Euroroute bypass (A75) & A780

High quality, budget accommodation ideal for both
families and business travellers. Spacious, en suite
bedrooms feature tea and coffee making facilities,
and Freeview TV in most hotels. Internet access and
Wi-fi are available for a small fee. The adjacent
family restaurant features a wide and varied menu.
See also the Hotel Groups pages.

Rooms 40

DUNDEE   Map 21 NO43
City of Dundee

DoubleTree by Hilton Dundee

★★★★ 76% ◉ HOTEL

☎ 01382 641122
Kingsway West DD2 5JT
e-mail: sales@thelandmarkdundee.co.uk
web: www.thelandmarkdundee.co.uk
dir: From A90 (Kingsway) at rdbt junct with A85,
follow hotel signs

Well located off Kingsway West with ample parking,
this hotel offers contemporary bedrooms that are
equipped with many thoughtful extras. The restaurant
overlooks the gardens which are a feature at this
hotel. A good leisure club includes a gym, steam room
and sauna. The hotel is a popular wedding venue.

Save on hotels. Book at **theAA.com/hotel**

DRY – DUN 513 SCOTLAND

D

Rooms 95 (11 fmly) (45 GF) ⚓ **Facilities** STV FTV
Wi-fi ⓢ supervised Gym Sauna Steam room Xmas
New Year **Conf** Class 50 Board 45 Thtr 100
Parking 140 **Notes** ⊗ Civ Wed 100

Apex City Quay Hotel & Spa

★★★★ 76% HOTEL

☎ 0845 365 0000 & 01382 202404
1 West Victoria Dock Rd DD1 3JP
e-mail: dundee.reservations@apexhotels.co.uk
web: www.apexhotels.co.uk
dir: A85/Riverside Drive to Discovery Quay. Exit rdbt
for City Quay

This stylish, purpose-built hotel occupies an enviable
position at the heart of Dundee's regenerated
quayside. Bedrooms, including a number of smart
suites, feature the very latest in design. Warm
hospitality and professional service are an integral
part of the hotel's appeal. Public areas are open-plan
with panoramic windows and contemporary dining
options. The luxurious Yu Spa completes the package.

Rooms 151 (17 fmly) ⚓ **Facilities** Spa FTV Wi-fi ⓢ HL
ⓢ Gym Steam room Sauna Xmas New Year
Conf Class 180 Board 120 Thtr 375 **Services** Lift
Parking 150 **Notes** ⊗ Civ Wed 300

Premier Inn Dundee Centre

BUDGET HOTEL

☎ 0871 527 8320
Discovery Quay, Riverside Dr DD1 4XA
web: www.premierinn.com
dir: Follow signs for Discovery Quay, hotel on
waterfront

High quality, budget accommodation ideal for both
families and business travellers. Spacious, en suite
bedrooms feature tea and coffee making facilities,
and Freeview TV in most hotels. Internet access and
Wi-fi are available for a small fee. The adjacent
family restaurant features a wide and varied menu.
See also the Hotel Groups pages.

Rooms 40

Premier Inn Dundee East

BUDGET HOTEL

☎ 0871 527 8322
**115-117 Lawers Dr, Panmurefield Village, Broughty
Ferry DD5 3UP**
web: www.premierinn.com
dir: From N: A92 (Dundee & Arbroath). Hotel 1.5m
after Sainsbury's. From S: A90. At end of dual
carriageway follow Dundee to Arbroath signs

Rooms 60

Premier Inn Dundee (Monifieth)

BUDGET HOTEL

☎ 0871 527 8318
Ethiebeaton Park, Arbroath Rd, Monifieth DD5 4HB
web: www.premierinn.com
dir: From A90 (Kingsway Rd) follow Carnoustie/
Arbroath (A92) signs

Rooms 40

Premier Inn Dundee North

BUDGET HOTEL

☎ 0871 527 8324
**Camperdown Leisure Park, Dayton Dr, Kingsway
DD2 3SQ**
web: www.premierinn.com
dir: 2m N of city centre on A90 at junct with A923,
adjacent to cinema. At entrance to Camperdown
Country Park

Rooms 78

Premier Inn Dundee West

BUDGET HOTEL

☎ 0871 527 8326
Kingsway West DD2 5JU
web: www.premierinn.com
dir: On A90 towards Aberdeen adjacent to Technology
Park rdbt

Rooms 64

DUNFERMLINE	Map 21 NT08
Fife	

King Malcolm Hotel

★★★ 74% HOTEL

☎ 01383 722611
Queensferry Rd KY11 8DS
e-mail: info@kingmalcolm-hotel-dunfermline.com
web: www.peelhotels.co.uk
dir: On A823, S of town

Located to the south of the city, this purpose-built
hotel remains popular with business clientele and is
convenient for access to both Edinburgh and Fife.
Public rooms include a smart foyer lounge and a
conservatory bar, as well as a restaurant. Bedrooms,
although not large, are well laid out and well
equipped.

Rooms 48 (2 fmly) (24 GF) **Facilities** Wi-fi ♬ Xmas
New Year **Conf** Class 60 Board 50 Thtr 150
Parking 60 **Notes** Civ Wed 120

Premier Inn Dunfermline

BUDGET HOTEL

☎ 0871 527 8328
4-12 Whimbrel Place, Fife Leisure Park KY11 8EX
web: www.premierinn.com
dir: M90 junct 3 (Forth Road Bridge exit) 1st left at
lights signed Duloch Park. 1st left into Fife Leisure
Park

High quality, budget accommodation ideal for both
families and business travellers. Spacious, en suite
bedrooms feature tea and coffee making facilities,
and Freeview TV in most hotels. Internet access and
Wi-fi are available for a small fee. The adjacent
family restaurant features a wide and varied menu.
See also the Hotel Groups pages.

Rooms 40

DUNOON	Map 20 NS17
Argyll & Bute	

Selborne Hotel

Leisureplex

★★ 74% HOTEL

☎ 01369 702761
Clyde St, West Bay PA23 7HU
e-mail: selborne.dunoon@alfatravel.co.uk
web: www.leisureplex.co.uk
dir: From Caledonian MacBrayne pier. Past castle, left
into Jane St, right into Clyde St

This holiday hotel is situated overlooking the West
Bay and provides unrestricted views of the Clyde
Estuary towards the Isles of Cumbrae. Tour groups
are especially well catered for in this good-value
establishment, which offers entertainment most
nights. Bedrooms are comfortable and many have sea
views.

Rooms 98 (6 fmly) (14 GF) ⚓ S £35-£50; D £56-£86
(incl. bkfst)* **Facilities** FTV Wi-fi HL Pool table Table
tennis ♬ Xmas New Year **Services** Lift **Parking** 30
Notes LB ⊗ Closed Dec-Feb (ex Xmas) RS Nov & Mar

E

EAST KILBRIDE
South Lanarkshire   Map 20 NS65

Macdonald Crutherland House

★★★★ 75% ◉◉ HOTEL

☎ 0844 879 9039
Strathaven Rd G75 0QZ
e-mail: crutherland@macdonald-hotels.co.uk
web: www.macdonaldhotels.co.uk/crutherland
dir: Follow A726 signed Strathaven, straight over Torrance rdbt, hotel on left after 250yds

This mansion is set in 37 acres of landscaped grounds two miles from the town centre. Behind its Georgian façade is a very relaxing hotel with elegant public areas plus extensive banqueting and leisure facilities. The bedrooms are spacious and comfortable. Staff provide good levels of attention and enjoyable meals are served in the restaurant. Macdonald Hotels is the AA Hotel Group of the Year 2013-14.

Rooms 75 (16 fmly) (16 GF) **Facilities** Spa STV Wi-fi ⊗ Gym Sauna Steam room Xmas New Year **Conf** Class 100 Board 50 Thtr 500 **Services** Lift **Parking** 200 **Notes** ⊗ Civ Wed 300

Premier Inn Glasgow East Kilbride

BUDGET HOTEL

☎ 0871 527 8446
5 Lee's Burn Court, Nerston G74 3XB
web: www.premierinn.com
dir: M74 junct 5, follow East Kilbride/A725 signs. Into right lane, follow Glasgow/A749 signs. At lights left onto A749 signed East Kilbride Town Centre (A725). Take slip road to Lee's Burn Court

High quality, budget accommodation ideal for both families and business travellers. Spacious, en suite bedrooms feature tea and coffee making facilities, and Freeview TV in most hotels. Internet access and Wi-fi are available for a small fee. The adjacent family restaurant features a wide and varied menu. See also the Hotel Groups pages.

Rooms 44

Premier Inn Glasgow East Kilbride Central

BUDGET HOTEL

☎ 0871 527 8450
Brunel Way, The Murray G75 0LD
web: www.premierinn.com
dir: M74 junct 5, follow East Kilbride A725 signs, then Paisley A726 signs, left at Murray Rdbt, left into Brunel Way

Rooms 40

Premier Inn Glasgow East Kilbride (Peel Park)

BUDGET HOTEL

☎ 0871 527 8448
Eaglesham Rd G75 8LW
web: www.premierinn.com
dir: 8m from M74 junct 5 on A726 at rdbt of B764

Rooms 42

EDDLESTON
Scottish Borders   Map 21 NT24

The Horseshoe Inn

RESTAURANT WITH ROOMS

☎ 01721 730225
EH45 8QP
e-mail: reservations@horseshoeinn.co.uk
web: www.horseshoeinn.co.uk
dir: A703, 5m N of Peebles

This inn is five miles north of Peebles and only 18 miles south of Edinburgh. Originally a blacksmith's shop, it has a very good reputation for its delightful atmosphere and excellent cuisine. There are eight luxuriously appointed and individually designed bedrooms.

Rooms 8 (1 fmly)

EDINBURGH
City of Edinburgh   Map 21 NT27

The Balmoral

★★★★★ ◉◉◉ HOTEL

☎ 0131 556 2414
1 Princes St EH2 2EQ
e-mail: reservations.balmoral@roccofortecollection.com
web: www.roccofortecollection.com
dir: Follow city centre signs. Hotel at E end of Princes St, adjacent to Waverley Station

This elegant hotel enjoys a prestigious address at the top of Princes Street, with fine views over the city and the castle. Bedrooms and suites are stylishly furnished and decorated, all boasting a thoughtful range of extras and impressive marble bathrooms. Hotel amenities include a Roman-style health spa, extensive function facilities, a choice of bars and two very different dining options - Number One offers inspired fine dining whilst Hadrians is a bustling, informal brasserie.

Rooms 188 (22 fmly) (15 smoking) **Facilities** Spa STV Wi-fi ⊗ Gym ♫ Xmas New Year **Conf** Class 180 Board 60 Thtr 350 **Services** Lift Air con **Parking** 100 **Notes** ⊗ Civ Wed 120

Save on hotels. Book at **theAA.com/hotel**

EAS – EDI 515 SCOTLAND

E

Prestonfield

★★★★★ ⚛⚛ TOWN HOUSE HOTEL

☎ 0131 225 7800
Priestfield Rd EH16 5UT
e-mail: reservations@prestonfield.com
web: www.prestonfield.com
dir: A7 towards Cameron Toll. 200mtrs beyond
Royal Commonwealth Pool, into Priestfield Rd

This centuries-old landmark has been lovingly
restored and enhanced to provide deeply
comfortable and dramatically furnished bedrooms.
The building demands to be explored: from the
tapestry lounge and the whisky room to the
restaurant, where the walls are adorned with
pictures of former owners. Facilities and services are
up-to-the-minute, and carefully prepared meals are
served in the award-winning Rhubarb restaurant.

Rooms 23 (6 GF) ⚘ **Facilities** STV FTV Wi-fi ⚑ ♪ 18
Putt green ⚘ Free bike hire Xmas New Year
Conf Class 500 Board 40 Thtr 700 **Services** Lift
Parking 250 **Notes** Civ Wed 350

The Caledonian, A Waldorf Astoria Hotel

★★★★★ 87% ⚛⚛⚛ HOTEL

☎ 0131 222 8888
Princes St EH1 2AB
e-mail: guest_caledonian@waldorfastoria.com

Known locally as "the Caley", the Caledonian was
built in the age of steam and has recently benefitted
from a £24 million transformation without losing any
of the charm and character that has made it famous.
Spacious bedrooms and en suites offer comfort and
luxury, and there is a choice of award-wining
restaurants and wonderful public areas. For further
details please see the AA website: theAA.com

Rooms 241 (10 fmly) ⚘ **S** £189-£1149;
D £189-£1149* **Facilities** Spa STV Wi-fi ⚑ HL ⚒ Gym
Sauna Steam room Xmas New Year **Conf** Class 120
Board 80 Thtr 300 Del from £229 to £389*
Services Lift Air con **Parking** 39 **Notes** LB ⊗
Civ Wed 300

Hotel Missoni Edinburgh

★★★★★ 85% ⚛⚛ HOTEL

☎ 0131 220 6666
1 George IV Bridge EH1 1AD
e-mail: info.edinburgh@hotelmissoni.com
dir: At corner of Royal Mile & George IV Bridge

Located on the corner of the George IV Bridge and the
Royal Mile in the heart of the old town, this hotel's
design is strikingly different. Bold use of black and
white and vivid colours together with strong patterns
creates a stunning impression. Stylish bedrooms,
some with great city views, have iPod/AV hook-up, Wi-
fi, coffee machines, and bathrooms with walk-in
showers as standard. The buzzing cocktail bar and
Cucina Missoni, for modern Italian cuisine, attract
locals and residents alike.

Rooms 136 **Facilities** Spa STV FTV Wi-fi ⚑ Gym Xmas
New Year **Conf** Class 24 Board 24 Thtr 63
Services Lift Air con **Parking** 13

The Howard

★★★★★ 83% ⚛ TOWN HOUSE HOTEL

☎ 0131 537 3500
34 Great King St EH3 6QH
e-mail: reserve@thehoward.com
web: www.thehoward.com
dir: E on Queen St, 2nd left, Dundas St. Through 3
lights, right, hotel on left

Quietly elegant and splendidly luxurious, The Howard
provides an intimate and high quality experience for
the discerning traveller. It comprises three linked
Georgian houses and is situated just a short walk
from Princes Street. The sumptuous bedrooms and
suites, in a variety of styles, have well-equipped
bathrooms and a host of thoughtful touches. Ornate
chandeliers and lavish drapes adorn the drawing
room, while the Atholl Dining Room contains unique
hand-painted murals dating from the 19th century.

Rooms 18 (3 fmly) (2 GF) ⚘ **Facilities** STV FTV Wi-fi
⚑ HL Xmas New Year **Conf** Class 28 Board 28 Thtr 28
Services Lift **Parking** 12 **Notes** ⊗ Civ Wed 28

The Scotsman Hotel

★★★★★ 82% ⚛ TOWN HOUSE HOTEL

☎ 0131 556 5565
20 North Bridge EH1 1TR
e-mail:
reservations@thescotsmanhotelgroup.co.uk
web: www.thescotsmanhotel.co.uk
dir: A8 to city centre, left onto Charlotte St. Right into
Queen St, right at rdbt onto Leith St. Straight on, left
onto North Bridge, hotel on right

Formerly the headquarters of The Scotsman
newspaper this is a stunning hotel conversion. The
classical elegance of the public areas, complete with
a marble staircase, blends seamlessly with the
contemporary bedrooms and their state-of-the-art
technology. The superbly equipped leisure club
includes a stainless steel swimming pool and large
gym. Dining arrangements can be made in the
popular North Bridge Brasserie where afternoon tea is
also served.

Rooms 69 (4 GF) **S** £99-£1125; **D** £99-£1125*
Facilities Spa STV Wi-fi ⚑ ⚒ supervised Gym Beauty
treatments Xmas New Year **Conf** Class 50 Board 40
Thtr 100 Del from £170 to £485* **Services** Lift
Notes LB ⊗ Civ Wed 70

The Sheraton Grand Hotel & Spa

★★★★★ 81% ⚛ HOTEL

☎ 0131 229 9131
1 Festival Square EH3 9SR
e-mail: grandedinburgh@sheraton.com
dir: Follow City Centre signs (A8). Through Shandwick
Place, right at lights into Lothian Rd. Right at next
lights. Hotel on left at next lights

This modern hotel boasts one of the best spas in
Scotland - the external top floor hydro pool is
definitely worth a look, while the thermal suite
provides a unique venue for serious relaxation. The
spacious bedrooms are available in a variety of
styles, and the suites prove very popular. There is a
wide range of dishes available in the One Square Bar
and Restaurant.

Rooms 269 ⚘ **D** £170-£300* **Facilities** Spa STV FTV
Wi-fi ⚑ ⚒ ⚒ Gym Indoor/outdoor hydropool Kinesis
studio Thermal suite Fitness studio ⚑ Xmas New
Year **Conf** Class 350 Board 120 Thtr 500
Del from £250 to £350* **Services** Lift Air con
Parking 122 **Notes** ⊗ Civ Wed 485

EDINBURGH *continued*

Norton House Hotel & Spa

★★★★ ◉◉◉ HOTEL

☎ 0131 333 1275
Ingliston EH28 8LX
e-mail: nortonhouse@handpicked.co.uk
web: www.handpickedhotels.co.uk/nortonhouse
dir: Off A8, 5m W of city centre

This extended Victorian mansion, set in 55 acres of parkland, is peacefully situated just outside the city and is convenient for the airport. The original building dates from 1840, and was bought nearly 40 years later by John Usher of the Scottish brewing family. Today both the contemporary bedrooms and the very spacious, traditional ones have an impressive range of accessories including large flat-screen satellite TVs, DVD/CD players and free high speed internet access. Executive rooms have more facilities, of course, including MP3 connection and 'tilevision' TVs at the end of the baths. Public areas take in a choice of lounges as well as dining options, with a popular brasserie and the intimate Ushers Restaurant. There is a health club, and a spa which offers a long list of treatments.

Rooms 83 (10 fmly) (20 GF) ✿ **S** £89–£499; **D** £99–£509 (incl. bkfst) **Facilities** Spa STV Wi-fi ➷ ◎ Gym Archery Laser Clay shooting Quad biking Xmas New Year **Conf** Class 100 Board 60 Thtr 300 Del from £139 to £220 **Services** Lift **Parking** 200 **Notes** LB ⊗ Civ Wed 140

Dalmahoy, A Marriott Hotel & Country Club

★★★★ 81% ◉ HOTEL

☎ 0131 333 1845
Kirknewton EH27 8EB
e-mail: mhrs.edigs.frontdesk@marriotthotels.com
web: www.marriottdalmahoy.co.uk
dir: A720 (Edinburgh City Bypass) onto A71 towards Livingston, hotel on left in 2m

The rolling Pentland Hills and beautifully kept parkland provide a stunning setting for this imposing Georgian mansion. With two championship golf courses and a health and beauty club, there is plenty here to occupy guests. Bedrooms are spacious and most have fine views, while public rooms offer a choice of formal and informal drinking and dining options.

Rooms 215 (172 annexe) (59 fmly) (6 smoking) ✿ **Facilities** Spa STV Wi-fi ➷ HL ◎ ᴢ 36 ⅁ Putt green Gym Health & beauty treatments Steam room Dance studio Driving range Golf lessons Xmas New Year **Conf** Class 200 Board 120 Thtr 300 **Services** Lift Air con **Parking** 350 **Notes** ⊗ Civ Wed 250

Hotel du Vin Edinburgh

★★★★ 80% ◉
TOWN HOUSE HOTEL

☎ 0131 247 4900
11 Bristo Place EH1 1EZ
dir: M8 junct 1, A720 (signed Kilmarnock/W Calder/ Edinburgh W). Right at fork, follow A720 signs, merge onto A720. Take exit signed A703. At rdbt take A702/ Biggar Rd. 3.5m. Right into Lauriston Pl which becomes Forrest Rd. Right at Bedlam Theatre. Hotel on right

This hotel offers very stylish and comfortable accommodation; all bedrooms display the Hotel du Vin trademark facilities - air conditioning, free Wi-fi, plasma TVs, monsoon showers and Egyptian cotton linen to name but a few. Public areas include a whisky snug, and a mezzanine bar that overlooks the brasserie where modern Scottish cuisine is served. For the wine connoisseur there's La Roche tasting room where wines from around the world can be appreciated.

Rooms 47 ✿ **Facilities** STV Wi-fi **Conf** Class 10 Board 26 Thtr 30 **Services** Lift Air con

Apex International Hotel

★★★★ 79% ◉◉ HOTEL

☎ 0845 365 0000 & 0131 300 3456
31/35 Grassmarket EH1 2HS
e-mail: edinburgh.reservations@apexhotels.co.uk
web: www.apexhotels.co.uk
dir: Into Lothian Rd at west end of Princes St. 1st left into King Stables Rd, leads into Grassmarket

A sister to the Apex City Hotel close by, the International lies in a historic yet trendy square in the shadow of Edinburgh Castle. It has a versatile business and conference centre, and also Yu Time leisure and fitness facility with a stainless steel ozone pool. Bedrooms are contemporary in style and very well equipped. The fifth-floor restaurant boasts stunning views of the castle.

Rooms 169 (99 fmly) ✿ **Facilities** FTV Wi-fi ◎ Gym Tropicarium Xmas New Year **Conf** Class 80 Board 40 Thtr 200 **Services** Lift **Parking** 60 **Notes** ⊗ Civ Wed 200

George Hotel Edinburgh

★★★★ 79% HOTEL

☎ 0131 225 1251
19-21 George St EH2 2PB
e-mail:
enquiries.thegeorge@principal-hayley.com
web: www.principal-hayley.com/thegeorge
dir: In city centre

A long-established hotel, the George enjoys a city centre location. The splendid public areas have many original features such as intricate plasterwork, a marble-floored foyer and chandeliers. The Tempus Bar offers menus that feature a wide range of dishes to suit most tastes. The elegant, modern bedrooms come in a mix of sizes and styles; the upper ones having fine city views.

Rooms 249 (20 fmly) (4 GF) **Facilities** STV Wi-fi ➷ HL Xmas New Year **Conf** Class 120 Board 50 Thtr 300 **Services** Lift **Notes** ⊗ Civ Wed 300

Apex City Hotel

★★★★ 78% ◉ HOTEL

☎ 0845 365 0000 & 0131 243 3456
61 Grassmarket EH1 2HJ
e-mail: edinburgh.reservations@apexhotels.co.uk
web: www.apexhotels.co.uk
dir: Into Lothian Rd at west end of Princes St. 1st left into King Stables Rd. Leads into Grassmarket

This modern, stylish hotel lies in a historic yet trendy square dominated by Edinburgh Castle above. The design-led bedrooms are fresh and contemporary and each has artwork by Richard Demarco. Agua Bar and Restaurant is a smart open-plan area in dark wood and chrome that serves a range of meals and cocktails. Residents can use the spa at a sister hotel, Apex International, which is nearby.

Rooms 119 Facilities FTV Wi-fi Complimentary use of leisure facilities at Apex International Hotel Xmas **Conf** Class 30 Board 34 Thtr 70 **Services** Lift **Notes** Civ Wed 60

Edinburgh Marriott Hotel

★★★★ 78% HOTEL

☎ 0131 334 9191
111 Glasgow Rd EH12 8NF
e-mail: edinburgh@marriotthotels.com
web: www.edinburghmarriott.co.uk
dir: M8 junct 1 for Gogar, at rdbt turn right for city centre, hotel on right

This smart, modern hotel is located on the city's western edge which is convenient for the bypass, airport, showground and business park. Public areas include an attractive marbled foyer, extensive conference facilities and a restaurant serving a range of international dishes. The air-conditioned bedrooms are spacious and equipped with a range of extras.

Rooms 245 (76 fmly) (64 GF) Facilities STV FTV Wi-fi Gym Steam room Sauna Massage & beauty treatment room Xmas New Year **Conf** Class 120 Board 50 Thtr 250 **Services** Lift Air con **Parking** 300 **Notes** Civ Wed 80

Novotel Edinburgh Centre

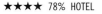

★★★★ 78% HOTEL

☎ 0131 656 3500
Lauriston Place, Lady Lawson St EH3 9DE
e-mail: H3271@accor.com
web: www.novotel.com
dir: From Edinburgh Castle right onto George IV Bridge from Royal Mile. Follow to junct, then right into Lauriston Place. Hotel 700mtrs on right

This modern hotel is located in the centre of the city, close to Edinburgh Castle. Smart and stylish public areas include a cosmopolitan bar, brasserie-style restaurant and indoor leisure facilities. The air-conditioned bedrooms feature a comprehensive range of extras and bathrooms with baths and separate shower cabinets.

Rooms 180 (146 fmly) Facilities STV Wi-fi HL Gym Sauna Steam room Xmas New Year **Conf** Class 50 Board 32 Thtr 80 **Services** Lift Air con **Parking** 15

Novotel Edinburgh Park

★★★★ 77% HOTEL

☎ 0131 446 5600
15 Lochside Av EH12 9DJ
e-mail: h6515@accor.com
dir: Near Hermiston Gate shopping area

Located just off the city by-pass and within minutes of the airport, this modern hotel offers bedrooms that are spacious and comfortable. The public areas include the open-plan lobby, bar and a restaurant offering diverse and informal dishes. A swimming pool and small gym are also available to the guests.

Rooms 170 (130 fmly) Facilities Wi-fi HL **Conf** Class 60 Board 40 Thtr 150 **Services** Lift **Parking** 96 **Notes** Civ Wed 90

See advert on page 501

Radisson Blu Hotel Edinburgh

★★★★ 77% HOTEL

☎ 0131 557 9797 & 557 6523
80 High St, The Royal Mile EH1 1TH
e-mail: sales.edinburgh@radissonblu.com
web: www.radissonblu.com/hotel-edinburgh
dir: On Royal Mile

Centrally located in the heart of the old town on the Royal Mile, the spacious and comfortable bedrooms cater well for both leisure and corporate guests. The staff provide very attentive service. Leisure facilities, parking and complimentary Wi-fi are all assets at this hotel.

Rooms 238 (5 fmly) **S** £95-£381; **D** £95-£381* Facilities STV FTV Wi-fi supervised Gym Saunas **Conf** Class 105 Board 52 Thtr 240 **Services** Lift Air con **Parking** 131 **Notes** LB Civ Wed 180

Apex Waterloo Place Hotel

★★★★ 76% HOTEL

☎ 0845 365 0000 & 0131 523 1819
23-27 Waterloo Place EH1 3BH
e-mail: edinburgh.reservations@apexhotels.co.uk
dir: At E end of Princes St. Telephone for detailed directions

This stunning hotel provides a state-of-the-art experience with slick interior design. Bedrooms, many with city views, are well appointed for both the business and leisure guest; stunning duplex suites provide extra space, surround-sound TV systems and luxurious feature bathrooms. The restaurant provides an appealing menu both at dinner and breakfast. There is also a well-equipped fitness centre and indoor pool. The hotel has direct, pedestrian access to Edinburgh's Waverley Station.

Rooms 186 (5 fmly) (15 GF) Facilities FTV Wi-fi Gym Sauna Steam rooms Xmas New Year **Conf** Class 70 Board 40 Thtr 150 **Services** Lift Air con **Notes** Civ Wed 80

Holiday Inn Edinburgh

★★★★ 76% HOTEL

☎ 0871 942 9026
Corstorphine Rd EH12 6UA
e-mail: edinburghhi@ihg.com
web: www.hiedinburghhotel.co.uk
dir: On A8, adjacent to Edinburgh Zoo

A modern hotel situated three miles west of Edinburgh and near Edinburgh Business Park. The hotel enjoys panoramic views of the Pentland Hills and makes a good base for visiting the attractions of the city. Bedrooms include family and executive rooms. The eating options are Traders Restaurant or Sampans Oriental Restaurant, as well as a café and bar. The Spirit Health and Fitness Club has a gym, swimming pool, sauna, spa and beauty treatments. There is also a conference centre.

Rooms 303 (76 fmly) **S** £39-£230; **D** £39-£230* Facilities Spa STV FTV Wi-fi HL supervised Gym New Year **Conf** Class 60 Board 45 Thtr 120 Del from £99 to £165* **Services** Lift Air con **Parking** 60 **Notes** LB Civ Wed 80

Macdonald Holyrood Hotel

★★★★ 76% HOTEL

☎ 0870 1942106
Holyrood Rd EH8 8AU
e-mail: general.holyrood@macdonald-hotels.co.uk
web: www.macdonaldhotels.co.uk/holyrood
dir: Parallel to Royal Mile, near Holyrood Palace & Dynamic Earth

Situated just a short walk from Holyrood Palace, this impressive hotel lies next to the Scottish Parliament building. Air-conditioned bedrooms are comfortably furnished, whilst the Club floor boasts a private lounge. Full business services complement the extensive conference suites. Macdonald Hotels is the AA Hotel Group of the Year 2013-14.

Rooms 156 (16 fmly) (13 GF) **D** £89-£245 Facilities Spa STV FTV Wi-fi Gym Sauna Steam room Library Xmas New Year **Conf** Class 100 Board 80 Thtr 200 Del from £130 to £210 **Services** Lift Air con **Parking** 38 **Notes** LB Civ Wed 100

E

EDINBURGH *continued*

Crowne Plaza Edinburgh - Royal Terrace

★★★★ 76% HOTEL

☎ 0131 557 3222
18 Royal Ter EH7 5AQ
e-mail: sales@royalterracehotel.co.uk
web: www.royalterracehotel.co.uk
dir: A8 to city centre, follow one-way system, left into Charlotte Sq. At end right into Queens St. Left at rdbt. At next island right into London Rd, right into Blenheim Place leading to Royal Terrace

Forming part of a quiet Georgian terrace in the heart of the city, this hotel offers bedrooms that successfully blend the historic architecture of the building with state-of-the-art facilities. Although most rooms afford lovely views, the top floor rooms provide excellent panoramas over the city to the Firth of Forth; for something unusual book an Ambassador Suite with a glass bathroom. The hotel's leisure club has a swimming pool, sauna and steam room, and award-winning dinners are served in the Terrace Brasserie.

Rooms 107 (13 fmly) (7 GF) **Facilities** Wi-fi ⓢ Gym Steam room Sauna Aromatherapy shower Xmas **New** Year **Conf** Class 40 Board 40 Thtr 100 **Services** Lift **Notes** ⊗ Civ Wed 80

The King James, Edinburgh   thistle

★★★★ 75% HOTEL

☎ 0871 376 9016
107 Leith St EH1 3SW
e-mail: edinburgh@thistle.co.uk
web: www.thistlehotels.com/edinburgh
dir: M8/M9 onto A8 signed city centre. Hotel at end of Princes St adjacent to St James shopping centre

This purpose-built hotel adjoins one of Edinburgh's premier shopping malls at the east end of Princes Street. The friendly team of staff are keen to please whilst stylish, well-equipped bedrooms provide excellent levels of comfort and good facilities. Public areas include a spacious restaurant, popular bar and an elegant lobby lounge.

Rooms 143 (12 fmly) ⓡ **Facilities** STV FTV Wi-fi HL Xmas New Year **Conf** Class 160 Board 50 Thtr 250 **Services** Lift **Parking** 18 **Notes** ⊗

The Roxburghe Hotel

★★★★ 75% HOTEL

☎ 0844 879 9063 & 0131 240 5500
38 Charlotte Square EH2 4HQ
e-mail: general.roxburghe@macdonald-hotels.co.uk
web: www.macdonaldhotels.co.uk/roxburghe
dir: On corner of Charlotte Sq & George St

This long-established hotel lies in the heart of the city overlooking Charlotte Square Gardens. Public areas are inviting and include relaxing lounges, a choice of bars (in the evening) and an inner concourse that looks onto a small lawned area. Smart bedrooms come in both classic and contemporary styles. There is a secure underground car park. Macdonald Hotels is the AA Hotel Group of the Year 2013-14.

Rooms 199 (3 fmly) **Facilities** Spa STV FTV Wi-fi ⓢ Gym Dance studio Sauna Steam room Xmas New Year **Conf** Class 160 Board 50 Thtr 300 **Services** Lift Air con **Parking** 20 **Notes** ⊗ Civ Wed 280

The Carlton Hotel

★★★★ 73% HOTEL

☎ 0131 472 3000
North Bridge EH1 1SD
e-mail: carlton@pumahotels.co.uk
web: www.pumahotels.co.uk
dir: On North Bridge which links Princes St to The Royal Mile

The Carlton occupies a city centre location just off the Royal Mile. Inside, it is modern and stylish in design, with an impressive open-plan reception/lobby, spacious first-floor lounge, bar and restaurant, plus a basement leisure club. Bedrooms, many air-conditioned, are generally spacious, with an excellent range of accessories.

Rooms 189 (20 fmly) **Facilities** Spa STV Wi-fi ⓢ supervised Gym Squash Dance studio Exercise classes Hair salon ♫ Xmas New Year **Conf** Class 110 Board 60 Thtr 220 **Services** Lift **Notes** Civ Wed 160

Malmaison Edinburgh

★★★ 86% ⊛ HOTEL

☎ 0844 693 0652
One Tower Place EH6 7DB
e-mail: edinburgh@malmaison.com
web: www.malmaison.com
dir: A900 from city centre towards Leith, at end of Leith Walk, through 3 sets of lights, left into Tower St. Hotel on right at end of road

The trendy Port of Leith is home to this stylish Malmaison. Inside, bold contemporary designs create a striking effect. Bedrooms are comprehensively equipped with CD players, mini-bars and loads of individual touches. Ask for one of the stunning superior rooms for a really memorable stay. The smart brasserie and a café bar are popular with the local clientele.

Rooms 100 (18 fmly) ⓡ **S** £89-£215; **D** £89-£215* **Facilities** STV FTV Wi-fi ⓢ Gym Xmas New Year **Conf** Class 32 Board 32 Thtr 80 Del from £170 to £210* **Services** Lift **Parking** 50 **Notes** LB Civ Wed 70

Apex European Hotel

★★★ 82% HOTEL

☎ 0845 365 0000 & 0131 474 3456
90 Haymarket Ter EH12 5LQ
e-mail: edinburgh.reservations@apexhotels.co.uk
web: www.apexhotels.co.uk
dir: A8 to city centre, 100m from Haymarket Railway Station

Lying just west of the city centre, close to Haymarket Station and handy for the Conference Centre, this modern hotel is popular with business travellers. Smart, stylish bedrooms offer an excellent range of facilities and have been designed with work requirements in mind. Public areas include Metro, an informal bistro. Service is friendly and pro-active.

Rooms 66 (3 GF) ⓡ **S** £60-£225; **D** £60-£225* **Facilities** FTV Wi-fi ⓢ New Year **Conf** Class 30 Board 36 Thtr 80 **Services** Lift **Parking** 10 **Notes** ⊗ Closed 24-27 Dec & 3-10 Jan

BEST WESTERN Braid Hills Hotel

★★★ 82% HOTEL

☎ 0131 447 8888 & 446 3003
134 Braid Rd EH10 6JD
e-mail: bookings@braidhillshotel.co.uk
web: www.braidhillshotel.co.uk
dir: 2.5m S A702, opposite Braid Burn Park

From its elevated position on the south side, this long-established hotel enjoys splendid panoramic views of the city and castle. Bedrooms are smart, stylish and well equipped. The public areas are comfortable and inviting, and guests can dine in either the restaurant or popular bistro/bar.

Rooms 67 (14 fmly) (14 GF) **Facilities** STV FTV Wi-fi Xmas New Year **Conf** Class 50 Board 30 Thtr 100 **Parking** 38 **Notes** ⊗ Civ Wed 100

Dalhousie Castle and Aqueous Spa

★★★ 81% ⊚⊚ HOTEL

☎ 01875 820153
Bonnyrigg EH19 3JB
e-mail: info@dalhousiecastle.co.uk
web: www.dalhousiecastle.co.uk
dir: A7 S from Edinburgh through Lasswade/ Newtongrange, right at Shell Garage (B704), hotel 0.5m from junct

A popular wedding venue, this imposing medieval castle sits amid lawns and parkland and even has a falconry. Bedrooms offer a mix of styles and sizes, including richly decorated themed rooms named after various historical figures. The Dungeon restaurant provides an atmospheric setting for dinner, and the less formal Orangery serves food all day. The spa offers many relaxing and therapeutic treatments and hydro facilities.

Rooms 36 (7 annexe) (3 fmly) 🐾 **Facilities** Spa FTV Wi-fi Fishing Falconry Clay pigeon shooting Archery Xmas New Year **Conf** Class 60 Board 45 Thtr 120 Del £125* **Parking** 110 **Notes** Civ Wed 100

DoubleTree by Hilton Edinburgh City Centre

★★★ 80% HOTEL

☎ 0131 221 5555
34 Bread St EH3 9AF
web: www.doubletree.com
dir: A71 to Haymarket Station. Straight on at junct & right on Torphichen St, left onto Morrison St, straight on to Bread St, hotel on right

Built in 1892 as a Co-op which once employed Sean Connery as a milkman, the hotel has won many awards for its design and presentation. Bedrooms are spacious and cater well for the needs of the modern guest. Open-plan public areas are enhanced with coloured lighting and an array of artwork. The Point Restaurant offers imaginative dishes. The Glass Box Penthouse conference room affords fantastic views of the city.

Rooms 139 (4 fmly) 🐾 **Facilities** FTV Wi-fi ⌕ **Conf** Class 60 Board 40 Thtr 120 **Services** Lift **Notes** ⊗ Civ Wed 90

BEST WESTERN Kings Manor

★★★ 79% HOTEL

☎ 0131 669 0444 & 468 8003
100 Milton Road East EH15 2NP
e-mail: reservations@kingsmanor.com
web: www.kingsmanor.com
dir: A720 E to Old Craighall junct, left into city, right at A1/A199 junct, hotel 400mtrs on right

Lying on the eastern side of the city and convenient for the by-pass, this hotel is popular with business guests, tour groups and for conferences. It boasts a fine leisure complex and a bright modern bistro, which complements the quality, creative cooking in the main restaurant.

Rooms 95 (8 fmly) (13 GF) 🐾 **S** £50-£80; **D** £60-£170 **Facilities** Spa STV FTV Wi-fi ⌕ ⊛ ⊰ Gym Health & beauty salon Steam room Sauna **Conf** Class 80 Board 60 Thtr 160 Del from £98 to £148 **Services** Lift **Parking** 130 **Notes** LB Civ Wed 100

Holiday Inn Edinburgh West

★★★ 78% HOTEL   *Holiday Inn*

☎ 0871 942 9025
107 Queensferry Rd EH4 3HL
e-mail: reservations-edinburghcitywest@ihg.com
web: www.holidayinn.co.uk
dir: On A90 approx 1m from city centre

Situated on the north-west side of the city, close to Murrayfield Stadium and just five miles from the airport, this purpose-built hotel has a bright contemporary look. The colourful, modern bedrooms are well equipped and three specifications are available - with two double beds; with a double bed and sofa; or with a double bed and separate lounge. Some have great views of the city too. There is limited free parking.

Rooms 101 (65 fmly) **S** £45-£180; **D** £50-£190* **Facilities** STV FTV Wi-fi ⌕ HL New Year **Conf** Class 60 Board 50 Thtr 140 Del from £79 to £149 **Services** Lift Air con **Parking** 80 **Notes** ⊗ Civ Wed 120

Old Waverley Hotel

★★★ 78% HOTEL

☎ 0131 556 4648
43 Princes St EH2 2BY
e-mail: reservations@oldwaverley.co.uk
web: www.oldwaverley.co.uk
dir: In city centre, opposite Scott Monument, Waverley Station & Jenners

Occupying a commanding position opposite Sir Walter Scott's famous monument on Princes Street, this hotel lies right in the heart of the city close to the station. The comfortable public rooms are all on first-floor level and along with front-facing bedrooms enjoy the fine views.

Rooms 85 (5 fmly) **Facilities** Wi-fi Leisure facilities at sister hotel **Services** Lift **Notes** ⊗

Mercure Edinburgh City - Princes Street Hotel

★★★ HOTEL

☎ 0844 815 9017
Princes St EH2 2DG
e-mail: info@mercureedinburgh.co.uk
web: www.jupiterhotels.co.uk
dir: opposite Scott Monument & Waverley Station. At east end of Princes St

Currently the rating for this establishment is not confirmed. This may be due to a change of ownership or because it has only recently joined the AA rating scheme.

Rooms 158 **Conf** Class 40 Board 27 Thtr 70

Holiday Inn Express Edinburgh City Centre

BUDGET HOTEL

☎ 0131 558 2300
Picardy Place EH1 3JT
e-mail: info@hieedinburgh.co.uk
web: www.hiexpress.com/edinburghcyct
dir: Follow signs to city centre & Greenside NCP. Hotel near E end of Princes St

A modern hotel ideal for families and business travellers. Fresh and uncomplicated, the spacious rooms include Sky TV, power shower and tea and coffee-making facilities. Continental buffet breakfast is included in the room rate; other meals may be taken at the nearby family pub or restaurant. See also the Hotel Groups pages.

Rooms 161 (53 fmly) (27 GF) (13 smoking) 🐾 **Conf** Class 8 Board 18 Thtr 20

E

E

EDINBURGH *continued*

Ibis Edinburgh Centre

BUDGET HOTEL

☎ 0131 240 7000
6 Hunter Square, off The Royal Mile EH1 1QW
e-mail: H2039@accor.com
web: www.ibishotel.com
dir: M8/M9/A1 over North Bridge (A7) & High St, take
1st right off South Bridge, into Hunter Sq

Modern, budget hotel offering comfortable
accommodation in bright and practical bedrooms.
Breakfast is self-service and dinner is available in
the restaurant. See also the Hotel Groups pages.

Rooms 99 (2 GF)

Premier Inn Edinburgh Airport (Newbridge)

BUDGET HOTEL

☎ 0871 527 9284
2A Kirkliston Rd, Newbridge EH28 8SL
web: www.premierinn.com
dir: M9 junct 1, A89 signed Broxburn. At lights turn
right, then 2nd right

High quality, budget accommodation ideal for both
families and business travellers. Spacious, en suite
bedrooms feature tea and coffee making facilities,
and Freeview TV in most hotels. Internet access and
Wi-fi are available for a small fee. The adjacent
family restaurant features a wide and varied menu.
See also the Hotel Groups pages.

Rooms 119

Premier Inn Edinburgh City Centre (Haymarket)

BUDGET HOTEL

☎ 0871 527 8368
1 Morrison Link EH3 8DN
web: www.premierinn.com
dir: Adjcent to Edinburgh International Conference
Centre

Rooms 281

Premier Inn Edinburgh City Centre (Princess St)

BUDGET HOTEL

☎ 0871 527 9358
122-123 Princess St EH2 4AD
web: www.premierinn.com
dir: From Edinburgh bypass (A720) onto A702, take
A700. NB Princes St is not accessible by car -it is
advisable to park in Castle Terrace Car Park (EH1
2EW)

Rooms 97

Premier Inn Edinburgh City Lauriston Place

BUDGET HOTEL

☎ 0871 527 8366
82 Lauriston Place, Lady Lawson St EH3 9DG
web: www.premierinn.com
dir: A8 onto A702 (Lothian Rd). Left into Lauriston
Place. Hotel on left

Rooms 112

Premier Inn Edinburgh East

BUDGET HOTEL

☎ 0871 527 8370
228 Willowbrae Rd EH8 7NG
web: www.premierinn.com
dir: M8 junct 1, A720 S for 12m, then A1. At Asda rdbt
turn left. In 2m, hotel on left before Esso garage

Rooms 39

Premier Inn Edinburgh (Inveresk)

BUDGET HOTEL

☎ 0871 527 8358
Carberry Rd, Inveresk, Musselburgh EH21 8PT
web: www.premierinn.com
dir: From A1 follow Dalkeith (A6094) signs. At rdbt
turn right, hotel 300yds on right

Rooms 40

Premier Inn Edinburgh (Leith)

BUDGET HOTEL

☎ 0871 527 8360
51-53 Newhaven Place, Leith EH6 4TX
web: www.premierinn.com
dir: From A1 follow coast road through Leith. Pass
Ocean Terminal, straight ahead at mini-rdbt, 2nd exit
signed Harry Ramsden's car park

Rooms 60

Premier Inn Edinburgh Park (The Gyle)

BUDGET HOTEL

☎ 0871 527 9336
**Edinburgh Park (Airport), 1 Lochside Court
EH12 9FX**
dir: M8 junct 1, A720 (city bypass). At Gogar rdbt 3rd
exit follow South Gyle/station signs. Into right lane
approaching Gyle rdbt, 3rd exit, follow Edinburgh Park
train station signs into Lochside Cres. Straight on at
2 rdbts, 400yds. Hotel on left

Rooms 120

INSPECTORS' CHOICE

21212

◉ ◉ ◉ ◉   RESTAURANT WITH ROOMS

☎ 0131 523 1030 & 0845 222 1212
3 Royal Ter EH7 5AB
e-mail: reservations@21212restaurant.co.uk

A real gem in Edinburgh's crown, this
establishment takes its name from the numbers of
choices at each course on the five-course dinner
menu. Located on the prestigious Royal Terrace this
is a light and airy, renovated Georgian townhouse
stretching over four floors. The four individually
designed bedrooms epitomise luxury living and the
bathrooms certainly have the wow factor. At the
heart of this restaurant with rooms is the creative,
award-winning cooking of Paul Kitching. Service
throughout is friendly and very attentive.

Rooms 4

INSPECTORS' CHOICE

The Witchery by the Castle

◉   RESTAURANT WITH ROOMS

☎ 0131 225 5613
352 Castlehill, The Royal Mile EH1 2NF
e-mail: mail@thewitchery.com
web: www.thewitchery.com
dir: Top of Royal Mile at gates of Edinburgh Castle

Originally built in 1595, The Witchery by the Castle
is situated in a historic building at the gates of
Edinburgh Castle. The two luxurious and
theatrically decorated suites, known as the Inner
Sanctum and the Old Rectory are located above the
restaurant and are reached via a winding stone
staircase. Filled with antiques, opulently draped
beds, large roll-top baths and a plethora of
memorabilia, this ancient and exciting
establishment is often described as one of the
country's most romantic destinations.

Rooms 8 (5 annexe)

Save on hotels. Book at theAA.com/hotel

EDI – FOR 521 SCOTLAND

ELGIN
Moray
Map 23 NJ26

Mansion House Hotel
★★★ 81% HOTEL

☎ 01343 548811
The Haugh IV30 1AW
e-mail: reception@mhelgin.co.uk
web: www.mansionhousehotel.co.uk
dir: Exit A96 into Haugh Rd, then 1st left

Set in grounds by the River Lossie, this baronial mansion is popular with leisure and business guests as well as being a lovely wedding venue. Bedrooms are spacious and many have views of the river. Extensive public areas include a choice of restaurants, with a bistro that contrasts nicely with the classical main restaurant. There is an indoor pool and a beauty and hair salon.

Rooms 23 (6 fmly) (5 GF) 🐾 **S** £97-£113;
D £154-£202 (incl. bkfst)* **Facilities** STV FTV Wi-fi 🏊
🏌 supervised Gym Hair studio Beauty treatment room New Year **Conf** Thtr 180 **Parking** 50 **Notes** ⊗
Civ Wed 160

Premier Inn Elgin
BUDGET HOTEL

☎ 0871 527 8372
15 Linkwood Way IV30 1HY
web: www.premierinn.com
dir: On A96, 1.5m E of city centre

High quality, budget accommodation ideal for both families and business travellers. Spacious, en suite bedrooms feature tea and coffee making facilities, and Freeview TV in most hotels. Internet access and Wi-fi are available for a small fee. The adjacent family restaurant features a wide and varied menu. See also the Hotel Groups pages.

Rooms 40

ERISKA
Argyll & Bute
Map 20 NM94

INSPECTORS' CHOICE

Isle of Eriska Hotel, Spa & Golf
★★★★★ COUNTRY HOUSE HOTEL

☎ 01631 720371
PA37 1SD
e-mail: office@eriska-hotel.co.uk
dir: Exit A85 at Connel, onto A828, 4m, follow hotel signs from N of Benderloch

Situated on its own private island with delightful beaches and walking trails, this hotel is in a tranquil setting, perfect for total relaxation. The spacious bedrooms are very comfortable and boast some fine antique pieces. The AA Rosette award for the Isle of Eriska Hotel is currently suspended due to a change of chef. AA Rosettes may be awarded once the inspectors have assessed the food created by the new kitchen regime.

Rooms 23 (6 fmly) (2 GF) 🐾 **S** £200-£300;
D £340-£500 (incl. bkfst)* **Facilities** Spa FTV Wi-fi
🏊 🏌 supervised ♨ 9 ⛳ Putt green Fishing 🏋 Gym
Squash Sauna Steam room Skeet shooting Nature trails Indoor tennis Badminton Xmas New Year
Conf Class 30 Board 30 Thtr 30 Del £400*
Parking 40 **Notes** LB Closed Jan Civ Wed 50

FALKIRK
Falkirk
Map 21 NS88

Premier Inn Falkirk Central
BUDGET HOTEL

☎ 0871 527 8388
Main St, Camelon FK1 4DS
web: www.premierinn.com
dir: From Falkirk A803 signed Glasgow. At mini-rdbt right, continue on A803. At Rosebank rdbt 2nd exit signed Glasgow & Stirling

High quality, budget accommodation ideal for both families and business travellers. Spacious, en suite bedrooms feature tea and coffee making facilities, and Freeview TV in most hotels. Internet access and Wi-fi are available for a small fee. The adjacent

family restaurant features a wide and varied menu. See also the Hotel Groups pages.

Rooms 31

Premier Inn Falkirk (Larbert)
BUDGET HOTEL

☎ 0871 527 8390
Glenbervie Business Park, Bellsdyke Rd, Larbert FK5 4EG
web: www.premierinn.com
dir: Just off A88. Approx 1m from M876 junct 2

Rooms 60

FINTRY
Stirling
Map 20 NS68

Culcreuch Castle Hotel & Estate
★★★ 80% HOTEL

☎ 01360 860555 & 860228
Kippen Rd G63 0LW
e-mail: info@culcreuch.com
web: www.culcreuch.com
dir: On B822, 17m W of Stirling

Peacefully located in 1,600 acres of parkland, this ancient castle dates back to 1296. Tastefully restored accommodation is in a mixture of individually themed castle rooms, some with four-poster beds, and more modern courtyard rooms which are suitable for families. Period style public rooms include a bar, serving light meals, an elegant lounge and a wood-panelled dining room.

Rooms 14 (4 annexe) (4 fmly) (4 GF) 🐾 **S** £76-£120;
D £102-£190 (incl. bkfst) **Facilities** STV FTV Wi-fi 🏊
Fishing New Year **Conf** Class 70 Board 30 Thtr 140
Del from £119 to £140 **Parking** 100 **Notes** LB ⊗
Closed 4-18 Jan & 25-26 Dec RS 19 Jan-mid Mar
Civ Wed 110

FORT AUGUSTUS
Highland
Map 23 NH30

The Lovat, Loch Ness
★★★ 87% ◉◉ HOTEL

☎ 01456 459250 & 0845 450 1100
Loch Ness Side PH32 4DU
e-mail: info@thelovat.com
web: www.thelovat.com
dir: A82 between Fort William & Inverness

This charming hotel enjoys an elevated position in the pretty town of Fort Augustus with views over Loch Ness. It has impressively styled bedrooms with a host of thoughtful extras. Inviting public areas include a comfortable lounge with a log fire, a stylish bar, and contemporary restaurant where food is cooked with

continued

F

F

FORT AUGUSTUS *continued*

skill and care. The hotel has an admirable green policy, and the hospitality and commitment to guest care will leave a lasting impression.

Rooms 28 (1 fmly) (7 GF) ✎ **S** £70–£185; **D** £70–£280 (incl. bkfst)* **Facilities** FTV Wi-fi ☙ Beauty treatment room Xmas New Year **Conf** Class 32 Board 24 Thtr 70 Del from £145 to £200* **Services** Lift **Parking** 30 **Notes** LB Civ Wed 150

Inchnacardoch Lodge Hotel

★★★ 74% ◉ SMALL HOTEL

☎ 01456 450900
Inchnacardoch Bay PH32 4BL
e-mail: happy@inchhotel.com
dir: On A82. Turn right before entering Fort Augustus from Inverness

This 150-year-old former hunting lodge is set on the hillside looking over the south end of Loch Ness, making it a perfect base for exploring the Highlands. Guests can expect the finest hospitality here from staff that are always eager to please. The bedrooms are very individual in style; the Bridal Suite is a very well appointed room with stunning views. The award-winning Yard Restaurant serves dishes based on the plentiful supply of local game and seafood.

Rooms 14 (2 fmly) **Facilities** FTV Wi-fi Fishing Xmas New Year **Conf** Class 30 Board 26 Thtr 45 Del from £95 to £200 **Parking** 30 **Notes** Civ Wed 35

FORTINGALL   Map 20 NN74
Perth & Kinross

Fortingall Hotel

★★★★ 81% ◉◉ SMALL HOTEL

☎ 01887 830367 & 830368
PH15 2NQ
e-mail: hotel@fortingallhotel.com
dir: B846 from Aberfeldy for 6m, left signed Fortingall for 3m. Hotel in village centre

Appointed to a very high standard, this hotel has plenty of charm. It lies at the foot of wooded hills in the heart of Glen Lyon. All the bedrooms are very well equipped and have an extensive range of thoughtful extras. The comfortable lounge, with its log fire, is ideal for pre-dinner drinks, and the small bar is full of character.

Rooms 10 (1 fmly) **S** £160–£200; **D** £250–£285 (incl. bkfst & dinner)* **Facilities** STV Wi-fi Fishing Deer stalking Grouse shoots ♫ Xmas New Year **Conf** Board 20 Thtr 40 Del £200* **Parking** 20 **Notes** LB Civ Wed 30

FORT WILLIAM   Map 22 NN17
Highland

Inverlochy Castle Hotel

★★★★★ ◉◉◉
COUNTRY HOUSE HOTEL

☎ 01397 702177
Torlundy PH33 6SN
e-mail: info@inverlochy.co.uk
web: www.inverlochycastlehotel.com
dir: Accessible from either A82 (Glasgow-Fort William) or A9 (Edinburgh-Dalwhinnie). Hotel 3m N of Fort William on A82, in Torlundy

With Ben Nevis as its backdrop, this imposing and gracious castle sits amidst extensive gardens and grounds overlooking the hotel's own loch. Lavishly appointed in classic country-house style, spacious bedrooms are extremely comfortable and boast flat-screen TVs and laptops with internet access. The sumptuous main hall and lounge provide the perfect setting for afternoon tea or a pre-dinner cocktail, while imaginative modern British cuisine is served in one of three dining rooms. A snooker room and DVD library are also available.

Rooms 17 (6 fmly) ✎ **S** £280–£695; **D** £335–£695 (incl. bkfst) **Facilities** STV FTV Wi-fi ⚲ Fishing ⚓ Fishing on loch Massage Riding Hunting Stalking Clay pigeon shooting Archery ♫ Xmas New Year **Conf** Class 20 Board 20 Thtr 50 Del £320* **Parking** 17 **Notes** Civ Wed 80

Moorings Hotel

★★★★ 74% ◉ HOTEL

☎ 01397 772797
Banavie PH33 7LY
e-mail: reservations@moorings-fortwilliam.co.uk
web: www.moorings-fortwilliam.co.uk
dir: Take A830 (N from Fort William), cross Caledonian Canal, 1st right

Located on the Caledonian Canal next to a series of locks known as Neptune's Staircase and close to Thomas Telford's house, this hotel has a dedicated team offering friendly service. Accommodation comes in two distinct styles and the newer rooms are particularly appealing. Meals can be taken in the bars or the spacious dining room.

Rooms 27 (2 fmly) (1 GF) ✎ **S** £70–£130; **D** £80–£150 (incl. bkfst)* **Facilities** STV Wi-fi Gym New Year **Conf** Class 60 Board 40 Thtr 140 Del from £110 to £150* **Parking** 60 **Notes** LB Closed 24-26 Dec Civ Wed 120

Lime Tree Hotel & Restaurant

★★★ 79% ◉◉ SMALL HOTEL

☎ 01397 701806
Lime Tree Studio, Achintore Rd PH33 6RQ
e-mail: info@limetreefortwilliam.co.uk
dir: On A82 at entrance to Fort William

A charming small hotel with an inspirational art gallery on the ground floor, and lots of original artwork displayed throughout. Evening meals can be enjoyed in the restaurant which has a loyal following. The hotel's comfortable lounges with their real fires are ideal for pre or post dinner drinks or maybe just to relax in. Individually designed bedrooms are spacious with some nice little personal touches, courtesy of the artist owner.

Rooms 9 (4 fmly) **S** £60-£110; **D** £80-£120 (incl. bkfst)* **Facilities** FTV Wi-fi New Year **Conf** Class 40 Board 30 Thtr 60 Del £149.95* **Parking** 9 **Notes** LB Closed 24-26 Dec

Alexandra Hotel

★★★ 73% HOTEL

☎ 01397 702241
The Parade PH33 6AZ
e-mail: salesalexandra@strathmorehotels.com
dir: Off A82. Hotel opposite railway station

This charming old hotel enjoys a prominent position in the town centre and is just a short walk from all the major attractions. Front-facing bedrooms have views over the town and the spectacular Nevis mountain range. There is a choice of restaurants, including a bistro serving meals until late, along with several stylish and very comfortable lounges.

Rooms 93 (2 fmly) **Facilities** Wi-fi Free use of nearby leisure club ♫ Xmas New Year **Conf** Class 100 Board 40 Thtr 120 **Services** Lift **Parking** 50

See advert on page 501

Ben Nevis Hotel & Leisure Club

★★ 75% HOTEL

☎ 01397 702331
North Rd PH33 6TG
e-mail: bennevismanager@strathmorehotels.com
dir: Off A82

This popular hotel is ideally situated on the outskirts of Fort William. It provides comfortable, well equipped bedrooms; many with views of the impressive Nevis mountains. The hotel's leisure centre is a firm favourite with guests at the hotel.

Rooms 119 (3 fmly) (30 GF) **Facilities** Wi-fi ⊗ supervised Gym Beauty salon ♫ Xmas New Year **Conf** Class 60 Board 40 Thtr 150 **Parking** 100 **Notes** Civ Wed 60

See advert on page 501

Croit Anna Hotel

★★ 71% HOTEL

☎ 01397 702268
Achintore Rd, Drimarben PH33 6RR
e-mail: croitanna.fortwilliam@alfatravel.co.uk
web: www.leisureplex.co.uk
dir: From Glencoe on A82 into Fort William, hotel 1st on right

Located on the edge of Loch Linnhe, just two miles out of town, this hotel offers some spacious bedrooms, many with fine views over the loch. There is a choice of two comfortable lounges and a large airy restaurant. The hotel appeals to coach parties and independent travellers alike.

Rooms 92 (5 fmly) (13 GF) **Facilities** FTV Pool table ♫ Xmas New Year **Parking** 25 **Notes** ⊗ Closed Dec-Jan (ex Xmas) RS Nov, Feb, Mar

Premier Inn Fort William

BUDGET HOTEL

☎ 0871 527 8402
Loch Iall, An Aird PH33 6AN
web: www.premierinn.com
dir: N end of Fort William Shopping Centre, just off A82 (ring road)

High quality, budget accommodation ideal for both families and business travellers. Spacious, en suite bedrooms feature tea and coffee making facilities, and Freeview TV in most hotels. Internet access and Wi-fi are available for a small fee. The adjacent family restaurant features a wide and varied menu. See also the Hotel Groups pages.

Rooms 40

FOYERS   Map 23 NH52
Highland

Craigdarroch House

◉ RESTAURANT WITH ROOMS

☎ 01456 486400
IV2 6XU
e-mail: info@hotel-loch-ness.co.uk
dir: Take B862 from either end of loch, then B852 signed Foyers

Craigdarroch is located in an elevated position high above Loch Ness on the south side. Bedrooms vary in style and size but all are comfortable and well equipped; those that are front-facing have wonderful views. The award-winning food is well worth staying in for, with the dining room or newly created lounge bar offering different dining options. Breakfasts are also memorable.

Rooms 8 (1 fmly)

GALASHIELS   Map 21 NT43
Scottish Borders

Kingsknowes Hotel

★★★ 79% HOTEL

☎ 01896 758375
Selkirk Rd TD1 3HY
e-mail: enq@kingsknowes.co.uk
web: www.kingsknowes.co.uk
dir: Exit A7 at Galashiels/Selkirk rdbt

An imposing turreted mansion, this hotel lies in attractive gardens on the outskirts of town close to the River Tweed. It boasts elegant public areas and many spacious bedrooms, some with excellent views. There is a choice of bars, one with a popular menu to supplement the restaurant.

Rooms 12 (2 fmly) ⟡ **S** fr £69; **D** fr £99 (incl. bkfst)* **Facilities** FTV Wi-fi HL **Conf** Class 40 Board 30 Thtr 80 **Parking** 65 **Notes** LB Civ Wed 75

G

GATEHOUSE OF FLEET
Dumfries & Galloway   Map 20 NX55

Cally Palace Hotel

★★★★ 77% ® COUNTRY HOUSE HOTEL

☎ 01557 814341
DG7 2DL
e-mail: info@callypalace.co.uk
web: www.callypalace.co.uk
dir: From M6 & A74, signed A75 Dumfries then
Stranraer. At Gatehouse-of-Fleet right onto B727, left
at Cally

A resort hotel with extensive leisure facilities, this
grand 18th-century building is set in 500 acres of
forest and parkland that incorporates its own golf
course. Bedrooms are spacious and well equipped,
while public rooms retain a quiet elegance. The short
dinner menu focuses on freshly prepared dishes; a
pianist plays most nights and the wearing of jacket
and tie is obligatory (for gentlemen).

Rooms 55 (7 fmly) (4 GF) ↑ **Facilities** STV FTV Wi-fi
⊕ ↓ 18 ♨ Putt green Fishing ♨ Gym Table tennis
Practice fairway Xmas New Year **Conf** Class 40
Board 25 Thtr 40 **Services** Lift **Parking** 100 **Notes** ⊗
Closed Jan-early Feb

GLASGOW
City of Glasgow   Map 20 NS56

See also Clydebank & Uplawmoor

Blythswood Square

★★★★★ 85% ®® HOTEL

☎ 0141 248 8888
11 Blythswood Square G2 4AD
e-mail: reserve@blythswoodsquare.com

Built in 1821, and restored to its former glory, this
was the headquarters of the Royal Scottish
Automobile Club which was the official start point for
the 1955 Monte Carlo Rally. The bedrooms and
bathrooms are sumptuous, and include suites and a
penthouse. Afternoon tea and cocktails are served in
the 35-metre, first-floor Salon Lounge, and the
award-winning restaurant occupies the old RSAC's
ballroom. The Spa includes a fantastic thermal suite.

Rooms 100 (5 GF) ↑ **S** £120-£200; **D** £160-£260
(incl. bkfst)* **Facilities** Spa STV Wi-fi ⊕ ⊕ Gym
Thermal experience Xmas New Year **Conf** Board 80
Thtr 130 Del £235* **Services** Lift Air con **Notes** LB
Civ Wed 80

INSPECTORS' CHOICE

Hotel du Vin at One Devonshire Gardens

★★★★ ®®® TOWN HOUSE HOTEL

☎ 0844 736 4256
1 Devonshire Gardens G12 0UX
e-mail: info.odg@hotelduvin.com
web: www.hotelduvin.com
dir: M8 junct 17, follow signs for A82, in 1.5m left
into Hyndland Rd, 1st right, right at mini rdbt, right
at end

Situated in a tree-lined Victorian terrace this luxury
'boutique' hotel has stunning, individually designed
bedrooms and suites that have the trademark
Egyptian linens and seriously good showers. The
oak-panelled Bistro offers a daily-changing menu
of both classic and modern dishes with a Scottish
influence. Naturally, wine is an important part of
the equation here, and knowledgeable staff can
guide guests around the impressive wine list.

Rooms 49 (7 GF) ↑ **D** £109-£195* **Facilities** STV
Wi-fi Gym Beauty treatment room Tennis & Squash
facilities at nearby club Xmas New Year
Conf Class 30 Board 30 Thtr 50 Del from £165 to
£275* **Notes** LB Civ Wed 70

Menzies Hotels - Glasgow

MenziesHotels

★★★★ 78% HOTEL

☎ 0141 222 2929 & 270 2323
27 Washington St G3 8AZ
e-mail: glasgow@menzieshotels.co.uk
web: www.menzieshotels.co.uk
dir: M8 junct 19, follow signs for SECC & Broomielaw.
Left at lights

Centrally located, this modern hotel is a short drive
from the airport and a short walk from the centre of
the city. Bedrooms are generally spacious and boast a
range of facilities, including high-speed internet
access. Facilities include a brasserie restaurant and
an impressive indoor leisure facility.

Rooms 141 (16 fmly) (15 smoking) **Facilities** STV FTV
Wi-fi ⊕ ⊕ supervised Gym Sauna Steam room Hair &

beauty salon Xmas New Year **Conf** Class 60 Board 70
Thtr 160 **Services** Lift Air con **Parking** 50
Notes Civ Wed 150

Beardmore Hotel

★★★★ 76% ® HOTEL

☎ 0141 951 6000
Beardmore St G81 4SA
e-mail: info@beardmore.scot.nhs.uk
web: www.thebeardmore.com

(For full entry see Clydebank)

Malmaison Glasgow

Malmaison

★★★★ 76% ® HOTEL

☎ 0844 693 0653
278 West George St G2 4LL
e-mail: reception.glasgow@malmaison.com
web: www.malmaison.com
dir: From S & E: M8 junct 18 (Charing Cross). From W
& N: M8 city centre

Built around a former church in the historic Charing
Cross area, this hotel is a smart, contemporary
establishment offering impressive levels of service
and hospitality. Bedrooms are spacious and feature a
host of modern facilities, such as CD players and
mini bars. Dining is a treat here, with French
brasserie-style cuisine, backed up by an excellent
wine list, served in the original crypt.

Rooms 72 (4 fmly) (19 GF) **D** £89-£159*
Facilities STV Wi-fi ⊕ Gym Cardiovascular equipment
New Year **Conf** Board 22 Thtr 30 **Services** Lift
Notes Civ Wed 60

Thistle Glasgow

thistle

★★★★ 76% HOTEL

☎ 0871 376 9043
36 Cambridge St G2 3HN
e-mail: glasgow@thistle.co.uk
web: www.thistle.com/glasgow
dir: In city centre, just off Sauchiehall St

Ideally located at the centre of Glasgow, and with
ample parking, this hotel is well presented with a
lobby area that gives a great impression on arrival. It
also benefits from having a well-presented leisure
club along with the largest ballroom in Glasgow.
Service is friendly and attentive.

Rooms 300 (38 fmly) (1 smoking) ↑ **Facilities** FTV
Wi-fi ⊕ HL ⊕ Gym Sauna Steam room Beauty
treatment room New Year **Conf** Class 800 Board 15
Thtr 1000 **Services** Lift Air con **Parking** 216 **Notes** ⊗
Civ Wed 720

Save on hotels. Book at **theAA.com/hotel**

GAT – GLA 525 SCOTLAND

Grand Central Hotel

★★★★ 75% HOTEL

☎ 0141 240 3700
99 Gordon St G1 3SF
e-mail: grandcentralhotel@principal-hayley.com
dir: M8 junct 19 towards city centre turn left at Hope St. Hotel 200mtrs on right

This is the place where John Logie Baird transmitted the world's first long-distance television pictures in 1927, and this 'grand old lady' of the Glasgow hotel scene is appointed to a very good standard. The decor is a blend of contemporary, art deco and original Victorian styles. Bedrooms are well equipped and suit business travellers especially. There is Champagne Central, a glamorous bar, the Tempus Bar and Restaurant, and Deli Central (with direct access to the Central Station) which is an eat-in deli and a take-away. Ample meeting facilities are available, and NCP car parks are nearby.

Rooms 186 (13 fmly) ⚑ **Facilities** FTV Wi-fi New Year **Conf** Class 350 Board 60 Thtr 500 Del from £135 to £195 **Services** Lift **Notes** ⊗ Civ Wed 500

Millennium Hotel Glasgow

★★★★ 74% HOTEL

☎ 0141 332 6711
George Square G2 1DS
e-mail: glasgow.reservations@millenniumhotels.co.uk
web: www.millenniumhotels.co.uk
dir: M8 junct 15 through 4 sets of lights, at 5th left into Hanover St. George Sq directly ahead, hotel on right

Right in the heart of the city, this hotel has pride of place overlooking George Square. Inside, the property has a contemporary air, with a spacious reception concourse and a glass veranda overlooking the square. There is a stylish brasserie and separate lounge bar, and bedrooms come in a variety of sizes.

Rooms 116 (17 fmly) ⚑ **Facilities** STV Wi-fi New Year **Conf** Class 24 Board 32 Thtr 40 **Services** Lift **Notes** ⊗ Closed 25 Dec Civ Wed 120

Novotel Glasgow Centre

★★★★ 71% HOTEL

☎ 0141 222 2775
181 Pitt St G2 4DT
e-mail: H3136@accor.com
web: www.novotel.com
dir: M8 junct 18 for Charing Cross. Follow to Sauchiehall St. 3rd right

Enjoying a convenient city centre location and with limited parking spaces, this hotel is ideal for both business and leisure travellers. Well-equipped bedrooms are brightly decorated and offer functional design. Modern public areas include a small fitness club and a brasserie serving a range of meals all day.

Rooms 139 (139 fmly) **Facilities** Wi-fi ⮧ Gym Sauna Steam room Xmas **Conf** Class 20 Board 20 Thtr 40 Del from £120 to £180 **Services** Lift Air con **Parking** 19

Mercure Glasgow City Hotel

★★★ HOTEL

☎ 0844 815 9017
201 Ingram St G1 1DQ
e-mail: info@mercureedinburgh.co.uk
web: www.jupiterhotels.co.uk
dir: M8 junct 15, straight through 4 lights, left at 5th into Hanover St, left into George Sq, right into Frederick St. Right at 2nd lights into Ingram St

This recently refurbished hotel enjoys a fantastic location in the heart of Glasgow with great access to shops, bars and restaurants. Bedrooms provide modern accommodation and a host of accessories including flat screen televisions and complimentary Wi-fi. Extensive conference facilities and the popular Bagio Café Bar mean you may not need to leave the hotel.

Rooms 91 **Conf** Class 40 Board 40 Thtr 60

Holiday Inn Glasgow City Centre - Theatreland

★★★ 83% ◉ HOTEL

☎ 0141 352 8300
161 West Nile St G1 2RL
e-mail: reservations@higlasgow.com
web: www.holidayinn.co.uk
dir: M8 junct 16, follow signs for Royal Concert Hall, hotel opposite

Built on a corner site close to the Theatre Royal Concert Hall and the main shopping areas, this contemporary hotel features the popular La Bonne Auberge French restaurant, a bar area and conservatory. Bedrooms are well equipped and

comfortable; suites are available. Staff are friendly and attentive.

Rooms 113 (20 fmly) (10 smoking) ⚑ **Facilities** STV FTV Wi-fi **Conf** Class 60 Board 60 Thtr 100 **Services** Lift Air con **Notes** ⊗

Uplawmoor Hotel

★★★ 81% ◉ SMALL HOTEL

THE CIRCLE

☎ 01505 850565
Neilston Rd G78 4AF
e-mail: info@uplawmoor.co.uk
web: www.uplawmoor.co.uk

(For full entry see Uplawmoor)

Campanile Glasgow

Campanile

BUDGET HOTEL

☎ 0141 287 7700
10 Tunnel St G3 8HL
e-mail: glasgow@campanile.com
web: www.campanile.com
dir: M8 junct 19, follow signs to SECC. Hotel adjacent to SECC

This modern building offers accommodation in smart, well-equipped bedrooms, all with en suite bathrooms. Refreshments may be taken at the informal bistro. See also the Hotel Groups pages.

Rooms 106 (2 fmly) (21 GF) **Conf** Class 60 Board 90 Thtr 150

Holiday Inn Express - Glasgow Theatreland

BUDGET HOTEL

☎ 0141 331 6800
165 West Nile St G1 2RL
e-mail: frontoffice.exp@higlasgow.com
web: www.hiexpressglasgow.co.uk
dir: Follow signs to Royal Concert Hall

A modern hotel ideal for families and business travellers. Fresh and uncomplicated, the spacious rooms include Sky TV, power shower and tea and coffee-making facilities. Continental buffet breakfast is included in the room rate; other meals may be taken at the nearby family pub or restaurant. See also the Hotel Groups pages.

Rooms 118 (34 fmly) (17 smoking) **Conf** Board 12 Thtr 20

G

GLASGOW *continued*

Ibis Glasgow

BUDGET HOTEL

☎ 0141 225 6000 & 619 9000
220 West Regent St G2 4DQ
e-mail: H3139@accor.com
web: www.ibis.com

Modern, budget hotel offering comfortable accommodation in bright and practical bedrooms. Breakfast is self-service and meals are also available in the café-bar 24 hours. See also the Hotel Groups pages.

Rooms 141 ☞ **S** £39-£170; **D** £39-£170

Premier Inn Glasgow (Bearsden)

BUDGET HOTEL

☎ 0871 527 8418
279 Milngavie Rd G61 3DQ
web: www.premierinn.com
dir: M8 junct 16, A81. Pass Asda on right. Hotel on left, behind The Burnbrae

High quality, budget accommodation ideal for both families and business travellers. Spacious, en suite bedrooms feature tea and coffee making facilities, and Freeview TV in most hotels. Internet access and Wi-fi are available for a small fee. The adjacent family restaurant features a wide and varied menu. See also the Hotel Groups pages.

Rooms 61

Premier Inn Glasgow (Bellshill)

BUDGET HOTEL

☎ 0871 527 8421
New Edinburgh Rd, Bellshill ML4 3PD
web: www.premierinn.com
dir: M74 junct 5, A725. Follow Bellshill A721 signs, bear left. At rdbt left, follow Tannochside sign. At next rdbt left into Bellziehill Rd. Hotel on right

Rooms 40

Premier Inn Glasgow (Cambuslang/ M74 Jct 1)

BUDGET HOTEL

☎ 0871 527 8422
Cambuslang Investment Park, Off London Rd G32 8YX
web: www.premierinn.com
dir: At end of M74, turn right at rdbt. At 1st lights turn right, at 2nd lights straight ahead. Hotel on right

Rooms 40

Premier Inn Glasgow City Centre

BUDGET HOTEL

☎ 0871 527 9360
St Andrew House, 141 West Nile St G1 2RN
web: www.premierinn.com
dir: Please telephone for detailed directions

Rooms 210

Premier Inn Glasgow City Centre Argyle St

BUDGET HOTEL

☎ 0871 527 8436
377 Argyle St G2 8LL
web: www.premierinn.com
dir: From S: M8 junct 19, at pedestrian lights left into Argyle St. Hotel 200yds on right

Rooms 121

Premier Inn Glasgow City Centre (Charing Cross)

BUDGET HOTEL

☎ 0871 527 8438
10 Elmbank Gardens G2 4PP
web: www.premierinn.com
dir: Telephone for directions

Rooms 278

Premier Inn Glasgow City Centre (George Square)

BUDGET HOTEL

☎ 0871 527 8440
187 George St G1 1YU
web: www.premierinn.com
dir: M8 junct 15, into Stirling Rd. Right into Cathedral St. At 1st lights left into Montrose St. Hotel after 1st lights

Rooms 239

Premier Inn Glasgow City Centre South

BUDGET HOTEL

☎ 0871 527 8442
80 Ballater St G5 0TW
web: www.premierinn.com
dir: M8 junct 21 follow East Kilbride signs, right onto A8 into Kingston St. Right into South Portland St, left into Norfolk St, through Gorbals St into Ballater St

Rooms 114

Premier Inn Glasgow East

BUDGET HOTEL

☎ 0871 527 8444
601 Hamilton Rd, Uddington G71 7SA
web: www.premierinn.com
dir: At entrance to Glasgow Zoo, adjacent to junct 4 of M73 & M74

Rooms 66

Holiday Inn Glasgow Airport

★★★ 77% HOTEL

☎ 0871 942 9031 & 0141 887 1266
Abbotsinch PA3 2TR
e-mail: operations-glasgow@ihg.com
web: www.higlasgowairporthotel.co.uk
dir: From E: M8 junct 28, follow hotel signs. From W: M8 junct 29, airport slip road to hotel

Located within the airport grounds and within walking distance of the terminal. Bedrooms are well appointed and cater for the needs of the modern traveller; all have mini bars. The open-plan public areas are relaxing as is the restaurant which offers a wide ranging a la carte menu. Wi-fi is available in the public areas.

Rooms 300 (6 fmly) **Facilities** STV FTV Wi-fi ☞
Conf Class 150 Board 75 Thtr 300 Del from £85 to £159* **Services** Lift Air con **Parking** 56
Notes Civ Wed 250

Save on hotels. Book at **theAA.com/hotel**

GLA – GRE 527 SCOTLAND

Premier Inn Glasgow Airport

BUDGET HOTEL

☎ 0871 527 8434
Whitecart Rd, Glasgow Airport PA3 2TH
web: www.premierinn.com
dir: M8 junct 28, follow airport signs for Long Stay &
Car Park 3 (Premier Inn signed). At 1st rdbt right into
St Andrews Drive. At next rdbt right into Whitecart Rd.
Under motorway. Left at garage. Hotel on right

High quality, budget accommodation ideal for both
families and business travellers. Spacious, en suite
bedrooms feature tea and coffee making facilities,
and Freeview TV in most hotels. Internet access and
Wi-fi are available for a small fee. The adjacent
family restaurant features a wide and varied menu.
See also the Hotel Groups pages.

Rooms 104

Premier Inn Glasgow (Paisley)

BUDGET HOTEL

☎ 0871 527 8432
Phoenix Retail Park PA1 2BH
web: www.premierinn.com
dir: M8 junct 28a, A737 signed Irvine, take 1st exit
signed Linwood, left at 1st rdbt to Phoenix Park

Rooms 40

GLENEAGLES

See **Auchterarder**

GLENFINNAN   Map 22 NM98
Highland

The Prince's House

★★★ 75% ◉◉ SMALL HOTEL

☎ 01397 722246
PH37 4LT
e-mail: princeshouse@glenfinnan.co.uk
web: www.glenfinnan.co.uk
dir: On A830, 0.5m on right past Glenfinnan
Monument. 200mtrs from railway station

This delightful hotel enjoys a well deserved reputation
for fine food and excellent hospitality. The hotel has
inspiring views and sits close to where 'Bonnie'
Prince Charlie raised the Jacobite standard.
Comfortably appointed bedrooms offer pleasing
decor. Excellent local game and seafood can be
enjoyed in the restaurant and the bar.

Rooms 9 ☏ **S** £65-£75; **D** £120-£150 (incl. bkfst)*
Facilities STV FTV Wi-fi Fishing New Year
Conf Class 20 Thtr 40 **Parking** 18 **Notes** LB ⊗ Closed
Xmas & Jan-Feb (ex New Year) RS Nov-Dec & Mar

GLENROTHES   Map 21 NO20
Fife

Holiday Inn Express Glenrothes

BUDGET HOTEL

☎ 01592 745509
Leslie Roundabout, Leslie Rd KY6 3EP
e-mail: reservations@hiexpressglenrothes.co.uk
web: www.hiexpress.com/glenrothes
dir: M90 junct 2A, onto A911 for Leslie. Through 4
rdbts, hotel on left

A modern hotel ideal for families and business
travellers. Fresh and uncomplicated, the spacious
rooms include Sky TV, power shower and tea and
coffee-making facilities. Continental buffet breakfast
is included in the room rate; other meals may be
taken at the nearby family pub or restaurant. See also
the Hotel Groups pages.

Rooms 49 (40 fmly) (21 GF) ☏ **Conf** Class 16
Board 16 Thtr 30

Premier Inn Glenrothes

BUDGET HOTEL

☎ 0871 527 8454
Beaufort Dr, Bankhead Roundabout KY7 4UJ
web: www.premierinn.com
dir: M90 junct 2a N'bound, A92 to Glenrothes. At 2nd
rbt (Bankhead) take 3rd exit. Hotel on left

High quality, budget accommodation ideal for
families and business travellers. Spacious, en suite
bedrooms feature tea and coffee making facilities,
and Freeview TV in most hotels. Internet access and
Wi-fi are available for a small fee. The adjacent
family restaurant features a wide and varied menu.
See also the Hotel Groups pages.

Rooms 41

GRANGEMOUTH   Map 21 NS98
Falkirk

The Grange Manor

★★★★ 78% HOTEL

☎ 01324 474836
Glensburgh FK3 8XJ
e-mail: info@grangemanor.co.uk
web: www.grangemanor.co.uk
dir: E: M9 junct 6, hotel 200mtrs to right. W: M9
junct 5, A905 for 2m

Located south of town and close to the M9, this
stylish hotel, popular with business and corporate
clientele, benefits from hands-on family ownership. It
offers spacious, high quality accommodation with
superb bathrooms. Public areas include a comfortable

foyer area, a lounge bar and a smart restaurant.
Cook's bar and restaurant is adjacent to the main
house in the converted stables. Staff throughout are
very friendly.

Rooms 36 (30 annexe) (6 fmly) (15 GF) **S** £70-£165;
D £70-£165 (incl. bkfst)* **Facilities** FTV Wi-fi Xmas
New Year **Conf** Class 68 Board 40 Thtr 120
Del from £100 to £200* **Services** Lift **Parking** 154
Notes ⊗ Civ Wed 120

GRANTOWN-ON-SPEY   Map 23 NJ02
Highland

Grant Arms Hotel

G

★★★ 79% HOTEL

☎ 01479 872526
25-27 The Square PH26 3HF
e-mail: info@grantarmshotel.com
web: www.grantarmshotel.com
dir: Exit A9 N of Aviemore onto A95

Conveniently located in the centre of the town, this
fine hotel is appointed to a high standard yet still
retains the building's traditional character. The
spacious bedrooms are stylishly presented and very
well equipped. The Garden Restaurant is a popular
venue for dinner, and lighter snacks can be enjoyed in
the comfortable bar. Modern conference facilities are
available and the hotel is very popular with
birdwatchers and wildlife enthusiasts.

Rooms 50 (7 fmly) ☏ **S** £85-£110; **D** £170-£220
(incl. bkfst & dinner) **Facilities** FTV Wi-fi ⌕
Birdwatching & Wildlife Club ♫ Xmas New Year
Conf Class 30 Board 16 Thtr 70 Del £95*
Services Lift **Notes** LB

GREENOCK   Map 20 NS27
Inverclyde

Holiday Inn Express Greenock

BUDGET HOTEL

☎ 01475 786666
Cartsburn PA15 1AE
e-mail: greenock@holidayinnexpress.org.uk
web: www.hiexpressgreenock.co.uk
dir: M8 junct 31, A8 to Greenock, right at 5th rdbt,
hotel on right

A modern hotel ideal for families and business
travellers. Fresh and uncomplicated, the spacious
rooms include Sky TV, power shower and tea and
coffee-making facilities. Continental buffet breakfast
is included in the room rate; other meals may be
taken at the nearby family pub or restaurant. See also
the Hotel Groups pages.

Rooms 71 (15 fmly) (6 GF) (20 smoking)
Conf Class 48 Board 32 Thtr 70

GREENOCK *continued*

Premier Inn Greenock

BUDGET HOTEL

☎ 0871 527 8476
The Point, 1-3 James Watt Way PA15 2AD
web: www.premierinn.com
dir: A8 to Greenock. At rdbt junct of East Hamilton St
& Main St (McDonalds visable on right) take 3rd exit.
Hotel on left

High quality, budget accommodation ideal for both
families and business travellers. Spacious, en suite
bedrooms feature tea and coffee making facilities,
and Freeview TV in most hotels. Internet access and
Wi-fi are available for a small fee. The adjacent
family restaurant features a wide and varied menu.
See also the Hotel Groups pages.

Rooms 17

GRETNA SERVICE AREA (A74(M))	Map 21 NY36
Dumfries & Galloway	

Days Inn Gretna Green - M74

BUDGET HOTEL

☎ 01461 337566
Welcome Break Service Area DG16 5HQ
e-mail: gretna.hotel@welcomebreak.co.uk
web: www.welcomebreak.co.uk
dir: Between junct 21 & 22 of A74(M) - accessible
from both N'bound & S'bound carriageways

This modern building offers accommodation in smart,
spacious and well-equipped bedrooms suitable for
families and business travellers, and all with en suite
bathrooms. Continental breakfast is available and
other refreshments may be taken at the nearby family
restaurant. See also the Hotel Groups pages.

Rooms 64 (54 fmly) (64 GF)

GRETNA (WITH GRETNA GREEN)	Map 21 NY36
Dumfries & Galloway	

Smiths at Gretna Green

★★★★ 80% ◎◎ HOTEL

☎ 01461 337007
Gretna Green DG16 5EA
e-mail: info@smithsgretnagreen.com
web: www.smithsgretnagreen.com
dir: From M74 junct 22 follow signs to Old
Blacksmith's Shop. Hotel opposite

Located next to the World Famous Old Blacksmith's
Shop Centre just off the motorway linking Scotland
and England. The bedrooms offer a spacious
environment, complete with flat-screen TVs, DVD
players and broadband. Family rooms feature a

separate children's area with bunk beds, each with
its own TV. Three suites and a penthouse apartment
are also available. Open-plan contemporary day
rooms lead to the brasserie restaurant; impressive
conference and banqueting facilities are provided.

Rooms 50 (8 fmly) 🐾 **S** £60-£140; **D** £70-£495 (incl.
bkfst)* **Facilities** STV FTV Wi-fi ↻ HL Treatment room
New Year **Conf** Class 100 Board 40 Thtr 250
Del from £115 to £165 **Services** Lift Air con
Parking 115 **Notes** Civ Wed 150

The Gables Hotel

★★★ 79% HOTEL

☎ 01461 338300
1 Annan Rd DG16 5DQ
e-mail: reservations@gables-hotel-gretna.co.uk
dir: M74 S or M6/M74 N follow signs for Gretna. At
rdbt at Gretna Gateway take exit onto Annan Rd, hotel
200yds on right

This Grade II listed hotel is located close to the Gretna
Gateway and is ideally located to explore both
Galloway and the Border City of Carlisle. Bedrooms
offer comfortable and well-appointed
accommodation. The main restaurant offers a carte
menu with a range of freshly prepared dishes, whilst
Saddlers bar provides light snacks and meals.

Rooms 31 (5 fmly) (10 GF) 🐾 **Facilities** FTV Wi-fi
Xmas New Year **Conf** Class 60 Board 48 Thtr 100
Parking 60 **Notes** ⊗ Civ Wed 100

HAMILTON	Map 20 NS75
South Lanarkshire	

Holiday Inn Express Hamilton

BUDGET HOTEL

☎ 01698 456300
Keith St ML3 7BL
e-mail: hamilton@holidayinnexpress.org.uk
web: www.hiexpress.com/hamilton
dir: 0.25m from M74 junct 6, in town centre (parking
available in Retail Unit)

A modern hotel ideal for families and business
travellers. Fresh and uncomplicated, the spacious
rooms include Sky TV, power shower and tea and
coffee-making facilities. Continental buffet breakfast
is included in the room rate; other meals may be
taken at the nearby family pub or restaurant. See also
the Hotel Groups pages.

Rooms 104 (68 fmly) (26 smoking) 🐾 **S** £49-£109;
D £49-£109 (incl. bkfst)* **Conf** Class 32 Board 36
Thtr 60 Del from £80 to £125*

HAWICK	Map 21 NT51
Scottish Borders	

Mansfield House Hotel

★★★ 81% HOTEL

☎ 01450 360400
Weensland Rd TD9 8LB
e-mail: reception@themansfieldhousehotel.co.uk
dir: A7 to Hawick onto A698 (Weensland Rd). Hotel
0.75m on right

This hotel is set in its own mature grounds at the top
of a hill with spectacular views over Hawick. The
bedrooms, located on the basement level and the first
floor, differ in size and include the fantastic Tower
Room accessed via a steep, narrow staircase - but
the climb is well worth the effort! Public areas are
welcoming and the style is in keeping with the age of
the building. The restaurant proudly uses local,
quality ingredients for the menus.

Rooms 16 (2 fmly) 🐾 **Facilities** FTV Wi-fi ↻ Xmas
New Year **Conf** Class 160 Board 60 Thtr 160
Parking 25 **Notes** ⊗ Civ Wed 120

INVERGARRY	Map 22 NH30
Highland	

Glengarry Castle Hotel

★★★ 82% ◎ COUNTRY HOUSE HOTEL

☎ 01809 501254
PH35 4HW
e-mail: castle@glengarry.net
web: www.glengarry.net
dir: On A82, 0.5m from A82/A87 junct

This charming country-house hotel is set in 50 acres
of grounds on the shores of Loch Oich. The spacious
day rooms include comfortable sitting rooms with lots
to read and board games to play. The classical dining
room boasts an innovative menu that showcases
local Scottish produce. The smart bedrooms vary in
size and style but all boast magnificent loch or
woodland views.

Rooms 26 (2 fmly) 🐾 **S** £75-£85; **D** £110-£195 (incl.
bkfst) **Facilities** FTV Wi-fi 🎣 Fishing **Parking** 30
Notes Closed mid Nov-mid Mar

Save on hotels. Book at **theAA.com/hotel**

GRE – INV 529 SCOTLAND

INVERGORDON — Map 23 NH76
Highland

Kincraig Castle Hotel

★★★★ 77% ◉ COUNTRY HOUSE HOTEL

☎ 01349 852587
IV18 0LF
e-mail: info@kincraig-house-hotel.co.uk
web: www.kincraig-house-hotel.co.uk
dir: Off A9 past Alness towards Tain. Hotel on left
0.25m past Rosskeen Church

This imposing castle is set in well-tended grounds in
an elevated position with views over the Cromarty
Firth. It offers smart, individually designed, well-
equipped bedrooms with satellite TVs, and inviting
public areas that retain the original features.
However, it is the friendly service and commitment to
guest care that will leave a lasting impression.

Rooms 15 (1 fmly) (1 GF) 🏌 **Facilities** STV Wi-fi ♘
Xmas New Year **Conf** Class 30 Board 24 Thtr 50
Parking 30 **Notes** Civ Wed 70

INVERKEILOR — Map 23 NO64
Angus

Gordon's

◉ ◉ ◉ RESTAURANT WITH ROOMS

☎ 01241 830364
Main St DD11 5RN
e-mail: gordonsrest@aol.com
dir: Exit A92 between Arbroath & Montrose into
Inverkeilor

It's worth a detour off the main road to this family-
run restaurant with rooms set in the centre of the
village. It has earned AA Rosettes for dinner, and the
excellent breakfasts are equally memorable. A huge
fire dominates the restaurant on cooler evenings, and
there is a small lounge with limited seating. The
attractive bedrooms are tastefully decorated and
thoughtfully equipped; the larger two are furnished in
pine.

Rooms 5 (1 annexe)

INVERNESS — Map 23 NH64
Highland

The New Drumossie Hotel

★★★★ 80% ◉◉ HOTEL

☎ 01463 236451 & 0870 194 2110
Old Perth Rd IV2 5BE
e-mail: stay@drumossiehotel.co.uk
dir: From A9 follow signs for Culloden Battlefield,
hotel on left after 1m

Set in nine acres of landscaped hillside grounds
south of Inverness, this hotel has fine views of the
Moray Firth towards Ben Wyvis. Art deco style
decoration together with a country-house atmosphere
are found throughout. Service is friendly and
attentive, the food imaginative and enjoyable and the
bedrooms spacious and well presented. The main
function room is probably the largest in this area.

Rooms 44 (10 fmly) (6 GF) 🏌 **Facilities** STV FTV Wi-fi
HL Fishing New Year **Conf** Class 200 Board 40
Thtr 500 **Services** Lift **Parking** 200 **Notes** ⊗
Civ Wed 400

Loch Ness Country House Hotel

★★★★ 79% ◉◉ SMALL HOTEL

☎ 01463 230512
Loch Ness Rd IV3 8JN
e-mail: info@lochnesscountryhousehotel.co.uk
web: www.lochnesscountryhousehotel.co.uk
dir: On A82, 1m from Inverness town boundary

Built in the Georgian era, this fine house is perfectly
situated in its own six acre private Highland estate.
The hotel has luxurious bedrooms, four of which are in
the garden suite cottages. The stylish restaurant
serves the best of local produce and guests have a
choice of cosy well-appointed lounges for after dinner
drinks. The garden terrace is ideal for relaxing and
has splendid views over the landscaped gardens
towards Inverness.

Rooms 13 (2 annexe) (8 fmly) (3 GF) **S** £70-£155;
D £80-£250 (incl. bkfst)* **Facilities** FTV Wi-fi Xmas
New Year **Conf** Class 40 Board 40 Thtr 100
Del from £120 to £195* **Parking** 50
Notes Civ Wed 150

Bunchrew House Hotel

★★★★ 75% ◉◉ COUNTRY HOUSE HOTEL

☎ 01463 234917
Bunchrew IV3 8TA
e-mail: welcome@bunchrewhousehotel.com
web: www.bunchrewhousehotel.com
dir: W on A862. Hotel 2m after canal on right

Overlooking the Beauly Firth this impressive mansion
house dates from the 17th century and retains much
original character. Individually styled bedrooms are
spacious and tastefully furnished. A wood-panelled
restaurant is the setting for artfully constructed
cooking and there is a choice of comfortable lounges
complete with real fires.

Rooms 16 (4 fmly) (1 GF) 🏌 **S** £110-£170;
D £120-£240 (incl. bkfst)* **Facilities** FTV Wi-fi
Fishing New Year **Conf** Class 30 Board 30 Thtr 80
Parking 40 **Notes** LB Closed 24-27 Dec Civ Wed 92

Glenmoriston Town House Hotel

★★★★ 75% ◉ TOWN HOUSE HOTEL

☎ 01463 223777
20 Ness Bank IV2 4SF
e-mail: reception@glenmoristontownhouse.com
web: www.glenmoristontownhouse.com
dir: On riverside opposite theatre

Bold contemporary designs blend seamlessly with the
classical architecture of this stylish hotel, situated on
the banks of the River Ness. Delightful day rooms
include a piano bar and two eating options. Abstract
Restaurant features accomplished modern Scottish
cuisine based on the finest Scottish produce, and
Contrast Brasserie is ideal for relaxed meals from
breakfast through to dinner, and when possible for
eating alfresco when the weather warms up. The
sleek, modern, individually designed bedrooms have
many facilities including free Wi-fi, DVD players and
flat-screen TVs.

Rooms 30 (15 annexe) (1 fmly) (6 GF) 🏌
Facilities STV FTV Wi-fi ♘ ♫ Xmas New Year
Parking 40 **Notes** ⊗ Civ Wed 70

INVERNESS *continued*

The Columba Hotel

★★★★ 74% HOTEL

☎ 08444 146 522
Ness Walk IV3 5NF
e-mail: reservations.columba@ohiml.com
web: www.oxfordhotelsandinns.com
dir: From A9, A96 follow signs to town centre, pass
Eastgate shopping centre into Academy St, at bottom
left into Bank St, right over bridge, hotel 1st left

Originally built in 1881 and with many original
features retained, the Columba Hotel lies in the heart
of Inverness overlooking the fast flowing River Ness.
The bedrooms are very stylish, and public areas
include a first-floor restaurant and lounge. A second
dining option is the ever popular McNabs bar bistro,
which is ideal for less formal meals.

Rooms 76 (4 fmly) **Facilities** FTV Wi-fi ♫ Xmas New
Year **Conf** Class 100 Board 60 Thtr 200 **Services** Lift
Notes Civ Wed 120

BEST WESTERN Inverness Palace Hotel & Spa

★★★ 78% HOTEL

☎ 01463 223243
8 Ness Walk IV3 5NG
e-mail: palace@miltonhotels.com
web: www.invernesspalacehotel.co.uk
dir: A82 Glenurquhart Rd onto Ness Walk. Hotel
300yds on right opposite Inverness Castle

Set on the north side of the River Ness close to the
Eden Court theatre and a short walk from the town,
this hotel has a contemporary look. Bedrooms offer
good levels of comfort and equipment, and a smart
leisure centre attracts a mixed market.

Rooms 88 (48 annexe) (3 fmly) ♦ **S** £69.90-£149.90;
D £79.90-£249.90 **Facilities** Spa FTV Wi-fi ❄
supervised Gym Beautician Hairdresser Sauna Steam
room Xmas New Year **Conf** Class 40 Board 30 Thtr 80
Del from £99.90 to £179.90 **Services** Lift **Parking** 18
Notes LB Civ Wed 100

Ramada Encore Inverness City Centre

★★★ 75% HOTEL

☎ 01463 228850
63 Academy St IV1 1LU
e-mail: reservations@encoreinverness.co.uk
web: www.encoreinverness.co.uk
dir: A9, A82, B865, hotel on right

This hotel is ideally located, as its name suggests,
close to the main shopping district, railway station

and the tourist attractions of Inverness. The
contemporary bedrooms have a bright stylish design
and all rooms are equipped with Wi-fi along with an
extensive choice of TV channels and movies. Public
areas include a modern restaurant and a light-filled
lounge area with comfortable seating. There is a
choice of ground-floor business suites which makes
the hotel very popular with corporate guests.

Rooms 90 (20 fmly) **Facilities** STV FTV Wi-fi
Conf Class 20 Board 20 Thtr 34 **Services** Lift
Notes ⊗

Thistle Inverness

thistle

★★★ 75% HOTEL

☎ 0871 376 9023
Millburn Rd IV2 3TR
e-mail: reception.inverness@thistle.co.uk
web: www.thistle.com/inverness
dir: From A9 take Raigmore Interchange exit (towards
Aberdeen), 3rd left towards centre. Hotel opposite

Well located within easy distance of the town centre,
this well-presented hotel offers modern bedrooms
including three suites. There is a well-equipped
leisure centre along with an informal brasserie and
open-plan bar and lounge. Ample parking is an added
benefit.

Rooms 118 ♦ **S** £40-£100; **D** £50-£150 (incl. bkfst)*
Facilities Wi-fi HL ❄ supervised Gym Sauna Steam
room Xmas New Year **Conf** Class 70 Board 50
Thtr 120 **Services** Lift **Parking** 80 **Notes** ⊗
Civ Wed 120

Royal Highland Hotel

★★★ 74% HOTEL

☎ 01463 231926 & 251451
Station Square, Academy St IV1 1LG
e-mail: info@royalhighlandhotel.co.uk
web: www.royalhighlandhotel.co.uk
dir: From A9 into town centre. Hotel next to rail
station & Eastgate Retail Centre

Built in 1858 adjacent to the railway station, this
hotel has the typically grand foyer of the Victorian era
with comfortable seating. The contemporary ASH
Brasserie and bar is a refreshing venue for both
eating and drinking throughout the day. The generally
spacious bedrooms are comfortably equipped
especially for the business traveller.

Rooms 85 (12 fmly) (2 GF) (10 smoking) ♦
Facilities FTV Wi-fi Xmas New Year **Conf** Class 80
Board 80 Thtr 200 **Services** Lift **Parking** 8
Notes Civ Wed 200

Mercure Inverness Hotel

★★★ HOTEL

☎ 0844 815 9006
Church St IV1 1DX
e-mail: info@mercureinverness.co.uk
web: www.jupiterhotels.co.uk
dir: From A9 junct A82 (Kessock Bridge) join A82
Inverness. At rdbt 2nd exit, rdbt straight ahead next
rdbt left onto B865. Right at lights continue past
church Hotel on left

The Mercure Inverness Hotel is situated in an ideal
location with the bustling Inverness city centre to one
side, and the attractive River Ness running the length
of the other. Spacious public areas, an inviting
leisure centre and comfortable bedrooms can all be
found here. The Brasserie serves a wide ranging
selection of dishes. On site parking and
complimentary Wi fi are added bonuses.

Rooms 106

Premier Inn Inverness Centre (Milburn Rd)

BUDGET HOTEL

☎ 0871 527 8544
Millburn Rd IV2 3QX
web: www.premierinn.com
dir: From A9 & A96 junct (Raigmore Interchange,
signed Airport/Aberdeen), take B865 towards town
centre, hotel 100yds after next rdbt

High quality, budget accommodation ideal for both
families and business travellers. Spacious, en suite
bedrooms feature tea and coffee making facilities,
and Freeview TV in most hotels. Internet access and
Wi-fi are available for a small fee. The adjacent
family restaurant features a wide and varied menu.
See also the Hotel Groups pages.

Rooms 55

Premier Inn Inverness Centre (River Ness)

BUDGET HOTEL

☎ 0871 527 9302
19-21 Huntly St IV3 5PR
web: www.premierinn.com
dir: Exit A9 at Longman rdbt, 1st exit into Longman
Rd (A82) follow Inverness/Fort William signs. Straight
on at 3 rdbts. At Telford St rdbt 1st exit into Wells St.
Right into Huntly St. Hotel on right

Rooms 98

Premier Inn Inverness East

BUDGET HOTEL

☎ 0871 527 8546
Beechwood Business Park IV2 3BW
web: www.premierinn.com
dir: From A9 follow Raigmore Hospital, Police HQ & Inshes Retail Park signs

Rooms 60

Premier Inn Inverness West

BUDGET HOTEL

☎ 0871 527 9338
Glenurquhart Rd IV3 5TD
web: www.premierinn.com
dir: From A9 exit at Kessock rdbt. At 4th rdbt 2nd exit into Kenneth St. Right at lights into Glenruquhart Rd, pass council offices, 1m, take A82 signed Fort William. Cross Caledonian Canal Bridge. Hotel on right

Rooms 76

| INVERURIE | Map 23 NJ72 |
| Aberdeenshire | |

Macdonald Pittodrie House

MACDONALD HOTELS & RESORTS

★★★★ 75% ◉ HOTEL

☎ 0870 1942111 & 01467 622 437
Chapel of Garioch, Pitcaple AB51 5HS
e-mail: gm.pittodrie@macdonald-hotels.co.uk
web: www.macdonald-hotels.com/pittodrie
dir: From A96 towards Inverness, pass Inverurie under bridge with lights. Turn left & follow signs

Set in extensive grounds this house dates from the 15th century and retains many historic features. Public rooms include a gracious drawing room, restaurant, and a cosy bar boasting an impressive selection of whiskies. The well-proportioned bedrooms are found in both the original house and in the extension that was designed to match the existing building. Macdonald Hotels is the AA Hotel Group of the Year 2013-14.

Rooms 27 (6 fmly) **S** £129-£400; **D** £129-£400*
Facilities STV FTV Wi-fi Clay pigeon shooting Quad biking Outdoor activities Xmas New Year
Conf Class 75 Board 50 Thtr 150 Del from £167*
Parking 200 **Notes** LB Civ Wed 120

| IRVINE | Map 20 NS33 |
| North Ayrshire | |

Menzies Irvine

MenziesHotels

★★★★ 77% HOTEL

☎ 01294 274272
46 Annick Rd KA11 4LD
e-mail: irvine@menzieshotels.co.uk
web: www.menzieshotels.co.uk
dir: From A78 at Warrix Interchange follow Irvine Central signs. At rdbt 2nd exit (town centre). At next rdbt right onto A71/Kilmarnock. Hotel 100mtrs on left

Situated on the edge of Irvine with good transportation links (including Prestwick Airport just seven miles away), this is a well-presented hotel that has an extremely friendly team with good customer care awareness. The decor is contemporary throughout, and there is a brasserie-style restaurant, cocktail bar and spacious lounge.

Rooms 128 (14 fmly) (64 GF) **Facilities** STV FTV Wi-fi ▷ Fishing Xmas New Year **Conf** Class 140 Board 100 Thtr 280 **Parking** 220 **Notes** Civ Wed 200

| KELSO | Map 21 NT73 |
| Scottish Borders | |

The Roxburghe Hotel & Golf Course

★★★★ 80% ◉◉ COUNTRY HOUSE HOTEL

☎ 01573 450331
Heiton TD5 8JZ
e-mail: hotel@roxburghe.net
web: www.roxburghe-hotel.com
dir: From A68 Jedburgh take A698 to Heiton, 3m SW of Kelso

Outdoor sporting pursuits are popular at this impressive Jacobean mansion owned by the Duke of Roxburghe, and set in 500 acres of woods and parkland bordering the River Teviot. Gracious public areas are the perfect settings for afternoon teas and carefully prepared meals. The elegant bedrooms are individually designed, some by the Duchess herself, and include superior rooms, some with four posters and log fires.

Rooms 22 (6 annexe) (3 fmly) (8 GF) **D** £109-£315 (incl. bkfst)* **Facilities** Spa STV FTV Wi-fi ▷ ♣ 18 Putt green Fishing ⬎ Clay shooting Health & beauty salon Mountain bike hire Falconry Archery Xmas New Year **Conf** Class 20 Board 20 Thtr 50 Del from £171 to £185* **Parking** 150 **Notes** LB Civ Wed 60

| KILCHRENAN | Map 20 NN02 |
| Argyll & Bute | |

Taychreggan Hotel

★★★★ 74% ◉◉ COUNTRY HOUSE HOTEL

☎ 01866 833211 & 833366
PA35 1HQ
e-mail: info@taychregganhotel.co.uk
web: www.taychregganhotel.co.uk
dir: W from Crianlarich on A85 to Taynuilt, S for 7m on B845 (single track) to Kilchrenan

Surrounded by stunning Highland scenery this stylish and superbly presented hotel, once a drover's cottage, enjoys an idyllic setting in 40 acres of wooded grounds on the shores of Loch Awe. The hotel has a smart bar with adjacent courtyard Orangerie and a choice of quiet lounges with deep, luxurious sofas. A well earned reputation has been achieved by the kitchen for the skilfully prepared dinners that showcase the local and seasonal Scottish larder. Families, and also dogs and their owners, are welcome.

Rooms 18 (1 fmly) **Facilities** FTV Wi-fi Fishing ⬎ Air rifle range Archery Clay pigeon shooting Falconry Mock deer stalk Xmas New Year **Conf** Class 15 Board 20 **Parking** 40 **Notes** Closed 3 Jan-9 Feb Civ Wed 70

K

K

KILCHRENAN *continued*

INSPECTORS' CHOICE

The Ardanaiseig Hotel

★★★ COUNTRY HOUSE HOTEL

☎ 01866 833333
by Loch Awe PA35 1HE
e-mail: info@ardanaiseig.com
dir: A85 at Taynuilt onto B845 to Kilchrenan. Left in front of pub (road very narrow) signed 'Ardanaiseig Hotel' & 'No Through Road'. Continue for 3m

Set amid lovely gardens and breathtaking scenery beside the shore of Loch Awe, this peaceful country-house hotel was built in a Scottish baronial style in 1834. Many fine pieces of furniture are evident in the bedrooms and charming day rooms, which include a drawing room, a library bar and an elegant dining room. The bedrooms are individually designed including some with four posters, some with loch views and some with access to the garden; standing on its own by the water is the Boat Shed, a delightful one bedroom suite.

Rooms 18 (4 fmly) (5 GF) **Facilities** FTV Wi-fi Fishing Boating Clay pigeon shooting Bikes for hire In house massage treatments Xmas New Year **Parking** 20 **Notes** Civ Wed 50

KILLIECRANKIE
Perth & Kinross

Map 23 NN96

INSPECTORS' CHOICE

Killiecrankie Hotel

★★★ ◉◉ SMALL HOTEL

☎ 01796 473220
PH16 5LG
e-mail: enquiries@killiecrankiehotel.co.uk
dir: Exit A9 at Killiecrankie onto B8079. Hotel 3m on right

Originally built in the 1840s, Killiecrankie sits in fours acres of wooded grounds with beautifully landscaped gardens; it enjoys a tranquil location by the Pass of Killiecrankie and the River Garry. Public areas include a wood-panelled bar and a cosy sitting room with original artwork, and a blazing fire in colder months. All of the bedrooms are individually decorated, well equipped and have wonderful countryside views.

Rooms 10 (2 GF) **S** £85-£115; **D** £170-£290 (incl. bkfst & dinner)* **Facilities** FTV Wi-fi Xmas New Year **Parking** 20 **Notes** Closed 3 Jan-12 Mar

---

KILLIN
Stirling

Map 20 NN53

The Ardeonaig Hotel & Restaurant

★★★★ 76% SMALL HOTEL

☎ 01567 820400
South Loch Tay Side FK21 8SU
e-mail: info@ardeonaighotel.co.uk
dir: From E via Kenmore take South Loch Tay Rd for 7m. From W via Killin take South Loch Tay Rd for 7m

Formerly a drover's inn as far back as the 16th century, this hotel has been refurbished to very good standards and now provides a high level of accommodation. Personal service from well trained and friendly staff makes guests feel like they are the only ones enjoying the tranquil setting and inspiring views. You can be assured of a memorable dining experience with dishes cooked with imagination and flair.

Rooms 17 (7 annexe) (14 GF) **D** £200-£360 (incl. bkfst & dinner)* **Facilities** Wi-fi Fishing Xmas New Year **Conf** Class 25 Board 25 Thtr 50 Del from £240 to £300* **Parking** 30 **Notes** LB Closed 7-24 Jan Civ Wed 50

KILMARNOCK
East Ayrshire

Map 20 NS43

The Fenwick Hotel

★★★ 85% HOTEL

☎ 01560 600478
Fenwick KA3 6AU
e-mail: info@thefenwickhotel.co.uk
web: www.thefenwickhotel.co.uk
dir: M77 junct 8, B7061 towards Fenwick, follow hotel signs

Benefiting from a great location alongside the M77 and offering easy links to Ayr, Kilmarnock and Glasgow. The spacious bedrooms are thoughtfully equipped; complimentary Wi-fi is available throughout the hotel. The bright restaurant offers both formal and informal dining and there are two bars to choose from.

Rooms 29 (2 fmly) (9 GF) **Facilities** STV FTV Wi-fi Xmas New Year **Conf** Class 280 Board 150 Thtr 280 **Services** Lift **Parking** 64 **Notes** Civ Wed 110

Premier Inn Kilmarnock

BUDGET HOTEL

☎ 0871 527 8566
Moorfield Roundabout, Annadale KA1 2RS
web: www.premierinn.com
dir: M74 junct 8 signed Kilmarnock (A71). From M77 onto A71 to Irvine. At next rdbt right onto B7064 signed Crosshouse Hospital. Hotel on right

High quality, budget accommodation ideal for both families and business travellers. Spacious, en suite bedrooms feature tea and coffee making facilities, and Freeview TV in most hotels. Internet access and Wi-fi are available for a small fee. The adjacent family restaurant features a wide and varied menu. See also the Hotel Groups pages.

Rooms 40

KINCARDINE	Map 21 NS98
Fife	

Premier Inn Falkirk North

BUDGET HOTEL

☎ 0871 527 8394
Bowtrees Roundabout, Houghs of Airth FK2 8PJ
web: www.premierinn.com
dir: From N: M9 junct 7 (or from S: M876) towards Kincardine Bridge. On rdbt at end of slip road

High quality, budget accommodation ideal for both families and business travellers. Spacious, en suite bedrooms feature tea and coffee making facilities, and Freeview TV in most hotels. Internet access and Wi-fi are available for a small fee. The adjacent family restaurant features a wide and varied menu. See also the Hotel Groups pages.

Rooms 40

KINCLAVEN	Map 21 NO13
Perth & Kinross	

Ballathie House Hotel

★★★★ 78% ◉◉ COUNTRY HOUSE HOTEL

☎ 01250 883268
PH1 4QN
e-mail: email@ballathiehousehotel.com
web: www.ballathiehousehotel.com
dir: From A9, 2m N of Perth, take B9099 through Stanley, follow signs. Or from A93 at Beech Hedge follow signs for hotel, 2.5m

Set in delightful grounds, this splendid Scottish mansion house combines classical grandeur with modern comfort. Bedrooms range from well-proportioned master rooms to modern standard rooms, and many boast antique furniture and art deco bathrooms. It might be worth requesting one of

the Riverside Rooms, a purpose-built development right on the banks of the river, complete with balconies and terraces. The elegant restaurant has views over the River Tay.

Rooms 41 (16 annexe) (2 fmly) (10 GF) ⚓ **S** fr £85; **D** fr £85 (incl. bkfst)* **Facilities** FTV Wi-fi Fishing ⚓ Xmas New Year **Conf** Class 20 Board 30 Thtr 50 **Services** Lift **Parking** 50 **Notes** Civ Wed 90

KINGUSSIE	Map 23 NH70
Highland	

INSPECTORS' CHOICE

The Cross

◉◉ RESTAURANT WITH ROOMS

☎ 01540 661166
Tweed Mill Brae, Ardbroilach Rd PH21 1LB
e-mail: relax@thecross.co.uk
dir: From lights in Kingussie centre take Ardbroilach Rd, 300yds left into Tweed Mill Brae

Built as a water-powered tweed mill in the late 19th century, The Cross is situated in the picturesque Cairngorm National Park and surrounded by four acres of riverside grounds with an abundance of wildlife. Comfortable lounges and a selection of well-appointed bedrooms are offered, and dinners are served by an open fire in the stone-walled and wood-beamed restaurant.

Rooms 8 (1 fmly)

KINLOCH RANNOCH	Map 23 NN65
Perth & Kinross	

Macdonald Loch Rannoch Hotel

★★★ 75% HOTEL

☎ 0844 879 9059 & 01882 632201
PH16 5PS
e-mail: loch_rannoch@macdonald-hotels.co.uk
web: www.macdonald-hotels.co.uk
dir: A9 onto B847 Calvine. Follow signs to Kinloch Rannoch, hotel 1m from village

Set deep in the countryside with elevated views across Loch Rannoch, this hotel is built around a 19th-century hunting lodge and provides a great base for exploring this beautiful area. The superior bedrooms have views over the loch. There is a choice of eating options - The Ptarmigan Restaurant and the Schiehallion Bar for informal eating. The hotel provides both indoor and outdoor activities. Macdonald Hotels is the AA Hotel Group of the Year 2013-14.

Rooms 47 (25 fmly) **Facilities** FTV Wi-fi HL ⚓ Fishing Gym Xmas New Year **Conf** Class 80 Board 50 Thtr 160 **Services** Lift **Parking** 52 **Notes** Civ Wed 130

KINROSS	Map 21 NO10
Perth & Kinross	

The Green Hotel Golf & Leisure Resort

★★★★ 74% HOTEL

☎ 01577 863467
2 The Muirs KY13 8AS
e-mail: reservations@green-hotel.com
web: www.green-hotel.com
dir: M90 junct 6, follow Kinross signs onto A922 for hotel

A long-established hotel offering a wide range of indoor and outdoor activities. Public areas include a classical restaurant, a choice of bars and a well-stocked gift shop. The comfortable, well-equipped bedrooms, most of which are generously proportioned, boast attractive colour schemes and smart modern furnishings.

Rooms 46 (1 annexe) (3 fmly) (12 GF) **S** £62-£92; **D** £72-£132 (incl. bkfst)* **Facilities** Spa STV FTV Wi-fi ⚓ ⚓ supervised ⚓ 36 ⚓ Putt green Fishing ⚓ Gym Petanque Curling (Sep-Apr) Cycling Shooting (Oct-Feb) Cycle hire Falconry ♫ Xmas New Year **Conf** Class 75 Board 60 Thtr 130 **Parking** 60 **Notes** Civ Wed 100

KIRKCALDY	Map 21 NT29
Fife	

Dean Park Hotel

★★★ 78% HOTEL

☎ 01592 261635
Chapel Level KY2 6QW
e-mail: reception@deanparkhotel.co.uk
dir: Signed from A92 (Kirkcaldy West junct)

Popular with both business and leisure guests, this hotel has extensive conference and meeting facilities. The bedrooms are spacious and comfortable, are well equipped and have modern decor and up-to-date amenities. Public areas include the Dukes Bar & Bistro, and the Windsor Restaurant which is renowned for its steaks.

Rooms 33 (2 fmly) (5 GF) ⚓ **S** £50-£60; **D** £65-£90 (incl. bkfst) **Facilities** STV FTV Wi-fi Xmas New Year **Conf** Class 125 Board 54 Thtr 250 **Services** Lift **Parking** 250 **Notes** LB ⊗ Civ Wed 200

K

KIRKCUDBRIGHT
Dumfries & Galloway   **Map 20 NX65**

Arden House Hotel
★★ 76% HOTEL

☎ 01557 330544
Tongland Rd DG6 4UU
dir: Exit A75, 4m W of Castle Douglas onto A711.
Follow Kirkcudbright signs, over Telford Bridge. Hotel
400mtrs on left

Set well back from the main road in extensive
grounds on the northeast side of town, this spotlessly
maintained hotel offers attractive bedrooms, a lounge
bar and adjoining conservatory serving a range of
popular dishes, which are also available in the dining
room. It boasts an impressive function suite in its
grounds.

Rooms 9 (7 fmly) 🐾 **S** £45-£55; **D** fr £65 (incl.
bkfst)* **Facilities** FTV Wi-fi **Conf** Class 175 Board 120
Thtr 175 Del from £100 to £125* **Parking** 70
Notes LB

LANARK
South Lanarkshire   **Map 21 NS84**

BEST WESTERN Cartland Bridge Hotel

★★★ 74% COUNTRY HOUSE HOTEL

☎ 01555 664426
Glasgow Rd ML11 9UF
e-mail: sales@cartlandbridge.co.uk
dir: A73 through Lanark towards Carluke. Hotel in
1.25m

Situated in wooded grounds on the edge of the town,
this Grade I listed mansion continues to be popular
with both business and leisure guests. Public areas
feature wood panelling, a gallery staircase and a
magnificent dining room. The well-equipped
bedrooms vary in size.

Rooms 18 (2 fmly) 🐾 **S** £50-£80; **D** £80-£130
Facilities FTV Wi-fi Xmas New Year **Conf** Class 180
Board 50 Thtr 250 **Parking** 120 **Notes** LB ⊗
Civ Wed 200

LANGBANK
Renfrewshire   **Map 20 NS37**

Gleddoch House Hotel
"bespoke"
★★★★ 73% HOTEL

☎ 01475 540711 & 0843 178 7120
PA14 6YE
e-mail: reservations.gleddochhouse@ohiml.com
web: www.oxfordhotelsandinns.com
dir: M8 to Greenock, onto A8, left at rdbt onto A789,
follow for 0.5m, turn right, 2nd on left

This hotel is set in spacious, landscaped grounds
high above the River Clyde with fine views. The period
house is appointed to a very high standard. The
modern extension is impressive and offers spacious
and very comfortable bedrooms. Warm hospitality and
attentive service are noteworthy along with the hotel's
parkland golf course and leisure club.

Rooms 70 (22 fmly) (17 GF) **Facilities** Spa FTV Wi-fi ♨
🐾 ♿ 18 Putt green Gym Steam room Sauna Xmas
New Year **Conf** Class 70 Board 40 Thtr 150
Del from £120 to £195* **Parking** 150
Notes Civ Wed 120

LARGS
North Ayrshire   **Map 20 NS25**

Willowbank Hotel
★★★ 73% HOTEL

☎ 01475 672311 & 675435
96 Greenock Rd KA30 8PG
e-mail: iaincsmith@btconnect.com
dir: On A78

A relaxed, friendly atmosphere prevails at this well
maintained hotel where hanging baskets are a
feature in summer months. The nicely decorated
bedrooms are, in general, spacious and offer
comfortable modern appointments. The public areas
include a large, well-stocked bar, a lounge and a
dining room.

Rooms 30 (4 fmly) **Facilities** STV ♬ Xmas New Year
Conf Class 100 Board 40 Thtr 200 **Parking** 40

LIVINGSTON
West Lothian   **Map 21 NT06**

Mercure Livingston Hotel
Mercure
★★★ HOTEL

☎ 0844 815 9102
Almondview EH54 6QB
e-mail: info@mercurelivingston.co.uk
dir: From M8 junct 3 take A899 towards Livingston,
exit at Centre Interchange, left at next rdbt, hotel on
left

This large, modern hotel is conveniently located in the
town centre with easy access to the M8. Bedrooms
offer the freedom of space and are comfortably
appointed for both business and leisure guests. There
is a large open-plan lobby and restaurant area,
complementary Wi-Fi throughout the hotel, and a
small but well appointed leisure club.

Rooms 120 **Conf** Class 55 Board 60 Thtr 100

Premier Inn Livingston M8 Jct 3

BUDGET HOTEL

☎ 0871 527 8632
Deer Park Av, Deer Park, Knightsbridge EH54 8AD
web: www.premierinn.com
dir: At M8 junct 3. Hotel opposite rdbt

High quality, budget accommodation ideal for both
families and business travellers. Spacious, en suite
bedrooms feature tea and coffee making facilities,
and Freeview TV in most hotels. Internet access and
Wi-fi are available for a small fee. The adjacent
family restaurant features a wide and varied menu.
See also the Hotel Groups pages.

Rooms 83

LOCHGILPHEAD
Argyll & Bute   **Map 20 NR88**

Cairnbaan Hotel
★★★ 78% ⊛ HOTEL

☎ 01546 603668
Crinan Canal, Cairnbaan PA31 8SJ
e-mail: info@cairnbaan.com
web: www.cairnbaan.com
dir: 2m N, A816 from Lochgilphead, hotel off B841

Located on the Crinan Canal, this small hotel offers
relaxed hospitality in a delightful setting. Bedrooms
are thoughtfully equipped, generally spacious and
benefit from stylish decor. Fresh seafood is a real
feature in both the formal restaurant and the

K

comfortable bar area. Alfresco dining is popular in the warmer months.

Rooms 12 **Facilities** Xmas **Conf** Class 100 Board 80 Thtr 160 **Parking** 53 **Notes** Civ Wed 120

LOCKERBIE　　　Map 21 NY18
Dumfries & Galloway

Kings Arms Hotel

★★ 80% HOTEL

☎ 01576 202410
High St DG11 2JL
e-mail: reception@kingsarmshotel.co.uk
web: www.kingsarmshotel.co.uk
dir: A74(M), 0.5m into town centre, hotel opposite town hall

Dating from the 17th century this former inn lies in the town centre. Now a family-run hotel, it provides attractive well-equipped bedrooms with Wi-fi access. At lunch a menu ranging from snacks to full meals is served in both the cosy bars and the restaurant at dinner.

Rooms 13 (2 fmly) ☞ **S** £57.50; **D** £90 (incl. bkfst)
Facilities FTV Wi-fi Xmas New Year **Conf** Class 40 Board 30 Thtr 80 **Parking** 8

Ravenshill House Hotel

★★ 75% HOTEL

☎ 01576 202882
12 Dumfries Rd DG11 2EF
e-mail:
aaenquiries@ravenshillhotellockerbie.co.uk
web: www.ravenshillhotellockerbie.co.uk
dir: From A74(M) Lockerbie junct 14 North or 18 South. Follow signs for A709 Dumfries. Hotel 0.5m on right

Set in spacious gardens on the fringe of the town, this friendly, family-run hotel offers cheerful service and good value, home-cooked meals. Bedrooms are generally spacious and comfortably equipped, including a two-room unit ideal for families.

Rooms 8 (2 fmly) ☞ **S** £40-£60; **D** £70-£80 (incl. bkfst)* **Facilities** FTV Wi-fi **Conf** Class 20 Board 12 Thtr 30 **Parking** 35 **Notes** LB Closed 1-7 Jan & 2 wks in Feb

LUSS　　　Map 20 NS39
Argyll & Bute

The Lodge on Loch Lomond

★★★★ 76% ⑩⑩ HOTEL

☎ 01436 860201
G83 8PA
e-mail: res@loch-lomond.co.uk
web: www.loch-lomond.co.uk
dir: Off A82, follow sign for hotel

This hotel is idyllically set on the shores of Loch Lomond. Public areas consist of an open-plan, split-level bar and fine dining restaurant overlooking the loch. The pine-finished bedrooms also enjoy the views and are comfortable, spacious and well equipped; some with saunas, DVDs and all with internet access. There is a stunning state-of-the-art leisure suite.

Rooms 47 (17 annexe) (20 fmly) (13 GF) ☞
Facilities Spa STV FTV Wi-fi ⓢ Fishing Boating Xmas New Year **Conf** Class 80 Board 60 Thtr 150 Del £180*
Parking 120 **Notes** Civ Wed 100

MELROSE　　　Map 21 NT53
Scottish Borders

Burt's Hotel

★★★ 78% ⑩⑩ HOTEL

☎ 01896 822285
Market Square TD6 9PL
e-mail: enquiries@burtshotel.co.uk
web: www.burtshotel.co.uk
dir: A6091, 2m from A68 3m S of Earlston

Recognised by its distinctive black and white façade and colourful window boxes, in the heart of a small market town, this hotel has been under the same family ownership for almost 40 years. The genuine warmth of hospitality is notable. The smart bedrooms have been individually styled and include Wi-fi. Food is important at Burt's, and the elegant restaurant is well complemented by the range of tasty meals in the bar.

Rooms 20 ☞ **S** £65-£85; **D** £126-£143 (incl. bkfst)*
Facilities STV FTV Wi-fi Salmon fishing Shooting New Year **Conf** Class 20 Board 20 Thtr 38 Del from £100 to £140* **Parking** 40 **Notes** Closed 24-26 Dec & 2-8 Jan

MILNGAVIE　　　Map 20 NS57
East Dunbartonshire

Premier Inn Glasgow (Milngavie)

BUDGET HOTEL

☎ 0871 527 8428
103 Main St G62 6JQ
web: www.premierinn.com
dir: M8 junct 16, follow Milngavie (A879) signs. Approx. 5m. Pass Murray Park Training Ground. Left at lights. Hotel on A81 adjacent to West Highland Gate Beefeater

High quality, budget accommodation ideal for both families and business travellers. Spacious, en suite bedrooms feature tea and coffee making facilities, and Freeview TV in most hotels. Internet access and Wi-fi are available for a small fee. The adjacent family restaurant features a wide and varied menu. See also the Hotel Groups pages.

Rooms 60

MOFFAT　　　Map 21 NT00
Dumfries & Galloway

Annandale Arms Hotel

★★★ 78% ⑩ HOTEL

☎ 01683 220013
High St DG10 9HF
e-mail: reception@annandalearmshotel.co.uk
web: www.annandalearmshotel.co.uk
dir: M74 junct 15, A701. Hotel on west side of central square that forms High St

With a history dating back 250 years, this family-run hotel in the heart of Moffat provides well-appointed, modern bedrooms and bathrooms, located away from the hustle and bustle of the high street. There is a welcoming bar and restaurant serving real ales and quality food. Wi-fi and off-road parking are added benefits.

Rooms 16 (2 fmly) (5 GF) ☞ **Facilities** FTV Wi-fi ⓢ New Year **Conf** Class 40 Board 40 Thtr 60 **Parking** 20 **Notes** Closed 25-26 Dec

M

MOTHERWELL	Map 21 NS75
North Lanarkshire	

Alona Hotel

★★★★ 77% HOTEL

☎ 01698 333888
Strathclyde Country Park ML1 3RT
e-mail: gm@alonahotel.co.uk
web: www.alonahotel.co.uk
dir: M74 junct 5, hotel approx 250yds on left

Alona is a Celtic word meaning 'exquisitely beautiful'. This hotel is situated within the idyllic beauty of Strathclyde Country Park, with tranquil views over the picturesque loch and surrounding forests. There is a very contemporary feel, from the open-plan public areas to the spacious and well-appointed bedrooms. Wi-fi is available throughout. M&D's, Scotland's Family Theme Park, is just next door.

Rooms 51 (24 fmly) (17 GF) ✎ **Facilities** FTV Wi-fi ♬
Xmas New Year **Conf** Class 100 Board 76 Thtr 400
Services Lift Air con **Parking** 100 **Notes** ⊗
Civ Wed 250

Premier Inn Glasgow (Motherwell)

BUDGET HOTEL

☎ 0871 527 8430
Edinburgh Rd, Newhouse ML1 5SY
web: www.premierinn.com
dir: From S: M74 junct 5, A725 towards Coatbridge. Take A8 towards Edinburgh, exit at junct 6, follow Lanark signs. Hotel 400yds on right

High quality, budget accommodation ideal for both families and business travellers. Spacious, en suite bedrooms feature tea and coffee making facilities, and Freeview TV in most hotels. Internet access and Wi-fi are available for a small fee. The adjacent family restaurant features a wide and varied menu. See also the Hotel Groups pages.

Rooms 40

MUIR OF ORD	Map 23 NH55
Highland	

Ord House Hotel

★★ 74% ⊕ SMALL HOTEL

☎ 01463 870492
IV6 7UH
e-mail: admin@ord-house.co.uk
dir: Exit A9 at Tore rdbt onto A832. 5m, through Muir of Ord. Left towards Ullapool (A832). Hotel 0.5m on left

Dating back to 1637, this country-house hotel is situated peacefully in wooded grounds and offers brightly furnished and well-proportioned accommodation. Comfortable day rooms reflect the character and charm of the house, with inviting lounges, a cosy snug bar and an elegant dining room where wide-ranging, creative menus are offered.

Rooms 12 (3 GF) ✎ **S** £60-£75; **D** £90-£130 (incl. bkfst)* **Facilities** Wi-fi ⅃ Putt green ⛳ Clay pigeon shooting **Parking** 30 **Notes** Closed Nov-Apr

---

MUTHILL	Map 21 NN81
Perth & Kinross	

Barley Bree Restaurant with Rooms

⊛ ⊛ RESTAURANT WITH ROOMS

☎ 01764 681451
6 Willoughby St PH5 2AB
e-mail: info@barleybree.com
dir: A9 onto A822 in centre of Muthill

Situated in the heart of the small village of Muthill, and just a short drive from Crieff, genuine hospitality and quality food are obvious attractions at this charming restaurant with rooms. The stylish bedrooms are appointed to a very high standard. The restaurant has a rustic feel with exposed stonework, wooden floors and a log-burning fire in the centre. Choices range from set, carte and tasting menus. Children are welcome too.

Rooms 6 (1 fmly)

NAIRN	Map 23 NH85
Highland	

Golf View Hotel & Spa

★★★★ 73% ⊕ HOTEL

☎ 01667 452301
The Seafront IV12 4HD
e-mail: golfview@crerarhotels.com
dir: Exit A96 into Seabank Rd, hotel at end on right

This fine hotel has wonderful sea views and overlooks the Moray Firth and the Black Isle beyond. The championship golf course at Nairn is adjacent to the hotel and guests have direct access to the long sandy beaches. Bedrooms are of a very high standard and the public areas are charming. A well-equipped leisure complex and swimming pool are also available.

Rooms 42 (6 fmly) **Facilities** Spa FTV Wi-fi ⊠ supervised ⌂ Gym Sauna Steam room Xmas New Year **Conf** Class 40 Board 40 Thtr 100 **Services** Lift **Parking** 40 **Notes** Civ Wed 100

Newton Hotel

★★★★ 72% ⊕ HOTEL

☎ 01667 453144
Inverness Rd IV12 4RX
e-mail: frontdesk.newton@bespokehotels.com
web: www.bespokehotels.com
dir: A96 from Inverness to Nairn, through 3 sets of lights, at 4th right to Newton Gate

This former mansion house, set in 21 acres of mature parkland and bordering Nairn's championship golf course, was a favourite with the actor Charlie Chaplin who often visited with his family. Originally built as a family home in 1872 the hotel has been extensively refurbished over the years, including the addition of the Highland Conference Centre. Bedrooms are of a high standard, and many of the front-facing rooms have splendid sea views.

Rooms 56 (4 fmly) ✎ **S** £49-£110; **D** £60-£150 (incl. bkfst) **Facilities** STV Wi-fi ⅃ Xmas New Year **Conf** Class 220 Board 90 Thtr 450 Del from £90 to £150 **Services** Lift **Parking** 150 **Notes** LB Civ Wed 250

INSPECTORS' CHOICE

Boath House

★★★ ◉◉◉◉ HOTEL

☎ 01667 454896
Auldearn IV12 5TE
e-mail: info@boath-house.com
web: www.boath-house.com
dir: 2m past Nairn on A96, E towards Forres, signed on main road

Standing in its own 20-acre grounds, this splendid Georgian mansion was built in 1825 for the Dunbar family but there has been has been occupation on is site since the 16th century. Guests are welcome to stroll around the gardens which have an ornamental lake, walled garden and secluded seating areas to relax in. The hospitality here is first class; the owners are passionate about what they do, and have an ability to establish a special relationship with their guests that will be particularly remembered. The food is also very memorable; head chef Charlie Lockley is devotee of slow and organic cooking which also includes using foraged produce. The five-course dinners are a culinary adventure, matched only by the excellence of breakfasts. The house itself is delightful, with inviting lounges and a dining room overlooking a trout loch. The bedrooms, with lake and woodland views, are striking and very comfortable; Orangerie Rooms have their own conservatory.

Rooms 8 (1 fmly) (1 GF) ⬧ **S** £270–£330;
D £345–£450 (incl. bkfst & dinner) **Facilities** FTV Wi-fi ⬧ Fishing ⬧ Beauty salon Treatment room Xmas New Year **Conf** Class 10 Board 10 Thtr 15 Del £295 **Parking** 20 **Notes** LB Civ Wed 28

NETHY BRIDGE   Map 23 NJ02
Highland

Nethybridge Hotel

★★★ 68% HOTEL

☎ 01479 821203
PH25 3DP
e-mail: salesnethybridge@strathmorehotels.com
dir: A9 onto A95, onto B970 to Nethy Bridge

This popular tourist and coaching hotel enjoys a central location amidst the majestic Cairngorm Mountains. Bedrooms are stylishly furnished in bold tartans whilst traditionally styled day rooms include two bars and a popular snooker room. Staff are friendly and keen to please.

Rooms 69 (3 fmly) (7 GF) **S** £35–£109; **D** £70–£168 (incl. bkfst)* **Facilities** Wi-fi Putt green Bowling green Beauty therapy room ♫ Xmas New Year **Conf** Thtr 100 **Services** Lift **Parking** 80 **Notes** LB

See advert on page 501

NEW LANARK   Map 21 NS84
South Lanarkshire

New Lanark Mill Hotel

★★★ 83% HOTEL

☎ 01555 667200
Mill One, New Lanark Mills ML11 9DB
e-mail: hotel@newlanark.org
web: www.newlanark.org
dir: Signed from major roads, M74 junct 7 & M8

Originally built as a cotton mill in the 18th century, this hotel forms part of a fully restored village, now a UNESCO World Heritage Site. There's a bright modern style throughout which contrasts nicely with features from the original mill. There is a comfortable foyer-lounge with a galleried restaurant above. The hotel enjoys stunning views over the River Clyde.

Rooms 38 (5 fmly) **S** £55–£85; **D** £59–£99 (incl. bkfst) **Facilities** STV Wi-fi ⬧ Gym Beauty room Steam room Sauna Aerobics studios Xmas New Year **Conf** Class 60 Board 40 Thtr 200 Del from £99 to £129 **Services** Lift **Parking** 75 **Notes** LB ⊗ Civ Wed 120

NEWTON MEARNS   Map 20 NS55
East Renfrewshire

Premier Inn Glasgow Newton Mearns (M77 Jct 4)

BUDGET HOTEL

☎ 0871 527 9304
Greenlaw Crookfur Rd G77 6NP
web: www.premierinn.com
dir: From N exit M77 junct 4 towards Newton Mearns. At rdbt 1st left. Hotel on left

High quality, budget accommodation ideal for both families and business travellers. Spacious, en suite bedrooms feature tea and coffee making facilities, and Freeview TV in most hotels. Internet access and Wi-fi are available for a small fee. The adjacent family restaurant features a wide and varied menu. See also the Hotel Groups pages.

Rooms 60

N

N

NEWTON STEWART · Map 20 NX46
Dumfries & Galloway

INSPECTORS' CHOICE
Kirroughtree House
★★★ ◉◉ COUNTRY HOUSE HOTEL

☎ 01671 402141
Minnigaff DG8 6AN
e-mail: info@kirroughtreehouse.co.uk
web: www.kirroughtreehouse.co.uk
dir: A75 onto A712, hotel entrance 300yds on left

This imposing mansion enjoys a peaceful location in eight acres of landscaped gardens near Galloway Forest Park. It is said that Robert Burns, a friend of the Heron family who owned the house at the time, sat on the staircase and recited his poems. The inviting day-rooms comprise a choice of lounges, and two elegant dining rooms where guests can enjoy the delightful cuisine which is firmly based on top quality, locally sourced ingredients. Well-proportioned, individually styled bedrooms include some suites and mini-suites, and many rooms enjoy lovely views. The service is very friendly and attentive. Stargazing and garden breaks are available.

Rooms 17 ♞ **S** £95-£125; **D** £160-£250 (incl. bkfst)* **Facilities** FTV Wi-fi ⛳ 9-hole pitch & putt Xmas New Year **Conf** Class 20 Board 20 Thtr 30 **Services** Lift **Parking** 50 **Notes** No children 10yrs Closed 2 Jan-1 Feb

The Bruce Hotel
★★★ 73% HOTEL

☎ 01671 402294
88 Queen St DG8 6JL
e-mail: mail@the-bruce-hotel.com
web: www.the-bruce-hotel.com
dir: Exit A75 at Newton Stewart rdbt towards town. Hotel 800mtrs on right

Named after the Scottish patriot Robert the Bruce, this welcoming hotel is just a short distance from the A75. One of the well-appointed bedrooms features a four-poster bed, and popular family suites contain separate bedrooms for children. Public areas include a traditional lounge, a formal restaurant and a lounge bar, both offering a good choice of dishes.

Rooms 20 (2 fmly) **S** £50-£65; **D** £50-£80 (incl. bkfst) **Facilities** FTV Wi-fi New Year **Conf** Class 50 Board 14 Thtr 100 Del from £65 to £85 **Parking** 14 **Notes** LB

NORTH BERWICK · Map 21 NT58
East Lothian

Macdonald Marine Hotel & Spa

★★★★ 82% ◉◉ HOTEL

☎ 0844 879 9130
Cromwell Rd EH39 4LZ
e-mail: sales.marine@macdonald-hotels.co.uk
web: www.macdonaldhotels.co.uk
dir: From A198 turn into Hamilton Rd at lights then 2nd right

This imposing hotel commands stunning views across the local golf course to the Firth of Forth. Stylish public areas provide a relaxing atmosphere; creative dishes are served in the restaurant and lighter bites in the lounge/bar. Bedrooms come in a variety of sizes and styles, all are well equipped and some are impressively large. The hotel boasts extensive leisure and conference facilities. Macdonald Hotels is the AA Hotel Group of the Year 2013-14.

Rooms 83 (4 fmly) (4 GF) **Facilities** Spa STV Wi-fi ♨ supervised Putt green Gym Indoor & outdoor salt water hydro pool Xmas New Year **Conf** Class 120 Board 60 Thtr 300 **Services** Lift **Parking** 50 **Notes** Civ Wed 150

OBAN · Map 20 NM82
Argyll & Bute

BEST WESTERN The Queens Hotel

★★★★ 72% ◉ HOTEL

☎ 01631 562505 & 570230
Corran Esplanade PA34 5AG
e-mail: thequeenshoteloban@hotmail.co.uk
dir: Into Oban on A85, down hill to mini rdbt. 2nd exit towards seafront. At next rdbt follow Ganavan Sands sign. Hotel 0.4m on right just after cathedral

The refurbished Queens Hotel enjoys a wonderful location with stunning views out over Oban Bay. The bedrooms are equipped with modern extras and some bathrooms feature chromatherapy spa baths. The Glen Campa restaurant serves award-winning food. A warm welcome is always forthcoming at this hotel.

Rooms 46 (2 fmly) ♞ **S** £50-£80; **D** £70-£150 (incl. bkfst)* **Facilities** FTV Wi-fi New Year **Services** Lift **Parking** 15 **Notes** Closed 3-31 Jan Civ Wed 60

Manor House Hotel
★★★ 85% ◉ HOTEL

☎ 01631 562087
Gallanach Rd PA34 4LS
e-mail: info@manorhouseoban.com
web: www.manorhouseoban.com
dir: Follow MacBrayne Ferries signs, pass ferry entrance for hotel on right

Handy for the ferry terminal and with views of the bay and harbour, this elegant Georgian residence was built in 1780 as the dower house for the family of the Duke of Argyll. Comfortable and attractive public rooms invite relaxation, while most of the well-equipped bedrooms are furnished with period pieces.

Rooms 11 (1 GF) ♞ **Facilities** FTV Wi-fi New Year **Parking** 20 **Notes** No children 12yrs Closed 25-26 Dec Civ Wed 30

Royal Hotel

★★★ 74% HOTEL

☎ 01631 563021
Argyll Sqaure PA34 4BE
e-mail: salesroyaloban@strathmorehotels.com
dir: A82 from Glasgow towards Loch Lomond &
Crianlarich then A85 (pass Loch Awe) to Oban

Well situated in the heart of Oban, just minutes from
the ferry terminal and with all the shops on its
doorstep, this hotel really is central. The comfortable
and well-presented bedrooms differ in size, and all
public areas are smart. There is a first-floor
restaurant overlooking the town square.

Rooms 91 (5 fmly) ✎ **Facilities** FTV Wi-fi 🎵 Xmas
New Year **Conf** Class 60 Board 30 Thtr 140
Services Lift **Parking** 25 **Notes** ⊗ Civ Wed 70

See advert on page 501

Falls of Lora Hotel

THE INDEPENDENTS
HOTEL ASSOCIATION

★★★ 73% HOTEL

☎ 01631 710483
PA37 1PB
e-mail: enquiries@fallsoflora.com
web: www.fallsoflora.com

(For full entry see Connel)

The Columba Hotel

★★★ 70% HOTEL

☎ 01631 562183
The Esplanade PA34 5QD
e-mail: columba@mckeverhotels.co.uk
dir: A85 to Oban, at 1st lights turn right

One of Oban's landmarks, this Victorian hotel is
located on the seafront, with stunning views out over
the Firth of Lorne to the Isle of Mull. The well-
appointed, contemporary bedrooms offer guests
comfortable accommodation. Alba Restaurant
provides a menu of modern Scottish dishes.

Rooms 49 (5 fmly) **Facilities** FTV Wi-fi 🎵 Xmas New
Year **Services** Lift **Parking** 6 **Notes** ⊗

Meldrum House Country Hotel & Golf Course

★★★★ 83% ◉◉ COUNTRY HOUSE HOTEL

☎ 01651 872294
AB51 0AE
e-mail: enquiries@meldrumhouse.co.uk
web: www.meldrumhouse.com
dir: 11m from Aberdeen on A947 (Aberdeen to Banff
road)

Set in 350 acres of wooded parkland this imposing
baronial country mansion has a golf course as its
centrepiece. Tastefully restored to highlight its
original character it provides a peaceful retreat.
Bedrooms are massive, and like the public rooms,
transport guests back to a bygone era, but at the
same time provide stylish modern amenities
including smart bathrooms.

Rooms 24 (13 annexe) (1 fmly) (6 GF) ✎
D £130-£300 (incl. bkfst)* **Facilities** FTV Wi-fi ⚴ 18
Putt green ⛳ Xmas New Year **Conf** Class 20
Board 30 Thtr 80 Del from £175 to £199* **Parking** 70
Notes LB Civ Wed 150

Onich Hotel

★★★ 73% HOTEL

☎ 01855 821214
PH33 6RY
e-mail: enquiries@onich-fortwilliam.co.uk
web: www.onich-fortwilliam.co.uk
dir: Beside A82, 2m N of Ballachulish Bridge

Genuine hospitality is part of the appeal of this hotel,
which lies right beside Loch Linnhe with gardens
extending to its shores. Nicely presented public areas
include a choice of inviting lounges and contrasting
bars, and views of the loch can be enjoyed from the
attractive restaurant. Bedrooms, with pleasing colour
schemes, are comfortably modern.

Rooms 26 (6 fmly) **Facilities** STV Wi-fi Games room
🎵 Xmas New Year **Conf** Board 40 Thtr 150
Parking 50 **Notes** Civ Wed 120

INSPECTORS' CHOICE

The Peat Inn

◉◉◉ RESTAURANT WITH ROOMS

☎ 01334 840206
KY15 5LH
e-mail: stay@thepeatinn.co.uk
dir: At junct of B940 & B941, 5m SW of St Andrews

This 300-year-old former coaching inn enjoys a
rural location, and is close to St Andrews. The Peat
Inn is spacious, very well appointed, and offers
rooms that all have lounge areas. The inn is
steeped in history and for years has proved a real
haven for food lovers. The three dining areas create
a romantic setting, and chef/owner Geoffrey
Smeddle produces excellent, award-winning dishes.
Expect welcoming open fires and a relaxed
ambiance. An extensive continental breakfast
selection is served to guests in their bedrooms each
morning.

Rooms 8 (8 annexe) (3 fmly)

P

PEEBLES   Map 21 NT24
Scottish Borders

AA HOTEL OF THE YEAR FOR SCOTLAND

INSPECTORS' CHOICE

Cringletie House

★★★★ ◎◎◎ COUNTRY HOUSE HOTEL

☎ 01721 725750
Edinburgh Rd EH45 8PL
e-mail: enquiries@cringletie.com
web: www.cringletie.com
dir: 2m N on A703

This romantic baronial mansion, built in 1861, is set in 28 acres of beautiful gardens and woodland; there is a walled garden with a 400-year-old yew hedge (perhaps the oldest in Scotland), a waterfall, sculptures and croquet lawn. In 1971 Scottish Heritage granted the property a Grade B listing, and in the same year the house became a hotel. The delightful public rooms, with welcoming fires, include a cocktail lounge with adjoining conservatory, and there are service bells in each room which still work. The award-winning, first-floor restaurant has a magnificent hand-painted ceiling. The individually designed bedrooms have grace and charm, and for the ultimate luxury there's the Selkirk Suite. Cringletie House is the AA Hotel of the Year for Scotland 2013-2014.

Rooms 13 (2 GF) ♪ **Facilities** FTV Wi-fi ⇘ HL Putt green ⚓ Petanque Giant chess & draughts In room therapy treatments Xmas New Year **Conf** Class 20 Board 24 Thtr 45 **Services** Lift **Parking** 30 **Notes** Closed 2-27 Jan Civ Wed 60

Macdonald Cardrona Hotel, Golf & Spa

★★★★ 77% ◎ HOTEL

☎ 01896 833600 & 0844 879 9024
Cardrona EH45 8NE
e-mail:
general.cardrona@macdonald-hotels.co.uk
web: www.macdonald-hotels.co.uk/cardrona
dir: On A72 between Peebles & Innerleithen, 3m S of Peebles

The rolling hills of the Scottish Borders are a stunning backdrop for this modern, purpose-built hotel. Spacious bedrooms are traditional in style, equipped with a range of extras, and most enjoy fantastic countryside. The hotel features some impressive leisure facilities, including an 18-hole golf course, 18-metre indoor pool and state-of-the-art gym. Macdonald Hotels is the AA Hotel Group of the Year 2013-14.

Rooms 99 (24 fmly) (16 GF) **Facilities** Spa FTV Wi-fi HL ⊗ ♨ 18 Putt green Fishing Gym Sauna Steam room Xmas New Year **Conf** Class 120 Board 90 Thtr 250 **Services** Lift **Parking** 200 **Notes** Civ Wed 200

PERTH   Map 21 NO12
Perth & Kinross

Murrayshall House Hotel & Golf Course

★★★★ 76% ◎◎ HOTEL

☎ 01738 551171
New Scone PH2 7PH
e-mail: info@murrayshall.co.uk
web: www.murrayshall.co.uk
dir: From Perth take A94 (Coupar Angus), 1m from Perth, right to Murrayshall just before New Scone

This imposing country house is set in 350 acres of grounds, including two golf courses, one of which is of championship standard. Bedrooms come in two distinct styles: modern suites in a purpose-built building contrast with more classic rooms in the main building. The Clubhouse bar serves a range of meals all day, whilst more accomplished cooking can be enjoyed in the Old Masters Restaurant.

Rooms 41 (14 annexe) (17 fmly) (5 GF) ♪ S £75-£150; **D** £140-£220 (incl. bkfst)* **Facilities** STV FTV Wi-fi HL ♨ 36 ⛳ Putt green Driving range New Year **Conf** Class 60 Board 30 Thtr 150 Del from £115 to £145* **Parking** 120 **Notes** LB Civ Wed 130

Parklands Hotel

★★★★ 74% ◎◎ SMALL HOTEL

☎ 01738 622451
2 St Leonards Bank PH2 8EB
e-mail: info@theparklandshotel.com
web: www.theparklandshotel.com
dir: M90 junct 10, in 1m left at lights at end of park area, hotel on left

Parklands Hotel is ideally located close to the centre of town, with open views over the South Inch. The enthusiastic proprietors continue to invest heavily in the business and the bedrooms have a smart contemporary feel. Public areas include a choice of restaurants, with a fine dining experience offered in 63@Parklands and more informal dining at the No. 1 The Bank Bistro.

Rooms 15 (3 fmly) (4 GF) ♪ **S** £92.50-£139; **D** £119-£189 (incl. bkfst) **Facilities** STV Wi-fi ⇘ **Conf** Class 18 Board 20 Thtr 24 Del from £127.50 to £149.50 **Parking** 30 **Notes** LB Closed 26 Dec-6 Jan Civ Wed 40

Mercure Perth Hotel

★★★ HOTEL

☎ 0844 815 9105
West Mill St PH1 5QP
e-mail: info@mercureperth.co.uk
web: www.jupiterhotels.co.uk
dir: A93/A989 to city centre, left into Caledonian Rd, right at lights onto Old High St, hotel on left

This former 15th-century watermill has been converted in to a modern hotel, yet still retains the original stream, now running through reception under a glass floor. Central to Perth, the hotel is an ideal location for visiting the area or further afield. Contemporary rooms include satellite TV and free Wi-fi. The hotel has extensive conference facilities and the Arts Grill where tempting meals are served.

Rooms 76 **Conf** Board 40 Thtr 120

P

The New County Hotel

★★★ 78% ◉◉ HOTEL

☎ 01738 623355
22-30 County Place PH2 8EE
e-mail: enquiries@newcountyhotel.com
web: www.newcountyhotel.com
dir: A9 junct 11 (Perth). Follow signs for town centre. Hotel on right after library

This is a smart hotel in the heart of the beautiful garden city of Perth. The bedrooms have a modern and stylish appearance and public areas include a popular bar and contemporary lounge area. No stay here is complete without a visit to the award-winning Opus One Restaurant, which has a well deserved reputation for fine dining.

Rooms 23 (4 fmly) 🐾 **S** £40-£80; **D** £60-£120 (incl. bkfst)* **Facilities** STV FTV Wi-fi New Year **Conf** Class 80 Board 24 Thtr 120 Del from £75 to £110* **Parking** 10 **Notes** LB ⊗

BEST WESTERN Lovat Hotel

★★★ 74% HOTEL

☎ 01738 636555
90-92 Glasgow Rd PH2 0LT
e-mail: enquiry@lovat.co.uk
dir: M90 junct 10, 3rd exit, straight through next 3 rdbts, hotel on right 0.5m after 3rd rdbt

The Lovat Hotel offers a comfortable and relaxing atmosphere just a short walk from the centre of Perth. Accommodation consists of comfortable, modern bedrooms, and guests can enjoy a great dining experience in the 1747 Restaurant and Bar. Residents can also enjoy complimentary access to leisure facilities at the hotel's nearby sister property. Deluxe rooms are available for those looking to splash out on a little extra luxury.

Rooms 30 (1 fmly) (10 GF) 🐾 **S** £45-£79; **D** £60-£92 (incl. bkfst)* **Facilities** FTV Wi-fi ⌂ Xmas New Year **Conf** Class 60 Board 30 Thtr 150 Del from £90 to £120* **Parking** 30 **Notes** ⊗ Civ Wed 150

BEST WESTERN Queens Hotel

★★★ 74% HOTEL

☎ 01738 442222
Leonard St PH2 8HB
e-mail: enquiry@queensperth.co.uk
dir: From M90 follow to 2nd lights, turn left. Hotel on right, opposite railway station

This popular hotel benefits from a central location close to both the bus and rail stations. Bedrooms vary in size and style with top floor rooms offering extra space and excellent views of the town. Public rooms include a smart leisure centre and versatile conference space. A range of meals is served in both the bar and restaurant.

Rooms 50 (4 fmly) **S** £75; **D** £110 (incl. bkfst)* **Facilities** STV FTV Wi-fi ⊙ Gym Steam room Xmas New Year **Conf** Class 70 Board 50 Thtr 200 **Services** Lift **Parking** 50 **Notes** LB ⊗ Civ Wed 220

Salutation Hotel

★★★ 71% HOTEL

☎ 01738 630066
South St PH2 8PH
e-mail: salessalutation@strathmorehotels.com
dir: At end of South St on right before River Tay

Situated at the heart of Perth, the Salutation is reputed to be one of the oldest hotels in Scotland and has been welcoming guests through its doors since 1699. It offers traditional hospitality with all the modern comforts. Bedrooms vary in size and are thoughtfully equipped. An extensive menu is available in the Adam Restaurant, with its impressive barrel-vaulted ceiling and original features.

Rooms 84 (5 fmly) 🐾 **S** £37-£89; **D** £58-£140 (incl. bkfst) **Facilities** Wi-fi ♫ Xmas New Year **Conf** Class 180 Board 60 Thtr 300 Del from £99 to £125 **Services** Lift **Notes** LB Civ Wed 100

See advert on page 501

PETERHEAD
Aberdeenshire
Map 23 NK14

Buchan Braes Hotel

★★★★ 75% ◉ HOTEL

☎ 01779 871471
Boddam AB42 3AR
e-mail: info@buchanbraes.co.uk
dir: From Aberdeen take A90, follow Peterhead signs. 1st right in Stirling signed Boddam. 50mtrs, 1st right

A contemporary hotel located in Boddam that is an excellent base for exploring the attractions of this wonderful part of Scotland. There is an open-plan lounge for drinks and snacks and the Grill Room with an open kitchen that offers a weekly changing, seasonal menu of locally sourced produce. All the bedrooms, including three suites, have 32" flat-screen TVs with satellite channels, king-sized beds and free Wi-Fi.

Rooms 47 (1 fmly) (26 GF) 🐾 **D** £85-£95 (incl. bkfst)* **Facilities** Wi-fi Xmas New Year **Conf** Class 100 Board 130 Thtr 250 Del £145* **Services** Lift **Parking** 40 **Notes** LB ⊗ Civ Wed 220

Palace Hotel

★★★ 80% HOTEL

☎ 01779 474821
Prince St AB42 1PL
e-mail: info@palacehotel.co.uk
web: www.palacehotel.co.uk
dir: A90 from Aberdeen, follow signs to Peterhead, on entering town turn into Prince St, then right into main car park

This town centre hotel is popular with business travellers and for social events. Bedrooms come in two styles, with the executive rooms being particularly smart and spacious. Public areas include a themed bar, an informal diner reached via a spiral staircase, and a brasserie restaurant and cocktail bar.

Rooms 64 (1 fmly) (14 GF) 🐾 **S** fr £60; **D** fr £70 (incl. bkfst)* **Facilities** STV FTV Wi-fi ♪ Snooker & pool table ♫ New Year **Conf** Class 100 Board 60 Thtr 250 **Services** Lift **Parking** 50 **Notes** Civ Wed 250

P

See also **Kinloch Rannoch**

Green Park Hotel

★★★★ 76% ◉ COUNTRY HOUSE HOTEL

☎ 01796 473248
Clunie Bridge Rd PH16 5JY
e-mail: bookings@thegreenpark.co.uk
web: www.thegreenpark.co.uk
dir: Exit A9 at Pitlochry, follow signs 0.25m through town

Guests return year after year to this lovely hotel, situated in a stunning setting on the shores of Loch Faskally. Most of the thoughtfully designed bedrooms, including a splendid wing, the restaurant and the comfortable lounges, enjoy these views. Dinner utilises fresh produce, much of it grown in the kitchen garden.

Rooms 51 (3 fmly) (16 GF) 🐾 **S** £73-£108;
D £146-£216 (incl. bkfst & dinner)* **Facilities** FTV
Wi-fi Putt green New Year **Services** Lift **Parking** 51
Notes LB

Knockendarroch House Hotel

★★★★ 74% ◉ SMALL HOTEL

☎ 01796 473473
Higher Oakfield PH16 5HT
e-mail: bookings@knockendarroch.co.uk
dir: Just off A9

This secluded hotel has outstanding views over the town and surrounding hills. The individually styled bedrooms are spacious and very well appointed - all have plasma TVs. The traditional, country-style public rooms have large sofas, welcoming open fires and an excellent whisky cabinet. Dinner is served every evening in the award-winning restaurant with only the best of Scottish produce being used. The staff are friendly and attentive.

Rooms 12 (1 GF) 🐾 **Facilities** FTV Wi-fi **Parking** 12
Notes No children 10yrs Closed Dec-Jan

Dundarach Hotel

★★★ 78% HOTEL

☎ 01796 472862
Perth Rd PH16 5DJ
e-mail: inbox@dundarach.co.uk
web: www.dundarach.co.uk
dir: S of town centre on main road

This welcoming, family-run hotel stands in mature grounds at the south end of town. Bedrooms come in a variety of styles, including a block of large purpose-built rooms that will appeal to business guests. Well-proportioned public areas feature inviting lounges and a conservatory restaurant giving fine views of the Tummel Valley.

Rooms 39 (19 annexe) (7 fmly) (12 GF) 🐾
Facilities FTV Wi-fi **Conf** Class 40 Board 40 Thtr 60
Parking 39 **Notes** ⊗ Closed Jan RS Dec & early Feb

The Plockton Hotel

★★★ 74% SMALL HOTEL

☎ 01599 544274
41 Harbour St IV52 8TN
e-mail: info@plocktonhotel.co.uk
web: www.plocktonhotel.co.uk
dir: A87 towards Kyle of Lochalsh. At Balmacara follow Plockton signs, 7m

This very popular hotel occupies an idyllic position on the waterfront of Loch Carron. Stylish bedrooms offer individual, pleasing decor and many have spacious balconies or panoramic views. There is a choice of three dining areas and seafood is very much a speciality. The staff and owners provide a relaxed and informal style of attentive service. A self-contained cottage is available for group bookings.

The Plockton Hotel

Rooms 15 (4 annexe) (1 fmly) (1 GF) 🐾 **Facilities** STV
Wi-fi ⚲ Pool table 🎵 New Year **Notes** ⊗ Closed
25 Dec & 1 Jan

Macdonald Inchyra Hotel and Spa

MACDONALD
HOTELS & RESORTS

★★★★ 75% HOTEL

☎ 01324 711911
Grange Rd FK2 0YB
e-mail: inchyra@macdonald-hotels.co.uk
web: www.macdonaldhotels.co.uk
dir: 2mins from M9 junct 5

Ideally placed for the M9 and Grangemouth terminal, this former manor house has been tastefully extended. The hotel provides comprehensive conference facilities and guests will find that The Scottish Steak Club serves the highest quality produce in a contemporary style. The bedrooms are comfortable and most are spacious. Macdonald Hotels is the AA Hotel Group of the Year 2013-14.

Rooms 98 (6 annexe) (35 fmly) (33 GF) **S** £87-£255;
D £97-£265 **Facilities** Spa FTV Wi-fi 🕓 ⚒ Gym
Steam room Sauna Aromatherapy shower Ice fountain
New Year **Conf** Class 300 Board 80 Thtr 750
Del from £135 to £175 **Services** Lift **Parking** 500
Notes LB ⊗ Civ Wed 450

Premier Inn Falkirk East

Premier Inn

BUDGET HOTEL

☎ 0871 527 8392
Beancross Rd FK2 0YS
web: www.premierinn.com
dir: M9 junct 5, Polmont A9 signs. Hotel on left

High quality, budget accommodation ideal for both families and business travellers. Spacious, en suite bedrooms feature tea and coffee making facilities, and Freeview TV in most hotels. Internet access and Wi-fi are available for a small fee. The adjacent family restaurant features a wide and varied menu. See also the Hotel Groups pages.

Rooms 40

Save on hotels. Book at **theAA.com/hotel**

PIT – PRE 543 SCOTLAND

PORT APPIN — Map 20 NM94
Argyll & Bute

INSPECTORS' CHOICE

Airds Hotel
★★★★ ◎◎◎ SMALL HOTEL

☎ 01631 730236
PA38 4DF
e-mail: airds@airds-hotel.com
web: www.airds-hotel.com
dir: From A828 (Oban to Fort William road), turn at Appin signed Port Appin. Hotel 2.5m on left

The views are stunning from this small, luxury hotel on the shores of Loch Linnhe and where the staff are delightful and nothing is too much trouble. The well-equipped bedrooms provide style and luxury whilst many bathrooms are furnished in marble and have power showers. Expertly prepared dishes, utilising the finest of ingredients, are served in the elegant dining room. Comfortable lounges with deep sofas and roaring fires provide the ideal retreat for relaxation. A real get-away-from-it-all experience.

Rooms 11 (3 fmly) (2 GF) ↟ **Facilities** STV FTV
Wi-fi ↳ Putt green ⛳ Xmas New Year
Conf Class 16 Board 16 Thtr 16 **Parking** 20
Notes LB RS Nov-Jan Civ Wed 40

The Pierhouse Hotel
★★★ 82% ◎ SMALL HOTEL

☎ 01631 730302 & 730622
PA38 4DE
e-mail: reservations@pierhousehotel.co.uk
web: www.pierhousehotel.co.uk
dir: A828 from Ballachulish to Oban. In Appin right at Port Appin & Lismore ferry sign. After 2.5m left after post office, hotel at end of road

Originally the residence of the Pier Master, with parts of the building dating back to the 19th century, this hotel is located on the shores of Loch Linnhe with picture-postcard views to the islands of Lismore and Mull. The beautifully appointed, individually designed bedrooms have Wi-fi access and include Arran Aromatics toiletries. The hotel has a Finnish sauna,

and also offers a range of treatments. Babysitting can be arranged.

Rooms 12 (2 fmly) (6 GF) ↟ **Facilities** FTV Wi-fi ↳
Aromatherapy Massage Sauna New Year
Conf Class 20 Board 20 Thtr 20 **Parking** 20
Notes Closed 25-26 Dec Civ Wed 80

PORTPATRICK — Map 20 NW95
Dumfries & Galloway

INSPECTORS' CHOICE

Knockinaam Lodge
★★★ ◎◎◎ HOTEL

☎ 01776 810471
DG9 9AD
e-mail: reservations@knockinaamlodge.com
web: www.knockinaamlodge.com
dir: From A77 or A75 follow signs to Portpatrick. Through Lochans. After 2m left at signs for hotel

Any tour of Dumfries and Galloway wouldn't be complete without a stay at this haven of tranquillity and relaxation. Knockinaam Lodge is an extended Victorian house set in an idyllic cove with its own pebble beach (ideal for a private swim in the summer) and sheltered by majestic cliffs and woodlands. Surrounded by 30 acres of delightful grounds, the lodge was the location for a meeting between Churchill and General Eisenhower in World War II. Today, a warm welcome is assured from the proprietors and their committed team, and much emphasis is placed on providing a sophisticated but intimate home-from-home experience. There are just ten suites - each individually designed and all with flat-screen TVs with DVD players, luxury toiletries and complimentary bottled water. The cooking is a real treat and showcases prime Scottish produce on the daily-changing, four-course set menus; guests can always discuss the choices in advance if they wish.

Rooms 10 (1 fmly) ↟ **S** £175-£340; **D** £285-£440
(incl. bkfst & dinner)* **Facilities** FTV Fishing
⛳ Shooting Walking Sea fishing Clay pigeon
shooting Xmas New Year **Conf** Class 10 Board 16
Thtr 30 **Parking** 20 **Notes** LB Civ Wed 40

POWFOOT — Map 21 NY16
Dumfries & Galloway

Powfoot Golf Hotel
★★★ 75% HOTEL

☎ 01461 700254 & 207580
Links Av DG12 5PN
e-mail: reception@thepowfootgolfhotel.co.uk
dir: A75 onto B721, through Annan. B724, approx 3m, left onto unclassified road

This hotel has well presented and comfortable modern bedrooms, many of which overlook the championship golf course. Public areas have panoramic views onto the Solway Firth and the Lakeland hills beyond. The service is friendly and relaxed, and quality food is served in a choice of locations.

Rooms 24 (9 fmly) (5 GF) ↟ **Facilities** FTV Wi-fi Xmas
New Year **Conf** Class 80 Board 80 Thtr 80 **Parking** 30
Notes ⊗ Civ Wed 100

PRESTWICK — Map 20 NS32
South Ayrshire

Parkstone Hotel
★★★ 77% HOTEL

☎ 01292 477286
Esplanade KA9 1QN
e-mail: info@parkstonehotel.co.uk
web: www.parkstonehotel.co.uk
dir: From Main St (A79) W to seafront, hotel in 600yds

Situated on the seafront in a quiet residential area only one mile from Prestwick Airport, this family-run hotel caters for business visitors as well as golfers. Bedrooms come in a variety of sizes; all are furnished in a smart, contemporary style. The attractive, modern look of the bar and restaurant is matched by an equally up-to-date menu.

Rooms 30 (2 fmly) (7 GF) ↟ **S** £59-£79; **D** £88-£98
(incl. bkfst) **Facilities** FTV Wi-fi Xmas New Year
Conf Thtr 100 **Parking** 34 **Notes** LB ⊗ Civ Wed 100

P

Hotels listed under Glasgow Airport

RHU
Argyll & Bute   Map 20 NS28

Rosslea Hall Hotel

★★★ 77% @ HOTEL

☎ 01436 439955
Ferry Rd G84 8NF
web: www.rossleahallhotel.co.uk
dir: On A814, opposite church

Overlooking the Firth of the Clyde and close to
Helensburgh, this imposing mansion is set in its own
well tended gardens. Bedrooms and bathrooms are of
a good size, are well appointed and cater well for the
modern traveller. The eating options include the
Conservatory Restaurant which offers dishes cooked
with imagination and flair, and overlooks the grounds
and the Clyde. The hotel is a popular wedding venue.

Rooms 30 (3 fmly) (2 GF) **Facilities** FTV Wi-fi Xmas
New Year **Conf** Class 60 Board 80 Thtr 150
Del from £110 to £148* **Parking** 30 **Notes** ⊗
Civ Wed 110

ROY BRIDGE   Map 22 NN28
Highland

BEST WESTERN Glenspean Lodge Hotel

★★★★ 73% SMALL HOTEL

☎ 01397 712223
PH31 4AW
e-mail: reservations@glenspeanlodge.co.uk
web: www.glenspeanlodge.com
dir: 2m E of Roy Bridge, exit A82 at Spean Bridge onto
A86

With origins as a hunting lodge dating back to the
Victorian era, this hotel sits in gardens in an elevated
position in the Spean Valley. Accommodation is
provided in well laid-out bedrooms, some suitable for
families. Inviting public areas include a comfortable
lounge bar and a restaurant that enjoys stunning
views of the valley.

Rooms 17 (4 fmly) **Facilities** Wi-fi Gym Sauna Xmas
New Year **Conf** Class 16 **Parking** 60 **Notes** Civ Wed 60

The Stronlossit Inn

★★★ 74% SMALL HOTEL

☎ 01397 712253
PH31 4AG
e-mail: stay@stronlossit.co.uk
web: www.stronlossit.co.uk
dir: Exit A82 at Spean Bridge onto A86, signed Roy
Bridge. Hotel on left

Appointed to modern standards with the character
and hospitality of a traditional hostelry, The
Stronlossit Inn is quite a draw for the discerning
Highland tourist. The spacious bar is the focal point,
with a peat burning fire providing a warm welcome in
cooler months; guests can eat in the attractive
restaurant. Bedrooms come in a mix of sizes and
styles, most being smartly modern and well equipped.

Rooms 10 (5 GF) **D** £86-£101 (incl. bkfst)
Facilities Wi-fi ⋈ **Conf** Class 12 Board 10 Thtr 20
Del from £100 to £125 **Parking** 30 **Notes** LB ⊗ No
children 17yrs Closed 1-15 Dec

ST ANDREWS   Map 21 NO51
Fife

The Old Course Hotel, Golf Resort & Spa

★★★★★ @@@ HOTEL

☎ 01334 474371
KY16 9SP
e-mail: reservations@oldcoursehotel.co.uk
dir: M90 junct 8, A91 to St Andrews

A haven for golfers, this internationally renowned
hotel sits adjacent to the 17th hole of the
championship course. Bedrooms vary in size and
style but all provide decadent levels of luxury. Day
rooms include intimate lounges, a bright
conservatory, a spa and a range of pro golf shops.
The fine dining Road Hole Restaurant, the Sands
Grill specialising in seafood and steaks, and the
informal Jigger Inn are all popular eating venues.
Staff throughout are friendly and services are
impeccably delivered.

Rooms 144 (5 fmly) (3 GF) **S** £215-£380;
D £245-£410 (incl. bkfst)* **Facilities** Spa STV FTV
Wi-fi ⋈ ⊗ ♨ 18 Putt green Gym Thermal suite 🎵
Xmas New Year **Conf** Class 473 Board 259 Thtr 950
Del from £249 to £495* **Services** Lift **Parking** 125
Notes LB ⊗ Civ Wed 180

Fairmont St Andrews, Scotland

★★★★★ 84% @@ HOTEL

☎ 01334 837000
KY16 8PN
e-mail: standrews.scotland@fairmont.com
dir: Approx 2m from St Andrews on A917 towards
Crail

Sitting just a few miles from St Andrews, overlooking
the rugged Fife coastline and the championship golf
courses, The Fairmont is situated on a 520-acre
estate. There are spacious bedrooms and bathrooms.
The eating options are The Squire for brasserie-style
food, Esperante for Mediterranean dishes, and The
Clubhouse and The Atrium with all-day menus. The

R

hotel has an impressive spa and health club. Good standards of service are found throughout.

Rooms 209 (209 fmly) (68 GF) 🐾 **Facilities** Spa STV FTV Wi-fi ⊗ ⊗ ♨ 36 Putt green Gym 106-seat cinema Nail salon Xmas New Year **Conf** Class 450 Board 168 Thtr 500 **Services** Lift Air con **Parking** 150 **Notes** Civ Wed 350

INSPECTORS' CHOICE

Rufflets Country House

★★★★ ◉◉ HOTEL

☎ 01334 472594
Strathkinness Low Rd KY16 9TX
e-mail: reservations@rufflets.co.uk
web: www.rufflets.co.uk
dir: 1.5m W on B939

Built in 1924 for a Dundee jute baron, this charming property is set in extensive gardens a few minutes' drive from the town centre. The stylish, spacious bedrooms are individually decorated, and include the Gilroy Suite, The Orchard Suite (separate from the main building), and Turret Rooms that have their own seating areas. Public rooms include a well-stocked bar, a choice of inviting lounges and the delightful Terrace Restaurant that serves imaginative, carefully prepared cuisine based on seasonal produce. Impressive conference and banqueting facilities are available in the adjacent Garden Suite. Families are very welcome, and the hotel is a popular wedding venue.

Rooms 24 (5 annexe) (2 fmly) (5 GF) 🐾
S £120-£240; **D** £130-£280 (incl. bkfst)*
Facilities STV FTV Wi-fi ⊗ Putt green ⛳ Golf driving net Children's outdoor games New Year **Conf** Class 60 Board 60 Thtr 200 Del from £150 to £250* **Parking** 50 **Notes** LB Civ Wed 130

Macdonald Rusacks Hotel

MACDONALD HOTELS & RESORTS

★★★★ 75% ◉◉◉ HOTEL

☎ 0844 879 9136 & 01334 474321
Pilmour Links KY16 9JQ
e-mail: general.rusacks@macdonald-hotels.co.uk
web: www.macdonald-hotels.co.uk
dir: From A91 W, straight on at rdbt into St Andrews. Hotel 220yds on left

This long-established hotel enjoys an almost unrivalled location with superb views across the famous golf course. Bedrooms, though varying in size, are comfortably appointed and well equipped. Classically styled public rooms include an elegant reception lounge and a modern restaurant and brasserie bar. Macdonald Hotels is the AA Hotel Group of the Year 2013-14.

Rooms 70 (1 annexe) 🐾 **S** £89-£590; **D** £99-£610 (incl. bkfst)* **Facilities** STV FTV Wi-fi New Year **Conf** Class 35 Board 20 Thtr 80 Del from £125 to £425* **Services** Lift **Parking** 21 **Notes** LB Civ Wed 60

BEST WESTERN Scores Hotel

Best Western

★★★ 81% HOTEL

☎ 01334 472451
76 The Scores KY16 9BB
e-mail: reception@scoreshotel.co.uk
web: www.bw-scoreshotel.co.uk
dir: M90 junct 2a, A92 E. Follow Glenrothes signs then St Andrews signs. Straight on at next 2 rdbts, left into Golf Place, right into The Scores

Enjoying views over St Andrews Bay, this well-presented hotel is situated only a short pitch from the first tee of the famous Old Course. Bedrooms are impressively furnished and come in various sizes; many are quite spacious. Smart public areas include Champions Grill, offering food all day from breakfast to dinner; Scottish High Teas are served here from 4.30-6.30pm. Alexander's Restaurant opens Thursday, Friday and Saturday evenings.

Rooms 36 (1 fmly) 🐾 **S** £94-£219; **D** £140-£350 (incl. bkfst) **Facilities** FTV Wi-fi HL Xmas New Year **Conf** Class 60 Board 40 Thtr 180 Del from £144 to £203 **Services** Lift **Parking** 12 **Notes** LB ⊗ Civ Wed 100

Russell Hotel

★★ 82% ◉ HOTEL

☎ 01334 473447
26 The Scores KY16 9AS
e-mail: russellhotel@talk21.com
web: www.russellhotelstandrews.co.uk
dir: From A91 left at 2nd rdbt into Golf Place, right in 200yds into The Scores, hotel in 300yds on left

Lying on the east bay, this friendly, family-run Victorian terrace hotel provides well appointed bedrooms in varying sizes; some enjoy fine sea views. Cosy public areas include a popular bar and an intimate restaurant, both offering a good range of freshly prepared dishes. Situated in St Andrews, said to be 'The Home of Golf', this hotel offers a comprehensive range of golfing breaks, and is convenient for visits to the castle, cathedral and university.

Rooms 10 (3 fmly) **Facilities** New Year **Notes** ⊗

S

ST BOSWELLS   Map 21 NT53
Scottish Borders

Dryburgh Abbey Hotel

★★★★ 73% ◎◎ COUNTRY HOUSE HOTEL

☎ 01835 822261
TD6 0RQ
e-mail: enquiries@dryburgh.co.uk
web: www.dryburgh.co.uk
dir: Exit A68 at St Boswells. B6356 signed Scott's
View & Earlston. Through Clintmains, 1.8m to hotel

This country house hotel, found in the heart of the
Scottish Borders, and sitting beside the ancient ruins
of Dryburgh Abbey and the majestic River Tweed,
dates from the mid-19th century, and offers
comfortable public areas and an array of bedrooms
and suites, each still displaying original features. The
award-winning Tweed Restaurant, overlooking the
river, showcases the chef's dedication to producing
modern Scottish cuisine, and The Abbey Bistro offers
food from noon until 9pm.

Rooms 38 (31 fmly) (8 GF) ✚ **S** £50-£210;
D £90-£320 (incl. bkfst)* **Facilities** FTV Wi-fi ↕ ☜
Putt green Fishing ☝ Sauna Xmas New Year
Conf Class 80 Board 60 Thtr 150 **Services** Lift
Parking 70 **Notes** Civ Wed 120

ST FILLANS   Map 20 NN62
Perth & Kinross

The Four Seasons Hotel

★★★ 85% ◎◎ HOTEL

☎ 01764 685333
Loch Earn PH6 2NF
e-mail: info@thefourseasonshotel.co.uk
web: www.thefourseasonshotel.co.uk
dir: On A85, towards W of village

Set on the edge of Loch Earn, this welcoming hotel
and many of its bedrooms benefit from fine views.
There is a choice of lounges, including a library,
warmed by log fires during winter. Local produce is
used to good effect in both the Meall Reamhar
restaurant and the more informal Tarken Room.

Rooms 18 (6 annexe) (7 fmly) ✚ **S** £54-£97;
D £108-£166 (incl. bkfst) **Facilities** FTV Wi-fi Xmas

New Year **Conf** Class 45 Board 38 Thtr 95
Del from £115.50 to £154.50* **Parking** 40 **Notes** LB
Closed 2 Jan-mid Feb RS Nov, Dec, Mar Civ Wed 80

SANQUHAR   Map 21 NS70
Dumfries & Galloway

Blackaddie House Hotel

★★★ 78% ◎◎ COUNTRY HOUSE HOTEL

☎ 01659 50270
Blackaddie Rd DG4 6JJ
e-mail: ian@blackaddiehotel.co.uk
dir: Exit A76 just N of Sanquhar at Burnside Service
Station. Take private road to hotel 300mtrs on right

Overlooking the River Nith and in two acres of
secluded gardens, this family run country house hotel
offers friendly and attentive hands-on service. The
bedrooms and suites, including family
accommodation, are all well presented and
comfortable with many useful extras provided as
standard. The award-winning food, served in the
restaurant, with its lovely garden views, is based on
prime Scottish ingredients.

Rooms 9 (3 annexe) (2 fmly) (3 GF) ✚ **S** £70-£75;
D £110-£190 (incl. bkfst)* **Facilities** FTV Wi-fi Xmas
New Year **Conf** Class 12 Board 16 Thtr 20 **Parking** 20
Notes LB Civ Wed 24

SCOURIE   Map 22 NC14
Highland

Scourie Hotel

★★★ 72% SMALL HOTEL

☎ 01971 502396
IV27 4SX
e-mail: patrick@scourie-hotel.co.uk
dir: N'bound on A894. Hotel in village on left

This well-established hotel is an angler's paradise
with extensive fishing rights available on a 25,000-
acre estate. Public areas include a choice of
comfortable lounges, a cosy bar and a smart dining
room offering wholesome fare. The bedrooms are
comfortable and generally spacious. The resident
proprietors and their staff create a relaxed and
friendly atmosphere.

Rooms 20 (2 annexe) (2 fmly) (5 GF) ✚ **S** £74-£85;
D £138-£158 (incl. bkfst & dinner)* **Facilities** Wi-fi
Fishing **Parking** 30 **Notes** LB Closed mid Oct-end Mar

SELKIRK   Map 21 NT42
Scottish Borders

BEST WESTERN Philipburn
Country House Hotel

★★★★ Ⓐ COUNTRY HOUSE HOTEL

☎ 01750 20747
Linglie Rd TD7 5LS
e-mail: info@philipburnhousehotel.co.uk
dir: From A7 follow signs for A72 & A707/Peebles &
Moffat. Hotel 1m from town centre

Ideally located in a tranquil setting on the outskirts of
Selkirk, this hotel dates back to 1751 and is
surrounded by gardens and woodland. Bedrooms are
individually designed and tastefully appointed to high
standards; some feature jacuzzi baths, and some
have a mezzanine floor and balcony dividing the
lounge from the sleeping area.

Rooms 14 (2 annexe) (2 fmly) ✚ **S** £95-£155;
D £125-£185 (incl. bkfst)* **Facilities** FTV Wi-fi ↕ ☝
Xmas New Year **Conf** Class 12 Board 24 Thtr 40
Del from £138 to £148 **Parking** 55 **Notes** LB ⊗
Closed 3-20 Jan Civ Wed 85

SHIEL BRIDGE   Map 22 NG91
Highland

Grants at Craigellachie

◎ RESTAURANT WITH ROOMS

☎ 01599 511331
Craigellachie, Ratagan IV40 8HP
e-mail: info@housebytheloch.co.uk
dir: From A87 exit for Glenelg, 1st right to Ratagan,
opposite Youth Hostel sign

Sitting on the tranquil shores of Loch Duich and
overlooked by the Five Sisters Mountains, Grants
really does occupy a stunning location. The restaurant
has a well deserved reputation for its cuisine, and the
bedrooms are stylish and have all the creature
comforts. Guests are guaranteed a warm welcome at
this charming house.

Rooms 4 (2 annexe)

Save on hotels. Book at **theAA.com/hotel**

ST – STI 547 SCOTLAND

INSPECTORS' CHOICE

Tigh an Eilean

★ ◉◉ HOTEL

☎ 01520 755251
IV54 8XN
e-mail: tighaneilean@keme.co.uk
dir: Exit A896 into Shieldaig, hotel in village centre

A splendid location by the sea, with views over the bay, is the icing on the cake for this delightful small hotel. It can be a long drive to reach Sheildaig, but guests remark that the journey is more than worth the effort. The brightly decorated bedrooms are comfortable though don't expect television, except in one of the lounges. For many, it's the food that attracts, with fish and seafood featuring strongly.

Rooms 11 (1 fmly) **Facilities** Wi-fi ↘ Birdwatching Kayaks Astronomical telescope Xmas New Year **Parking** 15 **Notes** RS late Oct-mid Mar

Premier Inn Edinburgh (Newcraighall)

BUDGET HOTEL

☎ 0871 527 8362
91 Newcraighall Rd, Newcraighall EH21 8RX
web: www.premierinn.com
dir: At junct of A1 & A6095 towards Musselburgh

High quality, budget accommodation ideal for both families and business travellers. Spacious, en suite bedrooms feature tea and coffee making facilities, and Freeview TV in most hotels. Internet access and Wi-fi are available for a small fee. The adjacent family restaurant features a wide and varied menu. See also the Hotel Groups pages.

Rooms 42

Premier Inn Edinburgh (South Queensferry)

BUDGET HOTEL

☎ 0871 527 8364
Builyeon Rd EH30 9YJ
web: www.premierinn.com
dir: M8 junct 2 follow M9 Stirling signs, exit at junct 1a take A8000 towards Forth Road Bridge, at 3rd rdbt 2nd exit into Builyeon Rd (NB do not go onto Forth Road Bridge)

Rooms 70

Smiddy House

◉◉ RESTAURANT WITH ROOMS

☎ 01397 712335
Roy Bridge Rd PH34 4EU
e-mail: enquiry@smiddyhouse.com
web: www.smiddyhouse.com
dir: In village centre, A82 onto A86

Set in the Great Glen which stretches from Fort William to Inverness, this was once the village smithy, and is now a very friendly establishment. The attractive bedrooms, named after places in Scotland, are comfortably furnished and well equipped. A relaxing garden room is available for guest use. Delicious evening meals are served in Russell's restaurant.

Rooms 4 (1 fmly)

Premier Inn Glasgow North East (Stepps)

BUDGET HOTEL

☎ 0871 527 8452
Crowwood Roundabout, Cumbernauld Rd G33 6HN
web: www.premierinn.com
dir: M8 junct 12, A80 (becomes dual carriageway) to Crowwood rdbt, 4th exit back onto A80, hotel 1st left. Or exit M80 at Crowwood rdbt, 3rd exit signed A80 West. Hotel 1st left

High quality, budget accommodation ideal for both families and business travellers. Spacious, en suite bedrooms feature tea and coffee making facilities, and Freeview TV in most hotels. Internet access and Wi-fi are available for a small fee. The adjacent family restaurant features a wide and varied menu. See also the Hotel Groups pages.

Rooms 80

The Stirling Highland Hotel

PUMA HOTELS
COLLECTION

★★★★ 75% ◉ HOTEL

☎ 01786 272727
Spittal St FK8 1DU
e-mail: stirling@pumahotels.co.uk
web: www.pumahotels.co.uk
dir: A84 into Stirling. Follow Stirling Castle signs to Albert Hall. Left, left again, follow Castle signs

Enjoying a location close to the castle and historic town, this atmospheric hotel was previously a high school. Public rooms have been converted from the original classrooms and retain many interesting features. Bedrooms are more modern in style and comfortably equipped. Scholars Restaurant serves traditional and international dishes, and the Headmaster's Study is the ideal venue for enjoying a drink.

Rooms 96 (4 fmly) **Facilities** Spa STV Wi-fi ⊛ supervised Gym Squash Steam room Dance studio Beauty therapist Xmas New Year **Conf** Class 80 Board 60 Thtr 100 **Services** Lift **Parking** 96 **Notes** Civ Wed 100

Premier Inn Stirling

BUDGET HOTEL

☎ 0871 527 9038
Glasgow Rd, Whins of Milton FK7 8EX
web: www.premierinn.com
dir: On A872, 0.25m from M9/M80 junct 9

High quality, budget accommodation ideal for both families and business travellers. Spacious, en suite bedrooms feature tea and coffee making facilities, and Freeview TV in most hotels. Internet access and Wi-fi are available for a small fee. The adjacent family restaurant features a wide and varied menu. See also the Hotel Groups pages.

Rooms 60

S

STRACHUR
Map 20 NN00
Argyll & Bute

The Creggans Inn
★★★ 80% ◉◉ HOTEL

☎ 01369 860279
PA27 8BX
e-mail: info@creggans-inn.co.uk
web: www.creggans-inn.co.uk
dir: A82 from Glasgow, at Tarbet take A83 towards
Cairndow, left onto A815 to Strachur

Benefiting from a superb location on the shores of
Loch Fyne, this well established family-run hotel
caters well for both the leisure and corporate market.
Many of the bedrooms are generous in size and enjoy
wonderful views of the loch. During the cooler months
open log fires are lit in the bar lounge and restaurant.
Wi-fi is available throughout.

Rooms 14 (2 fmly) ⚑ **Facilities** FTV Wi-fi New Year
Parking 16 **Notes** Civ Wed 80

STRANRAER
Map 20 NX06
Dumfries & Galloway

Corsewall Lighthouse Hotel
★★★ 80% ◉ HOTEL

☎ 01776 853220
Corsewall Point, Kirkcolm DG9 0QG
e-mail: lighthousehotel@btinternet.com
web: www.lighthousehotel.co.uk
dir: A718 from Stranraer to Kirkcolm (approx 8m).
Follow hotel signs for 4m

Looking for something completely different? This is a
unique hotel converted from buildings that adjoin a
Grade A listed, 19th-century lighthouse set on a rocky
coastline. Situated on the headland to the west of
Loch Ryan, the lighthouse beam still functions to
warn approaching ships. Bedrooms come in a variety
of sizes, some reached by a spiral staircase, and like
the public areas, are cosy and atmospheric. The
cottage suites in the grounds offer greater space. The
restaurant menus are based on Scottish produce such
as venison and salmon.

Rooms 11 (5 annexe) (4 fmly) (2 GF) (3 smoking) ⚑
S £140-£160; **D** £160-£270 (incl. bkfst & dinner)*
Facilities FTV Wi-fi Xmas New Year **Conf** Thtr 20
Parking 20 **Notes** LB ⊗ Civ Wed 28

STRATHAVEN
Map 20 NS74
South Lanarkshire

Rissons at Springvale
◉ RESTAURANT WITH ROOMS

☎ 01357 521131 & 520234
18 Lethame Rd ML10 6AD
e-mail: info@rissons.co.uk
dir: A71 into Strathaven, W of town centre off
Townhead St

Guests are assured of a warm welcome at this
charming establishment close to the town centre. The
bedrooms and bathrooms are stylish and well
equipped. The main attraction here is the food - a
range of interesting, well-prepared dishes served in
Rissons Restaurant.

Rooms 9 (1 fmly)

STRATHBLANE
Map 20 NS57
Stirling

Strathblane Country House
★★★ 78% COUNTRY HOUSE HOTEL

☎ 01360 770491
Milngavie Rd G63 9EH
e-mail: info@strathblanecountryhouse.co.uk
dir: On A81 (Milngavie Rd) S of Strathblane. Hotel
0.75m past Mugdock Country Park on right

Set in 10 acres of grounds, looking out on the
beautiful Campsie Fells, this majestic property, built
in 1874, offers a get-away-from-it-all experience, yet
is just a 20-minute drive from Glasgow. Lunch and
dinner are served in the relaxed Brasserie Restaurant,
and guests can visit the falconry or just kick back
and relax in front of the fire with a book and a dram
of whisky. Weddings are especially well catered for.

Rooms 10 (3 fmly) **S** £59-£90; **D** £59-£150 (incl.
bkfst) **Facilities** FTV Wi-fi Falconry ♫ Xmas New Year
Conf Class 60 Board 60 Thtr 180 **Parking** 120
Notes LB ⊗ Civ Wed 180

STRATHYRE
Map 20 NN51
Stirling

Creagan House
◉◉ RESTAURANT WITH ROOMS

☎ 01877 384638
FK18 8ND
e-mail: eatandstay@creaganhouse.co.uk
web: www.creaganhouse.co.uk
dir: 0.25m N of Strathyre on A84

Originally a farmhouse dating from the 17th
century, Creagan House has operated as a

restaurant with rooms for many years. The baronial-
style dining room provides a wonderful setting for
the cuisine which is classic French with some
Scottish influences. The warm hospitality and
attentive service are noteworthy.

Rooms 5 (1 fmly)

STRONTIAN
Map 22 NM86
Highland

Kilcamb Lodge Hotel
★★★ ◉◉ COUNTRY HOUSE HOTEL

☎ 01967 402257
PH36 4HY
e-mail: enquiries@kilcamblodge.co.uk
web: www.kilcamblodge.co.uk
dir: Off A861, via Corran Ferry

This historic house on the shores of Loch Sunart
was one of the first stone buildings in the area, and
was used as military barracks around the time of
the Jacobite uprising. It is situated on the beautiful
and peaceful Ardamurchan Peninsula where otters,
red squirrels and eagles can be spotted. The suites
and bedrooms, with either loch or garden views, are
stylishly decorated using designer fabrics and have
flat-screen TVs, DVD/CD players, plus bath robes,
iced water and even guest umbrellas. Accomplished
cooking, utilising much local produce, can be
enjoyed in the stylish dining room. Warm hospitality
is assured.

Rooms 10 (2 fmly) ⚑ **S** £120-£140; **D** £220-£375
(incl. bkfst & dinner)* **Facilities** FTV Wi-fi ⅋ Fishing
Boating Hiking Bird/whale/otter watching Stalking
Clay pigeon shooting Xmas New Year **Conf** Class 18
Board 18 Thtr 18 Del £155* **Parking** 20 **Notes** LB
No children 10yrs Closed 2 Jan-1 Feb Civ Wed 120

Save on hotels. Book at **theAA.com/hotel**

STR – TOR 549 SCOTLAND

TAIN	Map 23 NH78
Highland	

The Glenmorangie Highland Home at Cadboll

★★★ ◉◉ COUNTRY HOUSE HOTEL

☎ 01862 871671
Cadboll, Fearn IV20 1XP
e-mail: relax@glenmorangie.co.uk
web: www.theglenmorangiehouse.com
dir: A9 onto B9175 towards Nigg. Follow tourist signs

This historic highland home superbly balances top class service with intimate customer care. Evenings are dominated by the highly successful 'house party' where guests are introduced in the drawing room, sample whiskies then take dinner (a set six-course meal) together around one long table. Conversation can extend well into the evening. Stylish bedrooms are divided between the traditional main house and some cosy cottages in the grounds. This is an ideal base from which to enjoy the world famous whisky tours.

Rooms 9 (3 annexe) (4 fmly) (3 GF) ⚑
Facilities FTV Wi-fi ⚑ Archery Beauty treatments Clay pigeon shooting Falconry Xmas New Year **Conf** Board 12 **Parking** 60 **Notes** ⊗ No children 15yrs Civ Wed 60

TARBERT LOCH FYNE	Map 20 NR86
Argyll & Bute	

Stonefield Castle Hotel

★★★★ 74% ◉ HOTEL

☎ 01880 820836
PA29 6YJ
e-mail: reservations.stonefieldcastle@ohiml.com
web: www.oxfordhotelsandinns.com
dir: From Glasgow take M8 towards Erskine Bridge onto A82, follow Loch Lomond signs. From Arrochar follow A83 signs through Inveraray & Lochgilphead, hotel on left 2m before Tarbert

This fine baronial castle commands a superb lochside setting amidst beautiful woodland gardens renowned for their rhododendrons - visit in late spring to see them at their best. Elegant public rooms are a feature, and the picture-window restaurant offers unrivalled views across Loch Fyne. Bedrooms are split between the main house and a purpose-built wing.

Rooms 32 (2 fmly) (10 GF) **Facilities** Wi-fi Xmas New Year **Conf** Class 40 Board 50 Thtr 120 **Services** Lift **Parking** 50 **Notes** Civ Wed 100

THURSO	Map 23 ND16
Highland	

Forss House Hotel

★★★★ 76% ◉◉ SMALL HOTEL

☎ 01847 861201
Forss KW14 7XY
e-mail: anne@forsshousehotel.co.uk
web: www.forsshousehotel.co.uk
dir: On A836 between Thurso & Reay

This delightful country house is set in its own 20 acres of woodland and was originally built in 1810. The hotel offers a choice of bedrooms from the traditional styled rooms in the main house to the more contemporary annexe rooms in the grounds. All rooms are very well equipped and well appointed. The beautiful River Forss runs through the grounds and is a firm favourite with fishermen.

Rooms 14 (6 annexe) (1 fmly) (7 GF) ⚑ **S** £97-£130; **D** £130-£185 (incl. bkfst)* **Facilities** FTV Wi-fi ⚑ Fishing **Conf** Class 12 Board 14 Thtr 20 Del from £165 to £180* **Parking** 14 **Notes** Closed 23 Dec-3 Jan Civ Wed 26

TORRIDON	Map 22 NG95
Highland	

The Torridon

★★★★ ◉◉◉
COUNTRY HOUSE HOTEL

☎ 01445 791242
By Achnasheen, Wester Ross IV22 2EY
e-mail: info@thetorridon.com
web: www.thetorridon.com
dir: From A832 at Kinlochewe, A896 towards Torridon. (NB do not turn into village) 1m, hotel on right

Delightfully set amidst inspiring loch and mountain scenery, this elegant Victorian shooting lodge has been beautifully appointed to make the most of its many original features, and the 58 acres of surrounding parkland make it a perfect getaway destination. The attractive bedrooms are individually furnished and most enjoy stunning Highland views; expect to find Egyptian cotton sheets, duck down duvets, flat-screen satellite TVs, FM radios and iPod docks plus Victorian-style bathrooms; for complete privacy choose The Boathouse on the loch shore. Comfortable day rooms feature fine wood panelling and roaring fires in cooler months. Head chef Bruno Birckbeck creates award-winning menus based as much as possible on the locally sourced ingredients; the hotel has its own herd of cattle. The whisky bar is aptly named, boasting over 300 malts and in-depth tasting notes. Outdoor activities include shooting, cycling and walking.

Rooms 18 (2 GF) ⚑ **D** £340-£575 (incl. bkfst & dinner)* **Facilities** STV Wi-fi Fishing ⚑ Abseiling Archery Climbing Kayaking Mountain biking Clay pigeon shooting Xmas New Year **Conf** Board 16 Thtr 42 **Services** Lift **Parking** 20 **Notes** LB ⊗ Closed 2 Jan-9 Feb RS Nov-Mar Civ Wed 55

T

TROON	Map 20 NS33
South Ayrshire	

INSPECTORS' CHOICE

Lochgreen House Hotel

★★★★ ◉◉◉ COUNTRY HOUSE HOTEL

☎ 01292 313343
Monktonhill Rd, Southwood KA10 7EN
e-mail: lochgreen@costley-hotels.co.uk
web: www.costley-hotels.co.uk
dir: From A77 follow Prestwick Airport signs. 0.5m before airport take B749 to Troon. Hotel 1m on left

Set in immaculately maintained grounds, Lochgreen House is graced by tasteful extensions which have created stunning public rooms and spacious, comfortable and elegantly furnished bedrooms. Extra facilities include a coffee shop, gift shop and beauty treatments in The Retreat. The magnificent Tapestry Restaurant provides the ideal setting for dinners that are immaculately presented.

Rooms 38 (7 annexe) (17 GF) **Facilities** STV Wi-fi Beauty treatments Xmas New Year **Conf** Class 50 Board 50 Thtr 70 **Services** Lift **Parking** 50 **Notes** ⊗ Civ Wed 140

The Marine Hotel

★★★★ 78% ◉◉ HOTEL   PUMA HOTELS COLLECTION

☎ 01292 314444
Crosbie Rd KA10 6HE
e-mail: marine@pumahotels.co.uk
web: www.pumahotels.co.uk
dir: A77, A78, A79 onto B749. Hotel on left after golf course

A favourite with conference and leisure guests, this hotel overlooks Royal Troon's 18th fairway. The cocktail lounge and split-level restaurant enjoy panoramic views of the Firth of Clyde across to the Isle of Arran. Bedrooms and public areas are attractively appointed.

Rooms 89 **Facilities** Spa STV Wi-fi ⊛ supervised Gym Squash Steam room Beauty room Xmas New Year **Conf** Class 100 Board 40 Thtr 200 **Services** Lift **Parking** 200 **Notes** ⊗ Civ Wed 100

TURNBERRY	Map 20 NS20
South Ayrshire	

INSPECTORS' CHOICE

Turnberry Resort, Scotland

★★★★★ ◉◉◉ HOTEL

☎ 01655 331000
KA26 9LT
e-mail: turnberry@luxurycollection.com
web: www.turnberryresort.co.uk
dir: From Glasgow take A77, M77 S towards Stranraer, 2m past Kirkoswald follow signs for A719 & Turnberry. Hotel 500mtrs on right

Golf probably springs to mind when this hotel is mentioned, and with good reason. This famous establishment enjoys magnificent views over to Arran, Ailsa Craig, and the Mull of Kintyre. Facilities include a world-renowned golf course, the excellent Colin Montgomerie Golf Academy, a luxurious spa with pool, ESPA treatments and a techno fitness studio, as well as a host of outdoor pursuits for both adults and children. Some superbly modern rooms and more traditional, elegant bedrooms and suites are located in the main hotel, while adjacent lodges provide more space. The public areas are stunning and include the Grand Tea Lounge, Ailsa Bar and Lounge, the Duel in the Sun sports bar, 1906 restaurant, and the fine-dining James Miller room and chef's table.

Rooms 157 (40 annexe) (2 fmly) (12 GF) ⚑ **S** £165-£360; **D** £185-£380 (incl. bkfst)* **Facilities** Spa STV FTV Wi-fi ⊳ ⊛ supervised ⚐ 45 Putt green Fishing Gym Leisure club Outdoor activity centre Turnberry Performance Academy Xmas New Year **Conf** Class 145 Board 80 Thtr 300 Del from £179* **Services** Lift **Parking** 200 **Notes** Closed 1 wk Dec & 2 wks Jan Civ Wed 220

Malin Court

★★★ 83% HOTEL

☎ 01655 331457
KA26 9PB
e-mail: info@malincourt.co.uk
web: www.malincourt.co.uk
dir: On A74 to Ayr then A719 to Turnberry & Maidens

Forming part of the Malin Court Residential and Nursing Home Complex, this friendly and comfortable hotel enjoys delightful views over the Firth of Clyde and Turnberry golf courses. Standard and executive rooms are available; all are well equipped. Public areas are plentiful, with the restaurant serving high teas, dinners and light lunches.

Rooms 18 (9 fmly) **Facilities** STV Wi-fi Putt green **Conf** Class 60 Board 30 Thtr 200 **Services** Lift **Parking** 110 **Notes** ⊗ RS Oct-Mar Civ Wed 80

UPHALL	Map 21 NT07
West Lothian	

Macdonald Houstoun House

★★★★ 79% ◉◉ HOTEL

☎ 0844 879 9043
EH52 6JS
e-mail: houstoun@macdonald-hotels.co.uk
web: www.macdonaldhotels.co.uk
dir: M8 junct 3 follow Broxburn signs, straight over rdbt, at mini-rdbt turn right towards Uphall, hotel 1m on right

This historic 17th-century tower house lies in beautifully landscaped grounds and gardens, and features a modern leisure club and spa, a choice of dining options, a vaulted cocktail bar and extensive conference and meeting facilities. Stylish bedrooms, some located around a courtyard, are comfortably furnished and well equipped. Macdonald Hotels is the AA Hotel Group of the Year 2013-14.

Rooms 73 (47 annexe) (12 fmly) (12 GF) ⚑ **S** £61-£215; **D** £61-£215 **Facilities** Spa STV FTV Wi-fi ⊳ ⊛ ⚐ Gym Health & beauty salon Xmas New Year **Conf** Class 80 Board 80 Thtr 400 Del from £120 to £245 **Parking** 250 **Notes** LB Civ Wed 200

Save on hotels. Book at **theAA.com/hotel**

TRO – WIC 551 SCOTLAND

UPLAWMOOR
East Renfrewshire — Map 20 NS45

Uplawmoor Hotel

★★★ 81% SMALL HOTEL

THE CIRCLE

☎ 01505 850565
Neilston Rd G78 4AF
e-mail: info@uplawmoor.co.uk
web: www.uplawmoor.co.uk
dir: M77 junct 2, A736 signed Barrhead & Irvine.
Hotel 4m beyond Barrhead

Originally a coaching inn, this friendly hotel is set in a village off the Glasgow to Irvine road. The relaxed restaurant (with cocktail lounge adjacent) features imaginative dishes, whilst the separate lounge bar is popular for freshly prepared bar meals. The modern bedrooms are both comfortable and well equipped.

Rooms 14 (1 fmly) **S** £50-£65; **D** £80-£95 (incl. bkfst) **Facilities** STV Wi-fi **Conf** Class 12 Board 20 Thtr 40 Del from £125 to £135 **Parking** 40 **Notes** LB ⊗ Closed 26 Dec & 1 Jan

WHITEBRIDGE
Highland — Map 23 NH41

Whitebridge Hotel

★★ 69% HOTEL

☎ 01456 486226
IV2 6UN
e-mail: info@whitebridgehotel.co.uk
dir: A9 onto B851, follow signs to Fort Augustus. Or A82 onto B862 at Fort Augustus

Close to Loch Ness and set amid rugged mountain and moorland scenery, this hotel is popular with tourists, fishermen and deerstalkers. Guests have a choice of more formal dining in the restaurant or lighter meals in the popular cosy bar. Bedrooms are thoughtfully equipped and brightly furnished.

Rooms 12 (3 fmly) **Facilities** Wi-fi Fishing **Parking** 32 **Notes** Closed 11 Dec-9 Jan

WICK
Highland — Map 23 ND35

Mackay's Hotel

★★★ 74% HOTEL

☎ 01955 602323
Union St KW1 5ED
e-mail: info@mackayshotel.co.uk
dir: Opposite Caithness General Hospital

This well-established hotel is situated just outside the town centre overlooking the River Wick. MacKay's provides well-equipped, attractive accommodation, suited to both the business and leisure guest. There is a stylish bistro offering food throughout the day and the main bar offers a wide selection of whiskies.

Rooms 30 (2 fmly) ↖ **S** £86; **D** £110-£155 (incl. bkfst) **Facilities** FTV Wi-fi ↕ HL ♪ **Conf** Class 100 Board 60 Thtr 100 Del from £125 to £145 **Services** Lift **Notes** LB ⊗ Closed 24-26 Dec & 1-3 Jan Civ Wed 200

W

Scottish Islands

The Cuillin Hills and Loch Scavaig as seen from Elgol, Isle of Skye

ARRAN, ISLE OF

BLACKWATERFOOT — Map 20 NR92

BEST WESTERN Kinloch Hotel

★★★ 79% HOTEL

☎ 01770 860444
KA27 8ET
e-mail: reservations@kinlochhotel.eclipse.co.uk
web: www.bw-kinlochhotel.co.uk
dir: Ferry from Ardrossan to Brodick, follow signs for Blackwaterfoot, hotel in village centre

Well known for providing an authentic island experience, this long established stylish hotel is in an idyllic location. Smart public areas include a choice of lounges, popular bars and well-presented leisure facilities. Bedrooms vary in size and style but most enjoy panoramic sea views and several family suites offer excellent value. The spacious restaurant provides a wide ranging menu, and in winter when the restaurant is closed, the bar serves a choice of creative dishes.

Rooms 37 (7 fmly) (7 GF) ✆ **S** £35-£70; **D** £70-£140 (incl. bkfst)* **Facilities** STV Wi-fi ⌕ ⌚ Gym Squash New Year **Conf** Class 20 Board 40 Thtr 120 **Del** from £85 to £100* **Services** Lift **Parking** 2 **Notes** Civ Wed 150

BRODICK — Map 20 NS03

INSPECTORS' CHOICE

Kilmichael Country House Hotel

★★★ ◉ ◉ COUNTRY HOUSE HOTEL

☎ 01770 302219
Glen Cloy KA27 8BY
e-mail: enquiries@kilmichael.com
web: www.kilmichael.com
dir: From Brodick ferry terminal towards Lochranza for 1m. Left at golf course, follow signs

Reputed to be the oldest on the island, this lovely house lies in attractive gardens in a quiet glen less than five minutes' drive from the ferry terminal. It is a stylish, elegant country house, adorned with ornaments from around the world. The delightful bedrooms are furnished in classical style; some are contained in a pretty courtyard conversion. There are two inviting drawing rooms and a bright dining room where award-winning contemporary cuisine is served. The dishes include fresh eggs laid by the hotel's own ducks and hens, vegetables, fruit and herbs from the kitchen garden, and mushrooms and berries are foraged in season from the estate.

Rooms 8 (3 annexe) (7 GF) ✆ **S** £78-£98; **D** £130-£205 (incl. bkfst)* **Facilities** Wi-fi **Parking** 14 **Notes** LB No children 12yrs Closed Nov-Feb (ex for prior bookings)

BUTE, ISLE OF

ROTHESAY — Map 20 NS16

The Ardyne

Ⓤ

☎ 01700 502052
38 Mountstuart Rd PA20 9EB
e-mail: ardyne.hotel@virgin.net

Currently the rating for this establishment is not confirmed. This may be due to a change of ownership or because it has only recently joined the AA rating scheme. For further details please see the AA website: theAA.com

---

HARRIS, ISLE OF

SCARISTA (SGARASTA BHEAG) — Map 22 NG09

Scarista House

◉ ◉ RESTAURANT WITH ROOMS

☎ 01859 550238
HS3 3HX
e-mail: timandpatricia@scaristahouse.com
dir: On A859, 15m S of Tarbert

A former manse, Scarista House is a haven for food lovers who seek to explore this magnificent island. It enjoys breathtaking views of the Atlantic and is just a short stroll from miles of golden sandy beaches. The house is run in a relaxed country-house manner by the friendly hosts. Expect wellies in the hall and masses of books and CDs in one of two lounges. Bedrooms are cosy, and delicious set dinners and memorable breakfasts are provided.

Rooms 6 (3 annexe) (1 fmly)

TARBERT   Map 22 NB10

Hotel Hebrides

★★★★ 78% ⊛ HOTEL

☎ 01859 502364
Pier Rd HS3 3DG
e-mail: stay@hotel-hebrides.com
dir: To Tarbert via ferry from Uig (Isle of Skye); or ferry from Ullapool to Stornaway, A859 to Tarbert; or by plane to Stornaway from Glasgow, Edinburgh or Inverness

Benefiting from an elevated position overlooking the town this hotel is just a few minutes' walk from the centre. The small, hands-on team extend wonderful hospitality and customer care. The bedrooms are stylishly designed and include Wi-fi, high speed internet access and flat-screen TVs; the deluxe rooms have iPod docking stations and some rooms have loch and harbour views. Award-winning food is served in the Pierhouse Restaurant. A complimentary bus service is provided to the theatre in the summer months.

Rooms 21 (2 fmly) **Facilities** FTV Wi-fi ↳ ♫
Conf Class 35 Board 35 **Notes** ⊛

ISLAY, ISLE OF

PORT ASKAIG   Map 20 NR46

Port Askaig Hotel

★★ 63% SMALL HOTEL

☎ 01496 840245
PA46 7RD
e-mail: hotel@portaskaig.co.uk
web: www.portaskaig.co.uk
dir: At ferry terminal

The building of this endearing family-run hotel dates back to the 18th-century. The lounge provides fine views over the Sound of Islay to Jura, and there is a choice of bars that are popular with locals. Traditional dinners are served in the bright restaurant and a full range of bar snacks and meals is also available. The bedrooms are smart and comfortable.

Rooms 8 (1 fmly) (8 GF) **Parking** 21

MULL, ISLE OF

TOBERMORY   Map 22 NM55

INSPECTORS' CHOICE

Highland Cottage

★★★ ⊛⊛ SMALL HOTEL

☎ 01688 302030
Breadalbane St PA75 6PD
e-mail: davidandjo@highlandcottage.co.uk
web: www.highlandcottage.co.uk
dir: A848 Craignure/Fishnish ferry terminal, pass Tobermory signs, straight on at mini rdbt across narrow bridge, turn right. Hotel on right opposite fire station

Providing the highest level of natural and unassuming hospitality, this delightful little gem lies high above the island's capital. Don't be fooled by its side street location, a stunning view over the bay is just a few metres away. 'A country house hotel in town' it is an Aladdin's Cave of collectables and treasures, as well as masses of books and magazines. There are two inviting lounges, one with an honesty bar. The cosy dining room offers memorable dinners and splendid breakfasts. Bedrooms are individual; some have four-posters and all are comprehensively equipped to include TVs and music centres.

Rooms 6 (1 GF) **Facilities** FTV Wi-fi ↳ **Parking** 6
Notes LB No children 10yrs Closed Nov-Mar

ORKNEY

ST MARGARET'S HOPE   Map 24 ND49
Orkney

The Creel Restaurant with Rooms

⊛⊛ RESTAURANT WITH ROOMS

☎ 01856 831311
Front Rd KW17 2SL
e-mail: creelorkney@btinternet.com
web: www.thecreel.co.uk
dir: A961 into village, establishment on seafront

With wonderful sea views, The Creel enjoys a prominent position in the pretty fishing village of St Margaret's Hope. The award-winning restaurant has a well deserved reputation for the quality of its seafood and a window seat is a must in the charming restaurant. The stylish bedrooms are appointed to a high standard and most enjoy views over the bay. Breakfasts should not be missed, with local Orkney produce and freshly baked breads on the menu.

Rooms 3

SHETLAND

LERWICK   Map 24 HU44

Shetland Hotel

★★★ 77% HOTEL

☎ 01595 695515
Holmsgarth Rd ZE1 0PW
e-mail: reception@shetlandhotel.co.uk
dir: Opposite ferry terminal, on main road N from town centre

This purpose-built hotel is centrally located for both business and leisure guests, situated opposite the main ferry terminal. The spacious and comfortable bedrooms are on three floors and there are two dining options - the informal Beltramis Café Bar and The Waterfront Bar & Grill offering diverse, well executed and enjoyable dishes.

Rooms 64 (4 fmly) ♥ **S** £92; **D** £120 (incl. bkfst)*
Facilities FTV Wi-fi ↳ **Conf** Class 75 Board 50
Thtr 300 **Services** Lift **Parking** 150 **Notes** ⊛ Closed 25-26 Dec, 1-2 Jan

SCOTTISH ISLANDS

SCALLOWAY   Map 24 HU33

Scalloway Hotel

★★★ 75% ◉ SMALL HOTEL

☎ 01595 880444
Main St ZE1 0TR
e-mail: info@scallowayhotel.com
dir: 6m from main port of Lerwick on A970. Situated
in Scalloway Main St

Scalloway is the ancient capital of Shetland, and this
hotel sits overlooking the waterfront. It is currently
undergoing a full refurbishment using high quality
Shetland fabrics and materials, and good result have
been achieved to date. There is warm friendly service,
and award-winning cooking using the best produce
that the Shetland Larder has to offer.

Rooms 24 (1 fmly) ⬧ **S** £75; **D** £110 (incl. bkfst)
Facilities STV FTV Wi-fi ⬧ **Parking** 10 **Notes** LB

SKYE, ISLE OF

ARDVASAR   Map 22 NG60

Ardvasar Hotel

★★★ 74% SMALL HOTEL

☎ 01471 844223
Sleat IV45 8RS
e-mail: richard@ardvasar-hotel.demon.co.uk
web: www.ardvasarhotel.com
dir: From ferry, 500mtrs, left signed Ardvasar

The Isle of Skye is dotted with cosy, welcoming hotels
that make touring the island easy and convenient.
This hotel ranks highly amongst its peers thanks to
great hospitality and a preservation of community
spirit. The hotel sits less than five minutes' drive from
the Mallaig ferry and provides comfortable bedrooms
and a cosy bar lounge for residents. Seafood is
prominent on menus, and meals can be enjoyed in
either the popular bar or the attractive dining room.

Ardvasar Hotel

Rooms 10 (4 fmly) **Facilities** FTV Wi-fi ♫ Xmas New
Year **Conf** Board 24 Thtr 50 **Parking** 30

See advert on opposite page

COLBOST   Map 22 NG24

INSPECTORS' CHOICE

The Three Chimneys and House Over-By

◉ ◉ ◉ RESTAURANT WITH ROOMS

☎ 01470 511258
IV55 8ZT
e-mail: eatandstay@threechimneys.co.uk
dir: 4m W of Dunvegan village on B884 signed
Glendale

A visit to this delightful property will make a trip to
Skye even more memorable. The stunning food is
the result of a deft approach using quality local
ingredients. Breakfast is an impressive array of
local fish, meats and cheeses, served with fresh
home baking and home-made preserves. The stylish
lounge-breakfast area has the real wow factor.
Bedrooms, in the House Over-By, are creative and
thoughtfully equipped - all have spacious en suites
and wonderful views across Loch Dunvegan.

Rooms 6 (1 fmly) (6GF)

ISLEORNSAY   Map 22 NG71

Duisdale House Hotel

★★★★ 81% ◉ ◉ SMALL HOTEL

☎ 01471 833202
Sleat IV43 8QW
e-mail: info@duisdale.com
web: www.duisdale.com
dir: 7m S of Bradford on A851 towards Armadale. 7m
N of Armadale ferry

This grand Victorian house stands in its own
landscaped gardens overlooking the Sound of Sleat.
The hotel has a contemporary and chic style which
complements the original features of the house. Each
bedroom is individually designed and the superior
rooms have four-poster beds. The elegant lounge has
sumptuous sofas, original artwork and blazing log
fires in the colder months.

Rooms 18 (1 fmly) (1 GF) ⬧ **Facilities** STV Wi-fi ⬧
Private yacht Outdoor hydropool Xmas New Year
Conf Board 28 Thtr 50 **Parking** 30 **Notes** ⊗
Civ Wed 58

INSPECTORS' CHOICE

Kinloch Lodge

★★★ ◉◉◉ COUNTRY HOUSE HOTEL

☎ 01471 833214 & 833333
Sleat IV43 8QY
e-mail: reservations@kinloch-lodge.co.uk
web: www.kinloch-lodge.co.uk
dir: 6m S of Broadford on A851, 10m N of Armadale on A851

Owned and run in a hands-on fashion by Lord and Lady MacDonald and their family, this hotel enjoys a picture postcard location surrounded by hills and a sea loch. Bedrooms and bathrooms are well appointed and comfortable, and public areas boast numerous open fires and relaxing areas to sit. There is a cookery school run by Claire MacDonald and a shop that sells her famous cookery books and produce.

Rooms 15 (8 annexe) (1 GF) ☝ **Facilities** STV FTV Wi-fi Fishing Beauty treatment room Xmas New Year **Conf** Class 20 Board 20 Thtr 20 **Parking** 40

Toravaig House Hotel

★★★ 85% ◉◉ SMALL HOTEL

☎ 01471 820200 & 833231
Knock Bay, Sleat IV44 8RE
e-mail: info@skyehotel.co.uk
web: www.skyehotel.co.uk
dir: From Skye Bridge, left at Broadford onto A851, hotel 11m on left. Or from ferry at Armadale take A851, hotel 6m on right

Set in two acres and enjoying panoramic views to the Knoydart Hills, this hotel is a haven of peace, with stylish, well-equipped and beautifully decorated bedrooms. There is an inviting lounge complete with deep sofas and an elegant dining room where delicious meals are the order of the day. The hotel provides a sea-going yacht for guests' exclusive use from April to September.

Rooms 9 ☝ **Facilities** STV Wi-fi ☝ Daily excursions (Apr-Sep) on hotel yacht Xmas New Year **Conf** Board 10 Thtr 15 **Parking** 15 **Notes** ⊗ Civ Wed 25

Hotel Eilean Iarmain

★★★ 79% ◉◉ SMALL HOTEL   THE CIRCLE

☎ 01471 833332
Sleat IV43 8QR
e-mail: hotel@eileaniarmain.co.uk
web: www.eileaniarmain.co.uk
dir: From Skye Bridge take A87 towards Broadford. Left onto A851 signed Armadale. 8m, left to hotel. Or From Armadale ferry take A851 signed Broadford. 7m to hotel

A hotel of charm and character, this 19th-century former inn sits by the pier and enjoys fine views across the sea loch. Bedrooms are individual and retain a traditional style, and a stable block has been converted into four delightful suites. Public rooms are cosy and inviting, and the restaurant offers award-winning menus showcasing the island's best produce, especially seafood and game.

Rooms 16 (10 annexe) (4 fmly) (3 GF) **S** £75-£135; **D** £100-£250 (incl. bkfst)* **Facilities** FTV Wi-fi Fishing Shooting Art exhibitions Whisky tasting Tweed Shop ♫ Xmas New Year **Conf** Class 10 Board 14 Thtr 25 Del from £150 to £210 **Parking** 20 **Notes** LB Civ Wed 30

SCOTTISH ISLANDS

PORTREE   Map 22 NG44

Cuillin Hills Hotel

★★★★ 78% @@ HOTEL

☎ 01478 612003
IV51 9QU
e-mail: info@cuillinhills-hotel-skye.co.uk
web: www.cuillinhills-hotel-skye.co.uk
dir: Right 0.25m N of Portree off A855. Follow hotel signs

This imposing building enjoys a superb location overlooking Portree Bay and the Cuillin Hills. Accommodation is provided in smart, well-equipped rooms that are generally spacious; some rooms are found in an adjacent building. Public areas include comfortable lounges, a Malt Whisky Bar, The Cuillin Brasserie and a newly refurbished restaurant that takes advantage of the views - 'The View'. Service is particularly attentive.

Rooms 29 (7 annexe) (4 fmly) (10 GF) ✿
Facilities STV FTV Wi-fi HL Xmas New Year
Parking 56 **Notes** Civ Wed 45

Rosedale Hotel

★★★ 75% HOTEL

☎ 01478 613131
Beaumont Crescent IV51 9DF
e-mail: rosedalehotelsky@aol.com
web: www.rosedalehotelskye.co.uk
dir: Follow directions to village centre & harbour

The atmosphere is wonderfully warm at this delightful family-run waterfront hotel. A labyrinth of stairs and corridors connects the comfortable lounges, bar and charming restaurant - all are set on different levels. The restaurant has fine views of the bay. The modern bedrooms offer a good range of amenities.

Rooms 18 (1 fmly) (3 GF) **S** £40-£65; **D** £70-£150 (incl. bkfst) **Facilities** FTV Wi-fi **Parking** 2 **Notes** ⊗ Closed Nov-mid Mar

SKEABOST BRIDGE   Map 22 NG44

Skeabost Country House   "bespoke"

★★★ 75% @
COUNTRY HOUSE HOTEL

☎ 01470 532202 & 0843 178 7139
IV51 9NP
web: www.bespokehotels.com/skeabostcountryhouse
dir: From Skye Bridge on A87, through Portree towards Uig. Left onto A850, hotel on right

This delightful property stands in mature, landscaped grounds at the edge of Loch Snizort. Originally built as a hunting lodge by the MacDonalds and steeped in history, Skeabost offers a welcoming environment from the caring and helpful staff. The hotel provides award-winning food, charming day rooms and well appointed accommodation. The pretty grounds include a challenging 9-hole golf course, and there is salmon and trout fishing nearby. Wi-fi is available.

Rooms 14 (5 annexe) (5 GF) ✿ **D** £110-£255 (incl. bkfst)* **Facilities** FTV Wi-fi ⌁ 9 Fishing Xmas New Year **Conf** Class 20 Board 20 Thtr 40 Del from £130 to £275* **Parking** 40 **Notes** LB Civ Wed 120

STAFFIN   Map 22 NG46

Flodigarry Country House Hotel

★★★ 78% @ COUNTRY HOUSE HOTEL

☎ 01470 552203
IV51 9HZ
e-mail: info@flodigarry.co.uk
web: www.flodigarry.co.uk
dir: A855 from Portree, through Staffin to Flodigarry, hotel signed on right

This hotel is located in woodlands on The Quiraing in north-east Skye overlooking the sea towards the Torridon Mountains. The dramatic scenery is a real inspiration here, and this charming house was once the home of the Scotland's heroine, Flora MacDonald. Guests are assured of real Highland hospitality and there is an easy going atmosphere throughout. A full range of activities is offered, with mountain walks, fishing and boat trips proving to be the most popular.

Rooms 18 (7 annexe) (3 fmly) (4 GF) **Facilities** FTV Wi-fi Xmas New Year **Parking** 40 **Notes** Closed Nov-15 Dec & Jan Civ Wed 80

The Glenview

@@ RESTAURANT WITH ROOMS

☎ 01470 562248
Culnacnoc IV51 9JH
e-mail: enquiries@glenviewskye.co.uk
dir: 12m N of Portree on A855

The Glenview is located in one of the most beautiful parts of Skye with stunning sea views; it is close to the famous rock formation, The Old Man of Storr. The individually styled bedrooms are very comfortable and front-facing rooms enjoy the dramatic views. Evening meals should not to be missed as the restaurant has a well deserved reputation for its treatment of locally sourced produce.

Rooms 5

STRUAN   Map 22 NG33

Ullinish Country Lodge

RESTAURANT WITH ROOMS

☎ 01470 572214
IV56 8FD
e-mail: ullinish@theisleofskye.co.uk
dir: Take A863 N. Lodge signed on left

Set in some of Scotland's most dramatic landscape, with views of the Black Cuillin and MacLeoc's Tables, this lodge has lochs on three sides. Samuel Johnson and James Boswell stayed here in 1773 and were impressed with the hospitality even then. Hosts Brian and Pam hope to extend the same welcome to their guests today. As you would expect, all bedrooms have amazing views, and come with half-tester beds. The AA Rosette award for the Ullinish Country Lcdge is currently suspended due to a change in chef. AA Rosettes may be awarded once the inspectors have assessed the food created by the new kitchen regime.

Rooms 6

Save on hotels. Book at **theAA.com/hotel**

ISLE OF SKYE 559 SCOTLAND

SCOTTISH ISLANDS

Wales

Harlech Castle, Snowdonia

A

ABERAERON
Ceredigion
Map 8 SN46

INSPECTORS' CHOICE

Ty Mawr Mansion

◎ ◎ RESTAURANT WITH ROOMS

☎ 01570 470033
Cilcennin SA48 8DB
e-mail: info@tymawrmansion.co.uk
web: www.tymawrmansion.co.uk
dir: On A482 (Lampeter to Aberaeron road), 4m from Aberaeron

Surrounded by rolling countryside in its own naturally beautiful gardens, this fine country mansion house is a haven of peace and tranquillity. Careful renovation has restored it to its former glory and, combined with lush fabrics, top quality beds and sumptuous furnishings, the accommodation is spacious, superbly equipped and very comfortable. Award-winning chefs create mouth-watering dishes from local and seasonal produce. There is also a 27-seat cinema with all the authenticity of the real thing. Martin and Cath McAlpine offer the sort of welcome which makes every visit to Ty Mawr a memorable one.

Rooms 9 (1 annexe) (1 fmly)

ABERDARE
Rhondda Cynon Taff
Map 9 SO00

Premier Inn Aberdare

BUDGET HOTEL

☎ 0871 527 8002
Riverside Retail Park, Tirfounders Field CF44 0AH
web: www.premierinn.com
dir: M4 junct 32, A470 signed Merthyr Tydfil. In approx 10m take A4059 signed Aberdare. Straight on at 1st rdbt, 3rd exit at next rdbt into Ffordd Tirwaun signed Riverside Retail Park, hotel in park

High quality, budget accommodation ideal for both families and business travellers. Spacious, en suite bedrooms feature tea and coffee making facilities, and Freeview TV in most hotels. Internet access and Wi-fi are available for a small fee. The adjacent family restaurant features a wide and varied menu. See also the Hotel Groups pages.

Rooms 28

ABERGAVENNY
Monmouthshire
Map 9 SO21

Llansantffraed Court Hotel

WELSH RAREBITS Hooked Destination

★★★★ 78% ◎ ◎
COUNTRY HOUSE HOTEL

☎ 01873 840678
Llanvihangel Gobion, Clytha NP7 9BA
e-mail: reception@llch.co.uk
web: www.llch.co.uk
dir: At A465 & A40 Abergavenny junct take B4598 signed Usk (NB do not join A40). Towards Raglan, hotel on left in 4.5m

In a commanding position and in its own extensive grounds, this very impressive property - a privately owned country-house hotel - has enviable views of the Brecon Beacons. Extensive public areas include a relaxing lounge and a spacious restaurant offering imaginative and enjoyable award-winning dishes. Bedrooms vary in size and reflect the individuality of the building; all are comfortably furnished and provide some thoughtful extras. Extensive parking is available.

Rooms 21 (1 fmly) ⬥ **S** £90-£110; **D** £130-£185 (incl. bkfst)* **Facilities** STV FTV Wi-fi ⬥ Putt green Fishing ⬥ Clay pigeon shooting school Xmas New Year Child facilities **Conf** Class 120 Board 100 Thtr 220 Del from £150 to £190* **Services** Lift **Parking** 250 **Notes** LB Civ Wed 150

Angel Hotel

★★★ 80% ◎ HOTEL

☎ 01873 857121
15 Cross St NP7 5EN
e-mail: mail@angelabergavenny.com
web: www.angelabergavenny.com
dir: From A40 & A465 junct follow town centre signs, S of Abergavenny, past rail & bus stations

Once a coaching inn, this is a popular venue for both locals and visitors; the two traditional function rooms and a ballroom are in regular use. In addition there is a comfortable lounge, a relaxed bar and a smart restaurant. In warmer weather there is a central courtyard that is ideal for alfresco eating. The bedrooms include a four-poster room and some that are suitable for families.

Rooms 35 (4 annexe) (2 fmly) ⬥ **D** £101-£200* **Facilities** FTV Wi-fi ♫ New Year **Conf** Class 60 Board 60 Thtr 180 Del from £168* **Services** Lift **Parking** 30 **Notes** LB Closed 25 Dec RS 24 & 26-30 Dec Civ Wed 180

ABERGELE
Conwy
Map 14 SH97

Kinmel Manor Hotel

THE INDEPENDENTS
HOTEL ASSOCIATION

★★★ 75% HOTEL

☎ 01745 832014
St George's Rd LL22 9AS
e-mail: reception@kinmelmanorhotel.co.uk
dir: A55 junct 24, hotel entrance on rdbt

In a rural location at the end of a long drive leading from the A55, parts of this notable, family-run hotel date from the 16th century. The smart bedrooms vary from standard to superior and executive rooms. The public areas include a popular lounge bar, the stylish Seasons Brasserie, and leisure facilities which include a gym, indoor pool, jacuzzi, steam room and sauna.

Rooms 51 (3 fmly) (22 GF) ⬥ **S** £65-£85; **D** £90-£120 (incl. bkfst)* **Facilities** FTV Wi-fi ⬥ ⬥ Gym Steam room Sauna Spa bath Xmas New Year **Conf** Class 100 Board 100 Thtr 250 Del from £120.50 to £150* **Services** Lift **Parking** 120 **Notes** Civ Wed 250

The Kinmel Arms

◎ ◎ RESTAURANT WITH ROOMS

☎ 01745 832207
The Village, St George LL22 9BP
e-mail: info@thekinmelarms.co.uk
dir: From A55 junct 24a to St George. E on A55, junct 24. 1st left to Rhuddlan, 1st right into St George. 2nd right

This converted 17th-century coaching inn stands close to the church in the village of St George, in the beautiful Elwy Valley. The popular restaurant specialises in produce from Wales and north-west England, and friendly and helpful staff ensure you will have an enjoyable stay. The four attractive suites are luxuriously furnished and feature stunning bathrooms. Substantial continental breakfasts are served in the rooms.

Rooms 4

B

ABERSOCH   Map 14 SH32
Gwynedd

Porth Tocyn Hotel
★★★ 82% ◉◉ COUNTRY HOUSE HOTEL

☎ 01758 713303 & 07789 994942
Bwlch Tocyn LL53 7BU
e-mail: bookings@porthtocyn.fsnet.co.uk
web: www.porthtocynhotel.co.uk
dir: 2.5m S of Abersoch follow Porth Tocyn signs after Sarnbach

Located above Cardigan Bay with fine views over the area, Porth Tocyn is set in attractive gardens. Several elegantly furnished sitting rooms are provided and bedrooms are comfortably furnished. Children are especially welcome and a playroom is provided. Award-winning food is served in the restaurant.

Rooms 17 (1 fmly) (3 GF) **S** £75-£150; **D** £100-£180 (incl. bkfst)* **Facilities** FTV Wi-fi ↝ ⛳ Table tennis **Conf** Class 15 **Parking** 50 **Notes** LB Closed mid Nov-week before Easter

ABERYSTWYTH   Map 8 SN58
Ceredigion

Nanteos Mansion
RESTAURANT WITH ROOMS

☎ 01970 600522
Rhydyfelin SY23 4LU
e-mail: info@nanteos.com
dir: A487 onto A4120 signed Devil's Bridge then immediately right onto B4340 towards Trawscoed. Take 1st left fork, along narrow road, Nanteos Mansion signed

This historic mansion sits in delightfully peaceful countryside. The restaurant offers a good menu choice and a very pleasant wine list, and retains many of the grand features of the original house. Staff are keen to please and proud of the cuisine here. Bedrooms are splendid and well appointed and many offer very spacious accommodation. Public areas are also spacious and breakfast is taken in the Buttery, which is the restored original kitchen.

Rooms 14 (4 annexe) (4 fmly)

BANGOR   Map 14 SH57
Gwynedd

Premier Inn Bangor
BUDGET HOTEL

☎ 0871 527 8046
Parc Menai, Ffordd Y Parc LL57 4FA
web: www.premierinn.com
dir: A55 junct 9 (Holyhead, Ysbyty Gwynedd Hospital). Take 3rd exit off rdbt. Hotel next left

High quality, budget accommodation ideal for both families and business travellers. Spacious, en suite bedrooms feature tea and coffee making facilities, and Freeview TV in most hotels. Internet access and Wi-fi are available for a small fee. The adjacent family restaurant features a wide and varied menu. See also the Hotel Groups pages.

Rooms 40

BEAUMARIS   Map 14 SH67
Isle of Anglesey

The Bulkeley Hotel
★★★ 78% HOTEL

☎ 01248 810415
Castle St LL58 8AW
e-mail: reception@bulkeleyhotel.co.uk
web: www.bulkeleyhotel.co.uk
dir: A55 junct 8a to Beaumaris. Hotel in town centre

A Grade I listed hotel built in 1832, the Bulkeley is just 100 yards from the 13th-century Beaumaris Castle in the centre of town; the friendly staff create a relaxed atmosphere. Many rooms, including 18 of the bedrooms, have fine panoramic views across the Menai Straits to the Snowdonian Mountains. The well-equipped bedrooms and suites, some with four-posters, are generally spacious, and have pretty furnishings. There is a choice of bars, a coffee shop, a restaurant and bistro.

Rooms 43 (5 fmly) ⚑ **Facilities** FTV Wi-fi Xmas New Year **Conf** Class 40 Board 25 Thtr 180 **Services** Lift **Parking** 25 **Notes** Civ Wed 130

Bishopsgate House Hotel
★★ 85% ◉ SMALL HOTEL

☎ 01248 810302
54 Castle St LL58 8BB
e-mail: hazel@bishopsgatehotel.co.uk
dir: From Menai Bridge onto A545 to Beaumaris. Hotel on left in main street

This immaculately maintained, privately-owned and personally-run small hotel dates back to 1760. It features fine examples of wood panelling and a Chinese Chippendale staircase. Thoughtfully

furnished bedrooms are attractively decorated and two have four-poster beds. Quality cooking is served in the elegant restaurant and guests have a comfortable lounge and cosy bar to relax in.

Rooms 9 **S** £60-£70; **D** £99-£111 (incl. bkfst) **Facilities** FTV Wi-fi ↝ Xmas New Year **Parking** 8 **Notes** LB

BEDDGELERT   Map 14 SH54
Gwynedd

The Royal Goat Hotel
★★★ 78% HOTEL

THE CIRCLE
Selected Individual Hotels

☎ 01766 890224
LL55 4YE
e-mail: info@royalgoathotel.co.uk
web: www.royalgoathotel.co.uk
dir: On A498 at Beddgelert

An impressive building steeped in history, the Royal Goat provides well-equipped accommodation, and carries out an annual programme of refurbishment. Attractively appointed, comfortable public areas include a choice of bars and restaurants, a residents' lounge and function rooms.

Rooms 32 (4 fmly) **S** £60; **D** £85 (incl. bkfst)* **Facilities** FTV Wi-fi Fishing Xmas New Year **Conf** Class 40 Board 30 Thtr 70 **Services** Lift **Parking** 100 **Notes** LB Closed Jan-14 Feb

BETWS-Y-COED   Map 14 SH75
Conwy

See also Llanrwst

Craig-y-Dderwen Riverside Hotel
★★★★ 78% ◉ COUNTRY HOUSE HOTEL

☎ 01690 710293
LL24 0AS
e-mail: info@snowdoniahotel.com
web: www.snowdoniahotel.com
dir: A5 to Betws-y-Coed, cross Waterloo Bridge, take 1st left

This Victorian country-house hotel is set in well-maintained grounds alongside the River Conwy, at the end of a tree-lined drive. Views down the river can be enjoyed from the restaurant and deck. Many of the bedrooms have balconies, and the feature rooms include a four-poster bed and a hot tub. There are comfortable lounges and the atmosphere throughout is tranquil and relaxing.

Rooms 18 (2 fmly) (1 GF) (1 smoking) ⚑ **D** £120-£230 (incl. bkfst)* **Facilities** STV FTV Wi-fi ↝ Fishing ⚐ Badminton Volleyball New Year **Conf** Class 50 Board 50 Thtr 100 Del from £105 to £275* **Parking** 50 **Notes** Closed 23-26 Dec & 2 Jan-1 Feb Civ Wed 100

B

BETWS-Y-COED *continued*

Royal Oak Hotel

★★★ 86% ⚙ HOTEL

☎ 01690 710219
Holyhead Rd LL24 0AY
e-mail: royaloakmail@btopenworld.com
web: www.royaloakhotel.net
dir: On A5 in town centre, adjacent to St Mary's Church

Centrally situated in the village, this elegant, privately owned hotel started life as a coaching inn and now provides very comfortable bedrooms with smart, modern en suite bathrooms. The extensive public areas retain original charm and character. The choice of eating options includes the Grill Bistro, the Stables Bar which is much frequented by locals, and the more formal Llugwy Restaurant.

Rooms 27 (1 fmly) 🐾 **S** £77.50-£100; **D** £95-£185 (incl. bkfst)* **Facilities** FTV Wi-fi ↳ 𝄞 New Year **Conf** Class 40 Board 20 Thtr 80 Del from £100 to £130* **Parking** 90 **Notes** LB ⊗ Closed 25-26 Dec Civ Wed 60

See advert on opposite page

BEST WESTERN Waterloo Hotel

★★★ 80% HOTEL

Best Western

☎ 01690 710411
LL24 0AR
e-mail: reservations@waterloo-hotel.info
web: www.waterloo-hotel.info
dir: On A5, S of village centre

This long-established hotel, named after the nearby Waterloo Bridge, is ideally located for visiting Snowdonia. Stylish accommodation is split between rooms in the main hotel and modern, cottage-style rooms located in buildings to the rear. The attractive Garden Room Restaurant serves traditional Welsh specialities, and the vibrant Bridge Inn provides a wide range of food and drink throughout the day and evening.

Rooms 33 (22 annexe) (13 fmly) (29 GF) 🐾 **S** £92.50-£97.50; **D** £145-£155 (incl. bkfst)* **Facilities** FTV Wi-fi ↳ 𝄞 Gym Steam room Sauna Beauty salon New Year **Conf** Class 18 Board 12 Thtr 40 Del £110* **Parking** 100 **Notes** LB Closed 24-26 Dec

BODELWYDDAN
Denbighshire

Map 14 SJ07

Bodelwyddan Castle Hotel

Warner Leisure Hotels
JUST FOR GROWN-UPS

★★★ 73% HOTEL

☎ 01745 585088
LL18 5YA
dir: At A55 junct 25

This Grade II listed Victorian castle is located on the north Wales coast less than an hour from the Snowdonian mountains. The famous Bodelwyddan marble church, set in the valley below, can be seen from the grounds and The National Portrait Gallery is also situated on site. The hotel offers a great range of leisure facilities and numerous daily in-house and external activities. Packages range from a minimum two-night, half board stay. Please note that this is an adults-only (over 21 years) hotel.

Rooms 186 (51 GF) 🐾 **S** fr £100; **D** fr £200 (incl. bkfst & dinner)* **Facilities** Spa FTV Wi-fi ↳ HL 𝄞 supervised Putt green ⛳ Gym 𝄞 Xmas New Year **Services** Lift **Parking** 180 **Notes** ⊗ No children 21yrs

BRECON
Powys

Map 9 SO02

The Castle of Brecon Hotel

★★★ 75% HOTEL

☎ 01874 624611
Castle Square LD3 9DB
dir: In town centre

This former coaching inn occupies an elevated position overlooking the town and the River Usk, with the ruins of the 11th-century castle in the grounds. Lovely views can be enjoyed from the restaurant and some of the bedrooms. The remaining public areas are roomy and relaxed in a contemporary style. Function and meeting rooms are available and even incorporate one of the castle walls. There is ample parking to the front of the property.

Rooms 38 (8 annexe) (9 fmly) (2 GF) 🐾 **S** £65-£140; **D** £75-£150 (incl. bkfst)* **Facilities** FTV Wi-fi New Year **Conf** Class 100 Board 40 Thtr 140 Del £139* **Parking** 35 **Notes** LB ⊗ RS 24-26 Dec Civ Wed 120

Save on hotels. Book at **theAA.com/hotel**

BET – BRI 565 WALES

B

Peterstone Court

 RESTAURANT WITH ROOMS

☎ 01874 665387
Llanhamlach LD3 7YB
e-mail: info@peterstone-court.com
dir: 3m from Brecon on A40 towards Abergavenny

Situated on the edge of the Brecon Beacons, this establishment affords stunning views overlooking the River Usk. The atmosphere is friendly and informal; without any unnecessary fuss. No two bedrooms are alike, but all share comparable levels of comfort, quality and elegance. Public areas reflect similar standards, eclectically styled with a blend of the contemporary and the traditional. Quality produce is cooked with care in a range of enjoyable dishes.

Rooms 12 (4 annexe) (2 fmly)

BRIDGEND	Map 9 SS97
Bridgend	

BEST WESTERN Heronston Hotel

★★★ 76% HOTEL

☎ 01656 668811
Ewenny Rd CF35 5AW
e-mail:
reservations@bestwesternheronstonhotel.co.uk
web: www.bw-heronstonhotel.co.uk
dir: M4 junct 35, follow signs for Porthcawl, at 5th rdbt left towards Ogmore-by-Sea (B4265), hotel 200yds on left

Situated within easy reach of the town centre and the M4, this large modern hotel offers spacious well-equipped accommodation, including ground-floor rooms. Public areas include an open-plan lounge/bar, attractive restaurant and a smart leisure and fitness club. The hotel also has a choice of function and conference rooms, and ample parking is available.

Rooms 75 (4 fmly) (37 GF) ✿ **S** £69-£120; **D** £79-£130 (incl. bkfst) **Facilities** STV Wi-fi ఓ HL ⊙ Gym Steam room Sauna Spa pool New Year **Conf** Class 80 Board 60 Thtr 250 Del from £99 to £120 **Services** Lift **Parking** 160 **Notes** LB Civ Wed 200

Court Colman Manor

★★★ 72% ⑧ COUNTRY HOUSE HOTEL

☎ 01656 720212
Pen-y-Fai CF31 4NG
e-mail: experience@court-colman-manor.com
dir: M4 junct 36, A4063 towards Maesteg, after lights 1st exit to Bridgend, under motorway, next right, follow hotel signs

Dating back to the Tudor times this fine mansion is set in its own peaceful grounds outside Bridgend, and is just a short distance from the M4. The spacious, comfortable bedrooms include ten themed rooms inspired by an exotic location - India, Japan, Morocco etc. The award-winning food served in Bokhara Brasserie is imaginative, and Indian and Mediterranean dishes are included in the choices. Diners can see their meals being prepared in the open-plan kitchen.

Rooms 30 (2 fmly) ✿ **S** £51-£61; **D** £71-£121* **Facilities** FTV Wi-fi ఓ HL Xmas New Year **Conf** Class 60 Thtr 100 Del from £95* **Parking** 180 **Notes** ⊗ Civ Wed 150

Premier Inn Bridgend Central

Premier Inn

BUDGET HOTEL

☎ 0871 527 8146
The Derwen CF32 9ST
web: www.premierinn.com
dir: M4 junct 36, A4061 (signed Bridgend & Pen-y-Bont). Hotel at next rdbt

High quality, budget accommodation ideal for both families and business travellers. Spacious, en suite bedrooms feature tea and coffee making facilities, and Freeview TV in most hotels. Internet access and Wi-fi are available for a small fee. The adjacent family restaurant features a wide and varied menu. See also the Hotel Groups pages.

Rooms 68

Premier Inn Bridgend M4 Jct 35

BUDGET HOTEL

☎ 0871 527 8144
Pantruthyn Farm, Pencoed CF35 5HY
web: www.premierinn.com
dir: At M4 junct 35, behind petrol station & McDonalds

Rooms 40

B

BUILTH WELLS
Map 9 SO05
Powys

Caer Beris Manor Hotel
THE INDEPENDENTS
HOTEL ASSOCIATION

★★★ 77% COUNTRY HOUSE HOTEL

☎ 01982 552601
LD2 3NP
e-mail: caerberis@btconnect.com
web: www.caerberis.com
dir: From town centre follow A483/Llandovery signs.
Hotel on left

Guests can expect a relaxing stay at this friendly and
privately-owned boutique, country house hotel that
has extensive and attractive landscaped grounds.
Bedrooms are individually decorated and furnished to
retain an atmosphere of a bygone era. The spacious
and comfortable lounge, complete with log fire, and
lounge bar continue this theme. Dining is available in
the elegant 1896 Restaurant, complete with 16th-
century panelling. Those aiming for total relaxation
can also indulge in a well-being treatment including
massages and facials.

Rooms 23 (2 fmly) (3 GF) ⚓ **S** £78.95-£88.95;
D £139.90-£199.90 (incl. bkfst)* **Facilities** FTV Wi-fi
↘ Fishing ⚑ Clay pigeon shooting Birdwatching
Xmas New Year **Conf** Class 75 Board 50 Thtr 100
Parking 100 **Notes** LB Civ Wed 200

CAERNARFON
Map 14 SH46
Gwynedd

INSPECTORS' CHOICE

Seiont Manor Hotel

★★★ ◎◎
COUNTRY HOUSE HOTEL

☎ 01286 673366
Llanrug LL55 2AQ
e-mail: seiontmanor@handpicked.co.uk
web: www.handpickedhotels.co.uk/seiontmanor
dir: E on A4086, 2.5m from Caernarfon

A splendid hotel created from authentic farm
buildings, set in the tranquil countryside near
Snowdonia; the River Seiont flows through the 150-
acre grounds. The bedrooms, including junior
suites, are individually decorated and have
luxurious extra touches; each has either a balcony
or patio. The comfortable public rooms are cosy and
furnished in country-house style. The kitchen team
use the best local produce to provide exciting takes
on traditional dishes, and guests can choose to eat
in either the award-winning Llwyn y Brain
Restaurant or the conservatory brasserie.

Rooms 28 (2 fmly) (14 GF) ⚓ **S** £85-£155;
D £105-£245 (incl. bkfst)* **Facilities** STV FTV Wi-fi
↘ HL 🐟 Fishing Gym Xmas New Year **Conf** Class 40
Board 40 Thtr 100 **Parking** 60 **Notes** LB ⊗
Civ Wed 100

Celtic Royal Hotel

★★★ 80% HOTEL

☎ 01286 674477
Bangor St LL55 1AY
e-mail: reservations@celtic-royal.co.uk
web: www.celtic-royal.co.uk
dir: Exit A55 at Bangor, take A487 towards
Caernarfon

This large, impressive, privately owned hotel is
situated in the town centre. It provides attractively
appointed accommodation, which includes family
rooms and bedrooms for less able guests. The
spacious public areas include a bar, a choice of
lounges and a pleasant split-level restaurant. Guests
also have the use of the impressive health club.

Rooms 110 (12 fmly) ⚓ **S** £86-£105; **D** £120-£145
(incl. bkfst)* **Facilities** Wi-fi 🐟 Gym Steam room
Sauna ♬ Xmas New Year **Conf** Class 120 Board 120
Thtr 300 Del from £128 to £135* **Services** Lift
Parking 180 **Notes** LB ⊗ Civ Wed 200

Premier Inn Caernarfon

BUDGET HOTEL

☎ 0871 527 8180
Victioria Dock, Balaclava Rd LL55 1SQ
web: www.premierinn.com
dir: A55 junct 9, at rdbt 1st exit follow Caernarfon
signs. In Caernarfon at rdbt (Morrisons on right) 1st
exit, keep in right lane, at next rdbt 4th exit to mini
rdbt, hotel opposite

High quality, budget accommodation ideal for both
families and business travellers. Spacious, en suite
bedrooms feature tea and coffee making facilities,
and Freeview TV in most hotels. Internet access and
Wi-fi are available for a small fee. The adjacent
family restaurant features a wide and varied menu.
See also the Hotel Groups pages.

Rooms 49

CAERPHILLY   Map 9 ST18
Caerphilly

Premier Inn Caerphilly (Corbetts Lane)

BUDGET HOTEL

☎ 0871 527 8182
Corbetts Ln CF83 3HX
web: www.premierinn.com
dir: M4 junct 32, A470, 2nd left signed Caerphilly. At rdbt 4th exit, at next rdbt 2nd exit. Straight on at next rdbt & at Pwllypant Rdbt, hotel on left

High quality, budget accommodation ideal for both families and business travellers. Spacious, en suite bedrooms feature tea and coffee making facilities, and Freeview TV in most hotels. Internet access and Wi-fi are available for a small fee. The adjacent family restaurant features a wide and varied menu. See also the Hotel Groups pages.

Rooms 42

Premier Inn Caerphilly (Crossways)

BUDGET HOTEL

☎ 0871 527 8184
Crossways Business Park, Pontypandy CF83 3NL
web: www.premierinn.com
dir: M4 junct 32, A470 towards Merthyr Tydfil (junct 4 take A458 towards Caerphilly). At Crossways Business Park (5th rdbt). Hotel on right at McDonald's rdbt

Rooms 40

CAPEL CURIG   Map 14 SH75
Conwy

Cobdens Hotel

★★ 62% SMALL HOTEL

☎ 01690 720243
LL24 0EE
e-mail: info@cobdens.co.uk
dir: On A5, 4m N of Betws-y-Coed

Situated in the heart of Snowdonia, this hotel has been a centre for mountaineering and other outdoor pursuits for many years. A wide range of meals using local produce is served in the restaurant. There are two bars including the aptly named Mountain Bar, built in the side of the mountain. A sauna room is also available.

Rooms 17 (4 fmly) **Facilities** STV FTV Wi-fi ♭ Fishing Sauna Pool table New Year **Conf** Class 25 Board 30 Thtr 50 **Parking** 40 **Notes** Closed Jan RS 24-25 & 31 Dec

CARDIFF   Map 9 ST17
Cardiff

The St David's Hotel & Spa

★★★★★ 78% HOTEL

☎ 029 2045 4045
Havannah St CF10 5SD
e-mail: stdavids.reservations@principal-hayley.com
web: www.thestdavidshotel.com
dir: M4 junct 33, A4232 for 9m, follow Cardiff Bay signs, then Techniquest signs, at top exit slip road, 1st left at rdbt, 1st right

This imposing contemporary building sits in a prime position on Cardiff Bay and has a seven-storey atrium creating a dramatic impression. Leading from the atrium are the practically designed and comfortable bedrooms. Tides Restaurant, adjacent to the stylish cocktail bar, has views across the water to Penarth, and there is a quiet first-floor lounge for guests seeking peace and quiet. A well-equipped spa and extensive business areas complete the package.

Rooms 142 🐾 **Facilities** Spa FTV Wi-fi ♭ ☜ Gym Fitness studio Hydrotherapy pool Aerobics studio ♬ Xmas New Year **Conf** Class 110 Board 76 Thtr 270 Del from £149 to £299* **Services** Lift Air con **Parking** 60 **Notes** ⊗ Civ Wed 270

Park Plaza Cardiff

★★★★ 80% ⚜ HOTEL

☎ 029 2011 1111 & 2011 1101
Greyfriars Rd CF10 3AL
e-mail: ppcres@parkplazahotels.co.uk
web: www.parkplazacardiff.com
dir: From M4 follow city centre (A470) signs. Left into Boulevard de Nantes immediately left into Greyfriars Rd. Hotel on left by New Theatre

A smart hotel located in the city centre that features eye-catching, contemporary decor, a state-of-the-art indoor leisure facility, extensive conference and banqueting facilities and the spacious Laguna Kitchen and Bar. The bedrooms are also up-to-the-minute in style and feature a host of extras including a private bar, a safe and modem points.

Rooms 129 (20 fmly) 🐾 **S** £89-£230; **D** £89-£240* **Facilities** Spa FTV Wi-fi ♭ ☜ Gym Dance studio Steam room New Year **Conf** Class 80 Board 60 Thtr 150 Del from £145 to £175* **Services** Lift Air con **Notes** LB ⊗ Closed 24-26 Dec Civ Wed 120

Cardiff Marriott Hotel

★★★★ 79% ⚜ HOTEL

☎ 029 2039 9944
Mill Ln CF10 1EZ
web: www.cardiffmarriott.co.uk
dir: M4 junct 29, A48(M) E follow signs city centre & Cardiff Bay. 3m, right into Mill Lane

Centrally located in the Café Quarter of the city, this modern hotel has spacious public areas and a good range of services to suit both business and leisure guests. The eating options include the informal Chats Café Bar, and the Brasserie Centrale for contemporary French cuisine that uses locally sourced ingredients. The well-equipped bedrooms are comfortable and air conditioned. The leisure suite includes a multi-gym and a good size swimming pool.

Rooms 184 (68 fmly) 🐾 **Facilities** STV Wi-fi ♭ ☜ Gym Steam room Sauna Spa bath New Year **Conf** Class 200 Board 100 Thtr 400 Del from £140 to £180 **Services** Lift Air con **Parking** 146 **Notes** ⊗ Civ Wed 200

Mercure Cardiff Holland House Hotel & Spa

Mercure

★★★★ 76% HOTEL

☎ 029 2043 5000
24/26 Newport Rd CF24 0DD
e-mail: h6622@accor.com
web: www.mercure.com
dir: M4 junct 33, A4232 to city centre, right at lights facing prison, straight through next lights, hotel car park end of lane facing Magistrates Court

Conveniently located just a few minutes' walk from the city centre, this exciting hotel combines contemporary styling with a genuinely friendly welcome. Bedrooms, including five luxurious suites, are spacious and include many welcome extras. A state-of-the-art leisure club and spa is available in addition to a large function room. An eclectic menu provides a varied range of freshly prepared, quality dishes.

Rooms 165 (80 fmly) (8 smoking) **Facilities** Spa STV Wi-fi ☜ supervised Gym **Conf** Class 140 Board 42 Thtr 700 **Services** Lift Air con **Parking** 90 **Notes** Civ Wed 500

C

CARDIFF *continued*

The Parc Hotel, Cardiff   thistle

★★★★ 75% ◉ HOTEL

☎ 0871 376 9011
Park Place CF10 3UD
e-mail: cardiff@thistle.co.uk
web: www.thistle.com/theparchotel
dir: M4 junct 29, A48(M), 4th exit signed City Centre/
A470. At rdbt 2nd exit signed City Centre/A470

Ideally located in the very centre of Cardiff, this
bustling hotel retains an exterior of Victorian
splendour while the interior is contemporary. The
bedrooms are spacious, modern and well equipped,
and a range of dining options is available including
the Harlech Lounge & Bar and the modern Crown
Social Restaurant which offers quality food with
efficient service.

Rooms 140 (5 fmly) ₣ **Facilities** STV Wi-fi
Complimentary use of Vitality Gym opp hotel Xmas
New Year **Conf** Class 100 Board 50 Thtr 225
Services Lift Air con **Parking** 60 **Notes** ⊗
Civ Wed 225

Copthorne Hotel Cardiff-Caerdydd

★★★★ 73% HOTEL

☎ 029 2059 9100
Copthorne Way, Culverhouse Cross CF5 6DH
e-mail:
reservations.cardiff@millenniumhotels.co.uk
web: www.millenniumhotels.co.uk
dir: M4 junct 33, A4232 for 2.5m towards Cardiff
West. Take A48 W to Cowbridge

Nestled on the peaceful banks of its own ornamental
lake The Copthorne hotel is located a few minutes'
drive from the M4, the city centre and Cardiff Airport.
The hotel benefits from a complimentary car parking
for up to 225 cars and an in-house leisure club,
which features a 15-metre swimming pool, gym,
sauna, spa bath and steam room. For a memorable
dining experience, visit the Raglans Restaurant where
fresh produce takes centre stage. The Burgess Bar
and lounge area provides a relaxed environment for
drinks and light meals by the fireplace .

Rooms 135 (7 fmly) (27 GF) **Facilities** STV Wi-fi ⊗
Gym Sauna Steam room Xmas New Year
Conf Class 140 Board 80 Thtr 300 **Services** Lift
Parking 225 **Notes** Civ Wed 200

Novotel Cardiff Central

★★★★ 73% HOTEL

☎ 029 2047 5000
Schooner Way, Atlantic Wharf CF10 4RT
e-mail: h5982@accor.com
web: www.novotel.com
dir: M4 junct 29 onto A48(M), follow signs for city
centre

Situated in the heart of the city's development area,
this hotel is equally convenient for the centre and
Cardiff Bay. Bedrooms vary between standard rooms
in the modern extension and executive rooms in the
original wing. There is good seating space in public
rooms, and the hotel has a popular leisure club and
the Elements Restaurant innovative dining concept.

Rooms 138 (100 fmly) ₣ **S** £80-£395; **D** £95-£405
Facilities FTV Wi-fi ⊗ ⊗ Gym Sauna Steam room
Xmas New Year **Conf** Class 90 Board 65 Thtr 250
Del from £125 to £200* **Services** Lift Air con
Parking 120 **Notes** LB Civ Wed 250

The Angel Hotel

PUMA HOTELS
COLLECTION

★★★★ 70% HOTEL

☎ 029 2064 9200
Castle St CF10 1SZ
e-mail: angel@pumahotels.co.uk
web: www.pumahotels.co.uk
dir: Opposite Cardiff Castle

The Angel is a well-established hotel in the heart of
the city, overlooking the famous castle and almost
opposite the Millennium Stadium. All bedrooms offer
air conditioning and are appointed to a good
standard. Public areas include an impressive lobby, a
modern restaurant and a selection of conference
rooms. There is limited parking at the rear of the
hotel.

Rooms 102 (3 fmly) **Facilities** STV Wi-fi Xmas New
Year **Conf** Class 120 Board 50 Thtr 300 **Services** Lift
Air con **Parking** 60 **Notes** Civ Wed 200

Holiday Inn Cardiff City

Holiday Inn

★★★ 78% HOTEL

☎ 0800 405060 & 0871 942 9240
Castle St CF10 1XD
e-mail: cardiffcity@ihg.com
web: www.hicardiffcitycentre.co.uk
dir: M4 junct 29 E/A48(M), follow city centre signs,
onto A470. Turn left to hotel

This hotel has a fantastic location in the heart of the
city and is just a short walk from the Millennium
Stadium, Cardiff Castle and Cardiff Bay. There are
state-of-the-art conference and meeting facilities
available as well as banqueting. The air-conditioned
accommodation is modern with many guest extras

provided. The restaurant offers a good menu choice or
guests can take a snack in the lounge/bar area.

Rooms 157 (20 fmly) (10 smoking) **Facilities** STV FTV
Wi-fi ⊗ HL Xmas New Year **Conf** Class 60 Board 50
Thtr 180 **Services** Lift Air con **Parking** 85 **Notes** ⊗
Civ Wed 100

Park Inn by Radisson Cardiff City Centre

park inn
by Radisson

★★★ 77% HOTEL

☎ 029 2034 1441 & 2072 7026
Mary Ann St CF10 2JH
e-mail: info.cardiff-city@rezidorparkinn.com
dir: In city centre adjacent to John Lewis building &
Motorpoint Arena Cardiff. Follow signs to St Davids
car park adjacent to hotel

This hotel is ideal for both business travellers and
leisure guests, being situated in the centre of the city,
and close to the shops and the Millennium Stadium.
The accommodation has been appointed in a
contemporary style, with guest comfort as the key
consideration. The friendly restaurant provides a good
range of contemporary dishes, including grill
specialities. Limited secure parking is available.

Rooms 146 (9 fmly) ₣ **Facilities** STV Wi-fi ⊗
Arrangement with local gym nearby ♫ Xmas New
Year **Conf** Class 120 Board 50 Thtr 300 Del from £125
to £185* **Services** Lift **Parking** 40 **Notes** ⊗
Civ Wed 300

Park Inn by Radisson Cardiff North

park inn
by Radisson

★★★ 72% HOTEL

☎ 029 2058 9988
Circle Way East, Llanedeyrn CF23 9XF
e-mail: info.cardiff@rezidorparkinn.com
web: www.cardiff.parkinn.co.uk

This hotel is ideal for both business travellers and
leisure guests, being situated just a short distance
from the M4 and convenient for city-centre shopping
and the Millennium Stadium. The accommodation has
been appointed in a contemporary style, with comfort
as the key consideration. The friendly restaurant
provides a good range of dishes including their
specialities. There is a complimentary gym and
parking is extensive and secure.

Rooms 132 (16 fmly) (20 GF) **Facilities** STV FTV Wi-fi
⊗ supervised Gym Beauty treatment room Xmas New
Year **Conf** Class 160 Board 160 Thtr 200 **Services** Lift
Air con **Parking** 200 **Notes** ⊗ Civ Wed

The Legacy Cardiff International Hotel

★★★ 70% HOTEL

☎ 08444 119074 & 0330 333 2874
Merthyr Rd, Tongwynlais CF15 7LH
e-mail:
res-cardiffinternational@legacy-hotels.co.uk
dir: M4 junct 32, follow Tongwynlais A4054 signs at large rdbt, hotel on right

This modern hotel is conveniently located off the M4 and has easy access to Cardiff and the Millennium Stadium. Guests can enjoy the spacious open-plan public areas and relax in the well-proportioned and well-equipped bedrooms, which include some suites. A good range of meeting rooms makes this hotel a popular conference venue. There is ample parking in the area around the hotel.

Rooms 95 (38 fmly) (20 GF) **Facilities** FTV Wi-fi Xmas New Year **Conf** Class 120 Board 60 Thtr 180 **Services** Lift **Parking** 180 **Notes** Civ Wed

Sandringham Hotel

★★ 71% HOTEL

☎ 029 2023 2161
21 St Mary St CF10 1PL
e-mail: mm@sandringham-hotel.com
dir: M4 junct 29, follow 'city centre' signs. Opposite castle left into High St; leads to St Mary St (pedestrianised). Hotel on left

This friendly, privately owned and personally run hotel is near the Millennium Stadium and offers a convenient base for access to the city centre. Bedrooms are well equipped, and diners can relax in Café Jazz, the hotel's adjoining restaurant, where live music is provided most week nights. There is also a separate lounge/bar for residents, and an airy breakfast room.

Rooms 28 (1 fmly) **S** £33-£110; **D** £36-£155 (incl. bkfst) **Facilities** FTV Wi-fi ♫ **Conf** Class 70 Board 60 Thtr 100 Del from £75 to £165 **Notes** ⊗ Closed 24-26 Dec (pm)

Mercure Cardiff Centre Hotel

Ⓤ

☎ 029 2089 4000
Wharf Road East, Tyndall St CF10 4BB
e-mail: h6623@accor.com
web: www.mercure.com
dir: M4 juncts 29 & 33 follow city centre signs

Currently the rating for this establishment is not confirmed. We are working with the management / owners whilst works and changes take place to achieve an AA star rating. For further details please see the AA website: theAA.com

Rooms 100 (48 fmly) (27 GF) **S** £50-£250; **D** £50-£250* **Facilities** STV Wi-fi ♿ Leisure facilities at Mercure Holland House **Services** Lift Air con **Parking** 90

Holiday Inn Express Cardiff Airport

BUDGET HOTEL

☎ 01446 711117
Port Rd, Rhoose CF62 3BT
e-mail: sales@exhicardiffairport.co.uk
web: www.hiexpress.com/cardiffairport
dir: M4 junct 33, follow signs for Barry & Cardiff Airport. Hotel adjacent to airport terminal

A modern hotel ideal for families and business travellers. Fresh and uncomplicated, the spacious rooms include Sky TV, power shower and tea and coffee-making facilities. Continental buffet breakfast is included in the room rate; other meals may be taken at the nearby family pub or restaurant. See also the Hotel Groups pages.

Rooms 111 (60 fmly) (22 GF) (7 smoking) ♟ **S** £39.95-£54.95; **D** £39.95-£54.95 (incl. bkfst)* **Conf** Class 20 Board 20 Thtr 40 Del £69.95*

Holiday Inn Express Cardiff Bay

BUDGET HOTEL

☎ 029 2044 9000
Atlantic Wharf CF10 4EE
e-mail: reservations@exhicardiff.co.uk
web: www.hiexpresscardiff.co.uk
dir: M4 junct 33, A4232 through Queensgate Tunnel. Left at rdbt, into Hemmingway Rd, right into Schooner Way, 2nd right

Rooms 87 (49 fmly) (15 GF) ♟ **Conf** Class 12 Board 20 Thtr 30

Ibis Cardiff City Centre

BUDGET HOTEL

☎ 029 2064 9250
Churchill Way CF10 2HA
e-mail: H2936@accor.com
web: www.ibishotel.com
dir: M4 junct 29, to junct 29A, A48(M), A48, 2nd exit A4232. Follow signs to City Centre on Newport Rd, left after rail bridge, left after Queen St station

Modern, budget hotel offering comfortable accommodation in bright and practical bedrooms. Breakfast is self-service and dinner is available in the restaurant. See also the Hotel Groups pages.

Rooms 102 (19 GF)

Ibis Cardiff Gate

BUDGET HOTEL

☎ 029 2073 3222
Malthouse Av, Cardiff Gate Business Park, Pontprennau CF23 8RA
e-mail: H3159@accor.com
web: www.ibishotel.com
dir: M4 junct 30, follow Cardiff Service Station signs. Hotel on left

Rooms 78 (19 fmly) (22 GF) (7 smoking) **Conf** Class 24 Thtr 25

Premier Inn Barry Island (Cardiff Airport)

BUDGET HOTEL

☎ 0871 527 9370
Triangle Site, Fford Y Mileniwm, The Waterfront, Hood Rd CF62 5QN
web: www.premierinn.com
dir: M4 junct 33 A4232 signed A4050, pass through 8 rdbts left onto Trinity St, right onto A4055 Broad St. Left after 0.2m.

High quality, budget accommodation ideal for both families and business travellers. Spacious, en suite bedrooms feature tea and coffee making facilities, and Freeview TV in most hotels. Internet access and Wi-fi are available for a small fee. The adjacent family restaurant features a wide and varied menu. See also the Hotel Groups pages.

Rooms 80

CARDIFF *continued*

Premier Inn Cardiff City Centre

BUDGET HOTEL

☎ 0871 527 8196
Helmont House, 10 Churchill Way CF10 2NB
web: www.premierinn.com
dir: M4 junct 29 onto A48(M) towards Cardiff (East & South), 4.5m. Follow Cardiff (East), Docks & A4232 signs. Left at A4161 (Eastern Avenue North). At rdbt 2nd exit onto A4161 (Newport Rd). 2m, left into Station Terrace. Right into Churchill Way

Rooms 200

Premier Inn Cardiff City South

BUDGET HOTEL

☎ 0871 527 8198
Keen Rd CF24 5JT
web: www.premierinn.com
dir: Follow Cardiff Docks & Bay signs from A48(M), over flyover. At 5th rdbt 3rd exit. Hotel 1st right, 1st right again

Rooms 77

Premier Inn Cardiff East

BUDGET HOTEL

☎ 0871 527 8200
Newport Rd, Castleton CF3 2UQ
web: www.premierinn.com
dir: M4 junct 28, A48 signed Castleton. 3m, hotel on right

Rooms 49

Premier Inn Cardiff North

BUDGET HOTEL

☎ 0871 527 8202
Pentwyn Rd, Pentwyn CF23 7XH
web: www.premierinn.com
dir: W'bound: M4 junct 29, A48(M). (E'bound: M4 junct 30, A4232 signs, A48(M) towards Cardiff). Follow Pentwyn signs, 3rd exit at rdbt. Hotel 200yds on right

Rooms 142

Premier Inn Cardiff (Roath)

BUDGET HOTEL

☎ 0871 527 8194
Ipswich Rd, Roath CF23 9AQ
web: www.premierinn.com
dir: W'bound: M4 junct 29, A48(M) (or E'bound: M4 junct 30 A48(M)). Follow Cardiff (E) Docks & Cardiff Bay signs. Then follow brown signs for David Lloyd Tennis Centre. Into David Lloyd Leisure Club car park, follow hotel signs

Rooms 75

Premier Inn Cardiff West

BUDGET HOTEL

☎ 0871 527 8204
Port Rd, Nantisaf, Wenvoe CF5 6DD
web: www.premierinn.com
dir: M4 junct 33, S on A4232. Take 2nd exit (signed Airport), 3rd exit at Culverhouse Cross rdbt. Hotel 0.5m on Barry Rd (A4050)

Rooms 39

Ivy Bush Royal Hotel

★★★ 77% HOTEL

☎ 01267 235111
Spilman St SA31 1LG
e-mail: reception@ivybushroyal.co.uk
web: www.ivybushroyal.co.uk
dir: A48 to Carmarthen, over 1st rdbt, at 2nd rdbt right onto A4242. Straight over next 2 rdbts. Left at lights. Hotel on right at top of hill

This hotel offers spacious, well-equipped bedrooms and bathrooms, a relaxing lounge with outdoor patio seating and a comfortable restaurant serving a varied selection of carefully prepared meals. Weddings, meetings and conferences are all well catered for at this friendly, family-run establishment.

Rooms 70 (4 fmly) ♠ **Facilities** FTV Wi-fi ↘ Gym Xmas New Year **Conf** Class 50 Board 40 Thtr 200 **Services** Lift **Parking** 83 **Notes** ⊗ Civ Wed 150

Falcon Hotel

★★★ 74% HOTEL

☎ 01267 234959 & 237152
Lammas St SA31 3AP
e-mail: reception@falconcarmarthen.co.uk
web: www.falconcarmarthen.co.uk
dir: In town centre pass bus station, left, hotel 200yds on left

This friendly hotel has been owned and run by the Exton family for over 45 years, and it is located in the centre of the town. Bedrooms, some with four-poster beds, are tastefully decorated and have good facilities. There is a comfortable lounge with adjacent bar, and the restaurant offers a varied selection of enjoyable dishes at both lunch and dinner.

Rooms 16 (1 fmly) **Facilities** FTV ↘ **Conf** Class 50 Board 40 Thtr 80 **Parking** 36 **Notes** Closed 26 Dec RS Sun

St Pierre, A Marriott Hotel & Country Club

★★★★ 79% ⑳ COUNTRY HOUSE HOTEL

☎ 01291 625261
St Pierre Park NP16 6YA
e-mail: mhrs.cwlgs.frontdesk@marriotthotels.com
web: www.marriottstpierre.co.uk
dir: M48 junct 2, A466 for Chepstow. At next rdbt 1st exit signed Caerwent A48. Hotel approx 2m on left

This 14th-century property offers an extensive range of leisure and conference facilities. The comfortable bedrooms are well equipped and located in adjacent wings or in a lakeside cottage complex. The main bar, popular with golfers, overlooks the 18th green; diners can choose between an elegant, traditional restaurant or a modern brasserie.

Rooms 148 (16 fmly) (75 GF) **Facilities** Spa STV Wi-fi ⊛ ⅃ 36 ☙ Putt green Fishing ⅃ Gym Chipping green Floodlit driving range Sauna Steam room Xmas New Year **Conf** Class 120 Board 90 Thtr 240 **Parking** 440 **Notes** ⊗ Civ Wed 220

Save on hotels. Book at **theAA.com/hotel**

CAR – CRI 571 WALES

Castle View Hotel

★★★ 66% HOTEL

☎ 01291 620349
16 Bridge St NP16 5EZ
e-mail: castleviewhotel@btconnect.com
web: www.castleviewhotel.com
dir: M48 junct 2, A466 for Wye Valley, at 1st rdbt right onto A48 towards Gloucester. Follow 2nd sign to town centre, then to Chepstow Castle, hotel directly opposite

With a location just opposite the castle and the main car park, this hotel offers relaxed and welcoming hospitality and an informal atmosphere. Bedrooms and bathrooms offer a range of shapes and sizes, some with views of the castle. Dinner offers a good selection of well cooked and presented, mainly local, produce.

Rooms 13 (4 annexe) (7 fmly) **Facilities** Wi-fi Xmas New Year

CHIRK
Wrexham   Map 15 SJ23

Moreton Park Hotel

★★★ 75% HOTEL

☎ 01691 776666
Moreton Park, Gledrid LL14 5DG
e-mail: reservations@moretonpark.com
web: www.moretonpark.com
dir: 200yds from rdbt junct of A5 & B5070

Located on the town's outskirts and convenient for the A5, this very well maintained property provides a range of spacious, well-equipped bedrooms ideal for both business and leisure guests. Breakfast, lunch and dinner are available in the adjacent Lord Moreton Bar & Restaurant. Service is friendly and attentive.

Rooms 45 (20 fmly) **Facilities** STV Wi-fi Free use of facilities at sister hotel (0.5m) **Conf** Class 50 Board 20 Thtr 60 **Parking** 200 **Notes** ⊗

CONWY
Conwy   Map 14 SH77

Castle Hotel Conwy

★★★★ 79% ◉◉ TOWN HOUSE HOTEL

☎ 01492 582800
High St LL32 8DB
e-mail: mail@castlewales.co.uk
web: www.castlewales.co.uk
dir: A55 junct 18, follow town centre signs, cross estuary (castle on left). Right then left at mini-rdbts onto one-way system. Right at Town Wall Gate, right into Berry St then High St

This family-run, 16th-century hotel is one of Conwy's most distinguished buildings and offers a relaxed and friendly atmosphere. Bedrooms are appointed to an impressive standard and include a stunning suite. Public areas include a popular modern bar and the award-winning Shakespeare's restaurant.

Rooms 28 (2 fmly) ⚑ **S** £82-£95; **D** £130-£270 (incl. bkfst)* **Facilities** FTV Wi-fi ⌂ Xmas New Year **Conf** Class 20 Board 16 Thtr 30 Del from £109.50 to £119.50* **Parking** 34 **Notes** LB

CRICCIETH
Gwynedd   Map 14 SH43

Bron Eifion Country House Hotel

★★★★ 77% ◉ COUNTRY HOUSE HOTEL

☎ 01766 522385
LL52 0SA
e-mail: enquiries@broneifion.co.uk
dir: A497 between Porthmadog & Pwllheli, 0.5m from Criccieth, on right towards Pwhelli

This delightful country house built in 1883, is set in extensive grounds to the west of Criccieth. Now a privately owned and personally run hotel, it provides warm and very friendly hospitality as well as attentive service. The interior styling highlights the many retained period features. There is a choice of lounges and the very impressive central hall features a minstrels' gallery.

Rooms 18 (1 fmly) (1 GF) ⚑ **S** £95-£135; **D** £135-£185 (incl. bkfst)* **Facilities** FTV Wi-fi ⌂ Xmas New Year **Conf** Class 150 Board 60 Thtr 150 **Parking** 50 **Notes** LB ⊗ Civ Wed 150

George IV Hotel

Leisureplex

★★ 71% HOTEL

☎ 01766 522168
23-25 High St LL52 0BS
e-mail: georgeiv.criccieth@alfatravel.co.uk
web: www.leisureplex.co.uk
dir: On A497 in town centre

This hotel stands back from the A497 in the town centre. The bedrooms, which in general are spacious, are attractively furnished and well equipped to meet the needs of both business guests and holidaymakers. George's Brasserie serves a menu based on locally sourced ingredients.

Rooms 47 (11 fmly) **Facilities** FTV ♪ Xmas New Year **Services** Lift **Parking** 16 **Notes** ⊗ Closed Jan RS Nov & Feb-Mar

CRICKHOWELL
Powys   Map 9 SO21

Manor Hotel

★★★ 75% ◉ HOTEL

☎ 01873 810212
Brecon Rd NP8 1SE
e-mail: info@manorhotel.co.uk
web: www.manorhotel.co.uk
dir: On A40, 0.5m from Crickhowell

This impressive manor house, set in a stunning location, was the birthplace of Sir George Everest. The bedrooms and public areas are elegant, and there are extensive leisure facilities. The restaurant, with panoramic views, is the setting for exciting modern cooking.

Rooms 23 (2 fmly) **S** £69-£100; **D** £85-£160 (incl. bkfst)* **Facilities** STV FTV Wi-fi ⌂ ☉ Gym Fitness assessment Sunbed Xmas New Year **Conf** Class 250 Board 150 Thtr 300 Del from £120 to £140* **Parking** 200 **Notes** LB Civ Wed 150

C

CWMBRAN   Map 9 ST29
Torfaen

BEST WESTERN PLUS Parkway Hotel

★★★★ 79% HOTEL

☎ 01633 871199
Cwmbran Dr NP44 3UW
e-mail: enquiries@parkwayhotel.co.uk
web: www.bw-parkwayhotel.co.uk
dir: M4 junct 25a & 26, A4051 follow Cwmbran-Llantarnam Park signs. Right at rdbt, right for hotel

This purpose-built hotel, in over seven acres of grounds, offers comfortable bedrooms and public areas that will suit a wide range of guests. The coffee shop is an informal eating option throughout the day, and there is fine dining in Ravello's Restaurant. The bedrooms, including suites, interconnecting family rooms and wheelchair access rooms, are stylishly appointed. Additional facilities include a sports centre and conference and meeting facilities.

Rooms 70 (4 fmly) (34 GF) **S** £65-£125; **D** £80-£145 (incl. bkfst)* **Facilities** Spa STV FTV Wi-fi ⬇ ⓒ Gym Steam room Sauna Solaria ♫ Xmas New Year **Conf** Class 240 Board 100 Thtr 500 Del from £111 to £169* **Parking** 350 **Notes** LB ⊗ Civ Wed 250

Premier Inn Cwmbran

BUDGET HOTEL

☎ 0870 111 2851
Avondale Rd, Pontrhydyrun NP44 1DE
web: www.premierinn.com
dir: M4 junct 26, A4501 signed Cwmbran, straight on at next 5 rdbts. At 6th take Pontrhydyrun Rd exit, left into Avondale Rd

High quality, budget accommodation ideal for both families and business travellers. Spacious, en suite bedrooms feature tea and coffee making facilities, and Freeview TV in most hotels. Internet access and Wi-fi are available for a small fee. The adjacent family restaurant features a wide and varied menu. See also the Hotel Groups pages.

Rooms 40

DEGANWY   Map 14 SH77
Conwy

Quay Hotel & Spa
★★★★ 85% ⚙ HOTEL

☎ 01492 564100
Deganwy Quay LL31 9DJ
e-mail: info@quayhotel.com
web: www.quayhotel.co.uk
dir: M56, A494, A55 junct 18, straight across 2 rdbts. At lights bear left into The Quay. Hotel on right

This boutique hotel occupies a stunning position beside the estuary on Deganwy's Quay. What was once an area for railway storage is now a property of modern architectural design offering hotel-keeping of the highest standard. Spacious bedrooms, many with balconies and wonderful views, are decorated in neutral colours and boast a host of thoughtful extras, including up-to-the-minute communication systems. The friendly staff provide a fluent service in a charmingly informal manner.

Rooms 74 (15 fmly) (30 GF) **Facilities** Spa Wi-fi HL ⓒ supervised Gym Steam & sauna room Hydro therapy pool Xmas New Year **Conf** Class 240 Board 90 Thtr 240 **Services** Lift **Parking** 96 **Notes** LB Civ Wed 150

DEVIL'S BRIDGE   Map 9 SN77
Ceredigion

The Hafod Hotel
★★★ 70% HOTEL

☎ 01970 890232
SY23 3JL
e-mail: hafodhotel@btconnect.com
dir: Exit A44 in Ponterwyd signed Devil's Bridge/Pontarfynach onto A4120, 3m, over bridge. Hotel opposite

This former hunting lodge dates back to the 17th century and is situated in six acres of grounds. Now a family-owned and run hotel, it provides accommodation suitable for both business and leisure guests. Family rooms and a four-poster room are available. In addition to the dining area and lounge, there are tea rooms.

Rooms 17 (2 fmly) **Facilities** Wi-fi Xmas New Year **Conf** Class 70 Board 40 Thtr 100 **Parking** 200 **Notes** Civ Wed 40

DOLGELLAU   Map 14 SH71
Gwynedd

INSPECTORS' CHOICE

Penmaenuchaf Hall Hotel

★★★ ⚙⚙
COUNTRY HOUSE HOTEL

☎ 01341 422129
Penmaenpool LL40 1YB
e-mail: relax@penhall.co.uk
web: www.penhall.co.uk
dir: A470 onto A493 to Tywyn. Hotel approx 1m on left

Built in 1860, this impressive hall stands in 20 acres of formal gardens, grounds and woodland, and enjoys magnificent views across the River Mawddach. Sympathetic restoration has created a comfortable and welcoming hotel with spacious day rooms and thoughtfully furnished bedrooms, some with private balconies. Fresh produce cooked in modern British style is served in an elegant conservatory restaurant, overlooking the countryside.

Rooms 14 (2 fmly) ♞ **S** £118-£185; **D** £174-£268 (incl. bkfst) **Facilities** STV FTV Wi-fi ⬇ ⚘ Complimentary salmon & trout fishing Coracling Xmas New Year **Conf** Class 30 Board 22 Thtr 50 Del from £125 to £189* **Parking** 30 **Notes** LB No children 6yrs Civ Wed 65

Save on hotels. Book at **theAA.com/hotel**

CWM – GWB 573 | WALES

EBBW VALE
Blaenau Gwent
Map 9 SO10

Premier Inn Ebbw Vale
BUDGET HOTEL

☎ 0871 527 8356
Victoria Business Park, Waunllwyd NP23 8AN
web: www.premierinn.com
dir: M4 junct 28, A467 signed Risca, then Brynmawr.
At rdbt at Brynithel 1st exit onto A4046, signed Ebbw
Vale. At rdbt 3rd exit towards Waunllwyd. At rdbt 1st
exit, next left. Hotel adjacent

High quality, budget accommodation ideal for both
families and business travellers. Spacious, en suite
bedrooms feature tea and coffee making facilities,
and Freeview TV in most hotels. Internet access and
Wi-fi are available for a small fee. The adjacent
family restaurant features a wide and varied menu.
See also the Hotel Groups pages.

Rooms 44

EGLWYS FACH
Ceredigion
Map 14 SN69

INSPECTORS' CHOICE

Plas Ynyshir Hall Hotel
★★★ ◉◉◉
COUNTRY HOUSE HOTEL

☎ 01654 781209 & 781268
SY20 8TA
e-mail: ynyshir@relaischateaux.com
web: www.ynyshirhall.co.uk
dir: Exit A487, 5.5m S of Machynlleth, signed from
main road

Set in beautifully landscaped grounds and
surrounded by the RSPB Ynys-hir Nature Reserve,
Plas Ynyshir Hall is a haven of calm. The house was
once owned by Queen Victoria and it is surrounded
by mountain scenery. Lavishly styled bedrooms,
each individually themed around a great painter,
provide high standards of luxury and comfort. The
lounge and bar, adorned with an abundance of
fresh flowers, have different moods. The dining
room offers highly accomplished cooking using the
best, locally sourced ingredients including herbs,
soft fruit and vegetables from the hotel's own
kitchen garden, and wild foods gathered nearby.
This hotel makes an idyllic location for weddings.

Rooms 10 (3 annexe) (4 GF) 🐾 **S** £222.50-£495;
D £350-£695 (incl. bkfst)* **Facilities** Wi-fi 🏖 ☕
Xmas New Year **Conf** Class 20 Board 18 Thtr 25
Del from £230* **Parking** 20 **Notes** No children 9yrs
Closed 4-31 Jan Civ Wed 40

FISHGUARD
Pembrokeshire
Map 8 SM93

The Cartref Hotel
★★ 67% HOTEL

☎ 01348 872430 & 0781 330 5235
15-19 High St SA65 9AW
e-mail: cartrefhotel@btconnect.com
web: www.cartrefhotel.co.uk
dir: On A40 in town centre

Personally run by the proprietor, this friendly hotel
offers convenient access to the town centre and ferry
terminal. Bedrooms are well maintained and include
some family rooms. There is also a cosy lounge bar
and a welcoming restaurant that looks out onto the
high street.

Rooms 10 (2 fmly) 🐾 **S** £38-£45; **D** £70-£75 (incl.
bkfst)* **Facilities** FTV Wi-fi **Parking** 4

GWBERT-ON-SEA
Ceredigion
Map 14 SN69

The Cliff Hotel
★★★ 75% HOTEL

☎ 01239 613241
SA43 1PP
e-mail: reservations@cliffhotel.com
web: www.cliffhotel.com
dir: A487, into Cardigan, take B4548 towards Gwbert,
2m to hotel

Set in 30 acres of grounds with a 9-hole golf course,
this hotel commands superb sea views from its cliff-
top location overlooking Cardigan Bay. Bedrooms in
the main building have excellent views and there is
also a wing of modern rooms. Public areas are
spacious and comprise a choice of bars, lounges and
a fine dining restaurant. The spa offers a wide range
of up-to-the-minute leisure facilities.

Rooms 70 (6 fmly) (5 GF) 🐾 **Facilities** Spa FTV ⊗ ⳬ
9 Putt green Fishing Gym Xmas New Year
Conf Class 150 Board 140 Thtr 250 Del £99.50*
Services Lift **Parking** 100 **Notes** Civ Wed 200

G

H

The Swan-at-Hay Hotel

★★★ 74% HOTEL

☎ 01497 821188
Church St HR3 5DQ
e-mail: stay@swanathay.co.uk
web: www.swanathay.co.uk
dir: In town centre, on Brecon Road opposite cinema
bookshop

This former coaching inn, now a privately owned
hotel, has plenty of character and overlooks well-
tended gardens. The bedrooms are comfortable, and a
good range of guest extras are provided. The food,
based on fresh local ingredients, is offered on a well-
balanced menu. The Swan's location, between The
Black Mountains and the Brecon Beacons, is ideal for
walkers of course, but also convenient for leisure and
business guests visiting the area. Wi-fi is available.

Rooms 17 (1 fmly) (2 GF) **Facilities** FTV Wi-fi Xmas
New Year **Conf** Class 80 Board 60 Thtr 120
Parking 17 **Notes** RS Jan Civ Wed 80

Vale Resort

★★★★ 79% ⚛ HOTEL

☎ 01443 667800
Hensol Park CF72 8JY
e-mail: reservations@vale-hotel.com
web: www.vale-hotel.com
dir: M4 junct 34 towards Pendoylan, hotel signed
from junct

A wealth of leisure facilities is offered at this large
and modern, purpose-built complex, including two
golf courses and a driving range plus an extensive
health spa with a gym, swimming pool, squash
courts, orthopaedic clinic and a range of treatments.
Public areas are spacious and attractive, while
bedrooms, many with balconies, are well appointed.
Meeting and conference facilities are available.
Guests can dine in the traditional Vale Grill, a
brasserie-style restaurant serving quality fresh
ingredients.

Rooms 143 (114 annexe) (15 fmly) (36 GF) 🐾
S £75-£170; **D** £80-£180 (incl. bkfst)* **Facilities** Spa
STV Wi-fi ⓢ ♨ 36 ⚐ Putt green Fishing Gym
Squash Children's club (Sat am & school hols) Xmas
New Year **Conf** Class 280 Board 60 Thtr 700
Del from £125 to £160 **Services** Lift Air con
Parking 450 **Notes** LB ⊗ Civ Wed 700

Milebrook House Hotel

★★★ 79% ⚛⚛ COUNTRY HOUSE HOTEL

☎ 01547 528632
Milebrook LD7 1LT
e-mail: hotel@milebrook.co.uk
web: www.milebrookhouse.co.uk
dir: 2m E of Knighton, on A4113

Set in three acres of grounds and gardens in the
Teme Valley, this charming house dates back to 1760.
Over the years since its conversion into a hotel, it has
acquired a well-deserved reputation for its warm
hospitality, comfortable accommodation and the
quality of its cuisine, which uses local produce and
home-grown vegetables.

Rooms 10 (2 fmly) (2 GF) **S** £81.50-£88; **D** £140 (incl.
bkfst) **Facilities** Wi-fi ♨ Table tennis Trout fly fishing
Xmas New Year **Conf** Class 30 **Parking** 21 **Notes** LB
⊗ No children 8yrs RS Mon lunch

The Falcondale Hotel & Restaurant

★★★★ 76% ⚛⚛ COUNTRY HOUSE HOTEL

☎ 01570 422910
SA48 7RX
e-mail: info@thefalcondale.co.uk
web: www.thefalcondale.co.uk
dir: 800yds W of High St (A475) or 1.5m NW of
Lampeter (A482)

Built in the Italianate style, this charming Victorian
property is set in extensive grounds and beautiful
parkland. The individually-styled bedrooms are
generally spacious, well equipped and tastefully
decorated. Bars and lounges are similarly well
appointed with additional facilities including a
conservatory and terrace. The award-winning
restaurant, with a relaxed and friendly atmosphere,
offers menus based on the best seasonal, locally
sourced produce.

Rooms 19 (2 fmly) **Facilities** FTV Wi-fi ⓢ ♨ Xmas
New Year **Conf** Class 26 Board 26 Thtr 60
Services Lift **Parking** 60 **Notes** Civ Wed 200

Ty Mawr Hotel

★★ 78% SMALL HOTEL

☎ 01341 241440 & 07717 080171
LL45 2NH
e-mail: info@tymawrhotel.com
web: www.tymawrhotel.com
dir: From Barmouth A496 (Harlech road). In Llanbedr
turn right after bridge, hotel 50yds on left, follow
brown tourist sigs

Ty Mawr means 'Big House' in Welsh. Located in a
picturesque village within Snowdonia National Park,
this family-run hotel has a relaxed, friendly
atmosphere. The attractive grounds, opposite the
River Artro, provide a popular beer garden during fine
weather. The attractive, rustically furnished bar offers
a blackboard selection of food and a good choice of
real ales; a more formal menu is available in the
restaurant. Bedrooms are smart and brightly
decorated.

Rooms 10 (2 fmly) 🐾 **S** £50-£55; **D** £80-£85 (incl.
bkfst) **Facilities** STV FTV Wi-fi **Conf** Class 25
Parking 15 **Notes** LB Closed 24-26 Dec

The Royal Victoria Hotel Snowdonia   fOCUShotels

★★★ 68% HOTEL

☎ 01286 870253
LL55 4TY
e-mail: enquiries@theroyalvictoria.co.uk
web: www.theroyalvictoria.co.uk
dir: On A4086 (Caernarfon to Llanberis road) directly
opposite Snowdon Mountain Railway

This well-established hotel sits near the foot of
Snowdon, between the Peris and Padarn lakes. Pretty
gardens and grounds make an attractive setting for
the many weddings held here. Bedrooms are well
equipped. There are spacious lounges and bars, and
a large dining room with a conservatory looking out
over the lakes.

Rooms 106 (14 annexe) (7 fmly) 🐾 **Facilities** FTV
Wi-fi 𝄞 Xmas New Year **Conf** Class 60 Board 50
Thtr 100 **Services** Lift **Parking** 107
Notes Civ Wed 100

LLANDEILO
Carmarthenshire   Map 8 SN62

The Plough Inn

★★★★ 76% ◉ HOTEL

☎ 01558 823431
Rhosmaen SA19 6NP
e-mail: info@ploughrhosmaen.com
web: www.ploughrhosmaen.com
dir: 0.5m N of Llandeilo on A40

This privately-owned hotel has memorable views over the Towy Valley and the Black Mountains. Bedrooms, situated in a separate wing, are tastefully furnished, spacious and comfortable. The public lounge bar is popular with locals, as is the spacious restaurant where freshly prepared food can be enjoyed. There are also conference facilities, a gym and a sauna.

Rooms 23 (11 fmly) (8 GF) ↰ **S** £70-£90; **D** £90-£120 (incl. bkfst)* **Facilities** FTV Wi-fi Gym Sauna Xmas New Year **Conf** Class 60 Board 30 Thtr 100 Del £97.95* **Services** Air con **Parking** 70 **Notes** LB Civ Wed 120

White Hart Inn

★★ 72% HOTEL

☎ 01558 823419
36 Carmarthen Rd SA19 6RS
e-mail: info@whitehartinnwales.co.uk
web: www.whitehartinnwales.co.uk
dir: A40 onto A483, hotel 200yds on left

This privately-owned, 19th-century roadside hostelry is on the outskirts of town. The modern bedrooms are well equipped and tastefully furnished, and family rooms are available. Public areas include a choice of bars where a wide range of grilled dishes is available. There are several function rooms, including a large self-contained suite.

Rooms 11 (6 fmly) ↰ **S** £40-£45; **D** £60-£70 (incl. bkfst)* **Facilities** STV FTV Wi-fi New Year **Conf** Class 80 Board 40 Thtr 100 **Parking** 50 **Notes** ⊗ Civ Wed 70

LLANDRINDOD WELLS
Powys   Map 9 SO06

The Metropole

★★★★ 77% ◉ HOTEL   CLASSIC BRITISH HOTELS

☎ 01597 823700
Temple St LD1 5DY
e-mail: info@metropole.co.uk
web: www.metropole.co.uk
dir: On A483 in town centre

The centre of this famous spa town is dominated by The Metropole, a large Victorian hotel, which has been personally run by the same family for well over 100 years. The lobby leads to Spencers Bar and Brasserie, and to the comfortable and elegantly styled lounge. Bedrooms vary in style, but all are spacious and well equipped. Facilities include an extensive range of modern conference and function rooms, as well as the impressive leisure centre. Extensive parking is provided to the rear of the hotel.

Rooms 114 (11 fmly) **S** £85-£123; **D** £99-£159 (incl. bkfst)* **Facilities** Spa FTV Wi-fi ↕ ⓣ Gym Beauty & holistic treatments Sauna Steam room Xmas New Year **Conf** Class 200 Board 80 Thtr 300 **Services** Lift **Parking** 150 **Notes** LB Civ Wed 300

LLANDUDNO
Conwy   Map 14 SH78

INSPECTORS' CHOICE

Bodysgallen Hall and Spa

★★★★ ◉◉◉   PRIDE OF BRITAIN HOTELS

COUNTRY HOUSE HOTEL

☎ 01492 584466
LL30 1RS
e-mail: info@bodysgallen.com
web: www.bodysgallen.com
dir: A55 junct 19, A470 towards Llandudno. Hotel 2m on right

Situated in the idyllic surroundings of its own parkland and formal gardens, this 17th-century house is in an elevated position, with views towards Snowdonia and across to Conwy Castle. The lounges and dining room have fine antiques and great character. Accommodation is provided in the house, but also in delightfully converted cottages, together with a superb spa. Friendly and attentive service is discreetly offered, whilst the restaurant features fine local produce prepared with great skill.

Rooms 31 (16 annexe) (4 fmly) (4 GF) ↰ **S** £159-£349; **D** £179-£425 (incl. bkfst) **Facilities** Spa STV FTV Wi-fi ↕ ⓣ ⚑ Gym Beauty treatments Steam room Relaxation room Sauna Xmas New Year **Conf** Class 30 Board 22 Thtr 50 Del £174 **Parking** 50 **Notes** LB ⊗ No children 6yrs Civ Wed 50

Imperial Hotel

★★★★ 80% ◉ HOTEL   CLASSIC BRITISH HOTELS

☎ 01492 877466
The Promenade LL30 1AP
e-mail: reception@theimperial.co.uk
web: www.theimperial.co.uk
dir: A470 to Llandudno

The Imperial is a large and impressive hotel, situated on the promenade with lovely views out over the blue flag beaches to the bay, and within easy reach of the town centre and other amenities. Many of the bedrooms have sea views and there are also several suites available. The elegant Chantrey's Restaurant offers a fixed-price, monthly-changing menu that utilises local produce, and The Terrace is the place to relax and enjoy a leisurely lunch or a snack during the day.

Rooms 98 (10 fmly) ↰ **Facilities** FTV Wi-fi ↕ ⓣ Gym Beauty therapist Hairdressing ♪ Xmas New Year **Conf** Class 50 Board 50 Thtr 150 Del from £145 to £165* **Services** Lift **Parking** 25 **Notes** ⊗ Civ Wed 150

L

LLANDUDNO *continued*

St George's Hotel

★★★★ 80% ◉ HOTEL

☎ 01492 877544 & 862184
The Promenade LL30 2LG
e-mail: sales@stgeorgeswales.co.uk
web: www.stgeorgeswales.co.uk
dir: A55, A470, follow to promenade, 0.25m, hotel on corner

This large and impressive seafront property was the first hotel to be built in the town. Restored to its former glory, the accommodation is of very high quality. The many Victorian features include the splendid, ornate Wedgwood Room restaurant. The terrace restaurant and main lounges overlook the bay; hot and cold snacks are available all day. Many of the thoughtfully equipped bedrooms enjoy sea views.

Rooms 76 (13 fmly) ↸ **S** £90-£200; **D** £110-£245 (incl. bkfst)* **Facilities** STV FTV Wi-fi ᘔ In room beauty treatments Xmas New Year **Conf** Class 200 Board 45 Thtr 250 **Services** Lift Air con **Parking** 36 **Notes** LB ⊗ Civ Wed 200

See advert on opposite page

Empire Hotel & Spa

★★★★ 77% ◉ HOTEL

☎ 01492 860555
Church Walks LL30 2HE
e-mail: reservations@empirehotel.co.uk
web: www.empirehotel.co.uk
dir: From Chester, A55 junct 19 for Llandudno. Follow signs to Promenade, turn right at war memorial & left at rdbt. Hotel 100yds on right

Run by the same family for over almost 60 years, the Empire offers luxuriously appointed bedrooms with every modern facility. The 'Number 72' rooms in an adjacent house are particularly sumptuous. The indoor pool is overlooked by a lounge area where snacks are served all day, and in summer an outdoor pool and roof garden are available. The Watkins restaurant offers an interesting fixed-price menu.

Rooms 58 (8 annexe) (1 fmly) (2 GF) ↸ **S** £72.50-£110; **D** £102.50-£130 (incl. bkfst) **Facilities** Spa STV FTV Wi-fi ᘔ HL ⊗ ↖ Gym Sauna Steam room Fitness suite New Year **Conf** Class 20 Board 20 Thtr 24 Del from £100 to £130 **Services** Lift Air con **Parking** 57 **Notes** LB Closed 20-30 Dec

Osborne House

★★★ ◉ TOWN HOUSE HOTEL

☎ 01492 860330
17 North Pde LL30 2LP
e-mail: sales@osbornehouse.com
web: www.osbornehouse.com
dir: Exit A55 junct 19. Follow signs for Llandudno then Promenade. Continue to junct, turn right. Hotel on left opposite pier entrance

Built in 1832, this Victorian house was restored and converted into a luxurious townhouse by the Maddocks family. Spacious suites offer unrivalled comfort and luxury, combining antique furnishings with state-of-the-art technology and facilities. Each suite provides super views over the pier and bay. Osborne's café grill is open throughout the day and offers high quality food, while the bar blends elegance with plasma screens, dazzling chandeliers and gilt framed mirrors.

Rooms 7 (1 fmly) ↸ **S** £150-£160; **D** £150-£180 (incl. bkfst) **Facilities** STV FTV Wi-fi ᘔ Use of swimming pool & sauna at Empire Hotel (100yds) New Year **Services** Air con **Parking** 6 **Notes** ⊗ No children 11yrs Closed 22-30 Dec

St Tudno Hotel and Restaurant

★★★ 83% ◉◉ HOTEL

WELSH RAREBITS *Hotels of Distinction*

☎ 01492 874411
The Promenade LL30 2LP
e-mail: sttudnohotel@btinternet.com
web: www.st-tudno.co.uk
dir: On Promenade towards pier, hotel opposite pier entrance

An excellent family-owned hotel with friendly and attentive staff, that enjoys fine sea views. The stylish bedrooms are well equipped with mini-bars, robes, satellite TVs and many other thoughtful extras. Public rooms include a lounge, a welcoming bar and a small indoor pool. The Terrace Restaurant, where seasonal and daily-changing menus are offered, has a delightful Mediterranean atmosphere. Afternoon tea is a real highlight.

Rooms 18 (4 fmly) ☎ **S** £80-£110; **D** £98-£230 (incl. bkfst) **Facilities** FTV Wi-fi HL ⟳ Xmas New Year **Conf** Class 25 Board 20 Thtr 40 **Services** Lift **Parking** 12 **Notes** LB Civ Wed 70

Dunoon Hotel
★★★ 82% HOTEL

☎ 01492 860787
Gloddaeth St LL30 2DW
e-mail: reservations@dunoonhotel.co.uk
web: www.dunoonhotel.co.uk
dir: Exit Promenade at war memorial by pier into Gloddaeth St. Hotel 200yds on right

This impressive, privately owned hotel is centrally located and offers a variety of well-equipped bedrooms. Elegant public areas include a tastefully appointed restaurant where competently prepared dishes are served together with a good choice of notable, reasonably priced wines. The caring and attentive service is also noteworthy.

Dunoon Hotel

Rooms 49 (4 fmly) ☎ **S** £80-£114; **D** £138-£162 (incl. bkfst & dinner)* **Facilities** FTV Wi-fi Pool table **Services** Lift **Parking** 24 **Notes** LB Closed mid Dec-early Mar

Tynedale Hotel
★★★ 82% HOTEL

☎ 01492 877426
Central Promenade LL30 2XS
e-mail: enquiries@tynedalehotel.co.uk
web: www.tynedalehotel.co.uk
dir: On Promenade opposite bandstand

Tour groups are well catered for at this privately owned and personally run hotel, and regular live entertainment is a feature. Vibrant modern public areas create a unique and comfortable setting, and an attractive seafront patio garden is an additional asset. Bedrooms provide good comfort levels and the staff offer friendly and efficient service.

Rooms 54 (1 fmly) (10 GF) ☎ **S** £46-£64; **D** £88-£123 (incl. bkfst)* **Facilities** FTV Wi-fi ♬ ♪ Xmas New Year **Services** Lift **Parking** 15 **Notes** ⊗

Cae Mor Hotel
★★★ 75% HOTEL

☎ 01492 878101
5-6 Penrhyn Crescent LL30 1BA
e-mail: info@caemorhotel.co.uk
dir: Exit A55 junct 19, follow A470/Llandudno/Town Centre signs. Straight on at 3 rdbts, right at 4th. Into right lane, right at next rdbt, follow Promenade signs. Straight on at next rdbt, left at next rdbt onto Promenade. 200yds, pass Venue Cymru

Located in a stunning seafront position adjacent to Venue Cymru, this tastefully renovated Victorian hotel provides a range of thoughtfully furnished bedrooms in minimalist style with smart modern bathrooms. Public areas include a choice of lounges and a stylish restaurant, the setting for imaginative dinners featuring the best of local seasonal produce.

Rooms 23 (2 fmly) (2 GF) ☎ **S** £64-£102; **D** £85-£130 (incl. bkfst) **Facilities** FTV Wi-fi Xmas New Year **Conf** Board 28 Thtr 60 Del £127.50 **Services** Lift **Parking** 26 **Notes** LB Civ Wed 50

L

LLANDUDNO *continued*

Hydro Hotel

★★ 72% HOTEL

Leisureplex

☎ 01492 870101
Neville Crescent LL30 1AT
e-mail: hydro.llandudno@alfatravel.co.uk
web: www.leisureplex.co.uk
dir: Follow signs for theatre to seafront, towards pier

This large hotel is situated on the promenade overlooking the sea, and offers good, value-for-money, modern accommodation. Public areas are quite extensive and include a choice of lounges, a games/snooker room and a ballroom where entertainment is provided every night. The hotel is a popular venue for coach tour parties.

Rooms 120 (4 fmly) (9 GF) ☞ **Facilities** Wi-fi Table tennis Snooker ♬ Xmas New Year **Services** Lift **Parking** 10 **Notes** ⊗ Closed Jan-mid Feb RS Nov-Dec (ex Xmas) & mid Feb-Mar

Premier Inn Llandudno North (Little Orme)

Premier Inn

BUDGET HOTEL

☎ 0871 527 8636
Colwyn Rd LL30 3AL
web: www.premierinn.com
dir: A55 junct 20 follow Rhos-on-Sea/Llandrillo-Yn-Rhos/B5115 signs. Onto B5115 (Brompton Ave). Straight on at next 2 rdbts. Hotel on left

High quality, budget accommodation ideal for both families and business travellers. Spacious, en suite bedrooms feature tea and coffee making facilities, and Freeview TV in most hotels. Internet access and Wi-fi are available for a small fee. The adjacent family restaurant features a wide and varied menu. See also the Hotel Groups pages.

Rooms 19

The Lilly Restaurant with Rooms

◉ RESTAURANT WITH ROOMS

☎ 01492 876513
West Pde, West Shore LL30 2BD
e-mail: thelilly@live.co.uk
dir: Telephone for detailed directions

Located on the seafront on the West Shore with views over the Great Orme, this establishment has bedrooms that offer high standards of comfort and good facilities. Children are very welcome here, and a relaxed atmosphere can be found in Madhatters Brasserie, which takes its name from Lewis Caroll's *Alice in Wonderland* which was written on the West Shore. A fine dining restaurant is also available.

Rooms 5

LLANDUDNO JUNCTION Map 14 SH77
Conwy

Premier Inn Llandudno (Glan-Conwy)

Premier Inn

BUDGET HOTEL

☎ 0871 527 8634
Afon Conwy LL28 5LB
web: www.premierinn.com
dir: A55 junct 19. Exit rdbt at A470 (Betws-y-Coed). Hotel immediately on left, opposite petrol station

High quality, budget accommodation ideal for both families and business travellers. Spacious, en suite bedrooms feature tea and coffee making facilities, and Freeview TV in most hotels. Internet access and Wi-fi are available for a small fee. The adjacent family restaurant features a wide and varied menu. See also the Hotel Groups pages.

Rooms 41

LLANELLI Map 8 SN50
Carmarthenshire

BEST WESTERN Diplomat Hotel and Spa

Best Western

★★★ 79% HOTEL

☎ 01554 756156
Felinfoel SA15 3PJ
e-mail: reservations@diplomat-hotel-wales.com
web: www.diplomat-hotel-wales.com
dir: M4 junct 48, A4138 then B4303, hotel 0.75m on right

This Victorian mansion, set in mature grounds, has been extended over the years to provide a comfortable and relaxing hotel. The well-appointed bedrooms are located in the main house and there is also a wing of equally comfortable modern rooms. Public areas include Trubshaw's Restaurant, a large function suite and a modern leisure centre.

Rooms 50 (8 annexe) (2 fmly) (4 GF) **Facilities** FTV Wi-fi ↘ ☜ supervised Gym Sauna Steam room ♬ Xmas New Year **Conf** Class 150 Board 100 Thtr 450 **Services** Lift **Parking** 250 **Notes** Civ Wed 300

Ashburnham Hotel

★★ 76% HOTEL

☎ 01554 834343 & 834455
Ashburnham Rd, Pembrey SA16 0TH
e-mail: info@ashburnham-hotel.co.uk
web: www.ashburnham-hotel.co.uk
dir: M4 junct 48, A4138 to Llanelli, A484 W to Pembrey. Follow brown information signs

Amelia Earhart stayed at this friendly hotel after finishing her historic trans-Atlantic flight in 1928. Public areas include the brasserie restaurant and the conservatory lounge bar that serves an extensive range of bar meals. Bedrooms, varying from standard to superior, have modern furnishings and facilities. The hotel is licensed for civil ceremonies, and function and conference facilities are also available.

Rooms 13 (2 fmly) **Facilities** FTV Wi-fi ↘ **Conf** Class 150 Board 80 Thtr 150 **Parking** 100 **Notes** ⊗ RS 24-26 Dec Civ Wed 130

Premier Inn Llanelli Central East

Premier Inn

BUDGET HOTEL

☎ 0871 527 8638
Llandafen Rd SA14 9BD
web: www.premierinn.com
dir: M4 junct 48, A4138, approx 3m. Hotel on left

High quality, budget accommodation ideal for both families and business travellers. Spacious, en suite bedrooms feature tea and coffee making facilities, and Freeview TV in most hotels. Internet access and Wi-fi are available for a small fee. The adjacent family restaurant features a wide and varied menu. See also the Hotel Groups pages.

Rooms 50

Premier Inn Llanelli Central West

BUDGET HOTEL

☎ 0871 527 9342
Sandpiper Rd, Sandy Water Park SA15 4SG
web: www.premierinn.com
dir: M4 junct 48, A4138 towards Llanelli town centre. Then follow Carmarthen signs to Sandy Park rdbt. Hotel on left

Rooms 28

LLANGAMMARCH WELLS · Map 9 SN94
Powys

INSPECTORS' CHOICE
The Lake Country House & Spa

★★★ ◉◉ COUNTRY HOUSE HOTEL

☎ 01591 620202
LD4 4BS
e-mail: info@lakecountryhouse.co.uk
web: www.lakecountryhouse.co.uk
dir: W from Builth Wells on A483 to Garth (approx 6m). Left for Llangammarch Wells, follow hotel signs

Expect good old-fashioned values and hospitality at this Victorian country house hotel. In fact, the service is so traditionally English, guests may believe they have their own butler. The establishment offers a 9-hole, par 3 golf course, 50 acres of wooded grounds and a spa with a hot tub that overlooks the lake. Bedrooms, some located in an annexe, and some at ground-floor level, are individually styled and have many extra comforts. Traditional afternoon teas are served in the lounge, and award-winning cuisine is provided in the spacious and elegant restaurant.

Rooms 31 (12 annexe) (8 GF) 🐾 S £145-£210; D £195-£260 (incl. bkfst)* **Facilities** Spa FTV Wi-fi ⊗ ⚓ 9 ⚑ Putt green Fishing 🛶 Gym Archery Horse riding Mountain biking Quad biking Xmas New Year **Conf** Class 30 Board 25 Thtr 80 **Parking** 70 **Notes** LB No children 8yrs Civ Wed 100

LLANRWST · Map 14 SH86
Conwy

See also Betws-y-Coed

Maenan Abbey

★★★ 77% HOTEL

☎ 01492 660247
Maenan LL26 0UL
e-mail: reservations@manab.co.uk
dir: 3m N on A470

Set in its own spacious grounds, this privately owned hotel was built as an abbey in 1850 on the site of a 13th-century monastery. It is now a popular venue for weddings as the grounds and magnificent galleried staircase make ideal settings for photographs. Bedrooms include a large suite, and are equipped with modern facilities. Meals are served in the bar and restaurant.

Rooms 14 (3 fmly) (4 smoking) **Facilities** Wi-fi Fishing Guided mountain walks Xmas New Year **Conf** Class 30 Board 30 Thtr 50 **Parking** 60 **Notes** Civ Wed 55

LLANTRISANT · Map 9 ST39
Monmouthshire

Premier Inn Llantrisant

BUDGET HOTEL

☎ 0871 527 8640
Gwaun Elai, Magden Park CF72 8LL
web: www.premierinn.com
dir: M4 junct 34, A4119 towards Llantrisant & Rhondda. At 1st rdbt take 2nd exit. At 2nd rdbt take 1st exit

High quality, budget accommodation ideal for both families and business travellers. Spacious, en suite bedrooms feature tea and coffee making facilities, and Freeview TV in most hotels. Internet access and Wi-fi are available for a small fee. The adjacent family restaurant features a wide and varied menu. See also the Hotel Groups pages.

Rooms 51

LLANWDDYN · Map 15 SJ01
Powys

Lake Vyrnwy Hotel & Spa

★★★★ 76% ◉
COUNTRY HOUSE HOTEL

☎ 01691 870692
Lake Vyrnwy SY10 0LY
e-mail: info@lakevyrnwyhotel.co.uk
web: www.lakevyrnwy.com
dir: On A4393, 200yds past dam turn sharp right into drive

This elegant Victorian country-house hotel lies in 26,000 acres of woodland above Lake Vyrnwy, and provides a wide range of bedrooms, most with superb views and many with four-poster beds and balconies. Extensive public rooms retain many period features, and informal dining is available in the popular Tower Tavern. Relaxing and rejuvenating treatments are a feature of the stylish health spa.

Rooms 52 (12 fmly) 🐾 S £119-£235; D £144-£260 (incl. bkfst)* **Facilities** Spa STV FTV Wi-fi ⊗ 🏊 Gym Archery Birdwatching Canoeing Kayaking Clay shooting Sailing Fly fishing Cycling Xmas New Year **Conf** Class 80 Board 60 Thtr 200 **Services** Lift **Parking** 70 **Notes** LB Civ Wed 200

L

LLANWRTYD WELLS
Map 9 SN84
Powys

Carlton Riverside

◎◎ RESTAURANT WITH ROOMS

☎ 01591 610248
Irfon Crescent LD5 4SP
e-mail: info@carltonriverside.com
dir: In town centre beside bridge

Guests become part of the family at this character
property, set beside the river in Wales's smallest
town. Carlton Riverside offers award-winning cuisine
which Mary Ann Gilchrist produces using the very best
of local ingredients. The set menu is complemented
by a well-chosen wine list and dinner is served in the
stylish restaurant which offers a memorable blend of
traditional comfort, modern design and river views.
Four comfortable bedrooms have tasteful
combinations of antique and contemporary furniture,
along with welcome personal touches.

Rooms 4

Lasswade Country House

◎◎ RESTAURANT WITH ROOMS

☎ 01591 610515
Station Rd LD5 4RW
e-mail: info@lasswadehotel.co.uk
dir: Exit A483 into Irfon Terrace, right into Station Rd,
350yds on right

This friendly establishment on the edge of the town
has impressive views over the countryside. Bedrooms
are comfortably furnished and well equipped, while
the public areas consist of a tastefully decorated
lounge, an elegant restaurant with a bar, and an airy
conservatory which looks towards the neighbouring
hills. The kitchen utilises fresh, local produce to
provide an enjoyable dining experience.

Rooms 8 (1 fmly)

LLYSWEN
Map 9 SO13
Powys

AA HOTEL OF THE YEAR FOR WALES

INSPECTORS' CHOICE

Llangoed Hall

★★★★ ◎◎ COUNTRY HOUSE HOTEL

☎ 01874 754525
LD3 0YP
e-mail: enquiries@llangoedhall.com
dir: On A470 between Brecon & Builth Wells

Set against the stunning backdrop of the Black
Mountains and the Wye Valley, this imposing
country house is a haven of peace and quiet. The
interior is no less impressive, with a noteworthy art
collection complementing the many antiques in day
rooms and bedrooms. Comfortable, spacious
accommodation is matched by equally inviting
lounges. Llangoed Hall is the AA Hotel of the Year
for Wales 2013-2014.

Rooms 23 🅵 **Facilities** FTV Wi-fi ↘ ⚓ Snooker
table Outdoor chess Xmas New Year **Conf** Class 30
Board 30 Thtr 80 **Parking** 50 **Notes** ⊗ Civ Wed 80

MAESYCWMMER
Map 9 ST19
Caerphilly

Bryn Meadows Golf, Hotel & Spa

★★★★ 79% HOTEL

☎ 01495 225590
CF82 7SN
e-mail: reception@brynmeadows.co.uk
web: www.brynmeadows.com
dir: M4 junct 28, A467 signed Brynmawr, 10m to
Newbridge. Take A472 signed Ystrad Mynach. Hotel
off Crown rdbt signed 'golf course'. (NB for Sat Nav
use NP12 2BR)

Surrounded by its own mature parkland and 18-hole
golf course, this impressive hotel, golf, leisure and
function complex provides a range of high quality,
well-equipped bedrooms; several have their own
balconies or patio areas. The attractive public areas
include a pleasant restaurant which, like many of the
bedrooms, enjoys striking views of the golf course and

beyond. There are impressive function facilities and
the hotel is a popular venue for weddings.

Rooms 42 (4 fmly) (21 GF) 🅵 **Facilities** Spa FTV Wi-fi
🅢 supervised ⚽ 18 Putt green Gym Sauna Steam
room Aromatherapy suite Xmas New Year
Conf Class 70 Board 60 Thtr 120 **Services** Air con
Parking 120 **Notes** ⊗ Civ Wed 250

MANORBIER
Map 8 SS09
Pembrokeshire

Castlemead

RESTAURANT WITH ROOMS

☎ 01834 871358
SA70 7TA
e-mail: castlemeadhotel@aol.com
web: www.castlemeadhotel.com
dir: A4139 towards Pembroke, B4585 into village,
follow signs to beach & castle, establishment on left

Benefiting from a superb location with spectacular
views of the bay, the Norman church and Manorbier
Castle, this family-run business is friendly and
welcoming. Bedrooms, which include some in a
converted former coach house at ground floor level,
are generally quite spacious and have modern
facilities. Public areas include a sea-view residents'
lounge and a restaurant accessed by stairs, which is
available to non-residents, along with a cosy bar.
There are extensive gardens to the rear of the
property.

Rooms 8 (3 annexe) (2 fmly)

MERTHYR TYDFIL
Map 9 SO00
Merthyr Tydfil

Premier Inn Merthyr Tydfil

BUDGET HOTEL

☎ 0871 527 8768
Pentrebach CF48 4BB
web: www.premierinn.com
dir: M4 junct 32, A470 to Merthyr Tydfil. At rdbt right
to Pentrebach (A4060). At next rdbt 3rd exit signed
Abergavenny, (dual carriageway). Double back at next
rdbt by Pentrebach Co-op onto A4060 towards
Pentrebach. Left after layby, hotel adjacent to
Pentrebach House

High quality, budget accommodation ideal for both
families and business travellers. Spacious, en suite
bedrooms feature tea and coffee making facilities,
and Freeview TV in most hotels. Internet access and
Wi-fi are available for a small fee. The adjacent
family restaurant features a wide and varied menu.
See also the Hotel Groups pages.

Rooms 40

| **MISKIN** | **Map 9 ST08** |
| Rhondda Cynon Taff | |

Miskin Manor Country Hotel

★★★★ 75% ◉◉ COUNTRY HOUSE HOTEL

☎ 01443 224204
Pendoylan Rd CF72 8ND
e-mail: reservations@miskin-manor.co.uk
web: www.miskin-manor.co.uk
dir: M4 junct 34, A4119, signed Llantrisant, hotel 300yds on left

This historic manor house is peacefully located in 22-acre grounds, yet is only minutes away from the M4. Bedrooms are furnished to a high standard and include some located in converted stables and cottages. Public areas are spacious and comfortable and include a variety of function rooms. The relaxed atmosphere and the surroundings ensure this hotel remains popular for wedding functions as well as with business guests. There is a separate modern health and fitness centre which includes a gym, sauna, steam room and swimming pool.

Rooms 43 (9 annexe) (2 fmly) (7 GF) **Facilities** FTV Wi-fi ⊕ ⥮ Gym **Conf** Class 80 Board 65 Thtr 160 **Parking** 200 **Notes** Civ Wed 120

| **MOLD** | **Map 15 SJ26** |
| Flintshire | |

Beaufort Park Hotel

★★★ 78% HOTEL

☎ 01352 758646
Alltami Rd, New Brighton CH7 6RQ
e-mail: info@beaufortparkhotel.co.uk
web: www.beaufortparkhotel.co.uk
dir: A55, A494, through Alltami lights, over mini rdbt by petrol station towards Mold, A5119. Hotel 100yds on right

This large, modern hotel is conveniently located a short drive from the North Wales Expressway and offers various styles of spacious accommodation. There are extensive public areas, and several meeting and function rooms are available. There is a wide choice of meals in the formal restaurant and in the popular Arches bar.

Rooms 106 (8 fmly) (32 GF) **Facilities** FTV Wi-fi Squash ♫ Xmas New Year **Conf** Class 120 Board 120 Thtr 250 **Parking** 200 **Notes** Civ Wed 250

| **MONMOUTH** | **Map 10 SO51** |
| Monmouthshire | |

Bistro Prego

◉ RESTAURANT WITH ROOMS

☎ 01600 712600
7 Church St NP25 3BX
e-mail: enquiries@pregomonmouth.co.uk

Located in the middle of Monmouth, this Italian-style restaurant with rooms is open all day for a selection of teas, coffees, lunches and light snacks. At dinner, a delicious choice of dishes using local produce is available in the popular bistro-style dining area. Rooms are located above the dining room and come in a range of shapes and sizes.

Rooms 8 (2 fmly)

| **NARBERTH** | **Map 8 SN11** |
| Pembrokeshire | |

INSPECTORS' CHOICE

The Grove

◉◉ RESTAURANT WITH ROOMS

☎ 01834 860915
Molleston SA67 8BX
e-mail: info@thegrove-narberth.co.uk
web: www.thegrove-narberth.co.uk
dir: A48 to Carmarthen, A40 to Haverfordwest. At A478 rdbt 1st exit to Narberth, through town towards Tenby. At bottom of hill right, 1m, The Grove on right

The Grove is an elegant 18th-century country house set on a hillside in 24 acres of rolling countryside. The owners have lovingly restored the building with care, combining period features with excellent modern decor. There are bedrooms in the main house, and additional rooms in separate buildings; all are appointed with quality and comfort. Some bedrooms are on the ground floor, and most have fantastic views out over the Preseli Hills. There are two sumptuous lounge areas, one with an open fire and a small bar, and two separate dining rooms that offer award-winning cuisine. Self-catering cottages are available.

Rooms 20 (6 annexe) (3 fmly)

| **NEATH** | **Map 9 SS79** |
| Neath Port Talbot | |

Castle Hotel

★★★ 73% HOTEL

☎ 01639 641119
The Parade SA11 1RB
e-mail: info@castlehotelneath.co.uk
web: www.castlehotelneath.co.uk
dir: M4 junct 43, follow signs for Neath, 500yds past rail station, hotel on right. Car park on left in 50yds

Situated in the town centre, this Georgian property, once a coaching inn, has a wealth of history and plenty of character. Lord Nelson and Lady Hamilton are reputed to have stayed here, and it is where the Welsh Rugby Union was founded in 1881. The hotel provides well-equipped accommodation and pleasant public areas. Bedrooms include family bedded rooms and one with a four-poster. Green's restaurant provides a good range of dishes at both lunch and dinner. Function and meeting rooms are available.

Rooms 29 (3 fmly) (14 smoking) **Facilities** STV FTV Wi-fi ♤ ♫ Xmas New Year **Conf** Class 75 Board 50 Thtr 160 **Parking** 26 **Notes** ⊗ Civ Wed 120

| **NEWCASTLE EMLYN** | **Map 8 SN34** |
| Carmarthenshire | |

Gwesty'r Emlyn Hotel

WELSH RAREBITS *Hotels of Distinction*

★★★ 79% HOTEL

☎ 01239 710317
Bridge St SA38 9DU
e-mail: reception@gwestyremlynhotel.co.uk
web: www.gwestyremlynhotel.co.uk
dir: In town centre

This hotel, in the heart of a busy market town, dates back some 300 years. Appointed to a high standard, the stylish and comfortable bedrooms have luxury bathrooms. The public areas comprise a choice of bars, a cosy seating area and a modern restaurant offering dishes created from good, locally sourced ingredients. There is a gym, sauna and spa pool plus a large function suite for weddings and parties.

Rooms 24 (3 fmly) (1 GF) ↰ **S** £70-£80; **D** £90-£115 (incl. bkfst)* **Facilities** FTV Wi-fi Gym Sauna Splash pool Xmas New Year **Conf** Class 100 Board 50 Thtr 150 **Parking** 25 **Notes** LB ⊗ Civ Wed 150

N

NEWPORT
Newport
Map 9 ST38

See also Cwmbran

The Celtic Manor Resort

★★★★★ 85% ◉◉◉ HOTEL

☎ 01633 413000
Coldra Woods NP18 1HQ
e-mail: bookings@celtic-manor.com
web: www.celtic-manor.com
dir: M4 junct 24, take B4237 towards Newport. Hotel 1st on right

This hotel is part of the outstanding Celtic Manor Resort. Here there are three challenging golf courses including the Twenty Ten Course specifically designed for the 2010 Ryder Cup; a huge convention centre; superb leisure clubs and two hotels. This hotel has excellent bedrooms, with suites and two Presidential suites, offering good space and comfort; stylish extensive public areas are set around a spectacular atrium lobby that includes several eating options; Terry M is the award-winning, fine dining restaurant. There is a choice of shops and boutiques as well.

Rooms 334 (34 fmly) ☚ **S** £116-£218; **D** £138-£255 (incl. bkfst)* **Facilities** Spa STV FTV Wi-fi ⓑ ♨ 54 ⛳ Putt green Gym Golf Academy Clay pigeon shooting Mountain bike trails Games room Archery ♫ Xmas New Year Child facilities **Conf** Class 600 Board 60 Thtr 1500 Del from £150 to £240 **Services** Lift Air con **Parking** 1300 **Notes** LB ⊗ Civ Wed 100

The Manor House

★★★★ 74% ◉ HOTEL

☎ 01633 413000
The Celtic Manor Resort, Coldra Woods NP18 1HQ
e-mail: bookings@celtic-manor.com
web: www.celtic-manor.com
dir: M4 junct 24, B4237 towards Newport. Hotel 1st on right

Part of the complex of the Celtic Manor Resort, this hotel, built in the 19th century, offers country house charm combined with modern comforts. Sitting in beautiful landscaped gardens it has traditionally styled bedrooms, three with four-posters. Several eating options are available both at Manor House and

at the Celtic Manor Resort, where guests have access to all the hotel and leisure facilities; three challenging golf courses and superb leisure clubs among them.

Rooms 65 (3 fmly) ☚ **S** £67-£126; **D** £81-£145 (incl. bkfst)* **Facilities** Spa STV FTV Wi-fi ⓑ supervised ♨ 18 ⛳ Putt green Fishing Gym Golf academy Adventure golf Archery Clay pigeon shooting ♫ Xmas New Year Child facilities **Conf** Class 80 Board 40 Thtr 200 Del from £150 to £220 **Services** Lift Air con **Parking** 1000 **Notes** LB ⊗ Civ Wed 180

Premier Inn Newport South Wales

BUDGET HOTEL

☎ 0871 527 8814
Coldra Junction, Chepstow Rd, Langstone NP18 2NX
web: www.premierinn.com
dir: M4 junct 24, A48 to Langstone, at next rdbt return towards junct 24. Hotel 50mtrs on left

High quality, budget accommodation ideal for both families and business travellers. Spacious, en suite bedrooms feature tea and coffee making facilities, and Freeview TV in most hotels. Internet access and Wi-fi are available for a small fee. The adjacent family restaurant features a wide and varied menu. See also the Hotel Groups pages.

Rooms 63

NEWPORT
Pembrokeshire
Map 8 SN03

Llysmeddyg

◉◉ RESTAURANT WITH ROOMS

☎ 01239 820008
East St SA42 0SY
e-mail: contact@llysmeddyg.com
dir: On A487 in centre of town

Llysmeddyg is a Georgian townhouse offering a blend of old and new, with elegant furnishings, deep sofas and a welcoming fire. The owners of this property employed local craftsmen to create a lovely interior that has an eclectic style. The focus of the quality restaurant menu is the use of fresh, seasonal, locally sourced ingredients. The spacious bedrooms are comfortable and contemporary in design; bathrooms vary in style.

Rooms 8 (3 annexe) (3 fmly)

NORTHOP
Flintshire
Map 15 SJ26

Soughton Hall Hotel

★★★ 87% COUNTRY HOUSE HOTEL

☎ 01352 840811
CH7 6AB
e-mail: info@soughtonhall.co.uk
dir: A55/B5126, after 500mtrs turn left for Northop, left at lights (A5119-Mold). After 0.5m follow signs

Built as a bishop's palace in 1714, this elegant country house has magnificent grounds. Bedrooms are individually decorated and furnished with fine antiques and rich fabrics. There are several spacious day rooms furnished in keeping with the style of the house. The trendy Stables bar and restaurant offer a good range of dishes at both lunch and dinner. Understandably, the hotel is a very popular venue for weddings.

Rooms 15 (2 fmly) (2 GF) **Facilities** ⓑ ♨ Riding stables nearby Xmas **Parking** 100 **Notes** ⊗ Civ Wed 100

NORTHOP HALL
Flintshire
Map 15 SJ26

Holiday Inn A55 Chester West

★★★ 77% HOTEL

☎ 01244 550011
Westbound A55, Mold, nr Chester CH7 6HB
e-mail: bookings@holidayinnchesterwest.co.uk
web: www.holidayinnchesterwest.co.uk
dir: M6 junct 20, M56 to Queensferry, follow signs for A55/Conwy. Hotel 500yds past A494 slip road

This modern hotel is ideally situated to explore north Wales, and offers comfortable accommodation and warm hospitality. Facilities include a well-equipped gym. Hearty meals are served in the conservatory restaurant.

Rooms 81 (29 fmly) (31 GF) (5 smoking) **S** £29-£89; **D** £29-£89* **Facilities** STV Wi-fi ♨ HL Gym New Year **Conf** Class 130 Board 55 Thtr 220 Del from £99 to £104.50* **Services** Lift Air con **Parking** 200 **Notes** LB Closed 24-25 Dec Civ Wed 100

Save on hotels. Book at theAA.com/hotel

NEW – POR 583 | WALES

PEMBROKE — Pembrokeshire — Map 8 SM90

BEST WESTERN Lamphey Court Hotel & Spa

★★★★ 73% ⊛ HOTEL

☎ 01646 672273
Lamphey SA71 5NT
e-mail: info@lampheycourt.co.uk
web: www.lampheycourt.co.uk
dir: A477 to Pembroke. Left at Milton for Lamphey, hotel on right

This Georgian mansion, on an elevated site, is set in attractive countryside and is perfectly situated for exploring the stunning Pembrokeshire coast, the beaches and the Preseli Hills. Well-appointed bedrooms and family suites are situated in a converted coach house within the grounds. The elegant public areas include both formal and informal dining rooms that feature dishes inspired by the local produce. Leisure facilities include a state-of-the-art spa with a swimming pool, gym, sauna, treatment rooms and much more.

Rooms 38 (12 annexe) (7 fmly) (6 GF) **Facilities** Spa FTV Wi-fi ⇩ ☺ ⚲ Gym Yacht charter Xmas New Year **Conf** Class 40 Board 30 Thtr 60 **Parking** 50 **Notes** Civ Wed 80

Lamphey Hall Hotel

★★★ 77% HOTEL

☎ 01646 672394 & 07791 896191
Lamphey SA71 5NR
e-mail: andrewjones1990@aol.com
dir: From Carmarthen A40 to St Clears. Follow signs for A477, left at Milton

Set in a delightful village, this very friendly, privately owned and efficiently run hotel offers an ideal base from which to explore the surrounding countryside. Bedrooms are well equipped, comfortably furnished and include family rooms and ground floor rooms. Diners have a choice of three restaurant areas offering an extensive range of dishes. There is also a small lounge, a bar and attractive gardens.

Rooms 10 (1 fmly) (2 GF) **S** £49.50-£59.50; **D** £70-£89.50 (incl. bkfst)* **Facilities** FTV Wi-fi **Parking** 32

PONTYPOOL — Torfaen — Map 9 SO20

Premier Inn Pontypool

BUDGET HOTEL

☎ 0871 527 8890
Tyr'felin, Lower Mill Field NP4 0RH
web: www.premierinn.com
dir: At junct of A4042 & A472

High quality, budget accommodation ideal for both families and business travellers. Spacious, en suite bedrooms feature tea and coffee making facilities, and Freeview TV in most hotels. Internet access and Wi-fi are available for a small fee. The adjacent family restaurant features a wide and varied menu. See also the Hotel Groups pages.

Rooms 49

PONTYPRIDD — Rhondda Cynon Taff — Map 9 ST08

Llechwen Hall Hotel

★★★ 74% ⊛ COUNTRY HOUSE HOTEL

☎ 01443 742050 & 743020
Llanfabon CF37 4HP
e-mail: enquiries@llechwenhall.co.uk
dir: A470 N towards Merthyr Tydfil. At large rdbt take 3rd exit. At mini rdbt take 3rd exit, hotel signed 0.5m on left

Set on top of a hill with a stunning approach, this country house hotel has served many purposes in its 200-year-old history including a private school and a magistrates' court. The spacious, individually decorated bedrooms are well equipped; some are situated in the separate coach house nearby. There are ground-floor, twin, double and family bedrooms on offer. The Victorian-style public areas are attractively appointed and the hotel is a popular venue for weddings.

Rooms 20 (8 annexe) (6 fmly) (4 GF) **S** £99; **D** £119 (incl. bkfst)* **Facilities** FTV Wi-fi ⇩ Xmas New Year **Conf** Class 80 Board 40 Thtr 200 **Parking** 150 **Notes** Civ Wed 80

PORTHCAWL — Bridgend — Map 9 SS87

Seabank Hotel

★★ 64% HOTEL

Leisureplex

☎ 01656 782261
Esplanade CF36 3LU
e-mail: seabank@alfatravel.co.uk
web: www.leisureplex.co.uk
dir: M4 junct 37, A4229 to Porthcawl seafront

The Seabank Hotel stands in a prime location on the promenade of this seaside town, with panoramic sea views from the majority of bedrooms. Porthcawl has several beaches and coastal walks; the world famous Royal Porthcawl golf course is within easy distance and the cities of Swansea and Cardiff are only a short drive away. The spacious bedrooms are all en suite and there is a lift which serves most bedrooms. There is a spacious restaurant, a lounge bar and a choice of lounges with sea views. The hotel is a popular venue for coach tour parties, as well as weddings and conferences. There is ample parking around the hotel.

Rooms 89 (5 GF) ⚑ **S** £37-£54; **D** £60-£94 (incl. bkfst)* **Facilities** FTV Wi-fi ♫ Xmas New Year **Services** Lift **Parking** 100 **Notes** LB ⊗ Closed 2 Jan-10 Feb

PORTHMADOG — Gwynedd — Map 14 SH53

Royal Sportsman Hotel

★★★ 82% ⊛⊛ HOTEL

☎ 01766 512015
131 High St LL49 9HB
e-mail: enquiries@royalsportsman.co.uk
dir: At rdbt junct of A497 & A487

Ideally located in the centre of Porthmadog, this former coaching inn dates from the Victorian era and is a friendly, privately owned and personally run hotel. Bedrooms are tastefully decorated and well equipped, and some are in an annexe close to the hotel. There is a large comfortable lounge and a wide range of meals is served in the bar or restaurant.

Rooms 28 (9 annexe) (7 fmly) (9 GF) ⚑ **S** £63-£88; **D** £90-£104 (incl. bkfst)* **Facilities** STV FTV Wi-fi Xmas New Year **Conf** Class 50 Board 30 Thtr 50 **Parking** 17 **Notes** LB

P

PORTMEIRION
Gwynedd
Map 14 SH53

The Hotel Portmeirion

★★★★ 79% ◉◉ HOTEL

☎ 01766 770000 & 772440
LL48 6ET
e-mail: hotel@portmeirion-village.com
web: www.portmeirion-village.com
dir: 2m W, Portmeirion village is S off A487

Saved from dereliction in the 1920s by Clough Williams-Ellis, the elegant Hotel Portmeirion enjoys one of the finest settings in Wales, located beneath the wooded slopes of the village, overlooking the sandy estuary towards Snowdonia. Many bedrooms have private sitting rooms and balconies with spectacular views. The staff, mostly Welsh-speaking, provide a good mix of warm hospitality and efficient service.

Rooms 44 (30 annexe) (6 fmly) ⊀ **S** £99-£299; **D** £129-£349 (incl. bkfst & dinner)* **Facilities** Spa FTV Wi-fi ↩ ⌁ Xmas New Year **Conf** Class 40 Board 30 Thtr 100 **Services** Lift **Parking** 44 **Notes** ⊗ Civ Wed 130

Castell Deudraeth
★★★★ 79% ◉ HOTEL

☎ 01766 770000 & 772400
LL48 6EN
e-mail: castell@portmeirion-village.com
web: www.portmeirion-village.com
dir: Exit A4212 for Trawsfynydd/Porthmadog. 1.5m beyond Penrhyndeudraeth, hotel on right

A castellated mansion that overlooks Snowdonia and the famous Italianate village featured in 1960s cult TV series *The Prisoner*. An original concept, Castell Deudraeth combines traditional materials, such as oak and slate, with state-of-the-art technology and design. Dynamically styled bedrooms boast underfloor heating, real-flame gas fires, wide-screen TVs with DVDs and cinema surround-sound. The brasserie-themed dining room provides an informal option at dinner.

Rooms 11 (5 fmly) ⊀ **S** £99-£299; **D** £129-£349 (incl. bkfst & dinner)* **Facilities** Spa FTV Wi-fi ↩ ⌁ Xmas New Year **Conf** Class 18 Board 25 Thtr 30 **Services** Lift **Parking** 30 **Notes** ⊗ Closed Jan Civ Wed 30

PORT TALBOT
Neath Port Talbot
Map 9 SS78

BEST WESTERN Aberavon Beach Hotel

★★★ 80% HOTEL

☎ 01639 884949
Neath SA12 6QP
e-mail: sales@aberavonbeach.com
web: www.aberavonbeach.com
dir: M4 junct 41, A48 & follow signs for Aberavon Beach & Hollywood Park

This friendly, purpose-built hotel enjoys a prominent position on the seafront overlooking Swansea Bay. Bedrooms, many with sea views, are comfortably appointed and thoughtfully equipped. Public areas include an all-weather leisure suite with swimming pool, open-plan bar and restaurant plus a choice of function rooms.

Rooms 52 (6 fmly) ⊀ **Facilities** FTV Wi-fi ⌁ Sauna ♫ Xmas New Year **Conf** Class 200 Board 100 Thtr 300 **Services** Lift **Parking** 150 **Notes** Civ Wed 300

Premier Inn Port Talbot
BUDGET HOTEL

☎ 0871 527 8896
Baglan Rd, Baglan SA12 8ES
web: www.premierinn.com
dir: M4 junct 41 W'bound. Hotel just off 4th exit at rdbt. M4 junct 42 E'bound, left towards Port Talbot. Take 2nd exit off 2nd rdbt

High quality, budget accommodation ideal for both families and business travellers. Spacious, en suite bedrooms feature tea and coffee making facilities, and Freeview TV in most hotels. Internet access and Wi-fi are available for a small fee. The adjacent family restaurant features a wide and varied menu. See also the Hotel Groups pages.

Rooms 42

RAGLAN
Monmouthshire
Map 9 SO40

The Beaufort Raglan Coaching Inn & Brasserie
★★★ 77% ◉ HOTEL

☎ 01291 690412
High St NP15 2DY
e-mail: enquiries@beaufortraglan.co.uk
web: www.beaufortraglan.co.uk
dir: M4 junct 24, A449/A40 junct Monmouth/Abergavenny, 0.5m into village opposite church

This friendly, family-run village inn dating back to the 15th century has historic links with nearby Raglan Castle. The bright, stylish and beautifully appointed bedrooms in the main house are suitably equipped for both tourists and business guests. Food is served in either The Brasserie restaurant or traditional lounge, and both offer a relaxed service with an enjoyable selection of carefully prepared dishes.

Rooms 15 (5 annexe) (1 fmly) (5 GF) ⊀ **S** £60-£85; **D** £75-£115 (incl. bkfst)* **Facilities** FTV Wi-fi Use of facilities at golf club in village **Conf** Class 60 Board 30 Thtr 120 **Parking** 30 **Notes** LB ⊗ RS 25-26 Dec

REYNOLDSTON
Swansea
Map 8 SS48

INSPECTORS' CHOICE

Fairyhill
◉◉ RESTAURANT WITH ROOMS

☎ 01792 390139
SA3 1BS
e-mail: postbox@fairyhill.net
web: www.fairyhill.net
dir: M4 junct 47, A483, at next rdbt right onto A484. At Gowerton take B4295 for 10m

Peace and tranquillity are never far away at this charming Georgian mansion set in the heart of the beautiful Gower Peninsula. Bedrooms are furnished with care and are filled with many thoughtful extras. There is also a range of comfortable seating areas, with crackling log fires, to choose from, and the smart restaurant offers menus based on local produce and complemented by an excellent wine list.

Rooms 8

P

Save on hotels. Book at **theAA.com/hotel**

POR – SAU 585 | WALES

RHUDDLAN
Denbighshire | Map 15 SJ07

Premier Inn Rhuddlan

BUDGET HOTEL

☎ 0871 527 8932
Castle View Retail Park, Marsh Rd LL18 5UA
web: www.premierinn.com
dir: A55 junct 27, A525 signed Rhyl. At next rdbt 3rd exit into Station Rd. Next left into Marsh Rd. Hotel on left

High quality, budget accommodation ideal for both families and business travellers. Spacious, en suite bedrooms feature tea and coffee making facilities, and Freeview TV in most hotels. Internet access and Wi-fi are available for a small fee. The adjacent family restaurant features a wide and varied menu. See also the Hotel Groups pages.

Rooms 44

ROCKFIELD
Monmouthshire | Map 9 SO41

The Stonemill & Steppes Farm Cottages

◉ ◉ RESTAURANT WITH ROOMS

☎ 01600 775424
NP25 5SW
e-mail: bookings@thestonemill.co.uk
dir: A48 to Monmouth, take B4233 to Rockfield. 2.6m

Located in a small hamlet just west of Monmouth, close to the Forest of Dean and the Wye Valley, this operation offers accommodation comprising six very well-appointed cottages. The comfortable rooms (for self-catering or on a B&B basis) are architect designed and have been lovingly restored to retain many original features. In a separate, converted 16th-century barn is Stonemill Restaurant with oak beams, vaulted ceilings and an old cider press. Breakfast is served in the cottages on request. This establishment's location proves handy for golfers with a choice of many courses in the area.

Rooms 6 (6 fmly)

ROSSETT
Wrexham | Map 15 SJ35

BEST WESTERN Llyndir Hall Hotel

★★★ 83% HOTEL

☎ 01244 571648
Llyndir Ln LL12 0AY
e-mail: llyndirhallhotel@feathers.uk.com
dir: 5m S of Chester on B5445 follow Pulford signs

Located on the English/Welsh border within easy reach of Chester and Wrexham, this elegant manor house lies in several acres of mature grounds. The hotel is popular with both business and leisure guests, and facilities include conference rooms, an impressive leisure centre, a choice of comfortable lounges and a brasserie-style restaurant.

Rooms 48 (3 fmly) (17 GF) ⚲ **S** £49–£149; **D** £59–£159 (incl. bkfst) **Facilities** Spa FTV Wi-fi HL ⚘ supervised Gym Beauty salon Sauna Xmas New Year **Conf** Class 60 Board 40 Thtr 120 Del from £94 to £189 **Parking** 80 **Notes** ⊗ Civ Wed 120

SARN PARK
MOTORWAY SERVICE AREA (M4) Map 9 SS98
Bridgend

Days Inn Bridgend Cardiff - M4

BUDGET HOTEL

☎ 01656 659218
Sarn Park Services, M4 Junct 36 CF32 9RW
e-mail: sarn.hotel@welcomebreak.co.uk
web: www.welcomebreak.co.uk
dir: M4 junct 36

This modern building offers accommodation in smart, spacious and well-equipped bedrooms, suitable for families and business travellers, and all with en suite bathrooms. Continental breakfast is available and other refreshments may be taken at the nearby family restaurant. See also the Hotel Groups pages.

Rooms 40 (15 fmly) (20 GF) (8 smoking)

SAUNDERSFOOT
Pembrokeshire | Map 8 SN10

St Brides Spa Hotel

★★★★ 83% ◉ HOTEL

☎ 01834 812304
St Brides Hill SA69 9NH
e-mail: reservations@stbridesspahotel.com
web: www.stbridesspahotel.com
dir: A478 onto B4310 to Saundersfoot. Hotel above harbour

Set overlooking Carmarthen Bay this contemporary hotel and spa takes prime position. Many of the stylish, modern bedrooms enjoy sea views and have balconies; there are also luxury apartments in the grounds. The hotel is open plan and has excellent views of the bay from the split-level lounge areas. Fresh local seafood is a speciality in the modern airy restaurant, which has a terrace for dining alfresco when the weather allows. The destination spa enjoys some of the very best views from the double treatment room and spa pool.

Rooms 46 (12 annexe) (6 fmly) (9 GF) ⚲ **S** £125–£195; **D** £150–£290 (incl. bkfst)* **Facilities** Spa FTV Wi-fi ⚘ Gym Thermal suite Hydrotherapy pool Steam & herbal rooms Ice fountain Xmas New Year **Conf** Class 40 Board 34 Thtr 100 Del from £170 to £200* **Services** Lift **Parking** 65 **Notes** LB Civ Wed 90

S

INSPECTORS' CHOICE

The Bell at Skenfrith

◉ ◉   RESTAURANT WITH ROOMS

☎ 01600 750235
NP7 8UH
e-mail: enquiries@skenfrith.co.uk
web: www.skenfrith.co.uk
dir: On B4521 in Skenfrith, opposite castle

The Bell is a beautifully restored, 17th-century former coaching inn which still retains much original charm and character. It is peacefully situated on the banks of the Monnow, a tributary of the River Wye, and is ideally placed for exploring the numerous delights of the area. Natural materials have been used to create a relaxing atmosphere, while the bedrooms, which include full suites and rooms with four-poster beds, are stylish, luxurious and equipped with DVD players. Fresh produce from the garden is used by the kitchen brigade who produce award-winning food for relaxed dining in the welcoming restaurant.

Rooms 11 (2 fmly)

Crug-Glas Country House

RESTAURANT WITH ROOMS

☎ 01348 831302
Abereiddy SA62 6XX
e-mail: janet@crugglas.plus.com
dir: From Solva to St Davids on A487. From St Davids take A487 towards Fishguard. 1st left after Carnhedryn, house signed

This house, on a dairy, beef and cereal farm of approximately 600 acres, is situated about a mile from the coast on the St Davids peninsula. Comfort, relaxation and flawless attention to detail are provided by the charming host, Janet Evans. Each spacious bedroom has the hallmarks of assured design plus a luxury bathroom with both bath and shower; one suite on the top floor has great views. In addition there are two suites in separate buildings.

Rooms 7 (1 fmly)

See also **Port Talbot**

Swansea Marriott Hotel

★★★★ 80% HOTEL

☎ 0870 400 7282
The Maritime Quarter SA1 3SS
web: www.swanseamarriott.co.uk
dir: M4 junct 42, A483 to city centre past Leisure Centre, then follow signs to Maritime Quarter

Just opposite City Hall in the bustling Maritime Quarter, this busy hotel enjoys fantastic views over the bay and marina. The air-conditioned bedrooms are spacious and equipped with a range of extras. Public rooms include a popular leisure club with a gym, whirlpool, sauna and swimming pool; and The Bayside Grill restaurant which overlooks the marina. It is worth noting, however, that lounge seating is limited.

Rooms 119 (49 fmly) (11 GF) **Facilities** STV Wi-fi ⊛ Gym New Year **Conf** Class 120 Board 30 Thtr 300 **Services** Lift Air con **Parking** 122 **Notes** ⊛ Civ Wed 220

The Dragon Hotel

MACDONALD
HOTELS & RESORTS

★★★★ 77% ◉ HOTEL

☎ 01792 657100
The Kingsway Circle SA1 5LS
e-mail: info@dragon-hotel.co.uk
web: www.dragon-hotel.co.uk
dir: A483 follow signs for city centre. After lights at Sainsbury's right onto The Strand then left. Hotel straight ahead

This privately-owned hotel is located in the city centre and offers spacious modern accommodation with well-equipped, comfortable bedrooms. There is a bar and lounge facility on the first floor along with the dining room for breakfast. On the ground floor, the Dragons Brasserie provides award-winning food from a vibrant continental menu for both residents and non-residents. The health and fitness club offers an excellent choice of facilities and there is a good range of conference rooms. Macdonald Hotels is the AA Hotel Group of the Year 2013-14.

Rooms 106 (5 fmly) ☞ **S** £75-£129; **D** £75-£129* **Facilities** STV Wi-fi ⊹ HL ⊛ supervised Gym Beauty therapist Xmas New Year **Conf** Class 120 Board 60 Thtr 230 Del from £125* **Services** Lift Air con **Parking** 52 **Notes** LB ⊛ Civ Wed 200

Mercure Swansea Hotel

★★★ HOTEL

☎ 0844 815 9081
Phoenix Way SA7 9EG
e-mail: info@mercureswansea.co.uk
web: www.jupiterhotels.co.uk
dir: M4 junct 44, A48 (Llansamlet), left at 3rd lights, right at 1st mini rdbt, left into Phoenix Way at 2nd rdbt. Hotel 800mtrs on right

Currently the rating for this establishment is not confirmed. This may be due to a change of ownership or because it has only recently joined the AA rating scheme.

Rooms 119 **Conf** Class 80 Board 60 Thtr 200

Premier Inn Swansea City Centre

BUDGET HOTEL

☎ 0871 527 9060
Salubrious Place, Wind St SA1 1EE
web: www.premierinn.com
dir: M4 junct 42, A483 towards the city centre. Pass Sainsburys on left, right into Salubrious Place, 2nd right, then 3rd exit at mini rdbt

High quality, budget accommodation ideal for both families and business travellers. Spacious, en suite bedrooms feature tea and coffee making facilities, and Freeview TV in most hotels. Internet access and Wi-fi are available for a small fee. The adjacent family restaurant features a wide and varied menu. See also the Hotel Groups pages.

Rooms 116

Premier Inn Swansea North

BUDGET HOTEL

☎ 0871 527 9062
Upper Forest Way, Morriston SA6 8WB
web: www.premierinn.com
dir: M4 junct 45, A4067 towards Swansea. In 0.5m at 2nd exit left into Clase Rd. Hotel 400yds on left

Rooms 40

Premier Inn Swansea Waterfront

BUDGET HOTEL

☎ 0871 577 9212
The Waterfront Development, Langdon Rd SA1 8PL
web: www.premierinn.com
dir: M4 junct 42, A483 towards Swansea/Abertawe
(signed Fabian Way). Approx 4.5m. At 2nd lights, left
into SA1 Waterfront development. At rdbt take 2nd
exit into Langdon Rd. Hotel on left

Rooms 132

TENBY	Map 8 SN10
Pembrokeshire	

Atlantic Hotel

★★★ 81% HOTEL

☎ 01834 842881
The Esplanade SA70 7DU
e-mail: enquiries@atlantic-hotel.uk.com
web: www.atlantic-hotel.uk.com
dir: A478 into Tenby, follow town centre signs (keep
town walls on left) right at Esplanade, hotel on right

Expect a friendly welcome at this privately-owned and
personally-run hotel, which has an enviable position
looking out over South Beach towards Caldy Island.
Bedrooms vary in size and style, but all are well
equipped and tastefully appointed. The comfortable
public areas include a choice of restaurants and, in
fine weather guests can also enjoy the cliff-top
gardens.

Rooms 42 (11 fmly) (4 GF) **S** £82-£91; **D** £114-£194
(incl. bkfst) **Facilities** FTV Wi-fi ⌨ Steam room Spa
bath **Conf** Board 8 **Services** Lift **Parking** 25 **Notes** LB
Closed early Dec-late Jan

Clarence House

★★ 65% HOTEL

☎ 01834 844371
Esplanade SA70 7DU
e-mail: clarencehotel@freeuk.com
web: www.clarencehotel-tenby.co.uk
dir: From South Parade (by town walls) into St
Florence Parade & Esplanade

Owned by the same family for over 50 years, this hotel
has superb views from its elevated position. Many of
the bedrooms have sea views and all are comfortably
furnished. The bar leads to a sheltered rose garden
and a number of lounges. Entertainment is provided
in high season, and this establishment is particularly
popular with coach tour parties.

Rooms 76 (6 fmly) ⌨ **S** £35-£50; **D** £70-£100 (incl.
bkfst) **Facilities** FTV ♫ New Year **Services** Lift
Notes LB Closed 18-28 Dec

TINTERN PARVA	Map 4 SO50
Monmouthshire	

BEST WESTERN Royal George Hotel

★★★ 78% HOTEL

☎ 01291 689205
Wye Valley Rd NP16 6SF
e-mail: royalgeorgetintern@hotmail.com
web: www.bw-royalgeorgehotel.co.uk
dir: M48 junct 2, A466, 5m to Tintern, 2nd left

This privately owned and personally run hotel
provides comfortable, spacious accommodation,
including bedrooms with balconies overlooking the
well-tended garden; there are also a number of
ground-floor bedrooms. The public areas include a
lounge bar and a large function room, and a varied
and popular menu is available in either the bar or
restaurant. This hotel is an ideal base for exploring
the counties of Monmouthshire and Herefordshire.

Rooms 15 (14 annexe) (6 fmly) (10 GF) **Facilities** FTV
Wi-fi ⌨ Xmas New Year **Conf** Class 40 Board 30
Thtr 100 Del from £95 to £135 **Parking** 50
Notes Civ Wed 70

TREARDDUR BAY	Map 14 SH27
Isle of Anglesey	

Trearddur Bay Hotel

★★★ 82% HOTEL

☎ 01407 860301
LL65 2UN
e-mail: enquiries@trearddurbayhotel.co.uk
web: www.trearddurbayhotel.co.uk
dir: A55 junct 2, left, over 1st rdbt, left at 2nd rdbt,
right after approx 2m

This seaside hotel stands 100 yards from the Blue
Flag beach, offering stunning views of the bay. The
very comfortable bedrooms are well appointed and
have flat-screen TVs. Guests have a choice of dining
options: the more formal Bay Restaurant, or the Inn at
The Bay, which also has an outdoor area for summer
dining. Facilities include an indoor swimming pool
and a children's play area.

Rooms 43 (6 annexe) (6 fmly) (3 GF) ⌨ **S** £60-£150;
D £70-£220 (incl. bkfst) **Facilities** FTV Wi-fi ⌨ ⌨
Conf Class 80 Board 60 Thtr 200 Del from £90 to
£130 **Parking** 200 **Notes** LB Civ Wed 140

USK	Map 9 SO30
Monmouthshire	

Glen-yr-Afon House Hotel

★★★ 81% HOTEL

☎ 01291 672302 & 673202
Pontypool Rd NP15 1SY
e-mail: enquiries@glen-yr-afon.co.uk
web: www.glen-yr-afon.co.uk
dir: A472 through High St, over river bridge, follow to
right. Hotel 200yds on left

On the edge of this delightful old market town, Glen-
yr-Afon, a unique Victorian villa, offers all the
facilities expected of a modern hotel combined with
the warm atmosphere of a family home. Bedrooms are
furnished to a high standard and several overlook the
well-tended gardens. There is a choice of comfortable
sitting areas and a stylish and spacious banqueting
suite.

Rooms 28 (1 annexe) (2 fmly) ⌨ **S** £99-£123;
D £136-£159* **Facilities** STV FTV Wi-fi ⌨
Complimentary access to Usk Tennis Club New Year
Conf Class 200 Board 30 Thtr 100 Del from £140*
Services Lift **Parking** 151 **Notes** Civ Wed 150

The Three Salmons Hotel

★★★ 79% ⌨⌨ HOTEL

☎ 01291 672133
Bridge St NP15 1RY
e-mail: general@threesalmons.co.uk
dir: M4 junct 24, A449, 1st exit signed Usk. On
entering town, hotel on main road

The Three Salmons is a 17th-century coaching inn
located in the centre of a small market town with
friendly, efficient staff who help create a welcoming
atmosphere. The food in the contemporary restaurant
proves popular. Bedrooms are comfortable and a good
range of extras are provided. There is a large function
suite ideal for weddings and parties. Parking is
secure.

Rooms 24 (14 annexe) (3 fmly) (7 GF) **S** £80-£95;
D £100-£115 (incl. bkfst)* **Facilities** FTV Wi-fi
Conf Class 80 Board 40 Thtr 110 Del £135*
Parking 25 **Notes** LB Civ Wed 100

U

USK continued

Newbridge on Usk

◉ ◉ RESTAURANT WITH ROOMS

☎ 01633 451000 & 410262
Tredunnock NP15 1LY
e-mail: newbridgeonusk@celtic-manor.com
web: www.celtic-manor.com
dir: M4 junct 24, signed Newport, onto B4236. At Ship
Inn turn right, over mini-rdbt onto Llangybi/Usk road.
Turn right opposite Cwrt Bleddyn Hotel, signed
Tredunnock, through village & down hill

This cosy, gastro-pub is tucked away in a beautiful
village setting with the River Usk nearby. The well-
equipped bedrooms, in a separate building, provide
comfort and a good range of extras. Guests can eat at
rustic tables around the bar or in the upstairs dining
room where award-winning, seasonal food is served;
there is also a small private dining room. Breakfast is
one of the highlights of a stay with quality local
ingredients offered in abundance.

Rooms 6 (2 fmly)

WELSHPOOL Map 15 SJ20
Powys

Royal Oak Hotel

★★★ 77% HOTEL

☎ 01938 552217
The Cross SY21 7DG
e-mail: relax@royaloakhotel.info
web: www.royaloakhotel.info
dir: By lights at junct of A483 & A458

This traditional market town hotel dates back over
350 years. The public areas are furnished in a
minimalist style that highlights the many retained
period features, including exposed beams and open
fires. Three different bedroom styles provide good
comfort levels and imaginative food is served in the
elegant Red Room or in the adjacent all-day café/bar.

Rooms 25 (3 fmly) **Facilities** FTV Wi-fi Xmas New
Year **Conf** Class 60 Board 60 Thtr 150 **Parking** 19
Notes ⊗ Civ Wed

WOLF'S CASTLE Map 8 SM92
Pembrokeshire

Wolfscastle Country Hotel

★★★ 79% ◉
COUNTRY HOUSE HOTEL

☎ 01437 741225 & 741688
SA62 5LZ
e-mail: enquiries@wolfscastle.com
web: www.wolfscastle.com
dir: On A40 in village at top of hill. 6m N of
Haverfordwest

This large stone house, a former vicarage, dates back
to the mid-19th century and is now a friendly,
privately-owned and personally-run hotel. It provides
stylish, modern, well-maintained and well-equipped
bedrooms. There is a pleasant bar and an attractive
restaurant, which has a well deserved reputation for
its food.

Rooms 20 (2 fmly) ✿ **S** £82-£105; **D** £118-£150
(incl. bkfst & dinner)* **Facilities** STV Wi-fi New Year
Conf Class 100 Board 30 Thtr 100 Del from £140 to
£200* **Parking** 60 **Notes** Closed 24-26 Dec
Civ Wed 70

WREXHAM Map 15 SJ35
Wrexham

Premier Inn Wrexham

BUDGET HOTEL

☎ 0871 527 9190
Chester Rd, Gresford LL12 8PW
web: www.premierinn.com
dir: On B5445, just off A483 (dual carriageway) near
Gresford

High quality, budget accommodation ideal for both
families and business travellers. Spacious, en suite
bedrooms feature tea and coffee making facilities,
and Freeview TV in most hotels. Internet access and
Wi-fi are available for a small fee. The adjacent
family restaurant features a wide and varied menu.
See also the Hotel Groups pages.

Rooms 38

U

Save on hotels. Book at **theAA.com/hotel**

USK – WRE 589 WALES

Ireland

Dunluce Castle, Co Antrim

Additional Information for Northern Ireland & the Republic of Ireland

Licensing Regulations

Northern Ireland: Public houses open Mon-Sat 11.30-23.00. Sun 12.30-22.00. Hotels can serve residents without restriction. Non-residents can be served 12.30-22.00 on Christmas Day. Children under 18 are not allowed in the bar area and may neither buy nor consume liquor in hotels.

Republic of Ireland: General licensing hours are Mon-Thu 10.30-23.30, Fri & Sat 10.30-00.30. Sun 12.30-23.00 (or 00.30 if the following day is a Bank Holiday). There is no service (except for hotel residents) on Christmas Day or Good Friday.

The Fire Services (NI) Order 1984

This covers establishments accommodating more than six people, which must have a certificate from the Northern Ireland Fire Authority. Places accommodating fewer than six people need adequate exits. AA inspectors check emergency notices, fire fighting equipment and fire exits here.

The Republic of Ireland safety regulations are a matter for local authority regulations. For your own and others' safety, read the emergency notices and be sure you understand them.

Telephone numbers

Area codes for numbers in the Republic of Ireland apply only within the Republic. If dialling from outside check the telephone directory (from the UK the international dialling code is 00 353). Area codes for numbers in Britain and Northern Ireland cannot be used directly from the Republic.

For the latest information on the Republic of Ireland visit the AA Ireland's website: www.AAireland.ie

---

NORTHERN IRELAND

AGHADOWEY
Co Londonderry
Map 1 C6

Brown Trout Golf & Country Inn

IRISH COUNTRY HOTELS

★★★ 74% HOTEL

☎ 028 7086 8209
209 Agivey Rd BT51 4AD
e-mail: jane@browntroutinn.com
dir: At junct of A54 & B66 junct on road to Coleraine

Set alongside the Agivey River and featuring its own 9-hole golf course, this welcoming inn offers a choice of spacious accommodation. Comfortably furnished bedrooms are situated around a courtyard area whilst the cottage suites also have lounge areas. Home-cooked meals are served in the restaurant and lighter fare is available in the charming lounge bar which has entertainment at weekends.

Rooms 15 (11 fmly) (15 GF) ♠ **Facilities** STV FTV Wi-fi ⟲ ♨ 9 Putt green Gym Game fishing ♫ Xmas New Year **Conf** Class 24 Board 28 Thtr 40 **Parking** 80 **Notes** LB

ANTRIM
Co Antrim
Map 1 D5

Holiday Inn Express Antrim M2 Jct 1

 Holiday Inn Express

BUDGET HOTEL

☎ 028 9442 5500
Ballymena Rd BT4 1LL
e-mail: reception.antrim@holidayinnexpress.org.uk
web: www.hiexpress.com/antrim
dir: At Junction One Shopping Outlet

A modern hotel ideal for families and business travellers. Fresh and uncomplicated, the spacious rooms include Sky TV, power shower and tea and coffee-making facilities. Continental buffet breakfast is included in the room rate; other meals may be taken at the nearby family pub or restaurant. See also the Hotel Groups pages.

Rooms 90 (52 fmly) (10 GF) **Conf** Class 20 Board 20 Thtr 40

BALLYMENA
Co Antrim
Map 1 D5

Galgorm Resort & Spa

★★★★ 85% ◉◉ HOTEL

☎ 028 2588 1001
BT42 1EA
e-mail: mail@galgorm.com
dir: 1m from Ballymena on A42, between Galgorm & Cullybackey

Standing in 163 acres of private woodland and sweeping lawns beside the River Maine, this 19th-century mansion offers spacious, comfortable bedrooms. Public areas include a welcoming cocktail bar and elegant restaurant, as well as Gillies, a lively and atmospheric locals' bar. Also on the estate is an equestrian centre and a conference hall.

Rooms 75 (14 fmly) (8 GF) ♠ **S** £105-£245; **D** £105-£245 (incl. bkfst)* **Facilities** Spa FTV Wi-fi Fishing Clay pigeon shooting Archery Horseriding ♫ Xmas New Year **Conf** Class 170 Board 30 Thtr 500 Del from £150 to £165* **Services** Lift **Parking** 300 **Notes** LB ⊗ Civ Wed 500

Save on hotels. Book at theAA.com/hotel

AGH – BEL 593 IRELAND

BELFAST   Map 1 D5
Belfast

AA HOTEL OF THE YEAR FOR NORTHERN IRELAND

The Merchant Hotel

★★★★★ 85% ◉◉ HOTEL

☎ 028 9023 4888
16 Skipper St BT1 2DZ
e-mail: info@themerchanthotel.com
dir: In city centre, 2nd left at Albert Clock into Waring St. Hotel on left

A magnificent hotel situated in the historic Cathedral Quarter of the city centre. This Grade I listed building has been lovingly and sensitively restored to reveal its original architectural grandeur and interior opulence. All the bedrooms, including five suites, have air-conditioning, hi-speed internet access, flat-screen TVs and luxury bathrooms. There are several eating options including the grand and beautifully decorated Great Room Restaurant. The Merchant Hotel is the AA Hotel of the Year for Northern Ireland 2013-2014.

Rooms 62 (17 fmly) ⚑ **Facilities** Spa FTV Wi-fi ⌂ Gym ♫ Xmas New Year **Conf** Class 100 Board 60 Thtr 200 **Services** Lift Air con **Parking** 35 **Notes** LB ⊗ Civ Wed 130

Radisson Blu Hotel Belfast

★★★★ 77% HOTEL

☎ 028 9043 4065 & 9082 0107
3 Cromac Place BT7 2JB
e-mail: reservations.belfast@radissonblu.com
dir: On corner of Ormeau Rd & Cromac St

This modern hotel is in the centre of the regenerated urban area close to the city centre. The bedrooms are stylishly presented, well equipped and all have are air conditioning; there is a choice of business suites. Public areas include a spacious lounge bar and the Filini Restaurant, which serves good Italian and Sardinian cuisine. Ample secure parking, and free Wi-Fi (throughout the hotel) are available.

Rooms 120 (11 fmly) **S** £67-£359; **D** £67-£359 **Facilities** FTV Wi-fi ⌂ Access to LA Fitness Xmas New Year **Conf** Class 70 Board 50 Thtr 150 Del from £129 to £199* **Services** Lift Air con **Parking** 120 **Notes** LB Civ Wed 90

Malone Lodge Hotel

★★★★ 73% ◉ HOTEL

☎ 028 9038 8000
60 Eglantine Av BT9 6DY
e-mail: info@malonelodgehotel.com
web: www.malonelodgehotelbelfast.com
dir: At hospital rdbt exit towards Bouchar Rd, left at 1st rdbt, right at lights at top, then 1st left

Situated in the leafy suburbs of the university area of south Belfast, this stylish hotel forms the centrepiece of an attractive row of Victorian terraced properties. The unassuming exterior belies an attractive and spacious interior with a smart lounge, popular bar and stylish Green Door restaurant.

Rooms 54 (7 fmly) **Facilities** FTV Wi-fi **Conf** Class 100 Board 60 Thtr 190 **Services** Lift **Parking** 35 **Notes** ⊗ Civ Wed 140

Malmaison Belfast

★★★ 86% ◉ HOTEL

☎ 028 9022 0200
34-38 Victoria St BT1 3GH
e-mail: lsteele@malmaison.com
web: www.malmaison.com
dir: M1 along Westlink to Grosvenor Rd. Follow city centre signs. Pass City Hall on right, left onto Victoria St. Hotel on right

Situated in a former seed warehouse, this luxurious, contemporary hotel is ideally located for the city centre. Comfortable bedrooms boast a host of modern facilities, whilst the deeply comfortable, stylish public areas include a popular bar lounge. The 'Home Grown and Local' menu in the brasserie showcases local seasonal ingredients. The warm hospitality is notable.

Rooms 64 (8 fmly) **Facilities** STV Wi-fi Gym **Conf** Board 22 **Services** Lift

Holiday Inn Belfast

★★★ 81% HOTEL

☎ 0871 942 9005
22 Ormeau Av BT2 8HS
e-mail: belfast@ihg.com
web: www.holidayinn.co.uk
dir: M1/M2 onto West Link at Grosvenor Rd rdbt, follow city centre signs. 1st right, 2nd left into Hope St, at 2nd lights left into Bedford St, at next lights right into Ormeau Ave, hotel on right

This contemporary hotel is located in the heart of the city centre's 'golden mile' which makes it ideal for business visitors, for shopping and for exploring the tourist attractions. The air-conditioned bedrooms are modern in style and offer a comprehensive range of facilities. Public rooms include a staffed business centre and state-of-the-art health club.

Rooms 170 **Facilities** Spa Wi-fi ⌂ Gym ♫ **Services** Lift Air con

Ramada Encore Belfast City Centre

★★★ 81% HOTEL

☎ 028 9026 1800 & 9026 1809
20 Talbot St BT1 2LD
e-mail: reception@encorebelfast.co.uk
web: www.encorebelfast.co.uk
dir: On Dunbar Link behind St Annes Cathedral

This stylish modern hotel is ideally located in the city's Cathedral Quarter and is a short walk from the main shopping and business district. The open-plan public areas feature the SQ Bar & Grill, which is ideal for a relaxed lunch or an intimate dinner. The popular Hub Bar serves an extensive choice of cocktails and there's free Wi-fi in the bar area. The spacious bedrooms are very well appointed and have bathrooms with power showers.

Rooms 165 (20 fmly) ⚑ **Facilities** FTV Wi-fi ⌂ HL ♫ Xmas New Year **Conf** Class 75 Board 30 Thtr 110 **Services** Lift **Notes** ⊗

Park Inn by Radisson Belfast

★★★ 80% HOTEL

☎ 028 9067 7700
4 Clarence Street West BT2 7GP
e-mail: info.belfast@rezidorparkinn.com
dir: M1 into Belfast, which becomes A12 (Westlink). Right into Grosvenor Rd (B38), follow City Centre signs. Right into Durnham St (B503), left into Hope St, which becomes Bruce St. Left into Bedford St (A1). Left into Clarence St, hotel on left

This hotel is well located in the city centre and a short walk from the main shopping, entertainment and business districts. The contemporary bedrooms are stylishly presented and the ten spacious business rooms have complimentary Wi-fi. The hotel also provides the RBG Bar and Grill, a sauna, steam room and conference facilities.

Rooms 145 (5 fmly) **Facilities** FTV Wi-fi Gym Sauna Steam room ♫ Xmas New Year **Conf** Class 60 Board 44 Thtr 120 **Services** Lift Air con **Parking** 15 **Notes** ⊗

NORTHERN IRELAND

BELFAST *continued*

Premier Inn Belfast City Cathedral Quarter

BUDGET HOTEL

☎ 0871 527 8070
2-6 Waring St BT1 1XY
web: www.premierinn.com
dir: M1 or M2 to Westlink to Grosvenor Rd rdbt, signed city centre. Into Grosvenor Rd. At 2nd lights left, take right lane, right (pass City Hall on right). At end of Chichester St left into Victoria St. Through next 2 lights, left into Waring St. Hotel 300yds on right

High quality, budget accommodation ideal for both families and business travellers. Spacious, en suite bedrooms feature tea and coffee making facilities, and Freeview TV in most hotels. Internet access and Wi-fi are available for a small fee. The adjacent family restaurant features a wide and varied menu. See also the Hotel Groups pages.

Rooms 171

Premier Inn Belfast City Centre Alfred St

BUDGET HOTEL

☎ 0871 527 8068
Alfred St BT2 8ED
web: www.premierinn.com
dir: M1 or M2 to Westlink. Follow city centre signs. 1st right, 2nd left into Hope St. At 2nd lights left into Bedford St. At next lights right into Ormeau Ave. Left into Alfred St. Underground car park (chargeable) on left

Rooms 148

Premier Inn Belfast Titanic Quarter

BUDGET HOTEL

☎ 0871 527 9210
2A Queens Rd BT3 9FB
web: www.premierinn.com
dir: From all major routes follow Odyssey Arena signs. From M3 junct 1 exit onto Queens Island, to lights. Hotel on left

Rooms 102

BUSHMILLS   Map 1 C6
Co Antrim

Bushmills Inn Hotel

★★★★ 80% ◉ HOTEL

☎ 028 2073 3000 & 2073 2339
9 Dunluce Rd BT57 8QG
e-mail: mail@bushmillsinn.com
web: www.bushmillsinn.com
dir: On A2 in village centre

Enjoying a prominent position in the heart of the village, this hotel offers a range of bedroom styles including spacious, creatively designed rooms that have the latest technology and a small dressing room. The charming public areas feature inglenook turf-burning fires, cosy snugs along with a very popular traditional bar. The restaurant has a well deserved reputation for its food. The hotel is very popular with golfers; it is close to the Giants Causeway, Bushmills Distillery and the stunning scenery of the Antrim Coast.

Rooms 41 (2 fmly) (20 GF) **Facilities** Wi-fi ♫ New Year **Conf** Class 30 Board 18 Thtr 40 **Services** Lift **Parking** 70 **Notes** ⊗ Closed 25 Dec

---

CARNLOUGH   Map 1 D6
Co Antrim

Londonderry Arms Hotel

 IRISH COUNTRY HOTELS

★★★ 74% HOTEL

☎ 028 2888 5255
20 Harbour Rd BT44 0EU
e-mail: lda@glensofantrim.com
dir: 14m N from Larne on A2 (coast road)

This delightful hotel was built in the mid-19th century by Lady Londonderry, whose grandson, Winston Churchill, also owned it at one time. Today the hotel's Georgian architecture and rooms are still evident, and spacious bedrooms can be found in the modern extension. The hotel enjoys a prime location in this pretty fishing village overlooking the Antrim coast.

Rooms 35 (15 fmly) **S** £50-£65; **D** £60-£100 (incl. bkfst)* **Facilities** FTV Wi-fi Fishing New Year **Conf** Class 60 Board 40 Thtr 120 Del from £100 to £150* **Services** Lift **Parking** 50 **Notes** LB ⊗ Closed 24-25 Dec Civ Wed 60

CARRICKFERGUS   Map 1 D5
Co Antrim

Premier Inn Carrickfergus

BUDGET HOTEL

☎ 0871 527 8214
The Harbour, Alexandra Pier BT38 8BE
web: www.premierinn.com
dir: Exit at M2 junct 2, take M5 N onto A2 towards Carrickfergus. Follow Castle/Maritime Area signs. Right at rdbt adjacent to castle. Hotel straight ahead, adjacent to harbour

High quality, budget accommodation ideal for both families and business travellers. Spacious, en suite bedrooms feature tea and coffee making facilities, and Freeview TV in most hotels. Internet access and Wi-fi are available for a small fee. The adjacent family restaurant features a wide and varied menu. See also the Hotel Groups pages.

Rooms 49

COLERAINE   Map 1 C6
Co Londonderry

Premier Inn Coleraine

BUDGET HOTEL

☎ 0871 527 8262
3 Riverside Park North, Castleroe Rd BT51 3GE
web: www.premierinn.com
dir: A26 towards Colraine. At rdbt left on A29 (ring road) signed Cookstown/Garragh. At rdbt A54 (Castleroe Rd). Hotel on right

High quality, budget accommodation ideal for both families and business travellers. Spacious, en suite bedrooms feature tea and coffee making facilities, and Freeview TV in most hotels. Internet access and Wi-fi are available for a small fee. The adjacent family restaurant features a wide and varied menu. See also the Hotel Groups pages.

Rooms 49

Save on hotels. Book at **theAA.com/hotel**

BEL – ENN 595 IRELAND

CRAWFORDSBURN — Map 1 D5
Co Down

The Old Inn
★★★★ 82% ◉◉ HOTEL

☎ 028 9185 3255
15 Main St BT19 1JH
e-mail: info@theoldinn.com
web: www.theoldinn.com
dir: A2 from Belfast (pass Belfast City Airport & Transport Museum). 2m, left at lights onto B20. 1.2m to hotel

This delightful hotel enjoys a peaceful rural setting just a short drive from Belfast. The property dates from 1614, and many of the day rooms exude charm and character. Individually styled, comfortable bedrooms, some with feature beds, offer modern facilities. The popular bar and intimate restaurant both offer creative menus, and staff throughout are keen to please.

Rooms 31 (1 annexe) (7 fmly) (6 GF) ☎ **Facilities** STV FTV Wi-fi ⬙ In room spa/massage treatments ♫ Xmas New Year **Conf** Class 120 Board 40 Thtr 150 **Services** Lift **Parking** 84 **Notes** ⊗ RS 25 Dec Civ Wed 100

DUNGANNON — Map 1 C5
Co Tyrone

The Cohannon Inn & Auto Lodge
★★ 74% HOTEL

☎ 028 8772 4488
212 Ballynakilly Rd BT71 6HJ
e-mail: info@cohannon.com
dir: 400yds from M1 junct 14

Handy for the M1 and the nearby towns of Dungannon and Portadown, this hotel offers well-maintained bedrooms, located behind the inn complex in a smart purpose-built wing. Public areas are smartly furnished and wide-ranging menus are served throughout the day.

Rooms 42 (20 fmly) (21 GF) (5 smoking) **S** fr £40; **D** fr £54.95* **Facilities** FTV Wi-fi Hair & beauty salon New Year **Conf** Class 100 Board 40 Thtr 160 **Parking** 160 **Notes** LB RS 25 Dec

---

ENNISKILLEN — Map 1 C5
Co Fermanagh

Lough Erne Resort
★★★★★ 86% ◉◉ HOTEL

☎ 028 6632 3230
Belleek Rd BT93 7ED
e-mail: info@lougherneresort.com
web: www.lougherneresort.com
dir: A46 from Enniskillen towards Donegal, hotel in 3m

This delightful resort enjoys a peaceful and idyllic setting and boasts championship golf courses, a wonderful Thai spa and a host of outdoor and leisure pursuits. Bedrooms and en suites are spacious, particularly well appointed and include a number of luxury suites. Day rooms are spacious, luxurious and include lounges, bars and restaurants with splendid views. Service is friendly and extremely attentive.

Rooms 120 (61 annexe) **S** fr £85; **D** fr £110* **Facilities** Spa STV Wi-fi ◔ ⌁ 18 Fishing Gym ♫ Xmas New Year **Conf** Class 200 Board 80 Thtr 400 Del from £120* **Services** Lift **Parking** 240 **Notes** ⊗ Civ Wed 300

Manor House Country Hotel
★★★★ 80% ◉◉ COUNTRY HOUSE HOTEL

☎ 028 6862 2200
Killadeas BT94 1NY
e-mail: info@manorhouseresorthotel.com
dir: On B82, 7m N of Enniskillen

This charming country house hotel enjoys a stunning location on the banks of Lower Lough Erne and is a short drive from the busy town of Enniskillen. Bedrooms are equipped to a very high standard with front-facing rooms having the fabulous lough views. There is a choice of restaurants, and afternoon tea is served in the comfortable lounge with its open fire. The hotel has first-class business, conference and leisure facilities including its own air-conditioned cruiser for tours and corporate events.

Rooms 81 (12 fmly) (12 GF) ☎ **Facilities** FTV Wi-fi ⬙ ◔ Gym Sauna ♫ Xmas New Year **Conf** Class 120 Board 100 Thtr 400 **Services** Lift **Parking** 300 **Notes** ⊗ Civ Wed 300

Killyhevlin Hotel & Health Club
IRISH COUNTRY HOTELS
★★★★ 79% HOTEL

☎ 028 6632 3481
BT74 6RW
e-mail: info@killyhevlin.com
web: www.killyhevlin.com
dir: 2m S of Enniskillen, off A4

This modern, stylish hotel is situated on the shores of Lough Erne, south of the town. The well-equipped bedrooms are particularly spacious and enjoy fine views of the gardens and lake. The restaurant, informal bar and comfortable lounges all share the views. Staff are friendly and helpful. There are extensive leisure facilities and a spa.

Rooms 70 (42 fmly) (22 GF) ☎ **S** £60-£110; **D** £70-£160 (incl. bkfst)* **Facilities** Spa FTV Wi-fi ⬙ ◔ Fishing Gym Aerobic studio Steam room Sauna Hydrotherapy area ♫ New Year **Conf** Class 160 Board 100 Thtr 500 Del from £100 to £125 **Services** Lift **Parking** 500 **Notes** ⊗ Closed 25 Dec RS 24 & 26 Dec Civ Wed 250

LIMAVADY
Co Londonderry   Map 1 C6

Roe Park Resort

★★★★ 73% @ HOTEL

☎ 028 7772 2222
BT49 9LB
e-mail: reservations@roeparkresort.com
web: www.roeparkresort.com
dir: On A2 (Londonderry-Limavady road), 1m from
Limavady

This impressive, popular hotel is part of a modern
golf resort. The spacious, contemporary bedrooms are
well equipped and many have excellent views of the
fairways and surrounding estate. The Greens
Restaurant provides a refreshing dining experience
and the Coach House brasserie offers a lighter menu.
The leisure options are extensive.

Rooms 118 (15 fmly) (37 GF) (5 smoking) ⌀
S £70-£140; D £85-£155 (incl. bkfst)* **Facilities** Spa
FTV Wi-fi HL ⌀ supervised ⌀ 18 Putt green Fishing
Gym Driving range Indoor golf academy ♬ Xmas New
Year **Conf** Class 190 Board 140 Thtr 450 **Services** Lift
Parking 350 **Notes** LB ⊗ Civ Wed 300

LISBURN
Co Antrim   Map 1 D5

Premier Inn Lisburn

BUDGET HOTEL

☎ 0871 527 8606
136-144 Hillsborough Rd BT27 5QY
web: www.premierinn.com
dir: M1 onto A1 (Sprucefield Rd). Left into
Hillsborough Rd. Approx 1.5m, hotel on left

High quality, budget accommodation ideal for both
families and business travellers. Spacious, en suite
bedrooms feature tea and coffee making facilities,
and Freeview TV in most hotels. Internet access and
Wi-fi are available for a small fee. The adjacent
family restaurant features a wide and varied menu.
See also the Hotel Groups pages.

Rooms 60

LONDONDERRY
Co Londonderry   Map 1 C5

City Hotel

★★★★ 74% HOTEL

☎ 028 7136 5800
Queens Quay BT48 7AS
e-mail: reservations@cityhotelderry.com
dir: Follow city centre signs. Hotel on waterfront

In a central position overlooking the River Foyle, this
stylish, contemporary hotel will appeal to business
and leisure guests alike. All bedrooms have excellent
facilities including internet access; the executive
rooms make particularly good working environments.
Meeting and function facilities are extensive and
there are good leisure options.

Rooms 146 (16 fmly) ⌀ S £55-£138; D £55-£145*
Facilities FTV Wi-fi ⌀ ⌀ supervised Gym Steam room
♬ New Year **Conf** Class 150 Board 80 Thtr 350
Del from £99 to £210* **Services** Lift Air con
Parking 48 **Notes** LB ⊗ Closed 25 Dec Civ Wed 350

Premier Inn Derry / Londonderry

BUDGET HOTEL

☎ 0871 527 9414
Crescent Link BT47 6SA
web: www.premierinn.com
dir: Telephone for detailed directions

High quality, budget accommodation ideal for both
families and business travellers. Spacious, en suite
bedrooms feature tea and coffee making facilities,
and Freeview TV in most hotels. Internet access and
Wi-fi are available for a small fee. The adjacent
family restaurant features a wide and varied menu.
See also the Hotel Groups pages.

Rooms 60

ARDMORE
Co Waterford   MAP 1 C2

Cliff House Hotel

★★★★ 83% @@@@ HOTEL

☎ 024 87800 & 87801
e-mail: info@thecliffhousehotel.com
dir: From Dungarvan: N25, signed Cork. Left onto
R673. From Youghal: N25 signed Waterford. Right
onto R673 signed Ardmore. In Ardmore take Middle Rd
to hotel

This unique property, virtually sculpted into the cliff
face overlooking Ardmore Bay, is just a few minutes'
walk from the village. Most of the individually
designed bedroom suites and the public rooms enjoy
the spectacular views, as do the stunning spa and
leisure facilities. Dinner in the award-winning House
Restaurant is a particular highlight - the menus
feature imaginatively cooked, seasonal and local
produce.

Rooms 39 (8 fmly) (7 GF) **Facilities** Spa STV FTV Wi-fi
⌀ Fishing Gym Sauna Steam room Relaxation room
Outdoor pursuits New Year **Conf** Class 30 Board 20
Thtr 50 **Services** Lift Air con **Parking** 52 **Notes** ⊗
Closed 2 wks in Jan

REPUBLIC OF IRELAND

BALLINA
Co Mayo   Map 1 B4

Mount Falcon Estate
★★★★ 83% ◎◎ HOTEL

☎ 096 74472
Mount Falcon Estate
e-mail: info@mountfalcon.com
web: www.mountfalcon.com
dir: On N26, 6m from Foxford & 3m from Ballina.
Hotel on left

Dating from 1876, this house has been lovingly restored to its former glory, and has a bedroom extension that is totally in keeping with the original design. Relaxing lounges look out on the 100-acre estate, which has excellent salmon fishing on The Moy plus well-stocked trout lakes. Dinner is served in the original kitchen with choices from a varied and interesting menu; for lunch there is also the Boathole Bar. An air-conditioned gym is available.

Rooms 32 (3 fmly) ♠ **Facilities** Spa STV Wi-fi ♘ ⓣ supervised Fishing Gym Sauna Steam room Driving range New Year **Conf** Class 120 Board 80 Thtr 200 **Services** Lift **Parking** 260 **Notes** ⊗ Closed 24-27 Dec Civ Wed 200

Belleek Castle
★★★ 73% ◎◎ HOTEL

☎ 096 22400
Belleek
e-mail: info@belleekcastle.com
dir: In Belleek woods N of Ballina

This lovely manor house, formerly the ancestral home of the Earl of Arran, is set in wonderful parkland at the head of Belleek Wood on the River Moy estuary. The cosy public lounges are welcoming, and are complemented by a series of banqueting suites that are decorated in a nautical theme. Bedroom accommodation varies in style; all rooms are comfortably appointed. Dinner is the highlight of any visit, offered from a choice of Market or Gourmet set menus. The food is all locally sourced, and the chef has a keen eye for seasonality. The hotel is a popular wedding venue. There is also a museum specialising in armoury and memorabilia from the Spanish Armada.

Rooms 11 (2 fmly) **S** €50-€160; **D** €80-€220 (incl. bkfst)* **Facilities** STV FTV Wi-fi ♘ Xmas New Year **Conf** Class 60 Board 30 Thtr 100 Del from €80 to €300 **Parking** 200 **Notes** LB ⊗ Civ Wed 200

BALLINGEARY
Co Cork   Map 1 B2

Gougane Barra Hotel
★★★ 78% ◎ HOTEL

☎ 026 47069
Gougane Barra
e-mail: gouganebarrahotel@eircom.net
dir: On L4643. Exit R584 between N22 at Macroom & N71 at Bantry

This charming hotel, run by the Lucey family for over five generations, is in an idyllic location on the shores of Gougane Barra Lake, overlooking the tiny Oratory of St. Finbarr, a popular venue for intimate weddings. The bedrooms vary in size, but they are all well decorated, very comfortable and ideal for leisure guests. Chef Katie Lucey prepares menus based on the best local and seasonal ingredients, some from artisan producers. The ground floor includes cosy lounge areas and a traditional bar, with a marquee theatre in the summer months for an innovative experience known as Theatre by the Lake.

Rooms 26 (12 GF) ♠ **S** €49-€65; **D** €89-€115 (incl. bkfst) **Facilities** STV FTV Wi-fi Fishing Boating Cycling **Parking** 26 **Notes** LB ⊗ Closed 10 Oct-10 Apr Civ Wed

---

BALLYCOTTON
Co Cork   Map 1 C2

INSPECTORS' CHOICE

Bayview Hotel
★★★ ◎◎ HOTEL

☎ 021 4646746
e-mail: res@thebayviewhotel.com
dir: Exit N25 at Castlemartyr, through Ladysbridge & Garryvoe to Ballycotton

The gardens of this hotel seem to hang onto the cliffs overlooking the pier and Ballycotton Bay. The comfortable public rooms and bedrooms with balconies take in the breathtaking coastline views. Dinner in the Capricho Room is a special delight where guests will find locally-landed fish on the menu. More casual dining is available throughout the day in the bar. The warm and friendly team impress with their high standards of customer care.

Rooms 35 (5 GF) (10 smoking) **Facilities** STV Wi-fi Pitch and putt Sea angling Use of swimming pool at sister hotel **Conf** Class 30 Board 24 Thtr 60 **Services** Lift Air con **Parking** 40 **Notes** ⊗ Closed Nov-Apr Civ Wed 100

BALLYLICKEY	Map 1 B2
Co Cork	

INSPECTORS' CHOICE

Sea View House Hotel
★★★ ◉ ◉ HOTEL

☎ 027 50073 & 50462
e-mail: info@seaviewhousehotel.com
web: www.seaviewhousehotel.com
dir: 5km from Bantry, 11km from Glengarriff on N71

Colourful gardens and glimpses of Bantry Bay through the mature trees frame this delightful country house. Owner Kathleen O'Sullivan's team of staff are exceptionally pleasant, and there is a relaxed atmosphere in the cosy lounges. Guest comfort and good cuisine are top priorities. Bedrooms are spacious and individually styled, and some on the ground floor are appointed to suit less able guests.

Rooms 25 (3 fmly) (5 GF) ⚑ **Facilities** STV FTV Wi-fi **Conf** Class 30 Board 25 Thtr 25 **Parking** 32 **Notes** Closed mid Nov-mid Mar Civ Wed 75

BALLYLIFFIN	Map 1 C6
Co Donegal	

Ballyliffin Lodge & Spa
★★★★ 76% HOTEL

☎ 074 9378200
Shore Rd
e-mail: info@ballyliffinlodge.com
dir: From Derry take A2 towards Moville, exit for Carndonagh at Quigleys Point. Ballyliffin 10km

Located in the heart of the village, this property offers a range of very comfortable bedrooms, many of which enjoy panoramic views of Malin Head and the famed Ballyliffin Golf Club. Dinner is served in the open-plan Jacks bar and restaurant, and less formal meals are served in the bar throughout the day. Guests are welcome to use the leisure facilities in the adjoining Crystal Rock Spa, where there is also a hairdressing salon.

Rooms 40 (28 fmly) ⚑ **S** €70-€120; **D** €110-€190 (incl. bkfst)* **Facilities** Spa STV Wi-fi ⊙ supervised Gym Hair salon ♫ New Year Child facilities **Conf** Class 200 Board 100 Thtr 300 **Services** Lift **Parking** 80 **Notes** ⊗ Civ Wed 150

BALLYVAUGHAN	Map 1 B3
Co Clare	

INSPECTORS' CHOICE

Gregans Castle
★★★ ◉ ◉ ◉
COUNTRY HOUSE HOTEL

☎ 065 7077005
e-mail: stay@gregans.ie
dir: 3.5m S of Ballyvaughan on N67

This hotel is a hidden gem in The Burren area, and the delightful restaurant and bedrooms enjoy splendid views towards Galway Bay. The Haden family, together with their welcoming staff, offer a high level of personal service. Bedrooms are individually decorated; superior rooms and suites are particularly comfortable; some are on the ground floor and have patio gardens. There are welcoming fires in the comfortable drawing room and the cosy cocktail bar where afternoon tea is served. Dinner is a highlight of any visit; the chef shows a real passion for food which is evident in his cooking of top quality local and organic produce. The area is rich in archaeological, geological and botanical interest, and cycling and walking tours can be organised. There is a beautiful garden to relax in.

Rooms 21 (3 fmly) (7 GF) ⚑ **S** €155-€205; **D** €205-€325 (incl. bkfst)* **Facilities** Wi-fi ⇖ ⛵ **Conf** Class 25 Board 14 Thtr 25 **Parking** 25 **Notes** LB Closed Jan-12 Feb & 30 Nov-Dec Civ Wed 65

BALTIMORE	Map 1 B1
Co Cork	

Rolfs Country House
◉ RESTAURANT WITH ROOMS

☎ 028 20289
Baltimore Hill
e-mail: info@rolfscountryhouse.com
dir: Before village turn sharp left up hill. House signed

Situated on a hill above the fishing village of Baltimore, are the 400-year-old stone buildings that the Haffner family converted into accommodation. Available are ten traditionally furnished en suite bedrooms in an annexe building, a cosy bar with an open fire, and a rustic restaurant on two levels. Dinner is served nightly during the high season and at weekends in the winter months; the menu features quality meats, artisan cheeses and fish landed at the busy pier. This is a lovely place to stay and the hosts are very friendly.

Rooms 10 (10 annexe)

BANTRY	Map 1 B2
Co Cork	

Westlodge Hotel
★★★ 78% HOTEL

☎ 027 50360
e-mail: reservations@westlodgehotel.ie
web: www.westlodgehotel.ie
dir: N71 to Bantry

With a superb leisure and wellness centre and good children's facilities, this hotel is very popular with families; the friendly team of staff ensure a memorable visit. The bedrooms include standard and family rooms and there is one superior suite. Dinner menus include organic and local seafood. The hotel's location on the outskirts of Bantry makes it an ideal base for touring west Cork and south Kerry, and there are lovely walks in the grounds. Historical and archaeology tours of the Bantry can be booked.

Rooms 90 (20 fmly) (20 GF) **Facilities** STV Wi-fi ⊙ supervised ⚑ Putt green Gym Squash 2 beauty treatment rooms Pitch & putt ♫ New Year **Conf** Class 200 Board 24 Thtr 400 **Services** Lift Air con **Parking** 400 **Notes** ⊗ Closed 23-27 Dec Civ Wed 300

Save on hotels. Book at theAA.com/hotel

BAL – BLA 599 IRELAND

BARNA (BEARNA)
Co Galway
Map 1 B3

The Twelve

★★★★ 80% ◉◉ HOTEL

☎ 091 597000
Barna Village
e-mail: enquire@thetwelvehotel.ie
dir: Coast road Barna village, 10 mins from Galway

Located just ten minutes west of Galway city, this hotel looks as if it has been on the site for decades. However, once inside the decor is striking and contemporary. The bedrooms come in a number of different sizes, but all are furnished with taste and with guest comfort in mind. The Pins is a vibrant and popular bar and bistro where food is served throughout the day. West Restaurant opens during the evening, and features fine dining from a well-compiled menu of local and seasonal produce. Le Petit Spa offers treatments based on seaweed products.

The Twelve

Rooms 47 (12 fmly) ➟ **S** €80-€120; **D** €90-€130 (incl. bkfst) **Facilities** STV FTV Wi-fi ♨ Beauty treatment room Children's cookery programme Art classes Wine classes ♪ Xmas New Year **Conf** Class 70 Board 60 Thtr 80 **Services** Lift Air con **Parking** 140 **Notes** LB RS 22-27 Dec Civ Wed 100

See advert below

BELMULLET
Co Mayo
Map 1 A5

The Talbot Hotel

★★★★ 76% HOTEL

☎ 097 20484
Barrack St
e-mail: info@thetalbothotel.ie

In the heart of Belmullet town, this family operated boutique property has evolved from humble beginnings of a grocery store with a bar, to what is now a warm and welcoming hotel. The simple exterior belies the contemporary opulence that makes up the range of individually designed and decorated bedrooms and suites that make up this comfortable townhouse. The bar is a popular venue with the locals, where quality food is served throughout the day, with seafood a feature. The 1st floor Barony Restaurant opens at weekends and peak periods.

Rooms 21 (4 fmly) (8 GF) ➟ **S** €75-€180; **D** €160-€280 (incl. bkfst)* **Facilities** STV Wi-fi ♨ ♪ Xmas New Year **Conf** Class 100 Board 100 Thtr 180 Del from €120 to €215* **Services** Lift Air con **Notes** LB ⊗

BLARNEY
Co Cork
Map 1 B2

Blarney Golf Resort

★★★★ 78% HOTEL

☎ 021 4384477
Tower
e-mail: reservations@blarneygolfresort.com
dir: Exit N20 for Blarney, 4km to Tower, right into Old Kerry Rd. Hotel 2km on right

This resort includes a John Daly designed golf course. The hotel is situated close to Tower village and the famous Blarney Castle. Bedrooms are well equipped and comfortable; some have balconies and spacious lounges. Early Bird and carte dinner menus are served nightly in the Inniscarra Restaurant, with more casual dining available in the golf club bar. There are excellent leisure facilities in the Sentosa Spa.

Rooms 117 (56 annexe) (56 fmly) (30 GF) **Facilities** Spa FTV Wi-fi ⊙ supervised ♨ 18 Putt green Gym Steam room Sauna ♪ Xmas New Year **Conf** Class 150 Board 40 Thtr 300 **Services** Lift Air con **Parking** 250 **Notes** ⊗

REPUBLIC OF IRELAND

CARLOW — Map 1 C3
Co Carlow

Seven Oaks Hotel
★★★ 78% HOTEL

☎ 059 9131308
Athy Rd
e-mail: info@sevenoakshotel.com

This hotel is conveniently situated within walking distance of the town centre. Public areas include comfortable lounges, library, bar and a restaurant where food is available all day. There is a traditional Irish music session on Monday nights in the Oak Bar. Bedrooms are spacious and very well appointed. There are extensive leisure and banqueting facilities and a secure car park.

Rooms 89 (5 fmly) (7 GF) ⚡ **S** €59-€80; **D** €100-€139 (incl. bkfst)* **Facilities** STV Wi-fi ⌨ ⌘ supervised Gym Aerobic studio Steam room 🎵 **Conf** Class 150 Board 80 Thtr 400 **Services** Lift Air con **Parking** 200 **Notes** LB ⊗ Closed 25-26 Dec RS Good Fri Civ Wed 200

CARRICKMACROSS — Map 1 C4
Co Monaghan

Shirley Arms Hotel
★★★★ 76% ⊛ HOTEL

☎ 042 9673100
Main St
e-mail: reception@shirleyarmshotel.ie
dir: N2 to Derry, take Ardee Rd to Carrickmacross

Set at the top of the town, this long established hotel is an imposing stone building with a contemporary interior. Bedrooms, in a purpose-built block, are spacious and have clean, modern lines; there is also a comfortable suite in the original house overlooking the square. Food is an important element of the business here, with options available throughout the day.

Rooms 25 (2 fmly) ⚡ **Facilities** STV Wi-fi ⌨ 🎵 New Year **Conf** Class 150 Board 200 Thtr 200 **Services** Lift **Parking** 80 **Notes** ⊗ Closed 24-26 Dec RS 6 Apr Civ Wed 150

CASHEL — Map 1 A4
Co Galway

INSPECTORS' CHOICE

Cashel House Hotel
★★★ ⊛⊛ COUNTRY HOUSE HOTEL

☎ 095 31001
e-mail: res@cashel-house-hotel.com
web: www.cashel-house-hotel.com
dir: S off N59, 1.5km W of Recess, well signed

Cashel House is a mid-19th century property, standing at the head of Cashel Bay in the heart of Connemara, and set amidst secluded, award-winning gardens with woodland walks. Attentive service comes with the perfect balance of friendliness and professionalism from McEvilly family and their staff. The comfortable lounges have turf fires and antique furnishings. The restaurant offers local produce such as the famous Connemara lamb, and fish from the nearby coast.

Rooms 29 (4 fmly) (6 GF) (4 smoking) ⚡ **S** €70-€90; **D** €140-€180 (incl. bkfst)* **Facilities** STV FTV Wi-fi Garden school Cookery classes Xmas New Year **Parking** 40 **Notes** LB Closed Jan-10 Feb Civ Wed 80

CASTLEMARTYR — Map 1 C2
Co Cork

Castlemartyr Resort
★★★★★ 89% ⊛⊛ HOTEL

☎ 021 4219000
e-mail: reception@castlemartyrresort.ie
dir: N25, 3rd exit signed Rosslare. Continue past Carrigtwohill & Midleton exits. Right at lights in village

Castlemartyr Resort is an impressively restored 18th-century property, where old world grandeur and contemporary styles marry well. The individually decorated bedrooms in the Manor House make luxurious retreats, while the modern wing rooms are furnished in a more contemporary style to a very high standard. The hotel offers fine dining in the Bell Tower Restaurant featuring modern Irish cuisine and

more casual eating options in Knights Bar and the Golf Clubhouse nearby. The estate grounds of over 220 acres offer a myriad of outdoor pursuits including golf on the Ron Kirby designed inland links style course, cycling and boating on the lake. There are walking or jogging routes along the nature trails. There is also a stunning spa wellness and leisure facility available for guests.

Rooms 109 (98 annexe) (6 fmly) (30 GF) **Facilities** Spa STV FTV Wi-fi ⌨ ⌘ supervised ⚡ 18 ⛳ Gym Bicycles Horse & carriage rides Target archery Clay pigeon shooting 🎵 New Year **Conf** Class 150 Board 75 Thtr 250 **Services** Lift Air con **Parking** 200 **Notes** Closed 16-27 Dec Civ Wed 190

CAVAN — Map 1 C4
Co Cavan

Radisson Blu Farnham Estate Hotel
★★★★ 79% ⊛ HOTEL

☎ 049 4377700
Farnham Estate
e-mail: info.farnham@radissonblu.com
dir: From Dublin take N3 to Cavan. From Cavan take Killeshandra road for 4km

Situated on a 1,300 acre estate, this 16th-century Great House combines old-world grandeur with modern glamour. Interiors are light, airy and contemporary with a relaxing atmosphere. The spacious bedrooms and suites are in the newer building. Interesting dining options are available in the Botanica Restaurant and Wine Goose Cellar Bar. There are extensive banqueting facilities and the health spa offers a range of treatments.

Rooms 158 (50 GF) ⚡ **S** €99-€250; **D** €109-€320 (incl. bkfst)* **Facilities** Spa STV Wi-fi ⌨ ⌘ ⚡ ⚡ 18 Putt green Fishing ⛳ Gym 🎵 Xmas New Year **Conf** Class 200 Board 44 Thtr 380 Del from €159 to €175* **Services** Lift **Parking** 600 **Notes** ⊗ Civ Wed 150

CLAREMORRIS — Map 1 B4
Co Mayo

McWilliam Park Hotel
★★★★ 79% HOTEL

☎ 094 9378000
e-mail: info@mcwilliamparkhotel.ie
dir: Take Castlebar/Claremorris exit from N17, straight over rdbt. Hotel on right

This fine hotel is situated on the outskirts of Claremorris, approximately 20 minutes from the Marian Shrine at Knock and the airport. There are comfortable lounges together with extensive conference, leisure and health facilities. The

Save on hotels. Book at **theAA.com/hotel**

CAR – COR 601 IRELAND

bedrooms are spacious and well appointed, with good communication technology. Food is served all day in Kavanagh's bar, and dinner is available each night in J.G's Restaurant which also serves a popular Sunday lunch. Traditional music, dancing and other entertainment events are held on a regular basis in the McWilliam Suite.

Rooms 103 (19 fmly) (15 GF) (44 smoking) 🐾 **Facilities** Spa STV FTV Wi-fi ᕒ 🐾 Gym ♫ Xmas New Year **Conf** Class 250 Board 80 Thtr 600 **Services** Lift **Parking** 320 **Notes** ⊗ Civ Wed 200

CLIFDEN   Map 1 A4
Co Galway

Abbeyglen Castle Hotel

★★★★ 80% ⊛ HOTEL

☎ 095 21201
Sky Rd
e-mail: info@abbeyglen.ie
dir: N59 from Galway towards Clifden. Hotel 1km from Clifden on Sky Road

The tranquil setting overlooking Clifden, matched with the dedication of the Hughes's father and son team and their attentive staff, combine to create a magical atmosphere. Now into its 5th decade, Abbeyglen Castle has a well earned reputation, with many guests returning year after year. Well-appointed rooms and very comfortable suites are available, together with a range of relaxing lounge areas. The restaurant features a daily-changing menu of traditional and more modern dishes; many guests enjoy impromptu sessions around the piano in the bar following dinner. Treatment rooms are available.

Rooms 45 (9 GF) 🐾 **S** €98-€145; **D** €140-€240 (incl. bkfst)* **Facilities** STV Wi-fi ᕒ Putt green Beauty treatment & relaxation centre ♫ Xmas New Year **Conf** Class 50 Board 40 Thtr 100 Del from €190 to €220* **Services** Lift **Parking** 50 **Notes** LB ⊗ No children 10yrs Closed 5-30 Jan

---

CLONAKILTY   Map 1 B2
Co Cork

Inchydoney Island Lodge & Spa

★★★★ 83% ⊛⊛ HOTEL

☎ 023 8833143
e-mail: reservations@inchydoneyisland.com
dir: Follow N71 (West Cork road) to Clonakilty. At rdbt in Clonakilty take 2nd exit, follow signs to hotel

Benefiting from a stunning location on Inchydoney Island, this welcoming hotel has much to offer guests that are looking for a truly relaxing experience. All of the comfortably appointed bedrooms and suites have sea views with balconies or terraces. The public rooms are spacious and decorated with an interesting range of specially commissioned furniture and artwork. Guests can choose between the informal atmosphere of the popular Dunes pub and bistro, or The Gulfstream Restaurant where the emphasis is on locally landed seafood cooked with care. The Island Spa offers a range of thalassotherapy treatments, featuring sea water pumped daily from the shore.

Rooms 67 (24 fmly) (18 GF) **S** €125-€175; **D** €158-€250 (incl. bkfst) **Facilities** Spa STV Wi-fi 🐾 supervised Fishing Gym Sauna Steam room Snooker room Surfing Ocean safari ♫ Child facilities **Conf** Board 50 Thtr 300 **Services** Lift **Parking** 200 **Notes** LB ⊗ Closed 24-25 Dec Civ Wed 300

CLONMEL   Map 1 C2
Co Tipperary

Hotel Minella

★★★★ 79% HOTEL   MANOR HOUSE HOTELS

☎ 052 6122388
e-mail: frontdesk@hotelminella.ie
web: www.hotelminella.ie
dir: S of river in town

This family-run hotel is set in nine acres of well-tended gardens on the banks of the Suir River. The hotel originates from the 1860s, and the public areas include a cocktail bar and a range of lounges; some of the bedrooms are particularly spacious. The leisure centre in the grounds is noteworthy. Two-bedroom holiday homes are also available.

Rooms 90 (8 fmly) (14 GF) (10 smoking) 🐾 **S** €100-€140; **D** €120-€160 (incl. bkfst) **Facilities** FTV Wi-fi ᕒ 🐾 Fishing ⚓ Gym Beauty treatment room Sauna Steam room Child facilities **Conf** Class 300 Board 20 Thtr 500 Del from €120 to €140 **Services** Lift **Parking** 100 **Notes** LB ⊗ Closed 24-28 Dec

---

CONG   Map 1 B4
Co Mayo

Ashford Castle

★★★★★ 86% ⊛⊛ HOTEL

☎ 094 9546003
e-mail: ashford@ashford.ie
web: www.ashford.ie
dir: In Cross left at church onto R345 signed Cong. Left at hotel sign, through castle gates

Set in over 300 acres of rolling parklands, this magnificent castle, dating from 1228, occupies a stunning position on the edge of Lough Corrib. Bedrooms and suites vary in style but all benefit from a pleasing combination of character, charm and modern comforts. Dinner in the elegant George V Dining Room is a treat, with creative cookery of seasonal ingredients. Less formal dining is available in other locations on the estate during peak periods. The hotel offers an extensive range of both indoor and outdoor leisure pursuits including falconry, golf, shooting, fishing and an equestrian centre.

Rooms 83 (6 fmly) (22 GF) 🐾 **D** €275-€950 (incl. bkfst) **Facilities** Spa STV Wi-fi ᕒ 9 ⚓ Putt green Fishing Gym Archery Clay pigeon Falconry Horse riding Bike hire Lake cruises Water sports ♫ Xmas New Year **Conf** Class 65 Thtr 110 **Services** Lift **Parking** 200 **Notes** ⊗ Civ Wed 150

CORK   Map 1 B2
Co Cork

Maryborough Hotel & Spa

★★★★ 80% ⊛ HOTEL

☎ 021 4365555
Maryborough Hill, Douglas
e-mail: info@maryborough.com
dir: From Jack Lynch Tunnel 2nd exit signed Douglas. Right at 1st rdbt, follow Rochestown signs to fingerpost rdbt. Left, hotel on left in 0.5m

Dating from 1715, this house was renovated and extended to become a fine hotel with beautifully landscaped grounds featuring rare plant species. There are stylish suites in the main house and the bedrooms in the wing are comfortably furnished. The bar and lounge are very popular for the range of food served throughout the day; Zings restaurant offers a mix of classic and contemporary dishes. There are impressive spa, leisure and conference facilities, plus activities for children.

Rooms 93 (6 fmly) **S** €105-€250; **D** €130-€500 (incl. bkfst) **Facilities** Spa STV Wi-fi ᕒ 🐾 supervised Gym Sauna Steam room New Year **Conf** Class 250 Board 60 Thtr 500 **Services** Lift **Parking** 300 **Notes** LB ⊗ Closed 24-26 Dec Civ Wed 100

REPUBLIC OF IRELAND

CORK *continued*

Silver Springs Moran Hotel

★★★★ 78% HOTEL

☎ 021 4507533
Tivoli
e-mail: silverspringsres@moranhotels.com
web: www.silverspringsmoranhotel.com
dir: N8 S, take Silver Springs exit. Right, then right
again, hotel on left

Located on the main approach to the city this hotel
has spacious, contemporary public areas. The lobby
lounge is very popular for all-day dining, with more
formal meals served in the Watermarq Restaurant.
Bedrooms and suites are comfortable, many offering
good views over the River Lee. Excellent conference
and leisure facilities are available in separate
buildings in the grounds.

Rooms 109 (32 fmly) (12 smoking) S €89–€250;
D €109–€199 (incl. bkfst) **Facilities** Wi-fi
supervised Gym Squash Aerobics classes New
Year **Conf** Class 520 Board 30 Thtr 800 Del from €114
to €184 **Services** Lift **Parking** 325 **Notes** LB
Closed 24-27 Dec Civ Wed 500

DELGANY	Map 1 D3
Co Wicklow	

Glenview Hotel

★★★★ 77% HOTEL

☎ 01 2873399
Glen O' the Downs
e-mail: sales@glenviewhotel.com
dir: From Dublin city centre follow signs for N11, past
Bray on N11 S'bound, exit 9

This hotel is set in lovely terraced gardens overlooking
the Glen o' the Downs. The comfortable bedrooms are
spacious, and many enjoy the great views over the
valley. The impressive public areas include a
conservatory bar, lounge and choice of dining options
including the first-floor Woodlands Restaurant where
dinner is served. The hotel has an excellent range of
leisure and conference facilities. A championship golf
course and horse riding can be found nearby.

Rooms 70 (11 fmly) (16 GF) **Facilities** Spa STV
Wi-fi supervised Gym Aerobics studio Massage
Beauty treatment room Xmas New Year
Conf Class 100 Board 80 Thtr 270 Del from €300 to
€500* **Services** Lift **Parking** 200 **Notes**
Civ Wed 120

DINGLE (AN DAINGEAN)	Map 1 A2
Co Kerry	

Dingle Skellig Hotel & Peninsula Spa

★★★★ 80% HOTEL

☎ 066 9150200
e-mail: reservations@dingleskellig.com
dir: N86 to Dingle, hotel on harbour

This modern hotel, close to the town, overlooks Dingle
Bay and has spectacular views from many of the
comfortably furnished bedrooms and suites. Public
areas offer a spacious bar and lounge and a bright,
airy restaurant. There are extensive health and leisure
facilities, and many family activities are organised in
the Fungi Kids Club.

Rooms 113 (10 fmly) (31 GF) **Facilities** Spa STV
FTV Wi-fi supervised Gym New Year Child
facilities **Conf** Class 120 Board 100 Thtr 250
Services Lift **Parking** 110 **Notes** LB Closed Jan
RS Nov-Dec Civ Wed 250

Dingle Benners Hotel

★★★ 72% HOTEL

☎ 066 9151638
Main St
e-mail: info@dinglebenners.com
dir: In town centre

Located in the centre of the town with parking to the
rear, this long-established property has an old world
charm. There are a selection of relaxing lounges, open
turf fires and comfortable bedrooms that are
furnished with antique pine; some have four-poster
beds. Food is available in Mrs Benner's traditional
bar.

Rooms 52 (2 fmly) (9 GF) **Facilities** STV FTV Wi-fi
Services Lift **Parking** 32 **Notes** Closed 19-27 Dec
Civ Wed 90

DONABATE	Map 1 D4
Co Dublin	

The Waterside House Hotel

★★★ 73% HOTEL

☎ 01 8436153
e-mail: info@watersidehousehotel.ie
web: www.watersidehousehotel.ie
dir: Exit M1 junct 4 (Donabate/Portrane), 3rd exit at
rdbt, pass Newbridge House Demesne on left,
continue over rail bridge, right at sign for golf courses
& hotel. Hotel on left

This family run hotel is situated in an enviable
position right on Donabate beach in north Co. Dublin.
Overlooking Lambay Island, the public areas and
bedrooms are appointed in a contemporary style, with
the comfortable lounge bar and terrace taking
advantage of the breathtaking views. The Signal
Restaurant offers evening dining in a cosy
environment at weekends and during peak seasons.
Entertainment is provided on a regular basis, with
tribute shows during the summer months. A popular
wedding venue, it is close to Dublin Airport and a
number of golf courses.

Rooms 35 (8 fmly) (8 GF) S €40–€240; D €40–€240
Facilities STV FTV Wi-fi Xmas New Year
Conf Class 150 Board 100 Thtr 400 **Services** Lift
Air con **Parking** 100 **Notes** LB Civ Wed 250

DONEGAL	Map 1 B5
Co Donegal	

Harvey's Point Hotel

★★★★ 87% HOTEL

☎ 074 9722208
Lough Eske
e-mail: stay@harveyspoint.com
web: www.harveyspoint.com
dir: N56 from Donegal, then 1st right (Loch Eske/
Harvey's Point)

Situated by the shores of Lough Eske, a short drive
from Donegal, this welcoming hotel is an oasis of
relaxation; comfort and attentive guest care are the
norm here. A wide range of particularly spacious
suites and bedrooms is on offer, together with smaller
rooms in the courtyard annexe. The kitchen brigade
maintains consistently high standards in The
Restaurant at dinner, with less formal dining in the
sun lounge throughout the day. A very popular Sunday
buffet lunch is served weekly, with dinner and
cabaret entertainment on selected dates during the
summer. Breakfast is also a feature of a stay here.
Pet friendly accommodation is available.

Rooms 64 (8 annexe) (17 fmly) (28 GF)
S €209–€435; D €280–€580 (incl. bkfst)*
Facilities STV FTV Wi-fi Beauty treatment rooms
Bicycle hire Walking tours Xmas New Year

Save on hotels. Book at **theAA.com/hotel**

COR – DUB 603 | IRELAND

Conf Class 200 Board 50 Thtr 200 Del from €199*
Services Lift **Parking** 300 **Notes** LB Closed Mon &
Tue Nov-Mar Civ Wed 250

Mill Park Hotel

★★★★ 76% HOTEL

☎ 065 7074300
The Mullins, Donegal Town
e-mail: info@millparkhotel.com

The Mill Park is located within walking distance of
Donegal town. It is a family owned and operated
property, with a friendly and dedicated team that are
sure to please with their natural and warm approach.
All of the comfortable rooms and suites have been
recently renovated in stylish contemporary décor
schemes. All-day dining is available in the Café Bar,
a popular destination with the locals, with more
formal evening dining in the first floor Granary
Restaurant that overlooks the main lobby. There is a
spacious leisure centre available on a complimentary
basis to resident guests, together with treatments
and pampering in the Wellness Centre. The hotel has
an excellent reputation for its banqueting and
conference facilities.

Rooms 115

The Central Hotel Conference & Leisure Centre

★★★ 77% HOTEL

☎ 074 9721027
The Diamond
e-mail: info@centralhoteldonegal.com
dir: In town centre

Located right in the centre of the town, this long
established hotel is a gem. The public rooms are
decorated to a high standard; a popular carvery lunch
is served in The Just William, and an all-day menu of
European dishes and authentic Thai specialities is
available in the atmospheric Upper Deck Bar.
Afternoon tea is served on the first-floor mezzanine
from where guests can look down on the bustling
town below. Bedrooms vary in style and many have
views over Donegal Bay. There is also a contemporary
banqueting suite where occasional concerts are held.

Rooms 112 (26 fmly) **Facilities** STV FTV Wi-fi ⌨ ⏾
supervised Gym ♫ Xmas New Year **Conf** Class 160
Board 70 Thtr 380 **Services** Lift **Notes** ⊗ Civ Wed

DUBLIN   Map 1 D4
Dublin

INSPECTORS' CHOICE

The Merrion Hotel

★★★★★ ⓐⓐⓐⓐ HOTEL

☎ 01 6030600
Upper Merrion St
e-mail: info@merrionhotel.com
dir: At top of Upper Merrion St on left, beyond
Government buildings on right

This terrace of gracious Georgian buildings, reputed
to have been the birthplace of the Duke of
Wellington, embraces the character of many
changes of use over 200 years. Bedrooms and
suites are spacious, some in the original house;
others are in a modern wing overlooking the
gardens. They all offer great comfort and a wide
range of extra facilities. The lounges retain the
charm and opulence of days gone by, while the
Cellar bar area is a popular meeting point. Dining
options include The Cellar Restaurant specialising
in prime local ingredients and, for that very special
occasion, the award-winning Restaurant Patrick
Guilbaud is Dublin's finest. "Art Tea" is an
afternoon tea experience with a difference, where
delightful pastries are inspired by some of the
hotels vast art collection.

Rooms 142 (21 GF) (20 smoking) ⌨ **S** €485-€3350;
D €505-€3350* **Facilities** Spa STV FTV Wi-fi ⌨ ⏾
Gym Steam room Xmas New Year **Conf** Class 25
Board 25 Thtr 60 **Services** Lift Air con **Parking** 60
Notes ⊗ Civ Wed 50

INSPECTORS' CHOICE

The Shelbourne Dublin, a Renaissance Hotel

★★★★★ ⓐⓐ HOTEL

☎ 01 6634500
27 St Stephen's Green
e-mail: rhi.dubbr.reservations@renaissancehotels.
com
web: www.theshelbourne.ie
dir: M1 to city centre, along Parnell St to O'Connell
St towards Trinity College, 3rd right into Kildare St,
hotel on left

This Dublin landmark exudes elegance and a real
sense of history, having been established in 1824.
The public areas are spacious and offer a range of
dining and bar options. There is a selection of
bedroom styles and suites available, many with
commanding views over St. Stephen's Green. No 27
is a popular bar and lounge for casual dining. The
Saddle Room is the main restaurant featuring a
steak and seafood menu with a contemporary twist,
while afternoon tea is served in the elegant Lord
Mayor's Lounge. An extensive leisure and fitness
facility is now completed.

Rooms 265 (7 smoking) ⌨ **S** €219-€760;
D €239-€790 (incl. bkfst) **Facilities** Spa STV FTV
Wi-fi ⌨ ⏾ Gym Relaxtion room Thermal facilities
Dance studio ♫ Xmas **Conf** Class 240 Board 60
Thtr 400 **Services** Lift Air con **Notes** LB ⊗
Civ Wed 350

DUBLIN *continued*

The Westbury Hotel

★★★★★ 87% ◉◉ HOTEL

☎ 01 6791122
Grafton St
e-mail: westbury@doylecollection.com
dir: Adjacent to Grafton St, half way between Trinity College & Stephens Green

Located just off Grafton Street, Dublin's premier shopping district, this is an oasis of calm; guests are well cared for amid smart, contemporary surroundings. Spacious public areas include the relaxing Gallery Lounge where afternoon tea is popular with shoppers taking a break. Café Novo is the hotel's buzzing street-level brasserie bar, while Wilde-The Restaurant is an elegant grill with an emphasis on seasonal and artisan fare. A range of stylish suites and bedrooms is offered; many overlooking the roofs of the city. Valet parking is available.

Rooms 205 (9 fmly) ↝ **Facilities** STV FTV Wi-fi ⇘ Gym
Conf Class 100 Board 46 Thtr 200 **Services** Lift
Air con **Parking** 100 **Notes** ⊗ Civ Wed 120

AA HOTEL OF THE YEAR FOR THE REPUBLIC OF IRELAND

Castleknock Hotel & Country Club

★★★★ 82% ◉ HOTEL

☎ 01 6406300
Porterstown Rd, Castleknock
e-mail: info@chcc.ie
web: www.castleknockhotel.com
dir: M50 from airport. Exit at junct 6 (signed Navan, Cavan & M3) onto N3, becomes M3. Exit at junct 3. At top of slip road 1st left signed Consilla (R121). At T-junct left. 1km to hotel

This modern hotel is set on a golf course yet it is only 15 minutes from Dublin. The bedrooms are very comfortable, with all the expected modern guest facilities. The spacious public rooms have an airy feel, and some rooms open onto a terrace that overlooks the golf course. The range of food and beverage outlets includes The Park Room, a steak house, a busy all-day brasserie, and The Lime Tree which is open in the evening. Excellent conference and banqueting facilities are available, together with a popular leisure centre. Castleknock Hotel is the AA Hotel of the Year for the Republic of Ireland 2013-2014.

Rooms 138 (30 fmly) (5 smoking) ↝ **S** €59–€420;
D €59–€420* **Facilities** Spa FTV Wi-fi ⇘ ⊡
supervised ⚓ 18 Gym Sauna Steam room Children's
pool ♫ Xmas New Year **Conf** Class 140 Board 80
Thtr 500 **Services** Lift **Parking** 200 **Notes** LB ⊗
Closed 24-26 Dec Civ Wed 200

Clontarf Castle Hotel

★★★★ 80% HOTEL

☎ 01 8332321 & 8534336
Castle Av, Clontarf
e-mail: mlong@clontarfcastle.ie
dir: M1 towards centre, left at Whitehall Church, left at T-junct, straight on at lights, right at next lights into Castle Ave, hotel on right at rdbt

Dating back to the 12th century, this castle retains many historic architectural features which have been combined with contemporary styling in the well-equipped bedrooms. Public areas offer relaxing lounges, and modern cuisine is served in Fahrenheit Grill, Indigo Lounge and Knights Bar. The Great Hall is a versatile venue for banqueting and conferences.

Rooms 111 (7 fmly) (11 GF) (23 smoking) ↝
Facilities STV Wi-fi ⇘ Gym Xmas New Year
Conf Class 250 Board 90 Thtr 600 **Services** Lift
Air con **Parking** 134 **Notes** ⊗ Civ Wed 400

Crowne Plaza Hotel Dublin - Blanchardstown

CROWNE PLAZA
HOTELS & RESORTS

★★★★ 79% ◉ HOTEL

☎ 01 8977777
The Blanchardstown Centre
e-mail: info@cpireland.crowneplaza.com
dir: M50 junct 6 (Blanchardstown)

This landmark building is on the doorstep of a wide range of shops in Blanchardstown. Bedrooms are stylishly decorated with generously sized beds and well appointed en suites. The Sanctuary Bar serves an international range of informal dishes from lunchtime through to the evening, with Italian specialities (pasta dishes and pizzas) served in the evenings in Forchetta Restaurant. Secure underground parking is provided. There is a floor of dedicated boardrooms and meeting facilities, together with banqueting rooms. Secure underground parking is complimentary to resident guests.

Rooms 188 (60 fmly) (15 smoking) ↝ **S** €69–€320;
D €69–€380* **Facilities** STV FTV Wi-fi ⇘ HL Gym
Sauna New Year **Conf** Class 300 Board 300 Thtr 500
Del from €140 to €200* **Services** Lift Air con
Parking 250 **Notes** ⊗ Civ Wed 300

Stillorgan Park Hotel

★★★★ 78% ◉ HOTEL

☎ 01 2001800
Stillorgan Rd, Stillorgan
e-mail: info@stillorganpark.com
web: www.stillorganpark.com
dir: From N11 follow Wexford signs (pass RTE studios on left) through 5 sets of lights. Hotel on left

This modern hotel is situated on the southern outskirts of the city, close to UCD, Dundrum and Stillorgan shopping centres. Comfortable public areas include a spacious lobby, The Purple Sage Restaurant and a traditional style bar. There are extensive air-conditioned banqueting and conference facilities, a gym and a spa with treatment rooms.

Rooms 150 (8 fmly) (4 smoking) ↝ **S** fr €79
D fr €79* **Facilities** Spa STV Wi-fi ⇘ Gym ♫ New Year
Conf Class 220 Board 130 Thtr 500 Del from €170
Services Lift Air con **Parking** 300 **Notes** LB ⊗ Closed
25 Dec RS 24 Dec Civ Wed 300

Ashling Hotel, Dublin

★★★★ 77% HOTEL

☎ 01 6772324
Parkgate St
e-mail: info@ashlinghotel.ie
dir: Close to River Liffey, opposite Heuston Station

Situated on the banks of the River Liffey close to the city centre, railway station and law courts, this hotel is on the tram route and just a five-minute walk from Phoenix Park. The property is appointed to a high standard in a contemporary style. The bedrooms are comfortably furnished; the newer ones are more spacious. Food is available in the Iveagh Bar throughout the day and a popular carvery is served at lunchtime; Chesterfield's Brasserie offers a carte in the evening. Staff are very friendly and service is attentive and professional. Secure multi-storey parking is available.

Rooms 225 (23 fmly) (10 smoking) ↝ **S** €79–€275;
D €89–€380 **Facilities** STV Wi-fi **Conf** Class 110
Board 50 Thtr 220 **Services** Lift **Parking** 100
Notes LB ⊗ Closed 24-26 Dec

Red Cow Moran Hotel

MORAN
HOTELS

★★★★ 76% HOTEL

☎ 01 4593650
Red Cow Complex, Naas Rd
e-mail: redcowres@moranhotels.com
web: www.moranhotels.com
dir: At junct of M50 & N7 on city side of motorway

Located just off the M50, this hotel is 20 minutes from the airport and close to the city centre via the Luas light rail system. The dedicated team of staff

Save on hotels. Book at **theAA.com/hotel**

DUB 605   IRELAND

show a genuine willingness to create a memorable stay. Bedrooms are well equipped and comfortable, and the public areas and conference rooms are spacious. Ample free parking is available.

Rooms 123 (21 fmly) (13 smoking) **S** €79-€259; **D** €79-€259* **Facilities** FTV Wi-fi ☼ ♫ New Year **Conf** Class 350 Board 150 Thtr 750 Del from €99.50 to €139* **Services** Lift Air con **Parking** 700 **Notes** LB ⊗ Closed 24-26 Dec Civ Wed 400

Bewleys Hotel Ballsbridge

★★★ 77% HOTEL

☎ 01 6681111
Merrion Rd, Ballsbridge
e-mail: ballsbridge@bewleyshotels.com
dir: On corner of Merrion Rd & Simmonscourt Rd

This stylish hotel is a restored 19th-century Masonic school situated near the RDS, Aviva Stadium and the city centre. It offers comfortable, good-value, well-appointed accommodation. The Brasserie serves an interesting menu with a very popular carvery lunch and breakfast; snacks are available in Tom's Bar throughout the day. There is secure underground parking, and Thomas Prior Hall is a unique venue for banquets and conferences.

Rooms 304 (63 fmly) (45 GF) (24 smoking) ⌁ **D** €79-€399 **Facilities** Wi-fi ☼ Xmas New Year **Conf** Class 150 Board 80 Thtr 250 Del from €135 to €229 **Services** Lift **Parking** 220 **Notes** LB ⊗ Civ Wed 250

Sandymount Hotel

★★★ 77% HOTEL

☎ 01 614 2000
Herbert Rd, Sandymount
e-mail: info@sandymounthotel.ie
dir: Adjacent to Aviva Stadium, 200mtrs from Dart Rail Station

This hotel (previously known as the Mount Herbert Hotel) has been run by the Loughran family for three generations, and is located close to the Aviva Stadium, the RDS and Sandymount village. The comfortable bedrooms are well appointed, as are the lounge areas. The bistro restaurant and bar overlook the lovely garden. There are conference facilities and ample free parking is available.

Rooms 168 (3 fmly) (56 GF) **Facilities** STV Wi-fi **Conf** Class 60 Board 40 Thtr 100 **Services** Lift **Parking** 90 **Notes** ⊗ Closed 21-27 Dec

Bewleys Hotel Leopardstown

★★★ 75% HOTEL

☎ 01 2935000 & 2935001
Central Park, Leopardstown
e-mail: leop@bewleyshotels.com
dir: M50 junct 13/14, follow signs for Leopardstown. Hotel on right

This hotel is conveniently situated close to the Central Business Park and Leopardstown racecourse and is serviced by the Luas light rail system and Aircoach. The bedrooms are spacious and well appointed. Contemporary in style, the open-plan public areas include a spacious lounge bar with snack food available throughout the day, while lunch and dinner are served in the Brasserie. There is a gym and a choice of conference rooms including the Power Suite. Underground parking is available.

Rooms 354 (70 fmly) (50 smoking) ⌁ **S** €69-€199; **D** €69-€398* **Facilities** STV FTV Wi-fi ☼ Gym **Conf** Class 50 Board 50 Thtr 160 Del €149* **Services** Lift **Parking** 228 **Notes** LB ⊗ Closed 23-25 Dec

Cassidys Hotel

★★★ 75% HOTEL

☎ 01 8780555
6-8 Cavendish Row, Upper O'Connell St
e-mail: stay@cassidyshotel.com
dir: In city centre at N end of O'Connell St

This family-run hotel is located at the top of O'Connell Street, in a terrace of red-brick Georgian townhouses, directly opposite the famed Gate Theatre. The warm and welcoming atmosphere created by the hospitable team in Groomes Bar and Bistro adds to the traditional atmosphere. Bedrooms are individually styled and well appointed; many have air conditioning. A residents' gym, conference facilities and limited parking are all available.

Rooms 113 (26 annexe) (3 fmly) (12 GF) (30 smoking) **Facilities** STV Wi-fi Gym Fitness suite **Conf** Class 45 Board 45 Thtr 80 **Services** Lift **Parking** 8 **Notes** ⊗ Closed 24-26 Dec

Temple Bar Hotel

★★★ 74% HOTEL

☎ 01 6773333
Fleet St, Temple Bar
e-mail: reservations@tbh.ie
web: www.templebarhotel.com
dir: From Trinity College towards O'Connell Bridge. 1st left onto Fleet St. Hotel on right

This hotel is situated right in the heart of Dublin's Temple Bar area, and is close to the main shopping districts, restaurants and the nightlife of the city. Bedrooms are comfortable and well equipped, with more spacious executive rooms available at a small surcharge. Food is served throughout the day in Buskers themed bar, with the Rendezvous a more peaceful option. Alchemy is the smart night club which becomes a music venue at weekends and at other peak periods. Parking is available in a multi-storey opposite at a reduced rate for hotel guests.

Rooms 129 (6 fmly) (30 smoking) **Facilities** STV Wi-fi ☼ **Conf** Class 40 Board 40 Thtr 70 **Services** Lift **Notes** ⊗ Closed 23-25 Dec RS Good Fri

Bewleys Hotel Newlands Cross

★★★ 74% HOTEL

☎ 01 4640140 & 4123301
Newlands Cross, Naas Rd
e-mail: newlands@bewleyshotels.com
web: www.bewleyshotels.com
dir: M50 junct 9, N7 (Naas road). Hotel near junct of N7 & Belgard Rd

This modern hotel is situated on the N7 and close to the M50 and Luas light rail to the city. Bedrooms are spacious and the pricing structure proves popular with families. The Brasserie restaurant is open through the day for casual dining and serves a carvery lunch; more formal meals are served in the evening. The hotel also has a comfortable bar where snacks are available, conference rooms, a gym and ample free parking.

Rooms 297 (176 fmly) (61 GF) ⌁ **S** €59-€199; **D** €69-€199* **Facilities** STV Wi-fi ☼ Gym ♫ New Year **Conf** Class 18 Board 14 Thtr 50 Del from €94 to €194 **Services** Lift **Parking** 200 **Notes** LB ⊗ Closed 24-26 Dec

DUBLIN *continued*

Ibis Hotel Dublin West

BUDGET HOTEL

☎ 01 464 1480
Naas Rd, Monastery Rd, Clondalkin
e-mail: H0595@accor.com
dir: On Red Cow rdbt M50 junct 9 off Naas Rd on Monastery Rd

Close to Dublin airport and the M50, this hotel is modern in style. Bedrooms have contemporary furnishings including large desks. Public rooms include a restaurant and a lounge. Breakfast is self-service and a 24-hour snack service is also available. See also the Hotel Groups pages.

Rooms 150 (39 fmly) (35 GF) **S** €32-€99; **D** €32-€99
Conf Class 25 Board 18 Thtr 35 Del from €70 to €110

| DUBLIN AIRPORT | Map 1 D4 |
| Dublin | |

Crowne Plaza Dublin Northwood

★★★★ 80% ⊛ HOTEL

☎ 01 8628888
Northwood Park, Santry Demesne, Santry
e-mail: info@crowneplazadublin.ie
web: www.cpdublin.crowneplaza.com
dir: M50 junct 4, left into Northwood Park, 1km, hotel on left

Located within minutes of Dublin Airport, and served by a complimentary shuttle service, this modern hotel is located in Northwood Park, and benefits from an idyllic location overlooking 85 acres of mature woodlands of the former Santry Demesne. Bedrooms come in a variety of styles, and each is comfortable and well appointed. Guests in executive rooms have the use of a lounge facility where light breakfast is served. The hotel offers a range of dining options, including full room service and a lobby café. There are extensive conference and event rooms at this property, together with a secure multi-storey car park. Guests also have use of a well equipped gymnasium.

Rooms 204 (17 fmly) (5 smoking) ↱ **S** €90-€165; **D** €115-€185* **Facilities** STV FTV Wi-fi ↳ HL Gym Xmas New Year **Conf** Class 450 Board 100 Thtr 850 **Services** Lift Air con **Parking** 400 **Notes** LB ⊗ Civ Wed 300

Bewleys Hotel Dublin Airport

★★★ 75% HOTEL

☎ 01 8711000 & 8711200
Baskin Ln
e-mail: dublinairport@bewleyshotels.com
dir: At end of M50 N'bound, 2nd exit at rdbt (N32), left at next rdbt

Conveniently situated for Dublin Airport, this hotel has the added advantage of secure underground parking and a complimentary shuttle bus to the airport. Bedrooms are spacious and suitable for families; there is a comfortable lounge bar and brasserie with a wide selection of dishes on offer. Good quality meeting and banqueting rooms are available.

Rooms 469 (232 fmly) (36 smoking) ↱ **Facilities** FTV Wi-fi ↳ Fitness room Xmas **Conf** Class 150 Board 12 Thtr 300 Del from €85 to €234* **Services** Lift **Parking** 1150 **Notes** Civ Wed 250

Premier Inn Dublin Airport

BUDGET HOTEL

☎ 0871 527 8312
Airside Retail Park
web: www.premierinn.com
dir: M1 junct 2 for Dublin Airport. At main airport rdbt 3rd exit, follow Drogheda & Belfast signs. 2nd exit at Cloghran rdbt. Right at lights signed Airside Industrial Estate/Retail Park. Hotel on right

High quality, budget accommodation ideal for both families and business travellers. Spacious, en suite bedrooms feature tea and coffee making facilities, and Freeview TV in most hotels. Internet access and Wi-fi are available for a small fee. The adjacent family restaurant features a wide and varied menu. See also the Hotel Groups pages.

Rooms 155

| DUNBOYNE | Map 1 D4 |
| Co Meath | |

Dunboyne Castle Hotel & Spa

★★★★ 78% HOTEL

☎ 01 8013500
e-mail: ediaz@dunboynecastlehotel.com
dir: In Dunboyne take R157 towards Maynooth. Hotel on left

Located within walking distance of Dunboyne village, this fine property is a successful combination of the traditional and contemporary. Set on over two acres of mature woodland and well tended grounds, the original house is home to a number of meeting rooms, with the spacious bedrooms in a modern block to the

side. All day dining is offered in the Terrace Lounge, with evening dining and breakfast served in the newly refurbished Ivy Restaurant.

Rooms 145

| DUNDALK | Map 1 D4 |
| Co Louth | |

Ballymascanlon House Hotel

★★★★ 80% HOTEL

☎ 042 9358200
e-mail: info@ballymascanlon.com
dir: M1 junct 18 onto N52 signed Dundalk North/R173 at Carlingford. Exit at Faughart rdbt. 1st left at next rdbt. Hotel in approx 1km on left

This Victorian mansion is set in 130 acres of woodland and landscaped gardens at the foot of the Cooley Mountains. The elegant house and the modern extension make this a very comfortable hotel that has really stylish bedrooms. Public areas include a spacious restaurant, lounge and bar, together with relaxing reading rooms that retain many original architectural features. There is a well-equipped leisure centre, and The Oak Room banqueting facility proves to be very popular for weddings and family occasions.

Rooms 90 (11 fmly) (5 GF) (34 smoking) ↱ **Facilities** STV FTV Wi-fi ↳ ⊛ supervised ⅃ 18 ⅏ Putt green Gym Steam room Sauna Plunge pool ♫ Xmas New Year **Conf** Class 220 Board 100 Thtr 400 **Services** Lift **Parking** 250 **Notes** Civ Wed 300

| DUNFANAGHY | Map 1 C6 |
| Co Donegal | |

Arnold's Hotel

IRISH COUNTRY HOTELS

★★★ 75% ⊛ HOTEL

☎ 074 9136208
e-mail: enquiries@arnoldshotel.com
dir: N56 from Letterkenny, hotel on left on entering village

This family-owned and run hotel, situated in a coastal village overlooking sandy beaches and beautiful scenery, is noted for its warm welcome and good food. The public areas and bedrooms are very comfortable; there is a traditional cosy bar with turf fires, a popular bistro that serves food throughout the day, and Seascapes Restaurant where local seafood features on the menu. There are stables attached to the hotel, with preferential terms for residents. Photographic and painting breaks are available, as is links-based golf.

Rooms 30 (10 fmly) ↱ **S** €50-€85; **D** €100-€130 (incl. bkfst)* **Facilities** FTV Wi-fi ♫ New Year **Parking** 60 **Notes** ⊗ RS Nov-Apr Civ Wed 90

Save on hotels. Book at **theAA.com/hotel**

DUB – GAL 607 IRELAND

DUNGARVAN
Co Waterford

Map 1 C2

Lawlors Hotel

★★★ 70% HOTEL

☎ 058 41122
e-mail: info@lawlorshotel.com
dir: Off N25

This town centre hotel has very attractive and comfortable public areas with a busy bar where food is served throughout the day. A good value dinner menu is available in Davit's Restaurant. The bedrooms vary in size but all are well appointed. Conference and meeting rooms plus secure parking are available.

Rooms 89 (8 fmly) **Facilities** Wi-fi 𝕋𝕃 **New Year Conf** Class 215 Board 420 Thtr 420 **Services** Lift **Notes** Closed 25 Dec

DURRUS
Co Cork

Map 1 B2

Blairscove House & Restaurant

◉ ◉ RESTAURANT WITH ROOMS

☎ 027 61127
e-mail: mail@blairscove.ie
dir: From Durrus on R591 towards Crookhaven, 2.4km, house (blue gate) on right

Blairscove comprises four elegant suites located in the courtyard of a Georgian country house outside the pretty village of Durrus near Bantry; each room is individually decorated in a contemporary style and has stunning views over Dunmanus Bay and the mountains. The restaurant is renowned for its wide range of hors d'oeuvres and its open wood-fire grill. The piano playing and candle light add to a unique dining experience.

Rooms 4 (4 annexe) (1 fmly)

ENNIS
Co Clare

Map 1 B3

Temple Gate Hotel

★★★ 80% ◉ HOTEL

☎ 065 6823300
The Square
e-mail: info@templegatehotel.com
dir: Exit N18 onto Tulla Rd for 0.25m, hotel on left

This smart hotel is owned and run by the Madden family and is located in the centre of the town. It incorporates a 19th-century, Gothic-style Great Hall banqueting room. The public areas are well planned and include a comfortable library lounge, popular traditional pub and Legends Restaurant. Bedrooms are attractive and well equipped with some executive rooms and suites available.

Rooms 70 (3 fmly) (11 GF) (20 smoking) S €119-€149; D €139-€179* **Facilities** STV FTV Wi-fi ↳ 𝕋𝕃 **New Year Conf** Class 100 Board 80 Thtr 250 Del €170* **Services** Lift **Parking** 52 **Notes** LB ⊗ Closed 25-26 Dec RS 24 Dec **Civ Wed** 200

ENNISKERRY
Co Wicklow

Map 1 D3

The Ritz Carlton Powerscourt

★★★★★ 89% ◉ ◉ HOTEL

☎ 01 2748888
Powerscourt Estate
e-mail: powerscourtreservations@ritzcarlton.com
dir: From Dublin take M50, M11, then N11, follow Enniskerry signs. In Enniskerry left up hill, hotel on right

This very stylish hotel, built in the Palladian style, has a tranquil setting with stunning views over the gardens and woodlands to the Sugar Loaf. The bedrooms and suites are particularly spacious and well appointed with very impressive bathrooms that have TVs, deep tubs and walk-in showers. The luxuriously appointed public areas are airy and spacious with a variety of food options that includes the Gordon Ramsay at Powerscourt restaurant. The hotel also has a stunning spa, two golf courses, and includes fly fishing and equestrian pursuits among its many leisure facilities.

Rooms 200 (39 GF) **Facilities** Spa STV Wi-fi ↳ ⚄ ⚲ 36 Putt green Fishing ⚑ Gym Cycling Mega chess Xmas **New Year Conf** Class 240 Board 72 Thtr 500 **Services** Lift Air con **Parking** 384 **Notes** Civ Wed 400

GALWAY
Co Galway

Map 1 B3

The G Hotel

★★★★★ 87% ◉ ◉ HOTEL

☎ 091 865200
Wellpark, Dublin Rd
e-mail: info@theg.ie
dir: Telephone for detailed directions

Designed in association with the acclaimed milliner Philip Treacy who hails from the county, this hotel is the epitome of contemporary styling. The public areas include a series of eclectically furnished lounges, each with its own identity. The cutting-edge design is also apparent in the bedrooms and suites, which are very comfortable and appointed to a high standard. An interesting menu is on offer at dinner each evening in GiGi's, the atmospheric restaurant, and a very popular all-day menu is served in the lounges, including traditional afternoon tea. The hotel has a number of boardrooms, an events space and an Espa spa facility. Underground and valet parking is available.

Rooms 101 (2 fmly) 🐾 **Facilities** Spa STV FTV Wi-fi HL Gym **New Year Conf** Class 42 Board 40 Thtr 120 **Services** Lift Air con **Parking** 349 **Notes** ⊗ Closed 23-26 Dec **Civ Wed** 90

Ardilaun Hotel & Leisure Club

★★★★ 81% ◉ HOTEL

☎ 091 521433
Taylor's Hill
e-mail: info@theardilaunhotel.ie
web: www.theardilaunhotel.ie
dir: M6 to Galway City West, then follow signs for N59 Clifden, then N6 towards Salthill

This very smart country-house style hotel, appointed to a high standard, is located on the outskirts of the city near Salthill and has lovely landscaped gardens. The bedrooms have been thoughtfully appointed and the deluxe rooms and suites are particularly spacious. Public areas include a selection of comfortable lounges, the Camilaun Restaurant that overlooks the garden, Blazers bistro and bar, and extensive banqueting and leisure facilities.

Rooms 125 (17 fmly) (8 GF) (16 smoking) 🐾 S €69-€280; D €89-€390 (incl. bkfst)* **Facilities** Spa STV Wi-fi ⚄ supervised Gym Beauty treatment & analysis rooms Beauty salon 𝕋𝕃 **New Year Conf** Class 280 Board 100 Thtr 650 Del from €140 to €175* **Services** Lift **Parking** 380 **Notes** LB Closed 23 Dec pm & 24-26 Dec **Civ Wed** 650

REPUBLIC OF IRELAND

GALWAY *continued*

Park House Hotel & Restaurant

★★★★ 79% ◉ HOTEL

☎ 091 564924
Forster St, Eyre Square
e-mail: parkhousehotel@eircom.net
web: www.parkhousehotel.ie
dir: In city centre/Eyre Sq

Situated just off Eyre Square, this well established hotel offers comfortable facilities to suit business or leisure guests. Public areas and bedrooms are well appointed and attractively decorated. The Park Restaurant has been a popular spot for the people of Galway for many years; less formal food is available throughout the day in Boss Doyle's bar. Parking for hotel guests is available at the rear.

Rooms 84 (4 smoking) ✿ **Facilities** STV FTV Wi-fi ⌀ ♫ **Conf** Class 15 Board 15 Thtr 15 **Services** Lift Air con **Parking** 48 **Notes** ⊗ Closed 24-26 Dec

GARRYVOE
Co Cork
Map 1 C2

Garryvoe Hotel

IRISH COUNTRY HOTELS

★★★★ 79% ◉ HOTEL

☎ 021 4646718
Ballycotton Bay, Castlemartyr
e-mail: res@garryvoehotel.com
web: www.garryvoehotel.com
dir: N25 onto L72 at Castlemartyr (between Midleton & Youghal). 6km to hotel

In a delightful location facing the beach and overlooking Ballycotton Island and Bay, this is a comfortable, family-run hotel with caring staff. The bedrooms are appointed to a very high standard; some have balconies. The popular bar serves light meals throughout the day, and a more formal dinner menu is available in the dining room. There are extensive banqueting and excellent health club facilities.

Rooms 82 (17 fmly) (5 smoking) **Facilities** STV Wi-fi ⌀ ⊙ supervised Putt green Gym Sauna Steam room ♫ **Conf** Class 150 Board 12 Thtr 300 **Services** Lift **Parking** 100 **Notes** ⊗ Closed 24-25 Dec Civ Wed 150

GLASLOUGH
Co Monaghan
Map 1 C5

The Lodge at Castle Leslie Estate

★★★★ 80% ◉◉ HOTEL

☎ 047 88100
e-mail: info@castleleslie.com
dir: M1 junct 14, N2 to Monaghan, N12 to N185 to Glaslough

Set in 1,000 acres of rolling countryside dotted with mature woodland, the lodge is the social hub of the Castle Leslie Estate which has been in the Leslie family since the 1660s. The comfortably furnished bedrooms are in the original hunting lodge and the converted stable block. Resident guests have two dining options - Snaffles Restaurant and Connors Bar. There is a Victorian spa, a successful equestrian centre and a private fishing lake. For those who enjoy country pursuits this hotel is ideal for the many walks and interesting flora and fauna that the area has to offer.

Rooms 29 (2 fmly) (10 GF) ✿ **S** €100-€170; **D** €130-€200 (incl. bkfst)* **Facilities** Spa STV FTV Wi-fi ⌀ Fishing Equestrian centre **Conf** Class 25 Board 24 Thtr 40 **Services** Lift **Parking** 100 **Notes** ⊗ Closed 22-28 Dec Civ Wed 40

GLENDALOUGH
Co Wicklow
Map 1 D3

The Glendalough Hotel

★★★ 73% HOTEL

☎ 0404 45135
e-mail: info@glendaloughhotel.ie
dir: N11 to Kilmacongue, right onto R755, straight on at Laragh, right onto R756

Mountains and forest provide the setting for this long-established hotel at the edge of the famed monastic site, and many of the comfortably appointed bedrooms have superb forest views. Food is served daily in the very popular bar and on the terrace when weather permits. The renovated Glendasan River Restaurant is a stylish bistro where dinner is served, while the atmospheric Glendalough Tavern is a popular meeting place for visitors and locals alike.

Rooms 44 (3 fmly) **Facilities** STV Wi-fi Fishing ♫ **Conf** Class 150 Board 50 Thtr 200 **Services** Lift **Parking** 100 **Notes** ⊗ RS Dec-Jan, Mon-Fri

GOREY
Co Wexford
Map 1 D3

Amber Springs Hotel

★★★★ 80% ◉ HOTEL

☎ 053 9484000
Wexford Rd
e-mail: info@ambersprings.ie
dir: 500mtrs from Gorey by-pass at junct 23

This hotel, on the Wexford road, is within walking distance of the town. Bedrooms are spacious and very comfortable, and guests have full use of the leisure facilities. Dining in Kelby's Bistro is a highlight of a visit, with a combination of interesting food and really friendly service.

Rooms 80 (34 fmly) (24 GF) ✿ **Facilities** Spa STV Wi-fi ⌀ ⊙ supervised Gym Mini golf Petting farm Kids train ♫ New Year Child facilities **Conf** Class 450 Board 30 Thtr 700 **Services** Lift Air con **Parking** 178 **Notes** ⊗ Closed 25-26 Dec Civ Wed 700

Seafield Golf & Spa Hotel

★★★★ 78% ◉ HOTEL

☎ 053 942 4000
Ballymoney
e-mail: reservations@seafieldhotel.com
dir: M11 exit 22

This ultra-modern hotel is part of a village style resort that includes an 18-hole championship golf course, courtyard family suites and the award-winning Oceo Spa. Set in 225 acres of parkland with mature trees, river-side walks and access onto Ballymoney Beach, the hotel offers contemporary, spacious bedrooms and suites which have views of either the coastline or the golf course. There are two dining options - fine dining in the restaurant, and a more casual option in the bar or on the terrace.

Rooms 101 ✿ **S** €76-€155; **D** €92-€250 (incl. bkfst) **Facilities** Spa STV Wi-fi ⌀ ⊙ ⌁ 18 Putt green Gym Playground ♫ New Year Child facilities **Conf** Class 220 Board 40 Thtr 300 **Services** Lift **Parking** 200 **Notes** LB ⊗ Civ Wed 280

Ashdown Park Hotel

★★★★ 76% ◉ HOTEL

☎ 053 9480500
The Coach Rd
e-mail: info@ashdownparkhotel.com
web: www.ashdownparkhotel.com
dir: N11 junct 22, on approaching Gorey, 1st left (before railway bridge), hotel on left

Situated on an elevated position overlooking the town, this modern hotel has excellent health, leisure and banqueting facilities. There are comfortable lounge

Save on hotels. Book at **theAA.com/hotel**

GAL – KIL 609 IRELAND

areas and two dining options - Ivy, a popular carvery bar, and The Rowan Tree, the first-floor fine dining restaurant open in the evenings. Bedrooms are available in a number of styles; all are spacious and well equipped. Close to a number of golf courses, this property is popular with golfers, and also with families as it is near the beaches.

Rooms 79 (17 fmly) (22 GF) ⮝ **S** €65-€110; **D** €70-€170 (incl. bkfst)* **Facilities** Spa FTV Wi-fi ⮝ ⮝ supervised Gym Leisure centre Massage rooms ♫ New Year Child facilities **Conf** Class 315 Board 100 Thtr 800 Del from €110 to €125* **Services** Lift **Parking** 150 **Notes** LB ⮾ Closed 25 Dec Civ Wed 300

INSPECTORS' CHOICE
Marlfield House Hotel
★★★ ⊚ ⊚
COUNTRY HOUSE HOTEL

☎ 053 9421124
e-mail: info@marlfieldhouse.ie
web: www.marlfieldhouse.com
dir: N11 junct 23, follow signs for Courtown. At Courtown Rd rdbt left for Gorey. Hotel 1m on left

This Regency-style building has been gracefully extended and developed into an excellent hotel. An atmosphere of elegance and luxury permeates every corner of the house, underpinned by truly friendly and professional service led by the Bowe family who are always in evidence. The bedrooms are decorated in keeping with the style of the house, with some really spacious rooms and suites on the ground floor. Dinner in the restaurant is always a highlight of a stay at Marlfield.

Rooms 19 (3 fmly) (6 GF) ⮝ **Facilities** FTV Wi-fi ⮝ ⮝ Beauty treatment room **Conf** Board 24 Thtr 60 **Parking** 100 **Notes** LB Closed 2 Jan-28 Feb RS Nov-Dec & Mar-Apr Civ Wed 120

KENMARE   Map 1 B2
Co Kerry

INSPECTORS' CHOICE
Sheen Falls Lodge
★★★★★ ⊚ ⊚   COUNTRY HOUSE HOTEL

☎ 06466 41600
e-mail: info@sheenfallslodge.ie
dir: From Kenmare take N71 to Glengarriff over suspension bridge, take 1st left

This former fishing lodge has been developed into a beautiful hotel with a friendly team of professional staff. The cascading Sheen Falls are floodlit at night, forming a romantic backdrop to the enjoyment of award-winning cuisine in La Cascade Restaurant. Less formal dining is available in Oscar's Bistro, and the Sun Lounge serves refreshments and light snacks throughout the day. The bedrooms are very comfortably appointed; many of the suites are particularly spacious. The leisure centre and beauty therapy facilities offer a number of exclusive treatments, and outdoor pursuits include walking, fishing, tennis, horse riding and clay pigeon shooting.

Rooms 66 (14 fmly) (14 GF) ⮝ **S** €95-€280; **D** €138-€340 (incl. bkfst)* **Facilities** Spa STV Wi-fi ⮝ supervised ⮝ Fishing ⮝ Gym Table tennis Steam room Clay pigeon shooting Cycling Vintage car rides Library ♫ Xmas New Year **Conf** Class 65 Board 50 Thtr 120 **Services** Lift **Parking** 76 **Notes** ⮾ Closed 2 Jan-1 Feb Civ Wed 100

KILKENNY   Map 1 C3
Co Kilkenny

Kilkenny River Court Hotel
★★★★ 78% ⊚ HOTEL

☎ 056 7723388
The Bridge, John St
e-mail: reservations@rivercourthotel.com
dir: In town centre, opposite castle

Hidden behind archways on John Street, this is a very comfortable and welcoming establishment. The restaurant, bar and many of the well-equipped bedrooms command great views of Kilkenny Castle and the River Nore. Attentive, friendly staff ensure good service throughout the hotel. Excellent corporate and leisure facilities are provided.

Rooms 90 (4 fmly) **Facilities** Spa Wi-fi ⮝ supervised Gym Beauty salon & treatment rooms **Conf** Class 110 Board 45 Thtr 260 **Services** Lift **Parking** 84 **Notes** ⮾ Closed 23-26 Dec Civ Wed 250

Langton House Hotel
★★★★ 76% HOTEL

☎ 056 7765133 & 7721728
69 John St
e-mail: reservations@langtons.ie
dir: N9 & N10 from Dublin, follow city centre signs on outskirts of Kilkenny, left to Langtons. Hotel 500mtrs on left after lights

This hotel, situated in the heart of the Mediaeval city of Kilkenny, has long had a well-deserved reputation for its genuine hospitality as a vibrant and entertainment venue with many strings to its bow. There is a nightclub with free access for resident guests and up to seven bars to choose from. The most recent addition is the much talked about Set Theatre, where leading performers take to the stage. There is a range of bedroom options, many in the garden annexe; all are very comfortable and smartly decorated, with the junior suites in the main house being particularly well appointed. Eating options include The Langton, a busy restaurant serving dinner, and the more casual, all-day '67', a lively bar popular with visitors and locals that features live music groups most evenings. The elegant Tea Room is open throughout the day.

Rooms 34 (16 annexe) (4 fmly) (8 GF) (22 smoking) **Facilities** STV FTV Wi-fi ♫ New Year **Conf** Class 250 Board 30 Thtr 400 **Services** Air con **Parking** 60 **Notes** Closed 24-25 Dec Civ Wed 252

REPUBLIC OF IRELAND

KILLARNEY Map 1 B2
Co Kerry

Muckross Park Hotel & Cloisters Spa

★★★★ 85% ◉ HOTEL

☎ 064 6623400
Lakes of Killarney
e-mail: info@muckrosspark.com
dir: From Killarney take N71 towards Kenmare

Dating originally from 1795, this fine property offers spacious accommodation and excellent public areas. Most of the bedrooms are in a recently developed block to the rear, with some in the original building, retaining many of the original features. All of the rooms and suites are beautifully appointed, with high quality fabrics and furnishings. Casual dining is available throughout the day in the old world atmosphere of Molly Darcy's pub, with more formal dining in the Blue Pool or GB Shaw's Restaurants. The Cloisters Spa is an oasis of calm and tranquillity, with a wide range of treatments available.

Rooms 68 (3 fmly) **S** €79-€259; **D** €119-€299 (incl. bkfst)* **Facilities** Spa STV Wi-fi ⚓ ⚑ Gym Cycling Yoga Pilates Free bike hire Guided walks ♫ New Year **Conf** Class 250 Board 60 Thtr 350 Del from €125 to €295 **Services** Lift Air con **Parking** 80 **Notes** LB ⊛ Closed Nov-Jan wkdays Civ Wed 250

Cahernane House Hotel

★★★★ 80% ◉◉ HOTEL

☎ 064 6631895
Muckross Rd
e-mail: info@cahernane.com
web: www.cahernane.com
dir: On N22 to Killarney, take 1st exit off rdbt then left at church, 1st exit at next rdbt to Muckross Rd

This fine country mansion, the former home of the Earls of Pembroke, has a magnificent mountain backdrop and panoramic views from its lakeside setting, yet is only a ten minute walk from the town centre. Elegant period furniture is complemented by more modern pieces to create a comfortable hotel offering a warm atmosphere with a particularly friendly team dedicated to guest care. A number of accommodation options are available, some in the original house, others in a more recent building accessed by a stunning conservatory. Dinner in the Herbert Room is a highlight of a stay at this property, with more casual fare on offer in the cosy Cellar Bar.

Rooms 38 (26 annexe) ⚑ **Facilities** Wi-fi ⚓ Fishing ⚓ **Conf** Class 10 Board 10 Thtr 15 **Services** Lift Air con **Parking** 50 **Notes** LB ⊛ Closed 21 Dec-Jan Civ Wed 60

The Lake Hotel

★★★★ 75% ◉ HOTEL

☎ 064 6631035
Lake Shore, Muckross Rd
e-mail: info@lakehotel.com
dir: N22 to Killarney. Hotel 2km from town on Muckross Rd

Enjoying a delightful location on the shores of Killarney's lake shore, this hotel is run by a second generation of the Huggard family together with a dedicated and friendly team. There is a relaxed atmosphere with log fires and stunning views from the lounges and restaurant, and guests could be lucky enough to see a herd of red deer wander by. The smartly furnished bedrooms have either lake or woodland views; some have balconies and four-poster beds. The spa offers good facilities, and there are cycle paths and lovely walks to enjoy.

Rooms 130 (6 fmly) (23 GF) ⚑ **S** €75-€240; **D** €105-€360* **Facilities** Spa STV FTV Wi-fi ⚓ ⚓ Fishing ⚓ Gym Sauna Steam room ♫ **Conf** Class 60 Board 40 Thtr 80 Del from €125 to €230* **Services** Lift **Parking** 140 **Notes** ⊛ Closed 6 Dec-Jan Civ Wed 60

Castlerosse Hotel & Golf Resort

★★★ 79% HOTEL

☎ 064 6631144
Lakes of Killarney
e-mail: res@castlerosse.ie
web: www.castlerosse.ie
dir: From Killarney take R562 signed Killorglin & The Ring of Kerry. Hotel 2.5km from town on left

This hotel is situated on 6,000 acres overlooking the Lakes of Killarney with the Magillycuddy Mountains as a backdrop. At times guests may be able to spot deer in Killarney National Park. Bedrooms and junior suites are well appointed and comfortable. There is live entertainment most nights in Mulligan's pub. Leisure facilities include a 9-hole parkland golf course, tennis courts, a leisure centre and treatment rooms.

Rooms 120 (27 fmly) **Facilities** Spa STV FTV Wi-fi ⚓ supervised ⚓ 9 ⚓ Putt green Gym Golf & horse riding arranged ♫ **Conf** Class 100 Board 40 Thtr 200 **Services** Lift **Parking** 100 **Notes** ⊛ Closed Nov-Mar Civ Wed 80

KILLINEY Map 1 D4
Co Dublin

Fitzpatrick Castle Hotel

★★★★ 81% ◉ HOTEL

☎ 01 2305400
e-mail: reservations@fitzpatricks.com
web: www.fitzpatrickcastle.com
dir: From Dun Laoghaire port turn left, on coast road right at lights, left at next lights. Follow to Dalkey, right at Ivory Pub, immediate left, up hill, hotel at top

This family-owned, 18th-century castle is situated in lovely gardens with mature trees and spectacular views over Dublin Bay. The original castle rooms are appointed to a high standard and have four-poster beds, while the rooms in the modern wing are spacious and some have balconies. Lounges are comfortably furnished, and PJ's restaurant serves dinner on certain days of the week; more casual fare is available each night in the trendy Dungeon bar and grill. There are extensive leisure and conference facilities.

Rooms 113 (36 fmly) (12 smoking) **S** €120-€190; **D** €140-€300 **Facilities** STV Wi-fi ⚓ supervised Gym Beauty/hairdressing salon Sauna Steam room Fitness centre ♫ Xmas New Year **Conf** Class 250 Board 80 Thtr 500 Del from €180 to €260 **Services** Lift **Parking** 300 **Notes** LB ⊛ RS 25-Dec Civ Wed 400

KILMESSAN Map 1 C/D4
Co Meath

The Station House Hotel

★★★ 75% ◉ HOTEL

☎ 046 9025239 & 9025586
e-mail: info@thestationhousehotel.com
web: www.thestationhousehotel.com
dir: M50, N3 towards Navan. At Dunshaughlin left at end of village, follow signs

While the Station House saw its last train in the early sixties, it still retains much of its railway history and atmosphere. Some of the accommodation is located in the old carriage house, and the signal box is the bridal suite; the station itself hosts diners in the station master's office. The bedrooms are comfortably appointed, and the lounge areas are very relaxing. Set in attractively landscaped gardens and woodlands, this is a popular wedding venue. Dinner is always a highlight, featuring well-sourced ingredients cooked with both flair and care.

Rooms 20 (14 annexe) (3 fmly) (5 GF) ⚑ **S** €90; **D** €150* **Facilities** Wi-fi ⚓ ♫ Xmas New Year **Conf** Class 300 Board 100 Thtr 400 Del from €116 to €150 **Parking** 200 **Notes** LB ⊛ Civ Wed 100

Save on hotels. Book at **theAA.com/hotel**

KIL – LET 611 IRELAND

KINGSCOURT
Co Cavan

Map 1 C4

Cabra Castle Hotel
★★★★ 79% ◉ HOTEL

☎ 042 9667030
e-mail: sales@cabracastle.com
dir: R165 between Kingscourt & Carrickmacross

Nestled in over 100 acres of parkland and manicured gardens, this family run property offers a selection of accommodation styles. Some rooms are in the 19th century castle building, with the balance in a number of courtyard buildings at the rear. Weddings are a particular feature of the business of the castle, due to really spectacular facilities and an outstanding reputation. The Courtroom is the principal dining area of the castle, a series of first floor elegantly appointed rooms where dinner is a highlight of a visit. All day dining is offered in The Derby Bar, or on the Terrace when weather permits. Leisure pursuits on the grounds include 9-hole golf and tennis, with horse riding and fishing available nearby.

Rooms 105 (88 annexe) (10 fmly) (48 GF) 🐾
S €85-€142; **D** €110-€222 (incl. bkfst)*
Facilities Wi-fi ⚓ 9 ⛳ **Conf** Class 160 Board 60 Thtr 200 Del from €155 to €195* **Parking** 200 **Notes** ⊗ Closed 24-27 Dec Civ Wed 350

KINSALE
Co Cork

Map 1 B2

Carlton Hotel Kinsale
★★★★ 79% ◉ HOTEL

CARLTON
HOTEL GROUP

☎ 021 4706000
Rathmore Rd
e-mail: reservations.kinsale@carlton.ie
dir: R600 to Kinsale, turn left signed Charles Fort. 3kms, (pass rugby club), hotel on left

This recently-built hotel is set on an elevated position overlooking Oysterhaven Bay in 90 acres of mature parkland, approximately five kilometres from the town centre. All of the bedrooms are spacious and well appointed, many with spectacular views over the bay. Two-bedroom holiday apartment options are available in the grounds. The contemporary public rooms are on the first floor, with spacious terraces. They include the Rockpool Restaurant where guests can cook fine Angus steaks on lava stones at their table. The team at this property are all very guest focused, and make families particularly welcome.

Rooms 130 (20 fmly) (24 GF) **Facilities** Spa STV FTV Wi-fi ⊘ ⊛ supervised Gym New Year **Conf** Class 120 Board 40 Thtr 300 **Services** Lift Air con **Parking** 140 **Notes** ⊗ Closed 23-27 Dec Civ Wed 200

Blue Haven Hotel
★★★ 75% HOTEL

☎ 021 4772209
3/4 Pearse St
e-mail: info@bluehavenkinsale.com
web: www.bluehavenkinsale.com
dir: In town centre

At the heart of this historic town, this vibrant hotel offers a comfortable lounge and café, a very popular and stylish bar with an airy bistro plus an elegant restaurant. Live music is a feature seven days a week in high season, and five days in low season. Bedrooms vary in size and are furnished to a high standard.

Rooms 17 🐾 **Facilities** FTV Wi-fi ♫ New Year **Conf** Class 35 Board 25 Thtr 100 **Notes** ⊗ Closed 25 Dec Civ Wed 70

The White House
◉ RESTAURANT WITH ROOMS

☎ 021 4772125
Pearse St, The Glen
e-mail: whitehse@indigo.ie
dir: In town centre

Centrally located among the narrow, twisting streets of the charming maritime town of Kinsale, this restaurant with rooms dates from 1850. It is a welcoming hostelry with smart comfortably appointed contemporary bedrooms. The atmospheric bar and bistro are open for lunch and dinner, with Restaurant d'Antibes also open during the evenings. The varied menu features local fish and beef. The courtyard at the rear makes a perfect setting in summer and there is regular entertainment in the bar.

Rooms 10 (2 fmly)

LETTERKENNY
Co Donegal

Map 1 C5

Radisson Blu Hotel Letterkenny
★★★★ 79% ◉ HOTEL

☎ 074 9194444
Paddy Harte Rd
e-mail: info.letterkenny@radissonblu.com
dir: N14 into Letterkenny. At Polestar Rdbt take 1st exit, to hotel

Letterkenny is an ideal base for visiting the many peninsulas of County Donegal. Within walking distance of the town and the retail parks, this hotel offers a range of very comfortable rooms, with all the facilities that today's traveller expects. Guests can dine throughout the day in the popular Oakk Bar & Grill, or, in the evening, enjoy seafood delights and other good dishes in Brasserie TriBeCa. Well-equipped meeting rooms are available, together with a large conference and banqueting hall. The leisure facilities are complimentary to resident guests.

Rooms 114 (5 fmly) (6 smoking) **Facilities** STV Wi-fi ⊛ Gym Sauna Steam room Sunbed Olympic weights room Xmas New Year **Conf** Class 270 Thtr 600 **Services** Lift **Parking** 150 **Notes** ⊗ Civ Wed 600

Downings Bay Hotel
★★★ 75% HOTEL

☎ 074 9155586 & 9155770
Downings
e-mail: info@downingsbayhotel.com
dir: 23m N of Letterkenny on R245. Hotel in village centre

This friendly family-run hotel is situated on Sheephaven Bay in the picturesque village of Downings. There is a cosy lounge; JC's a traditional style bar where an extensive menu is available all day, and The Haven Restaurant which opens for dinner. The bedroom accommodation is spacious and all rooms are comfortable and well appointed. A popular location for families and within easy reach of a number of golf courses, this property hosts occasional musical events, and there is a nightclub open at weekends. Guests have complimentary use of the local leisure centre.

Rooms 40 (8 fmly) (4 smoking) 🐾 **S** €40-€80; **D** €80-€160 (incl. bkfst) **Facilities** Wi-fi ⊘ ⊛ supervised Gym Sauna Steam room Indoor adventure play area ♫ New Year Child facilities **Conf** Class 175 Board 50 Thtr 350 Del from €90 to €120 **Services** Lift Air con **Parking** 40 **Notes** LB ⊗ Closed 25-26 Dec Civ Wed 80

REPUBLIC OF IRELAND

LIMERICK — Co Limerick — Map 1 B3

Limerick Strand Hotel
★★★★ 79% @ HOTEL

☎ 061 421800
Ennis Rd
e-mail: info@strandlimerick.ie
dir: From Shannon/Galway follow N18 to Limerick. At
Coonagh rdbt follow Ennis road into city centre. Hotel
on right on banks of river

This hotel enjoys stunning views over the River
Shannon, and all bedrooms are spacious and fitted to
a high standard. The public areas make the most of
the views, with meeting rooms on the penthouse level.
All-day dining is available in the bar, with innovative
evening meals served in the River Restaurant. Secure
parking is available at a reduced rate for residents.

Rooms 184 (13 fmly) ❀ **Facilities** Spa STV Wi-fi ⓦ ⓧ
supervised Gym ♫ Xmas New Year **Conf** Class 400
Board 50 Thtr 600 **Services** Lift Air con **Parking** 203
Notes Civ Wed 450

LISDOONVARNA — Co Clare — Map 1 B3

Sheedy's Country House Hotel
★★★ 78% @@ HOTEL

☎ 065 7074026
e-mail: info@sheedys.com
dir: 200mtrs from The Square in town centre

Dating in part from the 17th century and set in an
unrivalled town centre location on the edge of The
Burren, this house is full of character and has an
intimate atmosphere. Fine cuisine can be enjoyed in
the contemporary restaurant, and the bedrooms are
spacious and well appointed. Sheedys makes an ideal
base for touring as it is close to Doolin, Lahinch Golf
Course, and the Cliffs of Moher.

Rooms 11 (1 fmly) (5 GF) ❀ **S** €75-€110; **D** €99-€180
(incl. bkfst)* **Facilities** STV FTV Wi-fi ⓦ **Parking** 40
Notes LB ⓧ Closed mid Oct-Apr

Wild Honey Inn
@@ RESTAURANT WITH ROOMS

☎ 065 7074300
Kincora
e-mail: info@wildhoneyinn.com

Set in a former hotel dating from the 1860s, when the
town prospered as a Spa, The Wild Honey Inn has
created a solid reputation for its cuisine. "Modern
bistro style" is Aidan Mc Grath's description of the
food on offer which is served in the comfortable
atmospheric bar area at both lunch and dinner. Great

attention is given to the provenance of the
ingredients, most of which are organic and sourced
as close to Co. Clare as possible. Reservations are not
taken. Bedrooms come in a number of styles, with the
garden rooms benefiting from private patios. Resident
guests have the use of a relaxing lounge, filled with
reading material, not surprisingly featuring food and
cookery. Breakfast is also a highlight of any visit,
with a range of interesting options sure to set one up
for the many walks and healthy pursuits of the Burren
region.

Rooms 14

LUCAN — Co Dublin — Map 1 D4

Finnstown Country House Hotel
★★★ 79% @ HOTEL

☎ 01 6010700 & 6010708
Newcastle Rd
e-mail: edwina@finnstown-hotel.ie
dir: From M1 onto M50 S'bound. 1st exit for N4. Take
slip road signed Newcastle/Adamstown. Straight on
at rdbt, through lights, hotel on right

Set in 45 acres of wooded grounds and paddocks,
Finnstown House is a calm and peaceful country
property in an urban setting. The elegant bar and
drawing room is where informal meals are served
throughout the day, with more formal dining at lunch
and dinner in the Peacock Restaurant. There is a wide
choice of bedroom styles, situated both in the main
house and in the annexes. The staff members are very
guest focussed, with a warm and friendly approach.
This is a very popular venue for small conferences
and family celebrations. A fitness centre is available
to resident guests.

Rooms 82 (54 annexe) (6 fmly) (9 GF) (12 smoking)
❀ **D** €69-€250 (incl. bkfst) **Facilities** STV Wi-fi ⓦ ⓧ
♨ Gym Steam room ♫ New Year **Conf** Class 150
Board 50 Thtr 300 Del €180 **Services** Lift Air con
Parking 300 **Notes** LB ⓧ Closed 24-26 Dec
Civ Wed 200

Lucan Spa Hotel
★★★ 67% HOTEL

☎ 01 6280494
e-mail: info@lucanspahotel.ie
web: www.lucanspahotel.ie
dir: At N4 junct 4a, approx 11km from city centre

Set in its own grounds and 20 minutes from Dublin
Airport, close to the M50, the Lucan Spa is a lovely
Georgian house with a modern extension. Bedrooms
vary in size and are well equipped. There are two
dining options; dinner is served in Honora D
Restaurant, and The Earl Bistro is for more casual
dining. A conference centre is also available.

Rooms 71 (15 fmly) (9 GF) ❀ **S** €45-€120;
D €65-€190 (incl. bkfst) **Facilities** STV FTV Wi-fi ⓦ
Access to Lucan Golf Club ♫ New Year Child
facilities **Conf** Class 250 Board 80 Thtr 600
Services Lift Air con **Parking** 200 **Notes** LB ⓧ Closed
24-25 Dec Civ Wed 250

MACREDDIN — Co Wicklow — Map 1 D3

BrookLodge & Wells Spa
★★★★ 87% @@ HOTEL

☎ 0402 36444
e-mail: info@brooklodge.com
web: www.brooklodge.com
dir: N11 to Rathnew, R752 to Rathdrum, R753 to
Aughrim, follow signs to Macreddin Village

A luxury country-house hotel in a village-style setting
which includes an 18-hole golf course, a pub, café
and food shop. There is a choice of dining options -
the award-winning Strawberry Tree Restaurant
specialising in organic and wild foods and a more
casual Italian restaurant. Bedrooms and lounges in
the original house are very comfortable; there are also
bedrooms in Brookhall, tailored for guests attending
weddings and conferences. The Wells Spa offers
extensive treatments and leisure facilities, and there
are many outdoor activities including horse riding
and off-road driving.

Rooms 86 (32 annexe) (27 fmly) (4 GF) **Facilities** Spa
STV FTV Wi-fi ⓦ ♒ ♨ 18 Putt green Gym Archery
Clay pigeon shooting Off road driving New Year
Conf Class 170 Board 150 Thtr 300 **Services** Lift
Air con **Parking** 200 **Notes** Closed 24-25 Dec
Civ Wed 200

MALAHIDE — Co Dublin — Map 1 D4

Grand Hotel
★★★★ 80% HOTEL

☎ 018 450000
e-mail: info@thegrand.ie
dir: In Malahide village along beach front overlooking
marina

Established in 1835, this fine hotel is in the vibrant
and bustling coastal town of Malahide. Family owned
and operated, there is a very friendly and welcoming
atmosphere throughout the hotel. It offers a range of
spacious and well-appointed bedrooms and suites,
including a penthouse. The hotel is well established
for hosting conference and banqueting events, with
an array of meeting rooms including a tiered
auditorium. Coast Restaurant is the main dining
room with picture windows overlooking the estuary;
less formal dining is available in the Palm Court
Carvery, and all day in Ryan's Bar. Guests are

Save on hotels. Book at **theAA.com/hotel**

LIM – NEW 613 | IRELAND

welcome to use the Arena Leisure Centre in the grounds. Ample parking is provided.

Rooms 203 (107 fmly) (14 smoking) 🐾 **Facilities** STV Wi-fi ⃟ ⃟ supervised Gym New Year **Conf** Class 285 Board 90 Thtr 500 **Services** Lift **Parking** 400 **Notes** ⊗ Closed 24-26 Dec Civ Wed 190

MALLOW
Co Cork

Map 1 B2

Springfort Hall Country House Hotel
★★★ 77% ⚙ HOTEL

☎ 022 21278
e-mail: stay@springfort-hall.com
web: www.springfort-hall.com
dir: N20 onto R581 at Two Pot House, hotel 500mtrs on right

This 18th-century country manor is tucked away amid tranquil woodlands located just six kilometres from Mallow. There is an attractive oval dining room, a cosy drawing room and lounge bar where bistro-style food is served. The spacious bedrooms are comfortably furnished. There are extensive banqueting and conference facilities. Local amenities include championship golf courses, fishing on the Blackwater and Ballyhass Lakes, and horseracing at Cork Race course.

Rooms 49 (5 fmly) (17 GF) **Facilities** STV FTV ♫ **Conf** Class 200 Board 50 Thtr 300 **Parking** 200 **Notes** ⊗ Closed 23-26 Dec Civ Wed 250

MOHILL
Co Leitrim

Map 1 C4

Lough Rynn Castle
★★★★ 78% ⚙⚙ HOTEL

☎ 071 9632700 & 9632714
e-mail: enquiries@loughrynn.ie

Once the ancestral home of Lord Leitrim, set in 300 acres of parkland, the castle offers a range of luxurious rooms and suites. The award-winning Sandstone Restaurant is an elegant dining option, and the many lounges are individually decorated; some feature antique furniture.

Rooms 43 (16 annexe) (5 fmly) (6 GF) 🐾 **D** €99-€195 (incl. bkfst)* **Facilities** STV FTV Wi-fi ⃟ ♫ Xmas New Year **Conf** Class 200 Board 30 Thtr 450 **Services** Air con **Notes** LB ⊗ Civ Wed 320

MOVILLE
Co Donegal

Map 1 C6

Redcastle Hotel, Golf & Spa Resort
★★★★ 79% ⚙ HOTEL

☎ 074 9385555
Inishowen Peninsula
e-mail: info@redcastlehotel.com
dir: On R238 between Derby & Greencastle

Perched beside the sea in mature parkland just outside Redcastle, this hotel has an enviable position on the Inishowen Peninsula with great views over Lough Foyle. Now refurbished, it offers spacious bedrooms that are well equipped; some on the ground floor and some with balconies. The public areas include a range of relaxing lounges with an atmospheric bar where food is served throughout the day, and a large terrace for relaxing when the weather permits. The Edge Restaurant is right on the water's edge, and offers a well thought out menu with interesting options. There is a conference centre and an extensive leisure club offering spa treatments. The hotel has its own private 9-hole golf course, with sea fishing available from the shore.

Rooms 93 (17 fmly) (16 GF) (8 smoking) 🐾 **S** €64-€104; **D** €78-€158 (incl. bkfst)* **Facilities** Spa STV FTV Wi-fi ⃟ ⃟ ⛳ 9 Putt green Fishing 🚣 Gym Thalasso therapy pool ♫ New Year **Conf** Class 150 Board 50 Thtr 300 Del from €109 to €159* **Services** Lift **Parking** 200 **Notes** LB ⊗ Civ Wed 250

MULRANY
Co Mayo

Map 1 B4

Mulranny Park Hotel
★★★★ 79% ⚙⚙ HOTEL

☎ 098 36000
e-mail: info@mulrannyparkhotel.ie
dir: R311 from Castlebar to Newport onto N59. Hotel on right

Set on an elevated site, this property has commanding views over Clew Bay. Originally a railway hotel dating from the late 1800s, it has a range of smart public rooms that retain many of the period features. Bedrooms vary in size but are comfortable and decorated in a contemporary style. Dinner in the Nephin Restaurant is a highlight of any stay, with casual dining available throughout the day in the Waterfront Bar. A programme of activities is offered weekly for resident guests, in addition to a well appointed leisure club.

Rooms 61 (25 fmly) 🐾 **S** €65-€110; **D** €55-€85 (incl. bkfst) **Facilities** Wi-fi ⃟ ⃟ supervised Gym Steam room Health & beauty Hairdressing Cycling ♫ New Year **Conf** Class 140 Board 50 Thtr 400 Del from €120 to €220 **Services** Lift **Parking** 200 **Notes** LB ⊗ Closed 4-21 Jan Civ Wed 150

NEWMARKET-ON-FERGUS
Co Clare

Map 1 B3

Dromoland Castle Hotel
★★★★★ ⚙⚙ HOTEL

☎ 061 368144
e-mail: sales@dromoland.ie
dir: N18 to Ennis/Galway from Shannon for 8km to 'Dromoland Interchange' signed Quin. Take slip road left, 4th exit at 1st rdbt, 2nd exit at 2nd rdbt. Hotel 500mtrs on left

Dromoland Castle, dating from the early 18th century, stands on a 375-acre estate and offers extensive indoor leisure activities and outdoor pursuits. The team are wholly committed to caring for guests. The thoughtfully equipped bedrooms and suites vary in style but all provide excellent levels of comfort, and the magnificent public rooms, warmed by log fires, are no less impressive. The hotel has several dining options - the elegant fine-dining Earl of Thomond, the less formal Fig Tree in the golf clubhouse, and The Gallery which offers a menu all day.

Rooms 99 (20 fmly) 🐾 **S** €245-€470; **D** €245-€470 **Facilities** Spa STV Wi-fi ⃟ ⃟ supervised ⛳ 18 ⛳ Putt green Fishing Gym Archery Clay shooting Mountain bikes Driven shoots Falconry Pony & trap ♫ Xmas New Year **Conf** Class 220 Board 80 Thtr 450 Del from €295 to €495 **Services** Lift **Parking** 120 **Notes** LB ⊗ Civ Wed 70

RATHMULLAN   Map 1 C6
Co Donegal

Rathmullan House

★★★★ 80% ◉◉ COUNTRY HOUSE HOTEL

☎ 074 9158188

e-mail: info@rathmullanhouse.com
dir: From Letterkenny, then Ramelton then Rathmullan, R243. Left at Mace shop, through village, hotel gates on right

Dating from the 18th century, this fine property has been operating as a country-house hotel for the last 50 years under the stewardship of the Wheeler family. It is in a magical setting leading right on the shores of Lough Swilly. Guests are welcome to wander around the well-planted grounds and the walled garden, from where many of the ingredients for the Weeping Elm Restaurant's seasonal menus are grown. The numerous lounges are relaxing and comfortable, many have welcoming log and turf fires. The bedrooms vary in size, but they are furnished to a high standard; many feature balconies and patio areas.

Rooms 34 (4 fmly) (9 GF) **Facilities** Wi-fi 🕸 🌙 🥏 Beauty treatment room New Year **Conf** Class 90 Board 40 Thtr 135 **Parking** 80 **Notes** Closed 11 Jan-5 Feb RS 15 Nov-12 Mar Civ Wed 135

RATHNEW   Map 1 D3
Co Wicklow

Tinakilly Country House & Restaurant

★★★★ 76% ◉◉ HOTEL

☎ 0404 69274

e-mail: info@tinakilly.ie
dir: Follow N11/M11 to Rathnew, then R750 towards Wicklow. Entrance to hotel approx 500mtrs from village on left

An elegant oak-lined avenue leads to Tinakilly House, a Victorian mansion steeped in history. It was built in 1884 for Captain Robert Halpin, Master Mariner and Commander of *SS Great Eastern* who laid the telegraphic cable joining Europe to America. There are lovely garden views from the lounges that have open log fires. Some of the comfortable bedrooms and suites enjoy views over the Irish Sea and bird sanctuary at Broadlough Costal Lagoon. Furnishings throughout reflect the Victorian period yet provide all modern comforts. Fine dining is available in the dining room, and snacks and afternoon tea are served in the drawing room.

Rooms 51 (15 fmly) (14 GF) 🐾 **S** €70-€160; **D** €80-€220 (incl. bkfst)* **Facilities** STV Wi-fi 🕸 🎵 New Year **Conf** Class 70 Board 35 Thtr 90 **Services** Lift **Parking** 60 **Notes** ⊗ Closed 24-26 Dec Civ Wed 100

Hunter's Hotel

★★★ 78% ◉ HOTEL

☎ 0404 40106

e-mail: reception@hunters.ie
dir: 1.5km from village off N11

One of Ireland's oldest coaching inns, this charming country house was built in 1720 and is full of character and atmosphere. The comfortable bedrooms have wonderful views over prize-winning gardens that border the River Vartry. The restaurant has a good reputation for carefully prepared dishes which make the best use of high quality local produce, including fruit and vegetables from the hotel's own garden.

Rooms 16 (2 fmly) (2 GF) **Conf** Class 40 Board 16 Thtr 40 **Parking** 50 **Notes** ⊗ Closed 24-26 Dec

RECESS (SRAITH SALACH)   Map 1 A4
Co Galway

INSPECTORS' CHOICE

Lough Inagh Lodge Hotel

★★★ ◉ COUNTRY HOUSE HOTEL

☎ 095 34706 & 34694
Inagh Valley
e-mail: inagh@iol.ie
dir: From Recess take R344 towards Kylemore

Dating from 1880, this former fishing lodge is akin to a family home, where guests are encouraged to relax and enjoy the peace. Overlooking Lough Inagh, and situated amid the mountains of Connemara, it is in an ideal location for those who enjoy walking and fishing. Bedrooms are individually decorated, some with spacious seating areas, and each is dedicated to an Irish literary figure. There are two cosy lounges where welcoming turf fires are often lit. Informal dining from a bar menu is available during the day. Dinner is a highlight of a visit to the lodge; the menus feature locally sourced produce cooked with care - seafood is a speciality.

Rooms 13 (1 fmly) (4 GF) **Facilities** Fly fishing Cycling **Conf** Class 20 Board 20 Thtr 20 **Services** Air con **Parking** 16 **Notes** Closed mid Dec-mid Mar

ROSAPENNA   Map 1 C6
Co Donegal

Rosapenna Hotel & Golf Resort

★★★★ 78% HOTEL

☎ 074 9155128

e-mail: reservations@rosapenna.ie

Adjoining the 800 acre Dunes System and a number of links golf courses, The Rosapenna Hotel has been welcoming guests for over a century. Bedrooms come in a number of styles, with some having balconies making the most of the wonderful rugged views. The public rooms all offer great space, with lots of comfortable relaxing lounge options. The Vardon Restaurant offers a well compiled menu, featuring the best of Donegal produce, and of course, the freshest of seafood.

Rooms 63 (6 fmly) (31 GF) **Facilities** STV FTV Wi-fi 🕸 🦢 supervised ⤢ 45 ⛳ Putt green Treatment room Snooker room Table tennis 🎵 **Services** Lift **Notes** Civ Wed 100

ROSCOMMON   Map 1 B4
Co Roscommon

Kilronan Castle Estate & Spa

★★★★ 78% ◉ HOTEL

☎ 071 9618000
Ballyfarnon
e-mail: enquiries@kilronancastle.ie

Located on the shores of Lough Meelagh, this recently restored Gothic revival castle dates from the early 19th century, and is set in almost 50 acres of rolling park and woodland. Great care has been taken in its restoration, with many of the fine bedrooms and suites in the adjoining sympathetically-built modern block. The Drawing Room is now a cosy lounge serving food throughout the day. The highlight however is dinner in the Douglas Hyde Restaurant, where the friendly professional team go to great lengths to offer fine food in elegant surroundings. The impressive Spa has a wide range of treatments on offer. There is also a leisure centre together with a wonderful events centre accessed by a tunnel from the main building.

Rooms 84 (9 fmly) **S** €89-€179; **D** €109-€209 (incl. bkfst) **Facilities** Spa Wi-fi 🕸 Gym 🎵 Xmas New Year **Conf** Class 360 Board 60 Thtr 500 Del from €119 to €189 **Services** Lift Air con **Notes** LB ⊗ Civ Wed

Save on hotels. Book at **theAA.com/hotel**

RAT – SLA 615 IRELAND

ROSSLARE
Co Wexford

Map 1 D2

Kelly's Resort Hotel & Spa

★★★★ ◉ HOTEL

☎ 053 9132114
e-mail: info@kellys.ie
dir: N25 onto Rosslare/Wexford road, signed Rosslare Strand

The Kelly family have been offering hospitality here since 1895, where together with a dedicated team, they provide very professional and friendly service. The resort overlooks the sandy beach and is within minutes of the ferry port at Rosslare. Bedrooms are thoughtfully equipped and comfortably furnished. The extensive leisure facilities include a smart spa, swimming pools, a crèche, young adults' programme and spacious well-tended gardens. Both the eating options, La Marine Bistro and Beaches restaurant, have been awarded an AA Rosette for the quality of their cuisine.

Rooms 118 (15 fmly) (20 GF) ⬧ **Facilities** Spa STV FTV Wi-fi ⬧ supervised ⬧ ⬧ Putt green ⬧ Gym Bowls Badminton Crazy golf Table tennis Snooker Sauna Steam room ⬧ **Conf** Class 30 Board 20 Thtr 30 **Services** Lift **Parking** 150 **Notes** ⬧ Closed early Dec-late Feb

SALTHILL

See **Galway**

SKIBBEREEN
Co Cork

Map 1 B2

West Cork Hotel

★★★ 75% HOTEL

☎ 028 21277
Ilen St
e-mail: info@westcorkhotel.com
dir: In Skibbereen, N71 into Bridge St, with Baby Hannah's pub on left to right into Ilen St, hotel on right. From Cork Road, N71 to Schull, left at next rdbt towards town centre, hotel on left

This charming hotel was built in 1902 and is family owned and run. It is located in the centre of town beside the River Ilen, where guests can enjoy an outdoor drink while sitting on the historic old West Cork railway bridge. There is a cosy lounge with log fire, and furnishings and decor that are a successful mix of the best of old and new. Food is available throughout the day in the Railway Bar and in the evening in Kennedy's Restaurant. Bedrooms vary in size and are comfortably furnished, some with riverside views. There are extensive banqueting facilities and ample car parking at the rear of the hotel.

Rooms 34 (4 fmly) ⬧ **Facilities** FTV Wi-fi Use of facilities at Skibbereen Sports Centre **Conf** Class 20 Board 24 Thtr 250 **Services** Lift **Parking** 100 **Notes** LB ⬧ Closed 24-28 Dec Civ Wed 300

SLANE
Co Meath

Map 1 D4

Conyngham Arms Hotel

★★★ 74% HOTEL

☎ 041 984444
Main St
e-mail: info@conynghamarms.ie
dir: From N2 north in village at x-rds take N51 (left), hotel 100yds on left

This 17th-century coaching inn has been beautifully refurbished to a high standard of comfort and quality, and is situated in the centre of Slane village, close to Slane Castle and the World Heritage site of Newgrange and many other historical sites. The bedrooms vary in size due to the age of the house and are very smartly appointed with guest comfort in mind. Food is bistro style featuring the best of local produce, and breads and confectionary from their own bakery, served throughout the day in the cosy bar with an open log fire. There is private off-street parking available.

Rooms 15 ⬧ **S** €55-€85; **D** €90-€140 (incl. bkfst)* **Facilities** FTV Wi-fi **Conf** Class 100 Board 50 Thtr 200 Del from €140 to €200* **Parking** 20 **Notes** LB ⬧ Civ Wed 200

REPUBLIC OF IRELAND

SLIGO
Co Sligo   Map 1 B5

Radisson Blu Hotel & Spa Sligo

★★★★ 79% @ HOTEL

☎ 071 9140008
Rosses Point Rd, Ballincar
e-mail: info.sligo@radissonblu.com
dir: From N4 into Sligo to main bridge. Take R291 on left. Hotel 1.5m on right

Located three kilometres north of the town overlooking Sligo Bay, this contemporary hotel offers standard and business class bedrooms which are all appointed with up-to-date facilities. The Benwiskin bar offers tasty casual dining throughout the day, and for formal dining in the evening there's Classiebawn Restaurant. Residents are welcome to use Healthstyles leisure club during their stay, and spa treatment facilities are also available. A range of eleven rooms are provided for meetings and events.

Rooms 132 (13 fmly) (32 GF) (19 smoking) **S** €250; **D** €250 (incl. bkfst)* **Facilities** Spa STV Wi-fi ☉ Gym Steam room Thermal suite Xmas New Year **Conf** Class 420 Board 40 Thtr 750 **Services** Lift Air con **Parking** 320 **Notes** ⊗ Civ Wed 750

The Glasshouse
★★★★ 78% HOTEL

☎ 071 9194300
Swan Point
e-mail: info@theglasshouse.ie
dir: From N4 right at 2nd junct. Left at Post Office into Wine St. Hotel on right

This landmark building in the centre of town makes a bold statement with its cutting edge design and contemporary decor. Bright cheerful colours are used throughout the hotel; the bedrooms have excellent facilities including LCD TVs, workspace and internet access. There is a café bar serving food throughout the day, with a board walk for alfresco riverside dining. More formal evening dining takes place in the Kitchen restaurant. Secure underground parking is complimentary to residents, and preferential terms have been arranged at a nearby leisure and fitness facility.

Rooms 116 **Facilities** STV FTV Wi-fi New Year **Conf** Class 100 Board 60 Thtr 120 **Services** Lift **Parking** 250 **Notes** ⊗ Closed 24-25 Dec Civ Wed 120

See advert below

Sligo Park Hotel & Leisure Club
★★★★ 76% HOTEL

☎ 071 9190400
Pearse Rd
e-mail: sligo@leehotels.com
dir: N4 to Sligo take exit S2 (Sligo Sth) Carrowroe/R287. Follow signs for Sligo. Hotel 1m on right

Set in seven acres on the southern side of town, this hotel is well positioned for visiting the many attractions of the north west and Yeats' Country. Bedrooms are spacious and appointed to a high standard. There are two dining options, plus good leisure and banqueting facilities.

Rooms 136 (10 fmly) (52 GF) (23 smoking) ⌘ **S** €65-€135; **D** €75-€149* **Facilities** Wi-fi ⊠ ☉ supervised ☺ Gym Holistic treatment suite Plunge pool Steam room ♫ Xmas New Year **Conf** Class 290 Board 80 Thtr 520 Del from €120 to €199* **Services** Lift **Parking** 200 **Notes** LB ⊗ RS 24-26 Dec Civ Wed 520

Save on hotels. Book at **theAA.com/hotel**

SLI – TRA 617 IRELAND

STRAFFAN Map 1 D4
Co Kildare

INSPECTORS' CHOICE

The K Club

★★★★★ COUNTRY HOUSE HOTEL

☎ 01 6017200
e-mail: sales@kclub.ie
dir: From Dublin take N4, exit for R406, hotel on right in Straffan

The K Club is set in 550 acres of rolling woodland. There are two magnificent championship golf courses, and a spa facility that complements the truly luxurious hotel that is the centrepiece of the resort. Public areas, suites and bedrooms are opulently furnished, and many have views of the formal gardens that lead down to the banks of the River Liffey. Dining options include the elegant River Room, with more informal dining options offered in Legends in the Golf Pavilion. There is also a Thai restaurant in the resort. The K Club was host to The Ryder Cup in 2006.

Rooms 69 (10 fmly) **Facilities** Spa Wi-fi ⊗ supervised ⅃ 36 Putt green Fishing ⛳ Gym Beauty salon Fishing tuition Clay pigeon shooting Horse riding Falconry ♫ Xmas New Year **Conf** Class 300 Board 160 Thtr 300 **Services** Lift **Parking** 205 **Notes** ⊗

Barberstown Castle

★★★★ 80% ◉◉ HOTEL

☎ 01 6288157
e-mail: info@barberstowncastle.ie
web: www.barberstowncastle.ie
dir: R406, follow signs for Barberstown

With parts dating from the 13th century, this castle hotel provides the very best in standards of comfort. The inviting public areas range from the original keep, which houses one of the restaurant areas, to the warmth of the drawing room and its cocktail bar. Bedrooms, some in a purpose-built wing, are elegantly appointed with relaxing seating areas. The airy Tea Room serves light meals throughout the day.

The Castle is a popular venue for weddings and other family occasions.

Rooms 57 (21 GF) ⤬ **S** €120-€200; **D** €168-€270 (incl. bkfst) **Facilities** STV Wi-fi ⊗ ♫ New Year **Conf** Class 100 Board 70 Thtr 200 Del from €155 to €185* **Services** Lift **Parking** 200 **Notes** LB ⊗ Closed 24-26 Dec & Jan Civ Wed 300

THOMASTOWN Map 1 C3
Co Kilkenny

INSPECTORS' CHOICE

Mount Juliet Hotel

★★★★ ◉◉◉ COUNTRY HOUSE HOTEL

☎ 056 7773000
e-mail: info@mountjuliet.ie
dir: M7 from Dublin, M9 towards Waterford, exit at junct 9/Danesfort for hotel

Mount Juliet is set in 1,500 acres of parkland with a Jack Nicklaus-designed golf course and an equestrian centre. The elegant and spacious public areas retain much of the original architectural features including ornate plasterwork and Adam fireplaces. Bedrooms in the main house are elegant and comfortably appointed to a high standard, with more compact rooms available in the Clubhouse annexe. Fine dining is on offer in the ornate Lady Helen restaurant overlooking the river; with French Brasserie cuisine in Kendal's located in the golf clubhouse. The President's Bar is the location for all-day dining. The hotel has an excellent spa and health club, with equestrian and other activities also available.

Rooms 59 (28 annexe) (14 GF) ⤬ **S** €144-€254; **D** €159-€269 (incl. bkfst)* **Facilities** Spa STV Wi-fi ⊗ supervised ⅃ 18 ⛳ Putt green Fishing ⛳ Gym Archery Cycling Clay pigeon shooting Equestrian Xmas New Year Child facilities **Conf** Class 40 Board 20 Thtr 75 Del from €234 to €289* **Parking** 200 **Notes** LB ⊗ Closed Sun-Wed eve Nov-1st wk Dec & Jan-Mar Civ Wed 60

THURLES Map 1 C3
Co Tipperary

Horse & Jockey Hotel

★★★★ 79% HOTEL

☎ 0504 44192
Horse & Jockey
e-mail: info@horseandjockeyhotel.com
dir: 800mtrs from M8 junct 6

Located just off the motorway, this hotel offers smart and well-appointed bedrooms which are very comfortable. Dining options are the Enclosure Bar with a varied menu, and for more formal dining in the evening there is Silks Restaurant. There is also a well-equipped leisure centre with spa treatments and an equestrian themed gift shop. The conference facilities include ten self-contained meeting rooms and a tiered auditorium seating 200 delegates.

Rooms 67 (4 fmly) (15 GF) (7 smoking) **S** €75-€95; **D** €99-€129 (incl. bkfst) **Facilities** Spa STV FTV Wi-fi ⊗ supervised Gym Sauna Steam room Hydrotherapy area **Conf** Class 24 Board 25 Thtr 200 Del from €110 to €150 **Services** Lift **Parking** 450 **Notes** LB ⊗ Closed 25 Dec RS 24 & 26 Dec

---

TRALEE Map 1 A2
Co Kerry

Ballygarry House Hotel and Spa

★★★★ 81% ◉ HOTEL

☎ 066 7123322
Killarney Rd
e-mail: info@ballygarryhouse.com
web: www.ballygarryhouse.com
dir: 1.5km from Tralee, on N21

This charming hotel offers the complete country house experience, where courtesy and care is paramount from the friendly team. Located a short drive from the town centre, there are comfortably furnished lounges with open log fires. Food is served throughout the day in the Leebrook Lounge and fine dining is available in the evening in Brooks Restaurant which overlooks the lovely six-acre gardens. Bedrooms and suites are spacious and elegantly decorated. Spa treatments and relaxation areas are offered in the Nadur Spa. A recent addition is The Pavilion, a party venue where the outdoors is seamlessly brought indoors.

Rooms 64 (11 fmly) (12 GF) ⤬ **D** €110-€310 (incl. bkfst) **Facilities** Spa STV Wi-fi ⊗ Steam room Sauna ♫ New Year **Conf** Class 100 Board 50 Thtr 200 Del from €117 to €132 **Services** Lift **Parking** 200 **Notes** LB ⊗ Closed 20-26 Dec Civ Wed 350

TRALEE *continued*

INSPECTORS' CHOICE

Ballyseede Castle

★★★ ◉ HOTEL

☎ 066 7125799
e-mail: info@ballyseedecastle.com
dir: On N21 just after junct of N21/N22

Ballyseede Castle is steeped in history dating back to 1590 and has been fought over, lived in and lovingly restored to a high standard which still pays homage to its ancient grandeur. The spacious bedrooms are elegantly decorated; some have four-poster beds and antique furnishings. There are gracious receptions rooms with original ornamental cornices and marble fireplaces, a carved oak library, a cosy bar and a splendid banqueting hall. The castle stands in its own grounds at the end of a winding drive through formal gardens and woodland.

Rooms 23 (4 fmly) (10 GF) ☏ **S** €95-€115;
D €109-€199 (incl. bkfst)* **Facilities** STV FTV Wi-fi
Parking 180 **Notes** ⊗ Closed Jan-3 Mar
Civ Wed 130

TRAMORE — Map 1 C2
Co Waterford

Majestic Hotel

★★★ 78% HOTEL

☎ 051 381761
e-mail: info@majestic-hotel.ie
dir: Exit N25 through Waterford onto R675 to Tramore. Hotel on right, opposite lake

A warm welcome awaits visitors to this long established, family friendly hotel in the holiday resort of Tramore. Many of the comfortable and well-equipped bedrooms have sea views; some have balconies. Public areas offer relaxing comfortable lounges, a smartly decorated bar, a garden patio and a spacious restaurant where guests can enjoy the spectacular sea views. A discounted rate at Splashworld across from the hotel is available to residents.

Rooms 60 (8 fmly) ☏ **S** €50-€80; **D** €80-€140 (incl. bkfst)* **Facilities** STV FTV Wi-fi ⌕ ♫ New Year **Conf** Class 100 Board 50 Thtr 100 Del from €80 to €100* **Services** Lift **Parking** 10 **Notes** LB ⊗ Civ Wed 250

TULLOW — Map 1 D3
Co Carlow

Mount Wolseley Hotel, Spa & Country Club

★★★★ 80% ◉ HOTEL

☎ 059 9180 100 & 9151 674
e-mail: info@mountwolseley.ie
dir: N7 from Dublin. In Naas, take N9 towards Carlow. In Castledermot left for Tullow

Located on a vast, well landscaped estate long associated with the Wolseley family of motoring fame, this hotel has much to offer. Public areas are very spacious with a large range of suites and bedrooms. Leisure pursuits include a championship golf course together with a popular health centre and Sanctuary Spa facilities. The hotel offers a number of dining options including Aaron's lounge, Fredrick's (1 AA Rosette), and The Wolseley Lounge in the Golf Pavillion.

Rooms 143 (10 fmly) (5 smoking) ☏ **S** €70-€125;
D €90-€220 (incl. bkfst)* **Facilities** Spa STV FTV Wi-fi ⌕ HL ⊛ supervised ⌕ 18 ⛳ Putt green Gym Childrens play area ♫ Xmas New Year Child facilities **Conf** Class 288 Board 70 Thtr 750 Del €129* **Services** Lift Air con **Parking** 160 **Notes** LB ⊗ Closed 25-26 Dec Civ Wed 450

WATERFORD — Map 1 C2
Co Waterford

INSPECTORS' CHOICE

Waterford Castle Hotel and Golf Resort

★★★★ ◉◉ HOTEL

☎ 051 878203
The Island
e-mail: info@waterfordcastle.com
dir: From city centre into Dunmore East Rd, 1.5m, pass hospital, 0.5m left after lights. Ferry at bottom of road

This enchanting and picturesque castle dates back to Norman times and is located on a 320-acre island just a five-minute journey from the mainland by chain-link ferry. Bedrooms vary in style and size, but all are individually decorated and offer high standards of comfort. Dinner is served in the oak-panelled Munster Room, with breakfast taken in the conservatory. The 18-hole golf course is set in beautiful parkland where deer can be seen.

Rooms 19 (2 fmly) (4 GF) **Facilities** Wi-fi ⌕ 18 ⛳ Putt green ⛵ Boules Archery Clay pigeon shooting In room treatments ♫ New Year **Conf** Class 48 Board 45 Thtr 120 Del from €220 to €250 **Services** Lift **Parking** 50 **Notes** ⊗ Closed 24-26 Dec Civ Wed 120

Save on hotels. Book at theAA.com/hotel

TRA – WES 619 IRELAND

Faithlegg House Hotel & Golf Resort

FBD Hotels & Resorts

★★★★ 78% ⊛ HOTEL

☎ 051 382000
Faithlegg
e-mail: reservations@fhh.ie
web: www.faithlegg.com
dir: From Waterford follow Dunmore East Rd then Cheekpoint Rd

This hotel is surrounded by a parkland championship golf course and overlooks the estuary of the River Suir. The house has 14 original bedrooms, and the others in a more contemporary style are in an adjacent modern block. There is a range of comfortable lounges together with comprehensive meeting facilities. The leisure and treatment rooms are the perfect way to work off the excesses of the food offered in the Roseville Restaurant. Lighter options are served throughout the day in the Piano Bar and in the golf Clubhouse.

Rooms 82 (6 fmly) (30 GF) **Facilities** FTV Wi-fi ⊗ supervised ⌖ 18 ⌗ Putt green Gym Sauna Steam room New Year **Conf** Class 90 Board 44 Thtr 180 **Services** Lift **Parking** 100 **Notes** ⊗ Closed 20-27 Dec Civ Wed

Granville Hotel

★★★ 80% HOTEL

☎ 051 305555
The Quay
e-mail: stay@granville-hotel.ie
web: www.granville-hotel.ie
dir: N25 to waterfront, hotel opposite clock tower

Centrally located on the quayside, this long established hotel was originally a coaching house. It is appointed to a very high standard, and retains much of its original character. The bedrooms come in a choice of standard or executive grades; all are well equipped and very comfortable. The Meagher Bar offers food throughout the day, and is a popular lunch venue with shoppers and the business community of Waterford. The Bianconi is an elegant restaurant where evening dinner is served. Friendliness and hospitality are hallmarks of a stay here.

Rooms 100 (5 fmly) (10 smoking) **S** €70-€110; **D** €90-€180 (incl. bkfst) **Facilities** STV ♪ New Year **Conf** Class 150 Board 30 Thtr 200 **Services** Lift **Parking** 300 **Notes** LB ⊗ Closed 25-26 Dec Civ Wed 200

Tower Hotel

★★★ 79% HOTEL

☎ 051 862300
The Mall
e-mail: info@thw.ie
web: www.towerhotelwaterford.com
dir: Opposite Reginald's Tower in town centre. Hotel at end of quay

With a commanding position on The Mall opposite Reginald's Tower, this well established hotel has much to offer. The spacious public areas include conference suites, a choice of dining options and a popular leisure club. Health and beauty treatments are available. A range of bedrooms is on offer; all are comfortably appointed and stylishly decorated. Secure parking is provided to the rear of the building.

Rooms 136 (9 fmly) **Facilities** STV FTV Wi-fi ⊗ supervised Gym Beauty treatment rooms ♪ New Year **Conf** Class 250 Board 80 Thtr 500 Del from €100 to €150* **Services** Lift **Parking** 100 **Notes** ⊗ Closed 24-28 Dec Civ Wed 400

Dooley's Hotel

★★★ 78% HOTEL

☎ 051 873531
30 The Quay
e-mail: hotel@dooleys-hotel.ie
dir: Adjacent to N25, on the Quay

This hotel has been family run for three generations. It is situated on the quay overlooking the River Suir at the harbour's mouth. Dinner is served in New Ship Restaurant and casual dining is available in the Dry Dock Bar. Bedrooms are attractively decorated and offer a good standard of comfort. There is a convenient public car park opposite the hotel.

Rooms 110 (3 fmly) (29 smoking) **S** €70-€140; **D** €80-€198 (incl. bkfst) **Facilities** STV Wi-fi ⌗ ♪ New Year **Conf** Class 150 Board 100 Thtr 240 Del from €110* **Services** Lift **Notes** ⊗ Closed 25-27 Dec RS 24 Dec

| WESTPORT | Map 1 B4 |
| Co Mayo | |

Knockranny House Hotel

MANOR HOUSE HOTELS

★★★★ 84% ⊛⊛ HOTEL

☎ 098 28600
e-mail: info@khh.ie
web: www.khh.ie
dir: On N5 (Westport-Castlebar road)

Perched on a height overlooking Westport, with Clew Bay and Croagh Patrick in the distance, this fine family-run property is set in well landscaped grounds. The reception rooms take full advantage of the stunning views, and include The Brehon, a lounge where food is served throughout the day, and La Fougére, the award-winning restaurant that is a real treat to visit. The comfortable furnishings create an inviting and relaxing atmosphere throughout the lounges, bar and restaurant. Bedrooms are very well appointed and come in a number of styles, with the newer ones being particularly spacious. Guests have complimentary use of extensive leisure facilities, with wellbeing treatments on offer in Spa Salveo. There are extensive banqueting and conference facilities.

Rooms 97 (4 fmly) (18 GF) **Facilities** Spa STV FTV Wi-fi ⌗ HL ⊗ Gym ♪ New Year **Conf** Class 350 Board 40 Thtr 600 **Services** Lift **Parking** 150 **Notes** ⊗ Closed 24-26 Dec Civ Wed 250

Hotel Westport Leisure, Spa & Conference

★★★★ 80% ⊛ HOTEL

☎ 098 25122 & 0870 876 5432
Newport Rd
e-mail: reservations@hotelwestport.ie
web: www.hotelwestport.ie
dir: N5 to Westport. Right at end of Castlebar St, 1st right before bridge, right at lights, left before church. Follow to end of street

Located in seven acres of woodlands and just a short riverside walk from the town, this hotel offers spacious public areas, including The Islands restaurant and the all-day Maple Bar. Bedrooms come in a range of styles, and are all comfortable and well appointed. Both leisure and business guests are well catered for by the enthusiastic and friendly team who go to great lengths to ensure residents enjoy their stay. This hotel is a popular choice with special interest groups and also families, who enjoy the leisure facilities, and in summer time, the children's club.

Rooms 129 (67 fmly) (42 GF) (12 smoking) **S** €140-€150; **D** €240-€280 (incl. bkfst)* **Facilities** Spa STV Wi-fi ⌗ HL ⊗ supervised Gym Children's pool Lounger pool Steam room Sauna Fitness suite ♪ Xmas New Year **Conf** Class 150 Board 60 Thtr 500 Del €160* **Services** Lift **Parking** 220 **Notes** LB ⊗ Civ Wed 350

REPUBLIC OF IRELAND

WESTPORT *continued*

The Wyatt Hotel

★★★ 74% HOTEL

☎ 098 25027
The Octagon
e-mail: info@wyatthotel.com
web: www.wyatthotel.com
dir: Follow one-way system in town. Hotel by tall monument at Octagon

This stylish, welcoming hotel is situated in the famous town-centre Octagon. Bedrooms are attractively decorated and well equipped. Public areas are very comfortable with open fires and include a lively, contemporary bar and the traditional Cobblers Bar. JW Bistro serves food all day, and in high season The Wyatt Restaurant offers more formal dining.

Rooms 51 (2 GF) (5 smoking) ♟ **Facilities** Wi-fi Complimentary use of nearby leisure park ♫ New Year **Conf** Class 200 Board 80 Thtr 300 **Services** Lift **Parking** 20 **Notes** ⊗ Closed 25-26 Dec Civ Wed 200

Mill Times Hotel Westport

★★★ 73% HOTEL

☎ 098 29200 & 29130
Mill St
e-mail: info@milltimeshotel.ie
web: www.milltimeshotel.ie
dir: N59 signed town centre, in Bridge St keep in left lane, into Mill St, hotel on left

This family run hotel is situated in the centre of Westport, close to the shops and many pubs of this bustling town. It is ideal for visiting north Mayo with its many beaches and golf courses, or as a base for climbing the pilgrimage mountain of Croagh Patrick. Bedrooms are traditional in style and public areas are comfortable. Uncle Sam's café bar is a lively venue with entertainment at weekends. Temptations Restaurant offers good value meals during the evening, and is where a hearty breakfast is served. Underground parking is provided.

Rooms 34 (6 fmly) **Facilities** Wi-fi ♫ New Year **Conf** Class 60 Board 60 Thtr 200 **Services** Lift Air con **Parking** 25 **Notes** ⊗ Closed 24-25 Dec Civ Wed 100

Whitford House Hotel Health & Leisure Club

★★★★ 77% ◉ HOTEL

☎ 053 9143444
New Line Rd
e-mail: info@whitford.ie
web: www.whitford.ie
dir: Just off N25 (Duncannon rdbt) take exit for R733 (Wexford), hotel immediately left

This is a friendly family-run hotel just three kilometres from the town centre and within easy reach of the Rosslare Ferry. Comfortable bedrooms range from standard to the spacious deluxe rooms. Public areas include a choice of lounges and the popular Forthside Bar Bistro where a carvery is served at lunch. More formal meals are on offer during the evening in the award-winning Seasons Restaurant. Leisure and fitness facilities are complimentary to resident guests.

Rooms 36 (28 fmly) (18 GF) **S** €59-€130; **D** €90-€190 (incl. bkfst)* **Facilities** Spa FTV Wi-fi ♨ ☀ supervised Gym Children's playground Football area Hairdresser ♫ Xmas New Year **Conf** Class 12 Board 25 Thtr 50 Del from €89.45 to €182* **Parking** 200 **Notes** LB ⊗ RS 24-27 Dec Civ Wed 100

Gibraltar

GIBRALTAR
O'Callaghan Eliott Hotel
★★★★ 79% HOTEL

☎ 00 350 200 70500 & 200 75905
2 Governor's Pde
e-mail: eliott@ocallaghanhotels.com
web: www.ocallaghanhotels.com

Located in the heart of the old town, this hotel provides a convenient central base for exploring the duty-free shopping district and other key attractions on foot. The bedrooms are stylish, spacious and well equipped. The roof-top restaurant provides stunning bay views, while guests can also take a swim in the roof-top pool.

Rooms 123 ↖ **S** £129-£240; **D** £139-£250 (incl. bkfst) **Facilities** STV Wi-fi ↲ Gym ♬ Xmas New Year **Conf** Class 80 Board 70 Thtr 180 Del from £165 to £250 **Services** Lift Air con **Parking** 17 **Notes** LB ⊗ Civ Wed 120

Caleta Hotel
★★★★ 78% ◉◉ HOTEL

☎ 00 350 200 76501
Sir Herbert Miles Rd, PO Box 73
e-mail: sales@caletahotel.gi
web: www.caletahotel.com
dir: Enter Gibraltar via Spanish border & cross runway. At 1st rdbt turn left, hotel in 2kms

For travellers arriving in Gibraltar by plane, the Caleta is an eye-catching coastal landmark that can be spotted from the air if arriving from the east. This imposing and stylish hotel sits on a cliff top and all sea-facing rooms enjoy panoramic views across the straights to Morocco. Bedrooms vary in size and style; some have spacious balconies, flat-screen TVs and mini bars. Several dining venues are available, but Nunos provides an award-winning, fine dining Italian experience. The staff are friendly and service is professional.

Rooms 161 (89 annexe) (13 fmly) (80 smoking) **Facilities** Spa STV FTV Wi-fi ↳ ↲ supervised Gym Health & beauty club Xmas New Year **Conf** Class 172 Board 85 Thtr 200 **Services** Lift Air con **Parking** 32 **Notes** ⊗ Civ Wed 300

The Rock Hotel
★★★★ 78% ◉ HOTEL

☎ 00 350 200 73000
Europa Rd
e-mail: rockhotel@gibtelecom.net
web: www.rockhotelgibraltar.com
dir: From airport follow tourist board signs. Hotel on left half way up Europa Rd

Enjoying a prime elevated location directly below the Rock, this long-established art deco styled hotel has been the destination of celebrities and royalty since it was built in 1932. The bedrooms are spacious and well equipped, and many boast stunning coastal views that stretch across the Mediterranean to Morocco. The staff are friendly and service is delivered with flair and enthusiasm. Creative dinners and hearty breakfasts can be enjoyed in the stylish restaurant.

Rooms 104 (25 smoking) **Facilities** STV Wi-f ↲ supervised Xmas New Year **Conf** Class 24 Board 30 Thtr 70 **Services** Lift Air con **Parking** 40 **Notes** RS 5 Oct-1 Apr Civ Wed 40

Acknowledgments

The Automobile Association would like to thank the following photographers, companies and picture libraries for their assistance in the preparation of this book.

Abbreviations for the picture credits are as follows – (t) top; (b) bottom; (c) centre; (l) left; (r) right; (AA) AA World Travel Library

England Opener AA/Nigel Hicks; London Opener AA/James Tims; Channel Islands Opener AA/Wyn Voysey; Scotland Opener AA/Karl Blackwell; Scottish Islands Opener AA/Stephen Whitehorne; Wales Opener AA/Mark Bauer; Ireland Opener AA/Chris Hill; Gibraltar Opener AA/James Tims.

001 © Tips Images / Tips Italia Srl a socio unico / Alamy; 002 © Hemis/Alamy; 003 AA/Karl Blackwell; 004 Courtesy of Dukes Hotel; 005 Courtesy of The Merchant Hotel; 009 AA/Karl Blackwell; 011l Courtesy of Gravetye Manor; 011r Courtesy of Dukes Hotel; 012l Courtesy of Cringletie; 012r Courtesy of Llangoed Hall; 013l Courtesy of The Merchant Hotel; 013r Courtesy of Castleknock Hotel & Country Club; 015c Courtesy of Macdonald Compleat Angler; 015b Courtesy of Gisborough Hall; 016t Courtesy of The Milestone Hotel; 016c Courtesy of The Chesterfield Mayfair; 019 Courtesy of Duisdale House Hotel; 020 Courtesy of Duisdale House Hotel; 021 (c) Adam White Photography/Hell Bay Hotel; 024l AA/Terence Carter; 024c Photodisc; 024r AA/Karl Blackwell; 025tl AA/Karl Blackwell; 025bc Photodisc; 025br AA/James Tims; 028 AA/Karl Blackwell; 029 AA/Karl Blackwell; 046 AA/Clive Sawyer.

Every effort has been made to trace the copyright holders, and we apologise in advance for any unintentional omissions or errors. We would be pleased to apply any corrections in a following edition of this publication

COUNTY MAPS

England

1 Bedfordshire
2 Berkshire
3 Bristol
4 Buckinghamshire
5 Cambridgeshire
6 Greater Manchester
7 Herefordshire
8 Hertfordshire
9 Leicestershire
10 Northamptonshire
11 Nottinghamshire
12 Rutland
13 Staffordshire
14 Warwickshire
15 West Midlands
16 Worcestershire

Scotland

17 City of Glasgow
18 Clackmannanshire
19 East Ayrshire
20 East Dunbartonshire
21 East Renfrewshire
22 Perth & Kinross
23 Renfrewshire
24 South Lanarkshire
25 West Dunbartonshire

Wales

26 Blaenau Gwent
27 Bridgend
28 Caerphilly
29 Denbighshire
30 Flintshire
31 Merthyr Tydfil
32 Monmouthshire
33 Neath Port Talbot
34 Newport
35 Rhondda Cynon Taff
36 Torfaen
37 Vale of Glamorgan
38 Wrexham

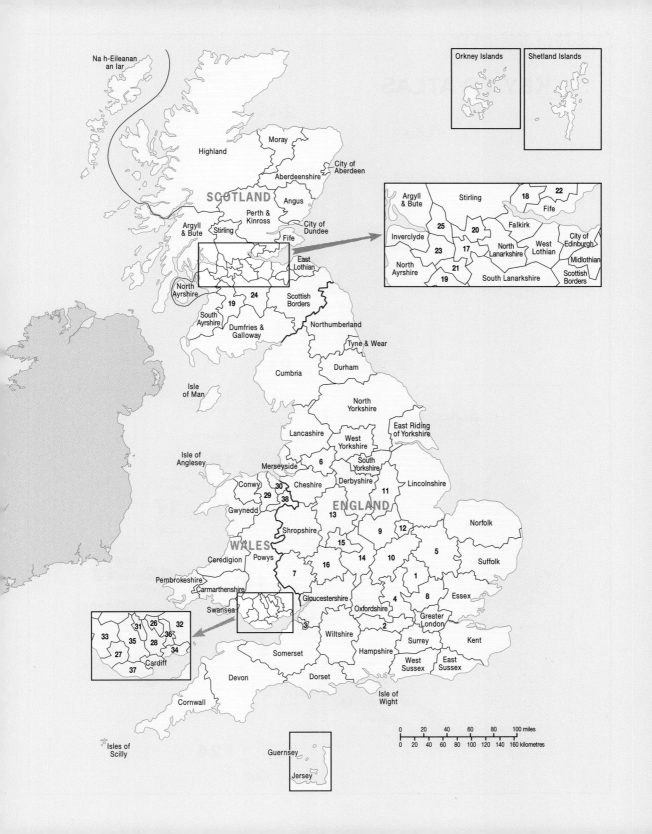

Na h-Eileanan
an Iar

Highland

Moray

City of
Aberdeen

SCOTLAND

Aberdeenshire

Angus

Perth &
Kinross

City of
Dundee

Argyll
& Bute

Stirling

Fife

North
Ayrshire

East
Lothian

South
Ayrshire

19

24

Scottish
Borders

Dumfries &
Galloway

Northumberland

Tyne & Wear

Cumbria

Durham

Isle
of Man

North
Yorkshire

Lancashire

East Riding
of Yorkshire

Isle of
Anglesey

West
Yorkshire

Merseyside

6

South
Yorkshire

Lincolnshire

Conwy

30

Cheshire

Derbyshire

11

29

38

Gwynedd

13

ENGLAND

Norfolk

Shropshire

9

12

Ceredigion

15

WALES

Powys

14

10

5

Suffolk

Pembrokeshire

7

16

1

Carmarthenshire

Swansea

Gloucestershire

4

8

Essex

Oxfordshire

3

2

Greater
London

26

32

Kent

31

36

Wiltshire

Surrey

33

35

28

34

Somerset

Hampshire

West
Sussex

East
Sussex

27

Cardiff

37

Devon

Dorset

Isle of
Wight

Cornwall

Isles of
Scilly

Guernsey

Jersey

Orkney Islands

Shetland Islands

Argyll
& Bute

Stirling

18

22

Fife

25

20

Falkirk

Inverclyde

17

North
Lanarkshire

West
Lothian

City of
Edinburgh

23

North
Ayrshire

21

Midlothian

19

South Lanarkshire

Scottish
Borders

0   20   40   60   80   100 miles
0 20 40 60 80 100 120 140 160 kilometres

KEY TO ATLAS

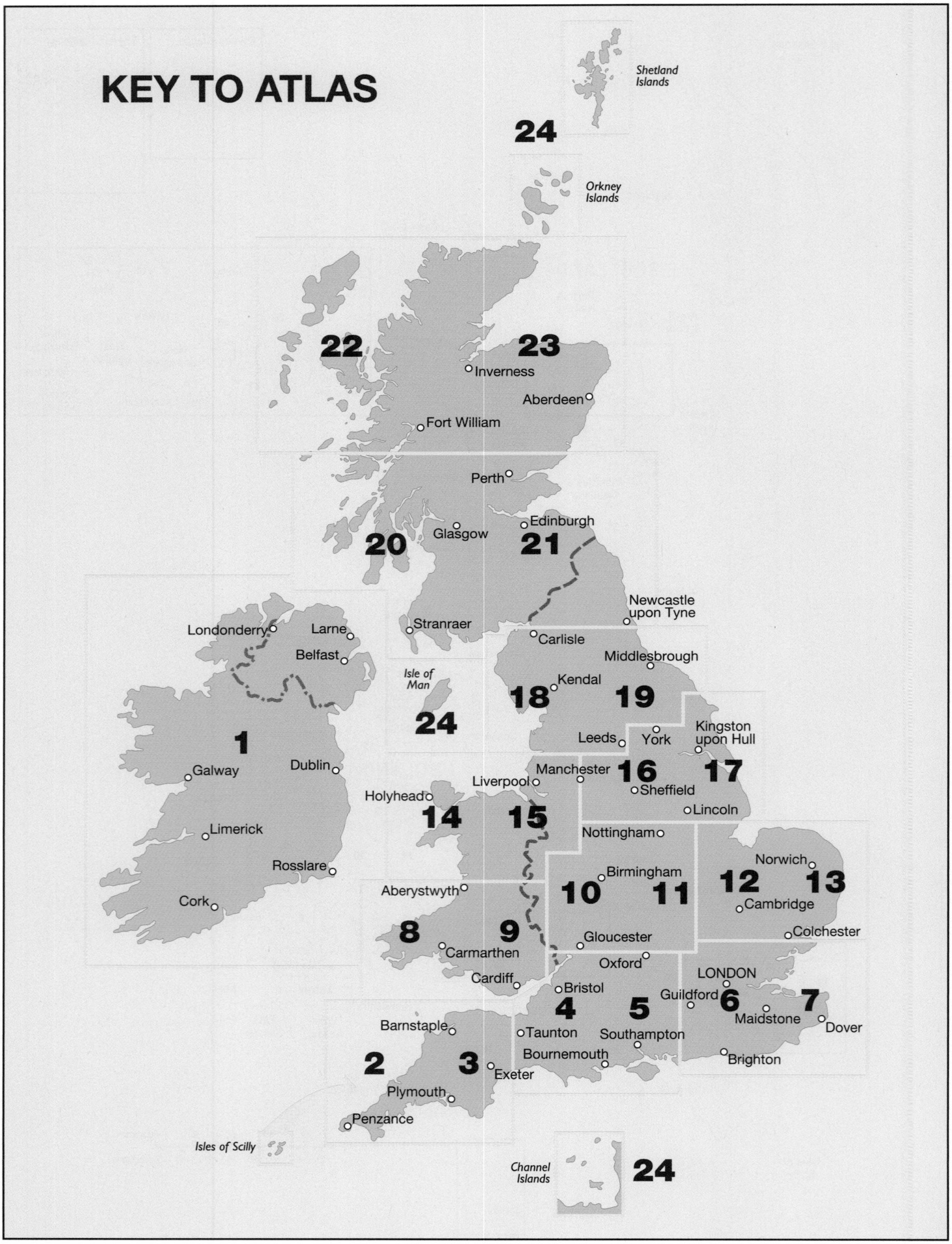

24 Shetland Islands

Orkney Islands

22   **23**
Inverness

Aberdeen

Fort William

Perth

20   **21**
Glasgow   Edinburgh

Stranraer

Newcastle upon Tyne

Carlisle

Middlesbrough

Londonderry   Larne

Belfast

Isle of Man

Kendal

18   **19**

24

Leeds   York   Kingston upon Hull

1

Galway   Dublin

Holyhead

Liverpool   Manchester

16   **17**
Sheffield

Lincoln

14   **15**

Limerick

Nottingham

Rosslare

Aberystwyth

Norwich

12   **13**

Cork

Birmingham

10   **11**

Cambridge

Colchester

8   **9**

Carmarthen

Gloucester

Oxford

LONDON

Cardiff

Bristol

Guildford   **6**

7

Barnstaple

4   **5**

Taunton   Southampton

Maidstone   Dover

2   **3**

Bournemouth

Brighton

Exeter

Plymouth

Penzance

Isles of Scilly

Channel Islands   **24**

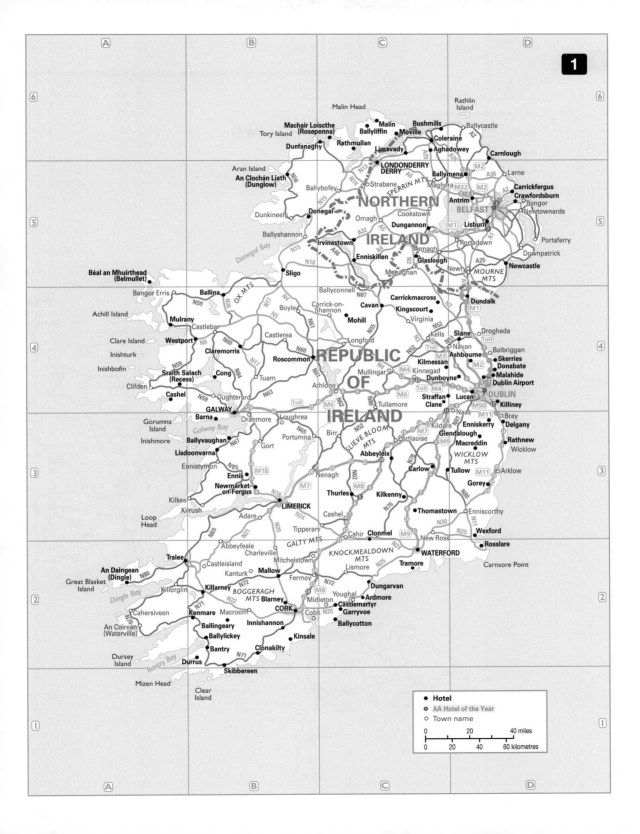

1

6
5
4
3
2
1

A
B
C
D

Malin Head
Rathlin Island

Machair Loiscthe (Rosepenna)
Tory Island
Malin
Bushmills
Ballycastle
Ballyliffin
Moville
Dunfanaghy
Rathmullan
Coleraine
Carnlough
Limavady
Aghadowey

Aran Island
An Clochán Liath (Dunglow)
LONDONDERRY DERRY
Strabane
Ballymena
Larne
Ballybofey
Maghera
M2
Carrickfergus
Crawfordsburn
SPERRIN MTS
A36
Antrim
Bangor
Donegal
M22
M2
Newtownards
Dunkineely
Cookstown
Omagh
Dungannon
BELFAST
Ballyshannon
M1
Lisburn
Portaferry
Irvinestown
Armagh
Portadown
Downpatrick
N15
A46
Enniskillen
Glaslough
Newry
A25
Newcastle
N16
Monaghan
MOURNE MTS
Sligo
Ballyconnell
N87
Carrickmacross
Dundalk
Bangor Erris
Ballina
OX MTS
Cavan
Kingscourt
M1
Boyle
Carrick-on-Shannon
Mulrany
N26
N17
Drogheda
Castlebar
N4
Mohill
Virginia
Slane
Toll
Westport
N5
N60
Claremorris
Roscommon
N5
Longford
Navan
Ashbourne
Balbriggan
Clare Island
N59
Castlerea
N52
Kells
M2
Skerries
Inishturk
N61
Kilmessan
Donabate
Inishbofin
Sraith Salach (Recess)
Cong
N84
Tuam
Mullingar
Kinnegad
Dunboyne
Malahide
Clifden
Oughterard
N63
Athlone
REPUBLIC OF IRELAND
M4
Dublin Airport
Cashel
N59
Toll
M4
Straffan
Lucan
DUBLIN
GALWAY
Loughrea
M6
Tullamore
Clane
M50
Killiney
Barna
Oranmore
N65
Birr
Naas
M11
Bray
Gorumna Island
N67
Gort
Portumna
SLIEVE BLOOM MTS
Kildare
Enniskerry
Delgany
Ballyvaughan
Portlaoise
M7
Glendalough
Inishmore
Lisdoonvarna
M9
Macreddin
Rathnew
Ennistymon
M18
Nenagh
Abbeyleix
WICKLOW MTS
Wicklow
Ennis
N62
Carlow
Tullow
Newmarket-on-Fergus
N18
Thurles
M8
Kilkenny
Gorey
Kilkee
M7
Arklow
Kilrush
LIMERICK
Cashel
N76
Enniscorthy
Loop Head
Adare
N24
Thomastown
Tipperary
N30
Cahir
Clonmel
Wexford
Abbeyfeale
GALTY MTS
M9
New Ross
N25
Rosslare
Tralee
Charleville
Mitchelstown
KNOCKMEALDOWN MTS
WATERFORD
Carnsore Point
Castleisland
Kanturk
Fermoy
Lismore
Tramore
An Daingean (Dingle)
N86
Killorglin
Mallow
N72
Dungarvan
Great Blasket Island
N72
Ardmore
Dingle Bay
Killarney
BOGGERAGH MTS
Blarney
Youghal
Castlemartyr
Cahersiveen
N22
Macroom
CORK
Midleton
Garryvoe
An Coireán (Waterville)
Kenmare
Innishannon
Cobh
N25
Ballycotton
Ballingeary
Kinsale
Ballylickey
N71
Clonakilty
Dursey Island
Bantry
Durrus
Skibbereen
Bantry Bay
Mizen Head
Clear Island

● Hotel
● AA Hotel of the Year
○ Town name

0   20   40 miles
0   20   40   60 kilometres

Legend

M6	Motorway/toll motorway	
	Motorway junction full/restricted. Service area	
A33	Primary route single/dual carriageway	
A34	Other A road single/dual carriageway	
B3400	B road	
	Unclassified road	
—V—	Vehicle ferry	
—C—	Fast vehicle ferry or catamaran	
● **Stamford**	Hotel
● **Llyswen**	AA Hotel of the Year
○ King's Cliffe	Town/Village name
	National boundary
ESSEX	English county name & boundary
CONWY	Welsh county name & boundary
MORAY	Scottish county name & boundary
	National Park

Lundy

Hartland Point
Hartland

Morwenstow

Kilkhampton

Bude
Bude Stra
Bay
Widemouth Bay

Crackington Haven
Week St Mary

Boscastle
Tintagel

Delabole
Camelford

Port Isaac
Polzeath
St Tudy
Bolventor
BODMIN MOOR
Pendoggett
Blisland
Rock
Harlyn
Padstow
A389
Wadebridge
Porthcothan
Bodmin
Lanivet
St Cleer
Mawgan Porth
St Mawgan
C O R N W A L L
St Keyne
St Columb Major
Dobwalls
Liske
Roche
Newquay
Bugle
Lostwithiel
West Pentire
Fraddon
St Blazey
Golant
Perranporth
Summercourt
St Austell
Pelynt
Ladock
St Stephen
Fowey
Lo
St Agnes
Marazanvose
Polruan
Polperro
Porthtowan
Grampound
Pentewan
Portreath
Carnon Downs
Tregony
Mevagissey
St Ives Bay
St Day
Truro
Gorran Haven
Gwithian
St Ives
Redruth
Portloe
Zennor
Camborne
St Just-in-Roseland
Veryan
Lelant
Hayle
St Mawes
Portscatho
Penryn
Constantine
St Just
Penzance
Falmouth
A3071
Marazion
Helston
Mawnan Smith
Land's End
Sennen
Newlyn
Gweek
Manaccan
Land's End
St Buryan
Mousehole
Praa Sands
St Keverne
Porthcurno
Treen
Mount's Bay
Porthleven
Mullion
Coverack
Cadgwith
Lizard
Lizard Point

ISLES OF SCILLY
Bryher
New Grimsby
○ Higher Town
Hugh Town
St Mary's
Middle Town
Old Town
SV

SW

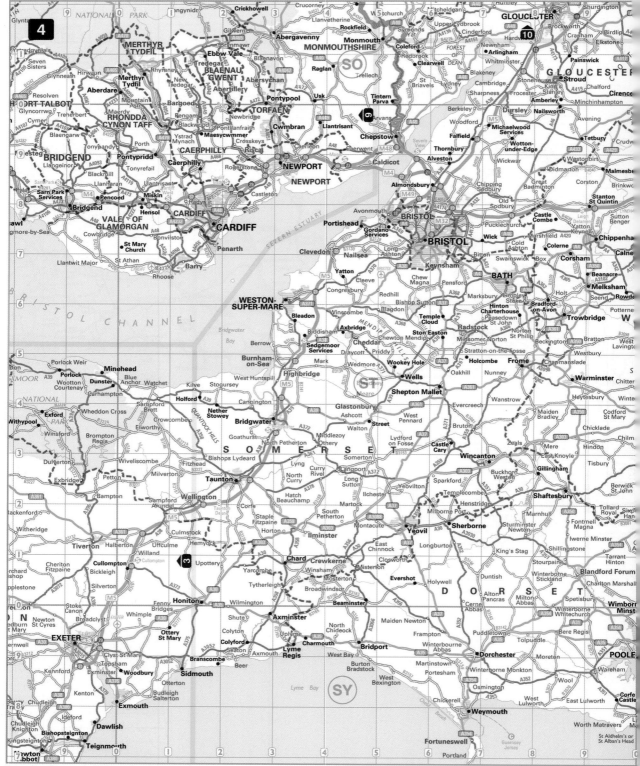

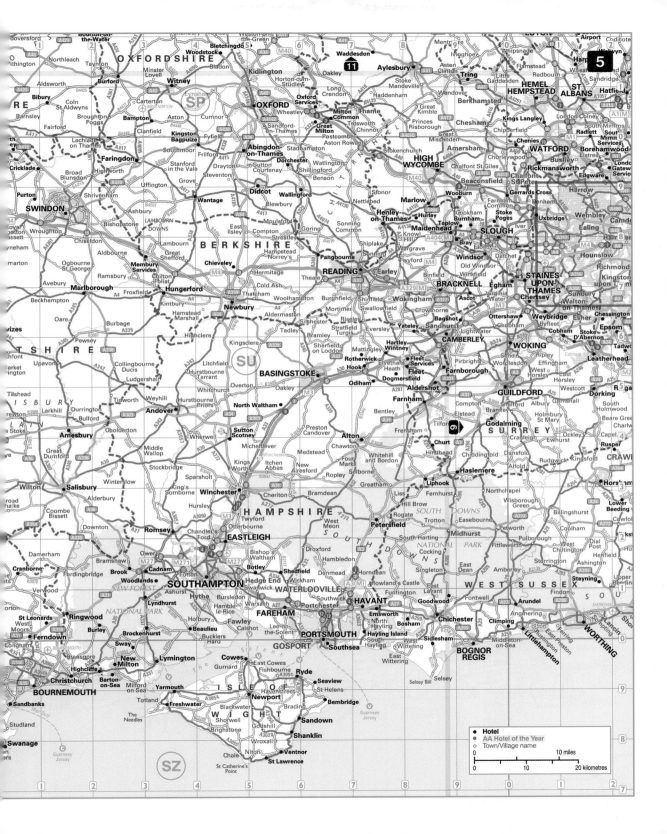

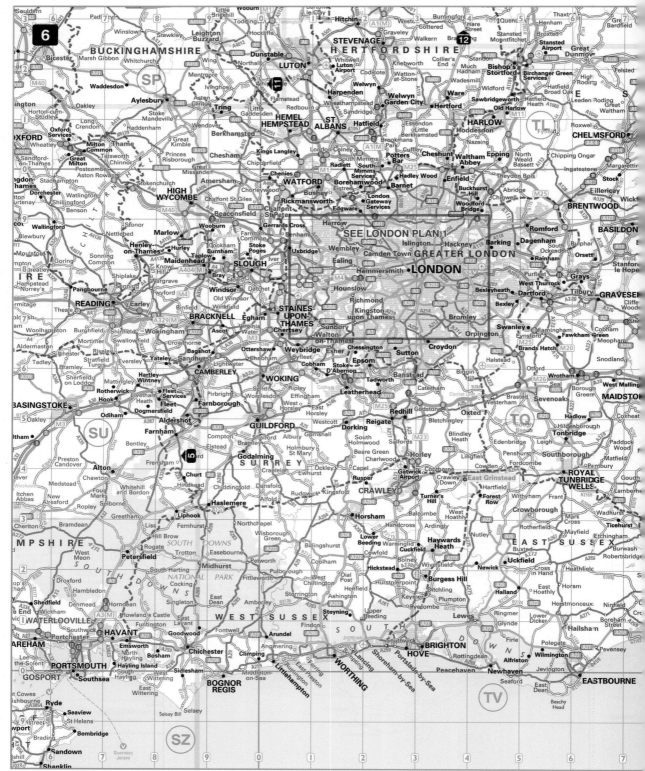

CARDIGAN BAY

CERE

SM

SN

PEMBROKESHIRE

CARMARTHENSHIRE

SR

SS

Legend:
- ● Hotel
- ● AA Hotel of the Year
- ○ Town/Village name

0 — 10 miles
0 — 10 — 20 kilometres

Aberdyfi
Llandre
Aberystwyth
Llanfarian
Llanrhystud
Llansantffraid
Aberarth
New Quay
Aberaeron
Temple Bar
Llangranog
Aberporth
Lampe
Tan-y-groes
Talgarreg
Blaenporth
Rhydowen
Gwbert-on-Sea
St Dogmaels
Cardigan
Llechryd
Llanybydder
Newcastle Emlyn
Llandysul
Llangeler
Strumble Head
Nevern
Newport
Eglwyswrw
Cynwyl Elfed
Brechfa
St David's Head
Letterston
Wolf's Castle
St Davids
Solva
Newgale
Roch
MYNYDD PRESELI
Llandissilio
Carmarthen
Nantgaredig
Llanarthne
St Brides Bay
PEMBROKESHIRE COAST NATIONAL PARK
Broad Haven
Haverfordwest
Robeston Wathen
Whitland
St Clears
Llanddarog
Cross Hands
Pontyberem
Johnston
Narberth
Red Roses
Laugharne
Llansteffan
Pontyates
Marloes
Kilgetty
Amroth
Pendine
Kidwelly
Broad Sound
Dale
Angle
Neyland
Pembroke
Carew
St Florence
Saundersfoot
Carmarthen Bay
Pembrey
Bury Port
Llanelli
Gorseinon
Pembroke Dock
Lamphey
Penally
Tenby
Castlemartin
PEMBROKESHIRE COAST NATIONAL PARK
Manorbier
Bosherston
Llangennith
SWANSEA
Llanrhidian
Gowerton
Dunvant
Reynoldston
Rhossili
Worms Head
Oxwich
Port Einon
Bishopston
Milford Haven
Lundy
Ilfracombe
Woo
Mortehoe
Lee
Combe Martin

For continuation pages refer to numbered arrows

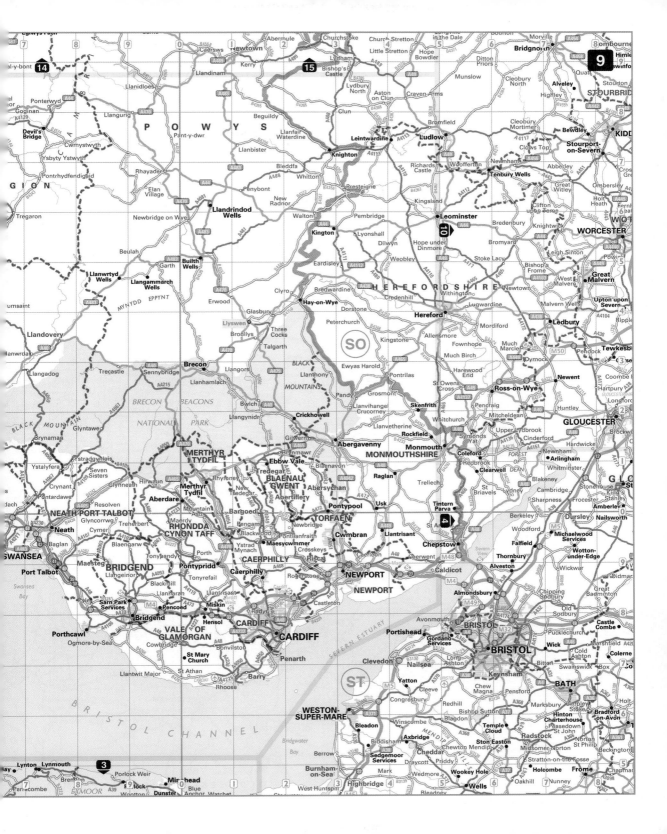

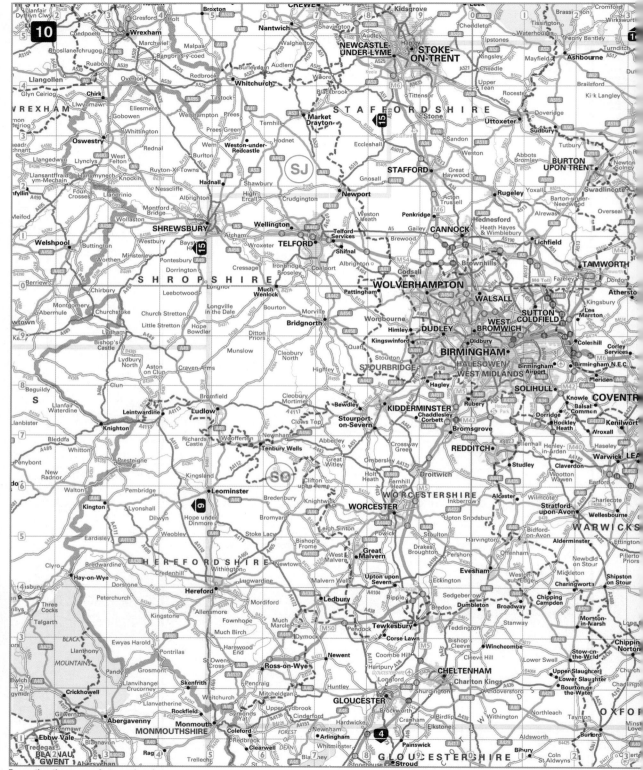

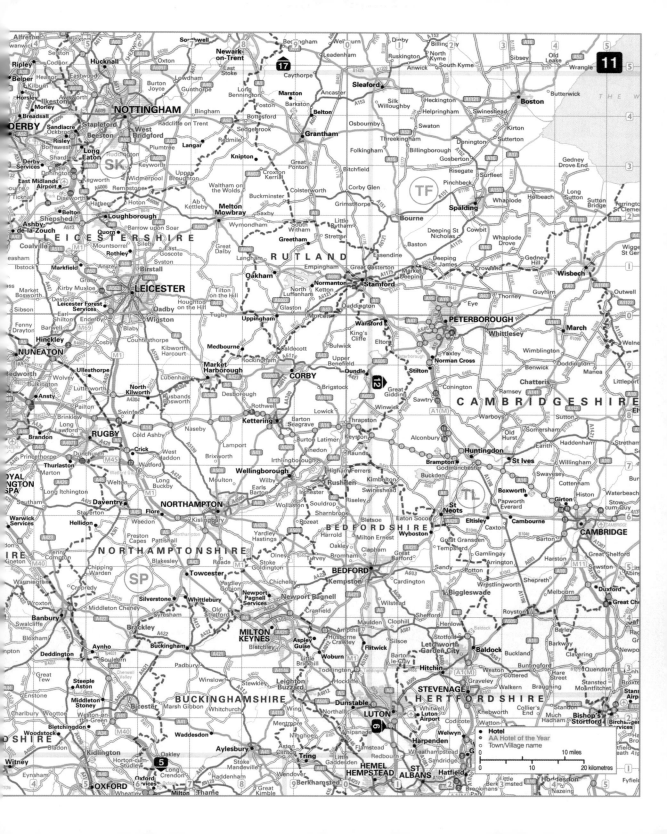

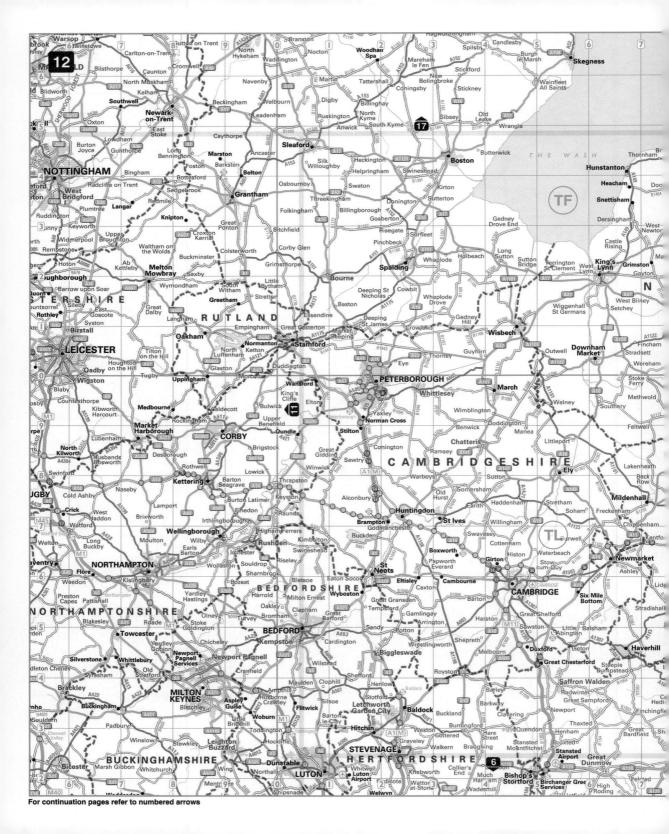

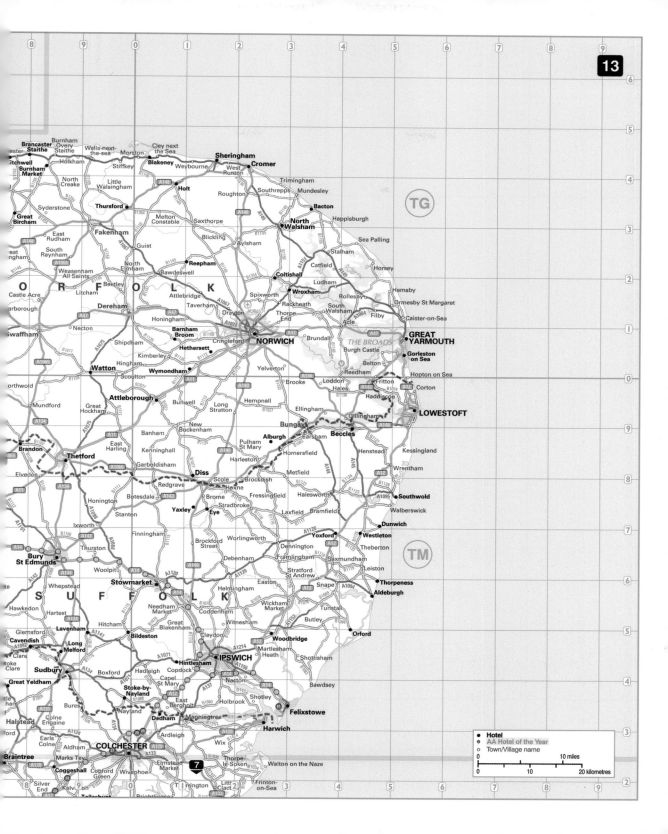

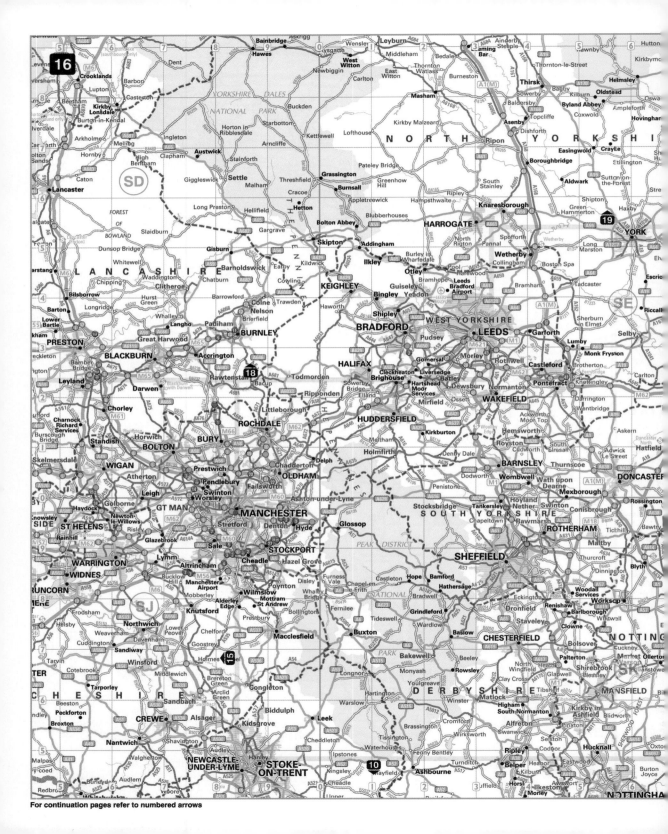

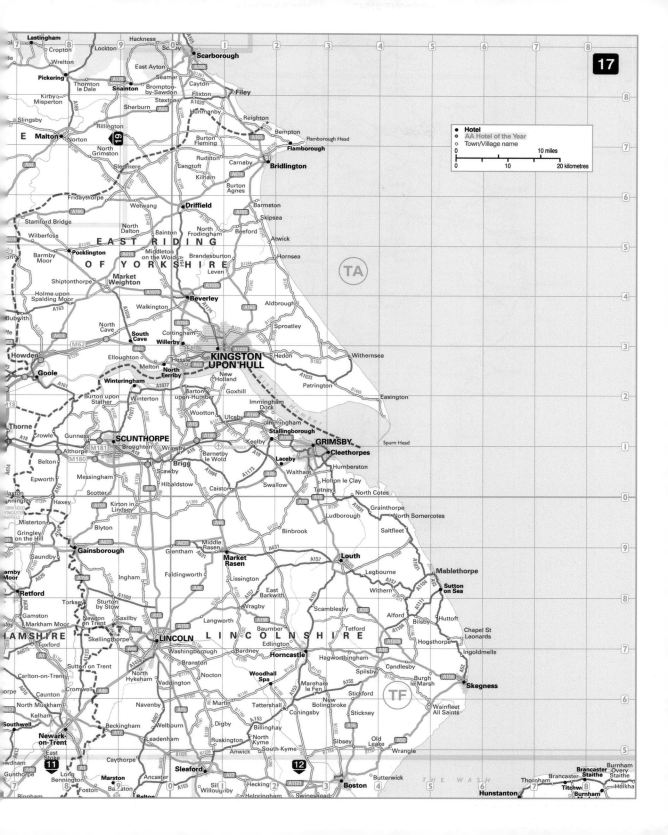

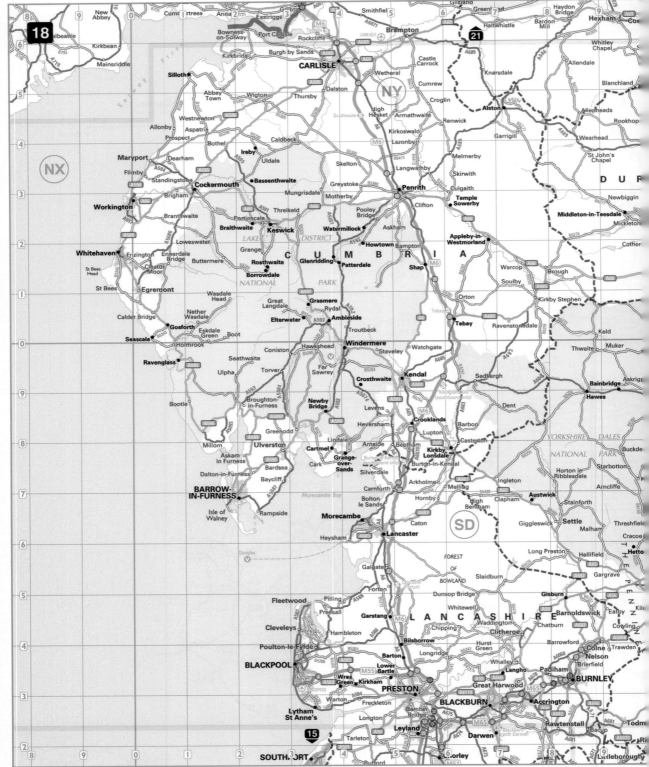

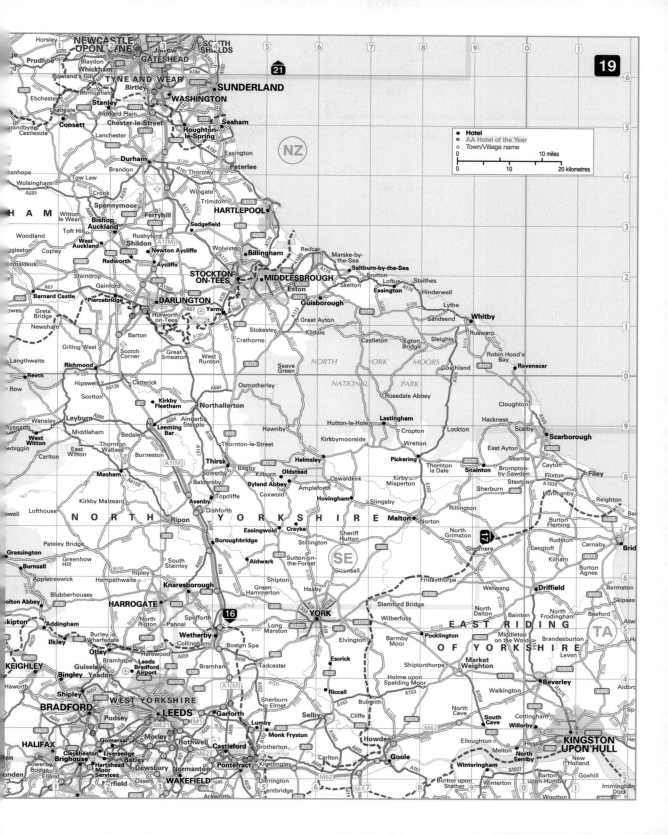

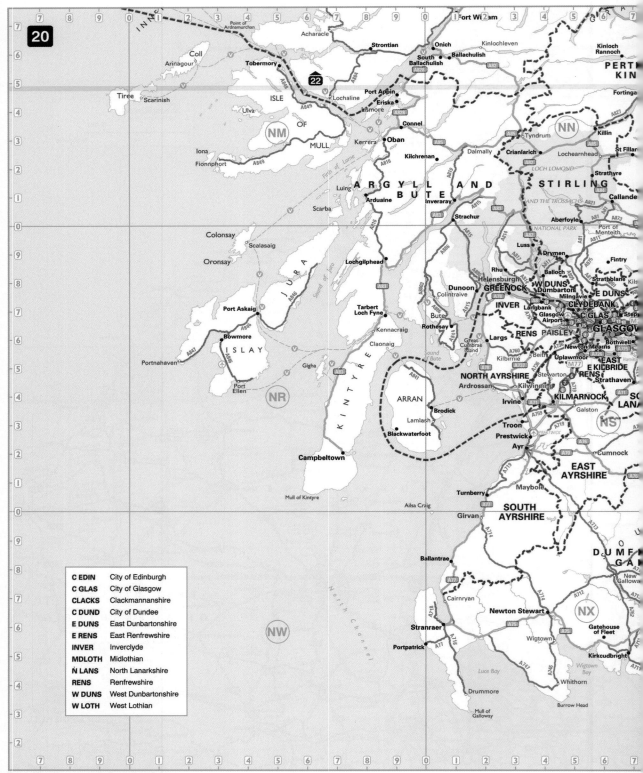

20

Point of Ardnamurchan
Acharacle
Arinagour
Coll
Tobermory
Tiree
Scarinish
Strontian
Onich
Ballachulish
South Ballachulish
Kinlochleven
Fort William
Kinloch Rannoch
PERTH KIN
ISLE
22
Lochaline
Port Appin
Eriska
Lismore
A82
Fortinga
Ulva
A849
OF
MULL
Kerrera
Connel
A85
Tyndrum
Killin
St Fillan
NM
NN
Iona
Fionnphort
A849
Oban
Kilchrenan
Dalmally
Crianlarich
Lochearnhead
Kerrera
LOCH LOMOND
Strathyre
Firth of Lorne
ARGYLL AND
STIRLING
Luing
Arduaine
BUTE
Inveraray
Strachur
AND THE TROSSACHS
Callande
Scarba
Aberfoyle
Port of Menteith
Colonsay
Scalasaig
NATIONAL PARK
Luss
Oronsay
Lochgilphead
Fintry
JURA
Rhu
Balloch
Strathblane
Helensburgh
W DUNS
Dunoon
GREENOCK
Dumbarton
E DUNS
Port Askaig
Colintraive
Milngavie
CLYDEBANK
Tarbert
Loch Fyne
INVER
Langbank
C GLAS
Step
Bowmore
Kennacraig
Bute
Glasgow Airport
GLASGOW
ISLAY
Claonaig
Rothesay
RENS PAISLEY
Portnahaven
Gigha
Great Cumbrae Island
Largs
Bothwell
Newton Mearns
EAST
Port Ellen
Sound of Bute
Uplawmoor
E KILBRIDE
NR
Kilbirnie
E RENS
NORTH AYRSHIRE
Stewarton
KINTYRE
ARRAN
Strathaven
Ardrossan
Kilwinning
SO
Irvine
KILMARNOCK
LANA
Brodick
Galston
NS
Lamlash
Troon
Blackwaterfoot
Prestwick
EAST
AYRSHIRE
Campbeltown
Ayr
Cumnock
Mull of Kintyre
Turnberry
Maybole
Ailsa Craig
SOUTH
AYRSHIRE
Girvan
DUMF
GA
Ballantrae
New Galloway
A77
Cairnryan
NW
North Channel
Newton Stewart
Stranraer
NX
Gatehouse of Fleet
Portpatrick
Wigtown
Wigtown Bay
Kirkcudbright
Luce Bay
Whithorn
Drummore
Burrow Head
Mull of Galloway

C EDIN	City of Edinburgh
C GLAS	City of Glasgow
CLACKS	Clackmannanshire
C DUND	City of Dundee
E DUNS	East Dunbartonshire
E RENS	East Renfrewshire
INVER	Inverclyde
MDLOTH	Midlothian
N LANS	North Lanarkshire
RENS	Renfrewshire
W DUNS	West Dunbartonshire
W LOTH	West Lothian

For continuation pages refer to numbered arrows

22

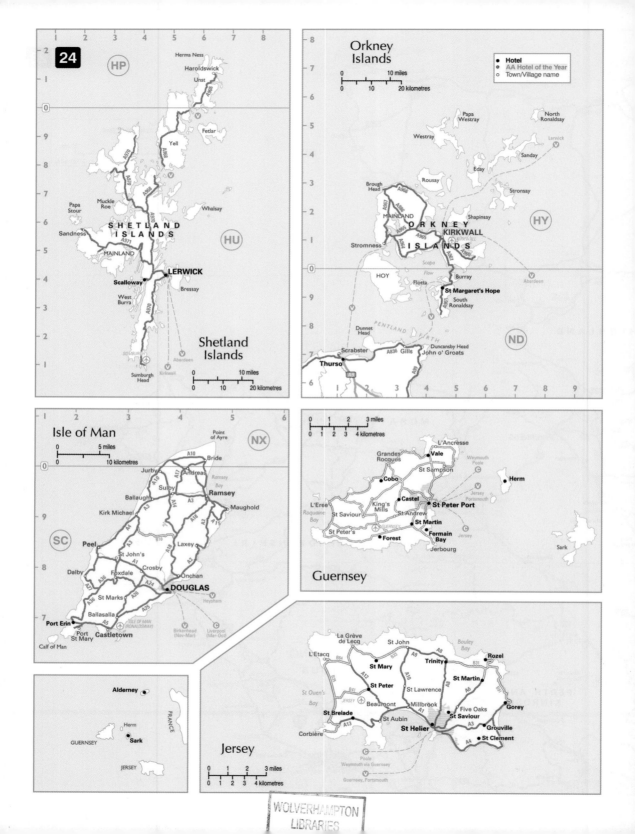

Readers' Report Form

Please send this form to:–
Editor, The Hotel Guide,
Lifestyle Guides,
AA Media,
Fanum House,
Basingstoke RG21 4EA

e-mail: lifestyleguides@theAA.com

Please use this form to recommend any hotel where you have stayed, whether it is included in the guide or not currently listed. You can also help us to improve the guide by completing the short questionnaire on the reverse.

Please note that the AA does not undertake to arbitrate between you and the hotel management, or to obtain compensation or engage in protracted correspondence.

Date

Your name (BLOCK CAPITALS)

Your address (BLOCK CAPITALS)

Post code

E-mail address

Name of hotel

Location

Comments

(please attach a separate sheet if necessary)

Please tick here ☐ if you DO NOT wish to receive details of AA offers or products   PTO

Readers' Report Form *continued*

Have you bought this guide before? ☐ YES ☐ NO

Do you regularly use any other, accommodation, restaurant, pub or food guides? ☐ YES ☐ NO
If YES, which ones?

_____

_____

Why did you buy this guide? (tick all that apply)
Holiday ☐   Short break ☐   Business travel ☐   Special occasion ☐
Overnight stop ☐   Find a venue for an event e.g. conference ☐
Other (please state) _____

How often do you stay in hotels? (tick one choice)
More than once a month ☐   Once a month ☐   Once in 2-3 months ☐
Once in six months ☐   Once a year ☐   Less than once a year ☐
Other (please state) _____

Please answer these questions to help us make improvements to the guide:
Which of these factors are the most important when choosing a hotel? (tick all that apply)
Price ☐   Location ☐   Awards/ratings ☐   Service ☐
Decor/surroundings ☐   Previous experience ☐   Recommendation ☐
Other (please state) _____

Do you read the editorial features in the guide? ☐ YES ☐ NO

Do you use the location atlas? ☐ YES ☐ NO

What elements of the guide do you find most useful when choosing somewhere to stay? (tick all that apply)
Description ☐   Photo ☐   Advertisement ☐   Star rating ☐

Is there any other information you would like to see added to this guide?

_____

_____

_____

_____

Readers' Report Form

Please send this form to:–
Editor, The Hotel Guide,
Lifestyle Guides,
AA Media,
Fanum House,
Basingstoke RG21 4EA

e-mail: lifestyleguides@theAA.com

Please use this form to recommend any hotel where you have stayed, whether it is included in the guide or not currently listed. You can also help us to improve the guide by completing the short questionnaire on the reverse.

Please note that the AA does not undertake to arbitrate between you and the hotel management, or to obtain compensation or engage in protracted correspondence.

Date

Your name (BLOCK CAPITALS)

Your address (BLOCK CAPITALS)

Post code

E-mail address

Name of hotel

Location

Comments

(please attach a separate sheet if necessary)

Please tick here ☐ if you DO NOT wish to receive details of AA offers or products

PTO

Readers' Report Form *continued*

Have you bought this guide before? ☐ YES ☐ NO

Do you regularly use any other, accommodation, restaurant, pub or food guides? ☐ YES ☐ NO
If YES, which ones?

Why did you buy this guide? (tick all that apply)

Holiday ☐   Short break ☐   Business travel ☐   Special occasion ☐
Overnight stop ☐   Find a venue for an event e.g. conference ☐
Other (please state)

How often do you stay in hotels? (tick one choice)

More than once a month ☐   Once a month ☐   Once in 2-3 months ☐
Once in six months ☐   Once a year ☐   Less than once a year ☐
Other (please state)

Please answer these questions to help us make improvements to the guide:

Which of these factors are the most important when choosing a hotel? (tick all that apply)

Price ☐   Location ☐   Awards/ratings ☐   Service ☐
Decor/surroundings ☐   Previous experience ☐   Recommendation ☐
Other (please state)

Do you read the editorial features in the guide? ☐ YES ☐ NO

Do you use the location atlas? ☐ YES ☐ NO

What elements of the guide do you find most useful when choosing somewhere to stay? (tick all that apply)

Description ☐   Photo ☐   Advertisement ☐   Star rating ☐

Is there any other information you would like to see added to this guide?

Readers' Report Form

Please send this form to:–
Editor, The Hotel Guide,
Lifestyle Guides,
AA Media,
Fanum House,
Basingstoke RG21 4EA

e-mail: lifestyleguides@theAA.com

Please use this form to recommend any hotel where you have stayed, whether it is included in the guide or not currently listed. You can also help us to improve the guide by completing the short questionnaire on the reverse.

Please note that the AA does not undertake to arbitrate between you and the hotel management, or to obtain compensation or engage in protracted correspondence.

Date

Your name (BLOCK CAPITALS)

Your address (BLOCK CAPITALS)

Post code

E-mail address

Name of hotel

Location

Comments

(please attach a separate sheet if necessary)

Please tick here ☐ if you DO NOT wish to receive details of AA offers or products

PTO

Readers' Report Form *continued*

Have you bought this guide before? ☐ YES ☐ NO

Do you regularly use any other, accommodation, restaurant, pub or food guides? ☐ YES ☐ NO
If YES, which ones?

_____

_____

Why did you buy this guide? (tick all that apply)

Holiday ☐   Short break ☐   Business travel ☐   Special occasion ☐

Overnight stop ☐   Find a venue for an event e.g. conference ☐

Other (please state) _____

How often do you stay in hotels? (tick one choice)

More than once a month ☐   Once a month ☐   Once in 2-3 months ☐

Once in six months ☐   Once a year ☐   Less than once a year ☐

Other (please state) _____

Please answer these questions to help us make improvements to the guide:

Which of these factors are the most important when choosing a hotel? (tick all that apply)

Price ☐   Location ☐   Awards/ratings ☐   Service ☐

Decor/surroundings ☐   Previous experience ☐   Recommendation ☐

Other (please state) _____

Do you read the editorial features in the guide? ☐ YES ☐ NO

Do you use the location atlas? ☐ YES ☐ NO

What elements of the guide do you find most useful when choosing somewhere to stay? (tick all that apply)

Description ☐   Photo ☐   Advertisement ☐   Star rating ☐

Is there any other information you would like to see added to this guide?

_____

_____

_____

_____